ESSENTIAL READINGS IN

WORLD

POLITICS

8TH EDITION

ESSENTIAL READINGS IN

WORLD POLITICS

8TH EDITION

Karen A. Mingst, Jack L. Snyder, and
Heather Elko McKibben

W. W. NORTON & COMPANY
Independent Publishers Since 1923

W. W. Norton & Company has been independent since its founding in 1923, when William Warder Norton and Mary D. Herter Norton first published lectures delivered at the People's Institute, the adult education division of New York City's Cooper Union. The firm soon expanded its program beyond the Institute, publishing books by celebrated academics from America and abroad. By midcentury, the two major pillars of Norton's publishing program—trade books and college texts—were firmly established. In the 1950s, the Norton family transferred control of the company to its employees, and today—with a staff of five hundred and hundreds of trade, college, and professional titles published each year—W. W. Norton & Company stands as the largest and oldest publishing house owned wholly by its employees.

Editor: Peter Lesser
Project Editors: Caitlin Moran, Thea Goodrich
Associate Editor: Anna Olcott
Managing Editor, College: Marian Johnson
Senior Production Manager: Sean Mintus
Marketing Manager, Political Science: Ashley Sherwood
Director of College Permissions: Megan Schindel
Permissions Associate: Patricia Wong
Composition: Westchester Publishing Services
Cartography: Mapping Specialists Limited
Manufacturing: Transcontinental

Permission to use copyrighted material is included in the credits section of this book, which begins on page 655.

Library of Congress Cataloging-in-Publication Data

Names: Mingst, Karen A., 1947–editor. | McKibben, Heather Elko, author. | Snyder, Jack L., author.
Title: Essential readings in world politics / Karen A. Mingst, Heather Elko McKibben, and Jack L. Snyder.
Description: 8th Edition. | New York : W.W. Norton & Company, [2022] |
Series: The Norton Series in World Politics | Previous edition: 2019. |
    Includes bibliographical references.
    Identifiers: LCCN 2021050490 | ISBN 9780393441710 (Paperback)
Subjects: LCSH: International relations. | World politics.
Classification: LCC JZ1305 .E85 2022 | DDC 327--dc23/eng/20211120
LC record available at https://lccn.loc.gov/2021050490

W. W. Norton & Company, Inc., 500 Fifth Avenue, New York, NY 10110
    wwnorton.com
W. W. Norton & Company Ltd., 15 Carlisle Street, London W1D 3BS

2 3 4 5 6 7 8 9 0

CONTENTS

10. HUMAN RIGHTS 555

11. THE ENVIRONMENT 606

PREFACE

This reader is the result of a collaborative effort between the three co-editors, with an evolving mix of classic and contemporary selections over eight editions.

The articles have been selected to meet several criteria. First, the collection is designed to augment and amplify the core text, *Essentials of International Relations,* Ninth Edition, by Karen A. Mingst and Heather Elko McKibben. The chapters in this book follow those in the text. Second, the selections are purposefully eclectic; that is, key theoretical articles are paired with contemporary pieces found in the literature. When possible, articles have been chosen to reflect diverse theoretical perspectives and policy viewpoints. Finally, the articles are intended to be both readable and engaging to undergraduates. The co-editors worked to maintain the integrity of challenging pieces while making them accessible to undergraduates at a variety of colleges and universities, in some cases working closely with authors to translate technical material into highly accessible yet precise prose.

Special thanks go to those individuals who provided reviews of this book and offered suggestions and reflections based on teaching experience. Our product benefited greatly from these evaluations, although had we included all the suggestions, the book would have been thousands of pages! Peter Lesser, our editor at W. W. Norton, guided part of the process, compiling thorough evaluations from users of earlier editions and providing suggestions. Anna Olcott kept us "on task" and offered excellent suggestions as the book took final shape. Their professionalism and understanding made this process much more rewarding. We also thank W. W. Norton's copyediting and production staff for their careful work on this book.

ABOUT THE AUTHORS

Karen A. Mingst is Professor Emeritus at the Patterson School of Diplomacy and International Commerce at the University of Kentucky. She holds a PhD in political science from the University of Wisconsin. A specialist in international organization, international law, and international political economy, Professor Mingst has conducted research in Western Europe, West Africa, and Yugoslavia. She is the author or editor of seven books and numerous academic articles.

Jack L. Snyder is the Robert and Renee Belfer Professor of International Relations in the Department of Political Science and the Saltzman Institute of War and Peace Studies at Columbia University. He is the editor of the Norton Series in World Politics and his books include *From Voting to Violence: Democratization and Nationalist Conflict*. Professor Snyder is a Fellow of the American Academy of Arts and Sciences and an elected member and chair of Columbia's Arts and Sciences Policy and Planning Committee.

Heather Elko McKibben is an associate professor in the Department of Political Science at the University of California, Davis. She received her PhD from the University of Pittsburgh in 2008 and held a postdoctorate position in the Niehaus Center for Globalization and Governance at Princeton University before coming to Davis. Her research interests lie in the study of international cooperation and international negotiations. She is the author of *State Strategies in International Bargaining: Play by the Rules or Change Them?* as well as multiple academic articles.

GUIDE TO THIS READER

Many of the selections included here are reprinted in their entirety. A number have been excerpted from longer works. A * * * indicates that word(s) or sentence(s) are omitted. A ■ ■ ■ indicates that paragraph(s) or section(s) are omitted. Brackets indicate text added by the editors for purposes of clarification. Complete bibliographic citations are included at the bottom of the first page of each selection. Readers who desire to delve deeper into the source material are encouraged to pursue these citations as well as those cited in the readings.

1 | APPROACHES TO INTERNATIONAL RELATIONS

In *Essentials of International Relations*, Ninth Edition, Karen A. Mingst and Heather Elko McKibben introduce theories and approaches used to study international relations. The readings in this section of *Essential Readings in World Politics* complement that introduction.

Many of the conceptual approaches that shape international relations thinking today have a long track record. Thucydides (460 BCE–c.395 BCE), in his history of the Peloponnesian War, presents a classic dialogue between Athenian imperialists and their Melian victims. The two sides debate the place of power and principle in international relations. The leaders of Melos ponder the fate of the island, deciding whether to risk defying the Athenians, and whether they can rely on the enemy of Athens, the Lacedaemonians (also known as Spartans), for protection. Today's "realist" school of thought views Thucydides as the founder of their intellectual lineage. They frequently quote his statement that the devastating Peloponnesian War was caused by the rising power of Athens and the fear it inspired in Sparta. Harvard's Graham Allison recently popularized the relevance of this to the rising power of contemporary China and the fear it inspires in the United States, calling this "the Thucydides trap." But it is not only realists who look back to Thucydides for insight. "Constructivist" scholars such as Alexander Wendt, Theodore Hopf, and Ned Lebow, who believe that international relations is constructed not only out of the raw facts of power but from persuasive discourse between countries, point out that the Melian dialogue is indeed an attempt at persuasion.

Thomas Hobbes's *Leviathan*, published in 1651 at the time of the English Civil War, explains how fear and greed lead to endemic conflict in situations of anarchy, where there is no sovereign power to provide protection and enforce laws. This work expresses the central insight of contemporary realists about the lack of an international sovereign as the root cause of war. This problem is often called "the security dilemma," a situation in which any effort by one state to increase its security will necessarily reduce the security of others.

Immanuel Kant's *Perpetual Peace*, published in 1795, foreshadows the key arguments of today's liberal approach to international relations theory: liberal states with representative governments are unlikely to fight wars against each other, because government policy is accountable to the average citizen who bears the costs of war. This creates the potential to form a cooperative league of liberal states, embodied nowadays in international organizations such as international economic institutions, the North Atlantic Treaty Organization, and the European Union, which were established to a large extent through the efforts of the liberal great powers.

Thucydides
MELIAN DIALOGUE

Introduction by Suresht Bald

It was the sixteenth year of the Peloponnesian War, but for the last six years the two great feuding empires headed by Athens and Sparta (Lacedaemon) had avoided open hostile action against each other. Ten years into the war they had signed a treaty of peace and friendship; however, this treaty did not dissipate the distrust that existed between them. Each feared the other's hegemonic designs on the Peloponnese and sought to increase its power to thwart the other's ambitions. Without openly attacking the other, each used persuasion, coercion, and subversion to strengthen itself and weaken its rival. This struggle for hegemony by Athens and Sparta was felt most acutely by small, hitherto "independent" states who were now being forced to take sides in the bipolar Greek world of the fifth century B.C. One such state was Melos.

Despite being one of the few island colonies of Sparta, Melos had remained neutral in the struggle between Sparta and Athens. Its neutrality, however, was unacceptable to the Athenians, who, accompanied by overwhelming military and naval power, arrived in Melos to pressure it into submission. After strategically positioning their powerful fleet, the Athenian generals sent envoys to Melos to negotiate the island's surrender.

The commissioners of Melos agreed to meet the envoys in private. They were afraid the Athenians, known for their rhetorical skills, might sway the people if allowed a public forum. The envoys came with an offer that if the Melians submitted and became part of the Athenian empire, their people and their possessions would not be harmed. The Melians argued that by the law of nations they had the right to remain neutral, and no nation had the right to attack without provocation. Having been a free state for seven hundred years they were not ready to give up that freedom. Thucydides captures the exchange between the Melian commissioners and the Athenian envoys:

* * * The Athenians * * * sent a fleet against the island of Melos. Thirty of the ships were their own, six were from Chios, and two were from Lesbos. Their own troops numbered twelve hundred hoplites, three hundred archers, and twenty mounted archers. There were also about fifteen hundred hoplites from their allies on the islands. The Melians are colonists from Sparta and would not submit to Athenian control like the other islanders. At first, they were neutral and lived peaceably, but they became openly hostile after Athens once tried to compel their obedience by ravaging their land. The generals Cleomedes, son of Lycomedes, and Tisias, son of Tisimachus, bivouacked on Melian territory with their troops, but before doing any injury to the land, they sent ambassadors to hold talks with the Melians. The Melian leadership, however, did not bring these men before the popular assembly. Instead, they asked them to discuss their mission with the council and the privileged voters. The Athenian ambassadors spoke as follows.

"We know that what you are thinking in bringing us before a few voters, and not before the popular assembly, is that now the people won't be deceived after listening to a single long, seductive, and unrefuted speech from us. Well, those of you who are sitting here can make things even safer

From Thucydides, *The Peloponnesian War,* trans. Walter Blanco, ed. Blanco and Jennifer Tolbert Roberts (New York: W. W. Norton, 1998). Introduction by Suresht Bald, Willamette University.

for yourselves. When we say something that seems wrong, interrupt immediately, and answer, not in a set speech, but one point at a time.—But say first whether this proposal is to your liking."

The Melian councillors said, "There can be no objection to the reasonableness of quiet, instructive talks among ourselves. But this military force, which is here, now, and not off in the future, looks different from instruction. We see that you have come as judges in a debate, and the likely prize will be war if we win the debate with arguments based on right and refuse to capitulate, or servitude if we concede to you."

ATHENIANS

Excuse us, but if you're having this meeting to make guesses about the future or to do anything but look at your situation and see how to save your city, we'll leave. But if that's the topic, we'll keep talking.

MELIANS

It's natural and understandable that in a situation like this, people would want to express their thoughts at length. But so be it. This meeting is about saving our city, and the format of the discussion will be as you have said.

ATHENIANS

Very well.

We Athenians are not going to use false pretenses and go on at length about how we have a right to rule because we destroyed the Persian empire, or about how we are seeking retribution because you did us wrong. You would not believe us anyway. And please do not suppose that you will persuade *us* when you say that you did not campaign with the Spartans although you were their colonists, or that you never did us wrong. No, each of us must exercise what power he really thinks he can, and we know and you know that in the human realm, justice is enforced only among those who can be equally constrained by it, and that those who have power use it, while the weak make compromises.

MELIANS

Since you have ruled out a discussion of justice and forced us to speak of expediency, it would be inexpedient, at least as we see it, for you to eradicate common decency. There has always been a fair and right way to treat people who are in danger, if only to give them some benefit for making persuasive arguments by holding off from the full exercise of power. This applies to you above all, since you would set an example for others of how to take the greatest vengeance if you fall.

ATHENIANS

We're not worried about the end of our empire, if it ever does end. People who rule over others, like the Spartans, are not so bad to their defeated enemies. Anyway, we're not fighting the Spartans just now. What is really horrendous is when subjects are able to attack and defeat their masters.—But you let us worry about all that. We are here to talk about benefiting our empire and saving your city, and we will tell you how we are going to do that, because we want to take control here without any trouble and we want you to be spared for both our sakes.

MELIANS

And just how would it be as much to our advantage to be enslaved, as for you to rule over us?

ATHENIANS

You would benefit by surrendering before you experience the worst of consequences, and we would benefit by not having you dead.

MELIANS

So you would not accept our living in peace, being friends instead of enemies, and allies of neither side?

ATHENIANS

Your hatred doesn't hurt us as much as your friendship. That would show us as weak to our other subjects, whereas your hatred would be a proof of our power.

MELIANS

Would your subjects consider you reasonable if you lumped together colonists who had no connection to you, colonists from Athens, and rebellious colonists who had been subdued?

ATHENIANS

They think there's justice all around. They also think the independent islands are strong, and that we are afraid to attack them. So aside from adding to our empire, your subjugation will also enhance our safety, especially since you are islanders and we are a naval power. Besides, you're weaker than the others—unless, that is, you show that you too can be independent.

MELIANS

Don't you think there's safety in our neutrality? You turned us away from a discussion of justice and persuaded us to attend to what was in your interest. Now it's up to us to tell you about what is to our advantage and to try to persuade you that it is also to yours. How will you avoid making enemies of states that are now neutral, but that look at what you do here and decide that you will go after them one day? How will you achieve anything but to make your present enemies seem more attractive, and to force those who had no intention of opposing you into unwilling hostility?

ATHENIANS

We do not think the threat to us is so much from mainlanders who, in their freedom from fear, will be continually putting off their preparations against us, as from independent islanders, like you, and from those who are already chafing under the restraints of rule. These are the ones who are most likely to commit themselves to ill-considered action and create foreseeable dangers for themselves and for us.

MELIANS

Well then, in the face of this desperate effort you and your slaves are making, you to keep your empire and they to get rid of it, wouldn't we, who are still free, be the lowest of cowards if we didn't try everything before submitting to slavery?

ATHENIANS

No, not if you think about it prudently. This isn't a contest about manly virtue between equals, or about bringing disgrace on yourself. You are deliberating about your very existence, about standing up against a power far greater than yours.

MELIANS

But we know that there are times when the odds in warfare don't depend on the numbers. If we give up, our situation becomes hopeless right away, but if we fight, we can still hope to stand tall.

ATHENIANS

In times of danger, hope is a comfort that can hurt you, but it won't destroy you if you back it up with plenty of other resources. People who gamble everything on it (hope is extravagant by nature, you see) know it for what it really is only after they have lost everything. Then, of course, when you can recognize it and take precautions, it's left you flat. You don't want to experience that. You Melians are weak, and you only have one chance. So don't be like all those people who could have saved themselves by their own efforts, but who abandoned their realistic hopes and turned in their hour of need to invisible powers—to prophecies and oracles and all the other nonsense that conspires with hope to ruin you.

MELIANS

As you well know, we too think it will be hard to fight both your power and the fortunes of war, especially with uneven odds. Still, we believe that our fortune comes from god, and that we will not be defeated because we take our stand as righteous men against men who are in the wrong. And what we lack in power will be made up for by the Spartan League. They will have to help us, if only because of our kinship with them and the disgrace they would feel if they didn't. So it's not totally irrational for us to feel hopeful.

ATHENIANS

Well, when it comes to divine good will, we don't think we'll be left out. We're not claiming anything or doing anything outside man's thinking about the gods or about the way the gods themselves behave. Given what we believe about the gods and know about men, we think that both are always forced by the law of nature to dominate everyone they can. We didn't lay down this law, it was there—and we weren't the first to make use of it. We took it as it was and acted on it, and we will bequeath it as a living thing to future generations, knowing full well that if you or anyone else had the same power as we, you would do the same thing. So we probably don't have to fear any disadvantage when it comes to the gods. And as to this opinion of yours about the Spartans, that you can trust them to help you because of their fear of disgrace—well, our blessings on your innocence, but we don't envy your foolishness. The Spartans do the right thing among themselves, according to their local customs. One could say a great deal about their treatment of others, but to put it briefly, they are more conspicuous than anyone else we know in thinking that pleasure is good and expediency is just. Their mindset really bears no relation to your irrational belief that there is any safety for you now.

MELIANS

But it's exactly because of this expediency that we trust them. They won't want to betray the Melians, their colonists, and prove themselves helpful to their enemies and unreliable to their well-wishers in Greece.

ATHENIANS

But don't you see that expediency is safe, and that doing the right and honorable thing is dangerous? On the whole, the Spartans are the last people to take big risks.

MELIANS

We think they'll take on dangers for us that they wouldn't for others and regard those dangers as less risky, because we are close to the Peloponnese from an operational point of view. Also, they can trust our loyalty because we are kin and we think alike.

ATHENIANS

Men who ask others to come to fight on their side don't offer security in good will but in real fighting power. The Spartans take this kind of thing more into consideration than others, because they have so little faith in their own resources that they even attack their neighbors with plenty of allies. So it's not likely that they'll try to make their way over to an island when we control the sea.

MELIANS

Then maybe they'll send their allies. The sea of Crete is large, and it is harder for those who control the sea to catch a ship than it is for the ship to get through to safety without being noticed. And if that doesn't work, they might turn against your territory or attack the rest of your allies, the ones Brasidas didn't get to. And then the fight would shift from a place where you have no interest to your own land and that of your allies.

ATHENIANS

It's been tried and might even be tried for you—though surely you are aware that we Athenians have never abandoned a siege out of fear of anyone.

But it occurs to us that after saying you were going to talk about saving yourselves, you haven't in any of this lengthy discussion mentioned anything that most people would rely on for their salvation. Your strongest arguments are in the future and depend on hope. What you've actually got is too meager to give you a chance of surviving the forces lined up against you now. You've shown a very irrational attitude—unless, of course, you intend to reach some more prudent conclusion than this after you send us away and begin your deliberations. For surely you don't mean to commit yourselves to that "honor" which has been so destructive to men in clear and present dangers involving "dishonor." Many men who could still see where it was leading them have been drawn on by the allure of this so-called "honor," this word with its seductive power, and fallen with open eyes into irremediable catastrophe, vanquished in their struggle with a fine word, only to achieve a kind of dishonorable honor because they weren't just unlucky, they were fools. You can avoid this, if you think things over carefully, and decide that there is nothing so disgraceful in being defeated by the greatest city in the world, which invites you to become its ally on fair terms—paying us tribute, to be sure, but keeping your land for yourselves. You have been given the choice between war and security. Don't be stubborn and make the wrong choice. The people who are most likely to succeed stand up to their equals, have the right attitude towards their superiors, and are fair to those beneath them.

We will leave now. Think it over, and always remember that you are making a decision about your country. You only have one, and its existence depends on this one chance to make a decision, right or wrong.

Then the Athenians withdrew from the discussion. The Melians, left to themselves, came to the conclusion that had been implied by their responses in the talks. They answered the Athenians as follows: "Men of Athens, our decision is no different from what it was at first. We will not in this brief moment strip the city we have lived in for seven hundred years of its freedom. We will try to save it, trusting in the divine good fortune that has preserved us so far and in the help we expect from the Spartans and from others. We invite you to be our friends, to let us remain neutral, and to leave our territory after making a treaty agreeable to us both."

That was the Melian response. The talks were already breaking up when the Athenians said, "Well, judging from this decision, you seem to us to be the only men who can make out the future more clearly than what you can see, and who gaze upon the invisible with your mind's eye as if it were an accomplished fact. You have cast yourselves on luck, hope, and the Spartans, and the more you trust in them, the harder will be your fall."

Then the Athenian envoys returned to the camp. Since the Melians would not submit, the Athenian generals immediately took offensive action and, after dividing their men according to the cities they came from, began to build a wall around Melos. Later the Athenians left a garrison of their own and allied men to guard the land and sea routes and then withdrew with most of their army. The men who were left behind remained there and carried on the siege.

At about this same time, the Argives invaded the territory of Phlius, where they fell into an ambush set by the Phliasians and the Argive exiles, who killed about eighty of them. The Athenian raiders on Pylos took a great deal of booty from Spartan territory, but despite even this, the Spartans did not renounce the treaty and declare war. They did, however, announce that if any of their people wished to raid Athenian territory, they could do so. The Corinthians made war on the Athenians over some private quarrels, but the rest of the Peloponnesians held their peace. The Melians staged a night attack on the part of the Athenian wall opposite their market and captured it. They killed some men and withdrew into the city carrying grain and as many other useful provisions as they could, taking no further action. The Athenians kept a better watch from then on. And so the summer came to an end.

The following winter, the Spartans were about to march into Argive territory, but the omens from sacrifices made before crossing the border were unfavorable and they turned back. This balked expedition led the Argives to suspect some of their citizens. They arrested some, but others managed to escape. At about the same time, the Melians again captured yet another part of the Athenian wall when only a few men were on guard duty. Because of this, another contingent later came from Athens, under the command of Philocrates, son of Demeas. By now, the Melians were completely cut off, and there were traitors within the city itself. So, on their own initiative, they agreed to terms whereby the Athenians could do with them as they liked. The Athenians thereupon killed all the males of fighting age they could capture and sold the women and children into slavery. The Athenians then occupied the place themselves and later sent out five hundred colonists.

Thomas Hobbes
FROM *LEVIATHAN*

Of the NATURAL CONDITION *of Mankind, as Concerning Their Felicity, and Misery*

Nature hath made men so equal, in the faculties of body, and mind; as that though there be found one man sometimes manifestly stronger in body, or of quicker mind then another; yet when all is reckoned together, the difference between man, and man, is not so considerable, as that one man can thereupon claim to himself any benefit, to which another may not pretend, as well as he. For as to the strength of body, the weakest has strength enough to kill the strongest, either by secret machination, or by confederacy with others, that are in the same danger with himself.

And as to the faculties of the mind (setting aside the arts grounded upon words, and especially that skill of proceeding upon general, and infallible rules, called science; which very few have, and but in few things; as being not a native faculty, born with us; nor attained, (as prudence), while we look after somewhat else), I find yet a greater equality amongst men, than that of strength. For prudence, is but experience; which equal time, equally bestowes on all men, in those things they equally apply themselves unto. That which may perhaps make such equality incredible, is but a vain conceit of one's own wisdom, which almost all men think they have in a greater degree, than the vulgar; that is, than all men but themselves, and a few

others, whom by fame, or for concurring with themselves, they approve. For such is the nature of men, that howsoever they may acknowledge many others to be more witty, or more eloquent, or more learned; yet they will hardly believe there be many so wise as themselves: for they see their own wit at hand, and other men's at a distance. But this proveth rather that men are in that point equal, than unequal. For there is not ordinarily a greater sign of the equal distribution of any thing, than that every man is contented with his share.

From this equality of ability, ariseth equality of hope in the attaining of our ends. And therefore if any two men desire the same thing, which nevertheless they cannot both enjoy, they become enemies; and in the way to their end (which is principally their own conservation, and sometimes their delectation only), endeavour to destroy, or subdue one an other. And from hence it comes to pass, that, where an invader hath no more to fear, than an other man's single power; if one plant, sow, build, or possess a convenient seat, others may probably be expected to come prepared with forces united, to dispossess, and deprive him, not only of the fruit of his labour, but also of his life, or liberty. And the invader again is in the like danger of another.

And from this diffidence of one another, there is no way for any man to secure himself, so reasonable, as anticipation; that is, by force, or wiles, to master the persons of all men he can, so long, till he see no other power great enough to endanger him: And this is no more than his own conservation requireth, and is generally allowed. Also because there be some, that taking pleasure in contemplating their own power in the acts of

From Thomas Hobbes, *Leviathan* (1651), ed. A. R. Waller (Cambridge: Cambridge University Press, 1904), 81–86. This excerpt has been edited to contemporary spelling and capitalization.

conquest, which they pursue farther than their security requires; if others, that otherwise would be glad to be at ease within modest bounds, should not by invasion increase their power, they would not be able, long time, by standing only on their defence, to subsist. And by consequence, such augmentation of dominion over men, being necessary to a man's conservation, it ought to be allowed him.

Again, men have no pleasure (but on the contrary a great deal of grief) in keeping company, where there is no power able to over-awe them all. For every man looketh that his companion should value him, at the same rate he sets upon himself: And upon all signs of contempt, or undervaluing, naturally endeavours, as far as he dares (which amongst them that have no common power to keep them in quiet, is far enough to make them destroy each other), to extort a greater value from his contemners, by dommage; and from others, by the example.

So that in the nature of man, we find three principal causes of quarrel. First, competition; secondly, diffidence; thirdly, glory.

The first, maketh men invade for gain; the second, for safety; and the third, for reputation. The first use violence, to make themselves masters of other men's persons, wives, children, and cattle; the second, to defend them; the third, for trifles, as a word, a smile, a different opinion, and any other sign of undervalue, either direct in their persons, or by reflexion in their kindred, their friends, their nation, their profession, or their name.

Hereby it is manifest, that during the time men live without a common power to keep them all in awe, they are in that condition which is called war; and such a war, as is of every man, against every man. For WAR, consisteth not in battle only, or the act of fighting; but in a tract of time, wherein the will to contend by battle is sufficiently known: and therefore the notion of *time,* is to be considered in the nature of war; as it is in the nature of weather. For as the nature of foul weather, lyeth not in a shower or two of rain; but in an inclination thereto of many days together; So the nature of war, consisteth not in actual fighting; but in the known disposition thereto, during all the *time* there is no assurance to the contrary. All other time is PEACE.

Whatsoever therefore is consequent to a time of war, where every man is enemy to every man; the same is consequent to the time, wherein men live without other security, than what their own strength, and their own invention shall furnish them withal. In such condition, there is no place for industry; because the fruit thereof is uncertain: and consequently no culture of the earth; no navigation, nor use of the commodities that may be imported by sea; no commodious building; no instruments of moving, and removing such things as require much force; no knowledge of the face of the earth; no account of time; no arts; no letters; no society; and which is worst of all, continual fear, and danger of violent death; And the life of man, solitary, poor, nasty, brutish, and short.

It may seem strange to some man, that has not well weighed these things; that nature should thus dissociate, and render men apt to invade, and destroy one another: and he may therefore, not trusting to this inference, made from the passions, desire perhaps to have the same confirmed by experience. Let him therefore consider with himself, when taking a journey, he arms himself, and seeks to go well accompanied; when going to sleep, he locks his doors; when even in his house he locks his chests; and this when he knows there be laws, and public officers, armed, to revenge all injuries shall be done him; what opinion he has of his fellow subjects, when he rides armed; of his fellow citizens, when he locks his doors; and of his children, and servants, when he locks his chests. Does he not there as much accuse mankind by his actions, as I do by my words? But neither of us accuse man's nature in it. The desires, and other passions of man, are in themselves no sin. No more are the actions, that proceed from those passions, till they know a law that forbids them: which till laws be made they cannot know: nor can any law be made, till they have agreed upon the person that shall make it.

It may peradventure be thought, there was never such a time, nor condition of war as this; and I believe it was never generally so, over all the world: but there are many places, where they live so now. For the savage people in many places of *America,* except the government of small families, the concord whereof dependeth on natural lust, have no government at all; and live at this day in that brutish manner, as I said before. Howsoever, it may be perceived what manner of life there would be, where there were no common power to fear; by the manner of life, which men that have formerly lived under a peaceful government, use to degenerate into, in a civil war.

But though there had never been any time, wherein particular men were in a condition of war one against another; yet in all times, kings, and persons of sovereign authority, because of their independency, are in continual jealousies, and in the state and posture of gladiators; having their weapons pointing, and their eyes fixed on one another; that is, their forts, garrisons, and guns upon the frontiers of their kingdoms, and continual spies upon their neighbours; which is a posture of war. But because they uphold thereby, the industry of their subjects; there does not follow from it,

that misery, which accompanies the liberty of particular men.

To this war of every man against every man, this also is consequent; that nothing can be unjust. The notions of right and wrong, justice and injustice have there no place. Where there is no common power, there is no law: where no law, no injustice. Force, and fraud, are in war, the two cardinal virtues. Justice, and injustice are none of the faculties neither of the body, nor mind. If they were, they might be in a man that were alone in the world, as well as his senses, and passions. They are qualities, that relate to men in society, not in solitude. It is consequent also to the same condition, that there be no propriety, no dominion, no *mine* and *thine* distinct; but only that to be every man's, that he can get; and for so long, as he can keep it. And thus much for the ill condition, which man by mere nature is actually placed in; though with a possibility to come out of it, consisting partly in the passions, partly in his reason.

The passions that incline men to peace, are fear of death; desire of such things as are necessary to commodious living; and a hope by their industry to obtain them. And reason suggesteth convenient articles of peace, upon which men may be drawn to agreement. These articles, are they, which otherwise are called the laws of nature. * * *

Immanuel Kant

FROM *PERPETUAL PEACE*

The state of peace among men living in close proximity is not the natural state * * *; instead, the natural state is a one of war, which does not just consist in open hostilities, but also in the constant and enduring threat of them. The state of peace must therefore be *established,* for the suspension of hostilities does not provide the security of peace, and unless this security is pledged by one neighbor to another (which can happen only in a state of *lawfulness*), the latter, from whom such security has been requested, can treat the former as an enemy.

First Definitive Article of Perpetual Peace: The Civil Constitution of Every Nation Should Be Republican

The sole established constitution that follows from the idea * * * of an original contract, the one on which all of a nation's just * * * legislation must be based, is republican. For, first, it accords with the principles of the *freedom* of the members of a society (as men), second, it accords with the principles of the *dependence* of everyone on a single, common [source of] legislation (as subjects), and third, it accords with the law of the equality of them all (as citizens). Thus, so far as [the matter of] right is concerned, republicanism is the original foundation of all forms of civil constitution. Thus, the only question remaining is this, does it also provide the only foundation for perpetual peace?

Now in addition to the purity of its origin, a purity whose source is the pure concept of right, the republican constitution also provides for this desirable result, namely, perpetual peace, and the reason for this is as follows: If (as must inevitably be the case, given this form of constitution) the consent of the citizenry is required in order to determine whether or not there will be war, it is natural that they consider all its calamities before committing themselves to so risky a game. (Among these are doing the fighting themselves, paying the costs of war from their own resources, having to repair at great sacrifice the war's devastation, and, finally, the ultimate evil that would make peace itself better, never being able—because of new and constant wars—to expunge the burden of debt.) By contrast, under a nonrepublican constitution, where subjects are not citizens, the easiest thing in the world to do is to declare war. Here the ruler is not a fellow citizen, but the nation's owner, and war does not affect his table, his hunt, his places of pleasure, his court festivals, and so on. Thus, he can decide to go to war for the most meaningless of reasons, as if it were a kind of pleasure party, and he can blithely leave its justification (which decency requires) to his diplomatic corps, who are always prepared for such exercises.

From Immanuel Kant, *Perpetual Peace [1795] and Other Essays on Politics, History, and Morals,* trans. Ted Humphrey (Indianapolis: Hackett Publishing Co., 1983), 107–17. The author's notes have been omitted.

Second Definitive Article for a Perpetual Peace: The Right of Nations Shall Be Based on a Federation of Free States

As nations, peoples can be regarded as single individuals who injure one another through their close proximity while living in the state of nature (i.e., independently of external laws). For the sake of its own security, each nation can and should demand that the others enter into a contract resembling the civil one and guaranteeing the rights of each. This would be a federation *of nations,* but it must not be a nation consisting of nations. The latter would be contradictory, for in every nation there exists the relation of *ruler* (legislator) to *subject* (those who obey, the people); however, many nations in a single nation would constitute only a single nation, which contradicts our assumption (since we are here weighing the rights of *nations* in relation to one another, rather than fusing them into a single nation).

Just as we view with deep disdain the attachment of savages to their lawless freedom—preferring to scuffle without end rather than to place themselves under lawful restraints that they themselves constitute, consequently preferring a mad freedom to a rational one—and consider it barbarous, rude, and brutishly degrading of humanity, so also should we think that civilized peoples (each one united into a nation) would hasten as quickly as possible to escape so similar a state of abandonment. Instead, however, each *nation* sees its majesty * * * to consist in not being subject to any external legal constraint, and the glory of its ruler consists in being able, without endangering himself, to command many thousands to sacrifice themselves for a matter that does not concern them. * * *

Given the depravity of human nature, which is revealed and can be glimpsed in the free relations among nations (though deeply concealed by governmental restraints in law governed civil-society), one must wonder why the word *right* has not been completely discarded from the politics of war as pedantic, or why no nation has openly ventured to declare that it should be. For while Hugo Grotius, Pufendorf, Vattel, and others whose philosophically and diplomatically formulated codes do not and cannot have the slightest legal force (since nations do not stand under any common external constraints), are always piously cited in justification of a war of aggression (and who therefore provide only cold comfort), no example can be given of a nation having foregone its intention [of going to war] based on the arguments provided by such important men. The homage that every nation pays (at least in words) to the concept of right proves, nonetheless, that there is in man a still greater, though presently dormant, moral aptitude to master the evil principle in himself (a principle he cannot deny) and to hope that others will also overcome it. For otherwise the word *right* would never leave the mouths of those nations that want to make war on one another, unless it were used mockingly, as when that Gallic prince declared, "Nature has given the strong the prerogative of making the weak obey them."

Nations can press for their rights only by waging war and never in a trial before an independent tribunal, but war and its favorable consequence, victory, cannot determine the right. And although a *treaty of peace* can put an end to some particular war, it cannot end the state of war (the tendency always to find a new pretext for war). (And this situation cannot straightforwardly be declared unjust, since in this circumstance each nation is judge of its own case.) * * * Nonetheless, from the throne of its moral legislative power, reason absolutely condemns war as a means of determining the right and makes seeking the state of peace a matter of unmitigated duty. But without a contract among nations peace can be neither inaugurated nor guaranteed. A league of a special sort must therefore be established, one that we can call a *league of peace (foedus pacificum)*, which will be distinguished from a *treaty of peace (pactum pacis)* because the latter seeks merely to stop *one* war, while the former seeks to end *all* wars forever. This league does not seek any power of the sort possessed by nations, but only the maintenance and security of each nation's own freedom, as well as that of the other nations leagued with it, without their having thereby to subject themselves to civil laws and their constraints (as men in the state of nature must do). It can be shown that this *idea of federalism* should eventually include all nations and thus lead to perpetual peace. For if good fortune should so dispose matters that a powerful and enlightened people should form a republic (which by its nature must be inclined to seek perpetual peace), it will provide a focal point for a federal association among other nations that will join it in order to guarantee a state of peace among nations that is in accord with the idea of the right of nations, and through several associations of this sort such a federation can extend further and further.

2

HISTORICAL CONTEXT

Core ideas about international politics, introduced in Chapter 2 of *Essentials of International Relations*, Ninth Edition, have emerged as responses to historic diplomatic challenges. The selections in this chapter were written at historical and intellectual turning points over the past century: the end of World War I, the end of the Cold War, and what is often called "the crisis of liberalism" attendant to the rise of China and of nationalist populism in the West. These events spawned many of the ideas and trends that still shape debates about contemporary international politics.

The post–World War I peace process led to a clear statement of the liberal perspective. The Fourteen Points, as described by U.S. president Woodrow Wilson in an address to Congress in January 1918, summarized some of the key ideas of liberal theory. Wilson blamed power politics, secret diplomacy, and autocratic leaders for the devastating world war. He suggested that the spread of democracy and the creation of a "league of nations" could stop aggression.

At the end of the Cold War in 1989, Francis Fukuyama published a controversial essay, "The End of History?," speculating whether the victory of liberal ideas over communism and fascism had left no significant rival ideology in sight. Samuel Huntington, in what is probably the most discussed essay on world politics in recent decades, begged to differ: he foresaw the emergence of a "clash of civilizations" pitting "the West against the rest." In Huntington's subsequent book, *The Clash of Civilizations and the Remaking of World Order* (1996), he somewhat modified his earlier claim, acknowledging that conflicts within civilizations remained more common than conflicts between them. Despite criticism from many scholarly experts and political analysts, his thesis attracted huge attention, seemed relevant in an era of rising terrorist attacks, and appealed even to some non-Westerners, such as Chinese nationalists who agreed that a clash of civilizations was coming.

A key question for the future is whether the rise of illiberal China represents a new ideological rival to liberalism based on the principles of national sovereignty, mercantilist economic strategies, cultural conservatism, and authoritarian politics. If so, will these principles attract adherents among other rising powers? Is history beginning again? The final selection by G. John Ikenberry on contemporary challenges facing the liberal international order asks whether the world is again at a decisive turning point.

Woodrow Wilson
THE FOURTEEN POINTS

It will be our wish and purpose that the processes of peace, when they are begun, shall be absolutely open and that they shall involve and permit henceforth no secret understandings of any kind. The day of conquest and aggrandizement is gone by; so is also the day of secret covenants entered into in the interest of particular governments and likely at some unlooked-for moment to upset the peace of the world. It is this happy fact, now clear to the view of every public man whose thoughts do not still linger in an age that is dead and gone, which makes it possible for every nation whose purposes are consistent with justice and the peace of the world to avow now or at any other time the objects it has in view.

We entered this war because violations of right had occurred which touched us to the quick and made the life of our own people impossible unless they were corrected and the world secured once and for all against their recurrence. What we demand in this war, therefore, is nothing peculiar to ourselves. It is that the world be made fit and safe to live in; and particularly that it be made safe for every peace-loving nation which, like our own, wishes to live its own life, determine its own institutions, be assured of justice and fair dealing by the other people of the world as against force and selfish aggression. All the peoples of the world are in effect partners in this interest, and for our own part we see very clearly that unless justice be done to others it will not be done to us. The program of the world's peace, therefore, is our program; and that program, the only possible program, as we see it, is this:

I. Open covenants of peace, openly arrived at, after which there shall be no private international understandings of any kind but diplomacy shall proceed always frankly and in the public view.

II. Absolute freedom of navigation upon the seas, outside territorial waters, alike in peace and in war, except as the seas may be closed in whole or in part by international action for the enforcement of international covenants

III. The removal, so far as possible, of all economic barriers and the establishment of an equality of trade conditions among all the nations consenting to the peace and associating themselves for its maintenance.

IV. Adequate guarantees given and taken that national armaments will be reduced to the lowest point consistent with domestic safety.

V. A free, open-minded, and absolutely impartial adjustment of all colonial claims, based upon a strict observance of the principle that in determining all such questions of sovereignty the interests of the populations concerned must have equal weight with the equitable claims of the government whose title is to be determined.

VI. The evacuation of all Russian territory and such a settlement of all questions affecting Russia as will secure the best and freest cooperation of the other nations of the world in obtaining for her an unhampered

From Woodrow Wilson's address to the U.S. Congress, January 8, 1918.

and unembarrassed opportunity for the independent determination of her own political development and national policy and assure her of a sincere welcome into the society of free nations under institutions of her own choosing; and, more than a welcome, assistance also of every kind that she may need and may herself desire. The treatment accorded Russia by her sister nations in the months to come will be the acid test of their good will, of their comprehension of her needs as distinguished from their own interests, and of their intelligent and unselfish sympathy.

VII. Belgium, the whole world will agree, must be evacuated and restored, without any attempt to limit the sovereignty which she enjoys in common with all other free nations. No other single act will serve as this will serve to restore confidence among the nations in the laws which they have themselves set and determined for the government of their relations with one another. Without this healing act the whole structure and validity of international law is forever impaired.

VIII. All French territory should be freed and the invaded portions restored, and the wrong done to France by Prussia in 1871 in the matter of Alsace-Lorraine, which has unsettled the peace of the world for nearly fifty years, should be righted, in order that peace may once more be made secure in the interest of all.

IX. A readjustment of the frontiers of Italy should be effected along clearly recognizable lines of nationality.

X. The peoples of Austria-Hungary, whose place among the nations we wish to see safeguarded and assured, should be accorded the freest opportunity of autonomous development.

XI. Rumania, Serbia, and Montenegro should be evacuated; occupied territories restored; Serbia accorded free and secure access to the sea; and the relations of the several Balkan states to one another determined by friendly counsel along historically established lines of allegiance and nationality; and international guarantees of the political and economic independence and territorial integrity of the several Balkan states should be entered into.

XII. The Turkish portions of the present Ottoman Empire should be assured a secure sovereignty, but the other nationalities which are now under Turkish rule should be assured an undoubted security of life and an absolutely unmolested opportunity of autonomous development, and the Dardanelles should be permanently opened as a free passage to the ships and commerce of all nations under international guarantees.

XIII. An independent Polish state should be erected which should include the territories inhabited by indisputably Polish populations, which should be assured a free and secure access to the sea, and whose political and economic independence and territorial integrity should be guaranteed by international covenant.

XIV. A general association of nations must be formed under specific covenants for the purpose of affording mutual guarantees of political independence and territorial integrity to great and small states alike.

In regard to these essential rectifications of wrong and assertions of right we feel ourselves to be intimate partners of all the governments and peoples associated together against the imperialists. We cannot be separated in interest or divided in purpose. We stand together until the end.

For such arrangements and covenants we are willing to fight and to continue to fight until they are achieved; but only because we wish the right to prevail and desire a just and stable peace such as can be secured only by removing the chief provocations to war, which this program does remove. We have no jealousy of German greatness, and there is nothing in this program that impairs it. We grudge her no achievement or distinction of learning or of pacific enterprise such as have made her record very bright and very enviable. We do not wish to injure her or to block in any way her legitimate influence or power. We do not wish to fight her either with arms or with hostile arrangements of trade if she is willing to associate herself with us and the other peace-loving nations of the world in covenants of justice and law and fair dealing. We wish her only to accept a place of equality among the peoples of the world—the new world in which we now live—instead of a place of mastery.

Neither do we presume to suggest to her any alteration or modification of her institutions. But it is necessary, we must frankly say, and necessary as a preliminary to any intelligent dealings with her on our part, that we should know whom her spokesmen speak for when they speak to us, whether for the Reichstag majority or for the military party and the men whose creed is imperial domination.

We have spoken now, surely, in terms too concrete to admit of any further doubt or question. An evident principle runs through the whole program I have outlined. It is the principle of justice to all peoples and nationalities, and their right to live on equal terms of liberty and safety with one another, whether they be strong or weak. Unless this principle be made its foundation no part of the structure of international justice can stand. The people of the United States could act upon no other principle; and to the vindication of this principle they are ready to devote their lives, their honor, and everything that they possess. The moral climax of this the culminating and final war for human liberty has come, and they are ready to put their own strength, their own highest purpose, their own integrity and devotion to the test.

Francis Fukuyama
THE END OF HISTORY?

In watching the flow of events over the past decade or so, it is hard to avoid the feeling that something very fundamental has happened in world history. The past year has seen a flood of articles commemorating the end of the Cold War, and the fact that "peace" seems to be breaking out in many regions of the world. Most of these analyses lack any larger conceptual framework for distinguishing between what is essential and what is contingent or accidental in world history, and are predictably superficial. If Mr. Gorbachev were ousted from the Kremlin or a new Ayatollah proclaimed the millennium from a desolate Middle Eastern capital, these same commentators would scramble to announce the rebirth of a new era of conflict.

And yet, all of these people sense dimly that there is some larger process at work, a process that gives coherence and order to the daily headlines. The twentieth century saw the developed world descend into a paroxysm of ideological violence, as liberalism contended first with the remnants of absolutism, then bolshevism and fascism, and finally an updated Marxism that threatened to lead to the ultimate apocalypse of nuclear war. But the century that began full of self-confidence in the ultimate triumph of Western liberal democracy seems at its close to be returning full circle to where it started: not to an "end of ideology" or a convergence between capitalism and socialism, as earlier predicted, but to an unabashed victory of economic and political liberalism.

The triumph of the West, of the Western *idea*, is evident first of all in the total exhaustion of viable systematic alternatives to Western liberalism. In the past decade, there have been unmistakable changes in the intellectual climate of the world's two largest communist countries, and the beginnings of significant reform movements in both. But this phenomenon extends beyond high politics and it can be seen also in the ineluctable spread of consumerist Western culture in such diverse contexts as the peasants' markets and color television sets now omnipresent throughout China, the cooperative restaurants and clothing stores opened in the past year in Moscow, the Beethoven piped into Japanese department stores, and the rock music enjoyed alike in Prague, Rangoon, and Tehran.

What we may be witnessing is not just the end of the Cold War, or the passing of a particular period of postwar history, but the end of history as such: that is, the end point of mankind's ideological evolution and the universalization of Western liberal democracy as the final form of human government. This is not to say that there will no longer be events to fill the pages of *Foreign Affairs*'s yearly summaries of international relations, for the victory of liberalism has occurred primarily in the realm of ideas or consciousness and is as yet incomplete in the real or material world. But there are powerful reasons for believing that it is the ideal that will govern the material world *in the long run*. To understand how this is so, we must first consider some theoretical issues concerning the nature of historical change.

I

The notion of the end of history is not an original one. Its best known propagator was Karl Marx,

From *The National Interest* 16 (Summer 1989): 3–18. Some of the author's notes have been omitted.

who believed that the direction of historical development was a purposeful one determined by the interplay of material forces, and would come to an end only with the achievement of a communist Utopia that would finally resolve all prior contradictions. But the concept of history as a dialectical process with a beginning, a middle, and an end was borrowed by Marx from his great German predecessor, Georg Wilhelm Friedrich Hegel.

For better or worse, much of Hegel's historicism has become part of our contemporary intellectual baggage. The notion that mankind has progressed through a series of primitive stages of consciousness on his path to the present, and that these stages corresponded to concrete forms of social organization, such as tribal, slave-owning, theocratic, and finally democratic-egalitarian societies, has become inseparable from the modern understanding of man. Hegel was the first philosopher to speak the language of modern social science, insofar as man for him was the product of his concrete historical and social environment and not, as earlier natural right theorists would have it, a collection of more or less fixed "natural" attributes. The mastery and transformation of man's natural environment through the application of science and technology was originally not a Marxist concept, but a Hegelian one. Unlike later historicists whose historical relativism degenerated into relativism *tout court*, however, Hegel believed that history culminated in an absolute moment—a moment in which a final, rational form of society and state became victorious.

It is Hegel's misfortune to be known now primarily as Marx's precursor, and it is our misfortune that few of us are familiar with Hegel's work from direct study, but only as it has been filtered through the distorting lens of Marxism. In France, however, there has been an effort to save Hegel from his Marxist interpreters and to resurrect him as the philosopher who most correctly speaks to our time. Among those modern French interpreters of Hegel, the greatest was certainly Alexandre Kojève, a brilliant Russian emigre who taught a highly influential series of seminars in Paris in the 1930s at the *Ecole Practique des Hautes Etudes*.[1] While largely unknown in the United States, Kojève had a major impact on the intellectual life of the continent. Among his students ranged such future luminaries as Jean-Paul Sartre on the Left and Raymond Aron on the Right; postwar existentialism borrowed many of its basic categories from Hegel via Kojève.

Kojève sought to resurrect the Hegel of the *Phenomenology of Mind*, the Hegel who proclaimed history to be at an end in 1806. For as early as this Hegel saw in Napoleon's defeat of the Prussian monarchy at the Battle of Jena the victory of the ideals of the French Revolution, and the imminent universalization of the state incorporating the principles of liberty and equality. Kojève, far from rejecting Hegel in light of the turbulent events of the next century and a half, insisted that the latter had been essentially correct. The Battle of Jena marked the end of history because it was at that point that the *vanguard* of humanity (a term quite familiar to Marxists) actualized the principles of the French Revolution. While there was considerable work to be done after 1806—abolishing slavery and the slave trade, extending the franchise to workers, women, blacks, and other racial minorities, etc.— the basic *principles* of the liberal democratic state could not be improved upon. The two world wars in this century and their attendant revolutions and upheavals simply had the effect of extending those principles spatially, such that the various provinces of human civilization were brought up to the level of its most advanced outposts, and of forcing those societies in Europe and North America at the vanguard of civilization to implement their liberalism more fully.

The state that emerges at the end of history is liberal insofar as it recognizes and protects through a system of law man's universal right to freedom, and democratic insofar as it exists only with the consent of the governed. For Kojève, this so-called "universal homogenous state" found real-life embodiment in the countries of postwar Western Europe—precisely those flabby, prosperous, self-satisfied, inward-looking, weak-willed states whose grandest project was nothing more heroic than the creation of the Common Market. But this was only to be expected. For human history and the conflict that characterized it was based on the existence of "contradictions": primitive man's quest for mutual recognition, the dialectic of the master and slave, the transformation and mastery of nature, the struggle for the universal recognition of rights, and the dichotomy between proletarian and capitalist. But in the universal homogenous state, all prior contradictions are resolved and all human needs are satisfied. There is no struggle or conflict over "large" issues, and consequently no need for generals or statesmen; what remains is primarily economic activity. * * *

II

For Hegel, the contradictions that drive history exist first of all in the realm of human consciousness, i.e., on the level of ideas—not the trivial election year proposals of American politicians, but ideas in the sense of large unifying world views that might best be understood under the rubric of ideology. Ideology in this sense is not restricted to the secular and explicit political doctrines we usually associate with the term, but can include religion, culture, and the complex of moral values underlying any society as well.

■ ■ ■

For Hegel, all human behavior in the material world, and hence all human history, is rooted in a prior state of consciousness—an idea similar to the one expressed by John Maynard Keynes when he said that the views of men of affairs were usually derived from defunct economists and academic scribblers of earlier generations. * * *

Hegel's idealism has fared poorly at the hands of later thinkers. Marx reversed the priority of the real and the ideal completely, relegating the entire realm of consciousness—religion, art, culture, philosophy itself—to a "superstructure" that was determined entirely by the prevailing material mode of production. Yet another unfortunate legacy of Marxism is our tendency to retreat into materialist or utilitarian explanations of political or historical phenomena, and our disinclination to believe in the autonomous power of ideas. A recent example of this is Paul Kennedy's hugely successful *The Rise and Fall of the Great Powers,* which ascribes the decline of great powers to simple economic overextension. Obviously, this is true on some level: an empire whose economy is barely above the level of subsistence cannot bankrupt its treasury indefinitely. But whether a highly productive modern industrial society chooses to spend 3 or 7 percent of its GNP on defense rather than consumption is entirely a matter of that society's political priorities, which are in turn determined in the realm of consciousness.

■ ■ ■

III

Have we in fact reached the end of history? Are there, in other words, any fundamental "contradictions" in human life that cannot be resolved in the context of modern liberalism, that would be resolvable by an alternative political-economic structure? If we accept the idealist premises laid out above, we must seek an answer to this question in the realm of ideology and consciousness. Our task is not to answer exhaustively the challenges to liberalism promoted by every crackpot messiah around the world, but only those that are embodied in important social or political forces and movements, and which are therefore part of world history. For our purposes, it matters very little what strange thoughts occur to people in Albania or Burkina Faso, for we are interested in what one could in some sense call the common ideological heritage of mankind.

In the past century, there have been two major challenges to liberalism, those of fascism and of communism. The former saw the political weakness, materialism, anomie, and lack of community of the West as fundamental contradictions in liberal societies that could only be resolved by a strong state that forged a new "people" on the basis of national exclusiveness. Fascism was destroyed as a living ideology by World War II. This was a defeat, of course, on a very material level, but it amounted to a defeat of the idea as well. What destroyed fascism as an idea was not universal moral revulsion against it, since plenty of people were willing to endorse the idea as long as it seemed the wave of the future, but its lack of success. After the war, it seemed to most people that German fascism as well as its other European and Asian variants were bound to self-destruct. There was no material reason why new fascist movements could not have sprung up again after the war in other locales, but for the fact that expansionist ultranationalism, with its promise of unending conflict leading to disastrous military defeat, had completely lost its appeal. The ruins of the Reich chancellory as well as the atomic bombs dropped on Hiroshima and Nagasaki killed this ideology on the level of consciousness as well as materially, and all of the proto-fascist movements spawned by the German and Japanese examples like the Peronist movement in Argentina or Subhas Chandra Bose's Indian National Army withered after the war.

The ideological challenge mounted by the other great alternative to liberalism, communism, was far more serious. Marx, speaking Hegel's language, asserted that liberal society contained a fundamental contradiction that could not be resolved within its context, that between capital and labor, and this contradiction has constituted the chief accusation against liberalism ever since. But surely, the class issue has actually been successfully resolved in the West. As Kojève (among others) noted, the egalitarianism of modern America represents the essential achievement of the classless society envisioned by Marx. This is not to say that there are not rich people and poor people in the United States, or that the gap between them has not grown in recent years. But the root causes of economic inequality do not have to do with the underlying legal and social structure of our society, which remains fundamentally egalitarian and moderately redistributionist, so much as with the cultural and social characteristics of the groups that make it up, which are in turn the historical legacy of premodern conditions. Thus black poverty in the United States is not the inherent product of liberalism, but is rather the "legacy of slavery and racism" which persisted long after the formal abolition of slavery.

As a result of the receding of the class issue, the appeal of communism in the developed Western world, it is safe to say, is lower today than any time since the end of the First World War. This can be measured in any number of ways: in the declining membership and electoral pull of the major European communist parties, and their overtly revisionist programs; in the corresponding electoral success of conservative parties from Britain and Germany to the United States and Japan, which are unabashedly pro-market and antistatist; and in an intellectual climate whose most "advanced" members no longer believe that bourgeois society is something that ultimately needs to be overcome. This is not to say that the opinions of progressive intellectuals in Western countries are not deeply pathological in any number of ways. But those who believe that the future must inevitably be socialist tend to be very old, or very marginal to the real political discourse of their societies.

One may argue that the socialist alternative was never terribly plausible for the North Atlantic world, and was sustained for the last several decades primarily by its success outside of this region. But it is precisely in the non-European world that one is most struck by the occurrence of major ideological transformations. Surely the most remarkable changes have occurred in Asia. Due to the strength and adaptability of the indigenous cultures there, Asia became a battleground for a variety of imported Western ideologies early in this century. Liberalism in Asia was a very weak reed in the period after World War I; it is easy today to forget how gloomy Asia's political future looked as recently as ten or fifteen years ago. It is easy to forget as well how momentous the outcome of Asian ideological struggles seemed for world political development as a whole.

The first Asian alternative to liberalism to be decisively defeated was the fascist one represented by Imperial Japan. Japanese fascism (like its German version) was defeated by the force of American arms in the Pacific war, and liberal democracy was imposed on Japan by a victorious United States. Western capitalism and political liberalism when transplanted to Japan were adapted and transformed by the Japanese in such a way as to be scarcely recognizable. Many Americans are now aware that Japanese industrial organization is very different from that prevailing in the United States or Europe, and it is questionable what relationship the factional maneuvering that takes place with the governing Liberal Democratic Party bears to democracy. Nonetheless, the very fact that the essential elements of economic and political liberalism have been so successfully grafted onto uniquely Japanese traditions and institutions guarantees their survival in the long run. More important is the contribution that Japan has made in turn to world history by following in the footsteps of the United States to create a truly universal consumer culture that has become both a symbol and an underpinning of the universal homogenous state. V. S. Naipaul travelling in Khomeini's Iran shortly after the revolution noted the omnipresent signs advertising the products of Sony, Hitachi, and JVC, whose appeal remained virtually irresistible and gave the lie to the regime's pretensions of restoring a state based on the rule of the *Shariah*. Desire for access to the consumer culture, created in large measure by Japan, has played a crucial role in fostering the spread of economic liberalism throughout Asia, and hence in promoting political liberalism as well.

The economic success of the other newly industrializing countries (NICs) in Asia following on the example of Japan is by now a familiar story. What is important from a Hegelian standpoint is that political liberalism has been following economic liberalism, more slowly than many had hoped but with seeming inevitability. Here again we see the victory of the idea of the universal homogenous state. South Korea had developed into a modern, urbanized society with an increasingly large and well-educated middle class that could not possibly be isolated from the larger democratic trends around them. Under these circumstances it seemed intolerable to a large part of this population that it should be ruled by an anachronistic military regime while Japan, only a decade or so ahead in economic terms, had parliamentary institutions for over forty years. Even the former socialist regime in Burma, which for so many decades existed in dismal isolation from the larger trends dominating Asia, was buffeted in the past year by pressures to liberalize both its economy and political system. It is said that unhappiness with strongman Ne Win began when a senior Burmese officer went to Singapore for medical treatment and broke down crying when he saw how far socialist Burma had been left behind by its ASEAN neighbors.

But the power of the liberal idea would seem much less impressive if it had not infected the largest and oldest culture in Asia, China. The simple existence of communist China created an alternative pole of ideological attraction, and as such constituted a threat to liberalism. But the past fifteen years have seen an almost total discrediting of Marxism-Leninism as an economic system. Beginning with the famous third plenum of the Tenth Central Committee in 1978, the Chinese Communist party set about decollectivizing agriculture for the 800 million Chinese who still lived in the countryside. The role of the state in agriculture was reduced to that of a tax collector, while production of consumer goods was sharply increased in order to give peasants a taste of the universal homogenous state and thereby an incentive to work. The reform doubled Chinese grain output in only five years, and in the process created for Deng Xiao-ping a solid political base from which he was able to extend the reform to other parts of the economy. Economic statistics do not begin to describe the dynamism, initiative, and openness evident in China since the reform began.

China could not now be described in any way as a liberal democracy. At present, no more than 20 percent of its economy has been marketized, and most importantly it continues to be ruled by a self-appointed Communist party which has given no hint of wanting to devolve power. Deng has made none of Gorbachev's promises regarding democratization of the political system and there is no Chinese equivalent of *glasnost*. The Chinese leadership has in fact been much more circumspect in criticizing Mao and Maoism than Gorbachev with respect to Brezhnev and Stalin, and the regime continues to pay lip service to Marxism-Leninism as its ideological underpinning. But anyone familiar with the outlook and behavior of the new technocratic elite now governing China knows that Marxism and ideological principle have become virtually irrelevant as guides to policy, and that bourgeois consumerism has a real meaning in that country for the first time since the revolution. The various slowdowns in the pace of reform, the campaigns against "spiritual pollution" and crackdowns on political dissent are more properly seen as tactical adjustments made in the process of managing what is an extraordinarily difficult political transition. By ducking the question of political reform while putting the economy on a new footing, Deng has managed to avoid the breakdown of authority that has accompanied Gorbachev's *perestroika*. Yet the pull of the liberal idea continues to be very strong as economic power devolves and the economy becomes more open to the outside world. There are currently over 20,000 Chinese students studying in the U.S. and other Western countries, almost all of them the children of the Chinese elite. It is hard to believe that when they return home to run the country they will be content for China to be the only country in Asia unaffected by the larger democratizing trend. The student demonstrations in Beijing that broke out first in December 1986 and recurred recently on the occasion of Hu Yaobang's death were only the beginning of what will inevitably be mounting pressure for change in the political system as well.

What is important about China from the standpoint of world history is not the present state of the reform or even its future prospects. The central issue is the fact that the People's Republic of China can no longer act as a beacon for illiberal forces around the world, whether they be guerrillas in some Asian jungle or middle class students in Paris. Maoism, rather than being the pattern for Asia's future, became an anachronism, and it was the mainland Chinese who in fact were decisively influenced by the prosperity and dynamism of their overseas co-ethnics—the ironic ultimate victory of Taiwan.

Important as these changes in China have been, however, it is developments in the Soviet Union—the original "homeland of the world proletariat"—that have put the final nail in the coffin of the Marxist-Leninist alternative to liberal democracy. It should be clear that in terms of formal institutions, not much has changed in the four years since Gorbachev has come to power: free markets and the cooperative movement represent only a small part of the Soviet economy, which remains centrally planned; the political system is still dominated by the Communist party, which has only begun to democratize internally and to share power with other groups; the regime continues to assert that it is seeking only to modernize socialism and that its ideological basis remains

Marxism-Leninism; and, finally, Gorbachev faces a potentially powerful conservative opposition that could undo many of the changes that have taken place to date. Moreover, it is hard to be too sanguine about the chances for success of Gorbachev's proposed reforms, either in the sphere of economics or politics. But my purpose here is not to analyze events in the short-term, or to make predictions for policy purposes, but to look at underlying trends in the sphere of ideology and consciousness. And in that respect, it is clear that an astounding transformation has occurred.

Emigres from the Soviet Union have been reporting for at least the last generation now that virtually nobody in that country truly believed in Marxism-Leninism any longer, and that this was nowhere more true than in the Soviet elite, which continued to mouth Marxist slogans out of sheer cynicism. The corruption and decadence of the late Brezhnev-era Soviet state seemed to matter little, however, for as long as the state itself refused to throw into question any of the fundamental principles underlying Soviet society, the system was capable of functioning adequately out of sheer inertia and could even muster some dynamism in the realm of foreign and defense policy. Marxism-Leninism was like a magical incantation which, however absurd and devoid of meaning, was the only common basis on which the elite could agree to rule Soviet society.

What has happened in the four years since Gorbachev's coming to power is a revolutionary assault on the most fundamental institutions and principles of Stalinism, and their replacement by other principles which do not amount to liberalism *per se* but whose only connecting thread is liberalism. This is most evident in the economic sphere, where the reform economists around Gorbachev have become steadily more radical in their support for free markets, to the point where some like Nikolai Shmelev do not mind being compared in public to Milton Friedman. There is a virtual consensus among the currently dominant school of Soviet economists now that central planning and the command system of allocation are the root cause of economic inefficiency, and that if the Soviet system is ever to heal itself, it must permit free and decentralized decision-making with respect to investment, labor, and prices. After a couple of initial years of ideological confusion, these principles have finally been incorporated into policy with the promulgation of new laws on enterprise autonomy, cooperatives, and finally in 1988 on lease arrangements and family farming. There are, of course, a number of fatal flaws in the current implementation of the reform, most notably the absence of a thoroughgoing price reform. But the problem is no longer a *conceptual* one: Gorbachev and his lieutenants seem to understand the economic logic of marketization well enough, but like the leaders of a Third World country facing the IMF, are afraid of the social consequences of ending consumer subsidies and other forms of dependence on the state sector.

In the political sphere, the proposed changes to the Soviet constitution, legal system, and party rules amount to much less than the establishment of a liberal state. Gorbachev has spoken of democratization primarily in the sphere of internal party affairs, and has shown little intention of ending the Communist party's monopoly of power; indeed, the political reform seeks to legitimize and therefore strengthen the CPSU's rule. Nonetheless, the general principles underlying many of the reforms—that the "people" should be truly responsible for their own affairs, that higher political bodies should be answerable to lower ones, and not vice versa, that the rule of law should prevail over arbitrary police actions, with separation of powers and an independent judiciary, that there should be legal protection for property rights, the need for open discussion of public issues and the right of public dissent, the empowering of the Soviets as a forum in which the whole Soviet people can participate, and of a political culture that is more tolerant and pluralistic—come from a source fundamentally alien to the USSR's Marxist-Leninist tradition, even if they are incompletely articulated and poorly implemented in practice.

■　■　■

If we admit for the moment that the fascist and communist challenges to liberalism are dead, are there any other ideological competitors left? Or put another way, are there contradictions in liberal society beyond that of class that are not resolvable? Two possibilities suggest themselves, those of religion and nationalism.

The rise of religious fundamentalism in recent years within the Christian, Jewish, and Muslim traditions has been widely noted. One is inclined to say that the revival of religion in some way attests to a broad unhappiness with the impersonality and spiritual vacuity of liberal consumerist societies. Yet while the emptiness at the core of liberalism is most certainly a defect in the ideology—indeed, a flaw that one does not need the perspective of religion to recognize—it is not at all clear that it is remediable through politics. Modern liberalism itself was historically a consequence of the weakness of religiously-based societies which, failing to agree on the nature of the good life, could not provide even the minimal preconditions of peace and stability. In the contemporary world only Islam has offered a theocratic state as a political alternative to both liberalism and communism. But the doctrine has little appeal for non-Muslims, and it is hard to believe that the movement will take on any universal significance. Other less organized religious impulses have been successfully satisfied within the sphere of personal life that is permitted in liberal societies.

The other major "contradiction" potentially unresolvable by liberalism is the one posed by nationalism and other forms of racial and ethnic consciousness. It is certainly true that a very large degree of conflict since the Battle of Jena has had its roots in nationalism. Two cataclysmic world wars in this century have been spawned by the nationalism of the developed world in various guises, and if those passions have been muted to a certain extent in postwar Europe, they are still extremely powerful in the Third World. Nationalism has been a threat to liberalism historically in Germany, and continues to be one in isolated parts of "post-historical" Europe like Northern Ireland.

But it is not clear that nationalism represents an irreconcilable contradiction in the heart of liberalism. In the first place, nationalism is not one single phenomenon but several, ranging from mild cultural nostalgia to the highly organized and elaborately articulated doctrine of National Socialism. Only systematic nationalisms of the latter sort can qualify as a formal ideology on the level of liberalism or communism. The vast majority of the world's nationalist movements do not have a political program beyond the negative desire of independence *from* some other group or people, and do not offer anything like a comprehensive agenda for socio-economic organization. As such, they are compatible with doctrines and ideologies that do offer such agendas. While they may constitute a source of conflict for liberal societies, this conflict does not arise from liberalism itself so much as from the fact that the liberalism in question is incomplete. Certainly a great deal of the world's ethnic and nationalist tension can be explained in terms of peoples who are forced to live in unrepresentative political systems that they have not chosen.

While it is impossible to rule out the sudden appearance of new ideologies or previously unrecognized contradictions in liberal societies, then, the present world seems to confirm that the fundamental principles of socio-political organization have not advanced terribly far since 1806. Many of the wars and revolutions fought since that time have been undertaken in the name of ideologies which claimed to be more advanced than liberalism, but whose pretensions were ultimately unmasked by history. In the meantime, they have helped to spread the universal homogenous state to the point where it could have a significant effect on the overall character of international relations.

IV

What are the implications of the end of history for international relations? Clearly, the vast bulk of the Third World remains very much mired in history, and will be a terrain of conflict for many years to come. But let us focus for the time being on the larger and more developed states of the world who after all account for the greater part of world politics. Russia and China are not likely to join the developed nations of the West as liberal societies any time in the foreseeable future, but suppose for a moment that Marxism-Leninism ceases to be a factor driving the foreign policies of these states—a prospect which, if not yet here, the last few years have made a real possibility. How will the overall characteristics of a de-ideologized world differ from those of the one with which we are familiar at such a hypothetical juncture?

The most common answer is—not very much. For there is a very widespread belief among many observers of international relations that underneath the skin of ideology is a hard core of great power national interest that guarantees a fairly high level of competition and conflict between nations. Indeed, according to one academically popular school of international relations theory, conflict inheres in the international system as such, and to understand the prospects for conflict one must look at the shape of the system—for example, whether it is bipolar or multipolar—rather than at the specific character of the nations and regimes that constitute it. This school in effect applies a Hobbesian view of politics to international relations, and assumes that aggression and insecurity are universal characteristics of human societies rather than the product of specific historical circumstances.

Believers in this line of thought take the relations that existed between the participants in the classical nineteenth-century European balance of power as a model for what a de-ideologized contemporary world would look like. Charles Krauthammer, for example, recently explained that if as a result of Gorbachev's reforms the USSR is shorn of Marxist-Leninist ideology, its behavior will revert to that of nineteenth-century imperial Russia. While he finds this more reassuring than the threat posed by a communist Russia, he implies that there will still be a substantial degree of competition and conflict in the international system, just as there was say between Russia and Britain or Wilhelmine Germany in the last century. This is, of course, a convenient point of view for people who want to admit that something major is changing in the Soviet Union, but do not want to accept responsibility for recommending the radical policy redirection implicit in such a view. But is it true?

In fact, the notion that ideology is a superstructure imposed on a substratum of permanent great power interest is a highly questionable proposition. For the way in which any state defines its national interest is not universal but rests on some kind of prior ideological basis, just as we saw that economic behavior is determined by a prior state of consciousness. In this century, states have adopted highly articulated doctrines with explicit foreign policy agendas legitimizing expansionism, like Marxism-Leninism or National Socialism.

The expansionist and competitive behavior of nineteenth-century European states rested on no less ideal a basis; it just so happened that the ideology driving it was less explicit than the doctrines of the twentieth century. For one thing, most "liberal" European societies were illiberal insofar as they believed in the legitimacy of imperialism, that is, the right of one nation to rule over other nations without regard for the wishes of the ruled. The justifications for imperialism varied from nation to nation, from a crude belief in the legitimacy of force, particularly when applied to non-Europeans, to the White Man's Burden and Europe's

Christianizing mission, to the desire to give people of color access to the culture of Rabelais and Molière. But whatever the particular ideological basis, every "developed" country believed in the acceptability of higher civilizations ruling lower ones—including, incidentally, the United States with regard to the Philippines. This led to a drive for pure territorial aggrandizement in the latter half of the century and played no small role in causing the Great War.

The radical and deformed outgrowth of nineteenth-century imperialism was German fascism, an ideology which justified Germany's right not only to rule over non-European peoples, but over *all* non-German ones. But in retrospect it seems that Hitler represented a diseased bypath in the general course of European development, and since his fiery defeat, the legitimacy of any kind of territorial aggrandizement has been thoroughly discredited. Since the Second World War, European nationalism has been defanged and shorn of any real relevance to foreign policy, with the consequence that the nineteenth-century model of great power behavior has become a serious anachronism. The most extreme form of nationalism that any Western European state has mustered since 1945 has been Gaullism, whose self-assertion has been confined largely to the realm of nuisance politics and culture. International life for the part of the world that has reached the end of history is far more preoccupied with economics than with politics or strategy.

The developed states of the West do maintain defense establishments and in the postwar period have competed vigorously for influence to meet a worldwide communist threat. This behavior has been driven, however, by an external threat from states that possess overtly expansionist ideologies, and would not exist in their absence. To take the "neo-realist" theory seriously, one would have to believe that "natural" competitive behavior would reassert itself among the OECD states were Russia and China to disappear from the face of the earth.

That is, West Germany and France would arm themselves against each other as they did in the 1930s, Australia and New Zealand would send military advisers to block each others' advances in Africa, and the U.S.-Canadian border would become fortified. Such a prospect is, of course, ludicrous: minus Marxist-Leninist ideology, we are far more likely to see the "Common Marketization" of world politics than the disintegration of the EEC into nineteenth-century competitiveness. Indeed, as our experience in dealing with Europe on matters such as terrorism or Libya prove, they are much further gone than we down the road that denies the legitimacy of the use of force in international politics, even in self-defense.

The automatic assumption that Russia shorn of its expansionist communist ideology should pick up where the czars left off just prior to the Bolshevik Revolution is therefore a curious one. It assumes that the evolution of human consciousness has stood still in the meantime, and that the Soviets, while picking up currently fashionable ideas in the realm of economics, will return to foreign policy views a century out of date in the rest of Europe. This is certainly not what happened to China after it began its reform process. Chinese competitiveness and expansionism on the world scene have virtually disappeared: Beijing no longer sponsors Maoist insurgencies or tries to cultivate influence in distant African countries as it did in the 1960s. This is not to say that there are not troublesome aspects to contemporary Chinese foreign policy, such as the reckless sale of ballistic missile technology in the Middle East; and the PRC continues to manifest traditional great power behavior in its sponsorship of the Khmer Rouge against Vietnam. But the former is explained by commercial motives and the latter is a vestige of earlier ideologically-based rivalries. The new China far more resembles Gaullist France than pre–World War I Germany.

The real question for the future, however, is the degree to which Soviet elites have assimilated the consciousness of the universal homogenous state that is post-Hitler Europe. From their writings and from my own personal contacts with them, there is no question in my mind that the liberal Soviet intelligentsia rallying around Gorbachev has arrived at the end-of-history view in a remarkably short time, due in no small measure to the contacts they have had since the Brezhnev era with the larger European civilization around them. "New political thinking," the general rubric for their views, describes a world dominated by economic concerns, in which there are no ideological grounds for major conflict between nations, and in which, consequently, the use of military force becomes less legitimate. As Foreign Minister Shevardnadze put it in mid-1988:

> The struggle between two opposing systems is no longer a determining tendency of the present-day era. At the modern stage, the ability to build up material wealth at an accelerated rate on the basis of front-ranking science and high-level techniques and technology, and to distribute it fairly, and through joint efforts to restore and protect the resources necessary for mankind's survival acquires decisive importance.

The post-historical consciousness represented by "new thinking" is only one possible future for the Soviet Union, however. There has always been a very strong current of great Russian chauvinism in the Soviet Union, which has found freer expression since the advent of *glasnost*. It may be possible to return to traditional Marxism-Leninism for a while as a simple rallying point for those who want to restore the authority that Gorbachev has dissipated. But as in Poland, Marxism-Leninism is dead as a mobilizing ideology: under its banner people cannot be made to work harder, and its adherents have lost confidence in themselves. Unlike the propagators of traditional Marxism-Leninism, however, ultra-nationalists in the USSR believe in their Slavophile cause passionately, and one gets

the sense that the fascist alternative is not one that has played itself out entirely there.

The Soviet Union, then, is at a fork in the road: it can start down the path that was staked out by Western Europe forty-five years ago, a path that most of Asia has followed, or it can realize its own uniqueness and remain stuck in history. The choice it makes will be highly important for us, given the Soviet Union's size and military strength, for that power will continue to preoccupy us and slow our realization that we have already emerged on the other side of history.

V

The passing of Marxism-Leninism first from China and then from the Soviet Union will mean its death as a living ideology of world historical significance. For while there may be some isolated true believers left in places like Managua, Pyongyang, or Cambridge, Massachusetts, the fact that there is not a single large state in which it is a going concern undermines completely its pretensions to being in the vanguard of human history. And the death of this ideology means the growing "Common Marketization" of international relations, and the diminution of the likelihood of large-scale conflict between states.

This does not by any means imply the end of international conflict *per se*. For the world at that point would be divided between a part that was historical and a part that was post-historical. Conflict between states still in history, and between those states and those at the end of history, would still be possible. There would still be a high and perhaps rising level of ethnic and nationalist violence, since those are impulses incompletely played out, even in parts of the post-historical world. Palestinians and Kurds, Sikhs and Tamils, Irish Catholics and Walloons, Armenians and Azeris, will continue to have their unresolved grievances. This implies that terrorism and wars of national liberation will continue to be an important item on the international agenda. But large-scale conflict must involve large states still caught in the grip of history, and they are what appear to be passing from the scene.

The end of history will be a very sad time. The struggle for recognition, the willingness to risk one's life for a purely abstract goal, the worldwide ideological struggle that called forth daring, courage, imagination, and idealism, will be replaced by economic calculation, the endless solving of technical problems, environmental concerns, and the satisfaction of sophisticated consumer demands. In the post-historical period there will be neither art nor philosophy, just the perpetual caretaking of the museum of human history. I can feel in myself, and see in others around me, a powerful nostalgia for the time when history existed. Such nostalgia, in fact, will continue to fuel competition and conflict even in the post-historical world for some time to come. Even though I recognize its inevitability, I have the most ambivalent feelings for the civilization that has been created in Europe since 1945, with its north Atlantic and Asian offshoots. Perhaps this very prospect of centuries of boredom at the end of history will serve to get history started once again.

NOTE

1. Kojève's best-known work is his *Introduction à la lecture de Hegel* (Paris: Editions Gallimard, 1947), which is a transcript of the *Ecole Practique* lectures from the 1930s. This book is available in English entitled *Introduction to the Reading of Hegel* arranged by Raymond Queneau, edited by Allan Bloom, and translated by James Nichols (New York: Basic Books, 1969).

Samuel P. Huntington
THE CLASH OF CIVILIZATIONS?

The Next Pattern of Conflict

Wor ld politics is entering a new phase, and intellectuals have not hesitated to proliferate visions of what it will be—the end of history, the return of traditional rivalries between nation states, and the decline of the nation state from the conflicting pulls of tribalism and globalism, among others. Each of these visions catches aspects of the emerging reality. Yet they all miss a crucial, indeed a central, aspect of what global politics is likely to be in the coming years.

It is my hypothesis that the fundamental source of conflict in this new world will not be primarily ideological or primarily economic. The great divisions among humankind and the dominating source of conflict will be cultural. Nation states will remain the most powerful actors in world affairs, but the principal conflicts of global politics will occur between nations and groups of different civilizations. The clash of civilizations will dominate global politics. The fault lines between civilizations will be the battle lines of the future.

Conflict between civilizations will be the latest phase in the evolution of conflict in the modern world. For a century and a half after the emergence of the modern international system with the Peace of Westphalia, the conflicts of the Western world were largely among princes—emperors, absolute monarchs, and constitutional monarchs attempting to expand their bureaucracies, their armies, their mercantilist economic strength, and,

From *Foreign Affairs* 72, no. 3 (Summer 1993): 22–49.

most important, the territory they ruled. In the process they created nation states, and beginning with the French Revolution the principal lines of conflict were between nations rather than princes. * * * [A]s a result of the Russian Revolution and the reaction against it, the conflict of nations yielded to the conflict of ideologies, first among communism, fascism-Nazism, and liberal democracy, and then between communism and liberal democracy. During the Cold War, this latter conflict became embodied in the struggle between the two superpowers, neither of which was a nation state in the classical European sense and each of which defined its identity in terms of its ideology.

* * * With the end of the Cold War, international politics moves out of its Western phase, and its centerpiece becomes the interaction between the West and non-Western civilizations and among non-Western civilizations. In the politics of civilizations, the peoples and governments of non-Western civilizations no longer remain the objects of history as targets of Western colonialism but join the West as movers and shapers of history.

The Nature of Civilizations

During the Cold War the world was divided into the First, Second, and Third Worlds. Those divisions are no longer relevant. It is far more meaningful now to group countries not in terms of their political or economic systems or in terms of their level of economic development but rather in terms of their culture and civilization.

What do we mean when we talk of a civilization? A civilization is a cultural entity. Villages, regions, ethnic groups, nationalities, religious groups, all have distinct cultures at different levels of cultural heterogeneity. The culture of a village in southern Italy may be different from that of a village in northern Italy, but both will share in a common Italian culture that distinguishes them from German villages. European communities, in turn, will share cultural features that distinguish them from Arab or Chinese communities. Arabs, Chinese, and Westerners, however, are not part of any broader cultural entity. They constitute civilizations. A civilization is thus the highest cultural grouping of people and the broadest level of cultural identity people have short of that which distinguishes humans from other species. It is defined both by common objective elements, such as language, history, religion, customs, institutions, and by the subjective self-identification of people. * * *

* * * Civilizations are nonetheless meaningful entities, and while the lines between them are seldom sharp, they are real. Civilizations are dynamic; they rise and fall; they divide and merge. And, as any student of history knows, civilizations disappear and are buried in the sands of time.

Westerners tend to think of nation states as the principal actors in global affairs. They have been that, however, for only a few centuries. The broader reaches of human history have been the history of civilizations. In *A Study of History*, Arnold Toynbee identified 21 major civilizations; only six of them exist in the contemporary world.

Why Civilizations Will Clash

Civilization identity will be increasingly important in the future, and the world will be shaped in large measure by the interactions among seven or eight major civilizations. These include Western, Confucian, Japanese, Islamic, Hindu, Slavic-Orthodox, Latin American, and possibly African civilization. The most important conflicts of the future will occur along the cultural fault lines separating these civilizations from one another.

Why will this be the case?

First, differences among civilizations are not only real; they are basic. Civilizations are differentiated from each other by history, language, culture, tradition and, most important, religion. The people of different civilizations have different views on the relations between God and man, the individual and the group, the citizen and the state, parents and children, husband and wife, as well as differing views of the relative importance of rights and responsibilities, liberty and authority, equality and hierarchy. These differences are the product of centuries. They will not soon disappear. * * *

Second, the world is becoming a smaller place. The interactions between peoples of different civilizations are increasing; these increasing interactions intensify civilization consciousness and awareness of differences between civilizations and commonalities within civilizations. * * *

Third, the processes of economic modernization and social change throughout the world are separating people from longstanding local identities. They also weaken the nation state as a source of identity. In much of the world, religion has moved in to fill this gap, often in the form of movements that are labeled "fundamentalist." Such movements are found in Western Christianity, Judaism, Buddhism, and Hinduism, as well as in Islam. * * * The "unsecularization of the world," George Weigel has remarked, "is one of the dominant social facts of life in the late twentieth century." * * *

Fourth, the growth of civilization-consciousness is enhanced by the dual role of the West. On the one hand, the West is at a peak of power. At the same time, however, and perhaps as a result, a return to the roots phenomenon is occurring among non-Western civilizations. Increasingly one hears references to trends toward a turning inward and "Asianization" in Japan, the end of the Nehru legacy and the "Hinduization" of India, the failure of Western ideas of socialism and nationalism and hence "re-Islamization" of the Middle East, and now a debate over Westernization versus Russianization in Boris Yeltsin's country. A West at the peak of its power confronts non-Wests that increasingly have the desire, the will, and the resources to shape the world in non-Western ways.

■ ■ ■

Fifth, cultural characteristics and differences are less mutable and hence less easily compromised and resolved than political and economic ones. In the former Soviet Union, communists can become democrats, the rich can become poor and the poor rich, but Russians cannot become Estonians and Azeris cannot become Armenians. * * * Even more than ethnicity, religion discriminates sharply and exclusively among people. A person can be half-French and half-Arab and simultaneously even a citizen of two countries. It is more difficult to be half-Catholic and half-Muslim.

Finally, economic regionalism is increasing. * * * On the one hand, successful economic regionalism will reinforce civilization-consciousness. On the other hand, economic regionalism may succeed only when it is rooted in a common civilization. The European Community rests on the shared foundation of European culture and Western Christianity. The success of the North American Free Trade Area depends on the convergence now underway of Mexican, Canadian, and American cultures. Japan, in contrast, faces difficulties in creating a comparable economic entity in East Asia because Japan is a society and civilization unique to itself. * * *

■ ■ ■

As people define their identity in ethnic and religious terms, they are likely to see an "us" versus "them" relation existing between themselves and people of different ethnicity or religion. The end of

ideologically defined states in Eastern Europe and the former Soviet Union permits traditional ethnic identities and animosities to come to the fore. Differences in culture and religion create differences over policy issues, ranging from human rights to immigration to trade and commerce to the environment. * * * Most important, the efforts of the West to promote its values of democracy and liberalism as universal values, to maintain its military predominance and to advance its economic interests engender countering responses from other civilizations. * * *

The clash of civilizations thus occurs at two levels. At the micro-level, adjacent groups along the fault lines between civilizations struggle, often violently, over the control of territory and each other. At the macro-level, states from different civilizations compete for relative military and economic power, struggle over the control of international institutions and third parties, and competitively promote their particular political and religious values.

The Fault Lines between Civilizations

The fault lines between civilizations are replacing the political and ideological boundaries of the Cold War as the flash points for crisis and bloodshed. The Cold War began when the Iron Curtain divided Europe politically and ideologically. The Cold War ended with the end of the Iron Curtain. As the ideological division of Europe has disappeared, the cultural division of Europe between Western Christianity, on the one hand, and Orthodox Christianity and Islam, on the other, has reemerged. The most significant dividing line in Europe, as William Wallace has suggested, may well be the eastern boundary of Western Christianity in the year 1500. This line runs along what are now the boundaries between Finland and Russia and between the Baltic states and Russia, cuts through Belarus and Ukraine separating the more Catholic western Ukraine from Orthodox eastern Ukraine, swings westward separating Transylvania from the rest of Romania, and then goes through Yugoslavia almost exactly along the line now separating Croatia and Slovenia from the rest of Yugoslavia. In the Balkans this line, of course, coincides with the historic boundary between the Hapsburg and Ottoman empires. The peoples to the north and west of this line are Protestant or Catholic; they shared the common experiences of European history—feudalism, the Renaissance, the Reformation, the Enlightenment, the French Revolution, the Industrial Revolution; they are generally economically better off than the peoples to the east; and they may now look forward to increasing involvement in a common European economy and to the consolidation of democratic political systems. The peoples to the east and south of this line are Orthodox or Muslim; they historically belonged to the Ottoman or Tsarist empires and were only lightly touched by the shaping events in the rest of Europe; they are generally less advanced economically; they seem much less likely to develop stable democratic political systems. The Velvet Curtain of culture has replaced the Iron Curtain of ideology as the most significant dividing line in Europe. As the events in Yugoslavia show, it is not only a line of difference; it is also at times a line of bloody conflict.

Conflict along the fault line between Western and Islamic civilizations has been going on for 1,300 years. * * *

■ ■ ■

This centuries-old military interaction between the West and Islam is unlikely to decline. It could become more virulent. The Gulf War left some Arabs feeling proud that Saddam Hussein had attacked Israel and stood up to the West. It also left many feeling humiliated and resentful of the West's military presence in the Persian Gulf, the West's overwhelming military dominance, and their apparent inability to shape their own destiny. Many Arab countries, in addition to the oil exporters, are reaching levels of economic and social development where autocratic forms of government become inappropriate and efforts to introduce democracy become stronger. Some openings in Arab political systems have already occurred. The principal beneficiaries of these openings have been Islamist movements. * * *

Those relations are also complicated by demography. The spectacular population growth in Arab countries, particularly in North Africa, has led to increased migration to Western Europe. The movement within Western Europe toward minimizing internal boundaries has sharpened political sensitivities with respect to this development. * * *

■ ■ ■

Historically, the other great antagonistic interaction of Arab Islamic civilization has been with the pagan, animist, and now increasingly Christian black peoples to the south. In the past, this antagonism was epitomized in the image of Arab slave dealers and black slaves. It has been reflected in the on-going civil war in the Sudan between Arabs and blacks, the fighting in Chad between Libyan-supported insurgents and the government, the tensions between Orthodox Christians and Muslims in the Horn of Africa, and the political conflicts, recurring riots and communal violence between Muslims and Christians in Nigeria. The modernization of Africa and the spread of Christianity are likely to enhance the probability of violence along this fault line. Symptomatic of the intensification of this conflict was Pope John Paul II's speech in Khartoum in February 1993 attacking the actions of the Sudan's Islamist government against the Christian minority there.

On the northern border of Islam, conflict has increasingly erupted between Orthodox and

Muslim peoples, including the carnage of Bosnia and Sarajevo, the simmering violence between Serb and Albanian, the tenuous relations between Bulgarians and their Turkish minority, the violence between Ossetians and Ingush, the unremitting slaughter of each other by Armenians and Azeris, the tense relations between Russians and Muslims in Central Asia. * * *

The conflict of civilizations is deeply rooted elsewhere in Asia. The historic clash between Muslim and Hindu in the subcontinent manifests itself now not only in the rivalry between Pakistan and India but also in intensifying religious strife within India between increasingly militant Hindu groups and India's substantial Muslim minority. The destruction of the Ayodhya mosque in December 1992 brought to the fore the issue of whether India will remain a secular democratic state or become a Hindu one. * * *

■   ■   ■

Groups or states belonging to one civilization that become involved in war with people from a different civilization naturally try to rally support from other members of their own civilization. * * *

■   ■   ■

Civilization rallying to date has been limited, but it has been growing, and it clearly has the potential to spread much further. As the conflicts in the Persian Gulf, the Caucasus, and Bosnia continued, the positions of nations and the cleavages between them increasingly were along civilizational lines. Populist politicians, religious leaders, and the media have found it a potent means of arousing mass support and of pressuring hesitant governments. In the coming years, the local conflicts most likely to escalate into major wars will be those, as in Bosnia and the Caucasus, along the fault lines between civilizations. The next world war, if there is one, will be a war between civilizations.

The West versus the Rest

The West is now at an extraordinary peak of power in relation to other civilizations. Its superpower opponent has disappeared from the map. Military conflict among Western states is unthinkable, and Western military power is unrivaled. Apart from Japan, the West faces no economic challenge. It dominates international political and security institutions and with Japan international economic institutions. Global political and security issues are effectively settled by a directorate of the United States, Britain, and France, world economic issues by a directorate of the United States, Germany, and Japan, all of which maintain extraordinarily close relations with each other to the exclusion of lesser and largely non-Western countries. Decisions made at the U.N. Security Council or in the International Monetary Fund that reflect the interests of the West are presented to the world as reflecting the desires of the world community. The very phrase "the world community" has become the euphemistic collective noun (replacing "the Free World") to give global legitimacy to actions reflecting the interests of the United States and other Western powers.[1] * * *

■   ■   ■

* * * V. S. Naipaul has argued that Western civilization is the "universal civilization" that "fits all men." At a superficial level much of Western culture has indeed permeated the rest of the world. At a more basic level, however, Western concepts differ fundamentally from those prevalent in other civilizations. Western ideas of individualism, liberalism, constitutionalism, human rights, equality, liberty, the rule of law, democracy, free markets, the separation of church and state often have little resonance in Islamic, Confucian, Japanese, Hindu, Buddhist, or Orthodox cultures. Western efforts to propagate such ideas produce instead a reaction against "human rights imperialism" and a reaffirmation of

indigenous values, as can be seen in the support for religious fundamentalism by the younger generation in non-Western cultures. The very notion that there could be a "universal civilization" is a Western idea, directly at odds with the particularism of most Asian societies and their emphasis on what distinguishes one people from another. Indeed, the author of a review of 100 comparative studies of values in different societies concluded that "the values that are most important in the West are least important worldwide."[2] In the political realm, of course, these differences are most manifest in the efforts of the United States and other Western powers to induce other peoples to adopt Western ideas concerning democracy and human rights. Modern democratic government originated in the West. When it has developed in non-Western societies it has usually been the product of Western colonialism or imposition.

The central axis of world politics in the future is likely to be, in Kishore Mahbubani's phrase, the conflict between "the West and the Rest" and the responses of non-Western civilizations to Western power and values.[3] Those responses generally take one or a combination of three forms. At one extreme, non-Western states can, like Burma and North Korea, attempt to pursue a course of isolation, to insulate their societies from penetration or "corruption" by the West, and, in effect, to opt out of participation in the Western-dominated global community. The costs of this course, however, are high, and few states have pursued it exclusively. A second alternative, the equivalent of "bandwagoning" in international relations theory, is to attempt to join the West and accept its values and institutions. The third alternative is to attempt to "balance" the West by developing economic and military power and cooperating with other non-Western societies against the West, while preserving indigenous values and institutions; in short, to modernize but not to Westernize.

■ ■ ■

Implications for the West

This article does not argue that civilization identities will replace all other identities, that nation states will disappear, that each civilization will become a single coherent political entity, that groups within a civilization will not conflict with and even fight each other. This paper does set forth the hypotheses that differences between civilizations are real and important; civilization-consciousness is increasing; conflict between civilizations will supplant ideological and other forms of conflict as the dominant global form of conflict; international relations, historically a game played out within Western civilization, will increasingly be de-Westernized and become a game in which non-Western civilizations are actors and not simply objects; successful political, security, and economic international institutions are more likely to develop within civilizations than across civilizations; conflicts between groups in different civilizations will be more frequent, more sustained, and more violent than conflicts between groups in the same civilization; violent conflicts between groups in different civilizations are the most likely and most dangerous source of escalation that could lead to global wars; the paramount axis of world politics will be the relations between "the West and the Rest"; the elites in some torn non-Western countries will try to make their countries part of the West, but in most cases face major obstacles to accomplishing this; a central focus of conflict for the immediate future will be between the West and several Islamic-Confucian states.

This is not to advocate the desirability of conflicts between civilizations. It is to set forth descriptive hypotheses as to what the future may be like. If these are plausible hypotheses, however, it is necessary to consider their implications for Western policy. These implications should be divided between short-term advantage and long-term accommodation. In the short term it is clearly in the interest of the West to promote greater cooperation and unity within its own civilization, particularly between its European and North American components; to incorporate into the West societies in Eastern Europe, and Latin America whose cultures are close to those of the West; to promote and maintain cooperative relations with Russia and Japan; to prevent escalation of local inter-civilization conflicts into major inter-civilization wars; to limit the expansion of the military strength of Confucian and Islamic states; to moderate the reduction of Western military capabilities and maintain military superiority in East and Southwest Asia; to exploit differences and conflicts among Confucian and Islamic states; to support in other civilizations groups sympathetic to Western values and interests; to strengthen international institutions that reflect and legitimate Western interests and values and to promote the involvement of non-Western states in those institutions.

In the longer term other measures would be called for. Western civilization is both Western and modern. Non-Western civilizations have attempted to become modern without becoming Western. To date only Japan has fully succeeded in this quest. Non-Western civilizations will continue to attempt to acquire the wealth, technology, skills, machines, and weapons that are part of being modern. They will also attempt to reconcile this modernity with their traditional culture and values. Their economic and military strength rela-

tive to the West will increase. Hence the West will increasingly have to accommodate these non-Western modern civilizations whose power approaches that of the West but whose values and interests differ significantly from those of the West. This will require the West to maintain the economic and military power necessary to protect its interests in relation to these civilizations. It will also, however, require the West to develop a more profound understanding of the basic religious and philosophical assumptions underlying other civilizations and the ways in which people in those civilizations see their interests. It will require an effort to identify elements of commonality between Western and other civilizations. For the relevant future, there will be no universal civilization, but instead a world of different civilizations, each of which will have to learn to coexist with the others.

NOTES

1. Almost invariably Western leaders claim they are acting on behalf of "the world community." One minor lapse occurred during the run-up to the Gulf War. In an interview on "Good Morning America," Dec. 21, 1990, British Prime Minister John Major referred to the actions "the West" was taking against Saddam Hussein. He quickly corrected himself and subsequently referred to "the world community." He was, however, right when he erred.

2. Harry C. Triandis, *The New York Times*, Dec. 25, 1990, p. 41, and "Cross-Cultural Studies of Individualism and Collectivism," *Nebraska Symposium on Motivation*, vol. 37, 1989, pp. 41–133.

3. Kishore Mahbubani, "The West and the Rest," *The National Interest*, Summer 1992, pp. 3–13.

G. John Ikenberry

THE CRISIS OF THE POST–COLD WAR LIBERAL ORDER

The Cold War ended suddenly and unexpectedly. The great geopolitical struggle between the United States and the Soviet Union ceased. One era of great-power relations ended and another began. But it was a historical turning point unlike the postwar moments of 1815, 1919, and 1945. In 1991, the old bipolar order collapsed without a great-power war. The Cold War ended not with a military victory but with a political and ideological triumph: the collapse of the Soviet Union—and with it, the political and ideological collapse of communism. Moreover, unlike what had occurred at past postwar moments, the global system was not overturned. Quite the contrary—the world that the United States and its allies created after World War II remained intact. The end of the Cold War simply consolidated and expanded this order. The Soviet bloc, estranged from the West for half a century, collapsed and fitfully sought a place within the West, at least for a while.

What followed in the 1990s was the closest the world has come to a "liberal moment." The great contest between liberal democracy and communism seemed to be settled. The American-led order was left standing, and no rival geopolitical or ideological challengers were in view. "While the collapse of communism did not bring an end of history," David A. Bell writes, "it did, briefly, seem to establish a worldwide consensus." The wars and upheavals of the twentieth century appeared to have rendered a verdict as to which social and political system was superior. "That system was what could be called the liberal ideal, constructed around representative democracy, human rights, and free-market capitalism complemented by a strong social safety net."[1] The world of the 1930s had been turned on its head. The question was not whether liberal democracies would survive, but how to organize relations within an expanding world of liberal democracies, unchallenged by grand ideological rivalries or competing centers of power.

During the first decade after the Cold War, democracy and markets flourished worldwide. The progressive forces of history that liberal internationalists had invoked since the nineteenth century seemed alive and well, and were working to reshape and expand the liberal democratic core of the global system. The North American Free Trade Agreement (NAFTA), the Asia-Pacific Economic Cooperation (APEC), and the World Trade Organization (WTO) signaled a strengthening of the world economy's rules and institutions. The European Union opened its doors to new members and continued on its path of political and economic integration. NATO expanded eastward and the US-Japan alliance was renewed. Russia became a quasi-member of the West, joining the G-7 process to create a new G-8, and China became Washington's "strategic partner." President Clinton's policy of building post–Cold War order around expanding markets, democracy, and institutions was the seeming embodiment of the liberal vision of international

From G. John Ikenberry, *A World Safe for Democracy: Liberal Internationalism and the Crises of Global Order* (New Haven: Yale University Press, 2020), 255–85, 381–89.

order. By the end of the 1990s, American officials were describing the United States as the world's "indispensable nation," using its power, ideas, and inheritance of institutions and partnerships to underwrite global order. For the first time in the modern era, scholars could talk about a unipolar world order.

But this moment did not last. Just two decades after the "liberal ideal" swept the world, liberal democracy and liberal internationalism were in retreat. The dark forces that were supposedly banished from the West—illiberalism, autocracy, nationalism, protectionism, spheres of influence, territorial revisionism—reasserted themselves. China and Russia dashed all hopes that they would quickly transition to democracy and support the liberal world order. To the contrary, they strengthened their authoritarian systems at home and flouted liberal norms abroad. Even more stunning, the United States and Great Britain seemed to step back from their role as champions of liberal international order. For the first time since the 1930s, the United States, with the election of Donald Trump in 2016, has had a president who was actively hostile to liberal internationalism. Trade, alliances, international law, multilateralism, torture and human rights—on all these issues, the American president made statements and pursued policies that, if fully realized, would effectively end the country's role as leader of the liberal international order. Britain's vote to leave the European Union (EU), and myriad other troubles besetting Europe, appeared to mark an end to the long postwar project of building a greater union. Meanwhile, liberal democracy came under threat in all corners of the globe, as varieties of authoritarianism rose to new salience in Hungary, Poland, the Philippines, Turkey, Brazil, and elsewhere. Across the liberal democratic world, populist, nationalist, and xenophobic strands of backlash politics proliferated.[2]

This is where we stand today. The worldwide consensus on the liberal ideal, if it ever truly existed, has vanished. What explains this reversal in fortunes? If the liberal international order is in crisis, what sort of crisis is it and what are its sources?

It is important to recall that the postwar liberal order did not begin as a global order. It was built "inside" half of a bipolar system as part of a larger geopolitical project of waging a global Cold War. Its original bargains, institutions, and social purposes were tied to the West, American leadership, and the global struggle against Soviet communism. When the Cold War ended, this inside order became the outside order. As the Soviet Union collapsed, the great rival of liberal internationalism was swept away, and the American-led order expanded outward. Liberal internationalism was globalized. Although this was seen as a moment of triumph of Western liberal democracies, the globalization of the liberal order put in motion two shifts that later became sources of crisis. First, it upended the political foundations of the liberal order. As new states entered the system, the old bargains and institutions that provided stability and governance were overrun. A wider array of states—with more diverse ideologies and agendas—were now part of the order. This triggered a crisis of authority: new bargains, roles, and responsibilities were now required at precisely the moment when the United States and its old allies were no longer in a position to assign them. These struggles over governance and authority continue today. Second, the globalization of the liberal order weakened its capacity to function as a security community. This can be called a crisis of social purpose. In its Cold War configuration, the liberal order was a sort of full-service security community, enhancing the capacity of Western governments to pursue policies of economic and social protection and advancement. As liberal internationalism became the platform for the wider global order, this shared social purpose eroded.

Taking all these elements together, the crisis of liberal order can be understood as a crisis of success, in the sense that its troubles emerged from its post–

Cold War expansion. Put differently, the troubles might be seen as a "Polanyi crisis"—turmoil and instability resulting from the rapid mobilization and spread of global capitalism, market society, and complex interdependence, all of which have overrun the political foundations that supported global capitalism's birth and development.[3] It is not, fundamentally, what might be called an "E. H. Carr crisis," in which liberal internationalism fails because of the return of great-power politics and the problems of anarchy.[4] Even though China and Russia are real and dangerous competitors, the troubles facing liberal internationalism are not primarily driven by a return of geopolitical conflict. The problems of liberal order are due less to the problems of anarchy and more to the problems of modernity—to the challenge of reestablishing stable foundations of liberal capitalist democracy.

I make this argument in four steps. First, I look at the restructuring of the international system after the Cold War and its implications for liberal order. Here the focus is on the globalization of liberal internationalism. The expansive nature of liberal order is rooted in its logic of multilateral and open relations. The American hegemonic political order in which liberal internationalism was embedded also contained a logic that facilitated the expansion of the order after the Cold War. Second, I offer an account of the sources of the liberal order's crisis, focusing on the erosion of its institutional and political foundations and the hollowing out of its social purposes. These are the twin crises of authority and community that have unfolded as liberal order has expanded. In effect, the liberal order has become wider but shallower. The erosion of domestic social supports within the Western liberal democracies—the system of embedded liberalism—is at the root of the breakdown. Third, I look at the ways in which China and Russia have responded to the post–Cold War globalization of liberal order. The bargains and partnerships that facilitated the integration of Germany and Japan into the postwar

liberal hegemonic order could not be extended to China and Russia on terms that either state could accept. Fourth, I identify the sources of stability and resilience in the contemporary liberal international order. While the Cold War–era liberal order took the form of a relatively coherent, if loosely organized, political community, the expanded post–Cold War liberal order is fragmented into various international realms. It has become less a matter of being either "in" or "out." This has allowed states—particularly illiberal states such as China and Russia—to pick and choose their connections to it. The globalized liberal order contains many layers and realms of order, each with its own logic and operation within the wider system. On one hand, this fragmentation weakens the liberal order. But on the other hand it has also created a more diverse array of constituencies and interests that support an open, rules-based system.

The Globalization of Liberalism

The end of the Cold War was a tale of two orders, both forged in the 1940s. One of these was built in response to the threats and imperatives that emerged in the struggle with the Soviet Union. This was the bipolar order organized around deterrence, containment, and ideological struggle between the two superpowers, and it ended with the fall of the Soviet Union. The other was the U.S.-led international order built inside the bipolar system; this is the Western liberal order. It was reinforced by the Cold War but was constructed, as we have seen, as a distinct project dating back to the early decades of the twentieth century. Under the cover of the Cold War, a revolution in relations among Western great powers rebuilt this order around binding security ties, managed open markets, social protections, multilateral cooperation, and American hegemonic leadership.

After the Cold War, this order provided the liberal logic for the wider international system.

The end of the Cold War was an "incredibly swift transition," Adam Roberts observes, "dramatic, decisive, and remarkably peaceful."[5] Earlier great wars had destroyed and discredited previous international orders and opened the way for sweeping negotiations over the basic rules and principles of a new order. But the American-led system not only survived the end of the Cold War but was widely seen as responsible for the West's triumph. The Cold War was a bipolar competition between two ways of organizing the modern world, and the collapse of the Soviet Union was seen to render a verdict. Western policy toward the Soviet Union was vindicated, as were the relations among the advanced industrial democracies. In this sense, the end of the Cold War was a conservative event. It entailed the peaceful capitulation of the Soviet Union—reluctant, to be sure, and not on the terms that Mikhail Gorbachev, the last Soviet premier, had hoped for. But the fall of the Soviet "pole" left in place the American "pole," and the American-led rules, institutions, and relationships that had been built during the Cold War became the core of the post–Cold War order.[6]

The end of the Cold War was felt most immediately and profoundly in West Germany, which saw the peaceful end of hostilities and the prospect of national reunification as a ratification of its western side's long postwar commitment to the European project and the Western rules-based order. The European Community and the Atlantic Alliance had provided the framework for West Germany to turn itself into a stable parliamentary democracy and pioneer its own distinctive social market society. They would now provide the framework for unifying Germany and integrating its eastern neighbors into a united Europe. In arguing for unification to a wary Europe and Russia in 1990, German foreign minister Hans-Dietrich Genscher quoted the novelist Thomas Mann: "What we seek is a European Germany, not a German Europe."[7]

The Western liberal order and the European project within it allowed Germany and Europe to solve a geopolitical problem that had remained elusive since the 1870s: reconciling a powerful Germany with a stable European state system. The German people mostly welcomed this transition because it let them see their country in a new light. After a dark past, they were now on the right side of history, offering a model to Europe and the world. "The unification of Germany and the more gradual unification of the European continent were seen as a template of the future for all other regions of the world," argues Thomas Bagger, a German diplomat. "It defined the prism through which Germans watched, analyzed and interpreted global events."[8]

America's first impulse after the Cold War was to build on the logic of this Western liberal order. President George H. W. Bush, who took office as the Soviet Union was breaking up, described the coming order in liberal internationalist terms. Its underpinnings would be democracy, open trade, and international law. "Great nations of the world are moving toward democracy through the door of freedom," Bush said in his 1989 inaugural address. "We know how to secure a more just and prosperous life for man on earth: through free markets, free speech, free elections, and the exercise of free will unhampered by the state."[9] In a speech later that year to the United Nations, he argued that democracy was on the march and commerce was a force for progress. In this "new world order," the United Nations and multilateral institutions were to play a critical role in "the central issue of our time," that "the nations of the world might come to agree that law, not force, shall govern."[10] The United States would stand at the center of this expanding world of liberal democracy and multilateral cooperation, in what Bush called a "widening circle of freedom." With the Cold War over, the United States invited the world into its Western liberal order.[11]

This liberal international vision was reflected in the work of the Bush administration, which sought to expand regional and global institutions in both security and economic cooperation. In relations toward Europe, State Department officials began a series of institutional steps: the evolution of NATO to include associate relations with countries to the east, the creation of more formal institutional relations with the European Community, and an expanded role for the Conference on Security Cooperation in Europe.[12] In the Western Hemisphere, the Bush administration pushed for the North American Free Trade Agreement and for closer ties with South America. In East Asia, it used the APEC forum to create more institutional links in the region, demonstrate American commitment, and ensure that Asian regionalism moved in a trans-Pacific direction. Bush's secretary of state, James Baker, later likened his administration's post–Cold War order-building strategy to the American strategy after 1945: "Men like Truman and Acheson were above all, though we sometimes forget it, institution builders. They fostered the economic institutions . . . that brought unparalleled prosperity. . . . At a time of similar opportunity and risk, I believed we should take a leaf from their book."[13]

This orientation toward expanding the Western liberal order continued under President Clinton, who tried to use multilateral institutions to stabilize and integrate the emerging market democracies into the advanced democratic world. Anthony Lake, Clinton's national security adviser, said the strategy was to "strengthen the community of market democracies" and "foster and consolidate new democracies and market economies where possible." The United States would help "democracy and market economies take root," which would in turn expand and strengthen the Western democratic order.[14] This strategy primarily targeted those parts of the world that were beginning the transition to market democracy: countries in Central and Eastern Europe and the Asia-Pacific region. Domestic reforms in these countries would be encouraged—and locked in if possible—through new trade pacts and security partnerships. In the formal statement of its strategy, the Clinton administration called for a multilateral approach to major foreign policy challenges like nuclear proliferation, regional instability, and unfair trade practices.[15] Multilateral cooperation would provide a foundation for an expanding liberal democratic world.[16]

By the end of the 1990s, the consolidation and expansion of the liberal international order appeared to be well under way. NATO was expanded eastward to include states that had previously been in the Warsaw Pact. This expansion was controversial, and caused leading American foreign policy figures to publicly warn that it could undermine fragile relations with Russia. But the Clinton administration wanted to show solidarity with countries making democratic transitions—and to institutionally embed these new entrants into the Western order.[17] Because they had no hostile intentions toward Russia, administration policymakers assumed Russia could be persuaded that NATO expansion was not a threat. NAFTA and APEC were also pursued as mechanisms to lock in the worldwide movement, begun in the 1980s, toward economic and trade liberalization. The creation of the World Trade Organization in 1995 was a further attempt to expand and strengthen the institutional foundations of liberal international order. Building on the old General Agreement on Tariffs and Trade, the WTO marked a major step in formalizing international trade law. An organization was established with an independent secretariat, a dispute-settlement mechanism, and an expanded framework for trade cooperation.[18] In an interview in 2006, Clinton made the point directly: "I was heavily influenced by the success of the post–World War II and Cold War multilateral organizations. . . . I saw that they worked, and at the end of the Cold War, I saw an opportunity for the first time in history to globalize them in a way that the East-West division had prevented."[19] The postwar era was not so much a "unipolar moment" as a "multilateral moment," an opportunity for the United States to shape the world in a way that would outlast momentary power advantages.[20]

The Clinton administration's decision to invite China to join the WTO was perhaps the capstone of this liberal internationalist strategy. Clinton saw China's rise as part of a rapidly unfolding globalization of the world system. The United States would gain in this globalizing world, China would be transformed, and its integration into the world economic system would be a win-win proposition. China's involvement in the trade system would have liberalizing effects on its society, creating domestic constituencies for openness and political reform. Once it became enmeshed in the WTO's liberal rules and practices and began to realize the benefits of trade and economic growth, incentives would be generated to liberalize its domestic economy and institutions. This was not a naive expectation that China would turn into a Western-style democracy. The assumption was that economic openness would have a liberalizing effect on Chinese society and that this would lead to bottom-up demands for political change.[21] In May 2000, Congress voted to award China permanent normal trade relations, and effectively backed China's bid for WTO membership. Clinton emphasized the liberal logic of this move. "By joining the WTO, China is not simply agreeing to import more of our products; it is agreeing to import one of democracy's most cherished values: economic freedom."[22] China was growing rapidly and its impact on the world economy was unavoidable. WTO membership would bias its ascent in the direction of Western norms and practices. At this transitional moment, globalization was seen as a liberalizing force and, as one administration official put it, Clinton "bet his presidency on globalization."[23]

This American engagement strategy with China extended into the George W. Bush administration. China would grow both economically and militarily, but through the dynamics of interdependence it would also become more democratic at home and cooperative abroad. "Open trade is a force for freedom in China. . . . Free trade has introduced new technologies that offer Chinese people access to uncensored information and democratic ideas," President George W. Bush argued in May 2001. "When we open trade, we open minds."[24] Several years later, Deputy Secretary of State Robert Zoellick provided an explicit statement of this logic in a speech urging China to take on the role of a "responsible stakeholder." Zoellick maintained that China was a major beneficiary of the American-led international order, and the United States expected it to act responsibly. China would gain voice and leadership in exchange for supporting the existing international order—and its Western-defined values and priorities. Zoellick urged China to "adjust to the rules developed over the last century." If it did, it could expect to become a leading state within this order: "It would work with us to sustain the international system that has enabled its success."[25] The door to China's integration into the Western liberal order was open.

Meanwhile, economic and political liberalism spread worldwide. Having watched in the 1980s as the diverging economic fortunes of the Soviet system and export-oriented capitalist states became increasingly apparent, governments in the 1990s increasingly engaged in market-oriented economic reforms—liberalization of their foreign economic policies, privatization, and deregulation. Economic liberalism was manifest in a wide range of policies. The privatization of state enterprises, as Beth Simmons, Frank Dobbin, and Geoffrey Garrett observe, "went from an iconoclastic policy idea in Margaret Thatcher's 1979 British election manifesto to a major element of economic policy in both the developed and developing world over the course of twenty years."[26] During the same period, countries increasingly opened their economies to cross-border flows of capital and trade. Internationally, the World Bank, the International Monetary Fund (IMF), and other financial institutions embraced the Washington Consensus, proscribing market-oriented policies for borrowing countries and governments pursuing economic reforms. IMF lending and world trade grew rapidly. By the turn of the century, developing countries accounted for 47 percent of world gross national product and a third of world trade.[27] Countries everywhere began to integrate into the world economy and operate within its expanding system of rules and institutions.

The 1980s and 1990s were also a period of political liberalization when a "third wave" of democratization and liberal constitutionalism spread around the world.[28] In what Simmons, Dobbin, and Garrett call the "headline statistic of the late twentieth century," the proportion of democratic countries more than doubled, rising from under 30 percent in the early 1980s to almost 60 percent in the first decade of the twenty-first century. (The number of sovereign states in the world also doubled in these decades.)[29] Political transitions to democracy manifested different patterns across regions. Latin American countries began to democratize in the 1970s, and East Asia and the Pacific followed in the 1980s. The fall of the Berlin Wall and the collapse of communism in the former Soviet bloc triggered a wave of democratization across Eastern Europe.[30] The end of Cold War polarization also undermined many military and one-party dictatorships that had previously been backed by one of the superpowers. Not all the resulting regime changes fully crossed the democratic threshold. Some authoritarian regimes used partial liberalization as a way of holding on to autocratic rule.[31] Other regimes, which did engage in more thoroughgoing democratic transitions, have since reverted to authoritarianism. But as the 1990s ended, democracy appeared to be on the march.[32]

The broad trends toward economic and political liberalism during the last decades of the twentieth century are captured in Figure 2.1, which tracks shifts in three indicators of liberalization from 1980 to 2004. The first indicator shows the percentage of government revenue that comes from the privatization of state ownership, which is an indicator of domestic economic liberalization. The second is a measure of the global average of financial openness—or capital account openness—which shows the degree of foreign economic liberalization. The third indicator shows the proportion of democratic countries in the world.

The confluence of these trends shows that the shifts toward liberal democracy and an open world economy were simultaneous and reinforcing during the decades. The spread of economic and political liberalism was driven by a variety of forces, including, importantly, that capitalist democracies were increasingly outperforming countries in the Soviet bloc. This was true well before the end of the Cold War. With the collapse of the Soviet Union, communism disappeared as a grand alternative to liberal capitalist democracy. In the meantime, the United States and the other leading capitalist states increasingly seemed to provide the world with an attractive model for domestic and foreign economic reform. The IMF, World Bank, and other institutions provided the policy ideas and resources that reinforced this liberalization movement. The United States put its unrivaled geopolitical and ideological weight behind the movement, supporting the expansion of regional and global institutions that would facilitate and lock in liberal economic and political transitions.[33] The Western liberal subsystem of the Cold War bipolar world was spreading outward, providing the ideals and institutions for a one-world global order.

As the twentieth century ended, the United States found itself at the center of an expanding liberal international order. In one sense, the spread of political and economic liberalism reflected the shifting distribution of power. The collapse of the Soviet Union left the United States as the unipolar power. This one nation possessed such a disproportionate share of material capabilities that it was

Figure 2.1. Spread of Economic and Political Liberalism

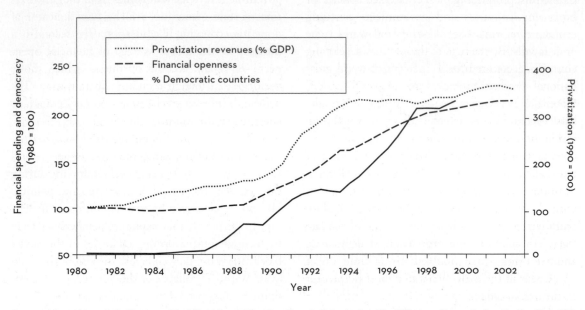

Financial spending and democracy (1980 = 100)

Privatization (1990 = 100)

- ············ Privatization revenues (% GDP)
- – – – Financial openness
- —— % Democratic countries

Year

unambiguously in a class by itself. Given its unipolar position, the spread of economic and political liberalism is easy to explain. The character of the international order reflected the orientation of its most powerful state. The United States used its commanding position to push liberalism outward into the world. There were no alternative centers of power and no other games in town. But the causal arrows also flow in the opposite direction. In important respects, unipolarity was not the cause but the consequence of liberal order. Unipolarity was created by a distinctive material distribution of capabilities, but also by the absence of other states attempting to become poles. A pole is not only an aggregation of power but a hub of institutions and relationships that states use to connect to other states.[34] What made the United States unipolar was not only its unrivaled possession of hard power, denominated in military, technological, and eco-

nomic assets; it was also that America was situated at the center of liberal international order that other states sought to join.[35] Power created order, but order also created power. Unipolarity emerged in the post–Cold War period because alternative poles, seen not just as projectors of power but as attractors of allegiance, fell away.[36]

Several features of the post–Cold War liberal order made it easier for states to join it rather than resist it or balance against it. First, the order was organized around multilateral rules and institutions. This made it relatively easy for states to make political and economic transitions and apply for membership. Multilateral economic organizations, starting with the Bretton Woods institutions, were designed to be expandable. The specific criteria for entry into regional and global institutions varied across the system. But the underlying logic of multilateralism was that states meeting the standards are welcome to join, which biased the post–Cold War transitional moment in favor of integration and expansion. Beyond this, the liberal order attracted transitioning states because it offered benefits and protections. In effect, it provided "goods and services" for states that affiliated with it. The most basic of these services was security protection. Other goods and services included access to markets, foreign aid, and technical assistance. To be inside the order was to gain favorable terms in an open system of trade and investment. Institutions like the IMF and the World Bank provided standby assistance when developing economies entered a crisis. In effect, the liberal order was an intergovernmental club in which membership had its privileges.[37] Third, to the extent that the United States and the other powerful states in the system also operated inside this order—respecting its rules and institutions—smaller states had some reassurance that these leading states would not simply coerce and dominate them. Obviously, the United States did sometimes employ coercion, intervention, and crude forms of power politics, but it was at least possible for states undergoing liberal transitions to see complexities and institutional restraints in the American exercise of hegemonic power. The institutional underpinnings of the liberal order made America's material power position both more durable and less threatening to other states. To join the liberal order was to gain voice opportunities and institutional access to the world's most powerful state.[38] In these ways, the liberal order biased the strategic direction of states toward integration and participation.

The world that emerged in the aftermath of the Cold War was both surprising and remarkable. It was surprising to many observers that the Western liberal order built during the Cold War survived the end of this bipolar struggle. Balance-of-power realists, in particular, predicted that NATO and the other Western institutions created in response to the Soviet threat would not remain in place—let alone expand—when that threat disappeared.[39] What these observers missed was that the Western liberal democracies' order-building project had begun before and had been pursued in the shadows of the Cold War. This was a product of the revolution in relations within postwar Europe and between Europe, the United States, and the wider world of liberal democracies. It was the project driven by the disasters of the 1930s and efforts to put the Western liberal capitalist countries on a more stable foundation. The order that undergirded the wider global system after the collapse of Soviet communism did not need to be constructed, unlike in 1815, 1919, and 1945, because it was already in place.

The Crisis of the Liberal Order

During the Cold War, the American-led liberal order was lodged and its foundation was laid within the Western side of the bipolar world system. After the collapse of the Soviet Union, as the nucleus of an expanding global system, this liberal order was freed from its Cold War foundations and became the platform for an expanding global system of liberal democracy, markets, and complex interdependence. A worldwide "liberal moment" had arrived. Yet at this very moment, the seeds of crisis were planted. The globalization of liberal order was more fraught than many liberal internationalists appreciated at the time. During the Cold War, the bipolar global system served to reinforce the roles, commitments, and community that were together manifest as the American-led international order. The Cold War-era Western order was not simply an alliance or a grouping of trading partners. It was a loosely functioning political order with institutions, bargains, and shared understandings of its social purposes. The crisis of liberal internationalism can be seen as a slow-motion reaction to the global expansion of this postwar Western order. The characteristics of the liberal order that made it stable and resilient during the Cold

War, and thus attractive to transitioning states after the Cold War, were eroded as it globalized.

Specifically, the expansion of liberal internationalism weakened and undermined two facets of the postwar liberal order. One was the order's governance logic: its political bargains, institutional commitments, and authority relations. The other was its social purposes and embedded liberal protections. In both these dimensions, the underpinnings of the postwar liberal order have given way. The order has lost the shared understanding of itself as a "security community," a group of like-minded states cooperating for mutual protection and advancement.[40] And it has become weaker, thinner, and less connected to the political and economic well-being of the societies and constituencies at its core. We can look at these two facets in turn.

Governance and Authority Relations

The globalization of the liberal order created problems of governance and authority. During the Cold War, the Western-oriented liberal order was led by the United States, Europe, and Japan, and organized around a complex array of bargains, working relationships, and institutions. In the early postwar years, most of the core agreements about trade, finance, and monetary relations were hammered out between the United States and Britain. West Germany and Japan later became "junior partners" in a Western-oriented trilateral system. These countries did not agree on everything, but relative to the rest of the world, they were a small and homogeneous group of states. Their economies converged, their interests were aligned, and they generally trusted each other. They were also on the same side of the Cold War, and the American-led alliance system reinforced cooperation. This system of alliances made it easier for the United States and its partners to make commitments and bear burdens and for European and Asian states to accept American leadership. In this sense, the Cold War liberal order reinforced the belief that the liberal democracies were involved in a common political project.

At the heart of this order was a set of strategic bargains between the United States and its economic and security partners, especially West Germany and Japan. As the leading state, the United States provided them with security protection and maintained a relatively open domestic market to absorb their exports. In return, these partners held US dollars, allowing the United States to run balance-of-payments deficits without facing the adjustment requirements of other states.[41] This arrangement allowed the United States to be a generous provider of both security and markets. The United States underwrote the rules and institutions of the order while reserving the right to act unilaterally to protect its own national interests. Its partners enjoyed the benefits of these bargains. They gained access to the American market and raw materials and were protected by American military power. Alliance-based security protection also allowed these states to devote greater resources to domestic economic growth and competitiveness.[42] The United States, as the dominant power, placed itself within a complex of institutions that gave its partners regular channels of access to Washington policymaking.[43] The United States played the role of liberal hegemon, supporting openness and stability across the order. In return, its partners supported the United States in the Cold War.

But since the Cold War ended, the set of bargains that held this core grouping together has slowly weakened. To be sure, these states' overall orientation has remained remarkably stable. Japan and Western Europe, led by Germany, continued through the 1990s and into the current period to be committed to open trade relations and alliance ties with the United States. The United States remained committed to leading—indeed expanding—the liberal order. But as Michael Mastanduno argues, the key sources of American leverage behind the Cold War–era hegemonic bargains—the security dependence of its partners, the unique position of the dollar, and the indispensability of its market—have eroded.[44] The end of the Cold War eliminated the common threat that had made NATO and the US-Japan alliance necessary. After the September 11 terrorist attacks and the American invasion of Iraq, the security challenges that had united the leading liberal democracies were less fully aligned. The expansion of the world economy, led by the rise of China, meant that the American market was no longer the indispensable engine of global economic growth. Germany and Japan remain tied to the American market, but both are increasingly integrated into their own regional trading and production systems; and because of this, they have found it less necessary to finance US deficits, by holding dollars, or to play the role of junior partners. In these various ways, the old security and economic bargains between the United States and its key partners have eroded.

Even if the old trilateral partnerships endure, they are no longer at the center of all markets and exchanges. The rise of China, in particular, has altered the center of gravity of the world economy. In 2010, China passed Japan to become the world's second-largest economy in market-exchange terms, and it is closing in on the United States. Since it began its market reforms, China's foreign trade has expanded rapidly, from approximately $20 billion in 1978 to $500 billion in 2000 to $3 trillion in 2016. In the past two decades, China has become the hub of fast-growing regional economies linked together by trade and manufacturing networks. When the Cold War ended, the United States was the leading trade partner with Japan, South Korea, and most of the countries of Southeast Asia. Three decades later, China holds this position. In 2015, it also became America's largest trading partner.[45] As its economy has grown, China has also increased its military capabilities and expanded its geopolitical ambitions in East Asia and around the world. It is now both a major player in the world economy and a rival of American hegemony in East Asia and beyond.

These new circumstances complicated American governance of the liberal international order. It is now China—not Germany and Japan—that the United States must engage in managing the world economy. But the trilateral economic and security bargains that underlay the Cold War liberal order and its expansion in the 1990s are not easily recreated in US-China relations. As I noted earlier, the United States did offer a hegemonic bargain to China. Beginning with George H. W. Bush, each post–Cold War American president—until Donald Trump—tried to entice China into the role of "responsible stakeholder." In the 1990s, China seemed to agree to this bargain. It joined the WTO and accepted the market-opening commitments that came with developing-country membership. In the decade after it entered the WTO, China's imports and exports expanded rapidly. It did not actively challenge the American security position in East Asia and it agreed to hold large quantities of US Treasury securities. China articulated a grand strategy of "peaceful rise," It integrated into the world trade and financial systems, and enjoyed rapid economic growth.[46] Seen from Washington, China was growing rapidly and becoming powerful, but it was doing so, at least loosely, within a framework of Western-oriented rules and institutions that would bias its political development in an open and liberal direction.

Over the past decade, this liberal hegemonic bargain began to break down. China got what it expected—access to the world trading system and achievement of rapid economic growth—but it did not undertake the liberal reforms that Western governments expected in return. Under President Xi, China became more illiberal, more nationalistic, and more assertive. Its military buildup, expansive maritime claims, and assertive economic diplomacy were increasingly seen by Washington as direct challenges to America's hegemony in the region. As Mastanduno argues, "Xi's China has acted less like a rule taker, even less as a responsible stakeholder, and more as a nascent rule maker."[47] Starting with the Obama administration, the United States responded by looking for ways to counter China's emerging rule-making role in Asia and the world economy. President Obama announced a "pivot to Asia," seeking to reassure allies of America's economic and security commitment to the region. At the center of this pivot was the Trans-Pacific Partnership (TPP), a framework for negotiating closer trade ties between the United States and its East Asian partners. While the TPP was expected to generate economic gains, Obama defended it as an initiative to help ensure that China would not "write the rules of the global economy."[48] It was also seen as a way to strengthen ties to allies and forge new ties with countries, which would be necessary to form a counterweight to growing Chinese power. By then, liberal anticipations that China would integrate itself into the liberal international order as a responsible stakeholder had all but disappeared.[49]

Given a pathway into the expanding post–Cold War liberal order, China achieved rapid and dramatic economic success. But this very success has undermined the hegemonic bargains holding the order together. As China has become an economic peer of the United States, it has been increasingly discontented with the role of a junior partner or rule taker. During the Cold War and the 1990s, the liberal international order was structured around bargains between the United States, Western Europe, and Japan, which were embedded in an alliance system that made it easier for these states to settle their differences. But China is growing powerful outside this alliance system, and its sheer size makes it a more independent player in the world economy. It thus sits both inside and outside the post–Cold War liberal international order. It is sufficiently large and integrated into the world economy to be critical to the stable functioning of this order. But it is also sufficiently outside it—and outside the liberal democratic world—to make agreements on the governance of the order very difficult.

The changing position of the United States has also unsettled the liberal order. American unipolarity after the Cold War did not trigger immediate efforts at great-power balancing in part because China and Russia were not yet in a position to challenge the United States. But the other powers also felt less need for balancing because the American-led order was built on a foundation of rules, institutions, and strategic bargains that shaped and restrained the way power was exercised. Nonetheless, the United States did not entirely escape reactions to its unrivaled power. As the world entered its unipolar moment, American power was increasingly an issue in world politics. During the Cold War, American power had a functional role in the system: it served as a balance against Soviet power. With the sudden emergence of unipolarity, American power was both less constrained and less functional. New debates emerged about American hegemonic power. What would restrain it? How credible was America's commitment to an open, rules-based international order?[50] The American war in Iraq and the Global War on Terror exacerbated these worries. The 2008 financial crisis, which began in the United States, also raised questions about the American economic model and its commitment to manage the open world system. With the Trump administration, the global reaction to American power has taken a new and dramatic turn. It is no longer a question of whether the United States will exercise power outside of a preexisting system of rules and institutions, but of how fully it is bent upon undermining that order. The entrance of the Trump administration has caused the political crisis of the liberal order to crescendo.[51]

The globalization of economic and political liberalism, in short, put in motion forces that undermined the governance logic of the order. As increasingly diverse states entered the order with new visions and agendas, the democratic world became no longer primarily Anglo-American or even Western. The liberal democratic world was expanding, but expansion made it a less coherent political community. The post–Cold War era also brought into play new and complex global issues, such as climate change, terrorism, weapons proliferation, and the growing challenges of interdependence. It was particularly hard for states in different regions, with different political orientations and levels of development, to reach consensus over these issues that raise fundamental questions of authority and governance. Who pays, who adjusts, who leads? How would authority across the expanding liberal order be redistributed among rising non-Western states? The old coalition—led by the United States, Europe, and Japan—built a postwar order on layers of bargains, institutions, and working relationships. But this old trilateral core is no longer as central to the global system as it once was. The crisis of liberal order today is partly a problem of how to reorganize its governance. The old foundations have weakened, but new bargains and governance relationships have yet to be negotiated.[52]

Social Purpose and Embedded Liberalism

It is also a crisis of social purpose and embedded liberalism. During the Cold War, the core states that formed the Western liberal order had a shared sense that they lived inside a community of liberal democracies—a political order that generated security and economic well-being for those within it. For most people, to be inside this order was to be better off than those outside it. Liberal democracies were able to reconcile economic openness and social protections within an organized system of multilateral cooperation. Together, the Western-oriented liberal order had features of what could be called a security community—a sort of mutual-protection society. But in more recent decades, as the liberal order has globalized, these security-community functions have eroded. The liberal order's social purposes—mutual protection and social advancement within a community of democratic states—have thinned out. It has come to look less like a security community and more like a platform of rules and institutions for capitalist transactions.[53]

During the Cold War, the economic foundations of this security community were organized around what John Ruggie has called "embedded liberalism."[54] * * * [T]his was the idea that the leading liberal democracies would seek to organize the world economy so as to reconcile market openness with social protections. The collapse of world markets in the 1930s was disastrous for the Western industrial societies; a central goal of policymakers was to reorganize and reopen the world economy while giving national governments the tools to promote economic stability. "Unlike the economic nationalism of the thirties," Ruggie argues, "it would be multilateral in character; unlike the liberalism of the gold standard and free trade, its multilateralism would be predicated upon domestic interventionism."[55] The compromise of embedded liberalism was aimed at taming the disruptive effects of market openness without eliminating the efficiency and welfare gains that came from open trade. Liberal democracies worked together to create rules and institutions that allowed states to stabilize and manage market risks. "National societies," Rawi Abdelal and John Ruggie argue, "shared the risks through varieties of safeguards and insurance schemes that composed, in part, the European welfare state or, in the ever-exceptional United States, the New Deal state."[56] This is why large segments of society across the liberal democratic world became constituencies for postwar liberal order.

The crisis of liberal order stems partly from the breakdown of this compromise. Beginning in the 1980s, the globalization of the liberal order entailed the liberalization of markets in both the advanced industrial and developing worlds. Policy elites in the United States and Europe championed the opening and deregulation markets—this was the so-called neoliberal policy agenda.[57] In trade, efforts at multilateral liberalization were extended to new areas, such as services, agriculture, international property rights, and regulatory harmonization. In the 1990s, the liberalization agenda was extended still further: the Clinton administration, in coordination with the IMF and the World Bank, tried to get developing countries to liberalize their closely guarded financial markets. Banking, stock, and bond markets were opened, and countries in Latin America, East Asia, and Central Europe moved from state-led economic growth strategies to reliance on market forces. In what became known as the Washington Consensus, the expansion of market society was widely seen by Western elites as the key to political liberalization and expansion as well as consolidation of the liberal world economy, thus opening up a new era of growth and social advancement.[58] Political and economic liberalism were seen as mutually reinforcing. But market expansion created new, sharp economic divides between winners and losers in Western societies, while weakening embedded liberal supports and protections. As Jeff Colgan and Robert Keohane argue, "the effects of a neoliberal economic agenda have eroded the social contract that had previously ensured crucial political support for the [liberal] order."[59]

The liberal order's social purposes have been undermined by rising economic insecurity and inequality across the advanced industrial world. Even before the 2008 financial crisis, the fortunes of workers and middle-class citizens in Europe and the United States had been stagnant for decades.[60] From the end of World War II to the 1970s, incomes grew rapidly in the United States for both lower- and upper-income classes, and the income gaps did not significantly widen. But this changed beginning in the 1970s. In the United States, almost all the growth in wealth since 1980 has gone to the top 20 percent of earners in society. Those without skills or a college education have increasingly fallen behind. Between 1974 and 2015, the real median household income for Americans without a college education declined by 24 percent, while median incomes for those with college degrees continued to gain. The concentration of income and wealth at the very top of society has risen to a level not seen since the 1920s.

Similar patterns played out at the global level. Branko Milanović has famously described the past two decades' differential gains across the global system as an "elephant curve." He finds that the vast bulk of gains in real per capita income have gone to two very different groups. One consists of workers in countries like China and India who have taken low-end manufacturing and service jobs at very low wage levels and have experienced dramatic gains—even if they remain at the lower end of the global income spectrum. Since 1990, more than a billion such people have moved out of extreme poverty—a remarkable shift in the life fortunes of a huge part of the global population.[61] This is the elephant's back. The other group is the top 1 percent—even top 0.01 percent—who have experienced massive increases in wealth. This is the elephant's trunk, extended upward.[62] Meanwhile, the middle and working classes in the advanced industrial countries have seen the fewest income gains. This stagnation in the economic fortunes of these middle segments of Western society has been reinforced by long-term shifts in technology, trade patterns, union organization, and manufacturing sites.[63] There have been great winners in the recent growth of the world economy—but the old constituencies of the Western liberal order are not among them.[64]

The security-community aspect of the liberal order has also been weakened by the simple expansion of the scope and diversity of the peoples and societies that make it up. The democratic world is now less Anglo-American, less Western. It includes most of the world—developed and developing, North and South, colonial and postcolonial, Asian and European. This too is a crisis born of success. But it brought an increasing divergence of views across the order about its members' place in the world and their historical legacies and grievances. The liberal world order now less resembled a community with a shared narrative of its past and future.[65] Expansion had weakened the shared identity—historical, geographic, and cultural—of the societies within it.

Taken together, the liberal order's social purposes are not what they once were. It is less obvious today that the liberal democratic world is a security community. What do citizens in Western democracies get from liberal internationalism? How does an open and loosely rules-based international order deliver physical and economic security to the great middle class? Throughout the twentieth century, liberal internationalism was tied to progressive and social democratic agendas within Western liberal democracies. It was not seen as the enemy of nationalism but as a tool permitting governments to pursue economic security and advancements at home. But in recent decades, this connection between social and economic advancement at home and liberal internationalism abroad has been broken.

The Limits and Durability of the Liberal Order

The expansion of the liberal order has revealed both its limits and its resiliency. The limits are most obvious in the order's increasingly fraught relations with China and Russia. Any hope that either country might become a "responsible stakeholder" in this order has been dashed. With Russia, the bargains between Washington and Moscow that ended the Cold War did not survive the 1990s. The expansion of NATO, disputes over energy pipelines, and the refusal to accommodate Russia's regional ambitions all helped break down relations.[66] The collapse of the Russian economy at the end of the Cold War left Russia weakened and resentful. The West's efforts to manage relations have also labored under the burden, centuries in the making, of antidemocratic and antiliberal Russian domestic politics. Russia's loss of empire and the West's encroachments on its traditional spheres of influence added to its grievances and rivalry.[67] The United States could have made more far-reaching concessions to Russia on security,

such as forgoing NATO enlargement. But this would have meant ignoring the desires of Eastern European states to join the Western alliance and European Union and to create an institutional basis for their transitions to liberal democracy. In any event, it is not clear that a more generous post–Cold War settlement would have put Russia on a path to Western-style reform and integration.[68] That path disappeared with the failure of Russia's transition to democracy in the 1990s.

China's reversal of its experiments with economic and political reform is a more recent and surprising development. For the first two decades after the Cold War, American leaders looked for ways to integrate China into the existing order. China, in turn, pursued ambitious programs of economic liberalization, joined the established global multilateral bodies, and became deeply integrated in the global system. It took over Taiwan's permanent seat on the UN Security Council. It participates in the WTO and plays a role in the IMF, the World Bank, and the G-20.[69] In ideology and vision, it slowly moved away from earlier decades' calls for a "new international order" and began calling for incremental reforms to global rules and institutions. Its discourse became more about fairness and justice in the organization of the global order—which meant, fundamentally, giving China a greater voice in running the existing global institutions. It now seeks to make the international order "more reasonable" by giving China a larger role in the IMF and the World Bank, more voice in international leadership forums such as the G-20, and, over the long term, making the renminbi a world reserve currency. These reforms all suggest a Chinese movement toward the center of the international economic order.

Yet under President Xi's leadership, China has signaled that its embrace of reform has limits. It has redoubled its commitment to one-party authoritarian political rule and begun to pursue ambitious regional economic programs—such as the Belt and Road Initiative. Now neither fully inside nor fully outside the post–Cold War liberal international order, it is actively pursuing its interests inside most of the leading global institutions, while also trying to move the world toward a post-Western order that is less tied to liberal economic and political values.[70] China had its most successful decades of economic growth and rising living standards during the era of American unipolarity, and it is now using its rapidly acquired wealth and power to challenge and reorient this order.

These developments help illuminate the limits of the global spread of liberal internationalism. First, the failure of the hegemonic bargain offered it by a succession of American presidents shows that China has become too big to be integrated into a US-led liberal international order. Unlike Japan and Germany, China rose up (or as the Chinese would say, reemerged) outside the United States alliance system. The security and economic bargains that provided the foundation for the Cold War–era liberal order are not transferable to China, which is increasingly a peer great power. Second, liberal internationalists assumed that as China liberalized its economy and integrated into the world economy, growing domestic and international pressures would compel it to liberalize its political institutions. This did not happen. Unlike South Korea, Taiwan, and other East Asian countries, China was large enough to resist international pressures and, absent a democratic transition, its autocratic state elites have incentives to resist the rules and norms that privilege liberal democracy. Finally, globalization has fragmented the liberal order. It was an amalgam of institutions and policy realms even during the Cold War, when it was more delimited in geopolitical space and membership. But as this "inside" order became the "outside" order, what was once a loose political community became a sprawling and fragmented system of rules, institutions, and relationships. This shift in its character has made it easier for states—particularly those like China that are ambivalent about liberal order—to pick and choose which parts of the order they wish to join. China can get the benefits of participating in an open and loosely rules-based order, without committing to domestic regime change or strategic partnership with the leading liberal states.

The expansion of the liberal order has also illuminated the sources of its durability.[71] First, it clearly has integrative tendencies. States of many sizes and types have found paths into the club. Germany and Japan were the first major states to reconstitute themselves—initially through coercive occupation—and integrate into postwar security and economic institutions. Some states joined the order as client states or frontline allies during the Cold War. After the Cold War, many former Soviet client states and some of the former Soviet republics joined the European Union and NATO. Many countries integrated into the order by making political and economic transitions. One can see this in the steady expansion of the Organization for Economic Cooperation and Development, a club of the developed market economies, which has grown from twenty countries at its founding in 1960 to thirty-four today.[72] The point is that a wide range of states outside the West have sought to get into this order so as to enjoy its benefits. The order's institutions and ideology—hegemonic and liberal internationalist—seem to facilitate this integration.

A second source of durability is the liberal order's hierarchical authority relations. Hierarchical orders can differ in the extent to which they are dominated by a single state. A leading state can organize and dominate, standing above other states, or else the order might consist of a coalition of major states that cooperatively exert leadership. In the latter case, the order is organized around an array of great powers, junior partners, client states, and other stakeholders. In the economic realm, authority and decision making are shared. The formal multilateral institutions—the IMF, the World Bank, and the WTO—are organized this way, as are the informal leadership groups like the G-7 and G-20. They are hierarchical institutions inhabited by coalitions of leading states. The United States and Western Europe remain overrepresented in many of these institutions, but they are not based on a fixed membership.[73] Doors are open, and bargains are on the table. That the G-20 has joined the G-7 as an important leadership forum is a reflection of this capacity of governance mechanisms to evolve and expand beyond the old Western great powers.[74]

A third source of durability is the way economic gains are spread across the international order. Orders can differ in their distribution of economic and other material rewards. In traditional imperial orders, the profits and gains flowed overwhelmingly to the imperial core. In colonial and informal empires, they flowed disproportionately to the wealthy and powerful states, classes, and social groupings that organized and ran the order. But the American-led liberal order, with its system of open trade and investment, distributed economic gains more widely.[75] Trade and investment across the system allowed states near and far to grow and advance and, often, to outpace the United States and its Western partners.[76] States around the world have integrated themselves into the existing system in pursuit of trade and growth.

A fourth feature of international order is the degree to which it accommodates diverse models of capitalism and economic development. In practice if not in ideology, the postwar global order has been relatively open to these differences.[77] There have been three general types of capitalist models: the Anglo-American neoliberal or market-fundamentalist model that has dominated economic debates in Western capitals from the end of the Cold War until the 2008 global financial crisis; an older postwar model of "embedded liberalism," which has emphasized the social welfare state and "managed" openness; and the statist model that has been pursued throughout East Asia and the developing world.[78] These models have tended to coexist and wax and wane across the decades. A recent study of the "distribution of identity" relating to models of political economy across major Western and non-Western countries revealed a remarkable convergence of ideological preferences for some combination of economic liberalism and social democracy. In all the countries surveyed, there was great skepticism about neoliberalism but widespread support for social democratic and liberal approaches.[79]

What makes the liberal international order resilient are the many constituencies and interests tied to it. Its relatively open and integrative features have led to a steady expansion of stakeholders but also to fragmentation.[80] As the social purposes and embedded liberal protections have eroded, the order has overrun its political foundations and lost political support within Western industrial societies. It is now a more complex system of semi-independent international institutions and cooperative relations. While this fragmentation has weakened the coherence of the order, it has also reduced the incentives for outright opposition. Liberal order is less like a castle with a drawbridge and walls and more like a shopping mall. It is easy for states to enter and exist and it is easier for them to resist or avoid its rules and institutions. By the same token, the order provides both less opportunity and less need for outright opposition to it.

Many of the institutions and regimes that make up the liberal international order are not uniquely liberal. Rather, they are Westphalian, in that they are designed to solve problems of sovereign states, whether democratic or authoritarian—and many of the key participants are not liberal or democratic. Even during the Cold War, when the liberal order was primarily an arrangement among liberal democracies, the Soviet Union often worked with these countries to help build international institutions. Moscow's committed antiliberalism did not stop it from partnering with Washington to create arms-control agreements or cooperating with the World Health Organization to spearhead a global campaign to eradicate smallpox. More recently, countries across the democratic and authoritarian divide have crafted global rules to guard against environmental destruction. The signatories of the Paris climate agreement, for example, include autocracies such as China, Iran, and Russia. Westphalian approaches have also led to agreements governing the oceans, the atmosphere, outer space, and Antarctica. The 1987 Montreal Protocol, for example, which reversed the destruction of the ozone layer, was supported by both democracies and authoritarian states. Westphalian internationalism involves agreements that do not challenge the sovereignty of states but embody collective measures to solve problems that states cannot address on their own.[81]

Most institutions in the liberal order do not demand that their backers be liberal democracies. They simply need to be status quo states that are capable of fulfilling their commitments. These institutions do not challenge the Westphalian system; they codify it. The United Nations, for example, enshrines the principle of state sovereignty and, through the permanent members of the Security Council, the notion of great-power decision making. All these factors make the order more durable. Because much international cooperation has nothing to do with liberalism and democracy, regimes that are hostile to liberal democracy can still retain their international agendas and support the order's core institutions. The persistence of Westphalian institutions provides a lasting foundation on which distinctively liberal and democratic institutions can be erected and defended.

Finally, the durability of a loosely organized system of open and rules-based order rests on the deep political imperatives that spring from rising economic and security interdependence. Liberal international ideas and projects have remained alive and evolved over the past two centuries because liberal democracies—and other states—have struggled to cope with the complex challenges of interdependence. As long as interdependence—economic, security-related, and environmental—continues to grow, peoples and governments everywhere will be compelled to work together to solve problems or else to suffer grievous harm. Growing interdependence creates incentives for political cooperation at the heart of the liberal international project. Liberal democratic capitalist societies have thrived and expanded because they have found a way to reconcile sovereignty and interdependence—exploiting the gains that come from modernity while protecting themselves from its dangers.

This dynamic of constant change and ever-increasing interdependence is only accelerating. Global capitalism has drawn more people and countries into cross-border webs of exchange, making virtually the entire world population dependent on the competent management of international finance and trade. The alternatives to a functioning liberal international order are not very attractive; even China, the most powerful illiberal state in the world, has no grand alternative vision of order to offer. If it is not possible to radically reduce the conditions of economic and security interdependence, then the alternative to liberal international order is simply a more chaotic and dangerous interdependent world. International order does not rise spontaneously and liberal order is not self-generating. But the interests and constituencies that have a stake in some sort of updated and reformed liberal international order are growing—not shrinking. This is the ultimate source of the resiliency of liberal international order: more people stand to lose from its undoing than stand to win.

In short, the same forces of globalization that brought large parts of the world into the Western liberal order also made that order less like a club and more like a public utility—a system of functional institutions and regimes to which states could variously attach themselves. At the same time, the stagnation of incomes and rising inequality in Western industrial societies eroded the order's ability to fulfill its old social purposes of economic and social protection. This is why a major "outside" power like China is able to embed itself only partially within the order: accepting the whole package is no longer either as necessary or as attractive as it once was.

Yet, even as the postwar liberal order has overrun its foundations, overturned its borders, and undermined its social purposes, its deep logic of open and rules-based cooperation remains intact. Indeed, the crisis has illuminated it. Liberal democracies still exist, as they always have, within a wider world of increasing economic and security interdependence. The current political backlash to these global realities is both inevitable and doomed to fail. There is no escape. Liberal democracies will find themselves doing what they have always done in moments of crisis—searching for ways to reestablish and reinforce the political foundations for liberal capitalist democracy.

NOTES

1. David A. Bell, "The Many Lives of Liberalism," *New York Review of Books,* 17 January 2019, https://www.nybooks.com/articles/2019/01/17/many-lives-of-liberalism/.

2. See Edward Luce, *The Retreat of Western Liberalism* (New York: Atlantic Monthly, 2017); and Bill Emmott, *The Fate of the West: The Battle to Save the World's Most Successful Political Idea* (New York: PublicAffairs, 2017).

3. Karl Polanyi, *The Great Transformation: The Political and Economic Origins of Our Times* (New York: Farrar and Rinehart, 1944).

4. E. H. Carr, *The Twenty Years' Crisis, 1919–1939* (London: Macmillan, 1940).

5. Adam Roberts, "An 'Incredibly Swift Transition': Reflections on the End of the Cold War," in Melvyn P. Leffler and Odd Arne Westad, eds., *The Cambridge History of the Cold War,* Vol. 3 (Cambridge: Cambridge University Press, 2010), p. 513.

6. For accounts of the end of the Cold War, see Robert Service, *The End of the Cold War: 1985–1991* (New York: PublicAffairs, 2015); Mary Elise Sarotte, *The Collapse: The Accidental Opening of the Berlin Wall* (New York: Basic Books, 2005); and Jacques Lévesque, *The Enigma of 1989: The USSR and the Liberation of Eastern Europe* (Berkeley: University of California Press, 1997). For portraits of American diplomacy at the end of the Cold War, see Robert D. Zelikow and Condoleezza Rice, *Germany Unified and Europe Transformed: A Study in Statecraft* (Cambridge, MA: Harvard University Press, 1995); and Robert L. Hutchings, *American Diplomacy and the End of the Cold War: An Insider's Account of U.S. Diplomacy in Europe, 1989–1992* (Baltimore: Johns Hopkins University Press, 1998).

7. Quoted in Daniel Hamilton, "A More European Germany, a More German Europe," *Journal of International Affairs,* Vol. 45, No. 1 (Summer 1991), pp. 127–49.

8. Thomas Bagger, "The World According to Germany: Reassessing 1989," *Washington Quarterly,* Vol. 41, No. 4 (Winter 2019), p. 54.

9. George H. W. Bush, "Inaugural Address," 20 January 1989, https://millercenter.org/the-presidency/presidential-speeches/january-20-1989-inaugural-address.

10. George H. W. Bush, "Address to the United Nations General Assembly," 25 September 1989, https://2009-2017.state.gov/p/io/potusunga/207266.htm.

11. Quoted in Tony Smith, *America's Mission: The United States and the Worldwide Struggle for Democracy* (Princeton, NJ: Princeton University Press, 1994), 315.

12. See Wallace J. Thies, *Why NATO Endures* (Cambridge: Cambridge University Press, 2009).

13. James A. Baker, *The Politics of Diplomacy: Revolution, War, and Peace, 1989–1992* (New York: Putnam, 1995), pp. 605–6.

14. Anthony Lake, "From Containment to Enlargement," *Vital Speeches of the Day,* Vol. 60, No. 1 (15 October 1993), pp. 13–19. See also Douglas Brinkley, "Democratic Enlargement: The Clinton Doctrine," *Foreign Policy,* No. 106 (Spring 1997), p. 116.

15. See White House, *A National Security Strategy of Engagement and Enlargement* (Washington, DC, July 1994).

16. For accounts of Clinton's strategy of expanding the community of market democracies, see Derek Chollet and James Goldgeier, *America between the Wars: From 11/9 to 9/11* (New York: PublicAffairs, 2008); and Smith, *America's Mission,* chap. 11.

17. See James Goldgeier, *Not Whether but When: The U.S. Decision to Enlarge NATO* (Washington, DC: Brookings Institution Press, 1999). For more recent evidence, see Mary Elise Sarotte, "How to Enlarge NATO: The Debate within the Clinton Administration, 1993–95," *International Security,* Vol. 41, No. 1 (Summer 2019), pp. 7–41.

18. On the creation of the WTO and its evolving relationship with China, see Paul Blustein, *Schism: China, America, and the Fracturing of the Global Trading System* (Waterloo, ON: CIGI Press, 2019).

19. Quoted in Strobe Talbott, *The Great Experiment: The Story of Ancient Empires, Modern States, and the Quest for a Global Nation* (New York: Simon and Schuster, 2008), p. 329.

20. See Talbott, *The Great Experiment,* pp. 329–30.

21. For a careful analysis of the assumptions and expectations behind the Clinton administration's engagement policy toward China, see Alastair Iain Johnston, "The Failures of the 'Failure of Engagement' with China," *Washington Quarterly,* Vol. 42, No. 2 (Summer 2019), pp. 99–114.

22. Bill Clinton, "Speech at the Paul H. Nitze School of Advanced International Studies," 8 March 2000, quoted in Michael Mandelbaum, *The Ideas That Conquered the World: Peace, Democracy, and Free Markets in the Twenty-First Century* (New York: PublicAffairs, 2002), p. 455.

23. Quoted in Chollet and Goldgeier, *America between the Wars,* p. 153.

24. George W. Bush, "Remarks to the Los Angeles World Affairs Council," 29 May 2001, https://www.govinfo.gov/content/pkg/PPP-2001-book1/pdf/PPP-2001-book1-doc-pg593.pdf.

25. Robert Zoellick, "Whither China? From Membership to Responsibility," remarks to the National Committee on US-China Relations, New York, 21 September 2005, https://2001-2009.state.gov/s/d/former/zoellick/rem/53682.htm.

26. Beth Simmons, Frank Dobbin, and Geoffrey Garrett, "Introduction: The Diffusion of Liberalization," in Simmons, Dobbin, and Garrett, eds., *The Global Diffusion of Markets and Democracy* (New York: Cambridge University Press, 2008), p. 3.

27. Anne O. Krueger, "The World Economy at the Start of the 21st Century," remarks by the first deputy managing director, International Monetary Fund (Annual Gilbert Lecture, Rochester University, New York), 6 April 2006, https://www.imf.org/en/News/Articles/2015/09/28/04/53/sp040606.

28. See Samuel P. Huntington, *The Third Wave: Democratization in the Late Twentieth Century* (Norman: University of Oklahoma Press, 1991).

29. Simmons, Dobbin, and Garrett, "Introduction," p. 3. See also Adam Przeworski, Michael E. Alvarez, José Antonio Cheibub, and Fernando Limongi, *Democracy and Development: Political Institutions and Material Well-Being in the World, 1950–1990* (Cambridge: Cambridge University Press, 2000).

30. The regional context is important in determining the incidence and success of democratic transitions. The greater the proportion of democracies already existing in a region, the greater the likelihood of democratic transitions by the remaining authoritarian regimes. See Kristian Skrede Gliditsch and Michael D. Ward, "Diffusion and the International Context of Democratization," *International Organization,* Vol. 60, No. 4 (2006), pp. 911–33.

31. See Stephan Haggard and Robert R. Kaufman, "Democratization during the Third Wave," *Annual Review of Political Science,* Vol. 19 (2016), p. 127.

32. Haggard and Kaufman emphasize the uniqueness of the international setting that facilitated the diffusion of liberalism and democracy. "The expectation of strong diffusion processes was associated with a particular moment in world history: the collapse of an authoritarian superpower, the dissolution of its empire, a brief moment of unchallenged American supremacy, and a strong belief in the combined power of economic interdependence, international institutions, and democracy." Haggard and Kaufman, "Democratization during the Third Wave," p. 137.

33. As Carles Boix finds, in historical periods when the international system is dominated by a liberal or authoritarian hegemon, the great powers are more likely to promote like-minded regimes. The most pronounced manifestation of this international setting occurred in the two decades after the end of the Cold War. See Boix, "Democracy, Development, and the International System," *American Political Science Review,* Vol. 105, No. 4 (2011), pp. 809–28.

34. On definitions of polarity, see G. John Ikenberry, Michael Mastanduno, and William C. Wohlforth, "Introduction: Unipolarity, State Behavior, and Systemic Consequences," in Ikenberry, Mastanduno, and Wohlforth, eds., *International Relations Theory and the Consequences of Unipolarity* (New York: Cambridge University Press, 2011), pp. 1–32.

35. Anne-Marie Slaughter argues that power and influence are created by countries that act as hubs of global networks. See Slaughter, *The Chessboard and the Web: Strategies of Connection in a Networked World* (New Haven, CT: Yale University Press, 2017).

36. G. John Ikenberry, "The Liberal Sources of American Unipolarity," in Ikenberry, Mastanduno, and Wohlforth, *International Relations Theory and the Consequences of Unipolarity,* pp. 216–51.

37. On the "club benefits" of liberal order, see Ikenberry, "The Liberal Sources of American Unipolarity"; and Daniel Drezner, *All Politics Is Global: Explaining International Regulatory Regimes* (Princeton, NJ: Princeton University Press, 2007).

38. This argument is made in G. John Ikenberry, *After Victory: Institutions, Strategic Restraint, and the Rebuilding of Order after Major War* (Princeton, NJ: Princeton University Press, 2001).

39. See John Mearsheimer, "Back to the Future: Instability in Europe after the Cold War," *International Security,* Vol. 15, No. 1 (Summer 1990), pp. 5–56; and my rebuttal in *After Victory,* chap. 7. For a survey of realist theories and their expectations about the post–Cold War international order, see Michael Mastanduno, "A Realist View: Three Images of the Coming International Order," in T.V. Paul and John A. Hall, eds., *International Order and the Future of World Politics* (London: Cambridge University Press, 1999), pp. 19–40. See also the debate in G. John Ikenberry, ed., *America Unrivaled: The Future of the Balance of Power* (Ithaca, NY: Cornell University Press, 2002).

40. The term *security community* was introduced by Karl Deutsch to capture the unique character of highly like-minded and consensual groupings of states. What defines a security community, according to Deutsch, is the complete absence of the perception of security threats between states within the community. See Deutsch, *Political Community and the North Atlantic Area: International Organization in the Light of Historical Experience* (Princeton, NJ: Princeton University Press, 1957). The term here is used slightly differently to refer to a political order in which its members actively establish institutions and agreements that create a community of shared risk and mutual protection. See also Emanuel Adler, "Seasons of Peace: Progress in Postwar International Security," in Emanuel Adler and Beverly Crawford, eds., *Progress in Postwar International Relations* (New York: Columbia University Press, 1991), pp. 128–73. Adler wrote this piece at the end of the Cold War and anticipated a progressive trajectory in which the Western security community would eventually expand to cover other regions of the world, especially Eastern Europe—though in perhaps less stable, less intimate arrangements (which he terms *common security*). It is interesting to note that Adler did not anticipate the weakening of the North Atlantic security community with its expansion.

41. Francis Gavin, *Gold, Dollars, and Power: The Politics of International Monetary Relations, 1958–71* (Chapel Hill: University of North Carolina Press, 2004).

42. See Michael Mastanduno, "System Maker and Privilege Taker: US Power and the International Political Economy," in Ikenberry, Mastanduno, and Wohlforth, *International Relations Theory and the Consequences of Unipolarity,* pp. 142–47; David Lake, *Entangling Relations: American Foreign Policy in Its Century* (Princeton, NJ: Princeton University Press, 1999), chaps. 5 and 6; and Lake, *Hierarchy in International Relations* (Ithaca, NY: Cornell University Press, 2011), which covers both the economic and security dimensions of American hegemony.

43. See G. John Ikenberry, *Liberal Leviathan: The Origins, Crisis, and Transformation of the American World Order* (Princeton, NJ: Princeton University Press, 2011), chap. 5.

44. Mastanduno, "System Maker and Privilege Taker," p. 171.

45. See Nicholas Lardy, *The State Strikes Back: The End of Economic Reform in China?* (Washington, DC: Peterson Institute for International Economics, 2019).

46. Avery Goldstein, *Rising to the Challenge: China's Grand Strategy and International Security* (Stanford, CA: Stanford University Press,

2005); and Thomas Christensen, *The China Challenge: Shaping the Choices of a Rising Power* (New York: Norton, 2016).

47. Michael Mastanduno, "Partner Politics: Russia, China, and the Challenge of Extending U.S. Hegemony after the Cold War," *Security Studies,* Vol. 28, No. 3 (Summer 2019), p. 501.

48. White House, "Statement by the President on the Trans-Pacific Partnership," 5 October 2015, https://obamawhitehouse.archives.gov/the-press-office/2015/10/05/statement-president-trans-pacific-partnership.

49. For a bellwether statement of this shifting view within the Washington foreign policy establishment about China, see Kurt M. Campbell and Ely Ratner, "The China Reckoning: How Beijing Defied American Expectations," *Foreign Affairs,* Vol. 97, No. 2 (March/April 2018), pp. 60–70.

50. See Ikenberry, *Liberal Leviathan.* For debates about American unipolarity, see Stephen Walt, *Taming American Power: The Global Response to US Primacy* (New York: Norton, 2005); and Stephen G. Brooks and William C. Wohlforth, *World Out of Balance: International Relations and the Challenge of American Primacy* (Princeton, NJ: Princeton University Press, 2008).

51. See Kori Schake, *America vs the West: Can the Liberal World Order Be Preserved?* (Sydney: Penguin, 2018).

52. For an overview of these governance challenges, see Amitav Acharya, *Why Govern? Rethinking Demand and Progress in Global Governance* (Cambridge: Cambridge University Press, 2016).

53. This idea of a security community as a response to mutual vulnerability is hinted at in the concept of the "risk society" put forward by the sociologists Ulrich Beck and Anthony Giddens. Their argument is that the rise of modernity—of an advanced and rapidly developing global system—has generated growing awareness of and responses to "risk." Modernization is an inherently unsettling march into the future. A risk society is, as Beck defines it, "a systematic way of dealing with hazards and insecurities induced and introduced by modernization itself." Beck, *Risk Society: Towards a New Modernity* (London: Sage, 1992). See also Anthony Giddens and Christopher Pierson, *Making Sense of Modernity: Conversations with Anthony Giddens* (Palo Alto, CA: Stanford University Press, 1998).

54. John G. Ruggie, "International Regimes, Transactions, and Change: Embedded Liberalism in the Postwar Economic Order," *International Organization,* Vol. 36, No. 2 (Spring 1982), pp. 379–415.

55. Ruggie, "International Regimes, Transactions, and Change," p. 393.

56. Rawi Abdelal and John G. Ruggie, "The Principles of Embedded Liberalism: Social Legitimacy and Global Capitalism," in David Moss and John Cisternino, eds., *New Perspectives on Regulation* (Cambridge, MA: Tobin Project, 2009), p. 153.

57. David Harvey, *A Brief History of Neoliberalism* (Oxford: Oxford University Press, 2005). For a sweeping historical portrait of transformations in Western industrial societies, beginning in the 1970s, and the rise of neoliberalism, broadly defined, see Simon Reid-Henry, *Empire of Democracy: The Remaking of the West since the Cold War, 1971–2017* (New York: Simon and Schuster, 2019). For a trenchant early critique of the neoliberal project, see Susan Strange, *Casino Capitalism* (Oxford: Basil Blackwell, 1986).

58. For a portrait and critique of the Washington Consensus, see Narcis Serra and Joseph E. Stiglitz, eds., *The Washington Consensus Reconsidered: Towards a New Global Governance* (Oxford: Oxford University Press, 2008). See also John Williamson, "The Strange History of the Washington Consensus," *Journal of Post Keynesian Economics,* Vol. 27, No. 2 (Winter 2004/5), pp. 195–206.

59. Jeff D. Colgan and Robert O. Keohane, "The Liberal Order Is Rigged: Fix It Now or Watch It Wither," *Foreign Affairs,* Vol. 96, No. 3 (May/June 2017), p. 37.

60. For evidence of stagnant and declining incomes among the working and middle class in the United States and Europe, and connections to the election of Donald Trump and Brexit, see Ronald Inglehart and Pippa Norris, "Trump, Brexit, and the Rise of Populism: Economic Have-Nots and Cultural Backlash," Research Working Paper 16-026 (Cambridge, MA: Harvard Kennedy School, 19 July 2016).

61. See "Decline of Global Extreme Poverty Continues but Has Slowed," World Bank, Washington, DC, 19 September 2018, https://www.worldbank.org/en/news/press-release/2018/09/19/decline-of-global-extreme-poverty-continues-but-has-slowed-world-bank.

62. Branko Milanović, *Global Inequality: A New Approach for the Age of Globalization* (Cambridge, MA: Harvard University Press, 2016), chap. 1.

63. On the unraveling of postwar social democratic coalitions, see Paul Collier, *The Future of Capitalism: Facing the New Anxieties* (London: Allen Lane, 2019), chap. 3; and Carles Boix, *Democratic Capitalism at the Crossroads: Technological Change and the Future of Politics* (Princeton, NJ: Princeton University Press, 2019).

64. See Mark Blyth, *Austerity: A History of a Dangerous Idea* (Oxford: Oxford University Press, 2013); and Blyth, "Capitalism in Crisis: What Went Wrong," *Foreign Affairs,* Vol. 95, No. 4 (July/August 2016), pp. 172–79. For a wider portrait of the economic and social consequences of neoliberalism and its impact on global political and Western grand strategy, see Adam Tooze, *Crashed: How a Decade of Financial Crises Changed the World* (New York: Viking, 2018).

65. See Daniel Deudney and G. John Ikenberry, "Democratic Internationalism: An American Grand Strategy for a Post-Exceptionalist Era," working paper (New York: Council on Foreign Relations, November 2012).

66. For arguments that the Western post–Cold War policies of NATO enlargement, democracy promotion, and other pressures and encroachments were responsible for Russia's illiberal turn, see Stephen F. Cohen, *Failed Crusade: America and the Tragedy of Post-Communist Russia* (New York: Norton, 2002); Cohen, *Soviet Fates and the Lost Alternatives: From Stalinism to the New Cold War* (New York: Columbia University Press, 2009); Dimitri K. Simes, "Losing Russia: The Costs of Renewed Confrontation," *Foreign Affairs,* Vol. 86, No. 6 (November/December 2007), pp. 36–52; and John Mearsheimer, "Why the Ukraine Crisis Is the West's Fault: The Liberal Delusions That Provoked Putin," *Foreign Affairs,* Vol. 93, No. 5 (September/October 2014), pp. 77–89. This is also the interpretation advanced by Mikhail Gorbachev in his recent memoir that retraces the history of post-Soviet Russia through the prism of international transformations in the early 1990s. See Gorbachev, *The New Russia* (Cambridge: Polity Press, 2016).

67. See Daniel Deudney and G. John Ikenberry, "The Unravelling of the Cold War Settlement," *Survival,* Vol. 51, No. 6 (December 2009/January 2010), pp. 39–62.

68. For a skeptical assessment of the role of Western policies on Russia's reversion to authoritarianism, see Kathryn Stoner and Michael

McFaul, "Who Lost Russia (This Time)? Vladimir Putin," *Washington Quarterly,* Vol. 38, No. 2 (2015), pp. 167–87.

69. See Rosemary Foot and Andrew Walter, *China, the United States, and Global Order* (New York: Cambridge University Press, 2011).

70. See Christopher A. McNally, "Sino-Capitalism: China's Reemergence and the International Political Economy," *World Politics,* Vol. 64, No. 4 (2012), pp. 741–76; and Jessica Weiss, "A World Safe for Autocracy? China's Rise and the Future of Global Politics," *Foreign Affairs,* Vol. 98, No. 4 (July/August 2019), pp. 92–98. For a study of China's institutional strategies, see Phillip Lipscy, *Renegotiating the World: Institutional Change in International Relations* (Cambridge: Cambridge University Press, 2017).

71. See G. John Ikenberry, "Why the Liberal World Order Will Survive," *Ethics and International Affairs,* Vol. 32, No. 1 (Spring 2018), pp. 17–29.

72. See Richard Woodward, *The Organization for Economic Co-operation and Development (OECD)* (New York: Palgrave, 2009).

73. On the difficulties of accommodating rising non-Western states in global institutions, see Robert Wade, "Protecting Power: Western States in Global Organization," in David Held and Charles Roger, eds., *Global Governance at Risk* (Cambridge: Polity Press, 2013), pp. 77–110.

74. For portraits of this expanding system of multilateral governance, see Fen Osler Hampson and Paul Heinbecker, "The 'New' Multilateralism of the Twenty-First Century," *Global Governance,* Vol. 17, No. 3 (July/September 2011), pp. 299–310; Dries Van Langenhove, "The Transformation of Multilateralism: Mode 1.0 to Mode 2.0," *Global Policy,* Vol. 1, No. 3 (October 2010), pp. 263–70; Richard Cooper, "The G-20 as an Improvised Crisis Committee and/or a Contested 'Steering Committee,'" *International Affairs,* Vol. 86, No. 3 (2010), pp. 741–57; and Andrew Cooper and Vincent Pouliot, "How Much Is Global Governance Changing? The G20 as International Practice," *Cooperation and Conflict,* Vol. 50, No. 3 (2015), pp. 334–50.

75. There is a literature that explores "who benefits" from empire. But there is less systematic work that explores the distribution of economic gains across the wider global and regional orders in different historical eras. D. K. Fieldhouse has done some of the best work on the economics of empire. See Fieldhouse, *Economics and Empire, 1830–1914* (London: Weidenfeld and Nicolson, 1973); and Fieldhouse, *The West and the Third World: Trade, Colonialism and Development* (Oxford: Blackwell, 1999). On the American case, see William Woodruff, *America's Impact on the World: A Study of the Role of the United States in the World Economy, 1750–1970* (London: Macmillan, 1975).

76. Arthur Stein argues that hegemonic leadership requires the hegemon to incur relative decreases to its economic growth to support the functioning of the broader order. See Stein, "The Hegemon's Dilemma: Great Britain, the United States, and the International Economic Order," *International Organization,* Vol. 38, No. 2 (Spring 1984), pp. 355–86.

77. For the classic portrait of the varieties of postwar capitalism, see Andrew Shonfield, *Modern Capitalism: The Changing Balance of Public and Private Power* (Oxford: Oxford University Press, 1965).

78. See Alice H. Amsden, *The Rise of the "Rest": Challenges to the West from Late-Industrializing Economies* (Oxford: Oxford University Press, 2001). For a discussion of the struggles between the United States and developing countries over development and economic policies, see Amsden, *Escape from Empire: The Developing World's Journey through Heaven and Hell* (Cambridge, MA: MIT Press, 2007).

79. See Bentley B. Allan, Srdjan Vucetic, and Ted Hopf, "The Distribution of Identity and the Future of International Order: China's Hegemonic Prospects," *International Organization,* Vol. 72, No. 4 (Fall 2018), pp. 839–69.

80. On the growing and diverse constituencies that are committed to the ongoing functioning of an open and multilateral governance system, see Miles Kahler, "Global Governance: Three Futures," *International Studies Review,* Vol. 20 (2018), pp. 239–46.

81. This argument is developed in Daniel Deudney and G. John Ikenberry, "Liberal World: The Resilient Order," *Foreign Affairs,* Vol. 97, No. 4 (July/August 2018), pp. 16–24.

3 INTERNATIONAL RELATIONS THEORIES

Over the past century, the most prominent perspectives for understanding the basic nature of international politics have included realism, liberalism, various forms of idealism, such as social constructivism, and economic radicalism, including Marxism. These viewpoints have vied for influence both in public debates and in academic arguments.

The readings in this chapter constitute some of the most concise and important statements of these theoretical traditions. Hans J. Morgenthau, the leading figure in the field of international relations in the period after World War II, presents a realist view of power politics. His influential book, *Politics Among Nations* (1948), excerpted here, played a central role in intellectually preparing Americans to exercise global power in the Cold War period and to reconcile power politics with the idealistic ethics that had often dominated American discussions about foreign relations.

In *The Tragedy of Great Power Politics* (2001), John J. Mearsheimer offers a contemporary interpretation of international politics that he calls "offensive realism." The chapter reprinted here is a marvel of clarity in describing international anarchy and its implications. States operate in a self-help system; to ensure their survival in that system, states must strive to become as powerful as possible. This competitive striving for security makes conflict the enduring and dominant feature of international relations, in Mearsheimer's view.

Michael W. Doyle, drawing inspiration from Kant, advances the liberal theory of the democratic peace. Before Doyle, some scholars had tried to argue that democracies are in general more peaceful than other kinds of states, but the facts showed that this was not true: democracies get into and start wars just as frequently as non-democracies. Doyle's 1986 article in the *American Political Science Review* moved this discussion in a more productive direction, pointing out that no two democracies had ever fought a war against each other—a finding that still holds true, as long as democracy is defined strictly enough. This sparked an ongoing debate among academics and public commentators on why this was the case, and whether it meant that the United States and other democracies should place efforts to promote the further spreading of democracy at the head of their foreign policy agendas.

Whereas realists like Mearsheimer argue that the condition of anarchy necessarily causes insecurity and fear among states, social constructivists such as Alexander Wendt insist that behavior in anarchy depends on the ideas, cultures, and identities that people and their states bring to the anarchical situation. The excerpt here is drawn from his seminal piece in that debate, which has spawned influential research on such topics as the taboo against using nuclear weapons, changing norms of humanitarian military intervention, and the rise of powerful transnational human rights networks, some of which we excerpt in later chapters. Ted Hopf's essay offers a crystal-clear statement of the constructivist approach and why it is important for understanding international relations.

In addition to realism, liberalism, and constructivism, thinking about international politics has also been shaped by radical critiques of global capitalism. These include Marxist-Leninist doctrines propounded by the Soviet Union and theories about dependent economic development advanced by voices in the Global South. Perhaps the most consequential radical theory of international relations is V. I. Lenin's *Imperialism, the Highest Stage of Capitalism,* published in 1917, just months before Lenin's Bolshevik party seized power in the Russian Revolution. Lenin's arguments about global inequality, the privileged position of finance capital, competition for resources and markets, and the consequent armed rivalries between great powers continue to resonate today. Not only leftist radicals but also realists can still find much of interest in Lenin's insights.

The liberal response to Leninist and other radical analyses of international economic rivalry points to the development of effective international institutions after World War II that succeeded in facilitating international economic cooperation. Robert O. Keohane, in his highly influential book *After Hegemony: Cooperation and Discord in the World Political Economy* (1984), lays out the theory of liberal institutionalism to explain how such institutions make cooperation possible despite the absence of a sovereign enforcement power standing above states. He explains that international institutions (or "international regimes") establish rules around which expectations converge. Rules reduce the costs of transactions, facilitate bargaining across different issue areas, and provide information that reduces the risk of cheating. Although the overwhelming power of a dominant liberal state, the United States, was needed to establish this system after 1945, Keohane argued that the system's strong institutions could keep it going despite the relative economic decline of its leading hegemonic power. The debate over this claim is now even more urgent than it was when Keohane first advanced it.

Hans J. Morgenthau

A REALIST THEORY OF INTERNATIONAL POLITICS

This book purports to present a theory of international politics. The test by which such a theory must be judged is not *a priori* and abstract but empirical and pragmatic. The theory, in other words, must be judged not by some preconceived abstract principle or concept unrelated to reality, but by its purpose: to bring order and meaning to a mass of phenomena which without it would remain disconnected and unintelligible. It must meet a dual test, an empirical and a logical one: Do the facts as they actually are lend themselves to the interpretation the theory has put upon them, and do the conclusions at which the theory arrives follow with logical necessity from its premises? In short, is the theory consistent with the facts and within itself?

The issue this theory raises concerns the nature of all politics. The history of modern political thought is the story of a contest between two schools that differ fundamentally in their conceptions of the nature of man, society, and politics. One believes that a rational and moral political order, derived from universally valid abstract principles, can be achieved here and now. It assumes the essential goodness and infinite-malleability of human nature, and blames the failure of the social order to measure up to the rational standards on lack of knowledge and understanding, obsolescent social institutions, or the depravity of certain isolated individuals or groups.

It trusts in education, reform, and the sporadic use of force to remedy these defects.

The other school believes that the world, imperfect as it is from the rational point of view, is the result of forces inherent in human nature. To improve the world one must work with those forces, not against them. This being inherently a world of opposing interests and of conflict among them, moral principles can never be fully realized, but must at best be approximated through the ever temporary balancing, of interests and the ever precarious settlement of conflicts. This school, then, sees in a system of checks and balances a universal principle for all pluralist societies. It appeals to historic precedent rather than to abstract principles, and aims at the realization of the lesser evil rather than of the absolute good.

■ ■ ■

*** Principles of Political Realism

*** Political realism believes that politics, like society in general, is governed by objective laws that have their roots in human nature. In order to improve society it is first necessary to understand the laws by which society lives. The operation of these laws being impervious to our preferences, men will challenge them only at the risk of failure.

Realism, believing as it does in the objectivity of the laws of politics, must also believe in the

From Hans J. Morgenthau, *Politics Among Nations: The Struggle for Power and Peace* (1948, repr. New York: Knopf, 1985), 3–5, 12, 31–34, 36–39. Some of the author's notes have been omitted.

possibility of developing a rational theory that reflects, however imperfectly and one-sidedly, these objective laws. It believes also, then, in the possibility of distinguishing in politics between truth and opinion—between what is true objectively and rationally, supported by evidence and illuminated by reason, and what is only a subjective judgment, divorced from the facts as they are and informed by prejudice and wishful thinking.

■ ■ ■

For realism, theory consists in ascertaining facts and giving them meaning through reason. It assumes that the character of a foreign policy can be ascertained only through the examination of the political acts performed and of the foreseeable consequences of these acts. Thus we can find out what statesmen have actually done, and from the foreseeable consequences of their acts we can surmise what their objectives might have been.

Yet examination of the facts is not enough. To give meaning to the factual raw material of foreign policy, we must approach political reality with a kind of rational outline, a map that suggests to us the possible meanings of foreign policy. In other words, we put ourselves in the position of a statesman who must meet a certain problem of foreign policy under certain circumstances, and we ask ourselves what the rational alternatives are from which a statesman may choose who must meet this problem under these circumstances (presuming always that he acts in a rational manner), and which of these rational alternatives this particular statesman, acting under these circumstances, is likely to choose. It is the testing of this rational hypothesis against the actual facts and their consequences that gives theoretical meaning to the facts of international politics.

* * * The main signpost that helps political realism to find its way through the landscape of international politics is the concept of interest defined in terms of power. This concept provides the link between reason trying to understand international politics and the facts to be understood. * * *

We assume that statesmen think and act in terms of interest defined as power, and the evidence of history bears that assumption out. That assumption allows us to retrace and anticipate, as it were, the steps a statesman—past, present, or future—has taken or will take on the political scene. We look over his shoulder when he writes his dispatches; we listen in on his conversation with other statesmen; we read and anticipate his very thoughts. Thinking in terms of interest defined as power, we think as he does, and as disinterested observers we understand his thoughts and actions perhaps better than he, the actor on the political scene, does himself.

■ ■ ■

* * * Political realism is aware of the moral significance of political action. It is also aware of the ineluctable tension between the moral command and the requirements of successful political action. And it is unwilling to gloss over and obliterate that tension and thus to obfuscate both the moral and the political issue by making it appear as though the stark facts of politics were morally more satisfying than they actually are, and the moral law less exacting than it actually is.

Realism maintains that universal moral principles cannot be applied to the actions of states in their abstract universal formulation, but that they must be filtered through the concrete circumstances of time and place. The individual may say for himself: "*Fiat justitia, pereat mundus* (Let justice be done, even if the world perish)," but the state has no right to say so in the name of those who are in its care. Both individual and state must judge political action by universal moral principles, such as that of liberty. Yet while the individual has a moral right to sacrifice himself in defense of such a moral principle, the state has no right to let its moral disapprobation of the infringement of liberty get in the way of successful political action, itself inspired by the moral principle of national survival. There can be no political morality without prudence; that is, without consideration of the political consequences of seemingly moral action. Realism, then, considers prudence—the weighing of the consequences of alternative political actions—to be the supreme virtue in politics. Ethics in the abstract judges action by its conformity with the moral law; political ethics judges action by its political consequences. * * *

■ ■ ■

POLITICAL POWER

What Is Political Power?

■ ■ ■

International politics, like all politics, is a struggle for power. Whatever the ultimate aims of international politics, power is always the immediate aim. Statesmen and peoples may ultimately seek freedom, security, prosperity, or power itself. They may define their goals in terms of a religious, philosophic, economic, or social ideal. They may hope that this ideal will materialize through its own inner force, through divine intervention, or through the natural development of human affairs. They may also try to further its realization through nonpolitical means, such as technical co-operation with other nations or international organizations. But whenever they strive to realize their goal by means of international politics, they do so by striving for power. The Crusaders wanted to free the holy places from domination by the Infidels; Woodrow Wilson wanted to make the world safe for democracy; the Nazis wanted to open Eastern Europe to German colonization, to dominate Europe, and to conquer the world. Since they all chose power to achieve these ends, they were actors on the scene of international politics.

■ ■ ■

* * * When we speak of power, we mean man's control over the minds and actions of other men. By political power we refer to the mutual relations of control among the holders of public authority and between the latter and the people at large.

Political power is a psychological relation between those who exercise it and those over whom it is exercised. It gives the former control over certain actions of the latter through the impact which the former exert on the latter's minds. That impact derives from three sources: the expectation of benefits, the fear of disadvantage, the respect or love for men or institutions. It may be exerted through orders, threats, the authority or charisma of a man or of an office, or a combination of any of these.

■ ■ ■

Political power must be distinguished from force in the sense, of the actual exercise of physical violence. The threat of physical violence in the form of police action, imprisonment, capital punishment, or war is an intrinsic element of politics. When violence becomes an actuality, it signifies the abdication of political power in favor of military or pseudo-military power. In international politics in particular, armed strength as a threat or a potentiality is the most important material factor making for the political power of a nation. If it becomes an actuality in war, it signifies the substitution of military for political power. The actual exercise of physical violence substitutes for the psychological relation between two minds, which is of the essence of political power, the physical relation between two bodies, one of which is strong enough to dominate the other's movements. It is for this reason that in the exercise of physical violence the psychological element of the political relationship is lost, and that we must distinguish between military and political power.

■   ■   ■

While it is generally recognized that the interplay of the expectation of benefits, the fear of disadvantages, and the respect or love for men or institutions, in ever changing combinations, forms the basis of all domestic politics, the importance of these factors for international politics is less obvious, but no less real. There has been a tendency to reduce political power to the actual application of force or at least to equate it with successful threats of force and with persuasion, to the neglect of charisma. That neglect * * * accounts in good measure for the neglect of prestige as an independent element in international politics. * * *

■   ■   ■

An economic, financial, territorial, or military policy undertaken for its own sake is subject to evaluation in its own terms. Is it economically or financially advantageous? * * *

When, however, the objectives of these policies serve to increase the power of the nation pursuing them with regard to other nations, these policies and their objectives must be judged primarily from the point of view of their contribution to national power. An economic policy that cannot be justified in purely economic terms might nevertheless be undertaken in view of the political policy pursued.

The insecure and unprofitable character of a loan to a foreign nation may be a valid argument against it on purely financial grounds. But the argument is irrelevant if the loan, however unwise it may be from a banker's point of view, serves the political policies of the nation. It may of course be that the economic or financial losses involved in such policies will weaken the nation in its international position to such an extent as to outweigh the political advantages to be expected. On these grounds such policies might be rejected. In such a case, what decides the issue is not purely economic and financial considerations but a comparison of the political chances and risks involved; that is, the probable effect of these policies upon the power of the nation.

■   ■   ■

The Depreciation of Political Power

The aspiration for power being the distinguishing element of international politics, as of all politics, international politics is of necessity power politics. While this fact is generally recognized in the practice of international affairs, it is frequently denied in the pronouncements of scholars, publicists, and even statesmen. Since the end of the Napoleonic Wars, ever larger groups in the Western world have been persuaded that the struggle for power on the international scene is a temporary phenomenon, a historical accident that is bound to disappear once the peculiar historic conditions that have given rise to it have been eliminated. * * * During the nineteenth century, liberals everywhere shared the conviction that power politics and war were residues of an obsolete system of government, and that the victory of democracy and constitutional government over absolutism and autocracy would assure the victory of international harmony and permanent peace over power politics and war. Of this liberal school of thought, Woodrow Wilson was the most eloquent and most influential spokesman.

In recent times, the conviction that the struggle for power can be eliminated from the international scene has been connected with the great attempts at organizing the world, such as the League of Nations and the United Nations. * * *

* * * [In fact,] the struggle for power is universal in time and space and is an undeniable fact of experience. It cannot be denied that throughout historic time, regardless of social, economic, and political conditions, states have met each other in contests for power. Even though anthropologists have shown that certain primitive peoples seem to be free from the desire for power, nobody has yet shown how their state of mind and the conditions under which they live can be recreated on a world-wide scale so as to eliminate the struggle for power from the international scene.[1] It would be useless and even self-destructive to free one or the other of the peoples of the earth from the desire for power while leaving it extant in others. If the desire for power cannot be abolished everywhere in the world, those who might be cured would simply fall victims to the power of others.

The position taken here might be criticized on the ground that conclusions drawn from the past are unconvincing, and that to draw such conclusions has always been the main stock in trade of the enemies of progress and reform. Though it is true that certain social arrangements and institutions have always existed in the past, it does not necessarily follow that they must always exist in the future. The situation is, however, different when we deal not with social arrangements and institutions created by man, but with those elemental bio-psychological drives by which in turn society is created. The drives to live, to propagate, and to dominate are common to all men.[2] Their relative strength is dependent upon social conditions that may favor one drive and tend to repress another, or that may withhold social approval from certain manifestations of these drives while they encourage others. Thus, to take examples only from the sphere of power, most societies condemn killing as a means of attaining power within society, but all societies encourage the killing of enemies in that struggle for power which is called war. * * *

■ ■ ■

NOTES

1. For an illuminating discussion of this problem, see Malcolm Sharp, "Aggression: A Study of Values and Law," *Ethics,* Vol. 57, No. 4, Part II (July 1947).
2. Zoologists have tried to show that the drive to dominate is found even in animals, such as chickens and monkeys, who create social hierarchies on the basis of will and the ability to dominate. See, e.g., Warder Allee, *Animal Life and Social Growth* (Baltimore: The Williams and Wilkens Company, 1932), and *The Social Life of Animals* (New York: W. W. Norton and Company, Inc., 1938).

John J. Mearsheimer

ANARCHY AND THE STRUGGLE FOR POWER

Great powers, I argue, are always searching for opportunities to gain power over their rivals, with hegemony as their final goal. This perspective does not allow for status quo powers, except for the unusual state that achieves preponderance. Instead, the system is populated with great powers that have revisionist intentions at their core.[1] This chapter presents a theory that explains this competition for power. Specifically, I attempt to show that there is a compelling logic behind my claim that great powers seek to maximize their share of world power. I do not, however, test offensive realism against the historical record in this chapter. That important task is reserved for later chapters.

Why States Pursue Power

My explanation for why great powers vie with each other for power and strive for hegemony is derived from five assumptions about the international system. None of these assumptions alone mandates that states behave competitively. Taken together, however, they depict a world in which states have considerable reason to think and sometimes behave aggressively. In particular, the system encourages states to look for opportunities to maximize their power vis-à-vis other states.

How important is it that these assumptions be realistic? Some social scientists argue that the assumptions that underpin a theory need not conform to reality. Indeed, the economist Milton Friedman maintains that the best theories "will be found to have assumptions that are wildly inaccurate descriptive representations of reality, and, in general, the more significant the theory, the more unrealistic the assumptions."[2] According to this view, the explanatory power of a theory is all that matters. If unrealistic assumptions lead to a theory that tells us a lot about how the world works, it is of no importance whether the underlying assumptions are realistic or not.

I reject this view. Although I agree that explanatory power is the ultimate criterion for assessing theories, I also believe that a theory based on unrealistic or false assumptions will not explain much about how the world works.[3] Sound theories are based on sound assumptions. Accordingly, each of these five assumptions is a reasonably accurate representation of an important aspect of life in the international system.

Bedrock Assumptions

The first assumption is that the international system is anarchic, which does not mean that it is chaotic or riven by disorder. It is easy to draw that conclusion, since realism depicts a world characterized by security competition and war. By itself, however, the realist notion of anarchy has nothing to do with conflict; it is an ordering principle, which says that the system comprises independent states that have no central authority above them.[4] Sovereignty, in

From John J. Mearsheimer, *The Tragedy of Great Power Politics* (New York: W. W. Norton, 2001), 29–54. Some of the author's notes have been edited.

other words, inheres in states because there is no higher ruling body in the international system.[5] There is no "government over governments."[6]

The second assumption is that great powers inherently possess some offensive military capability, which gives them the wherewithal to hurt and possibly destroy each other. States are potentially dangerous to each other, although some states have more military might than others and are therefore more dangerous. A state's military power is usually identified with the particular weaponry at its disposal, although even if there were no weapons, the individuals in those states could still use their feet and hands to attack the population of another state. After all, for every neck, there are two hands to choke it.

The third assumption is that states can never be certain about other states' intentions. Specifically, no state can be sure that another state will not use its offensive military capability to attack the first state. This is not to say that states necessarily have hostile intentions. Indeed, all of the states in the system may be reliably benign, but it is impossible to be sure of that judgment because intentions are impossible to divine with 100 percent certainty.[7] There are many possible causes of aggression, and no state can be sure that another state is not motivated by one of them.[8] Furthermore, intentions can change quickly, so a state's intentions can be benign one day and hostile the next. Uncertainty about intentions is unavoidable, which means that states can never be sure that other states do not have offensive intentions to go along with their offensive capabilities.

The fourth assumption is that survival is the primary goal of great powers. Specifically, states seek to maintain their territorial integrity and the autonomy of their domestic political order. Survival dominates other motives because, once a state is conquered, it is unlikely to be in a position to pursue other aims. Soviet leader Josef Stalin put the point well during a war scare in 1927: "We can and must build socialism in the [Soviet Union].

But in order to do so we first of all have to exist."[9] States can and do pursue other goals, of course, but security is their most important objective.

The fifth assumption is that great powers are rational actors. They are aware of their external environment and they think strategically about how to survive in it. In particular, they consider the preferences of other states and how their own behavior is likely to affect the behavior of those other states, and how the behavior of those other states is likely to affect their own strategy for survival. Moreover, states pay attention to the long term as well as the immediate consequences of their actions.

As emphasized, none of these assumptions alone dictates that great powers as a general rule *should* behave aggressively toward each other. There is surely the possibility that some state might have hostile intentions, but the only assumption dealing with a specific motive that is common to all states says that their principal objective is to survive, which by itself is a rather harmless goal. Nevertheless, when the five assumptions are married together, they create powerful incentives for great powers to think and act offensively with regard to each other. In particular, three general patterns of behavior result: fear, self-help, and power maximization.

State Behavior

Great powers fear each other. They regard each other with suspicion, and they worry that war might be in the offing. They anticipate danger. There is little room for trust among states. For sure, the level of fear varies across time and space, but it cannot be reduced to a trivial level. From the perspective of any one great power, all other great powers are potential enemies. This point is illustrated by the reaction of the United Kingdom and France to German reunification at the end of the Cold War. Despite the fact that these three states had been close allies for almost forty-five years, both the

United Kingdom and France immediately began worrying about the potential dangers of a united Germany.[10]

The basis of this fear is that in a world where great powers have the capability to attack each other and might have the motive to do so, any state bent on survival must be at least suspicious of other states and reluctant to trust them. Add to this the "911" problem—the absence of a central authority to which a threatened state can turn for help—and states have even greater incentive to fear each other. Moreover, there is no mechanism, other than the possible self-interest of third parties, for punishing an aggressor. Because it is sometimes difficult to deter potential aggressors, states have ample reason not to trust other states and to be prepared for war with them.

The possible consequences of falling victim to aggression further amplify the importance of fear as a motivating force in world politics. Great powers do not compete with each other as if international politics were merely an economic marketplace. Political competition among states is a much more dangerous business than mere economic intercourse; the former can lead to war, and war often means mass killing on the battlefield as well as mass murder of civilians. In extreme cases, war can even lead to the destruction of states. The horrible consequences of war sometimes cause states to view each other not just as competitors, but as potentially deadly enemies. Political antagonism, in short, tends to be intense, because the stakes are great.

States in the international system also aim to guarantee their own survival. Because other states are potential threats, and because there is no higher authority to come to their rescue when they dial 911, states cannot depend on others for their own security. Each state tends to see itself as vulnerable and alone, and therefore it aims to provide for its own survival. In international politics, God helps those who help themselves. This emphasis on self-help does not preclude states from forming alliances.[11] But alliances are only temporary marriages of convenience: today's alliance partner might be tomorrow's enemy, and today's enemy might be tomorrow's alliance partner. For example, the United States fought with China and the Soviet Union against Germany and Japan in World War II, but soon thereafter flip-flopped enemies and partners and allied with West Germany and Japan against China and the Soviet Union during the Cold War.

States operating in a self-help world almost always act according to their own self-interest and do not subordinate their interests to the interests of other states, or to the interests of the so-called international community. The reason is simple: it pays to be selfish in a self-help world. This is true in the short term as well as in the long term, because if a state loses in the short run, it might not be around for the long haul.

Apprehensive about the ultimate intentions of other states, and aware that they operate in a self-help system, states quickly understand that the best way to ensure their survival is to be the most powerful state in the system. The stronger a state is relative to its potential rivals, the less likely it is that any of those rivals will attack it and threaten its survival. Weaker states will be reluctant to pick fights with more powerful states because the weaker states are likely to suffer military defeat. Indeed, the bigger the gap in power between any two states, the less likely it is that the weaker will attack the stronger. Neither Canada nor Mexico, for example, would countenance attacking the United States, which is far more powerful than its neighbors. The ideal situation is to be the hegemon in the system. As Immanuel Kant said, "It is the desire of every state, or of its ruler, to arrive at a condition of perpetual peace by conquering the whole world, if that were possible."[12] Survival would then be almost guaranteed.[13]

Consequently, states pay close attention to how power is distributed among them, and they make a special effort to maximize their share of world power. Specifically, they look for opportunities to alter the balance of power by acquiring additional increments of power at the expense of potential rivals. States employ a variety of means—economic, diplomatic, and military—to shift the balance of power in their favor, even if doing so makes other states suspicious or even hostile. Because one state's gain in power is another state's loss, great powers tend to have a zero-sum mentality when dealing with each other. The trick, of course, is to be the winner in this competition and to dominate the other states in the system. Thus, the claim that states maximize relative power is tantamount to arguing that states are disposed to think offensively toward other states, even though their ultimate motive is simply to survive. In short, great powers have aggressive intentions.[14]

Even when a great power achieves a distinct military advantage over its rivals, it continues looking for chances to gain more power. The pursuit of power stops only when hegemony is achieved. The idea that a great power might feel secure without dominating the system, provided it has an "appropriate amount" of power, is not persuasive, for two reasons.[15] First, it is difficult to assess how much relative power one state must have over its rivals before it is secure. Is twice as much power an appropriate threshold? Or is three times as much power the magic number? The root of the problem is that power calculations alone do not determine which side wins a war. Clever strategies, for example, sometimes allow less powerful states to defeat more powerful foes.

Second, determining how much power is enough becomes even more complicated when great powers contemplate how power will be distributed among them ten or twenty years down the road. The capabilities of individual states vary over time, sometimes markedly, and it is often difficult to predict the direction and scope of change in the balance of power. Remember, few in the West anticipated the collapse of the Soviet Union before it happened. In fact, during the first half of the Cold War, many in the West feared that the Soviet economy would eventually generate greater wealth than the American economy, which would cause a marked power shift against the United States and its allies. What the future holds for China and Russia and what the balance of power will look like in 2020 is difficult to foresee.

Given the difficulty of determining how much power is enough for today and tomorrow, great powers recognize that the best way to ensure their security is to achieve hegemony now, thus eliminating any possibility of a challenge by another great power. Only a misguided state would pass up an opportunity to be the hegemon in the system because it thought it already had sufficient power to survive.[16] But even if a great power does not have the wherewithal to achieve hegemony (and that is usually the case), it will still act offensively to amass as much power as it can, because states are almost always better off with more rather than less power. In short, states do not become status quo powers until they completely dominate the system.

All states are influenced by this logic, which means that not only do they look for opportunities to take advantage of one another, they also work to ensure that other states do not take advantage of them. After all, rival states are driven by the same logic, and most states are likely to recognize their own motives at play in the actions of other states. In short, states ultimately pay attention to defense as well as offense. They think about conquest themselves, and they work to check aggressor states from gaining power at their expense. This inexorably leads to a world of constant security competition, where states are willing to lie, cheat, and use brute force if it helps them gain advantage over their rivals. Peace, if one defines that concept as a state of tranquility or mutual concord, is not likely to break out in this world.

The "security dilemma," which is one of the most well-known concepts in the international relations literature, reflects the basic logic of offensive realism. The essence of the dilemma is that the measures a state takes to increase its own security usually decrease the security of other states. Thus, it is difficult for a state to increase its own chances of survival without threatening the survival of other states. John Herz first introduced the security dilemma in a 1950 article in the journal *World Politics*.[17] After discussing the anarchic nature of international politics, he writes, "Striving to attain security from . . . attack, [states] are driven to acquire more and more power in order to escape the impact of the power of others. This, in turn, renders the others more insecure and compels them to prepare for the worst. Since none can ever feel entirely secure in such a world of competing units, power competition ensues, and the vicious circle of security and power accumulation is on."[18] The implication of Herz's analysis is clear: the best way for a state to survive in anarchy is to take advantage of other states and gain power at their expense. The best defense is a good offense. Since this message is widely understood, ceaseless security competition ensues. Unfortunately, little can be done to ameliorate the security dilemma as long as states operate in anarchy.

It should be apparent from this discussion that saying that states are power maximizers is tantamount to saying that they care about relative power, not absolute power. There is an important distinction here, because states concerned about relative power behave differently than do states interested in absolute power.[19] States that maximize relative power are concerned primarily with the distribution of material capabilities. In particular, they try to gain as large a power advantage as possible over potential rivals, because power is the best means to survival in a dangerous world. Thus, states motivated by relative power concerns are likely to forgo large gains in their own power, if such gains give rival states even greater power, for smaller national gains that nevertheless provide them with a power advantage over their rivals.[20] States that maximize absolute power, on the other hand, care only about the size of their own gains, not those of other states. They are not motivated by balance-of-power logic but instead are concerned with amassing power without regard to how much power other states control. They would jump at the opportunity for large gains, even if a rival gained more in the deal. Power, according to this logic, is not a means to an end (survival), but an end in itself.[21]

Calculated Aggression

There is obviously little room for status quo powers in a world where states are inclined to look for opportunities to gain more power. Nevertheless, great powers cannot always act on their offensive intentions, because behavior is influenced not only by what states want, but also by their capacity to realize these desires. Every state might want to be king of the hill, but not every state has the wherewithal to compete for that lofty position, much less achieve it. Much depends on how military might is distributed among the great powers. A great power that has a marked power advantage over its rivals is likely to behave more aggressively, because it has the capability as well as the incentive to do so.

By contrast, great powers facing powerful opponents will be less inclined to consider offensive action and more concerned with defending the existing balance of power from threats by their more powerful opponents. Let there be an opportunity for those weaker states to revise the balance in their own favor, however, and they will take advantage of it. Stalin put the point well at the end of World War II: "Everyone imposes his own system as far as his army can reach. It cannot be otherwise."[22] States might also have the capability to gain advantage over a rival power but nevertheless decide that the perceived costs of offense are too high and do not justify the expected benefits.

In short, great powers are not mindless aggressors so bent on gaining power that they charge headlong into losing wars or pursue Pyrrhic victories. On the contrary, before great powers take offensive actions, they think carefully about the balance of power and about how other states will react to their moves. They weigh the costs and risks of offense against the likely benefits. If the benefits do not outweigh the risks, they sit tight and wait for a more propitious moment. Nor do states start arms races that are unlikely to improve their overall position. As discussed at greater length in Chapter 3, states sometimes limit defense spending either because spending more would bring no strategic advantage or because spending more would weaken the economy and undermine the state's power in the long run.[23] To paraphrase Clint Eastwood, a state has to know its limitations to survive in the international system.

Nevertheless, great powers miscalculate from time to time because they invariably make important decisions on the basis of imperfect information. States hardly ever have complete information about any situation they confront. There are two dimensions to this problem. Potential adversaries have incentives to misrepresent their own strength or weakness, and to conceal their true aims.[24] For example, a weaker state trying to deter a stronger state is likely to exaggerate its own power to discourage the potential aggressor from attacking. On the other hand, a state bent on aggression is likely to emphasize its peaceful goals while exaggerating its military weakness, so that the potential victim does not build up its own arms and thus leaves itself vulnerable to attack. Probably no national leader was better at practicing this kind of deception than Adolf Hitler.

But even if disinformation was not a problem, great powers are often unsure about how their own military forces, as well as the adversary's, will perform on the battlefield. For example, it is sometimes difficult to determine in advance how new weapons and untested combat units will perform in the face of enemy fire. Peacetime maneuvers and war games are helpful but imperfect indicators of what is likely to happen in actual combat. Fighting wars is a complicated business in which it is often difficult to predict outcomes. Remember that although the United States and its allies scored a stunning and remarkably easy victory against Iraq in early 1991, most experts at the time believed that Iraq's military would be a formidable foe and put up stubborn resistance before finally succumbing to American military might.[25]

Great powers are also sometimes unsure about the resolve of opposing states as well as allies. For example, Germany believed that if it went to war against France and Russia in the summer of 1914, the United Kingdom would probably stay out of the fight. Saddam Hussein expected the United States to stand aside when he invaded Kuwait in August 1990. Both aggressors guessed wrong, but each had good reason to think that its initial judgment was correct. In the 1930s, Adolf Hitler believed that his great-power rivals would be easy to exploit and isolate because each had little interest in fighting Germany and instead was determined to get someone else to assume that burden. He guessed right. In short, great powers constantly find themselves confronting situations in which they have to make important decisions with incomplete information. Not surprisingly, they sometimes make faulty judgments and end up doing themselves serious harm.

Some defensive realists go so far as to suggest that the constraints of the international system are so powerful that offense rarely succeeds, and that aggressive great powers invariably end up being punished.[26] As noted, they emphasize that 1) threatened states balance against aggressors and ultimately crush them, and 2) there is an offense-defense balance that is usually heavily tilted toward the defense, thus making conquest especially difficult. Great powers, therefore, should be content with the existing balance of power and not try to change it by force. After all, it makes little sense for a state to initiate a war that it is likely to lose; that would be self-defeating behavior. It is better to concentrate instead on preserving the balance of power.[27] Moreover, because aggressors seldom succeed, states should understand that security is abundant, and thus there is no good strategic reason for wanting more power in the first place. In a world where conquest seldom pays, states should have relatively benign intentions toward each other. If they do not, these defensive realists argue, the reason is probably poisonous domestic politics, not smart calculations about how to guarantee one's security in an anarchic world.

There is no question that systemic factors constrain aggression, especially balancing by threatened states. But defensive realists exaggerate those restraining forces.[28] Indeed, the historical record provides little support for their claim that offense rarely succeeds. One study estimates that there were sixty-three wars between 1815 and 1980, and the initiator won thirty-nine times, which translates into about a 60 percent success rate.[29] Turning to specific cases, Otto von Bismarck unified Germany by winning military victories against Denmark in 1864, Austria in 1866, and France in 1870, and the United States as we know it today was created in good part by conquest in the nineteenth century. Conquest certainly paid big dividends in these cases. Nazi Germany won wars against Poland in 1939 and France in 1940, but lost to the Soviet Union between 1941 and 1945. Conquest ultimately did not pay for the Third Reich, but if Hitler had restrained himself after the fall of France and had not invaded the Soviet Union, conquest probably would have paid handsomely for the Nazis. In short, the historical record shows that offense sometimes succeeds and sometimes does not. The trick for a sophisticated power maximizer is to figure out when to raise and when to fold.[30]

Hegemony's Limits

Great powers, as I have emphasized, strive to gain power over their rivals and hopefully become hegemons. Once a state achieves that exalted position, it becomes a status quo power. More needs to be said, however, about the meaning of hegemony.

A hegemon is a state that is so powerful that it dominates all the other states in the system.[31] No other state has the military wherewithal to put up a serious fight against it. In essence, a hegemon is the only great power in the system. A state that is substantially more powerful than the other great powers in the system is not a hegemon, because it faces, by definition, other great powers. The United Kingdom in the mid-nineteenth century, for example, is sometimes called a hegemon. But it was not a hegemon, because there were four other great powers in Europe at the time—Austria, France, Prussia, and Russia—and the United Kingdom did not dominate them in any meaningful way. In fact, during that period, the United Kingdom considered France to be a serious threat to the balance of power. Europe in the nineteenth century was multipolar, not unipolar.

Hegemony means domination of the system, which is usually interpreted to mean the entire world. It is possible, however, to apply the concept of a system more narrowly and use it to describe particular regions, such as Europe, Northeast Asia, and the Western Hemisphere. Thus, one can distinguish between *global hegemons*, which dominate the world, and *regional hegemons*, which dominate distinct geographical areas. The United States has been a regional hegemon in the Western Hemisphere for at least the past one hundred years. No other state in the Americas has sufficient military might to challenge it, which is why the United States is widely recognized as the only great power in its region.

My argument, which I develop at length in subsequent chapters, is that except for the unlikely event wherein one state achieves clear-cut nuclear superiority, it is virtually impossible for any state to achieve global hegemony. The principal impediment to world domination is the difficulty of projecting power across the world's oceans onto the territory of a rival great power. The United States, for example, is the most powerful state on the planet today. But it does not dominate Europe and Northeast Asia the way it does the Western Hemisphere, and it has no intention of trying to conquer and control those distant regions, mainly because of the stopping power of water. Indeed, there is reason to think that the American military commitment to Europe and Northeast Asia might wither away over the next decade. In short, there has never been a global hegemon, and there is not likely to be one anytime soon.

The best outcome a great power can hope for is to be a regional hegemon and possibly control another region that is nearby and accessible over land. The United States is the only regional hegemon in modern history, although other states have fought major wars in pursuit of regional hegemony: imperial Japan in Northeast Asia, and Napoleonic France, Wilhelmine Germany, and Nazi Germany in Europe. But none succeeded. The Soviet Union, which is located in Europe and Northeast Asia, threatened to dominate both of those regions during the Cold War. The Soviet Union might also have attempted to conquer the oil-rich Persian Gulf region, with which it shared a border. But even if Moscow had been able to dominate Europe, Northeast Asia, and the Persian Gulf, which it never came close to doing, it still would have been unable to conquer the Western Hemisphere and become a true global hegemon.

States that achieve regional hegemony seek to prevent great powers in other regions from duplicating their feat. Regional hegemons, in other words, do not want peers. Thus the United States, for example, played a key role in preventing imperial Japan, Wilhelmine Germany, Nazi Germany, and the Soviet Union from gaining regional supremacy. Regional hegemons attempt to check aspiring hegemons in other regions because they fear that a rival great power that dominates its own region will be an especially powerful foe that is essentially free to cause trouble in the fearful great power's backyard. Regional hegemons prefer that there be at least two great powers located together in other regions, because their proximity will force them to concentrate their attention on each other rather than on the distant hegemon.

Furthermore, if a potential hegemon emerges among them, the other great powers in that region might be able to contain it by themselves, allowing the distant hegemon to remain safely on the sidelines. Of course, if the local great powers were unable to do the job, the distant hegemon would take the appropriate measures to deal with the threatening state. The United States, as noted, has assumed that burden on four separate occasions in the twentieth century, which is why it is commonly referred to as an "offshore balancer."

In sum, the ideal situation for any great power is to be the only regional hegemon in the world. That state would be a status quo power, and it would go to considerable lengths to preserve the existing distribution of power. The United States is in that enviable position today; it dominates the Western Hemisphere and there is no hegemon in any other area of the world. But if a regional hegemon is confronted with a peer competitor, it would no longer be a status quo power. Indeed, it would go to considerable lengths to weaken and maybe even destroy its distant rival. Of course, both regional hegemons would be motivated by that logic, which would make for a fierce security competition between them.

Power and Fear

That great powers fear each other is a central aspect of life in the international system. But as noted, the level of fear varies from case to case. For example, the Soviet Union worried much less about Germany in 1930 than it did in 1939. How much states fear each other matters greatly, because the amount of fear between them largely determines the severity of their security competition, as well as the probability that they will fight a war. The more profound the fear is, the more intense is the security competition, and the more likely is war. The logic is straightforward: a scared state will look especially hard for ways to enhance its security, and it will be disposed to pursue risky policies to achieve that end. Therefore, it is important to understand what causes states to fear each other more or less intensely.

Fear among great powers derives from the fact that they invariably have some offensive military capability that they can use against each other, and the fact that one can never be certain that other states do not intend to use that power against oneself. Moreover, because states operate in an anarchic system, there is no night watchman to whom they can turn for help if another great power attacks them. Although anarchy and uncertainty about other states' intentions create an irreducible level of fear among states that leads to power-maximizing behavior, they cannot account for why sometimes that level of fear is greater than at other times. The reason is that anarchy and the difficulty of discerning state intentions are constant facts of life, and constants cannot explain variation. The capability that states have to threaten each other, however, varies from case to case, and it is the key factor that drives fear levels up and down. Specifically, the more power a state possesses, the more fear it generates among its rivals. Germany, for example, was much more powerful at the end of the 1930s than it was at the decade's beginning, which is why the Soviets became increasingly fearful of Germany over the course of that decade.

This discussion of how power affects fear prompts the question, What is power? It is important to distinguish between potential and actual power. A state's potential power is based on the size of its population and the level of its wealth. These two assets are the main building blocks of military power. Wealthy rivals with large populations can usually build formidable military forces. A state's actual power is embedded mainly in its army and the air and naval forces that directly support it. Armies are the central ingredient of military power, because they are the principal instrument for conquering and controlling territory—the paramount political objective in a world of territorial states. In short, the key component of military might, even in the nuclear age, is land power.

Power considerations affect the intensity of fear among states in three main ways. First, rival states that possess nuclear forces that can survive a nuclear attack and retaliate against it are likely to fear each other less than if these same states had no nuclear weapons. During the Cold War, for example, the level of fear between the superpowers probably would have been substantially greater if nuclear weapons had not been invented. The logic here is simple: because nuclear weapons can inflict devastating destruction on a rival state in a short period of time, nuclear-armed rivals are going to be reluctant to fight with each other, which means that each side will have less reason to fear the other than would otherwise be the case. But as the Cold War demonstrates, this does not mean that war between nuclear powers is no longer thinkable; they still have reason to fear each other.

Second, when great powers are separated by large bodies of water, they usually do not have much offensive capability against each other, regardless of the relative size of their armies. Large bodies of water are formidable obstacles that cause significant power-projection problems for attacking armies. For example, the stopping power of water explains in good part why the United Kingdom and the United States (since becoming a great power in 1898) have never been invaded by another great power. It also explains why the United States has never tried to conquer territory in Europe or Northeast Asia, and why the United Kingdom has never attempted to dominate the European continent. Great powers located on the same landmass are in a much better position to attack and conquer each other. That is especially true of states that share a common border. Therefore, great powers separated by water are likely to fear each other less than great powers that can get at each other over land.

Third, the distribution of power among the states in the system also markedly affects the levels of fear.[32] The key issue is whether power is distributed more or less evenly among the great powers or whether there are sharp power asymmetries. The configuration of power that generates the most fear is a multipolar system that contains a potential hegemon—what I call "unbalanced multipolarity."

A potential hegemon is more than just the most powerful state in the system. It is a great power with so much actual military capability and so much potential power that it stands a good chance of dominating and controlling all of the other great powers in its region of the world. A potential hegemon need not have the wherewithal to fight all of its rivals at once, but it must have excellent prospects of defeating each opponent alone, and good prospects of defeating some of them in tandem. The key relationship, however, is the power gap between the potential hegemon and the second most powerful state in the system: there must be a marked gap between them. To qualify as a potential hegemon, a state must have—by some reasonably large margin—the most formidable army as well as the most latent power among all the states located in its region.

Bipolarity is the power configuration that produces the least amount of fear among the great powers, although not a negligible amount by any means. Fear tends to be less acute in bipolarity, because there is usually a rough balance of power between the two major states in the system. Multipolar systems without a potential hegemon, what I call "balanced multipolarity," are still likely to have power asymmetries among their members, although these asymmetries will not be as pronounced as the gaps created by the presence of an aspiring hegemon. Therefore, balanced multipolarity is likely to generate less fear than unbalanced multipolarity, but more fear than bipolarity.

This discussion of how the level of fear between great powers varies with changes in the distribution of power, not with assessments about each other's intentions, raises a related point. When a state surveys its environment to determine which states pose a threat to its survival, it focuses mainly on the offensive *capabilities* of potential rivals, not their intentions. As emphasized earlier, intentions are ultimately unknowable, so states worried about their survival must make worst-case assumptions about their rivals' intentions. Capabilities, however, not only can be measured but also determine whether or not a rival state is a serious threat. In short, great powers balance against capabilities, not intentions.[33]

Great powers obviously balance against states with formidable military forces, because that offensive military capability is the tangible threat to their survival. But great powers also pay careful attention to how much latent power rival states control, because rich and populous states usually can and do build powerful armies. Thus, great powers tend to fear states with large populations and rapidly expanding economies, even if these states have not yet translated their wealth into military might.

The Hierarchy of State Goals

Survival is the number one goal of great powers, according to my theory. In practice, however, states pursue non-security goals as well. For example, great powers invariably seek greater economic prosperity to enhance the welfare of their citizenry. They sometimes seek to promote a particular ideology abroad, as happened during the Cold War when the United States tried to spread democracy around the world and the Soviet Union tried to sell communism. National unification is another goal that sometimes motivates states, as it did with Prussia and Italy in the nineteenth century and Germany after the Cold War. Great powers also occasionally try to foster human rights around the globe. States might pursue any of these, as well as a number of other non-security goals.

Offensive realism certainly recognizes that great powers might pursue these non-security goals, but it has little to say about them, save for one important point: states can pursue them as long as the requisite behavior does not conflict with balance-of-power logic, which is often the case.[34] Indeed, the pursuit of these non-security goals sometimes complements the hunt for relative power. For example, Nazi Germany expanded into eastern Europe for both ideological and realist reasons, and the superpowers competed with each other during the Cold War for similar reasons. Furthermore, greater economic prosperity invariably means greater wealth, which has significant implications for security, because wealth is the foundation of military power. Wealthy states can afford powerful military forces, which enhance a state's prospects for survival. As the political economist Jacob Viner noted more than fifty years ago, "there is a long-run harmony" between wealth and power.[35] National unification is another goal that usually complements the pursuit of power. For example, the unified German state that emerged in 1871 was more powerful than the Prussian state it replaced.

Sometimes the pursuit of non-security goals has hardly any effect on the balance of power, one way or the other. Human rights interventions usually fit this description, because they tend to be small-scale operations that cost little and do not detract from a great power's prospects for survival. For better or for worse, states are rarely willing to expend blood and treasure to protect foreign populations from gross abuses, including genocide. For instance, despite claims that American foreign policy is infused with moralism, Somalia (1992–93) is the only instance during the past one hundred years in which U.S. soldiers were killed in action on a humanitarian mission. And in that

case, the loss of a mere eighteen soldiers in an infamous firefight in October 1993 so traumatized American policymakers that they immediately pulled all U.S. troops out of Somalia and then refused to intervene in Rwanda in the spring of 1994, when ethnic Hutu went on a genocidal rampage against their Tutsi neighbors.[36] Stopping that genocide would have been relatively easy and it would have had virtually no effect on the position of the United States in the balance of power.[37] Yet nothing was done. In short, although realism does not prescribe human rights interventions, it does not necessarily proscribe them.

But sometimes the pursuit of non-security goals conflicts with balance-of-power logic, in which case states usually act according to the dictates of realism. For example, despite the U.S. commitment to spreading democracy across the globe, it helped overthrow democratically elected governments and embraced a number of authoritarian regimes during the Cold War, when American policymakers felt that these actions would help contain the Soviet Union.[38] In World War II, the liberal democracies put aside their antipathy for communism and formed an alliance with the Soviet Union against Nazi Germany. "I can't take communism," Franklin Roosevelt emphasized, but to defeat Hitler "I would hold hands with the Devil."[39] In the same way, Stalin repeatedly demonstrated that when his ideological preferences clashed with power considerations, the latter won out. To take the most blatant example of his realism, the Soviet Union formed a non-aggression pact with Nazi Germany in August 1939—the infamous Molotov-Ribbentrop Pact—in hopes that the agreement would at least temporarily satisfy Hitler's territorial ambitions in eastern Europe and turn the Wehrmacht toward France and the United Kingdom.[40] When great powers confront a serious threat, in short, they pay little attention to ideology as they search for alliance partners.[41]

Security also trumps wealth when those two goals conflict, because "defence," as Adam Smith wrote in *The Wealth of Nations,* "is of much more importance than opulence."[42] Smith provides a good illustration of how states behave when forced to choose between wealth and relative power. In 1651, England put into effect the famous Navigation Act, protectionist legislation designed to damage Holland's commerce and ultimately cripple the Dutch economy. The legislation mandated that all goods imported into England be carried either in English ships or ships owned by the country that originally produced the goods. Since the Dutch produced few goods themselves, this measure would badly damage their shipping, the central ingredient in their economic success. Of course, the Navigation Act would hurt England's economy as well, mainly because it would rob England of the benefits of free trade. "The act of navigation," Smith wrote, "is not favorable to foreign commerce, or to the growth of that opulence that can arise from it." Nevertheless, Smith considered the legislation "the wisest of all the commercial regulations of England" because it did more damage to the Dutch economy than to the English economy, and in the mid-seventeenth century Holland was "the only naval power which could endanger the security of England."[43]

Creating World Order

The claim is sometimes made that great powers can transcend realist logic by working together to build an international order that fosters peace and justice. World peace, it would appear, can only enhance a state's prosperity and security. America's political leaders paid considerable lip service to this line of argument over the course of the twentieth century. President Clinton, for example, told an audience at the United Nations in September 1993 that "at the birth of this organization 48 years ago . . . a generation of gifted leaders from many nations stepped forward to organize the world's efforts on behalf of security and prosperity. . . .

Now history has granted to us a moment of even greater opportunity. . . . Let us resolve that we will dream larger. . . . Let us ensure that the world we pass to our children is healthier, safer and more abundant than the one we inhabit today."[44]

This rhetoric notwithstanding, great powers do not work together to promote world order for its own sake. Instead, each seeks to maximize its own share of world power, which is likely to clash with the goal of creating and sustaining stable international orders.[45] This is not to say that great powers never aim to prevent wars and keep the peace. On the contrary, they work hard to deter wars in which they would be the likely victim. In such cases, however, state behavior is driven largely by narrow calculations about relative power, not by a commitment to build a world order independent of a state's own interests. The United States, for example, devoted enormous resources to deterring the Soviet Union from starting a war in Europe during the Cold War, not because of some deep-seated commitment to promoting peace around the world, but because American leaders feared that a Soviet victory would lead to a dangerous shift in the balance of power.[46]

The particular international order that obtains at any time is mainly a by-product of the self-interested behavior of the system's great powers. The configuration of the system, in other words, is the unintended consequence of great-power security competition, not the result of states acting together to organize peace. The establishment of the Cold War order in Europe illustrates this point. Neither the Soviet Union nor the United States intended to establish it, nor did they work together to create it. In fact, each superpower worked hard in the early years of the Cold War to gain power at the expense of the other, while preventing the other from doing likewise.[47] The system that emerged in Europe in the aftermath of World War II was the unplanned consequence of intense security competition between the superpowers.

Although that intense superpower rivalry ended along with the Cold War in 1990, Russia and the

United States have not worked together to create the present order in Europe. The United States, for example, has rejected out of hand various Russian proposals to make the Organization for Security and Cooperation in Europe the central organizing pillar of European security (replacing the U.S.-dominated NATO). Furthermore, Russia was deeply opposed to NATO expansion, which it viewed as a serious threat to Russian security. Recognizing that Russia's weakness would preclude any retaliation, however, the United States ignored Russia's concerns and pushed NATO to accept the Czech Republic, Hungary, and Poland as new members. Russia has also opposed U.S. policy in the Balkans over the past decade, especially NATO's 1999 war against Yugoslavia. Again, the United States has paid little attention to Russia's concerns and has taken the steps it deems necessary to bring peace to that volatile region. Finally, it is worth noting that although Russia is dead set against allowing the United States to deploy ballistic missile defenses, it is highly likely that Washington will deploy such a system if it is judged to be technologically feasible.

For sure, great-power rivalry will sometimes produce a stable international order, as happened during the Cold War. Nevertheless, the great powers will continue looking for opportunities to increase their share of world power, and if a favorable situation arises, they will move to undermine that stable order. Consider how hard the United States worked during the late 1980s to weaken the Soviet Union and bring down the stable order that had emerged in Europe during the latter part of the Cold War.[48] Of course, the states that stand to lose power will work to deter aggression and preserve the existing order. But their motives will be selfish, revolving around balance-of-power logic, not some commitment to world peace.

Great powers cannot commit themselves to the pursuit of a peaceful world order for two reasons. First, states are unlikely to agree on a general formula for bolstering peace. Certainly, international relations scholars have never reached a consensus on what the blueprint should look like. In fact, it seems there are about as many theories on the causes of war and peace as there are scholars studying the subject. But more important, policymakers are unable to agree on how to create a stable world. For example, at the Paris Peace Conference after World War I, important differences over how to create stability in Europe divided Georges Clemenceau, David Lloyd George, and Woodrow Wilson.[49] In particular, Clemenceau was determined to impose harsher terms on Germany over the Rhineland than was either Lloyd George or Wilson, while Lloyd George stood out as the hard-liner on German reparations. The Treaty of Versailles, not surprisingly, did little to promote European stability.

Furthermore, consider American thinking on how to achieve stability in Europe in the early days of the Cold War.[50] The key elements for a stable and durable system were in place by the early 1950s. They included the division of Germany, the positioning of American ground forces in Western Europe to deter a Soviet attack, and ensuring that West Germany would not seek to develop nuclear weapons. Officials in the Truman administration, however, disagreed about whether a divided Germany would be a source of peace or war. For example, George Kennan and Paul Nitze, who held important positions in the State Department, believed that a divided Germany would be a source of instability, whereas Secretary of State Dean Acheson disagreed with them. In the 1950s, President Eisenhower sought to end the American commitment to defend Western Europe and to provide West Germany with its own nuclear deterrent. This policy, which was never fully adopted, nevertheless caused significant instability in Europe, as it led directly to the Berlin crises of 1958–59 and 1961.[51]

Second, great powers cannot put aside power considerations and work to promote international peace because they cannot be sure that their efforts will succeed. If their attempt fails, they are likely to pay a steep price for having neglected the balance of power, because if an aggressor appears at the door there will be no answer when they dial 911. That is a risk few states are willing to run. Therefore, prudence dictates that they behave according to realist logic. This line of reasoning accounts for why collective security schemes, which call for states to put aside narrow concerns about the balance of power and instead act in accordance with the broader interests of the international community, invariably die at birth.[52]

Cooperation Among States

One might conclude from the preceding discussion that my theory does not allow for any cooperation among the great powers. But this conclusion would be wrong. States can cooperate, although cooperation is sometimes difficult to achieve and always difficult to sustain. Two factors inhibit cooperation: considerations about relative gains and concern about cheating.[53] Ultimately, great powers live in a fundamentally competitive world where they view each other as real, or at least potential, enemies, and they therefore look to gain power at each other's expense.

Any two states contemplating cooperation must consider how profits or gains will be distributed between them. They can think about the division in terms of either absolute or relative gains (recall the distinction made earlier between pursuing either absolute power or relative power; the concept here is the same). With absolute gains, each side is concerned with maximizing its own profits and cares little about how much the other side gains or loses in the deal. Each side cares about the other only to the extent that the other side's behavior affects its own prospects for achieving maximum profits. With relative gains, on the other hand, each side considers not only its own individual gain, but also how well it fares compared to the other side.

Because great powers care deeply about the balance of power, their thinking focuses on relative gains when they consider cooperating with other states. For sure, each state tries to maximize its absolute gains; still, it is more important for a state to make sure that it does no worse, and perhaps better, than the other state in any agreement. Cooperation is more difficult to achieve, however, when states are attuned to relative gains rather than absolute gains.[54] This is because states concerned about absolute gains have to make sure that if the pie is expanding, they are getting at least some portion of the increase, whereas states that worry about relative gains must pay careful attention to how the pie is divided, which complicates cooperative efforts.

Concerns about cheating also hinder cooperation. Great powers are often reluctant to enter into cooperative agreements for fear that the other side will cheat on the agreement and gain a significant advantage. This concern is especially acute in the military realm, causing a "special peril of defection," because the nature of military weaponry allows for rapid shifts in the balance of power.[55] Such a development could create a window of opportunity for the state that cheats to inflict a decisive defeat on its victim.

These barriers to cooperation notwithstanding, great powers do cooperate in a realist world. Balance-of-power logic often causes great powers to form alliances and cooperate against common enemies. The United Kingdom, France, and Russia, for example, were allies against Germany before and during World War I. States sometimes cooperate to gang up on a third state, as Germany and the Soviet Union did against Poland in 1939.[56] More recently, Serbia and Croatia agreed to conquer and divide Bosnia between them, although the United States and its European allies prevented them from executing their agreement.[57] Rivals as well as allies cooperate. After all, deals can be struck that roughly reflect the distribution of power and satisfy concerns about cheating. The various arms control agreements signed by the superpowers during the Cold War illustrate this point.

The bottom line, however, is that cooperation takes place in a world that is competitive at its core—one where states have powerful incentives to take advantage of other states. This point is graphically highlighted by the state of European politics in the forty years before World War I. The great powers cooperated frequently during this period, but that did not stop them from going to war on August 1, 1914.[58] The United States and the Soviet Union also cooperated considerably during World War II, but that cooperation did not prevent the outbreak of the Cold War shortly after Germany and Japan were defeated. Perhaps most amazingly, there was significant economic and military cooperation between Nazi Germany and the Soviet Union during the two years before the Wehrmacht attacked the Red Army.[59] No amount of cooperation can eliminate the dominating logic of security competition. Genuine peace, or a world in which states do not compete for power, is not likely as long as the state system remains anarchic.

Conclusion

In sum, my argument is that the structure of the international system, not the particular characteristics of individual great powers, causes them to think and act offensively and to seek hegemony.[60] I do not adopt Morgenthau's claim that states invariably behave aggressively because they have a will to power hardwired into them. Instead, I assume that the principal motive behind great-power behavior is survival. In anarchy, however, the desire to survive encourages states to behave aggressively. Nor does my theory classify states as more or less aggressive on the basis of their economic or political systems. Offensive realism makes only a handful of assumptions about great powers, and these assumptions apply equally to all great powers.

Except for differences in how much power each state controls, the theory treats all states alike.

I have now laid out the logic explaining why states seek to gain as much power as possible over their rivals. * * *

NOTES

1. Most realist scholars allow in their theories for status quo powers that are not hegemons. At least some states, they argue, are likely to be satisfied with the balance of power and thus have no incentive to change it. See Randall L. Schweller, "Neorealism's Status-Quo Bias: What Security Dilemma?" *Security Studies* 5, No. 3 (Spring 1996, special issue on "Realism: Restatements and Renewal," ed. Benjamin Frankel), pp. 98–101; and Arnold Wolfers, *Discord and Collaboration: Essays on International Politics* (Baltimore, MD: Johns Hopkins University Press, 1962), pp. 84–86, 91–92, 125–26.

2. Milton Friedman, *Essays in Positive Economics* (Chicago: University of Chicago Press, 1953), p. 14. Also see Kenneth N. Waltz, *Theory of International Politics* (Reading, MA: Addison-Wesley, 1979), pp. 5–6, 91, 119.

3. Terry Moe makes a helpful distinction between assumptions that are simply useful simplifications of reality (i.e., realistic in themselves but with unnecessary details omitted), and assumptions that are clearly contrary to reality (i.e., that directly violate well-established truths). See Moe, "On the Scientific Status of Rational Models," *American Journal of Political Science* 23, No. 1 (February 1979), pp. 215–43.

4. The concept of anarchy and its consequences for international politics was first articulated by G. Lowes Dickinson, *The European Anarchy* (New York: Macmillan, 1916). For a more recent and more elaborate discussion of anarchy, see Waltz, *Theory of International Politics*, pp. 88–93. Also see Robert J. Art and Robert Jervis, eds., *International Politics: Anarchy, Force, Imperialism* (Boston: Little, Brown, 1973), pt. 1; and Helen Milner, "The Assumption of Anarchy in International Relations Theory: A Critique," *Review of International Studies* 17, No. 1 (January 1991), pp. 67–85.

5. Although the focus in this study is on the state system, realist logic can be applied to other kinds of anarchic systems. After all, it is the absence of central authority, not any special characteristic of states, that causes them to compete for power.

6. Inis L. Claude, Jr., *Swords into Plowshares: The Problems and Progress of International Organization*, 4th ed. (New York: Random House, 1971), p. 14.

7. The claim that states might have benign intentions is simply a starting assumption. I argue subsequently that when you combine the theory's five assumptions, states are put in a position in which they are strongly disposed to having hostile intentions toward each other.

8. My theory ultimately argues that great powers behave offensively toward each other because that is the best way for them to guarantee their security in an anarchic world. The assumption here, however, is that there are many reasons besides security for why a state might behave aggressively toward another state. In fact, it is uncertainty

about whether those non-security causes of war are at play, or might come into play, that pushes great powers to worry about their survival and thus act offensively. Security concerns alone cannot cause great powers to act aggressively. The possibility that at least one state might be motivated by non-security calculations is a necessary condition for offensive realism, as well as for any other structural theory of international politics that predicts security competition.

9. Quoted in Jon Jacobson, *When the Soviet Union Entered World Politics* (Berkeley: University of California Press, 1994), p. 271.

10. See Elizabeth Pond, *Beyond the Wall: Germany's Road to Unification* (Washington, DC: Brookings Institution Press, 1993), chap. 12; Margaret Thatcher, *The Downing Street Years* (New York: Harper-Collins, 1993), chaps. 25–26; and Philip Zelikow and Condoleezza Rice, *Germany Unified and Europe Transformed: A Study in State-craft* (Cambridge, MA: Harvard University Press, 1995), chap. 4.

11. Frederick Schuman introduced the concept of self-help in *International Politics: An Introduction to the Western State System* (New York: McGraw-Hill, 1933), pp. 199–202, 514, although Waltz made the concept famous in *Theory of International Politics*, chap. 6. On realism and alliances, see Stephen M. Walt, *The Origins of Alliances* (Ithaca, NY: Cornell University Press, 1987).

12. Quoted in Martin Wight, *Power Politics* (London: Royal Institute of International Affairs, 1946), p. 40.

13. If one state achieves hegemony, the system ceases to be anarchic and becomes hierarchic. Offensive realism, which assumes international anarchy, has little to say about politics under hierarchy. But as discussed later, it is highly unlikely that any state will become a global hegemon, although regional hegemony is feasible. Thus, realism is likely to provide important insights about world politics for the foreseeable future, save for what goes on inside in a region that is dominated by a hegemon.

14. Although great powers always have aggressive intentions, they are not always *aggressors*, mainly because sometimes they do not have the capability to behave aggressively. I use the term "aggressor" throughout this book to denote great powers that have the material wherewithal to act on their aggressive intentions.

15. Kenneth Waltz maintains that great powers should not pursue hegemony but instead should aim to control an "appropriate" amount of world power. See Waltz, "The Origins of War in Neorealist Theory," in Robert I. Rotberg and Theodore K. Rabb, eds., *The Origin and Prevention of Major Wars* (Cambridge: Cambridge University Press, 1989), p. 40.

16. The following hypothetical example illustrates this point. Assume that American policy-makers were forced to choose between two different power balances in the Western Hemisphere. The first is the present distribution of power, whereby the United States is a hegemon that no state in the region would dare challenge militarily. In the second scenario, China replaces Canada and Germany takes the place of Mexico. Even though the United States would have a significant military advantage over both China and Germany, it is difficult to imagine any American strategist opting for this scenario over U.S. hegemony in the Western Hemisphere.

17. John H. Herz, "Idealist Internationalism and the Security Dilemma," *World Politics* 2, No. 2 (January 1950), pp. 157–80. Although Dickinson did not use the term "security dilemma," its logic is clearly articulated in *European Anarchy*, pp. 20, 88.

18. Herz, "Idealist Internationalism," p. 157.

19. See Joseph M. Grieco, "Anarchy and the Limits of Cooperation: A Realist Critique of the Newest Liberal Institutionalism," *International Organization* 42, No. 3 (Summer 1988), pp. 485–507; Stephen D. Krasner, "Global Communications and National Power: Life on the Pareto Frontier," *World Politics* 43, No. 3 (April 1991), pp. 336–66; and Robert Powell, "Absolute and Relative Gains in International Relations Theory," *American Political Science Review* 85, No. 4 (December 1991), pp. 1303–20.

20. See Michael Mastanduno, "Do Relative Gains Matter? America's Response to Japanese Industrial Policy," *International Security* 16, No. 1 (Summer 1991), pp. 73–113.

21. Waltz maintains that in Hans Morgenthau's theory, states seek power as an end in itself; thus, they are concerned with absolute power, not relative power. See Waltz, "Origins of War," pp. 40–41; and Waltz, *Theory of International Politics*, pp. 126–27.

22. Quoted in Marc Trachtenberg, *A Constructed Peace: The Making of the European Settlement, 1945–1963* (Princeton, NJ: Princeton University Press, 1999), p. 36.

23. In short, the key issue for evaluating offensive realism is not whether a state is constantly trying to conquer other countries or going all out in terms of defense spending, but whether or not great powers routinely pass up promising opportunities to gain power over rivals.

24. See Richard K. Betts, *Surprise Attack: Lessons for Defense Planning* (Washington, DC: Brookings Institution Press, 1982); James D. Fearon, "Rationalist Explanations for War," *International Organization* 49, No. 3 (Summer 1995), pp. 390–401; Robert Jervis, *The Logic of Images in International Relations* (Princeton, NJ: Princeton University Press, 1970); and Stephen Van Evera, *Causes of War: Power and the Roots of Conflict* (Ithaca, NY: Cornell University Press, 1999), pp. 45–51, 83, 137–42.

25. See Joel Achenbach, "The Experts in Retreat: After-the-Fact Explanations for the Gloomy Predictions," *Washington Post*, February 28, 1991; and Jacob Weisberg, "Gulfballs: How the Experts Blew It, Big-Time," *New Republic*, March 25, 1991.

26. Jack Snyder and Stephen Van Evera make this argument in its boldest form. See Jack Snyder, *Myths of Empire: Domestic Politics and International Ambition* (Ithaca, NY: Cornell University Press, 1991), esp. pp. 1, 307–8; and Van Evera, *Causes of War*, esp. pp. 6, 9.

27. Relatedly, some defensive realists interpret the security dilemma to say that the offensive measures a state takes to enhance its own security force rival states to respond in kind, leaving all states no better off than if they had done nothing, and possibly even worse off. See Charles L. Glaser, "The Security Dilemma Revisited," *World Politics* 50, No. 1 (October 1997), pp. 171–201.

28. Although threatened states sometimes balance efficiently against aggressors, they often do not, thereby creating opportunities for successful offense. Snyder appears to be aware of this problem, as he adds the important qualifier "at least in the long run" to his claim that "states typically form balancing alliances to resist aggressors." *Myths of Empire*, p. 11.

29. John Arquilla, *Dubious Battles: Aggression, Defeat, and the International System* (Washington, DC: Crane Russak, 1992), p. 2. Also see Bruce Bueno de Mesquita, *The War Trap* (New Haven, CT: Yale University Press, 1981), pp. 21–22; and Kevin Wang and James Ray, "Beginners and Winners: The Fate of Initiators of Interstate Wars

Involving Great Powers since 1495," *International Studies Quarterly* 38, No. 1 (March 1994), pp. 139–54.

30. Although Snyder and Van Evera maintain that conquest rarely pays, both concede in subtle but important ways that aggression sometimes succeeds. Snyder, for example, distinguishes between expansion (successful offense) and overexpansion (unsuccessful offense), which is the behavior that he wants to explain. See, for example, his discussion of Japanese expansion between 1868 and 1945 in *Myths of Empire*, pp. 114–16. Van Evera allows for variation in the offense-defense balance, to include a few periods where conquest is feasible. See *Causes of War*, chap. 6. Of course, allowing for successful aggression contradicts their central claim that offense hardly ever succeeds.

31. See Robert Gilpin, *War and Change in World Politics* (Cambridge: Cambridge University Press, 1981), p. 29; and William C. Wohlforth, *The Elusive Balance: Power and Perceptions during the Cold War* (Ithaca, NY: Cornell University Press, 1993), pp. 12–14.

32. In subsequent chapters, the power-projection problems associated with large bodies of water are taken into account when measuring the distribution of power (see Chapter 4). Those two factors are treated separately here, however, simply to highlight the profound influence that oceans have on the behavior of great powers.

33. For an opposing view, see David M. Edelstein, "Choosing Friends and Enemies: Perceptions of Intentions in International Relations," Ph.D. diss., University of Chicago, August 2000; Andrew Kydd, "Why Security Seekers Do Not Fight Each Other," *Security Studies* 7, No. 1 (Autumn 1997), pp. 114–54; and Walt, *Origins of Alliances*.

34. See note 8 in this chapter.

35. Jacob Viner, "Power versus Plenty as Objectives of Foreign Policy in the Seventeenth and Eighteenth Centuries," *World Politics* I, No. 1 (October 1948), p. 10.

36. See Mark Bowden, *Black Hawk Down: A Story of Modern War* (London: Penguin, 1999); Alison Des Forges, *"Leave None to Tell the Story": Genocide in Rwanda* (New York: Human Rights Watch, 1999), pp. 623–25; and Gerard Prunier, *The Rwanda Crisis: History of a Genocide* (New York: Columbia University Press, 1995), pp. 274–75.

37. See Scott R. Feil, *Preventing Genocide: How the Early Use of Force Might Have Succeeded in Rwanda* (New York: Carnegie Corporation, 1998); and John Mueller, "The Banality of 'Ethnic War,'" *International Security* 25, No. 1 (Summer 2000), pp. 58–62. For a less sanguine view of how many lives would have been saved had the United States intervened in Rwanda, see Alan J. Kuperman, "Rwanda in Retrospect," *Foreign Affairs* 79, No. 1 (January–February 2000), pp. 94–118.

38. See David F. Schmitz, *Thank God They're on Our Side: The United States and Right-Wing Dictatorships, 1921–1965* (Chapel Hill: University of North Carolina Press, 1999), chaps. 4–6; Gaddis Smith, *The Last Years of the Monroe Doctrine, 1945–1993* (New York: Hill and Wang, 1994); Tony Smith, *America's Mission: The United States and the Worldwide Struggle for Democracy in the Twentieth Century* (Princeton, NJ: Princeton University Press, 1994); and Stephen Van Evera, "Why Europe Matters, Why the Third World Doesn't: American Grand Strategy after the Cold War," *Journal of Strategic Studies* 13, No. 2 (June 1990), pp. 25–30.

39. Quoted in John M. Carroll and George C. Herring, eds., *Modern American Diplomacy*, rev. ed. (Wilmington, DE: Scholarly Resources, 1996), p. 122.

40. Nikita Khrushchev makes a similar point about Stalin's policy toward Chinese nationalist leader Chiang Kai-shek during World War II.

41. See Walt, *Origins of Alliances*, pp. 5, 266–68.

42. Adam Smith, *An Inquiry into the Nature and Causes of the Wealth of Nations,* ed. Edwin Cannan (Chicago: University of Chicago Press, 1976), Vol. 1, p. 487. All the quotes in this paragraph are from pp. 484–87 of that book.

43. For an overview of the Anglo-Dutch rivalry, see Jack S. Levy, "The Rise and Decline of the Anglo-Dutch Rivalry, 1609–1689," in William R. Thompson, ed., *Great Power Rivalries* (Columbia: University of South Carolina Press, 1999), pp. 172–200; and Paul M. Kennedy, *The Rise and Fall of British Naval Mastery* (London: Allen Lane, 1976), chap. 2.

44. William J. Clinton, "Address by the President to the 48th Session of the United Nations General Assembly," United Nations, New York, September 27, 1993. Also see George Bush, "Toward a New World Order: Address by the President to a Joint Session of Congress," September 11, 1990.

45. Bradley Thayer examined whether the victorious powers were able to create and maintain stable security orders in the aftermath of the Napoleonic Wars, World War I, and World War II, or whether they competed among themselves for power, as realism would predict. Thayer concludes that the rhetoric of the triumphant powers notwithstanding, they remained firmly committed to gaining power at each other's expense. See Bradley A. Thayer, "Creating Stability in New World Orders," Ph.D. diss., University of Chicago, August 1996.

46. See Melvyn P. Leffler, *A Preponderance of Power: National Security, the Truman Administration, and the Cold War* (Stanford, CA: Stanford University Press, 1992).

47. For a discussion of American efforts to undermine Soviet control of Eastern Europe, see Peter Grose, *Operation Rollback: America's Secret War behind the Iron Curtain* (Boston: Houghton Mifflin, 2000); Walter L. Hixson, *Parting the Curtain: Propaganda, Culture, and the Cold War, 1945–1961* (New York: St. Martin's, 1997); and Gregory Mitrovich, *Undermining the Kremlin: America's Strategy to Subvert the Soviet Bloc, 1947–1956* (Ithaca, NY: Cornell University Press, 2000).

48. For a synoptic discussion of U.S. policy toward the Soviet Union in the late 1980s that cites most of the key sources on the subject, see Randall L. Schweller and William C. Wohlforth, "Power Test: Evaluating Realism in Response to the End of the Cold War," *Security Studies* 9, No. 3 (Spring 2000), pp. 91–97.

49. The editors of a major book on the Treaty of Versailles write, "The resulting reappraisal, as documented in this book, constitutes a new synthesis of peace conference scholarship. The findings call attention to divergent peace aims within the American and Allied camps and underscore the degree to which the negotiators considered the Versailles Treaty a work in progress." Manfred F. Boemeke, Gerald D. Feldman, and Elisabeth Glaser, eds., *The Treaty of Versailles: A Reassessment after 75 Years* (Cambridge: Cambridge University Press, 1998), p. 1.

50. This paragraph draws heavily on Trachtenberg, *Constructed Peace*; and Marc Trachtenberg, *History and Strategy* (Princeton, NJ: Princeton University Press, 1991), chaps. 4–5. Also see G. John Ikenberry, "Rethinking the Origins of American Hegemony," *Political Science Quarterly* 104, No. 3 (Autumn 1989), pp. 375–400.

51. The failure of American policymakers during the early Cold War to understand where the security competition in Europe was leading is summarized by Trachtenberg, "The predictions that were made pointed as a rule in the opposite direction: that Germany could not be kept down forever; that the Federal Republic would ultimately . . . want nuclear forces of her own; that U.S. troops could not be expected to remain in . . . Europe. . . . Yet all these predictions—every single one—turned out to be wrong." Trachtenberg, *History and Strategy*, pp. 231–32. Also see Trachtenberg, *Constructed Peace*, pp. vii–viii.

52. For more discussion of the pitfalls of collective security, see John J. Mearsheimer, "The False Promise of International Institutions," *International Security* 19, No. 3 (Winter 1994–95), pp. 26–37.

53. See Grieco, "Anarchy and the Limits of Cooperation," pp. 498, 500.

54. For evidence of relative gains considerations thwarting cooperation among states, see Paul W. Schroeder, *The Transformation of European Politics, 1763–1848* (Oxford: Clarendon, 1994), chap. 3.

55. Charles Lipson, "International Cooperation in Economic and Security Affairs," *World Politics* 37, No. 1 (October 1984), p. 14.

56. See Randall L. Schweller, "Bandwagoning for Profit: Bringing the Revisionist State Back In," *International Security* 19, No. 1 (Summer 1994), pp. 72–107. See also the works cited in note 59 in this chapter.

57. See Misha Glenny, *The Fall of Yugoslavia: The Third Balkan War*, 3d rev. ed. (New York: Penguin, 1996), p. 149; Philip Sherwell and Alina Petric, "Tudjman Tapes Reveal Plans to Divide Bosnia and Hide War Crimes," *Sunday Telegraph* (London), June 18, 2000; Laura Silber and Allan Little, *Yugoslavia: Death of a Nation*, rev. ed. (New York: Penguin, 1997), pp. 131–32, 213; and Warren Zimmerman, *Origins of a Catastrophe: Yugoslavia and Its Destroyers—America's Last Ambassador Tells What Happened and Why* (New York: Times Books, 1996), pp. 116–17.

58. See John Maynard Keynes, *The Economic Consequences of the Peace* (New York: Penguin, 1988), chap. 2; and J. M. Roberts, *Europe, 1880–1945* (London: Longman, 1970), pp. 239–41.

59. For information on the Molotov-Ribbentrop Pact of August 1939 and the ensuing cooperation between those states, see Alan Bullock, *Hitler and Stalin: Parallel Lives* (London: HarperCollins, 1991), chaps. 14–15; I.C.B. Dear, ed., *The Oxford Companion to World War II* (Oxford: Oxford University Press, 1995), pp. 780–82; Anthony Read and David Fisher, *The Deadly Embrace: Hitler, Stalin, and the Nazi-Soviet Pact, 1939–1941* (New York: Norton, 1988); Geoffrey Roberts, *The Unholy Alliance: Stalin's Pact with Hitler* (Bloomington: Indiana University Press, 1989), chaps. 8–10; and Adam B. Ulam, *Expansion and Coexistence: Soviet Foreign Policy, 1917–1973*, 2d ed. (New York: Holt, Rinehart, and Winston, 1974), chap. 6.

60. Waltz maintains that structural theories can explain international outcomes—i.e., whether war is more likely in bipolar or multipolar systems—but that they cannot explain the foreign policy behavior of particular states. A separate theory of foreign policy, he argues, is needed for that task. See *Theory of International Politics*, pp. 71–72, 121–23.

Michael W. Doyle

LIBERALISM AND WORLD POLITICS

Promoting freedom will produce peace, we have often been told. In a speech before the British Parliament in June of 1982, President Reagan proclaimed that governments founded on a respect for individual liberty exercise "restraint" and "peaceful intentions" in their foreign policy. He then announced a "crusade for freedom" and a "campaign for democratic development" (Reagan, June 9, 1982).

In making these claims the president joined a long list of liberal theorists (and propagandists) and echoed an old argument: the aggressive instincts of authoritarian leaders and totalitarian ruling parties make for war. Liberal states, founded on such individual rights as equality before the law, free speech and other civil liberties, private property, and elected representation are fundamentally against war this argument asserts. When the citizens who bear the burdens of war elect their governments, wars become impossible. Furthermore, citizens appreciate that the benefits of trade can be enjoyed only under conditions of peace. Thus the very existence of liberal states, such as the U.S., Japan, and our European allies, makes for peace.

Building on a growing literature in international political science, I reexamine the liberal claim President Reagan reiterated for us. I look at three distinct theoretical traditions of liberalism, attributable to three theorists: Schumpeter, a brilliant explicator of the liberal pacifism the president invoked;

Machiavelli, a classical republican whose glory is an imperialism we often practice; and Kant.

Despite the contradictions of liberal pacifism and liberal imperialism, I find, with Kant and other liberal republicans, that liberalism does leave a coherent legacy on foreign affairs. Liberal states are different. They are indeed peaceful, yet they are also prone to make war, as the U.S. and our "freedom fighters" are now doing, not so covertly, against Nicaragua. Liberal states have created a separate peace, as Kant argued they would, and have also discovered liberal reasons for aggression, as he feared they might. I conclude by arguing that the differences among liberal pacifism, liberal imperialism, and Kant's liberal internationalism are not arbitrary but rooted in differing conceptions of the citizen and the state.

Liberal Pacifism

There is no canonical description of liberalism. What we tend to call *liberal* resembles a family portrait of principles and institutions, recognizable by certain characteristics—for example, individual freedom, political participation, private property, and equality of opportunity—that most liberal states share, although none has perfected them all. Joseph Schumpeter clearly fits within this family when he considers the international effects of capitalism and democracy.

Schumpeter's "Sociology of Imperialisms," published in 1919, made a coherent and sustained argument concerning the pacifying (in the sense of

From *American Political Science Review* 80, no. 4 (December 1986): 1151–69. The author's notes have been omitted.

nonaggressive) effects of liberal institutions and principles (Schumpeter, 1955; see also Doyle, 1986, pp. 155–59). Unlike some of the earlier liberal theorists who focused on a single feature such as trade (Montesquieu, 1949, vol. I, bk. 20, chap. 1) or failed to examine critically the arguments they were advancing, Schumpeter saw the interaction of capitalism and democracy as the foundation of liberal pacifism, and he tested his arguments in a sociology of historical imperialisms.

He defines *imperialism* as "an objectless disposition on the part of a state to unlimited forcible expansion" (Schumpeter, 1955, p. 6). Excluding imperialisms that were mere "catchwords" and those that were "object-ful" (e.g., defensive imperialism), he traces the roots of objectless imperialism to three sources, each an atavism. Modern imperialism, according to Schumpeter, resulted from the combined impact of a "war machine," warlike instincts, and export monopolism.

Once necessary, the war machine later developed a life of its own and took control of a state's foreign policy: "Created by the wars that required it, the machine now created the wars it required" (Schumpeter, 1955, p. 25). Thus, Schumpeter tells us that the army of ancient Egypt, created to drive the Hyksos out of Egypt, took over the state and pursued militaristic imperialism. Like the later armies of the courts of absolutist Europe, it fought wars for the sake of glory and booty, for the sake of warriors and monarchs—wars *gratia* warriors.

A warlike disposition, elsewhere called "instinctual elements of bloody primitivism," is the natural ideology of a war machine. It also exists independently; the Persians, says Schumpeter (1955, pp. 25–32), were a warrior nation from the outset.

Under modern capitalism, export monopolists, the third source of modern imperialism, push for imperialist expansion as a way to expand their closed markets. The absolute monarchies were the last clear-cut imperialisms. Nineteenth-century imperialisms merely represent the vestiges of the imperialisms created by Louis XIV and Catherine

the Great. Thus, the export monopolists are an atavism of the absolute monarchies, for they depend completely on the tariffs imposed by the monarchs and their militaristic successors for revenue (Schumpeter, 1955, pp. 82–83). Without tariffs, monopolies would be eliminated by foreign competition.

Modern (nineteenth-century) imperialism, therefore, rests on an atavistic war machine, militaristic attitudes left over from the days of monarchical wars, and export monopolism, which is nothing more than the economic residue of monarchical finance. In the modern era, imperialists gratify their private interests. From the national perspective, their imperialistic wars are objectless.

Schumpeter's theme now emerges. Capitalism and democracy are forces for peace. Indeed, they are antithetical to imperialism. For Schumpeter, the further development of capitalism and democracy means that imperialism will inevitably disappear. He maintains that capitalism produces an unwarlike disposition; its populace is "democratized, individualized, rationalized" (Schumpeter, 1955, p. 68). The people's energies are daily absorbed in production. The disciplines of industry and the market train people in "economic rationalism"; the instability of industrial life necessitates calculation. Capitalism also "individualizes"; "subjective opportunities" replace the "immutable factors" of traditional, hierarchical society. Rational individuals demand democratic governance.

Democratic capitalism leads to peace. As evidence, Schumpeter claims that throughout the capitalist world an opposition has arisen to "war, expansion, cabinet diplomacy"; that contemporary capitalism is associated with peace parties; and that the industrial worker of capitalism is "vigorously anti-imperialist." In addition, he points out that the capitalist world has developed means of preventing war, such as the Hague Court and that the least feudal, most capitalist society—the United States—has demonstrated the least imperialistic tendencies (Schumpeter, 1955, pp. 95–96). An example of the lack of imperialistic tendencies in the U.S., Schumpeter thought, was our leaving over half of Mexico unconquered in the war of 1846–48.

Schumpeter's explanation for liberal pacifism is quite simple: Only war profiteers and military aristocrats gain from wars. No democracy would pursue a minority interest and tolerate the high costs of imperialism. When free trade prevails, "no class" gains from forcible expansion because

> foreign raw materials and food stuffs are as accessible to each nation as though they were in its own territory. Where the cultural backwardness of a region makes normal economic intercourse dependent on colonization it does not matter, assuming free trade, which of the "civilized" nations undertakes the task of colonization. (Schumpeter, 1955, pp. 75–76)

Schumpeter's arguments are difficult to evaluate. In partial tests of quasi-Schumpeterian propositions, Michael Haas (1974, pp. 464–65) discovered a cluster that associates democracy, development, and sustained modernization with peaceful conditions. However, M. Small and J. D. Singer (1976) have discovered that there is no clearly negative correlation between democracy and war in the period 1816–1965—the period that would be central to Schumpeter's argument (see also Wilkenfeld, 1968; Wright, 1942, p. 841).

* * * A recent study by R. J. Rummel (1983) of "libertarianism" and international violence is the closest test Schumpeterian pacifism has received. "Free" states (those enjoying political and economic freedom) were shown to have considerably less conflict at or above the level of economic sanctions than "nonfree" states. The free states, the partly free states (including the democratic socialist countries such as Sweden), and the nonfree states accounted for 24%, 26%, and 61%, respectively, of the international violence during the period examined.

These effects are impressive but not conclusive for the Schumpeterian thesis. The data are limited, in this test, to the period 1976 to 1980. It includes, for example, the Russo-Afghan War, the Vietnamese invasion of Cambodia, China's invasion of Vietnam, and Tanzania's invasion of Uganda but just misses the U.S., quasi-covert intervention in Angola (1975) and our not so covert war against Nicaragua (1981–). More importantly, it excludes the cold war period, with its numerous interventions, and the long history of colonial wars (the Boer War, the Spanish-American War, the Mexican Intervention, etc.) that marked the history of liberal, including democratic capitalist, states (Doyle, 1983b; Chan, 1984; Weede, 1984).

The discrepancy between the warlike history of liberal states and Schumpeter's pacifistic expectations highlights three extreme assumptions. First, his "materialistic monism" leaves little room for noneconomic objectives, whether espoused by states or individuals. Neither glory, nor prestige, nor ideological justification, nor the pure power of ruling shapes policy. These nonmaterial goals leave little room for positive-sum gains, such as the comparative advantages of trade. Second, and relatedly, the same is true for his states. The political life of individuals seems to have been homogenized at the same time as the individuals were "rationalized, individualized, and democratized." Citizens—capitalists and workers, rural and urban—seek material welfare. Schumpeter seems to presume that ruling makes no difference. He also presumes that no one is prepared to take those measures (such as stirring up foreign quarrels to preserve a domestic ruling coalition) that enhance one's political power, despite deterimental effects on mass welfare. Third, like domestic politics, world politics are homogenized. Materially monistic and democratically capitalist, all states evolve toward free trade and liberty together. Countries differently constituted seem to disappear from Schumpeter's analysis. "Civilized" nations govern "culturally backward" *regions*. These assumptions are not shared by Machiavelli's theory of liberalism.

Liberal Imperialism

Machiavelli argues, not only that republics are not pacifistic, but that they are the best form of state for imperial expansion. Establishing a republic fit for imperial expansion is, moreover, the best way to guarantee the survival of a state.

Machiavelli's republic is a classical mixed republic. It is not a democracy—which he thought would quickly degenerate into a tyranny—but is characterized by social equality, popular liberty, and political participation (Machiavelli, 1950, bk. 1, chap. 2, p. 112; see also Huliung, 1983, chap. 2; Mansfield, 1970; Pocock, 1975, pp. 198–99; Skinner, 1981, chap. 3). The consuls serve as "kings," the senate as an aristocracy managing the state, and the people in the assembly as the source of strength.

Liberty results from "disunion"—the competition and necessity for compromise required by the division of powers among senate, consuls, and tribunes (the last representing the common people). Liberty also results from the popular veto. The powerful few threaten the rest with tyranny, Machiavelli says, because they seek to dominate. The mass demands not to be dominated, and their veto thus preserves the liberties of the state (Machiavelli, 1950, bk. 1, chap. 5, p. 122). However, since the people and the rulers have different social characters, the people need to be "managed" by the few to avoid having their recklessness overturn or their fecklessness undermine the ability of the state to expand (Machiavelli, 1950, bk. 1, chap. 53, pp. 249–50). Thus the senate and the consuls plan expansion, consult oracles, and employ religion to manage the resources that the energy of the people supplies.

Strength, and then imperial expansion, results from the way liberty encourages increased population and property, which grow when the citizens know their lives and goods are secure from arbitrary seizure. Free citizens equip large armies and provide soldiers who fight for public glory and the common good because these are, in fact, their own

(Machiavelli, 1950, bk. 2, chap. 2, pp. 287–90). If you seek the honor of having your state expand, Machiavelli advises, you should organize it as a free and popular republic like Rome, rather than as an aristocratic republic like Sparta or Venice. Expansion thus calls for a free republic.

"Necessity"—political survival—calls for expansion. If a stable aristocratic republic is forced by foreign conflict "to extend her territory, in such a case we shall see her foundations give way and herself quickly brought to ruin"; if, on the other hand, domestic security prevails, "the continued tranquility would enervate her, or provoke internal disensions, which together, or either of them separately, will apt to prove her ruin" (Machiavelli, 1950, bk. 1, chap. 6, p. 129). Machiavelli therefore believes it is necessary to take the constitution of Rome, rather than that of Sparta or Venice, as our model.

Hence, this belief leads to liberal imperialism. We are lovers of glory, Machiavelli announces. We seek to rule or, at least, to avoid being oppressed. In either case, we want more for ourselves and our states than just material welfare (materialistic monism). Because other states with similar aims thereby threaten us, we prepare ourselves for expansion. Because our fellow citizens threaten us if we do not allow them either to satisfy their ambition or to release their political energies through imperial expansion, we expand.

There is considerable historical evidence for liberal imperialism. Machiavelli's (Polybius's) Rome and Thucydides' Athens both were imperial republics in the Machiavellian sense (Thucydides, 1954, bk. 6). The historical record of numerous U.S. interventions in the postwar period supports Machiavelli's argument (* * * Barnet, 1968, chap. 11), but the current record of liberal pacifism, weak as it is, calls some of his insights into question. To the extent that the modern populace actually controls (and thus unbalances) the mixed republic, its diffidence may outweigh elite ("senatorial") aggressiveness.

We can conclude either that (1) liberal pacifism has at least taken over with the further development of capitalist democracy, as Schumpeter predicted it would or that (2) the mixed record of liberalism—pacifism and imperialism—indicates that some liberal states are Schumpeterian democracies while others are Machiavellian republics. Before we accept either conclusion, however, we must consider a third apparent regularity of modern world politics.

Liberal Internationalism

Modern liberalism carries with it two legacies. They do not affect liberal states separately, according to whether they are pacifistic or imperialistic, but simultaneously.

The first of these legacies is the pacification of foreign relations among liberal states. * * *

Beginning in the eighteenth century and slowly growing since then, a zone of peace, which Kant called the "pacific federation" or "pacific union," has begun to be established among liberal societies. More than 40 liberal states currently make up the union. Most are in Europe and North America, but they can be found on every continent, as Appendix 1 indicates.

Here the predictions of liberal pacifists (and President Reagan) are borne out: liberal states do exercise peaceful restraint, and a separate peace exists among them. This separate peace provides a solid foundation for the United States' crucial alliances with the liberal powers, e.g., the North Atlantic Treaty Organization and our Japanese alliance. This foundation appears to be impervious to the quarrels with our allies that bedeviled the Carter and Reagan administrations. It also offers the promise of a continuing peace among liberal states, and as the number of liberal states increases, it announces the possibility of global peace this side of the grave or world conquest.

Of course, the probability of the outbreak of war in any given year between any two given states is low. The occurrence of a war between any two adjacent states, considered over a long period of time, would be more probable. The apparent absence of war between liberal states, whether adjacent or not, for almost 200 years thus may have significance. Similar claims cannot be made for feudal, fascist, communist, authoritarian, or totalitarian forms of rule (Doyle, 1983a, p. 222), nor for pluralistic or merely similar societies. More significant perhaps is that when states are forced to decide on which side of an impending world war they will fight, liberal states all wind up on the same side despite the complexity of the paths that take them there. These characteristics do not prove that the peace among liberals is statistically significant nor that liberalism is the sole valid explanation for the peace. They do suggest that we consider the possibility that liberals have indeed established a separate peace—but only among themselves.

Liberalism also carries with it a second legacy: international "imprudence" (Hume, 1963, pp. 346–47). Peaceful restraint only seems to work in liberals' relations with other liberals. Liberal states have fought numerous wars with nonliberal states. (For a list of international wars since 1816 see Appendix 2.)

Many of these wars have been defensive and thus prudent by necessity. Liberal states have been attacked and threatened by nonliberal states that do not exercise any special restraint in their dealings with the liberal states. Authoritarian rulers both stimulate and respond to an international political environment in which conflicts of prestige, interest, and pure fear of what other states might do all lead states toward war. War and conquest have thus characterized the careers of many authoritarian rulers and ruling parties, from Louis XIV and Napoleon to Mussolini's fascists, Hitler's Nazis, and Stalin's communists.

Yet we cannot simply blame warfare on the authoritarians or totalitarians, as many of our more enthusiastic politicians would have us do. Most wars arise out of calculations and miscalculations of interest, misunderstandings, and mutual suspicions, such as those that characterized the origins of World War I. However, aggression by the liberal state has also characterized a large number of wars. Both France and Britain fought expansionist colonial wars throughout the nineteenth century. The United States fought a similar war with Mexico from 1846 to 1848, waged a war of annihilation against the American Indians, and intervened militarily against sovereign states many times before and after World War II. Liberal states invade weak nonliberal states and display striking distrust in dealings with powerful nonliberal states (Doyle, 1983b).

Neither realist (statist) nor Marxist theory accounts well for these two legacies. While they can account for aspects of certain periods of international stability (* * * Russett, 1985), neither the logic of the balance of power nor the logic of international hegemony explains the separate peace maintained for more than 150 years among states sharing one particular form of governance—liberal principles and institutions. Balance-of-power theory expects—indeed is premised upon—flexible arrangements of geostrategic rivalry that include preventive war. Hegemonies wax and wane, but the liberal peace holds. Marxist "ultra-imperialists" expect a form of peaceful rivalry among capitalists, but only liberal capitalists maintain peace. Leninists expect liberal capitalists to be aggressive toward nonliberal states, but they also (and especially) expect them to be imperialistic toward fellow liberal capitalists.

Kant's theory of liberal internationalism helps us understand these two legacies. * * * *Perpetual Peace*, written in 1795 (Kant, 1970, pp. 93–130), helps us understand the interactive nature of international relations. Kant tries to teach us methodologically that we can study neither the systemic relations of states nor the varieties of state behavior in isolation from each other. Substantively, he anticipates for us the ever-widening pacification of

a liberal pacific union, explains this pacification, and at the same time suggests why liberal states are not pacific in their relations with nonliberal states. Kant argues that perpetual peace will be guaranteed by the ever-widening acceptance of three "definitive articles" of peace. When all nations have accepted the definitive articles in a metaphorical "treaty" of perpetual peace he asks them to sign, perpetual peace will have been established.

The First Definitive Article requires the civil constitution of the state to be republican. By *republican* Kant means a political society that has solved the problem of combining moral autonomy, individualism, and social order. A private property and market-oriented economy partially addressed that dilemma in the private sphere. The public, or political, sphere was more troubling. His answer was a republic that preserved juridical freedom— the legal equality of citizens as subjects—on the basis of a representative government with a separation of powers. Juridical freedom is preserved because the morally autonomous individual is by means of representation a self-legislator making laws that apply to all citizens equally, including himself or herself. Tyranny is avoided because the individual is subject to laws he or she does not also administer (Kant, *PP* [*Perpetual Peace*], pp. 99–102 * * *).

Liberal republics will progressively establish peace among themselves by means of the pacific federation, or union (*foedus pacificum*), described in Kant's Second Definitive Article. The pacific union will establish peace within a federation of free states and securely maintain the rights of each state. The world will not have achieved the "perpetual peace" that provides the ultimate guarantor of republican freedom until "a late stage and after many unsuccessful attempts" (Kant, *UH* [*The Idea for a Universal History with a Cosmopolitan Purpose*], p. 47). At that time, all nations will have learned the lessons of peace through right conceptions of the appropriate constitution, great and sad experience, and good will. Only then will individuals enjoy perfect republican rights or the full guarantee of a global and just peace. In the meantime, the "pacific federation" of liberal republics—"an enduring and gradually expanding federation likely to prevent war"—brings within it more and more republics—despite republican collapses, backsliding, and disastrous wars—creating an ever-expanding separate peace (Kant, *PP*, p. 105). Kant emphasizes that

> it can be shown that this idea of federalism, extending gradually to encompass all states and thus leading to perpetual peace, is practicable and has objective reality. For if by good fortune one powerful and enlightened nation can form a republic (which is by nature inclined to seek peace), this will provide a focal point for federal association among other states. These will join up with the first one, thus securing the freedom of each state in accordance with the idea of international right, and the whole will gradually spread further and further by a series of alliances of this kind. (Kant, *PP*, p. 104)

The pacific union is not a single peace treaty ending one war, a world state, nor a state of nations. Kant finds the first insufficient. The second and third are impossible or potentially tyrannical. National sovereignty precludes reliable subservience to a state of nations; a world state destroys the civic freedom on which the development of human capacities rests (Kant, *UH*, p. 50). Although Kant obliquely refers to various classical interstate confederations and modern diplomatic congresses, he develops no systematic organizational embodiment of this treaty and presumably does not find institutionalization necessary (Riley, 1983, chap. 5; Schwarz, 1962, p. 77). He appears to have in mind a mutual nonaggression pact, perhaps a collective security agreement, and the cosmopolitan law set forth in the Third Definitive Article.

The Third Definitive Article establishes a cosmopolitan law to operate in conjunction with the pacific union. The cosmopolitan law "shall be limited to conditions of universal hospitality." In this Kant calls for the recognition of the "right of a foreigner not to be treated with hostility when he arrives on someone else's territory." This "does not extend beyond those conditions which make it possible for them [foreigners] to attempt to enter into relations [commerce] with the native inhabitants" (Kant, *PP*, p. 106). Hospitality does not require extending to foreigners either the right to citizenship or the right to settlement, unless the foreign visitors would perish if they were expelled. Foreign conquest and plunder also find no justification under this right. Hospitality does appear to include the right of access and the obligation of maintaining the opportunity for citizens to exchange goods and ideas without imposing the obligation to trade (a voluntary act in all cases under liberal constitutions).

Perpetual peace, for Kant, is an epistemology, a condition for ethical action, and, most importantly, an explanation of how the "mechanical process of nature visibly exhibits the purposive plan of producing concord among men, even against their will and indeed by means of their very discord" (Kant, *PP*, p. 108; *UH*, pp. 44–45). Understanding history requires an epistemological foundation, for without a teleology, such as the promise of perpetual peace, the complexity of history would overwhelm human understanding (Kant, *UH*, pp. 51–53). Perpetual peace, however, is not merely a heuristic device with which to interpret history. It is guaranteed, Kant explains in the "First Addition" to *Perpetual Peace* ("On the Guarantee of Perpetual Peace"), to result from men fulfilling their ethical duty or, failing that, from a hidden plan. Peace is an ethical duty because it is only under conditions of peace that all men can treat each other as ends, rather than means to an end (Kant, *UH*, p. 50; Murphy, 1970, chap. 3). * * *

In the end, however, our guarantee of perpetual peace does not rest on ethical conduct. * * *

The guarantee thus rests, Kant argues, not on the probable behavior of moral angels, but on that of "devils, so long as they possess understanding" (*PP*, p. 112). In explaining the sources of each of the three definitive articles of the perpetual peace, Kant then tells us how we (as free and intelligent devils) could be motivated by fear, force, and calculated advantage to undertake a course of action whose outcome we could reasonably anticipate to be perpetual peace. Yet while it is possible to conceive of the Kantian road to peace in these terms, Kant himself recognizes and argues that social evolution also makes the conditions of moral behavior less onerous and hence more likely (*CF* [*The Contest of Faculties*], pp. 187–89; Kelly, 1969, pp. 106–13). In tracing the effects of both political and moral development, he builds an account of why liberal states do maintain peace among themselves and of how it will (by implication, has) come about that the pacific union will expand. He also explains how these republics would engage in wars with nonrepublics and therefore suffer the "sad experience" of wars that an ethical policy might have avoided.

* * *

Kant shows how republics, once established, lead to peaceful relations. He argues that once the aggressive interests of absolutist monarchies are tamed and the habit of respect for individual rights engrained by republican government, wars would appear as the disaster to the people's welfare that he and the other liberals thought them to be. The fundamental reason is this:

> If, as is inevitably the case under this constitution, the consent of the citizens is required to decide whether or not war should be declared, it is very natural that they will have a great hesitation in embarking on so dangerous an enterprise. For this would mean calling down on themselves all the miseries of war, such as doing the fighting themselves, supplying the costs of the war from their own resources, painfully making good the ensuing devastation, and, as the crowning evil, having to take upon themselves a burden of debts which will embitter peace itself and which can never be paid off on account of the constant threat of new wars. But under a constitution where the subject is not a citizen, and which is therefore not republican, it is the simplest thing in the world to go to war. For the head of state is not a fellow citizen, but the owner of the state, and war will not force him to make the slightest sacrifice so far as his banquets, hunts, pleasure palaces and court festivals are concerned. He can thus decide on war, without any significant reason, as a kind of amusement, and unconcernedly leave it to the diplomatic corps (who are always ready for such proposes) to justify the war for the sake of propriety. (Kant, *PP*, p. 100)

Yet these domestic republican restraints do not end war. If they did, liberal states would not be warlike, which is far from the case. They do introduce republican caution—Kant's "hesitation"—in place of monarchical caprice. Liberal wars are only fought for popular, liberal purposes. The historical liberal legacy is laden with popular wars fought to promote freedom, to protect private property, or to support liberal allies against nonliberal enemies. Kant's position is ambiguous. He regards these wars as unjust and warns liberals of their susceptibility to them (Kant, *PP*, p. 106). At the same time, Kant argues that each nation "can and ought to" demand that its neighboring nations enter into the pacific union of liberal states (*PP*, p. 102). * * *

* * *

* * * As republics emerge (the first source) and as culture progresses, an understanding of the

legitimate rights of all citizens and of all republics comes into play; and this, now that caution characterizes policy, sets up the moral foundations for the liberal peace. Correspondingly, international law highlights the importance of Kantian publicity. Domestically, publicity helps ensure that the officials of republics act according to the principles they profess to hold just and according to the interests of the electors they claim to represent. Internationally, free speech and the effective communication of accurate conceptions of the political life of foreign peoples is essential to establishing and preserving the understanding on which the guarantee of respect depends. Domestically just republics, which rest on consent, then presume foreign republics also to be consensual, just, and therefore deserving of accommodation. * * * Because nonliberal governments are in a state of aggression with their own people, their foreign relations become for liberal governments deeply suspect. In short, fellow liberals benefit from a presumption of amity; nonliberals suffer from a presumption of enmity. Both presumptions may be accurate; each, however, may also be self-confirming.

Lastly, cosmopolitan law adds material incentives to moral commitments. The cosmopolitan right to hospitality permits the "spirit of commerce" sooner or later to take hold of every nation, thus impelling states to promote peace and to try to avert war. Liberal economic theory holds that these cosmopolitan ties derive from a cooperative international division of labor and free trade according to comparative advantage. Each economy is said to be better off than it would have been under autarky; each thus acquires an incentive to avoid policies that would lead the other to break these economic ties. Because keeping open markets rests upon the assumption that the next set of transactions will also be determined by prices rather than coercion, a sense of mutual security is vital to avoid security-motivated searches for economic autarky. Thus, avoiding a challenge to

another liberal state's security or even enhancing each other's security by means of alliance naturally follows economic interdependence.

A further cosmopolitan source of liberal peace is the international market's removal of difficult decisions of production and distribution from the direct sphere of state policy. A foreign state thus does not appear directly responsible for these outcomes, and states can stand aside from, and to some degree above, these contentious market rivalries and be ready to step in to resolve crises. The interdependence of commerce and the international contacts of state officials help create cross-cutting transnational ties that serve as lobbies for mutual accommodation. According to modern liberal scholars, international financiers and transnational and transgovernmental organizations create interests in favor of accommodation. Moreover, their variety has ensured that no single conflict sours an entire relationship by setting off a spiral of reciprocated retaliation * * *. Conversely, a sense of suspicion, such as that characterizing relations between liberal and nonliberal governments, can lead to restrictions on the range of contacts between societies, and this can increase the prospect that a single conflict will determine an entire relationship.

No single constitutional, international, or cosmopolitan source is alone sufficient, but together (and only together) they plausibly connect the characteristics of liberal polities and economies with sustained liberal peace. Alliances founded on mutual strategic interest among liberal and nonliberal states have been broken; economic ties between liberal and nonliberal states have proven fragile; but the political bonds of liberal rights and interests have proven a remarkably firm foundation for mutual nonaggression. A separate peace exists among liberal states.

In their relations with nonliberal states, however, liberal states have not escaped from the insecurity caused by anarchy in the world political system considered as a whole. Moreover, the very constitutional restraint, international respect for individual rights, and shared commercial interests that establish grounds for peace among liberal states establish grounds for additional conflict in relations between liberal and nonliberal societies.

Conclusion

Kant's liberal internationalism, Machiavelli's liberal imperialism, and Schumpeter's liberal pacifism rest on fundamentally different views of the nature of the human being, the state, and international relations. Schumpeter's humans are rationalized, individualized, and democratized. They are also homogenized, pursuing material interests "monistically." Because their material interests lie in peaceful trade, they and the democratic state that these fellow citizens control are pacifistic. Machiavelli's citizens are splendidly diverse in their goals but fundamentally unequal in them as well, seeking to rule or fearing being dominated. Extending the rule of the dominant elite or avoiding the political collapse of their state, each calls for imperial expansion.

Kant's citizens, too, are diverse in their goals and individualized and rationalized, but most importantly, they are capable of appreciating the moral equality of all individuals and of treating other individuals as ends rather than as means. The Kantian state thus is governed publicly according to law, as a republic. Kant's is the state that solves the problem of governing individualized equals, whether they are the "rational devils" he says we often find ourselves to be or the ethical agents we can and should become. Republics tell us that

> in order to organize a group of rational beings who together require universal laws for their survival, but of whom each separate individual

is secretly inclined to exempt himself from them, the constitution must be so designed so that, although the citizens are opposed to one another in their private attitudes, these opposing views may inhibit one another in such a way that the public conduct of the citizens will be the same as if they did not have such evil attitudes. (Kant, *PP*, p. 113)

Unlike Machiavelli's republics, Kant's republics are capable of achieving peace among themselves because they exercise democratic caution and are capable of appreciating the international rights of foreign republics. These international rights of republics derive from the representation of foreign individuals, who are our moral equals. Unlike Schumpeter's capitalist democracies, Kant's republics—including our own—remain in a state of war with nonrepublics. Liberal republics see themselves as threatened by aggression from nonrepublics that are not constrained by representation. Even though wars often cost more than the economic return they generate, liberal republics also are prepared to protect and promote—sometimes forcibly—democracy, private property, and the rights of individuals overseas against nonrepublics, which, because they do not authentically represent the rights of individuals, have no rights to noninterference. These wars may liberate oppressed individuals overseas; they also can generate enormous suffering.

■   ■   ■

Perpetual peace, Kant says, is the end point of the hard journey his republics will take. The promise of perpetual peace, the violent lessons of war, and the experience of a partial peace are proof of the need for and the possibility of world peace. They are also the grounds for moral citizens and statesmen to assume the duty of striving for peace.

Appendix 1. Liberal Regimes and the Pacific Union, 1700–1982

PERIOD	PERIOD	PERIOD
18th Century	**1900–1945**	**1945–[b]**
Swiss Cantons[a]	Switzerland	Switzerland
French Republic, 1790–1795	United States	United States
United States,[a] 1776–	Great Britain	Great Britain
Total = 3	Sweden	Sweden
	Canada	Canada
1800–1850	Greece, –1911;	Australia
Swiss Confederation	1928–1936	New Zealand
United States	Italy, –1922	Finland
France, 1830–1849	Belgium, –1940	Ireland
Belgium, 1830–	Netherlands, –1940	Mexico
Great Britain, 1832–	Argentina, –1943	Uruguay, –1973
Netherlands, 1848–	France, –1940	Chile, –1973
Piedmont, 1848–	Chile, –1924; 1932–	Lebanon, –1975
Denmark, 1849–	Australia, 1901	Costa Rica,
Total = 8	Norway, 1905–1940	–1948; 1953–
	New Zealand, 1907–	Iceland, 1944–
1850–1900	Colombia, 1910–1949	France, 1945–
Switzerland	Denmark, 1914–1940	Denmark, 1945
United States	Poland, 1917–1935	Norway, 1945
Belgium	Latvia, 1922–1934	Austria, 1945–
Great Britain	Germany, 1918–1932	Brazil, 1945–1954;
Netherlands	Austria, 1918–1934	1955–1964
Piedmont, –1861	Estonia, 1919–1934	Belgium, 1946–
Italy, 1861–	Finland, 1919–	Luxembourg, 1946–
Denmark, –1866	Uruguay, 1919–	Netherlands, 1946–
Sweden, 1864–	Costa Rica, 1919–	Italy, 1946–
Greece, 1864–	Czechoslovakia,	Philippines,
Canada, 1867–	1920–1939	1946–1972
France, 1871–	Ireland, 1920–	India, 1947–1975; 1977–
Argentina, 1880–	Mexico, 1928–	Sri Lanka, 1948–1961;
Chile, 1891–	Lebanon, 1944–	1963–1971; 1978–
Total = 14	Total = 29	Ecuador, 1948–1963; 1979–

(continued)

Appendix 1. Liberal Regimes and the Pacific Union, 1700–1982 (Continued)

PERIOD

1945–[b] (cont.)

Israel, 1949–	Japan, 1951–	Malaysia, 1963–
West Germany, 1949–	Bolivia, 1956–1969; 1982–	Botswana, 1966–
Greece, 1950–1967; 1975–	Colombia, 1958–	Singapore, 1965–
Peru, 1950–1962; 1963–	Venezuela, 1959–	Portugal, 1976–
1968; 1980–	Nigeria, 1961–1964;	Spain, 1978–
El Salvador, 1950–1961	1979–1984	Dominican Republic, 1978–
Turkey, 1950–1960;	Jamaica, 1962–	Honduras, 1981–
1966–1971	Trinidad and Tobago, 1962–	Papua New Guinea, 1982–
	Senegal, 1963–	Total = 50

Note: I have drawn up this approximate list of "Liberal Regimes" according to the four institutions Kant described as essential: market and private property economies; polities that are externally sovereign; citizens who possess juridical rights; and "republican" (whether republican or parliamentary monarchy), representative government. This latter includes the requirement that the legislative branch have an effective role in public policy and be formally and competitively (either inter- or intra-party) elected. Furthermore, I have taken into account whether male suffrage is wide (i.e., 30%) or, as Kant (*MM* [*The Metaphysics of Morals* in *Kant's Political Writings*], p. 139) would have had it, open by "achievement" to inhabitants of the national or metropolitan territory (e.g., to poll-tax payers or householders). This list of liberal regimes is thus more inclusive than a list of democratic regimes, or polyarchies (Powell, 1982, p. 5). Other conditions taken into account here are that female suffrage is granted within a generation of its being demanded by an extensive female suffrage movement and that representative government is internally sovereign (e.g., including, and especially over military and foreign affairs) as well as stable (in existence for at least three years). Sources for these data are Banks and Overstreet (1983), Gastil (1985), *The Europa Yearbook, 1985* (1985), Langer (1968), U.K. Foreign and Commonwealth Office (1980), and U.S. Department of State (1981). Finally, these lists exclude ancient and medieval "republics," since none appears to fit Kant's commitment to liberal individualism (Holmes, 1979).

[a]There are domestic variations within these liberal regimes: Switzerland was liberal only in certain cantons; the United States was liberal only north of the Mason-Dixon line until 1865, when it became liberal throughout.

[b]Selected list, excludes liberal regimes with populations less than one million. These include all states categorized as "free" by Gastil and those "partly free" (four-fifths or more free) states with a more pronounced capitalist orientation.

Appendix 2. International Wars Listed Chronologically

British-Maharattan (1817–1818)	Russo-Persian (1826–1828)
Greek (1821–1828)	Russo-Turkish (1828–1829)
Franco-Spanish (1823)	First Polish (1831)
First Anglo-Burmese (1823–1826)	First Syrian (1831–1832)
Javanese (1825–1830)	Texas (1835–1836)

(continued)

Appendix 2. International Wars Listed Chronologically (Continued)

First British-Afghan (1838–1842)

Second Syrian (1839–1940)

Franco-Algerian (1839–1847)

Peruvian-Bolivian (1841)

First British-Sikh (1845–1846)

Mexican-American (1846–1848)

Austro-Sardinian (1848–1849)

First Schleswig-Holstein (1848–1849)

Hungarian (1848–1849)

Second British-Sikh (1848–1849)

Roman Republic (1849)

La Plata (1851–1852)

First Turco-Montenegran (1852–1853)

Crimean (1853–1856)

Anglo-Persian (1856–1857)

Sepoy (1857–1859)

Second Turco-Montenegran (1858–1859)

Italian Unification (1859)

Spanish-Moroccan (1859–1860)

Italo-Roman (1860)

Italo-Sicilian (1860–1861)

Franco-Mexican (1862–1867)

Ecuadorian-Colombian (1863)

Second Polish (1863–1864)

Spanish-Santo Dominican (1863–1865)

Second Schleswig-Holstein (1864)

Lopez (1864–1870)

Spanish-Chilean (1865–1866)

Seven Weeks (1866)

Ten Years (1868–1878)

Franco-Prussian (1870–1871)

Dutch-Achinese (1873–1878)

Balkan (1875–1877)

Russo-Turkish (1877–1878)

Bosnian (1878)

Second British-Afghan (1878–1880)

Pacific (1879–1883)

British-Zulu (1879)

Franco-Indochinese (1882–1884)

Mahdist (1882–1885)

Sino-French (1884–1885)

Central American (1885)

Serbo-Bulgarian (1885)

Sino-Japanese (1894–1895)

Franco-Madagascan (1894–1895)

Cuban (1895–1898)

Italo-Ethiopian (1895–1896)

First Philippine (1896–1898)

Greco-Turkish (1897)

Spanish-American (1898)

Second Philippine (1899–1902)

Boer (1899–1902)

Boxer Rebellion (1900)

Ilinden (1903)

Russo-Japanese (1904–1905)

Central American (1906)

Central American (1907)

Spanish-Moroccan (1909–1910)

Italo-Turkish (1911–1912)

First Balkan (1912–1913)

Second Balkan (1913)

World War I (1914–1918)

Russian Nationalities (1917–1921)

Russo-Polish (1919–1920)

(continued)

Appendix 2. International Wars Listed Chronologically (Continued)

Hungarian-Allies (1919)

Greco-Turkish (1919–1922)

Riffian (1921–1926)

Druze (1925–1927)

Sino-Soviet (1929)

Manchurian (1931–1933)

Chaco (1932–1935)

Italo-Ethiopian (1935–1936)

Sino-Japanese (1937–1941)

Changkufeng (1938)

Nomohan (1939)

World War II (1939–1945)

Russo-Finnish (1939–1940)

Franco-Thai (1940–1941)

Indonesian (1945–1946)

Indochinese (1945–1954)

Madagascan (1947–1948)

First Kashmir (1947–1949)

Palestine (1948–1949)

Hyderabad (1948)

Korean (1950–1953)

Algerian (1954–1962)

Russo-Hungarian (1956)

Sinai (1956)

Tibetan (1956–1959)

Sino-Indian (1962)

Vietnamese (1965–1975)

Second Kashmir (1965)

Six Day (1967)

Israeli-Egyptian (1969–1970)

Football (1969)

Bangladesh (1971)

Philippine-MNLF (1972–)

Yom Kippur (1973)

Turco-Cypriot (1974)

Ethiopian-Eritrean (1974–)

Vietnamese-Cambodian (1975–)

Timor (1975–)

Saharan (1975–)

Ogaden (1976–)

Ugandan-Tanzanian (1978–1979)

Sino-Vietnamese (1979)

Russo-Afghan (1979–)

Iran-Iraqi (1980–)

Note: This table is taken from Melvin Small and J. David Singer (1982, pp. 79–80). This is a partial list of international wars fought between 1816 and 1980. In Appendices A and B, Small and Singer identify a total of 575 wars during this period, but approximately 159 of them appear to be largely domestic, or civil wars.

This list excludes covert interventions, some of which have been directed by liberal regimes against other liberal regimes—for example, the United States' effort to destabilize the Chilean election and Allende's government. Nonetheless, it is significant that such interventions are not pursued publicly as acknowledged policy. The covert destabilization campaign against Chile is recounted by the Senate Select Committee to Study Governmental Operations with Respect to Intelligence Activities (1975, *Covert Action in Chile, 1963–74*).

Following the argument of this article, this list also excludes civil wars. Civil wars differ from international wars, not in the ferocity of combat, but in the issues that engender them. Two nations that could abide one another as independent neighbors separated by a border might well be the fiercest of enemies if forced to live together in one state, jointly deciding how to raise and spend taxes, choose leaders, and legislate fundamental questions of value. Notwithstanding these differences, no civil wars that I recall upset the argument of liberal pacification.

REFERENCES

Banks, Arthur, and William Overstreet, eds. 1983. *A Political Handbook of the World; 1982–1983*. New York: McGraw Hill.

Barnet, Richard. 1968. *Intervention and Revolution*. Cleveland: World Publishing Co.

Chan, Steve. 1984. Mirror, Mirror on the Wall . . . : Are Freer Countries More Pacific? *Journal of Conflict Resolution*, 28:617–48.

Doyle, Michael W. 1983a. Kant, Liberal Legacies, and Foreign Affairs: Part 1. *Philosophy and Public Affairs*, 12:205–35.

Doyle, Michael W. 1983b. Kant, Liberal Legacies, and Foreign Affairs: Part 2. *Philosophy and Public Affairs*, 12:323–53.

Doyle, Michael W. 1986. *Empires*. Ithaca: Cornell University Press.

The Europa Yearbook for 1985. 1985. 2 vols. London: Europa Publications.

Gastil, Raymond. 1985. The Comparative Survey of Freedom 1985. *Freedom at Issue*, 82:3–16.

Haas, Michael. 1974. *International Conflict*. New York: Bobbs-Merrill.

Holmes, Stephen. 1979. Aristippus in and out of Athens. *American Political Science Review*, 73:113–28.

Huliung, Mark. 1983. *Citizen Machiavelli*. Princeton: Princeton University Press.

Hume, David. 1963. Of the Balance of Power. *Essays: Moral, Political, and Literary*. Oxford: Oxford University Press.

Kant, Immanuel. 1970. *Kant's Political Writings*. Hans Reiss, ed. H. B. Nisbet, trans. Cambridge: Cambridge University Press.

Kelly, George A. 1969. *Idealism, Politics, and History*. Cambridge: Cambridge University Press.

Langer, William L., ed. 1968. *The Encyclopedia of World History*. Boston: Houghton Mifflin.

Machiavelli, Niccolo. 1950. *The Prince and the Discourses*. Max Lerner, ed. Luigi Ricci and Christian Detmold, trans. New York: Modern Library.

Mansfield, Harvey C. 1970. Machiavelli's New Regime. *Italian Quarterly*, 13:63–95.

Montesquieu, Charles de. 1949. *Spirit of the Laws*. New York: Hafner. (Originally published in 1748.)

Murphy, Jeffrie. 1970. *Kant: The Philosophy of Right*. New York: St. Martin's.

Pocock, J. G. A. 1975. *The Machiavellian Moment*. Princeton: Princeton University Press.

Powell, G. Bingham. 1982. *Contemporary Democracies*. Cambridge, MA: Harvard University Press.

Reagan, Ronald. June 9, 1982. Address to Parliament. *New York Times*.

Riley, Patrick. 1983. *Kant's Political Philosophy*. Totowa, NJ: Rowman and Littlefield.

Rummel, Rudolph J. 1983. Libertarianism and International Violence. *Journal of Conflict Resolution*, 27:27–71.

Russett, Bruce. 1985. The Mysterious Case of Vanishing Hegemony. *International Organization*, 39:207–31.

Schumpeter, Joseph. 1955. The Sociology of Imperialism. In *Imperialism and Social Classes*. Cleveland: World Publishing Co. (Essay originally published in 1919.)

Schwarz, Wolfgang. 1962. Kant's Philosophy of Law and International Peace. *Philosophy and Phenomenonological Research*, 23:71–80.

Skinner, Quentin. 1981. *Machiavelli*. New York: Hill and Wang.

Small, Melvin, and J. David Singer. 1976. The War-Proneness of Democratic Regimes. *The Jerusalem Journal of International Relations*, 1(4):50–69.

Small, Melvin, and J. David Singer. 1982. *Resort to Arms*. Beverly Hills: Sage Publications.

Thucydides. 1954. *The Peloponnesian War*. Rex Warner, ed. and trans. Baltimore: Penguin.

U.K. Foreign and Commonwealth Office. 1980. *A Yearbook of the Commonwealth 1980*. London: HMSO.

U.S. Congress. Senate. Select Committee to Study Governmental Operations with Respect to Intelligence Activities. 1975. *Covert Action in Chile, 1963–74*. 94th Cong., 1st sess., Washington, DC: U.S. Government Printing Office.

U.S. Department of State. 1981. *Country Reports on Human Rights Practices*. Washington, DC: U.S. Government Printing Office.

Weede, Erich. 1984. Democracy and War Involvement. *Journal of Conflict Resolution*, 28:649–64.

Wilkenfeld, Jonathan. 1968. Domestic and Foreign Conflict Behavior of Nations. *Journal of Peace Research*, 5:56–69.

Wright, Quincy. 1942. *A Study of History*. Chicago: University of Chicago Press.

Alexander Wendt

ANARCHY IS WHAT STATES MAKE OF IT
The Social Construction of Power Politics

The debate between realists and liberals has reemerged as an axis of contention in international relations theory.[1] Revolving in the past around competing theories of human nature, the debate is more concerned today with the extent to which state action is influenced by "structure" (anarchy and the distribution of power) versus "process" (interaction and learning) and institutions. Does the absence of centralized political authority force states to play competitive power politics? Can international regimes overcome this logic, and under what conditions? What in anarchy is given and immutable, and what is amenable to change?

■　■　■

* * * I argue that self-help and power politics do not follow either logically or causally from anarchy and that if today we find ourselves in a self-help world, this is due to process, not structure. There is no "logic" of anarchy apart from the practices that create and instantiate one structure of identities and interests rather than another; structure has no existence or causal powers apart from process. Self-help and power politics are institutions, not essential features of anarchy. *Anarchy is what states make of it.*

■　■　■

From *International Organization* 46, no. 2 (Spring 1992): 391–425. Some of the author's notes have been omitted.

Anarchy and Power Politics

Classical realists such as Thomas Hobbes, Reinhold Niebuhr, and Hans Morgenthau attributed egoism and power politics primarily to human nature, whereas structural realists or neorealists emphasize anarchy. The difference stems in part from different interpretations of anarchy's causal powers. Kenneth Waltz's work is important for both. In *Man, the State, and War,* he defines anarchy as a condition of possibility for or "permissive" cause of war, arguing that "wars occur because there is nothing to prevent them."[2] It is the human nature or domestic politics of predator states, however, that provide the initial impetus or "efficient" cause of conflict which forces other states to respond in kind.[3] Waltz is not entirely consistent about this, since he slips without justification from the permissive causal claim that in anarchy war is always possible to the active causal claim that "war may at any moment occur."[4] But despite Waltz's concluding call for third-image theory, the efficient causes that initialize anarchic systems are from the first and second images. This is reversed in Waltz's *Theory of International Politics,* in which first- and second-image theories are spurned as "reductionist," and the logic of anarchy seems by itself to constitute self-help and power politics as necessary features of world politics.[5]

This is unfortunate, since whatever one may think of first- and second-image theories, they have the virtue of implying that practices determine the character of anarchy. In the permissive view, only if human or domestic factors cause A to attack B will B have to defend itself. Anarchies may contain dynamics that lead to competitive power politics, but they also may not, and we can argue about when particular structures of identity and interest will emerge. In neorealism, however, the role of practice in shaping the character of anarchy is substantially reduced, and so there is less about which to argue: self-help and competitive power politics are simply given exogenously by the structure of the state system.

I will not here contest the neorealist description of the contemporary state system as a competitive, self-help world;[6] I will only dispute its explanation. I develop my argument in three stages. First, I disentangle the concepts of self-help and anarchy by showing that self-interested conceptions of security are not a constitutive property of anarchy. Second, I show how self-help and competitive power politics may be produced causally by processes of interaction between states in which anarchy plays only a permissive role. In both of these stages of my argument, I self-consciously bracket the first- and second-image determinants of state identity, not because they are unimportant (they are indeed important), but because like Waltz's objective, mine is to clarify the "logic" of anarchy. Third, I reintroduce first- and second-image determinants to assess their effects on identity-formation in different kinds of anarchies.

Anarchy, Self-Help, and Intersubjective Knowledge

Waltz defines political structure on three dimensions: ordering principles (in this case, anarchy), principles of differentiation (which here drop out), and the distribution of capabilities.[7] By itself, this definition predicts little about state behavior. It does not predict whether two states will be friends or foes, will recognize each other's sovereignty, will have dynastic ties, will be revisionist or status quo powers, and so on. These factors, which are fundamentally intersubjective, affect states' security interests and thus the character of their interaction under anarchy. In an important revision of Waltz's theory, Stephen Walt implies as much when he argues that the "balance of threats," rather than the balance of power, determines state action, threats being socially constructed.[8] Put more generally, without assumptions about the structure of identities and interests in the system, Waltz's definition of structure cannot predict the content or dynamics of anarchy. Self-help is one such intersubjective structure and, as such, does the decisive explanatory work in the theory. The question is whether self-help is a logical or contingent feature of anarchy. In this section, I develop the concept of a "structure of identity and interest" and show that no particular one follows logically from anarchy.

A fundamental principle of constructivist social theory is that people act toward objects, including other actors, on the basis of the meanings that the objects have for them.[9] States act differently toward enemies than they do toward friends because enemies are threatening and friends are not. Anarchy and the distribution of power are insufficient to tell us which is which. U.S. military power has a different significance for Canada than for Cuba, despite their similar "structural" positions, just as British missiles have a different significance for the United States than do Soviet missiles. The distribution of power may always affect states' calculations, but how it does so depends on the intersubjective understandings and expectations, on the "distribution of knowledge," that constitute their conceptions of self and other.[10] If society "forgets" what a university is, the powers and practices of professor and student cease to exist; if the United States and Soviet Union decide that they are no longer enemies, "the cold war is over." It is collective meanings that constitute the structures which organize our actions.

Actors acquire identities—relatively stable, role-specific understandings and expectations about self—by participating in such collective meanings.[11]

Identities are inherently relational: "Identity, with its appropriate attachments of psychological reality, is always identity within a specific, socially constructed world," Peter Berger argues.[12] Each person has many identities linked to institutional roles, such as brother, son, teacher, and citizen. Similarly, a state may have multiple identities as "sovereign," "leader of the free world," "imperial power," and so on.[13] The commitment to and the salience of particular identities vary, but each identity is an inherently social definition of the actor grounded in the theories which actors collectively hold about themselves and one another and which constitute the structure of the social world.

Identities are the basis of interests. Actors do not have a "portfolio" of interests that they carry around independent of social context; instead, they define their interests in the process of defining situations.[14] As Nelson Foote puts it: "Motivation . . . refer[s] to the degree to which a human being, as a participant in the ongoing social process in which he necessarily finds himself, defines a problematic situation as calling for the performance of a particular act, with more or less anticipated consummations and consequences, and thereby his organism releases the energy appropriate to performing it."[15] Sometimes situations are unprecedented in our experience, and in these cases we have to construct their meaning, and thus our interests, by analogy or invent them de novo. More often they have routine qualities in which we assign meanings on the basis of institutionally defined roles. When we say that professors have an "interest" in teaching, research, or going on leave, we are saying that to function in the role identity of "professor," they have to define certain situations as calling for certain actions. This does not mean that they will necessarily do so (expectations and competence do not equal performance), but if they do not, they will not get tenure. The absence or failure of roles makes defining situations and interests more difficult, and identity confusion may result. This seems to be happening today in the United States and the former Soviet Union: without the cold war's mutual attributions of threat and hostility to define their identities, these states seem unsure of what their "interests" should be.

An institution is a relatively stable set or "structure" of identities and interests. Such structures are often codified in formal rules and norms, but these have motivational force only in virtue of actors' socialization to and participation in collective knowledge. Institutions are fundamentally cognitive entities that do not exist apart from actors' ideas about how the world works.[16] This does not mean that institutions are not real or objective, that they are "nothing but" beliefs. As collective knowledge, they are experienced as having an existence "over and above the individuals who happen to embody them at the moment."[17] In this way, institutions come to confront individuals as more or less coercive social facts, but they are still a function of what actors collectively "know." Identities and such collective cognitions do not exist apart from each other; they are "mutually constitutive."[18] On this view, institutionalization is a process of internalizing new identities and interests, not something occurring outside them and affecting only behavior; socialization is a cognitive process, not just a behavioral one. Conceived in this way, institutions may be cooperative or conflictual, a point sometimes lost in scholarship on international regimes, which tends to equate institutions with cooperation. There are important differences between conflictual and cooperative institutions to be sure, but all relatively stable self-other relations—even those of "enemies"—are defined intersubjectively.

Self-help is an institution, one of various structures of identity and interest that may exist under anarchy. Processes of identity-formation under anarchy are concerned first and foremost with preservation or "security" of the self. Concepts of security therefore differ in the extent to which and the manner in which the self is identified cognitively with the other,[19] and, I want to suggest, it is upon this cognitive variation that the meaning of anarchy and the distribution of power depends. Let me illustrate with a standard continuum of security systems.[20]

At one end is the "competitive" security system, in which states identify negatively with each other's security so that ego's gain is seen as alter's loss. Negative identification under anarchy constitutes system of "realist" power politics: risk-averse actors that infer intentions from capabilities and worry about relative gains and losses. At the limit—in the Hobbesian war of all against all—collective action is nearly impossible in such a system because each actor must constantly fear being stabbed in the back.

In the middle is the "individualistic" security system, in which states are indifferent to the relationship between their own and others' security. This constitutes "neoliberal" systems: states are still self-regarding about their security but are concerned primarily with absolute gains rather than relative gains. One's position in the distribution of power is less important, and collective action is more possible (though still subject to free riding because states continue to be "egoists").

Competitive and individualistic systems are both "self-help" forms of anarchy in the sense that states do not positively identify the security of self with that of others but instead treat security as the individual responsibility of each. Given the lack of a positive cognitive identification on the basis of which to build security regimes, power politics within such systems will necessarily consist of efforts to manipulate others to satisfy self-regarding interests.

This contrasts with the "cooperative" security system, in which states identify positively with one another so that the security of each is perceived as the responsibility of all. This is not self-help in any interesting sense, since the "self" in terms of which interests are defined is the community; national interests are international interests.[21] In practice, of course, the extent to which states' identification with the community varies, from the limited form found in "concerts" to the full-blown

form seen in "collective security" arrangements.[22] Depending on how well developed the collective self is, it will produce security practices that are in varying degrees altruistic or prosocial. This makes collective action less dependent on the presence of active threats and less prone to free riding.[23] Moreover, it restructures efforts to advance one's objectives, or "power politics," in terms of shared norms rather than relative power.[24]

On this view, the tendency in international relations scholarship to view power and institutions as two opposing explanations of foreign policy is therefore misleading, since anarchy and the distribution of power only have meaning for state action in virtue of the understandings and expectations that constitute institutional identities and interests. Self-help is one such institution, constituting one kind of anarchy but not the only kind. Waltz's three-part definition of structure therefore seems underspecified. In order to go from structure to action, we need to add a fourth: the intersubjectively constituted structure of identities and interests in the system.

This has an important implication for the way in which we conceive of states in the state of nature before their first encounter with each other. Because states do not have conceptions of self and other, and thus security interests, apart from or prior to interaction, we assume too much about the state of nature if we concur with Waltz that, in virtue of anarchy, "international political systems, like economic markets, are formed by the coaction of self-regarding units."[25] We also assume too much if we argue that, in virtue of anarchy, states in the state of nature necessarily face a "stag hunt" or "security dilemma."[26] These claims presuppose a history of interaction in which actors have acquired "selfish" identities and interests; before interaction (and still in abstraction from first- and second-image factors) they would have no experience upon which to base such definitions of self and other. To assume otherwise is to attribute to states in the state of nature qualities that they can only possess in society.[27] Self-help is an institution, not a constitutive feature of anarchy.

What, then, *is* a constitutive feature of the state of nature before interaction? Two things are left if we strip away those properties of the self which presuppose interaction with others. The first is the material substrate of agency, including its intrinsic capabilities. For human beings, this is the body; for states, it is an organizational apparatus of governance. In effect, I am suggesting for rhetorical purposes that the raw material out of which members of the state system are constituted is created by domestic society before states enter the constitutive process of international society,[28] although this process implies neither stable territoriality nor sovereignty, which are internationally negotiated terms of individuality (as discussed further below). The second is a desire to preserve this material substrate, to survive. This does not entail "self-regardingness," however, since actors do not have a self prior to interaction with an other; how they view the meaning and requirements of this survival therefore depends on the processes by which conceptions of self evolve.

This may all seem very arcane, but there is an important issue at stake: are the foreign policy identities and interests of states exogenous or endogenous to the state system? The former is the answer of an individualistic or undersocialized systemic theory for which rationalism is appropriate; the latter is the answer of a fully socialized systemic theory. Waltz seems to offer the latter and proposes two mechanisms, competition and socialization, by which structure conditions state action.[29] The content of his argument about this conditioning, however, presupposes a self-help system that is not itself a constitutive feature of anarchy. As James Morrow points out, Waltz's two mechanisms condition behavior, not identity and interest.[30] This explains how Waltz can be accused of both "individualism" and "structuralism."[31] He is the former with respect to systemic constitutions of identity and interest, the latter with respect to systemic determinations of behavior.

Anarchy and the Social Construction of Power Politics

If self-help is not a constitutive feature of anarchy, it must emerge causally from processes in which anarchy plays only a permissive role.[32] This reflects a second principle of constructivism: that the meanings in terms of which action is organized arise out of interaction.[33] This being said, however, the situation facing states as they encounter one another for the first time may be such that only self-regarding conceptions of identity can survive; if so, even if these conceptions are socially constructed, neorealists may be right in holding identities and interests constant and thus in privileging one particular meaning of anarchic structure over process. In this case, rationalists would be right to argue for a weak, behavioral conception of the difference that institutions make, and realists would be right to argue that any international institutions which are created will be inherently unstable, since without the power to transform identities and interests they will be "continuing objects of choice" by exogenously constituted actors constrained only by the transaction costs of behavioral change.[34] Even in a permissive causal role, in other words, anarchy may decisively restrict interaction and therefore restrict viable forms of systemic theory. I address these causal issues first by showing how self-regarding ideas about security might develop and then by examining the conditions under which a key efficient cause—predation—may dispose states in this direction rather than others.

Conceptions of self and interest tend to "mirror" the practices of significant others over time. This principle of identity-formation is captured by the symbolic interactionist notion of the "looking-glass self," which asserts that the self is a reflection of an actor's socialization.

Consider two actors—ego and alter—encountering each other for the first time.[35] Each wants to survive and has certain material capabilities, but neither actor has biological or domestic imperatives for power, glory, or conquest (still bracketed), and there is no history of security or insecurity between the two. What should they do? Realists would probably argue that each should act on the basis of worst-case assumptions about the other's intentions, justifying such an attitude as prudent in view of the possibility of death from making a mistake. Such a possibility always exists, even in civil society; however, society would be impossible if people made decisions purely on the basis of worst-case possibilities. Instead, most decisions are and should be made on the basis of probabilities, and these are produced by interaction, by what actors *do*.

In the beginning is ego's gesture, which may consist, for example, of an advance, a retreat, a brandishing of arms, a laying down of arms, or an attack.[36] For ego, this gesture represents the basis on which it is prepared to respond to alter. This basis is unknown to alter, however, and so it must make an inference or "attribution" about ego's intentions and, in particular, given that this is anarchy, about whether ego is a threat.[37] The content of this inference will largely depend on two considerations. The first is the gesture's and ego's physical qualities, which are in part contrived by ego and which include the direction of movement, noise, numbers, and immediate consequences of the gesture.[38] The second consideration concerns what alter would intend by such qualities were it to make such a gesture itself. Alter may make an attributional "error" in its inference about ego's intent, but there is also no reason for it to assume a priori—before the gesture—that ego is threatening, since it is only through a process of signaling and interpreting that the costs and probabilities of being wrong can be determined.[39] Social threats are constructed, not natural.

Consider an example. Would we assume, a priori, that we were about to be attacked if we are ever contacted by members of an alien civilization? I think not. We would be highly alert, of course, but whether we placed our military forces on alert or launched an attack would depend on how we interpreted the import of their first gesture for our security—if only to avoid making an immediate enemy out of what may be a dangerous adversary. The possibility of error, in other words, does not force us to act on the assumption that the aliens are threatening: action depends on the probabilities we assign, and these are in key part a function of what the aliens do; prior to their gesture, we have no systemic basis for assigning probabilities. If their first gesture is to appear with a thousand spaceships and destroy New York, we will define the situation as threatening and respond accordingly. But if they appear with one spaceship, saying what seems to be "we come in peace," we will feel "reassured" and will probably respond with a gesture intended to reassure them, even if this gesture is not necessarily interpreted by them as such.[40]

This process of signaling, interpreting, and responding completes a "social act" and begins the process of creating intersubjective meanings. It advances the same way. The first social act creates expectations on both sides about each other's future behavior: potentially mistaken and certainly tentative, but expectations nonetheless. Based on this tentative knowledge, ego makes a new gesture, again signifying the basis on which it will respond to alter, and again alter responds, adding to the pool of knowledge each has about the other, and so on over time. The mechanism here is reinforcement; interaction rewards actors for holding certain ideas about each other and discourages them from holding others. If repeated long enough, these "reciprocal typifications" will create relatively stable concepts of self and other regarding the issue at stake in the interaction.[41]

It is through reciprocal interaction, in other words, that we create and instantiate the relatively enduring social structures in terms of which we define our identities and interests. Jeff Coulter sums up the ontological dependence of structure on process this way: "The parameters of social organization themselves are reproduced only in and through the orientations and practices of members engaged in social interactions over time. . . . Social configurations are not 'objective' like mountains or forests, but neither are they 'subjective' like dreams or flights of speculative fancy. They are, as most social scientists concede at the theoretical level, intersubjective constructions."[42]

The simple overall model of identity- and interest-formation proposed in Figure 3.1 applies to competitive institutions no less than to cooperative ones. Self-help security systems evolve from cycles of interaction in which each party acts in ways that the other feels are threatening to the self, creating expectations that the other is not to be trusted. Competitive or egoistic identities are caused by such insecurity; if the other is threatening, the self is forced to "mirror" such behavior in its conception of the self's relationship to that other.[43] Being treated as an object for the gratification of others precludes the positive identification with others necessary for collective security; conversely, being treated by others in ways that are empathic with respect to the security of the self permits such identification.[44]

Competitive systems of interaction are prone to security "dilemmas," in which the efforts of actors to enhance their security unilaterally threatens the security of the others, perpetuating distrust and alienation. The forms of identity and interest that constitute such dilemmas, however, are themselves ongoing effects of, not exogenous to, the interaction; identities are produced in and through "situated activity."[45] We do not *begin* our relationship with the aliens in a security dilemma; security dilemmas are not given by anarchy or nature. Of course, once institutionalized such a dilemma may be hard to change (I return to this below), but the point remains: identities and interests are constituted by collective meanings that are always in

Figure 3.1. The Codetermination of Institutions and Process

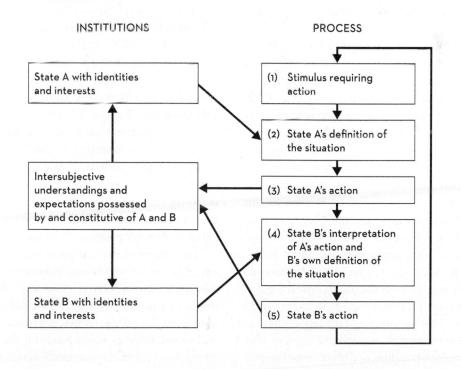

process. As Sheldon Stryker emphasizes, "The social process is one of constructing and reconstructing self and social relationships."[46] If states find themselves in a self-help system, this is because their practices made it that way. Changing the practices will change the intersubjective knowledge that constitutes the system.

Predator States and Anarchy as Permissive Cause

The mirror theory of identity-formation is a crude account of how the process of creating identities and interests might work, but it does not tell us why a system of states—such as, arguably, our own—would have ended up with self-regarding and not collective identities. In this section, I examine an efficient cause, predation, which, in conjunction with anarchy as a permissive cause, may generate a self-help system. In so doing, however, I show the key role that the structure of identities and interests plays in mediating anarchy's explanatory role.

The predator argument is straightforward and compelling. For whatever reasons—biology, domestic politics, or systemic victimization—some states may become predisposed toward aggression. The aggressive behavior of these predators or "bad apples" forces other states to engage in competitive power politics, to meet fire with fire, since failure to do so may degrade or destroy them. One predator will best a hundred pacifists because anarchy provides no guarantees. This argument is powerful in part because it is so weak: rather than making the strong assumption that all states are inherently power-seeking (a purely reductionist theory of power politics), it assumes that just one is power-seeking and that the others have to follow suit because anarchy permits the one to exploit them.

In making this argument, it is important to reiterate that the possibility of predation does not in itself force states to anticipate it a priori with competitive power politics of their own. The possibility of predation does not mean that "war may at any moment occur"; it may in fact be extremely unlikely. Once a predator emerges, however, it may condition identity- and interest-formation in the following manner.

In an anarchy of two, if ego is predatory, alter must either define its security in self-help terms or pay the price. This follows directly from the above argument, in which conceptions of self mirror treatment by the other. In an anarchy of many, however, the effect of predation also depends on the level of collective identity already attained in the system. If predation occurs right after the first encounter in the state of nature, it will force others with whom it comes in contact to defend themselves, first individually and then collectively *if* they come to perceive a common threat. The emergence of such a defensive alliance will be seriously inhibited if the structure of identities and interests has already evolved into a Hobbesian world of maximum insecurity, since potential allies will strongly distrust each other and face intense collective action problems; such insecure allies are also more likely to fall out amongst themselves once the predator is removed. If collective security identity is high, however, the emergence of a predator may do much less damage. If the predator attacks any member of the collective, the latter will come to the victim's defense on the principle of "all for one, one for all," even if the predator is not presently a threat to other members of the collective. If the predator is not strong enough to withstand the collective, it will be defeated and collective security will obtain. But if it is strong enough, the logic of the two-actor case (now predator and collective) will activate, and balance-of-power politics will reestablish itself.

The timing of the emergence of predation relative to the history of identity-formation in the community is therefore crucial to anarchy's explanatory role as a permissive cause. Predation will always lead victims to defend themselves, but whether defense will be collective or not depends on the history of interaction within the potential collective as much as on the ambitions of the predator. Will the disappearance of the Soviet threat renew old insecurities among the members of the North Atlantic Treaty Organization? Perhaps, but not if they have reasons independent of that threat for identifying their security with one another. Identities and interests are relationship-specific, not intrinsic attributes of a "portfolio"; states may be competitive in some relationships and solidary in others. "Mature" anarchies are less likely than "immature" ones to be reduced by predation to a Hobbesian condition, and maturity, which is a proxy for structures of identity and interest, is a function of process.[47]

The source of predation also matters. If it stems from unit-level causes that are immune to systemic impacts (causes such as human nature or domestic politics taken in isolation), then it functions in a manner analogous to a "genetic trait" in the constructed world of the state system. Even if successful, this trait does not select for other predators in an evolutionary sense so much as it teaches other states to respond in kind, but since traits cannot be unlearned, the other states will continue competitive behavior until the predator is either destroyed or transformed from within. However, in the more likely event that predation stems at least in part from prior systemic interaction—perhaps as a result of being victimized in the past (one thinks here of Nazi Germany or the Soviet Union)—then it is more a response to a learned identity and, as such, might be transformed by future social interaction in the form of appeasement, reassurances that security needs will be met, systemic effects on domestic politics, and so on. In this case, in other words, there is more hope that process can transform a bad apple into a good one.

The role of predation in generating a self-help system, then, is consistent with a systematic focus on process. Even if the source of predation is entirely exogenous to the system, it is what states *do* that determines the quality of their interactions under anarchy. In this respect, it is not surprising that it is classical realists rather than structural realists who emphasize this sort of argument. The former's emphasis on unit-level causes of power politics leads more easily to a permissive view of anarchy's explanatory role (and therefore to a processual view of international relations) than does the latter's emphasis on anarchy as a "structural cause";[48] neorealists do not need predation because the system is given as self-help.

This raises anew the question of exactly how much and what kind of role human nature and domestic politics play in world politics. The greater and more destructive this role, the more significant predation will be, and the less amenable anarchy will be to formation of collective identities. Classical realists, of course, assumed that human nature was possessed by an inherent lust for power or glory. My argument suggests that assumptions such as this were made for a reason: an unchanging Hobbesian man provides the powerful efficient cause necessary for a relentless pessimism about world politics that anarchic structure alone, or even structure plus intermittent predation, cannot supply. One can be skeptical of such an essentialist assumption, as I am, but it does produce determinate results at the expense of systemic theory. A concern with systemic process over structure suggests that perhaps it is time to revisit the debate over the relative importance of first-, second-, and third-image theories of state identity-formation.[49]

Assuming for now that systemic theories of identity-formation in world politics are worth pursuing, let me conclude by suggesting that the realist-rationalist alliance "reifies" self-help in the sense of treating it as something separate from the practices by which it is produced and sustained. Peter Berger and Thomas Luckmann define reification as follows: "[It] is the apprehension of the products of human activity *as if* they were something else than human products—such as facts of nature, results of cosmic laws, or manifestations of divine will. Reification implies that man is capable of forgetting his own authorship of the human world, and, further, that the dialectic between man, the producer, and his products is lost to consciousness. The reified world is . . . experienced by man as a strange facticity, an *opus alienum* over which he has no control rather than as the *opus proprium* of his own productive activity."[50] By denying or bracketing states' collective authorship of their identities and interests, in other words, the realist-rationalist alliance denies or brackets the fact that competitive power politics help create the very "problem of order" they are supposed to solve—that realism is a self-fulfilling prophecy. Far from being exogenously given, the intersubjective knowledge that constitutes competitive identities and interests is constructed every day by processes of "social will formation."[51] It is what states have made of themselves.

Institutional Transformations of Power Politics

Let us assume that processes of identity- and interest-formation have created a world in which states do not recognize rights to territory or existence—a war of all against all. In this world, anarchy has a "realist" meaning for state action: be insecure and concerned with relative power. Anarchy has this meaning only in virtue of collective, insecurity-producing practices, but if those practices are relatively stable, they do constitute a system that may resist change. The fact that worlds of power politics are socially constructed, in other words, does not guarantee they are malleable, for at least two reasons.

The first reason is that once constituted, any social system confronts each of its members as an objective social fact that reinforces certain behaviors and discourages others. Self-help systems, for example, tend to reward competition and punish altruism. The possibility of change depends on whether the exigencies of such competition leave room for actions that deviate from the prescribed script. If they do not, the system will be reproduced and deviant actors will not.[52]

The second reason is that systemic change may also be inhibited by actors' interests in maintaining relatively stable role identities. Such interests are rooted not only in the desire to minimize uncertainty and anxiety, manifested in efforts to confirm existing beliefs about the social world, but also in the desire to avoid the expected costs of breaking commitments made to others—notably domestic constituencies and foreign allies in the case of states—as part of past practices. The level of resistance that these commitments induce will depend on the "salience" of particular role identities to the actor.[53] The United States, for example, is more likely to resist threats to its identity as "leader of anticommunist crusades" than to its identity as "promoter of human rights." But for almost any role identity, practices and information that challenge it are likely to create cognitive dissonance and even perceptions of threat, and these may cause resistance to transformations of the self and thus to social change.[54]

For both systemic and "psychological" reasons, then, intersubjective understandings and expectations may have a self-perpetuating quality, constituting path-dependencies that new ideas about self and other must transcend. This does not change the fact that through practice agents are continuously producing and reproducing identities and interests, continuously "choosing now the preferences [they] will have later."[55] But it does mean that choices may not be experienced with meaningful degrees of freedom. This could be a constructivist justification for the realist position that only simple learning is possible in self-help systems. The realist might concede that such systems are socially constructed and still argue that after the corresponding identities and interests have become institutionalized, they are almost impossible to transform.

In the remainder of this article, I examine three institutional transformations of identity and security interest through which states might escape a Hobbesian world of their own making. In so doing, I seek to clarify what it means to say that "institutions transform identities and interests," emphasizing that the key to such transformations is relatively stable practice.

Sovereignty, Recognition, and Security

In a Hobbesian state of nature, states are individuated by the domestic processes that constitute them as states and by their material capacity to deter threats from other states. In this world, even if free momentarily from the predations of others, state security does not have any basis in social recognition—in intersubjective understandings or norms that a state has a right to its existence, territory, and subjects. Security is a matter of national power, nothing more.

The principle of sovereignty transforms this situation by providing a social basis for the individuality and security of states. Sovereignty is an institution, and so it exists only in virtue of certain intersubjective understandings and expectations; there is no sovereignty without an other. These understandings and expectations not only constitute a particular kind of state—the "sovereign" state—but also constitute a particular form of community, since identities are relational. The essence of this community is a mutual recognition of one another's right to exercise exclusive political authority within territorial limits. These reciprocal "permissions"[56] constitute a spatially rather than functionally differentiated world—a world in which fields of practice constitute and are organized around "domestic" and "international" spaces rather than around the performance of particular activities.[57] The location of the boundaries between these spaces is of course sometimes contested, war being one practice through which states negotiate the terms of their individuality. But this does not change the fact that it is only in virtue of mutual recognition that states have "territorial property rights."[58] This recognition functions as a form of "social closure" that disempowers nonstate actors and empowers and helps stabilize interaction among states.[59]

Sovereignty norms are now so taken for granted, so natural, that it is easy to overlook the extent to which they are both presupposed by and an ongoing artifact of practice. When states tax "their" "citizens" and not others, when they "protect" their markets against foreign "imports," when they kill thousands of Iraqis in one kind of war and then refuse to "intervene" to kill even one person in another kind, a "civil" war, and when they fight a global war against a regime that sought to destroy the institution of sovereignty and then give Germany back to the Germans, they are acting against the background of, and thereby reproducing, shared norms about what it means to be a sovereign state.

If states stopped acting on those norms, their identity as "sovereigns" (if not necessarily as "states") would disappear. The sovereign state is an ongoing accomplishment of practice, not a once-and-for-all creation of norms that somehow exist apart from practice.[60] Thus, saying that "the institution of sovereignty transforms identities" is shorthand for saying that "regular practices produce mutually constituting sovereign identities (agents) and their associated institutional norms (structures)." Practice is the core of constructivist resolutions of the agent-structure problem. This ongoing process may not be politically problematic in particular historical contexts and, indeed, once a community of mutual recognition is constituted, its members—even the disadvantaged ones[61]—may have a vested interest in reproducing it. In fact, this is part of what having an identity means. But this identity and institution remain dependent on what actors do: removing those practices will remove their intersubjective conditions of existence.

This may tell us something about how institutions of sovereign states are reproduced through social interaction, but it does not tell us why such a structure of identity and interest would arise in the first place. Two conditions would seem necessary for this to happen: (1) the density and regularity of interactions must be sufficiently high and (2) actors must be dissatisfied with preexisting forms of identity and interaction. Given these conditions, a norm of mutual recognition is relatively undemanding in terms of social trust, having the form of an assurance game in which a player will acknowledge the sovereignty of the others as long as they will in turn acknowledge that player's own sovereignty. Articulating international legal principles such as those embodied in the Peace of Augsburg (1555) and the Peace of Westphalia (1648) may also help by establishing explicit criteria for determining violations of the nascent social consensus.[62] But whether such a consensus holds depends on what states do. If they treat each other as if they were sovereign, then over time they will institutionalize that mode of subjectivity; if they do not, then that mode will not become the norm.

Practices of sovereignty will transform understandings of security and power politics in at least three ways. First, states will come to define their (and our) security in terms of preserving their "property rights" over particular territories. We now see this as natural, but the preservation of territorial frontiers is not, in fact, equivalent to the survival of the state or its people. Indeed, some states would probably be more secure if they would relinquish certain territories—the "Soviet Union" of some minority republics, "Yugoslavia" of Croatia and Slovenia, Israel of the West Bank, and so on. The fact that sovereignty practices have historically been oriented toward producing distinct territorial spaces, in other words, affects states' conceptualization of what they must "secure" to function in that identity, a process that may help account for the "hardening" of territorial boundaries over the centuries.[63]

Second, to the extent that states successfully internalize sovereignty norms, they will be more respectful toward the territorial rights of others.[64]

This restraint is *not* primarily because of the costs of violating sovereignty norms, although when violators do get punished (as in the Gulf War) it reminds everyone of what these costs can be, but because part of what it means to be a "sovereign" state is that one does not violate the territorial rights of others without "just cause." A clear example of such an institutional effect, convincingly argued by David Strang, is the markedly different treatment that weak states receive within and outside communities of mutual recognition.[65] What keeps the United States from conquering the Bahamas, or Nigeria from seizing Togo, or Australia from occupying Vanuatu? Clearly, power is not the issue, and in these cases even the cost of sanctions would probably be negligible. One might argue that great powers simply have no "interest" in these conquests, and this might be so, but this lack of interest can only be understood in terms of their recognition of weak states' sovereignty. I have no interest in exploiting my friends, not because of the relative costs and benefits of such action but because they are my friends. The absence of recognition, in turn, helps explain the Western states' practices of territorial conquest, enslavement, and genocide against Native American and African peoples. It is in *that* world that only power matters, not the world of today.

Finally, to the extent that their ongoing socialization teaches states that their sovereignty depends on recognition by other states, they can afford to rely more on the institutional fabric of international society and less on individual national means—especially military power—to protect their security. The intersubjective understandings embodied in the institution of sovereignty, in other words, may redefine the meaning of others' power for the security of the self. In policy terms, this means that states can be less worried about short-term survival and relative power and can thus shift their resources accordingly. Ironically, it is the great powers, the states with the greatest national means, that may have the hardest time learning this lesson; small powers do not have the luxury of relying on national means and may therefore learn faster that collective recognition is a cornerstone of security.

None of this is to say that power becomes irrelevant in a community of sovereign states. Sometimes states *are* threatened by others that do not recognize their existence or particular territorial claims, that resent the externalities from their economic policies, and so on. But most of the time, these threats are played out within the terms of the sovereignty game. The fates of Napoleon and Hitler show what happens when they are not.

Cooperation among Egoists and Transformations of Identity

We began this section with a Hobbesian state of nature. Cooperation for joint gain is extremely difficult in this context, since trust is lacking, time horizons are short, and relative power concerns are high. Life is "nasty, brutish, and short." Sovereignty transforms this system into a Lockean world of (mostly) mutually recognized property rights and (mostly) egoistic rather than competitive conceptions of security, reducing the fear that what states already have will be seized at any moment by potential collaborators, thereby enabling them to contemplate more direct forms of cooperation. A necessary condition for such cooperation is that outcomes be positively interdependent in the sense that potential gains exist which cannot be realized by unilateral action. States such as Brazil and Botswana may recognize each other's sovereignty, but they need further incentives to engage in joint action. One important source of incentives is the growing "dynamic density" of interaction among states in a world with new communications technology, nuclear weapons, externalities from industrial development, and so on.[66] Unfortunately, growing dynamic density does not ensure that states will in fact realize joint gains; interdependence also entails vulnerability and the risk of being "the sucker," which if exploited will become a source of conflict rather than cooperation.

This is the rationale for the familiar assumption that egoistic states will often find themselves facing prisoners' dilemma, a game in which the dominant strategy, if played only once, is to defect. As Michael Taylor and Robert Axelrod have shown, however, given iteration and a sufficient shadow of the future, egoists using a tit-for-tat strategy can escape this result and build cooperative institutions.[67] The story they tell about this process on the surface seems quite similar to George Herbert Mead's constructivist analysis of interaction, part of which is also told in terms of "games."[68] Cooperation is a gesture indicating ego's willingness to cooperate; if alter defects, ego does likewise, signaling its unwillingness to be exploited; over time and through reciprocal play, each learns to form relatively stable expectations about the other's behavior, and through these, habits of cooperation (or defection) form. Despite similar concerns with communication, learning, and habit-formation, however, there is an important difference between the game theoretic and constructivist analysis of interaction that bears on how we conceptualize the causal powers of institutions.

In the traditional game-theoretic analysis of cooperation, even an iterated one, the structure of the game—of identities and interests—is exogenous to interaction and, as such, does not change.[69] A "black box" is put around identity- and interest-formation, and analysis focuses instead on the relationship between expectations and behavior. The norms that evolve from interaction are treated as rules and behavioral regularities which are external to the actors and which resist change because of the transaction costs of creating new ones. The game-theoretic analysis of cooperation among egoists is at base behavioral.

A constructivist analysis of cooperation, in contrast, would concentrate on how the expectations produced by behavior affect identities and interests. The process of creating institutions is one of internalizing new understandings of self and other, of acquiring new role identities, not just of creating external constraints on the behavior of exogenously constituted actors.[70] Even if not intended as such, in other words, the process by which egoists learn to cooperate is at the same time a process of reconstructing their interests in terms of shared commitments to social norms. Over time, this will tend to transform a positive interdependence of *outcomes* into a positive interdependence of *utilities* or collective interest organized around the norms in question. These norms will resist change because they are tied to actors' commitments to their identities and interests, not merely because of transaction costs. A constructivist analysis of "the cooperation problem," in other words, is at base cognitive rather than behavioral, since it treats the intersubjective knowledge that defines the structure of identities and interests, of the "game," as endogenous to and instantiated by interaction itself.

The debate over the future of collective security in Western Europe may illustrate the significance of this difference. A weak liberal or rationalist analysis would assume that the European states' "portfolio" of interests has not fundamentally changed and that the emergence of new factors, such as the collapse of the Soviet threat and the rise of Germany, would alter their cost-benefit ratios for pursuing current arrangements, thereby causing existing institutions to break down. The European states formed collaborative institutions for good, exogenously constituted egoistic reasons, and the same reasons may lead them to reject those institutions; the game of European power politics has not changed. A strong liberal or constructivist analysis of this problem would suggest that four decades of cooperation may have transformed a positive interdependence of outcomes into a collective "European identity" in terms of which states increasingly define their "self"-interests.[71] Even if egoistic reasons were its starting point, the process of cooperating tends to redefine those reasons by reconstituting identities and interests in terms of

new intersubjective understandings and commitments. Changes in the distribution of power during the late twentieth century are undoubtedly a challenge to these new understandings, but it is not as if West European states have some inherent, exogenously given interest in abandoning collective security if the price is right. Their identities and security interests are continuously in process, and if collective identities become "embedded," they will be as resistant to change as egoistic ones.[72] Through participation in new forms of social knowledge, in other words, the European states of 1990 might no longer be the states of 1950.

Critical Strategic Theory and Collective Security

The transformation of identity and interest through an "evolution of cooperation" faces two important constraints. The first is that the process is incremental and slow. Actors' objectives in such a process are typically to realize joint gains within what they take to be a relatively stable context, and they are therefore unlikely to engage in substantial reflection about how to change the parameters of that context (including the structure of identities and interests) and unlikely to pursue policies specifically designed to bring about such changes. Learning to cooperate may change those parameters, but this occurs as an unintended consequence of policies pursued for other reasons rather than as a result of intentional efforts to transcend existing institutions.

A second, more fundamental, constraint is that the evolution of cooperation story presupposes that actors do not identify negatively with one another. Actors must be concerned primarily with absolute gains; to the extent that antipathy and distrust lead them to define their security in relativistic terms, it will be hard to accept the vulnerabilities that attend cooperation.[73] This is important because it is precisely the "central balance" in the state system that seems to be so often afflicted with such competitive thinking, and realists can therefore argue that the possibility of cooperation within one "pole" (for example, the West) is parasitic on the dominance of competition between poles (the East–West conflict). Relations between the poles may be amenable to some positive reciprocity in areas such as arms control, but the atmosphere of distrust leaves little room for such cooperation and its transformative consequences.[74] The conditions of negative identification that make an "evolution of cooperation" most needed work precisely against such a logic.

This seemingly intractable situation may nevertheless be amenable to quite a different logic of transformation, one driven more by self-conscious efforts to change structures of identity and interest than by unintended consequences. Such voluntarism may seem to contradict the spirit of constructivism, since would-be revolutionaries are presumably themselves effects of socialization to structures of identity and interest. How can they think about changing that to which they owe their identity? The possibility lies in the distinction between the social determination of the self and the personal determination of choice, between what Mead called the "me" and the "I."[75] The "me" is that part of subjectivity which is defined in terms of others; the character and behavioral expectations of a person's role identity as "professor," or of the United States as "leader of the alliance," for example, are socially constituted. Roles are not played in mechanical fashion according to precise scripts, however, but are "taken" and adapted in idiosyncratic ways by each actor.[76] Even in the most constrained situations, role performance involves a choice by the actor. The "I" is the part of subjectivity in which this appropriation and reaction to roles and its corresponding existential freedom lie.

The fact that roles are "taken" means that, in principle, actors always have a capacity for "character planning"—for engaging in critical self-reflection and choices designed to bring about changes in their lives.[77] But when or under what conditions can this creative capacity be exercised? Clearly, much of the time it cannot: if actors were constantly reinventing their identities, social order would be impossible, and the relative stability of identities and interests in the real world is indicative of our propensity for habitual rather than creative action. The exceptional, conscious choosing to transform or transcend roles has at least two preconditions. First, there must be a reason to think of oneself in novel terms. This would most likely stem from the presence of new social situations that cannot be managed in terms of preexisting self-conceptions. Second, the expected costs of intentional role change—the sanctions imposed by others with whom one interacted in previous roles—cannot be greater than its rewards.

When these conditions are present, actors can engage in self-reflection and practice specifically designed to transform their identities and interests and thus to "change the games" in which they are embedded. Such "critical" strategic theory and practice has not received the attention it merits from students of world politics (another legacy of exogenously given interests perhaps), particularly given that one of the most important phenomena in contemporary world politics, Mikhail Gorbachev's policy of "New Thinking," is arguably precisely that.[78] Let me therefore use this policy as an example of how states might transform a competitive security system into a cooperative one, dividing the transformative process into four stages.

The first stage in intentional transformation is the breakdown of consensus about identity commitments. In the Soviet case, identity commitments centered on the Leninist theory of imperialism, with its belief that relations between capitalist and socialist states are inherently conflictual, and on the alliance patterns that this belief engendered. In the 1980s, the consensus within the Soviet Union over the Leninist theory broke down for a variety of reasons, principal among which seem to have been the state's inability to meet the economic-technological-military challenge from the West, the government's decline of political legitimacy at home, and the reassurance from the West that it did not intend to invade the Soviet Union, a reassurance that reduced the external costs of role change.[79] These factors paved the way for a radical leadership transition and for a subsequent "unfreezing of conflict schemas" concerning relations with the West.[80]

The breakdown of consensus makes possible a second stage of critical examination of old ideas about self and other and, by extension, of the structures of interaction by which the ideas have been sustained. In periods of relatively stable role identities, ideas and structures may become reified and thus treated as things that exist independently of social action. If so, the second stage is one of denaturalization, of identifying the practices that reproduce seemingly inevitable ideas about self and other; to that extent, it is a form of "critical" rather than "problem-solving" theory.[81] The result of such a critique should be an identification of new "possible selves" and aspirations.[82] New Thinking embodies such critical theorizing. Gorbachev wants to free the Soviet Union from the coercive social logic of the cold war and engage the West in far-reaching cooperation. Toward this end, he has rejected the Leninist belief in the inherent conflict of interest between socialist and capitalist states and, perhaps more important, has recognized the crucial role that Soviet aggressive practices played in sustaining that conflict.

Such rethinking paves the way for a third stage of new practice. In most cases, it is not enough to rethink one's own ideas about self and other, since old identities have been sustained by systems of interaction with *other* actors, the practices of which remain a social fact for the transformative agent. In order to change the self, then, it is often necessary to change the identities and interests of the others that help sustain those systems of interaction. The vehicle for inducing such change is one's own practice and, in particular, the practice of

"altercasting"—a technique of interactor control in which ego uses tactics of self-presentation and stage management in an attempt to frame alter's definitions of social situations in ways that create the role which ego desires alter to play.[83] In effect, in altercasting ego tries to induce alter to take on a new identity (and thereby enlist alter in ego's effort to change itself) by treating alter *as if* it already had that identity. The logic of this follows directly from the mirror theory of identity-formation, in which alter's identity is a reflection of ego's practices; change those practices and ego begins to change alter's conception of itself.

What these practices should consist of depends on the logic by which the preexisting identities were sustained. Competitive security systems are sustained by practices that create insecurity and distrust. In this case, transformative practices should attempt to teach other states that one's own state can be trusted and should not be viewed as a threat to their security. The fastest way to do this is to make unilateral initiatives and self-binding commitments of sufficient significance that another state is faced with "an offer it cannot refuse."[84] Gorbachev has tried to do this by withdrawing from Afghanistan and Eastern Europe, implementing asymmetric cuts in nuclear and conventional forces, calling for "defensive defense," and so on. In addition, he has skillfully cast the West in the role of being morally required to give aid and comfort to the Soviet Union, has emphasized the bonds of common fate between the Soviet Union and the West, and has indicated that further progress in East–West relations is contingent upon the West assuming the identity being projected onto it. These actions are all dimensions of altercasting, the intention of which is to take away the Western "excuse" for distrusting the Soviet Union, which, in Gorbachev's view, has helped sustain competitive identities in the past.

Yet by themselves such practices cannot transform a competitive security system, since if they are not reciprocated by alter, they will expose ego to a "sucker" payoff and quickly wither on the vine. In order for critical strategic practice to transform competitive identities, it must be "rewarded" by alter, which will encourage more such practice by ego, and so on.[85] Over time, this will institutionalize a positive rather than a negative identification between the security of self and other and will thereby provide a firm intersubjective basis for what were initially tentative commitments to new identities and interests.[86]

Notwithstanding today's rhetoric about the end of the cold war, skeptics may still doubt whether Gorbachev (or some future leader) will succeed in building an intersubjective basis for a new Soviet (or Russian) role identity. There are important domestic, bureaucratic, and cognitive-ideological sources of resistance in both East and West to such a change, not the least of which is the shakiness of the democratic forces' domestic position. But if my argument about the role of intersubjective knowledge in creating competitive structures of identity and interest is right, then at least New Thinking shows a greater appreciation—conscious or not—for the deep structure of power politics than we are accustomed to in international relations practice.

Conclusion

All theories of international relations are based on social theories of the relationship between agency, process, and social structure. Social theories do not determine the content of our international theorizing, but they do structure the questions we ask about world politics and our approaches to answering those questions. The substantive issue at stake in debates about social theory is what kind of foundation offers the most fruitful set of questions and research strategies for explaining the revolutionary changes that seem to be occurring in the late twentieth century international system. Put simply, what should systemic theories of international relations look like? How should they con-

ceptualize the relationship between structure and process? Should they be based exclusively on "microeconomic" analogies in which identities and interests are exogenously given by structure and process is reduced to interactions within those parameters? Or should they also be based on "sociological" and "social psychological" analogies in which identities and interests and therefore the meaning of structure are endogenous to process? Should a behavioral-individualism or a cognitive-constructivism be the basis for systemic theories of world politics?

This article notwithstanding, this question is ultimately an empirical one in two respects. First, its answer depends in part on how important interaction among states is for the constitution of their identities and interests. On the one hand, it may be that domestic or genetic factors, which I have systematically bracketed, are in fact much more important determinants of states' identities and interests than are systemic factors. To the extent that this is true, the individualism of a rationalist approach and the inherent privileging of structure over process in this approach become more substantively appropriate for systemic theory (if not for first- and second-image theory), since identities and interests are *in fact* largely exogenous to interaction among states. On the other hand, if the bracketed factors are relatively unimportant or if the importance of the international system varies historically (perhaps with the level of dynamic density and interdependence in the system), then such a framework would not be appropriate as an exclusive foundation for general systemic theory.

Second, the answer to the question about what systemic theories should look like also depends on how easily state identities and interests can change as a result of systemic interaction. Even if interaction is initially important in constructing identities and interests, once institutionalized its logic may make transformation extremely difficult. If the meaning of structure for state action changes so slowly that it becomes a de facto parameter within which process takes place, then it may again be substantively appropriate to adopt the rationalist assumption that identities and interests are given (although again, this may vary historically).

We cannot address these empirical issues, however, unless we have a framework for doing systemic research that makes state identity and interest an issue for both theoretical and empirical inquiry. Let me emphasize that this is *not* to say we should never treat identities and interests as given. The framing of problems and research strategies should be question-driven rather than method-driven, and if we are not interested in identity- and interest-formation, we may find the assumptions of a rationalist discourse perfectly reasonable. Nothing in this article, in other words, should be taken as an attack on rationalism per se. By the same token, however, we should not let this legitimate analytical stance become a de facto ontological stance with respect to the content of third-image theory, at least not until after we have determined that systemic interaction does not play an important role in processes of state identity- and interest-formation. We should not choose our philosophical anthropologies and social theories prematurely. By arguing that we cannot derive a self-help structure of identity and interest from the principle of anarchy alone—by arguing that anarchy is what states make of it—this article has challenged one important justification for ignoring processes of identity- and interest-formation in world politics. As such, it helps set the stage for inquiry into the empirical issues raised above and thus for a debate about whether communitarian or individualist assumptions are a better foundation for systemic theory.

I have tried to indicate by crude example what such a research agenda might look like. Its objective should be to assess the causal relationship between practice and interaction (as independent variable) and the cognitive structures at the level of individual states and of systems of states which constitute identities and interests (as dependent

variable)—that is, the relationship between what actors *do* and what they *are*. We may have some a priori notion that state actors and systemic structures are "mutually constitutive," but this tells us little in the absence of an understanding of how the mechanics of dyadic, triadic, and *n*-actor interaction shape and are in turn shaped by "stocks of knowledge" that collectively constitute identities and interests and, more broadly, constitute the structures of international life. Particularly important in this respect is the role of practice in shaping attitudes toward the "givenness" of these structures. How and why do actors reify social structures, and under what conditions do they denaturalize such reifications?

The state-centrism of this agenda may strike some, particularly postmodernists, as "depressingly familiar."[87] The significance of states relative to multinational corporations, new social movements, transnationals, and intergovernmental organizations is clearly declining, and "postmodern" forms of world politics merit more research attention than they have received. But I also believe, with realists, that in the medium run sovereign states will remain the dominant political actors in the international system. Any transition to new structures of global political authority and identity—to "postinternational" politics—will be mediated by and path-dependent on the particular institutional resolution of the tension between unity and diversity, or particularism and universality, that is the sovereign state.[88] In such a world there should continue to be a place for theories of anarchic interstate politics, alongside other forms of international theory; to that extent, I am a statist and a realist. I have argued in this article, however, that statism need not be bound by realist ideas about what "state" must mean. State identities and interests can be collectively transformed within an anarchic context by many factors—individual, domestic, systemic, or transnational—and as such are an important dependent variable. Such a reconstruction of state-centric international theory is necessary if we are to theorize adequately about the emerging forms of transnational political identity that sovereign states will help bring into being. To that extent, I hope that statism, like the state, can be historically progressive.

■　■　■

NOTES

1. See, for example, Joseph Grieco, "Anarchy and the Limits of Cooperation: A Realist Critique of the Newest Liberal Institutionalism," *International Organization* 42 (Summer 1988), pp. 485–507; Joseph Nye, "Neorealism and Neoliberalism," *World Politics* 40 (January 1988), pp. 235–51; Robert Keohane, "Neoliberal Institutionalism: A Perspective on World Politics," in his collection of essays entitled *International Institutions and State Power* (Boulder, CO: Westview Press, 1989), pp. 1–20; John Mearsheimer, "Back to the Future: Instability in Europe after the Cold War," *International Security* 13 (Summer 1990), pp. 5–56.

2. Kenneth Waltz, *Man, the State, and War* (New York: Columbia University Press, 1959), p. 232.

3. Ibid., pp. 169–70.

4. Ibid., p. 232. This point is made by Hidemi Suganami in "Bringing Order to the Causes of War Debates," *Millennium* 19 (Spring 1990), p. 34, fn. 11.

5. Kenneth Waltz, *Theory of International Politics* (Boston: Addison-Wesley, 1979).

6. The neorealist description is not unproblematic. For a powerful critique, see David Lumsdaine, [*Moral Vision in International Politics:*] *The Foreign Aid Regime, 1949–1989* (Princeton, NJ: Princeton University Press, [1993]).

7. Waltz, *Theory of International Politics*, pp. 79–101.

8. Stephen Walt, *The Origins of Alliances* (Ithaca, NY: Cornell University Press, 1987).

9. See, for example, Herbert Blumer, "The Methodological Position of Symbolic Interactionism," in his *Symbolic Interactionism: Perspective and Method* (Englewood Cliffs, NJ: Prentice-Hall, 1969), p. 2. Throughout this article, I assume that a theoretically productive analogy can be made between individuals and states.

10. The phrase "distribution of knowledge" is Barry Barnes's, as discussed in his work *The Nature of Power* (Cambridge: Polity Press, 1988); see also Peter Berger and Thomas Luckmann, *The Social Construction of Reality* (New York: Anchor Books, 1966).

11. For an excellent short statement of how collective meanings constitute identities, see Peter Berger, "Identity as a Problem in the Sociology of Knowledge," *European Journal of Sociology*, vol. 7, no. 1, 1966, pp. 32–40.

12. Berger, "Identity as a Problem in the Sociology of Knowledge," p. 111.

13. While not normally cast in such terms, foreign policy scholarship on national role conceptions could be adapted to such identity language. See Kal Holsti, "National Role Conceptions in the Study of Foreign Policy," *International Studies Quarterly* 14 (September 1970), pp. 233–309; and Stephen Walker, ed., *Role Theory and Foreign Policy Analysis* (Durham, NC: Duke University Press, 1987). For an important effort to do so, see Stephen Walker, "Symbolic Interactionism and International Politics: Role Theory's Contribution to International Organization," in C. Shih and Martha Cottam, eds., *Contending Dramas: A Cognitive Approach to Post-War International Organizational Processes* (New York: Praeger, [1992]).

14. On the "portfolio" conception of interests, see Barry Hindess, *Political Choice and Social Structure* (Aldershot, UK: Edward Elgar, 1989), pp. 2–3. The "definition of the situation" is a central concept in interactionist theory.

15. Nelson Foote, "Identification as the Basis for a Theory of Motivation," *American Sociological Review* 16 (February 1951), p. 15. Such strongly sociological conceptions of interest have been criticized, with some justice, for being "oversocialized"; see Dennis Wrong, "The Oversocialized Conception of Man in Modern Sociology," *American Sociological Review* 26 (April 1961), pp. 183–93. For useful correctives, which focus on the activation of presocial but nondetermining human needs within social contexts, see Turner, *A Theory of Social Interaction*, pp. 23–69; and Viktor Gecas, "The Self-Concept as a Basis for a Theory of Motivation," in Judith Howard and Peter Callero, eds., *The Self-Society Dynamic* (Cambridge: Cambridge University Press, 1991), pp. 171–87.

16. In neo-Durkheimian parlance, institutions are "social representations." See Serge Moscovici, "The Phenomenon of Social Representations," in Rob Farr and Serge Moscovici, eds., *Social Representations* (Cambridge: Cambridge University Press, 1984), pp. 3–69.

17. Berger and Luckmann, *The Social Construction of Reality*, p. 58.

18. See Giddens, *Central Problems in Social Theory*; and Alexander Wendt and Raymond Duvall, "Institutions and International Order," in Ernst-Otto Czempiel and James Rosenau, eds., *Global Changes and Theoretical Challenges* (Lexington, MA: Lexington Books, 1989), pp. 51–74.

19. Proponents of choice theory might put this in terms of "interdependent utilities."

20. Security systems might also vary in the extent to which there is a functional differentiation or a hierarchical relationship between patron and client, with the patron playing a hegemonic role within its sphere of influence in defining the security interests of its clients. I do not examine this dimension here; for preliminary discussion, see Alexander Wendt, "The States System and Global Militarization," Ph.D. diss., University of Minnesota, Minneapolis, 1989; and Alexander Wendt and Michael Barnett, "The International System and Third World Militarization," unpublished manuscript, 1991.

21. This amounts to an "internationalization of the state." For a discussion of this subject, see Raymond Duvall and Alexander Wendt, "The International Capital Regime and the Internationalization of the State," unpublished manuscript, 1987. See also R. B. J. Walker, "Sovereignty, Identity, Community: Reflections on the Horizons of Contemporary Political Practice," in R. B. J. Walker and Saul Mendlovitz, eds., *Contending Sovereignties* (Boulder, CO: Lynne Rienner, 1990), pp. 159–85.

22. On the spectrum of cooperative security arrangements, see Charles Kupchan and Clifford Kupchan, "Concerts, Collective Security, and the Future of Europe," *International Security* 16 (Summer

1991), pp. 114–61; and Richard Smoke, "A Theory of Mutual Security," in Richard Smoke and Andrei Kortunov, eds., *Mutual Security* (New York: St. Martin's Press, 1991), pp. 59–111. These may be usefully set alongside Christopher Jencks' "Varieties of Altruism," in Jane Mansbridge, ed., *Beyond Self-Interest* (Chicago: University of Chicago Press, 1990), pp. 53–67.

23. On the role of collective identity in reducing collective action problems, see Bruce Fireman and William Gamson, "Utilitarian Logic in the Resource Mobilization Perspective," in Mayer Zald and John McCarthy, eds., *The Dynamics of Social Movements* (Cambridge, MA: Winthrop, 1979), pp. 8–44; Robyn Dawes et al., "Cooperation for the Benefit of Us—Not Me, or My Conscience," in Mansbridge, *Beyond Self-Interest*, pp. 97–110; and Craig Calhoun, "The Problem of Identity in Collective Action," in Joan Huber, ed., *Macro-Micro Linkages in Sociology* (Beverly Hills, CA: Sage, 1991), pp. 51–75.

24. See Thomas Risse-Kappen, "Are Democratic Alliances Special?" unpublished manuscript, Yale University, New Haven, CT, 1991.

25. Waltz, *Theory of International Politics*, p. 91.

26. See Waltz, *Man, the State, and War;* and Robert Jervis, "Cooperation Under the Security Dilemma," *World Politics* 30 (January 1978), pp. 167–214.

27. My argument here parallels Rousseau's critique of Hobbes. For an excellent critique of realist appropriations of Rousseau, see Michael Williams, "Rousseau, Realism, and Realpolitik," *Millennium* 18 (Summer 1989), pp. 188–204. Williams argues that far from being a fundamental starting point in the state of nature, for Rousseau the stag hunt represented a stage in man's fall. On p. 190, Williams cites Rousseau's description of man prior to leaving the state of nature: "Man only knows himself; he does not see his own well-being to be identified with or contrary to that of anyone else; he neither hates anything nor loves anything; but limited to no more than physical instinct, he is no one, he is an animal." For another critique of Hobbes on the state of nature that parallels my constructivist reading of anarchy, see Charles Landesman, "Reflections on Hobbes: Anarchy and Human Nature," in Peter Caws, ed., *The Causes of Quarrel* (Boston: Beacon, 1989), pp. 139–48.

28. Empirically, this suggestion is problematic, since the process of decolonization and the subsequent support of many Third World states by international society point to ways in which even the raw material of "empirical statehood" is constituted by the society of states. See Robert Jackson and Carl Rosberg, "Why Africa's Weak States Persist: The Empirical and the Juridical in Statehood," *World Politics* 35 (October 1982), pp. 1–24.

29. Waltz, *Theory of International Politics,* pp. 74–77.

30. See James Morrow, "Social Choice and System Structure in World Politics," *World Politics* 41 (October 1988), p. 89. Waltz's behavioral treatment of socialization may be usefully contrasted with the more cognitive approach taken by Ikenberry and the Kupchans in the following articles: G. John Ikenberry and Charles Kupchan, "Socialization and Hegemonic Power," *International Organization* 44 (Summer 1989), pp. 283–316; and Kupchan and Kupchan, "Concerts, Collective Security, and the Future of Europe." Their approach is close to my own, but they define socialization as an elite strategy to induce value change in others, rather than as a ubiquitous feature of interaction in terms of which all identities and interests get produced and reproduced.

31. Regarding individualism, see Richard Ashley, "The Poverty of Neorealism," *International Organization* 38 (Spring 1984), pp. 225–86; Wendt, "The Agent-Structure Problem in International Relations Theory"; and David Dessler, "What's at Stake in the Agent-Structure Debate?" *International Organization* 43 (Summer 1989), pp. 441–74. Regarding structuralism, see R. B. J. Walker, "Realism, Change, and International Political Theory," *International Studies Quarterly* 31 (March 1987), pp. 65–86; and Martin Hollis and Steven Smith, *Explaining and Understanding International Relations* (Oxford: Clarendon Press, 1989).

32. The importance of the distinction between constitutive and causal explanations is not sufficiently appreciated in constructivist discourse. See Wendt, "The Agent-Structure Problem in International Relations Theory," pp. 362–65; Wendt, "The States System and Global Militarization," pp. 110–13; and Wendt, "Bridging the Theory/Meta-Theory Gap in International Relations," *Review of International Studies* 17 (October 1991), p. 390.

33. See Blumer, "The Methodological Position of Symbolic Interactionism," pp. 2–4.

34. See Robert Grafstein, "Rational Choice: Theory and Institutions," in Kristen Monroe, ed., *The Economic Approach to Politics* (New York: Harper Collins, 1991), pp. 263–64. A good example of the promise and limits of transaction cost approaches to institutional analysis is offered by Robert Keohane in his *After Hegemony* (Princeton, NJ: Princeton University Press, 1984).

35. This situation is not entirely metaphorical in world politics, since throughout history states have "discovered" each other, generating an instant anarchy as it were.

36. Mead's analysis of gestures remains definitive. See Mead's *Mind, Self, and Society.* See also the discussion of the role of signaling in the "mechanics of interaction" in Turner's *A Theory of Social Interaction,* pp. 74–79 and 92–115.

37. On the role of attribution processes in the interactionist account of identity-formation, see Sheldon Stryker and Avi Gottlieb, "Attribution Theory and Symbolic Interactionism," in John Harvey et al., eds., *New Directions in Attribution Research,* vol. 3 (Hillsdale, NJ: Lawrence Erlbaum, 1981), pp. 425–58; and Kathleen Crittenden, "Sociological Aspects of Attribution," *Annual Review of Sociology*, vol. 9, 1983, pp. 425–46. On attributional processes in international relations, see Shawn Rosenberg and Gary Wolfsfeld, "International Conflict and the Problem of Attribution," *Journal of Conflict Resolution* 21 (March 1977), pp. 75–103.

38. On the "stagecraft" involved in "presentations of self," see Erving Goffman, *The Presentation of Self in Everyday Life* (New York: Doubleday, 1959). On the role of appearance in definitions of the situation, see Gregory Stone, "Appearance and the Self," in Arnold Rose, ed., *Human Behavior and Social Processes* (Boston: Houghton Mifflin, 1962), pp. 86–118.

39. This discussion of the role of possibilities and probabilities in threat perception owes much to Stewart Johnson's comments on an earlier draft of my article.

40. On the role of "reassurance" in threat situations, see Richard Ned Lebow and Janice Gross Stein, "Beyond Deterrence," *Journal of Social Issues,* vol. 43, no. 4, 1987, pp. 5–72.

41. On "reciprocal typifications," see Berger and Luckmann, *The Social Construction of Reality,* pp. 54–58.

42. Jeff Coulter, "Remarks on the Conceptualization of Social Structure," *Philosophy of the Social Sciences* 12 (March 1982), pp. 42–43.

43. The following articles by Noel Kaplowitz have made an important contribution to such thinking in international relations: "Psychopolitical Dimensions of International Relations: The Reciprocal Effects of Conflict Strategies," *International Studies Quarterly* 28 (December 1984), pp. 373–406; and "National Self-Images, Perception of Enemies, and Conflict Strategies: Psychopolitical Dimensions of International Relations," *Political Psychology* 11 (March 1990), pp. 39–82.

44. These arguments are common in theories of narcissism and altruism. See Heinz Kohut, *Self-Psychology and the Humanities* (New York: Norton, 1985); and Martin Hoffmann, "Empathy, Its Limitations, and Its Role in a Comprehensive Moral Theory," in William Kurtines and Jacob Gewirtz, eds., *Morality, Moral Behavior, and Moral Development* (New York: Wiley, 1984), pp. 283–302.

45. See C. Norman Alexander and Mary Glenn Wiley, "Situated Activity and Identity Formation," in Morris Rosenberg and Ralph Turner, eds., *Social Psychology: Sociological Perspectives* (New York: Basic Books, 1981), pp. 269–89.

46. Sheldon Stryker, "The Vitalization of Symbolic Interactionism," *Social Psychology Quarterly* 50 (March 1987), p. 93.

47. On the "maturity" of anarchies, see Barry Buzan, *People, States, and Fear* (Chapel Hill: University of North Carolina Press, 1983).

48. A similar intuition may lie behind Ashley's effort to reappropriate classical realist discourse for critical international relations theory. See Richard Ashley, "Political Realism and Human Interests," *International Studies Quarterly* 38 (June 1981), pp. 204–36.

49. Waltz has himself helped open up such a debate with his recognition that systemic factors condition but do not determine state actions. See Kenneth Waltz, "Reflections on *Theory of International Politics*: A Response to My Critics," in Robert Keohane, ed., *Neorealism and Its Critics* (New York: Columbia University Press, 1986), pp. 322–45. The growing literature on the observation that "democracies do not fight each other" is relevant to this question, as are two other studies that break important ground toward a "reductionist" theory of state identity: William Bloom's *Personal Identity, National Identity and International Relations* (Cambridge: Cambridge University Press, 1990) and Lumsdaine's *Ideals and Interests*.

50. See Berger and Luckmann, *The Social Construction of Reality*, p. 89. See also Douglas Maynard and Thomas Wilson, "On the Reification of Social Structure," in Scott McNall and Gary Howe, eds., *Current Perspectives in Social Theory*, vol. 1 (Greenwich, CT: JAI Press, 1980), pp. 287–322.

51. See Richard Ashley, "Social Will and International Anarchy," in Hayward Alker and Richard Ashley, eds., *After Realism*, work in progress, Massachusetts Institute of Technology, Cambridge, and Arizona State University, Tempe, 1992.

52. See Ralph Turner, "Role-Taking: Process Versus Conformity," in Rose, *Human Behavior and Social Processes*, pp. 20–40; and Judith Howard, "From Changing Selves toward Changing Society," in Howard and Callero, *The Self-Society Dynamic*, pp. 209–37.

53. On the relationship between commitment and identity, see Foote, "Identification as the Basis for a Theory of Motivation"; Howard Becker, "Notes on the Concept of Commitment," *American Journal of Sociology* 66 (July 1960), pp. 32–40; and Stryker, *Symbolic Interactionism*. On role salience, see Stryker, ibid.

54. On threats to identity and the types of resistance that they may create, see Glynis Breakwell, *Coping with Threatened Identities* (London: Methuen, 1986); and Terrell Northrup, "The Dynamic of Identity in Personal and Social Conflict," in Louis Kreisberg et al., eds., *Intractable Conflicts and Their Transformation* (Syracuse, NY: Syracuse University Press, 1989), pp. 55–82. For a broad overview of resistance to change, see Timur Kuran, "The Tenacious Past: Theories of Personal and Collective Conservatism," *Journal of Economic Behavior and Organization* 10 (September 1988), pp. 143–71.

55. James March, "Bounded Rationality, Ambiguity, and the Engineering of Choice," *Bell Journal of Economics* 9 (Autumn 1978), p. 600.

56. Haskell Fain, *Normative Politics and the Community of Nations* (Philadelphia: Temple University Press, 1987).

57. This is the intersubjective basis for the principle of functional nondifferentiation among states, which "drops out" of Waltz's definition of structure because the latter has no explicit intersubjective basis. In international relations scholarship, the social production of territorial space has been emphasized primarily by poststructuralists. See, for example, Richard Ashley, "The Geopolitics of Geopolitical Space: Toward a Critical Social Theory of International Politics," *Alternatives* 12 (October 1987), pp. 403–34; and Simon Dalby, *Creating the Second Cold War* (London: Pinter, 1990). But the idea of space as both product and constituent of practice is also prominent in structurationist discourse. See Giddens, *Central Problems in Social Theory*; and Derek Gregory and John Urry, eds., *Social Relations and Spatial Structures* (London: Macmillan, 1985).

58. See John Ruggie, "Continuity and Transformation in the World Polity: Toward a Neorealist Synthesis," *World Politics* 35 (January 1983), pp. 261–85.

59. For a definition and discussion of "social closure," see Raymond Murphy, *Social Closure* (Oxford: Clarendon Press, 1988).

60. See Richard Ashley, "Untying the Sovereign State: A Double Reading of the Anarchy Problematique," *Millennium* 17 (Summer 1988), pp. 227–62.

61. See, for example, Mohammed Ayoob, "The Third World in the System of States: Acute Schizophrenia or Growing Pains?" *International Studies Quarterly* 33 (March 1989), pp. 67–80.

62. See William Coplin, "International Law and Assumptions about the State System," *World Politics* 17 (July 1965), pp. 615–34.

63. See Anthony Smith, "States and Homelands: The Social and Geopolitical Implications of National Territory," *Millennium* 10 (Autumn 1981), pp. 187–202.

64. This assumes that there are no other, competing, principles that organize political space and identity in the international system and coexist with traditional notions of sovereignty; in fact, of course, there are. On "spheres of influence" and "informal empires," see Jan Triska, ed., *Dominant Powers and Subordinate States* (Durham, NC: Duke University Press, 1986); and Ronald Robinson, "The Excentric Idea of Imperialism, With or Without Empire," in Wolfgang Mommsen and Jurgen Osterhammel, eds., *Imperialism and After: Continuities and Discontinuities* (London: Allen & Unwin, 1986), pp. 267–89. On Arab conceptions of sovereignty, see Michael Barnett, "Sovereignty, Institutions, and Identity: From Pan-Arabism

to the Arab State System," unpublished manuscript, University of Wisconsin, Madison, 1991.

65. David Strang, "Anomaly and Commonplace in European Expansion: Realist and Institutional Accounts," *International Organization* 45 (Spring 1991), pp. 143–62.

66. On "dynamic density," see Ruggie, "Continuity and Transformation in the World Polity"; and Waltz, "Reflections on *Theory of International Politics.*" The role of interdependence in conditioning the speed and depth of social learning is much greater than the attention to which I have paid it. On the consequences of interdependence under anarchy, see Helen Milner, "The Assumption of Anarchy in International Relations Theory: A Critique," *Review of International Studies* 17 (January 1991), pp. 67–85.

67. See Michael Taylor, *Anarchy and Cooperation* (New York: Wiley, 1976); and Robert Axelrod, *The Evolution of Cooperation* (New York: Basic Books, 1984).

68. Mead, *Mind, Self, and Society.*

69. Strictly speaking, this is not true, since in iterated games the addition of future benefits to current ones changes the payoff structure of the game at T1, in this case from prisoners' dilemma to an assurance game. This transformation of interest takes place entirely within the actor, however, and as such is not a function of interaction with the other.

70. In fairness to Axelrod, he does point out that internalization of norms is a real possibility that may increase the resilience of institutions. My point is that this important idea cannot be derived from an approach to theory that takes identities and interests as exogenously given.

71. On "European identity," see Barry Buzan et al., eds., *The European Security Order Recast* (London: Pinter, 1990), pp. 45–63.

72. On "embeddedness," see John Ruggie, "International Regimes, Transactions, and Change: Embedded Liberalism in a Postwar Economic Order," in Krasner, *International Regimes,* pp. 195–232.

73. See Grieco, "Anarchy and the Limits of Cooperation."

74. On the difficulties of creating cooperative security regimes given competitive interests, see Robert Jervis, "Security Regimes," in Krasner, *International Regimes,* pp. 173–94; and Charles Lipson, "International Cooperation in Economic and Security Affairs," *World Politics* 37 (October 1984), pp. 1–23.

75. See Mead, *Mind, Self, and Society.*

76. Turner, "Role-Taking."

77. On "character planning," see Jon Elster, *Sour Grapes: Studies in the Subversion of Rationality* (Cambridge: Cambridge University Press, 1983), p. 117.

78. For useful overviews of New Thinking, see Mikhail Gorbachev, *Perestroika: New Thinking for Our Country and the World* (New York: Harper & Row, 1987); and Allen Lynch, *Gorbachev's International Outlook: Intellectual Origins and Political Consequences* (New York: Institute for East–West Security Studies, 1989).

79. For useful overviews of these factors, see Jack Snyder, "The Gorbachev Revolution: A Waning of Soviet Expansionism?" *World Politics* 12 (Winter 1987–88), pp. 93–121; and Stephen Meyer, "The Sources and Prospects of Gorbachev's New Political Thinking on Security," *International Security* 13 (Fall 1988), pp. 124–63.

80. See Daniel Bar-Tal et al., "Conflict Termination: An Epistemological Analysis of International Cases," *Political Psychology* 10 (June 1989), pp. 233–55.

81. See Robert Cox, "Social Forces, States and World Orders: Beyond International Relations Theory," in Keohane, *Neorealism and Its Critics,* pp. 204–55. See also Brian Fay, *Critical Social Science* (Ithaca, NY: Cornell University Press, 1987).

82. Hazel Markus and Paula Nurius, "Possible Selves," *American Psychologist* 41 (September 1986), pp. 954–69.

83. See Goffman, *The Presentation of Self in Everyday Life*; Eugene Weinstein and Paul Deutschberger, "Some Dimensions of Altercasting," *Sociometry* 26 (December 1963), pp. 454–66; and Walter Earle, "International Relations and the Psychology of Control: Alternative Control Strategies and Their Consequences," *Political Psychology* 7 (June 1986), pp. 369–75.

84. See Volker Boge and Peter Wilke, "Peace Movements and Unilateral Disarmament: Old Concepts in a New Light," *Arms Control* 7 (September 1986), pp. 156–70; Zeev Maoz and Daniel Felsenthal, "Self-Binding Commitments, the Inducement of Trust, Social Choice, and the Theory of International Cooperation," *International Studies Quarterly* 31 (June 1987), pp. 177–200; and V. Sakamoto, "Unilateral Initiative as an Alternative Strategy," *World Futures,* vol. 24, nos. 1–4, 1987, pp. 107–34.

85. On rewards, see Thomas Milburn and Daniel Christie, "Rewarding in International Politics," *Political Psychology* 10 (December 1989), pp. 625–45.

86. The importance of reciprocity in completing the process of structural transformation makes the logic in this stage similar to that in the "evolution of cooperation." The difference is one of prerequisites and objective: in the former, ego's tentative redefinition of self enables it to try and change alter by acting "as if" both were already playing a new game; in the latter, ego acts only on the basis of given interests and prior experience, with transformation emerging only as an unintended consequence.

87. Yale Ferguson and Richard Mansbach, "Between Celebration and Despair: Constructive Suggestions for Future International Theory," *International Studies Quarterly* 35 (December 1991), p. 375.

88. For excellent discussions of this tension, see Walker, "Sovereignty, Identity, Community"; and R. B. J. Walker, "Security, Sovereignty, and the Challenge of World Politics," *Alternatives* 15 (Winter 1990), pp. 3–27. On institutional path dependencies, see Stephen Krasner, "Sovereignty: An Institutional Perspective," *Comparative Political Studies* 21 (April 1988), pp. 66–94.

Ted Hopf

THE PROMISE OF CONSTRUCTIVISM IN INTERNATIONAL RELATIONS THEORY

A challenger to the continuing dominance of neorealism and neoliberal institutionalism in the study of international relations in the United States, constructivism is regarded with a great deal of skepticism by mainstream scholars.[1] While the reasons for this reception are many, three central ones are the mainstream's miscasting of constructivism as necessarily postmodern and antipositivist; constructivism's own ambivalence about whether it can buy into mainstream social science methods without sacrificing its theoretical distinctiveness; and, related to this ambivalence, constructivism's failure to advance an alternative research program. In this article, I clarify constructivism's claims, outline the differences between "conventional" and "critical" constructivism, and suggest a research agenda that both provides alternative understandings of mainstream international relations puzzles and offers a few examples of what constructivism can uniquely bring to an understanding of world politics.

Constructivism offers alternative understandings of a number of the central themes in international relations theory, including: the meaning of anarchy and balance of power, the relationship between state identity and interest, an elaboration of power, and the prospects for change in world politics. Constructivism itself should be understood in its *conventional* and *critical* variants, the latter being more closely tied to critical social theory. The conventional constructivist desire to present an alternative to mainstream international relations theory requires a research program. Such a program includes constructivist reconceptualizations of balance-of-threat theory, the security dilemma, neoliberal cooperation theory, and the democratic peace. The constructivist research program has its own puzzles that concentrate on issues of identity in world politics and the theorization of domestic politics and culture in international relations theory.

Conventional Constructivism and Issues in Mainstream International Relations Theory

Since constructivism is best defined in relation to the issues it claims to apprehend, I present its position on several of the most significant themes in international relations theory today.

From *International Security* 23, no. 1 (Summer 1998): 171–200.

Actors and Structures Are Mutually Constituted

How much do structures constrain and enable the actions of actors, and how much can actors deviate from the constraints of structure? In world politics, a structure is a set of relatively unchangeable constraints on the behavior of states.[2] Although these constraints can take the form of systems of material dis/incentives, such as a balance of power or a market, as important from a constructivist perspective is how an action does or does not reproduce both the actor and the structure.[3] For example, to the extent that U.S. appeasement in Vietnam was unimaginable because of U.S. identity as a great power, military intervention constituted the United States as a great power. Appeasement was an unimaginable act. By engaging in the "enabled" action of intervention, the United States reproduced its own identity of great power, as well as the structure that gave meaning to its action. So, U.S. intervention in Vietnam perpetuated the international intersubjective understanding of great powers as those states that use military power against others.

Meaningful behavior, or action,[4] is possible only within an intersubjective social context. Actors develop their relations with, and understandings of, others through the media of norms and practices. In the absence of norms, exercises of power, or actions, would be devoid of meaning. Constitutive norms define an identity by specifying the actions that will cause Others to recognize that identity and respond to it appropriately.[5] Since structure is meaningless without some intersubjective set of norms and practices, anarchy, mainstream international relations theory's most crucial structural component, is meaningless. Neither anarchy, that is, the absence of any authority above the state, nor the distribution of capabilities, can "socialize" states to the desiderata of the international system's structure absent some set of meaningful norms and practices.[6]

A story many use in first-year international relations courses to demonstrate the structural extreme, that is, a situation where no agency is imaginable, illustrates the point. The scenario is a fire in a theater where all run for the exits.[7] But absent knowledge of social practices or constitutive norms, structure, even in this seemingly overdetermined circumstance, is still indeterminate. Even in a theater with just one door, while all run for that exit, who goes first? Are they the strongest or the disabled, the women or the children, the aged or the infirm, or is it just a mad dash? Determining the outcome will require knowing more about the situation than about the distribution of material power or the structure of authority. One will need to know about the culture, norms, institutions, procedures, rules, and social practices that constitute the actors and the structure alike.

Anarchy as an Imagined Community

Given that anarchy is structural, it must be mutually constituted by actors employing constitutive rules and social practices, implying that anarchy is as indeterminate as Arnold Wolfers's fire. Alexander Wendt has offered a constructivist critique of this fundamental structural pillar of mainstream international relations theory.[8] But still more fundamentally, this move opens the possibility of thinking of anarchy as having multiple meanings for different actors based on their own communities of intersubjective understandings and practices. And if multiple understandings of anarchy are possible, then one can begin to theorize about different domains and issue areas of international politics that are understood by actors as more, or less, anarchic.

Self-help, the neorealist inference that all states should prefer security independence whenever possible, is a structurally determined behavior of an actor only to the extent that a single particular understanding of anarchy prevails.[9] If the implications of anarchy are not constant across all relationships and issue areas of international politics, then a continuum of anarchies is possible. Where there are catastrophic consequences for not being able to rely on one's own capacity to enforce an agreement, such as arms control in a world of offensive military advantage, neorealist conceptualizations of anarchy are most apt. But where actors do not worry much about the potential costs of ceding control over outcomes to other states or institutions, such as in the enforcement of trade agreements, this is a realm of world politics where neorealist ideas of anarchy are just imaginary.

Identities and Interests in World Politics

Identities are necessary, in international politics and domestic society alike, in order to ensure at least some minimal level of predictability and order.[10] Durable expectations between states require intersubjective identities that are sufficiently stable to ensure predictable patterns of behavior. A world without identities is a world of chaos, a world of pervasive and irremediable uncertainty, a world much more dangerous than anarchy. Identities perform three necessary functions in a society: they tell you and others who you are and they tell you who others are.[11] In telling you who you are, identities strongly imply a particular set of interests or preferences with respect to choices of action in particular domains, and with respect to particular actors.

The identity of a state implies its preferences and consequent actions.[12] A state understands others according to the identity it attributes to them, while simultaneously reproducing its own identity through daily social practice. The crucial observation here is that the producer of the identity is not in control of what it ultimately means to others; the intersubjective structure is the final arbiter of meaning. For example, during the Cold War, Yugoslavia and other East European countries often understood the Soviet Union as Russia, despite the fact that the Soviet Union was trying hard not to have that identity. Soviet control over its own identity was structurally constrained not only by East European understanding, but also by daily Soviet practice, which of course included conversing with East Europeans in Russian.

Whereas constructivism treats identity as an empirical question to be theorized within a historical context, neorealism assumes that all units in global politics have only one meaningful identity, that of self-interested states. Constructivism stresses that this proposition exempts from theorization the very fundamentals of international political life, the nature and definition of the actors. The neorealist assumption of self-interest presumes to know, a priori, just what is the self being identified. In other words, the state in international politics, across time and space, is assumed to have a single eternal meaning. Constructivism instead assumes that the selves, or identities, of states are a variable; they likely depend on historical, cultural, political, and social context.

Constructivism and neorealism share the assumption that interests imply choices, but neorealism further assumes that states have the same a priori interests. Such a homogenizing assumption is possible only if one denies that interests are the products of the social practices that mutually constitute actors and structures.[13] Given that interests are the product of identity, that is, having the identity "great power" implies a particular set of interests different from those implied by the identity "European Union member," and that identities are multiple, constructivist logic precludes acceptance of pregiven interests.[14]

By making interests a central variable, constructivism explores not only how particular interests come to be, but also why many interests do not. The tautological, and therefore also true, most common, and unsatisfying explanation is that interests are absent where there is no reason for them, where promised gains are too meager. Constructivism, instead, theorizes about the meaning of absent interests. Just as identities and interests are produced through social practices, missing interests are understood by constructivists as produced absences, omissions that are the understandable product of social practices and structure. The social practices that constitute an identity cannot imply interests that are not consistent with the practices and structure that constitute that identity. At the extreme, an actor would not be able to imagine an absent interest, even if presented with it.[15]

The consequences of this treatment of interests and identities work in the same direction as constructivism's account of structure, agency, and anarchy: states are expected to have (1) a far wider array of potential choices of action before them than is assumed by neorealism, and (2) these choices will be constrained by social structures that are mutually created by states and structures via social practices. In other words, states have more agency under constructivism, but that agency is not in any sense unconstrained. To the contrary, choices are rigorously constrained by the webs of understanding of the practices, identities, and interests of other actors that prevail in particular historical contexts.

The Power of Practice

Power is a central theoretical element for both mainstream and constructivist approaches to international relations theory, but their conceptualizations of power are vastly different. Neorealism and neoliberal institutionalism assume that material power, whether military or economic or both, is the single most important source of influence and authority in global politics.[16] Constructivism argues that both material and discursive power are necessary for any understanding of world affairs. I emphasize both because often

constructivists are dismissed as unRealistic for believing in the power of knowledge, ideas, culture, ideology, and language, that is, discourse.[17] The notion that ideas are a form of power, that power is more than brute force, and that material and discursive power are related is not new. Michel Foucault's articulation of the power/knowledge nexus, Antonio Gramsci's theory of ideological hegemony, and Max Weber's differentiation of coercion from authority are all precursors to constructivism's position on power in political life.[18] Empirical work exists in both international relations theory and security studies that demonstrates the need to appreciate both the material and the discursive aspects of power.[19] Given that the operation of the material side of power is familiar from the mainstream literature, here I concentrate on the discursive side, the power of practice in constructivism.

The power of social practices lies in their capacity to reproduce the intersubjective meanings that constitute social structures and actors alike. The U.S. military intervention in Vietnam was consistent with a number of U.S. identities: great power, imperialist, enemy, ally, and so on. Others observing the United States not only inferred U.S. identity from its actions in Vietnam, but also reproduced the intersubjective web of meaning about what precisely constituted that identity. To the extent, for example, that a group of countries attributed an imperialist identity to the United States, the meaning of being an imperialist state was reproduced by the U.S. military intervention. In this way, social practices not only reproduce actors through identity, but also reproduce an intersubjective social structure through social practice. A most important power of practice is its capacity to produce predictability and so, order. Social practices greatly reduce uncertainty among actors within a socially structured community, thereby increasing confidence that what actions one takes will be followed by certain consequences and responses from others.[20]

An actor is not even able to act as its identity until the relevant community of meaning, to paraphrase Karl Deutsch,[21] acknowledges the legitimacy of that action, by that actor, in that social context. The power of practice is the power to produce intersubjective meaning within a social structure. It is a short step from this authorizing power of practice to an understanding of practice as a way of bounding, or disciplining interpretation, making some interpretations of reality less likely to occur or prevail within a particular community.[22] The meanings of actions of members of the community, as well as the actions of Others, become fixed through practice; boundaries of understanding become well known. In this way, the ultimate power of practice is to reproduce and police an intersubjective reality.[23] Social practices, to the extent that they authorize, discipline, and police, have the power to reproduce entire communities, including the international community, as well as the many communities of identity found therein.[24]

State actions in the foreign policy realm are constrained and empowered by prevailing social practices at home and abroad. Richard Ashley, for example, writes of a foreign policy choice as being a kind of social practice that at once constitutes and empowers the state, defines its socially recognized competence, and secures the boundaries that differentiate the domestic and international economic and political spheres of practice and, with them, the appropriate domains in which specific actors may secure recognition and act competently. Finally, Ashley concludes, foreign policy practice depends on the existence of intersubjective "precedents and shared symbolic materials—in order to impose interpretations upon events, silence alternative interpretations, structure practices, and orchestrate the collective making of history."[25]

Although I have necessarily concentrated on articulating how discursive power works in this section, the power to control intersubjective understanding is not the only form of power relevant to a constructivist approach to world politics. Having resources that allow oneself to deploy discursive power—the economic and military wherewithal to sustain institutions necessary for the formalized reproduction of social practices—is almost always part of the story as well.

Change in World Politics

Constructivism is agnostic about change in world politics.[26] It restores much variety and difference to world affairs and points out the practices by which intersubjective order is maintained, but it does not offer any more hope for change in world politics than neorealism. Constructivism's insight that anarchy is what states make of it, for example, implies that there are many different understandings of anarchy in the world, and so state actions should be more varied than only self-help. But this is an observation of already-existing reality, or, more precisely, a set of hypotheses about the same. These different understandings of anarchy are still rooted in social structures, maintained by the power of practice, and quite impervious to change. What constructivism does offer is an account of how and where change may occur.

One aspect of constructivist power is the power to reproduce, discipline, and police. When such power is realized, change in world politics is very hard indeed. These intersubjective structures, however, although difficult to challenge, are not impregnable. Alternative actors with alternative identities, practices, and sufficient material resources are theoretically capable of effecting change. Robert Cox's account of British and American supremacy, for example, perhaps best illustrates the extraordinary staying power of a well-articulated ideological hegemony, but also its possible demise. And Walker rightly observes that constructivism, to the extent that it surfaces diversity, difference, and particularity, opens up at least potential alternatives to the current prevailing structures.[27] Constructivism conceives of the politics of identity as a continual contest for control over the power necessary to produce meaning in a social group. So long as there is difference, there is a potential for change.

Thus, contrary to some critics[28] who assert that constructivism believes that change in world politics is easy, that "bad" neorealist structures need only be thought away, in fact constructivism appreciates the power of structure, if for no other reason than it assumes that actors reproduce daily their own constraints through ordinary practice. Constructivism's conceptualization of the relationship between agency and structure grounds its view that social change is both possible and difficult. Neorealism's position that all states are meaningfully identical denies a fair amount of possible change to its theoretical structure.

In sum, neorealism and constructivism share fundamental concerns with the role of structure in world politics, the effects of anarchy on state behavior, the definition of state interests, the nature of power, and the prospects for change. They disagree fundamentally, however, on each concern. Contra neorealism, constructivism assumes that actors and structures mutually constitute each other; anarchy must be interpreted to have meaning; state interests are part of the process of identity construction; power is both material and discursive; and change in world politics is both possible and difficult.

Constructivisms: Conventional and Critical

To the degree that constructivism creates theoretical and epistemological distance between itself and its origins in critical theory, it becomes "conventional" constructivism. Although constructivism shares many of the foundational elements of critical theory, it also resolves some issues by adopting defensible rules of thumb, or conventions, rather than following critical theory all the way up the postmodern critical path.[29] I situate constructivism in this way to highlight both its commonalities with traditional international relations theory and its differences with the critical theory with which it is sometimes misleadingly conflated.[30] Below I sketch out the relationship between conventional constructivism and critical social theory by identifying both those aspects of critical theory that constructivism has retained and those it has chosen to conventionalize. The result, conventional constructivism, is a collection of principles distilled from critical social theory but without the latter's more consistent theoretical or epistemological followthrough. Both critical and conventional constructivism are on the same side of the barricades in Yosef Lapid's characterization of the battle zone: the fixed, natural, unitary, stable, and essence-like, on the one (mainstream international relations theory) hand, and the emergent, constructed, contested, interactive, and process-like, on the other (constructivist) one.[31]

Conventional and critical constructivism do share theoretical fundamentals. Both aim to "denaturalize" the social world, that is, to empirically discover and reveal how the institutions and practices and identities that people take as natural, given, or matter of fact, are, in fact, the product of human agency, of social construction.[32] Both believe that intersubjective reality and meanings are critical data for understanding the social world.[33] Both insist that all data must be "contextualized," that is, they must be related to, and situated within, the social environment in which they were gathered, in order to understand their meaning.[34] Both accept the nexus between power and knowledge, the power of practice in its disciplinary, meaning-producing, mode.[35] Both also accept the restoration of agency to human individuals. Finally, both stress the reflexivity of the self and society, that is, the mutual constitution of actor and structure.[36]

Perhaps where constructivism is most conventional is in the area of methodology and epistemology. The authors of the theoretical introduction to *The Culture of National Security*, for example, vigorously, and perhaps defensively, deny that their authors use "any special interpretivist methodology."[37] The authors are careful to stress that they do not depart from "normal science" in this volume, and none of the contributors either deviates from that ground or questions whether it is appropriate.[38] This position is anathema to critical theory which, as part of its constitutive epistemology, has a lengthy bill of particulars against positivism.

Conventional constructivism, while expecting to uncover differences, identities, and multiple understandings, still assumes that it can specify a set of conditions under which one can expect to see one identity or another. This is what Mark Hoffman has called "minimal foundationalism, accepting that a contingent universalism is possible and may be necessary." In contrast, critical theory rejects either the possibility or the desirability of a minimal or contingent foundationalism.[39] Ashley chides all noncritical approaches for "anticipating analysis coming to a close." In allowing for such premature closure, the analyst participates in the normalization or naturalization of what is being observed, and risks hiding the patterns of domination that might be revealed if closure could only be deferred.[40] To reach an intellectually satisfying point of closure, constructivism adopts positivist conventions about sample characteristics, methods of difference, process tracing, and spuriousness checks. In making this choice, critical theorists argue, constructivism can offer an understanding of social reality but cannot criticize the boundaries of its own understanding, and this is precisely what critical theory is all about.[41]

So, for example, Thomas Berger makes claims about Japanese and German national identities that imply a certain outcome for an indefinite period of time to come.[42] Such a claim requires the presumed nonexistence of relevant unobservables, as well as the assumption that the practices, institutions, norms, and power relations that underlay the production of those identities are somehow fixed or constant. Critical theorists would see this as an illusion of control; none of these factors can be so easily immobilized for either analysis or prediction.

This difference manifests itself as well in how critical and conventional constructivism understand identity. Conventional constructivists wish to discover identities and their associated reproductive social practices, and then offer an account of how those identities imply certain actions. But critical theorists have a different aim. They also wish to surface identities, not to articulate their effects, but to elaborate on how people come to believe in a single version of a naturalized truth. In other words, critical theory aims at exploding the myths associated with identity formation, whereas conventional constructivists wish to treat those identities as possible causes of action. Critical theory thus claims an interest in change, and a capacity to foster change, that no conventional constructivist could make.

In addition, and in a related vein, critical theorists self-consciously recognize their own participation in the reproduction, constitution, and fixing of the social entities they observe.[43] They realize that the actor and observer can never be separated. Conventional constructivists ignore this injunction, while largely adopting interpretivist understandings of the connectivity of subjects with other subjects in a web of intersubjective meaning. The observer never becomes a subject of the same self-reflective critical inquiry.

Conventional and critical constructivists also split over the origins of identity.[44] Whereas conventional constructivists accommodate a cognitive account for identity, or offer no account at all, critical constructivists are more likely to see some form of alienation driving the need for identity. As remarked above, conventional constructivism accepts the existence of identities and wants to understand their reproduction and effects, but critical constructivists use critical social theory to specify some understanding of the origin of identity.

Tzvetan Todorov and Ashis Nandy, for example, assume that European identities were incomplete (indeed, every self is incomplete without an other) until they encountered peoples in the Americas and India, respectively.[45] The necessity of difference with an other to produce one's own identity is found in Hegel's bondsman's tale, where the more powerful slaveowner can neither know his own identity nor exercise his superior power until his slave, his other, helps him construct that identity through practice. Perhaps conventional constructivism could accept this assumption: the need for others to construct oneself, but critical constructivism moves beyond this position with the aid of Nietzsche, Freud, and Lacan.[46] The former allows difference to reign, whereas the latter implies either the assimilation of the other, if deemed equal, or his oppression, if inferior.[47]

Critical theory's approach toward identity is rooted in assumptions about power.[48] Critical theorists see power being exercised in every social exchange, and there is always a dominant actor in that exchange. Unmasking these power relations is a large part of critical theory's substantive agenda; conventional constructivism, on the other hand, remains "analytically neutral" on the issue of power relations. Although conventional constructivists share the idea that power is everywhere, because they believe that social practices reproduce underlying power relations, they are not necessarily interested in interrogating those relations. Critical theory's assumption that all social relations are instances of hierarchy, subordination, or domination ironically appears similar to the expectations of realists and neorealists about world politics.[49] The different conceptualizations of power imply different theoretical agendas. Whereas conventional constructivism is aimed at the production of new knowledge and insights based on novel understandings, "critical theory analyzes social constraints and cultural understandings from a supreme human interest in enlightenment and emancipation."[50]

Although conventional and critical constructivism share a number of positions—mutual constitution of actors and structures, anarchy as a social construct, power as both material and discursive, and state identities and interests as variables—conventional constructivism does not accept critical theory's ideas about its own role in producing change and maintains a fundamentally different understanding of power.[51]

A Constructivist Research Agenda

This section aims at moving constructivism from the margins[52] by articulating a loosely Lakatosian research program for a constructivist study of international relations.[53] I present this research agenda in three sections. The first step is to show that constructivism offers competing understandings of some key puzzles from mainstream international relations theory. The second move is to suggest what new and innovative puzzles constructivism promises to raise. The last step is for constructivism to point out its own weaknesses.

Mainstream Puzzles, Constructivist Solutions

Constructivism can provide alternative accounts of the balance of threat, security dilemmas, neoliberal institutionalist accounts of cooperation under anarchy, and the liberal theory of the democratic peace.

BALANCE OF THREAT

Neorealism tells us that states ally against power. Steven Walt rightly observed that this is empirically wrong. He suggested, instead, that states ally against threats. The attempted fix was to claim that states will balance, not against power, but against particular kinds of power. The latter is the power possessed by a relatively capable, geographically proximate state with offensive military capabilities and perceived hostile intentions.[54] Whereas geographical proximity and offensive military capacity can be established a priori, perceived intentions threaten tautology. Several constructivist scholars have pointed to balance of threat as one of the mainstream accounts most susceptible to a constructivist alternative.[55] What is missing here is a theory of threat perception, and this is precisely what a constructivist account of identity offers.

Distribution of power cannot explain the alliance patterns that emerged after World War II; otherwise, the United States would have been balanced against, not the Soviet Union. Instead, the issue must be how France, Britain, Germany, and the United States came to understand Soviet military capabilities and geographical proximity as threatening. The neorealist account would be that the Soviet Union demonstrated by its behavior that it was an objective threat to Western Europe. A constructivist account would be that the state identities of Western Europe, the United States, and the Soviet Union, each rooted in domestic sociocultural milieus, produced understandings of one another based on differences in identity and practice. The potential advantage of this approach is that it is more likely to surface differences in how the Soviet threat was constructed in different sites than is the neorealist approach, which accords objective meaning to Soviet conduct.

Let us imagine, for example, that the United States balanced against the Soviet Union because of the latter's communist identity, and what that meant to the United States. If true, it means that other possible Soviet identities, such as an Asian, Stalinist, Russian, or authoritarian threat, were not operative. So what? First, how the United States understood the Soviet threat, as communist, not only explains the anticommunist direction of U.S.

actions in the Cold War, but it also tells us that the United States understood itself as the anticommunist protector of a particular set of values both at home and abroad. Second, how the United States constructed the Soviet communist threat needs to be understood in relation to how Western Europeans understood that threat. If, for example, France understood the Soviet threat as a Russian threat, as an instance of superior Russian power in Europe, then France would not readily join in U.S. anticommunist ventures against the Soviet Union. In particular, whereas the United States saw the third world during the Cold War as an arena for battling communism, as in Vietnam, Europeans very rarely understood it in those terms, instead regarding third world states as economic actors or as former colonies.

SECURITY DILEMMAS

Security dilemmas are the products of presumed uncertainty.[56] They are assumed to be commonplace in world politics because states presumably cannot know, with sufficient certainty or confidence, the intentions of others. But as important as the security dilemma is to understanding conflictual relations among states, we do not see much evidence of security dilemmas among many pairs or groups of states: members of the same alliance, members of the same economic institution, perhaps two peaceful states or two neutral states, and so on. In the study of world politics, uncertainty might be best treated as a variable, not a constant. Constructivism can provide an understanding of what happens most of the time in relations between states, namely, nothing threatening at all. By providing meaning, identities reduce uncertainty.[57]

States understand different states differently. Soviet and French nuclear capabilities had different meanings for British decision makers. But of course certainty is not always a source of security. Knowing that another state is an aggressor resolves the security dilemma, but only by replacing it with certain insecurity, an increased confidence that the other state is in fact threatening. As Richard Ashley, bowing generously to Karl Deutsch, pointed out, politics itself is impossible in the absence of "a background of mutual understandings and habitual practices that orients and limits the mutual comprehension of practices, the signification of social action."[58] Constructivism's empirical mission is to surface the "background" that makes uncertainty a variable to understand, rather than a constant to assume.

NEOLIBERAL COOPERATION

Neoliberalism offers compelling arguments about how states can achieve cooperation among themselves. Simple iterative interaction among states, even when they prefer to exploit one another, may still lead to cooperative outcomes. The conditions minimally necessary for such outcomes include transparency of action, capacity to monitor any noncooperative behavior and punish the same in a predictable fashion, a sufficiently low discount (high appreciation) rate for future gains from the relationship, and an expectation that the relationship will not end in the foreseeable future.[59]

International institutions, whether in the form of regimes, laws, treaties, or organizations, help provide these necessary conditions for cooperation. By having rules about what constitutes a violation of a relationship, institutions help increase the confidence of each state that it will not be exploited and that its own cooperative move will be reciprocated. By establishing formal mechanisms of surveillance, institutions enable states to see what other states are doing, again enhancing confidence that a defection will be seen and a cooperative action will be followed by the same. By creating rules and procedures for surveillance and sanction, all parties can have greater confidence that violations will be punished. By formalizing these relationships, institutions help reduce each state's discount rate for future gains while increasing each state's expectation that the relationship will continue into the future.[60]

Constructivism shares neoliberalism's conclusion that cooperation is possible under anarchy, but offers a very different account of how that outcome emerges. Robert Keohane presents as the heart of neoliberalism two fundamental assumptions: there are potentially beneficial agreements among states that have not been reached, and they are hard to achieve.[61] A constructivist approach might begin by investigating how states understand their interests within a particular issue area. The distribution of identities and interests of the relevant states would then help account for whether cooperation is possible. The assumption of exogenous interests is an obstacle to developing a theory of cooperation.

Sitting down to negotiate a trade agreement among friends (as opposed to adversaries or unknowns) affects a state's willingness to lead with a cooperative move. Perhaps it would no longer understand its interests as the unilateral exploitation of the other state. Instead it might see itself as a partner in pursuit of some value other than narrow strategic interest. In *Logic of Collective Action,* Mancur Olson bracketed a host of situations where cooperation was relatively easy, despite large numbers of players, the absence of a group large enough to provide a public good, but sufficiently small to avert coordination problems (a *k*-group), no hegemonic leadership, and so on. These were situations where communities of identity existed such that the players were not in a noncooperative game in the first place. Too little attention has been paid to this insight. A constructivist account of cooperation would reconstruct such intersubjective communities as a matter of course.

When a neoliberal writes of difficulty in reaching an agreement, she usually has one particular problem in mind: uncertainty. Many of the institutional mechanisms described above are aimed at reducing uncertainty among states: provision of transparency; facilitation of iteration; enabling of decomposition; and of course the development of rules, monitoring capabilities, and adjudication procedures. A constructivist would agree that these are all very important, but that a prior issue must be raised: Is it not likely that the level of certainty is a variable associated with identity and practice, and that, ceteris paribus, the less certainty one has, the more institutional devices are necessary to produce cooperation, the harder that cooperation will be to achieve, and the more likely it will be to break down?

Neoliberalism has concluded that an important part of ensuring compliance with agreements is the development of reputations for reliability.[62] One of the most important components of discursive power is the capacity to reproduce order and predictability in understandings and expectations. In this respect, identities are a congealed reputation, that is, the closest one can get in social life to being able to confidently expect the same actions from another actor time after time. Identities subsume reputation; being a particular identity is sufficient to provide necessary diagnostic information about a state's likely actions with respect to other states in particular domains.[63]

On the other side of the life cycle, neoliberals argue that institutions die when members no longer "have incentives to maintain them."[64] But one of the more enduring puzzles for neoliberals is why these institutions persist past the point that great powers have an apparent interest in sustaining them. Their answers include lags caused by domestic political resistance to adjustment, the stickiness of institutional arrangements, and the transaction costs entailed in the renegotiation of agreements and the establishment of a new order.[65] An alternative constructivist hypothesis would be that if the identities being reproduced by the social practices constituting that institution have gone beyond the strategic game-playing self-regarding units posited by neoliberals, and have developed an understanding of each other as partners in some common enterprise, then the institution will persist, even if apparent underlying power and interests have shifted.[66] Duncan Snidal, in his formal representation of what is most likely to happen as a hegemon falters, includes as an untheorized variable "interest in the regime," with the obvious positive relationship between interest in the regime and willingness to expend resources to maintain it after hegemonic decline.[67] Constructivist research, through exploring the nature of the norms, practices, and identities constituting membership in some institution, can provide some measurable substantive content for that variable.

Although constructivists and neoliberals agree that anarchy does not preclude cooperation among states, how they understand the emergence and reproduction of such cooperation yields very different accounts and research agendas.

THE DEMOCRATIC PEACE

The observation that democratic states have not fought each other is an empirical regularity in search of a theory. Neither structural nor normative accounts fare very well.[68] The former requires assuming a consistently bellicose executive being constrained by a pacific public and its duly-elected representative institutions—but only when democratic adversaries are about. The latter has more promise, but its naturalization of certain aspects of liberalism—the market, nonviolent resolution of differences, the franchise, the First Amendment—and its crucial assumption that these norms actually matter to decision makers in democratic states when making choices about war and peace with other democracies, are untenable and untested, respectively.

Constructivism is perfectly suited to the task of testing and fundamentally revising the democratic peace.[69] Its approach aims at apprehending how the social practices and norms of states construct the identities and interests of the same. Ergo, if democracies do not fight each other, then it must be because of the way they understand each other, their intersubjective accounts of each other, and the socio-international practices that accompany those accounts.[70] But constructivism could offer a more general account of zones of peace, one not limited to democracies. Different periods of the histories of both Africa and Latin America have been marked by long stretches of little or no warfare between states. These pacific periods are obviously not associated with any "objective" indicators of democracy. By investigating how African and Latin American states constructed themselves and others, it might be possible to understand these neglected zones of "authoritarian peace."

Constructivist Puzzles

Constructivism offers an account of the politics of identity.[71] It proposes a way of understanding how nationalism, ethnicity, race, gender, religion, and sexuality, and other intersubjectively understood communities, are each involved in an account of global politics. Understanding how identities are constructed, what norms and practices accompany their reproduction, and how they construct each other is a major part of the constructivist research program.

Although nationalism and ethnicity are receiving more attention in mainstream international relations theory, attention to gender, sexuality, race, and religion have received much less, and certainly none of them is part of either neorealist or neoliberal accounts of how the world works.[72] Constructivism promises to deal with these issues, not merely because they are topical or heretofore undervalued, but because as varieties of identity, they are central to how constructivism generates understandings of social phenomena. Constructivism assumes, a priori, that identities are potentially part of the constitutive practices of the state, and so, productive of its actions at home and abroad.[73]

One of the most important by-products of this concern with identity politics is the return of differences among states. The same state is, in effect, many different actors in world politics, and different states behave differently toward other states, based on the identities of each. If true, then we should expect different patterns of behavior across groups of states with different identities and interests.[74] Although it is tempting to assert that similarity breeds cooperation, it is impossible to make such an a priori claim. Identities have much more meaning for each state than a mere label. Identities offer each state an understanding of other states, its nature, motives, interests, probable actions, attitudes, and role in any given political context.

Understanding another state as one identity, rather than another, has consequences for the possible actions of both. For example, Michael Barnett has speculated that the failure of deterrence against Iraq in Kuwait in 1990 is because Saudi Arabia was seen as an "Arab," rather than a "sovereign," state. Iraq's understanding of Saudi Arabia as an Arab state implied that Riyadh would never allow U.S. forces to deploy on Arab territory. If, instead, Iraq had understood Saudi Arabia as a sovereign state, in a realist world, it would have perhaps expected Saudi balancing against Iraqi actions in Kuwait, including U.S. military intervention, and would have been deterred.[75] In other words, neorealist predictions of balancing behavior, such as that of Saudi Arabia, rely on a single particular identity being ascribed to that country by Iraq. But if alternative identities are possible, as constructivism suggests, the neorealist world is smaller than alleged.

Or another state may not be seen as another "state" at all, but instead as an ally, friend, enemy, co-guarantor, threat, a democracy, and so on.[76] Finally, constructivism's expectation of multiple identities for actors in world politics rests on an openness to local historical context. This receptivity to identities being generated and reproduced empirically, rather than resting on pregiven assumptions, opens up the study of world politics to different units altogether.[77] Hypothesizing differences among states allows for movement beyond the typical binary characterizations of mainstream international relations: democratic-nondemocratic, great power–non-great power, North-South, and so forth. While these common axes of analysis are certainly relevant, constructivism promises to explain many other meaningful communities of identity throughout world politics.

A third constructivist promise is to return culture and domestic politics to international relations theory. To the extent that constructivism is ontologically agnostic—that is, it does not include or exclude any particular variables as meaningful—it envisions no disciplinary divides between international relations and comparative subfields (or any fields for that matter). Constructivism has no inherent focus on "second image" accounts of world politics. In fact, an appropriate criticism would be that it has remained far too long at the systemic level of analysis.[78] Nevertheless, constructivism provides a promising approach for uncovering those features of domestic society, culture, and politics that should matter to state identity and state action in global politics. There are many different ways in which a constructivist account can operate at the domestic level. I mention only several here.

Any state identity in world politics is partly the product of the social practices that constitute that identity at home.[79] In this way, identity politics at home constrain and enable state identity, interests, and actions abroad. Ashis Nandy has written about the close connection between Victorian British generational and gender identities at home and the colonization of India. Victorian Britain drew a very strict line between the sexes and also between generations, differentiating the latter into young and old, productive and unproductive, respectively. British colonial dominance was understood as masculine in relationship to Indian's feminine sub-

mission, and Indian culture was understood as infantile and archaic. In these ways Victorian understandings of itself made India comprehensible to Britain in a particular way.[80] Whereas conventional accounts of colonialism and imperialism rely on disparities in relative material power to explain relations of domination and subordination, constructivists would add that no account of such hierarchical outcomes is complete without exploring how imperial identities are constructed both at home and with respect to the subordinated Other abroad.[81] Even if material power is necessary to produce imperialism, its reproduction cannot be understood without investigating the social practices that accompanied it and the discursive power, especially in the form of related identities, they wielded.

Within the state itself might exist areas of cultural practice, sufficiently empowered through institutionalization and authorization, to exert a constitutive or causative influence on state policy.[82] The state's assumed need to construct a national identity at home to legitimize the state's extractive authority has effects on state identity abroad. A more critical constructivist account might begin by positing the state's need for an Other in world politics, so as to justify its own rule at home.[83]

A last promise of constructivism concerns not so much research issues as research strategy. Constructivism offers a heterogamous research approach: that is, it readily combines with different fields and disciplines. Constructivism itself is the product of structural linguistics, postmodern political theory, critical theory, cultural and media studies, literary criticism, and no doubt others. Far from claiming primacy as a theory of international politics, constructivism lends itself to collaboration with other approaches, both within political science and outside. Literatures in decision making, political culture, socialization, and experimental cognitive and social psychology would seem to be most promising partners.

Constructivist Problems

A constructivist research program, like all others, has unexplained anomalies, but their existence need not necessitate the donning of protective belts of any sort. Conventional constructivism has one large problem that has several parts. Friedrich Kratochwil has observed that no theory of culture can substitute for a theory of politics.[84] Paul Kowert and Jeffrey Legro have pointed out that there is no causal theory of identity construction offered by any of the authors in the Katzenstein volume.[85] Both criticisms are as accurate as they are different, and imply different remedies.

Kratochwil's statement reinforces the point that constructivism is an approach, not a theory. And if it is a theory, it is a theory of process, not substantive outcome. In order to achieve the latter, constructivism must adopt some theory of politics to make it work. Critical theory is far more advanced in this regard than conventional constructivism, but it comes at a price, a price that one may or may not be willing to pay, depending on empirical, theoretical, and/or aesthetic interests. I have described how differently critical and conventional constructivism treat the origins of identity and the nature of power. It is here that critical theory finds its animating theory of politics. By assuming that the identities of the Self and Other are inextricably bound up in a relationship of power, and that the state is a dominating instrument, critical theorists can offer theoretically informed accounts of the politics of identity: at least along the dimensions specified, that of hierarchy, subordination, domination, emancipation, and state-society struggle.

The price paid for such theories of politics, however, is an ironic one that naturalizes certain "realities," privileging social relations of dominance and hierarchy. Of course, critical theory asserts its ultimate openness to variation and change, but the point here is that its theory of politics, a priori, is more closed than that of its conventional version, which stands accused of theoretical underspecification. The problem of underspecification exists because conventional constructivism, as a theory of process, does not specify the existence, let alone the precise nature or value, of its main causal/constitutive elements: identities, norms, practices, and social structures. Instead, constructivism specifies how these elements are theoretically situated vis-à-vis each other, providing an understanding of a process and an outcome, but no a priori prediction per se. The advantages of such an approach are in the nonpareil richness of its elaboration of causal/constitutive mechanisms in any given social context and its openness (and not just in the last instance, as in critical theory) to the discovery of other substantive theoretical elements at work. The cost here, however, is the absence of a causal theory of identity.

The dilemma is that the more conventional constructivism moves to furnish such a causal theory, the more it loses the possibility of maintaining the ontological openness that its interpretivist methods afford. But the dilemma is a continuum, not a binary opposition. Conventional constructivists can and do specify their theoretical elements in advance in practice. Just to take one example, not a single author in the Katzenstein volume assessed gender, class, or race in any of their analyses. This observation (not criticism) is intended to underline how conventional constructivists already bound their a priori theoretical domains according to empirical interest and theoretical priors. Moreover, conventional constructivists can make predictions, if they choose. Their only constraint is just how durable they believe the social structures to be that they have demonstrated are constraining the reproduction of identities, interests, norms, and practices, in some social context. For example, when Risse-Kappen argues that North Atlantic Treaty Organization (NATO) members regard each other as liberal allies, rather than as realist states balancing against a threat, he is making a prediction: if NATO members see each other as liberal allies, NATO will persist beyond the point where the threat disappears.

One obstacle to the development of a causal model of identity is conventional constructivism's silence on the issue of intentionality. Critical theorists confidently declare their indifference to the issue: establishing causality is an illusory goal. Kowert and Legro point out the failure of any author in the Katzenstein volume to establish more than a correlative relationship between an identity and an outcome. In fact, the authors do far more than that: they control for alternative explanations and they show the connection between norms and interests and outcomes. But what is missing is the decision based on the identity. Here again, constructivist heterogamy allows for an attempted fix. The answer may lie in trying to marry constructivist process to psychological process. Kowert and Legro discuss the possibility in terms of the experimental social psychological work of Marilyn Brewer and Jonathan Turner.[86] To the extent it is possible to establish a causal link between a particular identity, such as Japanese antimilitarism, and an interest in opposing Japanese military expenditures (or between belief in a norm, such as humanitarian interventionism, and an action to fulfill that norm), it might be attainable through ongoing work on the connection between identity and behavior in social psychology.

The last problem with constructivism is really not so much a problem as it is an advantage. Constructivism's theory of process and commitment to interpretivist thick description place extraordinary demands on the researcher to gather mountains of elaborate empirical data. To reconstruct the operation of identity politics, even in a limited domain for a short period, requires thousands of pages of reading, months of interviews and archival research, and a host of less conventional activities, such as riding public transportation, standing in lines, and going to bars and cafés to participate in local practices. (The latter need not be so onerous.) The point here is that the evidence necessary to develop an understanding of, say, a national identity, its relation to domestic identities, the practices that constitute both, implied interests of each, and the overall social structure is necessarily vast and varied. Constructivism is no shortcut.

The Constructivist Promise

The assumptions that underlay constructivism account for its different understanding of world politics. Since actors and structures are mutually constructed, state behavior in the face of different distributions of power or anarchy is unknowable absent a reconstruction of the intersubjective meaning of these structures and actors. Since actors have multiple identities, and these identities imply different interests, the a priori and exogenous attribution of identical interests to states is invalid. Since power is both material and discursive, patterned behavior over time should be understood as a result of material or economic power working in concert with ideological structures, social practices, institutionalized norms, and intersubjective webs of meaning. The greatest power of all is that which disciplines actors to naturally imagine only those actions that reproduce the underlying arrangements of power—material and discursive. Since constructivist social structures are both enduring and mutable, change in world politics is considered both difficult and possible.

A conventional constructivist recasting of mainstream international relations puzzles is based on the implications of its assumptions. Since what constitutes a threat can never be stated as an a priori, primordial constant, it should be approached as a social construction of an Other, and theorized at that level. Since identities, norms, and social practices reduce uncertainty, the security dilemma should not be the starting point for analyzing relations among states. Since states are already situated in multiple social contexts, any account of (non)cooperation among them should begin by exploring how their understandings of each other generate their relevant interests. Since communities of identity are expected to exist, patterns of behavior that spur scholars to consider a liberal peace should instead provoke us to consider zones of peace more generally.

A conventional constructivist account of politics operates between mainstream international relations and critical theory. Conventional constructivism rejects the mainstream presumption that world politics is so homogenous that universally valid generalizations can be expected to come of theorizing about it. It denies the critical constructivist position that world politics is so heterogeneous that we should presume to look for only the unique and the differentiating. Contrary to both these two approaches, conventional constructivism presumes we should be looking for communities of intersubjectivity in world politics, domains within which actors share understandings of themselves and each other, yielding predictable and replicable patterns of action within a specific context.

Mainstream international relations theory treats world politics as an integrated whole, undifferentiated by either time or territory. Critical theory regards world politics as an array of fragments that can never add up to a whole, and regards efforts to construct such a whole as a political move to impose some kind of rationalistic, naturalized order on irrepressible difference. Conventional constructivism, on the other hand, regards the world as a complicated and vast array of different domains, the apprehension of all of which could never yield a fully coherent picture of international politics. The failure to account for any one of them, however, will guarantee a theoretically unsatisfying understanding of the world. In effect, the promise of constructivism is to restore a kind of partial order and predictability to world politics that derives not from imposed homogeneity, but from an appreciation of difference.

NOTES

1. The canonical neorealist work remains Kenneth N. Waltz, *Theory of International Politics* (Reading, Mass.: Addison-Wesley, 1979). The debate between neorealism and neoliberal institutionalism is presented and summarized in David A. Baldwin, ed., *Neorealism and Neoliberalism* (New York: Columbia University Press, 1993). Constructivist challenges can be found in Nicholas Greenwood Onuf, *World of Our Making: Rules and Rule in Social Theory and International Relations* (Columbia: University of South Carolina Press, 1989); Peter J. Katzenstein, ed., *The Culture of National Security: Norms and Identity in World Politics* (New York: Columbia University Press, 1996); and Yosef Lapid and Friedrich V. Kratochwil, eds., *The Return of Culture and Identity in IR Theory* (Boulder, Colo.: Lynne Rienner, 1996).

2. Most important for this article, this is the neorealist conceptualization of international structure. All references to neorealism, unless otherwise noted, are from Waltz, *Theory of International Politics*.

3. Friedrich Kratochwil suggests that this difference in the understanding of structure is because structuralism entered international relations theory not through sociolinguistics, but through microeconomics. Friedrich V. Kratochwil, "Is the Ship of Culture at Sea or Returning?" in Lapid and Kratochwil, *The Return of Culture and Identity*, p. 211.

4. The critical distinction between action and behavior is made by Charles Taylor, "Interpretation and the Sciences of Man," in Paul Rabinow and William M. Sullivan, eds., *Interpretive Social Science: A Second Look* (Berkeley: University of California Press, 1987), pp. 33–81.

5. Ronald L. Jepperson, Alexander Wendt, and Peter J. Katzenstein, "Norms, Identity, and Culture in National Security," in Katzenstein, *The Culture of National Security*, p. 54.

6. David Dessler, "What's At Stake in the Agent-Structure Debate?" *International Organization*, Vol. 43, No. 3 (Summer 1989), pp. 459–460.

7. Arnold Wolfers, *Discord and Collaboration* (Baltimore, Md.: Johns Hopkins University Press, 1962).

8. Alexander Wendt, "Anarchy Is What States Make of It: The Social Construction of Power Politics," *International Organization*, Vol. 46, No. 2 (Spring 1992), 391–425.

9. Elizabeth Kier, for example, shows how the same "objective" external structural arrangement of power cannot account for French military strategy between the two world wars. Elizabeth Kier, "Culture and French Military Doctrine before World War II," in Katzenstein, *The Culture of National Security*, pp. 186–215.

10. The focus on identity does not reflect a lack of appreciation for other elements in the constructivist approach, such as norms, culture, and institutions. Insofar as identities are the most proximate causes of choices, preferences, and action, I concentrate on them, but with the full recognition that identities cannot be understood without a simultaneous account of normative, cultural, and institutional context.

11. Henri Tajfel, *Human Groups and Social Categories: Studies in Social Psychology* (Cambridge, U.K.: Cambridge University Press, 1981), p. 255. Although there are many accounts of the origin of identity,

I offer a cognitive explanation because it has minimal a priori expectations, assuming only that identities are needed to reduce complexity to some manageable level.

12. Dana Eyre and Mark Suchman, for example, find that, controlling for rational strategic need, domestic coalition politics, and super-power manipulation, countries in the third world prefer certain weapons systems over others because of their understanding of what it means to be "modern" in the twentieth century. Dana P. Eyre and Mark C. Suchman, "Status, Norms, and the Proliferation of Conventional Weapons: An Institutional Theory Approach," in Katzenstein, *The Culture of National Security*, pp. 73–113. Other examples of empirical research that have linked particular identities to particular sets of preferences are "civilized" identities driving attitudes toward weapons of mass destruction; notions of what constitutes "humanitarian" shaping decisions to intervene in other states; the identity of a "normal" state implying particular Soviet foreign policies; and "antimilitarist" identities in Japan and German shaping their post–World War II foreign policies. These arguments can be found in Richard Price and Nina Tannenwald, "Norms and Deterrence: The Nuclear and Chemical Weapons Taboos," pp. 114–152; Martha Finnemore, "Constructing Norms of Human-itarian Intervention," pp. 153–185; Robert Herman, "Identity, Norms, and National Security: The Soviet Foreign Policy Revolu-tion and the End of the Cold War," pp. 271–316; and Thomas U. Berger, "Norms, Identity, and National Security in Germany and Japan," pp. 317–356. All of the above are in Katzenstein, *The Culture of National Security*. On identity and mutual intelligibility, see Roxanne Lynn Doty, "The Bounds of 'Race' in International Relations," *Millennium: Journal of International Studies*, Vol. 22, No. 3 (Winter 1993), p. 454.

13. Robert Keohane calls the failure to contextualize interests one of the major weaknesses of mainstream international relations theory. Robert O. Keohane, "International Institutions: Two Approaches," *International Studies Quarterly*, Vol. 32, No. 4 (December 1988), pp. 390–391.

14. Jeffrey Legro, for example, has shown how the preferences of great powers before and during World War II with respect to the use and nonuse of strategic bombing, and chemical and submarine warfare, are unfathomable without first understanding the identities of the military organizations responsible for shaping those preferences. Jeffrey W. Legro, "Culture and Preferences in the International Cooperation Two-Step," *American Political Science Review*, Vol. 90, No. 1 (March 1996), pp. 118–137.

15. See, for example, Tannenwald, "Norms and Deterrence," and Kier, "Culture and French Military Doctrine before World War II," p. 203. For a brilliant account of how social structure enables and impedes the construction of identity and interest, see Jane K. Cowan, "Going Out for Coffee? Contesting the Grounds of Gendered Pleasures in Everyday Sociability," in Peter Loizos and Evthymios Papataxiarchis, eds., *Contested Identities: Gender and Kinship in Modern Greece* (Princeton, N.J.: Princeton University Press, 1991), pp. 196–197.

16. A rare effort in the mainstream literature to break away from this focus on material power is Judith Goldstein and Robert O. Keohane, eds., *Ideas and Foreign Policy* (Ithaca, N.Y.: Cornell University Press, 1993).

17. As R.B.J. Walker has clarified, "To suggest that culture and ideology are crucial for the analysis of world politics is not necessarily to take an idealist position. . . . On the contrary, it is important to recognize that ideas, consciousness, culture, and ideology are bound up with more immediately visible kinds of political, military, and economic power." In R.B.J. Walker, "East Wind, West Wind: Civilizations, Hegemonies, and World Orders," in Walker, ed., *Culture, Ideology, and World Order* (Boulder, Colo.: Westview Press, 1984), p. 3. See also Onuf, *World of Our Making*, p. 64. Joseph Nye's conceptualiza-tion of "soft" power could be usefully read through a constructivist interpretation. See Joseph S. Nye, Jr., *Bound to Lead: The Changing Nature of American Power* (New York: Basic Books, 1991), esp. pp. 173–201.

18. Colin Gordon, ed., *Power/Knowledge: Selected Interviews and Other Writings, 1972–1997, by Michel Foucault* (Brighton, Sussex, U.K.: Harvester Press, 1980); Antonio Gramsci, *Selections from the Prison Notebooks*, trans. and ed., Quinton Hoare and Geoffrey Nowell Smith (New York: International Publishers, 1992); and Max Weber, *From Max Weber*, ed., Hans Gerth and C. Wright Mills (New York: Oxford University Press, 1946).

19. Price and Tannenwald show that even power as material as nuclear missiles and chemical artillery had to be understood and interpreted before it had any meaning. In Price and Tannenwald, "Norms and Deterrence." Robert Cox has provided an account of the rise, repro-duction, and demise of nineteenth-century British supremacy, and the rise and reproduction of U.S. dominance in the twentieth century through a close reading of the interaction between material and discursive power. Robert W. Cox, "Social Forces, States, and World Orders: Beyond International Relations Theory," *Millennium: Journal of International Studies*, Vol. 10, No. 1 (Spring 1981), pp. 126–155.

20. Onuf sees these reproducible patterns of action as the product of "reflexive self-regulation," whereby agents refer to their own and other's past and anticipated actions in deciding how to act. Onuf, *World of Our Making*, p. 62.

21. Karl W. Deutsch, *Nationalism and Social Communication: An Inquiry into the Foundations of Nationality* (New York: MIT Press, 1953), pp. 60–80. Deutsch was a constructivist long ahead of his time to the extent that he argued that individuals could not engage in meaningful action absent some community-wide intersubjectivity. Another work constructivist in essence is Robert Jervis's *The Logic of Images in International Relations* (Princeton, N.J.: Princeton Univer-sity Press, 1970). Applying Erving Goffmann's self-presentation theory to international politics, Jervis pointed out that state actions, such as gunboat diplomacy, were meaningless unless situated in a larger intersubjective community of diplomatic practice.

22. See Doty, "The Bounds of Race," p. 454; and Carol Cohn, "Sex and Death in the Rational World of Defense Intellectuals," *Signs: Jour-nal of Women in Culture and Society*, Vol. 12, No. 32 (Summer 1987), pp. 687–718.

23. See Richard K. Ashley, "Untying the Sovereign State: A Double Reading of the Anarchy Problématique," *Millennium: Journal of International Studies*, Vol. 17, No. 2 (Summer 1988), p. 243, for a discussion of this process.

24. Richard K. Ashley, "The Geopolitics of Geopolitical Space: Toward a Critical Social Theory of International Politics," *Alternatives*, Vol. 12, No. 4 (October–December 1987), p. 409.

25. Richard K. Ashley, "Foreign Policy as Political Performance," *International Studies Notes* (1988), p. 53.

26. Critical constructivism denies this vigorously.

27. R.B.J. Walker, "Realism, Change, and International Political Theory," *International Studies Quarterly*, Vol. 31, No. 1 (March 1987), pp. 76–77.

28. See, for example, John J. Mearsheimer, "The False Promise of International Institutions," *International Security*, Vol. 19, No. 1 (Winter 1994/1995), pp. 5–49, esp. 37–47.

29. Jepperson, Wendt, and Katzenstein differentiate the kind of "sociological" analysis performed in their volume from the "radical constructivist position" of Richard Ashley, David Campbell, R.B.J. Walker, and Cynthia Weber. See Jepperson, Wendt, and Katzenstein, "Norms, Identity, and Culture," p. 46, notes 41 and 42.

30. As, for example, in Mearsheimer, "The False Promise of International Institutions," wherein constructivism, reflectivism, postmodernism, and poststructuralism are all reduced to "critical theory," p. 37, note 128.

31. Yosef Lapid, "Culture's Ship: Returns and Departures in International Relations Theory," in Lapid and Kratochwil, *The Return of Culture and Identity*, pp. 3–20.

32. Mark Hoffman, "Critical Theory and the Inter-Paradigm Debate," *Millennium: Journal of International Studies*, Vol. 16, No. 2 (Summer 1987), pp. 233–236.

33. Ashley, "The Geopolitics of Geopolitical Space," p. 403.

34. In this respect, both critical and conventional constructivism can be understood as sharing an interpretivist epistemology, more generally. See Taylor, "Interpretation and the Sciences of Man."

35. James Der Derian, *On Diplomacy. A Genealogy of Western Estrangement* (Oxford, U.K.: Basil Blackwell, 1987), p. 4.

36. R.B.J. Walker, "World Politics and Western Reason: Universalism, Pluralism, Hegemony," in Walker, *Culture, Ideology, and World Order*, p. 195; and Ashley, "The Geopolitics of Geopolitical Space," pp. 409–410.

37. Jepperson, Wendt, and Katzenstein, "Norms, Identity, and Culture," p. 67.

38. The only, even partial, exceptions are Price and Tannenwald, "Norms and Deterrence," and Michael N. Barnett, "Institutions, Roles, and Disorder: The Case of the Arab States System," *International Studies Quarterly*, Vol. 37, No. 3 (September 1993), pp. 271–296.

39. Mark Hoffman, "Restructuring, Reconstruction, Reinscription, Rearticulation: Four Voices in Critical International Theory," *Millennium: Journal of International Studies*, Vol. 20, No. 1 (Spring 1991), p. 170. David Campbell argues that no identity (or any other theoretical element for that matter) may be allowed to be fixed or final. It must be critically deconstructed as soon as it acquires a meaning. David Campbell, "Violent Performances: Identity, Sovereignty, Responsibility," in Lapid and Kratochwil, *The Return of Culture and Identity*, pp. 164–166. See also Stephen J. Rosow, "The Forms of Internationalization: Representation of Western Culture on a Global Scale," *Alternatives*, Vol. 15, No. 3 (July–September 1990), p. 289, for differences on this issue.

40. Ashley, "The Geopolitics of Geopolitical Space," p. 408.

41. Hoffman, "Restructuring, Reconstruction, Reinscription, Rearticulation," p. 232.

42. Berger, "Norms, Identity, and National Security in Germany and Japan."

43. Cynthia Weber points this out as a very important distinction between her approach to the state and more modernist approaches. Weber similarly separates conventional constructivists from critical theorists. Max Weber, *Simulating Sovereignty: Intervention, the State, and Symbolic Exchange* (Cambridge, U.K.: Cambridge University Press, 1995), p. 3.

44. For a review of this issue see Friedrich Kratochwil, "Is the Ship of Culture at Sea or Returning?" pp. 206–210.

45. The discussion of the work of Todorov and Nandy is in Naeem Inayatullah and David L. Blaney, "Knowing Encounters: Beyond Parochialism in International Relations Theory," in Lapid and Kratochwil, *The Return of Culture and Identity*, pp. 65–84.

46. For an account of identity based on these three theorists, see Anne Norton, *Reflections on Political Identity* (Baltimore, Md.: Johns Hopkins University Press, 1988).

47. Inayatullah and Blaney, "Knowing Encounters," pp. 65–66. For a very useful analysis of how different accounts of identity have made their way through feminist theorizing, see Allison Weir, *Sacrificial Logics: Feminist Theory and the Critique of Identity* (New York: Routledge, 1996).

48. My views on the differences separating critical and conventional constructivist positions on power were shaped in conversation with Jim Richter.

49. See Arturo Escobar, "Discourse and Power in Development: Michel Foucault and the Relevance of His Work to the Third World," *Alternatives*, Vol. 10, No. 4 (October–December 1984), esp. pp. 377–378.

50. This is taken from Andrew Linklater, "The Question of the Next Stage in International Relations Theory: A Critical-Theoretical Point of View," *Millennium: Journal of International Studies*, Vol. 21, No. 1 (Spring 1992), p. 91, and is based on his interpretation of Jürgen Habermas. For a view on precisely the point of the emancipator power of critical theory, see Chris Brown, "'Turtles All the Way Down': Anti-Foundationalism, Critical Theory, and International Relations," *Millennium: Journal of International Studies*, Vol. 23, No. 2 (Summer 1994), p. 219.

51. For an alternative account of international relations theory from a critical theory perspective in which conventional constructivism's positions can be found as well, see Richard K. Ashley, "Three Modes of Economism," *International Studies Quarterly*, Vol. 27, No. 4 (December 1983), pp. 477–491. On the construction of anarchy, in particular, see Ashley, "Untying the Sovereign State," p. 253. In addition, conventional constructivism is more willing to accept the ontological status of the state when theorizing, whereas critical theory demands that the state remain a zone of contestation, and should be understood as such; its autonomous existence should not be accepted. For the former conventional view, see Alexander Wendt, "Constructing International Politics," *International Security*, Vol. 20, No. 1 (Summer 1995), p. 72. For the critical view of the state, see Ashley, "Untying the Sovereign State," pp. 248–251.

52. For the challenge to constructivists to develop a research program or be marginalized, see Keohane, "International Institutions," p. 392. For criticism in a similar vein, see Thomas J. Biersteker, "Critical Reflections on Post-Positivism in International Relations,"

International Studies Quarterly, Vol. 33, No. 3 (September 1989), p. 266.

53. It is a loose adaptation because, while I adopt Lakatosian criteria for what constitutes a progressive and degenerative shift in a research program, I do not adopt his standards of falsificationism or their associated "protective belts" of auxiliary hypotheses. See Imre Lakatos, "Falsification and the Methodology of Scientific Research Programmes," in Imre Lakatos and Alan Musgrave, eds., *Criticism and the Growth of Knowledge* (Cambridge, U.K.: Cambridge University Press, 1970), pp. 91–196.

54. Stephen M. Waltz, *The Origins of Alliances* (Ithaca, N.Y.: Cornell University Press, 1987), p. 5. By acknowledging that "one cannot determine a priori . . . which sources of threat will be most important in any given case; one can say only that all of them are likely to play a role," Waltz does not offer a nontautological means for specifying threat. Quotation on p. 26.

55. See Thomas Risse-Kappen, "Collective Identity in a Democratic Community: The Case of NATO," in Katzenstein, *The Culture of National Security*, pp. 361–368; Barnett, "Identity and Alliances," pp. 401–404; Peter J. Katzenstein, "Introduction: Alternative Perspectives on National Security," in Katzenstein, *The Culture of National Security*, pp. 27–28; Jepperson, Wendt, and Katzenstein, "Norms, Identity, and Culture," p. 63; and Wendt, "Constructing International Politics," p. 78.

56. Robert Jervis, "Cooperation under the Security Dilemma," *World Politics*, Vol. 30, No. 2 (March 1978), pp. 167–214.

57. I thank Maria Fanis for bringing home to me the importance of thinking about world politics in this way.

58. Ashley, "Three Modes," p. 478; see also Ashley, "The Geopolitics of Geopolitical Space," p. 414.

59. Kenneth A. Oye, "Explaining Cooperation under Anarchy: Hypotheses and Strategies," in Kenneth A. Oye, ed., *Cooperation under Anarchy* (Princeton, N.J.: Princeton University Press, 1986), pp. 1–24.

60. The regimes literature is vast. For an early foundational volume that includes theoretical specification, empirical illustration, and some self-critique, see Stephen D. Krasner, ed., *International Regimes* (Ithaca, N.Y.: Cornell University Press, 1983). Elaboration of the market failure logic is in Robert O. Keohane, *After Hegemony* (Princeton, N.J.: Princeton University Press, 1984).

61. Keohane, "International Institutions," p. 386.

62. On the critical importance of a theory of reputation to account for economic transactions, such as contracts, see David M. Kreps, "Corporate Culture and Economic Theory," in James E. Alt and Kenneth A. Shepsle, eds., *Perspectives on Positive Political Economy* (Cambridge, U.K.: Cambridge University Press, 1990), pp. 90–143. Formal game-theoretic work on reputation consistently shows that it should matter, and it does, but only when assumed to do so. Empirical work in international relations has shown that reputations do not work as hypothesized by most international relations theory. See Jonathan Mercer, *Reputation and International Politics* (Ithaca, N.Y.: Cornell University Press, 1996); Ted Hopf, *Peripheral Visions: Deterrence Theory and American Foreign Policy in the Third World, 1965–1990* (Ann Arbor: University of Michigan Press, 1994); Richard Ned Lebow, *Between Peace and War: The Nature of International Crisis* (Baltimore, Md.: Johns

Hopkins University Press, 1981); and Jervis, *Logic of Images in International Relations*.

63. For a recognition that "shared focal points," à la Thomas Schelling, have much in common with intersubjective reality and its capacity to promote cooperative solutions to iterative games, see Geoffrey Garrett and Barry R. Weingast, "Ideas, Interests, and Institutions: Constructing the European Community's Internal Market," in Goldstein and Keohane, *Ideas and Foreign Policy*, pp. 173–206.

64. Keohane, "International Institutions," p. 387.

65. On lags and stickiness, see Stephen D. Krasner, "State Power and the Structure of International Trade," *World Politics*, Vol. 28, No. 3 (April 1976), pp. 317–343. On transaction costs, see Keohane, *After Hegemony*.

66. Another constructivist hypothesis offers itself here: institutionalized cooperation will be more likely to endure to the extent that the identities of the members of that institution are understood as common and they are reproduced by a thick array of social practices. This is meant as a continuum, with narrow self-interest being arrayed at one end of the spectrum, neoliberal institutionalization of self-interested cooperation in the middle, community of identity toward the other end, and harmony at the other pole.

67. Duncan Snidal, "The Limits of Hegemonic Stability Theory," *International Organization*, Vol. 39, No. 4 (Autumn 1985), esp. pp. 610–611.

68. For a comprehensive review of the most recent literature on the democratic peace, and an empirical test that shows that satisfaction with the status quo (a variable subject to constructivist interpretation) is the single most important factor affecting the use of force by democracies and authoritarian states alike, see David L. Rousseau, Christopher Gelpi, and Dan Reiter, "Assessing the Dyadic Nature of the Democratic Peace, 1918–1988," *American Political Science Review*, Vol. 90, No. 3 (September 1996), p. 527.

69. For a very well-developed research design to test constructivist versus mainstream accounts of the democratic peace, see Colin Kahl, "Constructing a Separate Peace: Constructivism, Collective Liberal Identity, and the Democratic Peace," *Security Studies*, Vol. 8, No. 2–3 (1998), pp. 94–144.

70. For accounts of the democratic peace that focus on its contextual intersubjective characters, see Ido Oren, "The Subjectivity of the 'Democratic' Peace: Changing U.S. Perceptions of Imperial Germany," *International Security*, Vol. 20, No. 2 (Fall 1995), pp. 147–184; Thomas Risse-Kappen, *Cooperation among Democracies*, p. 30; and Risse-Kappen, "Collective Identity in a Democratic Community," pp. 366–367.

71. I do not try to compile a comprehensive set of questions for constructivists, but instead merely elaborate general themes for research, themes that do not have a prominent place in mainstream international relations theory.

72. For a critical view of neorealism's belated efforts to capture nationalism, see Yosef Lapid and Friedrich Kratochwil, "Revisiting the 'National': Toward an Identity Agenda in Neorealism?" in Lapid and Kratochwil, *The Return of Culture and Identity*, pp. 105–126. For a most imaginative critical constructivist treatment of nationalism, see Daniel Deudney, "Ground Identity: Nature, Place, and Space in Nationalism," in ibid., pp. 129–145; see also Roxanne Lynn Doty, "Sovereignty and the Nation: Constructing the Bound-

aries of National Identity," in Thomas J. Biersteker and Cynthia Weber, eds., *State Sovereignty as Social Construct* (Cambridge, U.K.: Cambridge University Press, 1996) pp. 121–147.

73. For example, J. Ann Tickner observes that contemporary masculinized Western understandings of themselves lead to feminized portrayals of the South as "emotional and unpredictable." Tickner, "Identity in International Relations Theory: Feminist Perspectives," in Lapid and Kratochwil, *The Return of Culture and Identity*, pp. 147–162.

74. For example, Risse-Kappen, "Collective Identity in a Democratic Community," finds a common identity within the North Atlantic Treaty Organization; see also Iver B. Neumann and Jennifer M. Welsh, "The Other in European Self-Definition," *Review of International Studies*, Vol. 17, No. 4 (October 1991), pp. 327–348, for an exploration of "Christian" and "European" states versus "Islamic" "Asiatic" Turkey.

75. Michael N. Barnett, "Institutions, Roles, and Disorder: The Case of the Arab States System," *International Studies Quarterly*, Vol. 37, No. 3 (September 1993), pp. 271–296.

76. See Risse-Kappen, "Collective Identity in a Democratic Community," and Michael N. Barnett, "Sovereignty, Nationalism, and Regional Order in the Arab System," *International Organization*, Vol. 49, No. 3 (Summer 1995), pp. 479–510, for examples.

77. Yale Ferguson and Richard Mansbach, for example, offer a rich variety of "polities," such as city-states, civilizations, polis, empires, kingdoms, caliphates, each of which had and, in some cases, has and will have, meaningful identities in world politics. Ferguson and Mansbach, "Past as Prelude," pp. 22–28, and Sujata Chakrabarti Pasic, "Culturing International Relations Theory," both in Lapid and Kratochwil, *The Return of Culture and Identity*, pp. 85–104.

78. Keohane, in "International Institutions," p. 392, has made this observation about "reflectivist" scholarship. For similar laments, see Dessler, "What's At Stake," p. 471; and Barnett, "Institutions, Roles, and Disorder," p. 276. Alexander Wendt acknowledges he has "systematically bracketed" domestic factors in Wendt, "Anarchy Is What States Make of It," p. 423.

79. Two works that make the connection between domestic identity construction at home and state identity are Audie Klotz, *Norms in International Relations: The Struggle against Apartheid* (Ithaca, N.Y.: Cornell University Press, 1995); and Peter J. Katzenstein, *Cultural Norms and National Security* (Ithaca, N.Y.: Cornell University Press, 1996).

80. Inayatullah and Blaney, "Knowing Encounters," pp. 76–80.

81. Compare this, for example, to Richard Cottam's very interesting account of imperial British images of Egypt. The critical difference is that Cottam does not see British constructions of themselves or their society's parts as relevant to an understanding of British images of Egyptians, Richard Cottam, *Foreign Policy Motivation: A General Theory and Case Study* (Pittsburgh: University of Pittsburgh Press, 1977).

82. One might say this about the French military between World Wars I and II. See Kier, "Culture and French Military Doctrine before World War II."

83. This is done by David Campbell, *Writing Security: United States Foreign Policy and the Politics of Identity* (Minneapolis: University of Minnesota Press, 1992) and Jim George, *Discourses of Global Politics: A Critical (Re)Introduction to International Relations* (Boulder, Colo.: Lynne Rienner, 1994).

84. Kratochwil, "Is the Ship of Culture at Sea or Returning?" p. 206.

85. Paul Kowert and Jeffrey Legro, "Norms, Identity, and Their Limits: A Theoretical Reprise," in Katzenstein, *The Culture of National Security*, p. 469. For other critical reviews of constructivism and world politics, see Jeffrey T. Checkel, "The Constructivist Turn in International Relations Theory," *World Politics*, Vol. 50, No. 2 (January 1998), pp. 324–348, and Emanuel Adler, "Seizing the Middle Ground: Constructivism in World Politics," *European Journal of International Relations*, Vol. 3, No. 3 (1997), pp. 319–363.

86. Ibid., p. 479.

V. I. Lenin

FROM *IMPERIALISM, THE HIGHEST STAGE OF CAPITALISM*

■ ■ ■

Chapter V

The Division of the World among Capitalist Combines

Monopolist capitalist combines—cartels, syndicates, trusts—divide among themselves, first of all, the whole internal market of a country, and impose their control, more or less completely, upon the industry of that country. But under capitalism the home market is inevitably bound up with the foreign market. Capitalism long ago created a world market. As the export of capital increased, and as the foreign and colonial relations and the "spheres of influence" of the big monopolist combines expanded, things "naturally" gravitated towards an international agreement among these combines, and towards the formation of international cartels.

This is a new stage of world concentration of capital and production, incomparably higher than the preceding stages. Let us see how this super-monopoly develops.

■ ■ ■

From V. I. Lenin, *Imperialism, the Highest Stage of Capitalism: A Popular Outline* (1917, trans. and repr. New York: International Publishers, 1939). The order of some passages has been changed. The author's notes have been omitted.

Chapter X

The Place of Imperialism in History

We have seen that the economic quintessence of imperialism is monopoly capitalism. This very fact determines its place in history, for monopoly that grew up on the basis of free competition, and precisely out of free competition, is the transition from the capitalist system to a higher social-economic order. We must take special note of the four principal forms of monopoly, or the four principal manifestations of monopoly capitalism, which are characteristic of the epoch under review.

Firstly, monopoly arose out of the concentration of production at a very advanced stage of development. This refers to the monopolist capitalist combines, cartels, syndicates and trusts. We have seen the important part that these play in modern economic life. At the beginning of the twentieth century, monopolies acquired complete supremacy in the advanced countries. And although the first steps towards the formation of the cartels were first taken by countries enjoying the protection of high tariffs (Germany, America), Great Britain, with her system of free trade, was not far behind in revealing the same basic phenomenon, namely, the birth of monopoly out of the concentration of production.

Secondly, monopolies have accelerated the capture of the most important sources of raw materials, especially for the coal and iron industries, which are the basic and most highly cartelised industries in capitalist society. The monopoly of the most important sources of raw materials has enormously increased the power of big capital, and has sharpened the antagonism between cartelised and non-cartelised industry.

Thirdly, monopoly has sprung from the banks. The banks have developed from modest intermediary enterprises into the monopolists of finance capital. Some three or five of the biggest banks in each of the foremost capitalist countries have achieved the "personal union" of industrial and bank capital, and have concentrated in their hands the disposal of thousands upon thousands of millions which form the greater part of the capital and income of entire countries. A financial oligarchy, which throws a close net of relations of dependence over all the economic and political institutions of contemporary bourgeois society without exception—such is the most striking manifestation of this monopoly.

Fourthly, monopoly has grown out of colonial policy. To the numerous "old" motives of colonial policy, finance capital has added the struggle for the sources of raw materials, for the export of capital, for "spheres of influence," *i.e.*, for spheres for profitable deals, concessions, monopolist profits and so on; in fine, for economic territory in general. When the colonies of the European powers in Africa, for instance, comprised only one-tenth of that territory (as was the case in 1876), colonial policy was able to develop by methods other than those of monopoly—by the "free grabbing" of territories, so to speak. But when nine-tenths of Africa had been seized (approximately by 1900), when the whole world had been divided up, there was inevitably ushered in a period of colonial monopoly and, consequently, a period of particularly intense struggle for the division and the redivision of the world.

The extent to which monopolist capital has intensified all the contradictions of capitalism is generally known. It is sufficient to mention the high cost of living and the oppression of the cartels. This intensification of contradictions constitutes the most powerful driving force of the transitional period of history, which began from the time of the definite victory of world finance capital.

Monopolies, oligarchy, the striving for domination instead of the striving for liberty, the exploitation of an increasing number of small or weak nations by an extremely small group of the richest or most powerful nations—all these have given birth to those distinctive characteristics of imperialism which compel us to define it as parasitic or decaying capitalism. More and more prominently there emerges, as one of the tendencies of imperialism, the creation of the "bond-holding" (rentier) state, the usurer state, in which the bourgeoisie lives on the proceeds of capital exports and by clipping coupons. It would be a mistake to believe that this tendency to decay precludes the possibility of the rapid growth of capitalism. It does not. In the epoch of imperialism, certain branches of industry, certain strata of the bourgeoisie and certain countries betray, to a more or less degree, one or other of these tendencies. On the whole, capitalism is growing far more rapidly than before. But this growth is not only becoming more and more uneven in general; its unevenness also manifests itself, in particular, in the decay of the countries which are richest in capital (such as England).

■　　■　　■

When free competition in Great Britain was at its zenith, *i.e.,* between 1840 and 1860, the leading British bourgeois politicians were opposed to colonial policy and were of the opinion that the liberation of the colonies and their complete separation from Britain was inevitable and desirable. M. Beer, in an article, "Modern British Imperialism," published in 1898, shows that in 1852, Disraeli, a statesman generally inclined towards imperialism, declared: "The colonies are millstones round our necks." But at the end of the nineteenth century the heroes of the hour in England were Cecil

Rhodes and Joseph Chamberlain, open advocates of imperialism, who applied the imperialist policy in the most cynical manner.

It is not without interest to observe that even at that time these leading British bourgeois politicians fully appreciated the connection between what might be called the purely economic and the politico-social roots of modern imperialism. Chamberlain advocated imperialism by calling it a "true, wise and economical policy," and he pointed particularly to the German, American and Belgian competition which Great Britain was encountering in the world market. Salvation lies in monopolies, said the capitalists as they formed cartels, syndicates and trusts. Salvation lies in monopolies, echoed the political leaders of the bourgeoisie, hastening to appropriate the parts of the world not yet shared out. The journalist, Stead, relates the following remarks uttered by his close friend Cecil Rhodes, in 1895, regarding his imperialist ideas:

I was in the East End of London yesterday and attended a meeting of the unemployed. I listened to the wild speeches, which were just a cry for "bread," "bread," "bread," and on my way home I pondered over the scene and I became more than ever convinced of the importance of imperialism. . . . My cherished idea is a solution for the social problem, *i.e.,* in order to save the 40,000,000 inhabitants of the United Kingdom from a bloody civil war, we colonial statesmen must acquire new lands to settle the surplus population, to provide new markets for the goods produced by them in the factories and mines. The Empire, as I have always said, is a bread and butter question. If you want to avoid civil war, you must become imperialists.

This is what Cecil Rhodes, millionaire, king of finance, the man who was mainly responsible for the Boer War, said in 1895. * * *

■   ■   ■

* * * The unevenness in the rate of expansion of colonial possessions is very marked. If, for instance, we compare France, Germany and Japan, which do not differ very much in area and population, we will see that the first has annexed almost three times as much colonial territory as the other two combined. In regard to finance capital, also, France, at the beginning of the period we are considering, was perhaps several times richer than Germany and Japan put together. In addition to, and on the basis of, purely economic causes, geographical conditions and other factors also affect the dimensions of colonial possessions. However strong the process of levelling the world, of levelling the economic and living conditions in different countries, may have been in the past decades as a result of the pressure of large-scale industry, exchange and finance capital, great differences still remain; and among the six powers, we see, firstly, young capitalist powers (America, Germany, Japan) which progressed very rapidly; secondly, countries with an old capitalist development (France and Great Britain), which, of late, have made much slower progress than the previously mentioned countries; and, thirdly, a country (Russia) which is economically most backward, in which modern capitalist imperialism is enmeshed, so to speak, in a particularly close network of precapitalist relations.

■   ■   ■

Colonial policy and imperialism existed before this latest stage of capitalism, and even before capitalism. Rome, founded on slavery, pursued a colonial policy and achieved imperialism. But "general" arguments about imperialism, which ignore, or put into the background the fundamental difference of social-economic systems, inevitably degenerate into absolutely empty banalities, or into grandiloquent comparisons like "Greater Rome and Greater Britain." Even the colonial policy of capitalism in its *previous* stages is essentially different from the colonial policy of finance capital.

The principal feature of modern capitalism is the domination of monopolist combines of the big capitalists. These monopolies are most firmly established when *all* the sources of raw materials are controlled by the one group. And we have seen with what zeal the international capitalist combines exert every effort to make it impossible for their rivals to compete with them; for example, by buying up mineral lands, oil fields, etc. Colonial possession alone gives complete guarantee of success to the monopolies against all the risks of the struggle with competitors, including the risk that the latter will defend themselves by means of a law establishing a state monopoly. The more capitalism is developed, the more the need for raw materials is felt, the more bitter competition becomes, and the more feverishly the hunt for raw materials proceeds throughout the whole world, the more desperate becomes the struggle for the acquisition of colonies.

■   ■   ■

The bourgeois reformists, and among them particularly the present-day adherents of Kautsky, of course, try to belittle the importance of facts of this kind by arguing that it "would be possible" to obtain raw materials in the open market without a "costly and dangerous" colonial policy; and that it would be "possible" to increase the supply of raw materials to an enormous extent "simply" by improving agriculture. But these arguments are merely an apology for imperialism, an attempt to embellish it, because they ignore the principal feature of modern capitalism: monopoly. Free markets are becoming more and more a thing of the past; monopolist syndicates and trusts are restricting them more and more every day, and "simply" improving agriculture reduces itself to improving the conditions of the masses, to raising wages and reducing profits. Where, except in the

imagination of the sentimental reformists, are there any trusts capable of interesting themselves in the condition of the masses instead of the conquest of colonies?

Finance capital is not only interested in the already known sources of raw materials; it is also interested in potential sources of raw materials, because present-day technical development is extremely rapid, and because land which is useless today may be made fertile tomorrow if new methods are applied (to devise these new methods a big bank can equip a whole expedition of engineers, agricultural experts, etc.), and large amounts of capital are invested. This also applies to prospecting for minerals, to new methods of working up and utilising raw materials, etc., etc. Hence, the inevitable striving of finance capital to extend its economic territory and even its territory in general. In the same way that the trusts capitalise their property by estimating it at two or three times its value, taking into account its "potential" (and not present) returns, and the further results of monopoly, so finance capital strives to seize the largest possible amount of land of all kinds and in any place it can, and by any means, counting on the possibilities of finding raw materials there, and fearing to be left behind in the insensate struggle for the last available scraps of undivided territory, or for the repartition of that which has been already divided.

■   ■   ■

The necessity of exporting capital also gives an impetus to the conquest of colonies, for in the colonial market it is easier to eliminate competition, to make sure of orders, to strengthen the necessary "connections," etc., by monopolist methods (and sometimes it is the only possible way).

The non-economic superstructure which grows up on the basis of finance capital, its politics and its ideology, stimulates the striving for colonial conquest. "Finance capital does not want liberty, it wants domination," as Hilferding very truly says. * * *

■   ■   ■

Since we are speaking of colonial policy in the period of capitalist imperialism, it must be observed that finance capital and its corresponding foreign policy, which reduces itself to the struggle of the Great Powers for the economic and political division of the world, give rise to a number of *transitional* forms of national dependence. The division of the world into two main groups—of colony-owning countries on the one hand and colonies on the other—is not the only typical feature of this period; there is also a variety of forms of dependent countries; countries which, officially, are politically independent, but which are, in fact, enmeshed in the net of financial and diplomatic dependence. We have already referred to one form of dependence—the semi-colony. Another example is provided by Argentina.

"South America, and especially Argentina," writes Schulze-Gaevernitz in his work on British imperialism, "is so dependent financially on London that it ought to be described as almost a British commercial colony."

■   ■   ■

Chapter VII

Imperialism as a Special Stage of Capitalism

We must now try to sum up and put together what has been said above on the subject of imperialism. Imperialism emerged as the development and direct continuation of the fundamental attributes of capitalism in general. But capitalism only became capitalist imperialism at a definite and very high stage of its development, when certain of its fundamental attributes began to be transformed into their opposites; when the features of a period of transition from capitalism to a higher social and economic system began to take shape and reveal themselves all along the line. Economically, the main thing in this process is the substitution of capitalist monopolies for capitalist free competition. Free competition is the fundamental attribute of capitalism, and of commodity production generally. Monopoly is exactly the opposite of free competition; but we have seen the latter being transformed into monopoly before our very eyes, creating large-scale industry and eliminating small industry, replacing large-scale industry by still larger-scale industry, finally leading to such a concentration of production and capital that monopoly has been and is the result: cartels, syndicates and trusts, and merging with them, the capital of a dozen or so banks manipulating thousands of millions. At the same time monopoly, which has grown out of free competition, does not abolish the latter, but exists over it and alongside of it, and thereby gives rise to a number of very acute, intense antagonisms, friction and conflicts. Monopoly is the transition from capitalism to a higher system.

If it were necessary to give the briefest possible definition of imperialism we should have to say that imperialism is the monopoly stage of capitalism. Such a definition would include what is most important, for, on the one hand, finance capital is the bank capital of a few big monopolist banks, merged with the capital of the monopolist combines of manufacturers; and, on the other hand, the division of the world is the transition from a colonial policy which has extended without hindrance to territories unoccupied by any capitalist power, to a colonial policy of monopolistic possession of the territory of the world which has been completely divided up.

But very brief definitions, although convenient, for they sum up the main points, are nevertheless inadequate, because very important features of the phenomenon that has to be defined have to be especially deduced. And so, without forgetting the conditional and relative value of all definitions, which can never include all the concatenations of a phenomenon in its complete development, we must give a definition of imperialism that will embrace the following five essential features:

1. The concentration of production and capital developed to such a high stage that it created monopolies which play a decisive role in economic life.
2. The merging of bank capital with industrial capital, and the creation, on the basis of this "finance capital," of a "financial oligarchy."
3. The export of capital, which has become extremely important, as distinguished from the export of commodities.
4. The formation of international capitalist monopolies which share the world among themselves.
5. The territorial division of the whole world among the greatest capitalist powers is completed.

Imperialism is capitalism in that stage of development in which the dominance of monopolies and finance capital has established itself; in which the export of capital has acquired pronounced importance; in which the division of the world among the international trusts has begun; in which the division of all territories of the globe among the great capitalist powers has been completed.

■   ■   ■

Another special feature of imperialism, which is connected with the facts we are describing, is the decline in emigration from imperialist countries, and the increase in immigration into these countries from the backward countries where lower wages are paid. As Hobson observes, emigration from Great Britain has been declining since 1884. In

that year the number of emigrants was 242,000, while in 1900, the number was only 169,000. German emigration reached the highest point between 1880 and 1890, with a total of 1,453,000 emigrants. In the course of the following two decades, it fell to 544,000 and even to 341,000. On the other hand, there was an increase in the number of workers entering Germany from Austria, Italy, Russia and other countries. According to the 1907 census, there were 1,342,294 foreigners in Germany, of whom 440,800 were industrial workers and 257,329 were agricultural workers. In France, the workers employed in the mining industry are, "in great part," foreigners: Polish, Italian and Spanish. In the United States, immigrants from Eastern and Southern Europe are engaged in the most poorly paid occupations, while American workers provide the highest percentage of overseers or of the better paid workers. Imperialism has the tendency to create privileged sections even among the workers, and to detach them from the main proletarian masses.

It must be observed that in Great Britain the tendency of imperialism to divide the workers, to encourage opportunism among them and to cause temporary decay in the working class movement, revealed itself much earlier than the end of the nineteenth and the beginning of the twentieth centuries; for two important distinguishing features of imperialism were observed in Great Britain in the middle of the nineteenth century, *viz.,* vast colonial possessions and a monopolist position in the world market. Marx and Engels systematically traced this relation between opportunism in the labour movement and the imperialist features of British capitalism for several decades. For example, on October 7, 1858, Engels wrote to Marx:

The English proletariat is becoming more and more bourgeois, so that this most bourgeois of all nations is apparently aiming ultimately at the possession of a bourgeois aristocracy, and a bourgeois proletariat *as well as* a bourgeoisie.

For a nation which exploits the whole world—this is, of course, to a certain extent justifiable.

Almost a quarter of a century later, in a letter dated August 11, 1881, Engels speaks of ". . . the worst type of English trade unions which allow themselves to be led by men sold to, or at least, paid by the bourgeoisie." In a letter to Kautsky, dated September 12, 1882, Engels wrote:

> You ask me what the English workers think about colonial policy? Well, exactly the same as they think about politics in general. There is no workers' party here, there are only Conservatives and Liberal-Radicals, and the workers merrily share the feast of England's monopoly of the colonies and the world market. . . . [Engels expressed similar ideas in the press in his preface to the second edition of *The Condition of the Working Class in England,* which appeared in 1892.]

We thus see clearly the causes and effects. The causes are: 1) Exploitation of the whole world by this country. 2) Its monopolistic position in the world market. 3) Its colonial monopoly. The effects are: 1) A section of the British proletariat becomes bourgeois. 2) A section of the proletariat permits itself to be led by men sold to, or at least, paid by the bourgeoisie. The imperialism of the beginning of the twentieth century completed the division of the world among a handful of states, each of which today exploits (*i.e.,* draws super-profits from) a part of the world only a little smaller than that which England exploited in 1858. * * *

The distinctive feature of the present situation is the prevalence of economic and political conditions which could not but increase the irreconcilability between opportunism and the general and vital interests of the working class movement. Embryonic imperialism has grown into a dominant system; capitalist monopolies occupy first place in economics and politics; the division of the world has been completed. On the other hand, instead of an undisputed monopoly by Great Britain, we see a few imperialist powers contending for the right to share in this monopoly, and this struggle is characteristic of the whole period of the beginning of the twentieth century. Opportunism, therefore, cannot now triumph in the working class movement of any country for decades as it did in England in the second half of the nineteenth century. But, in a number of countries it has grown ripe, over-ripe, and rotten, and has become completely merged with bourgeois policy in the form of "social-chauvinism."

■   ■   ■

Chapter IX

The Critique of Imperialism

By the critique of imperialism, in the broad sense of the term, we mean the attiude towards imperialist policy of the different classes of society as part of their general ideology.

The enormous dimensions of finance capital concentrated in a few hands and creating an extremely extensive and close network of ties and relationships which subordinate not only the small and medium, but also even the very small capitalists and small masters, on the one hand, and the intense struggle waged against other national state groups of financiers for the division of the world and domination over other countries, on the other hand, cause the wholesale transition of the possessing classes to the side of imperialism. The signs of the times are a "general" enthusiasm regarding its prospects, a passionate defence of imperialism, and every possible embellishment of its real nature. The imperialist ideology also penetrates the working class. There is no Chinese Wall between it and the other classes. The leaders of the so-called "Social-Democratic"

Party of Germany are today justly called "social-imperialists," that is, socialists in words and imperialists in deeds; but as early as 1902, Hobson noted the existence of "Fabian imperialists" who belonged to the opportunist Fabian Society in England.

Bourgeois scholars and publicists usually come out in defence of imperialism in a somewhat veiled form, and obscure its complete domination and its profound roots; they strive to concentrate attention on partial and secondary details and do their very best to distract attention from the main issue by means of ridiculous schemes for "reform," such as police supervision of the trusts and banks, etc. Less frequently, cynical and frank imperialists speak out and are bold enough to admit the absurdity of the idea of reforming the fundamental features of imperialism.

■ ■ ■

Robert O. Keohane

FROM *AFTER HEGEMONY*
Cooperation and Discord in the World Political Economy

Realism, Institutionalism, and Cooperation

Impressed with the difficulties of cooperation, observers have often compared world politics to a "state of war." In this conception, international politics is "a competition of units in the kind of state of nature that knows no restraints other than those which the changing necessities of the game and the shallow conveniences of the players impose" (Hoffmann, 1965, p. vii). It is anarchic in the sense that it lacks an authoritative government that can enact and enforce rules of behavior. States must rely on "the means they can generate and the arrangements they can make for themselves" (Waltz, 1979, p. 111). Conflict and war result, since each state is judge in its own cause and can use force to carry out its judgments (Waltz, 1959, p. 159). The discord that prevails is accounted for by fundamental conflicts of interest (Waltz, 1959; Tucker, 1977).

Were this portrayal of world politics correct, any cooperation that occurs would be derivative from overall patterns of conflict. Alliance cooperation would be easy to explain as a result of the operation of a balance of power, but system-wide patterns of cooperation that benefit many countries without being tied to an alliance system

directed against an adversary would not. If international politics were a state of war, institutionalized patterns of cooperation on the basis of shared purposes should not exist except as part of a larger struggle for power. The extensive patterns of international agreement that we observe on issues as diverse as trade, financial relations, health, telecommunications, and environmental protection would be absent.

At the other extreme from these "Realists" are writers who see cooperation as essential in a world of economic interdependence, and who argue that shared economic interests create a demand for international institutions and rules (Mitrany, 1975). Such an approach, which I refer to as "Institutionalist" because of its adherents' emphasis on the functions performed by international institutions, runs the risk of being naive about power and conflict. Too often its proponents incorporate in their theories excessively optimistic assumptions about the role of ideals in world politics, or about the ability of statesmen to learn what the theorist considers the "right lessons." But sophisticated students of institutions and rules have a good deal to teach us. They view institutions not simply as formal organizations with headquarters buildings and specialized staffs, but more broadly as "recognized patterns of practice around which expectations converge" (Young, 1980, p. 337). They regard these patterns of practice as significant because they affect state behavior. Sophisticated institutionalists do not expect cooperation always to prevail, but they are aware of the malleability of

From Robert O. Keohane, *After Hegemony: Cooperation and Discord in the World Political Economy* (Princeton, NJ: Princeton University Press, 1984), chaps. 1, 6, 7. Some of the author's notes have been omitted.

interests and they argue that interdependence creates interests in cooperation.

During the first twenty years or so after World War II, these views, though very different in their intellectual origins and their broader implications about human society, made similar predictions about the world political economy, and particularly about the subject of this [discussion], the political economy of the advanced market-economy countries. Institutionalists expected successful cooperation in one field to "spill over" into others (Haas, 1958). Realists anticipated a relatively stable international economic order as a result of the dominance of the United States. Neither set of observers was surprised by what happened, although they interpreted events differently.

Institutionalists could interpret the liberal international arrangements for trade and international finance as responses to the need for policy coordination created by the fact of interdependence. These arrangements, which we will call "international regimes," contained rules, norms, principles, and decisionmaking procedures. Realists could reply that these regimes were constructed on the basis of principles espoused by the United States, and that American power was essential for their construction and maintenance. For Realists, in other words, the early postwar regimes rested on the *political hegemony* of the United States. Thus Realists and Institutionalists could both regard early postwar developments as supporting their theories.

After the mid-1960s, however, U.S. dominance in the world political economy was challenged by the economic recovery and increasing unity of Europe and by the rapid economic growth of Japan. Yet economic interdependence continued to grow, and the pace of increased U.S. involvement in the world economy even accelerated after 1970. At this point, therefore, the Institutionalist and Realist predictions began to diverge. From a strict Institutionalist standpoint, the increasing need for coordination of policy, created by interdependence, should have led to more cooperation. From

a Realist perspective, by contrast, the diffusion of power should have undermined the ability of anyone to create order.

On the surface, the Realists would seem to have made the better forecast. Since the late 1960s there have been signs of decline in the extent and efficacy of efforts to cooperate in the world political economy. As American power eroded, so did international regimes. The erosion of these regimes after World War II certainly refutes a naive version of the Institutionalist faith in interdependence as a solvent of conflict and a creator of cooperation. But it does not prove that only the Realist emphasis on power as a creator of order is valid. It might be possible, after the decline of hegemonic regimes, for more symmetrical patterns of cooperation to evolve after a transitional period of discord. Indeed, the persistence of attempts at cooperation during the 1970s suggests that the decline of hegemony does not necessarily sound cooperation's death knell.

International cooperation and discord thus remain puzzling. Under what conditions can independent countries cooperate in the world political economy? In particular, can cooperation take place without hegemony and, if so, how? This [project] is designed to help us find answers to these questions. I begin with Realist insights about the role of power and the effects of hegemony. But my central arguments draw more on the Institutionalist tradition, arguing that cooperation can under some conditions develop on the basis of complementary interests, and that institutions, broadly defined, affect the patterns of cooperation that emerge.

Hegemonic leadership is unlikely to be revived in this century for the United States or any other country. Hegemonic powers have historically only emerged after world wars; during peacetime, weaker countries have tended to gain on the hegemon rather than vice versa (Gilpin, 1981). It is difficult to believe that world civilization, much less a complex international economy, would survive such a war in the nuclear age. Certainly no prosperous hegemonic power is likely to emerge from such a cataclysm. As long as a world political economy persists, therefore, its central political dilemma will be how to organize cooperation without hegemony.

■ ■ ■

A Functional Theory of International Regimes

* * * [I]nternational regimes could be created and emphasized their value for overcoming what could be called "political market failure." * * * [Following is a] detailed examination of this argument by exploring why political market failure occurs and how international regimes can help to overcome it. This investigation will help us understand both why states often comply with regime rules and why international regimes can be maintained even after the conditions that facilitated their creation have disappeared. The functional theory developed in this chapter will therefore suggest some reasons to believe that even if U.S. hegemonic leadership may have been a crucial factor in the creation of some contemporary international economic regimes, the continuation of hegemony is not necessarily essential for their continued viability.

Political Market Failure and the Coase Theorem

Like imperfect markets, world politics is characterized by institutional deficiencies that inhibit mutually advantageous cooperation. * * * [I]n this self-help system, [there are] conflicts of interest between actors. In economic terms, these conflicts can be regarded as arising in part from the existence of externalities: actors do not bear the full costs, or receive the full benefits, of their own actions.[1] Yet in a famous article Ronald Coase (1960) argued that the presence of externalities

alone does not necessarily prevent effective coordination among independent actors. Under certain conditions, declared Coase, bargaining among these actors could lead to solutions that are Pareto-optimal regardless of the rules of legal liability.

To illustrate the Coase theorem and its counter-intuitive result, suppose that soot emitted by a paint factory is deposited by the wind onto clothing hanging outdoors in the yard of an old-fashioned laundry. Assume that the damage to the laundry is greater than the $20,000 it would cost the laundry to enclose its yard and install indoor drying equipment; so if no other alternative were available, it would be worthwhile for the laundry to take these actions. Assume also, however, that it would cost the paint factory only $10,000 to eliminate its emissions of air pollutants. Social welfare would clearly be enhanced by eliminating the pollution rather than by installing indoor drying equipment, but in the absence of either governmental enforcement or bargaining, the egoistic owner of the paint factory would have no incentive to spend anything to achieve this result.

It has frequently been argued that this sort of situation requires centralized governmental authority to provide the public good of clean air. Thus if the laundry had an enforceable legal right to demand compensation, the factory owner would have an incentive to invest $10,000 in pollution control devices to avoid a $20,000 court judgment. Coase argued, however, that the pollution would be cleaned up equally efficiently even if the laundry had no such recourse. If the law, or the existence of a decentralized self-help system, gave the factory a right to pollute, the laundry owner could simply pay the factory owner a sum greater than $10,000, but less than $20,000, to install anti-soot equipment. Both parties would agree to some such bargain, since both would benefit.

In either case, the externality of pollution would be eliminated. The key difference would not be one of economic efficiency, but of distribution of benefits between the factory and the laundry. In a self-help system, the laundry would have to pay between $10,000 and $20,000 and the factory would reap a profit from its capacity to pollute. But if legal liability rules were based on "the polluter pays principle," the laundry would pay nothing and the factory would have to invest $10,000 without reaping a financial return. Coase did not dispute that rules of liability could be evaluated on grounds of fairness, but insisted that, given his assumptions, efficient arrangements could be consummated even where the rules of liability favored producers of externalities rather than their victims.

The Coase theorem has frequently been used to show the efficacy of bargaining without central authority, and it has occasionally been applied specifically to international relations (Conybeare, 1980). The principle of sovereignty in effect establishes rules of liability that put the burden of externalities on those who suffer from them. The Coase theorem could be interpreted, therefore, as predicting that problems of collective action could easily be overcome in international politics through bargaining and mutual adjustment—that is, through cooperation * * *. The further inference could be drawn that the discord observed must be the result of fundamental conflicts of interest rather than problems of coordination. The Coase theorem, in other words, could be taken as minimizing the importance of [Mancur] Olson's [1965] perverse logic of collective action or of the problems of coordination emphasized by game theory. However, such a conclusion would be incorrect for two compelling sets of reasons.

In the first place, Coase specified three crucial conditions for his conclusion to hold. These were: a legal framework establishing liability for actions, presumably supported by governmental authority; perfect information; and zero transaction costs (including organization costs and the costs of making side-payments). It is absolutely clear that none of these conditions is met in world politics. World government does not exist, making property rights and rules of legal liability fragile; information is

extremely costly and often held unequally by different actors; transaction costs, including costs of organization and side-payments, are often very high. Thus an *inversion* of the Coase theorem would seem more appropriate to our subject. In the absence of the conditions that Coase specified, coordination will often be thwarted by dilemmas of collective action.

Second, recent critiques of Coase's argument reinforce the conclusion that it cannot simply be applied to world politics, and suggest further interesting implications about the functions of international regimes. It has been shown on the basis of game theory that, with more than two participants, the Coase theorem cannot necessarily be demonstrated. Under certain conditions, there will be no stable solution: any coalition that forms will be inferior, for at least one of its members, to another possible coalition. The result is an infinite regress. In game-theoretic terminology, the "core" of the game is empty. When the core is empty, the assumption of zero transaction costs means that agreement is hindered rather than facilitated: "in a world of zero transaction costs, the inherent instability of all coalitions could result in endless recontracting among the firms" (Aivazian and Callen, 1981, p. 179; Veljanovski, 1982).

What do Coase and his critics together suggest about the conditions for international cooperation through bargaining? First, it appears that approximating Coase's first two conditions—that is, having a clear legal framework establishing property rights and low-cost information available in a roughly equal way to all parties—will tend to facilitate cooperative solutions. But the implications of reducing transaction costs are more complex. If transaction costs are too high, no bargains will take place; but if they are too low, under certain conditions an infinite series of unstable coalitions may form.

Inverting the Coase theorem allows us to analyze international institutions largely as responses to problems of property rights, uncertainty, and transaction costs. Without consciously designed institutions, these problems will thwart attempts to cooperate in world politics even when actors' interests are complementary. From the deficiency of the "self-help system" (even from the perspective of purely self-interested national actors) we derive a need for international regimes. Insofar as they fill this need, international regimes perform the functions of establishing patterns of legal liability, providing relatively symmetrical information, and arranging the costs of bargaining so that specific agreements can more easily be made. Regimes are developed in part because actors in world politics believe that with such arrangements they will be able to make mutually beneficial agreements that would otherwise be difficult or impossible to attain.

This is to say that the architects of regimes anticipate that the regimes will facilitate cooperation. Within the functional argument being constructed here, these expectations explain the formation of the regimes: the *anticipated effects* of the regimes account for the actions of governments that establish them. Governments believe that *ad hoc* attempts to construct particular agreements, without a regime framework, will yield inferior results compared to negotiations within the framework of regimes. Following our inversion of the Coase theorem, we can classify the reasons for this belief under the categories of legal liability (property rights), transaction costs, and problems of uncertainty. We will consider these issues in turn.

LEGAL LIABILITY

Since governments put a high value on the maintenance of their own autonomy, it is usually impossible to establish international institutions that exercise authority over states. This fact is widely recognized by officials of international organizations and their advocates in national governments as well as by scholars. It would therefore be mistaken to regard international regimes, or the organizations that constitute elements of them, as characteristically unsuccessful attempts to institutionalize centralized authority in world politics. They cannot establish patterns of legal liability that are as solid as those developed within well-ordered societies, and their architects are well aware of this limitation.

Of course, the lack of a hierarchical structure of world politics does not prevent regimes from developing bits and pieces of law (Henkin, 1979, pp. 13–22). But the principal significance of international regimes does not lie in their formal legal status, since any patterns of legal liability and property rights established in world politics are subject to being overturned by the actions of sovereign states. International regimes are more like the "quasi-agreements" that William Fellner (1949) discusses when analyzing the behavior of oligopolistic firms than they are like governments. These quasi-agreements are legally unenforceable but, like contracts, help to organize relationships in mutually beneficial ways (Lowry, 1979, p. 276) Regimes also resemble conventions: practices, regarded as common knowledge in a community, that actors conform to not because they are uniquely best, but because others conform to them as well (Hardin, 1982; Lewis, 1969; Young, 1983). What these arrangements have in common is that they are designed not to implement centralized enforcement of agreements, but rather to establish stable mutual expectations about others' patterns of behavior and to develop working relationships that will allow the parties to adapt their practices to new situations. Contracts, conventions, and quasi-agreements provide information and generate patterns of transaction costs: costs of reneging on commitments are increased, and the costs of operating within these frameworks are reduced.

Both these arrangements and international regimes are often weak and fragile. Like contracts and quasi-agreements, international regimes are frequently altered: their rules are changed, bent, or broken to meet the exigencies of the moment. They are rarely enforced automatically, and they are not self-executing. Indeed, they are often matters for negotiation and renegotiation. As [Donald] Puchala has argued, "attempts to enforce EEC regulations open political cleavages up and down the supranational-to-local continuum and spark intense politicking along the cleavage lines" (1975, p. 509).

TRANSACTION COSTS

Like oligopolistic quasi-agreements, international regimes alter the relative costs of transactions. Certain agreements are forbidden. Under the provisions of the General Agreement on Tariffs and Trade (GATT), for instance, it is not permitted to make discriminatory trade arrangements except under specific conditions. Since there is no centralized government, states can nevertheless implement such actions, but their lack of legitimacy means that such measures are likely to be costly. Under GATT rules, for instance, retaliation against such behavior is justified. By elevating injunctions to the level of principles and rules, furthermore, regimes construct linkages between issues. No longer does a specific discriminatory agreement constitute merely a particular act without general significance; on the contrary, it becomes a "violation of GATT" with serious implications for a large number of other issues. In the terms of Prisoners' Dilemma, the situation has been transformed from a single-play to an iterated game. In market-failure terms, the transaction costs of certain possible bargains have been increased, while the costs of others have been reduced. In either case, the result is the same: incentives to violate regime principles are reduced. International regimes reduce transaction costs of legitimate bargains and increase them for illegitimate ones.

International regimes also affect transaction costs in the more mundane sense of making it cheaper for governments to get together to negotiate agreements. It is more convenient to make agreements within a regime than outside of one. International economic regimes usually incorporate international organizations that provide forums for meetings and secretariats that can act as catalysts for agreement. Insofar as their principles and rules can be applied to a wide variety of particular issues, they are efficient: establishing the rules and principles at the outset makes it unnecessary to renegotiate them each time a specific question arises.

International regimes thus allow governments to take advantage of potential economics of scale. Once a regime has been established, the marginal cost of dealing with each additional issue will be lower than it would be without a regime. * * * [I]f a policy area is sufficiently dense, establishing a regime will be worthwhile. Up to a point there may even be what economists call "increasing returns to scale." In such a situation, each additional issue could be included under the regime at lower cost than the previous one. As [Paul] Samuelson notes, in modern economies, "increasing returns is the prime case of deviations from perfect competition" (1967, p. 117). In world politics, we should expect increasing returns to scale to lead to more extensive international regimes.

In view of the benefits of economies of scale, it is not surprising that specific agreements tend to be "nested" within regimes. For instance, an agreement by the United States, Japan, and the European Community in the Multilateral Trade Negotiations to reduce a particular tariff will be affected by the rules and principles of GATT—that is, by the trade regime. The trade regime, in turn, is nested within a set of other arrangements, including those for monetary relations, energy, foreign investment, aid to developing countries, and other issues, which together constitute a complex and interlinked pattern of relations among the advanced market-economy countries. These, in turn, are related to military-security relations among the major states.[2]

The nesting patterns of international regimes affect transaction costs by making it easier or more difficult to link particular issues and to arrange side-payments, giving someone something on one issue in return for her help on another.[3] Clustering of issues under a regime facilitates side-payments among these issues: more potential *quids* are available for the *quo*. Without international regimes linking clusters of issues to one another, side-payments and linkages would be difficult to arrange in world politics; in the absence of a price system for the exchange of favors, institutional barriers would hinder the construction of mutually beneficial bargains.

Suppose, for instance, that each issue were handled separately from all others, by a different governmental bureau in each country. Since a side-payment or linkage always means that a government must give up something on one dimension to get something on another, there would always be a bureaucratic loser within each government. Bureaus that would lose from proposed side-payments, on issues that matter to them, would be unlikely to bear the costs of these linkages willingly on the basis of other agencies' claims that the national interest required it.

Of course, each issue is not considered separately by a different governmental department or bureau. On the contrary, issues are grouped together, in functionally organized departments such as Treasury, Commerce, and Energy (in the United States). Furthermore, how governments organize themselves to deal with foreign policy is affected by how issues are organized internationally; issues considered by different regimes are often dealt with by different bureaucracies at home. Linkages and side-payments among issues grouped in the same regime thus become easier, since the necessary internal tradeoffs will tend to take place within rather than across bureaus; but linkages among issues falling into different regimes will remain difficult, or even become more so (since the natural linkages on those issues will be with issues within the same regime).

Insofar as issues are dealt with separately from one another on the international level, it is often hard, in simply bureaucratic terms, to arrange for them to be considered together. There are bound to be difficulties in coordinating policies of different international organizations—GATT, the IMF [International Monetary Fund], and the IEA [International Energy Agency] all have different memberships and different operating styles—in addition to the resistance that will appear to such a move within member governments. Within regimes, by contrast, side-payments are facilitated by the fact that regimes bring together negotiators to consider sets of issues that may well lie within the negotiators' bureaucratic bailiwicks at home. GATT negotiations, as well as deliberations on the international monetary system, have been characterized by extensive bargaining over side-payments and the politics of issue-linkage (Hutton, 1975). The well-known literature on "spillover" in bargaining, relating to the European Community and other integration schemes, can also be interpreted as concerned with side-payments. According to these writings, expectations that an integration arrangement can be expanded to new issue-areas permit the broadening of potential side-payments, thus facilitating agreement (Haas, 1958).

We conclude that international regimes affect the costs of transactions. The value of a potential agreement to its prospective participants will depend, in part, on how consistent it is with principles of legitimacy embodied in international regimes. Transactions that violate these principles will be costly. Regimes also affect bureaucratic costs of transactions: successful regimes organize issue-areas so that productive linkages (those that facilitate agreements consistent with the principles of the regime) are facilitated, while destructive linkages and bargains that are inconsistent with regime principles are discouraged.

UNCERTAINTY AND INFORMATION

From the perspective of market-failure theories, the informational functions of regimes are the most important of all. * * * [W]hat Akerlof [1970] called "quality uncertainty" was the crucial problem in [a] "market for lemons" example. Even in games of pure coordination with stable equilibria, this may be a problem. Conventions—commuters meeting under the clock at Grand Central Station, suburban families on a shopping trip "meeting at the car"—become important. But in simple games of coordination, severe information problems are not embedded in the structure of relationships, since actors have incentives to reveal information and their own preferences fully to one another. In these games the problem is to reach some point of agreement; but it may not matter much which of several possible points is chosen (Schelling, 1960/1978). Conventions are important and ingenuity may be required, but serious systemic impediments to the acquisition and exchange of information are lacking (Lewis, 1969; Young, 1983).

Yet as we have seen in * * * discussions of collective action and Prisoners' Dilemma, many situations—both in game theory and in world politics—are characterized by conflicts of interest as well as common interests. In such situations, actors have to worry about being deceived and double-crossed, just as the buyer of a used car has to guard against purchasing a "lemon." The literature on market failure elaborates on its most fundamental contention—that, in the absence of appropriate institutions, some mutually advantageous bargains will not be made because of uncertainty—by pointing to three particularly important sources of difficulty: *asymmetrical information; moral hazard;* and *irresponsibility.*

ASYMMETRICAL INFORMATION   Some actors may know more about a situation than others. Expecting that the resulting bargains would be unfair, "outsiders" will be reluctant to make agreements with "insiders" (Williamson, 1975, pp. 31–33). This is essentially the problem of "quality uncertainty" as discussed by Akerlof. Recall that this is a problem not merely of insufficient information, but rather of *systematically biased* patterns of information, which are recognized in advance of any agreement both by the holder of more information (the seller of the used car) and by its less well-informed prospective partner (the potential buyer of the "lemon" or "creampuff," as the case may be). Awareness that others have greater knowledge than oneself, and are therefore capable of manipulating a relationship or even engaging successful deception and double-cross, is a barrier to making agreements. When this suspicion is unfounded—that is, the agreement would be mutually beneficial—it is an obstacle to improving welfare through cooperation.

This problem of asymmetrical information only appears when dishonest behavior is possible. In a society of saints, communication would be open and no one would take advantage of superior information. In our imperfect world, however, asymmetries of information are not rectified simply by communication. Not all communication reduces uncertainty, since communication may lead to asymmetrical or unfair bargaining outcomes as a result of deception. Effective communication is not measured well by the amount of talking that used-car salespersons do to customers or that governmental officials do to one another in negotiating international regimes! The information that is required in entering into an international regime is not merely information about other governments' resources and formal negotiating positions, but also accurate knowledge of their future positions. In part, this is a matter of estimating whether they will keep their commitments. As the "market for lemons" example suggests, and as we will see in more detail below, a government's reputation therefore becomes an important asset in persuading others to enter into agreements with it. International regimes help governments to assess others' reputations by providing standards of behavior against which performance can be measured, by linking these standards to specific issues, and by providing forums, often through international organizations, in which these evaluations can be made.[4] Regimes may also include international organizations whose secretariats act not only as mediators but as providers of unbiased information that is made available, more or less equally to all members. By reducing asymmetries of information through a process of upgrading the general level of available information, international regimes reduce uncertainty. Agreements based on misapprehension and deception may be avoided; mutually beneficial agreements are more likely to be made.

Regimes provide information to members, thereby reducing risks of making agreements. But the information provided by a regime may be insufficiently detailed. A government may require precise information about its prospective partners' internal evaluations of a particular situation, their intentions, the intensity of their preferences, and their willingness to adhere to an agreement even in adverse future circumstances. Governments also need to know whether other participants will follow the spirit as well as the letter of agreements, whether they will share the burden of adjustment to unexpected adverse change, and whether they are likely to seek to strengthen the regime in the future.

The significance of asymmetrical information and quality uncertainty in theories of market failure therefore calls attention to the importance not only of international regimes but also of variations in the degree of closure of different states' decisionmaking processes. Some governments maintain secrecy much more zealously than others. American officials, for example, often lament that the U.S. government leaks information "like a sieve" and claim that this openness puts the United States at a disadvantage vis-à-vis its rivals.

Surely there are disadvantages in openness. The real or apparent incoherence in policy that often accompanies it may lead the open government's partners to view it as unreliable because its top leaders, whatever their intentions, are incapable of carrying out their agreements. A cacophony of messages may render all of them uninterpreta-ble. But some reflection on the problem of making agreements in world politics suggests that there are advantages for the open government that cannot be duplicated by countries with more tightly closed bureaucracies. Governments that cannot provide detailed and reliable information about their intentions—for instance, because their decisionmaking processes are closed to the outside world and their officials are prevented from developing frank informal relationships with their foreign counterparts—may be unable convincingly to persuade their potential partners of their commitment to the contemplated arrangements. Observers from other countries will be uncertain about the genuineness of officials' enthusiasm or the depth of their support for the cooperative scheme under consideration. These potential partners will therefore insist on discounting the value of prospective agreements to take account of their uncertainty. As in the "market for lemons," some potential agreements, which would be beneficial to all parties, will not be made because of "quality uncertainty"—about the quality of the closed government's commitment to the accord.[5]

MORAL HAZARD Agreements may alter incentives in such a way as to encourage less cooperative behavior. Insurance companies face this problem of "moral hazard." Property insurance, for instance, may make people less careful with their property and therefore increase the risk of loss (Arrow, 1974). The problem of moral hazard arises quite sharply in international banking. The solvency of a major country's largest banks may be essential to its financial system, or even to the stability of the entire international banking network. As a result, the country's central bank may have to intervene if one of these banks is threatened. The U.S. Federal Reserve, for instance, could hardly stand idly by while the Bank of America or Citibank became unable to meet its liabilities. Yet this responsibility creates a problem of moral hazard, since the largest banks, in effect, have automatic insurance against disastrous consequences of risky but (in the short-run at least) profitable loans. They have incentives to follow risk-seeking rather than risk-averse behavior at the expense of the central bank (Hirsch, 1977).

IRRESPONSIBILITY Some actors may be irresponsible, making commitments that they may not be able to carry out. Governments or firms may enter into agreements that they intend to keep, assuming that the environment will continue to be benign; if adversity sets in, they may be unable to keep their commitments. Banks regularly face this problem, leading them to devise standards of creditworthiness. Large governments trying to gain adherents to international agreements may face similar difficulties: countries that are enthusiastic about cooperation are likely to be those that expect to gain more, proportionately, than they contribute. This is a problem of self-selection, as discussed in the market-failure literature. For instance, if rates are not properly adjusted, people with high risks of heart attack will seek life insurance more avidly than those with longer life expectancies; people who purchased "lemons" will tend to sell them earlier on the used-car market than people with "creampuffs" (Akerlof, 1970; Arrow, 1974). In international politics, self-selection means that for certain types of activities—such as sharing research and development information—weak states (with much to gain but little to give) may have more incentive to participate than strong ones, but less incentive actually to spend funds on research and development.[6] Without the strong states, the enterprise as a whole will fail.

From the perspective of the outside observer, irresponsibility is an aspect of the problem of public goods and free-riding; but from the standpoint of the actor trying to determine whether to rely on a potentially irresponsible partner, it is a problem of uncertainty. Either way, informational costs and asymmetries may prevent mutually beneficial agreement.

REGIMES AND MARKET FAILURE

International regimes help states to deal with all of these problems. As the principles and rules of a regime reduce the range of expected behavior, uncertainty declines, and as information becomes more widely available, the asymmetry of its distribution is likely to lessen. Arrangements within regimes to monitor actors' behavior * * * mitigate problems of moral hazard. Linkages among particular issues within the context of regimes raise the costs of deception and irresponsibility, since the consequences of such behavior are likely to extend beyond the issue on which they are manifested. Close ties among officials involved in managing international regimes increase the ability of governments to make mutually beneficial agreements, because intergovernmental relationships characterized by ongoing communication among working-level officials, informal as well as formal, are inherently more conducive to exchange of information than are traditional relationships between closed bureaucracies. In general, regimes make it more sensible to cooperate by lowering the likelihood of being double-crossed. Whether we view this problem through the lens of game theory or that of market failure, the central conclusion is the same: international regimes can facilitate cooperation by reducing uncertainty. Like international law, broadly defined, their function is "to make human actions conform to predictable patterns so that contemplated actions can go forward with some hope of achieving a rational relationship between means and ends" (Barkun, 1968, p. 154).

Thus international regimes are useful to governments. Far from being threats to governments (in which case it would be hard to understand why they exist at all), they permit governments to attain objectives that would otherwise be unattainable. They do so in part by facilitating intergovernmental agreements. Regimes facilitate agreements by raising the anticipated costs of violating others' property rights, by altering transaction costs through the clustering of issues, and by providing reliable information to members. Regimes are relatively efficient institutions, compared with the alternative of having a myriad of unrelated agreements, since their principles, rules, and institutions create linkages among issues that give actors incentives to reach mutually beneficial agreements. They thrive in situations where states have common as well as conflicting interests on multiple, overlapping issues and where externalities are difficult but not impossible to deal with through bargaining. Where these conditions exist, international regimes can be of value to states.

We have seen that it does not follow from this argument that regimes necessarily increase global welfare. They can be used to pursue particularistic and parochial interests as well as more widely shared objectives. Nor should we conclude that all potentially valuable regimes will necessarily be instituted. * * * [E]ven regimes that promise substantial overall benefits may be difficult to invent.

■　　■　　■

Bounded Rationality and Redefinitions of Self-Interest

The perfectly rational decisionmaker * * * may face uncertainty as a result of the behavior of others, or the forces of nature, but she is assumed to make her own calculations costlessly. Yet this individual, familiar in textbooks, is not made of human flesh and blood. Even the shrewdest speculator or the most brilliant scientist faces limitations on her capacity for calculation. To imagine that all available information will be used by a decisionmaker is to exaggerate the intelligence of the human species.

Decisionmakers are in practice subject to limitations on their own cognitive abilities, quite apart from the uncertainties inherent in their environ-

ments. Herbert Simon has made this point with his usual lucidity (1982, p. 162):

> Particularly important is the distinction between those theories that locate all the conditions and constraints in the environment, outside the skin of the rational actor, and those theories that postulate important constraints arising from the limitations of the actor himself as an information processor. Theories that incorporate constraints on the information-processing capacities of the actor may be called *theories of bounded rationality*.

Actors subject to bounded rationality cannot maximize in the classical sense, because they are not capable of using all the information that is potentially available. They cannot compile exhaustive lists of alternative courses of action, ascertaining the value of each alternative and accurately judging the probability of each possible outcome (Simon, 1955/1979a, p. 10). It is crucial to emphasize that the source of their difficulties in calculation lies not merely in the complexity of the external world, but in their own cognitive limitations. In this respect, behavioral theories of bounded rationality are quite different from recent neoclassical theories, such as the theories of market failure * * *, which retain the assumption of perfect maximization:

> [In new neoclassical theories] limits and costs of information are introduced, not as psychological characteristics of the decision maker, but as part of his technological environment. Hence, the new theories do nothing to alleviate the computational complexities facing the decision maker—do not see him coping with them by heroic approximation, simplifying and satisficing, but simply magnify and multiply them. Now he needs to compute not merely the shapes of his supply and demand curves, but in addition, the costs and benefits of computing those shapes to greater accuracy as well. Hence, to some extent,

the impression that these new theories deal with the hitherto ignored phenomena of uncertainty and information transmission is illusory. (Simon, 1979b, p. 504)

In Simon's own theory, people "satisfice" rather than maximize. That is, they economize on information by searching only until they find a course of action that falls above a satisfactory level—their "aspiration level." Aspiration levels are adjusted from time to time in response to new information about the environment (Simon, 1972, p. 168). In view of people's knowledge of their own cognitive limitations, this is often a sensible strategy; it is by no means irrational and may well be the best way to make most decisions.

In ordinary life, we satisfice all the time. We economize on information by developing habits, by devising operating rules to simplify calculation in situations that repeat themselves, and by adopting general principles that we expect, in the long run, to yield satisfactory results. I do not normally calculate whether to brush my teeth in the morning, whether to hit a tennis ball directed at me with my backhand or my forehand, or whether to tell the truth when asked on the telephone whether Robert Keohane is home. On the contrary, even apart from any moral scruples I might have (for instance, about lying), I assume that my interests will be furthered better by habitually brushing my teeth, applying the rule "when in doubt, hit it with your forehand because you have a lousy backhand," and adopting the general principle of telling the truth than by calculating the costs and benefits of every alternative in each case. I do not mean to deny that I might occasionally be advantaged by pursuing a new idea at my desk rather than brushing my teeth, hitting a particular shot with my backhand, or lying to an obnoxious salesman on the telephone. If I could costlessly compute the value of each alternative, it might indeed be preferable to make the necessary calculations each time I faced a choice. But since this is not feasible, given the costs of processing information, it is in my long-run interest to eschew calculation in these situations.

Simon's analysis of bounded rationality bears some resemblance to the argument made for rule-utilitarianism in philosophy, which emphasizes the value of rules in contributing to the general happiness.[7] Rule-utilitarianism was defined by John Austin in a dictum: "Our rules would be fashioned on utility; our conduct, on our rules" (Mackie, 1977, p. 136). The rule-utilitarian adopts these rules, or "secondary principles," in John Stuart Mill's terms, in the belief that they will lead, in general, to better results than a series of *ad hoc* decisions based each time on first principles.[8] A major reason for formulating and following such rules is the limited calculating ability of human beings. In explicating his doctrine of utilitarianism, Mill therefore anticipated much of Simon's argument about bounded rationality (1861/1951, p. 30):

> Nobody argues that the art of navigation is not founded on astronomy, because sailors cannot wait to calculate the Nautical Almanack. Being rational creatures, they go to sea with it ready calculated; and all rational creatures go out upon the sea of life with their minds made up on the common questions of right and wrong, as well as on many of the far more difficult questions of wise and foolish. And this, as long as foresight is a human quality, it is to be presumed they will continue to do.

If individuals typically satisfice rather than maximize, all the more so do governments and other large organizations (Allison, 1971; Steinbruner, 1974; Snyder and Diesing, 1977). Organizational decision-making processes hardly meet the requirements of classical rationality. Organizations have multiple goals, defined in terms of aspiration levels; they search until satisfactory courses of action are found; they resort to feedback rather than systematically forecasting future conditions; and they use "standard operating procedures and rules of thumb" to make and implement decisions (Cyert and March, 1963, p. 113; March and Simon, 1958).

The behavioral theory of the firm has made it clear that satisficing does not constitute aberrant behavior that should be rectified where possible; on the contrary, it is intelligent. The leader of a large organization who demanded that the organization meet the criteria of classical rationality would herself be foolish, perhaps irrationally so. An organization whose leaders behaved in this way would become paralyzed unless their subordinates found ways to fool them into believing that impossible standards were being met. This assertion holds even more for governments than for business firms, since governments' constituencies are more varied, their goals more diverse (and frequently contradictory), and success or failure more difficult to measure. Assumptions of unbounded rationality, however dear they may be to the hearts of classical Realist theorists (Morgenthau, 1948/1966) and writers on foreign policy, are idealizations. A large, complex government would tie itself in knots by "keeping its options open," since middle-level bureaucrats would not know how to behave and the top policymakers would be overwhelmed by minor problems. The search for complete flexibility is as quixotic as looking for the Holy Grail or the fountain of youth.

If governments are viewed as constrained by bounded rationality, what are the implications for the functional argument * * * about the value of international regimes? * * * [U]nder rational-choice assumptions, international regimes are valuable to governments because they reduce transaction costs and particularly because they reduce uncertainty in the external environment. Each government is better able, with regimes in place, to predict that its counterparts will follow predictably cooperative policies. According to this theory, governments sacrifice the ability to maximize their myopic self-interest by making calculations on each issue as it arises, in return for acquiring greater certainty about others' behavior.

Under bounded rationality, the inclination of governments to join or support international regimes will be reinforced by the fact that the alternatives to regimes are less attractive than they would be if the assumptions of classical rationality were valid. Actors laboring under bounded rationality cannot calculate the costs and benefits of each alternative course of action on each issue. On the contrary, they need to simplify their own decisionmaking processes in order to function effectively at all. The rules of thumb they devise will not yield better, and will generally yield worse, results (apart from decisionmaking costs) than classically rational action—whether these rules of thumb are adopted unilaterally or as part of an international regime. Thus a comparison between the value of a unilateral rule of thumb and that of a regime rule will normally be more favorable to the regime rule than a comparison between the value of costless, perfectly rational calculation and the regime rule.

When we abandon the assumption of classical rationality, we see that it is not international regimes that deny governments the ability to make classically rational calculations. The obstacle is rather the nature of governments as large, complex organizations composed of human beings with limited problem-solving capabilities. The choice that governments actually face with respect to international regimes is not whether to adhere to regimes at the expense of maximizing utility through continuous calculation, but rather on what rules of thumb to rely. Normally, unilateral rules will fit the individual country's situation better than rules devised multilaterally. Regime rules, however, have the advantage of constraining the actions of others. The question is whether the value of the constraints imposed on others justifies the costs of accepting regime rules in place of the rules of thumb that the country would have adopted on its own.

Thus if we accept that governments must adopt rules of thumb, the costs of adhering to international regimes appear less severe than they would be if classical rationality were a realistic possibility. Regimes merely substitute multilateral rules (presumably somewhat less congenial per se) for unilateral ones, with the advantage that other actors' behavior thereby becomes more predictably cooperative. International regimes neither enforce hierarchical rules on governments nor substitute their own rules for autonomous calculation; instead, they provide rules of thumb in place of those that governments would otherwise adopt.

* * * [W]e can see how different our conception of international regimes is from the self-help system that is often taken as revealing the essence of international politics. In a pure self-help system, each actor calculates its interests on each particular issue, preserving its options until that decision has been made. The rational response to another actor's distress in such a system is to take advantage of it by driving a hard bargain, demanding as much as "the traffic will bear" in return for one's money, one's oil, or one's military support. Many such bargains are in fact struck in world politics, especially among adversaries; but one of the key features of international regimes is that they limit the ability of countries in a particularly strong bargaining position (however transitory) to take advantage of that situation. This limitation, as we have stressed, is not the result of altruism but of the fact that joining a regime changes calculations of long-run self-interest. To a government that values its ability to make future agreements, reputation is a crucial resource; and the most important aspect of an actor's reputation in world politics is the belief of others that it will keep its future commitments even when a particular situation, myopically viewed, makes it appear disadvantageous to do so. Thus even classically rational governments will sometimes join regimes and comply with their rules. To a government seeking to economize on decisionmaking costs, the regime is also valuable for providing rules of thumb; discarding it would require establishing a new set of rules to guide one's bureaucracy. The convenience of rules of thumb combines with the superiority of long-run calculations of self-interest over myopic ones to reinforce adherence to rules by egoistic governments, particularly when they labor under the constraints of bounded rationality.

■ ■ ■

NOTES

1. For an elaborated version of this definition, see Davis and North (1971, p. 16).

2. For the idea of "nesting," I am indebted to Aggarwal (1981). Snidal (1981) also relies on this concept, which was used in a similar context some years ago by Barkun (1968, p. 17).

3. On linkage, see especially the work of Kenneth A. Oye (1979, 1983). See also Stein (1980) and Tollison and Willett (1979).

4. This point was suggested to me by reading Elizabeth Colson's account of how stateless societies reach consensus on the character of individuals: through discussions and gossip that allow people to "apply the standards of performance in particular roles in making an overall judgement about the total person; this in turn allows them to predict future behavior" (1974, p. 53).

5. In 1960 Thomas Schelling made a similar argument about the problem of surprise attack. Asking how we would prove that we were not planning a surprise attack if the Russians suspected we were, he observed that "evidently it is not going to be enough just to tell the truth. . . . There has to be some way of authenticating certain facts, the facts presumably involving the disposition of forces" (p. 247). To authenticate facts requires becoming more open to external monitoring as a way of alleviating what Akerlof [1970] later called "quality uncertainty."

6. Bobrow and Kudrle found evidence of severe problems of collective goods in the IEA's energy research and development program, suggesting that "commercial interests and other national rivalries appear to have blocked extensive international cooperation" (1979, p. 170).

7. In philosophy, utilitarianism refers to an ethical theory that purports to provide generalizable principles for moral human action. Since my argument here is a positive one, seeking to explain the behavior of egoistic actors rather than to develop or criticize an ethical theory, its relationship to rule-utilitarianism in philosophy, as my colleague Susan Okin has pointed out to me, is only tangential.

8. John Mackie argues that even act-utilitarians "regularly admit the use of rules of thumb," and that whether one follows rules therefore does not distinguish act- from rule-utilitarianism (1977, p. 137). Conversely, Joseph Nye has pointed out to me that even rule-utilitarians must depart at some point from their rules for consequentialist reasons. The point here is not to draw a hard-and-fast dichotomy between the two forms of utilitarianism, but rather to point out the similarities between Mill's notion of relying on rules and Simon's conception of bounded rationality. If all utilitarians have to resort to rules of thumb to some extent, this only strengthens

the point I am making about the importance of rules in affecting, but not determining, the behavior of governments. For a succinct discussion of utilitarianism in philosophy, see Urmson (1968).

REFERENCES

* * * *Where a date is given for an original as well as a later edition, the latter was used; page references in the text refer to it.*

Aggarwal, Vinod, 1981. Hanging by a Thread: International Regime Change in the Textile/Apparel System, 1950–1979 (Ph.D. dissertation. Stanford University).

Aivazian, Varouj A., and Jeffrey L. Callen, 1981. The Coase theorem and the empty core. *Journal of Law and Economics*, vol. 24, no. 1 (April), pp. 175–81.

Akerlof, George A., 1970. The market for "lemons." *Quarterly Journal of Economics*, vol. 84, no. 3 (August), pp. 488–500.

Allison, Graham, 1971. *Essence of Decision: Explaining the Cuban Missile Crisis* (Boston: Little, Brown).

Arrow, Kenneth J., 1974. *Essays in the Theory of Risk-Bearing* (New York: North-Holland/American Elsevier).

Barkun, Michael, 1968. *Law without Sanctions: Order in Primitive Societies and the World Community* (New Haven: Yale University Press).

Bobrow, Davis W., and Robert Kudrle, 1979. Energy R & D: in tepid pursuit of collective goods *International Organization*, vol. 33, no. 2 (Spring), pp. 149–76.

Coase, Ronald, 1960. The problem of social cost. *Journal of Law and Economics*, vol. 3, pp. 1–44

Colson, Elizabeth, 1974. *Tradition and Contract: The Problem of Order* (Chicago: Aldine Publishing Company).

Conybeare, John A.C., 1980. International organization and the theory of property rights. *International Organization*, vol. 34, no. 3 (Summer), pp. 307–34.

Cyert, Richard, and James G. March, 1963. *The Behavioral Theory of the Firm* (Englewood Cliffs, NJ: Prentice-Hall).

Davis, Lance, and Douglass C. North, 1971. *Institutional Change and American Economic Growth* (Cambridge: Cambridge University Press).

Fellner, William, 1949. *Competition among the Few* (New York: Knopf).

Gilpin, Robert, 1981, *War and Change in World Politics* (Cambridge: Cambridge University Press).

Haas, Ernst B., 1958. *The Uniting of Europe* (Stanford: Stanford University Press).

Hardin, Russell, 1982. *Collective Action* (Baltimore: The Johns Hopkins University Press for Resources for the Future).

Henkin, Louis, 1979. *How Nations Behave: Law and Foreign Policy*, 2nd edition (New York: Columbia University Press for the Council on Foreign Relations).

Hirsch, Fred, 1977. The Bagehot problem. *The Manchester School*, vol. 45, no. 3 (September), pp. 241–57.

Hoffmann, Stanley, 1965. *The State of War: Essays on the Theory and Practice of International Politics* (New York: Praeger).

Hutton, Nicholas, 1975. The salience of linkage in international economic negotiations. *Journal of Common Market Studies*, vol. 13, nos. 1–2, pp. 136–60.

Lewis, David K., 1969. *Convention: A Philosophical Study* (Cambridge: Harvard University Press).

Lowry, S. Todd, 1979. Bargain and contract theory in law and economics. In Samuels, 1979, pp. 261–82.

Mackie, J. L., 1977. *Ethics: Inventing Right and Wrong* (Harmondsworth, England: Penguin Books).

March, James G., and Herbert Simon, 1958. *Organizations* (New York: John Wiley & Sons).

Mill, John Stuart, 1861/1951. *Utilitarianism* (New York: E. P. Dutton).

Mitrany, David, 1975. *The Functional Theory of Politics* (London: St. Martin's Press for the London School of Economics and Political Science).

Morgenthau, Hans J., 1948/1966. *Politics among Nations*, 4th edition (New York: Knopf).

Olson, Mancur, 1965. *The Logic of Collective Action* (Cambridge: Harvard University Press).

Oye, Kenneth A., 1979. The domain of choice. In Oye et al., 1979, pp. 3–33.

Oye, Kenneth A., 1983. Belief Systems, Bargaining and Breakdown: International Political Economy 1929–1934 (Ph.D. dissertation, Harvard University).

Puchala, Donald J., 1975. Domestic politics and regional harmonization in the European Communities. *World Politics*, vol. 27, no. 4 (July), pp. 496–520.

Samuelson, Paul A., 1967. The monopolistic competition revolution. In R. E. Kuenne, ed., *Monopolistic Competition Theory* (New York: John Wiley & Sons)

Schelling, Thomas C., 1960/1980, *The Strategy of Conflict* (Cambridge: Harvard University Press).

Schelling, Thomas C., 1978. *Micromotives and Macrobehavior* (New York: W. W. Norton).

Simon, Herbert A., 1955. A behavioral model of rational choice. *Quarterly Journal of Economics*, vol. 69, no. 1 (February), pp. 99–118. Reprinted in Simon, 1979a, pp. 7–19.

Simon, Herbert A., 1972. Theories of bounded rationality. In Radner and Radner, 1972, pp. 161–76. Reprinted in Simon, 1982, pp. 408–23.

Simon, Herbert A., 1979a. *Models of Thought* (New Haven: Yale University Press).

Simon, Herbert A., 1979b. Rational decision making in business organizations. *American Economic Review*, vol. 69, no. 4 (September), pp. 493–513. Reprinted in Simon, 1982, pp. 474–94.

Simon, Herbert A., 1982. *Models of Bounded Rationality*, 2 vols. (Cambridge: MIT Press).

Snidal, Duncan, 1981. Interdependence, Regimes and International Cooperation (unpublished manuscript).

Snyder, Glenn H., and Paul Diesing, 1977. *Conflict among Nations: Bargaining, Decision making, and System Structure in International Crises* (Princeton: Princeton University Press).

Stein, Arthur A., 1980. The politics of linkage. *World Politics*, vol. 33, no. 1 (October), pp. 62–81.

Steinbruner, John D., 1974. *The Cybernetic Theory of Decision: New Dimensions of Political Analysis* (Princeton: Princeton University Press).

Tollison, Robert D., and Thomas D. Willett, 1979. An economic theory of mutually advantageous issue linkages in international negotiations. *International Organization*, vol. 33, no. 4 (Autumn), pp. 425–49.

Tucker, Robert W., 1977. *The Inequality of Nations* (New York: Basic Books).

Urmson, J. O., 1968. Utilitarianism. *International Encyclopedia of the Social Sciences* (New York: Macmillan), pp. 224–29.

Veljanovski, Cento G., 1982. The Coase theorems and the economic theory of markets and law. *Kyklos*, vol. 35, fasc. 1, pp. 53–74.

Waltz, Kenneth, 1959. *Man, the State and War* (New York: Columbia University Press).

Waltz, Kenneth, 1979. *Theory of World Politics* (Reading, MA: Addison-Wesley).

Williamson, Oliver, 1975. *Markets and Hierarchies: Analysis and Anti-Trust Implications* (New York: The Free Press).

Young, Oran R., 1980. International regimes: problems of concept formation. *World Politics*, vol. 32, no. 3 (April), pp. 331–56.

Young, Oran R., 1983. Regime dynamics: the rise and fall of international regimes. In Krasner, 1983, pp. 93–114.

4 LEVELS OF ANALYSIS

A typical framework for organizing the different theoretical traditions is the "levels of analysis." These levels are arrayed on a continuum starting with the international system as a whole, then continuing down through the type of domestic political system of individual states (democratic or authoritarian), the various interest groups and bureaucracies within the state, and finally individual decision making and psychology.

Different theoretical traditions place different bets on which level is likely to explain more about international politics. Realists such as Hans J. Morgenthau, Kenneth Waltz, and John Mearsheimer normally start by looking as the structure of the international system as a whole. Morgenthau writes in *Politics Among Nations* that the international system is characterized by competition among states, each seeking to enhance its power. As a consequence of this competition, a balance of power tends to emerge. In the selection in this chapter, Morgenthau discusses what states can do to stabilize the balance. Waltz makes the bold argument that nuclear proliferation is one way to stabilize the balance, even in the hard case of a country like Iran that has an undemocratic regime, a militant political culture, and the potential for volatile civil-military relations.

As we saw in the previous chapters, liberal theorists such as Michael Doyle prioritize the domestic regime type of states and the distinctive patterns of diplomatic relations this creates, most notably the absence of war between democracies. The liberal multilateralist G. John Ikenberry prioritizes the distinctive pattern of international organizations that are created by powerful liberal states to sustain cooperation among them. Jessica Chen Weiss and Jeremy Wallace examine the frictions that occur when a rising illiberal power like China does not fit easily into the rules of the liberal economic order.

One of the most consequential tasks of political judgment is inferring the intentions of a state's adversaries. In her article "In the Eye of the Beholder," Keren Yarhi-Milo surveys three theories of how leaders and their intelligence services approach this problem. The first two are based on variants of a rational theory of decision making: the first posits that actors base their judgments on the adversary's costly behavior, ignoring "cheap talk," while the second expects them to focus mainly on the adversary's capabilities. Yarhi-Milo proposes a third theory based on psychological research about selective attention to information. In case studies of the Carter administration's response to the Soviet invasion of Afghanistan and the Reagan administration's response to Mikhail Gorbachev's diplomacy, she finds that leaders focus inordinately on vivid information gained in personal encounters, whereas intelligence services focus narrowly on data that can be compiled routinely, such as weapons capabilities.

Hans J. Morgenthau

THE BALANCE OF POWER

The aspiration for power on the part of several nations, each trying either to maintain or overthrow the status quo, leads of necessity to a configuration that is called the balance of power[1] and to policies that aim at preserving it. We say "of necessity" advisedly. For here again we are confronted with the basic misconception that has impeded the understanding of international politics and has made us the prey of illusions. This misconception asserts that men have a choice between power politics and its necessary outgrowth, the balance of power, on the one hand, and a different, better kind of international relations on the other. It insists that a foreign policy based on the balance of power is one among several possible foreign policies and that only stupid and evil men will choose the former and reject the latter.

It will be shown * * * that the international balance of power is only a particular manifestation of a general social principle to which all societies composed of a number of autonomous units owe the autonomy of their component parts; that the balance of power and policies aiming at its preservation are not only inevitable but are an essential stabilizing factor in a society of sovereign nations; and that the instability of the international balance of power is due not to the faultiness of the principle but to the particular conditions under which the principle must operate in a society of sovereign nations.

From Hans J. Morgenthau, *Politics Among Nations: The Struggle for Power and Peace* (1948, repr. New York: Knopf, 1985), 187–89, 198–201, 213–14, 222, 227–28. Some of the author's notes have been omitted.

Social Equilibrium

Balance of Power as Universal Concept

The concept of "equilibrium" as a synonym for "balance" is commonly employed in many sciences—physics, biology, economics, sociology, and political science. It signifies stability within a system composed of a number of autonomous forces. Whenever the equilibrium is disturbed either by an outside force or by a change in one or the other elements composing the system, the system shows a tendency to re-establish either the original or a new equilibrium. Thus equilibrium exists in the human body. While the human body changes in the process of growth, the equilibrium persists as long as the changes occurring in the different organs of the body do not disturb the body's stability. This is especially so if the quantitative and qualitative changes in the different organs are proportionate to each other. When, however, the body suffers a wound or loss of one of its organs through outside interference, or experiences a malignant growth or a pathological transformation of one of its organs, the equilibrium is disturbed, and the body tries to overcome the disturbance by re-establishing the equilibrium either on the same or a different level from the one that obtained before the disturbance occurred.[2]

The same concept of equilibrium is used in a social science, such as economies, with reference to the relations between the different elements of the economic system, e.g., between savings and investments, exports and imports, supply and demand, costs and prices. Contemporary capitalism itself has been described as a system of "countervailing power."[3] It also applies to society as a whole. Thus we search for a proper balance between different geographical regions, such as the East and the West, the North and the South; between different kinds of activities, such as agriculture and industry, heavy and light industries, big and small businesses, producers and consumers, management and labor; between different functional groups, such as city and country, the old, the middle-aged, and the young, the economic and the political sphere, the middle classes and the upper and lower classes.

Two assumptions are at the foundation of all such equilibriums: first, that the elements to be balanced are necessary for society or are entitled to exist and, second, that without a state of equilibrium among them one element will gain ascendancy over the others, encroach upon their interests and rights, and may ultimately destroy them.

Consequently, it is the purpose of all such equilibriums to maintain the stability of the system without destroying the multiplicity of the elements composing it. If the goal were stability alone, it could be achieved by allowing one element to destroy or overwhelm the others and take their place. Since the goal is stability plus the preservation of all the elements of the system, the equilibrium must aim at preventing any element from gaining ascendancy over the others. The means employed to maintain the equilibrium consist in allowing the different elements to pursue their opposing tendencies up to the point where the tendency of one is not so strong as to overcome the tendency of the others, but strong enough to prevent the others from overcoming its own. * * *

■ ■ ■

DIFFERENT METHODS OF THE BALANCE OF POWER

The balancing process can be carried on either by diminishing the weight of the heavier scale or by increasing the weight of the lighter one.

Divide and Rule

The former method has found its classic manifestation, aside from the imposition of onerous conditions in peace treaties and the incitement to treason and revolution, in the maxim "divide and rule." It has been resorted to by nations who tried to make or keep their competitors weak by dividing them or keeping them divided. The most consistent and important policies of this kind in modern times are the policy of France with respect to Germany and the policy of the Soviet Union with respect to the rest of Europe. From the seventeenth century to the end of the Second World War, it has been an unvarying principle of French foreign policy either to favor the division of the German Empire into a number of small independent states or to prevent the coalescence of such states into one unified nation. * * * Similarly, the Soviet Union from the twenties to the present has consistently opposed all plans for the unification of Europe, on the assumption that the pooling of the divided strength of the European nations into a "Western bloc" would give the enemies of the Soviet Union such power as to threaten the latter's security.

The other method of balancing the power of several nations consists in adding to the strength of the weaker nation. This method can be carried out by two different means: Either B can increase its power sufficiently to offset, if not surpass, the power of A, and vice versa; or B can pool its power with the power of all the other nations that pursue identical policies with regard to A, in which case A will pool its power with all the nations pursuing identical policies with respect to B. The former alternative is exemplified by the policy of compensations and the armament race as well as by disarmament; the latter, by the policy of alliances.

Compensations

Compensations of a territorial nature were a common device in the eighteenth and nineteenth centuries for maintaining a balance of power which had been, or was to be, disturbed by the territorial acquisitions of one nation. The Treaty of Utrecht of 1713, which terminated the War of the Spanish Succession, recognized for the first time expressly the principle of the balance of power by way of territorial compensations. It provided for the division of most of the Spanish possessions, European and colonial, between the Hapsburgs and the Bourbons *"ad conservandum in Europa equilibrium,"* as the treaty put it.

■   ■   ■

In the latter part of the nineteenth and the beginning of the twentieth century, the principle of compensations was again deliberately applied to the distribution of colonial territories and the delimitation of colonial or semicolonial spheres of influence. Africa, in particular, was during that period the object of numerous treaties delimiting spheres of influence for the major colonial powers. Thus the competition between France, Great Britain, and Italy for the domination of Ethiopia was provisionally resolved * * * by the treaty of 1906, which divided the country into three spheres of influence for the purpose of establishing in that region a balance of power among the nations concerned. * * *

Even where the principle of compensations is not deliberately applied, however, * * * it is nowhere absent from political arrangements, territorial or other, made within a balance-of-power system. For, given such a system, no nation will agree to concede political advantages to another nation without the expectation, which may or may not be well founded, of receiving proportionate advantages in return. The bargaining of diplomatic negotiations, issuing in political compromise, is but the principle of compensations in its most general form, and as such it is organically connected with the balance of power.

Armaments

The principal means, however, by which a nation endeavors with the power at its disposal to maintain or re-establish the balance of power are armaments. The armaments race in which Nation A tries to keep up with, and then to outdo, the armaments of Nation B, and vice versa, is the typical instrumentality of an unstable, dynamic balance of power. The necessary corollary of the armaments race is a constantly increasing burden of military preparations devouring an ever greater portion of the national budget and making for ever deepening fears, suspicions, and insecurity. The situation preceding the First World War, with the naval competition between Germany and Great Britain and the rivalry of the French and German armies, illustrates this point.

It is in recognition of situations such as these that, since the end of the Napoleonic Wars, repeated attempts have been made to create a stable balance of power, if not to establish permanent peace, by means of the proportionate disarmament of competing nations. The technique of stabilizing the balance of power by means of a proportionate reduction of armaments is somewhat similar to the technique of territorial compensations. For both techniques require a quantitative evaluation of the influence that the arrangement is likely to exert on the respective power of the individual nations. The difficulties in making such a quantitative evaluation—in correlating, for instance, the military strength of the French army of 1932 with the military power represented by the industrial potential of Germany—have greatly contributed to the failure of most attempts at creating a stable balance of power by means of disarmament. The only outstanding success of this kind was the Washington Naval Treaty of 1922, in which Great Britain, the United States, Japan, France, and Italy agreed to a proportionate reduction and limitation of naval armaments. Yet it must be noted that this treaty was part of an over-all political and territorial settlement in the Pacific which sought to stabilize the power relations in that region on the foundation of Anglo-American predominance.

Alliances

The historically most important manifestation of the balance of power, however, is to be found not in the equilibrium of two isolated nations but in the relations between one nation or alliance of nations and another alliance.

■　■　■

Alliances are a necessary function of the balance of power operating within a multiple-state system. Nations A and B, competing with each other, have three choices in order to maintain and improve their relative power positions. They can increase their own power, they can add to their own power the power of other nations, or they can withhold the power of other nations from the adversary. When they make the first choice, they embark upon an armaments race. When they choose the second and third alternatives, they pursue a policy of alliances.

Whether or not a nation shall pursue a policy of alliances is, then, a matter not of principle but of expediency. A nation will shun alliances if it believes that it is strong enough to hold its own unaided or that the burden of the commitments resulting from the alliance is likely to outweigh the advantages to be expected. It is for one or the other or both of these reasons that, throughout the better part of their history, Great Britain and the United States have refrained from entering into peacetime alliances with other nations.

■　■　■

The "Holder" of the Balance

Whenever the balance of power is to be realized by means of an alliance—and this has been generally so throughout the history of the Western world—two possible variations of this pattern have to be distinguished. To use the metaphor of the balance, the system may consist of two scales, in each of which are to be found the nation or nations identified with the same policy of the status quo or of imperialism. The continental nations of Europe have generally operated the balance of power in this way.

The system may, however, consist of two scales plus a third element, the "holder" of the balance or the "balancer." The balancer is not permanently identified with the policies of either nation or group of nations. Its only objective within the system is the maintenance of the balance, regardless of the concrete policies the balance will serve. In consequence, the holder of the balance will throw its weight at one time in this scale, at another time in the other scale, guided only by one consideration—the relative position of scales. Thus it will put its weight always in the scale that seems to be higher than the other because it is lighter. The balancer may become in a relatively short span of history consecutively the friend and foe of all major powers, provided they all consecutively threaten the balance by approaching predominance over the others and are in turn threatened by others about to gain such predominance. To paraphrase a statement of Palmerston: While the holder of the balance has no permanent friends, it has no permanent enemies either; it has only the permanent interest of maintaining the balance of power itself.

The balancer is in a position of "splendid isolation." It is isolated by its own choice; for, while the two scales of the balance must vie with each other to add its weight to theirs in order to gain the overweight necessary for success, it must refuse to enter into permanent ties with either side. The holder of the balance waits in the middle in watchful detachment to see which scale is likely to sink. Its isolation is "splendid"; for, since its support or lack of support is the decisive factor in the struggle for power, its foreign policy, if cleverly managed, is able to extract the highest price from those whom it supports. But since this support, regardless of the price paid for it, is always uncertain and shifts from one side to the other in accordance with the movements of the balance, its policies are resented and subject to condemnation on moral grounds. Thus it has been said of the outstanding balancer in modern times, Great Britain, that it lets others fight its wars, that it keeps Europe divided in order to dominate the continent, and that the fickleness of its policies is such as to make alliances with Great Britain impossible. "Perfidious Albion" has become a byword in the mouths of those who either were unable to gain Great Britain's support, however hard they tried, or else lost it after they had paid what seemed to them too high a price.

The holder of the balance occupies the key position in the balance-of-power system, since its position determines the outcome of the struggle for power. It has, therefore, been called the "arbiter" of the system, deciding who will win and who will lose. By making it impossible for any nation or combination of nations to gain predominance over the others, it preserves its own independence as well as the independence of all the other nations, and is thus a most powerful factor in international politics.

The holder of the balance can use this power in three different ways. It can make its joining one or the other nation or alliance dependent upon certain conditions favorable to the maintenance or restoration of the balance. It can make its support of the peace settlement dependent upon similar conditions. It can, finally, in either situation see to it that the objectives of its own national policy, apart from the maintenance of the balance of power, are realized in the process of balancing the power of others.

■　　■　　■

EVALUATION OF THE BALANCE OF POWER

■ ■ ■

The Unreality of the Balance of Power

[The] uncertainty of all power calculations not only makes the balance of power incapable of practical application but leads also to its very negation in practice. Since no nation can be sure that its calculation of the distribution of power at any particular moment in history is correct, it must at least make sure that its errors, whatever they may be, will not put the nation at a disadvantage in the contest for power. In other words, the nation must try to have at least a margin of safety which will allow it to make erroneous calculations and still maintain the balance of power. To that effect, all nations actively engaged in the struggle for power must actually aim not at balance—that is, equality—of power, but at superiority of power in their own behalf. And since no nation can foresee how large its miscalculations will turn out to be, all nations must ultimately seek the maximum of power obtainable under the circumstances. Only thus can they hope to attain the maximum margin of safety commensurate with the maximum of errors they might commit. The limitless aspiration for power, potentially always present * * * in the power drives of nations, finds in the balance of power a mighty incentive to transform itself into an actuality.

Since the desire to attain a maximum of power is universal, all nations must always be afraid that their own miscalculations and the power increases of other nations might add up to an inferiority for themselves which they must at all costs try to avoid. Hence all nations who have gained an apparent edge over their competitors tend to consolidate that advantage and use it for changing the distribution of power permanently in their favor. This can be done through diplomatic pressure by bringing the full weight of that advantage to bear upon the other nations, compelling them to make the concessions that will consolidate the temporary advantage into a permanent superiority. It can also be done by war. Since in a balance-of-power system all nations live in constant fear lest their rivals deprive them, at the first opportune moment, of their power position, all nations have a vital interest in anticipating such a development and doing unto the others what they do not want the others to do unto them. * * *

NOTES

1. The term "balance of power" is used in the text with four different meanings: (1) as a policy aimed at a certain state of affairs, (2) as an actual state of affairs, (3) as an approximately equal distribution of power, (4) as any distribution of power. Whenever the term is used without qualification, it refers to an actual state of affairs in which power is distributed among several nations with approximate equality. * * *

2. Cf., for instance, the impressive analogy between the equilibrium in the human body and in society in Walter B. Cannon, *The Wisdom of the Body* (New York: W. W. Norton and Company, 1932), pp. 293, 294: "At the outset it is noteworthy that the body politic itself exhibits some indications of crude automatic stabilizing processes. In the previous chapter I expressed the postulate that a certain degree of constancy in a complex system is itself evidence that agencies are acting or are ready to act to maintain that constancy. And moreover, that when a system remains steady it does so because any tendency towards change is met by increased effectiveness of the factor or factors which resist the change. Many familiar facts prove

that these statements are to some degree true for society even in its present unstabilized condition. A display of conservatism excites a radical revolt and that in turn is followed by a return to conservatism. Loose government and its consequences bring the reformers into power, but their tight reins soon provoke restiveness and the desire for release. The noble enthusiasms and sacrifices of war are succeeded by moral apathy and orgies of self-indulgence. Hardly any strong tendency in a nation continues to the stage of disaster; before that extreme is reached corrective forces arise which check the tendency and they commonly prevail to such an excessive degree as themselves to cause a reaction. A study of the nature of these social swings and their reversal might lead to valuable understanding and possibly to means of more narrowly limiting the disturbances. At this point, however, we merely note that the disturbances are roughly limited, and that this limitation suggests, perhaps, the early stages of social homeostasis."
(Reprinted by permission of the publisher. Copyright 1932, 1939, by Walter B. Cannon.)

3. John K. Galbraith, *American Capitalism, the Concept of Countervailing Power* (Boston: Houghton Mifflin, 1952).

Robert Jervis
HYPOTHESES ON MISPERCEPTION

In determining how he will behave, an actor must try to predict how others will act and how their actions will affect his values. The actor must therefore develop an image of others and of their intentions. This image may, however, turn out to be an inaccurate one; the actor may, for a number of reasons, misperceive both others' actions and their intentions. * * * I wish to discuss the types of misperceptions of other states' intentions which states tend to make. * * *

■   ■   ■

Theories—Necessary and Dangerous

* * * The evidence from both psychology and history overwhelmingly supports the view (which may be labeled Hypothesis 1) that decision-makers tend to fit incoming information into their existing theories and images. Indeed, their theories and images play a large part in determining what they notice. In other words, actors tend to perceive what they expect. Furthermore (Hypothesis 1a), a theory will have greater impact on an actor's interpretation of data (a) the greater the ambiguity of the data and (b) the higher the degree of confidence with which the actor holds the theory.[1]

■   ■   ■

From *World Politics* 20, no. 3 (April 1968): 454–79. Some of the author's notes have been omitted.

* * * Hypothesis 2: scholars and decision-makers are apt to err by being too wedded to the established view and too closed to new information, as opposed to being too willing to alter their theories. Another way of making this point is to argue that actors tend to establish their theories and expectations prematurely. In politics, of course, this is often necessary because of the need for action. But experimental evidence indicates that the same tendency also occurs on the unconscious level. * * *

However, when we apply these and other findings to politics and discuss kinds of misperception, we should not quickly apply the label of cognitive distortion. We should proceed cautiously for two related reasons. The first is that the evidence available to decision-makers almost always permits several interpretations. It should be noted that there are cases of visual perception in which different stimuli can produce exactly the same pattern on an observer's retina. Thus, for an observer using one eye the same pattern would be produced by a sphere the size of a golf ball which was quite close to the observer, by a baseball-sized sphere that was further away, or by a basketball-sized sphere still further away. Without other clues, the observer cannot possibly determine which of these stimuli he is presented with, and we would not want to call his incorrect perceptions examples of distortion. Such cases, relatively rare in visual perception, are frequent in international relations. The evidence available to decision-makers is almost always very ambiguous since accurate clues to others' intentions are surrounded by noise[2] and deception. In most cases, no matter how long, deeply, and "objectively" the evidence is analyzed, people can differ in their interpretations, and there are no general rules to indicate who is correct.

The second reason to avoid the label of cognitive distortion is that the distinction between perception and judgment, obscure enough in individual psychology, is almost absent in the making of inferences in international politics. Decision-makers who reject information that contradicts their views—or who develop complex interpretations of it—often do so consciously and explicitly. Since the evidence available contains contradictory information, to make any inferences requires that much information be ignored or given interpretations that will seem tortuous to those who hold a different position.

Indeed, if we consider only the evidence available to a decision-maker at the time of decision, the view later proved incorrect may be supported by as much evidence as the correct one—or even by more. Scholars have often been too unsympathetic with the people who were proved wrong. On closer examination, it is frequently difficult to point to differences between those who were right and those who were wrong with respect to their openness to new information and willingness to modify their views. Winston Churchill, for example, did not open-mindedly view each Nazi action to see if the explanations provided by the appeasers accounted for the data better than his own beliefs. Instead, like Chamberlain, he fitted each bit of ambiguous information into his own hypotheses. That he was correct should not lead us to overlook the fact that his methods of analysis and use of theory to produce cognitive consistency did not basically differ from those of the appeasers.

A consideration of the importance of expectations in influencing perception also indicates that the widespread belief in the prevalence of "wishful thinking" may be incorrect, or at least may be based on inadequate data. The psychological literature on the interaction between affect and perception is immense and cannot be treated here,

but it should be noted that phenomena that at first were considered strong evidence for the impact of affect on perception often can be better treated as demonstrating the influence of expectations.[3] Thus, in international relations, cases like the United States' misestimation of the political climate in Cuba in April 1961, which may seem at first glance to have been instances of wishful thinking, may instead be more adequately explained by the theories held by the decision-makers (e.g., Communist governments are unpopular). Of course, desires may have an impact on perception by influencing expectations, but since so many other factors affect expectations, the net influence of desires may not be great.

There is evidence from both psychology[4] and international relations that when expectations and desires clash, expectations seem to be more important. The United States would like to believe that North Vietnam is about to negotiate or that the USSR is ready to give up what the United States believes is its goal of world domination, but ambiguous evidence is seen to confirm the opposite conclusion, which conforms to the United States' expectations. Actors are apt to be especially sensitive to evidence of grave danger if they think they can take action to protect themselves against the menace once it has been detected.

Safeguards

Can anything then be said to scholars and decision-makers other than "Avoid being either too open or too closed, but be especially aware of the latter danger"? Although decision-makers will always be faced with ambiguous and confusing evidence and will be forced to make inferences about others which will often be inaccurate, a number of safeguards may be suggested which could enable them to minimize their errors. First, and most obvious, decision-makers should be aware that they do not make "unbiased" interpretations of each new bit of incoming information, but rather are inevitably heavily influenced by the theories they expect to be verified. They should know that what may appear to them as a self-evident and unambiguous inference often seems so only because of their preexisting beliefs. To someone with a different theory the same data may appear to be unimportant or to support another explanation. Thus many events provide less independent support for the decision-makers' images than they may at first realize. Knowledge of this should lead decision-makers to examine more closely evidence that others believe contradicts their views.

Second, decision-makers should see if their attitudes contain consistent or supporting beliefs that are not logically linked. These may be examples of true psycho-logic. While it is not logically surprising nor is it evidence of psychological pressures to find that people who believe that Russia is aggressive are very suspicious of any Soviet move, other kinds of consistency are more suspect. For example, most people who feel that it is important for the United States to win the war in Vietnam also feel that a meaningful victory is possible. And most people who feel defeat would neither endanger U.S. national security nor be costly in terms of other values also feel that we cannot win. Although there are important logical linkages between the two parts of each of these views (especially through theories of guerrilla warfare), they do not seem strong enough to explain the degree to which the opinions are correlated. Similarly, in Finland in the winter of 1939, those who felt that grave consequences would follow Finnish agreement to give Russia a military base also believed that the Soviets would withdraw their demand if Finland stood firm. And those who felt that concessions would not lead to loss of major values also believed that Russia would fight if need be.[5] In this country, those who favored a nuclear test ban tended to argue that fallout was very harmful, that only limited improvements in technology would flow from further testing, and that a test ban would increase the chances for peace and security. Those who opposed the test ban were apt to disagree on all three points. This does not mean, of course, that the people holding such sets of supporting views were necessarily wrong in any one element. The Finns who wanted to make concessions to the USSR were probably correct in both parts of their argument. But decision-makers should be suspicious if they hold a position in which elements that are not logically connected support the same conclusion. This condition is psychologically comfortable and makes decisions easier to reach (since competing values do not have to be balanced off against each other). The chances are thus considerable that at least part of the reason why a person holds some of these views is related to psychology and not to the substance of the evidence.

Decision-makers should also be aware that actors who suddenly find themselves having an important shared interest with other actors have a tendency to overestimate the degree of common interest involved. This tendency is especially strong for those actors (e.g., the United States, at least before 1950) whose beliefs about international relations and morality imply that they can cooperate only with "good" states and that with those states there will be no major conflicts. On the other hand, states that have either a tradition of limited cooperation with others (e.g., Britain) or a strongly held theory that differentiates occasionally from permanent allies[6] (e.g., the Soviet Union) find it easier to resist this tendency and need not devote special efforts to combating its danger.

A third safeguard for decision-makers would be to make their assumptions, beliefs, and the predictions that follow from them as explicit as possible. An actor should try to determine, before events occur, what evidence would count for and against his theories. By knowing what to expect he would know what to be surprised by, and surprise could indicate to that actor that his beliefs needed reevaluation.[7]

A fourth safeguard is more complex. The decision-maker should try to prevent individuals and organizations from letting their main task, political future, and identity become tied to specific theories and images of other actors.[8] If this occurs, subgoals originally sought for their contribution to higher ends will take on value of their own, and information indicating possible alternative routes to the original goals will not be carefully considered. For example, the U.S. Forest Service was unable to carry out its original purpose as effectively when it began to see its distinctive competence not in promoting the best use of lands and forests but rather in preventing all types of forest fires.[9]

Organizations that claim to be unbiased may not realize the extent to which their definition of their role has become involved with certain beliefs about the world. Allen Dulles is a victim of this lack of understanding when he says, "I grant that we are all creatures of prejudice, including CIA officials, but by entrusting intelligence coordination to our central intelligence service, which is excluded from policy-making and is married to no particular military hardware, we can avoid, to the greatest possible extent, the bending of facts obtained through intelligence to suit a particular occupational viewpoint."[10] This statement overlooks the fact that the CIA has developed a certain view of international relations and of the cold war which maximizes the importance of its information-gathering, espionage, and subversive activities. Since the CIA would lose its unique place in the government if it were decided that the "back alleys" of world politics were no longer vital to U.S. security, it is not surprising that the organization interprets information in a way that stresses the continued need for its techniques.

Fifth, decision-makers should realize the validity and implications of Roberta Wohlstetter's argument that "a willingness to play with material from different angles and in the context of unpopular as well as popular hypotheses is an essential ingredient of a good detective, whether the end is the solution of a crime or an intelligence estimate."[11] However, it is often difficult, psychologically and politically, for any one person to do this. Since a decision-maker usually cannot get "unbiased" treatments of data, he should instead seek to structure conflicting biases into the decision-making process. The decision-maker, in other words, should have devil's advocates around. Just as, as Neustadt points out,[12] the decision-maker will want to create conflicts among his subordinates in order to make appropriate choices, so he will also want to ensure that incoming information is examined from many different perspectives with many different hypotheses in mind. To some extent this kind of examination will be done automatically through the divergence of goals, training, experience, and information that exists in any large organization. But in many cases this divergence will not be sufficient. The views of those analyzing the data will still be too homogeneous, and the decision-maker will have to go out of his way not only to cultivate but to create differing viewpoints.

While all that would be needed would be to have some people examining the data trying to validate unpopular hypotheses, it would probably be more effective if they actually believed and had a stake in the views they were trying to support. If in 1941 someone had had the task of proving the view that Japan would attack Pearl Harbor, the government might have been less surprised by the attack. And only a person who was out to show that Russia would take objectively great risks would have been apt to note that several ships with especially large hatches going to Cuba were riding high in the water, indicating the presence of a bulky but light cargo that was not likely to be anything other than strategic missiles. And many people who doubt the wisdom of the administration's Vietnam policy would be somewhat reassured if there were people in the government who searched the statements and actions of both sides in an effort to prove that North Vietnam was willing to negotiate and that the official interpretation of such moves as the Communist activities during the Tết truce of 1967 was incorrect.

Of course all these safeguards involve costs. They would divert resources from other tasks and would increase internal dissension. Determining whether these costs would be worth the gains would depend on a detailed analysis of how the suggested safeguards might be implemented. Even if they were adopted by a government, of course, they would not eliminate the chance of misperception. However, the safeguards would make it more likely that national decision-makers would make conscious choices about the way data were interpreted rather than merely assuming that they can be seen in only one way and can mean only one thing. Statesmen would thus be reminded of alternative images of others just as they are constantly reminded of alternative policies.

These safeguards are partly based on Hypothesis 3: actors can more easily assimilate into their established image of another actor information contradicting that image if the information is transmitted and considered bit by bit than if it comes all at once. In the former case, each piece of discrepant data can be coped with as it arrives and each of the conflicts with the prevailing view will be small enough to go unnoticed, to be dismissed as unimportant, or to necessitate at most a slight modification of the image (e.g., addition of exceptions to the rule). When the information arrives in a block, the contradiction between it and the prevailing view is apt to be much clearer and the probability of major cognitive reorganization will be higher.

Sources of Concepts

An actor's perceptual thresholds—and thus the images that ambiguous information is apt to produce—are influenced by what he has experienced and learned about.[13] If one actor is to perceive that another fits in a given category he must first have, or develop, a concept for that category. We can usefully distinguish three levels at which a concept can be present or absent. First, the concept can be completely missing. The actor's cognitive structure may not include anything corresponding to the phenomenon he is encountering. This situation can occur not only in science fiction, but also in a world of rapid change or in the meeting of two dissimilar systems. Thus China's image of the Western world was extremely inaccurate in the mid-nineteenth century, her learning was very slow, and her responses were woefully inadequate. The West was spared a similar struggle only because it had the power to reshape the system it encountered. Once the actor clearly sees one instance of the new phenomenon, he is apt to recognize it much more quickly in the future.[14] Second, the actor can know about a concept but not believe that it reflects an actual phenomenon. Thus Communist and Western decision-makers are each aware of the other's explanation of how his system functions, but do not think that the concept corresponds to reality. Communist elites, furthermore, deny that anything *could* correspond to the democracies' description of themselves. Third, the actor may hold a concept, but not believe that another actor fills it at the present moment. Thus the British and French statesmen of the 1930's held a concept of states with unlimited ambitions. They realized that Napoleons were possible, but they did not think Hitler belonged in that category. Hypothesis 4 distinguishes these three cases: misperception is most difficult to correct in the case of a missing concept and least difficult to correct in the case of a recognized but presumably unfilled concept. All other things being equal (e.g., the degree to which the concept is central to the actor's cognitive structure), the first case requires more cognitive reorganization than does the second, and the second requires more reorganization than the third.

However, this hypothesis does not mean that learning will necessarily be slowest in the first case, for if the phenomena are totally new the actor may make such grossly inappropriate responses that he will quickly acquire information clearly indicating that he is faced with something he does not understand. And the sooner the actor realizes that things are not—or may not be—what they seem, the sooner he is apt to correct his image.[15]

Three main sources contribute to decision-makers' concepts of international relations and of other states and influence the level of their perceptual thresholds for various phenomena. First, an actor's beliefs about his own domestic political system are apt to be important. In some cases, like that of the USSR, the decision-makers' concepts are tied to an ideology that explicitly provides a frame of reference for viewing foreign affairs. Even where this is not the case, experience with his own system will partly determine what the actor is familiar with and what he is apt to perceive in others. Louis Hartz claims, "It is the absence of the experience of social revolution which is at the heart of the whole American dilemma. . . . In a whole series of specific ways it enters into our difficulty of communication with the rest of the world. We find it difficult to understand Europe's 'social question'. . . . We are not familiar with the deeper social struggles of Asia and hence tend to interpret even reactionary regimes as 'democratic.'"[16] Similarly, George Kennan argues that in World War I the Allied powers, and especially America, could not understand the bitterness and violence of others' internal conflicts: ". . . The inability of the Allied statesmen to picture to themselves the passions of the Russian civil war [was partly caused by the fact that] we represent . . . a society in which the manifestations of evil have been carefully buried and sublimated in the social behavior of people, as in their very consciousness. For this reason, probably, despite our widely traveled and outwardly cosmopolitan lives, the mainsprings of political behavior in such a country as Russia tend to remain concealed from our vision."[17]

Second, concepts will be supplied by the actor's previous experiences. An experiment from another field illustrates this. Dearborn and Simon presented business executives from various divisions (e.g., sales, accounting, production) with the same hypothetical data and asked them for an analysis and recommendations from the standpoint of what would be best for the company as a whole. The executives' views heavily reflected their departmental perspectives.[18] William W. Kaufmann shows how the perceptions of Ambassador Joseph Kennedy were affected by his past: "As befitted a former chairman of the Securities Exchange and Maritime Commissions, his primary interest lay in economic matters. . . . The revolutionary character of the Nazi regime was not a phenomenon that he could easily grasp. . . . It was far simpler, and more in accord with his own premises, to explain German aggressiveness in economic terms. The Third Reich was dissatisfied, authoritarian, and expansive largely because her economy was unsound."[19] Similarly it has been argued that Chamberlain was slow to recognize Hitler's intentions partly because of the limiting nature of his personal background and business experiences. The impact of training and experience seems to be demonstrated when the background of the appeasers is compared to that of their opponents. One difference stands out: "A substantially higher percentage of the anti-appeasers (irrespective of class origins) had the kind of knowledge which comes from close acquaintance, mainly professional, with foreign affairs."[20] Since members of the diplomatic corps are responsible for meeting threats to the nation's security before these grow to major proportions and since they have learned about cases in which aggressive states were not recognized as such until very late, they may be prone to interpret ambiguous data as showing that others are aggressive. It should be stressed that we cannot say that the professionals of the 1930s were more apt to make accurate judgments of other states. Rather, they may have been more sensitive to the chance that others were aggressive. They would then rarely take an aggressor for a status-quo power, but would more often make the opposite error. Thus in the years before World War I the permanent officials in the British Foreign Office overestimated German aggressiveness.[21]

A parallel demonstration in psychology of the impact of training on perception is presented by an experiment in which ambiguous pictures were shown to both advanced and beginning police-administration students. The advanced group perceived more violence in the pictures than did the beginners. The probable explanation is that "the law enforcer may come to accept crime as a familiar personal experience, one which he himself is not surprised to encounter. The acceptance of crime as a familiar experience in turn increases the ability or readiness to perceive violence where clues to it are potentially available."[22] This experiment lends weight to the view that the British diplomats' sensitivity to aggressive states was not totally a product of personnel selection procedures.

A third source of concepts, which frequently will be the most directly relevant to a decision-maker's perception of international relations, is international history. As Henry Kissinger points out, one reason why statesmen were so slow to recognize the threat posed by Napoleon was that previous events had accustomed them only to actors who wanted to modify the existing system, not overthrow it.[23] The other side of the coin is even more striking: historical traumas can heavily influence future perceptions. They can either establish a state's image of the other state involved or can be used as analogies. An example of the former case is provided by the fact that for at least ten years after the Franco-Prussian War most of Europe's statesmen felt that Bismarck had aggressive plans when in fact his main goal was to protect the status quo. Of course the evidence was ambiguous. The post-1871 Bismarckian maneuvers, which were designed to keep peace, looked not unlike the pre-1871 maneuvers designed to set the stage for war. But that the post-1871 maneuvers were seen as indicating aggressive plans is largely attributable to the impact of Bismarck's earlier actions on the statesmen's image of him.

A state's previous unfortunate experience with a type of danger can sensitize it to other examples of that danger. While this sensitivity may lead the state to avoid the mistake it committed in the past, it may also lead it mistakenly to believe that the present situation is like the past one. Santayana's maxim could be turned around: "Those who remember the past are condemned to make the opposite mistakes." As Paul Kecskemeti shows, both defenders and critics of the unconditional surrender plan of the Second World War thought in terms of the conditions of World War I.[24] Annette Baker Fox found that the Scandinavian countries' neutrality policies in World War II were strongly influenced by their experiences in the previous war, even though vital aspects of the two situations were different. Thus "Norway's success [during the First World War] in remaining non-belligerent though pro-Allied gave the Norwegians confidence that their country could again stay out of war."[25] And the lesson drawn from the unfortunate results of this policy was an important factor in Norway's decision to join NATO.

The application of the Munich analogy to various contemporary events has been much commented on, and I do not wish to argue the substantive points at stake. But it seems clear that the probabilities that any state is facing an aggressor who has to be met by force are not altered by the career of Hitler and the history of the 1930s. Similarly the probability of an aggressor's announcing his plans is not increased (if anything, it is decreased) by the fact that Hitler wrote *Mein Kampf*. Yet decision-makers are more sensitive to these possibilities, and thus more apt to perceive ambiguous evidence as indicating they apply to a given case, than they would have been had there been no Nazi Germany.

Historical analogies often precede, rather than follow, a careful analysis of a situation (e.g., Truman's initial reaction to the news of the invasion of South Korea was to think of the Japanese invasion of Manchuria). Noting this precedence, however, does not show us which of many analogies will come to a decision-maker's mind. Truman could have thought of nineteenth-century European wars that were of no interest to the United States. Several factors having nothing to do with the event under consideration influence what analogies a decision-maker is apt to make. One factor is the number of cases similar to the analogy with which the decision-maker is familiar. Another is the importance of the past event to the political system of which the decision-maker is a part. The more times such an event occurred and the greater its consequences were, the more a decision-maker will be sensitive to the particular danger involved and the more he will be apt to see ambiguous stimuli as indicating another instance of this kind of event. A third factor is the degree of the decision-maker's personal involvement in the past case—in time, energy, ego, and position. The last-mentioned variable will affect not only the event's impact on the decision-maker's cognitive structure, but also the way he perceives the event and the lesson he draws. Someone who was involved in getting troops into South Korea after the attack will remember the Korean War differently from someone who was involved in considering the possible use of nuclear weapons or in deciding what messages should be sent to the Chinese. Greater personal involvement will usually give the event greater impact, especially if the decision-maker's own views were validated by the event. One need not accept a total application of learning theory to nations to believe that "nothing fails like success."[26] It also seems likely that if many critics argued at the time that the decision-maker was wrong, he will be even more apt to see other situations in terms of the original event. For example, because Anthony Eden left the government on account of his views and was later shown to have been correct, he probably was more apt to see as Hitlers other leaders with whom he had conflicts (e.g., Nasser). A fourth factor is the degree to which the analogy is compatible with the rest of his belief system. A fifth is the absence of alternative concepts and analogies. Individuals and states vary in the amount of direct or indirect political experience they have had which can provide different ways of interpreting data. Decision-makers who are aware of multiple possibilities of states' intentions may be less likely to seize on an analogy prematurely. The perception of citizens of nations like the United States which have relatively little history of international politics may be more apt to be heavily influenced by the few major international events that have been important to their country.

The first three factors indicate that an event is more apt to shape present perceptions if it occurred in the recent rather than the remote past. If it occurred recently, the statesman will then know about it at first hand even if he was not involved in the making of policy at the time. Thus if generals are prepared to fight the last war, diplomats may be prepared to avoid the last war. Part of the Anglo-French reaction to Hitler can be explained by the prevailing beliefs that the First World War was to a large extent caused by misunderstandings and could have been avoided by farsighted and nonbelligerent diplomacy. And part of the Western perception of Russia and China can be explained by the view that appeasement was an inappropriate response to Hitler.[27]

The Evoked Set

The way people perceive data is influenced not only by their cognitive structure and theories about other actors but also by what they are concerned with at the time they receive the information. Information is evaluated in light of the small part of the person's memory that is presently active—the "evoked set." My perceptions of the dark streets I pass walking home from the movies will be different if the film I saw had dealt with spies than if it had been a comedy. If I am working on aiding a country's education system and I hear someone talk about the need for economic development in that state, I am apt to think he is concerned with education, whereas if I had been working on, say, trying to achieve political stability in that country, I would have placed his remarks in that framework.[28]

Thus Hypothesis 5 states that when messages are sent from a different background of concerns and information than is possessed by the receiver, misunderstanding is likely. Person A and person B will read the same message quite differently if A has seen several related messages that B does not know about. This difference will be compounded if, as is frequently the case, A and B each assume that the other has the same background he does. This means that misperception can occur even when deception is neither intended nor expected. Thus Roberta Wohlstetter found not only that different parts of the United States government had different perceptions of data about Japan's intentions and messages partly because they saw the incoming information in very different contexts, but also that officers in the field misunderstood warnings from Washington: "Washington advised General Short [in Pearl Harbor] on November 27 to expect 'hostile action' at any moment, by which it meant 'attack on American possessions from without,' but General Short understood this phrase to mean 'sabotage.'"[29] Washington did not realize the extent to which Pearl Harbor considered the danger of sabotage to be primary, and furthermore it incorrectly believed that General Short had received the intercepts of the secret Japanese diplomatic messages available in Washington which indicated that surprise attack was a distinct possibility. Another implication of this hypothesis is that if important information is known to only part of the government of state A and part of the government of state B, international messages may be misunderstood by those parts of the receiver's government that do not match, in the information they have, the part of the sender's government that dispatched the message.[30]

Two additional hypotheses can be drawn from the problems of those sending messages. Hypothesis 6 states that when people spend a great deal of time drawing up a plan or making a decision, they tend to think that the message about it they wish to convey will be clear to the receiver.[31] Since they are aware of what is to them the important pattern in their actions, they often feel that the pattern will be equally obvious to others, and they overlook the degree to which the message is apparent to them only because they know what to look for. Those who have not participated in the endless meetings may not understand what information the sender is trying to convey. George Quester has shown how the German and, to a lesser extent, the British desire to maintain target limits on bombing in the first eighteen months of World War II was undermined partly by the fact that each side knew the limits it was seeking and its own reasons for any apparent "exceptions" (e.g., the German attack on Rotterdam) and incorrectly felt that these limits and reasons were equally clear to the other side.[32]

Hypothesis 7 holds that actors often do not realize that actions intended to project a given image may not have the desired effect because the actions themselves do not turn out as planned. Thus even without appreciable impact of different cognitive structures and backgrounds, an action may convey an unwanted message. For example, a country's representatives may not follow instructions and so may give others impressions contrary to those the home government wished to convey. The efforts of Washington and Berlin to settle their dispute over Samoa in the late 1880s were complicated by the provocative behavior of their agents on the spot. These agents not only increased the intensity of the local conflict, but led the decision-makers to become more suspicious of the other state because they tended to assume that their agents were obeying instructions and that the actions of the other side represented official policy. In such cases both sides will believe that the other is reading hostility into a policy of theirs which is friendly. Similarly, Quester's study shows that the attempt to limit bombing referred to above failed partly because neither side was able to bomb as accurately as it thought it could and thus did not realize the physical effects of its actions.[33]

Further Hypotheses from the Perspective of the Perceiver

From the perspective of the perceiver several other hypotheses seem to hold. Hypothesis 8 is that there is an overall tendency for decision-makers to see other states as more hostile than they are.[34] There seem to be more cases of statesmen incorrectly believing others are planning major acts against their interest than of statesmen being lulled by a potential aggressor. There are many reasons for this which are too complex to be treated here (e.g., some parts of the bureaucracy feel it is their responsibility to be suspicious of all other states; decision-makers often feel they are "playing it safe" to believe and act as though the other state were hostile in questionable cases; and often, when people do not feel they are a threat to others, they find it difficult to believe that others may see them as a threat). It should be noted, however, that decision-makers whose perceptions are described by this hypothesis would not necessarily further their own values by trying to correct for this tendency. The values of possible outcomes as well as their probabilities must be considered, and it may be that the probability of an unnecessary arms-tension cycle arising out of misperceptions, multiplied by the costs of such a cycle, may seem less to decision-makers than the probability of incorrectly believing another state is friendly, multiplied by the costs of this eventuality.

Hypothesis 9 states that actors tend to see the behavior of others as more centralized, disciplined, and coordinated than it is. This hypothesis holds true in related ways. Frequently, too many complex events are squeezed into a perceived pattern. Actors are hesitant to admit or even see that particular incidents cannot be explained by their theories.[35] Those events not caused by factors that are important parts of the perceiver's image are often seen as though they were. Further, actors see others as more internally united than they in fact are and generally overestimate the degree to which others are following a coherent policy. The degree to which the other side's policies are the product of internal bargaining,[36] internal misunderstandings, or subordinates' not following instructions is underestimated. This is the case partly because actors tend to be unfamiliar with the details of another state's policy-making processes. Seeing only the finished product, they find it simpler to try to construct a rational explanation for the policies, even though they know that such an analysis could not explain their own policies.[37]

Familiarity also accounts for Hypothesis 10: because a state gets most of its information about the other state's policies from the other's foreign office, it tends to take the foreign office's position for the stand of the other government as a whole. In many cases this perception will be an accurate one, but when the other government is divided or when the other foreign office is acting without specific authorization, misperception may result. For example, part of the reason why in 1918 Allied governments incorrectly thought "that the Japanese were preparing to take action [in Siberia], if need be, with agreement with the British and French alone, disregarding the absence of American consent,"[38] was that Allied ambassadors had talked mostly with Foreign Minister Motono, who was among the minority of the Japanese favoring this policy. Similarly, America's NATO allies may have gained an inaccurate picture of the degree to which the American government was committed to the MLF because they had greatest contact with parts of the government that strongly favored the MLF. And states that tried to get information about Nazi foreign policy from German diplomats were often misled because these officials were generally ignorant of or out of sympathy with Hitler's plans. The Germans and the Japanese sometimes purposely misinformed their own ambassadors in order to deceive their enemies more effectively.

Hypothesis 11 states that actors tend to overestimate the degree to which others are acting in response to what they themselves do when the others behave in accordance with the actor's desires; but when the behavior of the other is undesired, it is usually seen as derived from internal forces. If the *effect* of another's action is to injure or threaten the first side, the first side is apt to believe that such was the other's *purpose*. An example of the first part of the hypothesis is provided by Kennan's account of the activities of official and unofficial American representatives who protested to the new Bolshevik government against several of its actions. When the Soviets changed their position, these representatives felt it was largely because of their influence.[39] This sort of interpretation can be explained not only by the fact that it is gratifying to the individual making it, but also, taking the other side of the coin mentioned in Hypothesis 9, by the fact that the actor is most familiar with his own input into the other's decision and has less knowledge of other influences. The second part of Hypothesis 11 is illustrated by the tendency of actors to believe that the hostile behavior of others is to be explained by the other side's motives and not by its reaction to the first side. Thus Chamberlain did not see that Hitler's behavior was related in part to his belief that the British were weak. More common is the failure to see that the other side is reacting out of fear of the first side, which can lead to self-fulfilling prophecies and spirals of misperception and hostility.

This difficulty is often compounded by an implication of Hypothesis 12: when actors have intentions that they do not try to conceal from others, they tend to assume that others accurately perceive these intentions. Only rarely do they believe that others may be reacting to a much less favorable image of themselves than they think they are projecting.[40]

For state A to understand how state B perceives A's policy is often difficult because such understanding may involve a conflict with A's image of itself. Raymond Sontag argues that Anglo-German relations before World War I deteriorated partly because "the British did not like to think of themselves as selfish, or unwilling to tolerate 'legitimate' German expansion. The Germans did not like to think of themselves as aggressive, or unwilling to recognize 'legitimate' British vested interest."[41]

Hypothesis 13 suggests that if it is hard for an actor to believe that the other can see him as a menace, it is often even harder for him to see that issues important to him are not important to others. While he may know that another actor is on an opposing team, it may be more difficult for him to realize that the other is playing an entirely different game. This is especially true when the game he is playing seems vital to him.[42]

The final hypothesis, Hypothesis 14, is as follows: actors tend to overlook the fact that evidence consistent with their theories may also be consistent with other views. When choosing between two theories we have to pay attention only to data that cannot be accounted for by one of the theories. But it is common to find people claiming as proof of their theories data that could also support alternative views. This phenomenon is related to the point made earlier that any single bit of information can be interpreted only within a framework of hypotheses and theories. And while it is true that "we may without a vicious circularity accept some datum as a fact because it conforms to the very law for which it counts as another confirming instance, and reject an allegation of fact because it is already excluded by law,"[43] we should be careful lest we forget that a piece of information seems in many cases to confirm a certain hypothesis only because we already believe that hypothesis to be correct and that the information can with as much validity support a different hypothesis. For example, one of the reasons why the German attack on Norway took both that country and England by surprise, even though they had detected German ships moving toward Norway, was that they expected not an attack but an attempt by the Germans to break through the British blockade and reach the Atlantic. The initial course of the ships was consistent with either plan, but the British and Norwegians took this course to mean that their predictions were being borne out.[44] This is not to imply, that the interpretation made was foolish, but only that the decision-makers should have been aware that the evidence was also consistent with an invasion and should have had a bit less confidence in their views.

The longer the ships would have to travel the same route whether they were going to one or another of two destinations, the more information would be needed to determine their plans. Taken as a metaphor, this incident applies generally to the treatment of evidence. Thus as long as Hitler made demands for control only of ethnically German areas, his actions could be explained either by the hypothesis that he had unlimited ambitions or by the hypothesis that he wanted to unite all the Germans. But actions against non-Germans (e.g., the takeover of Czechoslovakia in March 1938) could not be accounted for by the latter hypothesis. And it was this action that convinced the appeasers that Hitler had to be stopped. It is interesting to speculate on what the British reaction would have been had Hitler left Czechoslovakia alone for a while and instead made demands on Poland similar to those he eventually made in the summer of 1939. The two paths would then still not have diverged, and further misperception could have occurred.

NOTES

1. Floyd Allport, *Theories of Perception and the Concept of Structure* (New York 1955), 382; Ole Holsti, "Cognitive Dynamics and Images of the Enemy," in David Finlay, Ole Holsti, and Richard Fagen, *Enemies in Politics* (Chicago 1967), 70.
2. For a use of this concept in political communication, see Roberta Wohlstetter, *Pearl Harbor* (Stanford 1962).
3. See, for example, Donald Campbell, "Systematic Error on the Part of Human Links in Communications Systems," *Information and Control*, 1 (1958), 346–50; and Leo Postman, "The Experimental Analysis of Motivational Factors in Perception," in Judson S. Brown, ed., *Current Theory and Research in Motivation* (Lincoln, Neb., 1953), 59–108.
4. Dale Wyatt and Donald Campbell, "A Study of Interviewer Bias as Related to Interviewer's Expectations and Own Opinions," *International Journal of Opinion and Attitude Research*, IV (Spring 1950), 77–83.
5. Max Jacobson, *The Diplomacy of the Winter War* (Cambridge, MA, 1961), 136–39.
6. Raymond Aron, *Peace and War* (Garden City 1966), 29.
7. [Thomas] Kuhn, *The Structure of Scientific Revolution* [(Chicago 1964)], 65.
8. See Philip Selznick, *Leadership in Administration* (Evanston 1957).
9. Ashley Schiff, *Fire and Water: Scientific Heresy in the Forest Service* (Cambridge, MA, 1962)
10. *The Craft of Intelligence* (New York 1963), 53.
11. P. 302. See Beveridge, 93, for a discussion of the idea that the scientist should keep in mind as many hypotheses as possible when conducting and analyzing experiments.
12. *Presidential Power* (New York 1960).
13. Most psychologists argue that this influence also holds for perception of shapes. For data showing that people in different societies differ in respect to their predisposition to experience certain optical illusions and for a convincing argument that this difference can be explained by the societies' different physical environments, which have led their people to develop different patterns of drawing inferences from ambiguous visual cues, see Marshall Segall, Donald Campbell, and Melville Herskovits, *The Influence of Culture on Visual Perceptions* (Indianapolis 1966).
14. Thus when Bruner and Postman's subjects first were presented with incongruous playing cards (i.e., cards in which symbols and colors of the suits were not matching, producing red spades and black diamonds), long exposure times were necessary for correct identification. But once a subject correctly perceived the card and added this type of card to his repertoire of categories, he was able to identify other incongruous cards much more quickly. For an analogous example—in this case, changes in the analysis of aerial reconnaissance photographs of an enemy's secret weapons-testing facilities produced by the belief that a previously unknown object may be present—see David Irving, *The Mare's Nest* (Boston 1964), 66–67, 274–75.
15. [Jerome Bruner and Leo Postman, "On the Perceptions of Incongruity: A Paradigm," in Jerome Bruner and David Krech, eds., *Perception and Personality* (Durham, NC, 1949).]

16. *The Liberal Tradition in America* (New York 1955), 306.

17. *Russia and the West Under Lenin and Stalin* (New York 1962), 142–43.

18. DeWitt Dearborn and Herbert Simon, "Selective Perception: A Note on the Departmental Identification of Executives," *Sociometry*, XXI (June 1958), 140–44.

19. "Two American Ambassadors: Bullitt and Kennedy," in [Gordon Craig and Felix Gilbert, eds., *The Diplomats*, Vol. 3 (New York 1963)], 358–59.

20. [Donald Lammers, *Explaining Munich* (Stanford 1966)], 15.

21. George Monger, *The End of Isolation* (London 1963).

22. Hans Toch and Richard Schulte, "Readiness to Perceive Violence as a Result of Police Training," *British Journal of Psychology*, LII (November 1961), 392 (original italics omitted). It should be stressed that one cannot say whether or not the advanced police students perceived the pictures "accurately." The point is that their training predisposed them to see violence in ambiguous situations. * * * For an experiment showing that training can lead people to "recognize" an expected stimulus even when that stimulus is in fact not shown, see Israel Goldiamond and William F. Hawkins, "Vexierversuch: The Log Relationship Between Word-Frequency and Recognition Obtained in the Absence of Stimulus Words," *Journal of Experimental Psychology*, LVI (December 1958), 457–63.

23. *A World Restored* (New York 1964), 2–3.

24. *Strategic Surrender* (New York 1964), 215–41.

25. *The Power of Small States* (Chicago 1959), 81.

26. William Inge, *Outspoken Essays,* First Series (London 1923), 88.

27. Of course, analogies themselves are not "unmoved movers." The interpretation of past events is not automatic and is informed by general views of international relations and complex judgments. And just as beliefs about the past influence the present, views about the present influence interpretations of history. It is difficult to determine the degree to which the United States' interpretation of the reasons it went to war in 1917 influenced American foreign policy in the 1920s and 1930s and how much the isolationism of that period influenced the histories of the war.

28. For some psychological experiments on this subject, see Jerome Bruner and A. Leigh Minturn, "Perceptual Identification and Perceptual Organization," *Journal of General Psychology*, LIII (July 1955), 22–28; Seymour Feshbach and Robert Singer, "The Effects of Fear Arousal and Suppression of Fear Upon Social Perception," *Journal of Abnormal and Social Psychology*, LV (November 1957), 283–88; and Elsa Sippoal, "A Group Study of Some Effects of Preparatory Sets," *Psychology Monographs*, XLVI, No. 210 (1935), 27–28. For a general discussion of the importance of the perceiver's evoked set, see Postman, 87.

29. Pp. 73–74.

30. For example, Roger Hilsman points out, "Those who knew of the peripheral reconnaissance flights that probed Soviet air defenses during the Eisenhower administration and the U-2 flights over the Soviet Union itself . . . were better able to understand some of the things the Soviets were saying and doing than people who did not know of these activities" (*To Move a Nation* [Garden City 1967], 66). But it is also possible that those who knew about the U-2 flights at times misinterpreted Soviet messages by incorrectly believing that the sender was influenced by, or at least knew of, these flights.

31. I am grateful to Thomas Schelling for discussion on this point.

32. *Deterrence Before Hiroshima* (New York 1966), 105–22.

33. Ibid.

34. For a slightly different formulation of this view, see [Ole Holsti, "Cognitive Dynamics and Images of the Enemy," in David Finlay, Ole Holsti, and Richard Fagen, *Enemies in Politics* (Chicago 1967)], 27.

35. The Soviets consciously hold an extreme version of this view and seem to believe that nothing is accidental. See the discussion in Nathan Leites, *A Study of Bolshevism* (Glencoe 1953), 67–73.

36. A. W. Marshall criticizes Western explanations of Soviet military posture for failing to take this into account. See his "Problems of Estimating Military Power," a paper presented at the 1966 Annual Meeting of the American Political Science Association, 16.

37. It has also been noted that in labor-management disputes both sides may be apt to believe incorrectly that the other is controlled from above, either from the international union office or from the company's central headquarters (Robert Blake, Herbert Shepard, and Jane Mouton, *Managing Intergroup Conflict in Industry* [Houston 1964], 182). It has been further noted that both Democratic and Republican members of the House tend to see the other party as the one that is more disciplined and united (Charles Clapp, *The Congressman* [Washington 1963], 17–19).

38. George Kennan, *Russia Leaves the War* (New York 1967), 484.

39. Ibid., 404, 408, 500.

40. Herbert Butterfield notes that these assumptions can contribute to the spiral of "Hobbesian fear. . . . You yourself may vividly feel the terrible fear that you have of the other party, but you cannot enter into the other man's counter-fear, or even understand why he should be particularly nervous. For you know that you yourself mean him no harm, and that you want nothing from him save guarantees for your own safety; and it is never possible for you to realize or remember properly that since he cannot see the inside of your mind, he can never have the same assurance of your intentions that you have" (*History and Human Conflict* [London 1951], 20).

41. *European Diplomatic History 1871–1932* (New York 1933), 125. It takes great mental effort to realize that actions which seem only the natural consequence of defending your vital interests can look to others as though you are refusing them any chance of increasing their influence. In rebutting the famous Crowe "balance of power" memorandum of 1907, which justified a policy of "containing" Germany on the grounds that she was a threat to British national security, Sanderson, a former permanent undersecretary in the Foreign Office, wrote, "It has sometimes seemed to me that to a foreigner reading our press the British Empire must appear in the light of some huge giant sprawling all over the globe, with gouty fingers and toes stretching in every direction, which cannot be approached without eliciting a scream" (quoted in Monger, 315). But few other Englishmen could be convinced that others might see them this way.

42. George Kennan makes clear that in 1918 this kind of difficulty was partly responsible for the inability of either the Allies or the new Bolshevik government to understand the motivations of the other

side: "There is . . . nothing in nature more egocentrical than the embattled democracy. . . . It . . . tends to attach to its own cause an absolute value which distorts its own vision of everything else. . . . It will readily be seen that people who have got themselves into this frame of mind have little understanding for the issues of any contest other than the one in which they are involved. The idea of people wasting time and substance on any *other* issue seems to them preposterous" (*Russia and the West*, 11–12).

43. [Abraham Kaplan, *The Conduct of Inquiry* (San Francisco 1964)], 89.
44. Johan Jorgen Hoist, "Surprise, Signals, and Reaction: The Attack on Norway," *Cooperation and Conflict*, No. 1 (1966), 34. The Germans made a similar mistake in November 1942 when they interpreted the presence of an Allied convoy in the Mediterranean as confirming their belief that Malta would be resupplied. They thus were taken by surprise when landings took place in North Africa (William Langer, *Our Vichy Gamble* [New York 1966], 365).

Keren Yarhi-Milo

IN THE EYE OF THE BEHOLDER
How Leaders and Intelligence Communities
Assess the Intentions of Adversaries

How do policymakers infer the long-term political intentions of their states' adversaries? This question has important theoretical, historical, and political significance. If British decisionmakers had understood the scope of Nazi Germany's intentions for Europe during the 1930s, the twentieth century might have looked very different. More recently, a Brookings report observes that "[t]he issue of mutual distrust of long-term intentions . . . has become a central concern in U.S.–China relations."[1] Statements by U.S. and Chinese officials confirm this suspicion. U.S. Ambassador to China Gary Locke noted "a concern, a question mark, by people all around the world and governments all around the world as to what China's intentions are."[2] Chinese officials, similarly, have indicated that Beijing regards recent U.S. policies as a "sophisticated ploy to frustrate China's growth."[3]

Current assessments of the threat posed by a rising China—or for that matter, a possibly nuclear-armed Iran, or a resurgent Russia—depend on which indicators observers use to derive predictions about a potential adversary's intentions. Surprisingly, however, little scholarship exists to identify which indicators leaders and the state's intelligence apparatus tasked with estimating threats use to assess intentions. For example, disputes among American analysts over the military capabilities of the Soviet Union dominated

From *International Security* 38, no. 1 (Summer 2013): 7–51. Some of the author's notes have been omitted.

debates on the Soviet threat throughout the Cold War, yet there has been little examination of the extent to which such calculations shaped or reflected U.S. political decisionmakers' assessments of Soviet intentions. Analyzing how signals are filtered and interpreted by the state's decisionmakers and its intelligence apparatus can lead to better understanding of the types of signals that tend to prompt changes in relations with adversaries, as well as help to develop useful advice for policymakers on how to deter or reassure an adversary more effectively.

In this article, I compare two prominent rationalist approaches in international relations theory about how observers can be expected to infer adversaries' political intentions, with a third approach that I develop and term the "selective attention thesis." First, the behavior thesis asserts that observers refer to certain noncapability-based actions—such as the adversary's decision to withdraw from a foreign military intervention or join binding international organizations—to draw conclusions regarding that adversary's intentions. This approach focuses on the role of costly information in influencing state behavior. Actions are considered costly if they require the state to expend significant, unrecoverable resources or if they severely constrain its future decisionmaking. The basic intuition behind this approach is that an action that costs nothing could equally be taken by actors with benign or with malign intentions, and thus it provides no credible information about the actor's likely plans.[4] Observers should therefore ignore "cheap talk."[5] Second, the capabilities thesis, drawing on insights from realism as well as costly signaling, asserts that states should consider an adversary's military capabilities in assessing its intentions. Of particular importance would be significant changes in armament policies, such as a unilateral reduction in military capabilities. Such changes reveal credible information about an adversary's ability to engage in warfare and thus its intention to do so.[6]

Drawing on insights from psychology, neuroscience, and organizational theory, I develop a third approach, the selective attention thesis. This thesis posits that individual perceptual biases and organizational interests and practices influence which types of indicators observers regard as credible signals of the adversary's intentions. Thus, the thesis predicts differences between a state's political leaders and its intelligence community in their selection of which signals to focus on and how to interpret those signals. In particular, decisionmakers often base their interpretations on their own theories, expectations, and needs, sometimes ignoring costly signals and paying more attention to information that, though less costly, is more vivid (i.e., personalized and emotionally involving). The thesis also posits that organizational affiliations and roles matter: intelligence organizations predictably rely on different indicators than civilian decisionmakers do to determine an adversary's intentions. In intelligence organizations, the collection and analysis of data on the adversary's military inventory typically receive priority. Over time, intelligence organizations develop substantial knowledge of these material indicators that they then use to make predictions about an adversary's intentions.

To test the competing theses, I examined * * * U.S. assessments of Soviet intentions under the administration of President Jimmy Carter (a period when détente collapsed) [and] U.S. assessments of Soviet intentions in the years leading to the end of the Cold War during the second administration of President Ronald Reagan. * * * My findings are based on review of more than 30,000 archival documents and intelligence reports, as well as interviews with former decisionmakers and intelligence officials. The cases yield findings more consistent with the selective attention thesis than with either the behavior or capabilities thesis, as I explain in the conclusion.

Before proceeding, it is important to note what lies outside the scope of this study. First, I am concerned primarily with the perceptions of an adversary's long-term political intentions because these are most likely to affect a state's foreign policy and strategic choices. Second, I do not address whether observers correctly identified the intentions of their adversaries. Addressing this question would require that we first establish what the leaders of * * * the Soviet Union during the periods examined here genuinely believed their own intentions to be at the time. Third, elsewhere I address the effects of perceived intentions on the collective policies of the states.[7] Rather, the focus of this article is on the indicators that leaders and intelligence organizations tend to privilege or ignore in their assessments of an adversary's political intentions. * * *

Theories of Intentions and the Problem of Attention

The three theses I outline below provide different explanations as to how observers reach their assessments about the adversary's political intentions. The term "political intentions" refers to beliefs about the foreign policy plans of the adversary with regard to the status quo.[8] I divide assessments of political intentions into three simple categories: expansionist, opportunistic, or status quo.[9] Expansionist adversaries exhibit strong determination to expand their power and influence beyond their territorial boundaries. Opportunistic states desire a favorable change in the distribution of power with either a limited or an unlimited geographical scope, but do not actively seek change. They may have contingent plans to seize opportunities to achieve this objective, but they will not pursue their revisionist goals when the cost of doing so appears high.[10] Status quo powers want only to maintain their relative power position.

The Selective Attention Thesis

Information about intentions can be complex, ambiguous, and potentially deceptive, and thus requires much interpretive work. Cognitive, affective, and organizational practices impede individuals' ability to process this information. To distinguish between signals and noise, individuals use a variety of heuristic inference strategies.[11] These simplified models of reality, however, can have the unintended effect of focusing excessive attention on certain pieces of information and away from others. The selective attention thesis recognizes that individual decisionmakers and bureaucratic organizations, such as an intelligence community, process information differently. The thesis yields two hypotheses: the subjective credibility hypothesis explains the inference process of decisionmakers, and the organizational expertise hypothesis describes that of intelligence organizations.

THE SUBJECTIVE CREDIBILITY HYPOTHESIS

The subjective credibility hypothesis predicts that decisionmakers will not necessarily detect or interpret costly actions as informative signals.[12] This psychology-based theory posits that both the degree of credence given to evidence and the interpretation of evidence deemed credible will depend on a decisionmaker's expectations about the links between the adversary's behavior and its under-lying characteristics; his or her own theories about which signals are indicative of the adversary's type; and the vividness of the information.[13]

First, the attention paid to costly actions hinges on observers' expectations about the adversary.[14] Observers are likely to vary in their prior degree of distrust toward an adversary and the extent to which they believe its intentions are hostile. This variation in decisionmakers' beliefs and expectations affects their selection and reading of signals in predictable ways. Given cognitive assimilation mechanisms and the human tendency to try to maintain cognitive consistency, decisionmakers who already hold relatively more hawkish views about the adversary's intentions when they assume power are less likely to perceive and categorize even costly reassuring actions as credible signals of benign intent. They are likely to reason, for example, that the adversary's actions are intended to deceive observers into believing that it harbors no malign intentions. Or they may believe that the adversary's reassuring signals merely reflect its economic or domestic political interests, and thus should not be seen as signaling more benign foreign policy goals. In contrast, those with relatively less hawkish views of an adversary's intentions are more likely to interpret reassuring signals as conforming with their current beliefs and, therefore, are more likely to see such signals as benign. Hawks are likely to focus on costly actions that indicate malign intentions, because such actions are consistent with their existing beliefs about the adversary's intentions.[15]

Second, decisionmakers' interpretations are also guided by their theories about the relationship between an adversary's behavior and its underlying characteristics. As Robert Jervis points out, different observers will interpret even costly behavior differently, "because some of them saw a certain correlation while others either saw none or believed that the correlation was quite different."[16] If, for instance, a decisionmaker believes in the logic of diversionary war, he or she is likely to pay attention to indicators of an adversary state's domestic social unrest and see them as evidence that its leadership is about to embark on a revisionist foreign policy. Thus, social unrest serves as an index of intention, one that the adversary is unlikely to manipulate to project a false image. Those within the administration who do not share this theory of diversionary war will view social unrest as an unreliable indicator of future intentions.

Third, the subjective credibility hypothesis expects decisionmakers to focus on information that, even if perhaps costless, is vivid. Vividness refers to the "emotional interest of information, the concreteness and imaginability of information, and the sensory, spatial, and temporal proximity of information."[17] One "vivid" indicator that is particularly salient to the issues studied in this article consists of a decisionmaker's impressions from personal interactions with members of the adversary's leadership.[18] Recent work in psychology and political science has shown that our emotional responses in face-to-face meetings shape the certainty of our beliefs and preferences for certain choices.[19] As Eugene Borgida and Richard Nisbett argued, "[T]here may be a kind of 'eyewitness' principle of the weighing of evidence, such that firsthand, sense-impression data is assigned greater validity."[20] Accordingly, information about intentions that is vivid, personalized, and emotionally involving is more likely to be remembered, and hence to be disproportionately available for influencing inferences. Conversely, decisionmakers will be reluctant to rely on evidence that is abstract, colorless, objective, or less tangible—such as measurements of the adversary's weapon inventory or the contents of its doctrinal manuals—even if such evidence could be regarded as extremely reliable. This kind of information is not nearly as engaging as the vivid, salient, and often emotionally laden personal responses that leaders take away from meeting with their opponents.[21]

A few clarifications about the selective attention thesis are in order. First, the importance of prior beliefs in assimilating new information is central to both psychological and some rationalist approaches.[22] In Bayesian learning models, observers evaluating new evidence are not presumed to possess identical prior beliefs. The prediction that distinguishes Bayesian models from biased-learning models concerns whether observers with identical prior beliefs and levels of uncertainty will be similarly affected by new information revealed by costly signals.[23] In contrast, the subjective credibility hypothesis claims that a process of updating might not occur even in the face of costly signals, and that vivid, noncostly actions can also be seen as informative. Further, the concept of Bayesian updating suggests that disconfirming data will always lead to some belief change, or at least to lowered confidence. The subjective credibility hypothesis, however, recognizes that some decisionmakers will not revise their beliefs even when confronted with valuable and costly information for reasons described above, such as a strong confirmation bias, the colorless nature of the information, or incongruity with the decisionmaker's theories. This study also asks a set of questions about the importance of costly actions that Bayesian models tend to ignore: that is, do different observers select different kinds of external indicators to update their beliefs?

THE ORGANIZATIONAL EXPERTISE HYPOTHESIS

The bureaucratic-organizational context in which intelligence analysts operate has specific effects that do not apply to political decisionmakers. As a collective, intelligence organizations tend to analyze their adversary's intentions through the prism of their relative expertise. Intelligence organizations tend to devote most of their resources to the collection, production, and analysis of information about the military inventory of the adversary, which can be known and tracked over time. As Mark Lowenthal writes, "[T]he regularity and precision that govern each nation's military make it susceptible to intelligence collection."[24] Quantified inventories can also be presented in a quasi-scientific way to decisionmakers.

Over time, the extensive monitoring of the adversary's military inventory creates a kind of narrow-mindedness that influences the inference process. To use Isaiah Berlin's metaphor, extensive monitoring creates hedgehogs: "[T]he intellectually aggressive hedgehogs knew one big thing and sought, under the banner of parsimony, to expand the explanatory power of that big thing to 'cover' new cases."[25] This is not to argue that intelligence organizations know only how to count an adversary's missiles and military divisions. Rather, the organizational expertise hypothesis posits that, because analyzing intentions is one central issue with which intelligence organizations are explicitly tasked, and because there is no straightforward or easy way to predict the adversary's intentions, a state's intelligence apparatus has strong incentives to use the relative expertise that it has, which emphasizes careful empirical analysis of military capabilities. Unlike the capabilities thesis, the organizational expertise hypothesis sees the logic of relying on capabilities as arising from bureaucratic and practical reasons specific to intelligence organizations.[26]

The Capabilities Thesis

The capabilities thesis posits that observers should infer an adversary's intentions based on indexes of its military power. This thesis draws on several realist theories that suggest that a state's intentions reveal, or are at least constrained by, its military capabilities. Two pathways link military power and perceived intentions.[27] First, according to John Mearsheimer's theory of offensive realism, decisionmakers in an anarchic international system must "assume the worst" about adversaries' intentions.[28] How aggressive a state can (or will) be is essentially a function of its power. A second pathway relies on the logic of costly actions, according to which the size of an incremental increase or decrease in an adversary's military capabilities, in combination with how powerful the observing country sees it to be, can serve as a credible signal of aggressive or benign intentions.[29]

Drawing on these insights, the capabilities hypothesis predicts that observers in a state will infer an adversary's intentions from perceived trends in the level of the adversary's military capabilities compared with its own military capabilities. Under conditions of uncertainty about states' intentions, a perception that an adversary is devoting more resources to building up its military capabilities is likely to be seen as a costly signal of hostile intentions. As Charles Glaser puts it, "[A] state's military buildup can change the adversary's beliefs about the state's motives, convincing the adversary that the state is inherently more dangerous than it had previously believed. More specifically, the state's buildup could increase the adversary's assessment of the extent to which it is motivated by the desire to expand for reasons other than security."[30] Conversely, a perception of a freeze or a decrease in the adversary's military capabilities or its investment in them is likely to be seen as a costly and reassuring signal of more benign intentions. At the same time, realists have long emphasized that a state's perception of security or threat depends on how its military power compares with the power of the adversary, that is, on the balance of military power. Thus, in the process of discerning intentions, assessments of the balance of military capabilities are also likely to affect interpretations of benign or hostile intent. For example, if the adversary already enjoys military superiority over the observer, then observers will perceive an increase in the adversary's military capabilities as clear evidence of hostile intentions.

The Behavior Thesis

The behavior thesis posits that certain kinds of noncapability-based actions are also useful in revealing information about political intentions, because undertaking them requires the adversary either to sink costs or to commit itself credibly by tying its own hands. I evaluate the potential causal role of three types of such "costly" actions. The first is a state's decision to join or withdraw from binding international institutions.[31] Some institutions can impose significant costs on states, and they are thus instrumental in allowing other states to discern whether a state has benign or malign intentions.[32] The structural version of the democratic peace, for instance, posits that the creation of democratic domestic institutions—because of their constraining effects, transparency, and ability to generate audience costs—should make it easier for others to recognize a democratic state's benign intentions.[33]

The second costly signal involves foreign interventions in the affairs of weaker states, or withdrawals from such interventions. A state's decision to spill blood and treasure in an effort to change the status quo, for example, is likely to be viewed as a costly, hence credible, signal of hostile intentions.

A third type of behavioral signal involves arms control agreements. Scholars have pointed out that, when offensive and defensive weapons are distinguishable, arms control agreements—especially those that limit offensive deployment and impose effective verification—provide an important and reassuring signal of benign intentions.[34] Cheating or reneging on arms control agreements would lead others to question the intentions of that state. It is important to differentiate indicators such as the signing of arms control agreements as a behavioral signal of intentions from indicators associated with the capabilities thesis. Although both theses ultimately deal with the relationship between a state's military policy and others' assessments of its intentions, they have different predictions. If the capabilities thesis is correct, a change in perceived intentions should occur only when the implementation of the agreement results in an actual decrease in the adversary's capabilities. Policymakers should refer to the actual change in capabilities as the reason for a change in their perceptions of the adversary's intentions. If the behavior thesis is correct, perceptions of intentions should shift when the arms control agreement is signed, and policymakers should refer to the action of signing the agreement as a critical factor. Evidence indicating that changes in assessments of intentions occurring at the time of the signing of a treaty in response to expectations of future shifts in capabilities, or reasoning pointing to both the symbolic and the actual value of a treaty, confirms both theses.

■   ■   ■

Research Design

To evaluate the selective attention, capabilities, and behavior theses, I examine, first, the perceptions of key decisionmakers and their closest senior advisers on the foreign policy of a particular adversary and, second, the coordinated assessments of the intelligence community.[35] In addition to variation on the dependent variable—perceptions of political intentions—the cases also provide useful variation on the explanatory variables.

To test the propositions offered by the selective attention thesis, I examine how the primary decisionmakers—President Jimmy Carter [and] President Ronald Reagan * * * and their senior advisers—varied in their initial assessments of the enemy. Also, all three key decisionmakers were engaged in personal meetings with the adversary's leadership, albeit to various degrees.

The cases also allow testing of the capabilities thesis, because both the initial balance of capabilities and the magnitude of change in the adversary's capabilities during the period of interaction vary across the cases. Both Cold War cases assume relative equality in military capabilities between the superpowers with a moderate increase (the collapse of détente case) or decrease (the end of the Cold War case) in Soviet capabilities during the interaction period. In contrast, the German military was vastly inferior to the British military, but an unprecedented increase in German military capabilities during the mid-to-late 1930s shifted the balance of power in Germany's favor. Thus, the interwar case should be an easy test case for the capabilities thesis, as the dramatic increase in German military capabilities and the shift in the balance of power during the period should have led observers to focus on this indicator as a signal of intentions.

The cases are also useful in testing the predictions of the behavior thesis. In particular, the end of the Cold War case is an easy test for the behavior thesis, given that the Soviet leader, Mikhail Gorbachev, took a series of extremely costly actions. This should have had a significant reassuring influence on observers' perceptions.

In each case, I subject the evidence to two probes. First, I look for covariance between changes in the independent variables cited in each thesis and changes in the dependent variable of perceptions of intentions. A finding of no correlation between the predictions of a thesis and the time or direction in which perceptions of intentions change is evidence against that thesis. Second, through process tracing, I examine whether decisionmakers or collective intelligence reports explicitly cited the adversary's capabilities or its behavior, for example, as relevant evidence in their assessments of the adversary's intentions. This step provides a further check against mistaking correlation for causation. Third, in each case I test the predictions of the selective attention framework by comparing decisionmakers' assessments with those of the intelligence communities, as well as

by tracing the process by which the selective attention criteria account for the variation among decisionmakers in how they categorized credible signals, and the timing of changes in their perceived intentions.

The Collapse of Détente, 1977–80

Jimmy Carter began his presidency with great optimism about relations with the Soviet Union. But by his last year in office, the U.S.-Soviet détente had collapsed: Carter did not meet with Soviet leaders; he increased the defense budget; he withdrew the Strategic Arms Limitation Talks (SALT) II Treaty from Senate consideration; and he announced the Carter Doctrine, which warned against interference with U.S. interests in the Middle East. In this case, I briefly outline trends in Soviet military capabilities and costly actions during that period that inform the capabilities and behavior theses, respectively. Then I show how the main decisionmakers in the Carter administration—President Jimmy Carter, National Security Adviser Zbigniew Brzezinski, and Secretary of State Cyrus Vance[36]— assessed Soviet intentions in a manner that is most consistent with the subjective credibility hypothesis of the selective attention thesis. This is followed by a discussion of the U.S. intelligence community's assessments which, I argue, are in line with both the capabilities thesis and the selective attention thesis's organizational expertise hypothesis.

The U.S. consensus during this period was that the Soviet Union was building up and modernizing its military capabilities and that the correlation of military forces was shifting in its favor.[37] The Soviets were expanding their already large conventional ground and theater air forces and introducing modern systems that were equal or superior to those of NATO.[38] The deployment of Soviet intermediate-range ballistic missiles in Europe produced a growing concern over the potential threat of Soviet continental strategic superiority.[39] While the United States maintained what it called "asymmetric equivalence" with the Soviet Union,[40] the U.S. defense establishment was especially worried about increases in Soviet nuclear counterforce capability. The Soviets were steadily improving the survivability and flexibility of their strategic forces, which had reached the potential to destroy about four-fifths of the U.S. Minuteman silos by 1980 or 1981.[41] In mid-1979, the National Security Council (NSC) cautioned that the strategic nuclear balance was deteriorating faster than the United States had expected two years earlier, and would get worse into the early 1980s.

The Soviets took two kinds of costly actions that fit the criteria of the behavior thesis. The first was signing the SALT II Treaty in June 1979, which called for reductions in U.S. and Soviet strategic forces to 2,250 in all categories of delivery vehicles.[42] The second was Soviet interventions in crises around the world. The Soviets intervened in twenty-six conflicts during 1975–80.[43] Unlike previous interventions during that period, however, the 1978 Soviet intervention in Ethiopia was direct, not simply through Cuban proxies, and the Soviet invasion of Afghanistan in late 1979 was a full-scale application of Soviet military power. The United States feared that the pattern of Soviet actions would expand beyond the "arc of crisis" to include additional regions and countries more important to U.S. interests. The Soviet invasion of Afghanistan, in particular, significantly intensified this fear, because it was the first direct use of Soviet force beyond the Warsaw Pact nations to restore a pro-Soviet regime. In addition to these two interventions, reports in 1979 that the Soviets had placed a combat brigade in Cuba created a sense of panic in Washington that subsided only when American decisionmakers realized that the brigade had been in Cuba since 1962.[44]

Carter Administration Assessments of Soviet Intentions

In what follows I show that, consistent with the subjective credibility hypothesis derived from the selective attention thesis, Carter and his advisers did not agree on the informative value of Soviet costly actions. Rather, they debated the importance of various indicators in inferring intentions, and interpreted costly Soviet behavior markedly differently from one another. Specifically, their initial beliefs and theories about the Soviet Union affected the degree of credibility that each of the three decisionmakers attached to various Soviet actions.

Prior to becoming national security adviser, Brzezinski had held a more negative impression of the Soviet Union than either Carter or Vance.[45] During their first year in office, Carter and Vance perceived Soviet intentions as, at worst, opportunistic.[46] Brzezinski's private weekly memoranda to Carter reveal that, even though he was more skeptical than the president about Soviet intentions, he, too, was hopeful that the Soviets would remain relatively cooperative.[47] As conflicts in the third world grew in scope, intensity, and importance throughout 1978, however, Brzezinski concluded that the Soviet involvement in Africa was expansionist, not merely opportunistic. In January 1978, he maintained that "either by design or simply as a response to an apparent opportunity, the Soviets have stepped up their efforts to exploit African turbulence to their own advantage."[48] Soon after, he cautioned Carter that the "Soviet leaders may be acting merely in response to an apparent opportunity, or the Soviet actions may be part of a wider strategic design."[49] On February 17, Brzezinski provided Carter with a rare, explicit account of his impressions of Soviet intentions, including a table that divided Soviet behavior into three categories: benign, neutral, and malignant.[50] Brzezinski described Soviet objectives as seeking "selective détente,"[51] and explained that his revised assessments about Soviet intentions "emerge from Soviet behavior and statements since the election."[52] The table is particularly illuminating because it provides no mention of Soviet military capabilities, only of Soviet behavior, although the latter was not confined to Soviet interventionism or costly actions alone. During February and March, Cuban and Soviet forces backed the government of Ethiopia in its effort to expel the defeated Somali army; Brzezinski believed that the Soviet Union was in Ethiopia "because it has a larger design in mind."[53] He reiterated these conclusions in subsequent reports to the president.[54]

In contrast, Secretary of State Vance believed that the Soviet Union's actions in Africa were not "part of a grand Soviet plan, but rather attempts to exploit targets of opportunity,"[55] and that they were "within the bounds of acceptable competition."[56] Alarmed by Carter's growing skepticism about Soviet motivations and objectives, Vance requested a formal review of U.S.–Soviet relations in May 1978. "Many are asking whether this Administration has decided to make a sharp shift in its foreign policy priorities," Vance noted, expressing alarm about the more hawkish Brzezinski's influence on the president's view of the Soviet Union.[57] Indeed, Carter's growing distrust of Soviet intentions, ignited by the Soviet involvement in the Horn of Africa, had become apparent in a series of public statements depicting the Soviets as less trustworthy and calling for the adoption of a harsher U.S. stance.[58] Yet Carter continued to see the Soviet Union's actions in the Horn as opportunistic.[59]

By mid-1978, Brzezinski and Vance found themselves in opposing camps while Carter vacillated. Brzezinski summarized the differences:

> One view . . . was that "the Soviets have stomped all over the code of détente." They continue to pursue a selective détente. Their action reflects growing assertiveness in Soviet foreign policy generally. Brezhnev's diminished control permits

the natural, historical, dominating impulse of the regime to assert itself with less restraint.

> Another view . . . was that the record of Soviet action is much more mixed and has to be considered case-by-case. The Soviets are acting on traditional lines and essentially reacting to U.S. steps.[60]

Convinced by early 1979 that the Soviets were pursuing an expansionist "grand design," Brzezinski continued to press Carter to act more assertively. He wrote to Carter that the recent pattern in Soviet interventions revealed revisionist intentions.[61] Although alarmed, the president continued to reject Brzezinski's calls to "deliberately toughen both the tone and the substance of our foreign policy."[62] The issue of Soviet intentions resurfaced in the fall of 1979 during the uproar over the Soviet brigade in Cuba. Brzezinski saw this as another credible indicator of Soviet expansionist intentions, but Carter and Vance were unpersuaded.[63]

The Soviet invasion of Afghanistan in December 1979 caused Carter to re-evaluate his perceptions of Soviet intentions. On January 20, 1980, he declared that it had made "a more dramatic change in my opinion of what the Soviets' ultimate goals are than anything they've done in the previous time that I've been in office."[64] Carter now viewed the Soviet Union as expansionist, not necessarily because of the financial or political costs incurred by the Soviets, but because the invasion represented a qualitative shift in Soviet behavior. Explaining this shift, Carter adopted Brzezinski's line of reasoning, saying, "[I]t is obvious that the Soviets' actual invasion of a previously nonaligned country, an independent, freedom-loving country, a deeply religious country, with their own massive troops is a radical departure from the policy or actions that the Soviets have pursued since the Second World War."[65] Consequently, he warned that the invasion of Afghanistan was "an extremely serious threat to peace because of the threat of further Soviet expansion into neighboring countries."[66]

The invasion was seen as an informative indicator of intention not solely because it was a "costly" action, but also because of the emotional response it invoked in Carter. Indeed, the reason he saw the invasion as indicative of Soviet intentions can also be explained, as Richard Ned Lebow and Janice Stein point out, by the "egocentric bias" that led Carter to exaggerate the extent to which he, personally, was the target of Soviet actions.[67] In particular, the invasion contradicted the frank rapport and the understanding that he felt he had achieved with Brezhnev during their meeting in June 1979 in Vienna.[68] Indeed, during that summit meeting, Carter spoke of "continuing cooperation and honesty in our discussions," and upon his return he had proudly reported to Congress that "President Brezhnev and I developed a better sense of each other as leaders and as men."[69] Brezhnev's justification for the invasion—which asserted that the Soviet troops were sent in response to requests by the Afghan government—infuriated Carter, as he interpreted it as an "insult to his intelligence."[70] Finally, Brezhnev's betrayal also suggested that the Soviet leader could not be trusted to be a partner for détente. As Carter explained, "[T]his is a deliberate aggression that calls into question détente and the way we have been doing business with the Soviets for the past decade. It raises grave questions about Soviet intentions and destroys any chance of getting the SALT Treaty through the Senate. And that makes the prospects for nuclear war even greater."[71] Carter wrote in his diary, "[T]he Soviet invasion sent a clear indication that they were not to be trusted."[72]

Vance's reactions to and interpretation of the Soviet invasion differed dramatically from Carter's. He did not see the invasion as significant and costly, and thus informative of Soviet intentions. Rather, he considered it an "aberration" from past behavior, and "largely as an expedient reaction to opportunities rather than as a manifestation of a more sustained trend."[73] Vance understood why others might view the invasion as a significant signal of expansionist intentions, but he believed that "the primary motive for the Soviet actions was defensive, [and] that the Soviets do not have long-term regional ambitions beyond Afghanistan."[74] Indeed, Vance continued to view Soviet intentions as opportunistic long after the invasion of Afghanistan.[75]

In sum, the evidence presented provides strong support for the selective attention thesis. The support for the capabilities thesis is weak: the significant Soviet military buildup did not lead all U.S. observers to see Soviet intentions as becoming more hostile throughout this period. More important, none of the decisionmakers referred to the Soviet military buildup in explaining his assessment of Soviet political intentions. Brzezinski's writings rarely discussed the recent Soviet military buildup, even though it would have bolstered the hawkish case.[76] The evidence for the behavior thesis is moderate. Both Carter and Brzezinski used Soviet military interventions to infer political intentions. Yet the behavior thesis does not explain why, unlike Brzezinski, Carter and Vance did not infer hostile or expansionist motives from Soviet involvement in the Horn of Africa; it also does not explain why the invasion of Afghanistan triggered such a dramatic change in Carter's beliefs about Soviet intentions but had no such effect on Vance. Finally, the behavior thesis fails to account for the differences between the decisionmakers' inference processes—which largely relied on assessments of Soviet actions, albeit not necessarily "costly" ones—and the U.S. intelligence community's inference process, which, as described in the next section, largely relied on assessments of Soviet capabilities.

U.S. Intelligence Community Assessments of Soviet Intentions

The bulk of the integrated national intelligence estimates (NIEs) on the Soviet Union throughout the Cold War focused on aspects of the Soviet military arsenal. As Raymond Garthoff stated, "Estimates of Soviet capabilities were the predominant focus of attention and received virtually all of the intelligence collection, analysis, and estimative effort."[77] Former Director of Central Intelligence George Tenet noted that "from the mid-1960s on to the Soviet collapse, we knew roughly how many combat aircraft or warheads the Soviets had, and where. But why did they need that many or that kind? What did they plan to do with them? To this day, Intelligence is always much better at counting heads than divining what is going on inside them. That is, we are very good at gauging the size and location of militaries and weaponry. But for obvious reasons, we can never be as good at figuring out what leaders will do with them."[78]

During the mid-to-late 1970s, various agencies within the U.S. intelligence community held differing views about Soviet intentions. For example, the State Department's Bureau of Intelligence and Research and the Central Intelligence Agency (CIA) saw the Soviets as opportunistic. The military intelligence agencies and the Defense Intelligence Agency (part of the Department of Defense) viewed Soviet intentions as expansionist. The reasoning described in the integrated NIEs shows that all U.S. intelligence agencies viewed measures of Soviet current and projected strategic power as the most important indicator of Soviet political intentions. For example, NIE 11-4-78 estimated that "more assertive Soviet international behavior" was "likely to persist as long as the USSR perceives that Western strength is declining and its own strength is steadily increasing." It judged that "if the new [Soviet] leaders believe the 'correlation of forces' to be favorable, especially if they are less impressed than Brezhnev with U.S. military might and more impressed with their own, they might employ military power even more assertively in pursuit of their global ambitions."[79] The centrality of Soviet capabilities and the balance of capabilities as indicators of intentions also dominated NIE 11-3/8-79, in which Director of Central Intelligence Stansfield Turner asserted that "as they [the Soviets] see this [military] superiority increase during the next three to five years, they will probably attempt to secure maximum political advantage from their military arsenal in anticipation of U.S. force modernization programs."[80]

* * *

Interagency disagreements about Soviet military strength and the evolving correlation of forces shaped readings of Soviet intentions. Agencies that perceived the Soviet Union as highly confident in its power also predicted that Soviet foreign policy would become more aggressive. Agencies that perceived Soviet capabilities as weaker also saw Soviet intentions as less aggressive and Soviet objectives as more moderate.[81] Bureaucratic interests did sometimes influence interpretations of Soviet capabilities and intentions, but whatever the parochial motives of analysts from different agencies and in spite of their disagreements about Soviet intentions, all of the intelligence agencies grounded their estimates of intentions in Soviet capabilities. Furthermore, in stark contrast to the Carter administration's decisionmakers, the intelligence community made almost no references to presumably costly noncapabilities-based actions to support the inferences they were drawing about their political intentions.[82]

In sum, the review of the NIEs on the Soviet Union reveals that unlike Carter, Brzezinski, and Vance, the U.S. intelligence community did not assess Soviet political intentions on the basis of behavioral or vivid indicators, but rather on their reading of Soviet military capabilities. This finding is consistent with both the capabilities thesis and the selective attention thesis's organizational expertise hypothesis. The marked differences between evaluations by the civilian decisionmakers and those of the intelligence community, as well as the substantial number of NIEs dedicated to assessing Soviet military capabilities, provide further support for the selective attention thesis.

The End of the Cold War, 1985–88

During his first term, President Ronald Reagan perceived Soviet intentions as expansionist. His views changed dramatically, however, during his second administration. Following the Moscow summit in May 1988, Reagan asserted that his characterization of the Soviet Union five years earlier as an "evil empire" belonged to "another time, another era."[83] When asked if he could declare the Cold War over, the president responded, "I think right now, of course."[84] This section explores the indicators that President Reagan, Secretary of State George Shultz, and Secretary of Defense Caspar Weinberger used to assess Soviet political intentions during Reagan's second term, and how the U.S. intelligence community analyzed similar indicators to infer Gorbachev's intentions during the same period. The discussion that follows begins with some background information about trends in Soviet capabilities and costly action. This is followed by an analysis of how Reagan and his advisers perceived Soviet intentions. The final section evaluates the inference process that the coordinated assessments of the U.S. intelligence community used to judge Soviet intentions during the same period.

Realist accounts of the end of the Cold War point to the decline in Soviet power relative to that of the United States during the late 1980s.[85] Yet archival documents show that at this time, the U.S. defense establishment estimated that the Soviet Union's military power was growing; that the Soviets were modernizing their strategic force comprehensively;[86] and that the Warsaw Pact had a strong advantage over NATO in almost all categories of forces as a result of its continuing weapons production.[87] In addition, prior to the signing of the Intermediate Nuclear Forces (INF) Treaty, the United States perceived the theater nuclear balance of power as extremely threatening, given the Soviet Union's vigorous modernization and initial deployment of intermediate-range ballistic missiles in Europe. Although the INF Treaty, which took effect in June 1988, substantially limited Soviet medium-range and intermediate-range ballistic missile forces, the U.S. intelligence community believed that it did not diminish the Soviets' ability to wage a nuclear war.[88] Then, in December 1988, Soviet Head of State Mikhail Gorbachev announced a unilateral and substantial reduction in Soviet conventional forces in Eastern Europe. Even so, U.S. perceptions of the balance of capabilities did not change until late 1989, following initial implementation of the Soviet force reductions. The announcement itself did not result in U.S. recognition of any significant diminution of Soviet capabilities in either size or quality.[89]

As for Soviet behavioral signals, Gorbachev's proposals during 1985 and 1986 were not sufficiently "costly."[90] During 1987 and 1988, however, the Soviet Union offered additional and significant reassurances to the United States. Especially costly were the Soviet acceptance of asymmetric reductions in the INF in 1987, the withdrawal of Soviet troops from Afghanistan announced publicly in February 1988,[91] and a series of other actions that Gorbachev undertook throughout 1988 aimed at restructuring the political system in the Soviet Union.[92]

Second Reagan Administration's Assessments of Soviet Intentions

A review of the historical record shows that Reagan, Shultz, and Weinberger disagreed on which Soviet actions they categorized as costly. Their interpretation of signals was shaped by their expectations, theories, and vivid, costless information.

To be sure, all three decisionmakers shared similar hawkish views of the Soviet Union, but they exhibited important differences in outlook. Weinberger held much more hawkish views than Reagan and Shultz at the start of Reagan's second administration.[93] Shultz was far less hawkish and did not believe, prior to 1985, that the Soviet Union desired global domination. Reagan's views were closer to those of Weinberger than Shultz. During his first term, Reagan had repeatedly referred to the Soviet Union as an ideologically motivated power bent on global hegemony.[94] Until mid-1987, Reagan continued to view Soviet intentions as expansionist. In December 1985, Reagan stated both in public and in private his belief that Gorbachev was still dedicated to traditional Soviet goals and that he had yet to see a break from past Soviet behavior.[95] In 1986, although Reagan had begun to view Gorbachev's policies as signaling a positive change in attitude, he still asserted that he had no illusions about the Soviets or their ultimate intentions."[96]

Reagan and Shultz began to gradually reevaluate their perceptions of Gorbachev's intentions during 1987. The Soviet leader's acceptance of the U.S. proposal on INF was a major contributing factor. In 1987 Reagan reflected on his evolving characterization of the Soviet Union: "With regard to the evil empire. I meant it when I said it [in 1983], because under previous leaders they have made it evident that . . . their program was based on expansionism."[97] Still, neither Reagan nor Shultz expected Gorbachev to signal a genuine change in Soviet foreign policy objectives. Reagan wrote, "[I]n the spring of 1987 we were still facing a lot of uncertainty regarding the Soviets. . . . It was evident something was up in the Soviet Union, but we still didn't know what it was."[98]

Two events in the spring of 1988 persuaded Reagan and Shultz of a change in Soviet intentions. First, the initial Soviet withdrawal from Afghanistan in April symbolized to both that the Brezhnev Doctrine was dead.[99] Shultz explained that the dominant perception in the administration was that "if the Soviets left Afghanistan, the Brezhnev Doctrine would be breached, and the principle of 'never letting go' would be violated."[100] In a private conversation with Gorbachev, Reagan acknowledged that the withdrawal "was a tangible step in the right direction," and took note of Gorbachev's statement that "the settlement could serve as a model for ending other regional conflict."[101] The second event occurred during the 19th Communist Party Conference, at which Gorbachev proposed major domestic reforms such as the establishment of competitive elections with secret ballots; term limits for elected officials; separation of powers with an independent judiciary; and provisions for freedom of speech, assembly, conscience, and the press. The proposals signaled to many in the Reagan administration that Gorbachev's domestic reforms were meant to make revolutionary and irreversible changes. Ambassador Jack Matlock described these proposals as "nothing short of revolutionary in the Soviet context," adding that they "provided evidence that Gorbachev was finally prepared to cross the Rubicon and discard the Marxist ideology that had defined and justified the Communist Party dictatorship in the Soviet Union."[102]

Reagan also paid significant attention to some "costless" actions and viewed them as credible signals of changed intentions given their vividness. Reagan repeatedly cited his positive impressions of Gorbachev from their private interactions in four summit meetings as persuading him that Gorbachev was genuinely seeking to reduce U.S.-Soviet tensions.[103] Emphasizing his growing conviction of Gorbachev's trustworthiness,[104] Reagan began increasingly to refer to Gorbachev as a friend who was "very sincere about the progressive ideas that he is introducing there [in the Soviet Union] and the changes that he thinks should be made."[105] * * * The president wrote, "It's clear that there was a chemistry between Gorbachev and me that produced something very close to a friendship. He was a tough, hard bargainer. . . . I liked Gorbachev even though he was a dedicated Communist."[106] * * *

Other members of Reagan's administration noticed the importance of vivid information in shaping his views. Matlock thus notes, "Once he [Reagan] and Shultz started meeting with Gorbachev they relied on their personal impressions and personal instincts." * * * Reagan's personality—specifically his openness to contradictory information, his belief in his power of persuasion, and his emotional intelligence[107]—allowed him to rely heavily on his personal impressions of Gorbachev. As Barbara Farnham puts it, for Reagan, "[p]ersonal experience counted for everything."[108] Reagan's confidants have pointed to his tendency to reduce issues to personalities: "If he liked and trusted someone, he was more prone to give credence to the policies they espoused."[109]

■ ■ ■

As for the role of Soviet capabilities, both Reagan and Shultz saw a connection between the Soviet Union's capabilities, its actions, and its political intentions. In their eyes, Soviet expansionist conduct during the 1970s occurred at a time when the United States had lost its superiority over the Soviet Union in strategic nuclear weapons.[110] They made it clear, however, that it was Soviet behavior during that period, rather than the Soviet military buildup, that was the decisive evidence of Soviet aggressive intentions. In fact, one of Reagan's favorite quotations was that "nations do not mistrust each other because they are armed; they are armed because they mistrust each other."[111] Reagan similarly acknowledged that the adversary's capabilities by themselves are not good indicators of its intentions; instead they are a by-product of how each state perceives the other's intentions.

■ ■ ■

In conclusion, the series of Gorbachev's costly actions should make this an easy case for the behavior thesis, yet, the empirical evidence lends only moderate support. While Reagan and Shultz relied on costly behavior signals to infer intentions, they also focused significantly on behavioral actions such as their own personal impressions of Gorbachev. Further, the behavior thesis fails to explain

Weinberger's inference process: the secretary of defense stated explicitly that he did not regard any of Gorbachev's costly actions as credible reassuring indicators of intentions. As a result, his assessments of Soviet intentions did not change at all, even after leaving office. These aspects in the inference processes underscore the subjective nature of credibility. The support for the capabilities thesis is weak. Given the perceived trends in Soviet capabilities described at the beginning of this section, one would have expected the perceived intentions of the Soviet Union to have remained hostile until mid-1988. This thesis, therefore, cannot explain the radical change in Reagan's and Shultz's perceptions, and why the president and his secretary of state rarely focused on the Soviet military arsenal as an indicator that shaped their assessments of Soviet political intentions during the period under examination.

U.S. Intelligence Community's Assessment of Soviet Intentions

The U.S. intelligence community's National Intelligence Estimates focused on markedly different indicators of Soviet intentions from 1985 to 1988 than did Reagan, Shultz, and Weinberger.[112] It gave greatest weight to the Soviet Union's military capabilities in judging Soviet political intentions. The U.S. intelligence community, as is now known, overestimated Soviet strategic forces and defense spending during the 1980s; this overestimation was an important contributing factor to the community's tendency to overstate Soviet hostility.[113]

Intelligence estimates from 1985 to 1987 concluded that Gorbachev was seeking détente with the West to reduce U.S. challenges to Soviet interests and to decrease U.S. defense efforts. His long-term goal was said to be to "preserve and advance the USSR's international influence and its relative military power."[114] Recognition by the Soviet leadership that the correlation of forces would soon shift against the Soviet Union and a relative decline in Soviet economic power were offered as the leading explanations for Gorbachev's cooperative initiatives.[115] A 1985 NIE stated, "Moscow has long believed that arms control must first and foremost protect the capabilities of Soviet military forces relative to their opponents. The Soviets seek to limit U.S. force modernization through both the arms control process and any resulting agreements."[116] A Special NIE in 1986 pointed to Soviet concerns about the Reagan administration's Strategic Defense Initiative as the primary motive behind Gorbachev's pursuit of a détente-like policy vis-à-vis the West. The NIEs portrayed Gorbachev's arms control initiatives as propaganda aimed at bolstering his campaign of deception.[117] The intelligence community's working assumption was that, despite serious economic problems since the mid-1970s, Soviet objectives remained unchanged.[118]

By mid-1988, Reagan's and Shultz's assessments of Soviet intentions had undergone a fundamental change, but the available NIEs indicate that the U.S. intelligence community did not revise its estimates of Soviet objectives until mid-1989.[119] Throughout 1987 and 1988, the community continued to hold that Gorbachev's foreign policy initiatives were merely tactical, and that no significant discontinuity in Soviet traditional goals and expectations could be anticipated.[120] For instance, in describing Gorbachev's "ultimate goal[s]," a late-1987 NIE repeated earlier assertions that Gorbachev was pursuing a clever plan to pursue communism, not through the use of blunt force, but through a deceiving posture of accommodation with the West that was intended to win more friends in the underdeveloped world.[121] Soviet modernization efforts toward greater "warfighting" capabilities, coupled with calculations as to how economic difficulties would affect the strategic balance of power, were said to provide the most reliable guides to Soviet objectives.[122]

In conclusion, consistent with the expectations of the selective attention thesis's organizational expertise hypothesis, as well as with those of the capabilities thesis, the intelligence community's

NIEs inferred Soviet political intentions primarily from its military capabilities. Throughout this period, the community did not update its assessments in response to Gorbachev's costly actions of reassurance, and it rarely used costly Soviet behavior to draw inferences about Soviet foreign policy goals. It saw Gorbachev's policies on arms limitations, for example, as rooted in the need to increase Soviet relative economic capabilities, a task that could be accomplished only by reducing pressure to allocate more resources to defense. Engaging NATO in arms control agreements was merely a ploy to undercut support in the West for NATO's weapons modernization efforts.[123] Thus, the support for the behavior thesis is weak.

Interestingly, the intelligence community's reluctance to revise its estimates of Soviet intentions led to repeated clashes between Director of Central Intelligence Robert Gates and Secretary of State Shultz, the latter saying later that he had little confidence in the community's intelligence reports on the Soviet Union.[124] Nevertheless, intelligence assessments had only limited impact on Reagan and Shultz, who drew conclusions about Soviet intentions largely from their personal impressions and insights from meetings with Gorbachev. As Matlock explains, "They are very experienced people and experienced politicians and it meant much more to them what they were experiencing."[125] Paul Pillar contends that Reagan and his advisers, apart from Shultz, "brushed aside as irrelevant any careful analysis of Soviet intentions, just as Carter and Brzezinski had brushed aside the question of the Soviets' reason for intervening in Afghanistan."[126]

■   ■   ■

In sum, the findings imply that any study on the efficacy of signals that fails to consider how signals are perceived and interpreted may be of little use to policymakers seeking to deter or reassure an adversary. They also suggest that policymakers should not assume that their costly signals will be understood clearly by their state's adversaries. They should not fear that others are necessarily making worst-case assumptions about their intentions on the basis of their military capabilities, but they should be aware that the adversary's intelligence apparatus is likely to view such an indicator as a credible signal of intentions. Decisionmakers' inclination to rely on their own judgments and subjective reading of signals to infer political intentions is pervasive and universal, but these individuals should be wary: getting inside the mind of the adversary is perhaps one of the most difficult tasks facing intelligence organizations, and perhaps most susceptible to bias and bureaucratic interests. * * *

NOTES

1. Kenneth Lieberthal and Wang Jisi, "Addressing U.S.-China Strategic Distrust" (Washington, DC: Brookings Institution, 2012), p. vi.

2. Gary Locke, "China Is a Country of Great Contrasts," National Public Radio, January 18, 2012, http://www.npr.org/2012/01/18/145384412/ambassador-locke-shares-his-impressions-of-china.

3. Jeffrey A. Bader, Obama and China's Rise. An Insider's Account of America's Asia Strategy (Washington, DC: Brookings Institution Press, 2012).

4. In the context of foreign policy intentions, see James D. Fearon, "Signaling Foreign Policy Interests: Tying Hands versus Sinking Costs," Journal of Conflict Resolution, Vol. 41, No. 1 (February 1997), pp. 68–90; Andrew Kydd, Trust and Mistrust in International Relations (Princeton, NJ: Princeton University Press, 2005); and Robert F. Trager, "Diplomatic Calculus in Anarchy: How Communication Matters," American Political Science Review, Vol. 104, No. 2 (May 2010), pp. 347–68.

5. Thomas C. Schelling, The Strategy of Conflict (Cambridge, Mass.: Harvard University Press, 1980); and Fearon, "Signaling Foreign Policy Interests." On when and how "cheap talk" could matter, see Trager, "Diplomatic Calculus in Anarchy"; Joseph Farrell and Robert Gibbons, "Cheap Talk Can Matter in Bargaining," Journal of Economic Theory, Vol. 48, No. 1 (June 1989), pp. 221–37; and Anne E. Sartori, Deterrence by Diplomacy (Princeton, NJ: Princeton University Press, 2005).

6. Charles L. Glaser, Rational Theory of International Politics: The Logic of Competition and Cooperation (Princeton, NJ: Princeton University Press, 2010).

7. For the effects of perceived intentions on policies, see Keren Yarhi-Milo, Knowing [the] Adversary: Leaders, Intelligence, and Assessments of Intentions in International Relations (Princeton, NJ: Princeton University Press, [2014]).

8. Intention should be distinguished from states' motives for keeping or changing the status quo. On motives, see Glaser, Rational Theory of International Politics, pp. 38–39.

9. The scope of the revisionist intentions in expansionist and opportunistic states can be limited or unlimited. For a similar typology, see Keith L. Shimko, Images and Arms Control: Perceptions of the Soviet Union in the Reagan Administration (Ann Arbor: University of Michigan Press, 1991).

10. Douglas Seay, "What Are the Soviets' Objectives in Their Foreign, Military, and Arms Control Policies?" in Lynn Eden and Steven E. Miller, eds., Nuclear Arguments: Understanding the Strategic Nuclear Arms and Arms Control Debates (Ithaca, NY: Cornell University Press, 1989), pp. 47–108; and Robert Jervis, Perception and Misperception in International Politics (Princeton, NJ: Princeton University Press, 1976).

11. Amos Tversky and Daniel Kahneman, "Availability: A Heuristic for Judging Frequency and Probability," Cognitive Psychology, Vol. 5, No. 2 (September 1973), pp. 207–32; and Thomas Gilovich, Dale Griffin, and Daniel Kahneman, eds., Heuristics and Biases: The Psychology of Intuitive Judgment (Cambridge: Cambridge University Press, 2002).

12. Robert Jervis, "Signaling and Perception: Drawing Inferences and Projecting Images," in Kristen Monroe, ed., Political Psychology (Mahwah, NJ: Lawrence Erlbaum, 2002); and Jonathan Mercer, "Emotional Beliefs," International Organization, Vol. 64, No. 1 (January 2010), pp. 1–31.

13. The literature on such biases is vast. For important works and good summaries, see Jervis, Perception and Misperception in International Politics; Ole Holsti, "The Belief System and National Images: A Case Study," Journal of Conflict Resolution, Vol. 6, No. 3 (September 1962), pp. 244–52; and Philip E. Tetlock, "Social Psychology and World Politics," in Susan T. Fiske, Daniel T. Gilbert, and Gardner Lindzey, eds., Handbook of Social Psychology, 4th ed. (New York: McGraw-Hill, 1998), pp. 868–914.

14. Robert Jervis, "Understanding Beliefs," Political Psychology, Vol. 27, No. 5 (October 2006), pp. 641–63.

15. This hypothesis cannot indicate a priori when observers will change their assessments about intentions, but it can predict the possibility of change in perceived intentions relative to those of other observers on the basis of their initial beliefs about the intentions of the adversary.

16. Peer Schouten, "Theory Talk #12: Robert Jervis on Nuclear Weapons, Explaining the Non Realist Politics of the Bush Administration and U.S. Military Presence in Europe," Theory Talks, January 24, 2008, http://www.theory-talks.org/2008/07/theory-talk-12.html.

17. Richard E. Nisbett and Lee Ross, Human Inference: Strategies and Shortcomings of Social Judgment (Englewood Cliffs, NJ: Prentice Hall, 1980), p. 62.

18. On the importance of personal meetings in inferring leaders' sincerity, see Todd Hall and Keren Yarhi-Milo, "The Personal Touch: Leaders' Impressions, Costly Signaling, and Assessments of Sincerity in International Affairs," International Studies Quarterly, Vol. 56, No. 3 (September 2012), pp. 560–73.

19. See, for example, Mercer, "Emotional Beliefs"; and Rose McDermott, "The Feeling of Rationality: The Meaning of Neuroscientific Advances for Political Science," Perspectives on Politics, Vol. 2, No. 4 (December 2004), pp. 691–706.

20. Borgida and Nisbett, "Differential Impact of Abstract vs. Concrete Information," p. 269.

21. Nisbett and Ross, *Human Inference,* pp. 188–91; Fiske and Taylor, *Social Cognition,* pp. 278–79; Tversky and Kahneman, "Availability"; Kaufmann, "Out of the Lab and into the Archives"; and Rose McDermott, Jonathan Cowden, and Stephen Rosen, "The Role of Hostile Communications in a Simulated Crisis Game," *Peace and Conflict: Journal of Peace Psychology,* Vol. 14, No. 2 (2008), p. 156.

22. For a debate on the role of "common prior beliefs" in bargaining models, see Alastair Smith and Allan Stam, "Bargaining and the Nature of War." *Journal of Conflict Resolution,* Vol. 50, No. 6 (December 2004), pp. 783–813; and Mark Fey and Kristopher W. Ramsay, "The Common Priors Assumption: A Comment on 'Bargaining and the Nature of War,' " *Journal of Conflict Resolution,* Vol. 50, No. 4 (2006), pp. 607–13.

23. Alan Gerber and Donald P. Green, "Rational Learning and Partisan Attitudes," *American Journal of Political Science,* Vol. 42, No. 3 (July 1998), pp. 189–210; and Charles S. Taber and Milton Lodge, "Motivated Skepticism in the Evaluation of Political Beliefs," *American Journal of Political Science,* Vol. 50, No. 3 (July 2006), pp. 755–69.

24. As Mark M. Lowenthal writes, "Deployed conventional and strategic forces . . . are difficult to conceal, as they tend to exist in identifiable garrisons and must exercise from time to time. They also tend to be garrisoned or deployed in large numbers, which makes hiding them or masking them impractical at best." Lowenthal, *Intelligence: From Secrets to Policy* (Washington, DC: CQ Press, 2009), pp. 234–35.

25. Philip E. Tetlock, *Expert Political Judgment: How Good Is It? How Can We Know?* (Princeton, NJ: Princeton University Press, 2005), pp. 20–21.

26. For analyses of how organizations influence information processes, see Martha S. Feldman and James G. March, "Information in Organizations as Signal and Symbol," *Administrative Science Quarterly,* Vol. 26, No. 2 (June 1981), pp. 171–86.

27. A third pathway concerns the offensive or defensive nature of the military capabilities as a signal of intentions. On the little impact that such indicators had on the inference processes of decisionmakers during these periods, see Yarhi-Milo, *Knowing [the] Adversary.*

28. John J. Mearsheimer, *The Tragedy of Great Power Politics* (New York: W. W. Norton, 2001), p. 31.

29. Kydd, *Trust and Mistrust in International Relations;* and Glaser, *Rational Theory of International Politics.*

30. Charles L. Glaser, "The Security Dilemma Revisited," *World Politics,* Vol. 50, No. 1 (October 1997), p. 178.

31. On the role of institutions in signaling intentions, see Robert O. Keohane, *After Hegemony: Cooperation and Discord in the World Political Economy* (Princeton, NJ: Princeton University Press, 1984); G. John Ikenberry, *After Victory: Institutions, Strategic Restraint, and the Rebuilding of Order after Major Wars* (Princeton, NJ: Princeton University Press, 2001); Seth Weinberger, "Institutional Signaling and the Origins of the Cold War," *Security Studies,* Vol. 12, No. 4 (Summer 2003), pp. 80–115.

32. The usefulness of international institutions in revealing information about intentions depends on institutional characteristics such as the nature of enforcement, the effects of veto points on state decision-making, and the institution's effects on member states' domestic political institutions.

33. For a summary of how domestic institutions can be a signal of intentions, see Mark L. Haas, "The United States and the End of the Cold War: Reactions to Shifts in Soviet Power, Policies, or Domestic Politics?" *International Organization,* Vol. 61, No. 1 (Winter 2007), p. 152; and James D. Fearon, "Domestic Political Audiences and the Escalation of International Disputes," *American Political Science Review,* Vol. 88, No. 3 (September 1994), pp. 577–92.

34. Glaser, "The Security Dilemma Revisited"; and Charles L. Glaser, *Analyzing Strategic Nuclear Policy* (Princeton, NJ: Princeton University Press, 1991).

35. For the U.S. cases, I use the declassified National Intelligence Estimates (NIEs) on the Soviet Union. NIEs, which are produced by the National Intelligence Council, are the most authoritative product of the intelligence community. The community regularly assessed Soviet intentions in the 11-4 and 11-8 series of NIEs, supplemented by occasional Special NIEs (SNIEs). In all NIEs, I analyze only those sections that deal with the question of intentions. In the British case, the main focus of the analysis is the coordinated Chiefs of Staff reports and memoranda, because these represent the integrated analysis of all three military service intelligence agencies.

36. On the relationship between the three decisionmakers, see Jerel A. Rosati, *The Carter Administration's Quest for Global Community: Beliefs and Their Impact on Behavior* (Columbia: University of South Carolina Press, 1987); and Betty Glad, *An Outsider in the White House: Jimmy Carter, His Advisors, and the Making of American Foreign Policy* (Ithaca, NY: Cornell University Press, 2009).

37. Zbigniew Brzezinski, memo, "Comprehensive Net Assessment, 1978," p. 8; and Harold Brown, "Report of Secretary of Defense Harold Brown to the Congress on the FY 1979 Budget, FY Authorization Request, and FY 1979–1983 Defense Programs," January 23, 1978, pp. 65–66.

38. Office of Strategic Research, "The Development of Soviet Military Power: Trends since 1965 and Prospects for the 1980s," SR 81-10035X (Washington, DC: National Foreign Research Center, April 1981), pp. xiii–xv.

39. NIE 11-6-78, pp. 2–3.

40. National Security Council (NSC) meeting, June 4, 1979, quoted in Zbigniew Brzezinski, *Power and Principle: Memoirs of the National Security Advisor, 1977–1981* (New York: Farrar, Straus and Giroux, 1983), pp. 334–36. The conventional military balance in Europe was perceived as favoring the Warsaw Pact forces. See National Foreign Assessment Center, "The Balance of Nuclear Forces in Central Europe," SR 78-10004 (Washington, DC: Central Intelligence Agency, January 1978); and "Comprehensive Net Assessment, 1978."

41. NIE 11-3/8-79, pp. 2, 4. Soviet damage-limitation capabilities were, however, still judged to be poor despite a large, ongoing Soviet investment. NIE 11-3/8-78, pp. 5–6, 11. See also Harold Brown, "Report of Secretary of Defense Harold Brown, on the FY 1979 Budget," pp. 65–66; and Harold Brown, "Department of Defense Annual Report, Fiscal Year 1980," January 25, 1979, p. 70.

42. As a result of the Soviet invasion of Afghanistan, Carter decided to table SALT II. NSC Weekly Report 123, December 28, 1979.

43. The Soviet Union had low-level involvement in eleven crises and conducted covert or semi-military activities in thirteen crises, in addition to using direct military force in Ethiopia and Afghanistan.

See International Conflict Behavior Project dataset, http://www.cidcm.umd.edu/icb/.

44. On the episode of the Soviet brigade in Cuba, see Cyrus R. Vance, *Hard Choices: Critical Years in America's Foreign Policy* (New York: Simon and Schuster, 1983), pp. 360–61; Brzezinski, *Power and Principle*, p. 347; and NSC Weekly Report 98, May 25, 1979; NSC Weekly Report 103, July 20, 1979; NSC Weekly Report 104, July 27, 1979; and NSC Weekly Report 109, September 13, 1979.

45. Rosati, *The Carter Administration's Quest for Global Community*; Melchiore Laucella, "A Cognitive-Psychodynamic Perspective to Understanding Secretary of State Cyrus Vance's Worldview," *Presidential Studies Quarterly*, Vol. 34, No. 2 (June 2004), pp. 227–71.

46. See, for example, *Public Papers of the President of the United States* [hereafter *PPP*] (Washington, DC: Government Printing Office, June 30, 1977), p. 1198; and *PPP*, December 15, 1977, p. 2119.

47. NSC Weekly Report 18, June 24, 1977.

48. NSC Weekly Report 42, January 13, 1978.

49. Quoted in Brzezinski, *Power and Principle*, p. 181.

50. NSC Weekly Report 47, February 17, 1978.

51. Ibid.

52. NSC Weekly Report 2, February 26, 1977.

53. Zbigniew Brzezinski, memo for the president, "The Soviet Union and Ethiopia: Implications for U.S. Soviet Relations," March 3, 1978.

54. NSC Weekly Report 55, April 21, 1978; and NSC Weekly Report 57, May 5, 1978.

55. Vance, *Hard Choices*, p. 84.

56. Ibid., p. 101.

57. Vance, memo to President Jimmy Carter, May 29, 1978. Document released to author under the Freedom of Information Act, July 2007.

58. *PPP*, May 20, 1978, pp. 872, 940; and *PPP*, May 25, 1978, p. 977. See also Brzezinski, *Power and Principle*, pp. 188–89; and Richard C. Thornton, *The Carter Years: Toward a New Global Order* (New York: Paragon House, 1991), p. 185.

59. *PPP*, November 13, 1978, p. 2017.

60. NSC Weekly Report 65, June 30, 1978.

61. NSC Weekly Report 84, January 12, 1979.

62. NSC Weekly Report 109, September 13, 1979.

63. Brzezinski, *Power and Principle*, pp. 347–51.

64. Jimmy Carter, interview, *Meet the Press*, January 20, 1980. See also Jimmy Carter, *Keeping Faith: Memoirs of a President* (Fayetteville: University of Arkansas Press, 1995), p. 480; "Message for Brezhnev from Carter Regarding Afghanistan," December 28, 1979; and Brzezinski, *Power and Principle*, p. 429.

65. *PPP*, January 20, 1980, p. 11. For a similar line of reasoning, see also pp. 308, 329.

66. *U.S. Department of State Bulletin (DSB)*, Vol. 80, No. 2034 (January 1980).

67. Richard Ned Lebow and Janice Gross Stein, "Afghanistan, Carter, and Foreign Policy Change: The Limits of Cognitive Models," in Dan Caldwell and Timothy J. McKeown, eds., *Diplomacy, Force, and Leadership: Essays in Honor of Alexander L. George* (Boulder, CO: Westview, 1993), p. 112.

68. Raymond L. Garthoff, *Détente and Confrontation: American-Soviet Relations from Nixon to Reagan*, rev. ed. (Washington, DC: Brookings Institution Press, 1994), p. 1059.

69. Quoted in ibid.

70. Ibid.

71. Hamilton Jordan, *Crisis: The Last Year of the Carter Presidency* (New York: G. P. Putnam's Sons, 1982), p. 99.

72. Jimmy Carter, *White House Diary* (New York: Farrar, Straus and Giroux, 2010), p. 383.

73. Ibid. For a similar logic, see Marshall Shulman, memorandum for Warren Christopher, "Notes on SU/Afghanistan," January 22, 1980; and Vance, *Hard Choices*, p. 388.

74. NSC Weekly Report 134, March 28, 1980.

75. See interviews with Vance and Shulman in Melchiore Laucella, "Cyrus Vance's Worldview: The Relevance of the Motivated Perspective," Ph.D. dissertation, Union Institute, 1996.

76. In only a few statements did the decisionmakers link Soviet intentions to the buildup. For example, in a report to Carter, Brzezinski wrote: "Soviet defense programs are going beyond the needs of legitimate deterrence and are increasingly pointing towards the acquisition of something which might approximate a war-fighting capability. While we do not know why the Soviets are doing this (intentions?), we do know that their increased capabilities have consequences for our national security." This statement does not, however, lend support to the capabilities thesis, as Brzezinski explicitly says that he cannot infer Soviet intentions from these indicators.

77. In this section, I rely in part on interviews I conducted with William Odom, head of the National Security Agency at the time, and Fritz Ermarth, Raymond Garthoff, Melvin Goodman, and Douglas MacEachin, all former CIA analysts of the Soviet Union. Raymond L. Garthoff, "Estimating Soviet Intentions and Capabilities," in Gerald K. Haines and Robert E. Leggett, eds., *Watching the Bear: Essays on CIA's Analysis of the Soviet Union* (Washington, DC: Center for the Study of Intelligence Publications, 2003), chap. 5, https://www.cia.gov/library/center-for-the-study-of-intelligence/csi-publications/books-and-monographs/watching-the-bear-essays on-cias-analysis-of-the-soviet-union.

78. "Speeches Delivered at the Conference," in ibid., chap. 8.

79. NIE 11-4-78, p. 6.

80. NIE 11-3/8-79, p. 4.

81. See, for example, NIE 11-4-77; NIE 11-3/8-79; and NIE 11-3/8-80.

82. NIE 11-4-78 made some references to current Soviet actions with respect to SALT and détente. This line of reasoning, however, was rarely invoked. NIE 4-1-78, pp. ix, x, 17.

83. Quoted in Raymond L. Garthoff, *The Great Transition: American-Soviet Relations and the End of the Cold War* (Washington, DC: Brookings Institution Press, 1994), p. 352.

84. President's news conference, Spaso House, Moscow, *DSB*, June 1988, p. 32.

85. William C. Wohlforth, "Realism and the End of the Cold War," *International Security*, Vol. 19, No. 3 (Winter 1994/95), pp. 91–129.

86. See, for example, NIE 11-3/8-86; NIE 11-3/8-87; and NIE 11-3/8-88.

87. Frank Carlucci, "Annual Report to the President and Congress, 1989" (Washington, DC: Government Printing Office, February 18, 1988), p. 29.

88. NIE 11-3/8-88, p. 5. The Department of Defense reached a similar conclusion. U.S. Department of Defense, Office of the Secretary of Defense, "Soviet Military Power" (Washington, DC: U.S.

Department of Defense, 1989), p. 7; and U.S. Department of Defense, Office of the Secretary of Defense, "Soviet Military Power" (Washington, DC: Government Printing Office, 1990), pp. 54–55.

89. National Intelligence Council (NIC), "Status of Soviet Unilateral Withdrawal," M 89-10003 (Washington, DC: NIC, October 1989).

90. Jack F. Matlock, *Reagan and Gorbachev: How the Cold War Ended* (New York: Random House, 2004), pp. 275–76; and Garthoff, *The Great Transition*, p. 334. For an analysis of Gorbachev's costly actions and their effects on perceived intentions, see Haas, "The United States and the End of the Cold War"; and Kydd, *Trust and Mistrust in International Relations*.

91. Soviet Foreign Minister Eduard Shevardnadze informed Shultz of the decision to withdraw from Afghanistan in September 1987. Gorbachev publicly confirmed this decision in February 1988.

92. Some decisionmakers in the United States did recognize the significance of Gorbachev's efforts to institute glasnost (openness, or transparency) within the Soviet Union during 1987. It was only from mid-1988, however, that his actions seemed aimed at fundamental institutional change. Both Shultz and Matlock argue that Gorbachev's actions had not, as of the end of 1987, signified fundamental reforms. George Shultz, *Turmoil and Triumph: My Years as Secretary of State* (New York: Charles Scribner's Sons, 1993), p. 1081; and Matlock, *Reagan and Gorbachev*, pp. 295–96. By mid-1988, however, Reagan had begun to praise Gorbachev for initiating true "democratic reform." He said that Gorbachev's efforts were "cause for shaking the head in wonder," leading him to view Gorbachev as "a serious man seeking serious reform." *DSB*, Vol. 2137 (1988), pp. 37–38.

93. In his comprehensive study on perceptions of the Soviet Union during the Reagan administration, Keith Shimko noted that "Weinberger's views of the Soviet Union were about as hard-line as one could get." Shimko, *Images and Arms Control*, p. 233.

94. Ibid., pp. 235–37.

95. See, for example, *DSB*, November 1985, p. 11; and *PPP*, 1985, p. 415.

96. *PPP*, 1986, p. 1369.

97. *PPP*, 1987, pp. 1508–09.

98. Ronald Reagan, *An American Life* (New York: Simon and Schuster, 1990), p. 683.

99. The Brezhnev Doctrine, announced in 1968, asserted the Soviet Union's right to use Warsaw Pact forces to intervene in any Eastern bloc nation that was seen as compromising communist rule and Soviet domination, either by trying to leave the Soviet sphere of influence or even by attempting to moderate Moscow's policies.

100. Shultz, *Turmoil and Triumph*, p. 1086.

101. Transcripts of the Washington Summit, June 1, 1988, 10:05 A.M.–11:20 A.M.; and *PPP*, 1988, pp. 632, 726.

102. Matlock, *Reagan and Gorbachev*, pp. 295–96.

103. Reagan and Gorbachev interacted during four summit meetings: the Geneva Summit (November 1985), the Reykjavik Summit (October 1986), the Washington Summit (December 1987), and the Moscow Summit (May 1988). During these summits, the two held long, private meetings, as a result of which Reagan gained a positive impression of the Soviet leader. Yarhi-Milo, *Knowing* [the] *Adversary*.

104. *PPP*, June 1, 1987, pp. 594–95; *PPP*, June 11, 1987, p. 624; *PPP*, June 12, 1987, pp. 635–36; *PPP*, August 29, 1987, p. 988; and *PPP*, September 16, 1987, p. 1038.

105. *PPP*, May 24, 1988, p. 649.

106. Reagan, *An American Life*, p. 707.

107. For an excellent analysis of Reagan's personality traits that allowed him to revise his beliefs about the Soviet threat, see Barbara Farnham, "Reagan and the Gorbachev Revolution: Perceiving the End of Threat," *Political Science Quarterly*, Vol. 116, No. 2 (Summer 2001), pp. 225–52; and Fred I. Greenstein, "Ronald Reagan, Mikhail Gorbachev, and the End of the Cold War: What Difference Did They Make?" in William C. Wolforth, ed., *Witnesses to the End of the Cold War* (Baltimore, MD: Johns Hopkins University Press, 1996).

108. Farnham, "Reagan and the Gorbachev Revolution," p. 248.

109. "Leadership and the End of the Cold War," in Richard K. Herrmann and Richard Ned Lebow, eds., *Ending the Cold War: Interpretations, Causation, and the Study of International Relations* (Basingstoke, UK: Palgrave Macmillan, 2004), p. 183.

110. *PPP*, 1985, pp. 650, 1287–88.

111. See, for example, Ronald Reagan, speech given at Moscow State University, May 31, 1988; and *DSB*, August 1988.

112. In addition to NIEs, I relied on the interviews that I conducted with Ermath, Garthoff, Goodman, MacEachin, and Odom.

113. The CIA's Office of Soviet Analysis had become increasingly concerned that estimates of projected Soviet strategic weapons systems were inflated. See, for example, MacEachin, memorandum to deputy director for intelligence, "Force Projections," NIE 11-3/8, April 22, 1986.

114. SNIE 11-9-86, p. 4; and NIE 11-18-87, pp. 3–4.

115. NIE 11-3/8-86; NIE 11-8-87; SNIE 11-16-88; and NIE 11-3/8-88.

116. NIE 11-3/8-85, p. 18. This line of reasoning is repeated in NIE 11-16-85, pp. 3–9.

117. See NIE 11-16-85, p. 13; and SNIE 11-8-86, pp. 15–17.

118. NIE 11-3/8-86, pp. 2, 18.

119. In an estimate published five days after the fall of the Berlin Wall, the intelligence community still viewed Warsaw Pact intentions as hostile, and warned of the possibility of an unprovoked attack on Western Europe. NIE 11-14-89, p. iii.

120. "NIE 11-18-87; SNIE, "Soviet Policy during the Next Phase of Arms Control in Europe"; Robert Gates, memorandum, "Gorbachev's Gameplan: The Long View," November 24, 1987; and NIE 11-3-8-88.

121. NIE 11-3/8-88.

122. Ibid. On the INF Treaty, see ibid., p. 6.

123. Shultz, *Turmoil and Triumph*, p. 864. See also "Nomination of Robert M. Gates," p. 481.

124. Author phone interview with Jack Matlock.

125. Paul Pillar, *Intelligence and U.S. Foreign Policy: Iraq, 9/11, and Misguided Reform* (New York: Columbia University Press, 2011), p. 116.

126. Mercer, "Emotional Beliefs," p. 14.

Kenneth N. Waltz

WHY IRAN SHOULD GET THE BOMB

Nuclear Balancing Would Mean Stability

The past several months have witnessed a heated debate over the best way for the United States and Israel to respond to Iran's nuclear activities. As the argument has raged, the United States has tightened its already robust sanctions regime against the Islamic Republic, and the European Union announced in January that it will begin an embargo on Iranian oil on July 1. Although the United States, the EU, and Iran have recently returned to the negotiating table, a palpable sense of crisis still looms.

It should not. Most U.S., European, and Israeli commentators and policymakers warn that a nuclear-armed Iran would be the worst possible outcome of the current standoff. In fact, it would probably be the best possible result: the one most likely to restore stability to the Middle East.

Power Begs to Be Balanced

The crisis over Iran's nuclear program could end in three different ways. First, diplomacy coupled with serious sanctions could convince Iran to abandon its pursuit of a nuclear weapon. But this outcome is unlikely: the historical record indicates that a country bent on acquiring nuclear weapons can rarely be dissuaded from doing so. Punishing a state through economic sanctions does not inexorably derail its nuclear program. Take North Korea, which succeeded in building its weapons despite countless rounds of sanctions and UN Security Council resolutions. If Tehran determines that its security depends on possessing nuclear weapons, sanctions are unlikely to change its mind. In fact, adding still more sanctions now could make Iran feel even more vulnerable, giving it still more reason to seek the protection of the ultimate deterrent.

The second possible outcome is that Iran stops short of testing a nuclear weapon but develops a breakout capability, the capacity to build and test one quite quickly. Iran would not be the first country to acquire a sophisticated nuclear program without building an actual bomb. Japan, for instance, maintains a vast civilian nuclear infrastructure. Experts believe that it could produce a nuclear weapon on short notice.

Such a breakout capability might satisfy the domestic political needs of Iran's rulers by assuring hard-liners that they can enjoy all the benefits of having a bomb (such as greater security) without the downsides (such as international isolation and condemnation). The problem is that a breakout capability might not work as intended.

The United States and its European allies are primarily concerned with weaponization, so they might accept a scenario in which Iran stops short of a nuclear weapon. Israel, however, has made it clear that it views a significant Iranian enrichment capacity alone as an unacceptable threat. It is possible, then, that a verifiable commitment from Iran

From *Foreign Affairs* 91, no. 4 (July/August 2012): 2–5.

to stop short of a weapon could appease major Western powers but leave the Israelis unsatisfied. Israel would be less intimidated by a virtual nuclear weapon than it would be by an actual one and therefore would likely continue its risky efforts at subverting Iran's nuclear program through sabotage and assassination—which could lead Iran to conclude that a breakout capability is an insufficient deterrent, after all, and that only weaponization can provide it with the security it seeks.

The third possible outcome of the standoff is that Iran continues its current course and publicly goes nuclear by testing a weapon. U.S. and Israeli officials have declared that outcome unacceptable, arguing that a nuclear Iran is a uniquely terrifying prospect, even an existential threat. Such language is typical of major powers, which have historically gotten riled up whenever another country has begun to develop a nuclear weapon of its own. Yet so far, every time another country has managed to shoulder its way into the nuclear club, the other members have always changed tack and decided to live with it. In fact, by reducing imbalances in military power, new nuclear states generally produce more regional and international stability, not less.

Israel's regional nuclear monopoly, which has proved remarkably durable for the past four decades, has long fueled instability in the Middle East. In no other region of the world does a lone, unchecked nuclear state exist. It is Israel's nuclear arsenal, not Iran's desire for one, that has contributed most to the current crisis. Power, after all, begs to be balanced. What is surprising about the Israeli case is that it has taken so long for a potential balancer to emerge.

Of course, it is easy to understand why Israel wants to remain the sole nuclear power in the region and why it is willing to use force to secure that status. In 1981, Israel bombed Iraq to prevent a challenge to its nuclear monopoly. It did the same to Syria in 2007 and is now considering similar action against Iran. But the very acts that have allowed Israel to maintain its nuclear edge in the short term have prolonged an imbalance that is unsustainable in the long term. Israel's proven ability to strike potential nuclear rivals with impunity has inevitably made its enemies anxious to develop the means to prevent Israel from doing so again. In this way, the current tensions are best viewed not as the early stages of a relatively recent Iranian nuclear crisis but rather as the final stages of a decades-long Middle East nuclear crisis that will end only when a balance of military power is restored.

Unfounded Fears

One reason the danger of a nuclear Iran has been grossly exaggerated is that the debate surrounding it has been distorted by misplaced worries and fundamental misunderstandings of how states generally behave in the international system. The first prominent concern, which undergirds many others, is that the Iranian regime is innately irrational. Despite a widespread belief to the contrary, Iranian policy is made not by "mad mullahs" but by perfectly sane ayatollahs who want to survive just like any other leaders. Although Iran's leaders indulge in inflammatory and hateful rhetoric, they show no propensity for self-destruction. It would be a grave error for policymakers in the United States and Israel to assume otherwise.

Yet that is precisely what many U.S. and Israeli officials and analysts have done. Portraying Iran as irrational has allowed them to argue that the logic of nuclear deterrence does not apply to the Islamic Republic. If Iran acquired a nuclear weapon, they warn, it would not hesitate to use it in a first strike against Israel, even though doing so would invite massive retaliation and risk destroying everything the Iranian regime holds dear.

Although it is impossible to be certain of Iranian intentions, it is far more likely that if Iran desires nuclear weapons, it is for the purpose of providing for its own security, not to improve its offensive capabilities (or destroy itself). Iran may be intransigent at the negotiating table and defiant in the face of sanctions, but it still acts to secure its own preservation. Iran's leaders did not, for example, attempt to close the Strait of Hormuz despite issuing blustery warnings that they might do so after the EU announced its planned oil embargo in January. The Iranian regime clearly concluded that it did not want to provoke what would surely have been a swift and devastating American response to such a move.

Nevertheless, even some observers and policymakers who accept that the Iranian regime is rational still worry that a nuclear weapon would embolden it, providing Tehran with a shield that would allow it to act more aggressively and increase its support for terrorism. Some analysts even fear that Iran would directly provide terrorists with nuclear arms. The problem with these concerns is that they contradict the record of every other nuclear weapons state going back to 1945. History shows that when countries acquire the bomb, they feel increasingly vulnerable and become acutely aware that their nuclear weapons make them a potential target in the eyes of major powers. This awareness discourages nuclear states from bold and aggressive action. Maoist China, for example, became much less bellicose after acquiring nuclear weapons in 1964, and India and Pakistan have both become more cautious since going nuclear. There is little reason to believe Iran would break this mold.

As for the risk of a handoff to terrorists, no country could transfer nuclear weapons without running a high risk of being found out. U.S. surveillance capabilities would pose a serious obstacle, as would the United States' impressive and growing ability to identify the source of fissile material. Moreover, countries can never entirely control or even predict the behavior of the terrorist groups they sponsor. Once a country such as Iran acquires a nuclear capability, it will have every reason to maintain full control over its arsenal. After all, building a bomb is costly and dangerous. It would

make little sense to transfer the product of that investment to parties that cannot be trusted or managed.

Another oft-touted worry is that if Iran obtains the bomb, other states in the region will follow suit, leading to a nuclear arms race in the Middle East. But the nuclear age is now almost 70 years old, and so far, fears of proliferation have proved to be unfounded. Properly defined, the term "proliferation" means a rapid and uncontrolled spread. Nothing like that has occurred; in fact, since 1970, there has been a marked slowdown in the emergence of nuclear states. There is no reason to expect that this pattern will change now. Should Iran become the second Middle Eastern nuclear power since 1945, it would hardly signal the start of a landslide. When Israel acquired the bomb in the 1960s, it was at war with many of its neighbors. Its nuclear arms were a much bigger threat to the Arab world than Iran's program is today. If an atomic Israel did not trigger an arms race then, there is no reason a nuclear Iran should now.

Rest Assured

In 1991, the historical rivals India and Pakistan signed a treaty agreeing not to target each other's nuclear facilities. They realized that far more worrisome than their adversary's nuclear deterrent was the instability produced by challenges to it. Since then, even in the face of high tensions and risky provocations, the two countries have kept the peace. Israel and Iran would do well to consider this precedent. If Iran goes nuclear, Israel and Iran will deter each other, as nuclear powers always have. There has never been a full-scale war between two nuclear-armed states. Once Iran crosses the nuclear threshold, deterrence will apply, even if the Iranian arsenal is relatively small. No other country in the region will have an incentive to acquire its own nuclear capability, and the current crisis will finally dissipate, leading to a Middle East that is more stable than it is today.

For that reason, the United States and its allies need not take such pains to prevent the Iranians from developing a nuclear weapon. Diplomacy between Iran and the major powers should continue, because open lines of communication will make the Western countries feel better able to live with a nuclear Iran. But the current sanctions on Iran can be dropped: they primarily harm ordinary Iranians, with little purpose.

Most important, policymakers and citizens in the Arab world, Europe, Israel, and the United States should take comfort from the fact that history has shown that where nuclear capabilities emerge, so, too, does stability. When it comes to nuclear weapons, now as ever, more may be better.

Jessica Chen Weiss and Jeremy L. Wallace

DOMESTIC POLITICS, CHINA'S RISE, AND THE FUTURE OF THE LIBERAL INTERNATIONAL ORDER

With the future of liberal internationalism in question, how will China's growing power and influence reshape world politics? The question of whether a rising China can be peacefully integrated into existing international institutions and norms is not new. Yet many studies have taken for granted the presence of a stable or liberalizing international order, one that the United States as the leading power would seek to preserve or deepen, rather than relinquish or dismantle.

New uncertainties about the willingness of the United States to support the Liberal International Order (LIO) have amplified anxieties over China's rise.[1] Some say that the system is resilient and will outlast a decline in U.S. power, as rising powers such as China have derived significant benefits from the LIO and can prosper within it[2] as long as their economic aspirations are not stymied.[3] To the extent that participation in international organizations has socialized and habituated their participants,[4] rising powers such as China may strive for greater authority and rights within the LIO rather than overturning its core principles.[5]

We argue that views of the LIO as integrative and resilient have been too optimistic, for two reasons. First, China's ability to profit from within the system has shaken the domestic consensus in the United States on preserving the existing LIO. As the LIO expanded after the Cold War, it grew to include many illiberal states.[6] But only China's rise has fused economic and security concerns about the consequences of letting an illiberal state prosper within the system. China's persistent illiberalism and growing military and economic power have helped call into question the adequacy of existing institutions, from the World Health Organization to the World Trade Organization (WTO).

Second, the literature has not adequately addressed how the rise of a nationalist, authoritarian power such as China will reshape the LIO, given the very different "social purpose," identity, and institutions that characterize state–society relations in the People's Republic of China (PRC).[7] Both illiberal and liberal states, including the United States, have selectively chosen which international institutions to join and be bound to.[8] That variation, along with variation in the willingness of the United States and other core democratic members to champion the more liberal components of the international order, makes it difficult to summarize China's approach to international order as either "revisionist" or "status quo."[9]

In this article, we propose a research agenda for understanding how China's domestic characteristics infuse its international efforts vis-à-vis the rules, norms, and institutions of the existing order. Major features of Chinese Communist Party (CCP) rule include a prioritization of the state over the individual, rule by law rather than rule of law, and a renewed emphasis on ethnic rather than civic nationalism. These features chafe against many of the fundamental principles of the LIO, but could coexist with a

From *International Organization* 75, no. 2 (Spring 2021): 635–664.

return to Westphalian principles and markets that are "embedded" in domestic systems of control.

The LIO has always been less liberal in practice than in theory,[10] reflecting persistent tensions between liberal norms and the Westphalian emphasis on noninterference into the domestic affairs of sovereign states.[11] Rather than being a frontal challenge to the existing international order, greater Chinese influence will likely shift the international order in a more Westphalian direction, as Beijing continues to support the principles enshrined in the UN charter of state sovereignty, equality, and noninterference, while circumscribing the liberal emphasis on individual political freedoms and movement toward more intrusive international institutions.[12]

To illuminate the domestic parameters of China's interests and efforts across the variety of issues, norms, and institutions that make up the international order, we suggest and illustrate a framework that highlights two domestic variables: centrality and heterogeneity. In so doing, we sketch an agenda for researchers to examine where China's rise entails more incremental or more fundamental challenges to the existing international order.

The rest of this article proceeds as follows. First, we discuss the twin challenges that China's rise has posed for the LIO. Second, we present the implications of centrality and heterogeneity for China's international efforts across different issue areas, illustrated with examples of China's approach to climate change, trade and exchange rates, Internet governance, territorial sovereignty, arms control, and humanitarian intervention. Finally, we conclude by considering how the international order might evolve in the shadow of China's influence.

China's Rise and the LIO

Canonical accounts of the LIO were optimistic that rising powers such as China could be peacefully integrated into the system and discouraged from overturning it. As Ikenberry notes, the LIO was designed to allow "rising countries on the periphery of this order—to advance their economic and political goals inside it."[13] As China joined dozens of international organizations and multilateral agreements, its behavior was also shaped by social pressures, helping explain Chinese cooperation even absent obvious material benefits.[14] China's stature within these institutions was also expected to constrain and shape China's choices, encouraging Beijing to channel its grievances into "rules-based revolution" rather than a violent bid for hegemony.[15] Many officials who supported China's accession to the WTO argued that greater trade and economic interdependence would have politically liberalizing effects.[16]

In our view, these accounts have given insufficient attention to the role of domestic politics, both in the rising state (China) and in the globally preponderant power (the United States). Centering the role of domestic politics leads to a more varied, and relatively less optimistic, set of expectations about China's rise and the future of the LIO.

A Shaken Consensus

Growing concerns about China's domestic and international trajectory have undermined support for continued engagement with China and institutional agreements that facilitated China's rapid economic growth. A surge in Chinese exports after its accession to the WTO helped fuel a backlash against globalization in developed democracies across the West, although scholars have debated whether economic hardship or perceptions of status threat was the dominant driver of electoral support for isolationist politicians.[17] In the United States, both Republican and Democratic officials charged China with unfair trade practices, poor compliance with WTO rulings, and exploiting open markets and scientific exchange to gain an advantage in next-generation technologies with national security implications.[18] China's persistent and increasingly personalistic form of authoritarianism led some in the U.S. policy community to concede that China's increased integration had not produced greater political or economic liberalization.[19]

The political cohort that took office under the Trump administration linked this disenchantment to broader attacks on the premise of the LIO.[20] Playing to widespread social, economic, and racial anxiety, Donald Trump won the 2016 presidential election on a nativist, America-first platform.[21] In office, not only did the Trump administration seek to alter the bilateral trading relationship by levying successive rounds of tariffs on virtually all Chinese-made goods, it also moved to expand the set of commercial activities deemed a risk to national security, accused the WTO of showing favoritism toward China, and began "decoupling" the supply chains of the two countries. By invoking national security to restrict trade, blocking WTO appellate appointments, and withdrawing from a range of multilateral agreements on climate, arms control, health, and trade, the Trump administration mounted a frontal assault on the once-U.S. led international order.

Without reference to U.S. domestic politics, theorists of liberal internationalism have difficulty explaining why the United States chose to undermine the best way to protect its values and interests even as China closed the relative power gap with the United States. Although recognizing that the leading state may not want to bind itself to rules that others do not follow, Ikenberry predicted that the United States as global hegemon would continue to invest in the LIO in order to create "a favorable institutional environment for the lead state as its relative power declines."[22] Despite a wave of new research into the domestic sources of unraveling U.S. support for liberal internationalism, these studies have not focused on concerns about China's rise.[23]

Yet it is important to note that the U.S.-led attack on the LIO was not an inevitable outcome but a choice by the Trump administration. A counterfactual U.S. administration led by Hillary Clinton would have been more likely to use multilateral pressure and institutional levers to confront and constrain China, as the United States had under President Obama.[24] Indeed, bipartisan concerns over China's ability to flout the rules while maintaining other privileges within the international system suggest that different political coalitions could succeed in making the case for renewed U.S. investment in multilateral leadership, with more stringent requirements on China should it wish to enjoy the benefits of access.[25] Alternatively, U.S. policies to encourage firms and laboratories to decouple their supply chains and research efforts could herald a return to more closed or preferential economic blocs reminiscent of the Cold War.[26] In short, domestic coalitions, identities, and ideological beliefs matter in shaping the choices of the leading state.[27]

China's Persistent Illiberalism and Tensions with the LIO

How do the domestic politics of an authoritarian state such as the PRC affect whether it seeks to engage or reshape the international order as it grows in power and influence? Do the CCP's ambitions extend beyond changing "the distribution of authority and rights" to challenging the "underlying principles of liberal order," as Ikenberry asks?[28] At a basic level, the PRC is likely to follow the United States in privileging its own domestic interests and relative power within the global hierarchy.[29] Yet the PRC is undeniably different from the United States in a number of ways that put it at odds with core principles of the LIO.[30] On the one hand, the PRC has been a staunch defender of Westphalian principles of respect for territorial sovereignty as well as the UN charter, the principle of non-intervention, and the present configuration of the UN Security

Council (UNSC). The PRC also helped shape, and ultimately signed on to, a more narrow conception of the "Responsibility To Protect" (R2P) principle authorizing international intervention to prevent genocide and crimes against humanity.[31] On the other hand, four characteristics of contemporary CCP rule are at odds with the LIO as a rules-based order that privileges democracy, free enterprise, and individual political freedoms.

First, the CCP has emphasized the role of the state over private enterprise, even though it was the introduction of markets and economic liberalization after Mao's death that unleashed China's economic miracle. China's brand of state capitalism—including subsidies, non-market barriers, and other preferential policies that have curtailed reciprocal market access—has been responsible for much of the international backlash against China's trade practices and participation in the WTO. China has also made financial, technical, and infrastructural assistance available to governments that do not meet the liberal political and economic conditions set by traditional lenders.[32]

Second, the CCP has opposed the elevation of individual political rights and has regarded civil society organizations and transnational nongovernmental organizations (NGOs) and activists with suspicion, fearing that they might challenge the CCP's domestic rule. In opposing the 1997 Ottawa Treaty banning land mines, for example, the Chinese government viewed the involvement of NGOs in the negotiation of a key document with distrust.[33] In the development arena, Chinese loans and grants have also sought to enhance state capacity. As one study of China's information and communications technology (ICT) investments in Africa noted, other donors typically select the most appropriate actors to advance a particular development objective, "be it a local NGO, a private company, or a specific ministry," whereas China "has preferred an actor-based approach, seeking to increase the capacity of the state"—including the installation of AI-powered surveillance systems.[34]

Third, the CCP has demonstrated a clear preference for "rule by law" over "rule of law." Laws in China have proliferated, but the CCP has redoubled its commitment to using the law to carry out its objectives rather than allowing the law to constrain its discretion.[35] On June 30, 2020, following a months-long standoff with a broadly popular movement for the defense of Hong Kong's freedoms, the PRC National People's Congress passed a national security law penalizing secession, subversion, organization and perpetration of terrorist activities, and collusion with foreign actors, including acts committed by anyone, anywhere in the world. By operating above the Basic Law, Hong Kong's mini-constitution, the National Security Law has been widely regarded as ending the "one country, two systems" model that was expected to provide Hong Kong with a "high degree of autonomy" until 2047.[36] In response to British accusations that China had violated its commitments under the 1984 Joint Declaration, Chinese Ambassador Liu Xiaoming insisted that China has always upheld its international obligations and that "the copyright of 'one country, two systems' belongs to Chinese former leader Deng Xiaoping, not the Sino-British Joint Declaration.[37] As developments in Hong Kong show, the CCP's willingness to rewrite and reinterpret its legal commitments indicates that it is unlikely that the CCP will use rule-based restraints to legitimize its international leadership.

Fourth, the CCP has promoted a more ethnonationalist vision of its rule: suppressing expressions of ethnic and religious identity with foreign ties, particularly Islam and Christianity, and appealing to foreign citizens of Chinese descent to love the motherland. This turn toward ethnic nativism rather than civic nationalism raises concerns about the CCP's willingness to tolerate individual differences and identities[38] and respect foreign governments' sovereignty over their putative citizens. And it feeds doubts that a hegemonic China will want to preserve an interconnected world in which international actors and ideas have opportunities to "penetrate" the leading state and shape its choices in ways that render them more acceptable to other states.[39]

These attributes suggest that the CCP's interests fundamentally conflict with the more demanding components of *political liberalism*, particularly the elevation of individual political rights above state sovereignty. That said, the leaders of post-Mao China have not sought to export a universal ideology or form of government, avoiding an irreconcilable conflict between China's rise and the defense of democracy.[40] As for *economic liberalism*, there are greater tensions between China's state-led mode of authoritarian capitalism and the first form of economic liberalism, premised on unfettered domestic markets, free trade between countries, and few constraints on international capital and foreign investment. But a form of re-"embedded" liberalism in which states have discretion to cushion the impacts of free trade could be more compatible with the CCP's desire for a stronger state role in the economy.[41] Finally, with regard to liberal institutionalism— governance via principled multilateralism—China has had a mixed record, working within some institutions to advance its interests (the World Bank, International Monetary Fund [IMF], UNSC, WTO, for example) while flouting others (including the rejection of the International Tribunal for the Law of the Sea [ITLOS] ruling on the South China Sea).[42] The CCP's preference for bilateral negotiations over multilateralism suggests that although China may become an increasingly ambitious stakeholder within existing institutions, its major new international initiatives, such as the Belt and Road Initiative, are unlikely to take the form of self-binding multilateral agreements that limit sovereign discretion.[43]

Although some might see persistent differences between China's interests and the LIO as a failure of socialization, Johnston allows that these international processes do not necessarily subsume domestic interests.[44] Moreover, one must also consider the patterns of appropriate behavior into which

China has been socialized. Namely, China has risen within a considerably less liberal version of international order in East Asia, where "American-led order is hierarchical but with much fainter liberal characteristics."[45] Finally, as Lake, Martin, and Risse note in this issue [see note 1], China is not the only state to reject many international intrusions on sovereignty; all states—liberal and illiberal—pick and choose which parts of the LIO to uphold.

Authoritarian Domestic Politics and International Order: Centrality and Heterogeneity

How does an illiberal state like China pick and choose the shape and extent of its engagement with the international order? What does China want from the array of structures, norms, and expectations that constitute the international system? Following Moravcsik, we consider state preferences—the outcomes that a state seeks in the international system—to be shaped predominantly by domestic interests, ideas, and the institutions that aggregate them.[46] State preferences cannot be deduced from the structure of the system or the distribution of power and capabilities but are determined first and foremost by domestic politics.[47]

Authoritarian regimes are not monolithic, coherent, or static polities. As Wallace notes, the character of authoritarian politics at any given time is affected by "*who* is in power, *how* do they rule, and *why* they do so."[48] Just as U.S. investment in the LIO has been buffeted and shaped by shifting domestic coalitions and ideas as well as by systemic changes in the distribution of power in the system,[49] so are Chinese politics subject to domestic and international contestation.[50]

The international context can also create incentives to alter domestic institutions and practices and foster the diffusion of norms and ideas.[51] International interactions have domestic consequences and can sometimes trigger domestic realignments.[52] Developments at the international level can create opportunities that empower certain domestic interests and ideas. International pressures can help accelerate domestic reforms but also generate domestic backlash, thereby strengthening hard-liners.[53] Ultimately, domestic structures and state–society relations condition how international ideas and practices are perceived and adopted.[54]

Research on China's approach to international order has largely focused on the extent of China's compliance and integration with existing institutions and norms, although more recent work has examined China's impact on international institutions.[55] Crucially, these works have not systematically focused on what a rising authoritarian power such as China will seek to achieve, nor have they systematically examined the role of domestic politics in shaping these interests and strategies. Where and on what issues will China lead a "rules-based revolution," in Goddard's terms?[56]

We argue that two characteristics—centrality and heterogeneity—shape the domestic politics of a given international issue area in an authoritarian state. In the next section, we discuss each characteristic of the general framework and then discuss its implications for China.

Centrality

Centrality describes how closely an authoritarian government sees an issue affecting its survival prospects. Issues that are readily linked to a government's self-identified pillars of domestic support are more central than those that are not. Central issues are more likely to galvanize mass attention and conflict among regime elites, jeopardizing the regime's survival. Because authoritarian regimes can be challenged or ousted at any time, the leadership places high priority on preempting or extin-guishing threats as they emerge, using a mix of repression and performance to suppress or placate domestic grievances. The costs of repression and the risk that it backfires increase with the centrality of an issue, giving authoritarian regimes more reason to rely on performance to address central issues. Performance can include policies that change outcomes, side payments to losers, and symbolic or rhetorical appeals that signal the regime's morality and affinity with domestic constituents.

Importantly, the centrality of any particular issue to the regime's pillars of support is contested. One of the leadership's main preoccupations is anticipating, pre-empting, or responding to links between seemingly minor issues and central pillars of regime support. Aggrieved individuals and interest groups often couch their demands in the same language that the regime uses to present its rule as legitimate.[57] By borrowing from and mirroring the regime's language, political entrepreneurs and activists magnify the resonance of their claims. In addition, a major challenge for the leadership is managing issues that touch upon multiple sources of regime support. Many policy choices involve trade-offs that may bolster support in one domain but harm it in another.

International issues vary in how closely they affect these pillars of regime support. A government is more likely to devote resources and attention to international issues that are domestically central than to those that are not. The greater the domestic centrality of an international issue, the more likely the government is to pursue unilateral policies that serve its domestic interests in shoring up these pillars.[58] In addition, international pressure is more likely to backfire when the changes demanded threaten to topple these central pillars of regime support. The greater the domestic centrality of an international issue, the harder it is for the government to concede internationally without suffering a potentially destabilizing domestic backlash.

In turn, the domestic centrality of an issue affects the government's bargaining position at the international level, in the spirit of a two-level game.[59] On central issues, a government that is more willing to "go it alone" in breach of existing norms and institutions is more likely to have leverage to demand international reforms on that issue or to build its own like-minded coalition of states to advance its views in an alternative set of institutions.[60] Ultimately, whether these investments entail greater cooperation or conflict depends on the prevailing norms and practices within a given issue area and the willingness of other stakeholders to make concessions to the government's domestic imperatives.

We next define the central pillars of CCP rule and then illustrate how the domestic positionality of different international issues have affected China's behavior. During the first 25 years of CCP rule, adherence to Mao's interpretation of communism and nationalism was the central pillar of regime support; potential challengers were deemed counterrevolutionaries or revisionists. With Mao's death and the move away from a planned economy in the 1970s, the CCP staked its legitimacy on three pillars: nationalism, economic growth, and public safety.

NATIONALISM

The CCP's ability to secure the nation's defense and territorial integrity has been critical to justifying its rule since the founding of the PRC, when Mao declared that "ours will no longer be a nation subject to insult and humiliation. We have stood up."[61] As the last two Chinese regimes were ousted by nationalist movements, CCP leaders are especially concerned about defending the nation's sovereignty against foreign encroachment and returning to China the status and privileges of a great power.

ECONOMIC GROWTH

The CCP has used growth and a litany of economic statistics, gross domestic product (GDP) in particular, to claim competence and justify its rule in the post-Mao era. Under Deng, the CCP moved away from communist ideology as a barometer of good performance, instead touting slogans such as "To get rich is glorious" and "black or white, as long as it catches mice it is a good cat." In addition to creating opportunities for rents and patronage, economic growth has funded the levers of CCP rule, particularly the coercive apparatus and information control systems that undergird domestic support, enabling the regime to stamp out challenges, co-opt potential rivals, or prevent alternative centers of influence from emerging.

PUBLIC SAFETY

The CCP's ability to keep its citizens safe from disease, disaster, crime, and terror has also been a central pillar of its rule. Public health issues commonly trigger domestic outcry and social mobilization, particularly when government malfeasance or inattention leads to the deaths of innocents.[62] The Chinese government's initial failure to disclose and act on the danger posed by the 2002–2003 Severe Acute Respiratory Syndrome (SARS) outbreak triggered a wave of public concern and what the political scientist Yanzhong Huang has called "the most severe socio-political crisis for the Chinese leadership since the 1989 Tiananmen crackdown."[63] The COVID-19 pandemic retraced these steps, with the government's initial delays in confirming evidence of human-to-human transmission, and the silencing of local doctors who tried to inform their colleagues about a new SARS-like virus, eliciting sharp critiques of Chinese-style authoritarianism and calls on Chinese social media for Xi Jinping to step down.[64] Only by silencing domestic critics and outperforming the many other countries that struggled to contain the virus did the Chinese government turn the tide of domestic discontent.[65]

Many international issues are unlikely to impact these central domestic pillars. At the United Nations, most issues are peripheral to these domestic pillars of support. Even though China became a veto-wielding member of the UNSC in

1971, Beijing was relatively slow to take on an active role at the United Nations, reluctant to use its veto power, and often willing to compromise or cooperate with existing frameworks.[66] Some issues, such as sovereignty, have been more domestically sensitive. But even an issue such as sovereignty bundles a number of issues,[67] some of which are more central than others.

Our framework expects that the CCP will invest in and insist rigidly on facets of sovereignty that are more closely linked to central pillars of regime support, particularly the defense of the nation's territorial integrity and activity within its borders, and that are more likely to show flexibility and invest less in other facets, such as peacekeeping and international intervention.[68]

Sovereignty over Taiwan is central to the CCP's nationalist claim that the island is rightfully part of China and that its de facto separation reflects an unfinished civil war. Taiwan is the major unresolved legacy of what party propagandists have termed China's "Century of Humiliation" at the hands of foreign powers, dating from the Opium Wars of the mid-1800s to the state's founding in 1949. As such, the leadership has regarded any moves that would make it appear "soft" on Taiwan independence as potential political liabilities. As Shirk notes, "No matter what public opinion actually is on this matter, the widespread belief that the CCP leaders would not survive politically if they did not fight to prevent Taiwan independence creates its own reality."[69] Johnston concurs: "The party leadership appears to have calculated its more concrete 'interests' in retaining power: Anyone who 'loses' Taiwan not only will encourage a domestic domino effect among unassimilated minorities in Xinjiang and Tibet, but also will lose power."[70]

Given the domestic centrality of the Taiwan issue, the Chinese government has invested heavily in keeping Taiwan out of the international system. It has opposed official participation by Taiwan in international organizations, worked to peel away

Taipei's diplomatic allies, and sought to limit the character of U.S. diplomatic and military relations with Taiwan. Beijing reacted angrily to advanced U.S. arms sales and staged live-fire missile exercises to protest the visit of former Taiwan President Lee Teng-hui to give a speech at his alma mater, Cornell University, in 1995. Beijing has made its economic assistance to third-party states conditional on adherence to "one China." Beijing has also forced foreign corporations, particularly airlines and the Marriott hotel chain, to avoid language on their websites that could be construed as treating Taiwan as a country, allowing "Taipei" instead.

Internet governance also directly affects the CCP's survival prospects and sovereignty over activity within its borders.[71] Xi Jinping has publicly framed the issue of cyber security and cyber sovereignty as necessary to defend the nation from internal and external threats and to ensure a stable economy: "Without web security there's no national security, there's no economic and social stability, and it's difficult to ensure the interests of the broader masses."[72] The CCP has also portrayed the Internet as a modern battleground against foreign efforts to weaken and divide the nation. As Xi put it, "Western anti-China forces have continuously tried in vain to use the internet to 'pull down' China."[73] The Chinese leadership has made clear that controlling activity on the Internet in China is a matter of life or death, regarding it as "the main battleground of struggle over public opinion" and warning that "winning or losing public support is an issue that concerns the CPC's survival or extinction."[74]

Given the domestic centrality of the Internet, the Chinese government has been determined to embed "respect for cyber sovereignty" into international discussions of Internet governance. Xi Jinping laid out China's position at the 2015 World Internet Conference in Wuzhen, where he emphasized "respect for cyber sovereignty" as the first principle needed to advance "the transformation of the global Internet governance system."[75] China's 2016 national cyber strategy also listed "respecting and protecting sovereignty in cyberspace" as the first principle. Support for state sovereignty in cyberspace is not uniquely Chinese; the independent Tallinn Manuals also agree that "the principle of sovereignty applies to cyberspace."[76] But at the fourth meeting of the UN Group of Governmental Experts on Developments in the Field of Information and Telecommunications in the Context of International Security, China worked with Russia to "expand the statement of the sovereignty norm."[77]

On less central facets of sovereignty, such as humanitarian intervention and peacekeeping, the CCP has been more willing to compromise. On peacekeeping, Wuthnow writes that China's stance evolved from "principled opposition in the 1970s, to begrudging acceptance in the 1980s, to limited participation in the 1990s, to active contributions in the early 21st century."[78] On international intervention, China dropped its initial opposition to the R2P principle, ultimately endorsing its application in multiple countries, including Darfur, Libya, Yemen, and Mali.[79] In Syria, Beijing supported a number of UNSC resolutions and abstained on several others, initially reserving its veto for actions it associated with the threat of forcible regime change, and later seeking to preserve host state consent.[80] As Börzel and Zürn note, this "pushback is different from full rejection or even dissidence."[81] Along with Russia, China has sought to defend the authority of the UNSC as an institution, while countering the most intrusive applications of the R2P principle, particularly after the 2011 intervention in Libya led to the extrajudicial killing of its long-standing dictator, Muammar al-Qaddafi.

That there are international issues that touch on central pillars of regime support does not necessarily mean that the government is unable to make concessions, particularly as part of an international agreement that helps the government's interest regarding another central issue. For example, Fravel shows that the CCP has been willing to make territorial compromises with neighboring states in order to shore up domestic security and

control over minority populations.[82] Similarly, many international issues affect multiple pillars of regime support, meaning that shifting conditions and emerging crises can galvanize unexpected changes in the government's strategy.

China's changing stance in international discussions on carbon emissions is a prime example of an international issue that touches on two central pillars: economic growth and public health. Initially, the CCP viewed international efforts to limit carbon emissions as threatening to domestic economic growth. Chinese negotiators echoed the developing world's chief refrain: that rich countries bear primary responsibility because of their historical emissions.[83] China's resistance to bearing the costs associated with carbon limits persisted through the Copenhagen meetings in December 2009, where its behavior "appeared calculated to frustrate progress."[84] During this period, the domestic centrality of growth imperatives drove China's international opposition to binding emissions targets.

As high levels of air pollution threatened public health, the Chinese government strenuously tried to repress domestic awareness of the issue. In 2007, the World Bank estimated the number of Chinese killed every year by pollution to be 750,000, but this figure was scrubbed from initial public pronouncement after pressure from Chinese government officials.[85] It was not until the scale of the catastrophe was revealed and galvanized mass and elite outrage that the Chinese government shifted strategies, emphasizing public welfare over growth and investing in international efforts to limit carbon emissions.

In April 2008, the U.S. Embassy began collecting samples of small particulate matter and publishing the results hourly on Twitter, ignoring the Chinese government's objections that this was "interfering in the internal affairs" of the PRC. In October 2010, the account tweeted that Beijing's air was "crazy bad," twenty times the World Health Organization's guidelines. Programmers had jokingly coded that label for scores beyond index, not expecting it to be triggered.[86] In the fall of 2011, the U.S. Embassy's monitoring equipment again registered scores so polluted that they were "beyond index," even though the Beijing city government had only reported that the air was "slightly polluted."[87] Real estate developer Pan Shiyi sent multiple messages to more than 16,000,000 followers on Weibo calling for the Chinese government to monitor $PM_{2.5}$ rather than just PM_{10}, including a poll in which more than 90 percent of 40,000 respondents agreed. Days later, Premier Wen Jiabao acceded, saying that the government needed to improve its environmental monitoring and bring its results closer to people's perceptions.[88] The government added $PM_{2.5}$ to a more restrictive set of standards in February 2012, with monitoring stations broadcasting hourly reports installed in dozens of cities by the end of that year.[89]

The domestic centrality of air pollution as a public health crisis spurred the Chinese government to shift gears. As Xi Jinping explicitly noted: "our environmental problems have reached such severe levels that the strictest measures are required . . . If not handled well they most often easily incite mass incidents."[90] A documentary on the health consequences of China's toxic air by former CCTV journalist Chai Jing garnered more than 100,000,000 views in 48 hours before being abruptly censored by Chinese authorities.[91]

Because sources of smog—principally coal— also emit substantial amounts of carbon dioxide, the Chinese government's efforts to combat air pollution simultaneously sought to reduce carbon emissions.[92] As Wu put it, China "shifted from a climate free-rider to a climate protector."[93] In November 2014, Presidents Barack Obama and Xi Jinping reached a historic agreement setting "new targets for carbon emissions reductions by the United States and a first-ever commitment by China to stop its emissions from growing by 2030."[94] Leading up to the Paris Conference of Parties (COP)-21 meetings, bilateral cooperation between the two largest emitters continued with the United States–China Joint Presidential Statement on Climate Change. China's support was indispensable to making the Paris meetings successful, as countries promised to make nationally determined contributions (NDCs) without a punishment process.

China's climate strategy shifted again as concerns about economic growth came to the fore in 2018, following the United States–China trade war and efforts to constrain credit expansion. These economic pressures pushed the Chinese government to loosen regulations on industrial pollution, leading firms in Beijing's environs to increase production, and Beijing's air pollution returned with a vengeance in the winter of 2018.[95]

Seen through our framework, China's international climate leadership is less the result of a principled stance than the byproduct of shifting domestic imperatives between growth and public health.[96] Curbing emissions became a critical task for the government once Chinese citizens identified smog as air pollution rather than "fog." The quantification of air pollution provided a focal point for mass and elite criticism. Growing social pressure on the government to protect public health, even at the expense of slower economic growth, helps explain China's about-face on climate change within a span of 10 years. Yet as the Chinese economy slowed in 2018 and then contracted for the first time in decades with the onset of COVID-19, the government refocused its efforts and prioritized domestic growth and employment over clean development.

Heterogeneity

Heterogeneity describes the degree of domestic division and contestation over government policy regarding a given international issue. Divergent interests and ideas about how to achieve those preferences can arise at both the mass and at the elite level, often rooted in geographic, economic, institutional, and ideological differences.[97] Even in authoritarian regimes, one can discern heterogeneity in surveys of public opinion, private and public commentary by policy elites and experts, and the statements and actions of state-owned and private industries, local governments, and central ministries. Leaked documents and archival material indicate that divisions within the regime's inner circle or politburo are often critical to authoritarian decisions, but may not become publicly available until much later.

Although most subnational actors in authoritarian systems lack formal veto power, their preferences and the implicit or explicit threat of noncompliance or disruptive protest may still affect the leadership's decision making, constrain implementation, and require side payments to minimize opposition. Even in authoritarian systems such as China's, power is fragmented and contested.[98] Central and local leaders face distinct incentives and possess different levels of information, making principal-agent problems pervasive.[99] Central decisions must be interpreted and implemented by multiple agents of the state at various levels of government, who in turn face the challenge of curbing the behavior of powerful industries and economic interests. In addition, when state leaders set out a general direction but leave the specifics to be hashed out, concentrated domestic interests can dominate both the design and implementation stages of the policy process. For example, Xi Jinping's signature Belt and Road Initiative has provided an encompassing but vague slogan that "makes it easy for domestic interest groups to use a national policy as cover to pursue their own agenda."[100]

The heterogeneity of domestic interests varies widely across international issue areas. An issue characterized by low domestic heterogeneity means that there is relatively little contestation over what the government should do at the international level. Low heterogeneity can arise when there is a mass–elite consensus in favor of a particular outcome, with minimal or weak dissent. Low heterogeneity also characterizes issues about which a small set of actors has an outsized stake in the outcome, and the majority is indifferent. In such cases, concentrated domestic interests can dominate or capture the policy process without opposition. In turn, the preferences of those concentrated interests can directly shape the government's international stance.

On issues characterized by high heterogeneity, both masses and elites may be divided over what international outcome the government should seek to achieve, with multiple stakeholders arguing at cross purposes. The higher the heterogeneity of domestic preferences and mobilized interests, the greater the likelihood that policies benefit some at the expense of others, whose opposition may need to be defused with side payments. On issues with high domestic heterogeneity, international commitments are likely to face compliance and enforcement challenges. As such, the anticipation of partial implementation may be necessary in order for national-level negotiators to reach international agreements.[101]

Low- and high-heterogeneity issues carry different domestic risks and rewards for the regime. Issues that unite a mass–elite consensus make it difficult for the government to show flexibility in the face of foreign pressure, as it risks a wider domestic backlash and defection or punishment of other elites. But international success on a low-heterogeneity issue can also give the government a larger boost in domestic support, as masses and elites are united in supporting that outcome.

In contrast, issues characterized by significant domestic divisions are challenging because some constituency will feel aggrieved that the government did not prioritize its interests. Side payments may defuse some of this opposition in the short run, but also give those actors resources and reasons to continue their efforts to lobby, petition, or protest in the future. If the government instead uses targeted repression against disgruntled losers, it can clear short-term obstacles but increase long-term resentment. In short, the downside risk to the regime is typically lower when an issue is characterized by high heterogeneity, as domestic divisions reduce the likelihood of a united challenge to its rule. But the upside rewards are also lower for high heterogeneity issues, as the government must use costly side payments or targeted repression.

Turning now to China's international interactions, a number of issues are characterized by low domestic heterogeneity. The reunification of Taiwan with mainland China is a goal that unites both masses and elites in China. Involvement in UN peacekeeping operations and the safety of Chinese citizens overseas are also issues on which there is relatively little domestic disagreement. On these issues, the Chinese government has set policy without much mass or elite dissent. As for low-heterogeneity issues about which a concentrated domestic interest dominates the policy process, a prime example is China's refusal to join the Ottawa Treaty banning landmines. As Johnston notes, it was the Chinese military's interest in continuing to use land-mines that drove the government's refusal to sign the treaty despite international pressure.[102]

On many other international issues, the Chinese government faces substantial domestic divisions. For example, export-oriented industries that benefitted from a stable, undervalued RMB have fought against revaluation, arguing that it would undermine social stability by leaving millions of Chinese workers without jobs. To pursue RMB appreciation, the Chinese leadership had to placate these interests with subsidies and other preferential policies.[103] On cyber sovereignty, the strength of domestic interests in having access to an open and unfiltered Internet has meant partial and porous implementation of Chinese government efforts to control cyber activity within its borders.[104] The government has tolerated widespread use of VPNs to jump the Great Firewall. Periodic crackdowns have made it harder for users with Chinese-made VPNs to access the outside Internet, while still allowing elites with access to foreign-made and purchased VPNs to browse freely.[105] And some intensive forms of monitoring, such as real-name IP registration and mandatory "Green Dam" filtering software on new computers, were stymied by opposition from the public and private businesses.[106]

High domestic heterogeneity has also characterized China's engagement with international efforts to address climate change, with particular opposition from polluting industries and the local governments that benefit from those revenues. These divisions have caused difficulties with the implementation and enforcement of China's international environmental commitments. Local officials have often resisted central directives to shut down polluting firms, as economic development remains of primary significance in cadre promotion evaluations.[107] Chinese officials and industries are also adept at gaming the system and providing as-if compliance with environmental regulations and incentives. Two examples are fudging pollution counterfactuals to gain resources through the Clean Development Mechanism (CDM) as well as cheating on chlorofluorocarbon (CFC) agreements. One study found that more than 85 percent of CDM projects had a low likelihood of "emission reductions being real, measurable, and additional."[108] China is also a party to the Montreal Protocol banning the production of CFC-11, which depletes atmospheric ozone and has "a global warming potential 4,750 times that of carbon dioxide." However, international investigators in 2018 traced an increase in CFC-11 to numerous chemical plants in China, which had resorted to producing the banned substance because its replacement was more expensive and less effective.[109]

At the same time, the interests of China's renewable energy industries have shaped its efforts to combat climate change in more positive ways. China's investments in renewables served to help its firms establish a leading position in a growing sector, but these policies have also generated positive externalities to help global efforts to combat climate change. In 2017, China accounted for more than half of global solar installations and 37 percent of wind turbines, and China's dominance is even stronger in manufacturing.[110] Because of the falling cost of Chinese-subsidized renewables, other countries have become "more confident that a gradual shift towards a low-carbon economy will not necessarily harm their long-term growth strategies."[111]

Nevertheless, the type of renewable energy technology that China is exporting has more to do with its industries' interests than with what is needed abroad. Take, for example, China's global promotion of ultra-high-voltage electricity grids developed by one of its gargantuan state-owned enterprises, State Grid. Although lauded from a climate change angle as a potential solution for reducing intermittency problems of renewables by linking more distant power sources with less wasted current, the actual grids being constructed are mostly in countries where fossil fuels dominate.[112]

As these examples illustrate, heterogeneity does not have a straightforward relationship with international cooperation or confrontation. Rather, it helps explain the nature of the domestic constraints and incentives that a government brings to the international table. Greater heterogeneity is likely to produce tougher and more drawn-out international negotiations as well as increasing the likelihood of implementation failure, requiring more monitoring and possibly enforcement in international agreements. Partial compliance may in turn make it more difficult for other governments to assess Beijing's intentions to determine whether Beijing reneged

after negotiating in bad faith or simply lacked the capacity to bring wayward domestic actors in line.

Centrality and Heterogeneity: Malleability and Movement

As Table 4.1 illustrates, centrality and heterogeneity do not map neatly onto one another. Some highly central issues are also highly heterogeneous, such as cyber sovereignty and climate change. Some highly central issues are characterized by relatively low heterogeneity, such as Taiwan. Some issues are characterized by low centrality and low heterogeneity, such as most issues before the United Nations and China's involvement in international peacekeeping. Finally, some low-centrality issues are characterized by a high degree of heterogeneity, like nonproliferation agreements to halt the spread of weapons of mass destruction (WMD) and related missile technology. These are not issues that directly affect the core pillars of regime legitimacy; therefore, China has not invested much international effort in addressing them,[113] but national-level cooperation has been undermined by subnational Chinese actors with a strong countervailing interest. For example, Johnston notes that China "played an

Table 4.1. Domestic Centrality and Heterogeneity in China's International Approach

	LOW HETEROGENEITY	HIGH HETEROGENEITY
High centrality	• "Homeland" issues; e.g., Taiwan, Hong Kong, Tibet, Xinjiang • Maritime and island disputes	• Internet governance • Climate change • Trade • Belt and Road Initiative • Exchange rates • Iran nuclear deal
Low centrality	• Most issues before the United Nations; e.g., peacekeeping • Ottawa Treaty banning landmines	

important role in the 2015 Iran nuclear deal (helping redesign a key reactor to reduce Iran's future plutonium output)," but also failed to halt the export of ballistic missile technology to Iran.[114]

Yet no static representation (as in Table 4.1) depicts the malleability and movement of issues, as domestic actors try to manipulate the apparent centrality and heterogeneity of a given issue. For example, subnational actors may link their demands to a central pillar in order to increase the likelihood of side payments or loopholes that protect them from international commitments. In a bidding war for government attention, subnational actors that amplify the centrality of their interests are more likely to succeed than those whose interests remain peripheral and parochial.

For example, during protracted negotiations over China's admission to the WTO, an array of industries, ministries, and provincial governments lobbied heavily for continued protection, some more successfully than others. The telecommunications industry and its affiliated ministry, the Ministry of Information Industries, succeeded by linking demands for protection to the national interest rather than a desire to avoid market competition. As Pearson notes, "Industry officials claimed foreign Internet providers would use access to China's Internet markets to steal economic information, disseminate propaganda via email, and use the Internet to support dissidents or undermine the party. Such arguments tapped into deep worries about loss of Chinese sovereignty to foreign powers. Widespread fear of social unrest made such arguments especially potent."[115]

In addition, the government may also try to increase the centrality of an international issue in order to reduce domestic dissent and demonstrate resolve in international negotiations. For example, by framing resistance in Hong Kong and the United States–China trade war as part of a national struggle reminiscent of the Opium War, Korean War, and other protracted disputes in which China eventually prevailed, the Chinese government has built public support for the costs of conflict, raised the domestic cost of international concessions, and signaled its intent to stand firm against foreign pressure. As Shi and Zhu note, the Chinese government has used its propaganda powers to frame the United States–China trade war as an existential struggle for the Chinese nation's development. When framed as a geopolitical struggle with the United States, Chinese survey respondents were much more supportive of the government's handling of the trade war than when the trade war's economic costs were mentioned.[116]

Conclusion

Can the LIO survive the challenge of China's growing influence and desire to reshape global governance? China's authoritarian character is at odds with key aspects of the system, particularly the emphasis on political liberalism and rules-based multilateralism. At the same time, the CCP has not spent significant energy defeating these liberal principles internationally except where they threaten its domestic survival and sovereignty. China has profited from its participation in the LIO and remains a staunch defender of the Westphalian order on which it was built. Indeed, at times the Chinese government has appeared more invested in preserving existing arrangements than the United States has, hence the irony of Xi Jinping defending free trade at Davos and COVID-19 cooperation at the World Health Assembly.[117]

The CCP has behaved strategically, investing in reshaping or rejecting international arrangements in issue areas that are central to its domestic rule and being more willing to free ride or defer to international practices on issues that are more peripheral. China's domestic "social purpose" does not require the wholesale destruction of the existing international order, although it favors a more conservative version that emphasizes Westphalian norms of sovereignty and noninterference. Within the United Nations, for example, China has sought to alter international obligations on human rights to emphasize the primacy of state sovereignty, oversight of civil society, and economic development.[118] At the same time, under international pressure, the Chinese-led Asian Infrastructure Investment Bank adopted rhetoric about the environmental and social consequences of its policies similar to those led by developed countries. And the IMF applauded China's announcement of a debt-sustainability framework in response to international criticism of the Belt and Road Initiative.

To understand the variation in China's approach to international order, we have proposed a framework grounded in the domestic politics of authoritarian rule. Two factors, centrality and heterogeneity, shape the PRC's approach to various issues in the area of international order. The more closely an international issue touches upon one or more of the central pillars of the regime's rule, the more the regime will invest internationally in that issue and resist international pressure. The greater the heterogeneity of domestic interests regarding an international issue, the more the regime will face competing demands from different subnational actors, requiring offsetting policies and partial implementation to appease countervailing interests. Although these characteristics are distinct, they can be strategically linked. For example, the CCP's nationalistic framing of the trade war aimed to reduce domestic heterogeneity by increasing its centrality.

Foregrounding the role of domestic politics is essential for understanding why and on what issues a powerful state chooses to invest in international leadership, and when it might choose to walk away from or shirk previous commitments. Our framework suggests that China's international leadership is more likely to be a byproduct of the CCP's domestic self-interest than a principled effort to provide public goods, although that was often the case for the United States. Acknowledging the primacy of domestic drivers also cautions against optimism that naming and shaming will lead to greater Chinese convergence with the LIO or hopes for a ratcheting-up of voluntary commitments and compliance.[119]

Domestic politics affect a state's preferences and negotiating strategies in ways that system-level factors, such as the balance of outside options or position within international networks of influence, cannot wholly predict. The strategic setting matters, but these system-level attributes are often endogenous to domestic calculations.[120] Although developed here in reference to authoritarian states, centrality and heterogeneity can provide a generalized framework to study the domestic pressures that governments across the spectrum of regime types face in relation to the LIO.

The future of the international order will depend on domestic political shifts not only in China but also in the United States and other leading members. China is not alone in shifting toward more ethno-nationalist policies; such trends are also apparent in democracies from India to Israel.[121] And many countries, including the United States, share China's ambivalence about some of the more intrusive elements of the liberal order, such as the International Criminal Court and International Court of Justice.[122]

On the other hand, the United States and other "like-minded" democracies could choose to build an enhanced but less universal set of institutions, with demanding standards of membership that would likely exclude China and other illiberal states.[123] China might be willing to change its practices in order to participate in some of these new arrangements, but only if the domestic price was not too high.

Our framework suggests that China would be more likely to show flexibility on issues that are less central and more heterogeneous. But even on issues that are highly central, such as trade, investment, intellectual property, technology, and the environment, their high heterogeneity means that the CCP may still be willing and able to make progress toward a set of international commitments; these negotiations are likely to be difficult and would require domestic side payments and risk partial enforcement to accommodate competing domestic interests. In contrast, on issues that are more central and less heterogeneous, the CCP is more likely to go it alone, forge an alternative coalition of states,[124] or work to shift norms in a less liberal direction.

Illiberal pressures from leading authoritarian states, along with populist challenges from within leading democratic states, might combine to produce a more minimalist version of the LIO. Reweighting international norms to privilege national sovereignty would require tolerating more political and ideological diversity than the "postnational liberalism" that blossomed after the Cold War.[125] A less domestically intrusive but still open and rules-based international order would help satisfy the Chinese government's desire for a world safe for autocracy alongside democracy.[126] Without such modifications, China's growing influence will likely lead to more conflict outside the system than competition over the rules inside it.

NOTES

1. For a definition of the LIO and its contested components, see Lake, Martin, and Risse, 2021.
2. Ikenberry 2008, 2011.
3. See Monteiro 2014; Deudney and Ikenberry 2018 also argue that the institutions of the liberal order will strengthen as long as economic interdependence grows.
4. Johnston 2008.
5. Schweller and Pu 2011 note that China seeks to grow and contest the existing international order from within.
6. Standards for certifying liberal practices have also become more stringent. See Towns 2010; Lake, Martin, and Risse, 2021.
7. Ruggie 1982; Simmons and Goemans (2021) also urge greater attention to "spatialized" identities and preferences for understanding domestic "social purposes."
8. Lake, Martin, and Risse 2021.
9. Johnston 2019a argues that international order is better conceptualized not as a coherent system but rather as the emergent properties of state-level interactions in different domains.
10. See Graham Allison, "The Myth of the Liberal Order," *Foreign Affairs*, 14 June 2018, available at <https://www.foreignaffairs.com /articles/2018-06-14/myth-liberal-order>; Barma, Ratner, and Weber 2013; Colgan and Keohane 2017; Rebecca Friedman Lissner and Mira Rapp-Hooper, "The Liberal Order Is More Than a Myth," *Foreign Affairs*, 31 July 2018, available at <https://www

.foreignaffairs.com/articles/world/2018-07-31/liberal-order-more -myth>.
11. Lake, Martin, and Risse, 2021. Others have criticized the hypocrisy of a liberal order that emphasizes sovereign equality while failing to acknowledge or level historical hierarchies. See Adler-Nissen and Zarakol 2020.
12. On the growing intrusiveness of international institutions after the end of the Cold War, see Börzel and Zürn, this issue. Foot 2020 argues that China promotes a triadic model of a strong state, social stability, and economic development, in contrast to the prevailing UN emphases on international peace and security, human rights, and development.
13. Ikenberry 2011, 135.
14. Johnston 2008.
15. Goddard 2018.
16. But see Johnston 2019a.
17. On the "China shock," see Colantone and Stanig 2018a, 2018b; Autor, Dorn, and Hanson 2013. On the 2016 US election and perceptions of China as a threat to US global dominance, see Mutz 2018. On the mobilization of mass discontent against international cooperation, see De Vries, Hobolt, and Walter 2021.
18. A chief concern for many US policymakers and scholars had been China's tendency to free ride or cheat on the rules. Christensen 2015.
19. Campbell and Ratner 2018.
20. For a different argument about China's rise and the unraveling of the LIO, see Mearsheimer 2019, who argues that the liberal order facilitated China's rise and hence a return to multipolarity, which in his view cannot sustain the liberal order.
21. See also Broz, Frieden, and Weymouth 2021 and Flaherty and Rogowski 2021.
22. Ikenberry 2011, 153, 155–56, 316.
23. See, for example, Musgrave 2019; in this issue, Rogowski and Flaherty show that the "China shock" is associated with increased support for populist parties only in countries with high levels of income inequality.
24. As Obama said of the Trans-Pacific Partnership, "we can't let countries like China write the rules of the global economy." White House, "Statement by the President on the Trans-Pacific Partnership." 5 October 2015. Available at <https://obamawhitehouse .archives.gov/the-press-office/2015/10/05/statement-president-trans -pacific-partnership>. Accessed 21 September 2020.
25. See, for example, Kurt M. Campbell and Jake Sullivan, "Competition Without Catastrophe," *Foreign Affairs*, 21 September 2019. Available at <https://www.foreignaffairs.com/articles/china /competition-with-china-without-catastrophe>.
26. Lake 2018.
27. See Kaufmann and Pape 1999; Snyder, Shapiro, and Bloch-Elkon 2009.
28. Ikenberry 2011, 27, 282.
29. Kupchan 2012.
30. Still, these differences in identity, particularly nationalism, are what Allan, Vucetic, and Hopf 2018 argue will prevent China from forging an effective counter-hegemonic bloc.
31. On humanitarianism and liberal intrusiveness, see Börzel and Zürn 2021. Foot 2020 notes that Beijing supports a state-centric version

of R2P that provides for the protection of civilians in armed conflict under host state consent.

32. Kaplan 2016.

33. Johnston 2008, 139.

34. Gagliardone 2019.

35. Minzner 2011.

36. Emily Feng, "Five Takeaways From China's Hong Kong National Security Law," NPR, 1 July 2020. Available at <https://www.npr.org/2020/07/01/885900989/5-takeaways-from-chinas-hong-kong-national-security-law>. Accessed 5 August 2020.

37. "Ambassador Liu Xiaoming Holds an On-Line Press Conference on Law on Safeguarding National Security in HKSAR." Available at <http://www.chinese-embassy.org.uk/eng/dshdjjh/t1796269.htm>. Accessed 5 August 2020.

38. See also Buzas 2021. Ironically, the intellectual architects behind China's assimilationist turn toward eliminating markers of religious and ethnic difference, particularly in Tibet and Xinjiang, have cited the US "melting pot" as inspiration. Gerry Shih, "Boiling Us Like Frogs: China's Muslim Clampdown Creeps into the Heartland, Targeting Hui Minority," *Washington Post*, 20 September 2019. Available at <https://www.washingtonpost.com/world/asia_pacific/boiling-us-like-frogs-chinas-clampdown-on-muslims-creeps-into-the-heartland-finds-new-targets/2019/09/20/25c8bb08-ba94-11e9-aeb2-a101a1fb27a7_story.html>. Accessed 21 September 2020.

39. Ikenberry 2011.

40. Weiss 2019.

41. Ruggie 1982. On embedded liberalism and contemporary challenges, see Mansfield and Rudra 2021, as well as Goodman and Pepinsky 2021.

42. Beijing has also used its economic and political clout as diplomatic leverage to garner support for its positions within existing institutions. See Flores-Macías and Kreps 2013; Foot 2020.

43. On transactional networks as the emerging basis of a parallel international order, see Barma et al. 2009.

44. Johnston 2008.

45. Ikenberry 2011, 26–27; see also Kang 2003; Katzenstein 2005.

46. Moravcsik 1997, 518.

47. Risse-Kappen 1991.

48. Wallace n.d.

49. See Chaudoin, Milner, and Tingley 2010; Kupchan and Trubowitz 2007; Musgrave 2019; Snyder, Shapiro, and Bloch-Elkon 2009.

50. For example, see Yan 2018 on competing political values and ideological strands in Chinese foreign policy.

51. See Finnemore and Sikkink 1998; Risse-Kappen 1994; including elections (Hyde 2011), protests (Weiss 2013), and the geographic distribution of ethnic minority populations (McNamee and Zhang 2019).

52. Putnam 1988.

53. Weiss and Wichowsky 2018; on backlash, see Terman 2016.

54. Risse-Kappen 1994.

55. See Foot and Walter 2011; Johnston 2003; 2008.

56. Goddard 2018. As Kastner, Pearson, and Rector (2018, 43) put it, their theory of Chinese behavior "abstracts away from domestic political dynamics within China, even though it is certain that factors such as public and elite opinion and bureaucratic interests

have, at times, influenced Beijing's approach to international regimes."

57. On the politicization of international issues and the process by which public contestation constrains decision making in a democratic context, see De Vries, Hobolt, and Walter 2021.

58. On normative dimensions of centrality, see Foot and Walter 2013, who argue that when a global norm is domestically salient—or central—the degree of normative fit between global and domestic norms informs Chinese behavior.

59. Putnam 1988.

60. As Kastner, Pearson, and Rector 2018 put it, a rising power's "outside options" and "indispensability" determine whether it will invest in, demand changes to, or passively accept a particular sector of global governance. Similarly, Goddard 2018 argues that a dissatisfied state's position within international networks determines whether it will integrate, exit, reform, or violently challenge the system.

61. Opening address at the First Plenary Session of the Chinese People's Political Consultative Conference, 21 September 1949, Selected Works of Mao Zedong, available at <https://www.marxists.org/reference/archive/mao/selected-works/volume-5/mswv5_01.htm> accessed 28 November 2020. (The full record is available at: <https://doi.org/10.1016/B978-0-08-022984-3.50005-0>.)

62. Throughout Chinese history, natural disasters such as earthquakes have often been regarded as portents of the government's downfall and the loss of the "mandate of heaven," particularly when they reflect poorly on the government's competence or morality. The shoddy construction of schoolhouses that collapsed in the 2008 Sichuan earthquake and killed tens of thousands of children remains a potent symbol of the regime's fecklessness. See Sorace 2017; Xu 2017.

63. Huang 2004.

64. See, for example, Xu Zhangrun. 4 February 2020. 许志永. "劝退书." 美好中国(blog) ["Dear Chairman Xi, It's Time for You to Go," translated by Geremie Barmé, <https://www.chinafile.com/reporting-opinion/viewpoint/dear-chairman-xi-its-time-you-go>, last accessed 28 November 2020]. Available at <https://cmcn.blog/2020/02/04/%e5%8a%9d%e9%80%80%e4%b9%a6/>. Accessed 11 August 2020; Josh Rudolph, "Sensitive Words: 'Where Is That Person? Everyday I Pray for Green Jade,'" *China Digital Times*, 11 February 2020. Available at <https://chinadigitaltimes.net/2020/02/sensitive-words-where-is-that-person-everyday-i-pray-for-green-jade/>. Accessed 11 August 2020.

65. Jessica Chen Weiss, "No 'Beijing Consensus': Why the US Risks a Pyrrhic Victory in Confronting China," SupChina, 29 June 2020. Available at <https://supchina.com/2020/06/29/no-beijing-consensus-the-u-s-risks-a-pyrrhic-victory/>. Accessed 21 September 2020; Yanzhong Huang, "Xi Jinping Won the Coronavirus Crisis," *Foreign Affairs*, 20 April 2020. Available at <https://www.foreignaffairs.com/articles/china/2020-04-13/xi-jinping-won-coronavirus-crisis>. Accessed 21 September 2020.

66. Johnston 2008.

67. Krasner 1999.

68. On the propensity of states to "re-border," particularly among autocracies, see Simmons and Goemans 2021.

69. Shirk 2006.

70. Johnston 2008, 210.

71. On authoritarian perceptions and responses to the challenges posed by the Liberal International Information Order (LIIO), see Farrell and Newman 2021.

72. "Xi Jinping Calls for Tighter Grip on Internet to Ensure Stability," *South China Morning Post*, 21 April 2018. Available at <https:// www.scmp.com/news/china/policies-politics/article/2142758 /chinese-president-xi-jinping-calls-tighter-grip>. Accessed 21 September 2020.

73. Speech at the National Propaganda Work Conference, 19 August 2013 [in Chinese]. Available at <http://theory.people.com .cn/n1/2018/1204/c40531-30440415.html>. Accessed 21 September 2020.

74. "Study History, Be Close to the People," *China Daily*, 25 July 2013. Available at <https://www.chinadaily.com.cn/opinion/2013-07/09 /content_16749701.htm>. Accessed 21 September 2020.

75. "Remarks by President of the People's Republic of China Xi Jinping at the Opening Ceremony of the Second World Internet Conference," 16 December 2015, Ministry of Foreign Affairs of the People's Republic of China. Available at <https://www.fmprc.gov.cn /mfa_eng/wjdt_665385/zyjh_665391/t1327570.shtml>. Accessed 21 September 2020.

76. Jensen 2017.

77. Segal 2017, 7.

78. Wuthnow 2013, 13.

79. Fung 2016.

80. Foot 2020; Fung 2018.

81. Börzel and Zürn 2021.

82. Fravel 2008.

83. Lewis 2008, 162.

84. Christoff 2010, 639.

85. David Barboza, "China Reportedly Urged Omitting Pollution-Death Estimates," *New York Times*, 5 July 2007. Available at <https://www.nytimes.com/2007/07/05/world/asia/05china.html>. Accessed 21 September 2020. Note that the World Bank's report also includes water pollution.

86. Barbara Demick, "US Embassy Air Quality Data Undercut China's Own Assessments," *Los Angeles Times*, 29 October 2011. Available at <https://www.latimes.com/archives/la-xpm-2011-oct-29-la-fg -chin-aair-quality-20111030-story.html>. Accessed 21 September 2020.

87. Ibid.

88. China Council for International Cooperation on Environment and Development 2012; Oliver 2014.

89. Oliver 2014.

90. 习近平关于总体国家安全观论述摘编[Excerpts from Xi Jinping's Views on Overall National Security], The Central Party History and Literature Research Institute of the Communist Party of China, 2018, 181–82.

91. Celia Hatton, "Under the Dome: The Smog Film Taking China by Storm," BBC, 2 March 2015. Available at <https://www.bbc.com /news/blogs-china-blog-31689232>. Accessed 21 September 2020.

92. In contrast, developed countries such as the United States had largely resolved air pollution as a political issue before climate science developed. In addition, natural resource endowments factored into Chinese decision makers' calculus. Whereas hydraulic fracturing (fracking) shifted US energy production to natural gas and away from coal, Chinese fracking efforts have yet to take off, in part because of a combination of poor geology and limited water resources as well as weak intellectual property protections that have dampened interest from the technologically leading US firms.

93. Wu 2016.

94. Mark Landler, "US and China Reach Climate Accord After Months of Talks," *New York Times*, 21 December 2017. Available at <https://www.nytimes.com/2014/11/12/world/asia/china-us-xi -obama-apec.html>. Accessed 21 September 2020.

95. Ministry of Ecology and Environment of the People's Republic of China, "生态环境部通报重点区域2018年10月-2019 年 1 月环境空气质量有关情况[The Ministry of Ecology and Environment notified the key areas from October 2018 to January 2019 on ambient air quality]", 20 February 2019, <http://www.mee.gov.cn/xxgk2018/xxgk /xxgk15/201902/t20190220_693001.html>, last accessed 28 November 2020. The increase is less drastic if one expands the time frame to March 2019, although it still shows a reversal after years of consistent progress. Lauri Myllyvirta, "Air Pollution Around Beijing Rebounds As Coal Consumption Rises by 13 Percent," *Unearthed* (blog), 22 May 2019. Available at <https://unearthed.greenpeace .org/2019/05/22/air-pollution-china-beijing-coal-2018/>. Accessed 21 September 2020.

96. On the political contestation between "climate vulnerable" and "climate forcing" actors and constituencies, see Colgan, Green, and Hale 2020.

97. On ideological heterogeneity in a democratic context, see, for example, De Vries, Hobolt, and Walter, 2021.

98. On the variety of constraints that leaders of different regime types face in foreign policy, see Hyde and Saunders 2020; Weeks 2008, 2012, 2014.

99. Lieberthal and Oksenberg 1988.

100. Yuen Yuen Ang, "Demystifying Belt and Road," *Foreign Affairs*, May/June 2019. Available at <https://www.foreignaffairs.com /articles/china/2019-05-22/demystifying-belt-and-road>.

101. Mertha and Pahre 2005.

102. Johnston 2008, 138–39.

103. Steinberg and Shih 2012.

104. Roberts 2018.

105. James Palmer, "China Is Trying to Give the Internet a Death Blow," *Foreign Policy* (blog), 25 August 2017. Available at <https:// foreignpolicy.com/2017/08/25/china-is-trying-to-give-the-internet -a-death-blow-vpn-technology/>. Accessed 30 May 2019.

106. Guobin Yang, "'Green Dam' as a Case of Online Activism in China," Columbia University Press (blog), 1 July 2009. Available at <https://www.cupblog.org/2009/07/01/green-dam-as-a-case-of -online-activism-in-china/>. Accessed 21 September 2020.

107. See Kostka and Hobbs 2012; Lorentzen, Landry, and Yasuda 2014.

108. Cames et al. 2016, 152.

109. Environmental Investigation Agency, "CFC-11 Illegal Production and Use in China: Blowing It," Environmental Investigation Agency, 9 July 2018. Available at <https://eia-international.org /report/blowing-it/>. Accessed 21 September 2020.

110. See "Global Market Outlook for Solar Power (2018-2022)" report, available at <https://www.solarpowereurope.org/global-market-outlook-2018-2022/>, accessed 21 September 2020; Global Wind Energy Council statistics and wind report, available at <http://gwec.net/global-figures/graphs/> and <https://gwec.net/global-wind-report-2018/>, accessed 21 September 2020. Nine of the ten largest solar exporters are Chinese, with the tenth being a Chinese-Canadian joint venture. David Kirton, "China's Solar-Panel Makers Dominate Global Exports," *Caixin Global*, 24 January 2019. Available at <https://www.caixinglobal.com/2019-01-24/chinas-solar-panel-makers-dominate-global-exports-101374069.html>. Accessed 21 September 2020.

111. Falkner 2016.

112. James Temple, "China's Giant Transmission Grid Could Be the Key to Cutting Climate Emissions," *MIT Technology Review*. 8 November 2018. Available at <https://www.technologyreview.com/2018/11/08/138280/chinas-giant-transmission-grid-could-be-the-key-to-cutting-climate-emissions/>. Accessed 21 September 2020.

113. As Kastner, Pearson, and Rector note, China has "generally complied with the regime since the late 1980s without investing significant resources in organizing or sustaining cooperation." Kastner, Pearson, and Rector 2018, 139.

114. Johnston 2019a, 29.

115. Pearson 2001, 362–63.

116. Shi and Zhu 2019,

117. Peter S. Goodman, "In Era of Trump, China's President Champions Economic Globalization," *New York Times*, 17 January 2017, Available at <https://www.nytimes.com/2017/01/17/business/dealbook/world-economic-forum-davos-china-xi-globalization.html.> Accessed 21 September 2020. Michael Bociurkiw, "Is China the New Leader on the World Health Stage?" CNN, 20 May 2020. Available at <https://www.cnn.com/2020/05/20/opinions/world-health-assembly-xi-trump-bociurkiw/index.html>. Accessed 21 September 2020.

118. Foot 2020; Piccone 2018.

119. Anne-Marie Slaughter, "The Paris Approach to Global Governance," *Project Syndicate* (blog), 28 December 2015. Available at <https://www.project-syndicate.org/commentary/paris-agreement-model-for-global-governance-by-anne-marie-slaughter-2015-12?barrier=accesspaylog>. Accessed 21 September 2020.

120. For example, Kastner, Pearson, and Rector attribute China's growing interest in multilateral climate change cooperation to public consciousness around air pollution, a domestic shift that made China's "outside options" less favorable. Kastner, Pearson, and Rector 2018, chapter 7.

121. See also Buzas 2021.

122. Lake, Martin, and Risse, 2021.

123. See Hart and Magsamen 2019; Ikenberry 2020.

124. Lake 2018.

125. Börzel and Zürn 2021. See also Kupchan 2014.

126. Weiss 2019.

REFERENCES

Adler-Nissen, Rebecca, and Ayşe Zarakol. 2020. Struggles for Recognition: The Liberal International Order and the Merger of Its Discontents. *International Organization* 75 (2). <https://doi.org/10.1017/S0020818320000454>.

Allan, Bentley B., Srdjan Vucetic, and Ted Hopf. 2018. The Distribution of Identity and the Future of International Order: China's Hegemonic Prospects. *International Organization* 72 (4):839–69.

Autor, David H., David Dorn, and Gordon H. Hanson. 2013. The China Syndrome: Local Labor Market Effects of Import Competition in the United States. *American Economic Review* 103 (6): 2121–68.

Barma, Naazneen, Giacomo Chiozza, Ely Ratner, and Steven Weber. 2009. A World Without the West? Empirical Patterns and Theoretical Implications. *Chinese Journal of International Politics* 2 (4):525–44.

Barma, Naazneen, Ely Ratner, and Steven Weber. 2013. The Mythical Liberal Order. *The National Interest* 124 (Mar/April):56–68.

Börzel, Tanja, and Michael Zürn. 2021. Contestations of the Liberal International Order: From Liberal Multilateralism to Postnational Liberalism. *International Organization* 75 (2). <https://doi.org/10.1017/S0020818320000570>.

Bröz, J. Lawrence, Jeffry Frieden, and Stephen Weymouth, 2021. Populism in Place: The Economic Geography of the Globalization Backlash. *International Organization* 75 (2). <https://doi.org/10.1017/S0020818320000314>.

Buzas, Zoltan. 2021. Racism and Antiracism in the Liberal International Order. *International Organization* 75 (2). <https://doi.org/10.1017/S0020818320000521>.

Cames, Martin, Ralph O. Harthan, Jürg Füssler, Michael Lazarus, C. Lee, Peter Erickson, and Randall Spalding-Fecher. 2016. How Additional Is the Clean Development Mechanism? Analysis of Application of Current Tools and Proposed Alternatives. Oeko-Institut EV CLIMA. B 3. Available at <https://ec.europa.eu/clima/sites/clima/files/ets/docs/clean_dev_mechanism_en.pdf.>

Campbell, Kurt M. and Ely Ratner. 2018. The China Reckoning. *Foreign Affairs* 97 (March/April):60–70.

Chaudoin, Stephen, Helen V. Milner, and Dustin H. Tingley. 2010. The Center Still Holds: Liberal Internationalism Survives. *International Security* 35 (1):75–94.

China Council for International Cooperation on Environment and Development. 2012. CCICED 2011 Annual Report. China Environmental Science Press. Available at <http://www.cciced.net/ccicedPhoneEN/PolicyResearch/research/201609/P020160921527145484340.pdf>. Accessed 21 September 2020.

Christensen, Thomas J. 2015. *The China Challenge: Shaping the Choices of a Rising Power.* W. W. Norton.

Christoff, Peter. 2010. Cold Climate in Copenhagen: China and the United States at COP15. *Environmental Politics* 19 (4):637–56.

Colantone, Italo, and Piero Stanig. 2018a. Global Competition and Brexit. *American Political Science Review* 112 (2):201–18.

Colantone, Italo, and Piero Stanig. 2018b The Trade Origins of Economic Nationalism: Import Competition and Voting Behavior in Western Europe. *American Journal of Political Science* 62 (4): 936–53.

Colgan, Jeff D., Jessica F. Green, and Thomas N. Hale. 2020. Asset Revaluation and the Existential Politics of Climate Change. *International Organization* 75 (2). <https://doi.org/10.1017/S00208183 20000296>.

Colgan, Jeff D., and Robert O. Keohane. 2017. The Liberal Order Is Rigged. *Foreign Affairs* 96 (May/June):36–44.

Deudney, Daniel, and G. John Ikenberry. 2018. Liberal World: The Resilient Order. *Foreign Affairs* 97 (July/August):16–24.

De Vries, Catherine E., Sara B. Hobolt and Stefanie Walter. 2021. Politicizing International Cooperation: The Mass Public, Political Entrepreneurs, and Political Opportunity Structures. *International Organization* 75 (2). <https://doi.org/10.1017/S002081832 0000491>.

Falkner, Robert. 2016. The Paris Agreement and the New Logic of International Climate Politics. *International Affairs* 92 (5):1107–25.

Farrell, Henry, and Abraham L. Newman. 2021. The Janus Face of the Liberal International Information Order: When Global Institutions Are Self-Undermining. *International Organization* 75 (2). <https://doi.org/10.1017/S0020818320000302>.

Finnemore, Martha, and Kathryn Sikkink. 1998. International Norm Dynamics and Political Change. *International Organization* 52 (4):887–917.

Flaherty, Thomas M., and Ronald Rogowski. 2021. Rising Inequality As a Threat to the Liberal International Order. *International Organization* 75 (2). <https://doi.org/10.1017/S0020818321000163>.

Flores-Macías, Gustavo A., and Sarah E. Kreps. 2013. The Foreign Policy Consequences of Trade: China's Commercial Relations with Africa and Latin America, 1992–2006. *The Journal of Politics* 75 (2): 357–71.

Foot, Rosemary. 2020. *China, the UN, and Human Protection: Beliefs, Power, Image.* Oxford University Press.

Foot, Rosemary, and Andrew Walter. 2011. *China, the United States, and Global Order.* Cambridge University Press.

Foot, Rosemary, and Andrew Walter. 2013. Global Norms and Major State Behavior: The Cases of China and the United States. *European Journal of International Relations* 19 (2):329–52.

Fravel, M. Taylor. 2008. *Strong Borders, Secure Nation: Cooperation and Conflict in China's Territorial Disputes.* Princeton University Press.

Fung, Courtney J. 2016. China and the Responsibility to Protect: From Opposition to Advocacy. United States Institute of Peace. United States Institute of Peace, 8 June. Available at <https://www.usip.org /publications/2016/06/china-and-responsibility-protect-opposition -advocacy>. Accessed 21 September 2020.

Fung, Courtney J. 2018. Separating Intervention from Regime Change: China's Diplomatic Innovations at the UN Security Council Regarding the Syria Crisis. *The China Quarterly* 235:693–712.

Gagliardone, Iginio. 2019. *China, Africa, and the Future of the Internet.* Zed Books.

Goddard, Stacie E. 2018. Embedded Revisionism: Networks, Institutions, and Challenges to World Order. *International Organization* 72 (4):763–97.

Goodman, Sara Wallace, and Thomas B. Pepinsky. Forthcoming. The Exclusionary Foundations of Embedded Liberalism. *International*

Organization 75 (2):<https://doi.org/10.1017/S002081832 0000478>.

Hart, Melanie, and Kelly Magsamen. 2019. Limit, Leverage, and Compete: A New Strategy on China. Center for American Progress, 3 April. Available at <https://www.americanprogress.org/issues /security/reports/2019/04/03/468136/limit-leverage-compete-new -strategy-china/>. Accessed 11 August 2020.

Huang, Yanxhong. 2004. The SARS Epidemic and Its Aftermath in China: A Political Perspective. In *Learning from SARS: Preparing for the Next Disease Outbreak*, edited by Adel Mahmoud, Laura Sivitz, Alison Mack, Stanley Lemon, Katherine Oberholtzer, Stacey Knobler. National Academies Press. Available at <https://www.ncbi .nlm.nih.gov/books/NBK92479/> Accessed 21 September 2020.

Hyde, Susan D. 2011. *The Pseudo-Democrat's Dilemma: Why Election Observation Became an International Norm.* Cornell University Press.

Hyde, Susan D., and Elizabeth N. Saunders. 2020. Recapturing Regime Type in International Relations: Leaders, Institutions, and Agency Space. *International Organization* 74 (2):363–95.

Ikenberry, G. John. 2008. The Rise of China and the Future of the West: Can the Liberal System Survive Changing China? *Foreign Affairs* 87 (January/February)1:23–37.

Ikenberry, G. John. 2011. *Liberal Leviathan: The Origins, Crisis, and Transformation of the American World Order.* Princeton University Press

Ikenberry, G. John. 2020. The Next Liberal Order. *Foreign Affairs* 99 (July/August):133–142.

Jensen, Eric Talbot. 2017. The Tallinn Manual 2.0: Highlights and Insights. *Georgetown Journal of International Law* 48:740–41.

Johnston, Alastair Iain. 2003. Is China a Status Quo Power? *International Security* 27 (4):5–56.

Johnston, Alastair I. 2008. *Social States: China in International Institutions, 1980–2000.* Princeton University Press.

Johnston, Alastair Iain. 2019a. China and a World of Orders. *International Security* 44 (2):9–60.

Johnston, Alastair Iain. 2019b. The Failures of the "Failure of Engagement" with China. *The Washington Quarterly* 42 (2):99–114.

Kang, David C. 2003. Getting Asia Wrong: The Need for New Analytical Frameworks. *International Security* 27 (4):57–85.

Kaplan, Stephen B. 2016. Banking Unconditionally: The Political Economy of Chinese Finance in Latin America. *Review of International Political Economy* 23 (4):643–76.

Kastner, Scott L., Margaret M. Pearson, and Chad Rector. 2018. *China's Strategic Multilateralism: Investing in Global Governance.* Cambridge University Press.

Katzenstein, Peter J. 2005. *A World of Regions: Asia and Europe in the American Imperium.* Cornell University Press.

Kaufmann, Chaim D., and Robert A. Pape. 1999. Explaining Costly International Moral Action: Britain's Sixty-Year Campaign Against the Atlantic Slave Trade. *International Organization* 53 (4):631–68.

Kostka, Genia, and William Hobbs. 2012. Local Energy Efficiency Policy Implementation in China: Bridging the Gap Between National Priorities and Local Interests. *The China Quarterly* 211:765–85.

Krasner, Stephen D. 1999. *Sovereignty: Organized Hypocrisy*. Princeton University Press.

Kupchan, Charles A. 2012. *No One's World: The West, the Rising Rest, and the Coming Global Turn*. Oxford University Press.

Kupchan, Charles A. 2014. The Normative Foundations of Hegemony and The Coming Challenge to Pax Americana. *Security Studies* 23 (2):219–57.

Kupchan, Charles A., and Peter L. Trubowitz. 2007. Dead Center: The Demise of Liberal Internationalism in the United States. *International Security* 32 (2):7–44.

Lake, David A. 2018. Economic Openness and Great Power Competition: Lessons for China and the United States. *The Chinese Journal of International Politics* 11 (3):237–70.

Lake, David A., Lisa L. Martin, and Thomas Risse. 2021. Challenges to the Liberal Order: Reflections on International Organization. *International Organization* 75 (2). <https://doi.org/10.1017/S0020818320000636>.

Lewis, Joanna I. 2008. China's Strategic Priorities in International Climate Change Negotiations. *The Washington Quarterly* 31 (1):155–74.

Lieberthal, Kenneth, and Michel Oksenberg. 1988. *Policy Making in China: Leaders, Structures, and Processes*. Princeton University Press.

Lorentzen, Peter, Pierre Landry, and John Yasuda. 2014. Undermining Authoritarian Innovation: The Power of China's Industrial Giants. *The Journal of Politics* 76 (1):182–94.

Mansfield, Edward, and Nita Rudra. 2021. Embedded Liberalism in the Digital Era. *International Organization* 75 (2). https://doi.org/10.1017/S0020818320000569>.

Martin, Lisa L. 2000. *Democratic Commitments: Legislatures and International Cooperation*. Princeton University Press.

McNamee, Lachlan, and Anna Zhang. 2019. Demographic Engineering and International Conflict: Evidence from China and the Former USSR. *International Organization* 73 (2):291–327.

Mearsheimer, John J. 2019. Bound to Fail: The Rise and Fall of the Liberal International Order. *International Security* 43 (4):7–50.

Mertha, Andrew, and Robert Pahre. 2005. Patently Misleading: Partial Implementation and Bargaining Leverage in Sino-American Negotiations on Intellectual Property Rights. *International Organization* 59 (3):695–729.

Minzner, Carl F. 2011. China's Turn Against Law. *The American Journal of Comparative Law* 59 (4):935–84.

Monteiro, Nuno P. 2014. *Theory of Unipolar Politics*. Cambridge University Press.

Moravcsik, Andrew. 1997. Taking Preferences Seriously: A Liberal Theory of International Politics. *International Organization* 51 (4):513–53.

Musgrave, Paul. 2019. International Hegemony Meets Domestic Politics: Why Liberals Can Be Pessimists. *Security Studies* 28 (3):451–78.

Mutz, Diana C. 2018. Status Threat, Not Economic Hardship, Explains the 2016 Presidential Vote. *Proceedings of the National Academy of Sciences* 115 (19):E4330–39.

Oliver, Steven. 2014. The Politics of Poor Air Quality in Contemporary China. PhD diss., University of California, San Diego.

Pearson, Margaret M. 2001. The Case of China's Accession to GATT/WTO. In *The Making of Chinese Foreign and Security Policy in the Era of Reform*, edited by David M. Lampton, 337–70. Stanford University Press.

Piccone, Ted. 2018. *China's Long Game on Human Rights at the United Nations*. Brookings.

Putnam, Robert D. 1988. Diplomacy and Domestic Politics: The Logic of Two-Level Games. *International Organization* 42 (3):427–60.

Risse-Kappen, Thomas. 1991. Public Opinion, Domestic Structure, and Foreign Policy in Liberal Democracies. *World Politics* 43 (4):479–512.

Risse-Kappen, Thomas. 1994. Ideas Do Not Float Freely: Transnational Coalitions, Domestic Structures, and the End of the Cold War. *International Organization* 48 (2):185–214.

Roberts, Margaret E. 2018. *Censored: Distraction and Diversion Inside China's Great Firewall*. Princeton University Press.

Ruggie, John Gerard. 1982. International Regimes, Transactions, and Change: Embedded Liberalism in the Postwar Economic Order. *International Organization* 36 (2):379–415.

Schweller, Randall L., and Xiaoyu Pu. 2011. After Unipolarity: China's Visions of International Order in an Era of US Decline. *International Security* 36 (1):41–72.

Segal, Adam. 2017. *Chinese Cyber Diplomacy in a New Era of Uncertainty*. Aegis Paper Series No. 1703, Stanford, California, Hoover Institution.

Shi, Weiyi, and Boliang Zhu. 2019. Managing International Tensions in Autocracies: Evidence from the Ongoing US-China Trade War. Paper presented at the Annual Meeting of the American Political Science Association. Washington, DC.

Shirk, Susan. 2006. Trends in PRC-Taiwan Relations and United States Policy Responses. In *Sources Of Conflict And Cooperation In The Taiwan Strait*, edited by Yong-nian, Zheng, and Wu Raymond Raykuo, 169–76. World Scientific.

Simmons, Beth A., and Hein Goemans. 2021. Built on Borders: Tensions with the Institution Liberalism (Thought It) Left Behind. *International Organization* 75 (2). <https://doi.org/10.1017/S0020818320000600>.

Snyder, Jack, Robert Y. Shapiro, and Yaeli Bloch-Elkon. 2009. Free Hand Abroad, Divide and Rule at Home. *World Politics* 61 (1):155–87.

Sorace, Christian P. 2017. *Shaken Authority: China's Communist Party and the 2008 Sichuan Earthquake*. Cornell University Press.

Steinberg, David A., and Victor C. Shih. 2012. Interest Group Influence in Authoritarian States: The Political Determinants of Chinese Exchange Rate Policy. *Comparative Political Studies* 45 (11):1405–34.

Terman, Rochelle. 2016. Backlash: Defiance, Human Rights, and the Politics of Shame. PhD diss., University of California, Berkeley.

Towns, Ann E. 2010. *Women and States: Norms and Hierarchies in International Society*. Cambridge University Press.

Wallace, Jeremy L. n.d. Seeking Truth, Hiding Facts: Information, Ideology, and Authoritarianism in China. Manuscript. Available at <http://www.jeremywallace.org/research.html>.

Weeks, Jessica L. 2008. Autocratic Audience Costs: Regime Type and Signaling Resolve. *International Organization* 62 (1):35–64.

Weeks, Jessica L. 2012. Strongmen and Straw Men: Authoritarian Regimes and the Initiation of International Conflict. *American Political Science Review* 106 (2):326–47.

Weeks, Jessica L. P. 2014. *Dictators at War and Peace.* Cornell University Press.

Weiss, Jessica Chen. 2013. Authoritarian Signaling, Mass Audiences, and Nationalist Protest in China. *International Organization* 67 (1):1–35.

Weiss, Jessica Chen. 2019. A World Safe for Autocracy? *Foreign Affairs* 98 (July/August):92–108.

Weiss, Jessica Chen, and Amber Wichowsky. 2018. External Influence on Exchange Rates: An Empirical Investigation of US Pressure and the Chinese RMB. *Review of International Political Economy* 25 (5): 596–623.

Wu, Fuzuo. 2016. Shaping China's Climate Diplomacy: Wealth, Status, and Asymmetric Interdependence. *Journal of Chinese Political Science* 21 (2):199–215.

Wuthnow, Joel. 2013. *Chinese Diplomacy and the UN Security Council: Beyond the Veto.* Routledge.

Xu, Bin. 2017. *The Politics of Compassion: The Sichuan Earthquake and Civic Engagement in China.* Stanford University Press.

Yan, Xuetong. 2018. Chinese Values vs. Liberalism: What Ideology Will Shape the International Normative Order? *Chinese Journal of International Politics* 11 (1):1–22.

5

THE STATE AND THE TOOLS OF STATECRAFT

States are key actors in international relations, and how they act depends, in part, on domestic political considerations, as explained in Chapter 5 of *Essentials of International Relations*. In a widely cited article, Robert D. Putnam explains the entanglements between international and domestic factors during negotiations, using the metaphor and the language of the two-level game. Negotiators consider not only what the other state wants but also what the domestic constituencies in each state will accept. This approach connects the disciplines of international relations and comparative politics.

Also examining the borders between domestic and international politics is Barry Posen's essay on ethnic conflict and the security dilemma. At the end of the Cold War, many communist regimes collapsed, in some cases leading to the breakdown of the states into anarchy. Some African regimes that had been sustained by communist Russia and Cold War rivalry also collapsed at this time. Posen, a realist international relations scholar, put the theory of the causes of war in international anarchy to the task of explaining the rise of ethnic conflict in postcommunist anarchy. In this piece, he draws on Robert Jervis's seminal article on the security dilemma in anarchy, which is reprinted in Chapter 7.

Robert D. Putnam

DIPLOMACY AND DOMESTIC POLITICS
The Logic of Two-Level Games

Introduction: The Entanglements of Domestic and International Politics

Domestic politics and international relations are often somehow entangled, but our theories have not yet sorted out the puzzling tangle. It is fruitless to debate whether domestic politics really determine international relations, or the reverse. The answer to that question is clearly "Both, sometimes." The more interesting questions are "When?" and "How?" This article offers a theoretical approach to this issue, but I begin with a story that illustrates the puzzle.

One illuminating example of how diplomacy and domestic politics can become entangled culminated at the Bonn summit conference of 1978.[1] In the mid-1970s, a coordinated program of global reflation, led by the "locomotive" economies of the United States, Germany, and Japan, had been proposed to foster Western recovery from the first oil shock.[2] This proposal had received a powerful boost from the incoming Carter administration and was warmly supported by the weaker countries, as well as the Organization for Economic Co-operation and Development (OECD) and many private economists, who argued that it would overcome international payments imbalances and speed growth all around. On the other hand, the Germans and the Japanese protested that prudent and successful economic managers should not be asked to bail out spendthrifts. Meanwhile, Jimmy Carter's ambitious National Energy Program remained deadlocked in Congress, while Helmut Schmidt led a chorus of complaints about the Americans' uncontrolled appetite for imported oil and their apparent unconcern about the falling dollar. All sides conceded that the world economy was in serious trouble, but it was not clear which was more to blame, tight-fisted German and Japanese fiscal policies or slack-jawed U.S. energy and monetary policies.

At the Bonn summit, however, a comprehensive package deal was approved, the clearest case yet of a summit that left all participants happier than when they arrived. Helmut Schmidt agreed to additional fiscal stimulus, amounting to 1 percent of GNP, Jimmy Carter committed himself to decontrol domestic oil prices by the end of 1980, and Takeo Fukuda pledged new efforts to reach a 7 percent growth rate. Secondary elements in the Bonn accord included French and British acquiescence in the Tokyo Round trade negotiations; Japanese undertakings to foster import growth and restrain exports; and a generic American promise to fight inflation. All in all, the Bonn summit produced a balanced agreement of unparalleled breadth and specificity.

From *International Organization* 42, no. 3 (Summer 1988): 427–60. Some of the author's notes have been omitted.

More remarkably, virtually all parts of the package were actually implemented.

Most observers at the time welcomed the policies agreed to at Bonn, although in retrospect there has been much debate about the economic wisdom of this package deal. However, my concern here is not whether the deal was wise economically, but how it became possible politically. My research suggests, first, that the key governments at Bonn adopted policies different from those that they would have pursued in the absence of international negotiations, but second, that agreement was possible only because a powerful minority within each government actually favored on domestic grounds the policy being demanded internationally.

Within Germany, a political process catalyzed by foreign pressures was surreptitiously orchestrated by expansionists inside the Schmidt government. Contrary to the public mythology, the Bonn deal was not forced on a reluctant or "altruistic" Germany. In fact, officials in the Chancellor's Office and the Economics Ministry, as well as in the Social Democratic party and the trade unions, had argued privately in early 1978 that further stimulus was domestically desirable, particularly in view of the approaching 1980 elections. However, they had little hope of overcoming the opposition of the Finance Ministry, the Free Democratic party (part of the government coalition), and the business and banking community, especially the leadership of the Bundesbank. Publicly, Helmut Schmidt posed as reluctant to the end. Only his closest advisors suspected the truth: that the chancellor "let himself be pushed" into a policy that he privately favored, but would have found costly and perhaps impossible to enact without the summit's package deal.

Analogously, in Japan a coalition of business interests, the Ministry of Trade and Industry (MITI), the Economic Planning Agency, and some expansion-minded politicians within the Liberal Democratic Party pushed for additional domestic stimulus, using U.S. pressure as one of their prime arguments against the stubborn resistance of the Ministry of Finance (MOF). Without internal divisions in Tokyo, it is unlikely that the foreign demands would have been met, but without the external pressure, it is even more unlikely that the expansionists could have overridden the powerful MOF. "Seventy percent foreign pressure, 30 percent internal politics," was the disgruntled judgment of one MOF insider. "Fifty-fifty," guessed an official from MITI.[3]

In the American case, too, internal politicking reinforced, and was reinforced by, the international pressure. During the summit preparations American negotiators occasionally invited their foreign counterparts to put more pressure on the Americans to reduce oil imports. Key economic officials within the administration favored a tougher energy policy, but they were opposed by the president's closest political aides, even after the summit. Moreover, congressional opponents continued to stymie oil price decontrol, as they had under both Nixon and Ford. Finally, in April 1979, the president decided on gradual administrative decontrol, bringing U.S. prices up to world levels by October 1981. His domestic advisors thus won a postponement of this politically costly move until after the 1980 presidential election, but in the end, virtually every one of the pledges made at Bonn was fulfilled. Both proponents and opponents of decontrol agree that the summit commitment was at the center of the administration's heated intramural debate during the winter of 1978–79 and instrumental in the final decision.[4]

In short, the Bonn accord represented genuine international policy coordination. Significant policy changes were pledged and implemented by the key participants. Moreover—although this counterfactual claim is necessarily harder to establish—those policy changes would very probably not have been pursued (certainly not the same scale and within the same time frame) in the absence of the international agreement. Within each country, one faction supported the policy shift being demanded of its country internationally, but that faction was initially outnumbered. Thus, international pressure was a necessary condition for these policy shifts. On the other hand, without domestic resonance, international forces would not have sufficed to produce the accord, no matter how balanced and intellectually persuasive the overall package. In the end, each leader believed that what he was doing was in his nation's interest—and probably in his own political interest, too, even though not all his aides agreed.[5] Yet without the summit accord he probably would not (or could not) have changed policies so easily. In that sense, the Bonn deal successfully meshed domestic and international pressures.

Neither a purely domestic nor a purely international analysis could account for this episode. Interpretations cast in terms either of domestic causes and international effects ("Second Image"[6]) or of international causes and domestic effects ("Second Image Reversed"[7]) would represent merely "partial equilibrium" analyses and would miss an important part of the story, namely, how the domestic politics of several countries became entangled via an international negotiation. The events of 1978 illustrate that we must aim instead for "general equilibrium" theories that account simultaneously for the interaction of domestic and international factors. This article suggests a conceptual framework for understanding how diplomacy and domestic politics interact.

Domestic-International Entanglements: The State of the Art

Much of the existing literature on relations between domestic and international affairs consists either of ad hoc lists of countless "domestic influences" on foreign policy or of generic observations that national and international affairs are somehow "linked."[8]

■ ■ ■

We need to move beyond the mere observation that domestic factors influence international affairs and vice versa, and beyond simple catalogs of instances of such influence, to seek theories that integrate both spheres, accounting for the areas of entanglement between them.

Two-Level Games: A Metaphor for Domestic-International Interactions

Over two decades ago Richard E. Walton and Robert B. McKersie offered a "behavioral theory" of social negotiations that is strikingly applicable to international conflict and cooperation.[9] They pointed out, as all experienced negotiators know, that the unitary-actor assumption is often radically misleading. As Robert Strauss said of the Tokyo Round trade negotiations: "During my tenure as Special Trade Representative, I spent as much time negotiating with domestic constituents (both industry and labor) and members of the U.S. Congress as I did negotiating with our foreign trading partners."[10]

The politics of many international negotiations can usefully be conceived as a two-level game. At the national level, domestic groups pursue their interests by pressuring the government to adopt favorable policies, and politicians seek power by constructing coalitions among those groups. At the international level, national governments seek to maximize their own ability to satisfy domestic pressures, while minimizing the adverse consequences of foreign developments. Neither of the two games can be ignored by central decision-makers, so long as their countries remain interdependent, yet sovereign.

Each national political leader appears at both game boards. Across the international table sit his foreign counterparts, and at his elbows sit diplomats and other international advisors. Around the domestic table behind him sit party and parliamentary figures, spokespersons for domestic agencies, representatives of key interest groups, and the leader's own political advisors. The unusual complexity of this two-level game is that moves that are rational for a player at one board (such as raising energy prices, conceding territory, or limiting auto imports) may be impolitic for that same player at the other board. Nevertheless, there are powerful incentives for consistency between the two games. Players (and kibitzers) will tolerate some differences in rhetoric between the two games, but in the end either energy prices rise or they don't.

The political complexities for the players in this two-level game are staggering. Any key player at the international table who is dissatisfied with the outcome may upset the game board, and conversely, any leader who fails to satisfy his fellow players at the domestic table risks being evicted from his seat. On occasion, however, clever players will spot a move on one board that will trigger realignments on other boards, enabling them to achieve otherwise unattainable objectives. This "two-table" metaphor captures the dynamics of the 1978 negotiations better than any model based on unitary national actors.

* * * Probably the most interesting empirically based theorizing about the connection between domestic and international bargaining is that of Glenn Snyder and Paul Diesing. Though working in the neo-realist tradition with its conventional assumption of unitary actors, they found that, in fully half of the crises they studied, top decision-makers were *not* unified. They concluded that prediction of international outcomes is significantly improved by understanding internal bargaining, especially with respect to minimally acceptable compromises.[11]

Metaphors are not theories, but I am comforted by Max Black's observation that "perhaps every science must start with metaphor and end with algebra; and perhaps without the metaphor there would never have been any algebra."[12] Formal analysis of any game requires well-defined rules, choices, payoffs, players, and information, and even then, many simple two-person, mixed-motive games have no determinate solution. Deriving analytic solutions for two-level games will be a difficult challenge. In what follows I hope to motivate further work on that problem.

Towards a Theory of Ratification: The Importance of "Win-Sets"

Consider the following stylized scenario that might apply to any two-level game. Negotiators representing two organizations meet to reach an agreement between them, subject to the constraint that any tentative agreement must be ratified by their respective organizations. The negotiators might be heads of government representing nations, for example, or labor and management representatives, or party leaders in a multiparty coalition, or a finance minister negotiating with an IMF team, or leaders of a House-Senate conference committee, or ethnic-group leaders in a consociational democracy. For the moment, we shall presume that each side is represented by a single leader or "chief negotiator," and that this individual has no independent policy preferences, but seeks simply to achieve an agreement that will be attractive to his constituents.[13]

It is convenient analytically to decompose the process into two stages:

1. bargaining between the negotiators, leading to a tentative agreement; call that Level I.
2. separate discussions within each group of constituents about whether to ratify the agreement; call that Level II.

This sequential decomposition into a negotiation phase and a ratification phase is useful for purposes of exposition, although it is not descriptively accurate. In practice, expectational effects will be quite important. There are likely to be prior consultations and bargaining at Level II to hammer out an initial position for the Level I negotiations. Conversely, the need for Level II ratification is certain to affect the Level I bargaining. In fact, expectations of rejection at Level II may abort negotiations at Level I without any formal action at Level II. For example, even though both the American and Iranian governments seem to have favored an arms-for-hostages deal, negotiations collapsed as soon as they became public and thus liable to de facto "ratification." In many negotiations, the two-level process may be iterative, as the negotiators try out possible agreements and probe their constituents' views. In more complicated cases, as we shall see later, the constituents' views may themselves evolve in the course of the negotiations. Nevertheless, the requirement that any Level I agreement must, in the end, be ratified at Level II imposes a crucial theoretical link between the two levels.

"Ratification" may entail a formal voting procedure at Level II, such as the constitutionally required two-thirds vote of the U.S. Senate for ratifying treaties, but I use the term generically to refer to any decision-process at Level II that is required to endorse or implement a Level I agreement, whether formally or informally. It is sometimes convenient to think of ratification as a parliamentary function, but that is not essential. The actors at Level II may represent bureaucratic agencies, interest groups, social classes, or even "public opinion." For example, if labor unions in a debtor country withhold necessary cooperation

from an austerity program that the government has negotiated with the IMF, Level II ratification of the agreement may be said to have failed; ex ante expectations about that prospect will surely influence the Level I negotiations between the government and the IMF.

Domestic ratification of international agreements might seem peculiar to democracies. As the German Finance Minister recently observed, "The limit of expanded cooperation lies in the fact that we are democracies, and we need to secure electoral majorities at home."[14] However, ratification need not be "democratic" in any normal sense. For example, in 1930 the Meiji Constitution was interpreted as giving a special role to the Japanese military in the ratification of the London Naval Treaty;[15] and during the ratification of any agreement between Catholics and Protestants in Northern Ireland, presumably the IRA would throw its power onto the scales. We need only stipulate that, for purposes of counting "votes" in the ratification process, different forms of political power can be reduced to some common denominator.

The only formal constraint on the ratification process is that since the identical agreement must be ratified by both sides, a preliminary Level I agreement cannot be amended at Level II without reopening the Level I negotiations. In other words, final ratification must be simply "voted" up or down; any modification to the Level I agreement counts as a rejection, unless that modification is approved by all other parties to the agreement.[16] Congresswoman Lynn Martin captured the logic of ratification when explaining her support for the 1986 tax reform bill as it emerged from the conference committee: "As worried as I am about what this bill does, I am even more worried about the current code. The choice today is not between this bill and a perfect bill; the choice is between this bill and the death of tax reform."[17]

Given this set of arrangements, we may define the "win-set" for a given Level II constituency as the set of all possible Level I agreements that would "win"—that is, gain the necessary majority among the constituents—when simply voted up or down.[18] For two quite different reasons, the contours of the Level II win-sets are very important for understanding Level I agreements.

First, **larger win-sets make Level I agreement more likely**, *ceteris paribus*.[19] By definition, any successful agreement must fall within the Level II win-sets of each of the parties to the accord. Thus, agreement is possible only if those win-sets overlap, and the larger each win-set, the more likely they are to overlap. Conversely, the smaller the win-sets, the greater the risk that the negotiations will break down. For example, during the prolonged pre-war Anglo-Argentine negotiations over the Falklands/Malvinas, several tentative agreements were rejected in one capital or the other for domestic political reasons; when it became clear that the initial British and Argentine win-sets did not overlap at all, war became virtually inevitable.[20]

■ ■ ■

The second reason why win-set size is important is that **the relative size of the respective Level II win-sets will affect the distribution of the joint gains from the international bargain**. The larger the perceived win-set of a negotiator, the more he can be "pushed around" by the other Level I negotiators. Conversely, a small domestic win-set can be a bargaining advantage: "I'd like to accept your proposal, but I could never get it accepted at home." Lamenting the domestic constraints under which one must operate is (in the words of one experienced British diplomat) "the natural thing to say at the beginning of a tough negotiation."[21]

This general principle was, of course, first noted by Thomas Schelling nearly thirty years ago:

The power of a negotiator often rests on a manifest inability to make concessions and meet demands. . . . When the United States

Government negotiates with other governments . . . if the executive branch negotiates under legislative authority, with its position constrained by law, . . . then the executive branch has a firm position that is visible to its negotiating partners. . . . [Of course, strategies such as this] run the risk of establishing an immovable position that goes beyond the ability of the other to concede, and thereby provoke the likelihood of stalemate or breakdown.[22]

Writing from a strategist's point of view, Schelling stressed ways in which win-sets may be manipulated, but even when the win-set itself is beyond the negotiator's control, he may exploit its leverage. A Third World leader whose domestic position is relatively weak (Argentina's Alfonsin?) should be able to drive a better bargain with his international creditors, other things being equal, than one whose domestic standing is more solid (Mexico's de la Madrid?).[23] The difficulties of winning congressional ratification are often exploited by American negotiators. During the negotiation of the Panama Canal Treaty, for example, "the Secretary of State warned the Panamanians several times . . . that the new treaty would have to be acceptable to at least sixty-seven senators," and "Carter, in a personal letter to Torrijos, warned that further concessions by the United States would seriously threaten chances for Senate ratification."[24] Precisely to forestall such tactics, opponents may demand that a negotiator ensure himself "negotiating room" at Level II before opening the Level I negotiations.

■ ■ ■

Determinants of the Win-Set

It is important to understand what circumstances affect win-set size. Three sets of factors are especially important:

- Level II preferences and coalitions
- Level II institutions
- Level I negotiators' strategies

Let us consider each in turn.

1. *The size of the win-set depends on the distribution of power, preferences, and possible coalitions among Level II constituents.*

Any testable two-level theory of international negotiation must be rooted in a theory of domestic politics, that is, a theory about the power and preferences of the major actors at Level II. This is not the occasion for even a cursory evaluation of the relevant alternatives, except to note that the two-level conceptual framework could in principle be married to such diverse perspectives as Marxism, interest group pluralism, bureaucratic politics, and neo-corporatism. For example, arms negotiations might be interpreted in terms of a bureaucratic politics model of Level II politicking, while class analysis or neo-corporatism might be appropriate for analyzing international macroeconomic coordination.

Abstracting from the details of Level II politics, however, it is possible to sketch certain principles that govern the size of the win-sets. For example, the lower the cost of "no-agreement" to constituents, the smaller the win-set.[25] Recall that ratification pits the proposed agreement, *not* against an array of other (possibly attractive) alternatives, but only against "no-agreement."[26] No-agreement often represents the status quo, although in some cases no-agreement may in fact lead to a worsening situation; that might be a reasonable description of the failed ratification of the Versailles Treaty.

Some constituents may face low costs from no-agreement, and others high costs, and the former will be more skeptical of Level I agreements than the latter. * * * The size of the win-set (and thus the negotiating room of the Level I negotiator) depends on the relative size of the "isolationist" forces (who oppose international cooperation in general) and the "internationalists" (who offer "all-purpose" support). All-purpose support for international agreements is probably greater in smaller, more dependent countries with more open economies, as compared to more self-sufficient countries, like the United States, for most of whose citizens the costs of no-agreement are generally lower. *Ceteris paribus*, more self-sufficient states with smaller win-sets should make fewer international agreements and drive harder bargains in those that they do make.

In some cases, evaluation of no-agreement may be the *only* significant disagreement among the Level II constituents, because their interests are relatively homogeneous. For example, if oil imports are to be limited by an agreement among the consuming nations—the sort of accord sought at the Tokyo summit of 1979, for example—then presumably every constituent would prefer to maximize his nation's share of the available supply, although some constituents may be more reluctant than others to push too hard, for fear of losing the agreement entirely. * * * Other international examples in which domestic interests are relatively homogeneous except for the evaluation or no-agreement might include the SALT talks, the Panama Canal Treaty negotiations, and the Arab-Israeli conflict. A negotiator is unlikely to face criticism at home that a proposed agreement reduces the opponents' arms too much, offers too little compensation for foreign concessions, or contains too few security guarantees for the other side, although in each case opinions may differ on how much to risk a negotiating deadlock in order to achieve these objectives.

The distinctive nature of such "homogeneous" issues is thrown into sharp relief by contrasting them to cases in which constituents' preferences are more heterogeneous, so that any Level I agreement bears unevenly on them. Thus, an internationally coordinated reflation may encounter domestic opposition *both* from those who think it goes too far (bankers, for example) *and* from those who think it does not go far enough (unions, for example). In 1919, some Americans opposed the Versailles Treaty because it was too harsh on the defeated powers and others because it was too lenient.[27] Such patterns are even more common, as we shall shortly see, where the negotiation involves multiple issues, such as an arms agreement that involves tradeoffs between seaborne and airborne weapons, or a labor agreement that involves tradeoffs between take-home pay and pensions. (Walton and McKersie term these "factional" conflicts, because the negotiator is caught between contending factions within his own organization.)

The problems facing Level I negotiators dealing with a *homogeneous* (or "boundary") conflict are quite different from those facing negotiators dealing with a *heterogeneous* (or "factional") conflict. In the former case, the more the negotiator can win at Level I—the higher his national oil allocation, the deeper the cuts in Soviet throw-weight, the lower the rent he promises for the Canal, and so on—the better his odds of winning ratification. In such cases, the negotiator may use the implicit threat from his own hawks to maximize his gains (or minimize his losses) at Level I, as Carter and Vance did in dealing with the Panamanians. Glancing over his shoulder at Level II, the negotiator's main problem in a homogeneous conflict is to manage the discrepancy between his constituents' expectations and the negotiable outcome. Neither negotiator is likely to find much sympathy for the enemy's demands among his own constituents, nor much support for his constituents' positions in the enemy camp. The effect of domestic division, embodied in hard-line opposition from hawks, is to raise the risk of involuntary defection and thus to impede agreement at Level I. The common belief that domestic politics is inimical to international cooperation no doubt derives from such cases.

The task of a negotiator grappling instead with a heterogeneous conflict is more complicated, but potentially more interesting. Seeking to maximize the chances of ratification, he cannot follow a simple "the more, the better" rule of thumb; imposing more severe reparations on the Germans in 1919 would have gained some votes at Level II but lost others, as would hastening the decontrol of domestic oil prices in 1978. In some cases, these lines of cleavage within the Level II constituencies will cut across the Level I division, and the Level I negotiator may find silent allies at his opponent's domestic table. German labor unions might welcome foreign pressure on their own government to adopt a more expansive fiscal policy, and Italian bankers might welcome international demands for a more austere Italian monetary policy. Thus transnational alignments may emerge, tacit or explicit, in which domestic interests pressure their respective governments to adopt mutually supportive policies. This is, of course, my interpretation of the 1978 Bonn summit accord.

In such cases, domestic divisions may actually improve the prospects for international cooperation. * * *

Thus far we have implicitly assumed that all eligible constituents will participate in the ratification process. In fact, however, participation rates vary across groups and across issues, and this variation often has implications for the size of the win-set. For example, when the costs and/or benefits of a proposed agreement are relatively concentrated, it is reasonable to expect that those constituents whose interests are most affected will exert special influence on the ratification process.[28] One reason why Level II games are more important for trade negotiations than in monetary matters is that the "abstention rate" is higher on international monetary issues than on trade issues.[29]

The composition of the active Level II constituency (and hence the character of the win-set) also varies with the politicization of the issue. Politicization often activates groups who are less worried about the costs of no-agreement, thus reducing the effective win-set. For example, politicization of the Panama Canal issue seems to have reduced the negotiating flexibility on both sides of the diplomatic table.[30] This is one reason why most professional diplomats emphasize the value of secrecy to successful negotiations. However, Woodrow Wilson's transcontinental tour in 1919 reflected the opposite calculation, namely, that by expanding the active constituency he could ensure ratification of the Versailles Treaty, although in the end this strategy proved fruitless.[31]

Another important restriction of our discussion thus far has been the assumption that the negotiations involve only one issue. Relaxing this assumption has powerful consequences for the play at both levels.[32] Various groups at Level II are likely to have quite different preferences on the several issues involved in a multi-issue negotiation. As a general rule, the group with the greatest interest in a specific issue is also likely to hold the most extreme position on that issue. In the Law of the Sea negotiations, for example, the Defense Department felt most strongly about sea-lanes, the Department of the Interior about sea-bed mining rights, and so on.[33] If each group is allowed to fix the Level I negotiating position for "its" issue, the resulting package is almost sure to be "non-negotiable" (that is, non-ratifiable in opposing capitals).[34]

Thus, the chief negotiator is faced with tradeoffs across different issues: how much to yield on mining rights in order to get sea-lane protection, how much to yield on citrus exports to get a better deal on beef, and so on. * * * The central point is simple: the possibility of package deals opens up a rich array of strategic alternatives for negotiators in a two-level game.

One kind of issue linkage is absolutely crucial to understanding how domestic and international politics can become entangled.[35] Suppose that a majority of constituents at Level II oppose a given policy (say, oil price decontrol), but that some members of that majority would be willing to switch their vote on that issue in return for more jobs (say, in export industries). If bargaining is limited to Level II, that tradeoff is not technically feasible, but if the chief negotiator can broker an international deal that delivers more jobs (say, via faster growth abroad), he can, in effect, overturn the initial outcome at the domestic table. Such a transnational issue linkage was a crucial element in the 1978 Bonn accord.

Note that this strategy works not by changing the preferences of any domestic constituents, but rather by creating a policy option (such as faster export growth) that was previously beyond domestic control. Hence, I refer to this type of issue linkage at Level I that alters the feasible outcomes at Level II as *synergistic linkage*. For example, "in the Tokyo Round . . . nations used negotiation to achieve internal reform in situations where constituency pressures would otherwise prevent action without the pressure (and tradeoff benefits) that an external partner could provide."[36] Economic interdependence multiplies the opportunities for altering domestic coalitions (and thus policy outcomes) by expanding the set of feasible alternatives in this way—in effect, creating political entanglements across national boundaries. Thus, we should expect synergistic linkage (which is, by definition, explicable only in terms of two-level analysis) to become more frequent as interdependence grows.

2. *The size of the win-set depends on the Level II political institutions.*

Ratification procedures clearly affect the size of the win-set. For example, if a two-thirds vote is required for ratification, the win-set will almost certainly be smaller than if only a simple majority is required. As one experienced observer has written: "Under the Constitution, thirty-four of the one hundred senators can block ratification of any treaty. This is an unhappy and unique feature of our democracy. Because of the effective veto power of a small group, many worthy agreements have been rejected, and many treaties are never considered for ratification."[37] As noted earlier, the U.S. separation of powers imposes a tighter constraint on the American win-set than is true in many other countries. This increases the bargaining power of American negotiators, but it also reduces the scope for international cooperation. It raises the odds for involuntary defection and makes potential partners warier about dealing with the Americans.

■   ■   ■

Not all significant ratification practices are formalized; for example, the Japanese propensity for seeking the broadest possible domestic consensus before acting constricts the Japanese win-set, as contrasted with majoritarian political cultures. Other domestic political practices, too, can affect the size of the win-set. Strong discipline within the governing party, for example, increases the win-set by widening the range of agreements for which the Level I negotiator can expect to receive backing. For example, in the 1986 House-Senate conference committee on tax reform, the final bill was closer to the Senate version, despite (or rather, *because of*) Congressman Rostenkowski's greater control of his delegation, which increased the House win-set. Conversely, a weakening of party discipline across the major Western nations would, *ceteris paribus*, reduce the scope for international cooperation.

The recent discussion of "state strength" and "state autonomy" is relevant here. The greater the autonomy of central decision-makers from their Level II constituents, the larger their win-set and thus the greater the likelihood of achieving international agreement. For example, central bank insulation from domestic political pressures in effect increases the win-set and thus the odds for international monetary cooperation; recent proposals for an enhanced role for central bankers

in international policy coordination rest on this point.[38] However, two-level analysis also implies that, *ceteris paribus*, the stronger a state is in terms of autonomy from domestic pressures, the weaker its relative bargaining position internationally. For example, diplomats representing an entrenched dictatorship are less able than representatives of a democracy to claim credibly that domestic pressures preclude some disadvantageous deal.[39] This is yet another facet of the disconcerting ambiguity of the notion of "state strength."

■   ■   ■

3. *The size of the win-set depends on the strategies of the Level I negotiators.*

Each Level I negotiator has an unequivocal interest in maximizing the other side's win-set, but with respect to his own win-set, his motives are mixed. The larger his win-set, the more easily he can conclude an agreement, but also the weaker his bargaining position vis-à-vis the other negotiator. This fact often poses a tactical dilemma. For example, one effective way to demonstrate commitment to a given position in Level I bargaining is to rally support from one's constituents (for example, holding a strike vote, talking about a "missile gap," or denouncing "unfair trading practices" abroad). On the other hand, such tactics may have irreversible effects on constituents' attitudes, hampering subsequent ratification of a compromise agreement.[40] Conversely, preliminary consultations at home, aimed at "softening up" one's constituents in anticipation of a ratification struggle, can undercut a negotiator's ability to project an implacable image abroad.

Nevertheless, disregarding these dilemmas for the moment and assuming that a negotiator wishes to expand his win-set in order to encourage ratification of an agreement, he may exploit both conventional side-payments and generic "good will." The use of side-payments to attract marginal supporters is, of course, quite familiar in game theory, as well as in practical politics. For example, the Carter White House offered many inducements (such as public works projects) to help persuade wavering Senators to ratify the Panama Canal Treaty.[41] In a two-level game the side-payments may come from unrelated domestic sources, as in this case, or they may be received as part of the international negotiation.

The role of side-payments in international negotiations is well known. However, the two-level approach emphasizes that the value of an international side-payment should be calculated in terms of its marginal contribution to the likelihood of ratification, rather than in terms of its overall value to the recipient nation. What counts at Level II is not total national costs and benefits, but their *incidence, relative to existing coalitions and proto-coalitions.* An across-the-board trade concession (or still worse, a concession on a product of interest to a committed free-trade congressman) is less effective than a concession (even one of lesser intrinsic value) that tips the balance with a swing voter. Conversely, trade retaliation should be targeted, neither at free-traders nor at confirmed protectionists, but at the uncommitted.

An experienced negotiator familiar with the respective domestic tables should be able to maximize the cost-effectiveness (to him and his constituents) of the concessions that he must make to ensure ratification abroad, as well as the cost-effectiveness of his own demands and threats, by targeting his initiatives with an eye to their Level II incidence, both at home and abroad. In this endeavor Level I negotiators are often in collusion, since each has an interest in helping the other to get the final deal ratified. In effect, they are moving jointly towards points of tangency between their respective political indifference curves. The empirical frequency of such targeting in trade negotiations and trade wars, as well as in other international negotiations, would be a crucial test of the relative merits of conventional unitary-actor analysis and the two-level approach proposed here.[42]

In addition to the use of specific side-payments, a chief negotiator whose political standing at home is high can more easily win ratification of his foreign initiatives. Although generic good will cannot guarantee ratification, as Woodrow Wilson discovered, it is useful in expanding the win-set and thus fostering Level I agreement, for it constitutes a kind of "all-purpose glue" for his supporting coalition. * * *

Note that each Level I negotiator has a strong interest in the popularity of his opposite number, since Party A's popularity increases the size of his win-set, and thus increases both the odds of success and the relative bargaining leverage of Party B. Thus, negotiators should normally be expected to try to reinforce one another's standing with their respective constituents.

Partly for this reason and partly because of media attention, participation on the world stage normally gives a head of government a special advantage vis-à-vis his or her domestic opposition. Thus, although international policy coordination is hampered by high transaction costs, heads of government may also reap what we might term "transaction benefits." Indeed, the recent evolution of Western summitry, which has placed greater emphasis on publicity than on substance, seems designed to appropriate these "transaction benefits" without actually seeking the sort of agreements that might entail transaction costs.[43]

Higher status negotiators are likely to dispose of more side-payments and more "good will" at home, and hence foreigners prefer to negotiate with a head of government than with a lower official. In purely distributive terms, a nation might have a bargaining advantage if its chief negotiator were a mere clerk. Diplomats are acting rationally, not merely symbolically, when they refuse to negotiate with a counterpart of inferior rank. America's negotiating partners have reason for concern whenever the American president is domestically weakened.

Uncertainty and Bargaining Tactics

Level I negotiators are often badly misinformed about Level II politics, particularly on the opposing side. In 1978, the Bonn negotiators were usually wrong in their assessments of domestic politics abroad; for example, most American officials did not appreciate the complex domestic game that Chancellor Schmidt was playing over the issue of German reflation. Similarly, Snyder and Diesing report that "decision makers in our cases only occasionally attempted such assessments, and when they tried they did pretty miserably. . . . Governments generally do not do well in analyzing each other's internal politics in crises [and, I would add, in normal times], and indeed it is inherently difficult."[44] Relaxing the assumption of perfect information to allow for uncertainty has many implications for our understanding of two-level games. Let me illustrate a few of these implications.

Uncertainty about the size of a win-set can be both a bargaining device and a stumbling block in two-level negotiation. In purely distributive Level I bargaining, negotiators have an incentive to understate their own win-sets. Since each negotiator is likely to know more about his own Level II than his opponent does, the claim has some plausibility. * * *

On the other hand, uncertainty about the opponent's win-set increases one's concern about the risk of involuntary defection. Deals can only be struck if each negotiator is convinced that the proposed deal lies within his opposite number's win-set and thus will be ratified. Uncertainty about party A's ratification lowers the expected value of the agreement to party B, and thus party B will demand more generous side-payments from party A than would be needed under conditions of certainty. In fact, party B has an incentive to feign doubt about party A's ability to deliver, precisely in order to extract a more generous offer.[45]

Thus, a utility-maximizing negotiator must seek to convince his opposite number that his own win-set is "kinky," that is, that the proposed deal is certain to be ratified, but that a deal slightly more favorable to the opponent is unlikely to be ratified. * * *

The analysis of two-level games offers many illustrations of Zartman's observation that all negotiation involves "the controlled exchange of partial information."[46]

Restructuring and Reverberation

Formally speaking, game-theoretic analysis requires that the structure of issues and payoffs be specified in advance. In reality, however, much of what happens in any bargaining situation involves attempts by the players to restructure the game and to alter one another's perceptions of the costs of no-agreement and the benefits of proposed agreements. Such tactics are more difficult in two-level games than in conventional negotiations, because it is harder to reach constituents on the other side with persuasive messages. Nevertheless, governments do seek to expand one another's win-sets. Much ambassadorial activity—wooing opinion leaders, establishing contact with opposition parties, offering foreign aid to a friendly, but unstable government, and so on—has precisely this function. When Japanese officials visit Capitol Hill, or British diplomats lobby Irish-American leaders, they are seeking to relax domestic constraints that might otherwise prevent the administration from cooperating with their governments.

■ ■ ■

In some instances, perhaps even unintentionally, international pressures "reverberate" within domestic politics, tipping the domestic balance and thus influencing the international negotiations. Exactly this kind of reverberation characterized the 1978 summit negotiations. Dieter Hiss, the German sherpa and one of those who believed that a stimulus program was in Germany's own interest, later wrote that summits change national policy

> only insofar as they mobilize and/or change public opinion and the attitude of political groups. . . . Often that is enough, if the balance of opinion is shifted, providing a bare majority for the previously stymied actions of a strong minority. . . . No country violates its own interests, but certainly the definition of its interests can change through a summit with its possible tradeoffs and give-and-take.[47]

From the point of view of orthodox social-choice theory, reverberation is problematic, for it implies a certain interconnectedness among the utility functions of independent actors, albeit across different levels of the game. Two rationales may be offered to explain reverberation among utility-maximizing egoists. First, in a complex, interdependent, but often unfriendly world, offending foreigners may be costly in the long run. "To get along, go along" may be a rational maxim. This rationale is likely to be more common the more dependent (or interdependent) a nation, and it is likely to be more persuasive to Level II actors who are more exposed internationally, such as multinational corporations and international banks.

A second rationale takes into account cognitive factors and uncertainty. It would be a mistake for political scientists to mimic most economists' disregard for the suasive element in negotiations.[48] Given the pervasive uncertainty that surrounds many international issues, messages from abroad can change minds, move the undecided, and hearten those in the domestic minority. * * *

Suasive reverberation is more likely among countries with close relations and is probably more frequent in economic than in political–military negotiations. Communiqués from the Western summits are often cited by participants to domestic audiences as a way of legitimizing their policies. After one such statement by Chancellor Schmidt, one of his aides privately characterized the argument as "not intellectually valid, but politically useful." Conversely, it is widely believed by summit participants that a declaration contrary to a government's current policy could be used profitably by its opponents. Recent congressional proposals to ensure greater domestic publicity for international commentary on national economic policies (including hitherto confidential IMF recommendations) turn on the idea that reverberation might increase international cooperation.[49]

Reverberation as discussed thus far implies that international pressure expands the domestic win-set and facilitates agreement. However, reverberation can also be negative, in the sense that foreign pressure may create a domestic backlash. Negative reverberation is probably less common empirically than positive reverberation, simply because foreigners are likely to forgo public pressure if it is recognized to be counterproductive. Cognitive balance theory suggests that international pressure is more likely to reverberate negatively if its source is generally viewed by domestic audiences as an adversary rather than an ally. Nevertheless, predicting the precise effect of foreign pressure is admittedly difficult, although empirically, reverberation seems to occur frequently in two-level games.

■ ■ ■

The Role of the Chief Negotiator

In the stylized model of two-level negotiations outlined here, the chief negotiator is the only formal link between Level I and Level II. Thus far, I have assumed that the chief negotiator has no independent policy views, but acts merely as an honest broker, or rather as an agent on behalf of his constituents. That assumption powerfully simplifies the analysis of two-level games. However, as principal-agent theory reminds us, this assumption is unrealistic.[50] Empirically, the preferences of the chief negotiator may well diverge from those of his constituents. Two-level negotiations are costly and risky for the chief negotiator, and they often interfere with his other priorities, so it is reasonable to ask what is in it for him.

The motives of the chief negotiator include:

1. Enhancing his standing in the Level II game by increasing his political resources or by minimizing potential losses. * * *
2. Shifting the balance of power at Level II in favor of domestic policies that he prefers for exogenous reasons. International negotiations sometimes enable government leaders to do what they privately wish to do, but are powerless to do domestically. * * *
3. To pursue his own conception of the national interest in the international context. * * *

It is reasonable to presume, at least in the international case of two-level bargaining, that the chief negotiator will normally give primacy to his domestic calculus, if a choice must be made, not least because his own incumbency often depends on his standing at Level II. Hence, he is more likely to present an international agreement for ratification, the less of his own political capital he expects to have to invest to win approval, and the greater the likely political returns from a ratified agreement.

This expanded conception of the role of the chief negotiator implies that he has, in effect, a veto over possible agreements. Even if a proposed deal lies within his Level II win-set, that deal is unlikely to be struck if he opposes it.[51] Since this proviso applies on both sides of the Level I table, the actual international bargaining set may be narrower—perhaps much narrower—than the overlap between the Level II win-sets. Empirically, this additional constraint is often crucial to the outcome of two-level games. One momentous example is the fate of the Versailles Treaty. The best evidence suggests, first, that perhaps 80 percent of the American public *and* of the Senate in 1919 favored ratification of the treaty, if certain reservations were attached, and second, that those reservations were acceptable to the other key signatories, especially Britain and France. In effect, it was Wilson himself who vetoed this otherwise ratifiable package, telling the dismayed French Ambassador, "I shall consent to nothing."[52]

Yet another constraint on successful two-level negotiation derives from the leader's existing domestic coalition. Any political entrepreneur has a fixed investment in a particular pattern of policy positions and a particular supporting coalition. If a proposed international deal threatens that investment, or if ratification would require him to construct a different coalition, the chief negotiator will be reluctant to endorse it, even if (judged abstractly) it could be ratified. Politicians may be willing to risk a few of their normal supporters in the cause of ratifying an international agreement, but the greater the potential loss, the greater their reluctance.

In effect, the fixed costs of coalition-building thus imply this constraint on the win-set: How great a realignment of prevailing coalitions at Level II would be required to ratify a particular proposal? For example, a trade deal may expand export opportunities for Silicon Valley, but harm Aliquippa. This is fine for a chief negotiator (for example, Reagan?) who can easily add Northern California yuppies to his support coalition and who has no hope of winning Aliquippa steelworkers anyhow. But a different chief negotiator with a different support coalition (for example, Mondale?) might find it costly or even impossible to convert the gains from the same agreement into politically usable form. * * *

Relaxing the assumption that the chief negotiator is merely an honest broker, negotiating on behalf of his constituents, opens the possibility that the constituents may be more eager for an agreement (or more worried about "no-agreement") than he is.

Empirical instances are not hard to find: in early 1987, European publics were readier to accept Gorbachev's "double-zero" arms control proposal than European leaders, just as in the early 1970s the American public (or at least the politically active public) was more eager for a negotiated end to the Vietnam War than was the Nixon administration. As a rule, the negotiator retains a veto over any proposed agreement in such cases. However, if the negotiator's own domestic standing (or indeed, his incumbency) would be threatened if he were to reject an agreement that falls within his Level II win-set, and if this is known to all parties, then the other side at Level I gains considerable leverage. Domestic U.S. discontent about the Vietnam War clearly affected the agreement reached at the Paris talks.[53] Conversely, if the constituents are (believed to be) hard-line, then a leader's domestic weakness becomes a diplomatic asset. * * *

■   ■   ■

Conclusion

The most portentous development in the fields of comparative politics and international relations in recent years is the dawning recognition among practitioners in each field of the need to take into account entanglements between the two. Empirical illustrations of reciprocal influence between domestic and international affairs abound. What we need now are concepts and theories that will help us organize and extend our empirical observations.

Analysis in terms of two-level games offers a promising response to this challenge. Unlike state-centric theories, the two-level approach recognizes the inevitability of domestic conflict about what the "national interest" requires. Unlike the "Second Image" or the "Second Image Reversed," the two-level approach recognizes that central decision-makers strive to reconcile domestic and international imperatives simultaneously. As we have seen, states-

men in this predicament face distinctive strategic opportunities and strategic dilemmas.

This theoretical approach highlights several significant features of the links between diplomacy and domestic politics, including:

- the important distinction between voluntary and involuntary defection from international agreements;
- the contrast between issues on which domestic interests are homogeneous, simply pitting hawks against doves, and issues on which domestic interests are more heterogeneous, so that domestic cleavage may actually foster international cooperation;
- the possibility of synergistic issue linkage, in which strategic moves at one game-table facilitate unexpected coalitions at the second table;
- the paradoxical fact that institutional arrangements which strengthen decision-makers at home may weaken their international bargaining position, and vice versa;
- the importance of targeting international threats, offers, and side-payments with an eye towards their domestic incidence at home and abroad;
- the strategic uses of uncertainty about domestic politics, and the special utility of "kinky win-sets";
- the potential reverberation of international pressures within the domestic arena;
- the divergences of interest between a national leader and those on whose behalf he is negotiating, and in particular, the international implications of his fixed investments in domestic politics.

Two-level games seem a ubiquitous feature of social life, from Western economic summitry to diplomacy in the Balkans and from coalition politics in Sri Lanka to legislative maneuvering on Capitol Hill. Far-ranging empirical research is needed now to test and deepen our understanding of how such games are played.

NOTES

1. The following account is drawn from Robert D. Putnam and C. Randall Henning, "The Bonn Summit of 1978: How Does International Economic Policy Coordination Actually Work?" *Brookings Discussion Papers in International Economics,* no. 53 (Washington, DC: Brookings Institution, October 1986), and Robert D. Putnam and Nicholas Bayne, *Hanging Together: Cooperation and Conflict in the Seven-Power Summits,* rev. ed. (Cambridge, MA: Harvard University Press, 1987), pp. 62–94.

2. Among interdependent economies, most economists believe, policies can often be more effective if they are internationally coordinated. For relevant citations, see Putnam and Bayne, *Hanging Together,* p. 24.

3. For a comprehensive account of the Japanese story, see I. M. Destler and Hisao Mitsuyu, "Locomotives on Different Tracks; Macroeconomic Diplomacy, 1977–1979," in I. M. Destler and Hideo Sato, eds., *Coping with U.S.-Japanese Economic Conflicts* (Lexington, MA: Heath, 1982).

4. For an excellent account of U.S. energy policy during this period, see G. John Ikenberry, "Market Solutions for State Problems: The International and Domestic Politics of American Oil Decontrol," *International Organization* 42 (Winter 1988).

5. It is not clear whether Jimmy Carter fully understood the domestic implications of his Bonn pledge at the time. See Putnam and Henning, "The Bonn Summit," and Ikenberry, "Market Solutions for State Problems."

6. Kenneth N. Waltz, *Man, the State, and War: A Theoretical Analysis* (New York: Columbia University Press, 1959).

7. Peter Gourevitch, "The Second Image Reversed: The International Sources of Domestic Politics," *International Organization* 32 (Autumn 1978), pp. 881–911.

8. I am indebted to Stephen Haggard for enlightening discussions about domestic influences on international relations.

9. Richard E. Walton and Robert B. McKersie, *A Behavioral Theory of Labor Negotiations: An Analysis of a Social Interaction System* (New York: McGraw-Hill, 1965).

10. Robert S. Strauss, "Foreword," in Joan E. Twiggs, *The Tokyo Round of Multilateral Trade Negotiations: A Case Study in Building Domestic Support for Diplomacy* (Washington, DC: Georgetown University Institute for the Study of Diplomacy, 1987), p. vii. Former Secretary of Labor John Dunlop is said to have remarked that "bilateral negotiations usually require three agreements—one across the [t]able and one on each side of the table," as cited in Howard Raiffa, *The Art and Science of Negotiation* (Cambridge, MA: Harvard University Press, 1982), p. 166.

11. Glenn H. Snyder and Paul Diesing, *Conflict Among Nations: Bargaining, Decision Making, and System Structure in International Crises* (Princeton: Princeton University Press, 1977), pp. 510–25.

12. Max Black, *Models and Metaphors* (Ithaca, NY: Cornell University Press, 1962), p. 242, as cited in Duncan Snidal, "The Game Theory of International Politics," *World Politics* 38 (October 1985), p. 36n.

13. To avoid unnecessary complexity, my argument throughout is phrased in terms of a single chief negotiator, although in many cases some of his responsibilities may be delegated to aides. Later in this article I relax the assumption that the negotiator has no independent preferences.

14. Gerhardt Stoltenberg, *Wall Street Journal Europe*, 2 October 1986, as cited in C. Randall Henning, *Macroeconomic Diplomacy in the 1980s: Domestic Politics and International Conflict Among the United States, Japan, and Europe,* Atlantic Paper No. 65 (New York: Croom Helm, for the Atlantic Institute for International Affairs, 1987), p. 1.

15. Ito Takashi, "Conflicts and Coalition in Japan, 1930: Political Groups and the London Naval Disarmament Conference," in Sven Groennings et al., eds., *The Study of Coalition Behavior* (New York: Holt, Rinehart, & Winston, 1970); Kobayashi Tatsuo, "The London Naval Treaty, 1930," in James W. Morley, ed., *Japan Erupts: The London Naval Conference and the Manchurian Incident, 1928–1932* (New York: Columbia University Press, 1984), pp. 11–117. I am indebted to William Jarosz for this example.

16. This stipulation is, in fact, characteristic of most real-world ratification procedures, such as House and Senate action on conference committee reports, although it is somewhat violated by the occasional practice of appending "reservations" to the ratification of treaties.

17. *New York Times*, 26 September 1986.

18. For the conception of win-set, see Kenneth A. Shepsle and Barry R. Weingast, "The Institutional Foundations of Committee Power," *American Political Science Review* 81 (March 1987), pp. 85–104. I am indebted to Professor Shepsle for much help on this topic.

19. To avoid tedium, I do not repeat the "other things being equal" proviso in each of the propositions that follow. Under some circumstances an expanded win-set might actually make practicable some outcome that could trigger a dilemma of collective action. See Vincent P. Crawford, "A Theory of Disagreement in Bargaining," *Econometrica* 50 (May 1982), pp. 607–37.

20. The Sunday Times Insight Team, *The Falklands War* (London: Sphere, 1982); Max Hastings and Simon Jenkins, *The Battle for the Falklands* (New York: Norton, 1984); Alejandro Dabai and Luis Lorenzano, *Argentina: The Malvinas and the End of Military Rule* (London: Verso, 1984). I am indebted to Louise Richardson for these citations.

21. Geoffrey W. Harrison, in John C. Campbell, ed., *Successful Negotiation: Trieste 1954* (Princeton: Princeton University Press, 1976), p. 62.

22. Thomas C. Schelling, *The Strategy of Conflict* (Cambridge, MA: Harvard University Press, 1960), pp. 19–28.

23. I am grateful to Lara Putnam for this example. For supporting evidence, see Robert R. Kaufman, "Democratic and Authoritarian Responses to the Debt Issue: Argentina, Brazil, Mexico," *International Organization* 39 (Summer 1985), pp. 473–503.

24. W. Mark Habeeb and I. William Zartman, *The Panama Canal Negotiations* (Washington, DC: Johns Hopkins Foreign Policy Institute, 1986), pp. 40, 42.

25. Thomas Romer and Howard Rosenthal, "Political Resource Allocation, Controlled Agendas, and the Status Quo," *Public Choice* 33 (no. 4, 1978), pp. 27–44.

26. In more formal treatments, the no-agreement outcome is called the "reversion point." A given constituent's evaluation of no-agreement corresponds to what Raiffa terms a seller's "walk-away price," that is, the price below which he would prefer "no deal." (Raiffa, *Art and Science of Negotiation.*) No-agreement is equivalent to what Snyder and Diesing term "breakdown," or the expected cost of war. (Snyder and Diesing, *Conflict Among Nations.*)

27. Thomas A. Bailey, *Woodrow Wilson and the Great Betrayal* (New York: Macmillan, 1945), pp. 16–37.

28. See James Q. Wilson, *Political Organization* (New York: Basic Books, 1975) on how the politics of an issue are affected by whether the costs and the benefits are concentrated or diffuse.

29. Another factor fostering abstention is the greater complexity and opacity of monetary issues; as Gilbert R. Winham ("Complexity in International Negotiation," in Daniel Druckman, ed., *Negotiations: A Social-Psychological Perspective* [Beverly Hills: Sage, 1977], p. 363) observes, "complexity can strengthen the hand of a negotiator vis-à-vis the organization he represents."

30. Habeeb and Zariman, *Panama Canal Negotiations*.

31. Bailey, *Wilson and the Great Betrayal*.

32. I am grateful to Ernst B. Haas and Robert O. Keohane for helpful advice on this point.

33. Ann L. Hollick, *U.S. Foreign Policy and the Law of the Sea* (Princeton: Princeton University Press, 1981), especially pp. 208–37, and James K. Sebenius, *Negotiating the Law of the Sea* (Cambridge, MA: Harvard University Press, 1984), especially pp. 74–78.

34. Raiffa, *Art and Science of Negotiation*, p. 175.

35. I am grateful to Henry Brady for clarifying this point for me.

36. Gilbert R. Winham, "The Relevance of Clausewitz to a Theory of International Negotiation," prepared for delivery at the 1987 annual meeting of the American Political Science Association.

37. Jimmy Carter, *Keeping Faith: Memoirs of a President* (New York: Bantam Books, 1982), p. 225.

38. Michael Artis and Sylvia Ostry, *International Economic Policy Coordination*, Chatham House Papers: 30 (London: Routledge & Kegan Paul, 1986), pp. 75–76. Of course, whether this is desirable in terms of democratic values is quite another matter.

39. Schelling, *Strategy of Conflict*, p. 28.

40. Walton and McKersie, *A Behavioral Theory of Labor Negotiations*, p. 345.

41. Carter, *Keeping Faith*, p. 172. See also Raiffa, *Art and Science of Negotiation*, p. 183.

42. The strategic significance of targeting at Level II is illustrated in John Conybeare, "Trade Wars: A Comparative Study of Anglo-Hanse, Franco-Italian, and Hawley-Smoot Conflicts," *World Politics* 38 (October 1985), p. 157. Retaliation in the Anglo-Hanse trade wars did not have the intended deterrent effect, because it was not (and perhaps could not have been) targeted at the crucial members of the opposing Level II coalition. Compare Snyder and Diesing, *Conflict Among Nations*, p. 552: "If one faces a coercive opponent, but the opponent's majority coalition includes a few wavering members inclined to compromise, a compromise proposal that suits their views may cause their defection and the formation of a different majority coalition. Or if the opponent's strategy is accommodative, based on a tenuous soft-line coalition, one knows that care is required in implementing one's own coercive strategy to avoid the opposite kind of shift in the other state."

43. Transaction benefits may be enhanced if a substantive agreement is reached, although sometimes leaders can benefit domestically by loudly rejecting a proffered international deal.

44. Snyder and Diesing, *Conflict Among Nations*, pp. 516, 522–23. Analogous misperceptions in Anglo-American diplomacy are the focus of Richard E. Neustadt, *Alliance Politics* (New York: Columbia University Press, 1970).

45. I am grateful to Robert O. Keohane for pointing out the impact of uncertainty on the expected value of proposals.

46. William Zartman, *The 50% Solution* (Garden City, NJ: Anchor Books, 1976), p. 14. The present analysis assumes that constituents are myopic about the other side's Level II, an assumption that is not unrealistic empirically. However, a fully informed constituent would consider the preferences of key players on the other side, for if the current proposal lies well within the other side's win-set, then it would be rational for the constituent to vote against it, hoping for a second-round proposal that was more favorable to him and still ratifiable abroad; this might be a reasonable interpretation of Senator Lodge's position in 1919 (Bailey, *Wilson and the Great Betrayal*). Consideration of such strategic voting at Level II is beyond the scope of this article.

47. Dieter Hiss, "Weitwirtschaftsgipfel: Betrachtungen eines Insiders [World Economic Summit: Observations of an Insider]," in Joachim Frohn and Reiner Staeglin, eds., *Empirische Wirtschaftsforschung* (Berlin: Duncker and Humblot, 1980), pp. 286–87.

48. On cognitive and communications explanations of international cooperation, see, for example, Ernst B. Haas, "Why Collaborate? Issue-Linkage and International Regimes," *World Politics* 32 (April 1980), pp. 357–405; Richard N. Cooper, "International Cooperation in Public Health as a Prologue to Macroeconomic Cooperation," *Brookings Discussion Papers in International Economics* 44 (Washington, DC: Brookings Institution, 1986); and Zartman, *50% Solution*, especially Part 4.

49. Henning, *Macroeconomic Diplomacy in the 1980s*, pp. 62–63.

50. For overviews of this literature, see Terry M. Moe, "The New Economics of Organization," *American Journal of Political Science* 28 (November 1984), pp. 739–77; John W. Prati and Richard J. Zeckhauser, eds., *Principals and Agents: The Structure of Business* (Boston, MA: Harvard Business School Press, 1985); and Barry M. Mitnick, "The Theory of Agency and Organizational Analysis," prepared for delivery at the 1986 annual meeting of the American Political Science Association. This literature is only indirectly relevant to our concerns here, for it has not yet adequately addressed the problems posed by multiple principals (or constituents, in our terms). For one highly formal approach to the problem of multiple principals, see R. Douglas Bernheim and Michael D. Whinston, "Common Agency," *Econometrica* 54 (July 1986), pp. 923–42.

51. This power of the chief negotiator is analogous to what Shepsle and Weingast term the "penultimate" or "ex post veto" power of the members of a Senate-House conference committee. (Shepsle and Weingast, "Institutional Foundations of Committee Power.")

52. Bailey, *Wilson and the Great Betrayal*, quotation at p. 15.

53. I. William Zartman, "Reality, Image, and Detail: The Paris Negotiations, 1969–1973," in Zartman, *50% Solution*, pp. 372–98.

Barry R. Posen

THE SECURITY DILEMMA AND ETHNIC CONFLICT

The end of the Cold War has been accompanied by the emergence of nationalist, ethnic and religious conflict in Eurasia. However, the risks and intensity of these conflicts have varied from region to region: Ukrainians and Russians are still getting along relatively well; Serbs and Slovenians had a short, sharp clash; Serbs, Croats and Bosnian Muslims have waged open warfare; and Armenians and Azeris seem destined to fight a slow-motion attrition war. The claim that newly released, age-old antipathies account for this violence fails to explain the considerable variance in observable intergroup relations.

The purpose of this article is to apply a basic concept from the realist tradition of international relations theory, 'the security dilemma', to the special conditions that arise when proximate groups of people suddenly find themselves newly responsible for their own security. A group suddenly compelled to provide its own protection must ask the following questions about any neighbouring group: Is it a threat? How much of a threat? Will the threat grow or diminish over time? Is there anything that must be done immediately? The answers to these questions strongly influence the chances for war.

This article assesses the factors that could produce an intense security dilemma when imperial order breaks down, thus producing an early resort to violence. The security dilemma is then employed to analyse * * * the break-up of Yugoslavia * * * to illustrate its utility. Finally, some actions are suggested to ameliorate the tendency towards violence.

The Security Dilemma

The collapse of imperial regimes can be profitably viewed as a problem of 'emerging anarchy'. The longest standing and most useful school of international relations theory—realism—explicitly addresses the consequences of anarchy—the absence of a sovereign—for political relations among states.[1] In areas such as the former Soviet Union and Yugoslavia, 'sovereigns' have disappeared. They leave in their wake a host of groups—ethnic, religious, cultural—of greater or lesser cohesion. These groups must pay attention to the first thing that states have historically addressed—the problem of security—even though many of these groups still lack many of the attributes of statehood.

Realist theory contends that the condition of anarchy makes security the first concern of states. It can be otherwise only if these political organizations do not care about their survival as independent entities. As long as some do care, there will be competition for the key to security—power. The competition will often continue to a point at which the competing entities have amassed more power than needed for security and, thus, consequently begin to threaten others. Those threatened will respond in turn.

From *Survival* 35, no. 1 (Spring 1993): 27–47. Some of the author's notes have been omitted.

Relative power is difficult to measure and is often subjectively appraised; what seems sufficient to one state's defence will seem, and will often be, offensive to its neighbours. Because neighbours wish to remain autonomous and secure, they will react by trying to strengthen their own positions. States can trigger these reactions even if they have no expansionist inclinations. This is the security dilemma: what one does to enhance one's own security causes reactions that, in the end, can make one less secure. Cooperation among states to mute these competitions can be difficult because someone else's 'cheating' may leave one in a militarily weakened position. All fear betrayal.

Often statesmen do not recognize that this problem exists: they do not empathize with their neighbours; they are unaware that their own actions can seem threatening. Often it does not matter if they know of this problem. The nature of their situation compels them to take the steps they do.

The security dilemma is particularly intense when two conditions hold. First, when offensive and defensive military forces are more or less identical, states cannot signal their defensive intent—that is, their limited objectives—by the kinds of military forces they choose to deploy. Any forces on hand are suitable for offensive campaigns. For example, many believe that armoured forces are the best means of defence against an attack by armoured forces. However, because armour has a great deal of offensive potential, states so outfitted cannot distinguish one another's intentions. They must assume the worst because the worst is possible.

A second condition arises from the effectiveness of the offence versus the defence. If offensive operations are more effective than defensive operations, states will choose the offensive if they wish to survive. This may encourage pre-emptive war in the event of a political crisis because the perceived superiority of the offensive creates incentives to strike first whenever war appears likely. In addition, in the situation in which offensive capability is strong, a modest superiority in numbers will appear to provide greatly increased prospects for military success. Thus, the offensive advantage can cause preventive war if a state achieves a military advantage, however fleeting.

The barriers to cooperation inherent in international politics provide clues to the problems that arise as central authority collapses in multiethnic empires. The security dilemma affects relations among these groups, just as it affects relations among states. Indeed, because these groups have the added problem of building new state structures from the wreckage of old empires, they are doubly vulnerable.

Here it is argued that the process of imperial collapse produces conditions that make offensive and defensive capabilities indistinguishable and make the offence superior to the defence. In addition, uneven progress in the formation of state structures will create windows of opportunity and vulnerability. These factors have a powerful influence on the prospects for conflict, regardless of the internal politics of the groups emerging from old empires. Analysts inclined to the view that most of the trouble lies elsewhere, either in the specific nature of group identities or in the short-term incentives for new leaders to 'play the nationalist card' to secure their power, need to understand the security dilemma and its consequences. Across the board, these strategic problems show that very little nationalist rabble-rousing or nationalistic combativeness is required to generate very dangerous situations.

The Indistinguishability of Offence and Defence

Newly independent groups must first determine whether neighbouring groups are a threat. They will examine one another's military capabilities to do so. Because the weaponry available to these groups will often be quite rudimentary, their offensive military capabilities will be as much a function of the quantity and commitment of the soldiers they can mobilize as the particular characteristics of the weapons they control. Thus, each group will have to assess the other's offensive military potential in terms of its cohesion and its past military record.

The nature of military technology and organization is usually taken to be the main factor affecting the distinguishability of offence and defence. Yet, clear distinctions between offensive and defensive capabilities are historically rare, and they are particularly difficult to make in the realm of land warfare. For example, the force structures of armed neutrals such as Finland, Sweden and Switzerland are often categorized as defensive. These countries rely more heavily on infantry, which is thought to have weak offensive potential, than on tanks and other mechanized weaponry, which are thought to have strong offensive potential. However, their weak offensive capabilities have also been a function of the massive military power of what used to be their most plausible adversary, the former Soviet Union. Against states of similar size, similarly armed, all three countries would have considerable offensive capabilities—particularly if their infantries were extraordinarily motivated—as German and French infantry were at the outset of World War I, as Chinese and North Vietnamese infantry were against the Americans and as Iran's infantry was against the Iraqis.

Ever since the French Revolution put the first politically motivated mass armies into the field, strong national identity has been understood by both scholars and practitioners to be a key ingredient of the combat power of armies.[2] A group identity helps the individual members cooperate to achieve their purposes. When humans can readily cooperate, the whole exceeds the sum of the parts, creating a unit stronger relative to those groups with a weaker identity. Thus, the 'groupness' of the ethnic, religious, cultural and linguistic collectivities that emerge from collapsed empires gives each of them an inherent offensive military power.

The military capabilities available to newly independent groups will often be less sophisticated; infantry-based armies will be easy to organize, augmented by whatever heavier equipment is inherited or seized from the old regime. Their offensive potential will be stronger the more cohesive their sponsoring group appears to be. Particularly in the close quarters in which these groups often find themselves, the combination of infantry-based, or quasi-mechanized, ground forces with strong group solidarity is likely to encourage groups to fear each other. Their capabilities will appear offensive.

The solidarity of the opposing group will strongly influence how each group assesses the magnitude of the military threat of the others. In general, however, it is quite difficult to perform such assessments. One expects these groups to be 'exclusive' and, hence, defensive. Frenchmen generally do not want to turn Germans into Frenchmen, or the reverse. Nevertheless, the drive for security in one group can be so great that it produces near-genocidal behaviour towards neighbouring groups. Because so much conflict has been identified with 'group' identity throughout history, those who emerge as the leaders of any group and who confront the task of self-defence for the first time will be sceptical that the strong group identity of others is benign.

What methods are available to a newly independent group to assess the offensive implications of another's sense of identity?[3] The main mechanism that they will use is history: how did other groups behave the last time they were unconstrained? Is there a record of offensive military activity by the other? Unfortunately, the conditions under which this assessment occurs suggest that these groups are more likely to assume that their neighbours are dangerous than not.

The reason is that the historical reviews that new groups undertake rarely meet the scholarly standards that modern history and social science hold as norms (or at least as ideals) in the West.

First, the recently departed multi-ethnic empires probably suppressed or manipulated the facts of previous rivalries to reinforce their own rule; the previous regimes in the Soviet Union and Yugoslavia lacked any systemic commitment to truth in historical scholarship. Second, the members of these various groups no doubt did not forget the record of their old rivalries; it was preserved in oral history. This history was undoubtedly magnified in the telling and was seldom subjected to critical appraisal. Third, because their history is mostly oral, each group has a difficult time divining another's view of the past. Fourth, as central authority begins to collapse and local politicians begin to struggle for power, they will begin to write down their versions of history in political speeches. Yet, because the purpose of speeches is domestic political mobilization, these stories are likely to be emotionally charged.

The result is a worst-case analysis. Unless proven otherwise, one group is likely to assume that another group's sense of identity, and the cohesion that it produces, is a danger. Proving it to be otherwise is likely to be very difficult. Because the cohesion of one's own group is an essential means of defence against the possible depredations of neighbours, efforts to reinforce cohesion are likely to be undertaken. Propagandists are put to work writing a politicized history of the group, and the mass media are directed to disseminate that history. The media may either willingly, or under compulsion, report unfolding events in terms that magnify the threat to the group. As neighbouring groups observe this, they do the same.

In sum, the military capability of groups will often be dependent on their cohesion, rather than their meagre military assets. This cohesion is a threat in its own right because it can provide the emotional power for infantry armies to take the offensive. An historical record of large-scale armed clashes, much less wholesale mistreatment of unarmed civilians, however subjective, will further the tendency for groups to see other groups as

threats. They will all simultaneously 'arm'— militarily and ideologically—against each other.

The Superiority of Offensive over Defensive Action

Two factors have generally been seen as affecting the superiority of offensive over defensive action—technology and geography. Technology is usually treated as a universal variable, which affects the military capabilities of all the states in a given competition. Geography is a situational variable, which makes offence particularly appealing to specific states for specific reasons. This is what matters most when empires collapse.

In the rare historical cases in which technology has clearly determined the offence–defence balance, such as World War I, soldiers and statesmen have often failed to appreciate its impact. Thus, technology need not be examined further, with one exception: nuclear weapons. If a group inherits a nuclear deterrent, and its neighbours do as well, 'groupness' is not likely to affect the security dilemma with as much intensity as would be the case in non-nuclear cases. Because group solidarity would not contribute to the ability of either side to mount a counterforce nuclear attack, nationalism is less important from a military standpoint in a nuclear relationship.

Political geography will frequently create an 'offence-dominant world' when empires collapse. Some groups will have greater offensive capabilities because they will effectively surround some or all of the other groups. These other groups may be forced to adopt offensive strategies to break the ring of encirclement. Islands of one group's population are often stranded in a sea of another. Where one territorially concentrated group has 'islands' of settlement of its members distributed across the nominal territory of another group (irredenta), the protection of these islands in the event of hostile action can seem extremely difficult. These islands may not be able to help one another; they may be subject to blockade and siege, and by virtue of their numbers relative to the surrounding population and because of topography, they may be militarily indefensible. Thus, the brethren of the stranded group may come to believe that only rapid offensive military action can save their irredenta from a horrible fate.[4]

The geographic factor is a variable, not a constant. Islands of population can be quite large, economically autonomous and militarily defensible. Alternatively, they can have large numbers of nearby brethren who form a powerful state, which could rescue them in the event of trouble. Potentially, hostile groups could have islands of another group's people within their states; these islands could serve as hostages. Alternatively, the brethren of the 'island' group could deploy nuclear weapons and thus punish the surrounding group if they misbehave. In short, it might be possible to defend irredenta without attacking or to deter would-be aggressors by threatening to retaliate in one way or another.

Isolated ethnic groups—ethnic islands—can produce incentives for preventive war. Theorists argue that perceived offensive advantages make preventive war more attractive: if one side has an advantage that will not be present later and if security can best be achieved by offensive military action in any case, then leaders will be inclined to attack during this 'window of opportunity'.[5] For example, if a surrounding population will ultimately be able to fend off relief attacks from the home territory of an island group's brethren, but is currently weak, then the brethren will be inclined to attack sooner rather than later.

In disputes among groups interspersed in the same territory, another kind of offensive advantage exists—a tactical offensive advantage. Often the goal of the disputants is to create ever-growing areas of homogeneous population for their brethren. Therefore, the other group's population must be induced to leave. The Serbs have introduced the term 'ethnic cleansing' to describe this objective, a term redolent with the horrors of 50 years earlier. The offence has tremendous tactical military advantages in operations such as these. Small military forces directed against unarmed or poorly armed civilians can generate tremendous terror. This has always been true, of course, but even simple modern weapons, such as machine guns and mortars, increase the havoc that small bands of fanatics can wreak against the defenceless: Consequently, small bands of each group have an incentive to attack the towns of the other in the hopes of driving the people away.[6] This is often quite successful, as the vast populations of war refugees in the world today attest.

The vulnerability of civilians makes it possible for small bands of fanatics to initiate conflict. Because they are small and fanatical, these bands are hard to control. (This allows the political leadership of the group to deny responsibility for the actions those bands take.) These activities produce disproportionate political results among the opposing group—magnifying initial fears by confirming them. The presence or absence of small gangs of fanatics is thus itself a key determinant of the ability of groups to avoid war as central political authority erodes. Although almost every society produces small numbers of people willing to engage in violence at any given moment, the rapid emergence of organized bands of particularly violent individuals is a sure sign of trouble.

The characteristic behaviour of international organizations, especially the United Nations (UN), reinforces the incentives for offensive action. Thus far, the UN has proven itself unable to anticipate conflict and provide the credible security guarantees that would mitigate the security dilemma. Once there is politically salient trouble in an area, the UN may try to intervene to 'keep the peace'. However, the conditions under which peacekeeping is attempted are favourable to the party that has had the most military success. As a general rule, the UN does not make peace: it negotiates cease-fires. Two parties in dispute generally agree to a cease-fire only because one is successful and happy with its gains, while the other has lost, but fears even worse to come. Alternatively, the two sides have fought to a bloody stalemate and would like to rest. The UN thus protects, and to some extent legitimates, the military gains of the winning side, or gives both a respite to recover. This approach by the international community to intervention in ethnic conflict, helps create an incentive for offensive military operations.

Windows of Vulnerability and Opportunity

Where central authority has recently collapsed, the groups emerging from an old empire must calculate their power relative to each other at the time of collapse and make a guess about their relative power in the future. Such calculations must account for a variety of factors. Objectively, only one side can be better off. However, the complexity of these situations makes it possible for many competing groups to believe that their prospects in a war would be better earlier, rather than later. In addition, if the geographic situation creates incentives of the kind discussed earlier, the temptation to capitalize on these windows of opportunity may be great. These windows may also prove tempting to those who wish to expand for other reasons.

The relative rate of state formation strongly influences the incentives for preventive war. When central authority has collapsed or is collapsing, the groups emerging from the political rubble will try to form their own states. These groups must choose leaders, set up bureaucracies to collect taxes and provide services, organize police forces for internal security and organize military forces for external security. The material remnants of the old state (especially weaponry, foreign currency reserves, raw material stocks and industrial capabilities) will be unevenly distributed across the territories of the old empire. Some groups may have had a privileged position in the old system. Others will be less well placed.

The states formed by these groups will thus vary greatly in their strength. This will provide immediate military advantages to those who are further along in the process of state formation. If those with greater advantages expect to remain in that position by virtue of their superior numbers, then they may see no window of opportunity. However, if they expect their advantage to wane or disappear, then they will have an incentive to solve outstanding issues while they are much stronger than the opposition.

This power differential may create incentives for preventive expropriation, which can generate a spiral of action and reaction. With military resources unevenly distributed and perhaps artificially scarce for some due to arms embargoes, cash shortages or constrained access to the outside world, small caches of armaments assume large importance. Any military depot will be a tempting target, especially for the poorly armed. Better armed groups also have a strong incentive to seize these weapons because this would increase their margin of superiority.

In addition, it matters whether or not the old regime imposed military conscription on all groups in society. Conscription makes arms theft quite easy because hijackers know what to look for and how to move it. Gains are highly cumulative because each side can quickly integrate whatever it steals into its existing forces. High cumulativity of conquered resources has often motivated states in the past to initiate preventive military actions.

Expectations about outside intervention will also affect preventive war calculations. Historically, this usually meant expectations about the intervention of allies on one side or the other, and the value of such allies. Allies may be explicit or tacit. A group may expect itself or another to find friends abroad. It may calculate that the other group's natural allies are temporarily preoccupied, or a group may calculate that it or its adversary has many other adversaries who will attack in the event of conflict. The greater the number of potential allies for all groups, the more complex this calculation will be and the greater the chance for error. Thus, two opposing groups could both think that the expected behaviour of others makes them stronger in the short term.

A broader window-of-opportunity problem has been created by the large number of crises and conflicts that have been precipitated by the end of the Cold War. The electronic media provide free global strategic intelligence about these problems to anyone for the price of a shortwave radio, much less a satellite dish. Middle and great powers, and international organizations, are able to deal with only a small number of crises simultaneously. States that wish to initiate offensive military actions, but fear outside opposition, may move quickly if they learn that international organizations and great powers are preoccupied momentarily with other problems.

Croats and Serbs

Viewed through the lens of the security dilemma, the early stages of Yugoslavia's disintegration were strongly influenced by the following factors. First, the parties identified the re-emerging identities of the others as offensive threats. The last time these groups were free of constraint, during World War II, they slaughtered one another with abandon. In addition, the Yugoslav military system trained most men for war and distributed infantry armament widely across the country. Second, the offensive appeared to have the advantage, particularly against Serbs 'marooned' in Croatian and Muslim territory. Third, the new republics were not equally powerful. Their power assets varied in terms of people and economic resources; access to the wealth and military assets of the previous regime; access to external allies; and possible outside ene-

mies. Preventive war incentives were consequently high. Fourth, small bands of fanatics soon appeared on the scene. Indeed, the political and military history of the region stressed the role of small, violent, committed groups; the resistance to the Turks; the Ustashe in the 1930s; and the Ustashe state and Serbian Chetniks during World War II.

Serbs and Croats both have a terrifying oral history of each other's behaviour. This history goes back hundreds of years, although the intense Croat–Serb conflict is only about 125 years old. The history of the region is quite warlike: the area was the frontier of the Hapsburg and Turkish empires, and Croatia had been an integral part of the military apparatus of the Hapsburg empire. The imposition of harsh Hungarian rule in Croatia in 1868; the Hungarian divide-and-conquer strategy that pitted Croats and Serbs in Croatia against each other; the rise of the independent Serbian nation-state out of the Ottoman empire, formally recognized in Europe in 1878; and Serbian pretensions to speak for all south Slavs were the main origins of the Croat–Serb conflict. When Yugoslavia was formed after World War I, the Croats had a very different vision of the new state than the Serbs. They hoped for a confederal system, while the Serbs planned to develop a centralized nation-state.[7] The Croats did not perceive themselves to be treated fairly under this arrangement, and this helped stimulate the development of a violent resistance movement, the Ustashe, which collaborated with the Fascist powers during the 1930s.

The Serbs had some reasons for assuming the worst about the existence of an independent Croatian state, given Croatian behaviour during World War II. Ustashe leadership was established in Croatia by Nazi Germany. The Serbs, both communist and non-communist, fought the Axis forces, including the Croats, and each other. (Some Croats also fought in Josef Tito's communist partisan movement against the Nazis.) Roughly a million people died in the fighting—some 5.9%

of Yugoslavia's pre-war population.[8] The Croats behaved with extraordinary brutality towards the Serbs, who suffered nearly 500,000 dead, more than twice as many dead as the Croats.[9] (Obviously, the Germans were responsible for many Serbian deaths as well.) Most of these were not killed in battle; they were civilians murdered in large-scale terrorist raids.

The Croats themselves suffered some 200,000 dead in World War II, which suggests that depredations were inflicted on many sides. (The noncommunist, 'nationalist' Chetniks were among the most aggressive killers of Croats, which helps explain why the new Croatian republic is worried by the nationalist rhetoric of the new Serbian republic.) Having lived in a pre- and post-war Yugoslavia largely dominated by Serbs, the Croats had reason to suspect that the demise of the Yugoslavian Communist Party would be followed by a Serbian bid for hegemony. In 1971, the Croatian Communist Party had been purged of leaders who had favoured greater autonomy. In addition, the historical record of the Serbs during the past 200 years is one of regular efforts to establish an ever larger centralized Serbian national state on the Balkan Peninsula. Thus, Croats had sufficient reason to fear the Serbs.

Serbs in Croatia were scattered in a number of vulnerable islands; they could only be 'rescued' by offensive action from Serbia. Such a rescue, of course, would have been enormously complicated by an independent Bosnia, which in part explains the Serbian war there. In addition, Serbia could not count on maintaining absolute military superiority over the Croats forever: almost twice as many Serbs as Croats inhabit the territory of what was once Yugoslavia, but Croatia is slightly wealthier than Serbia.[10] Croatia also has some natural allies within former Yugoslavia, especially Bosnian Muslims, and seemed somewhat more adept at winning allies abroad. As Croatia adopted the trappings of statehood and achieved international recognition, its military power was expected to grow. From the Serbian point of view, Serbs in Croatia were insecure and expected to become more so as time went by.

From a military point of view, the Croats probably would have been better off postponing their secession until after they had made additional military preparations. However, their experience in 1971, more recent political developments and the military preparations of the Yugoslav army probably convinced them that the Serbs were about to strike and that the Croatian leadership would be rounded up and imprisoned or killed if they did not act quickly.

Each side not only had to assess the other's capabilities, but also its intentions, and there were plenty of signals of malign intent. Between 1987 and 1990, Slobodan Milosevic ended the administrative autonomy within Serbia that had been granted to Kosovo and Vojvodina in the 1974 constitution.[11] In August 1990, Serbs in the Dalmatia region of Croatia held a cultural autonomy referendum, which they defended with armed roadblocks against expected Croatian interference.[12] By October, the Yugoslav army began to impound all of the heavy weapons stored in Croatia for the use of the territorial defence forces, thus securing a vast military advantage over the nascent armed forces of the republic.[13] The Serbian window of opportunity, already large, grew larger. The Croats accelerated their own military preparations.

It is difficult to tell just how much interference the Croats planned, if any, in the referendum in Dalmatia. However, Croatia had stoked the fires of Serbian secessionism with a series of ominous rulings. In the spring of 1990, Serbs in Croatia were redefined as a minority, rather than a constituent nation, and were asked to take a loyalty oath. Serbian police were to be replaced with Croats, as were some local Serbian officials. No offer of cultural autonomy was made at the time. These Croatian policies undoubtedly intensified Serbian fears about the future and further tempted them to exploit their military superiority.

It appears that the Croats overestimated the reliability and influence of the Federal Republic of Germany as an ally due to some combination of World War II history, the widespread misperception created by the European media and by Western political leaders of Germany's near-superpower status, the presumed influence of the large Croatian émigré community in Germany, and Germany's own diplomacy, which was quite favourable to Croatia even before its June 1991 declaration of independence.[14] These considerations may have encouraged Croatia to secede. Conversely, Serbian propaganda was quick to stress the German–Croatian connection and to speculate on future German ambitions in the Balkans.[15] Fair or not, this prospect would have had an impact on Serbia's preventive war calculus.

■   ■   ■

Conclusion

Three main conclusions follow from the preceding analysis. First, the security dilemma and realist international relations theory more generally have considerable ability to explain and predict the probability and intensity of military conflict among groups emerging from the wreckage of empires.

Second, the security dilemma suggests that the risks associated with these conflicts are quite high. Several of the causes of conflict and war highlighted by the security dilemma operate with considerable intensity among the groups emerging from empires. The kind of military power that these groups can initially develop and their competing versions of history will often produce mutual fear and competition. Settlement patterns, in conjunction with unequal and shifting power, will often produce incentives for preventive war. The cumulative effect of conquered resources will encourage preventive grabs of military equipment and other assets.

Finally, if outsiders wish to understand and perhaps reduce the odds of conflict, they must assess the local groups' strategic view of their situation. Which groups fear for their physical security and why? What military options are open to them? By making these groups feel less threatened and by reducing the salience of windows of opportunity, the odds of conflict may be reduced.

Because the international political system as a whole remains a self-help system, it will be difficult to act on such calculations. Outsiders rarely have major material or security interests at stake in regional disputes. It is difficult for international institutions to threaten credibly in advance to intervene, on humanitarian grounds, to protect groups that fear for the future. Vague humanitarian commitments will not make vulnerable groups feel safe and will probably not deter those who wish to repress them. In some cases, however, such commitments may be credible because the conflict has real security implications for powerful outside actors.

Groups drifting into conflict should be encouraged to discuss their individual histories of mutual relations. Competing versions of history should be reconciled if possible. Domestic policies that raise bitter memories of perceived past injustices or depredations should be examined. This exercise need not be managed by an international political institution; non-governmental organizations could play a role. Discussions about regional history would be an intelligent use of the resources of many foundations. A few conferences will not, of course, easily undo generations of hateful, politicized history, bolstered by reams of more recent propaganda. The exercise would cost little and, therefore, should be tried.

In some cases, outside powers could threaten not to act; this would discourage some kinds of aggressive behaviour. For example, outside powers could make clear that if a new state abuses a minority and then gets itself into a war with that minority and its allies, the abuser will find little sympathy abroad if it begins to lose. To accomplish this, however, outside powers must have a way of detecting mistreatment of minorities.

In other cases, it may be reasonable for outside powers to provide material resources, including armaments, to help groups protect themselves. However, this kind of hard-bitten policy is politically difficult for liberal democratic governments now dominating world politics to pursue, even on humanitarian grounds. In addition, it is an admittedly complicated game in its own right because it is difficult to determine the amount and type of military assistance needed to produce effective defensive forces, but not offensive capabilities. Nevertheless, considerable diplomatic leverage may be attained by the threat to supply armaments to one side or the other.

■　■　■

It will frequently prove impossible, however, to arrange military assets, external political commitments and political expectations so that all neighbouring groups are relatively secure and perceive themselves as such. War is then likely. These wars will confirm and intensify all the fears that led to their initiation. Their brutality will tempt outsiders to intervene, but peace efforts originating from the outside will be unsuccessful if they do not realistically address the fears that triggered the conflicts initially. In most cases, this will require a willingness to commit large numbers of troops and substantial amounts of military equipment to troubled areas for a very long time.

NOTES

1. The following realist literature is essential for those interested in the analysis of ethnic conflict: Kenneth Waltz, *Theory of International Politics* (Reading, MA: Addison Wesley, 1979), Chapters 6 and 8; Robert Jervis, 'Cooperation under the security dilemma', *World Politics*, no. 2, January 1978, pp. 167–213; Robert Jervis, *Perception and Misperception in International Politics* (Princeton, NJ: Princeton University Press, 1976), Chapter 3; Thomas C. Schelling, *Arms and Influence* (New Haven, CT: Yale University Press, 1966, 1976), Chapters 1 and 6.

2. See Carl Von Clausewitz, *On War* (Princeton, NJ: Princeton University Press, 1984), pp. 591–92; Robert Gilpin, 'The Richness of the Tradition of Political Realism', in Robert E. Keohane, *Neorealism and Its Critics* (New York: Columbia University Press, 1986), pp. 300–21, especially pp. 304–308.

3. This problem shades into an assessment of 'intentions', another very difficult problem for states in international politics. This issue is treated as a capabilities problem because the emergence of anarchy forces leaders to focus on military potential, rather than on intentions. Under these conditions, every group will ask whether neighbouring groups have the cohesion, morale and martial spirit to take the offensive if their leaders call on them to do so.

4. It is plausible that the surrounding population will view irredenta in their midst as an offensive threat by the outside group. They may be perceived as a 'fifth column', that must be controlled, repressed or even expelled.

5. See Stephen Van Evera, 'The cult of the offensive and the origins of the First World War', *International Security*, vol. 9, no. 1, Summer 1984, pp. 58–107.

6. Why do they not go to the defence of their own, rather than attack the other? Here, it is hypothesized that such groups are scarce relative to the number of target towns and villages, so they cannot 'defend' their own with any great confidence.

7. James Gow, 'Deconstructing Yugoslavia', *Survival*, vol. 33, no. 4, July/August 1991, p. 292; J.B. Hoptner, *Yugoslavia in Crisis 1934–1941* (New York: Columbia University Press, 1962), pp. 1–9.

8. Ivo Banac, 'Political change and national diversity', *Daedalus*, vol. 119, no. 1, Winter 1990, pp. 145–150, estimates that 487,000 Serbs, 207,000 Croats, 86,000 Bosnian Muslims and 60,000 Jews died in Yugoslavia during the war.

9. Aleksa Djilas, *The Contested Country* (Cambridge, MA: Harvard University Press, 1991), pp. 103–28. See especially, Chapter 4, 'The National State and Genocide: The Ustasha Movement, 1929–1945', especially pp. 120–27, which vividly describes large-scale Croatian murders of Serbs, as well as Jews and Gypsies; however, Djilas does not explain how 200,000 Croats also died.

10. See Sabrina Ramet, *Nationalism and Federalism in Yugoslavia 1962–1991* (Bloomington, IN: Indiana University Press, 2nd ed., 1992), Appendix 2, p. 286.

11. Gow, *op. cit.* in note 7, p. 294. Vojvodina contains the only petroleum and gas in Yugoslavia proximate to Serbia, so this act probably had a strategic motive; see Central Intelligence Agency, *Atlas of Eastern Europe* (Washington, DC: US Government Printing Office, August 1990), p. 10.

12. International Institute for Strategic Studies, *Strategic Survey 1990–1991* (London: Brassey's for the IISS, 1991), p. 167.

13. Gow, *op. cit.* in note 7, p. 299.

14. See John Newhouse, 'The diplomatic round', *The New Yorker*, 24 August 1992, especially p. 63. See also John Zametica, *The Yugoslav Conflict*, Adelphi Paper 270 (London: Brassey's for the IISS, 1992), pp. 63–65.

15. Ramet, *op. cit.* in note 10, p. 265.

6 WAR AND SECURITY

Warfare and military intervention continue to be central problems of international relations. Two of the readings in this section address a core issue: the relationship between the use of force and politics. Excerpts from classic books by Carl von Clausewitz, *On War* (originally published in the 1830s), and Thomas C. Schelling, *Arms and Influence* (1966), remind us that warfare is not simply an exercise of brute force; war needs to be understood as a continuation of political bargaining. In the most influential treatise on warfare ever written, Prussian general Clausewitz reminded the generation that followed the devastating Napoleonic Wars that armed conflict should not be considered a blind, all-out struggle governed by the logic of military operations. Rather, he said, the conduct of war had to be subordinated to its political objectives.

These ideas resonated strongly with American strategic thinkers of Schelling's era, who worried that military plans for total nuclear war would outstrip the ability of political leaders to control them. Schelling, a Harvard professor who also advised the U.S. Air Force on its nuclear weapons strategy, explained that political bargaining and risk-taking, not military victory, lay at the heart of the use and threat of force in the nuclear era. Erica Borghard and Shawn Lonergan apply Schelling's ideas to an analysis of the contemporary problem of cyber conflict. One of Schelling's major concerns was that an international crisis could escalate to the use of nuclear weapons if one or both sides worried that their nuclear deterrent forces had become vulnerable to a surprise attack. Caitlin Talmadge lays out a scenario in which successful U.S. air attacks on Chinese command and control centers in a non-nuclear battle over Taiwan could convince the Chinese military to use their vulnerable nuclear forces before they would be rendered useless.

James D. Fearon's 1995 article, "Rationalist Explanations for War," explores the puzzle of why two rational states would ever fight a costly war rather than settle their dispute more cheaply through peaceful bargaining. He shows that three problems can hinder the achievement of bargains that would benefit both sides: first, states may have private information (such as their military capabilities) that leads the sides to make different estimates as to who would prevail in a fight; second, side A may be unable to convince side B that it would live up to their bargain in the future; third, it may be impossible to divide up the stakes that lie at the heart of the dispute.

In other work, Fearon has argued that democracies may be able to bargain more effectively than authoritarian regimes because their leaders can tie their hands by issuing public threats that would be costly in domestic politics to back away from. Jessica Weeks has found that some authoritarian regimes are also responsive to domestic opinion. In the article reprinted here, she shows that domestically unaccountable "personalistic" leaders tend to be more war-prone than are military and single-party dictatorships.

While terrorism has long been used as a means of achieving political objectives, the attention of international relations researchers has been drawn to this phenomenon following the September 11, 2001, attacks. Virginia Page Fortna brings an exemplary research design to bear on the question "Do Terrorists Win?"

Carl von Clausewitz

WAR AS AN INSTRUMENT
OF POLICY

■　■　■

* * * *War is only a part of political intercourse, therefore by no means an independent thing in itself.*

We know, certainly, that War is only called forth through the political intercourse of Governments and Nations; but in general it is supposed that such intercourse is broken off by War, and that a totally different state of things ensues, subject to no laws but its own.

We maintain, on the contrary, that War is nothing but a continuation of political intercourse, with a mixture of other means. We say mixed with other means in order thereby to maintain at the same time that this political intercourse does not cease by the War itself, is not changed into something quite different, but that, in its essence, it continues to exist, whatever may be the form of the means which it uses, and that the chief lines on which the events of the War progress, and to which they are attached, are only the general features of policy which run all through the War until peace takes place. And how can we conceive it to be otherwise? Does the cessation of diplomatic notes stop the political relations between different Nations and Governments? Is not War merely another kind of writing and language for political thoughts? It has certainly a grammar of its own, but its logic is not peculiar to itself.

Accordingly, War can never be separated from political intercourse, and if, in the consideration of the matter, this is done in any way, all the threads of the different relations are, to a certain extent, broken, and we have before us a senseless thing without an object.

This kind of idea would be indispensable even if War was perfect War, the perfectly unbridled element of hostility, for all the circumstances on which it rests, and which determine its leading features, viz. our own power, the enemy's power, Allies on both sides, the characteristics of the people and their Governments respectively, etc.— are they not of a political nature, and are they not so intimately connected with the whole political intercourse that it is impossible to separate them? But this view is doubly indispensable if we reflect that real War is no such consistent effort tending to an extreme, as it should be according to the abstract idea, but a half-and-half thing, a contradiction in itself; that, as such, it cannot follow its own laws, but must be looked upon as a part of another whole—and this whole is policy.

Policy in making use of War avoids all those rigorous conclusions which proceed from its nature; it troubles itself little about final possibilities, confining its attention to immediate probabilities. If such uncertainty in the whole action ensues therefrom, if it thereby becomes a sort of game, the policy of each Cabinet places its confidence in the belief that in this game it will surpass its neighbour in skill and sharp-sightedness.

Thus policy makes out of the all-overpowering element of War a mere instrument, changes the tremendous battle-sword, which should be lifted with both hands and the whole power of the body

From Carl von Clausewitz, *On War* (1832; trans. J. J. Graham [1873], repr. Harmondsworth: Penguin Books, 1968), bk. 5, chap. 6. The author's notes have been omitted.

to strike once for all, into a light handy weapon, which is even sometimes nothing more than a rapier to exchange thrusts and feints and parries.

Thus the contradictions in which man, naturally timid, becomes involved by War may be solved, if we choose to accept this as a solution.

If War belongs to policy, it will naturally take its character from thence. If policy is grand and powerful, so also will be the War, and this may be carried to the point at which War attains to *its absolute form.*

In this way of viewing the subject, therefore, we need not shut out of sight the absolute form of War, we rather keep it continually in view in the background.

Only through this kind of view War recovers unity; only by it can we see all Wars as things of *one* kind; and it is only through it that the judgement can obtain the true and perfect basis and point of view from which great plans may be traced out and determined upon.

It is true the political element does not sink deep into the details of War. Vedettes are not planted, patrols do not make their rounds from political considerations; but small as is its influence in this respect, it is great in the formation of a plan for a whole War, or a campaign, and often even for a battle.

For this reason we were in no hurry to establish this view at the commencement. While engaged with particulars, it would have given us little help, and, on the other hand, would have distracted our attention to a certain extent; in the plan of a War or campaign it is indispensable.

There is, upon the whole, nothing more important in life than to find out the right point of view from which things should be looked at and judged of, and then to keep to that point; for we can only apprehend the mass of events in their unity from *one* standpoint; and it is only the keeping to one point of view that guards us from inconsistency.

If, therefore, in drawing up a plan of a War, it is not allowable to have a two-fold or three-fold point of view, from which things may be looked at, now with the eye of a soldier, then with that of an administrator, and then again with that of a politician, etc., then the next question is, whether *policy* is necessarily paramount and everything else subordinate to it.

That policy unites in itself, and reconciles all the interests of internal administrations, even those of humanity, and whatever else are rational subjects of consideration is presupposed, for it is nothing in itself, except a mere representative and exponent of all these interests towards other States. That policy may take a false direction, and may promote unfairly the ambitious ends, the private interests, the vanity of rulers, does not concern us here; for, under no circumstances can the Art of War be regarded as its preceptor, and we can only look at policy here as the representative of the interests generally of the whole community.

The only question, therefore, is whether in framing plans for a War the political point of view should give way to the purely military (if such a point is conceivable), that is to say, should disappear altogether, or subordinate itself to it, or whether the political is to remain the ruling point of view and the military to be considered subordinate to it.

That the political point of view should end completely when War begins is only conceivable in contests which are Wars of life and death, from pure hatred: as Wars are in reality, they are, as we before said, only the expressions or manifestations of policy itself. The subordination of the political point of view to the military would be contrary to common sense, for policy has declared the War; it is the intelligent faculty, War only the instrument, and not the reverse. The subordination of the military point of view to the political is, therefore, the only thing which is possible.

If we reflect on the nature of real War, and call to mind what has been said, *that every War should be viewed above all things according to the probability of its character, and its leading features as they are to be deduced from the political forces and proportions,* and that often—indeed we may safely affirm, in our days, *almost* always—War is to be regarded as an organic whole, from which the single branches are not to be separated, in which therefore every individual activity flows into the whole, and also has its origin in the idea of this whole, then it becomes certain and palpable to us that the superior standpoint for the conduct of the War, from which its leading lines must proceed, can be no other than that of policy.

From this point of view the plans come, as it were, out of a cast; the apprehension of them and the judgement upon them become easier and more natural, our convictions respecting them gain in force, motives are more satisfying and history more intelligible.

At all events from this point of view there is no longer in the nature of things a necessary conflict between the political and military interests, and where it appears it is therefore to be regarded as imperfect knowledge only. That policy makes demands on the War which it cannot respond to, would be contrary to the supposition that it knows the instrument which it is going to use, therefore, contrary to a natural and indispensable supposition. But if policy judges correctly of the march of military events, it is entirely its affair to determine what are the events and what the direction of events most favourable to the ultimate and great end of the War.

In one word, the Art of War in its highest point of view is policy, but, no doubt, a policy which fights battles instead of writing notes.

According to this view, to leave a great military enterprise or the plan for one, to *a purely military judgement and decision* is a distinction which cannot be allowed, and is even prejudicial; indeed, it is an irrational proceeding to consult professional soldiers on the plan of a War, that they may give a *purely military opinion* upon what the Cabinet ought to do; but still more absurd is the demand of Theorists that a statement of the available means of War should be laid before the General, that he may draw out a purely military plan for the War or for a campaign in accordance with those means. Experience in general also teaches us that notwithstanding the multifarious branches and scientific character of military art in the present day, still the leading outlines of a War are always determined by the Cabinet, that is, if we would use technical language, by a political not a military organ.

This is perfectly natural. None of the principal plans which are required for a War can be made without an insight into the political relations; and, in reality, when people speak, as they often do, of the prejudicial influence of policy on the conduct of a War, they say in reality something very different to what they intend. It is not this influence but the policy itself which should be found fault with. If policy is right, that is, if it succeeds in hitting the object, then it can only act with advantage on the War. If this influence of policy causes a divergence from the object, the cause is only to be looked for in a mistaken policy.

It is only when policy promises itself a wrong effect from certain military means and measures, an effect opposed to their nature, that it can exercise a prejudicial effect on War by the course it prescribes. Just as a person in a language with which he is not conversant sometimes says what he does not intend, so policy, when intending right, may often order things which do not tally with its own views.

This has happened times without end, and it shows that a certain knowledge of the nature of War is essential to the management of political intercourse.

But before going further, we must guard ourselves against a false interpretation of which this is very susceptible. We are far from holding the opinion that a War Minister smothered in official papers, a scientific engineer, or even a soldier who has been well tried in the field, would, any of them, necessarily make the best Minister of State where the Sovereign does not act for himself; or, in other words, we do not mean to say that this acquaintance with the nature of War is the principal qualification for a War Minister; elevation, superiority of mind, strength of character, these are the principal qualifications which he must possess; a knowledge of War may be supplied in one way or the other. * * *

■   ■   ■

We shall now conclude with some reflections derived from history.

In the last decade of the past century, when that remarkable change in the Art of War in Europe took place by which the best Armies found that a part of their method of War had become utterly unserviceable, and events were brought about of a magnitude far beyond what any one had any previous conception of, it certainly appeared that a false calculation of everything was to be laid to the charge of the Art of War. * * *

■   ■   ■

But is it true that the real surprise by which men's minds were seized was confined to the conduct of War, and did not rather relate to policy itself? That is: Did the ill success proceed from the influence of policy on the War, or from a wrong policy itself?

The prodigious effects of the French Revolution abroad were evidently brought about much less through new methods and views introduced by the French in the conduct of War than through the changes which it wrought in state-craft and civil administration, in the character of Governments, in the condition of the people, etc. That other Governments took a mistaken view of all these things; that they endeavoured, with their ordinary means, to hold their own against forces of a novel kind and overwhelming in strength—all that was a blunder in policy.

Would it have been possible to perceive and mend this error by a scheme for the War from a purely military point of view? Impossible. For if

there had been a philosophical strategist, who merely from the nature of the hostile elements had foreseen all the consequences, and prophesied remote possibilities, still it would have been practically impossible to have turned such wisdom to account.

If policy had risen to a just appreciation of the forces which had sprung up in France, and of the new relations in the political state of Europe, it might have foreseen the consequences which must follow in respect to the great features of War, and it was only in this way that it could arrive at a correct view of the extent of the means required as well as of the best use to make of those means.

We may therefore say, that the twenty years' victories of the Revolution are chiefly to be ascribed to the erroneous policy of the Governments by which it was opposed.

It is true these errors first displayed themselves in the War, and the events of the War completely disappointed the expectations which policy entertained. But this did not take place because policy neglected to consult its military advisers. That Art of War in which the politician of the day could believe, namely, that derived from the reality of War at that time, that which belonged to the policy of the day, that familiar instrument which policy had hitherto used—*that* Art of War, I say, was naturally involved in the error of policy, and therefore could not teach it anything better. It is true that War itself underwent important alterations both in its nature and forms, which brought it nearer to its absolute form; but these changes were not brought about because the French Government had, to a certain extent, delivered itself from the leading-strings of policy; they arose from an altered policy, produced by the French Revolution, not only in France, but over the rest of Europe as well. This policy had called forth other means and other powers, by which it became possible to conduct War with a degree of energy which could not have been thought of otherwise.

Therefore, the actual changes in the Art of War are a consequence of alterations in policy; and, so far from being an argument for the possible separation of the two, they are, on the contrary, very strong evidence of the intimacy of their connexion.

Therefore, once more: War is an instrument of policy; it must necessarily bear its character, it must measure with its scale: the conduct of War, in its great features, is therefore policy itself, which takes up the sword in place of the pen, but does not on that account cease to think according to its own laws.

Thomas C. Schelling

THE DIPLOMACY OF VIOLENCE

The usual distinction between diplomacy and force is not merely in the instruments, words or bullets, but in the relation between adversaries—in the interplay of motives and the role of communication, understandings, compromise, and restraint. Diplomacy is bargaining: it seeks outcomes that, though not ideal for either party, are better for both than some of the alternatives. In diplomacy each party somewhat controls what the other wants, and can get more by compromise, exchange, or collaboration than by taking things in his own hands and ignoring the other's wishes. The bargaining can be polite or rude, entail threats as well as offers, assume a status quo or ignore all rights and privileges, and assume mistrust rather than trust. But whether polite or impolite, constructive or aggressive, respectful or vicious, whether it occurs among friends or antagonists and whether or not there is a basis for trust and goodwill, there must be some common interest, if only in the avoidance of mutual damage, and an awareness of the need to make the other party prefer an outcome acceptable to oneself.

With enough military force a country may not need to bargain. Some things a country wants it can take, and some things it has it can keep, by sheer strength, skill and ingenuity. It can do this *forcibly*, accommodating only to opposing strength, skill, and ingenuity and without trying to appeal to an enemy's wishes. Forcibly a country can repel and expel, penetrate and occupy, seize, exterminate, disarm and disable, confine, deny access, and directly frustrate intrusion or attack. It can, that

is, if it has enough strength. "Enough" depends on how much an opponent has.

There is something else, though, that force can do. It is less military, less heroic, less impersonal, and less unilateral; it is uglier, and has received less attention in Western military strategy. In addition to seizing and holding, disarming and confining, penetrating and obstructing, and all that, military force can be used *to hurt*. In addition to taking and protecting things of value it can *destroy* value. In addition to weakening an enemy militarily it can cause an enemy plain suffering.

Pain and shock, loss and grief, privation and horror are always in some degree, sometimes in terrible degree, among the results of warfare; but in traditional military science they are incidental, they are not the object. If violence can be done incidentally, though, it can also be done purposely. The power to hurt can be counted among the most impressive attributes of military force.

Hurting, unlike forcible seizure or self-defense, is not unconcerned with the interest of others. It is measured in the suffering it can cause and the victims' motivation to avoid it. Forcible action will work against weeds or floods as well as against armies, but suffering requires a victim that can feel pain or has something to lose. To inflict suffering gains nothing and saves nothing directly; it can only make people behave to avoid it. The only purpose, unless sport or revenge, must be to influence somebody's behavior, to coerce his decision or choice. To be coercive, violence has to be anticipated. And it has to be avoidable by accommodation. The power to hurt is bargaining power. To exploit it is diplomacy—vicious diplomacy, but diplomacy.

From Thomas C. Schelling, *Arms and Influence* (New Haven, CT: Yale University Press, 1966), pp. 1–10, 12–13, 18–19, 21–24, 33–34.

The Contrast of Brute Force with Coercion

There is a difference between taking what you want and making someone give it to you, between fending off assault and making someone afraid to assault you, between holding what people are trying to take and making them afraid to take it, between losing what someone can forcibly take and giving it up to avoid risk or damage. It is the difference between defense and deterrence, between brute force and intimidation, between conquest and blackmail, between action and threats. It is the difference between the unilateral, "undiplomatic" recourse to strength, and coercive diplomacy based on the power to hurt.

The contrasts are several. The purely "military" or "undiplomatic" recourse to forcible action is concerned with enemy strength, not enemy interests; the coercive use of the power to hurt, though, is the very exploitation of enemy wants and fears. And brute strength is usually measured relative to enemy strength, the one directly opposing the other, while the power to hurt is typically not reduced by the enemy's power to hurt in return. Opposing strengths may cancel each other; pain and grief do not. The willingness to hurt, the credibility of a threat, and the ability to exploit the power to hurt will indeed depend on how much the adversary can hurt in return; but there is little or nothing about an adversary's pain or grief that directly reduces one's own. Two sides cannot both overcome each other with superior strength; they may both be able to hurt each other. With strength they can dispute objects of value; with sheer violence they can destroy them.

And brute force succeeds when it is used, whereas the power to hurt is most successful when held in reserve. It is the *threat* of damage, or of more damage to come, that can make someone yield or comply. It is *latent* violence that can influence someone's choice—violence that can still be withheld or inflicted, or that a victim believes can be withheld or inflicted. The threat of pain tries to structure someone's motives, while brute force tries to overcome his strength. Unhappily, the power to hurt is often communicated by some performance of it. Whether it is sheer terroristic violence to induce an irrational response, or cool premeditated violence to persuade somebody that you mean it and may do it again, it is not the pain and damage itself but its influence on somebody's behavior that matters. It is the expectation of *more* violence that gets the wanted behavior, if the power to hurt can get it at all.

To exploit a capacity for hurting and inflicting damage one needs to know what an adversary treasures and what scares him and one needs the adversary to understand what behavior of his will cause the violence to be inflicted and what will cause it to be withheld. The victim has to know what is wanted, and he may have to be assured of what is not wanted. The pain and suffering have to appear *contingent* on his behavior; it is not alone the threat that is effective—the threat of pain or loss if he fails to comply—but the corresponding assurance, possibly an implicit one, that he can avoid the pain or loss if he does comply. The prospect of certain death may stun him, but it gives him no choice.

Coercion by threat of damage also requires that our interests and our opponent's not be absolutely opposed. If his pain were our greatest delight and our satisfaction his greatest woe, we would just proceed to hurt and to frustrate each other. It is when his pain gives us little or no satisfaction compared with what he can do for us, and the action or inaction that satisfies us costs him less than the pain we can cause, that there is room for coercion. Coercion requires finding a bargain, arranging for him to be better off doing what we want—worse off not doing what we want—when he takes the threatened penalty into account.

It is this capacity for pure damage, pure violence, that is usually associated with the most vicious labor disputes, with racial disorders, with civil uprisings and their suppression, with racketeering. It is also the power to hurt rather than brute force that we use in dealing with criminals; we hurt them afterward, or threaten to, for their misdeeds rather than protect ourselves with cordons of electric wires, masonry walls, and armed guards. Jail, of course, can be either forcible restraint or threatened privation; if the object is to keep criminals out of mischief by confinement, success is measured by how many of them are gotten behind bars, but if the object is to *threaten* privation, success will be measured by how few have to be put behind bars and success then depends on the subject's understanding of the consequences. Pure damage is what a car threatens when it tries to hog the road or to keep its rightful share, or to go first through an intersection. A tank or a bulldozer can force its way regardless of others' wishes; the rest of us have to threaten damage, usually mutual damage, hoping the other driver values his car or his limbs enough to give way, hoping he sees us, and hoping he is in control of his own car. The threat of pure damage will not work against an unmanned vehicle.

This difference between coercion and brute force is as often in the intent as in the instrument. To hunt down Comanches and to exterminate them was brute force; to raid their villages to make them behave was coercive diplomacy, based on the power to hurt. The pain and loss to the Indians might have looked much the same one way as the other; the difference was one of purpose and effect. If Indians were killed because they were in the way, or somebody wanted their land, or the authorities despaired of making them behave and could not confine them and decided to exterminate them, that was pure unilateral force. If *some* Indians were killed to make *other* Indians behave, that was coercive violence—or intended to be, whether or not it was effective. The Germans at Verdun perceived themselves to be chewing up hundreds of thousands of French soldiers in a gruesome "meat-grinder." If the purpose was to eliminate a military obstacle—the French infantryman, viewed as a military "asset" rather than as a warm human being—the offensive at Verdun was a unilateral exercise of military force. If instead the object was to make the loss of young men—not of impersonal "effectives," but of sons, husbands, fathers, and the pride of French manhood—so anguishing as to be unendurable, to make surrender a welcome relief and to spoil the foretaste of an Allied victory, then it was an exercise in coercion, in applied violence, intended to offer relief upon accommodation. And of course, since any use of force tends to be brutal, thoughtless, vengeful, or plain obstinate, the motives themselves can be mixed and confused. The fact that heroism and brutality can be either coercive diplomacy or a contest in pure strength does not promise that the distinction will be made, and the strategies enlightened by the distinction, every time some vicious enterprise gets launched.

The contrast between brute force and coercion is illustrated by two alternative strategies attributed to Genghis Khan. Early in his career he pursued the war creed of the Mongols: the vanquished can never be the friends of the victors; their death is necessary for the victor's safety. This was the unilateral extermination of a menace or a liability. The turning point of his career, according to Lynn Montross, came later when he discovered how to use his power to hurt for diplomatic ends. "The great Khan, who was not inhibited by the usual mercies, conceived the plan of forcing captives—women, children, aged fathers, favorite sons—to march ahead of his army as the first potential victims of resistance."[1] Live captives have often proved more valuable than enemy dead; and the technique discovered by the Khan in his maturity remains contemporary. North Koreans and Chinese were reported to have quartered prisoners of war near strategic targets to inhibit bombing attacks by United Nations aircraft. Hostages represent the power to hurt in its purest form.

Coercive Violence in Warfare

This distinction between the power to hurt and the power to seize or hold forcibly is important in modern war, both big war and little war, hypothetical war and real war. For many years the Greeks and the Turks on Cyprus could hurt each other indefinitely but neither could quite take or hold forcibly what they wanted or protect themselves from violence by physical means. The Jews in Palestine could not expel the British in the late 1940s but they could cause pain and fear and frustration through terrorism, and eventually influence somebody's decision. The brutal war in Algeria was more a contest in pure violence than in military strength; the question was who would first find the pain and degradation unendurable. The French troops preferred—indeed they continually tried—to make it a contest of strength, to pit military force against the nationalists' capacity for terror, to exterminate or disable the nationalists and to screen off the nationalists from the victims of their violence. But because in civil war terrorists commonly have access to victims by sheer physical propinquity, the victims and their properties could not be forcibly defended and in the end the French troops themselves resorted, unsuccessfully, to a war of pain.

Nobody believes that the Russians can take Hawaii from us, or New York, or Chicago, but nobody doubts that they might destroy people and buildings in Hawaii, Chicago, or New York. Whether the Russians can conquer West Germany in any meaningful sense is questionable; whether they can hurt it terribly is not doubted. That the United States can destroy a large part of Russia is universally taken for granted; that the United States can keep from being badly hurt, even devastated, in return, or can keep Western Europe from being devastated while itself destroying Russia, is at best arguable; and it is virtually out of the question that

we could conquer Russia territorially and use its economic assets unless it were by threatening disaster and inducing compliance. It is the power to hurt, not military strength in the traditional sense, that inheres in our most impressive military capabilities at the present time [1966]. We have a Department of *Defense* but emphasize *retaliation*—"to return evil for evil" (synonyms: requital, reprisal, revenge, vengeance, retribution). And it is pain and violence, not force in the traditional sense, that inheres also in some of the least impressive military capabilities of the present time—the plastic bomb, the terrorist's bullet, the burnt crops, and the tortured farmer.

War appears to be, or threatens to be, not so much a contest of strength as one of endurance, nerve, obstinacy, and pain. It appears to be, and threatens to be, not so much a contest of military strength as a bargaining process—dirty, extortionate, and often quite reluctant bargaining on one side or both—nevertheless a bargaining process.

The difference cannot quite be expressed as one between the *use* of force and the *threat* of force. The actions involved in forcible accomplishment, on the one hand, and in fulfilling a threat, on the other, can be quite different. Sometimes the most effective direct action inflicts enough cost or pain on the enemy to serve as a threat, sometimes not. The United States threatens the Soviet Union with virtual destruction of its society in the event of a surprise attack on the United States; a hundred million deaths are awesome as pure damage, but they are useless in stopping the Soviet attack—especially if the threat is to do it all afterward anyway. So it is worth while to keep the concepts distinct—to distinguish forcible action from the threat of pain—recognizing that some actions serve as both a means of forcible accomplishment and a means of inflicting pure damage, some do not. Hostages tend to entail almost pure pain and damage, as do all forms of reprisal after the fact. Some modes of self-defense may exact so little in blood or treasure as to entail negligible violence; and some forcible actions entail so much violence that their threat can be effective by itself.

The power to hurt, though it can usually accomplish nothing directly, is potentially more versatile than a straightforward capacity for forcible accomplishment. By force alone we cannot even lead a horse to water—we have to drag him—much less make him drink. Any affirmative action, any collaboration, almost anything but physical exclusion, expulsion, or extermination, requires that an opponent or a victim *do* something, even if only to stop or get out. The threat of pain and damage may make him want to do it, and anything he can do is potentially susceptible to inducement. Brute force can only accomplish what requires no collaboration. The principle is illustrated by a technique of unarmed combat: one can disable a man by various stunning, fracturing, or killing blows, but to take him to jail one has to exploit the man's own efforts. "Come-along" holds are those that threaten pain or disablement, giving relief as long as the victim complies, giving him the option of using his own legs to get to jail.

We have to keep in mind, though, that what is pure pain, or the threat of it, at one level of decision can be equivalent to brute force at another level. Churchill was worried, during the early bombing raids on London in 1940, that Londoners might panic. Against people the bombs were pure violence, to induce their undisciplined evasion; to Churchill and the government, the bombs were a cause of inefficiency, whether they spoiled transport and made people late to work or scared people and made them afraid to work. Churchill's decisions were not going to be coerced by the fear of a few casualties. Similarly on the battlefield: tactics that frighten soldiers so that they run, duck their heads, or lay down their arms and surrender represent coercion based on the power to hurt; to the top command, which is frustrated but not coerced, such tactics are part of the contest in military discipline and strength.

The fact that violence—pure pain and damage—can be used or threatened to coerce and to deter, to intimidate and to blackmail, to demoralize and to paralyze, in a conscious process of dirty bargaining, does not by any means imply that violence is not often wanton and meaningless or, even when purposive, in danger of getting out of hand. Ancient wars were often quite "total" for the loser, the men being put to death, the women sold as slaves, the boys castrated, the cattle slaughtered, and the buildings leveled, for the sake of revenge, justice, personal gain, or merely custom. If an enemy bombs a city, by design or by carelessness, we usually bomb his if we can. In the excitement and fatigue of warfare, revenge is one of the few satisfactions that can be savored; and justice can often be construed to demand the enemy's punishment, even if it is delivered with more enthusiasm than justice requires. When Jerusalem fell to the Crusaders in 1099 the ensuing slaughter was one of the bloodiest in military chronicles. "The men of the West literally waded in gore, their march to the church of the Holy Sepulcher being gruesomely likened to 'treading out the wine press'. . . . ," reports Montross (p. 138), who observes that these excesses usually came at the climax of the capture of a fortified post or city. "For long the assailants have endured more punishment than they were able to inflict; then once the walls are breached, pent up emotions find an outlet in murder, rape and plunder, which discipline is powerless to prevent." The same occurred when Tyre fell to Alexander after a painful siege, and the phenomenon was not unknown on Pacific islands in the Second World War. Pure violence, like fire, can be harnessed to a purpose; that does not mean that behind every holocaust is a shrewd intention successfully fulfilled.

But if the occurrence of violence does not always bespeak a shrewd purpose, the absence of pain and destruction is no sign that violence was idle. Violence is most purposive and most successful when it is threatened and not used. Successful threats are those that do not have to be carried out. By European standards, Denmark was virtually unharmed in the Second World War; it was violence that made the Danes submit. Withheld violence—successfully threatened violence—can look clean, even merciful. The fact that a kidnap victim is returned unharmed, against receipt of ample ransom, does not make kidnapping a nonviolent enterprise. * * *

■ ■ ■

The Strategic Role of Pain and Damage

Pure violence, nonmilitary violence, appears most conspicuously in relations between unequal countries, where there is no substantial military challenge and the outcome of military engagement is not in question. Hitler could make his threats contemptuously and brutally against Austria; he could make them, if he wished, in a more refined way against Denmark. It is noteworthy that it was Hitler, not his generals, who used this kind of language; proud military establishments do not like to think of themselves as extortionists. Their favorite job is to deliver victory, to dispose of opposing military force and to leave most of the civilian violence to politics and diplomacy. But if there is no room for doubt how a contest in strength will come out, it may be possible to bypass the military stage altogether and to proceed at once to the coercive bargaining.

A typical confrontation of unequal forces occurs at the *end* of a war, between victor and vanquished. Where Austria was vulnerable before a shot was fired, France was vulnerable after its military shield had collapsed in 1940. Surrender negotiations are the place where the threat of civil violence can come to the fore. Surrender negotiations are often so one-sided, or the potential violence so unmistakable, that bargaining succeeds and the violence remains in reserve. But the fact that most of the actual damage was done during the military stage of the war, prior to victory and defeat, does not mean that violence was idle in the aftermath, only that it was latent and the threat of it successful.

Indeed, victory is often but a prerequisite to the exploitation of the power to hurt. When Xenophon was fighting in Asia Minor under Persian leadership, it took military strength to disperse enemy soldiers and occupy their lands; but land was not what the victor wanted, nor was victory for its own sake.

> Next day the Persian leader burned the villages to the ground, not leaving a single house standing, so as to strike terror into the other tribes to show them what would happen if they did not give in. . . . He sent some of the prisoners into the hills and told them to say that if the inhabitants did not come down and settle in their houses to submit to him, he would burn up their villages too and destroy their crops, and they would die of hunger.[2]

Military victory was but the *price of admission*. The payoff depended upon the successful threat of violence.

■ ■ ■

The Nuclear Contribution to Terror and Violence

Man has, it is said, for the first time in history enough military power to eliminate his species from the earth, weapons against which there is no conceivable defense. War has become, it is said, so destructive and terrible that it ceases to be an instrument of national power. "For the first time in human history," says Max Lerner in a book whose title, *The Age of Overkill*, conveys the point, "men have bottled up a power . . . which they have thus far not dared to use."[3] And Soviet military authorities, whose party dislikes having to accommodate an entire theory of history to a single technological event, have had to reexamine a set of principles that had been given the embarrassing name of "permanently operating factors" in warfare. Indeed, our era is epitomized by words like "the first time in human history," and by the abdication of what was "permanent."

For dramatic impact these statements are splendid. Some of them display a tendency, not at all necessary, to belittle the catastrophe of earlier wars. They may exaggerate the historical novelty of deterrence and the balance of terror. More important, they do not help to identify just what is new about war when so much destructive energy can be packed in warheads at a price that permits advanced countries to have them in large numbers. Nuclear warheads are incomparably more devastating than anything packaged before. What does that imply about war?

It is not true that for the first time in history man has the capability to destroy a large fraction, even the major part, of the human race. Japan was defenseless by August 1945. With a combination of bombing and blockade, eventually invasion, and if necessary the deliberate spread of disease, the United States could probably have exterminated the population of the Japanese islands without nuclear weapons. It would have been a gruesome, expensive, and mortifying campaign; it would have taken time and demanded persistence. But we had the economic and technical capacity to do it; and, together with the Russians or without them, we could have done the same in many populous parts of the world. Against defenseless people there is not much that nuclear weapons can do that cannot be done with an ice pick. And it would not have strained our Gross National Product to do it with ice picks.

It is a grisly thing to talk about. We did not do it and it is not imaginable that we would have done it. We had no reason; if we had had a reason, we would not have the persistence of purpose,

once the fury of war had been dissipated in victory and we had taken on the task of executioner. If we and our enemies might do such a thing to each other now, and to others as well, it is not because nuclear weapons have for the first time made it feasible.

■ ■ ■

* * * In the past it has usually been the victors who could do what they pleased to the enemy. War has often been "total war" for the loser. With deadly monotony the Persians, Greeks, or Romans "put to death all men of military age, and sold the women and children into slavery," leaving the defeated territory nothing but its name until new settlers arrived sometime later. But the defeated could not do the same to their victors. The boys could be castrated and sold only after the war had been won, and only on the side that lost it. The power to hurt could be brought to bear only after military strength had achieved victory. The same sequence characterized the great wars of this century; for reasons of technology and geography, military force has usually had to penetrate, to exhaust, or to collapse opposing military force—to achieve military victory—before it could be brought to bear on the enemy nation itself. The Allies in World War I could not inflict coercive pain and suffering directly on the Germans in a decisive way until they could defeat the German army; and the Germans could not coerce the French people with bayonets unless they first beat the Allied troops that stood in their way. With two-dimensional warfare, there is a tendency for troops to confront each other, shielding their own lands while attempting to press into each other's. Small penetrations could not do major damage to the people; large penetrations were so destructive of military organization that they usually ended the military phase of the war.

Nuclear weapons make it possible to do monstrous violence to the enemy without first achieving victory. With nuclear weapons and today's means of delivery, one expects to penetrate an enemy homeland without first collapsing his military force. What nuclear weapons have done, or appear to do, is to promote this kind of warfare to first place. Nuclear weapons threaten to make war less military, and are responsible for the lowered status of "military victory" at the present time. *Victory is no longer a prerequisite for hurting the enemy.* And it is no assurance against being terribly hurt. One need not wait until he has won the war before inflicting "unendurable" damages on his enemy. One need not wait until he has lost the war. There was a time when the assurance of victory—false or genuine assurance—could make national leaders not just willing but sometimes enthusiastic about war. Not now.

Not only *can* nuclear weapons hurt the enemy before the war has been won, and perhaps hurt decisively enough to make the military engagement academic, but it is widely assumed that in a major war that is *all* they can do. Major war is often discussed as though it would be only a contest in national destruction. If this is indeed the case—if the destruction of cities and their populations has become, with nuclear weapons, the primary object in an all-out war—the sequence of war has been reversed. Instead of destroying enemy forces as a prelude to imposing one's will on the enemy nation, one would have to destroy the nation as a means or a prelude to destroying the enemy forces. If one cannot disable enemy forces without virtually destroying the country, the victor does not even have the option of sparing the conquered nation. He has already destroyed it. Even with blockade and strategic bombing it could be supposed that a country would be defeated before it was destroyed, or would elect surrender before annihilation had gone far. In the Civil War it could be hoped that the South would become too weak to fight before it became too weak to survive. For "all-out" war, nuclear weapons threaten to reverse this sequence.

So nuclear weapons do make a difference, marking an epoch in warfare. The difference is not just in the amount of destruction that can be accomplished but in the role of destruction and in the decision process. Nuclear weapons can change the speed of events, the control of events, the sequence of events, the relation of victor to vanquished, and the relation of homeland to fighting front. Deterrence rests today on the threat of pain and extinction, not just on the threat of military defeat. We may argue about the wisdom of announcing "unconditional surrender" as an aim in the last major war, but seem to expect "unconditional destruction" as a matter of course in another one.

Something like the same destruction always *could* be done. With nuclear weapons there is an expectation that it *would* be done. It is not "overkill" that is new; the American army surely had enough 30 caliber bullets to kill everybody in the world in 1945, or if it did not it could have bought them without any strain. What is new is plain "kill"—the idea that major war might be just a contest in the killing of countries, or not even a contest but just two parallel exercises in devastation.

That is the difference nuclear weapons make. At least they *may* make that difference. They also may not. If the weapons themselves are vulnerable to attack, or the machines that carry them, a successful surprise might eliminate the opponent's means of retribution. That an enormous explosion can be packaged in a single bomb does not by itself guarantee that the victor will receive deadly punishment. Two gunfighters facing each other in a Western town had an unquestioned capacity to kill one another; that did not guarantee that both would die in a gunfight—only the slower of the two. Less deadly weapons, permitting an injured one to shoot back before he died, might have been more conducive to a restraining balance of terror, or of caution. The very efficiency of nuclear weapons could make them ideal for starting war, if they can suddenly eliminate the enemy's capability to shoot back.

And there is a contrary possibility: that nuclear weapons are not vulnerable to attack and prove not to be terribly effective against each other, posing no need to shoot them quickly for fear they will be destroyed before they are launched, and with no task available but the systematic destruction of the enemy country and no necessary reason to do it fast rather than slowly. Imagine that nuclear destruction *had* to go slowly—that the bombs could be dropped only one per day. The prospect would look very different, something like the most terroristic guerilla warfare on a massive scale. It happens that nuclear war does not have to go slowly; but it may also not have to go speedily. The mere existence of nuclear weapons does not itself determine that everything must go off in a blinding flash, any more than that it must go slowly. Nuclear weapons do not simplify things quite that much.

■   ■   ■

War no longer looks like just a contest of strength. War and the brink of war are more a contest of nerve and risk-taking, of pain and endurance. Small wars embody the threat of a larger war; they are not just military engagements but "crisis diplomacy." The threat of war has always been somewhere underneath international diplomacy, but for Americans it is now much nearer the surface. Like the threat of a strike in industrial relations, the threat of divorce in a family dispute, or the threat of bolting the party at a political convention, the threat of violence continuously circumscribes international politics. Neither strength nor goodwill procures immunity.

Military strategy can no longer be thought of, as it could for some countries in some eras, as the science of military victory. It is now equally, if not more, the art of coercion, of intimidation and deterrence. The instruments of war are more punitive than acquisitive. Military strategy, whether we like it or not, has become the diplomacy of violence.

NOTES

1. Lynn Montross, *War Through the Ages* (3d ed. New York, Harper and Brothers, 1960), p. 146.
2. Xenophon, *The Persian Expedition*, Rex Warner, transl. (Baltimore, Penguin Books, 1949), p. 272. "The 'rational' goal of the threat of violence," says H. L. Nieburg, "is an accommodation of interests, not the provocation of actual violence. Similarly the 'rational' goal of actual violence is demonstration of the will and capability of action, establishing a measure of the credibility of future threats, not the exhaustion of that capability in unlimited conflict." "Uses of Violence," *Journal of Conflict Resolution, 7* (1963), 44.
3. New York, Simon and Schuster, 1962, p. 47.

Erica D. Borghard and Shawn W. Lonergan

THE LOGIC OF COERCION IN CYBERSPACE

Cyberspace has definitively emerged as the latest frontier of militarized interactions between nation-states. Governments, as they are wont to do in an anarchic international system, have already invested considerable resources to develop offensive and defensive military capabilities in cyberspace. It remains to be seen, however, how and to what extent these tools can be employed to achieve desired political objectives. Put simply, what is the logic of coercion in cyberspace? Can governments use cyber power to deter state adversaries from taking undesirable actions or compel them to bend to their wills and, if so, how and under what conditions?[1] This analysis draws on the large corpus of coercion theory to assess the extent to which existing frameworks can shed light on the dynamics of coercion in cyberspace. The article proceeds as follows. First, we outline the theoretical logic of coercion theory and identify the factors necessary for successful coercion. Each element of coercion is immediately followed by a discussion of how it applies to the cyber domain and an assessment of how the particularities of the domain reflect on the requirements of successful coercion. We demonstrate that, based on current capabilities, cyber power has limited effectiveness as an independent tool of coercion. Second, we explore the extent to which cyber power could be used as part of a warfighting strategy to target an adversary's ability or willingness to resist and suggest which

strategies are likely to be more versus less effective.[2] We assert that, based on current capabilities, attrition, denial, and decapitation strategies are most likely to be effective in cyberspace. Finally, we conclude with recommendations for policymaking and further research.

Coercion Theory

As Thomas C. Schelling so eloquently articulated, coercion is fundamentally about affecting an adversary's behavior using the threat or limited application of military force; "[i]t is the *threat* of damage, or of more damage to come, that can make someone yield or comply."[3] Coercion involves producing a desired behavior or outcome on the part of an adversary by forcing her to confront a cost–benefit calculus, such that the adversary believes it is less costly to concede to the threatener's preferred course of (in)action than to defy the latter's demands.[4] Coercion is distinct from brute force. In the latter case, one state defeats another militarily and then imposes a political settlement on the defeated power; in the former case, the target of coercion retains the military capacity to resist or concede, and the coercer seeks to achieve a political settlement short of full-scale war by manipulating the cost–benefit calculus of the target state.[5] While coercion has always been a fundamental element of the exercise of state power, the advent of nuclear weapons and mutual assured destruction has made coercion even more critical. As Schelling explains, the prospect of

From *Security Studies* 26, no. 3 (2017): 452–81. Some of the authors' notes have been omitted.

civilization-ending nuclear warfare, coupled with advances in technology making it possible to target an enemy's population centers and hold its society at risk without first defeating its armed forces, has turned statecraft into the diplomacy of violence.[6] The significance of coercion for interstate relations has not decreased with the advent of cyber warfare; if anything, it has increased. Indeed, like nuclear weapons, cyber weapons enable governments to target adversary populations while bypassing the latter's military forces. For example, cyber weapons could be employed to target a state's critical infrastructure to render key pieces of a state's military systems inoperable at decisive times, as was allegedly the case when Syrian air defense systems failed to respond to an Israeli bombing operation against a purported Syrian nuclear enrichment facility in 2007.[7]

Notwithstanding the central role coercion plays in states' strategies, successful coercion—both its deterrent and compellent varieties—is difficult to achieve.[8] There is a large body of empirical literature that assesses the reasons for failed coercion, particularly focusing on examples of failed coercion in American foreign policy during the Vietnam War and through the use of air power in the post–Cold War international system.[9] In general, using the threat or limited application of military force to affect an adversary's behavior is difficult to accomplish because there are many factors that are necessary conditions for successful coercion, some of which are in tension with others. Moreover, if coercion is difficult to achieve through the threat or use of conventional military power, we argue that it is even more challenging in cyberspace. The literature on coercion suggests that four fundamental conditions must be met for coercion to succeed: the coercive threat must be clearly communicated; it must be linked to a cost–benefit calculus such that the target's costs of conceding are less than the costs of not complying; it must be credible; and there must be an element of reassurance.[10]

Communication

The essence of successful coercion is clear communication.[11] The target of a coercive threat has to know precisely the behavior in which the coercing state wants the target state to engage (or refrain from engaging), the timeframe in which the coercing state expects the target to comply, and the costs associated with cooperation versus defection. The target state must understand "what behavior of his will cause the violence to be inflicted and what will cause it to be withheld."[12] Ideally, coercion takes the form of an ultimatum: if State B does not do action X within timeframe Y, State A will take specified action Z. However, in the vast majority of international crises, political leaders default to ambiguity, rather than clarity, of threats; leaders often prefer to retain flexibility to escape from costly or imprudent commitments or be adaptive in their responses to an adversary's behavior, especially if they lack domestic political support.[13] The fundamental fact of anarchy complicates clear communication because it leads to poor, fragmentary information and creates incentives to misrepresent private information—indeed, this is a cause of war.[14] Beyond incentives for strategic ambiguity, clear signaling is complicated by misperceptions stemming from both cultural differences and cognitive limitations.[15] Insights from cognitive psychology have demonstrated that recipients of a signal tend to fit incoming information into preexisting beliefs, interpret signals based on implicit theories about their meaning, prefer simplicity over complexity, and are influenced by motivated biases.[16] Put simply, signaling often fails "because the perceiver does not understand what message the actor is trying to communicate."[17] Communication is facilitated when actors can agree on a shared meaning of a particular type or vehicle of signaling (such as diplomatic language). In the case of diplomatic language, for example, clarity is easier to achieve because "both the signaler and the perceiver agree as to the message that the former is trying to convey."[18]

Communication in Cyberspace

Understanding intent is exceptionally difficult in the cyber domain. Many scholars and U.S. government–sponsored studies have noted that cyber operations create a high probability of misunderstanding the coercing state's intentions.[19] Unlike diplomatic channels, in cyberspace there is no agreed-upon language that guides policymakers to a common understanding that helps divine the meaning behind a cyber signal. Moreover, in cyberspace, most operations are interactions between humans and machines facilitated by code for which there are few, if any, norms governing the exchange.[20] That many high-level decision makers lack even a basic understanding of the cyber domain and, therefore, are likely to be intellectually unprepared during a time of crisis, compounds this uncertainty. Furthermore, the signaler may be uncertain about what kind of cyber tool she should select to communicate in cyberspace because the actual effects of a cyber attack may be unpredictable ex ante—even to the signaler.

Signaling in cyberspace is the most problematic of all the domains (land, sea, air, space, and cyber) because the signal may go unrealized. In other words, in cyberspace only the initiator may perceive the engagement.[21] Moreover, even if a target state realizes it has been attacked, it is difficult to infer the intent behind a cyber signal based solely on an observed incursion. This ambiguity has the potential to trigger unintended escalation because it is difficult to distinguish between hostile and benign intentions when an outside actor is perceived to have accessed a critical system.[22] In a hypothetical example, Japan may have an intelligence requirement to monitor the uranium enrichment efforts of North Korea. However, Japan's access to a network at a North Korean enrichment facility does not

necessarily suggest that it intends to destroy North Korea's nuclear ambitions through cyber means; Japan could simply be monitoring the program to meet its own defensive requirements, which is widely accepted by international convention to be a necessary state practice.[23] Actors could exploit this uncertainty to their advantage, but it may also lead to unintended conflict.[24] Herbert Lin notes this ambiguity in cyberspace and concludes that the cyber domain presents an increased risk of accidental escalation: "In the absence of direct contact with those conducting such operations—sometimes even in the presence of such contact—determining intent is likely to be difficult and may rest heavily on inferences made on the basis of whatever attribution is possible. Thus, attempts to send signals to an adversary through limited and constrained military actions—problematic even in kinetic warfare—are likely to be even more problematic when cyber attacks are involved."[25]

Attribution problems complicate effective communication in cyberspace because they create problems for both target and initiator. From the perspective of the target state, a fundamental impediment to deciphering the intent behind a cyber signal is the difficulty of identifying the actor who sent it. This presents a challenge to policymakers because, if a cyber action is uncovered, the true meaning of the signal may not be ascertained without attribution. While some actions in themselves may send a clear signal without attribution, typically the identity of the signaling state is critical for coercion to succeed. For instance, in the prior scenario we assumed North Korea attributed the cyber incursion to Japan. However, what if North Korea were unable to attribute the access to Japan and had to surmise the intent of the incursion devoid of attribution? The spectrum of possible motivations of such an incursion ranges from a preparation for a preemptive attack from a rival such as Japan or the United States on one end of the spectrum, to a benign case of espionage from an ally such as China on the other. In this hypothetical case, not only is the signal obfuscated because intent cannot be deduced without attribution, but North Korea also does not know what is an appropriate response and against whom to respond. If these conditions are not met, coercion is by definition not possible.

There are, however, several methods to assign attribution following a cyber incursion.[26] The easiest ascription approach is when the perpetrator publically accepts responsibility for the action and the target state believes that the self-identified attacker possessed both the capability and motivation to carry it out. Another attribution technique mandates that the target state had access to the attacker's network from which the incursion originated and either witnessed the operation in real time or recorded it. This second method is difficult because it requires that the target state had access to the specific network from which the aggressor initiated an attack; that they observed the onslaught developing in real time and intentionally refrained from establishing tailored defenses or engaging in a preemptive attack to block the assault; or that they had complete intelligence collection of all cyber operations from the adversary's network, which is typically technically difficult to consistently collect. However, in some instances governments may decide that the intelligence value of maintaining access outweighs the likely damage from the attack. Another attribution method is when sensors placed either at Internet service providers or key nodes in the Internet run algorithms that analyze raw data flows and scan for anomalies and variants of known attack signatures. However, the real-time use of such technology is still in a nascent stage and there is currently no guarantee that, once detected, the source of the malware could be traced back to the true originator.[27] The final method of assigning attribution occurs when the signature of the attack (the coding) is so unique that it could be traced to a specific actor or threat network. Yet, this method heightens the risk of falling victim to deceptive techniques, such as embedding remarks in a foreign language of a noninvolved party, which may confound forensic experts seeking to assign attribution. Recently, however, there have been advances in signature recognition software designed to scour millions of lines of code to compile unique profiles of the developers.[28] Moreover, from the target's perspective, even if she is able to successfully attribute an attack to a particular actor, she may be hesitant to reveal her ability to do so because it would likely require going public with valuable information that could compromise her own capabilities and accesses. For instance, the United States' decision to quickly attribute the Sony hack in late 2014 to North Korea likely revealed and compromised American accesses to other governments' cyber infrastructure.

Attribution issues create problems not only for the target state attempting to infer the intent behind a signal, but also for the coercing state seeking to send a clear signal. The conventional wisdom on cyber operations posits that states typically seek to avoid attribution when conducting cyber exploitation and espionage operations. However, coercion in cyberspace requires attribution to be effective. A coercing state may employ several methods to ensure attribution. First, a state could couple the action in cyberspace with a formal diplomatic message, elucidating the meaning the signal (the cyber attack) was intended to convey.[29] Coupling a cyber operation with a diplomatic message may be the least costly method to ensure ascription for the coercer, but it must also be credible. This technique was observed in March 2016 when Secretary of Defense Ashton Carter, in a formal public statement, acknowledged that the United States conducted a cyber attack against the Islamic State of Iraq and Syria's command and control systems in Mosul, Iraq.[30] However, a coercing state must ensure that the target believes its self-declared attribution. This could present a problem for the coercing state if, in order to demonstrate that it was the one sending a signal, it had to reveal capabilities and accesses that it may prefer to keep private. Second, if coupling is not an available avenue, some have postulated several technical methods to ensure attribution, such as embedding unique signatures in code.[31] This type of ascription technique demands that some trace of the cyber operation remain on the target's machines.

This suggests that simply gaining access to a network and conducting cyber espionage is not sufficient to send a coercive signal in cyberspace—even if such accesses may be necessary to support a coercive signal.[32] While much of the discussion in the public domain conflates cyber espionage and cyber military operations, these are in fact distinct, just as they are in conventional domains. All forms of espionage, whether conducted in cyberspace or elsewhere, are fundamentally about collecting private information against another actor. Conversely, to be coercive, a cyber signal must be attributable and aim to disrupt, deny, degrade, and/or destroy data resident on computers and computer networks, or the systems themselves.

Cost-Benefit Calculus

Coercion theory assumes that states are rational actors who make cost–benefit calculations when determining how to respond to threats and inducements posed by other actors in the international system. The benefit side of the calculus involves how much the adversary values a particular course of action, while the cost side entails the price she anticipates paying in order to carry it out.[33] Coercion, put simply, forces the target state to choose between "making concessions or suffering the consequences."[34] Therefore, to be effective, a coercing state must issue a threat such that the target perceives it to be more costly to suffer those consequences than to concede.[35] To succeed, the coercer must know what the target state values and, therefore, what it can hold at risk to get the target to comply. * * * More important than an objective measure of costs versus benefits, however, is how

the adversary perceives them, which stems from "the magnitude of the dangers and profits the adversary sees ahead for a given path and the probability of their occurrence."[36] At its core, therefore, coercion is the manipulation of the target's perceptions of the cost–benefit balance of a particular course of action.[37]

Affecting an adversary's cost–benefit calculus may seem deceptively simple; in practice, it could fail across multiple dimensions. Coercion could fail because the target does not understand what the adversary values and, therefore, does not know how to appropriately tilt the cost–benefit calculus. This could stem from poor intelligence or, more fundamentally, from the fact that leaders are not always rational, utility-maximizing economic individuals. It may be difficult to quantify what a target state values if it involves something intangible (such as prestige) and, therefore, hard to assign a numerical value to the cost a coercer must threaten to impose to achieve a desired behavior. Relatedly, coercion could fail because states are not unitary actors and, therefore, there may be domestic political or bureaucratic organizational considerations that factor into what a target state values, how it perceives costs versus benefits, and acceptable levels of risk that the coercing state does not take into account. Moreover, even if the coercer knew what the adversary values, it could be politically difficult to make a sufficiently costly threat. Finally, coercion could fail due to cognitive limitations on the part of the target. Insights gleaned from prospect theory, for instance, have illustrated that individuals often fail to make rational, cost–benefit calculations when assessing risk (such as being more averse to losses than gains) and misunderstand sunk costs.[38]

Cost-Benefit Calculus in Cyberspace

In cyberspace, the state issuing a coercive threat must calculate what target to go after and the effect it seeks to deliver against it. Similarly, the target must also calculate whether it can absorb the cost and, if so, whether the coercer can ratchet up the cost to the target while avoiding too much cost itself. There are several categories of targets a state may consider attacking in cyberspace to coerce another state. Generally speaking, the class of target that inflicts the highest level of cost, a state's critical infrastructure, is typically the hardest to gain access to due to the technical complexities stemming from custom, tailored uses and advanced physical and virtual defensive measures commonly emplaced around these vital capabilities. The United States Department of Homeland Security has defined these crucial nodes as "... systems and assets, whether physical or virtual, so vital that the incapacity or destruction of such may have a debilitating impact on the security, economy, public health or safety, environment, or any combination of these matters."[39] This category includes critical infrastructure that is essential for everything from the safeguarding of nuclear regulatory systems to gas pipelines, and control systems that enable communication systems to work.[40] In the United States, many of these critical systems are run by private industry, but in states with parastatal enterprises (such as China), they remain centrally controlled by the government. Not all pieces of critical infrastructure, however, are universally valued across states. For instance, diverging state opinions over the ideal relationship between the citizen and the Internet has changed what states may consider critical infrastructure. Indeed, one accomplished Chinese academic with senior-level party connections noted to the authors that their "Great Fire Wall," which restricts citizen access to Western media sources, is considered part of China's critical infrastructure.[41] In this case, attacking a vital node that the state links to regime stability would be significantly costlier for China than the destruction of other types of critical infrastructure. Similarly, the recent hack of the U.S. Democratic

National Committee, allegedly committed by Russia or Russian-sponsored groups, is an example of how a state could target a critical component of a democratic regime—its electoral system.[42] This creates the potential for unintended escalation dynamics if the coercing state did not accurately calculate the extent to which the target values its electoral process.

Military capabilities may also be targeted by cyber attacks. These targets include everything from software running on advanced avionic platforms, to air defense assets, communication systems, and satellites tied into the Global Positioning System (GPS). Setting one's cyber sights on these military systems is similar in terms of costliness to targeting civilian critical infrastructure in that both are custom engineered and are typically difficult to gain access to and, therefore, mandate a highly tailored capability to exploit. Additionally, given that military systems are designed to be used during times of conflict, they tend to be more secure than civilian infrastructure because they are created with the expectation that they may be attacked via cyber means and, therefore, there is a greater emphasis placed on survivability and resilience early on in the development cycle.

From the target's perspective, attacks against critical national infrastructure and military capabilities are the most costly types of attacks, precisely because governments rely on these to survive in the international system and perform their basic functions. Coercing states may also choose to target the corporate sector of another state, depending on permissibility allowed by its own domestic legal regimes. Targets could include the online banking ability of a particular bank, the network of a leading defense contractor, or consumer information held by retailers. There is variation in terms of the cost to a coercer of targeting a particular company or sector of the economy, and this variation is largely a function of the resiliency and defenses that private actors choose to incorporate into their networks and systems. However, in terms of the perceived cost to the target state, generally speaking, cyber attacks against a private company are of a lower magnitude than attacks against critical national infrastructure and military capability, including command and control capabilities. Therefore, these kinds of attacks would only be useful to coerce a target state into conceding on relatively minor issues, if at all. This is analogous to conventional domains—dropping ordnance on a Walmart is fundamentally different from dropping ordnance on a communications node. However, there are two important caveats to this analysis. First, there may be some reputational costs a target may incur if attacks against certain private sectors actors are perceived to undermine the legitimacy of the regime. Second, there is likely to be important variation stemming from regime type, because some kleptocratic states may rely on the support of key industries or even companies to maintain regime stability. In these cases, attacks against business or industry may be comparable in terms of perceived cost to attacks against critical national infrastructure.

Regardless of the nature of the target, when sending a coercive signal in cyberspace, a policymaker must decide if she wants to produce a disruptive or destructive effect, the most salient distinction in the domain. Thus, a policymaker employing cyber attacks as a coercive instrument of state power must make a calculation of what effect is necessary to achieve the desired outcome. Destructive cyber attacks take two forms: the rare cyber attacks that generate an effect felt in the physical world, and the more common destruction of digital information, which can be almost as dire as a physical attack for many pieces of infrastructure. Disruptive attacks, conversely, seek to operationally diminish a system to the point that a user lacks confidence in its ability to perform some function. The latter may be more appealing to a coercing government because disruptive attacks enable functionality of the affected system to be restored once the attack is ceased and, thus, may aid in reassuring the target state, as will be discussed in a later

section. Notwithstanding the above discussion, states may be unable to perfectly tailor a cyber signal to affect a target's cost–benefit calculus. In other words, the technical complexities of certain types of costly operations may force less capable states into sending less costly signals that don't sufficiently alter the target's calculations. Governments may find cheap, fast, and easy cyber operations appealing even when they are less effective for the purposes of coercion. Put simply, governments may hit what they can get, rather than the optimal target, to coerce another state.

Credibility

Beyond being costly, a coercer's threat must be credible—the target must believe that the coercer will actually carry it out. A threat is credible if it is in a state's interests to carry it out and if that state has both the capability and the resolve, or political will, to do so.[43]*** A target may doubt a coercer's resolve because it doesn't believe that it is in the latter's interests to carry out the threat (this was particularly important in the context of nuclear deterrence); or because it doubts that the leader has sufficient domestic political support to carry out the threat;[44] or because the coercer has not established a reputation for carrying out past threats.[45] How individuals actually assess credibility, however, is poorly understood.[46]

Because credibility is difficult to convey but essential for coercion, states attempt to enhance the credibility of their threats by making them costly—through sending costly signals. James D. Fearon asserts that, "to be credible, a threat must have some cost or risk attached to it that might discourage an unresolved state from making it."[47] That's because talk is cheap: "words are cheap, not inherently credible when they emanate from an adversary, and sometimes too intimate a mode of expression."[48] There are two mechanisms states can employ to generate costly and, therefore, credible signals. First, states can tie their hands, limiting their choices and increasing the costs of backing down in the event the target of coercion does not comply with the terms of the threat. Second, states can sink costs, taking actions that are costly up front, such as mobilizing troops.[49] Using a similar framework, Robert Jervis describes how states can use indices to generate costly signals. Indices are "behaviors (either verbal or nonverbal) that the perceiver believes are inextricably linked to a characteristic that helps predict what the actor will do in the future."[50] Democracies, it has been argued, may have an advantage in costly signaling because they can more easily tie their hands through incurring audience costs.[51] Generating costly signals does not come without risks—indeed, costly signaling, paradoxically, is designed to increase the risk of war through locking in coercers to the use of force in order to (hopefully) avoid it.[52] Furthermore, there are myriad reasons states may seek to avoid a perfectly committing threat through sending an unambiguous costly signal, as previously noted.

Credibility in Cyberspace

* * * Credibility in cyberspace could be established via two mechanisms. First, establishing indices could create a venue for states to better communicate and demonstrate capability. However, indices of cyber power do not yet exist and are likely to be difficult to form. Therefore, at present, credibility is most likely to be inferred through costly signaling.

Cyber Power Indices

Establishing indices of cyber power contributes to the credibility of threats in cyberspace because it helps ascertain a state's capability.[53] Perfect information of another state's cyber capabilities does not exist; therefore, indices facilitate a state's assessment of another state's ability to carry out threats. In cyberspace, these indices include bud-

gets, growing and training cyber forces, establishing commands, and advertising participation in major cyber exercises.[54] When assessing capabilities in cyberspace, it is also critical to analyze how the latter would be employed. In particular, states in this domain may feel less constrained by international laws and norms (or even the threat of assured retaliation because, as this analysis demonstrates, these threats are difficult to credibly convey). This is because actors in the cyber domain tend to prefer to obfuscate their identities, leading some state actors to be more willing to act in ways that they would not otherwise be willing to on a battlefield or via formal diplomatic channels.

Estimating the capability of a cyberspace actor is a conundrum that has challenged scholars because the opaque nature of the domain confounds measurement efforts.[55] In the nuclear and chemical warfare arenas, there are methods to estimate the stockpiles of arms a nation holds and for which there exist treaties, accords, and international oversight institutions that monitor and limit the quantities of these weapons. However, in the cyber world there is no measure of relative strength; one cannot simply count the number of cyber tools the way one can count the number of warheads or the pounds of poison gas a country possesses. This is because offensive cyber capabilities are not universally lethal. A shroud of secrecy surrounds a nation-state's cyber capability and, therefore, creates a situation of imperfect information from which a policymaker must judge another state's actions and intent. Unlike in the conventional or nuclear realms, where states can reveal their capabilities to bolster credibility (or where the technology necessitates public tests to assess their effectiveness, such as nuclear tests), in the cyber realm states typically prefer to—and can—keep capabilities secret because revealing them would enable adversaries to defend against them and render the capabilities impotent. In other words, it is harder for states to reveal private information in cyberspace to enhance the credibility of their threats.

Moreover, governments face unique difficulties deriving intent based on observed capabilities because many states in the cyber domain find themselves coercing with the weapons they have, rather than the ones they may want or need. In other words, there may be a large gap between capabilities and intent. A distinction should be made here between what a state can measure about its own cyber capabilities and what its adversaries can assess. Measuring a rival's military strength has always been more difficult than introspective assessment due to military secrecy. However, the difference in cyberspace is that self-assessments of cyber capabilities (at least currently) also happen to be much harder to conduct because effective metrics have yet to be devised. This, in turn, makes assessing another state's cyber-military might even more difficult than for other domains and types of weapons.

Furthermore, measures of cyber power include factors beyond raw estimates of the size of cyber forces. While human capital and skill levels are important contributors to capability in the conventional domain, they are arguably even more vital in the cyber domain. Simply counting the number of cyber forces that a country may openly report as an assessment of cyber power does not take into account the differences in skill levels and a state's relative depth of cyber operations. A lack of homogeneity of material resources and technically proficient human capital across states means that one cannot precisely compare cyber capabilities between states. Comparing quantities of cyber forces is akin to comparing quantities of ships in a navy without distinguishing between tugboats and aircraft carriers. Regime type also factors into capabilities. Some states, such as Russia and China, place a greater emphasis on developing cyber forces to monitor their citizenry to detect unrest and preserve regime stability. From a technical standpoint, these operations are markedly different from conducting a destructive cyber attack against a state adversary. Democratic states have the advantage of devoting fewer cyber resources to population monitoring and, therefore, are freer to invest in adversary-centric capabilities.[56] Finally, what matters for capability in cyberspace is having the right operator, armed with the right capability, with access to a vulnerable target, rather than a numerical advantage. Capability and access imply that, regardless of how skilled an individual operator is, she will always be constrained by the cyber tools with which she has been equipped.

Cyber Operations as Costly Signals

In order to bolster the credibility of a threat, states often engage in costly signaling that ranges from national leaders' threats and troop mobilizations, to onshore trip wires, to the movement of aircraft carriers during times of crises.[57] All of these serve to demonstrate a state's capability and willingness to follow through with the terms of a threat. The greater the cost to the initiating state of producing a given signal, ceteris paribus, the more effective the signal is as an indication of the initiating state's resolve. Therefore, leaders could use cyber operations to convey their commitment to a particular course of action if they are sufficiently costly to produce.[58] Not all cyber operations are equally costly for the coercing state, however. Some operations are resource intensive, whereas other types of operations, such as a Distributed Denial of Service (DDoS) attacks and website defacements, can be conducted using minimal resources. In this regard, it is helpful to conceptualize interstate cyber signaling as existing along a spectrum where the greater the resource requirements, the costlier the signal is to produce, and the more resolve it demonstrates.

States can send signals via five broad categories of cyber attacks that are increasingly costly. The cheapest way to attack another entity is to conduct a DDoS attack. This is an operation where multiple compromised systems are directed by a central computer to flood another computer with information requests. When enough compromised computers are connected together they act as one botnet (a network of enslaved information technology devices that can be centrally controlled) and, if the network is large enough, it may overwhelm the processing capabilities of the intended target and force it to shut down. Examples of this include the alleged Iranian-based DDoS attacks against the U.S. financial sector in 2013, which took down the retail pages of over twenty-six corporations over a four-month time span.[59] These operations are on the far left of the spectrum because they are not inherently expensive to conduct (even though they may force the target to absorb high costs). The current going rate for a 24-hour DDoS attack is approximately $400–800 USD on the black market, depending on the size of the botnet being employed.[60] Furthermore, these operations are access agnostic in that, in order to conduct the operation, the attacker does not have to be pre-positioned with a back door into the target's network to facilitate the attack.

To send a costlier signal, a state could engage in operations designed to hack user accounts, including email and social media accounts. These are slightly costlier than DDoS attacks because they involve acquiring the credentials of an individual with access to the specific target (unless, in the unlikely scenario, the perpetrator can guess the target account's password). A well-known example of this is the 2013 hack of the Associated Press's Twitter feed, where hackers tweeted that there were two explosions in the White House and that the president was injured, prompting volatility in the stock market.[61]

Website defacement represents an additional level of cost for several reasons. First, it requires a minimal level of knowledge of webpage design coding. Second, website defacements involve delivering an effect to produce the observed defacement or redirection. Third, it is dependent on gaining access to the website administrator's account. Notable examples include the defacement of the United States Army's official website in 2015 and the Syrian Electronic Army's hack of a *Washington Post* website in 2015.[62]

Even more costly is gaining privileged access to internal networks for the purposes of data theft. This is more difficult than gaining access to a typical end user's account because it often relies on gaining access to internal systems and data repositories to which end users typically lack access. Most companies limit privileged accesses of this nature and compartmentalize this kind of information due to the potential consequences of a breach perpetrated against even a single actor with such extraordinary accesses (or by the actor herself). There is also an element of scale in these types of cases because attackers can acquire large amounts of private information, such as the contents of corporate email servers, billing records, personally identifiable information, and confidential information and documents pertaining to corporate strategy and development efforts. Two well-publicized examples of this kind of attack include the hack of the Department of Defense's Office of Personnel Management in 2015, allegedly committed by China, which compromised the personal information of nearly twenty-two million federal employees and their friends and family; and the 2014 attack against Sony Pictures Entertainment, attributed by the U.S. government to North Korea, which released embarrassing corporate communications, policies, and personally identifiable information of employees.[63]

The costliest type of signaling is a cyber attack that requires gaining access to well-defended or closed networks and seeks to disrupt or destroy key systems. Within this category, there is wide variation in the resources required to conduct these operations. The cost depends on the complexity of the attack and the relative difficulty of gaining access to the targeted systems. Since these types of operations disrupt or destroy data, they require customized tools that will produce the desired effect once inside the network. Furthermore, transacting in what is often a well-defended, restricted area is difficult not only because of the code-based language of exchange, but also because gaining access to closed and defended networks requires a significant investment of materiel resources and human capital. This investment includes not only the development of cyber tools to gain access to specific systems, but also the development of capabilities to exfiltrate information resident on the system and/or, more invasively, to completely subjugate the targeted machine. This investment extends beyond the development of cyber arms; it also requires extensive testing against a mockup of the intended target for both the developer and eventual cyber operator. The combination of technical know-how with financial resources severely limits the number of states that can be called genuine cyber powers—particularly since such investments may be long-term commitments without guaranteed successful outcomes. Indeed, some cyber operations may take years from the time the concept is conceived until the operation is implemented. Operations that involve gaining access to hardened systems that use closed networks not connected to the open Internet, such as the Stuxnet attack against Iran to delay its uranium enrichment program, are significantly costly. In the case of Stuxnet, custom-engineered cyber capabilities containing over fifteen thousand lines of code were required to manipulate Iran's customized Supervisory Control and Data Acquisition (SCADA) systems; this would certainly be costlier than a cyber attack that simply deleted information from servers to which an actor had gained access.[64] In this example, the Stuxnet attack would be significantly more costly to conduct than the 2012 Saudi Aramco breach, which destroyed data resident on over thirty thousand corporate computers, due to the time, material, and personnel requirements that would be mandated by the former compared to the later. Finally, this category of cyber attacks could require incurring the additional cost of gaining physical access to a network, particularly if it is closed, through using human operators.[65]

Operating militarily in cyberspace requires a skill set that is not uniformly distributed across all states and takes years to develop. Moreover, unlike traditional means of signaling, sending a signal via cyberspace is uniquely costly because, once an attack capability is used, it often cannot be used again. While it may be possible to replicate a capability, as already noted, there is little universality of cyber capabilities. Most critical targets are unique, and potential victims can prevent exploitation once the threat signature has been identified and incorporated into their defenses, which also compounds the difficulty of a sustained assault. Furthermore, once these tools are deployed they have a limited lifespan as routine defensive techniques and vulnerability patching may render a tool that took years to develop obsolete within seconds of employment.

Governments can also generate costly signals through manipulating the shared risk of war. This concept was championed by Schelling, who submits that credibility can be enhanced by exhibiting risky behavior, particularly during times of crisis.[66] States can demonstrate resolve through acting in a manner that increases the risk of war and/or increases political costs to the party issuing the threat, but falls short of initiating an attack. For instance, a state can raise the alert status of its forces or move naval fleets into close proximity of an area of hostiles. Neither of these signals is inherently costly; however, during a time of increased tension, such maneuvers increase the likelihood of war due to the potential misperception of intent and miscalculation. Furthermore, leaders can generate political costs through tying hands. In other words, politicians that are subjected to electoral sanctioning may generate self-imposed reputational costs by committing themselves to a course of action, which could put their political future in jeopardy if they waiver from it.[67]

In cyberspace, risk generation occurs by acting in overt ways that ensure the receiver perceives the signal, but falls short of a cyber attack. These types of actions include actively scanning networks, pinging pieces of key infrastructure, and perhaps even deploying beacons on compromised infrastructure. These operations can increase the risk of war because their intent cannot be surmised and could be interpreted as a precursory step to offensive cyber operations. However, these operations generate tradeoffs between intelligence collection and coercion strategies that policymakers should take into account.

Reassurance

Finally, to succeed, a coercive threat must have an element of reassurance, such that the target is made to believe that compliance with the terms of the threat will ensure the coercer does not mete out the threatened punishment regardless.[68] In other words, "the pain and suffering have to appear contingent on his behavior; it is not alone the threat that is effective—the threat of pain or loss if he fails to comply—but the corresponding assurance, possibly an implicit one, that he can avoid the pain or loss if he does comply."[69] Related to reassurance, Schelling also describes the importance of saving face—leaving a backdoor that enables that adversary to back down without paying too high a price in its own reputation and integrity. Coercers should therefore deliver the threat in a way that "decouple[s] an adversary's prestige and reputation from a dispute."[70]

Reassurance is also a difficult aspect of coercion. Todd S. Sechser argues that great powers encounter problems reassuring weaker states that are the targets of compellent threats because the very military capability that enhances the credibility of the stronger state's coercive threat makes it more difficult for the target to believe that the stronger state won't simply make more demands following the former's compliance with the initial threat.[71] This sheds light on the inherent tension

between the actions that enhance credibility versus those that buttress reassurance; the more a target believes the coercer will actually carry out a threat (credibility), the less likely the target believes the coercer will refrain from doing so in the event she complies (reassurance). * * *

Reassurance in Cyberspace

Assuring a target state that, once it capitulates to the aggressor's demands, the punishment will cease is perhaps the greatest obstacle to successful coercion in cyberspace. Effective command and control of a cyber attack are essential for reassurance. However, this is often exceedingly difficult in cyberspace depending on how and by whom an attack is carried out. For instance, 128 distinct cyber attacks were recorded against Estonian websites during May 2007 in response to the Estonian government's decision to relocate a Soviet-era war monument.[72] Since these assaults lacked a centralized controller, it would have been difficult for a unitary actor to provide the Estonian government with a credible assurance that the attacks would cease if the statue were returned to its original location (if we can assume this was the objective of the attacks). Furthermore, many states choose to employ cyber proxies to conduct cyber operations because they may not have the means to conduct the operation themselves or desire plausible deniability. Proxies may not act in the way a government desires depending on the proxy's incentives for participating in the attack and a government's ability to incentivize good behavior.[73] Furthermore, once the attack tool is released, it may be exceedingly difficult to stop. For instance, the Stuxnet computer virus was presumably never intended to propagate beyond Iranian nuclear centrifuges, but it infected over 100,000 computers worldwide before it could be stopped.[74] Due to the technical complexities of cyber capabilities and the collective action issues that may surround command and control of a cyber attack, a rational actor would be wise to second guess a reassurance that an assault will stop in exchange for submission.

A unique paradox occurs as an implication of this analysis. The ideal means to reassure a target is to engage in a disruptive cyber attack. Disruptive attacks are easily reversible and can, therefore, be credibly revoked if a target complies with a coercer's demands. However, disruptive attacks are not particularly costly and, therefore, are less credible than a destructive attack. A destructive attack can deliver an immediate effect, and it also generates irreversible costs to the target that can increase over time. Together, this implies that a coercive cyber attack that both reassures and maximizes costs for the target may be unachievable.

Assessing Warfighting Strategies in Cyberspace[75]

As the above discussion illustrates, cyber power is not an ideal independent tool of coercion. Nevertheless, governments may still choose to use cyber power to pursue warfighting strategies aimed at eroding a target's ability or willingness to resist due to the perceived ease or cost effectiveness of conducting cyber operations as opposed to conventional ones, particularly under conditions of conventional asymmetry—as well as their destructive nature in many cases.[76] * * *

Viable and Effective Strategies

Currently, we argue that there are three warfighting strategies that are likely to succeed using cyber power: attrition, denial, and decapitation. We claim that governments are most likely to achieve desired objectives using these strategies because the technical requirements and capabilities for carrying out these operations in cyberspace exist and because they can generate sufficient costs (in theory) to force a target government to concede. However, it is imperative to note that this discussion remains theoretical and its efficacy in practice is highly context dependent—whether a given government will concede to the demands of a coercing state will depend on the particular cost–benefit calculus it makes for a specific situation. While attrition, denial, and decapitation have different logics, what unites them is their discrete military application— these strategies are generally employed against military targets—and they are most likely to be successful when coupled with conventional military operations and/or diplomacy. In other words, the use of cyber power to undermine a government's ability or willingness to resist is not as effective in isolation from other instruments of state power.

ATTRITION

Attrition strategies seek to erode the adversary's military capability such that the target can no longer resist. Within the cyber domain, this strategy could include attacks that both degrade and destroy government or private networks and systems, depending on the latter's military utility. In cyberspace, the successful application of an attrition strategy would force a target to abandon a network or system through destroying it or building up a user's mistrust in it such that the target is forced to abandon its operation. A notable attribute of attrition strategies is that they seek to exhaust a target state's resources as it is forced to dedicate assets to protect or replicate capabilities in different and more secure manners. In particular, cyber raiding—targeting an enemy in its weakest areas—is a common tactic of attrition, where data is the equivalent of an enemy's provisions. Conventionally, raiding refers to stealing or destroying an enemy's provisions or equipment. These forays are commonly conducted behind an adversary's lines and are directed against their supply convoys and depots. In cyberspace, destroying or corrupting servers that handle military plans, air or ship tasking orders, or even defense developmental efforts, can prevent certain actions from occurring at the time they are urgently needed. More importantly, if they persist they will eventually erode a state's confidence in its networks and the data resident on them. It is difficult, if not impossible, to destroy a state's military capabilities through the exercise of cyber power alone. However, it is theoretically possible to force a state to suffer the gradual erosion of its capabilities—especially of its confidence in them—as vulnerable targets are attacked and as governments are forced to divert considerable resources to investigating and repairing them until the cost of continued resistance becomes unbearable.

DENIAL

A denial strategy involves increasing the costs to an adversary such that achieving a military objective—such as taking a piece of territory—becomes prohibitive or impossible.[77] As such, it could involve both a defensive component (increasing one's own defenses such that an adversary cannot go on the offense without incurring significant costs), as well as an offensive one (actively taking out enemy capabilities to deny the adversary the ability to achieve an objective).[78] In cyberspace, the targets of denial strategies mirror those of traditional domains of warfare, except that the effect achieved is delivered via a cyber operation. An adversary's Integrated Air Defense Systems (IADS), command and control apparatuses, and air traffic control systems are all examples of legitimate targets for a state pursuing a denial strategy. An example of using cyber means (coupled, in this case, with conventional military power) to target an adversary's air defense systems is the alleged 2007 Israeli air attack against Syria's nuclear facilities.[79] Unlike conventional approaches to denial, in cyber-

space, due to the increasing reliance of embedded technology in many modern battlefield systems, the surface from which these systems can be attacked has significantly increased. For instance, in conventional warfare the only way to remove tanks from a battlefield is to destroy them piecemeal from the air or ground. However, theoretically, it may be possible in the not too distant future (if not already) to use a cyber attack to render entire fleets of weapon systems inert at a critical moment. This concern has already been realized by many policymakers and is evident in the discussion over Chinese cyber espionage of the research and development of the Joint Strike Fighter.[80] On the other hand, the length of the timeframe under consideration could affect assessments of the potential costliness of denial strategies in cyberspace. For instance, cyber instruments could be used to disable, rather than destroy, an adversary's weapons systems or command and control, rendering an attack costly in the short term but less costly than the ostensibly permanent destruction of those systems through conventional means.[81]

DECAPITATION

Decapitation strategies seek to achieve strategic paralysis by targeting command and control centers, leadership, critical economic nodes, and key weapons systems.[81] Currently, it is technically possible to use cyber attacks to shut down a command and control node. However, given that most states employ secondary and tertiary redundant systems (for example, analogue or even courier-based communication), as well as separate communication networks (for example, multiple classified and unclassified networks), the impact of this type of operation could be short lived. Nevertheless, successfully targeting a critical command and control node, such as the U.S. government's Secure Internet Protocol Router Network (SIPRNET) or Joint Worldwide Intelligence Communications System

(JWICS), would have immediate and significant material and psychological effects. Therefore, governments should either take into account temporal limitations when targeting command and control networks, or ensure that they also target all additional means of adversary communication. Conventional military operations that target command and control facilities can wipe out entire communications networks, for example, through dropping ordnance on a facility. In contrast, cyber operations can typically target a single or limited number of communications nodes or networks due to the compartmentalized nature of each network. This would therefore require multiple distinct cyber operations to achieve near-complete command and control paralysis. Furthermore, even if cyber attacks could be used to successfully target a government's primary communications networks, backup systems would likely need to be defeated through traditional forms of electronic warfare or conventional operations (for example, jamming transmissions, capturing carriers, or cutting telephone lines or undersea cables). Altogether, this analysis implies that one is more likely to observe decapitation strategies employed at lower echelons of command, such as troops in the field, where there are typically fewer redundant systems, or against less-capable state adversaries.

Viable and Ineffective Strategies

Warfighting strategies in cyberspace can be technically viable but ineffective because they cannot force the adversary to incur sufficiently high costs to prompt a change in her behavior. Much of the activity that currently occurs in cyberspace falls into this category—actors can harass, annoy, or otherwise inconvenience each other. Indeed, those who claim that the threat of a cyber Armageddon is exaggerated focus on these kinds of cyber attacks.[82]

INTIMIDATION

An intimidation strategy is designed to directly address a state's domestic audiences and sometimes, national policymakers. Actions as part of an intimidation strategy do not cause significant damage and are typically tailored to undermine a government's legitimacy or convince domestic audiences that the government is powerless, prompting a loss of confidence by the public.[83] In cyberspace, intimidation typically takes the form of website defacement and email spamming campaigns. While these operations are technically easy to conduct because they involve fewer resources and a lower skill set compared to other types of operations, they cause minimal cost to the recipient. The effect these attacks produce is typically perceived as an annoyance, rather than a strategic message, because these types of attacks are fairly common and easy from which to recover. Therefore, they are unlikely to be sufficiently costly to force targeted governments to change their behavior. Indeed, observed intimidation strategies, such as the 2008 defacements of Georgian government websites portraying President Mikheil Saakashvili as Adolf Hitler, have had no real effect.[84]

Nonviable and Ineffective Strategies

The two paradigmatic strategies of traditional coercion that currently have the least utility in cyberspace are punishment and risk. While there has been considerable brouhaha in public and even government spheres regarding the potentially dire consequences of a "World War 3.0" or a "cyber Pearl Harbor," these are largely unrealistic given the current state of the domain.[85] However, as we will describe below, changes in modern societies' interconnectivity and reliance on automated systems, as well as advances in military cyber technologies, could change the value of these strategies.[86]

PUNISHMENT

Originally stemming from the work of Giulio Douhet, an Italian general and early proponent of the strategic use of air power, punishment strategies are designed to inflict sudden, large-scale pain and devastation on an adversary's civilian population until the panic-stricken citizenry demands an end to the war.[87] Indeed, Douhet envisioned that a single successful air raid on an enemy's population center could " . . . spread terror through the nation and quickly break down [a state's] material and moral resistance."[88] This concept was further refined by Schelling and modern coercion theorists, who applied it to the strategic use of nuclear weapons; holding an adversary's population at risk of extreme destruction is the foundation of modern deterrence theory.[89]

In theory, inflicting punishment in cyberspace would involve the use of cyber power to cause virtual and physical damage to civilian infrastructure and population centers. This could entail attacks against essential services, such as water treatment facilities, transportation, air traffic control systems, nuclear power plants, electrical grids, food safety systems, waste management systems, etc. However, in practice, there are two critical elements of punishment that cannot be sustained given the current nature of the cyber domain: first, the immediate and sudden nature of an attack; and second, the scale and scope of the pain. Put simply, governments cannot kill a lot of people in a very short period of time using cyber weapons; the magnitude of the pain states are currently capable of inflicting via the cyber domain alone is hardly comparable to the devastation wrought by conventional or nuclear attacks against cities. Access requirements and the cus-

tomized nature of cyber capabilities render it nearly impossible to launch a time-dependent, highly coordinated cyber campaign of the scale required to inflict severe costs on enemy populations. The scope is also nearly impossible to achieve because it would require an extraordinarily large number of discrete and distinct cyber attacks. As discussed in prior sections, there is limited universal lethality of cyber weapons, which means that governments would have to develop unique accesses and distinct tools for each targeted system. Moreover, there is no guarantee that an effect can be delivered as planned. Additionally, it is difficult to envision a government entity being able to sustain a cyber assault against multiple key pieces of infrastructure in order to push a society to a breaking point before the target moves to mitigate the onslaught through preestablished redundant mechanisms and/or cyber or kinetic military operations.

MANIPULATION OF RISK

Punishment and risk are fundamentally related—both involve targeting an adversary's population centers to force the government to concede to the coercer's demands. However, unlike punishment strategies that call for immediate and decisive destruction, risk strategies entail gradually escalating the intensity and scope of attacks against civilian targets.[90] There is a critical psychological element to the manipulation of risk in that what drives concessions is the threat and prospect of future pain. This requires that the coercing state can sustain and ratchet up an assault over time.

Like punishment, the manipulation of risk does not translate well into cyberspace. Carrying out a comprehensive, tiered cyber campaign plan to create the ratcheting effect of punishment that Schelling proscribes is exceedingly difficult for reasons already articulated. To wit, this would require a significant planning effort and mandate a costly access and capability development program. Furthermore, risk strategies do not rely upon the sudden and intense destruction that are envisioned by punishment strategies, but instead are designed to be employed over time. In order to be effective, the attack would have to be maintained against an adversary that would likely be active in trying to stop or mitigate the effects of the onslaught. Presumably, if a state is at the technical level where it is susceptible to large-scale cyber attacks, it also has the wherewithal to defend against them over time. Finally, the effective employment of a risk strategy in cyberspace would require an impossibly high level of control by the coercing government over the cyber tools it would employ against an adversary. According to Schelling, risk is most likely to succeed when an action, "once initiated, causes minimal harm if compliance is forthcoming and great harm if compliance is not forthcoming, is consistent with the time schedule of feasible compliance, is beyond recall once initiated, and cannot be stopped by the party that started it but *automatically* stops upon compliance, with all this fully understood by the adversary."[91] Indeed, the risks of using cyber power—effects getting beyond the control of the initiating state in unanticipated and potentially undesirable ways—are precisely the opposite of the calibrated manipulation of risk Schelling envisions.

Future Trends in Viability and Effectiveness

The negligible utility of punishment and risk strategies rests on the current state of technology and the dependence (and, therefore, vulnerability) of modern societies on cyber-enabled essential services. Changes along either of these dimensions—

technical viability and/or the costs that can be imposed on civilian populations—would alter the feasibility and effectiveness of these strategies. For instance, the dawn of the "Internet of Things" (a concept that depicts a not-too-distant future where everything from an individual's toaster and refrigerator to a city's garbage collection and other essential services are automated and connected to the Internet) could make it possible for governments to impose high and devastating costs on society through cyber means.[92] Moreover, it is conceivable that, as societies remove human redundancy through increased automation and become more dependent on interconnected networks of services, punishment and risk strategies could become more effective as the attack surface expands and more targets become vulnerable to a cyber attack.

Additionally, punishment and risk strategies could become more viable due to better investment in human capital, decreasing costs of planning and conducting large-scale cyber campaigns, increased government spending on developing cyber capabilities, and gaining and maintaining accesses to potential target sets, and the unknown unknowns of potentially disruptive technological innovations that make these attacks easier.

Strategic Implications of the Coercive Use of Cyber Power

This analysis explores the applicability of traditional theories of coercion to the cyber domain. We identify four key elements of coercion—communication, cost–benefit calculus, credibility, and reassurance—and assess how each manifests itself in cyberspace. We then analyze the utility of various warfighting strategies that seek to undermine an adversary's ability and/or willingness to resist and find that, based on the current state of the field, only three—attrition, denial, and decapitation—are likely to be useful for aspiring coercers in cyberspace. However, even these strategies are most useful in conjunction with conventional instruments of power and/or diplomacy; cyber power is rarely, if ever, independently decisive. For policymakers, this suggests that, especially if a coercing state has an asymmetrical advantage in other elements of national power, using cyber power to enable espionage, sabotage, and other shaping operations to support a cross-domain coercive strategy may be a more effective use of cyber capabilities than employing it as an independent instrument of state power.

This framework also highlights the importance of indices and developing an understanding of another state's intentions in cyberspace due to the high risk of misperception, which can lead to unintended outcomes and inadvertent escalation. A policy implication of this is that states should focus intelligence-collection efforts on developing an advanced understanding of the cyber capabilities and aspirations of potential adversaries. In addition to indices, states may also send signals through the use of cyber attacks. However, since neither of these signaling mechanisms is inherently clear, the most likely way to convey the intent behind an action in cyberspace is to ensure attribution and couple the event with a diplomatic message or place it within the context of a conventional military operation. Furthermore, for cyber power to be an effective coercive tool, the target needs to believe that an attack will cease once she complies with the coercer's demands. This would require assurances that would have to come via established means that often do not yet exist. Providing a credible reassurance is difficult because many types of cyber attacks, such as DDoS attacks, can come from numerous users and make it difficult for the threatening state to credibly demonstrate it exerts control over a decentralized network of attackers. This leads to a paradox in which the type of cyber attack that is most likely to aid in reassuring a victim may

also not be able to generate the punishment that would be necessary for capitulation.

Cyber power can be used as a coercive instrument of state power but, once the theory of coercion meets the reality of cyber operations, many attractive targets may become too costly and out of reach for a state to attack in a timely manner. Therefore, governments are more likely to pursue coercive strategies that allow for a wide variety of targets that are more easily accessible than hardened critical infrastructure. In other words, long development timelines and access constraints often mean that policymakers cannot attack their ideal target(s) in a timely manner and, therefore, are more likely to pursue warfighting strategies that do not necessitate sudden and intense devastation but, rather, inflict costs against vulnerable public and private interests. Given current levels of dependency on technology, this type of attack would provide damaging, but limited, effects. This has unique and potentially troubling implications. Since the end of the Second World War, many states have sought to limit their coercive attacks to key pieces of government and military infrastructure out of ethical and legal concerns surrounding targeting civilian infrastructure (and due to the domestic and international political costs of doing so). However, given that in cyberspace much of the vulnerable infrastructure is owned by private industry, policymakers may reevaluate norms against targeting these systems as they pursue attrition, denial, or decapitation strategies. Cyber warfighting strategies that intentionally target civilian infrastructure, such as punishment and risk, are currently nonviable and ineffective. However, as technology evolves and the Internet of Things makes societies both more interconnected and vulnerable, states may find strategies that explicitly aim to wreak havoc on civilian populations more effective. Together, this suggests that, at the domestic level, governments should strive to continue to build resiliency into civilian networks and, at the international level, norms governing appropriate targeting in the cyber domain are urgently needed.

NOTES

1. Thomas C. Schelling makes the important distinction between compellence and deterrence. The former involves the threat or limited application of force to change an adversary's behavior, while the latter involves the threat of force (or pain, in Schelling's parlance), to preserve the status quo. See Thomas C. Schelling, *The Strategy of Conflict* (Cambridge, MA: Harvard University Press, 1960) and idem., *Arms and Influence* (New Haven, CT: Yale University Press, 2008), 69–86. Robert J. Art elaborates on this concept. See Robert J. Art, "To What Ends Military Power?" *International Security* 4, no. 4 (Spring 1980): 3–35.

2. The authors are grateful to Jack Snyder for pointing out the distinction between coercion and warfighting strategies.

3. Schelling, *Arms and Influence*, 3. Emphasis in the original. Alexander L. George et al. also emphasize that coercion can involve both the threat or limited application of military power. See Alexander L. George, David K. Hall, and William R. Simons, eds., *The Limits of Coercive Diplomacy: Laos, Cuba, Vietnam* (Boston: Little, Brown and Company, 1971), 2, 18. Lawrence Freedman distinguishes between coercion, as defined by Schelling, and "strategic coercion," which is "the deliberate and purposive use of overt threats to influence another's strategic choices." See Lawrence Freedman, "Strategic Coercion," in *Strategic Coercion: Concepts and Cases*, ed. Lawrence Freedman (Oxford: Oxford University Press, 1998), 15.

4. Robert A. Pape, *Bombing to Win: Air Power and Coercion in War* (Ithaca, NY: Cornell University Press, 1996), 4. It is important to note, however, that Pape's reference to coercion in this context is distinct from deterrence; Schelling uses the umbrella term "coercion" to refer to both compellence and deterrence. See also Daniel L. Byman and Matthew Waxman, *The Dynamics of Coercion: American Foreign Policy and the Limits of Military Might* (Cambridge: Cambridge University Press, 2002), 3.

5. Schelling, *Arms and Influence*, 2–6. Pape, *Bombing to Win*, 13.

6. Schelling, *Arms and Influence*, 18–34. Schelling links technological advances in the power to hurt with the increased "importance of war and threats of war as techniques of influence, not of destruction; of coercion and deterrence, not of conquest and defense; of bargaining and intimidation," 33.

7. Richard A. Clarke and Robert K. Knake, *Cyber War: The Next Threat to National Security and What to Do About It* (New York: Ecco, 2012), 1–8.

8. It is widely accepted that deterrence may be easier to achieve, but harder for social scientists to observe due its negative object (for example, we only observe deterrence failures). Conversely, compellence is easy to observe but more difficult to achieve for precisely the same reason—there are reputational costs associated with being seen to back down and concede to an adversary's demands. Leaders who are successfully deterred could point to a variety of reasons they chose to not alter the status quo without losing face. See the discussion in Schelling, *Arms and Influence*, 74–75; Robert J. Art, "Coercive Diplomacy: What Do We Know?" in *The United States and Coercive Diplomacy*, ed. Robert J. Art and Patrick M. Cronin (Washington, DC: United States Institute of Peace Press, 2003), 361–62.

9. See, for example, Pape, *Bombing to Win*; Todd S. Sechser, "Goliath's Curse: Coercive Threats and Asymmetric Power," *International Organization* 64, no. 4 (October 2010): 627–60; Wallace J. Thies, *When Governments Collide: Coercion and Diplomacy in the Vietnam Conflict, 1964–1968* (Berkeley: University of California Press, 1980); Alexander L. George, *Forceful Persuasion: Coercive Diplomacy as an Alternative to War* (Washington, DC: United States Institute of Peace Press, 1991); Art, "Coercive Diplomacy," Alexander L. George and William E. Simons, eds., *The Limits of Coercive Diplomacy*, 2nd ed. (Boulder, CO: Westview Press, 1990); Byman and Waxman, *Dynamics of Coercion*; Thomas J. Christensen, *Worse Than a Monolith: Alliance Politics and Problems of Coercive Diplomacy in Asia* (Princeton, NJ: Princeton University Press, 2011).

10. Of course, this is not an exhaustive list of all of the factors that contribute to successful coercion. For example, George and Simons identify nine conditions that favor coercive diplomacy: clarity of objective, strong motivation, asymmetry of motivation, sense of urgency, strong leadership, domestic support, international support, fear of unacceptable escalation, and clarity of terms. See George and Simons, eds., *Limits of Coercive Diplomacy*, 279–91. However, we propose that these various lists and factors could be grouped into the four main conditions identified above.

11. However, it is important to note a caveat that, in some instances, sending ambiguous signals can be advantageous for the purposes of coercion. Particularly in the context of nuclear bargaining, the threat that leaves something to chance—precisely because the risk of nuclear war generates extraordinary costs—may help a coercing state. See Schelling, *Strategy of Conflict*, chap. 8.

12. Idem., *Arms and Influence*, 3–4.

13. Jack Snyder and Erica D. Borghard, "The Cost of Empty Threats: A Penny, Not a Pound," *American Political Science Review* 105, no. 3 (August 2011): 429; Robert Jervis, "Deterrence Theory Revisited," *World Politics* 31, no. 2 (January 1979): 303; Richard Ned Lebow, *Between Peace and War: The Nature of International Crises* (Baltimore, MD: Johns Hopkins University Press, 1981), 29–27; Glen H. Snyder and Paul Diesing, *Conflict Among Nations: Bargaining, Decision Making, and System Structure in International Crises* (Princeton, NJ: Princeton University Press, 1977), 213–15, 220. Even Schelling acknowledges that "most commitments are ultimately ambiguous in detail," *Arms and Influence*, 67.

14. Freedman, "Strategic Coercion," 18; James D. Fearon, "Rationalist Explanations for War," *International Organization* 49, no. 3 (Summer 1995): 379–414.

15. Robert Jervis, *Perception and Misperception in International Politics* (Princeton, NJ: Princeton University Press, 1976).

16. Ibid., 117–202. Robert Jervis, "Signaling and Perception: Drawing Inferences and Projecting Images," in *Political Psychology*, ed. Kristen Renwick Monroe (Mahwah, NJ: Lawrence Erlbaum Associates, 2002), 306–8. See also Robert Jervis, *The Logic of Images in International Relations* (New York: Columbia University Press, 1970).

17. Jervis, "Signaling and Perception," 304.

18. Ibid., 300.

19. For further reference, see Andru E. Wall, "Demystifying the Title 10-Title 50 Debate: Distinguishing Military Operations, Intelligence Activities & Covert Action," *Harvard National Security Journal* 3 (December 2011): 85–142.

20. For more on norms and international law as they pertain to the cyber domain, see Catherine Lotrionte, "A Better Defense: Examining the United States' New Norms-Based Approach to Cyber Deterrence," *Georgetown Journal of International Affairs* 8, no. 10 (April 2014): 75–88; Martha Finnemore, "Cultivating International Cyber Norms," in *America's Cyber Future: Security and Prosperity in the Information Age,* ed. Kristin M. Lord and Travis Sharp (Washington, DC: Center for a New American Security, 2011).

21. For instance, it is easy to imagine how a single signal could get lost in the over eighty-eight thousand petabytes of IP traffic that are estimated to transverse the Internet per month.

22. For further discussion of risks surrounding the ambiguity of intent in cyberspace, see Shawn W. Lonergan, "Cooperation under the Cybersecurity Dilemma," in *Confronting Inequality: Wealth, Rights, and Power,* ed. Hugh Liebert, Thomas Sherlock, and Cole Pinheiro (New York: Sloan, 2016).

23. Geoffrey B. Demarest, "Espionage in International Law," *Denver Journal of International Law and Policy* 24 (1995): 321–48.

24. Jervis, *Logic of Images in International Relations,* 86–87.

25. Herbert Lin, "Escalation Dynamics and Conflict Termination in Cyberspace," *Strategic Studies Quarterly* 47 (2012): 57.

26. For further reference on attribution, see Thomas Rid and Ben Buchanan, "Attributing Cyber Attacks," *Journal of Strategic Studies* 38, no. 1–2 (2015): 4–37; Jon R. Lindsay, "Tipping the Scales: The Attribution Problem and the Feasibility of Deterrence against Cyberattack," *Journal of Cybersecurity* 1, no. 1 (2015): 1–15.

27. Gerhard Munz and Georg Carle, "Real-Time Analysis of Flow Data for Network Attack Detection" (paper presented at the 10th IFIP/IEEE International Symposium on Integrated Network Management, Munich, Germany, 21 May 2007).

28. Developing unique signatures of attackers and code developers is becoming more common as exploits become increasingly sophisticated and threat data is shared among cyber security practitioners. Leon Panetta, "Remarks by Secretary Panetta on Cybersecurity to the Business Executives for National Security, New York City," 11 October 2012, http://archive.defense.gov/transcripts/transcript.aspx?transcriptid=5136. For a review of Panetta's speech, see Jack Goldsmith, "The Significance of Panetta's Cyber Speech and the Persistent Difficulty of Deterring Cyberattacks," *Lawfare,* 15 October 2012.

29. Jervis, *The Logic of Images in International Relations,* 139–44.

30. Damian Paletta and Felicia Schwartz, "Pentagon Deploys Cyberweapons against Islamic State," *Wall Street Journal,* 29 February 2016.

31. Goldsmith, "Panetta's Cyber Speech."

32. This, of course, creates something of a paradox for a coercing state because it may need to gain prior access to a system or network (which requires obfuscation and avoiding attribution) to send a subsequently attributable coercive signal. The one caveat to this is that cyber espionage could be used to conduct a data breach of sensitive information that can later be released to embarrass or otherwise intimidate some actor.

33. Byman and Waxman, *Dynamics of Coercion,* 11.

34. Pape, *Bombing to Win,* 12.

35. Byman and Waxman, *Dynamics of Coercion,* 10. Pape, *Bombing to Win,* 15–16.

36. Byman and Waxman, *Dynamics of Coercion,* 11.

37. George, *Forceful Persuasion,* 11–14. George also points out that the more expansive or extreme the demands of the coercing state are, the costlier the threat must be to secure compliance.

38. Byman and Waxman, *Dynamics of Coercion,* 10–14. Schelling, *Arms and Influence,* 86. Jack S. Levy, "Prospect Theory, Rational Choice, and International Relations," *International Studies Quarterly* 41, no. 1 (March 1997): 87–112.

39. "National Infrastructure Protection Plan: Partnering to Enhance Protection and Resiliency," *Department of Homeland Security,* 2009, https://www.dhs.gov/xlibrary/assets/NIPP_Plan.pdf.

40. Control systems are defined as, "Computer-based systems used within many infrastructure and industries to monitor and control sensitive processes and physical functions. These systems typically collect measurement and operational data from the field, process and display the information, and relay control commands to local or remote equipment or human-machine interfaces (operators)," ibid., 109.

41. Professor at Peking University, Beijing, China, in discussion with the authors, 17 June 2015.

42. David E. Sanger and Eric Schmitt, "Spy Agency Consensus Grows That Russia Hacked D.N.C.," *New York Times,* 26 July 2016.

43. Schelling, *Arms and Influence,* 36.

44. Randall L. Schweller, *Unanswered Threats: Political Constraints on the Balance of Power* (Princeton, NJ: Princeton University Press, 2008).

45. Schelling asserts that a country's image—others' expectations about how it is likely to behave—is "one of the few things worth fighting for." This is due to what Schelling describes as the interdependence of threats. See Schelling, *Arms and Influence,* 124, 55–59. Also see Herman Kahn, *On Thermonuclear War* (Princeton, NJ: Princeton University Press, 1960), 566. For a critique of the importance of having a reputation for resolve, see Jonathan Mercer, *Reputation and International Politics* (Ithaca, NY: Cornell University Press, 1996).

46. Robert Jervis, "Deterrence and Perception," *International Security* 7, no. 3 (Winter 1982–1983): 9.

47. James D. Fearon, "Signaling Foreign Policy Interests: Tying Hands Versus Sinking Costs," *Journal of Conflict Resolution* 41, no. 1 (February 1997): 69.

48. Schelling, *Arms and Influence,* 150.

49. Fearon, "Signaling Foreign Policy Interests," 70. Schelling also refers to these dynamics in his discussion of commitment through the use of bridge burning, trip wire forces, plate glass windows, and engaging a nation's honor and prestige through public commitments. Schelling, *Arms and Influence,* 44–49.

50. Jervis, "Signaling and Perception," 300.

51. The idea that democracies have an advantage in costly signaling has been the conventional wisdom in the literature, although Jessica L. Weeks argues that autocratic regimes are also capable of generating audience costs. Jessica L. Weeks, "Autocratic Audience Costs: Regime Type and Signaling Resolve," *International Organization* 62, no. 1 (Winter 2008): 35–64. For a different critique of audience costs logic, see Snyder and Borghard, "The Cost of Empty Threats."

52. Fearon, "Signaling Foreign Policy Interests," 82–83.

53. Robert Jervis, *The Logic of Images in International Relations*, 26–28.

54. In a general sense, it may be easier for democracies to showcase their level of cyber power due to greater institutionalized transparency over military organizations and budgets compared to authoritarian regimes.

55. For example, see H. J. Seo, Yoon-Cheol Choy, and SoonJa Hong, "A Study on the Methodology to Evaluate the Level of Nation's Capability for Cyber War" (paper presented at the 12th Annual International Workshop on Information Security Applications, Korea, August 2011).

56. Authoritarian states have gone to extensive efforts to institute hierarchies in their Internet infrastructure so that they can keep their citizens from accessing material that they deem may threaten regime stability. However, the West has pursued a free and open Internet that is largely devoid of state censorship. These conflicting visions for the Internet were evident in the 2012 breakdown of the United Nations' International Telecommunications Union's World Conference on International Communication (WCIT) when, in the wake of Arab Spring, many Middle Eastern states joined a voting bloc led by China and Russia to press for a treaty that limited the openness of the Internet and removed protections on free speech and human rights. In response, Canada, the United States, and many European states refused to ratify the treaty. This divide has given rise to extensive debates about Internet governance, state sovereignty in cyberspace, and the "Balkanization" of the Internet. See James D. Fielder, "The Internet and Dissent in Authoritarian State," in *Conflict and Cooperation in Cyberspace: The Challenge to National Security*, ed. Panayotis A. Yannakogeorgos and Adam B. Lowther (Boca Raton, FL: Taylor and Francis, 2014); Stephen K. Gourley, "Cyber Sovereignty," in *Conflict and Cooperation in Cyberspace*; Michael N. Schmitt, ed., *Tallinn Manual on the International Law Applicable to Cyber Warfare* (Cambridge: Cambridge University Press, 2013); Dana Polatin-Reuben and Joss Wright, "An Internet with Brics Characteristics: Data Sovereignty and the Balkanisation of the Internet" (paper presented at the 4th USENIX Workshop on Free and Open Communications on the Internet, San Diego, CA, 18 August 2014).

57. Fearon, "Signaling Foreign Policy Interests." Schelling, *Arms and Influence*. Christian Le Mière, *The Return of Gunboat Diplomacy*," *Survival* 53, no. 5 (October–November 2011): 53–68.

58. Though nonstate actors may engage in these activities, the scope of this article is limited to state-to-state exchanges. Furthermore, while Fearon discusses both tying hands and sinking costs as mechanisms for generating costly signals, we focus on cyber operations as sunk costs because the tying hands logic is a poor fit for the cyber domain. The only likely allegory to tying hands in cyberspace is the ability, in some instances, to create automaticity by initiating an autonomous offensive cyber response.

59. Deloitte CIO Journal, "DDoS Attacks on U.S. Banks: Worst Yet to Come?" *Wall Street Journal*, 19 February 2013.

60. Data comes from black markets accessed on the Dark Net on 17 March 2016. We are grateful to "BillyBear" for his assistance with this.

61. David Jackson, "AP Twitter Feed Hacked; No Attack at White House," *USA Today*, 23 April 2013.

62. Polly Mosendz, "Syrian Electronic Army Claims to Have Hacked U.S. Army Website," *Newsweek*, 8 June 2015. Brain Fung, "The Syrian Electronic Army Just Hacked the *Washington Post*, Again," *Washington Post*, 14 May 2015.

63. Julie Hirschfeld Davis, "Hacking of Government Computers Exposed 21.5 Million People," *New York Times*, 9 July 2015. David E. Sanger and Nicole Perlroth, "U.S. Said to Find North Korea Ordered Cyberattack on Sony" *New York Times*, 17 December 2014.

64. Langner, "Stuxnet's Secret Twin." Eric Oliver, "Stuxnet: A Case Study in Cyberwarfare," in *Conflict and Cooperation in Cyberspace*. Jon R. Lindsay, "Stuxnet and the Limits of Cyber Warfare," *Security Studies* 22, no. 3 (July–September 2013): 365–404.

65. Owens, Dam, and Lin, eds., *Cyberattack Capabilities*, 83–89.

66. Schelling, *Arms and Influence*, chap. 3.

67. Fearon, "Signaling Foreign Policy Interests." For an alternative point of view, see Snyder and Borghard, "The Cost of Empty Threats."

68. For a broader discussion of assurance strategies, see Jeffrey W. Knopf, "Varieties of Assurance," *Journal of Strategic Studies* 35, no. 3 (April 2002): 375–399.

69. Schelling, *Arms and Influence*, 4.

70. Ibid., 125.

71. Sechser, "Goliath's Curse,"

72. Andreas Schmidt, "The Estonian Cyberattacks," in *A Fierce Domain: Conflict in Cyberspace, 1986 to 2012*, ed. Jason Healey (Vienna, VA: Cyber Conflict Studies Association, 2013), 182.

73. For further reference, see Erica D. Borghard and Shawn W. Lonergan, "Can States Calculate the Risks of Using Cyber Proxies?" *Orbis* 60, no. 3 (Summer 2016): 395–416.

74. Kim Zetter, "Report: Obama Ordered Stuxnet to Continue After Bug Caused It to Spread Wildly," *Wired*, 1 June 2012.

75. For further discussion of the likely impact of cyber on strategy in general, see Joseph S. Nye, Jr., "Nuclear Lessons for Cyber Security?" *Strategic Studies Quarterly* (Winter 2011): 18–36.

76. Anti-Access/Area-Denial strategies currently pursued by states to thwart the movement and maneuver of conventionally superior militaries in a theater of operations typically contain a strong element of cyber power. See, for example, Erica D. Borghard and Shawn W. Lonergan, "Will Air-Sea Battle Be 'Sunk' by Cyberwarriors?" *National Interest*, 8 December 2014.

77. Robert Pape defines coercion by denial as "using military means to prevent the target from attaining its political objectives or territorial goals." *Bombing to Win*, 13.

78. Byman and Waxman, *Dynamics of Coercion*, 78–82.

79. Clarke and Knake, *Cyber War*, 1–8.

80. David E. Sanger, "With Spy Charges, U.S. Draws a Line That Few Others Recognize," *New York Times*, 19 May 2014.

81. Pape, *Bombing to Win*, 79.

82. Thomas Rid, *Cyber War Will Not Take Place* (Oxford: Oxford University Press, 2013), xiv–xv.

83. Andrew H. Kydd, and Barbara F. Walter, "The Strategies of Terrorism," *International Security* 31, no. 1 (Summer 2006): 66,

84. Jeffrey Carr, *Inside Cyber Warfare*, 2nd ed. (Sebastopol, CA: O'Reilly, 2012), 183–84. Andreas Hagen, "The Russo-Georgian War 2008," *A Fierce Domain*, ed. Healy. Ronald J. Deibert,

Rafal Rohozinski, and Masashi Crete–Nishihata, "Cyclones in Cyberspace: Information Shaping and Denial in the 2008 Russia–Georgia War," *Security Dialogue* 43, no. 1 (February 2012): 3–24.

85. See Michael Joseph Gross, "World War 3.0," *Vanity Fair,* 30 March 2012; Erik Gartzke, "The Myth of Cyberwar: Bringing War in Cyberspace Back Down to Earth," *International Security* 38, no. 2 (Fall 2013): 41–73.

86. The utility of punishment or risk strategies in general is beyond the scope of this discussion.

87. Giulio Douhet, *The Command of the Air,* trans. Dino Ferrari (New York: Coward-McCann, 1942), 57–58.

88. Ibid., 57.

89. Beyond Schelling, see, for instance, Patrick M. Morgan, *Deterrence: A Conceptual Analysis* (Beverly Hills, CA: Sage Publications, 1977); Robert Powell, *Nuclear Deterrence Theory: The Search for Credibility* (Cambridge: Cambridge University Press, 1990); Kahn, *On Thermonuclear War.*

90. Schelling, *Arms and Influence,* 3. Also see Pape's discussion of manipulation of risk in *Bombing to Win,* 66–69.

91. Schelling, *Arms and Influence,* 89. Italics in the original.

92. Jayavardhana Gubbi et al., "Internet of Things (IoT): A Vision, Architectural Elements, and Future Directions," *Future Generation Computer Systems* 29, no. 4 (September 2013): 1645–60.

Caitlin Talmadge

WOULD CHINA GO NUCLEAR?
Assessing the Risk of Chinese Nuclear Escalation in a Conventional War with the United States

Despite China's longstanding no-first-use pledge, both U.S. and Chinese experts have recently raised concerns about the possibility of Chinese nuclear escalation in the event of a conventional war with the United States—particularly if the United States employs concepts of operation that emphasize early attacks on Chinese command and control (C2) networks, ballistic missile submarines (SSBNs), mobile land-based missiles, missile bases, and air defense networks. These "escalation pessimists," as I call them, stand in contrast to a group of "escalation optimists," who are significantly less concerned about the potential nuclear pressures that a conventional war with the United States might place on China.

In general, a conventional war between the two countries is unlikely, much less Chinese nuclear escalation within that war. Certainly, Chinese nuclear escalation seems less likely than escalation by states such as Russia or Pakistan, which advertise a willingness to use nuclear weapons first. Nevertheless, the consequences of Chinese nuclear escalation would be so significant that the potential danger merits careful assessment. Unfortunately, the conflicting views of escalation optimists and pessimists remain a significant impediment to this assessment.

This impasse has two main sources. One is the lack of systematic, open-source military-technical analysis of the extent to which plausible U.S. conventional military operations are likely to threaten China's nuclear retaliatory capability. The other is a failure to incorporate perceptual variables that are likely to shape both how China will view threats to its nuclear arsenal after conventional deterrence fails and the purposes that China might believe nuclear escalation could serve under such conditions.

This article examines both these military-technical and perceptual factors in order to assess the risk of Chinese nuclear escalation. It finds that the pressures emphasized by pessimists are plausible, though not inevitable. Notably, the danger stems less from the purely military-technical threat that a U.S. conventional campaign would pose to China's nuclear arsenal, which pessimists may at times overestimate, than from what China is likely to believe these military-technical developments signal about broader U.S. intentions once a conventional war is under way, which optimists too often overlook. Optimism is therefore unwarranted, but some of the strongest reasons for pessimism are not the ones identified in the current debate. These reasons also differ in important ways from concerns about possible Soviet nuclear escalation against NATO in the late Cold War, a scenario that has explicitly and implicitly shaped much recent analysis of China without rigorous attention to the possible limits of the analogy. This analysis thus clarifies and helps resolve key points of disagreement in the current debate over China while also highlighting the critical factors that have influenced or could influence nuclear escalation risk in other scenarios.

From *International Security* 41, no. 4 (Spring 2017): 50–92.

To preview the main claims, the article's military-technical analysis finds that, consistent with the worries of the escalation pessimists, plausible U.S. conventional military operations in the event of war with China almost certainly would erode significant components of China's nuclear or nuclear-relevant capabilities even if this were not the U.S. goal. Crucially, however, a U.S. conventional campaign would be extremely unlikely to inadvertently eliminate China's nuclear arsenal outright. The key question is how China would then assess the survivability of its degraded nuclear force.

China's assessment is likely to be much less confident amid the fog and suspicions of a major war than it would be in peacetime. Indeed, the generally relaxed beliefs about nuclear escalation currently espoused by China's strategic community seem unlikely to persist in a world where the outbreak of an intense conventional war would have recently proven many of this community's other working assumptions incorrect. Chinese leaders could reasonably come to believe that the United States was seeking to pursue conventional counterforce—that is, the erosion or destruction of China's nuclear arsenal without U.S. use of nuclear weapons—or even nuclear counterforce. Under such circumstances, Chinese leaders might see limited nuclear escalation as their least bad option, using nuclear weapons for purposes of military advantage or coercive leverage or both, for reasons I outline further in this article.

The article proceeds in four sections. The first section frames the debate between escalation optimists and pessimists. The second section draws on some of the suggestions in this debate as well as logical deduction, past scholarship, and historical evidence to produce a general framework for assessing the threat that one country's conventional military operations might pose to an opponent's nuclear retaliatory capability and how the opponent might respond to this threat, based on both military-technical and perceptual variables. The third section uses this framework to evaluate the extent to which plausible U.S. conventional operations might erode China's nuclear retaliatory capability during a war and the extent to which such operations might in sum appear to China as the prelude to or an attempt at a counterforce campaign, possibly prompting Chinese nuclear escalation. The conclusion summarizes the findings and identifies areas for further research.

The Debate over Chinese Nuclear Escalation

In general, escalation from conventional to nuclear war could occur through a variety of pathways. These include preemption, as well as the dangers of unauthorized use, accidental launch based on faulty warning, and deliberate nuclear escalation to stalemate a conventional military attack.[1] With respect to China, the country's minimal nuclear posture, combined with its centralized control over nuclear weapons and long-standing no-first-use pledge, make these scenarios fairly implausible.[2] For example, a recent RAND analysis of U.S.-China conflict scenarios confidently excludes the problem of nuclear escalation all together. Capturing the general consensus, the report notes, "We assess the probability to be very low and so do not include the effects of nuclear warfare in our analysis of losses and costs. The general reason for this is that *mutual deterrence* prevails in the Sino-U.S. strategic-nuclear relationship."[3]

Recently, however, intensified security competition between the United States and China has prompted the United States to adopt conventional concepts of operation that some argue raise a distinct set of so-called inadvertent nuclear risks: namely, that China might mistake U.S. conventional operations for an attempt at or prelude to counterforce, creating pressures on Chinese leaders to escalate to nuclear use. The United States maintains that its conventional force planning efforts are not aimed at any particular country. Nevertheless, the U.S. approach is explicitly designed to counter adversaries with antiaccess, area-denial capabilities of the type the United States commonly asserts China is developing.

In particular, the U.S. concept known as AirSea Battle, though vague and promulgated as much outside the Pentagon as within it, reportedly envisioned rapid, large-scale U.S. attacks on the Chinese mainland in the event of war. According to analysis from an influential think tank closely associated with the Pentagon, U.S. targets in an AirSea Battle–style campaign were to include Chinese command and control networks, missile sites, intelligence, surveillance, and reconnaissance (ISR) assets, air defense systems, and submarines, with the goal of "executing a blinding campaign against PLA [People's Liberation Army] battle networks."[4] Although the Pentagon has since folded AirSea Battle into the broader U.S. Joint Operational Access Concept and renamed it the Joint Concept for Access and Maneuver in the Global Commons, the core ideas endure and reflect an expansive U.S. approach to conventional warfighting evident since at least 1991.[5]

Escalation Pessimists

Escalation pessimists worry that the U.S. approach could lead inadvertently to Chinese nuclear use. Their arguments echo Barry Posen's contention that NATO's approach to conventional warfighting in the late Cold War could have generated pressures for Soviet nuclear use by unintentionally infringing upon vital components of the Soviet retaliatory capability, such as its SSBN force and ground-based early warning radars.[6] For example, Thomas Christensen writes that Posen's analysis "should apply even more clearly to attacks on the Chinese homeland in a future U.S.-China conflict."[7] As Christensen explains, "China is simultaneously developing conventional and nuclear coercive capa-

bilities that overlap significantly." He points in particular to the dual nuclear and conventional relevance of Chinese submarines, missiles, space assets, and command and control systems, emphasizing that "if strikes by the United States on China's conventional coercive capabilities or their critical command and control nodes and supporting infrastructure were to appear in Beijing as a conventional attack on its nuclear retaliatory capability or as a precursor to a nuclear first strike, even a China that generally adheres to a No-First-Use posture might escalate to the nuclear level."[8]

Avery Goldstein, too, argues that a U.S.-China conventional war could inadvertently escalate to the nuclear level. In his view, the use of conventional force is inherently unpredictable, and as two nuclear-armed states using force to bargain at the conventional level, the United States and China might miscalculate in ways that could eventually lead to "unanticipated nuclear catastrophe." A particular danger stems from the possibility that the United States might mistakenly sink a Chinese SSBN during the course of a conventional war, "inviting Chinese nuclear retaliation."[9] Furthermore, Goldstein argues that both the United States and China are generally overconfident about their ability to control escalation, which exacerbates the risk.

Other experts also rate escalatory risks as high. For example, Joshua Rovner notes that there is a strong chance of inadvertent escalation given the targets that the United States likely would attack in a conventional first strike against China. "The targets . . . would include China's ballistic missiles and fixed and mobile launchers, as well as space- and ground-based facilities for targeting and guidance," he writes. "While U.S. planners might be confident that they can distinguish conventional from nuclear targets, Chinese officials might not be, especially because their ballistic missile stockpiles would be at the top of the target list."[10]

Similarly, Wu Riqiang writes that "because of the co-mingling of Chinese conventional and nuclear weapons and the difficulty of discriminating between them, the U.S. military might attack China's nuclear weapons inadvertently in a conventional war, which would drive China's confidence of retaliation lower. Therefore, Chinese leaders would face high use-it-or-lose-it pressure, and might lose confidence, leading to a decision to escalate." Wu identifies three types of intermingling as particularly worrisome. First, China mounts both nuclear and conventional warheads on its medium-range DF-21 missiles, which could lead to the United States unintentionally targeting China's nuclear arsenal in an attempt to suppress China's conventional missile threat. Second, Wu notes that the United States might have difficulty distinguishing between China's attack submarines and its SSBNs, resulting in the sinking of the latter, which could look to China like the prelude to counter-force. Third, Wu worries that U.S. efforts to degrade Chinese command and control over its conventional forces also could degrade China's ability to control or use its nuclear deterrent. In the larger context of what Wu sees as a vulnerable land-based Chinese intercontinental ballistic missile (ICBM) force, he worries that China might fear that it would soon lose its nuclear deterrent.[11]

Other escalation pessimists express similar concerns. For example, Christopher Twomey notes that China's "conventional systems rely on command and control systems that also perform a role in nuclear operations. . . . Chinese long-range over-the-horizon radars used to find U.S. carriers for attack by conventional ballistic missiles might also provide early warning capabilities. China's Second Artillery Force is responsible for both conventional and nuclear-armed missiles. The separation of command and control links between the two sides of the force is unclear."[12] Likewise, a second recent RAND study that is less alarmist about nuclear risks overall than the one previously mentioned still frets about China's decision to mount both nuclear and conventional warheads on the DF-21. As Eric Heginbotham and his coauthors warn, "The hunt

for conventionally armed missiles could result in the attrition of China's nuclear-capable missile force," which "could ultimately create a 'use-them-or-lose-them' dilemma . . . , particularly if other parts of China's strategic system (such as SSBNs) were under attack."[13] Some pessimists are so concerned that they have proposed entirely different U.S. concepts of operation for war in the Western Pacific.[14]

Escalation Optimists

Escalation optimists rate the risk of Chinese nuclear escalation as substantially lower—certainly too low to provide a reason to abandon AirSea Battle or its progeny. For example, Elbridge Colby, a former Pentagon official, acknowledges that a U.S. conventional campaign would attack targets on the Chinese mainland, raising some inherent risks of nuclear escalation. Nevertheless, he contends that U.S. policymakers are sensitized to the dangers and can manage the problem through the careful design of military campaigns.[15] Vincent Manzo, a Pentagon analyst, also soberly recognizes escalatory risk but argues that a U.S. campaign can be designed to limit the possibility that China would view it as threatening the country's nuclear deterrent. For example, the United States could geographically circumscribe the range of its operations on Chinese territory or conduct most of its attacks with stand-off weapons that would reduce the need to suppress Chinese air defenses.[16] My own conversations and interviews with numerous other current and former U.S. government officials, both military and civilian, suggest that many share Colby's and Manzo's views.[17] On occasion these views have surfaced publicly, as when former Director of National Intelligence and retired Commander of U.S. Pacific Command Adm. Dennis Blair recently described the possibility of nuclear escalation between the United States and China as "somewhere between zero and nil."[18]

Many Chinese analysts echo this relaxed view. As Fiona Cunningham and Taylor Fravel report, "China's strategic community does not share U.S. concerns about nuclear escalation from the implementation of the AirSea Battle Concept. Its members understand that the aim of the AirSea Battle Concept is to defeat Chinese 'antiaccess' capabilities and involves a blinding campaign. Nevertheless, most sources . . . did not believe that the AirSea Battle was relevant to Chinese nuclear weapons."[19]

Cunningham and Fravel do not accept these optimistic Chinese views uncritically, however. They note that Chinese confidence that an AirSea Battle–style campaign would not lead to nuclear escalation is in tension with stated Chinese concerns about how U.S. missile defenses and conventional prompt global strike might affect China's nuclear retaliatory capabilities.[20] Nevertheless, Cunningham and Fravel do question some of the pessimists' concerns. For example, Cunningham and Fravel show that "the majority of China's nuclear missiles are not colocated with conventional ones."[21] Hence they argue that the chance that the United States might mistakenly target Chinese nuclear missiles in a campaign against the conventional ones is lower than often assumed. Cunningham and Fravel also echo Chinese doubts about whether U.S. attacks on China's conventional command and control would impinge on China's nuclear command and control; the two types of launch brigades use different command chains, and Chinese command and control systems exhibit significant redundancy.[22]

Ultimately, both pessimists and optimists acknowledge some nontrivial potential for inadvertent nuclear escalation in the course of a conventional war. They disagree, however, on the seriousness of the risk. This disagreement stems largely from differing assumptions about which targets the United States would attack in a conventional military campaign against China, and whether China would view attacks on those targets as seriously eroding its nuclear retaliatory capabilities. The next section provides a general framework to help probe these two sets of assumptions systematically in the China case and beyond.

A Framework for Assessing Inadvertent Nuclear Escalation Risk

Two pathways could lead to inadvertent nuclear escalation.[23] First, a state could believe that its opponent was using conventional attack as a prelude to nuclear attack—that conventional operations were being used to "soften up" the target for a subsequent nuclear counterforce campaign, in a manner that would make that campaign more successful than if it occurred as a bolt from the blue. Or, even if such conventional operations did not objectively increase the likely effectiveness of a subsequent nuclear counterforce campaign, the target state might believe that operations of this sort strongly signaled that such a campaign was imminent, much more so than would have been credible in peacetime. Second, the target state might fear that the opponent was seeking to attrite the target's nuclear force through conventional counterforce—counterforce attacks below the nuclear threshold—and that it might soon be successful.[24]

In both of these scenarios, the key question would not be whether the target state expected to suffer complete nuclear disarmament at the hands of a nuclear or conventional counterforce attack. Rather, the issue would be whether the target state feared the erosion of its nuclear capabilities past some threshold considered vital to its security. That threshold most obviously would encompass retention of the state's ability to inflict unacceptable damage in a retaliatory second strike, but it also could include the ability to perform other tasks, such as providing a nuclear umbrella for allies or deterring third parties.[25] Under such circumstances, the target state might decide that it was better off escalating to nuclear use before it suffered nuclear disarmament or degradation past that key threshold.

Two broad rationales could motivate such use. First, a state could escalate for purposes of military advantage. In the extreme, a state that felt certain its adversary was in the process of launching a nuclear first strike might launch its own first strike in an effort to limit damage. Although massive, such escalation could seem like the least bad option in a world where all-out nuclear war appeared inevitable.[26] Even in a world where such conflict did not appear inevitable, though, a state could seek military advantage by using nuclear weapons in more limited form to halt the components of the opposing conventional campaign that posed the greatest threat to the target's nuclear forces.[27] Nuclear weapons could achieve these effects more rapidly than conventional forces, and a state might believe that such use would not invite all-out retaliation.

Second, a state might engage in limited nuclear escalation to try to generate coercive leverage, signaling its resolve to make the opponent pay significant costs until the counterforce campaign was either suspended or completed. Nothing says "you've crossed my red line" quite like a mushroom cloud. This attempt at bargaining would hold more promise if the escalating state believed that the opponent had not yet fully committed itself to a counterforce campaign, or if the escalating state anticipated that the opponent's campaign would take considerable time to be successful, or both. Escalation in the form of a demonstration strike or an attack on a purely military target might change the opponent's calculations during that window and lead it to back down.[28]

Admittedly, these escalatory logics might seem counterintuitive to those who associate nuclear weapons with stability. Nuclear weapons are said to mitigate the security dilemma because they are not very useful for conquering others' territory, but they are very effective in deterring attacks on one's own, assuming a state has a secure second-strike capability. Hence the presence of nuclear weapons can induce a situation of defensive advantage that should be conducive to peace.[29] Precisely because of the importance that states attach to their nuclear arsenals, however, states are likely to treat threats to those arsenals with the highest possible concern. Put another way, although the threat *of* nuclear weapons may inhibit escalation from peace to war, threats *to* nuclear weapons may provide reasons for intra-war escalation.

Inadvertent escalatory pressures should not arise automatically in conventional wars between nuclear-armed states, however. The emergence and intensity of these pressures should vary depending on observable features of the opponent's military campaign, the degree of nuclear-conventional intermingling in the target state, the target state's nuclear force posture and doctrine, and the target state's information about the opponent's nuclear force posture and doctrine. Below I flesh out these military-technical factors before discussing two additional wartime perceptual dynamics that could lead the target state to view the military-technical balance especially pessimistically, heightening escalatory pressure.

Military-Technical Drivers of Wartime Escalation Risk

Declaratory statements, known elements of force posture and campaign plans, past conventional military campaigns—all can offer clues as to whether and how one state might end up targeting the nuclear-relevant assets of another in a conventional war aimed at achieving only conventional objectives. Nuclear-relevant targets generally fall into four categories: (1) nuclear weapons or nuclear weapons components, such as mobile transporter erector launchers (TELs) armed with nuclear missiles, nuclear silos, tactical nuclear weapons, or nuclear warhead storage facilities; (2) the platforms used to deliver nuclear weapons, such as nuclear-capable aircraft or submarines armed with nuclear torpedoes or ballistic missiles; (3) the conventional forces used to protect or support nuclear forces, such as air defense systems that protect land-based missiles; attack submarines and land-based naval infrastructure that protect SSBNs; or infantry forces that guard the locations of nuclear weapons, warheads, or nuclear-relevant platforms; and (4) the command, control, communication, and computer (C4) networks and ISR assets relevant to detecting an incoming nuclear attack, as well as to targeting one's own nuclear weapons, such as early warning radars based in space, at sea, or on land; or fiber optic cables or radio transmitters.[30]

Two characteristics of the target state's military are crucial in assessing the likelihood that these nuclear-relevant targets might come under attack in a conventional war. First, if the target state physically colocates its nuclear forces with conventional weapons, extensively employs dual-capable platforms, relies heavily on conventional forces to protect or support nuclear forces, or bases nuclear weapons or related infrastructure in areas physically proximate to conventional battlefields, the odds that a conventional attack could implicate the state's nuclear capabilities will be higher.[31] Second, if the target state has tight, extensive inter-linkages between the C4ISR used to issue orders and communicate with forces in the field responsible for both conventional and nuclear operations, it is more likely that conventional operations seeking to disrupt the target's conventional capabilities will also have nuclear ramifications.

Even in this scenario, however, the target state might not view conventional attacks as constituting a counterforce threat. Not all nuclear-relevant targets are equally essential to a target state's retaliatory capability, so losing them should not generate equally strong pressures to use what remains. A state that believes it has a wide margin of safety for the survivability of its secure second-strike forces can afford to take a slightly more relaxed view of conventional military operations that affect nuclear assets, at least as compared to a state that sees its nuclear arsenal as highly vulnerable to counter-

force. For example, the significance of the destruction of a state's early warning radars during the course of a conventional war could vary dramatically depending on whether the state relies on those radars for a launch-on-warning posture. A state that expects to possess survivable second-strike forces even in the absence of warning of an incoming nuclear first strike is unlikely to view the conventional destruction of early warning radars with the same degree of alarm as a state whose nuclear forces are so vulnerable that they must be launched on warning if they are to be used at all.

Similarly, a state with mobile, hard-to-find ICBMs or submarine-launched ballistic missiles (SLBMs) that can survive the opponent's anti-submarine warfare (ASW) efforts has little reason to suddenly escalate if some of its tactical nuclear weapons are captured or destroyed in a conventional war, unless the state envisioned a vital mission that only tactical nuclear weapons could perform. The state's battlefield fortunes might not be as favorable at that point, but the state would still retain a nuclear retaliatory capability. By contrast, a target state reliant solely on tactical nuclear weapons for its nuclear deterrent (an unlikely case, but possible), or whose tactical nuclear weapons were backstopped only by highly vulnerable, silo-based ICBMs, or SLBMs not protected by a robust ASW capability, would have much more cause for concern in the event that a conventional war started to implicate those tactical nuclear weapons.

Likewise, a state possessing hardened, redundant, nuclear-dedicated C4ISR is less likely to feel pressure to escalate even in the event that a conventional war starts to infringe on some of the channels or methods it uses for commanding, controlling, and communicating with its nuclear forces. For example, a state could have multiple types of nuclear weapons and multiple ways of delivering launch orders to the operators of those different weapons. Even if some of these methods overlapped with those for conventional forces and were attacked as a way of neutralizing conventional forces in a conventional war, or did not overlap but were attacked by mistake in a conventional war, the state would still have a residual nuclear capacity. Although such a scenario would not be comforting, the target state's position would clearly be more secure than that of a state with fragile C4ISR shared between nuclear and conventional forces.

The target state's own estimates of the requirements of nuclear deterrence are critical as well. If the target state envisions a circumscribed role for nuclear weapons in its strategy, and in particular if the target state believes that the threshold for inflicting unacceptable retaliatory damage on an opponent is relatively low, then the state's ability to tolerate some conventional erosion of its nuclear capabilities will be higher. Put another way, a state that believes that the survival of only one or a handful of nuclear weapons is enough to induce nuclear restraint in its opponent can afford to be less worried about conventional counterforce. By contrast, if the target state believes that the threshold for inflicting unacceptable retaliatory damage on an opponent is relatively high, then the state has to be much more worried about the conventional erosion of its nuclear capabilities. Credibly threatening to destroy, say, 25 percent of an opponent's industrial base and kill half its population usually requires much more than a stray surviving warhead, especially if the opponent is believed to have the ability to limit damage, for example through missile defenses.

The target state's information regarding the nuclear doctrine of its opponent is also important. If the opponent is known to have a counterforce doctrine and credible counterforce capabilities, this knowledge is likely to foment a more suspicious interpretation of the opponent's conventional military operations.[32] By contrast, the conventional military operations of an opponent that has disavowed counterforce and that appears to lack counterforce capabilities will be less threatening even if this opponent attacks the same set of targets.

Ultimately, the upward curve of escalatory pressure is likely to look more exponential than linear as these various military-technical indicators of a possible counterforce campaign multiply. An isolated instance of conventional attack on a nuclear-relevant target can probably be distinguished from an attempt at or prelude to counterforce. If, however, a target state starts to experience multiple simultaneous or rapidly successive conventional attacks that seem to have nuclear implications, the interpretation may become more ominous. Even something as dramatic as the sinking of an SSBN could have vastly different meanings for the target state depending on the context of other events. Imagine, for example, a situation in which an SSBN had been sunk during the course of a conventional ASW campaign, but all of the target state's other nuclear weapons and nuclear-relevant C4 remained secure and physically distant from the site of conventional fighting. Such a scenario would look very different from a situation in which an SSBN had been sunk and these other nuclear-relevant targets were also under conventional attack. The target state could probably dismiss the potential counterforce implications of the sinking in the first scenario but might find it dramatically harder to do so in the second, where the sinking appeared to confirm a pattern.

Additional Perceptual Sources of Wartime Pessimism

Two wartime perceptual dynamics could add further pessimism to a target state's assessment of the nuclear implications of a conventional war, tilting its reasoning toward worst-case assumptions. First, the fact that a conventional war has broken out at all means that deterrence has failed once already and that the target state has entered a realm of profound uncertainty. In peacetime, it might have been easy for the target state's leadership to reassure itself that the opponent would never pursue a counterforce campaign: the costs would be too great, the chances of success too low, and so on. However, these are also arguably all reasons that an opponent should never have allowed a conventional war to happen either. If the target state's leadership now finds itself in a world where the conventional Rubicon has been crossed, a radical reassessment of the opponent's intentions and capabilities in the nuclear realm may follow. Is the opponent willing to take other actions that previously were considered unthinkable? If conventional deterrence failures are possible, why not nuclear ones? Is the opponent fighting a limited war, as perhaps assumed at the outset, or is the opponent bent on larger ambitions such as regime change, which could provide a motive for targeting the country's nuclear arsenal?

This reasoning alone is unlikely to generate nuclear escalatory pressure, but it may create a strong presumption of insecurity as the target state evaluates the military-technical variables that could generate such pressure. Indeed, dramatic wartime revision of peacetime assessments of adversary intentions is not unusual. Prior to the 1973 Arab-Israeli War, for example, Israel was supremely confident about its conventional superiority over its Arab neighbors. Within days of the war's outbreak, however, Israeli leaders came to fear that their country would be overrun. Although Arab ambitions were more limited—mainly to force Israel to negotiate the return of territory lost in 1967—Israeli leaders did not know this at the time and began making preparations for the use of their nuclear weapons as a means of ending the war. Fortunately, the war concluded for other reasons before this scenario came to pass, but the incident shows that the outbreak of an unexpectedly high-intensity conventional war can lead even previously secure states to rapidly infer that their adversaries' objectives are unlimited, resulting in preparations for nuclear use that would have seemed unthinkable only days earlier.[33]

Second, the fog of war is likely to degrade the target state's ability to perform this military-technical evaluation accurately, and missing or ambiguous information may be interpreted as highly threatening.[34] Accurate information about which targets the adversary has attacked may be in short supply, and incorrect information about some attacks could dramatically change the context in which the state interprets correct information about other attacks. Does lack of contact with an SSBN mean that the SSBN has been sunk, or does it mean that communications systems are not working or that the submarine has gone quiet to evade ASW efforts? In a world where the target state has reliable information that its other nuclear weapons are secure, losing contact with an SSBN would not by itself be likely to induce panic. Ambiguous information about the status of an SSBN might look far more alarming, however, in a world where the state was also receiving mistaken reports that its nuclear-relevant C4 was under threat, in addition to confirmed reports that other nuclear-relevant assets had been attacked.

Ambiguous and inaccurate reports are endemic to war, as is pessimistic decisionmaking in response to limited information. This is why there are repeated instances of military forces engaged in hostilities mistakenly shooting down civilian airliners.[35] Errors are almost inevitable and will tend to exacerbate rather than inhibit escalatory pressures arising from the objective military-technical situation. Such tendencies do not make escalation automatic, but they are likely to create additional sources of target state insecurity even when a strict military-technical evaluation might imply a more relaxed assessment.

Chinese Nuclear Escalation with the United States

This section uses the framework just outlined to assess the risk of Chinese nuclear escalation in a conventional war with the United States. First, it defines the likely scope of a plausible U.S. conventional campaign against China. Second, it examines the threat that such a campaign might pose to China's nuclear arsenal. Third, it assesses the survivability of the residual nuclear forces that China likely would retain once such a campaign got under way. Fourth, it moves beyond military-technical analysis to a discussion of the perceptual variables that might influence how China would respond to its new circumstances.

Likely Contours of a U.S. Conventional Campaign Against China

Despite the two countries' mutual interests in peace, several issues could plausibly embroil the United States and China in a major conventional war, notably Taiwan.[36] In the event of a Chinese effort to attack or coerce Taiwan, the United States would face strong pressure to intervene, possibly resulting in direct conflict with China.[37] As such, I use a notional war over Taiwan as a baseline scenario to illustrate some of the key conventional Chinese military capabilities that a U.S. conventional campaign might seek to suppress or destroy. The goal of this approach is not to accurately predict how an actual war between the United States and China would break out, or what the combat outcomes of specific battles might be. Rather, the scenario is a heuristic, providing a means of estimating the upward bound of nuclear escalation risk in the event that Chinese and U.S. conventional capabilities interact in an intense conflict with high political stakes for China.

How might such a war unfold? Open-source assessments generally remain pessimistic about China's ability to launch an outright invasion of Taiwan.[38] War is more likely to begin with Chinese efforts to coerce Taiwan by imposing economic and military damage and civilian suffering, with the threat of more to follow. Such coercion would require China to be able to credibly threaten to deny the United States control of the air and waters surrounding Taiwan. In addition, it likely would involve some combination of actual or threatened Chinese air and missile attacks and cyberattacks, along with a naval blockade involving submarines, mines, surface ships, and anti-ship cruise missiles. The goal would be to pressure Taiwan into accepting reunification, in part by making commercial traffic to Taiwan prohibitively costly even if attacks on Taiwan itself were limited.

Several studies have concluded that Chinese efforts to blockade or bombard Taiwan in these ways could result in rapid Chinese victory, suggesting that U.S. intervention to halt such an outcome would have to be extensive and swift.[39] Although U.S. officials often refer to China's "counter-intervention" strategy, it is China that would be projecting power in a Taiwan scenario.[40] The U.S. campaign therefore likely would seek to deny China this ability by (1) contesting China's efforts to control the air and waters surrounding Taiwan, as well as around U.S. military bases or forces in the region that were supporting the defense of Taiwan; (2) suppressing, attriting, or eliminating the weapons systems that China could use to strike Taiwan or U.S. military bases or forces in the region; and (3) paralyzing or destroying the Chinese C4ISR that would underlie China's campaign.

The potential target set for executing this type of campaign would be expansive. The United States likely would conduct both air-to-air and air-to-ground operations to prevent China's air force, the PLAAF, from being able to sortie over the strait, either to attack Taiwan directly (e.g., through operations to destroy Taiwan's air force, navy, and military infrastructure) or to enforce blockade efforts (e.g., through operations to attack ships seeking to bypass a blockade).[41] In addition, the United States would have to neutralize PLAAF airborne command and control platforms.

The United States also would want to render inoperable the thirty-nine Chinese air bases within unrefueled combat range of Taiwan, striking those bases' runways, fuel storage, hangars, and command facilities (see Map 6.1).[42] To con-

Map 6.1. Chinese Air Bases Relevant to a Taiwan Conflict

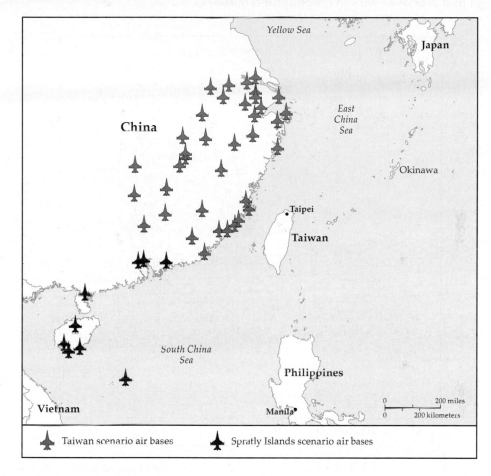

Source: Eric Heginbotham et al., *The U.S.-China Military Scorecard: Forces, Geography, and the Evolving Balance of Power, 1000–2017* (Arlington, VA: RAND Corporation, 2015), 138.

duct such attacks, the United States probably would rely heavily on cruise missiles launched from the stand-off ranges provided by submarines, surface ships, regional bases, and aircraft.[43] This approach would be preferable to traditional direct aerial attacks because it would minimize the need to suppress or destroy Chinese ship- and land-based air defenses.

Nevertheless, the United States also might want to attack these bases with manned bombers, which would in turn necessitate varying levels of air defense suppression or destruction. This latter campaign could result in additional missile and aerial attacks on Chinese surface vessels and the mainland. For example, China has extensive ship-based air defenses, including eight modern destroyers with surface-to-air missiles (SAMs).[44] In addition, China possesses dozens of land-based, long-range air defense batteries capable of launching an estimated 1,000 SAMs.[45] At least some of these batteries are

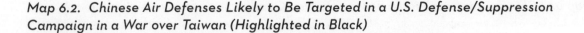

Map 6.2. *Chinese Air Defenses Likely to Be Targeted in a U.S. Defense/Suppression Campaign in a War over Taiwan (Highlighted in Black)*

● Within 1,000 km of Taipei   ○ Within 1,300 km of Thitu Island

Source: Eric Heginbotham et al., *The U.S.-China Military Scorecard: Forces, Geography, and the Evolving Balance of Power, 1996–2017* (Arlington, VA: RAND Corporation, 2015), 110.

mobile and designed to resist jamming.[46] A recent RAND study estimated that, in total, mainland China houses 823 air defense sites within 1,000 kilometers of Taiwan (see Map 6.2).[47]

Some U.S. aircraft, such as the F-22 and possibly the F-35, should be able to penetrate these defenses, but the United States would need to devote considerable effort to suppressing and destroying them given the limited inventory of fifth-generation platforms. The suppression campaign would consist largely of electronic warfare

efforts to jam the communications and radar systems on which China's integrated air defenses rely. The U.S. Navy and Marine Corps' EA-18G "Growler" aircraft is a modified Super Hornet dedicated expressly to this mission. The U.S. Air Force's EC-130H "Compass Call" platform is similarly designed to disrupt communications. In addition, both services have aircraft that can carry missiles designed to find and physically destroy air defense radars.[48] The Air Force's F-16CJ and the Navy and Marine Corps' EA-18G both carry high-speed anti-radiation missiles (HARMs).[49] The F-22's extremely powerful radar can assist in this process as well, by detecting radar emissions.[50] Nevertheless, the outcome would depend considerably on the skill and discipline of Chinese air defense crews.[51]

In addition to contesting Chinese control of the air, the United States likely would want to prevent the PLAN from operating freely within the first island chain.[52] This effort would be a prerequisite to any attempt to restore the flow of trade to Taiwan or to engage in mine clearance operations in Taiwanese harbors. Beyond the aforementioned fleet air defense capabilities, all of China's major surface vessels can launch anti-ship cruise missiles that would pose a threat to potential U.S. operations in the strait. China also possesses approximately three dozen conventionally powered attack submarines (SS) capable of launching anti-ship cruise missiles, and it is in the process of acquiring a fleet of modern nuclear-attack submarines (SSN) and a guided-missile attack submarine that could potentially launch torpedoes, anti-ship cruise missiles, and land-attack munitions.[53] Notably, China's diesel attack submarines could be used not only to conduct attacks with torpedoes and mines but also as cueing platforms for other Chinese attacks.[54] The United States would want to prevent all of these vessels from escaping to the deeper waters outside the first island chain, where they could threaten U.S. carrier battle groups.[55] In addition, China has significant shore-based naval assets, including coastal defense anti-ship cruise missiles and the land-based, medium-range DF-21D anti-ship ballistic missile.[56]

U.S. Aegis cruisers and destroyers do have robust organic defenses against such missiles, but saturated attacks could overwhelm them. As a result, the United States likely would seek to sink Chinese surface vessels and attack submarines. It also would want to eliminate shore-based naval infrastructure such as military ports, submarine pens, and ammunition depots, particularly for the East Sea Fleet based at Ningbo and South Sea Fleet based at Zhanjiang.[57] Again, the United States likely would try to use stand-off weapons where possible. U.S. attack submarines likely would launch torpedoes against Chinese surface vessels, as well as conduct ASW against Chinese attack submarines within the first island chain. The United States' maritime patrol aircraft and tactical auxiliary general ocean surveillance ships would join these efforts if China no longer controlled the air.

In addition, the United States almost certainly would target key components of the PLA Rocket Force (PLARF), formerly known as the Second Artillery.[58] Its arsenal of approximately 1,200 conventional short-range ballistic missiles (SRBMs) would be a major tool for coercing Taiwan, and China has stationed all such missiles within range of the island.[59] These short-range missiles also could pose a potential threat to U.S. surface or air forces operating in or near the strait, and likely to U.S. bases in South Korea and Japan. As such, the missiles' suppression or destruction would be a prerequisite to other operations, such as aerial ASW patrols or mine clearance.

Beyond its SRBMs, China's primary medium-range conventional ballistic missile (MRBM), the DF-21C, also could pose a substantial threat to U.S. bases in Japan and South Korea. China is believed to have thirty-six DF-21C launchers, with the number of missiles unknown. In addition, China has several hundred conventional ground-launched cruise missiles based in southwest and south-central China that could threaten Taiwan and U.S. forces.[60] Finding or disabling these short- and medium-range conventional missiles would be challenging, though not impossible. The base locations, as well as the general areas of operation for the individual missile brigades that fan out from the bases, are known with some confidence (see Map 6.3).[61]

It is likely that in addition to targeting China's conventional missile brigades, especially the launch elements, the United States would seek to target the

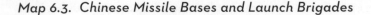

Map 6.3. Chinese Missile Bases and Launch Brigades

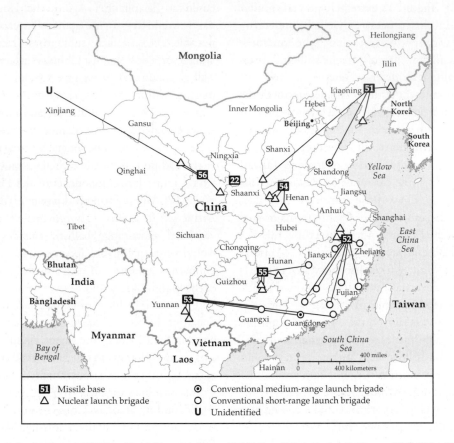

Legend:
- **51** Missile base
- △ Nuclear launch brigade
- U Unidentified
- ◉ Conventional medium-range launch brigade
- ○ Conventional short-range launch brigade

Source: Fiona S. Cunningham and M. Taylor Fravel, "Assuring Assured Retaliation: China's Nuclear Posture and U.S.-China Strategic Stability," *International Security* 40, no. 2 (Fall 2015): 43.

bases that provide staff support for these brigades, for three reasons. First, in contrast to the missiles themselves, the bases are fixed, readily identifiable targets—the sort the United States has routinely attacked in comparable air operations in Vietnam, Iraq, and elsewhere.[62] Second, the bases may house substantial stockpiles of additional missiles and spare parts, as well as repair, maintenance, and fuel facilities. Third, the bases may contain command and control facilities crucial to China's direction of a missile campaign, although much of this command and control may also be dispersed at other sites.

Locating launchers out of garrison would depend significantly on the quality of U.S. prewar intelligence about patrol routes and prepared launch sites, drawn mostly from satellite imagery and signals intelligence. The medium-range missiles are significantly larger than most other road traffic, cannot safely travel off road, require solid ground for launching to avoid debris kicked up by the rocket engine, and need significant numbers of personnel and vehicles to function properly—all of which would provide location clues.[63] In addition, U.S. satellites could detect infrared signatures from missile launches themselves as a means of narrowing search areas, and the United States might be able to detect additional communications between missile launch brigades and their headquarters.[64]

Locating and destroying the launchers, however, would require the United States to control the airspace over significant areas of mainland China, or to accept sortie attrition rates not seen since the Christmas bombings in Vietnam or even the battles over Europe to defeat the German night fighter force in 1944.[65] Unmanned aerial vehicles (UAVs) with dual-mode radar are well equipped to provide detailed images of search areas that could be passed to tactical aircraft, and some armed UAVs could potentially target the missiles themselves, but these platforms are unlikely to be survivable in heavily defended airspace. Similarly, U.S. fourth- and fifth-generation combat aircraft cued by UAV or satellite imagery could plausibly find and destroy Chinese mobile missiles and have some ability to evade air defenses, but eastern and coastal China are heavily defended—much more so than other theaters where the United States has conducted recent operations, such as Iraq, Afghanistan, Libya, and Serbia. Furthermore, it is almost inconceivable that the United States would send large, scarce, visible, vulnerable platforms such as AWACS, JSTARS, the U-2, or Global Hawk into this sort of environment. However, these are the mobile airborne radar platforms that would most aid combat aircraft in narrowing their missile search areas, especially in combination with equally vulnerable airborne electronic intelligence platforms such as the RC-135 and EP-3.[66]

Lastly, the United States likely would seek to interfere with Chinese C4ISR. It would want to deny China the ability to direct and communicate with its forces and to maintain awareness of U.S. operations. The United States probably would use both kinetic and non-kinetic means to target China's known air and naval operations command facilities; its command and control platforms in the air and at sea; and the computer, fiber-optic, and radio networks that connect these commanders to their various forces. China's coastal radio transmitters and over-the-horizon radar system, known as Skywave, would be particularly vulnerable, because they are large, fixed, emitting targets essential to cueing Chinese submarines and longer-range missiles.[67] In addition, the U.S. air defense suppression campaign would seek to neutralize Chinese radars used to detect and target incoming aircraft.[68] It is possible that the United States could seek to target Chinese satellites as well, or to jam Chinese space-based communication systems, although China would be less dependent on these in a Taiwan campaign because most of its land-based systems would be within theater range.[69]

The U.S. Conventional Threat to Nuclear-Relevant Targets

The earlier framework identified four categories of nuclear-relevant targets that could come under threat during a conventional war. Analysis of China's force structure and the contours of a likely U.S. campaign to defend Taiwan suggests that Chinese assets in all four categories could come under U.S. attack. Here I review them in turn, grouping the first two because they are tightly linked in this case.

NUCLEAR WEAPONS, COMPONENTS, AND DELIVERY PLATFORMS

A U.S. campaign to find, suppress, and destroy China's short- and medium- range conventional missiles would almost certainly take place in areas where China also has stationed some of its medium-range and intercontinental nuclear-tipped ballistic missiles. Of China's six operational missile bases, Bases 52, 53, and 55 are all located in southeast China relatively close to Taiwan. All oversee both nuclear and conventional missile brigades, although it is important to remember that these brigades and many of their supporting elements are dispersed from the bases themselves, which function essentially as staff offices.

According to open sources, Base 52 mostly oversees brigades of short-range conventional missiles such as the DF-11 but also has responsibility for at least one medium-range nuclear missile brigade of the DF-21A and one medium-range ballistic missile brigade of the conventional DF-21C. It also has substantial nuclear warhead storage and handling responsibilities. Similarly, Base 53 appears to oversee both conventional and nuclear missile brigades (probably one nuclear DF-21A brigade, one conventional DF-21D brigade, and one DF-21C or DF-31 nuclear brigade), as well as a conventional cruise missile brigade of DH-10s and a short-range conventional ballistic missile brigade of DF-11s. Likewise, Base 55 probably oversees two silo-based nuclear ICBM D-5A brigades but also a mobile, nuclear DF-31A brigade and a conventional cruise missile brigade of DH-10s.[70]

In addition, Base 51, located in northeastern China, appears to oversee a mix of both conventional and nuclear DF-21 brigades.[71] Although these brigades are located at substantial distances from Taiwan, their assets are ideally positioned to thwart U.S. forces in South Korea or Japan that might help defend Taiwan. As such, U.S. military operations in the vicinity of the nuclear DF-21 brigades are not unthinkable, depending on how China chooses to employ the conventional DF-21 brigades.

The nuclear and conventional missiles supported by these bases do not appear to be intermingled at the launch-brigade level, so in theory the United States could take care to attack only conventional launch brigades and their associated headquarters.[72] Threading this needle may prove difficult in the case of the DF-21, though. As mentioned, the DF-21 can carry either a nuclear or conventional warhead. China has at least four or five brigades that carry some form of the DF-21,[73]

and distinguishing from the air or at significant distances which DF-21s are conventional versus nuclear may not be possible. Prepared launch sites, surely a U.S. target, would look identical. As one authority notes, "The distinction between ballistic missiles equipped with nuclear and conventional payloads is becoming increasingly blurred."[74]

In addition, the wartime patrol routes of the nuclear and conventional brigades could overlap, especially given that a typical brigade comprises six battalions with two companies each.[75] These are unlikely to remain in a tightly confined area given that the point of such a structure is to enable mobility and dispersal. Multiple support elements are attached to each launch brigade, sometimes spread out within a radius of as much as 200 kilometers.[76] Furthermore, there is substantial open-source uncertainty about which missile brigades operate where and little detailed information at the battalion level or lower. Analysts who follow these matters also report regular and frequent changes in China's missile deployment patterns, which could increase the challenge of distinguishing nuclear from conventional targets.[77]

Moreover, if the areas of operation overlap, nuclear and conventional missile brigades might rely on the same transportation networks to reach launch sites or receive support. The PLARF relies heavily on surreptitious circulation of nuclear warheads along road and especially rail networks to improve survivability in a crisis or war, but this approach raises the risk that U.S. efforts to stymie movements of the conventional missile brigades could have a similar effect on the nuclear brigades.[78] At the very least, as Cunningham and Fravel note, "a conventional attack on a Chinese conventional missile brigade would send a very strong signal to China of an adversary's ability to threaten China's nuclear forces."[79]

As escalation pessimists have noted, an ASW campaign is the other pathway by which the United States might directly target Chinese nuclear weapons in the course of a conventional campaign. It is plausible that the United States could sink an SSBN in the process of hunting Chinese attack submarines. Historically, the correct classification of undersea targets has been one of the most challenging aspects of ASW, which is why the most robust approaches have relied on integrating multiple sources of information from passive sonar and signals intelligence. During the Cold War, for example, the United States relied on passive sonar in tactical engagements to help identify particular types of Soviet submarines based on the distinctive sounds (known as tonals) created by propellers and internal machinery rotating at particular frequencies. This method worked, however, only because the United States maintained highly accurate libraries identifying the signatures of every Soviet submarine.[80]

Advances in computing have since greatly improved U.S. target classification abilities, but the process can still prove difficult. A particular challenge is likely to arise from the fact that China will probably send its SSBNs to sea only if they are accompanied by an SSN or SS for protection. Chinese SLBMs lack the range to hit the continental United States from close to China's coasts, so defending SSBNs on the journey through U.S. acoustic barriers around the edges of the first island chain to the open ocean (most likely via the Philippine Sea) would be essential.[81] Furthermore, even if China were not trying to get its SSBNs to the open ocean, it might send them to sea within the first island chain so that they would not be destroyed in port. Hence protecting the SSBNs would be a key task for China's attack submarines, much as it was for Soviet attack submarines in the Barents Sea during the Cold War.[82]

Close Chinese SSN escorts of SSBNs are likely to complicate target differentiation for the United States, because U.S. attack submarines approaching Chinese submarines within attack or trail range in shallow water likely would lose the ability to keep the two targets distinct acoustically. To be clear, the United States is likely to be able to initially find China's SSBNs because they are distinctively noisy.[83]

But even if a U.S. attack submarine ascertained that China had both an SSBN and SSN close by (say, 5 miles ahead), maintaining clarity regarding which target track was associated with which enemy signature could be hard as the U.S. vessel closed in. The relevant waters in this scenario are also likely to be crowded and noisy, further complicating target classification, and in the most critical early stages of the campaign, the United States is unlikely to control the air such that it might be able to bring other ASW assets to assist.[84]

As a result, the United States might face a difficult choice: attacking both targets, knowing one might be an SSBN, or letting both the SSBN and attack submarine continue to roam. Sinking an SSBN in this scenario would not be truly inadvertent in the sense of mistaking an enemy SSBN for an attack submarine; it would be a known risk. But the scenario nevertheless points to the nuclear dangers that could arise from the standard course of conventional operations, even if the United States did not set out to aggressively sink Chinese SSBNs.[85] Beyond any dangers arising from the likely attacks on China's MRBMs as described above, the U.S. ASW campaign clearly would pose a direct threat to some of China's nuclear weapons, nuclear weapons components, and delivery platforms, much as the pessimists fear.

CONVENTIONAL FORCES USED TO PROTECT OR SUPPORT NUCLEAR FORCES

A U.S. conventional campaign on the scale described above also would involve attacks on Chinese conventional targets relevant to the protection or support of at least some nuclear forces. Three factors make it likely that such attacks would render those forces highly vulnerable or nonfunctional even if they remained physically intact.

First, the U.S. air defense suppression/destruction campaign would take place over largely the same territory that houses the missile bases and elements that oversee and support both nuclear and conventional launch brigades—especially Bases 55 and 52, which are closest to Taiwan and whose brigades operate under a heavy concentration of Chinese air defense assets (see Map 6.2). By definition, if the United States seeks to degrade the air defenses that protect conventional missile launch brigades, and nuclear missile launch brigades patrol and operate in the same or nearby locations, both conventional and nuclear missile launch brigades will lose some protection from aerial attack.[86]

This outcome is especially likely given that sophisticated air defense systems such as China's operate as an integrated network of radars and shooters rather than simply a point defense.[87] For example, U.S. attacks on detection and tracking radars along the coast would start to reduce warning for the SAM batteries that protect Chinese mobile SRBMs and MRBMs farther inland, potentially including nuclear MRBMs, even if the objective was to denude only the conventional missiles of protection. Similarly, U.S. attacks on Chinese air bases as part of the conventional fight would reduce China's ability to sortie aircraft that might otherwise protect airspace surrounding nuclear missile launch brigades just as much as the areas surrounding conventional missile launch brigades.

Second, as mentioned, in combating China's SRBMs and MRBMs, the United States would face strong incentives to attack Chinese missile bases and base elements directly—at least for Bases 55 and 52, and possibly Bases 53 and 51, though they are farther from Taiwan. All of these bases support conventional missile launch brigades that would be relevant in a Taiwan contingency. However, these same bases also support nuclear missile brigades by overseeing regiments dedicated to "transportation, warhead storage and inspection, repair and maintenance, and communications."[88] Under these circumstances, it is unlikely that the United States would attack these bases and nearby elements in a manner that would disrupt activities relevant to conventional missile operations only.

Third, even if the United States avoided sinking Chinese SSBNs, U.S. efforts to sink or constrain Chinese attack submarines—a virtual certainty given these vessels' offensive conventional capabilities—would render Chinese SSBNs significantly more vulnerable. Given the vulnerability of China's SSBNs, China would have to know that the loss of its attack submarines would enable the United States to destroy China's SLBM force virtually at will.[89] In addition, likely U.S. attacks on Chinese shore-based naval infrastructure and ports, discussed above, could dramatically undermine the functioning and survival of China's SSBNs even if they were not attacked directly. The East Sea Fleet oversees eighteen of China's diesel attack submarines, while the South Sea Fleet contains sixteen additional diesel attack submarines, two nuclear attack submarines, and all four (likely soon to be five) of China's Jin-class submarines that carry the JL-2 SLBM.[90] One can imagine a scenario in which the United States had not actually attacked any Chinese SSBNs but had set them adrift with no protection, no ports, and, as I discuss below, no ability to send or receive communications.

C4ISR RELEVANT TO NUCLEAR WARNING OR OPERATIONS

U.S. attacks on China's conventionally relevant C4ISR networks could also impede China's nuclear-relevant C4ISR. One problem is that the degree of Chinese comingling between nuclear and conventional missile command and control systems is not well understood, at least in the open-source literature. As noted above, many Western experts believe that systems for the two types of missiles are interlinked, whereas many Chinese experts insist that the two are separate.[91] If the Western experts are right, then there may be no way to degrade China's conventional C4ISR without nuclear implications. Even if the Chinese experts are right, however, the United States would need excellent intelligence about which C4ISR components are designated for conventional or nuclear activities to avoid the latter while targeting the former. Without this level of knowledge about China's command arrangements, the United States could destroy nuclear-relevant C4 during a conventional campaign even absent comingling.

C4ISR comingling could be a problem in the naval realm as well. China uses the same very low frequency transmitters to communicate with both its SSNs and SSBNs. The United States is likely to target these transmitters because of their vulnerability and their importance for conventional naval warfare.[92] In so doing, however, the United States would substantially degrade, if not eliminate, China's ability to communicate with its SSBNs at sea.

The Survivability of China's Residual Nuclear Forces

Despite the scope of the U.S. campaign just described, it is not obvious that China would immediately come to fear the impending destruction of its nuclear arsenal. For one thing, the conventional war would not afford the United States significant counterforce advantages over China beyond what the United States already enjoys in peacetime. U.S. satellites and nuclear weapons would do the bulk of the heavy lifting in a true counterforce scenario and would not suddenly become more effective because of a conventional war against China.[93] If anything, a first strike against China would probably be easier for the United States in peacetime, when China had not dispersed its TELs as it would during a crisis or war.

This situation notably differs from that of the late Cold War. In that era, the Soviets had real reason to fear that a conventional war could have served as the cloak behind which the United States would gain military advantages in executing a nuclear counterforce strike.[94] For example, NATO's offensive efforts to gain sea control in a conventional war also would have given NATO a leg up in destroying the Soviet SSBN force before it could reach the locations where it would most threaten the United States. Similarly, NATO conventional air operations would have involved electronic and kinetic attacks on Soviet ground-based early warning radars, which were critical to the Soviet ability to detect the initial stages of a nuclear attack, especially if that attack began with low-flying bombers or cruise missiles launched from the Soviet periphery. Such degradation would have nullified any Soviet hope of launching on warning, rendering the country's silo-based nuclear forces highly vulnerable. It also could have hampered Soviet nuclear command and control more generally.

As a result, the Soviets might have escalated out of a fear that the conventional war was delivering distinct and irreversible counterforce advantages to the United States, and in the belief that going first could limit damage or rapidly halt the components of the conventional campaign that posed the greatest nuclear threats, or both.[95] Yet militating against this escalatory danger was the very high baseline survivability of the Soviet nuclear arsenal, which through its sheer size might have provided some insurance against escalatory pressures on Soviet leaders.

Today's situation with respect to China is distinct. China does not appear to rely on its SSBN force or on early warning in the same ways the Soviets did, so the implications of conventional attacks that might impinge on those assets may be more benign. China also has virtually no ability to limit damage by going first. Furthermore, China's arsenal is smaller and inherently more vulnerable to counterforce even in peacetime, especially given improved U.S. capabilities since the Cold War. As a result, a conventional war with the United States would not alter the nuclear balance to nearly the degree that was possible in the Cold War case.

Indeed, many analysts note that China already recognizes the vulnerability of its sea-based deterrent forces.[96] Some go so far as to describe China's

Jin-class program as "puzzling" given the platforms' lack of survivability, and note that China seems much more focused on "modernizing and hiding its land-based missiles" as the main bulwark against nuclear attack.[97] It is possible, for example, that China's efforts to develop SSBNs are rooted in bureaucratic or domestic political motives rather than in a belief that these platforms functionally enhance China's nuclear deterrent. If that is true, then China's loss of its SSBNs might not be as threatening, because Chinese leaders may have already calculated their requirements for deterrence on the assumption that they will not be able to rely on SLBMs.

If this logic is correct, then the real question is how secure China's leaders assess their land-based nuclear forces to be (see Map 6.3). Here, too, China might remain relatively insulated from nuclear escalatory pressures. For example, even if the United States destroyed all of China's DF-21 missiles, both nuclear and conventional, within range of Taiwan, China would retain other land-based nuclear missiles. These would include other DF-21 launch brigades hundreds of miles farther inland, attached to Base 56 deep in China's interior.[98] Although currently positioned to deter India and Russia, these mobile missiles could relocate to areas from which they could threaten U.S. bases or forces in Asia.

Under the Taiwan scenario, China also would retain its approximately twenty silo-based, liquid-fueled DF-5A or DF-5B ICBMs, the latter of which the Pentagon now reports as carrying multiple independently targeted reentry vehicles.[99] Although vulnerable to counterforce attacks given their immobility and the need for fueling prior to launch, the DF-5A certainly would not be mistaken for a DF-21. Furthermore, the DF-5As have known, fixed locations that the United States could avoid (even though some of these may be decoy silos). As mentioned, China does station two brigades of DF-5A missiles near Base 55, which likely would be involved in a Taiwan campaign. The other DF-5As are attached to Base 54, however, which is farther from Taiwan and also appears to support exclu-sively nuclear brigades.[100] As a result, the United States and China likely could keep this latter base and its related elements fairly clear of the conventional fight. China also likely would retain its single brigade of the older, road-mobile, liquid-fueled DF-4 ICBMs, comprising about ten warheads and believed to be based in caves.[101]

Most importantly, China's DF-31 and DF-31A missiles—the road-mobile, intercontinental backbone of the country's nuclear deterrent—appear to be spread across a variety of locations, only some of which might be physically touched by the conventional fight. Open sources suggest that China probably has about eight DF-31 TELs and about the same number of warheads, with a range of about 7,000 kilometers. Estimates of the DF-31A suggest about twenty-five TELs and the same number of warheads, with a range of about 11,000 kilometers.[102] The two DF-31 missile brigades appear to be attached to Base 54 and possibly Base 53, while the three DF-31A brigades are likely attached to Bases 51, 55, and 56.[103]

Two features of this deployment pattern stand out. First, none of these ICBM brigades are attached to Base 52, which is the base with the greatest conventional missile capability and closest proximity to Taiwan. This suggests that the most intense and aggressive U.S. conventional operations are unlikely to pose a direct physical threat to China's core ICBM force.

Second, the mobile ICBM brigades are distributed across China's other operational missile bases in a notable effort at dispersion that should afford varying degrees of insulation from conventional warfare.[104] This use of strategic depth to improve survivability is a long-standing theme in China's nuclear strategy.[105] Some of these bases and associated brigades, such as the DF-31A brigade attached to Base 55, could still be affected by the conventional fight because of the bases' conventional missiles (whose areas of operation might overlap with those of the nuclear brigades) and the bases' and base elements' general proximity to Taiwan. This is also true to a lesser degree of the DF-31 brigade possibly attached to Base 53 in southern China. These bases are farther from Taiwan but also oversee conventional capabilities that could become relevant in a conventional conflict.

Even under those circumstances, however, China would still retain another DF-31 brigade attached to Base 54, which is located well inland and whose capabilities appear to be entirely nuclear and are therefore unlikely to be involved in a Taiwan scenario. In addition, China still would have a final DF-31A brigade attached to Base 56, located hundreds of miles away in western China. This brigade could be especially reassuring given that the longer range of the DF-31A as compared to the DF-31 would enable the brigade to hold more U.S. targets at risk. In general, these deployment patterns suggest that China should have reasonable confidence in the survivability of at least some of its mobile nuclear ICBM brigades even in the event of a conventional war over Taiwan.

In addition to the physical separation of some of these bases and nuclear launch brigades from the likely locus of conventional conflict, the PLARF's central warhead storage base is located deep inside China in the Qinling mountain range.[106] It is virtually inconceivable that the United States could somehow inadvertently threaten or destroy Base 22 while conducting the conventional campaign described earlier; it would be challenging even to do so deliberately. Although it is at least plausible that in the course of a war over Taiwan the United States might attack conventional targets well inside eastern China, such as elements attached to Bases 52 or 55, U.S. forces would have to travel hundreds of miles still farther into the Chinese interior before reaching Base 22.

The physical separation of many of China's nuclear launch brigades from areas likely to see conventional conflict with Taiwan also reduces the possibility that U.S. attacks on Chinese conventional C4ISR would eliminate China's nuclear retaliatory capacity. For example, even if the United

States attacked bases or base elements closer to Taiwan, possibly destroying some nuclear-relevant C4ISR in the process, it is highly unlikely that these attacks would prevent China from launching nuclear weapons from brigades attached to bases located elsewhere. Furthermore, China likely has built significant redundancies into its command and control arrangements for nuclear weapons, including by building back-up command and control capability into the extensive, virtually impenetrable complex at Base 22.[107] This development is far more important for nuclear stability than whether nuclear and conventional systems are interlinked. Even if interlinkages exist, redundancies could mean that conventional fighting would not necessarily create sudden, catastrophic escalatory nuclear pressures.

This is not to say that Chinese nuclear command and control is invulnerable. Command and control posed significant challenges for the United States and the Soviet Union throughout the Cold War, and China appears to recognize it as a serious concern today.[108] For example, Charles Glaser and Steve Fetter conclude that although developing truly survivable nuclear C2 is probably within China's reach, China has not yet achieved it.[109] Crucially, however, their analysis assesses the survivability of China's nuclear C2 in a nuclear war, not a conventional war. The question motivating their analysis is whether the United States can achieve or should pursue a damage-limitation capability against China—that is, the ability to preemptively destroy as much of China's nuclear arsenal as possible in a scenario where the United States anticipates a looming Chinese nuclear first strike. Such a scenario presupposes a dedicated effort to systematically destroy China's nuclear-relevant C2, including through the use of U.S. nuclear weapons. Glaser and Fetter are optimistic that China will eventually obtain survivable C2 even though the bar for survivability under the conditions they examine is dramatically higher than it would be in a conventional war of the type analyzed here.

In sum, the optimists have military-technical grounds for believing that a U.S. conventional campaign would not eliminate China's nuclear retaliatory capability, though significant erosion along the lines the pessimists fear does seem likely. The key question is how China interprets this erosion.

China's Likely Views of the Survivability of Its Nuclear Forces

China's long-standing belief in the minimal requirements of nuclear deterrence is reassuring.[110] Even with only a small number of remaining weapons, China might still believe that it had some insurance against a first strike. That said, if China believed that the U.S. conventional campaign was evolving into an attempt at conventional counterforce, or signaled that the United States would soon launch a nuclear counterforce attack, escalatory pressures could still arise. Chinese writings and statements remain deliberately ambiguous about whether China's no-first-use pledge would hold in the event that conventional attacks started to degrade China's nuclear retaliatory capabilities and about what sorts of conventional attacks China believes would cross this threshold.[111]

Furthermore, if China believes that the United States possesses a damage-limitation capability (or if China believes that the United States believes that it possesses a damage-limitation capability, whether the United States actually does or not), then the threshold above which China will believe it has enough survivable nuclear forces to deter a U.S. first strike is likely to rise.[112] China's persistent concern about U.S. missile defenses and conventional prompt global strike implies that China is indeed worried about whether it would have an adequate survivable nuclear force to impose unacceptable damage after a U.S. first strike.[113] In fact, China's pursuit of SLBMs may stem in part from the desire to thwart these U.S. efforts, because these

missiles could be more difficult for U.S. defenses to intercept.[114]

After all, China could reasonably expect failures in some proportion of its surviving nuclear missiles, no matter their type. For example, during the Cold War the United States routinely made conservative estimates of only 0.8 reliability for its missiles (that is, that out of every ten missiles it tried to launch, two would experience some sort of technical failure), even though actual reliability was probably at least 0.9.[115] China seems likely to make estimates that are at least as conservative given the relative immaturity of its nuclear forces. As such, it might view the destruction of its nuclear forces during the course of a conventional war as more threatening than peacetime statements about the minimal requirements of deterrence would imply, because China cannot assume that all of its surviving missiles will function properly.

Regardless, China continues to express general concerns about the survivability of its nuclear forces in the face of U.S. technological advancements, and the country's leaders are likely aware of considerable open-source evidence regarding U.S. counterforce capabilities.[116] Whether the United States could succeed in disarming China in a first strike remains the subject of considerable disagreement, of course. This is primarily a question of whether the United States would be able to find China's mobile land-based nuclear missiles. Li Bin, a physicist and expert on China's nuclear forces, has offered one of the most detailed analyses of the problem, arguing that the United States likely cannot develop the capability to find all of China's mobile missiles, as long as China undertakes some basic efforts at deception and dispersal.[117] Glaser and Fetter similarly conclude that "China's mobile missiles are likely highly survivable if deployed in the field with nuclear weapons relatively early in a crisis . . . ; if China could launch its mobile missiles from unprepared or unidentified sites; and if Chinese missile forces adopt best practices to avoid detection while in the field."[118] These arguments are consistent with a more generally skeptical view of the U.S. ability to locate mobile targets, drawn in part from the failed Scud missile hunt in the 1991 Gulf War.[119]

Other scholars have presented a more confident assessment of U.S. counterforce capabilities, however. Keir Lieber and Daryl Press argue that long-gestating technological trends rooted in the computer revolution have produced dramatic improvements in the accuracy and remote sensing required to conduct counterforce strikes, undermining the value of the hardening, concealment, and redundancy that states have typically pursued to ensure the survivability of their nuclear weapons. In particular, Lieber and Press posit that U.S. satellites can now use synthetic aperture radar to hunt mobile missiles much more effectively than in the past, which could have significant implications for the survivability of China's arsenal.[120]

Austin Long and Brendan Green come to a similar conclusion through retrospective analysis, showing that even in the Cold War U.S. intelligence capabilities relevant to potential counterforce operations were much better than commonly understood and are probably quite a bit better today given continuing investments.[121] Although Long and Green do not focus specifically on China, their analysis implies that the United States probably could use a combination of signals intelligence detected by satellites plus imagery intelligence provided by stealthy, high-altitude UAVs to locate Chinese mobile ICBMs, especially given that these missiles are substantially slower, larger, and more constrained in their movements and launch locations than Scud missiles were. They also are fewer in number and likely would have been monitored much more closely in peacetime.[122] Long and Green note, for example, that "mobile ICBMs are not typically operated as single transporter erector launchers (TELs). There is a mobile command center, a support vehicle carrying supplies and a field kitchen for the crew, a massive fuel tanker, and at least one security vehicle. Communications between these vehicles can . . . potentially be intercepted and used to locate the vehicles."[123]

Furthermore, in an all-out counterforce scenario the United States likely would be targeting these ICBMs with its own ICBMs, which move much faster to a target and have much lower accuracy requirements than the conventional munitions delivered by fighter-bombers in the Scud hunt.[124] The United States also is continuing to develop and refine a variety of techniques that could enable it to pursue even more sophisticated approaches to hunting Chinese mobile missiles in the future. These include covertly attaching tagging, tracking, and location devices to TELs or related vehicles, and emplacing on likely transportation routes unattended ground sensors that could detect passing TELs and communicate the information to U.S. satellites using burst transmissions that would be hard to intercept.[125] The implication is that hunting China's mobile ICBMs would not be impossible and that this is a contingency for which the United States has prepared for several decades.

Less important than whether this analysis is objectively correct is whether Chinese leaders might believe that it could be correct, regarding both the assessment of raw U.S. technological capabilities and what the pursuit of these capabilities signals about U.S. intentions. In other words, even if the capabilities and trajectory that these scholars identify do not prove definitively that the United States could find and destroy all Chinese mobile missiles, or that the United States would try to do so, the posited developments would make it significantly harder for a Chinese leader to confidently dismiss such possibilities during a war. The contest will come down to whether China believes it can hide a couple of dozen mobile missiles from the United States—or, more precisely, whether China believes that the United States believes that China can hide these missiles.

That story may become progressively harder for Chinese leaders to tell themselves as more and more of their conventional and nuclear or nuclear-relevant assets come under threat during a conventional war. If China interprets those developments as signs that the United States either is attempting conventional counterforce or is more willing to engage in nuclear counterforce than previously understood, China could come to see first use of nuclear weapons as a means of halting the most threatening components of the conventional campaign, or signaling resolve and forcing the United States to reconsider, or both. For example, if China's conventional military capabilities had been significantly degraded, China might see the limited use of nuclear weapons against a U.S. carrier strike group launching attacks on Chinese missile forces or supporting attacks on China's submarine force as the most expeditious means of stopping those potential threats to its nuclear arsenal. Even absent this sort of military utility, however, if China simply believed that the United States was in the process of probing for Chinese resistance, without having fully committed to counterforce yet, and that a counterforce campaign would take some time to be successful, China might see a window in which nuclear use—perhaps beginning with a demonstration strike—could impose enough costs on the United States to cause it to back down. Either or both of these types of motives could lead to use.

Wartime perceptual dynamics are likely to exacerbate fearful Chinese assessments of the security of their nuclear arsenal under these circumstances as well. It is one thing to be confident about the deterrence provided by even small numbers of nuclear weapons in a world where conventional deterrence is also holding steady and the prospect of an adversary attempt at damage limitation is remote. It is more difficult to be confident in a world where those nuclear weapons already have failed to deter the onset and escalation of a massive conventional war on one's home territory, and many of the state's nuclear weapons have been disabled or destroyed.

The mere fact that such a war is occurring could cause significant Chinese reassessment of U.S. intentions. Indeed, circumstantial military-technical evidence of possible U.S. preparation for nuclear counterforce strikes or of U.S. efforts at conventional counterforce may appear cumulatively more ominous during the course of a hot war than they would as a series of isolated hypotheticals in peacetime. In addition, China's ability to assess the scope and implications of U.S. conventional military operations in real time is likely to be limited, in part because U.S. military operations will deliberately seek to circumscribe China's situational awareness. Both of these factors could lead Chinese leaders to fear the worst in the face of an ambiguous military-technical assessment, even if the war had not produced real changes in the U.S. ability to destroy China's arsenal.

China's only past nuclear crisis during a conventional war lends some credence to this possibility. The 1969 border war with the Soviet Union began when Chinese troops ambushed Soviet border guards in a disputed area in an attempt to deter further Soviet incursions in the area as well as any broader Soviet intervention into Chinese politics.[126] The conflict quickly escalated beyond what Chinese leaders had expected and resulted in Moscow brandishing the threat of invasion as well as nuclear attack on China's nascent nuclear program.[127] Although China initially dismissed the nuclear threats, once Chinese leaders learned that the Soviets had been discussing such plans with other countries, the Chinese radically upgraded their assessment of the threats' credibility.[128]

According to a recent study, Chinese leaders suddenly "began to worry, albeit based on little reliable evidence, that Moscow would use the border negotiations as a 'smokescreen' for a nuclear 'sneak attack'." Three separate times during the fall of 1969, Chinese leaders were sure that a Soviet nuclear attack was imminent, to the point that they believed that aircraft transporting Soviet representatives to Beijing for talks on settling the war might actually be armed with nuclear weapons or part of a ruse to insert special operations forces.[129] Chinese leaders left Beijing and ordered preparations for the large-scale evacuation of Chinese civilians, as well as the dispersal of industrial facilities, digging of air-raid shelters, and stockpiling of key supplies.[130] Most importantly, Chinese leaders test-fired a thermonuclear weapon at Lop Nor and placed the country's nuclear forces on a months-long alert for the first and only time in China's history—a risky move given the reliance on liquid-fueled missiles and relatively untested command and control procedures at the time.[131] After numerous preparations for nuclear attacks that never came, China finally agreed to negotiations.

China is a different country today than it was in the time of Mao Zedong, and its arsenal is now better developed, which should induce caution in efforts to discern lessons from the earlier era. Nevertheless, this episode highlights several points with enduring relevance regarding the nuclear implications of conventional wars. China initiated a war in which it believed nuclear weapons would be irrelevant, despite the vast nuclear asymmetry between itself and its opponent. China then radically updated its assessment of the possibility of nuclear attack to a degree bordering on paranoia once the conventional war did not go as expected. Everything the Soviets did—even sending representatives to negotiate, or not launching a nuclear strike on a day that the Chinese expected it—only fed the narrative among Chinese leaders that a nuclear attack was imminent, even though archival evidence now suggests that the Soviets never intended to follow through on their threat.[132] Most worryingly, China prepared to use its nuclear weapons, even though it had to expect devastating retaliation and that merely the preparations to launch raised serious risks of accidental or unauthorized use. Fortunately, China's fears in this case eventually led it to de-escalate the crisis. It is an open question whether a similarly uneventful denouement would occur today in the event of a much larger-scale conventional war involving actual destruction of components of the country's nuclear arsenal and stakes radically more significant than uninhabited islands in the Ussuri River.

Conclusion

Chinese nuclear escalation in the event of a conventional war with the United States is a significant risk, although for reasons not fully surfaced in the existing debate. A U.S. conventional campaign would indeed pose a large, though not total, threat to China's nuclear arsenal. More important than the purely military-technical implications of the U.S. campaign, however, is what China is likely to believe the campaign signals about U.S. intentions in a world where conventional deterrence has just failed. Reasonable Chinese fears that the United States might be attempting conventional counterforce, or considering or preparing for nuclear counterforce, could lead China to engage in limited nuclear escalation to gain military advantage or coercive leverage—despite China's no-first-use policy.

This conclusion, derived from the article's general framework, raises a host of questions for further research. One of the most important is whether China's efforts to alert its nuclear forces during a crisis in order to improve survivability could look to the United States like preparation for escalation, leading the United States to launch what it saw as a damage-limitation strike even if it had originally not intended to engage in counterforce at all.[133] This possibility points to additional escalatory dynamics that might emerge in a future U.S.-China conflict, arising from U.S. interpretations of Chinese actions, especially as Chinese nuclear capabilities expand. Some expansion could be stabilizing, however. If China eventually develops a larger and more survivable nuclear arsenal, the threshold at which U.S. conventional operations could start to seriously erode that arsenal would increase, reassuring Chinese leaders in wartime. Whether such a development would be a net positive for the United States would depend among other things on how China's nuclear expansion affected other aspects of China's behavior, but on the escalation question, it could be beneficial.

More broadly, analysis of the China case raises the question of why the United States might adopt conventional military strategies that could increase risks of opponent nuclear escalation in the first place. Optimists often simply do not address the underlying drivers of such policies, whereas pessimists tend to characterize them as the inadvertent product of U.S. military planning run amok of civilian guidance.[134] It seems more likely that such policies are not inadvertent, at least not in the sense that senior civilian policymakers are blindly unaware of the escalatory risks these policies entail. Rather, my interviews and conversations with senior policymakers, both military and civilian, suggest that they have long been generally cognizant of the fact that U.S. conventional military operations have the potential to create nuclear pressures on opponents.[135]

Some U.S. policymakers view these pressures as regrettable but unavoidable, a necessary evil that should be minimized where possible. Others view these escalatory pressures as affirmatively useful—a means of improving general deterrence and making both conventional and nuclear war less likely. This divide mirrors an old debate.[136] In the Cold War, for example, RAND analysts noted that "those who would emphasize reducing the risk that a deep crisis might lead to nuclear war would give priority to enhancing first-strike stability," that is, to improving the chances that neither side will have an incentive to launch nuclear weapons first in a crisis. But "conversely," these analysts noted, "those who would stress the goal of deterring the Soviets, through the presence of strategic nuclear forces, from provoking a deep crisis in the first place would give priority to strengthening extended deterrence," including by developing policies that would deliberately undermine first-strike stability and threaten nuclear escalation if a crisis did break out.[137] "Obviously," they wrote, "the objective of extended deterrence contradicts that of first-strike stability."[138]

Today, most escalation pessimists would err on the side of strengthening what those analysts called first-strike stability, while escalation optimists tend to think first-strike instability will not be a problem or even to see it as beneficial. Aaron Friedberg has articulated this latter view most clearly with respect to China: "If PLA planners believe that the US would respond to a [conventional] first strike with a blinding campaign, and if they recognize that this could force them to contemplate using or losing their own nuclear weapons, their desire to avoid being put in such a situation might cause them to refrain from launching an [antiaccess/area-denial] campaign in the first place. In short, those who warn of ASB's escalatory potential may be right; but this very fact could actually enhance its deterrent utility."[139] Indeed, the fact that members of China's strategic community insist that they do not see a path from conventional to nuclear war could be read as an effort to deny the United States this "deterrent utility"—to convince the United States that adopting escalatory conventional strategies will not improve general deterrence, because China does not appreciate the nuclear risks that would inhere in a conventional war.[140]

The ultimate question is which of these views is correct. Should the United States do everything in its power to tamp down nuclear escalatory risks that might arise amid conventional war, even if this means sacrificing some conventional military advantages? Or should the United States leverage or even heighten these risks as a means of reducing the likelihood that war ever breaks out? Could there be a middle ground, some set of policies that would achieve what RAND analysts once called "an optimal amount of instability"—"enough to deter the [adversary] from precipitating a crisis, but not enough to cause a crisis to spiral out of control should it occur"?[141]

This article does not answer those enduring questions, but it does provide a foundation that could be used to perform the necessary analysis, both in the U.S.-China context and beyond. These trade-offs will remain challenging as the United States shapes its conventional military strategies toward other potential adversaries that have tight interlinkages between nuclear and conventional forces, such as Russia and North Korea. Future research should examine the extent to which such interlinkages may themselves be the product of deliberate strategic choices on the part of opponents.[142]

NOTES

1. On preemption, see Marc Trachtenberg, *History and Strategy* (Princeton, N.J.: Princeton University Press, 1991), chap. 1; Charles L. Glaser, *Analyzing Strategic Nuclear Policy* (Princeton, N.J.: Princeton University Press, 1990); and Robert Jervis, *The Meaning of the Nuclear Revolution: Statecraft and the Prospect of Armageddon* (Ithaca, N.Y.: Cornell University Press, 1990), especially chap. 5. On unauthorized or accidental launch, see Bruce G. Blair, *Strategic Command and Control: Redefining the Nuclear Threat* (Washington, D.C.: Brookings Institution Press, 1989); Scott D. Sagan, *The Limits of Safety: Organizations, Accidents, and Nuclear Weapons* (Princeton, N.J.: Princeton University Press, 1995); and Peter D. Feaver, *Guarding the Guardians: Civilian Control of Nuclear Weapons in the United States* (Ithaca, N.Y.: Cornell University Press, 1992). On deliberate escalation, see Keir A. Lieber and Daryl G. Press, "Coercive Nuclear Campaigns in the 21st Century: Understanding Adversary Incentives and Options for Nuclear Escalation," PASCC report number 2013-001 (Monterey, Calif.: Naval Postgraduate School, March 2013); Jasen Castillo, "Deliberate Escalation: Nuclear Strategies to Deter or Stop Conventional Attacks," Texas A&M University, October 2014, available from the author upon request; and Vipin Narang, *Nuclear Strategy in the Modern Era: Regional Powers and International Conflict* (Princeton, N.J.: Princeton University Press, 2014).

2. M. Taylor Fravel and Evan S. Medeiros, "China's Search for Assured Retaliation: The Evolution of Chinese Nuclear Strategy and Force Structure," *International Security*, Vol. 35, No. 2 (Fall 2010), pp. 48–87; and Avery Goldstein, *Deterrence and Security in the 21st Century: China, Britain, France, and the Enduring Legacy of the Nuclear Revolution* (Stanford, Calif.: Stanford University Press, 2000), chaps. 3–4.

3. David C. Gompert, Astrid Stuth Cevallos, and Cristina L. Garafola, *War with China: Thinking through the Unthinkable* (Santa Monica, Calif.: RAND Corporation, 2016), p. 29 (emphasis in the original).

4. Jan van Tol et al., "AirSea Battle," Microsoft PowerPoint slides, May 18, 2010, p. xiii, available from the author upon request.

5. Sam LaGrone, "Pentagon Drops Air Sea Battle Name, Concept Lives On," *U.S. Naval Institute News*, January 20, 2015, http://news

.usni.org/2015/01/20/pentagon-drops-air-sea-battle-name-concept-lives; and Michael R. Gordon and Bernard E. Trainor, *The Generals' War: The Inside Story of the Conflict in the Gulf* (New York: Little, Brown, 1995), pp. 137, 408, 414, 418, 423, 442.

6. Barry R. Posen, *Inadvertent Escalation: Conventional War and Nuclear Risks* (Ithaca, N.Y.: Cornell University Press, 1991).

7. Thomas J. Christensen, "The Meaning of the Nuclear Evolution: China's Strategic Modernization and U.S.-China Security Relations," *Journal of Strategic Studies*, Vol. 35, No. 4 (August 2012), p. 470 fn. 54.

8. Ibid., p. 453.

9. Avery Goldstein, "First Things First: The Pressing Danger of Crisis Instability in U.S.-China Relations," *International Security*, Vol. 37, No. 4 (Spring 2013), pp. 49–89, especially pp. 70–72, 88.

10. Joshua Rovner, "AirSea Battle and Escalation Risks," policy brief 12 (San Diego: University of California Institute on Global Conflict and Cooperation, January 2012), p. 4.

11. Wu Riqiang, "Sino-U.S. Inadvertent Nuclear Escalation," Renmin University, 2016, pp. 6, 10, 13–17, 30, 33–35, available from the author upon request.

12. Christopher P. Twomey, "Asia's Complex Strategic Environment: Nuclear Multipolarity and Other Dangers," *Asia Policy*, January 2011, p. 64.

13. Eric Heginbotham et al., *The U.S.-China Military Scorecard: Forces, Geography, and the Evolving Balance of Power, 1996–2017* (Arlington, Va.: RAND Corporation, 2015), p. 353.

14. T.X. Hammes, "Offshore Control: A Proposed Strategy for an Unlikely Conflict," Strategic Forum No. 278 (Washington, D.C.: Institute for National Strategic Studies, National Defense University, June 2012); and Jeffrey E. Kline and Wayne P. Hughes Jr., "Between Peace and the Air-Sea Battle: A War at Sea Strategy," *Naval War College Review*, Vol. 65, No. 4 (Autumn 2012), pp. 34–41.

15. Elbridge Colby, "Don't Sweat AirSea Battle," *National Interest*, July 31, 2013, http://nationalinterest.org/commentary/dont-sweat-airsea-battle-8804.

16. Vincent A. Manzo, "After the First Shots: Managing Escalation in Northeast Asia," *Joint Forces Quarterly*, 2nd Quarter 2015, especially pp. 96–97.

17. Discussions and interviews conducted with nearly three dozen current and former mid-level to senior civilians and military officers with experience serving in the Department of Defense (Office of the Secretary of Defense, Joint Staff, Service Staffs, Strategic Command, Pacific Command, and European Command), Department of State, and intelligence community, fall 2014–summer 2016. Participants requested anonymity.

18. Blair was responding to a question from William Norris during the Carnegie International Nuclear Policy Conference, Washington, D.C., March 23–24, 2015.

19. Fiona S. Cunningham and M. Taylor Fravel, "Assuring Assured Retaliation: China's Nuclear Posture and U.S.-China Strategic Stability," *International Security*, Vol. 40, No. 2 (Fall 2015), pp. 40–41.

20. Ibid., pp. 17–19, 41.

21. Ibid., p. 42.

22. Ibid., p. 44.

23. I draw here on Posen, *Inadvertent Escalation*, especially chap. 1.

24. Ibid., p. 2.

25. Ibid.

26. For critical analysis of damage-limitation logics, see Glaser, *Analyzing Strategic Nuclear Policy;* and Jervis, *The Meaning of the Nuclear Revolution.*

27. See some of the examples in Posen, *Inadvertent Escalation,* pp. 143–146, 154.

28. On limited nuclear use for coercive purposes under conditions of mutual vulnerability, see Robert Powell, "Theoretical Foundations of Strategic Nuclear Deterrence," *Political Science Quarterly,* Vol. 100, No. 1 (Spring 1985), pp. 75–96; and Robert Jervis, "Why Nuclear Superiority Doesn't Matter," *Political Science Quarterly,* Vol. 94, No. 4 (Winter 1979/80), pp. 628–629.

29. Glaser, *Analyzing Strategic Nuclear Policy;* Jervis, *The Meaning of the Nuclear Revolution;* and Waltz's chapters in Scott D. Sagan and Kenneth N. Waltz, *The Spread of Nuclear Weapons: A Debate* (New York: W. W. Norton, 1997).

30. Posen provides a similar but more abbreviated list. See Posen, *Inadvertent Escalation,* p. 3.

31. Ibid.

32. Ibid., pp. 3, 9.

33. Elbridge Colby et al., *The Israeli "Nuclear Alert" of 1973: Deterrence and Signaling in Crisis* (Washington, D.C.: Center for Naval Analyses, April 2013), pp. 13, 29–49; and Narang, *Nuclear Strategy in the Modern Era,* p. 289.

34. Posen, *Inadvertent Escalation,* pp. 19–23.

35. Examples include the downing of a Malaysian Air jet over Ukraine in 2014, the U.S. downing of an Iran Air flight in 1988, and the Soviet intercept of a Korean Air flight in 1983.

36. Scott L. Kastner, "Is the Taiwan Strait Still a Flashpoint? Rethinking the Prospects for Armed Conflict between China and Taiwan," *International Security,* Vol. 40, No. 3 (Winter 2015/16), pp. 54–92; Samuel J. Locklear, prepared statement, Department of Defense Authorization of Appropriations for Fiscal Year 2014 and the Future Years Defense Program, U.S. Senate, Committee on Armed Services, April 9, 2013, p. 420, http://www.armed-services.senate.gov/imo/media/doc/pacom_fullcomm_hearing_040913.pdf; and Bernard D. Cole, *Asian Maritime Strategies: Navigating Troubled Waters* (Annapolis: Naval Institute Press, 2013), p. 99. Conflicts in the South or East China Seas or on the Korean Peninsula are also possible, though unlikely to be as intense.

37. Charles L. Glaser, "A U.S.-China Grand Bargain? The Hard Choice between Military Competition and Accommodation," *International Security,* Vol. 39, No. 4 (Spring 2015), pp. 49–90.

38. James Steinberg and Michael E. O'Hanlon, *Strategic Reassurance and Resolve: U.S.-China Relations in the Twenty-first Century* (Princeton, N.J.: Princeton University Press, 2014), pp. 131–132; and Heginbotham et al., *The U.S.-China Military Scorecard,* chap. 8. On the likelihood of coercion, see Office of the Secretary of Defense, *Military and Security Developments Involving the People's Republic of China 2014,* annual report to Congress (Washington, D.C.: U.S. Department of Defense, 2014), http://archive.defense.gov/pubs/2014_DoD_China_Report.pdf; and Office of Naval Intelligence, *A Modern Navy with Chinese Characteristics* (Suitland, Md.: Office of Naval Intelligence, August 2009).

39. James Dobbins et al., *Conflict with China: Prospects, Consequences, and Strategies for Deterrence* (Washington, D.C.: RAND Corpora-

tion, 2011), pp. 3, 5; and Craig Murray, with Kyle Churchman, "Taiwan's Declining Defense Spending Could Jeopardize Military Preparedness" (Washington, D.C.: U.S.-China Economic and Security Review Commission, June 11, 2013), http://www.uscc.gov/Research/taiwan%E2%80%99s-declining-defense-spending-could-jeopardize-military-preparedness.

40. Roger Cliff, "Anti-Access Measures in Chinese Defense Strategy," testimony presented before the U.S.-China Economic and Security Review Commission (Santa Monica, Calif.: RAND Corporation, January 27, 2011), p. 2; M. Taylor Fravel and Christopher P. Twomey, "Projecting Strategy: The Myth of Chinese Counter-intervention," *Washington Quarterly,* Vol. 37, No. 4 (Winter 2015), pp. 171–187; and Stephen Biddle and Ivan Oelrich, "Future Warfare in the Western Pacific: Chinese Antiaccess/Area Denial, U.S. AirSea Battle, and Command of the Commons in East Asia," *International Security,* Vol. 41, No. 1 (Summer 2016), pp. 7–48.

41. Heginbotham et al., *The U.S.-China Military Scorecard,* pp. 31, 75.

42. Ibid., pp. xxv, 33, 139.

43. Ibid., p. xxv.

44. Ibid., p. 29.

45. Ibid., p. 32.

46. Ibid., p. 99.

47. Ibid., pp. 109–111.

48. Ibid., pp. 102–104.

49. The Growler, however, will eventually be replaced by the F-35, which, like other fifth-generation aircraft, is not large enough to carry the HARM internally while maintaining stealth. To attack enemy air defenses, fifth-generation aircraft will have to use subsonic glide weapons, which may not be as effective. See ibid., p. 124.

50. Ibid., p. 103.

51. States have exhibited considerable variation in this regard. See Stephen Biddle and Robert Zirkle, "Technology, Civil-Military Relations, and Warfare in the Developing World," *Journal of Strategic Studies,* Vol. 19, No. 2 (June 1996), pp. 171–212; and Barry R. Posen, "The War for Kosovo: Serbia's Political-Military Strategy," *International Security,* Vol. 24, No. 4 (Spring 2000), pp. 39–84.

52. Heginbotham et al., *The U.S.-China Military Scorecard,* pp. 153–200.

53. Ibid., p. 29; and Office of the Secretary of Defense, *Military and Security Developments Involving the People's Republic of China 2014,* p. 40.

54. Owen R. Coté Jr., "Assessing the Undersea Balance between the U.S. and China" (Cambridge, Mass.: Security Studies Program, Massachusetts Institute of Technology, February 2011), p. 2.

55. See Goldstein, "First Things First," pp. 69–73.

56. Heginbotham et al., *The U.S.-China Military Scorecard,* p. 30. For a discussion of the challenges that China may face in attempting to target this missile over the horizon, see ibid., pp. 156–171; and Coté, "Assessing the Undersea Balance between the U.S. and China," pp. 16–17.

57. Office of Naval Intelligence, *The PLA Navy: New Capabilities and Missions for the 21st Century* (Suitland, Md.: Office of Naval Intelligence, April 2015), p. 14.

58. Kelsey Davenport, "China Elevates Nuclear Rocket Force," *Arms Control Today,* March 2016, https://www.armscontrol.org/ACT/2016_03/News/China-Elevates-Nuclear-Rocket-Force.

59. Heginbotham et al., *The U.S.-China Military Scorecard,* pp. 28, 47.

60. Ibid., pp. 28, 50; Mark A. Stokes, prepared statement before the U.S.-China Economic and Security Review Commission, U.S. Senate, 114th Cong., 1st sess., April 1, 2015, pp. 6–17, http://origin.www.uscc.gov/sites/default/files/transcripts/April%2001,%202015_Hearing%20 Transcript_0.pdf; and Mark A. Stokes and Ian Easton, "Evolving Aerospace Trends in the Asia-Pacific Region: Implications for Stability in the Taiwan Strait and Beyond" (Arlington, Va.: Project 2049 Institute, 2010), p. 12.

61. Cunningham and Fravel, "Assuring Assured Retaliation," p. 43; Mark A. Stokes, "China's Nuclear Warhead Storage and Handling System" (Arlington, Va.: Project 2049 Institute, March 12, 2010); and Mark A. Stokes, "Second Artillery Unit and Leadership Directory" (Arlington, Va.: Project 2049 Institute, January 2, 2014), available from the author upon request.

62. On Vietnam, see Marshall L. Michel III, *The Eleven Days of Christmas: America's Last Vietnam Battle* (New York: Encounter Books, 2001); and Marshall L. Michel III, *Clashes: Air Combat over North Vietnam, 1965–1972* (Annapolis: Naval Institute Press, 2007). On Iraq, see Gordon and Trainor, *The Generals' War*, especially p. 201; and Thomas A. Keaney and Eliot A. Cohen, *Gulf War Airpower Survey: Summary Report* (Washington, D.C.: Department of the Air Force, 1993), especially p. 32.

63. Hans M. Kristensen, "DF-21C Missile Deploys to Central China" (Washington, D.C.: Federation of American Scientists, September 28, 2010), https://fas.org/blogs/security/2010/09/df21c/.

64. Caitlin Talmadge, "Closing Time: Assessing the Iranian Threat to the Strait of Hormuz," *International Security*, Vol. 33, No. 1 (Summer 2008), pp. 107–108, especially fn. 95; and Austin Long and Brendan Rittenhouse Green, "Stalking the Secure Second Strike: Intelligence, Counterforce, and Nuclear Strategy," *Journal of Strategic Studies*, Vol. 38, Nos. 1–2 (2015), pp. 15–16.

65. Michel, *The Eleven Days of Christmas*; William R. Emerson, "Operation POINTBLANK: A Tale of Bombers and Fighters," U.S. Air Force Academy Memorial Lecture No. 4 (Colorado Springs, Colo.: U.S. Air Force Academy, 1962), http://www.usafa.edu/df/dfh/docs/Harmon04.pdf; and Frank W. Heilenday, *Daylight Raids by the U.S. Eighth Air Force: Lessons Learned and Lingering Myths from World War II* (Santa Monica, Calif.: RAND Corporation, 1995), pp. 3–4.

66. Talmadge, "Closing Time," pp. 107–108; and Coté, "Assessing the Undersea Balance between the U.S. and China," p. 21.

67. Heginbotham et al., *The U.S.-China Military Scorecard*, p. xxv; and Coté, "Assessing the Undersea Balance between the U.S. and China," pp. 16–17.

68. Heginbotham et al., *The U.S.-China Military Scorecard*, p. 98.

69. Ibid., chap. 9, especially pp. 238, 240–241.

70. Jeffrey Lewis, *Paper Tigers: China's Nuclear Posture*, Adelphi Paper No. 446 (London: International Institute for Strategic Studies, 2014), p. 116; and Stokes, "Second Artillery Unit and Leadership Directory," pp. 10, 11, 20, 26.

71. Lewis, *Paper Tigers*, p. 116.

72. Cunningham and Fravel, "Assuring Assured Retaliation," pp. 42–45; and Ron Christman, "China's Second Artillery Force: Capabilities and Missions for the Near Seas," in Peter Dutton, Andrew S. Erickson, and Ryan Martinson, eds., *China's Near Seas Combat Capabilities* (Newport, R.I.: Naval War College, 2014), p. 35.

73. Stokes, prepared statement before the U.S.-China Economic and Security Review Commission, p. 9; and Lewis, *Paper Tigers*, p. 116.

74. Stokes, "China's Nuclear Warhead Storage and Handling System," p. 3.

75. Stokes, prepared statement before the U.S.-China Economic and Security Review Commission, pp. 4, 9.

76. Stokes, "Second Artillery Unit and Leadership Directory," p. 10.

77. See, for example, Stokes and Easton, "Evolving Aerospace Trends in the Asia-Pacific Region," pp. 8, 13; and Christman, "China's Second Artillery Force," p. 39.

78. Stokes, "China's Nuclear Warhead Storage and Handling System," p. 8.

79. Cunningham and Fravel, "Assuring Assured Retaliation," p. 45.

80. Owen R. Coté Jr., *The Third Battle: Innovation in the U.S. Navy's Silent Cold War Struggle with Soviet Submarines* (Newport, R.I.: Naval War College, 2003), especially pp. 25–26.

81. Wu Riqiang, "Survivability of China's Sea-Based Nuclear Forces," *Science and Global Security*, Vol. 19, No. 2 (2011), pp. 91–120; and Coté, "Assessing the Undersea Balance between the U.S. and China," especially pp. 12–14.

82. Coté, *The Third Battle*, p. 75.

83. Office of Naval Intelligence, *A Modern Navy with Chinese Characteristics*, p. 22. On likely Chinese efforts to pursue quieting, see Steven Mufson, "Obama's Quiet Nuclear Deal with China Raises Proliferation Concerns," *Washington Post*, May 10, 2015.

84. Wu, "Survivability of China's Sea-Based Nuclear Forces," p. 98. For background, see Scott R. Thompson, "Sound Propagation Considerations for a Deep-Ocean Acoustic Network," master's thesis, Naval Postgraduate School, 2009.

85. This problem is not new. See John J. Mearsheimer, "A Strategic Misstep: The Maritime Strategy and Deterrence in Europe," *International Security*, Vol. 11, No. 2 (Fall 1986), pp. 12, 40–41.

86. China is clearly aware of this threat and has added electronic countermeasure battalions to its missile brigades in response. See Stokes, "Second Artillery Unit and Leadership Directory," p. 9.

87. Office of the Secretary of Defense, *Military and Security Developments Involving the People's Republic of China 2014*, pp. 10, 33, 69.

88. Stokes, "China's Nuclear Warhead Storage and Handling System," p. 3.

89. Heginbotham et al., *The U.S.-China Military Scorecard*, pp. 315–316; and Wu, "Survivability of China's Sea-Based Nuclear Forces."

90. Office of Naval Intelligence, *The PLA Navy*, pp. 14–15; and Hans M. Kristensen and Robert S. Norris, "Chinese Nuclear Forces, 2015," *Bulletin of the Atomic Scientists*, Vol. 71, No. 4 (2015), p. 81.

91. Cunningham and Fravel, "Assuring Assured Retaliation," p. 42. Some Western analysts, such as Stokes, do believe that the systems are separate. See Stokes, prepared statement before the U.S.-China Economic and Security Review Commission, p. 11.

92. Wu, "Sino-U.S. Inadvertent Escalation," pp. 33–35.

93. Keir A. Lieber and Daryl G. Press, "The New Era of Counterforce: Technological Change and the Future of Deterrence," *International Security*, Vol. 41, No. 4 (Spring 2017), pp. 9–49.

94. Posen, *Inadvertent Escalation*, pp. 13–15, and chap. 2.

95. Ibid., pp. 2, 15, 28–29, and chap. 4, especially pp. 129–132; Benjamin B. Fischer, "The Soviet-American War Scare of the

1980s," *International Journal of Intelligence and Counterintelligence,* Vol. 19, No. 3 (2006), pp. 499–501, 504; Pavel Podvig, "History and the Current Status of the Russian Early-Warning System," *Science and Global Security,* Vol. 10 (2002), pp. 21–60; and interviews with A.S. Kalashnikov and Andrian Danilevich in John G. Hines, Ellis M. Mishulovich, and John F. Shull, *Soviet Intentions, 1965–1985,* Vol. 2: *Soviet Post–Cold War Testimonial Evidence* (McLean, Va.: BDM, 1995), pp. 31, 33–35, 41, 46, 57, 64, 88–90.

96. China likely is already planning to develop a next-generation SSBN and SLBM. See Michael S. Chase and Arthur Chan, "China's Evolving Strategic Deterrence Concepts and Capabilities," *Washington Quarterly,* Vol. 39, No. 1 (Spring 2016), p. 125.

97. Kristensen and Norris, "Chinese Nuclear Forces, 2015," p. 82.

98. Lewis, *Paper Tigers,* p. 116.

99. Office of the Secretary of Defense, *Military and Security Developments Involving the People's Republic of China 2015,* annual report to Congress (Washington, D.C.: U.S. Department of Defense, 2015), p. 8; and Kristensen and Norris, "Chinese Nuclear Forces, 2015," pp. 78–79. I exclude the DF-3 because China is likely phasing it out. See ibid.; and Lewis, *Paper Tigers,* p. 116.

100. Stokes, "Second Artillery Unit and Leadership Directory," p. 24.

101. Kristensen and Norris, "Chinese Nuclear Forces, 2015," p. 79. Kristensen and Norris note that this missile is in the process of being replaced by the DF-31.

102. Ibid., pp. 78–80. For background, see Heginbotham et al., *The U.S.-China Military Scorecard,* p. 28.

103. Lewis, *Paper Tigers,* p. 116.

104. Stokes, "Second Artillery Unit and Leadership Directory," pp. 12, 26; and Lewis, *Paper Tigers,* p. 116.

105. M. Taylor Fravel, "China's Nuclear Strategy," Massachusetts Institute of Technology, 2016, chap. 6.

106. Stokes, "China's Nuclear Warhead Storage and Handling System," p. 4.

107. Stokes, "Second Artillery Unit and Leadership Directory," p. 3; and Stokes, "China's Nuclear Warhead Storage and Handling System," p. 6.

108. Ashton B. Carter, John D. Steinbruner, and Charles A. Zraket, eds., *Managing Nuclear Operations* (Washington, D.C.: Brookings Institution Press, 1987); Blair, *Strategic Command and Control;* and Gregory Kulacki, "The Chinese Military Updates China's Nuclear Strategy" (Cambridge, Mass.: Union of Concerned Scientists, March 2015), http://www.ucsusa.org/sites/default/files/attach/2015/03/chinese-nuclear-strategy-full-report.pdf.

109. Charles L. Glaser and Steve Fetter, "Should the United States Reject MAD? Damage Limitation and U.S. Nuclear Strategy toward China," *International Security,* Vol. 41, No. 1 (Summer 2016), pp. 72–74.

110. Fravel and Medeiros, "China's Search for Assured Retaliation"; and Fravel, "China's Nuclear Strategy."

111. Fravel and Medeiros, "China's Search for Assured Retaliation," p. 80; and Christensen, "The Meaning of the Nuclear Evolution," pp. 454, 475–477. This ambiguity is a long-standing theme in Chinese nuclear strategy. See Goldstein, *Deterrence and Security in the 21st Century,* pp. 129–136.

112. Glaser and Fetter, "Should the United States Reject MAD?"; and Chase and Chan, "China's Evolving Strategic Deterrence Concepts and Capabilities," p. 130.

113. Cunningham and Fravel, "Assuring Assured Retaliation," pp. 15, 19–20; Heginbotham et al., *The U.S.-China Military Scorecard,* p. 315; and Theodore Postol, "Is a U.S. Missile Defense Aimed at China?" presentation at the Carnegie Endowment for International Peace, Washington, D.C., October 15, 2015, http://carnegieendowment.org/2015/10/15/is-u.s.-missile-defense-aimed-at-china-event-5026.

114. Andrew S. Erickson and Lyle J. Goldstein, "China's Future Nuclear Submarine Force: Insights from Chinese Writings," *Naval War College Review,* Vol. 60, No. 1 (Winter 2007), pp. 65–66.

115. Joshua M. Epstein, *The 1988 Defense Budget* (Washington, D.C.: Brookings Institution Press, 1987), p. 22; and Theodore Postol "The Trident and Strategic Stability," *Oceanus,* Vol. 28, No. 3 (Summer 1985), p. 51.

116. Keir A. Lieber and Daryl G. Press, "The End of MAD? The Nuclear Dimension of U.S. Primacy," *International Security,* Vol. 30, No. 4 (Spring 2006), pp. 7–44.

117. Li Bin, "Tracking Chinese Strategic Mobile Missiles," *Science and Global Security,* Vol. 15 (2007), pp. 1–30.

118. Glaser and Fetter, "Should the United States Reject MAD?" p. 70.

119. See, for example, David Ochmanek and Lowell H. Schwartz, *The Challenge of Nuclear-Armed Regional Adversaries* (Santa Monica, Calif.: RAND Corporation, 2008).

120. Lieber and Press, "The New Era of Counterforce."

121. Long and Green, "Stalking the Secure Second Strike," especially pp. 5–9.

122. Ibid., pp. 21–23.

123. Ibid., pp. 14–18.

124. Ibid., pp. 21–23.

125. Ibid., pp. 26–27.

126. M. Taylor Fravel, *Strong Borders, Secure Nation: Cooperation and Conflict in China's Territorial Disputes* (Princeton, N.J.: Princeton University Press, 2008), pp. 211–217; and Lorenz M. Lüthi, "Restoring Chaos to History: Sino-Soviet-American Relations, 1969," *China Quarterly,* June 2012, pp. 378–397.

127. Fravel, *Strong Borders, Secure Nation,* p. 213; Michael Gerson et al., *The Sino-Soviet Border Conflict: Deterrence, Escalation, and the Threat of Nuclear War in 1969* (Washington, D.C.: Center for Naval Analyses, November 2010), p. 27; Lüthi, "Restoring Chaos to History," p. 383; John Wilson Lewis and Litai Xue, *Imagined Enemies: China Prepares for Uncertain War* (Stanford, Calif.: Stanford University Press, 2006), p. 52; and Lyle J. Goldstein, *Preventive Attack and Weapons of Mass Destruction: A Comparative Historical Analysis* (Stanford, Calif.: Stanford University Press, 2006), pp. 78–83.

128. Lüthi, "Restoring Chaos to History," pp. 390–391; Gerson et al., *The Sino-Soviet Border Conflict,* pp. 28–40; and Lewis and Xue, *Imagined Enemies,* p. 56.

129. Gerson et al., *The Sino-Soviet Border Conflict,* pp. 46, 50. See also Lewis and Xue, *Imagined Enemies,* pp. 58–64.

130. Lüthi, "Restoring Chaos to History," pp. 391–394; Gerson et al., *The Sino-Soviet Border Conflict,* pp. 40–41; and Lewis and Xue, *Imagined Enemies,* pp. 54, 57.

131. In fact, there is evidence that senior Chinese leaders did not fully understand the primitive state of some of the missiles ordered to alert status. See Gerson et al., *The Sino-Soviet Border Conflict,* p. 4; Fravel, *Strong Borders, Secure Nation,* p. 215; and Lewis and Xue, *Imagined Enemies,* pp. 45, 59–72.

132. Gerson et al., *The Sino-Soviet Border Conflict*, pp. 46–52.

133. I owe my understanding of this point to Charles Glaser and Avery Goldstein.

134. See, for example, Christensen, "The Meaning of the Nuclear Evolution," p. 482; and Posen, *Inadvertent Escalation*, especially chap. 6.

135. See footnote 17.

136. Mearsheimer, "A Strategic Misstep," especially pp. 7–8, 46–54.

137. Glenn A. Kent and David E. Thaler, *First-Strike Stability: A Methodology for Evaluating Strategic Forces* (Santa Monica, Calif.: RAND Corporation, 1989), p. 5.

138. Ibid., pp. 45–46.

139. Aaron Friedberg, *Beyond Air-Sea Battle: The Debate over U.S. Military Strategy in Asia*, Adelphi Paper No. 444 (London: International Institute of Strategic Studies, April 2014), pp. 89–90.

140. I owe my understanding of this point to George Quester.

141. Kent and Thaler, *First-Strike Stability*, p. 46.

142. Opponents may adopt such strategies in an effort to wield "the threat that leaves something to chance." Thomas C. Schelling, *The Strategy of Conflict* (Cambridge, Mass.: Harvard University Press, 1960), chap. 8. See also Robert Powell, "Nuclear Brinkmanship, Limited War, and Military Power," *International Organization*, Vol. 69, No. 3 (Summer 2015), especially pp. 593–597.

James D. Fearon

RATIONALIST EXPLANATIONS FOR WAR

The central puzzle about war, and also the main reason we study it, is that wars are costly but nonetheless wars recur. Scholars have attempted to resolve the puzzle with three types of argument. First, one can argue that people (and state leaders in particular) are sometimes or always irrational. They are subject to biases and pathologies that lead them to neglect the costs of war or to misunderstand how their actions will produce it. Second, one can argue that the leaders who order war enjoy its benefits but do not pay the costs, which are suffered by soldiers and citizens. Third, one can argue that even rational leaders who consider the risks and costs of war may end up fighting nonetheless.

This article focuses on arguments of the third sort, which I will call rationalist explanations.[1] Rationalist explanations abound in the literature on international conflict, assuming a great variety of specific forms. Moreover, for at least two reasons many scholars have given rationalist explanations a certain pride of place. First, historians and political scientists who have studied the origins of particular wars often have concluded that war can be a rational alternative for leaders who are acting in their states' interest—they find that the expected benefits of war sometimes outweigh the expected costs, however unfortunate this may be. Second, the dominant paradigm in international relations theory, neorealism, is thought to advance or even to depend on rationalist arguments about the causes of war. Indeed, if no rationalist explanation for war is theoretically or empirically tenable, then neither is neorealism. The causes of war would then lie in the defects of human nature or particular states rather than in the international system, as argued by neorealists. What I refer to here as "rationalist explanations for war" could just as well be called "neorealist explanations."[2]

This article attempts to provide a clear statement of what a rationalist explanation for war is and to characterize the full set of rationalist explanations that are both theoretically coherent and empirically plausible. It should be obvious that this theoretical exercise must take place prior to testing rationalist explanations against alternatives—we cannot perform such tests unless we know what a rationalist explanation really is. Arguably, the exercise is also foundational for neorealism. Despite its prominence, neorealist theory lacks a clearly stated and fully conceived explanation for war. As I will argue below, it is not enough to say that under anarchy nothing stops states from using force, or that anarchy forces states to rely on self-help, which engenders mutual suspicion and (through spirals or the security dilemma) armed conflict. Neither do diverse references to miscalculation, deterrence failure because of inadequate forces or incredible threats, preventive and preemptive considerations, or free-riding in alliances amount to theoretically coherent rationalist explanations for war.

My main argument is that on close inspection none of the principal rationalist arguments

From *International Organization* 49, no. 3 (Summer 1995): 379–410. Some technical material has been moved to the notes.

advanced in the literature holds up as an explanation because none addresses or adequately resolves the central puzzle, namely, that war is costly and risky, so rational states should have incentives to locate negotiated settlements that all would prefer to the gamble of war. The common flaw of the standard rationalist arguments is that they fail either to address or to explain adequately what prevents leaders from reaching *ex ante* (prewar) bargains that would avoid the costs and risks of fighting. A coherent rationalist explanation for war must do more than give reasons why armed conflict might appear an attractive option to a rational leader under some circumstances—it must show why states are unable to locate an alternative outcome that both would prefer to a fight.

To summarize what follows, the article will consider five rationalist arguments accepted as tenable in the literature on the causes of war. Discussed at length below, these arguments are given the following labels: (1) anarchy; (2) expected benefits greater than expected costs; (3) rational preventive war; (4) rational miscalculation due to lack of information; and (5) rational miscalculation or disagreement about relative power. I argue that the first three arguments simply do not address the question of what prevents state leaders from bargaining to a settlement that would avoid the costs of fighting. The fourth and fifth arguments do address the question, holding that rational leaders may miss a superior negotiated settlement when lack of information leads them to miscalculate relative power or resolve. However, as typically stated, neither argument explains what prevents rational leaders from using diplomacy or other forms of communication to avoid such costly miscalculations.

If these standard arguments do not resolve the puzzle on rationalist terms, what does? I propose that there are three defensible answers, which take the form of general mechanisms, or causal logics, that operate in a variety of more specific international contexts.[3] In the first mechanism, rational leaders may be unable to locate a mutually preferable negotiated settlement due to *private information* about relative capabilities or resolve and *incentives to misrepresent* such information. Leaders know things about their military capabilities and willingness to fight that other states do not know, and in bargaining situations they can have incentives to misrepresent such private information in order to gain a better deal. I show that given these incentives, communication may not allow rational leaders to clarify relative power or resolve without generating a real risk of war. This is not simply a matter of miscalculation due to poor information but rather of specific strategic dynamics that result from the combination of asymmetric information and incentives to dissemble.

Second, rationally led states may be unable to arrange a settlement that both would prefer to war due to *commitment problems*, situations in which mutually preferable bargains are unattainable because one or more states would have an incentive to renege on the terms. While anarchy (understood as the absence of an authority capable of policing agreements) is routinely cited as a cause of war in the literature, it is difficult to find explanations for exactly why the inability to make commitments should imply that war will sometimes occur. That is, what are the specific, empirically identifiable mechanisms by which the inability to commit makes it impossible for states to strike deals that would avoid the costs of war? I identify three such specific mechanisms, arguing in particular that preventive war between rational states stems from a commitment problem rather than from differential power growth per se.

The third sort of rationalist explanation I find less compelling than the first two, although it is logically tenable. States might be unable to locate a peaceful settlement both prefer due to *issue indivisibilities*. Perhaps some issues, by their very natures, simply will not admit compromise.

Though neither example is wholly convincing, issues that might exhibit indivisibility include abortion in domestic politics and the problem of which prince sits on the throne of, say, Spain, in eighteenth- or nineteenth-century international politics. Issue indivisibility could in principle make war rational for the obvious reason that if the issue allows only a finite number of resolutions, it might be that none falls within the range that both prefer to fighting. However, the issues over which states bargain typically are complex and multidimensional; side-payments or linkages with other issues typically are possible; and in principle states could alternate or randomize among a fixed number of possible solutions to a dispute. War-prone international issues may often be *effectively* indivisible, but the cause of this indivisibility lies in domestic political and other mechanisms rather than in the nature of the issues themselves.

In the first section of the article I discuss the puzzle posed by the fact that war is costly. Using a simple formalization of the bargaining problem faced by states in conflict, I show that under very broad conditions bargains will exist that genuinely rational states would prefer to a risky and costly fight. The second section argues that rational miscalculations of relative power and resolve must be due to private information and then considers how war may result from the combination of private information and incentives to misrepresent that information in bargaining. In the third section, I discuss commitment problems as the second class of defensible rationalist explanations for war. Throughout, I specify theoretical arguments with simple game-theoretic representations and assess plausibility with historical examples.

Before beginning, I should make it clear that I am not presenting either commitment problems or private information and incentives to misrepresent as wholly novel explanations for war that are proposed here for the first time. The literature on the causes of war is massive, and these ideas, mixed with myriad others, can be found in it in various guises. The main theoretical task facing students of war is not to add to the already long list of arguments and conjectures but instead to take apart and reassemble these diverse arguments into a coherent theory fit for guiding empirical research. Toward this end, I am arguing that when one looks carefully at the problem of explaining how war could occur between genuinely rational, unitary states, one finds that there are really only two ways to do it. The diverse rationalist or neorealist explanations commonly found in the literature fail for two reasons. First, many do not even address the relevant question—what prevents states from locating a bargain both sides would prefer to a fight? They do not address the question because it is widely but incorrectly assumed that rational states can face a situation of deadlock, wherein no agreements exist that both sides would prefer to a war.[4] Second, the rationalist arguments that do address the question—such as (4) and (5) above—do not go far enough in answering it. When fully developed, they prove to be one of the two major mechanisms developed here, namely, either a commitment problem or a problem arising from private information and incentives to misrepresent. These two mechanisms, I will argue, provide the foundations for a rationalist or neorealist theory of war.

The Puzzle

Most historians and political scientists who study war dismiss as naive the view that all wars must be unwanted because they entail destruction and suffering. Instead, most agree that while a few wars may have been unwanted by the leaders who brought them about—World War I is sometimes given as an example—many or perhaps most wars were simply wanted. The leaders involved viewed war as a costly but worthwhile gamble.[5]

Moreover, many scholars believe that wanted wars are easily explained from a rationalist perspective. Wanted wars are thought to be Pareto-efficient—they occur when no negotiated settlements exist that both sides would prefer to the gamble of military conflict. Conventional wisdom holds that while this situation may be tragic, it is entirely possible between states led by rational leaders who consider the costs and risks of fighting. Unwanted wars, which take place despite the existence of settlements both sides preferred to conflict, are thought to pose more of a puzzle, but one that is resolvable and also fairly rare.

The conventional distinction between wanted and unwanted wars misunderstands the puzzle posed by war. The reason is that the standard conception does not distinguish between two types of efficiency—*ex ante* and *ex post*. As long as both sides suffer some costs for fighting, then war is always inefficient *ex post*—both sides would have been better off if they could have achieved the same final resolution without suffering the costs (or by paying lower costs). This is true even if the costs of fighting are small, or if one or both sides viewed the potential benefits as greater than the costs, since there are still costs. Unless states enjoy the activity of fighting for its own sake, as a consumption good, then war is inefficient *ex post*.

From a rationalist perspective, the central puzzle about war is precisely this *ex post* inefficiency. Before fighting, both sides know that war will entail some costs, and even if they expect offsetting benefits they still have an incentive to avoid the costs. The central question, then, is what prevents states in a dispute from reaching an *ex ante* agreement that avoids the costs they know will be paid *ex post* if they go to war? Giving a rationalist explanation for war amounts to answering this question.

Three of the most common and widely employed rationalist arguments in the literature do not directly address or answer the question. These are arguments from anarchy, preventive war, and positive expected utility.

Anarchy

Since Kenneth Waltz's influential *Man, the State, and War,* the anarchical nature of the international realm is routinely cited as a root cause of or explanation for the recurrence of war. Waltz argued that under anarchy, without a supranational authority to make and enforce law, "war occurs because there is nothing to prevent it. . . . Among states as among men there is no automatic adjustment of interests. In the absence of a supreme authority there is then the constant possibility that conflicts will be settled by force."[6]

The argument focuses our attention on a fundamental difference between domestic and international politics. Within a well-ordered state, organized violence as a strategy is ruled out—or at least made very dangerous—by the potential reprisals of a central government. In international relations, by contrast, no agency exists that can credibly threaten reprisal for the use of force to settle disputes.[7] The claim is that without such a credible threat, war will sometimes appear the best option for states that have conflicting interests.

While I do not doubt that the condition of anarchy accounts for major differences between domestic and international politics, and that anarchy encourages both fear of and opportunities for military conflict, the standard framing of the argument is not enough to explain why wars occur and recur. Under anarchy, nothing stops states from using force if they wish. But if using force is a costly option regardless of the outcome, then why is it ever employed? How exactly does the lack of a central authority prevent states from negotiating agreements both sides would prefer to fighting? As it is typically stated, the argument that anarchy provides a rationalist explanation for war does not address this question and so does not solve the problem posed by war's *ex post* inefficiency.

Neither, it should be added, do related arguments invoking the security dilemma, the fact that under anarchy one state's efforts to make itself more secure can have the undesired but unavoidable effect of making another state less secure.[8] By itself this fact says nothing about the availability or feasibility of peaceful bargains that would avoid the costs of war. More elaborate arguments are required, and those that are typically given do not envision bargaining and do not address the puzzle of costs. Consider, for instance, a spiral scenario in which an insecure state increases its arms, rendering another so insecure that it decides to attack. If the first state anticipated the reaction producing war, then by itself this is a deadlock argument; I argue against these below. If the first state did not anticipate war and did not want it, then the problem would seem to be miscalculation rather than anarchy, and we need to know why signaling and bargaining could not have solved it. As Robert Jervis has argued, anarchy and the security dilemma may well foster arms races and territorial competition.[9] But with the exception of occasional references to the preemptive war problem, the standard security dilemma arguments do not explicitly address the question of why the inability to make commitments should necessarily make for war between rational states.[10]

Below I will argue that anarchy is indeed implicated as a cause of specific sorts of military conflict (e.g., preventive and preemptive war and in some cases war over strategic territory). In contrast to the standard arguments, however, showing how anarchy figures in a coherent rationalist explanation entails describing the specific mechanism by which states' inability to write enforceable contracts makes peaceful bargains both sides would prefer unattainable.

Preventive War

It frequently is argued that if a declining power expects it might be attacked by a rising power in the future, then a preventive war in the present may be rational. Typically, however, preventive war arguments do not consider whether the rising and declining powers could construct a bargain, perhaps across time, that would leave both sides better off than a costly and risky preventive war would.[11] The incentives for such a deal surely exist. The rising state should not want to be attacked while it is relatively weak, so what stops it from offering concessions in the present and the future that would make the declining state prefer not to attack? Also, if war is inefficient and bargains both sides prefer to a fight will exist, why should the declining power rationally fear being attacked in the future? The standard argument supposes that an anticipated shift in the balance of power can by itself be enough to make war rational, but this is not so.

Positive Expected Utility

Perhaps the most common informal rationalist explanation found in the literature is that war may occur when two states each estimate that the expected benefits of fighting outweigh the expected costs. As Bruce Bueno de Mesquita argued in an influential formalization of this claim, war can be rational if both sides have positive expected utility for fighting; that is, if the expected utility of war (expected benefits less costs) is greater than the expected utility of remaining at peace.[12]

Informal versions of the expected utility argument typically fail to address the question of how or under what conditions it can be possible for two states both to prefer the costly gamble of war to any negotiated settlement. Formal versions have tended to avoid the question by making various restrictive and sometimes nonrationalist assumptions. To support these claims, I need to be more precise about the expected utility argument.

When Will There Exist Bargains Both Sides Prefer to War?

This section considers the question of whether and when two rationally led states could both prefer war to any negotiated settlement.

Consider two states, A and B, who have preferences over a set of issues represented by the interval $X = [0, 1]$. State A prefers issue resolutions closer to 1, while B prefers outcomes closer to 0.* * * For concreteness we might think of x as representing the proportion of all territory between A and B that is controlled by A. [Thus, a point X in the interval represents the situation where state A controls all the territory from ϕ to X, while state B controls all the territory from X to 1.][13]

In order to say whether the set X contains negotiated settlements that both sides would prefer to conflict, it must be possible to say how the states evaluate the military option versus those outcomes. Almost all analysts of war have stressed that war is a gamble whose outcome may be determined by random or otherwise unforeseeable events.[14] As Bueno de Mesquita argued, this makes expected utility a natural candidate.[15] Suppose that if the states fight a war, state A prevails with probability $p \in [0, 1]$, and that the winner gets to choose its favorite outcome in the issue space. * * * [Thus, A's expected utility for war is $p - c$, since A gets all the territory, which is worth 1, with probability p, loses everything with probability $1 - p$, and pays a cost for fighting c_A in either event.] Similarly, state B's expected utility for war will be $1 - p - c_B$. Since we are considering rationalist theories for war, we assume that c_A and c_B are both positive. War is thus represented as a costly lottery.[16] * * *

We can now answer the question posed above. The following result is easily demonstrated: given the assumptions stated in the last two paragraphs, there always exists a set of negotiated settlements that both sides prefer to fighting. * * *

[For example, in the special case where each state's value for an additional increment of territory is constant, the two states will both prefer any division of territory in the range from $p - c_A$ to $p + c_B$ over fighting a war. This interval represents the bargaining range, with $p - c_A$ and $p + c_B$ as the reservation levels that delimit it. This case of "risk neutral" states is depicted in Figure 6.1.]

This simple but important result is worth belaboring with some intuition. Suppose that two people (or states) are bargaining over the division of $100—if they can agree on a split they can keep what they agree to. However, in contrast to the usual economic scenarios, in this international relations example the players also have an outside option.[17] For a price of $20, they can go to war, in which case each player has a 50-percent chance of winning the whole $100. This implies that the expected value of the war option is $30 ($0.5 \cdot 100 + 0.5 \cdot 0 - 20$) for each side, so that if the players are risk-neutral, then neither should be willing to accept less than $30 in the bargaining. But notice that there is still a range of peaceful, bargained outcomes from ($31, $69) to ($69, $31) that make both sides strictly better off than the war option. Risk aversion will tend to increase the range yet further; indeed, even if the leaders pay no costs for war, a set of agreements both sides prefer to a fight will still exist provided both are risk-averse over the issues. In effect, the costs and risks of fighting open up a "wedge" of bargained solutions that risk-neutral or risk-averse states will prefer to the gamble of conflict. The existence of this *ex ante* bargaining range derives from the fact that war is inefficient *ex post*.

Three substantive assumptions are needed for the result, none of which seems particularly strong. First, the states know that there is some true probability p that one state would win in a military contest. As discussed below, it could be that the states have conflicting estimates of the likelihood of victory, and if both sides are optimistic about their chances this can obscure the bargaining range.

Figure 6.1. The Bargaining Range

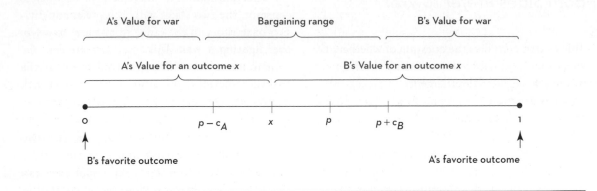

But even if the states have private and conflicting estimates of what would happen in a war, if they are rational, they should know that there can be only one true probability that one or the other will prevail (perhaps different from their own estimate). Thus rational states should know that there must in fact exist a set of agreements all prefer to a fight.

Second, it is assumed that the states are risk-averse or risk-neutral over the issues. Because risk attitude is defined relative to an underlying metric (such as money in economics), the substantive meaning of this assumption depends on the bargaining context. Loosely, it says that the states prefer a fifty-fifty split or share of whatever is at issue (in whatever metric it comes, if any) to a fifty-fifty chance at all or nothing, where this refers to the value of winning or losing a war. In effect, the assumption means that leaders do not like gambling when the downside risk is losing at war, which seems plausible given the presumption that state leaders normally wish to retain territory and power. A risk-acceptant leader is analogous to a compulsive gambler—willing to accept a sequence of gambles that has the expected outcome of eliminating the state and regime. Even if we admitted such a leader as rational, it seems doubtful that many have held such preferences (Hitler being a possible exception).

Finally, it was assumed that a continuous range of peaceful settlements (from 0 to 1) exists. In other words, the issues in dispute are perfectly divisible, so that there are always feasible bargains between the states' reservation levels $p - c_A$ and $p + c_B$. This third assumption immediately suggests a tenable rationalist explanation for war. Perhaps something about the nature of some international issues, such as which successor will sit on a throne, does not admit finely graded divisions and compromise. If so, then small costs for fighting and bad luck may make for rational war over such issues.

But we would immediately like to know what about the nature of an issue makes it impossible to divide up. On more thought, this seems empirically implausible. In the first place, most issues states negotiate over are quite complex—they have many dimensions of concern and allow many possible settlements. Second, if states can simply pay each other sums of money or goods (which they can, in principle), or make linkages with other issues, then this should have the effect of making any issues in dispute perfectly divisible. Before the age of nationalism, princes often bought, sold, and partitioned land.[18] In the nineteenth century the United States purchased the Louisiana Territory from France, and Alaska from Russia, and as late as 1898 President McKinley explored the possibility of buying Cuba from Spain in order to avoid a war over it.[19] Third, if something about the nature of an issue means that it can be settled in only, say, two ways, then some sort of random allocation or alternation between the two resolutions could in principle serve to create intermediate bargains. Mafia dons, for example, apparently have avoided costly internal wars by using lotteries to allocate construction contracts among families.[20]

In practice, creating intermediate settlements with cash, with linkages to other issues, or with randomization or alternation often seems difficult or impossible for states engaged in a dispute. For example, the immediate issue that gave rise to the Franco–Prussian war was a dispute over which prince would take the Spanish throne. It doubtless occurred to no one to propose that the two candidates alternate year by year, or three years for the Hapsburg and one for the Hohenzollern, or whatever. In this case as in many others, the issue could in principle have been made more continuous and was not for other reasons—here, alternating kings would have violated so many conventions and norms as to have been domestically unworkable. To give a more realistic example, nineteenth- and twentieth-century leaders cannot divide up and trade territory in international negotiations as easily as could rulers in the seventeenth and eighteenth centuries, due in part to domestic political consequences of the rise of nationalism; contrast, for example, the Congress of Vienna with the negotiations following World War I.

So in principle the indivisibility of the issues that are the subject of international bargaining can provide a coherent rationalist explanation for war. However, the real question in such cases is what prevents leaders from creating intermediate settlements, and the answer is likely to be other mechanisms (often domestic political) rather than the nature of the issues themselves.[21] Both the intrinsic complexity and richness of most matters over which states negotiate and the availability of linkages and side-payments suggest that intermediate bargains typically will exist.

It is thus not sufficient to say that positive expected utility by itself supplies a coherent or compelling rationalist explanation for war. Provided that the issues in dispute are sufficiently divisible, or that side-payments are possible, there should exist a set of negotiated agreements that have greater utility for both sides than the gamble of war does. The reason is that the *ex post* inefficiency of war opens up an *ex ante* bargaining range.

So, to explain how war could occur between rationally led states, we need to answer the following question. Given the existence of an *ex ante* bargaining range, why might states fail either to locate or to agree on an outcome in this range, so avoiding the costs and risks of war?

War Due to Private Information and Incentives to Misrepresent

Two commonly employed rationalist explanations in the literature directly address the preceding question. Both turn on the claim that war can be and often is the product of rational miscalculation. One explanation holds that a state's leaders may rationally overestimate their chance of military victory against an adversary, so producing a disagreement about relative power that only war can resolve. The other argues that rationally led states may lack information about an adversary's willingness to fight over some interest and so may challenge in the mistaken belief that war will not follow.

In this section I argue that while these ideas point toward a tenable rationalist explanation for war, neither goes far enough and neither works by itself. Both neglect the fact that states can in principle communicate with each other and so avoid a costly miscalculation of relative power or will. The cause of war cannot be simply lack of information, but whatever it is that prevents its disclosure. I argue that the fact that states have incentives to misrepresent their positions is crucial here, explaining on rationalist terms why diplomacy may not allow rational states to clarify disagreements about relative power or to avoid the miscalculation of resolve.

The mainstream international relations literature recognizes the existence of both private information and incentives to misrepresent, but typically views them as background conditions to be taken for granted rather than as key elements of an explanation of how rationally led states might end up at war. For example, Jack Levy's impressive review of the literature on the causes of war contains nothing on the role of incentives to misrepresent and discusses private information largely in the context of misperceptions of other states' intentions (which are linked to psychological biases). This is an accurate reflection of where these factors stand in the mainstream literature.[22]

Disagreements about Relative Power

Geoffrey Blainey's well-known and often-cited argument is that "wars usually begin when two nations disagree on their relative strength."[23] It is easy to see how a disagreement about relative strength—understood as conflicting estimates of the likelihood of military victory—can eliminate any *ex ante* bargaining range. Recall the example given above, where two states bargain over the division of $100, and each has the outside option of going to war. If each expects that it surely would prevail at war, then each side's expected value for the war option is $80 ($1 \cdot 100 + 0 \cdot 0 - 20$). So given these expectations, neither side will accept less than $80 in the bargaining, implying that no negotiated outcome is mutually preferred to war. More generally, suppose that state A expects to win with probability p, state B expects to win with probability r, and p and r sum to greater than one. Such conflicting expectations will certainly shrink and could eliminate any *ex ante* bargaining range.

But how could rationally led states have conflicting expectations about the likely outcome of military conflict? In the extreme case, how could both sides rationally expect to win? The literature barely addresses this question in explicit terms. Blainey, whom the literature views as advancing a rationalist explanation for war, in fact explains disagreements about relative power as a consequence of human *ir*rationality. He says that mutual optimism about victory in war is the product of "moods which cannot be grounded in fact" and which "permeate what appear to be rational assessments of the relative military strength of two contending powers." Mutual optimism is said to result from a "process by which nations evade reality," which hardly sounds like a rationalist explanation.[24]

Conflicting expectations about the likely outcome of military conflict may be explained in three ways. First, as Blainey suggests, emotional commitments could irrationally bias leaders' military estimates. They might, for instance, come to believe nationalist rhetoric holding that their soldiers are more courageous and spirited than those of the adversary.[25] Second, the world is a very complex place, and for this reason military analysts in different states could reach different conclusions about the likely impact of different technologies, doctrines, and tactics on the expected course of battle. Third, state leaders might have private information about militarily relevant factors—military capabilities, strategy, and tactics; the population's willingness to prosecute a long war; or third-state intentions. If a state has superior (and so private) information about any such factor, then its estimate of the probable course of battle may differ from that of an adversary.

Under a strict but standard definition of rationality, only the third explanation qualifies as an account of how rationally led states could have conflicting estimates of the probability of winning in war. As argued by John Harsanyi, if two rational agents have the same information about an uncertain event, then they should have the same beliefs about its likely outcome.[26] The claim is that given identical information, truly rational agents should reason to the same conclusions about the probability of one uncertain outcome or another. Conflicting estimates should occur only if the agents have different (and so necessarily private) information.[27]

It follows that the second explanation for disagreements about relative power listed above—the complexity of the world—is not a rationalist account. Instead, it is an account that explains conflicting military estimates as a consequence of bounded rationality. In this view, leaders or military analysts with the same information about military technology, strategy, political will, etc., might reason to different conclusions about the likely course of a war because of differential ability to cope with complexity of the problem. This is entirely plausible, but it is a bounded rationality explanation rather than a fully rationalist one.[28]

The rationalist account of how disagreements about the probability of winning might arise also seems empirically plausible. States certainly have private information about factors affecting the likely course of battle—for example, they jealously guard military secrets and often have superior information about what an ally will or will not fight for. Nonetheless, while private information about militarily relevant capabilities provides a first step, it does not provide a coherent rationalist explanation for war. The problem is that even if leaders have such private information, they should understand that their own estimates based on this information are suspect because they do not know the other side's private information. In principle, both sides could gain by sharing information, which would yield a consensus military estimate (absent bounded rationality). And, as shown above, doing so could not help but reveal bargains that both would prefer to a fight.[29]

So the question of how rationally led states can disagree about relative power devolves to the question of what prevents states from sharing private information about factors that might affect the course of battle. Before turning to this question, I will consider the second common explanation for how a rational miscalculation may produce war.

War Due to the Miscalculation of an Opponent's Willingness to Fight

Many wars have been given the following so-called rationalist explanation: state A transgressed some interest of state B in the erroneous belief that B would not fight a war over the matter. Though rationally led, state A lacked information about B's willingness to fight and simply happened to guess wrong, causing a war. Thus, some say that Germany miscalculated Russian and/or British willingness to fight in 1914; Hitler miscalculated Britain and France's willingness to resist his drive to the east; Japanese leaders in 1941 miscalculated U.S. willingness to fight a long war over control in the South Pacific; North Korea miscalculated U.S. willingness to defend South Korea; the United States miscalculated China's willingness to defend North Korea; and so on. In each case, the argument would hold that lack of information led a more-or-less rational actor to guess wrong about the extent of the bargaining range.

Blainey has argued that if states agree on relative power they are very unlikely to go to war against each other.[30] It is worth pointing out that in the preceding argument, war can occur despite complete agreement on relative power across states. To show how and for later use, I will introduce a simple model of international bargaining. As in the empirical examples just mentioned, in the model one state unilaterally chooses some revision of the status quo. The second state can then either acquiesce to the revision or can go to war to reverse it.

Formally, suppose there is a status quo resolution of the issues [represented as number q between 0 and 1] and that state A has the opportunity to choose any outcome x [between 0 and 1], presenting state B with a fait accompli. On observing what state A did (which might be nothing, i.e., $x = q$), state B can choose whether to go to war or to acquiesce to A's revision of the status quo.

If neither state has any private information, so that all payoffs are common knowledge, state A does best to push the outcome just up to B's reservation level $p + c_B$, which makes B just willing to acquiesce rather than go to war. With complete information, then, the states avoid the inefficient outcome of war.[31] On the other hand, if state B has private information about either its capabilities (which affect p) or its value for the issues at stake relative to the costs of conflict (c_B), then state A may not know whether a particular "demand" x will yield war or peace. Lacking this information, state A faces a trade-off in deciding whether and how much territory to "grab": The larger the grab, the greater the risk of war, but the better off A will be if state B acquiesces.

Suppose, for example, that A and B share a common estimate of p—they agree about relative power—but that A is unsure about B's costs for fighting. Under very broad conditions, if A cannot learn B's private information and if A's own costs are not too large, then state A's optimal grab produces a positive chance of war. Intuitively, if A is not too fearful of the costs of war relative to what might be gained in bargaining, it will run some risk of war in hopes of gaining on the ground. So Blainey's suggestion that a disagreement about relative power is necessary for war is incorrect—all that is necessary is that the states in dispute be unable to locate or agree on some outcome in the bargaining range. Since the bargaining range is determined not just by relative power but also by states' values for the issues at stake relative to the costs of fighting, uncertainty about the latter can (and apparently does) produce war.

Once again, it is entirely plausible that state leaders have private information about their value for various international interests relative to their costs of fighting over them.[32] Thus it seems we have a second tenable rationalist explanation for war, again based on the concept of private information. But as in the case of disagreements about relative power, the explanation fails as given because it does not explain why states cannot avoid miscalculating a potential opponent's willingness to fight. In the model, why cannot state A simply ask state B whether it would fight rather than acquiesce to a particular demand? To give a concrete example, why did German leaders in 1914 not simply ask their British and Russian counterparts what they would do if Austria were to attack Serbia? If they could have done so and if the answers could have been believed, the Germans might not have miscalculated concerning Russian and, more importantly, British willingness to fight. In consequence they might have avoided the horrendous costs of World War I.

To recap, I have argued that in a rationalist framework, disagreements about relative power and uncertainty about a potential opponent's willingness to fight must have the same source: leaders' private information about factors affecting the likely course of a war or their resolve to fight over specific interests. In order to avoid war's *ex post* inefficiency, leaders have incentives to share any such private information, which would have the effect of revealing peaceful settlements that lie within the bargaining range. So, to explain how war could occur between states led by rational leaders who consider the costs of fighting, we need to explain what would prevent them from sharing such private information.

Incentives to Misrepresent in Bargaining

Prewar bargaining may fail to locate an outcome in the bargaining range because of strategic incentives to withhold or misrepresent private information. While states have an incentive to avoid the costs of war, they also wish to obtain a favorable resolution of the issues. This latter desire can give them an incentive to exaggerate their true willingness or capability to fight, if by doing so they might deter future challenges or persuade the other side to make concessions. States can also have an incentive to conceal their capabilities or resolve, if they are concerned that revelation would make them militarily (and hence politically) vulnerable or would reduce the chances for a successful first strike. Similarly, states may conceal their true willingness to fight in order to avoid appearing as the aggressor.

Combined with the fact of private information, these various incentives to misrepresent can explain why even rational leaders may be unable to avoid the miscalculations of relative will and power that can cause war. This section first considers why this is so theoretically and then discusses two empirical examples.

A drawback of the simple bargaining model given above was that state B had no opportunity to try to communicate its willingness to fight to state A. It is easy to imagine that if communication were possible—say, if B could announce what interests in X it considered vital enough to fight over—this might at least lower the chance of war by miscalculation. To check this, we give state B an initial opportunity to make a foreign policy announcement f, which can be any statement about its foreign policy or what it considers to be vital or peripheral interests. (Assume as before that A is uncertain about B's capabilities or costs for fighting.)

If the announcement itself has no effect on either side's payoffs, then it can be shown that in any equilibrium in which state A does not choose randomly among demands, A will make the same demand regardless of what state B says, and the *ex ante* risk of war will remain the same as in the game without communication by state B. To gain an intuition for these results, suppose that A conditioned its behavior on f, grabbing more or less depending on what B announced. Then regardless of B's true willingness to fight, B does best to make the announcement that leads to the smallest grab by A—that is, B has an incentive to misrepresent its actual willingness to resist. But then A learns nothing from the announcement.[33]

This conclusion is slightly altered if the leaders of B can render the announcement f costly to make.[34] In practice, five common methods include building weapons, mobilizing troops, signing alliance treaties, supporting troops in a foreign land, and creating domestic political costs that would be paid if the announcement proves false. Of course, signaling by means of domestic political audience costs lies outside a purely unitary rational-actor framework, since this presumes a state run by an agent on behalf of a principal (the "audience") rather than a unitary state with a perfectly secure leadership. In the latter case, leaders may be able to make foreign policy announcements credible only by engaging an international reputation, taking financially costly mobilization measures, or bearing the costs and risks of limited military engagements.[35]

Even when the signal is costly, however, this will not in general completely eliminate all risk of war by miscalculation—indeed, it may even increase it. The reason concerns the nature of the signals that states have incentives to send. To be genuinely informative about a state's actual willingness or ability to fight, a signal must be costly in such a way that a state with lesser resolve or capability might not wish to send it. Actions that generate a real risk of war—for example, troop mobilizations that engage a leadership's reputation before international or domestic audiences—can easily satisfy this constraint, since states with high resolve are less fearful of taking them. In other words, a rational state may choose to run a real risk of (inefficient) war in order to signal that it will fight if not given a good deal in bargaining.[36]

The July crisis of World War I provides several examples of how incentives to misrepresent can make miscalculations of resolve hard to dispel. Soon after German leaders secretly endorsed Austrian plans to crush Serbia, they received both direct and indirect verbal indications from St. Petersburg that Russia would fight rather than acquiesce.[37] For example, on 21 July, the Russian Foreign Minister told the German ambassador that "Russia would not be able to tolerate Austria-Hungary's using threatening language to Serbia or taking military measures."[38] Such verbal statements had little effect on German leaders' beliefs, however, since they knew Russian leaders had a strategic incentive to misrepresent. On 18 July in a cable explaining Berlin's policy to Ambassador Lichnowsky in London, Secretary of State Jagow wrote that "there is certain to be some blustering in St. Petersburg."[39] Similarly, when on 26 July Lichnowsky began to report that Britain might join with France and Russia in the event of war, German Chancellor Bethmann Hollweg told his personal assistant of the "danger that France and England will commit their support to Russia in order not to alienate it, perhaps without really believing that for us mobilization means war, thinking of it as a bluff which they answer with a counterbluff."[40]

At the same time, the Chancellor had an incentive to misrepresent the strength and nature of German support for Austria's plans. Bethmann correctly anticipated that revealing this information would make Germany appear the aggressor, which might undermine Social Democratic support for his policies in Germany as well as turn British public opinion more solidly against his state.[41] This incentive led the Chancellor to avoid making direct or pointed inquiries about England's

attitude in case of war. The incentive also led him to pretend to go along with the British Foreign Secretary's proposals for a conference to mediate the dispute.[42] In consequence, Lord Grey may not have grasped the need for a stronger warning to Germany until fairly late in the crisis (on 29 July), by which time diplomatic and military actions had made backing off more difficult for both Austria and Germany.

In July 1914, incentives to misrepresent private information fostered and supported miscalculations of willingness to fight. Miscalculations of relative power can arise from this same source. On the one hand, states at times have an incentive to exaggerate their capabilities in an attempt to do better in bargaining. On the other hand, they can also have the well-known incentive to withhold information about capabilities and strategy. Presumably because of the strongly zero-sum aspect of military engagements, a state that has superior knowledge of an adversary's war plans may do better in war and thus in prewar bargaining—hence, states rarely publicize war plans. While the theoretical logic has not been worked out, it seems plausible that states' incentives to conceal information about capabilities and strategy could help explain some disagreements about relative power.

The 1904 war between Japan and Russia serves to illustrate this scenario. On the eve of the war, Russian leaders believed that their military could almost certainly defeat Japan.[43] In this conviction they differed little from the view of most European observers. By contrast, at the imperial council of 4 February that decided for war, the Japanese chief of staff estimated a fifty-fifty chance of prevailing, if their attack began immediately.[44] Thus Japanese and Russian leaders disagreed about relative power—their estimates of the likelihood of victory summed to greater than 1.

Moreover, historical accounts implicate this disagreement as a major cause of the war: Russia's refusal to compromise despite repeated offers by the Japanese was motivated in large measure by their belief that Japan would not dare attack them. The Japanese Cabinet finally decided for war after the Tsar and his advisers failed to make any real compromises over Korea or Manchuria in a series of proposals exchanged in 1903. The Tsar and his top advisers were hardly eager to fight, not because they expected to lose but because they saw an Asian war as a costly diversion of resources to the wrong theater.[45] Nonetheless, they refused to make concessions from what they viewed as a position of great military strength. They believed that Japan would have to settle for less, given its relative military weakness.[46]

The disagreement arose in substantial part from Japanese private information about their military capabilities and how they compared with Russia's. A far superior intelligence service had provided the Japanese military with a clear picture of Russian strengths and weaknesses in Northeast Asia and enabled them to develop an effective offensive strategy. According to John Albert White, due to this intelligence "the Japanese government apparently faced the war with a far more accurate conception of their task than their enemy had."[47] In addition, compared with the Russians or indeed with any European power, Japanese leaders had much better knowledge of the fighting ability of the relatively untested Japanese army and of the effect of the reforms, training, and capital development of the previous decade.[48]

If by communicating this private information the Japanese could have led the Russians to see that their chances of victory were smaller than expected, they might have done so. Almost all historians who have carefully examined the case agree that the Japanese government was not bent on war for its own sake—they were willing to compromise if the Russians would as well.[49] However, it was unthinkable for the Japanese to reveal such information or convince the Russians even if they did. In the first place, the Japanese could not simply make announcements about the quality of their forces, since the Russians would have had no

reason to believe them. Second, explaining how they planned to win a war might seriously compromise any such attempt by changing the likelihood that they would win; there is a trade-off between revealing information about resolve or capabilities to influence bargaining and reducing the advantages of a first strike.

In sum, the combination of private information about relative power or will and the strategic incentive to misrepresent these afford a tenable rationalist explanation for war. While states always have incentives to locate a peaceful bargain cheaper than war, they also always have incentives to do well in the bargaining. Given the fact of private information about capabilities or resolve, these incentives mean that states cannot always use quiet diplomatic conversations to discover mutually preferable settlements. It may be that the only way to surmount this barrier to communication is to take actions that produce a real risk of inefficient war.

This general mechanism operates in at least two other empirically important ways to produce conflict in specific circumstances. First, private information about the costs of fighting or the value leaders place on international interests can give them an incentive to cultivate a reputation for having lower costs or more far-flung vital interests than they actually do. If cutting a deal in one dispute would lead other states to conclude the leader's costs for using force are high, then the leader might choose a costly war rather than suffer the depredations that might follow from making concessions. The U.S. interventions in Korea and Vietnam are sometimes explained in these terms, and states surely have worried about such inferences drawn by other states for a long time.[50] The same logic operates when a small state or group (for example, Finland or the Chechens) chooses to fight a losing war against a larger one (for example, the Soviet Union or Russia) in order to develop a reputation for being hard to subjugate. In both cases, states employ war itself as a costly signal of privately known and otherwise unverifiable information about willingness to fight.

Second, since incentives to misrepresent military strength can undermine diplomatic signaling, states may be forced to use war as a credible means to reveal private information about their military capabilities. Thus, a rising state may seek out armed conflict in order to demonstrate that it is more powerful than others realize, while a state in apparent decline may fight in hope of revealing that its capabilities remain better than most believe. In both instances, the inefficient outcome of war derives from the fact that states have private information about their capabilities and a strategic incentive to misrepresent it to other states.

War as a Consequence of Commitment Problems

This section considers a second and quite different rationalist mechanism by which war may occur even though the states in dispute share the same assessment of the bargaining range. Even if private information and incentives to misrepresent it do not tempt states into a risky process of discovery or foster costly investments in reputation, states may be unable to settle on an efficient bargained outcome when for structural reasons they cannot trust each other to uphold the deal.

In this class of explanations, the structural condition of anarchy reemerges as a major factor, although for nonstandard reasons. In the conventional argument, anarchy matters because no hegemonic power exists to threaten states with "jail" if they use force. Without this threat, states become suspicious and worried about other states' intentions; they engage in self-help by building weapons; and somehow uncertainty-plus-weapons leads them ultimately to attack each other (the security dilemma or spiral model). Below, I show that anarchy does indeed matter but for more specific reasons and in more specific contexts. Anarchy matters when an unfortunate combination of state preferences and opportunities for action imply that one or both sides in a dispute have incentives to renege on peaceful bargains which, if they were enforceable, would be mutually preferred to war. I will consider three such unfortunate situations that can claim some empirical plausibility.

It should be stressed that in standard security dilemma and spiral model arguments the suspicions and lack of trust engendered by anarchy are understood to originate either from states' inability to observe each other's motivations (that is, from private information about greed or desire for conquest) or from the knowledge that motivations can change.[51] By contrast, in the arguments given below, states have no private information and motivations never change; thus states understand each other's motivations perfectly. This is not to argue that private information about the value a leadership places on expansion is unimportant in international politics—it surely is. Indeed, private information about motivation and various incentives to misrepresent it might exacerbate any of the three specific commitment problems discussed below. However, when they do so this is a matter of an interaction between informational and commitment problems rather than of anarchy per se. Our first task should be to isolate and specify the mechanisms by which anarchy itself might cause war.

Preemptive War and Offensive Advantages

Consider the problem faced by two gunslingers with the following preferences. Each would most prefer to kill the other by stealth, facing no risk of retaliation, but each prefers that both live in peace to a gunfight in which each risks death. There is a bargain here that both sides prefer to "war"—namely, that each leaves the other alone—but without the enforcement capabilities of a third party, such as an effective sheriff, they may not be able to attain it. Given their preferences, neither person can credibly commit not to defect from the bargain by trying to shoot the other in the back. Note that no matter how far the shadow of the future extends, iteration (or repeat play) will not make cooperation possible in strategic situations of this sort. Because being the "sucker" here may mean being permanently eliminated, strategies of conditional cooperation such as tit-for-tat are infeasible.[52] Thus, if we can find a plausible analogy in international relations, this example might afford a coherent rationalist explanation for war.

Preemptive war scenarios provide the analogy. If geography or military technology happened to create large first-strike or offensive advantages, then states might face the same problem as the gunslingers. To demonstrate this theoretically, I consider how offensive advantages affect the bargaining range between two states engaged in a dispute.

There are at least three ways of interpreting offensive advantages in a formal context. First, an offensive advantage might mean that a state's odds of winning are better if it attacks rather than defends. Second, an offensive advantage might mean that the costs of fighting are lower for an attacking state than for a defending state. It can be shown that no commitment problem operates in this second case, although lowering the costs of war for attackers does narrow the de facto bargaining range. Third, offensive advantages might mean that military technology and doctrine increase the variance of battlefield outcomes. That is, technology and doctrine might make total victory or total defeat more likely, while rendering stalemate and small territorial changes less likely. In this case, offensive advantages can actually reduce the expected utility of war for both sides, thus increasing the bargaining range and perhaps making war less rather than more likely. Intuitively, if states care most of all about security (understood as sur-

vival), then offensive advantages make war less safe by increasing the risk of total defeat.[53]

A commitment problem of the sort faced by the gunslingers arises only under the first interpretation, in which "offensive advantage" refers to an increase in a state's military prospects if it attacks rather than defends. To demonstrate this, let p_f be the probability that state A wins a war if A attacks; p_s the probability that A wins if A strikes second or defends; and p the chance that A wins if both states mobilize and attack at the same time. Thus, an offensive advantage exists when $p_f > p > p_s$.

Since states can always choose to attack if they wish, a peaceful resolution of the issues is feasible only if neither side has an incentive to defect unilaterally by attacking. * * * [It is easy to show that there will exist stable outcomes both sides prefer to conflict only if there is a de facto bargaining range represented by issue resolutions between $p_f - c_A$ and $p_s + c_B$. One end of the range is determined by A's value for attacking with a first strike advantage, and the other by B's.]

Notice that as p_f increases above p, and p_s decreases below it, this interval shrinks and may even disappear. Thus, first-strike advantages narrow the de facto bargaining range, while second-strike (or defensive) advantages increase it. The reason is that when first-strike advantages are large, both states must be given more from the peacetime bargain in order to allay the greater temptation of unilateral attack.

In the extreme case, [if the first-strike advantage is sufficiently large relative to the total costs of fighting,] no self-enforcing peaceful outcomes exist [$p_f - c_A$ is greater than $p_s + c_B$]. This does not mean that no bargains exist that both sides would prefer to war. Since by definition both states cannot enjoy the advantage of going first, agreements that both sides prefer to fighting are always available in principle. The problem is that under anarchy, large enough first-strike incentives (relative to cost-benefit ratios) can make all of these agreements unenforceable and incredible as bargains.

Does this prisoners' dilemma logic provide an empirically plausible explanation for war? Though I lack the space to develop the point, I would argue that first-strike and offensive advantages probably are an important factor making war more likely in a few cases, but not because they make mobilization and attack a dominant strategy, as in the extreme case above. In the pure preemptive war scenario leaders reason as follows: "The first-strike advantage is so great that regardless of how we resolve any diplomatic issues between us, one side will always want to attack the other in an effort to gain the (huge) advantage of going first." But even in July 1914, a case in which European leaders apparently held extreme views about the advantage of striking first, we do not find leaders thinking in these terms.[54] It would be rather surprising if they did, since they had all lived at peace but with the same military technology prior to July 1914. Moreover, in the crisis itself military first-strike advantages did not become a concern until quite late, and right to the end competed with significant political (and so strategic) disadvantages to striking first.[55]

Rather than completely eliminating enforceable bargains and so causing war, it seems more plausible that first-strike and offensive advantages exacerbate other causes of war by narrowing the bargaining range. If for whatever reason the issues in dispute are hard to divide up, then war will be more likely the smaller the set of enforceable agreements both sides prefer to a fight. Alternatively, the problems posed by private information and incentives to misrepresent may be more intractable when the de facto bargaining range is small.[56] For example, in 1914 large perceived first-strike advantages meant that relatively few costly signals of intent were sufficient to commit both sides to war (chiefly, for Germany/Austria and Russia). Had leaders thought defense had the advantage, the set of enforceable agreements both would have preferred would have been larger, and this may have made costly signaling less likely to have destroyed the bargaining range.

I should note that scholars have sometimes portrayed the preemptive war problem differently, assuming that neither state would want to attack unilaterally but that each would want to attack if the other was expected to also. This is a coordination problem known as "stag hunt" that would seem easily resolved by communication. At any rate, it seems farfetched to think that small numbers of states (typically dyads) would have trouble reaching the efficient solution here, if coordination were really the only problem.[57]

Preventive War as a Commitment Problem

Empirically, preventive motivations seem more prevalent and important than preemptive concerns. In his diplomatic history of Europe from 1848 to 1918, A.J.P. Taylor argued that "every war between the Great Powers [in this period] started as a preventive war, not a war of conquest."[58] In this subsection I argue that within a rationalist framework, preventive war is properly understood as arising from a commitment problem occasioned by anarchy and briefly discuss some empirical implications of this view.[59]

The theoretical framework used above is readily adapted for an analysis of the preventive war problem. Whatever their details, preventive war arguments are necessarily dynamic—they picture state leaders who think about what may happen in the future. So, we must modify the bargaining model to make it dynamic as well. Suppose state A will have the opportunity to choose the resolution of the issues in each of an infinite number of successive periods. For periods $t = 1, 2, \ldots$, state A can attempt a fait accompli to revise the status quo, choosing a demand x_t. On seeing the demand x_t, state B can either acquiesce or go to war, which state A is assumed to win with probability p_t. * * *

This model extends the one-period bargaining game considered above to an infinite-horizon case in which military power can vary over time. An important observation about the multiperiod model is that war remains a strictly inefficient outcome. * * * It is straightforward to show that there will always exist peaceful settlements in X such that both states would prefer to see one of these settlements implemented in every period from t forward rather than go to war.[60]

The strategic dilemma is that without some third party capable of guaranteeing agreements, state A may not be able to commit itself to future foreign policy behavior that makes B prefer not to attack at some point. Consider the simple case in which A's chance of winning a war begins at p_1 and then will increase to $p_2 > p_1$ in the next period, where it will remain for all subsequent periods. Under anarchy, state A cannot commit itself not to exploit the greater bargaining leverage it will have starting in the second period. * * * [At that time, A will choose a resolution of the issues that makes state B just willing to acquiesce, given the new distribution of military power. This means that in the first period, when state B is still relatively strong, B is choosing between going to war and acquiescing to A's first period demand, which gives it some value today plus the issue equivalent of fighting a war at a disadvantage in the next period. The most state A could possibly do for B in the first period would be to cede B's most preferred outcome ($x_1 = 0$). However, if the change in relative military power is large enough, this concession can still be too small to make accepting it worthwhile for state B. B may prefer to "lock in" what it gets from war when it is relatively strong, to one period of concessions followed by a significantly worse deal when it is militarily weaker. In sum,] if B's expected decline in military power is too large relative to B's costs for war, then state A's inability to commit to restrain its foreign policy demands after it gains power makes preventive attack rational for state B.[61] Note also that A's commitment problem meshes with a parallel problem facing B. If B could commit to fight in the second period rather than accept the rising state's increased demands, then B's bargaining power would not fall in the second period, so that preventive war would be unnecessary in the first.

Several points about this rationalist analysis of preventive war are worth stressing. First, preventive war occurs here despite (and in fact partially because of) the states' agreement about relative power. Preventive war is thus another area where Blainey's argument misleads. Second, contrary to the standard formulation, the declining state attacks not because it fears being attacked in the future but because it fears the peace it will have to accept after the rival has grown stronger. To illustrate, even if Iraq had moved from Kuwait to the conquest of Saudi Arabia, invasion of the United States would not have followed. Instead, the war for Kuwait aimed to prevent the development of an oil hegemon that would have had considerable bargaining leverage due to U.S. reliance on oil.[62]

Third, while preventive war arises here from states' inability to trust each other to keep to a bargain, the lack of trust is not due to states' uncertainty about present or future motivations, as in typical security-dilemma and spiral-model accounts. In my argument, states understand each other's motivations perfectly well—there is no private information—and they further understand that each would like to avoid the costs of war—they are not ineluctably greedy. Lack of trust arises here from the situation, a structure of preferences and opportunities, that gives one party an incentive to renege. For example, regardless of expectations about Saddam Hussein's future motivation or intentions, one could predict with some confidence that decreased competition among sellers of oil would have led to higher prices. My claim is not that uncertainty about intentions is unimportant in such situations—it surely is—but that commitment and informational problems are distinct mechanisms and that a rationalist preventive war argument turns crucially on a commitment problem.

Finally, the commitment problem behind preventive war may be undermined if the determinants of military power can reliably be transferred between states. In the model, the rising state can actually have an incentive to transfer away or otherwise limit the sources of its new strength, since by doing so it may avoid being attacked. While such transfers might seem implausible from a realist perspective, the practice of "compensation" in classical balance-of-power politics may be understood in exactly these terms: states that gained territory by war or other means were expected to (and sometimes did) allow compensating gains in order to reduce the incentive for preventive war against them.[63]

Preventive motivations figured in the origins of World War I and are useful to illustrate these points. One of the reasons that German leaders were willing to run serious risks of global conflict in 1914 was that they feared the consequences of further growth of Russian military power, which appeared to them to be on a dangerous upward trajectory.[64] Even if the increase in Russian power had not led Russia to attack Austria and Germany at some point in the future—war still being a costly option—greater Russian power would have allowed St. Petersburg to pursue a more aggressive foreign policy in the Balkans and the Near East, where Austria and Russia had conflicting interests. Austrian and German leaders greatly feared the consequences of such a (pro-Slav) Russian foreign policy for the domestic stability of the Austro-Hungarian Empire, thus giving them incentives for a preventive attack on Russia.[65]

By the argument made above, the states should in principle have had incentives to cut a multiperiod deal both sides would have preferred to preventive war. For example, fearing preventive attack by Austria and Germany, Russian leaders might have wished to have committed themselves not to push so hard in the Balkans as to endanger the Dual Monarchy. But such a deal would be so obviously unenforceable as to not be worth proposing.

Leaving aside the serious monitoring difficulties, once Russia had become stronger militarily, Austria would have no choice but to acquiesce to a somewhat more aggressive Russian policy in the Balkans. And so Russia would be drawn to pursue it, regardless of its overall motivation or desire for conquest of Austria-Hungary.

While German leaders in July 1914 were willing to accept a very serious risk that Russia might go to war in support of Serbia, they seem to have hoped at the start of the crisis that Russia would accept the Austrian demarche.[66] Thus, it is hard to argue that the preventive logic itself produced the war. Rather, as is probably true for other cases in which these concerns appear, the preventive logic may have made war more likely in combination with other causes, such as private information, by making Berlin much more willing to risk war.[67] How preventive concerns impinge on international bargaining with private information is an important topic for future research.

Commitment, Strategic Territory, and the Problem of Appeasement

The objects over which states bargain frequently are themselves sources of military power. Territory is the most important example, since it may provide economic resources that can be used for the military or be strategically located, meaning that its control greatly increases a state's chances for successful attack or defense. Territory is probably also the main issue over which states fight wars.[68]

In international bargaining on issues with this property, a commitment problem can operate that makes mutually preferable negotiated solutions unattainable. The problem is similar to that underlying preventive war. Here, both sides might prefer some package of territorial concessions to a fight, but if the territory in question is strategically vital or economically important, its transfer could radically increase one side's future bargaining leverage (think of the Golan Heights). In principle, one state might prefer war to the status quo but be unable to commit not to exploit the large increase in bargaining leverage it would gain from limited territorial concessions. Thus the other state might prefer war to limited concessions (appeasement), so it might appear that the issues in dispute were indivisible. But the underlying cause of war in this instance is not indivisibility per se but rather the inability of states to make credible commitments under anarchy.[69]

As an example, the 1939 Winter War between Finland and the Soviet Union followed on the refusal of the Finnish government to cede some tiny islands in the Gulf of Finland that Stalin seems to have viewed as necessary for the defense of Leningrad in the event of a European war. One of the main reasons the Finns were so reluctant to grant these concessions was that they believed they could not trust Stalin not to use these advantages to pressure Finland for more in the future. So it is possible that Stalin's inability to commit himself not to attempt to carry out in Finland the program he had just applied in the Baltic states may have led or contributed to a costly war both sides clearly wished to avoid.[70]

Conclusion

The article has developed two major claims. First, under broad conditions the fact that fighting is costly and risky implies that there should exist negotiated agreements that rationally led states in dispute would prefer to war. This claim runs directly counter to the conventional view that rational states can and often do face a situation of deadlock, in which war occurs because no mutually preferable bargain exists.

Second, essentially two mechanisms, or causal logics, explain why rationally led states are sometimes unable to locate or agree on such a bargain:

(1) the combination of private information about resolve or capability and incentives to misrepresent these, and (2) states' inability, in specific circumstances, to commit to uphold a deal. Historical examples were intended to suggest that both mechanisms can claim empirical relevance.

I conclude by anticipating two criticisms. First, I am not saying that explanations for war based on irrationality or "pathological" domestic politics are less empirically relevant. Doubtless they are important, but we cannot say how so or in what measure if we have not clearly specified the causal mechanisms making for war in the "ideal" case of rational unitary states. In fact, a better understanding of what the assumption of rationality really implies for explaining war may actually raise our estimate of the importance of particular irrational and second-image factors.

For example, once the distinction is made clear, bounded rationality may appear a more important cause of disagreements about relative power than private information about military capabilities. If private information about capabilities was often a major factor influencing the odds of victory, then we would expect rational leaders to update their war estimates during international crises; a tough bargaining stand by an adversary would signal that the adversary was militarily stronger than expected. Diplomatic records should then contain evidence of leaders reasoning as follows: "The fact that the other side is not backing down means that we are probably less likely to win at war than we initially thought." I do not know of a single clear instance of this sort of updating in any international crisis, even though updating about an opponent's resolve, or willingness to fight, is very common.

Second, one might argue that since both anarchy and private information plus incentives to misrepresent are constant features of international politics, neither can explain why states fail to strike a bargain preferable to war in one instance but not another. This argument is correct. But the task of specifying the causal mechanisms that explain the occurrence of war must precede the identification of factors that lead the mechanisms to produce one outcome rather than another in particular settings. That is, specific models in which commitment or information problems operate allow one to analyze how different variables (such as power shifts and cost-benefit ratios in the preventive war model) make for war in some cases rather than others.

This is the sense in which these two general mechanisms provide the foundations for a coherent rationalist or neorealist theory of war. A neorealist explanation for war shows how war could occur given the assumption of rational and unitary ("billiard ball") states, the assumption made throughout this article. Consider any particular factor argued in the literature to be a cause of war under this assumption—for example, a failure to balance power, offensive advantages, multipolarity, or shifts in relative power. My claim is that showing how any such factor could cause war between rational states requires showing how the factor can occasion an unresolvable commitment or information problem in specific empirical circumstances. Short of this, the central puzzle posed by war, its costs, has not been addressed.

NOTES

1. Of course, arguments of the second sort may and often do presume rational behavior by individual leaders; that is, war may be rational for civilian or military leaders if they will enjoy various benefits of war without suffering costs imposed on the population. While I believe that "second-image" mechanisms of this sort are very important empirically, I do not explore them here. A more accurate label for the subject of the article might be "rational unitary-actor explanations," but this is cumbersome.

2. For the founding work of neorealism, see Kenneth Waltz, *Theory of International Politics* (Reading, MA: Addison-Wesley, 1979). For examples of theorizing along these lines, see Robert Jervis, "Cooperation Under the Security Dilemma," *World Politics* 30 (January 1978), pp. 167–214; Stephen Walt, *The Origins of Alliances* (Ithaca, NY: Cornell University Press, 1987); John J. Mearsheimer, "Back to the Future: Instability in Europe After the Cold War," *International Security* 15 (Summer 1990), pp. 5–56; and Charles Glaser, "Realists as Optimists: Cooperation as Self-Help," *International Security* 19 (Winter 1994/95), pp. 50–90.

3. The sense of "mechanism" is similar to that proposed by Elster, although somewhat broader. See Jon Elster, *Political Psychology* (Cambridge: Cambridge University Press, 1993), pp. 1–7; and Jon Elster, *Nuts and Bolts for the Social Sciences* (Cambridge: Cambridge University Press, 1989), chap. 1.

4. For an influential example of this common assumption see Glenn Snyder and Paul Diesing, *Conflict among Nations* (Princeton, NJ: Princeton University Press, 1977).

5. See, for examples, Geoffry Blainey, *The Causes of War* (New York: Free Press, 1973); Michael Howard, *The Causes of Wars* (Cambridge, MA: Harvard University Press, 1983), especially chap. 1; and Arthur Stein, *Why Nations Cooperate: Circumstance and Choice in International Relations* (Ithaca, NY: Cornell University Press, 1990), pp. 60–64. Even the case of World War I is contested; an important historical school argues that this was a wanted war. See Fritz Fisher, *Germany's Aims in the First World War* (New York: Norton, 1967).

6. The quotation is drawn from Kenneth Waltz, *Man, the State, and War: A Theoretical Analysis* (New York: Columbia University Press, 1959), p. 188.

7. For a careful analysis and critique of this standard argument on the difference between the international and domestic arenas, see R. Harrison Wagner, "The Causes of Peace," in Roy A. Licklider, ed., *Stopping the Killing: How Civil Wars End* (New York: New York University Press, 1993), pp. 235–68 and especially pp. 251–57.

8. See John H. Herz, "Idealist Internationalism and the Security Dilemma," *World Politics* 2 (January 1950), pp. 157–80; and Jervis, "Cooperation Under the Security Dilemma." Anarchy is implicated in the security dilemma externality by the following logic: but for anarchy, states could commit to use weapons only for nonthreatening, defensive purposes.

9. Jervis, "Cooperation under the Security Dilemma."

10. For an analysis of the security dilemma that takes into account signaling, see Andrew Kydd, "The Security Dilemma, Game Theory, and World War I," paper presented at the annual meeting of the American Political Science Association, Washington, DC, 2–5 September 1993.

11. The most developed exception I know of is found in Stephen Van Evera, "Causes of War," Ph.D. diss., University of California, Berkeley, 1984, pp. 61–64.

12. See Bruce Bueno de Mesquita, *The War Trap* (New Haven, CT: Yale University Press, 1981), and "The War Trap Revisited: A Revised Expected Utility Model," *American Political Science Review* 79 (March 1985), pp. 157–76. For a generalization that introduces the idea of a bargaining range, see James D. Morrow, "A Continuous-Outcome Expected Utility Theory of War," *Journal of Conflict Resolution* 29 (September 1985), pp. 473–502. Informal versions of the expected utility argument are everywhere. For example, Waltz's statement that "A state will use force to attain its goals if, after assessing the prospects for success, it values those goals more than it values the pleasures of peace" appears in different ways in a great many works on war. See Waltz, *Man, the State, and War,* p. 60.

13. Let the states' utilities for the outcome $x \in X$ be $u_A(x)$ and $u_B (1 - x)$, and assume for now that $u_A(\cdot)$ and $u_B(\cdot)$ are continuous, increasing,

and weakly concave (that is, risk-neutral or risk-averse). Without losing any generality, we can set $u_i(1) = 1$ and $u_i(0) = 0$ for both states ($i = A, B$).

14. See, for classic examples, Thucydides, *The Peloponnesian War* (New York: Modern Library, 1951), pp. 45 and 48; and Carl von Clausewitz, *On War* (Princeton, NJ: Princeton University Press, 1984), p. 85.

15. Bueno de Mesquita, *The War Trap.*

16. Note that in this formulation the terms c_A and c_B capture not only the states' values for the costs of war but also the value they place on winning or losing on the issues at stake. That is, c_A reflects state A's costs for war relative to any possible benefits. For example, if the two states see little to gain from winning a war against each other, then c_A and c_B would be large even if neither side expected to suffer much damage in a war.

17. On the theory of bargaining with outside options, see Martin J. Osborne and Ariel Rubinstein, *Bargaining and Markets* (New York: Academic Press, 1990), chap. 3; Motty Perry, "An Example of Price Formation in Bilateral Situations," *Econometrica* 50 (March 1986), pp. 313–21; and Robert Powell, "Bargaining in the Shadow of Power" (University of California, Berkeley, 1993, mimeographed). See also the analyses in R. Harrison Wagner, "Peace, War, and the Balance of Power," *American Political Science Review* 88 (September 1994), pp. 593–607; and Wagner, "The Causes of Peace."

18. See, for example, Evan Luard, *War in International Society* (New Haven, CT: Yale University Press, 1992), p. 191. Schroeder notes that "patronage, bribes, and corruption" were "a major element" of eighteenth-century international relations. See Paul Schroeder, *The Transformation of European Politics, 1763–1848* (Oxford: Oxford University Press, 1994), p. 579.

19. On Cuba, see Ernest May, *Imperial Democracy* (New York: Harper and Row, 1961), pp. 149–50. On the Louisiana Purchase, military threats raised in the U.S. Senate apparently made Napoleon more eager to negotiate the sale. See E. Wilson Lyon, *Louisiana in French Diplomacy* (Norman: University of Oklahoma Press, 1934), pp. 179 and 214ff.

20. Diego Gambetta, *The Sicilian Mafia: The Business of Private Protection* (Cambridge, MA: Harvard University Press, 1993), p. 214.

21. In one of the only articles on this problem, Morrow proposes a private information explanation for states' failures to link issues in many disputes. See James D. Morrow, "Signaling Difficulties with Linkage in Crisis Bargaining," *International Studies Quarterly* 36 (June 1992), pp. 153–72.

22. See Jack Levy, "The Causes of War: A Review of Theories and Evidence," in Philip E. Tetlock et al., eds., *Behavior, Society, and Nuclear War,* vol. 1 (Oxford: Oxford University Press, 1989), pp. 209–333. Recent work using limited-information game theory to analyze crisis bargaining places the strategic consequences of private information at the center of the analysis. See, for examples, Bruce Bueno de Mesquita and David Lalman, *War and Reason* (New Haven, CT: Yale University Press, 1992); James D. Fearon, "Domestic Political Audiences and the Escalation of International Disputes," *American Political Science Review* 88 (September 1994), pp. 577–92; James D. Morrow, "Capabilities, Uncertainty, and Resolve: A Limited Information Model of Crisis Bargaining," *American Journal of Political Science* 33 (November 1989), pp. 941–72; Barry Nalebuff, "Brinkmanship and Nuclear Deterrence: The Neutrality of Escalation," *Conflict Management and Peace Science* 9 (Spring 1986), pp. 19–30; and Robert Powell, *Nuclear Deterrence Theory: The Problem of Credibility* (Cambridge: Cambridge University Press, 1990).

23. Blainey, *The Causes of War,* p. 246.

24. Ibid., p. 54. Blainey also blames patriotic and nationalistic fervor, leaders' (irrational) tendency to surround themselves with yes-men, and crowd psychology.

25. See Ralph K. White, *Nobody Wanted War: Misperception in Vietnam and Other Wars* (New York: Doubleday/Anchor), chap. 7; Blainey, *The Causes of War,* p. 54; and Richard Ned Lebow, *Between Peace and War: The Nature of International Crises* (Baltimore, MD: Johns Hopkins University Press, 1981), p. 247.

26. John C. Harsanyi, "Games with Incomplete Information Played by 'Bayesian' Players, Part III," *Management Science* 14 (March 1968), pp. 486–502.

27. Aumann observed an interesting implication of this doctrine: genuinely rational agents cannot "agree to disagree," in the sense that it cannot be commonly known that they are rational and that they hold different estimates of the likelihood of some uncertain event. See Robert Aumann, "Agreeing to Disagree," *The Annals of Statistics* 4 (November 1976), pp. 1236–39. Emerson Niou, Peter Ordeshook, and Gregory Rose note that this implies that rational states cannot agree to disagree about the probability that one or the other would win in a war in *The Balance of Power: Stability in the International System* (Cambridge: Cambridge University Press, 1989), p. 59.

28. On bounded rationality, see Herbert A. Simon, "A Behavioral Model of Rational Choice," *Quarterly Journal of Economics* 69 (February 1955), pp. 99–118.

29. This analysis runs exactly parallel to work in law and economics on pretrial bargaining in legal disputes. Early studies explained costly litigation as resulting from divergent expectations about the likely trial outcome, while in more recent work such expectations derive from private information about the strength of one's case. For a review and references, see Robert D. Cooter and Daniel L. Rubinfeld, "Economic Analysis of Legal Disputes and Their Resolution," *Journal of Economic Literature* 27 (September 1989), pp. 1067–97.

30. Blainey, *The Causes of War.*

31. This take-it-or-leave-it model of international bargaining is proposed and analyzed under conditions of both complete and incomplete information in James D. Fearon, "Threats to Use Force: The Role of Costly Signals in International Crises," Ph.D. diss., University of California, Berkeley, 1992, chap. 1. Similar results for more elaborate bargaining structures are given in my own work in progress. See James D. Fearon, "Game-Theoretic Models of International Bargaining: An Overview," University of Chicago, 1995. Powell has analyzed an alternative model in which both sides must agree if the status quo is to be revised. See Powell, "Bargaining in the Shadow of Power."

32. For examples and discussion on this point, see Fearon, "Threats to Use Force," chap. 3.

33. * * * Cheap talk announcements can affect outcomes in some bargaining contexts. For an example from economics, see Joseph

Farrell and Robert Gibbons, "Cheap Talk Can Matter in Bargaining," *Journal of Economic Theory* 48 (June 1989), pp. 221–37. These authors show how cheap talk might credibly signal a willingness to negotiate seriously that then affects subsequent terms of trade. For an example from international relations, see James D. Morrow, "Modeling the Forms of International Cooperation: Distribution Versus Information," *International Organization* 48 (Summer 1994), pp. 387–423.

34. The conclusion is likewise altered if the possibility of repeated interactions in sufficiently similar contexts is great enough that reputation building can be supported.

35. On signaling costs in crises and audience costs in particular, see Fearon, "Threats to Use Force," and "Domestic Political Audiences and the Escalation of International Disputes." For an excellent analysis of international signaling in general, see Robert Jervis, *The Logic of Images in International Relations* (Princeton, NJ: Princeton University Press, 1970).

36. For developed models that make this point, see James Fearon, "Deterrence and the Spiral Model: The Role of Costly Signals in Crisis Bargaining," paper presented at the annual meeting of the American Political Science Association, 30 August–2 September 1990, San Francisco, Calif.; Fearon, "Domestic Political Audiences and the Escalation of International Disputes"; Morrow, "Capabilities, Uncertainty, and Resolve"; Nalebuff, "Brinkmanship and Nuclear Deterrence"; and Powell, *Nuclear Deterrence Theory.*

37. Luigi Albertini, *The Origins of the War of 1914*, vol. 2 (London: Oxford University Press, 1953), pp. 183–87.

38. Ibid., p. 187.

39. Ibid., p. 158. For the full text of the cable, see Karl Kautsky, comp., *German Documents Relating to the Outbreak of the World War* (New York: Oxford University Press, 1924), doc. no. 71, p. 130.

40. Konrad Jarausch, "The Illusion of Limited War: Chancellor Bethmann Hollweg's Calculated Risk," *Central European History* 2 (March 1969), pp. 48–76. The quotation is drawn from p. 65.

41. See L. C. F. Turner, *Origins of the First World War* (New York: Norton, 1970), p. 101; and Jarausch, "The Illusion of Limited War," p. 63. Trachtenberg writes that "one of Bethmann's basic goals was for Germany to avoid coming across as the aggressor." See Marc Trachtenberg, *History and Strategy* (Princeton, NJ: Princeton University Press, 1991), p. 90.

42. Albertini concludes that "on the evening of the 27th all the Chancellor sought to do was to throw dust in the eyes of Grey and lead him to believe that Berlin was seriously trying to avert a conflict, that if war broke out it would be Russia's fault and that England could therefore remain neutral." See Albertini, *The Origins of the War of 1914*, vol. 1, pp. 444–45. See also Turner, *Origins of the First World War*, p. 99.

43. See J. A. White, *The Diplomacy of the Russo–Japanese War* (Princeton, NJ: Princeton University Press, 1964), pp. 142–43; and Ian Nish, *The Origins of the Russo–Japanese War* (London: Longman, 1985), pp. 241–42.

44. J. N. Westwood, *Russia against Japan, 1904–5: A New Look at the Russo–Japanese War* (Albany: State University of New York Press, 1986), p. 22. Estimates varied within the Japanese leadership, but with the exception of junior-level officers, few seem to have been

highly confident of victory. For example, as the decision for war was taken the Japanese navy requested a two-week delay to allow it to even the odds at sea. See Nish, *The Origins of the Russo–Japanese War*, pp. 197–200 and 206–7.

45. See, for example, David Walder, *The Short Victorious War: The Russo–Japanese Conflict, 1904–5* (London: Hutchinson, 1973), pp. 53–56; and Nish, *The Origins of the Russo–Japanese War*, p. 253.

46. See White, *The Diplomacy of the Russo–Japanese War*, chaps. 6–8; Nish, *The Origins of the Russo–Japanese War*, p. 241; and Lebow, *Between Peace and War*, pp. 244–46.

47. White, *The Diplomacy of the Russo–Japanese War*, p. 139. Nish writes that "many Russians certainly took a view of [the Japanese military] which was derisory in comparison with themselves. It may be that this derived from a deliberate policy of secrecy and concealment which the Japanese army applied because of the historic coolness between the two countries." See Nish, *The Origins of the Russo–Japanese War*, p. 241.

48. The British were the major exception, who as recent allies of Japan had better knowledge of its capabilities and level of organization. See Nish, *The Origins of the Russo–Japanese War*, p. 241.

49. See, for example, William Langer, "The Origins of the Russo–Japanese War," in Carl Schorske and Elizabeth Schorske, eds., *Explorations in Crisis* (Cambridge, MA: Harvard University Press, 1969), p. 44.

50. For some examples, see Fearon, "Threats to Use Force," chap. 3. For a formal version of reputational dynamics due to private information, see Barry Nalebuff, "Rational Deterrence in an Imperfect World," *World Politics* 43 (April 1991), pp. 313–35.

51. See, for examples, Robert Jervis, *Perception and Misperception in International Politics* (Princeton, NJ: Princeton University Press, 1976), pp. 62–67; Barry Posen, *The Sources of Military Doctrine* (Ithaca, NY: Cornell University Press, 1984), pp. 16–17; and Charles Glaser, "The Political Consequences of Military Strategy," *World Politics* 44 (July 1992), p. 506.

52. For dynamic game models that demonstrate this, see Robert Powell, "Absolute and Relative Gains in International Relations Theory," *American Political Science Review* 85 (December 1991), pp. 1303–20; and James D. Fearon, "Cooperation and Bargaining Under Anarchy," (University of Chicago, 1994, mimeographed). On tit-for-tat and the impact of the shadow of the future, see Robert Axelrod, *The Evolution of Cooperation* (New York: Basic Books, 1984); and Kenneth Oye, ed., *Cooperation under Anarchy* (Princeton, NJ: Princeton University Press, 1986).

53. This argument about military variance runs counter to the usual hypothesis that offensive advantages foster war. For a discussion and an empirical assessment, see James D. Fearon, "Offensive Advantages and War since 1648," paper presented at the annual meeting of the International Studies Association, 21–25 February 1995. On the offense–defense balance and war, see Jervis, "Cooperation under the Security Dilemma"; and Van Evera, "Causes of War," chap. 3.

54. For the argument about leaders' views on first-strike advantages in 1914, see Stephen Van Evera, "The Cult of the Offensive and the Origins of the First World War," *International Security* 9 (Summer 1984), pp. 58–107.

55. See, for example, Trachtenberg, *History and Strategy*, p. 90.

56. This is suggested by results in Roger Myerson and Mark Satterthwaite, "Efficient Mechanisms for Bilateral Trading," *Journal of Economic Theory* 29 (April 1983), pp. 265–81.

57. Schelling suggested that efficient coordination in stag hunt–like preemption problems might be prevented by a rational dynamic of "reciprocal fear of surprise attack." See Thomas Schelling, *The Strategy of Conflict* (Cambridge, MA: Harvard University Press, 1960), chap. 9. Powell has argued that no such dynamic exists between rational adversaries. See Robert Powell, "Crisis Stability in the Nuclear Age," *American Political Science Review* 83 (March 1989), pp. 61–76.

58. Taylor, *The Struggle for Mastery in Europe, 1848–1918* (London: Oxford University Press, 1954), p. 166. Carr held a similar view: "The most serious wars are fought in order to make one's own country militarily stronger or, more often, to prevent another country from becoming militarily stronger." See E. H. Carr, *The Twenty Years' Crisis, 1919–1939* (New York: Harper and Row, 1964), pp. 111–12.

59. To my knowledge, Van Evera is the only scholar whose treatment of preventive war analyzes at some length how issues of credible commitment intervene. The issue is raised by both Snyder and Levy. See Van Evera, "Causes of War," pp. 62–64; Jack Snyder, "Perceptions of the Security Dilemma in 1914," in Robert Jervis, Richard Ned Lebow, and Janice Gross Stein, eds., *Psychology and Deterrence* (Baltimore, MD: Johns Hopkins University Press, 1985), p. 160; and Jack Levy, "Declining Power and the Preventive Motivation for War," *World Politics* 40 (October 1987), p. 96.

60. If the states go to war in period t, expected payoffs from period t on are $(p_t/(1 - \delta)) - c_A$ for state A and $((1 - p_t)/(1 - \delta)) - c_B$ for state B [where δ is the time discount factor that both states apply to payoffs to be received in the next period].

61. The formal condition for preventive war is δ
$p_2 - p_1 > c_B (1 - \delta)^2$.

62. According to Hiro, President Bush's main concern at the first National Security Council meeting following the invasion of Kuwait was the potential increase in Iraq's economic leverage and its likely influence on an "already gloomy" U.S. economy.

See Dilip Hiro, *Desert Shield to Desert Storm: The Second Gulf War* (London: Harper-Collins, 1992), p. 108.

63. On compensation, see Edward V. Gulick, *Europe's Classical Balance of Power* (New York: Norton, 1955), pp. 70–72; and Paul W. Schroeder, *The Transformation of European Politics, 1763–1848*, pp. 6–7.

64. See Trachtenberg, *History and Strategy*, pp. 56–59; Albertini, *The Origins of the War of 1914*, vol. 2, pp. 129–30; Turner, *Origins of the First World War*, chap. 4; James Joll, *The Origins of the First World War* (London: Longman, 1984), p. 87; and Van Evera, "The Cult of the Offensive and the Origins of the First World War," pp. 79–85.

65. Samuel Williamson, "The Origins of World War I," *Journal of Interdisciplinary History* (Spring 1988), pp. 795–818 and pp. 797–805 in particular; and D. C. B. Lieven, *Russia and the Origins of the First World War* (New York: St. Martin's, 1983), pp. 38–49.

66. Jack S. Levy, "Preferences, Constraints, and Choices in July 1914," *International Security* 15 (Winter 1990/91), pp. 234–36.

67. Levy argues that preventive considerations are rarely themselves sufficient to cause war. See Levy, "Declining Power and the Preventive Motivation for War."

68. See, for example, Kalevi J. Holsti, *Peace and War: Armed Conflicts and International Order, 1648–1989* (Cambridge: Cambridge University Press, 1991); and John Vasquez, *The War Puzzle* (Cambridge: Cambridge University Press, 1993).

69. The argument is formalized in work in progress by the author, where it is shown that the conditions under which war will occur are restrictive: the states must be unable to continuously adjust the odds of victory by dividing up and trading the land. In other words, the smallest feasible territorial transfer must produce a discontinuously large change in a state's military chances for war to be possible. See also Wagner, "Peace, War, and the Balance of Power," p. 598, on this commitment problem.

70. See Max Jakobson, *The Diplomacy of the Winter War: An Account of the Russo-Finnish Conflict, 1939–1940* (Cambridge, MA: Harvard University Press, 1961), pp. 135–39; and Van Evera, "Causes of War," p. 63. Private information and incentives to misrepresent also caused problems in the bargaining here. See Fearon, "Threats to Use Force," chap. 3.

Jessica L. Weeks

STRONG MEN AND STRAW MEN
Authoritarian Regimes and the Initiation of International Conflict

A dolf Hitler, Saddam Hussein, and Idi Amin—these are names synonymous not only with domestic repression but also with international conflict. In fact, the record of international violence committed by such tyrants has fostered the impression that authoritarianism is inexorably linked to war and other international tensions. Policy makers have drawn on this view to recommend democratization and even regime change in the name of international peace.

Yet are all dictatorships equally belligerent? The historical record suggests that some authoritarian regimes have been much less conflict-prone than the headline-grabbing Kims and Husseins of recent history. China after Mao, Tanzania under Nyerere, Kenya under Kenyatta, Mexico under the PRI, and even the former Soviet Union have all been relatively cautious in their decisions to threaten or use military force.[1] What makes some authoritarian regimes less likely to initiate military conflicts than others? What *specific* political institutions in dictatorships encourage leaders to initiate military disputes abroad, and why?

Surprisingly little scholarship exists on these important questions. The scant research that has emerged in recent years has made some progress toward answering them by identifying potential correlates of greater conflict initiation in autocracies: for example, the size of the leader's support-ing coalition (Bueno de Mesquita et al. 2003; Peceny and Butler 2004; see also Peceny and Beer 2003; Peceny, Beer, and Sanchez-Terry 2002) or whether the regime is led by military officers (Lai and Slater 2006; Sechser 2004). Yet although this scholarship contains important insights, I show in this article that existing theoretical frameworks do not adequately explain patterns of dispute initiation among autocracies. We still have much to learn about why some dictatorships are more likely to initiate military conflicts than others and how their behavior compares to that of democracies.

This article attempts to shed light on the conflict behavior of authoritarian regimes by synthesizing insights from the study of comparative authoritarianism with those on conflict initiation, resulting in a theoretical framework that explains why some dictatorships are more belligerent than others and how their behavior compares to that of democracies. I begin by laying out a simple framework that highlights the factors affecting a leader's decision to initiate conflict. The framework highlights the potential costs of using military force—the costs of defeat, the costs of fighting—as well as the potential benefits. Together, these costs and benefits shape preferences over the use of force and therefore behavior.

The framework draws attention to three questions crucial to understanding why some types of regimes initiate more international military conflicts than others. First, does the leader face a domestic audience able to punish him or her for decisions about international conflict? Some dicta-

From *American Political Science Review* 106, no. 2 (May 2021): 326–339, 342–345.

torships do not face powerful domestic audiences, notably "personalist" dictatorships such as North Korea or Iraq under Saddam Hussein, where the leader has eliminated potential rivals and personally controls the state apparatus (Geddes 2003). Contrary to the conventional wisdom, however, nonpersonalist authoritarian leaders typically face powerful domestic audiences composed of regime elites (Weeks 2008). Despite the absence of elections or formally institutionalized procedures for removing leaders, leaders of nonpersonalist autocracies have strong incentives to attend to the preferences of their domestic audience—more so than the bulk of the international relations literature suggests.[2] The existence or absence of a domestic audience—that is, whether or not the regime is personalistic—is thus a first dimension affecting leaders' decisions to initiate military conflict.

This leads to the second question: What are the preferences of the domestic audience? In contrast to existing perspectives such as selectorate theory, I argue that even in dictatorships with relatively small winning coalitions, domestic audiences often have strong incentives to punish leaders who behave recklessly or incompetently in international affairs. Autocratic audiences consisting primarily of civilians are scarcely more likely to forgive unnecessary or failed uses of force than democratic domestic audiences made up of ordinary voters. However, autocratic audiences composed primarily of military officers are more likely to view force as necessary and appropriate than audiences consisting mostly of civilians, primarily because of military officers' particular belief structures regarding the use of military force. The military or civilian background of the domestic audience is therefore a second dimension affecting decisions to start military disputes.

Finally, what behavior can we expect from personalist leaders, who do not face a powerful domestic audience? Given personalist leaders' supremacy in international and domestic affairs, we must inquire into the preferences and tendencies of these kinds of leaders, rather than of their audiences. I argue that the challenges of attaining and maintaining absolute power mean that personalist regimes tend to "select for" leaders who are particularly drawn to the use of military force as a policy option. Combined with the fact that personalist dictators face few domestic consequences for defeat or for starting fights unwisely, this selection process means that personalists, on average, initiate more military conflicts than nonpersonalist leaders.

After developing these arguments, I carry out an extensive empirical analysis on a new dataset of authoritarian institutions that allows me to test these predictions against the expectations of existing theories. Existing measures of authoritarian institutions either conflate the two dimensions I highlight—personalism and military leadership— or do not measure them accurately. Using my new, finer grained measures, I carry out a battery of statistical analyses that provide strong support for my arguments, but do not match the expectations of other existing theories. The findings have many implications for the study of domestic politics and international conflict, and they also suggest valuable lessons for policy makers and statesmen confronting autocracies abroad.

Existing Literature on Dictatorships and International Conflict

To date, only a handful of studies have explored variation in the conflict behavior of autocracies. A series of early studies by Mark Peceny and colleagues (Peceny and Beer 2003; Peceny, Beer, and Sanchez-Terry 2002; Peceny and Butler 2004) concluded that personalist dictatorships, in which the leader depends on only a small coterie of supporters, are more likely to initiate conflicts than both democracies and other authoritarian regime types. Peceny and Butler (2004) attribute this pattern to Bueno de Mesquita et al.'s (2003) selectorate theory, arguing that personalist regimes are more likely to initiate conflicts than single-party regimes because of their small coalition size.[3] Selectorate theory posits that when the winning coalition (the group of regime insiders whose support is necessary to sustain the leader in office) is small relative to the selectorate (the group of individuals who have a role in selecting the leader), members of the winning coalition have strong incentives to stay loyal to the leader regardless of his or her performance in providing public goods, such as national security. In contrast, when the winning coalition (w) is large relative to the selectorate (s), or w/s is large, as it is in democracies, members of the winning coalition have greater incentives to evaluate leaders based on public goods provision. These factors combine to imply that large-coalition leaders have incentives to initiate only those military disputes that they are likely to win at low cost, which depresses their rates of dispute initiation.

However, there are problems with using selectorate theory to explain why personalist regimes might be more belligerent than nonpersonalist regimes.[4] First, selectorate theory assumes that small-coalition regime insiders lack tools to mitigate the uncertainty they face about their likely survival under a new ruler. Instead, selectorate theory assumes that small-w/s regime insiders believe that their survival is inextricably connected to the survival of the incumbent, which drives them to remain loyal even in the face of bad policy. An equally plausible assumption is that these individuals hold their privileged economic, social, or military positions for material or historical reasons that make them very difficult to replace even when a new leader comes to power. Indeed, rational elites would attempt to coordinate to prevent the leader from attaining such great power over their political futures (Magaloni 2008;

Svolik 2009). If elites can succeed in limiting the leader's power of appointment, the probability of surviving under a new leader would not be closely related to w/s.

Many real-world examples support this alternative assumption. Even in relatively small-coalition regimes such as post-Stalin USSR, modern China, and Argentina and Brazil under their military juntas, regime insiders knew that they could jettison an incompetent or reckless leader and survive politically, just as most of the members of Khrushchev's Politburo did after they ousted their premier. In fact, members of the winning coalition often coordinate to establish and maintain norms against arbitrarily dismissing top officials, precisely because such rules help regime insiders credibly constrain the leader in the future. In many dictatorships, therefore, leaders are not insulated by loyalty in the way assumed by selectorate theory, and the conclusion that they do not care greatly about foreign policy outcomes does not necessarily follow. In sum, selectorate theory relies on a key assumption that at best holds only in some authoritarian regimes.

A second potential weakness of selectorate theory is that it assumes that the payoffs and costs from international settlements and wars are public goods, meaning that leaders primarily perceive a benefit to winning if the regime's institutions incentivize them to care about the public welfare. However, this overlooks the fact that leaders may also perceive private benefits to winning, such as economic payoffs or even personal glory. If different types of regimes empower actors with different perceptions of the private benefits of fighting, this could affect the bargaining range and alter the conclusions of selectorate theory.

In contrast to selectorate theory, a second line of argument focuses not on coalition size, but rather on the fact that different authoritarian regimes have different sources of "infrastructural power," defined as "institutions to help manage elite factionalism and curb mass dissent" (Lai and Slater 2006, 114). This argument is built on two core assumptions. First, it assumes that leaders start international conflicts primarily as a way to deflect attention from domestic troubles. Second, it assumes that military-led regimes have less infrastructural power than party-based regimes. Combining these assumptions implies that military regimes are more likely to use (diversionary) force, because it meets their need for domestic support and legitimacy (117).[5]

However, existing scholarship casts doubt on both of these assumptions. First, diversionary gambles typically only make sense when the leader is highly insecure (Downs and Rocke 1994). This condition probably does not hold often enough to drive overall levels of dispute initiation, even if it can explain isolated cases. Moreover, potential targets of diversion may deliberately avoid conflict, thus short-circuiting the mechanism (Clark 2003; Leeds and Davis 1997; Smith 1996). Perhaps for these reasons, empirical evidence that diversionary motives drive patterns of conflict initiation is at best mixed.[6]

Second, even if diversion is common enough to explain variation in belligerence, it is not clear that infrastructural power would cause military regimes to engage in diversion more frequently than other types of regimes. Democracies and civilian autocracies also suffer the crises of legitimacy that supposedly motivate diversion, particularly in tough economic times. In fact, some argue that because democratic leaders lack other options for stabilizing their rule, diversionary war is most common in democracies (Gelpi 1997).[7] Given these issues, it is unsurprising that studies have failed to find evidence that military regimes engage in more diversionary force than civilian regimes. Indeed, recent empirical work on diversion in authoritarian regimes finds that it occurs most frequently in single-party regimes (Pickering and Kisangani 2010).

Domestic Institutions and International Conflict: A Theoretical Framework

To build a framework for understanding conflict initiation by dictatorships, I draw on the large literature on how domestic institutions constrain leaders' decisions to initiate international military disputes[8] and combine it with new insights into the domestic politics of authoritarian regimes. Constraints can take the form of either ex ante constraints in implementing policy decisions or ex post accountability for a leader's decisions. First, ex ante constraints could prevent leaders from initiating certain policies at all (Reiter and Stam 2002). However, even in democracies, executives can often circumvent ex ante constraints, particularly for short-term military activities. Many scholars have therefore focused on the second type of constraint: ex post accountability that deters leaders from choosing unpopular or risky policies. I adopt this approach.

Of course, knowing whether leaders can be punished for their decisions is not enough. We must also understand the preferences of the actors who could punish them, thus creating the constraint. Thus we turn our attention to the preferences of the *domestic audience*, if one exists—the group with the means to punish leaders, for example, by removing them from office. In democracies, domestic audiences are powerful and typically consist of voters or some subset of the electorate. In autocracies, as I argue in greater detail later, audiences often exist as well, though they typically consist of a much smaller group of regime insiders.[9] When no powerful audience exists, we must focus instead on the individual leader's preferences and perceptions.

It is also important to consider whether and why an audience might actually be motivated to punish or reward a leader for foreign policy decisions. The most plausible argument is that the audience draws inferences about the leader's competence or preferences by comparing the outcome of an international dispute to what would have happened had the leader acted differently, a form of "sophisticated retrospection."[10] Most studies of domestic politics and crisis bargaining indicate that if audiences care about competence and the costs of removing leaders are not too great, they will punish leaders for policy failures (however defined) and reward leaders for policy successes.

This leads to the question of how different audiences, or in the absence of an audience, leaders, define success and failure in international politics.[11] In my framework the leader chooses whether to initiate a military dispute with another state or rather to stick with the status quo. If the leader initiates a dispute, this action leads to some probability of victory or defeat, which results in some division of international goods or resolution of the issue at stake. Each possible outcome entails some combination of costs and benefits, be they material or normative; the question is then how the relevant actors perceive these costs and benefits and hence how they define success and failure.

The framework highlights the various preferences and perceptions that are central to understanding decisions to initiate conflict. First, the relevant actors perceive the *costs of fighting,* whether or not the country wins the dispute. Audiences and leaders could be averse to using force because it is either materially costly or because it is morally undesirable. For example, drawing on Kant's early insight, many scholars have argued that voters (the audience in democracies) are more sensitive to the material or moral costs of military conflict than are leaders or other elites.

In addition to generic views about force, audiences and leaders could perceive additional *costs of defeat* in a military challenge. In fact, many scholars have argued that defeat in international disputes is one of the cardinal sins of international politics (Goemans 2000). The costs of defeat could be either direct, in the form of lost military and economic resources, or more indirect. For example, defeat could invite future attacks by revealing military weakness.

Next, actors form views about the value of *international goods* such as territory, economic rights, or the removal of an external threat, compared to the status quo. On the one hand, holding constant the costs of using military force, some actors are more "greedy" in that they desire more goods.[12] On the other hand, the attractiveness of sticking with the status quo depends on actors' assessments of how threatening the international environment is. Leaders or audiences may fear that failure to act today will invite a costly future attack, or they might feel perfectly safe. If actors form an ominous view of maintaining the status quo, they might wish to initiate conflict today even if victory is not assured.[13] If they find the status quo acceptable, they would be more hesitant to initiate conflict.

The above discussion provides a framework for making predictions about the relative conflict initiation propensities of different kinds of regimes. We must first determine whether the leader faces a powerful domestic audience, or is relatively free of such constraints. When leaders do face strong audiences, we must understand that audience's views about the costs of fighting, the costs of defeat, and the relative benefits of winning, because unhappy audiences will punish leaders who deviate from their preferred policies. In contrast, when leaders are more autonomous, as they are in some dictatorships, we must inquire into their personal preferences and perceptions. For example, holding constant all other factors, actors who view the use of military force as costly would be motivated to initiate fewer military conflicts than other actors. Greedy leaders who desperately wish to attain international goods, fearful leaders who worry about the continuation of the status quo, or leaders facing audiences with those characteristics, would in contrast tend to initiate more disputes. The following section examines how these parameters vary among authoritarian regimes and what this variation means for regime type and constraints on the initiation of international conflict.

Audiences, Preferences, and Authoritarian Leaders' Initiation of Conflict

Modern scholarship has identified two dimensions central to understanding the internal logic of authoritarian regimes: whether the regime is led by civilians or the military, and the degree of personal power of the leader (Geddes 2003).[14] The following discussion shows that the two dimensions of militarism and personalism form natural cleavages when explaining variation in constraints and preferences across dictatorships. Because regimes can have any combination of these two characteristics, the two dimensions combine to form four ideal types of dictatorships, shown in Figure 6.2.[15] I adopt Slater's (2003) labels, distinguishing among nonpersonalist civilian regimes (*machines*), nonpersonalist military regimes (*juntas*), personalist civilian regimes (*bosses*), and personalist military regimes (*strongmen*).[16]

Domestic Audiences: Personalist versus Elite-constrained Dictators

The first question is what types of regimes face a powerful domestic audience that can punish or, at the extreme, remove leaders who do not represent their interests. Scholars have shown empirically that most authoritarian leaders lose power at the hands of government insiders (Svolik 2009). Yet dictatorships vary enormously in the extent to which regime insiders have the opportunity and incentives to oust their leader, giving them influence over policy.

At one end of the spectrum are despotic, sultanistic, or, here, "personalistic" regimes, in which one individual controls the instruments of state such as the military forces, any ruling party, or the state bureaucracy (Chehabi and Linz 1998; Geddes 2003; Weber 1997). Not only is the leader insulated

Figure 6.2. Typology of Authoritarian Regimes

	Civilian Audience or Leader	Military Audience or Leader
Nonpersonalist (Elite-constrained) Leader	Machine	Junta
Personalist (Unconstrained) Leader	Bose	Strongman

from free and fair elections but he or she is typically able to appoint friends, relatives, and cronies to important offices. These handpicked regime insiders have strong incentives to remain loyal to and uncritical of the leader, lest they risk their own political demise (Bratton and Van de Walle 1994). Therefore a defining feature of personalist regimes such as North Korea under the Kims, Iraq under Saddam Hussein, the Soviet Union under Stalin, Syria under the Assads, and Libya under Gaddafi is that their leaders do not face a strong, organized domestic audience able to exert ex ante or ex post constraints on their policy choices.[17]

This lack of a domestic audience in personalist dictatorships contrasts greatly with the powerful domestic audiences found in nonpersonalist autocracies. Unlike their counterparts in personalist dictatorships, government insiders in nonpersonalist autocracies often have both the will and the means to punish their leader. In nonpersonalist party-based machines such as contemporary China and the post-Stalin Soviet Union, government insiders rise through the ranks based in significant part on merit and seniority, rather than personal or family relationships to the paramount leader. Moreover, in these regimes the leaders cannot typically spy on subordinates and dispose of them if they detect disloyalty. Regime insiders' loyalty to the incumbent is thus more tenuous; if regime elites do succeed in ousting an incompetent leader, they are likely to survive.

The ability to punish or oust the leader is not limited to single-party regimes. In many military dictatorships—many of which are in Latin America, as well as the former military regimes of Algeria, South Korea, and Thailand—the officer corps and other junta members do not depend on the incumbent for their own political survival. Just as the Argentine junta ousted Galtieri after the Falklands debacle, high-ranking officers in nonpersonalist military dictatorships often punish or even oust the leader for policy failures. Officers in the Argentine military acted as a "constituency to which the junta remained attentive . . . much evidence exists to support the notion that a very real form of political constraint was exercised on Argentina's putative rulers" at the hands of these officers (Arquilla and Rasmussen 2001, 762). In sum, government insiders serve as a powerful domestic audience in nonpersonalist regimes.

Of course, even nonpersonalist dictators tend to be more secure in office than democratic leaders (Frantz 2008), reducing the likelihood of punishment.[18] Yet this greater likelihood of remaining in power could be offset by the leaders' fear of their post-ouster fates (Debs and Goemans 2010; Goemans 2000). Some lucky ousted nonpersonalist dictators (such as Khrushchev) go into a "retirement" of house arrest, but other ex-dictators face physical violence or exile. Thus, even if autocrats are less likely to lose office than democrats, they may fear the possibility of punishment more acutely.

The distinction between severe and nonsevere punishment raises the question whether personalist dictators, although less likely to be punished than non-personalist leaders, are more likely to be punished severely. If so, the small threat of the "ultimate punishment" could induce just as much caution in personalist as nonpersonalist leaders (Goemans 2008). Indeed, there is some evidence that personalist leaders are more likely to face severe punishment (such as exile or death) than leaders of machines, who more often face a quiet, if forced, retirement (Debs and Goemans 2010). Yet, given the historically low probability that personalist leaders will lose office even when their nation is defeated militarily, these fears are unlikely to overwhelm the relative lack of accountability that personalists enjoy. Elsewhere, I show that of the personalistic leaders who lost wars, only 12.5% lost office within two years (Weeks 2009), a much lower rate than both democrats and nonpersonalist dictators, for whom military defeat usually spelled ouster. Importantly, the differences in punishment received by democrats and nonpersonalist dictators were small. Absent a reliable threat of punishment, personalist leaders do not suffer the same extra cost of defeat as do democrats and non-personalist dictators and consequently can take greater risks.[19]

Thus, one way to measure the first dimension—whether the leader faces a powerful domestic audience with the ability to punish or depose—is whether or not a regime is ruled by a personalist dictator. Personalist dictators are particularly unlikely to face an effective domestic audience. In contrast, nonpersonalist dictators must reckon with powerful domestic audiences. When combined with the potentially unattractive fate of being deposed, nonpersonalist dictators' fear of removal at the hands of regime insiders can strongly condition their behavior. The preferences of domestic audiences in nonpersonalistic dictatorships are therefore important.

The Content of Constraints: Audience and Leader Preferences

The second question then is, What are audience preferences concerning the initiation of military conflict? These preferences derive from actors' evaluations of the relative costs and benefits of using military force, including the costs of fighting, the costs of defeat, and the benefits of winning. I argue that these preferences vary according to the composition of the audience, with important differences between military and civilian regimes. In personalist regimes without an effective domestic audience, I look instead at the preferences of the dictator. The discussion of each of the dictatorial types compares the preferences of the autocratic audience to those of a typical democratic audience (voters).

PEACEFUL MACHINES: ELITE-CONSTRAINED DICTATORSHIPS WITH CIVILIAN AUDIENCES

What are the preferences of the civilian elites comprising audiences in nonpersonalist civilian machines? These elites are typically officials in a dominant party, as in contemporary China, though they could also potentially be family members in a non-personalistic monarchy, such as Saudi Arabia, or high-level officials in an autocracy with limited multiparty competition. Contrary to the conventional wisdom, I argue later that civilian regime insiders in autocracies are not substantially more enthusiastic about initiating military force, on average, than democratic voters. In addition, selectorate theory's assumption that small-coalition regime insiders are dependent on the leader's survival for their own survival does not usually hold in nonpersonalist autocracies. The relatively small size of the winning coalition in machines therefore does not imply that these elites are bound to the leader by loyalty, overlooking foreign policy failures.

First, many scholars have argued that the perceived costs of fighting are lower for autocratic than for democratic audiences. The most obvious perceived costs are the material costs of fighting to which Kant alludes: Authoritarian elites might be more insulated from the direct costs of war than ordinary citizens. Yet despite the long pedigree of the Kantian argument, there are reasons to doubt it. Except in the most serious conflicts involving mass conscription, most wars involve the mobilization of only a very small proportion of the population. Moreover, democratic governments often adopt policies that minimize the costs of war to their constituents (Valentino, Huth, and Croco 2010); the direct personal costs for any individual citizen are therefore likely to be low. In autocracies the direct costs of war may be no lower for elites than for the general population.[20] In fact enemy governments often target high-level officials in their wartime efforts. For example, the United States used this kind of decapitation strategy in the recent Iraq and Afghanistan wars. Unlike the paramount leader, most audience members do not enjoy personal security details or have access to multiple secret underground bunkers to protect them and their families, much less their land or property.

Of course, other costs of war accrue to citizens off the battlefield, for example disruptions in the economy. Most scholars assume that ordinary citizens are more vulnerable to these economic costs than are wealthier elites, who can absorb a drop in income. However, the logic of authoritarianism actually suggests that only a very narrow circle of the elite would ignore such costs when it comes to evaluating the leader. Elites' economic interests are likely to be hard hit by a conflict, which can both destroy infrastructure and disrupt trade. In addition, elites cannot simply compensate themselves by taxing the public at a higher rate. As Wintrobe (2000) argues, most autocratic regimes stay in power through a combination of repression and loyalty. Defeat in war damages an important instrument of repression—the military—and taxing the citizens at higher rates to compensate for wartime losses is likely to reduce the regime's other resource, the loyalty of the public. In other words, when resources are destroyed in war, the only way that elites could insulate themselves economically would be to take steps that imperil the regime's stability, and thus their own survival. In sum, it is not clear that autocratic elites are substantially more insulated from the direct or indirect material costs of fighting than are ordinary citizens.

Alternatively, normative or moral concerns could raise the perceived costs of fighting.[21] Perhaps elites in autocracies are socialized to view military force as a more appropriate way to settle disputes than are leaders or citizens in democracies. Although I return to this issue in the discussion of military officers, there is at best weak evidence that *civilian* elites in dictatorships are more likely than their democratic counterparts to see war as morally appropriate. Most literature suggests that democracies apply pacific norms only when the opponent is also a democracy; existing research points to dyadic, rather than monadic, beliefs about the appropriateness of using force (Dixon 1994; Maoz and Russett 1993). Little scholarship demonstrates monadic differences in norms between democracies and autocracies, and in fact many scholars have commented on democracies' willingness to use force even against innocent civilians (Downes 2008). Even when scholars have found monadic differences in the willingness of democracies to refrain from certain practices, such as abusing enemy combatants, they have attributed them to strategic rather than normative factors (Wallace 2010). In sum, there is little existing evidence that civilian autocratic audiences view the costs of fighting as systematically lower than do democratic audiences.

A second possibility is that high-level officials in autocratic regimes are less concerned with the costs of defeat. However, this argument is also flawed. Outright military occupation and immediate regime change aside, defeat in war or even lower level disputes could weaken domestic support for the regime by providing a focal point for citizen discontent. Or defeated soldiers might turn against their own regime, as many Arab soldiers did in the aftermath of a humiliating defeat to Israel in 1948. Given the drastic consequences of regime change, the audience would be wary of a leader who takes what seems to be a foolish or selfish risk in this regard and so might jettison him or her to stave off citizen discontent. Defeat could also reveal or even increase a country's military vulnerability and make it more open to future invasion by hostile neighbors. Because of their greater understanding of international affairs, political and military elites might be especially attuned to the perils of exposing their military weaknesses or losing strategic territory. Unlike the ordinary public, authoritarian elites have their own access to information about the details of the war outcome and are not vulnerable to favorable framing by the leader. The consequences of defeat should therefore loom as large in the minds of autocratic audiences as of democratic audiences.

What about the value of the status quo compared to the value of international goods such as territory, economic rights, or the removal of an external threat? Although I return to this issue in the discussion of military regimes, there are no clear reasons to think that ordinary authoritarian elites are more paranoid or view other states as more threatening than do voters in democracies. The value of the status quo should not therefore be substantially lower for civilian autocratic elites than for democratic audiences. Alternatively, perhaps autocratic audiences are more likely to favor conflict because they have a greater desire for the potential benefits of victory, or "international goods." The most prominent formulation of this argument is that, because authoritarian elites can keep the spoils rather than sharing them with the population, military conquest may seem more attractive to autocrats than to democrats (Lake 1992). Yet the autocratic expansionism argument hinges on whether conquering foreign territory disproportionately benefits elites or the public; if the latter, we might actually expect authoritarian audiences to be better off directly consuming the resources that it would take to successfully conquer foreign territory (Bueno de Mesquita et al. 2003), leading to an anti-expansionist bias. Absent evidence that expansion and war disproportionately benefit the elite, this argument would not imply that autocrats start more wars.

In sum, this discussion suggests that civilian authoritarian audiences—even when they are small and not representative of the broader public—tend to view the initiation of military conflict with the same trepidation as democratic audiences. Although these autocratic audiences may approve of using force if the benefits outweigh the material or moral costs, they are no less wary of the possibility of defeat than their democratic counterparts and do not see systematically greater gains from fighting. In turn the fear of ex post punishment induces the leaders of these machines to heed the audience's preferences.

This conclusion is at odds with much of the conventional wisdom: One might expect that it is much easier for a leader to convince a small coalition of elites to forgive him or her for launching a foolish war than it would be to assuage Congress or voters, and that even nonpersonalist autocrats would therefore feel less constrained by the views of their audi-

ences.[22] However, for the reasons provided earlier, the conventional wisdom underestimates the vulnerability of nonpersonalist autocrats. First, the lonely post-tenure fates of leaders of machines may encourage even greater caution than in democracies, even if the odds of losing office are slightly lower. Second, leaders of machines may find it much more difficult to massage domestic opinion when the audience consists of high-level officials—themselves often active in foreign policy and with no special appetite for force—than a "rationally ignorant" mass public (Downs 1957). Even long after the fall of Baghdad, for example, voters had substantial misperceptions about the threat that Iraq had posed (Kull, Ramsay, and Lewis 2003). Together, these factors combine to produce, on average, no greater incentives for leaders of machines to initiate conflicts than for leaders of democracies.

H1:   Machines are no more likely to initiate military conflicts than democracies.

MILITANT JUNTAS: ELITE-CONSTRAINED DICTATORSHIPS WITH MILITARY AUDIENCES

Having discussed civilian non-personalist machines, I now turn to military juntas in which the leader faces an audience composed primarily of military officers.[23] Some of the arguments about elite audiences in nonpersonalist civilian autocracies apply to military regimes as well; for example, as in machines, elites in military juntas are not insulated from the costs of defeat. However an important exception exists in regard to the regime's perceived costs of fighting, and the value of the status quo. Military officers have been selected for, and socialized to hold, specific beliefs about the utility and appropriateness of military force as an instrument of politics. Specifically, military officers are more likely than civilians to form ominous views of the status quo, and to view military force as effective and routine.[24] These views raise the perceived net benefits of winning and lower the perceived costs of using force.

The argument emphasizes military officers' deeply engrained beliefs about the role of military force in international affairs.[25] Many scholars have argued that pre-existing beliefs can systematically affect actors' preferences over actions by defining expectations about, for example, cause and effect or the intentions of other actors.[26] Pre-existing beliefs are particularly likely to influence perceptions of military action, where cause and effect are so distant that individuals cannot learn from direct experience. To scholars of public opinion, it is unsurprising that there may be systematic differences among individuals in their perceptions of the utility and costs of armed conflict. For example, researchers regularly find that beliefs about the use of force vary by gender and education, even when there is no tangible link to the individual's personal well-being.[27]

As many scholars have argued, the result of military training is to inculcate individuals with systematic beliefs about the necessity, effectiveness, and appropriateness of using military force abroad (Sechser 2004). First, military officers are particularly likely to view the status quo as threatening. In his seminal work on the beliefs of military officers, Huntington (1957) argues that there is a "military ethic" that "views conflict as a universal pattern throughout nature and sees violence rooted in the permanent biological and psychological nature of men" (64).[28] Moreover, soldiers base their perceptions of threats on information not about the political intentions of the other state, but on the state's military capabilities: "Human nature being what it is, a stronger state should never be trusted even if it proclaims the friendliest intentions" (66), and soldiers are socialized to "view with alarm the potency and immediacy of the security threats to the state" (66). Because officers are less likely, on average, to feel comfortable with the status quo, they perceive higher net benefits of winning.

Second, military officers view the use of military force as routine, appropriate, and therefore relatively low-cost. Professional officers become so "function-ally specialized" (Posen 1984, 57) that they "forget that other means can also be used toward the same end" (Snyder 1984, 28). Over time, these tendencies may even harden into offensive doctrines (Posen 1984; Snyder 1984).[29] As Brecher (1996) puts it, "Violence is normal behavior for the military in power, for the military generally achieves and sustains power through violence and tends to use this technique in all situations of stress, internal or external. They also see violence as legitimate and effective" (220). In officers' Hobbesian worldview, resort to force is unavoidable and therefore morally acceptable, further reducing its perceived costs. In contrast officers view diplomacy as costly, because it wastes precious time and could allow civilians to meddle in what are properly military matters. In sum, in addition to viewing force as necessary because of the costs of inaction, officers become habituated to the role of force in international politics. Whereas their material costs of fighting may be no lower than for civilian autocratic elites or ordinary citizens, officers' *perceived* costs of fighting are lower. Consistent with these arguments, Horowitz and Stam (2011) find cross-national evidence that leaders with military experience are significantly more likely to initiate armed conflict, even when controlling for a host of confounding factors.

A potential counterargument is that military officers' Hobbesian views are offset by otherwise conservative tendencies.[30] Although Huntington saw military leaders as prone to exaggerating external threats, he ultimately believed that professional soldiers favor war only rarely, because "war at any time is an intensification of the threats to the military security of the state" (69).[31] Feaver and Gelpi (2004) report a similar conclusion in their study of the beliefs of American military officers, and Richard Betts (1977) finds that in the context of Cold War crises, U.S. military officers did not uniformly advocate more aggressive policies than civilian officials.

Importantly, however, these studies do not necessarily imply that officers in military juntas are less aggressive than elites in machines or ordinary citizens. First, they report on military officers in democracies with strong civil-military relations, usually the United States. In contrast, the military officers who rule military dictatorships have shaken off civilian control and declared the military's right to intervene in domestic politics. Even if it were true that military officers in the United States are relatively cautious, military juntas explicitly select for groups of officers who are decidedly not conservative about using force to settle political questions.

Second, even if we do believe that the American experience sheds light on the attitudes and preferences of military officers in dictatorships, the existing empirical evidence does not in fact favor the military conservatism hypothesis. For example, although Betts (1977) is often cited as evidence that military officers are not more hawkish than civilians, his conclusion was actually that military opinion was often divided and that the hawkish military officers rarely influenced U.S. policy. In fact, Betts' own data showed that during Cold War crises, military officers advocated more hawkish policy positions than civilians 21% of the time, equally hawkish positions 65% of the time, and were less hawkish only 14% of the time (216).[32] When it came to tactical escalation decisions after an intervention, military officers were *never* less aggressive than civilians.

Moreover, Feaver and Gelpi's (2004) surveys of American military and civilian elites suggest that military officers are only more conservative about using force when the mission involves "interventionist" goals such as spreading democracy or protecting human rights. In fact, when it comes to *realpolitik* questions such as the rise of China or WMD proliferation, military officers display patterns of beliefs consistent with the arguments made here. Military officers in the Feaver and Gelpi surveys were more likely than civilians to perceive external threats stemming from China, nuclear weapons, and the spread of arms; less likely to perceive diplomacy and diplomatic tools as important; and more likely to view the military as an important instrument of for-

eign policy.[33] This distinction matters because the United States, as a liberal superpower, is relatively unique among countries in its ability to use force to pursue nonsecurity goals. When it comes to the types of *realpolitik* security situations that most countries face, the evidence from the United States actually seems to suggest that military officers are more hawkish than civilians.

In sum, due to the background and training of military officers, autocratic audiences composed primarily of military men should tend to be more supportive of using military force than civilian audiences. Military officers' training leads them to view force as a routine and appropriate policy option, to be wary of diplomacy, and to fear the consequences if they do not act. As a result they perceive increased benefits from using force. Leaders facing such a "constituency" will therefore be more likely to initiate military conflicts than counterparts who face a civilian audience.

H2: Juntas are more likely to initiate military conflicts than machines and democracies.

PERSONALIST DICTATORS: AMBITIOUS AND UNCONSTRAINED

Finally, what behavior should we expect from personalist regimes, led by civilian bosses and military strongmen? Since the leaders of these regimes do not face a powerful domestic audience, we must investigate their personal views on the costs and benefits of using force. There are several reasons why we should expect these leaders to be prone to initiating military conflicts. I first discuss the two types of leaders together and then comment on how strongmen may differ from bosses due to their military backgrounds.

First, personalist dictators are, like military officers, particularly likely to view military force as necessary, effective, and hence net less costly than do either democratic voters or civilian officials in nonpersonalist regimes. One reason is that unlike elites in machines, who are typically bureaucrats who have risen through the civilian ranks, many personalist dictators, such as Stalin, Mao, Saddam Hussein, and Idi Amin, attained their personal status through violent means such as revolution, civil war, or a violent coup. These types of leaders have learned that force is an effective and even necessary means of dispute resolution, lowering their perception of its costs (Colgan 2010; Gurr 1988; Horowitz and Stam 2011).

Second, these leaders are more likely to desire international goods, or are more "revisionist," than typical audience members in a democracy, machine, or junta. Personalist regimes select for leaders who are particularly likely to cherish grand international ambitions. One way to think of personalist leaders is as individuals with "tyrannical" personalities who managed, through force and luck, to create domestic political conditions (personalist regimes) that feed this desire to dominate others. Rosen (2005) draws on classical works by Xenophon and others to argue that tyrants are particularly likely to crave supremacy over others (156–57), and Glad argues that many tyrants are narcissists who attempt to "buttress [their] exalted self-image" by placing themselves above others (Glad 2002, 26). Psychological studies of tyrants (i.e., the types of individuals who are particularly likely to become personalist dictators) in turn consistently highlight these leaders' need for absolute domination and their consequent grandiose ambitions.[34] One of Saddam Hussein's many aspirations, for example, was to establish a pan-Arab caliphate—with himself, of course, as caliph. As the heir of Nebuchadnezzar and Saladin, it was only natural that Saddam would order the construction of an ostentatious palace in Babylon—with his own initials inscribed on each brick (Woods et al. 2006). Muammar Gaddafi of Libya notoriously dubbed himself the "King of Kings," in 2008, gathering together more than 200 African tribal rulers and monarchs and declaring his hope for a single African government over which he would presumably preside.

Although leaders of other regime types may also be prone to visions of empire (Snyder 1991), in personalist dictatorships, the sycophants surrounding the dictator are particularly unwilling to rein in the leader's excessive ambition.[35] In the Kremlin under Stalin, "There was a clear etiquette: it was deadly to disagree too much. . . . Silence was often a virtue and veterans advised neophytes on how to behave and survive" (Montefiore 2004, 341). Although even subordinates in democracies may find it difficult to disabuse the leader of unrealistic goals, these tendencies are exacerbated in personalist autocracies, in which the leader is so unusually powerful.

Finally, the costs of defeat will be lower for personalist dictators compared not only to voters in democracies but also to audiences in nonpersonalist dictatorships. Personalist dictators have extraordinary resources at their disposal to protect themselves from harm during wartime, compared to other regime elites. In addition, their ability to disrupt coordination among regime elites means that even if defeat harms others in the regime, personalist leaders do not face the same threat of domestic punishment.

In sum, the internal logic of personalist dictatorships points clearly toward greater conflict initiation by personalist dictators compared to leaders of democracies or machines. First, the path toward becoming a personalist dictator selects for leaders who both have grand international ambitions and who view force as an effective long-term strategy, raising its net benefits and reducing its net costs. Second, personalist dictators are less vulnerable to the costs of defeat than audiences in nonpersonalist regimes. This increases their willingness to initiate disputes that they have only a low likelihood of winning and inflates their overall rate of dispute initiation. The implication for conflict initiation is that strongmen and bosses tend to, on average, initiate more military disputes than more constrained leaders.

H3: *Bosses and strongmen are more likely to initiate military conflicts than machines and democracies.*

STRONGMEN: MORE BELLIGERENT THAN BOSSES OR JUNTAS?

A final question is whether the effects of personalism and militarism are additive or redundant. Are personalistic strongmen more likely to initiate conflict than nonpersonalistic juntas? Are strongmen—personalist leaders with a military background who are surrounded by military advisors—more likely to embrace international conflict than (civilian) bosses? I consider each comparison—strongmen vs. juntas, and strongmen vs. bosses—in turn.

First, are strongmen more belligerent than juntas? The argument about juntas was that even though leaders of juntas must please a domestic audience, that audience, consisting of military officers, is more likely than a civilian audience to view force as a sound long-term strategy and to perceive the status quo ominously. These perceptions raise the anticipated net benefits of using force. Like militarism, one of the effects of personalism is that, because of selection, personalist leaders tend to believe that military force is necessary, effective, and superior to diplomacy. However, unlike personalist dictators, leaders of juntas cannot insulate themselves from the costs of defeat. Personalist strongmen should therefore be more likely to initiate conflict than nonpersonalist juntas, although the difference should be smaller than the differences between bosses and machines, where *both* beliefs and accountability are different.

Second, are strongmen more belligerent than bosses? Given that both are personalist regimes in which the leader faces few consequences from a domestic audience, the question is whether the military background of a strongman would favor the initiation of conflict. Because a substantial proportion of bosses must have a predilection for violence to survive their ascent to power and then keep their job, they will be attracted to violent strategies even if they do not have formal military training. In strongman regimes, the leader's military experience is largely redundant given that all

personalist regimes select for highly violent and ambitious leaders. On the margins, we would expect military strongmen to be more belligerent on average than civilian bosses, although the difference is likely smaller than between other regime types. In sum, there are reasons to expect that, although the effects of personalism and militarism are additive, there is some redundancy when both attributes are present.

H4: *The effects of personalism and militarism are partially redundant. Strongmen are only somewhat more likely to initiate military conflicts than juntas and only marginally more likely than bosses.*

Measuring Authoritarian Regime Type

Assessing these four hypotheses requires data that capture to what extent the paramount leader faces a powerful domestic audience, and whether the leader and the audience stem from civilian or military ranks. Previous attempts to measure these concepts, however, suffer from important shortcomings. For example, Lai and Slater (2006) rely on a combination of the Polity executive constraints (*xconst*) variable (Marshall and Jaggers 2002) and the Banks Cross-National Time Series "regime type" variable, which identifies whether the government is controlled by a civilian or military elite (Banks 2007).[36] However, the xconst variable is problematic for measuring political constraints in authoritarian regimes because it focuses on formal institutional constraints and "regular" limitations on the executive's power, explicitly excluding "irregular limitations such as the threat or actuality of coups and assassinations" (Marshall and Jaggers 2002, 23). It overlooks the possibility that the threat of coups, including both military coups and palace coups at the hands of political elites, is more predictable and credible in some regimes than others.[37]

Other scholars have used Geddes' (2003) typology, which distinguishes among military, single-party, and personalist regimes. An advantage of this classification is that it does not rely purely on formal institutions. However, the Geddes typology does not distinguish between military personalists (strongmen such as Pinochet or Idi Amin) and civilian personalists (bosses such as Saddam Hussein or North Korea under the Kims), so as Lai and Slater point out, we cannot assess whether personalist regimes are more conflict-prone because they are personalist, led by the military, or both. Moreover, Geddes counts quite personalistic leaders, such as Stalin and Mao, as single-party leaders because of the party institutions that undergird the regime. In contrast, the framework presented here refers to the personal power of the *leader*, indicating that Stalin and Mao should be considered bosses rather than machines.

A different approach allows me to draw on the strengths of the Geddes data while classifying regimes according to both personalism and military background. As part of her research, Geddes gathered information about a large number of domestic political variables for each regime. Three groups of questions reflected the characteristics of three regime types (personalist, single party, and military); Geddes aggregated the answers from each group of yes/no questions and assigned three regime-type categories based on these subscores. One attractive feature of the raw data is that many of the variables vary within the regime over time, unlike the tripartite regime typologies. For example, the raw data distinguish between the USSR under Stalin, which I code as a "boss," and the post-Stalin Soviet Union, which I code as a "machine." Both of these are coded as single-party regimes in the Geddes typology that other scholars have used, but the raw data indicate that, for example, Stalin chose most of the members of the Politburo and that the Politburo acted primarily as a rubber stamp, whereas in the post-Stalin era, neither of these were true.

Because of these advantages, I used the raw Geddes regime-type data to create both independent measures of the two dimensions (personalism and military leadership) and indicator variables for each of the four regime types: machine, junta, strongman, and boss. To measure the personalist dimension, I created an index of eight variables, including whether access to high government office depends on the personal favor of the leader, whether country specialists viewed the politburo or equivalent as a rubber stamp for the leader's decisions, and whether the leader personally controlled the security forces.[38] To measure the military dimension, I used five questions: whether the leader was a current or former high-ranking military officer,[39] whether officers hold cabinet positions not related to the armed forces, whether the military high command is consulted primarily about security (as opposed to political) matters, whether most members of the cabinet or politburo-equivalent are civilians, and whether the Banks dataset considers the government to be "military" or "military-civilian."

I first created indices representing the proportion of "yes" answers.[40] I then created dummy variables for each of the four regime types, using a cutoff of .5 to classify countries as either personalist or nonpersonalist, or military or civilian, and combining the two dimensions to create four regime types.[41] For example, I coded a country-year as a strongman if it scored more than .5 on the personalist index and .5 on the military index. Choosing the particular cutoff of .5 did not affect the substantive results, nor did weighting certain important subcomponents of the index more heavily than others or revising the components of the index in reasonable ways. I also show later that the results are similar whether one uses the indices or the categories, and I describe two ways to score democracies on these indices. * * *

Finally, Geddes did not code monarchies, theocracies, or unconsolidated regimes in her research. Although these types of regimes could in principle be coded according to my measures, lacking that data I created additional dummy variables to identify "other" nondemocracies (regimes that have

Figure 6.3. Examples of Authoritarian Regime Type, 1946-1999

	Civilian Audience or Leader	Military Audience or Leader
Elite-constrained Leaders	**"Machine"** 717 country-years China (after Mao) Kenya Malaysia Mexico (until 1997) Poland Senegal Tanzania USSR (after Stalin) (North) Vietnam	**"Junta"** 410 country-years Algeria Argentina Brazil Greece Myanmar (after 1988) Nigeria Rwanda South Korea Thailand
Personalistic Leaders	**"Boss"** 691 country-years China (Mao) Cuba (Castro) Egypt (Sadat, Mubarak) Indonesia (Sukarno) Iraq (Saddam) Libya (Qaddafi) North Korea (Kims) Portugal (Salazar) Romania (Ceausescu) USSR (Stalin)	**"Strongman"** 637 country-years Chile (Pinochet) Egypt (Nasser) Indonesia (Suharto) Iraq (Qasim, al-Bakr) Myanmar (until 1988) Pakistan (Ayub Khan) Paraguay (Stroessner) Somalia (Siad Barre) Spain (Franco) Uganda (Idi Amin)

Polity scores of 5 or lower, but no Geddes regime-type data). Figure 6.3 summarizes the distribution of machines, bosses, juntas, and strongmen for the 1946–99 period and provides examples of each category.

■ ■ ■

Results

I started the analysis by estimating the models with the regime-type dummy variables. Although less flexible, these results are more straightforward to interpret than the results using the raw indices; as I show later, the two approaches produce the same inferences. These analyses set the base regime-type category for Side A as democracy; we would expect junta, boss, and strongman to have positive and significant coefficients, with strongmen being the most belligerent of all. Machines should not initiate significantly more conflict than democracies according to the arguments.

The results support these predictions. * * * I begin by estimating an extremely parsimonious model in which the only control variables other than regime type are each side's raw military capabilities and major power status, both of which affect a regime's ability to project power. In these models, as well as the subsequent model that controls for additional covariates, the coefficients on junta, boss, and strongman are positive and significant at the .05 level or greater. Machines, in contrast, are not more likely to initiate conflicts than democracies; indeed in the cross-sectional model controlling for the full set of covariates, machines are slightly *less* likely to initiate conflicts than democracies, although this result does not hold in all of the analyses. * * *

Not only are there significant differences between democracies, on the one hand, and juntas, bosses, and strongmen, on the other hand, but there are also significant differences *among* authoritarian regime types. Tests of equality between coefficients indicate that juntas, bosses, and strongmen are all statistically different from machines.

■   ■   ■

The results in the more demanding fixed-effects analysis again strongly support the hypothesis that juntas, bosses, and strongmen are more likely to initiate conflicts than machines and, to a somewhat lesser extent, democracies. Machines, again, are no more belligerent than democracies. The one unexpected result in the fixed-effects models is that the coefficient on strongman is smaller—although not significantly so—than the coefficient on either boss or junta, which contradicts H4.

■   ■   ■

Finally, the findings indicate that the evidence does not support existing arguments about variation in the conflict propensity of dictatorships. First, it does not bear out the expectations of Lai and Slater's (2006) infrastructural-power theory of conflict. According to their arguments, bosses should be no more conflict-prone than machines, because what matters is not the level of personalism of the regime, but rather whether the regime has a party infrastructure to provide stability and co-opt dissent. With the improved measures of auto-cratic institutions that I present here—including the improved ability to distinguish juntas from strongmen—their argument is not supported.[42]

Second, the evidence appears inconsistent with selectorate theory. Previous research assessing the ability of selectorate theory to explain conflict among autocracies, such as Peceny and Butler (2004), relied on less accurate measures of autocratic institutions; for example, classifying Mao and Stalin as single-party rather than personalist leaders. Earlier research designs also made it difficult to gain a picture of overall patterns of dispute initiation by the initiator's regime type. Although selectorate theory's predictions are usually dyadic (i.e., they take into account the interaction between the regime types of the initiator and target), we would still expect that, averaging across all of the types of dyads, small-coalition regimes should initiate more conflict than large-coalition regimes.[43] Instead, we find that machines—which have small winning coalitions both in absolute size and relative to the selectorate (w/s)[44]—are no more belligerent and, indeed sometimes less belligerent than democracies, which have much larger coalitions and w/s scores. Moreover, small-coalition bosses do not initiate significantly more conflicts than juntas, which should also have a larger w/s.[45] Existing theoretical perspectives, in sum, cannot explain the findings.[46]

Conclusions

This article raises the possibility that conventional views of the relationship between regime type and foreign policy, including the argument that democracies are in general more selective about initiating international conflict than nondemocracies,[47] are, at best, incomplete and, at worst, wrong. Focusing myopically on the usual dichotomy between democracy and authoritarianism could lead to faulty inferences about the effect of regime type on foreign relations. The combination of better data and theoretical arguments that draw on recent advances in the study of comparative authoritarianism reveals that there are substantial differences in the tendency of different types of authoritarian regimes to initiate international conflicts.

The framework introduced here not only helps us understand how authoritarian regimes vary in their conflict behavior but also opens new avenues for creative theorizing about how domestic institutions affect both preferences and constraints, which combine to affect states' foreign policy behaviors more generally. The first task is to be more specific about what kinds of domestic constraints matter; here a first question is whether the leader faces any domestic audience that could punish him or her for decisions about international conflict. I argue that, contrary to the conventional wisdom, many authoritarian leaders face powerful domestic audiences composed of regime elites. Like democratic leaders, many autocracies must therefore be attentive to the preferences of these domestic constituents, more so than the existing literature suggests.

This, however, leads to a second question: What are the interests and preferences of that domestic audience in matters of war and peace? I first argue that, contra selectorate theory, even small-coalition audiences such as those in machines have strong incentives to jettison a leader who deviates from their preferred policies. However, audience members' backgrounds affect their preferences and therefore their conclusions about whether the use of force was warranted. Specifically, the military officers who form the leader's constituency in junta regimes tend to view the world more ominously than their counterparts in civilian nonpersonalist regimes. They fear the consequences of inaction and they view the use of force to settle political matters as business as usual. They thus favor the initiation of international conflict more frequently than their civilian counterparts in machines.

Finally, in personalist regimes in which leaders have eliminated rivals and consolidated power into their own hands, conflict initiation depends on the whims of those paramount leaders. Unfortunately, given the treacherous road to power in a personalist dictatorship, these unconstrained leaders are often precisely the types of individuals who seek out international conflict and can survive defeat, only to repeat the cycle.

In sum, in addition to the central point that differences among authoritarian regimes matter just as much for explaining international conflict as differences between democracies and dictatorships, this article has three theoretical implications. First, it suggests that we cannot simply deduce how leaders will behave by focusing on the presence or absence of "constraints." Rather, the impact of constraints or accountability depends on the preferences of the audience with the power to impose those constraints.

Second, we should not assume that preferences can be deduced simply from the relative size of the domestic audience or winning coalition. Rather, this article suggests that scholars should focus more on understanding the sources of preferences and how different institutional structures make those preferences salient. For example, my argument suggests that the background experiences of domestic audiences matter by shaping views about the use of force. This approach of blending measurable features of institutions with more sociological or constructivist insights about the sources of foreign policy preferences suggests productive lines of future research.

Third, the analysis suggests a way to integrate "first-image" theories, which focus on the behavior of individuals, with "second-image" theories about the importance of domestic political institutions. For example, I argue that the background experiences of individual leaders may be especially important for understanding behavior when the regime is personalist and the leader faces fewer domestic constraints (Byman and Pollack 2001). This claim leads to a whole host of propositions that can potentially be tested with new data sources (Horowitz and Stam 2011). Scholars of all theoretical orientations would do well to understand what shapes the worldviews and therefore preferences of influential actors in both democratic and authoritarian regimes.

The findings also suggest policy-relevant lessons for diplomacy with dictatorships, painting different pictures of the conflict behavior of machines, juntas, and personalists. For example, China's civilian, elite-constrained government has been the quintessential "machine" for at least the last two decades. The evidence here suggests that, although countries like China repress public participation in politics, they tend to be more cautious than other authoritarian regime types when it comes to international conflict. Like democratic leaders, machines face domestic audiences that are not systematically predisposed toward using force, and can punish the leader for costly or foolish decisions. This could be good news for deterrent strategies, because like democracies, these regimes tend to avoid starting fights that they cannot win. However, this feature also implies that, when machines do resort to military force, their efforts will be intense because their leaders cannot afford failure.

The implications for juntas are somewhat different. If the arguments laid out here are correct, policy makers should consider that military leaders in elite-constrained juntas often use force not because they necessarily desire expansion for its own sake, but because the military officers staffing these governments are socialized to see military force as standard operating procedure, to view powerful countries as inherently hostile, and to fear the costs of compromise. To persuade military dictators that threats are not imminent, diplomats may need to devise ways to assuage such fears. In contrast, strong shows of force will sometimes be necessary to convince military juntas of the high costs of using force.

Personalistic bosses like Kim Jong Il and Saddam Hussein, as well as strongmen like Pinochet, Idi Amin, and Nasser, have also been especially belligerent, although for slightly different reasons.

Personalist regimes tend to select for leaders with extreme international ambitions, and because personalist leaders are unusually insulated from the consequences of policy failures, they can act on these preferences and take risky gambles that more constrained leaders would eschew. The findings therefore suggest that one way to deter personalists is to emphasize that conflict may lead to regime change, whereas peace will reduce the likelihood of external interference. Given that personalist dictators are typically surrounded by sycophants who are afraid to communicate unwelcome news, face-to-face meetings may be necessary to ensure that the message is received by the person who matters most.

Finally, understanding what aspects of authoritarianism are most detrimental to peace could help guide policy makers toward promoting reform in cases where democratization seems unlikely. For example, they might make aid conditional on the leader allowing collective, civilian oversight of appointments and security organs (although they should expect stiff resistance from the leader). Indeed, given their leaders' greater sensitivity to the potential downsides of defeat, even juntas may be more desirable than personalist dictatorships on national security grounds. Either way, the evidence here suggests that scholars should pay careful attention to the type of regime most likely to emerge after foreign intervention or regime change, designing interventions and state-building activities to lower the likelihood that belligerent regimes emerge from the rubble.

NOTES

1. Indeed, scholars such as Oren and Hays (1997) have noted that single-party states seem more peaceful than other authoritarian regime types. Weart (1994) shows that oligarchies are also relatively peaceful. See also Sobek (2005).
2. For an exception, see Debs and Goemans (2010).
3. Others discuss some additional possible theoretical explanations, but do not develop and test one core argument (Peceny and Beer 2003; Peceny, Beer, and Sanchez-Terry 2002).

4. See also Clarke and Stone (2008), Ezrow and Frantz (2011), Haber (2006), Kennedy (2009), and Magaloni (2006) for additional critiques of selectorate theory and the evidence supporting it.

5. See also Debs and Goemans (2010) for an argument about military regimes that rests on the technology of leadership removal.

6. See for example Chiozza and Goemans (2003) and James (1987). Tir (2010) suggests that diversionary arguments may apply only to the subset of conflicts with high public salience.

7. Other research finds that only mature democracies and "consolidating" autocracies show evidence of diversion (Kisangani and Pickering 2009; Pickering and Kisangani 2005). See also Chiozza and Goemans (2003; 2004) on regime type and diversion.

8. Among many, see Dixon (1994), Howell and Pevehouse (2007), Maoz and Russett (1993), Morgan and Campbell (1991), Ray (1995), and Schultz (1999).

9. See Kinne (2005) for an argument about autocratic domestic audiences drawing on "poliheuristic theory," Weiss (2008; n.d.) on mass audiences in authoritarian regimes, and Kirshner (2007) on financial elites.

10. Fearon (1999), Johns (2006), and Smith (1998). Alternatively, the audience could wish to incentivize future behavior, or the audience could wish to rehabilitate the country's international reputation; see for example Fearon (1994) and Guisinger and Smith (2002).

11. A more complicated strategic model could also model the audience's reaction, but the central points can be illustrated by focusing on the leader's decision.

12. See for example Lake (1992) and Snyder (1991) on expansionist motives, Schweller (1994) on revisionist states, and Glaser (2010) on "greedy" states.

13. Finally, independent of the audience's preferences, the leader must reach some assessment of the probability that the country will win the dispute. Although it is possible that some types of leaders make systematically biased estimates of victory, I assume for simplicity that all leaders make unbiased (if imperfect) estimates. See, however, Frantz (2008).

14. Space does not permit exploring the merits of alternative ways of differentiating among authoritarian regimes, but see Arendt (1951), Brooker (2000), Brownlee (2007), Cheibub, Gandhi, and Vreeland (2010), Ezrow and Frantz (2011), Friedrich and Brzezinski (1956), Gandhi (2008), Gandhi and Przeworski (2006), Hadenius and Teorell (2007), Linz (2000), Magaloni (2006; 2008), O'Donnell (1978), Pepinsky (2009), and Wintrobe (2000).

15. Most previous work has used a three-part typology that does not allow separate examination of the military and personalist dimensions; for example, Peceny and Beer (2003) group strongmen and bosses together as "personalists."

16. See also Lai and Slater (2006). A possible point of confusion is that although I use Slater's labels, I argue that the military dimension is important because it conditions how decision makers interpret threats and opportunities, not because lower levels of "infrastructural power" in military regimes lead to diversion.

17. These constraints can be formal or informal. Often, the degree of constraints in authoritarian regimes does not reflect the letter of the law. See also Wright (2008) on how legislatures can constrain authoritarian rulers.

18. A few scholars would dispute this conventional claim about democracies. Chiozza and Goemans (2003; 2004) argue that democracies, typically viewed as the most accountable regime type, are less sensitive to conflict outcomes than nondemocracies. Debs and Goemans (2010) and Chiozza and Goemans (2011) suggest that modes of leadership removal affect leaders' sensitivity to conflict outcomes.

19. Is retrospective punishment credible in these autocracies? Earlier I argued that audiences draw inferences about the leader's competence or preferences by comparing the outcome of a dispute to the audience's expectations had the leader acted differently. Faced with the rotten fruits of a leader's decision, audiences may conclude that the leader is either unable or unwilling to further their policy interests and that a new leader would improve their well-being. The question then becomes whether other concerns, such as the fear of losing insider status, overwhelm audience members' desire for a competent leader who does not make poor foreign policy choices. Earlier I argued that audience members in nonpersonalist autocracies can usually assure themselves that they can hold on to their positions even under a new leader. They should therefore wish to replace leaders who make unwelcome foreign policy decisions.

20. In fact, the expectation that war will destabilize the enemy is common enough that many belligerents fight wars with this express goal in mind; see Holsti (1991).

21. I define norms broadly as standards of appropriate behavior shared by a particular community—in this case, a domestic community of policy makers. The norms could either involve moral beliefs about what is right or could refer simply to standard behaviors. See Goldstein and Keohane (1993), Katzenstein (1996), Mercer (1995), Risse-Kappen (1995), and Wendt (1992).

22. I thank an anonymous reviewer for putting it this way.

23. On military regimes, see Gandhi and Przeworski (2006), Geddes (2003), Nordlinger (1977), and Remmer (1989).

24. This argument reaches a similar conclusion as Debs and Goemans' (2010), who argue that military officers are often punished for making peaceful concessions. However, their mechanism relies on the technology of leadership removal rather than officers' perceptions of the necessity of using force.

25. Parochial interests could encourage these beliefs, for example by ingraining offensive doctrines, which increase institutional prestige and require larger budgets (Posen 1984; Snyder 1984).

26. See for example Adler (1992), Dafoe and Caughey (2011), Finnemore (1996), Goldstein and Keohane (1993), Horowitz and Stam (2011), Johnston (1995), Lake (2010), Legro (1996), Saunders (2011), and Snyder (1984).

27. For example, in a nationally-representative survey featuring a hypothetical scenario in which a state was developing nuclear weapons, Tomz and Weeks (2011) found significant differences across demographic groups in support for military strikes, threat perception, expectations of costs and success, and moral concerns.

28. See also Snyder (1984, 28).

29. Vagts (1958, 263) expresses a similar view, although see also Kier (1997).

30. For a helpful overview of this literature, see Sechser (2004).

31. Andreski (1992) reaches a similar conclusion, arguing that sending the army abroad for military adventures renders it unavailable for internal policing (105), and politicizing the army undermines its

war-fighting effectiveness. However, Andreski's evidence is purely anecdotal, and his argument should apply to any regime in which the military is important to the stability of the country, not only military dictatorships.

32. Author's calculation from Table A in Betts (1977).

33. For more detail, see the Online Appendix at http://falcon.arts .cornell.edu/jlw338/research.htm.

34. See, for example, Glad (2002) and Post (2004). Moreover, many personalist dictators are revolutionary leaders who wish to change the status quo both domestically and internationally (Colgan n.d.; Walt 1996).

35. For a related argument about the effects of personalist dictatorship on variation in intelligence quality, see Frantz and Ezrow (2009). See also Biddle (2004), Bratton and Van de Walle (1994), Brooks (1998), Egorov and Sonin (2009), and Geddes (2003) on the tradeoffs that dictators make between loyalty and military competence. For related logic pertaining to military technology and combat ability, see Biddle and Zirkle (1996) and Quinlivan (1999).

36. Variable S20F7—"Type of Regime" in the Banks (2007) dataset.

37. In fact, of the four examples Lai and Slater provide of juntas—Burma, Algeria, Greece (pre-1974), and Argentina (pre-1983)—their empirical analysis counts all four as strongmen because these regimes score low on formal "institutional constraints" according to the xconst measure.

38. The five other questions were (1) If there is a supporting party, does the leader choose most of the members of the politburo-equivalent?; (2) Was the successor to the first leader, or is the heir apparent, a member of the same family, clan, tribe, or minority ethnic group as the first leader?; (3) Has normal military hierarchy been seriously disorganized or overturned, or has the leader created new military forces loyal to him personally?; (4) Have dissenting officers or officers from different regions, tribes, religions, or ethnic groups been murdered, imprisoned, or forced into exile?; and (5) If the leader is from the military, has the officer corps been marginalized from most decision making?

39. I use the Cheibub, Gandhi, and Vreeland (2010) indicator for the effective leader's military background.

40. I code the index as "missing" when I have data on fewer than four of the subquestions.

41. For constructing the personalist dummy variable, I used the following rules to deal with missing values. If there were at least four nonmissing answers, I counted a country as personalist if it received a "yes" on more than 50% of the questions. In the few cases where two or three of the questions were answered, I counted a country as personalist if it scored yes on *all* of those answers, and as not personalist if it scored no on *all* of those answers. Otherwise, I coded nondemocratic observations as missing on the personalist dummy variable. I also experimented with other cutoffs, or basing the cutoffs on a weighted version of the index, or increasing the threshold for coding an observation as "missing;" such changes did not affect the substantive results. I coded democracies as nonpersonalist. I followed similar procedures for the military dummy variable; additional details are available in the Online Appendix.

42. Lai and Slater report monadic analyses in which the country-year is the unit of analysis, whereas I analyze directed dyad-years because

of the greater measurement precision that doing so allows. However, I did not find support for their hypotheses when I replicated their modeling approach using my data.

43. Indeed, Bueno de Mesquita et al. (2003, 245) suggest this finding.

44. See for example Bueno de Mesquita et al. (2003, 440).

45. See Peceny and Butler (2004) for a discussion of selectorate size and authoritarian regime type. Although Peceny and colleagues (2002; 2003; 2004) and Reiter and Stam (2003) operationalized regime type dyadically, my findings appear consistent with theirs in that personalist regimes (roughly comparable to my bosses and strongmen) or military regimes (roughly comparable to my juntas) are more belligerent against some types of targets than single-party regimes (roughly comparable to my machines) or democracies.

46. Another question is whether these findings are consistent with Weeks (2008), who finds that personalist regimes are the least able to signal credibly, whereas nonpersonalist regimes—including juntas—tend to be no different from democracies. If the costs of war are lower for strongmen, bosses, and juntas, as I have argued, then we might expect them to do *better* in crisis bargaining because it is credible that they will use force. One possibility is that the extremely low accountability of personalist leaders offsets their greater "inherent" credibility due to their lower costs for war. As for juntas, the combination of lower costs for war and high accountability of the leader to a domestic audience could imply a signaling advantage, which was not evident in Weeks's (2008) analysis. Future research could attempt to reconcile these findings, perhaps by considering whether the commitment problems created by the anticipation of future military conflict affects reciprocation rates in the present.

47. Gelpi and Griesdorf (2002), Reiter and Stam (2002), Schultz (2001).

REFERENCES

Adler, Emanuel. 1992. "The Emergence of Cooperation: National Epistemic Communities and the International Evolution of the Idea of Nuclear Arms Control." *International Organization* 46 (1): 101–45.

Andreski, Stanislav. 1992. *Wars, Revolutions, Dictatorships: Studies of Historical and Contemporary Problems from a Comparative Viewpoint.* London: F. Cass.

Arendt, Hannah. 1951. *The Origins of Totalitarianism.* New York: Harcourt Brace.

Arquilla, John, and Maria Moyano Rasmussen. 2001. "The Origins of the South Atlantic War." *Journal of Latin American Studies* 33 (4): 739–75.

Banks, Arthur S. 2007. *Cross-national Time-Series Data Archive.* Jerusalem: Databanks International.

Betts, Richard K. 1977. *Soldiers, Statesmen, and Cold War Crises.* Cambridge, MA: Harvard University Press.

Biddle, Stephen D. 2004. *Military Power: Explaining Victory and Defeat in Modern Battle.* Princeton, NJ: Princeton University Press.

Biddle, Stephen, and Robert Zirkle. 1996. "Technology, Civil-Military Relations, and Warfare in the Developing World." *Journal of Strategic Studies* 19 (2): 171–212.

Bratton, Michael, and Nicholas Van de Walle. 1994. "Neopatrimonial Regimes and Political Transitions in Africa." *World Politics* 46 (4): 453–89.

Brecher, Michael. 1996. "Crisis Escalation: Model and Findings." *International Political Science Review* 17 (2): 215–30.

Brooker, Paul. 2000. *Non-democratic Regimes: Theory, Government, and Politics*. New York: St. Martin's Press.

Brooks, Risa. 1998. *Political-Military Relations and the Stability of Arab Regimes*. 324th ed. London: International Institute for Strategic Studies.

Brownlee, Jason. 2007. *Authoritarianism in an Age of Democratization*. New York: Cambridge University Press.

Bueno de Mesquita, Bruce, Alastair Smith, Randolph M. Siverson, and James D. Morrow. 2003. *The Logic of Political Survival*. Cambridge, MA: MIT Press.

Byman, Daniel L., and Kenneth M. Pollack. 2001. "Let Us Now Praise Great Men: Bringing the Statesman Back In." *International Security* 25 (4): 107–46.

Chehabi, Houchang E., and Juan J. Linz. 1998. *Sultanistic Regimes*. Baltimore: Johns Hopkins University Press.

Cheibub, Jose A., Jennifer Gandhi, and James R. Vreeland. 2010. "Democracy and Dictatorship Revisited." *Public Choice* 143 (1): 67–101.

Chiozza, Giacomo, and H. E. Goemans. 2003. "Peace through Insecurity: Tenure and International Conflict." *Journal of Conflict Resolution* 47 (4): 443–67.

Chiozza, Giacomo, and H. E. Goemans. 2004. "International Conflict and the Tenure of Leaders: Is War Still Ex Post Inefficient?" *American Journal of Political Science* 48 (3): 604–19.

Chiozza, Giacomo, and H. E. Goemans. 2011. *Leaders and International Conflict*. New York: Cambridge University Press.

Clark, David H. 2003. "Can Strategic Interaction Divert Diversionary Behavior? A Model of U.S. Conflict Propensity." *Journal of Politics* 65 (4): 1013–39.

Clarke, Kevin A., and Randall W. Stone. 2008. "Democracy and the Logic of Political Survival." *American Political Science Review* 102 (3): 387–92.

Colgan, Jeff. 2010. "Oil and Revolutionary Governments: Fuel for International Conflict." *International Organization* 64 (4): 661–94.

Colgan, Jeff. N.d. *Petro-aggression: How Oil Causes War*. New York: Cambridge University Press. Forthcoming.

Dafoe, Allan, and Devin M. Caughey. 2011. "Honor and War: Using Southern Presidents to Identify Reputational Effects in International Conflict." University of California, Berkeley. Unpublished manuscript.

Debs, Alexandre, and H. E. Goemans. 2010. "Regime Type, the Fate of Leaders, and War." *American Political Science Review* 104: 430–45.

Dixon, William J. 1994. "Democracy and the Peaceful Settlement of International Conflict." *American Political Science Review* 88 (1): 14–32.

Downes, Alexander B. 2008. *Targeting Civilians in War*. Ithaca, NY: Cornell University Press.

Downs, Anthony. 1957. *An Economic Theory of Democracy*. New York: Harper.

Downs, George W., and David M. Rocke. 1994. "Conflict, Agency, and Gambling for Resurrection: The Principal-Agent Problem Goes to War." *American Journal of Political Science* 38 (2): 362–80.

Egorov, Georgy, and Konstantin Sonin. 2011. "Dictators and Their Viziers: Endogenizing the Loyalty-Competence Tradeoff." *Journal of the European Economic Association* 9 (5): 903–30.

Ezrow, Natasha M., and Frantz Erica. 2011. *Dictators and Dictatorships: Understanding Authoritarian Regimes and Their Leaders*. New York: Continuum.

Fearon, James D. 1994. "Domestic Political Audiences and the Escalation of International Disputes." *American Political Science Review* 88 (3): 577–92.

Fearon, James D. 1999. "Electoral Accountability and the Control of Politicians: Selecting Good Types versus Sanctioning Poor Performance." In *Democracy, Accountability, and Representation*, eds. Bernard Manin, Adam Przeworski, and Susan Stokes. Cambridge: Cambridge University Press, 55–97.

Feaver, Peter, and Christopher Gelpi. 2004. *Choosing Your Battles: American Civil-Military Relations and the Use of Force*. Princeton, NJ: Princeton University Press.

Finnemore, Martha. 1996. *National Interests in International Society*. Ithaca, NY: Cornell University Press.

Frantz, Erica. 2008. "Tying the Dictator's Hands: Elite Coalitions in Authoritarian Regimes." Ph.D. diss. University of California, Los Angeles.

Frantz, Erica, and Natasha M. Ezrow. 2009. "'Yes Men' and the Likelihood of Foreign Policy Mistakes across Dictatorships." Presented at the Annual Meeting of the American Political Science Association, Toronto.

Friedrich, Carl J., and Zbigniew K. Brzezinski. 1956. *Totalitarian Dictatorship and Autocracy*. Cambridge, MA: Harvard University Press.

Gandhi, Jennifer, and Adam Przeworski. 2006. "Cooperation, Cooptation, and Rebellion under Dictatorships." *Economics and Politics* 18 (1): 1–26.

Gandhi, Jennifer. 2008. *Political Institutions under Dictatorship*. Cambridge: Cambridge University Press.

Geddes, Barbara. 2003. *Paradigms and Sand Castles: Theory Building and Research Design in Comparative Politics*. Ann Arbor: University of Michigan Press.

Gelpi, Christopher. 1997. "Democratic Diversions: Governmental Structure and the Externalization of Domestic Conflict." *Journal of Conflict Resolution* 41 (2): 255–82.

Gelpi, Christopher F., and Michael Griesdorf. 2002. "Winners or Losers? Democracies in International Crisis, 1918–94." *American Political Science Review* 95 (3): 633–47.

Glad, Betty. 2002. "Why Tyrants Go Too Far: Malignant Narcissism and Absolute Power." *Political Psychology* 23 (1): 1–2.

Glaser, Charles L. 2010. *Rational Theory of International Politics: The Logic of Competition and Cooperation*. Princeton, NJ: Princeton University Press.

Goemans, Hein Erich. 2000. *War and Punishment: The Causes of War Termination and the First World War*. Princeton, NJ: Princeton University Press.

Goemans, H. E. 2008. "Which Way Out? The Manner and Consequences of Losing Office." *Journal of Conflict Resolution* 52 (6): 771–94.

Goldstein, Judith, and Robert O. Keohane. 1993. *Ideas and Foreign Policy: Beliefs, Institutions, and Political Change*. Ithaca, NY: Cornell University Press.

Green, Donald P., Soo Yeon Kim, and David H. Yoon. 2001. "Dirty Pool." *International Organization* 55 (2): 441–68.

Guisinger, A., and A. Smith. 2002. "Honest Threats: The Interaction of Reputation and Political Institutions in International Crises." *Journal of Conflict Resolution* 46 (2): 175–200.

Gurr, Ted Robert. 1988. "War, Revolution, and the Growth of the Coercive State." *Comparative Political Studies* 21 (1): 45–65.

Haber, Stephen. 2006. "Authoritarian Government." In *The Oxford Handbook of Political Economy,* eds. Barry R. Weingast and Donald A. Wittman. Oxford: Oxford University Press, 693–707.

Hadenius, Axel, and Jan Teorell. 2007. "Pathways from Authoritarianism." *Journal of Democracy* 18 (1): 143–57.

Holsti, K. J. 1991. *Peace and War: Armed Conflicts and International Order, 1648–1989.* New York: Cambridge University Press.

Horowitz, Michael C., and Allan C. Stam. 2011. "How Prior Military Experience Influences the Future Militarized Behavior of Leaders." University of Pennsylvania. Unpublished manuscript.

Howell, William G, and Jon C. Pevehouse. 2007. *While Dangers Gather: Congressional Checks on Presidential War Powers.* Princeton, NJ: Princeton University Press.

Huntington, Samuel P. 1957. *The Soldier and the State: The Theory and Politics of Civil-Military Relations.* Cambridge, MA: Belknap Press of Harvard University Press.

James, Patrick. 1987. "Conflict and Cohesion: A Review of the Literature and Recommendations for Future Research." *Cooperation and Conflict* 22 (1): 21–33.

Johns, Leslie. 2006. "Knowing the Unknown." *Journal of Conflict Resolution* 50 (2): 228–52.

Johnston, Alastair Iain. 1995. "Thinking about Strategic Culture." *International Security* 19 (4): 32–64.

Katzenstein, Peter J., ed. 1996. The *Culture of National Security: Norms and Identity in World Politics.* New York: Columbia University Press.

Kennedy, Ryan. 2009. "Survival and Accountability: An Analysis of the Empirical Support for 'Selectorate Theory.'" *International Studies Quarterly* 53 (3): 695–714.

Kier, Elizabeth. 1997. *Imagining War: French and British Military Doctrine between the Wars.* Princeton, NJ: Princeton University Press.

Kinne, Brandon J. 2005. "Decision Making in Autocratic Regimes: A Poliheuristic Perspective." *International Studies Perspectives* 6 (1): 114–28.

Kirshner, Jonathan. 2007. *Appeasing Bankers: Financial Caution on the Road to War.* Princeton, NJ: Princeton University Press.

Kisangani, Emizet F., and Jeffrey Pickering. 2009. "The Dividends of Diversion: Mature Democracies' Proclivity to Use Diversionary Force and the Rewards They Reap from It." *British Journal of Political Science* 39 (3): 483–515.

Kull, Steven, Clay Ramsay, and Evan Lewis. 2003. "Misperceptions, the Media, and the Iraq War." *Political Science Quarterly* 118 (4): 569–98.

Lai, Brian, and Dan Slater. 2006. "Institutions of the Offensive: Domestic Sources of Dispute Initiation in Authoritarian Regimes, 1950–1992." *American Journal of Political Science* 50 (1): 113–26.

Lake, David A. 1992. "Powerful Pacifists: Democratic States and War." *American Political Science Review* 86 (1): 24–37.

Lake, David A. 2010. "Two Cheers for Bargaining Theory: Assessing Rationalist Explanations of the Iraq War." *International Security* 35 (3): 7–52.

Leeds, Brett Ashley, and David R. Davis. 1997. "Domestic Political Vulnerability and International Disputes." *Journal of Conflict Resolution* 41 (6): 814–34.

Legro, Jeffrey W. 1996. "Culture and Preferences in the International Cooperation Two-step." *American Political Science Review* 90 (1): 118–37.

Linz, Juan J. 2000. *Totalitarian and Authoritarian Regimes.* Boulder, CO: Lynne Rienner.

Magaloni, Beatriz. 2006. *Voting for Autocracy: Hegemonic Party Survival and Its Demise in Mexico.* Cambridge: Cambridge University Press.

Magaloni, Beatriz. 2008. "Credible Power-sharing and the Longevity of Authoritarian Rule." *Comparative Political Studies* 41 (4/5): 715–41.

Maoz, Zeev, and Bruce Russett. 1993. "Normative and Structural Causes of Democratic Peace, 1946–1986." *American Political Science Review* 87 (3): 624–38.

Marshall, Monty G., and Keith Jaggers. 2002. *POLITY IV Project, Political Regime Characteristics and Transitions, 1800–2002, Dataset Users' Manual.* College Park: Center for International Development and Conflict Management, University of Maryland.

Mercer, Jonathan. 1995. "Anarchy and Identity." *International Organization* 49 (2): 229–52.

Montefiore, Simon Sebag. 2004. *Stalin: The Court of the Red Tsar.* New York: Knopf.

Morgan, T. Clifton, and Sally Howard Campbell. 1991. "Domestic Structure, Decisional Constraints, and War." *Journal of Conflict Resolution* 35 (2): 187–211.

Nordlinger, Eric A. 1977. *Soldiers in Politics: Military Coups and Governments.* Englewood Cliffs, NJ: Prentice-Hall.

O'Donnell, Guillermo. 1978. "Reflections on the Patterns of Change in the Bureaucratic-Authoritarian State." *Latin American Research Review* 13 (1): 3–38.

Oren, Ido, and Jude Hays. 1997. "Democracies May Rarely Fight One Another, but Developed Socialist States Rarely Fight at All." *Alternatives* 22: 493–521.

Peceny, Mark, and Caroline C. Beer. 2003. "Peaceful Parties and Puzzling Personalists." *American Political Science Review* 97 (2): 339–42.

Peceny, Mark, Caroline C. Beer, and Shannon Sanchez-Terry. 2002. "Dictatorial Peace?" *American Political Science Review* 96 (1): 15–26.

Peceny, Mark, and Christopher K. Butler. 2004. "The Conflict Behavior of Authoritarian Regimes." *International Politics* 41 (4): 565–81.

Pepinsky, Thomas B. 2009. *Economic Crises and the Breakdown of Authoritarian Regimes: Indonesia and Malaysia in Comparative Perspective.* New York: Cambridge University Press.

Pickering, Jeffrey, and Emizet F. Kisangani. 2005. "Democracy and Diversionary Military Intervention: Reassessing Regime Type and the Diversionary Hypothesis." *International Studies Quarterly* 49 (1): 23–44.

Pickering, Jeffrey, and Emizet F. Kisangani. 2010. "Diversionary Despots? Comparing Autocracies' Propensities to Use and to Benefit from Military Force." *American Journal of Political Science* 54 (2): 477–93.

Posen, Barry. 1984. *The Sources of Military Doctrine: France, Britain, and Germany between the World Wars.* Ithaca, NY: Cornell University Press.

Post, Jerrold M. 2004. Leaders *and Their Followers in a Dangerous World: The Psychology of Political Behavior.* Ithaca, NY: Cornell University Press.

Quinlivan, James T. 1999. "Coup-proofing: Its Practice and Consequences in the Middle East." *International Security* 24 (2): 131–65.

Ray, James Lee. 1995. *Democracy and International Conflict: An Evaluation of the Democratic Peace Proposition*. Columbia: University of South Carolina Press.

Reiter, Dan, and Allan C. Stam. 2002. *Democracies at War*. Princeton, NJ: Princeton University Press.

Remmer, Karen L. 1989. *Military Rule in Latin America*. Boston: Unwin Hyman.

Risse-Kappen, Thomas. 1995. "Democratic Peace—Warlike Democracies? A Social Constructivist Interpretation of the Liberal Argument." *European Journal of International Relations* 1 (4): 491–517.

Rosen, Stephen Peter. 2005. *War and Human Nature*. Princeton, NJ: Princeton University Press.

Saunders, Elizabeth N. 2011. *Leaders at War: How Presidents Shape Military Interventions*. Ithaca, NY: Cornell University Press.

Schultz, Kenneth. 1999. "Do Democratic Institutions Constrain or Inform? Contrasting Two Institutional Perspectives on Democracy and War." *International Organization* 53 (2): 233–66.

Schultz, Kenneth A. 2001. *Democracy and Coercive Diplomacy*. New York: Cambridge University Press.

Schweller, Randall L. 1994. "Bandwagoning for Profit: Bringing the Revisionist State Back In." *International Security* 19 (1): 72–107.

Sechser, Todd S. 2004. "Are Soldiers Less War-prone than Statesmen?" *Journal of Conflict Resolution* 48 (5): 746–74.

Slater, Dan. 2003. "Iron Cage in an Iron Fist: Authoritarian Institutions and the Personalization of Power in Malaysia." *Comparative Politics* 36 (1): 81–101.

Smith, Alastair. 1996. "Diversionary Foreign Policy in Democratic Systems." *International Studies Quarterly* 40 (1): 133–53.

Smith, Alastair. 1998. "International Crises and Domestic Politics." *American Political Science Review* 92 (3): 623–38.

Snyder, Jack L. 1984. *The Ideology of the Offensive: Military Decision Making and the Disasters of 1914*. Ithaca, NY: Cornell University Press.

Snyder, Jack L. 1991. *Myths of Empire: Domestic Politics and International Ambition*. Ithaca, NY: Cornell University Press.

Sobek, David. 2005. "Machiavelli's Legacy: Domestic Politics and International Conflict." *International Studies Quarterly* 49 (2): 179–204.

Svolik, Milan W. 2009. "Power Sharing and Leadership Dynamics in Authoritarian Regimes." *American Journal of Political Science* 53 (2): 477–94.

Tir, Jaroslav. 2010. "Territorial Diversion: Diversionary Theory of War and Territorial Conflict." *Journal of Politics* 72 (2): 413–25.

Tomz, Michael, and Jessica Weeks. 2011. "An Experimental Investigation of the Democratic Peace." Ppresented at the Annual Meeting of the American Political Science Association, Seattle.

Vagts, Alfred. 1958. *Defense and Diplomacy: The Soldier and the Conduct of Foreign Relations*. New York: King's Crown Press.

Valentino, Benjamin A., Paul K. Huth, and Sarah E. Croco. 2010. "Bear Any Burden? How Democracies Minimize the Costs of War." *Journal of Politics* 72 (2): 528–44.

Wallace, Geoffrey. 2010. "Surrendering the Higher Ground: The Abuse of Combatants during War." Ph.D. diss. Cornell University.

Walt, Stephen M. 1996. *Revolution and War*. Ithaca, NY: Cornell University Press.

Weart, Spencer R. 1994. "Peace among Democratic and Oligarchic Republics." *Journal of Peace Research* 31 (3): 299–316.

Weber, Max. 1997. *The Theory of Social and Economic Organization*. Glencoe, IL: Free Press.

Weeks, Jessica L. 2008. "Autocratic Audience Costs: Regime Type and Signaling Resolve." *International Organization* 62 (1): 35–64.

Weeks, Jessica L. 2009. "Leaders, Accountability, and Foreign Policy in Non-democracies." Ph.D. diss. Stanford University.

Weiss, Jessica Chen. 2008. "Powerful Patriots: Nationalism, Diplomacy, and the Strategic Logic of Anti-foreign Protest in China." Ph.D. diss. University of California, San Diego.

Weiss, Jessica Chen. N.d. "Autocratic Signaling, Mass Audiences, and Nationalist Protest in China." *International Organization*. Forthcoming.

Wendt, Alexander. 1992. "Anarchy Is What States Make of It: The Social Construction of Power Politics." *International Organization* 46 (2): 391–425.

Wintrobe, Ronald. 2000. *The Political Economy of Dictatorship*. New York: Cambridge University Press.

Woods, Kevin M., Michael R. Pease, Mark E. Stout, Williamson Murray, and James G. Lacey. 2006. *Iraqi Perspectives Project: A View of Operation Iraqi Freedom from Saddam's Senior Leadership*. Norfolk, VA: United States Joint Forces Command, Joint Center for Operational Analysis.

Wright, Joseph. 2008. "Do Authoritarian Institutions Constrain? How Legislatures affect Economic Growth and Investment." *American Journal of Political Science* 52 (2): 322–43.

Virginia Page Fortna

DO TERRORISTS WIN?
Rebels' Use of Terrorism and Civil War Outcomes

■ ■ ■

How effective is terrorism? This question has generated lively scholarly debate and is of obvious importance to policymakers. However, most existing studies of terrorism are not well equipped to answer this question for a simple reason—they lack an appropriate comparison. Few studies of terrorism have compared conflicts in which terrorism is used with those in which it is not. This article examines the outcomes of civil wars to assess whether rebel groups that use terrorism fare better than those who eschew this tactic.[1] I argue that terrorism is not a particularly effective tactic for winning outright, nor for obtaining concessions at the bargaining table. On balance, terrorists undermine rather than enhance their military effectiveness by attacking civilians indiscriminately. If it does not help rebels achieve their ultimate political goals, one might reasonably ask why rebels ever employ terrorism? A second finding of this research provides a possible answer. Wars in which terrorism is used last longer than others, suggesting that terrorism enhances rebel organizations' survival. Rebels thus appear to face a dilemma: what helps them survive comes at the expense of the larger political goals for which they ostensibly fight.

In the next section I review the literature and debate over the effectiveness of terrorism and argue that civil wars provide a fruitful testing ground for evaluating the relative success of terrorism. I then present definitions and explain how "terrorist" rebel groups are distinguished from others, as well as how I use war outcomes to gauge "success." Next I examine the strategic uses of terrorism to evaluate theoretically its advantages and disadvantages, and to generate hypotheses about its effects on war outcomes. In the following section I discuss how selection effects and endogeneity issues affect this study. After describing the data, I turn to empirical findings. * * * The data support hypotheses that although civil wars involving terrorism last longer than other wars, terrorist rebel groups are less likely than those who eschew terrorism to achieve outright victory or concessions at the negotiating table. Terrorism may be somewhat less ineffective against democracies, but even in this context, terrorists do not win.

State of the Debate

A number of authors have argued that terrorism works. Pape, for example, argues that suicide terrorism is on the rise because terrorists have learned that it pays, generating "gains for the terrorists' political cause" about half the time.[2] Similarly, Kydd and Walter argue that terrorism

From *International Organization* 69 (Summer 2015): 519–56.
Some of the author's notes have been omitted.

more generally "is a form of costly signaling" and that "terrorism often works."[3] Thomas argues that terrorism gives rebels the "power to hurt," inducing governments to negotiate and make concessions.[4] Some scholars suggest that although terrorism can sometimes backfire and effects may be nonlinear, it is, on balance, effective.[5]

Others, however, maintain that terrorism is not particularly effective. Abrahms argues that the prevailing view of terrorism as a potent coercive strategy rests on scant empirical footing, and that campaigns of violence that primarily target civilians almost never succeed.[6] Jones and Libicki conclude that "there is rarely a causal link between the use of terrorism and the achievement of [group] goals."[7] Merari and Cronin both argue that, although terrorist groups may achieve partial or tactical (for example, recruitment) objectives, they almost never achieve their strategic goals in full.[8]

Some of this debate hinges on what one counts as success: only full achievement of the group's goals, or any political concession, or achievement of intermediate goals meant eventually to help a group achieve its goals—an issue I return to below.[9] Whether terrorism is considered effective also depends on what the chances of success, however defined, are if terrorism is not used. Not surprisingly, terrorists achieve higher levels of success when groups have limited objectives that do not impinge on the core interests of the target state.[10] So perhaps terrorism only "works" when achieving political change is relatively easy. Success rates cannot be judged without some sort of context.

Claims that terrorism "works" or "does not work" reflect a causal argument; that terrorism leads, or does not lead, to political change in favor of the group using it. Implicit in any causal argument is an argument about variation: using terrorism leads to more change (or no more change) than not using terrorism. But few empirical studies examine variation on the independent variable; most look only at terrorist organizations, with no comparison with otherwise similar groups that do not use terrorism.[11]

I use data on civil wars to introduce variation. Civil wars represent a universe of cases in which a group has a serious enough perceived grievance against the state to launch a violent rebellion in which some groups choose to use terrorism as part of their repertoire of tactics whereas others do not. Data on civil wars are relatively well developed, allowing me to explore and control for a number of factors that are likely to affect both this tactical choice and the outcome I wish to explain.

The study of terrorism and the study of civil wars have generally proceeded in isolation from one another.[12] However, if one thinks of prominent cases such as the LTTE in Sri Lanka, the PLO or Hamas in Palestine, the IRA in Northern Ireland, the PKK in Turkey, or the MNLF and MILF in the Philippines, it is clear that much terrorism takes place in the context of civil war. Indeed, the vast majority—75 to 85 percent by most estimates—of all terrorism is domestic.[13] This article merges insights from the two literatures.

This raises the thorny question of the definition of terrorism, however, because some scholars maintain that in the Venn diagram of political violence, terrorism and civil war do not overlap, whereas for others they overlap completely.

Definitions

"Terrorist" Rebel Groups

Defining terrorism is notoriously difficult; as the cliché goes, one person's terrorist is another's freedom fighter, and this is particularly true in the context of civil wars. Because it is such a loaded term, its definition is highly contested.[14] I define *terrorist rebel groups* as those who employ a systematic campaign of indiscriminate violence against public civilian targets to influence a wider audience. The ultimate aim of this type of violence is to coerce the government to make political concessions, up to and including conceding outright defeat. This definition allows for distinctions among rebel groups and does not include in the definition other variables whose relationship to terrorism I wish to examine.[15]

For many scholars of terrorism, though by no means all,[16] a defining characteristic of terrorism is that it deliberately attacks civilians.[17] This distinguishes terrorism from "normal" rebel attacks on military targets. However, civilian targeting is ubiquitous; almost all rebel groups (and almost all governments involved in civil wars) target individuals as a form of "control" to force cooperation and deter civilians from providing aid to the opponents.[18] Violence against civilians is thus too broad a criterion by itself to distinguish terrorist rebel groups from others. Moreover, this type of selective violence against civilians to punish or deter collaboration with the other side is not what most people think of when they think of "terrorism."

By narrowing the definition to deliberately indiscriminate violence, I exclude this more common form of violence and focus on that which makes terrorism so terrifying: its randomness; and so outrageous: the intentional targeting of innocent civilians (as opposed to collaborators). This definition also captures what the literature often refers to as the "symbolic" nature of terrorism: that it aims not to influence the victims of the violence but to send a political message to a wider audience.[19] Stanton distinguishes strategies of "coercion" from the above-mentioned control by focusing on "the use of violence as a means of forcing the opponent to take a particular desired action—to agree to negotiations, to reduce its war aims, to make concessions, to surrender." This strategy is "intended not to coerce civilians themselves, but to coerce *the opponent* into making concessions."[20] An attack on a public market, for example, is intended to influence the government, not shoppers.

Stanton's strategies of "destabilization" and "cleansing," which she distinguishes from coercion, also sound like terrorism to some degree. These involve attacks on civilians intended to destabilize a country or to force people to flee by terrorizing the population. However, Stanton's operational coding of these strategies involve massacres and "scorched earth" campaigns (burning homes and crops), which, although terrifying to their victims are farther from our intuitive understanding of terrorism than the indiscriminate attacks she codes under coercion.[21] Thus, not all who "terrify" a population are "terrorist" as I use the term here—groups such as the RUF in Sierra Leone or the Lord's Resistance Army in Uganda are not coded as terrorist under my definition, for example. Some terrorist groups (such as the FMLN or the IRA, depending on one's political leanings) might thus be considered morally preferable to some nonterrorist groups.[22] Indeed, it is important not to let judgments of the morality of a group's cause influence the use of the term *terrorism*.

War Outcomes and Relative Success

Civil wars end in one of four ways: either the government or the rebels win outright, or they reach a peace agreement of some sort, or the rebellion peters out. These possibilities can be thought of as representing a continuum of success for the rebel group. Government victory and rebel victory obviously lie at opposite ends of this continuum, as depicted in Figure 6.4. Peace agreements represent a second-best outcome from the rebels' perspective. Agreements entail concessions and compromise by both sides, but since rebels fight to change the status quo, whereas governments fight to maintain it, government concessions represent at least partial political victory for rebels. Moreover, agreements require the government to accept rebels as legitimate negotiating partners, itself a significant concession. Indeed,

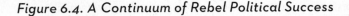

Figure 6.4. A Continuum of Rebel Political Success

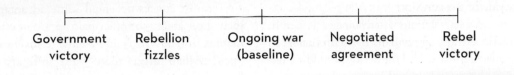

| Government victory | Rebellion fizzles | Ongoing war (baseline) | Negotiated agreement | Rebel victory |

many civil wars coded as ending in an agreement could easily be considered rebel victories in political if not military terms. For example, the peace agreement between South Africa and the ANC represented the fulfillment of that group's primary goal, the end of apartheid.[23]

Second worst from the rebels' perspective are wars that end when a formerly full-scale rebellion fizzles out with violence ending or dropping to such low levels that the conflict is no longer considered ongoing. Although the rebel group may still exist, it is not causing much trouble at this low level of violence. Most rebellions in this category have been largely defeated, though not eliminated outright.[24] Examples include Sendero Luminoso in Peru, which ended its fight after the capture of its leader; and the MQM in Pakistan, which "decided to pursue a peaceful strategy rather than a violent one" after the Pakistani military dealt "a serious blow to the militants."[25]

Scholars in the effectiveness debate differ on how to treat conflicts that have not yet ended. Should ongoing conflict count as failure because rebels have not yet achieved their goals,[26] or success because they have avoided defeat?[27] In relation to a group's ultimate political objectives, one can treat ongoing conflict as a baseline category of intermediate success; neither side has been able to defeat the other, no significant concessions have been agreed to, and the rebels continue to inflict pain on the country. However, rebel groups are organizations, and as such they seek to survive.[28] Ongoing war therefore represents success on that dimension. As I shall show, the goals of political change and organizational survival may be in tension.

Advantages and Disadvantages of Terrorism

Terrorism has both advantages and disadvantages. I argue that the advantages tend to help rebels survive rather than to win, whereas the disadvantages make it harder for terrorists to achieve political concessions or to win outright. Much of the literature considers the usefulness of terrorism in isolation. The implicit comparison is thus effectiveness relative to doing nothing. But how effective is terrorism relative to other tactics a rebel organization could employ? All rebel groups attack military targets; terrorist rebel groups, as defined here, are distinguished by the fact that they also purposely attack civilians indiscriminately to influence a wider audience.[29]

There are several potential audiences to consider. The primary audience is the government, which rebels hope to induce to make concessions or to give up the fight. There are also secondary audiences, those whose support rebels attempt to win, and those rebels hope to induce to put pressure on the government. Within the country, there is an "aggrieved" population on whose behalf the rebel organization claims to fight.[30] There are also civilians on the other side of the conflict—those who support the government or generally consent to be governed by it. For lack of a better term, I refer to this group as the "mainstream." It includes both those who benefit from and support the state and its use of violence against the rebel group and "fence-sitters." Finally, there are international audiences—particularly those (great or regional powers, neighboring states, relevant diasporas) in a position to aid or pressure either side of the conflict.

Terrorism has obvious disadvantages as a military tactic. Attacking civilians indiscriminately in public places is not useful for taking or holding territory or the capital. It is thus much less effective than other tactics for winning outright. Unlike attacks on the government's military forces, or even other types of attacks on civilians (such as ethnic cleansing of territory, or attacks to prevent collaboration with the enemy), indiscriminate attacks on public targets such as markets or buses have no direct military value.

The terrorism literature identifies a number of less direct ways through which it is thought to "work." These include (1) attrition, (2) advertising the cause, (3) provocation, (4) outbidding, and (5) spoiling.[31] Of these, attrition is arguably the most important because it entails the most direct (or least indirect) link between rebel actions and the achievement of political goals. The other strategies aim at intermediate goals, including mobilizing support, and/or preserving organizational survival, often in competition among groups claiming to represent the same aggrieved population. I discuss each of these strategies in turn, considering both the advantages and disadvantages of terrorism for the rebels' larger military effort.[32]

Attrition

Terrorism is used as part of an attrition strategy, meant to inflict pain on the other side so as to undermine the adversary's will, rather than its capacity, to fight.[33] However, terrorist attacks are not the only way to fight a war of attrition. Insurgency or guerrilla warfare tactics classically employ hit-and-run attacks to dog the adversary's forces and undermine its will to continue the fight. Unlike other forms of insurgency, terrorism, by definition, does not target military forces,

and thus does not degrade the government's military capacity.

Terrorist attacks do entail some advantages in their sheer ability to inflict pain in a cost-effective manner. It is less costly (in material terms) to attack "soft" civilian targets than "hard" military ones. Because terrorism attacks targets that are inherently hard to defend, preventing every single attack is difficult. As Condoleezza Rice described counterterrorism efforts (paraphrasing the IRA): "They only have to be right once. We have to be right 100 percent of the time."[34] It takes relatively few people to organize and carry out a terrorist attack, making full elimination of terrorist groups difficult; mere remnants can continue to inflict damage.

Terrorism is also a relatively cheap way to impose costs on civilians such that the mainstream population pressures its government to give in to terrorist demands. There is some evidence that this can be effective, up to a point,[35] perhaps particularly so in democracies (see hypothesis 4). However, terrorism can also induce pressure on the government not to concede by rallying the mainstream population around the flag. Moreover, many governments have a stated policy never to negotiate with terrorists. This is often observed only in the breach, and governments are always reluctant to negotiate with and grant concessions to any rebel group. The rhetoric of nonnegotiation with terrorists can nonetheless make it especially politically difficult to do so.

Terrorism is also thought to be a communication device, meant to signal strength and resolve, to convince the opponent that the war of attrition will be long and costly.[36] Compared with not attacking at all, terrorism may indeed be effective as a costly signal, but compared with attacks against the military, the effectiveness of terrorism as a signal of resolve is unclear at best, whereas terrorism signals weakness rather than strength.

Terrorism signals a willingness to use extreme tactics that violate widely held norms and this may be interpreted as a signal of resolve. However, extremism and resolve are not necessarily the same thing. Willingness to attack civilians signals willingness to impose these costs in the future. To the extent that the government cares more about the loss of civilian life than the loss of soldiers' lives, this may provide a signaling advantage to terrorist tactics.

There are also downsides to sending such signals, however. By deliberately violating the norm against targeting noncombatants, terrorists place themselves beyond the pale, painting themselves as untrustworthy—likely to break their promises rather than abide by a negotiated agreement.[37] The targets of terrorism may also infer from the extreme nature of the tactics used that the groups' demands are also extreme; that terrorists seek to destroy their society.[38] Opponents will therefore view negotiations as an act of appeasement. Use of extreme tactics may credibly signal resolve to carry on the fight, but it undermines the credibility of promises to reward concessions with peace.

Terrorism can also make it harder for rebels to accept concessions. Terrorist rebel groups may be particularly suspicious of the government in any potential negotiations to end the conflict. This may be, in part, because of a selection effect if only particularly hardline groups choose terrorist tactics. But it could also be induced by this choice. Having committed terrorist attacks, rebels may not believe that they will be accepted into a peaceful postwar political order.[39] Government promises of amnesty or of a power-sharing role for rebels may therefore not be credible to terrorist rebel groups. Mistrust and problems of credible commitment plague all civil wars,[40] but terrorism makes them even worse. For a number of reasons, then, signaling extremism can make one's would-be negotiating partner less, rather than more, willing to make political concessions.

As a signal of strength, moreover, terrorist attacks are clearly inferior. Despite the empirical (non)finding presented shortly, the deeply embedded conventional wisdom is that terrorism is a "weapon of the weak." To be credible, signals have to be costly. Precisely because it is less costly to attack "soft" civilian targets than hardened military ones, terrorism signals military impotence rather than strength.

In sum, terrorism is a cheap way to inflict costs in a war of attrition, and is hard to eliminate fully, fostering organizational survival. On the other hand, it creates pressures on the government not to concede, and its very affordability undermines its value as a credible signal.

Rebellion, particularly insurgency or guerrilla warfare, as Mao famously stressed, requires a supportive population.[41] Though Mao would disagree, the terrorism literature generally maintains that terrorism is a strategy used to mobilize support.[42] Do indiscriminate attacks on civilians enhance or undermine popular support?[43]

Advertising the Cause

One way terrorism is thought to mobilize support is by publicizing grievances—"propaganda of the deed"—to put the cause on the political agenda.[44] Because they are more outrageous, terrorist attacks usually generate more publicity than attacks against the military. This attention can create a sense of urgency about resolving a political issue.

At whom is such a strategy aimed? Publicizing grievances probably plays less of a role in situations that have escalated to the level of civil war than in lower-level conflicts. In civil wars, both the aggrieved and the mainstream population are already aware of the grievances. Terrorism can, however, publicize grievances to international audiences; or in some conflicts over secession or autonomy, to advertise the plight of an aggrieved population whose lives are quite remote to citizens in other parts of the country.

The disadvantages of targeting civilians to generate their support are obvious. Those who see such attacks as justified given their view of the righteousness of the cause, are those most likely already to support the rebellion. Terrorism "preaches to the choir." Those potential supporters who remain to be mobilized—less radical or politicized members of the aggrieved population, "fence-sitters," and the international community—are more likely to feel revulsion at the taking of innocent life.[45] Moreover, as Abrahms argues, the publicity gained by terrorism often focuses on the "senseless" or irrational nature of the violence rather than the grievances or demands the terrorist group wishes to make.[46] In the battle for legitimacy and "hearts and minds," terrorism is counterproductive.[47]

Provocation

The literature also suggests that terrorism can be used to mobilize support by provoking the state to overreact.[48] This strategy hopes to induce the government to crack down on the aggrieved population, creating new grievances and exacerbating old ones, causing an increase in support for the rebel organization. Because they violate norms of warfare, terrorist attacks may be more likely than attacks on military targets to provoke an overreaction. However, using terrorism for this purpose is risky for two reasons. First, successful provocation requires that the aggrieved will blame the government for the crackdown, rather than the rebel group that provoked it.[49] Second, by attacking civilians, terrorist attacks make it easier for the government to justify—both domestically and internationally—draconian measures to crush the rebellion. The opprobrium directed against a government that employs extreme measures will be lower when it is fighting a terrorist rebel group than a nonterrorist rebel group.[50] For provocation to work, the rebels must be able to goad the government into a "middling level of brutality."[51] A government strongly committed to human rights is difficult to provoke, whereas one willing to employ extreme brutality in its fight will be able to wipe out the rebels and the constituency they claim to represent.[52] In this Goldilocks equation, terrorism may induce governments to move from "too soft" to "just right," but can also make governments "too hard," allowing them to justify measures to crush the rebels rather than creating a backlash of support in their favor.

Outbidding

Terrorism is thought useful as a means of competing with other rival groups that claim to represent the same aggrieved population. Outbidding is intended to mobilize popular support for a group by demonstrating commitment to the cause and ability to fight for the interests of the aggrieved.[53] But why should the aggrieved population support groups that use terrorism over those who do not? Kydd and Walter respond that it is advantageous to be represented by an agent who will drive a harder bargain than oneself, and extreme tactics signal a tougher negotiating stance.[54] This argument discounts the cost of continued conflict to the aggrieved population, however. Supporting a group whose reservation price is higher than one's own by definition rules out settlements one would prefer to ongoing conflict. If one fears the government will never compromise (Kydd and Walter's second answer), then one should prefer not a more extreme agent, but a militarily more competent one. Given that terrorism signals military weakness rather than strength, it is unclear how attacking civilians rather than military targets might win political support.[55] Although competition among groups and factions is undoubtedly an important motive for rebel behavior, it is questionable how terrorism serves these competitive purposes better than other tactics.

Spoiling

Spoiling is another manifestation of competition among rebel groups. It occurs when a more extreme group is threatened by the prospect of peace between the government and a more moderate group. By launching a terrorist attack and inducing doubt about the moderates' ability or willingness to control terrorism, extremists can derail peace.[56] This can help ensure the survival of an extremist group that might otherwise become obsolete in the face of peace. Spoilers presumably hope for an eventual outcome more favorable to their cause than the one moderates were willing to accept, but spoiling does nothing to ensure this more favorable outcome rather than a less favorable one. Terrorism driven by spoiling thus contributes to survival but does nothing to help a group achieve its political goals.

Hypotheses

This evaluation of the pros and cons of terrorism relative not to inaction but to other types of attacks (notably attacks on military targets), leads to several hypotheses. On balance, terrorism generally undermines military effectiveness. It has no direct value for winning the war outright; it does not degrade the government's military capability, nor can it be used to take and hold territory. It is a cheap way to inflict costs on the enemy and may help signal resolve, but its low cost also signals weakness. It may help advertise the cause, but it also drives potential supporters away. It can provoke a government into self-destructive overreaction, but it can also help the government justify draconian measures in their fight against rebels.

H1:   Terrorist rebels are less likely than nonterrorist rebels to achieve military victory.

Terrorism also makes the second-best outcome for rebels less likely. Governments will grant fewer concessions to a less militarily effective opponent. Moreover, rebels' use of extreme tactics makes it harder for the government to negotiate an agreement and exacerbates the problems of trust and credible commitment that plague all civil wars.

H2:   Rebels using terrorism are less likely than those who eschew terrorism to achieve negotiated settlements.

There are, however, some advantages to terrorism for organizational survival. Terrorist rebel groups are hard to eliminate entirely, and spoiling can prevent peace with more moderate groups from making extremist groups obsolete. For both these reasons, and because terrorism prevents negotiated settlements that would otherwise end the war more quickly, terrorism should increase civil war duration.

H3:   Wars involving terrorist rebels are likely to last longer than those involving nonterrorist rebels.

I argue that terrorism is, on balance, ineffective for achieving political goals. But there are several reasons to think that terrorism might be relatively more effective against democracies than against autocracies. First, democratic governments are likely more sensitive to civilian loss of life.[57] If terrorism works by inflicting pain on civilians who then pressure their government to make concessions, then it stands to reason that the more accountable the government is to popular pressure, the more likely this strategy will work.

Second, democracies are thought to have trouble repressing or preventing and policing terrorist groups.[58] Because they start on the "soft" end of the spectrum, democracies should be more likely provoked into the "just right" level of brutality discussed earlier, whereas nondemocracies will be provoked into a response that is "too hard" and that brutally but effectively represses rebellion.

Terrorism may also be less likely to backfire by undermining support among the aggrieved when its victims are seen as "complicitous" in government policy because they have voted the government into power in democratic elections.[59]

H4: *Terrorism will be more effective against democratic governments than against nondemocratic governments.*

Selection and Potential Confounders

Because I look at the use of terrorism only in the context of civil wars, this study does not cover all terrorist organizations, raising issues of selection bias. The analysis excludes transnational terrorist groups that attack primarily across borders rather than in their home state.[60] It also excludes organizations involved in conflicts that do not meet the standard 1,000 battle death threshold of a civil war.[61] The smallest and weakest groups are thus excluded.[62] Focusing on the deadliest groups is defensible on policy grounds and is necessary for empirical comparison with nonterrorist groups. It does, however, limit generalizability because I evaluate terrorism by only groups capable of mounting civil war, not terrorism relative to other options for those without this capability. The notion that terrorism is used only by those with no other option is belied, however, by the terrorist rebel groups examined in this study, who by definition can mount a civil war.

The selection of organizations involved in civil wars likely overrepresents ethno-nationalist organizations, which are more likely to have clear political or territorial goals that are more easily negotiable than the goals of other types of terrorist organizations.[63] The data used here also exclude coups,[64] which are quite unlikely to involve terrorism and which may be more often successful than other types of rebellion. All of these selection issues bias the study toward finding terrorism successful, and against my own argument.

The temporal bounds of the data used in this study (post-1989) do not cover the era of decolonization, and therefore exclude a set of highly successful rebellions; virtually all of these cases led to independence. Some notable cases of terrorist success (for example, Algeria) are thus omitted. If terrorism was used disproportionally in anticolonial wars of this era (an open empirical question), excluding this era will bias the results away from finding terrorism effective. On the other hand, anticolonial struggles enjoyed particular legitimacy; relationships in that era may not apply to more recent conflicts.

Arguably more important as a concern than selection bias are the thorny issues of endogeneity and spuriousness for although terrorism inflicts random violence, it is not a tactic chosen at random. To assess its effectiveness accurately, I must therefore pay particular attention to any variables that might affect both the use of terrorism and the outcome of the war. The literature on the causes of terrorism, particularly on why terrorism appears in some places rather than others, suggests several potential confounders. I explore the relationships between these factors and the use of terrorism in greater depth elsewhere, but I discuss them briefly here.[65]

The most obvious potential confounding variable is the strength of the rebel group relative to the government. If, as is commonly asserted, terrorism is a "weapon of the weak,"[66] failure to take this into account will make terrorism look less effective than it really is.

The relationship between democracy and terrorism has generated significant theoretical and empirical debate.[67] Many see a positive relationship between democracy and terrorism, in part because terrorism is thought to be more effective against democracies, as discussed earlier.

Terrorism is also thought to be a tactic used by groups with particularly extreme aims. This argument is often tautological: groups that use extreme tactics such as terrorism are considered extremist, therefore extremist groups use terrorism. But it is possible to assess group aims independent of their tactics by focusing on how far rebels' stated aims are from the status quo. I argue elsewhere that in wars over a particular region, secessionist rebels can be considered more extreme than those fighting for autonomy, whereas in wars over control of the state, those who seek to transform society in fundamental ways (for example, by instituting Sharia in a secular state, or communism in a capitalist state, or vice versa) are more extreme than those merely engaged in a power struggle to take the reins of power (the fight between Lissouba and Sassou Nguesso in Congo–Brazzaville is a good example).[68]

Secessionist aims are particularly important to consider because scholars such as Pape and Stanton suggest that terrorism should be especially likely in secessionist conflicts.[69] Fazal suggests just the opposite, however; because separatists desire to become accepted members of the international system, they have incentives to avoid targeting civilians indiscriminately.[70] Scholars have also noted links between religious conflict and terrorism,[71] and between population and/or gross domestic product (GDP) per capita and terrorism.[72] Terrorism as defined here may be less likely in Africa than elsewhere,[73] and may be more likely where rebels do not have the advantage of rough terrain that enables other forms of insurgency.[74] The outbidding argument suggests that terrorism is more likely when there are several rebel groups active as part of the same struggle.[75]

This set of variables by no means exhausts the list of factors that might make rebel groups more likely to choose terrorism—this is obviously an important questions in its own right. For the purposes of this article, however, my focus is on variables that likely also affect the outcome of war, and whose omission could thus lead to spurious findings about the effectiveness of terrorism.[76]

The Data

The data analyzed here consist of 104 rebel groups involved in full-scale civil wars active between 1989 and 2004. Much of the data come from Cunningham, Gleditsch, and Salehyan's Non-State Actor data set (hereafter CGS),[77] which builds on and expands the well-known Uppsala-PRIO Armed Conflict Data (hereafter UCDP)[78] by identifying each nonstate (or rebel) actor.[79] These data are particularly useful for several reasons. First, the unit of analysis is the government-rebel group dyad, rather than the conflict as is common in many data sets on civil war. Second, the relative strength of the government and each rebel group is coded. The CGS data are time varying, allowing for variables that change over the course of the conflict, for example, changes in the relative strength of the actors, or changes in democracy or economic variables.

The dependent variable is war outcome for each dyad, covering the five possibilities discussed here: government victory, rebel victory, agreement (including peace agreements and ceasefire agreements), wars that fizzle out to "low or no activity" by dropping below twenty-five battle deaths per year, and ongoing conflicts. Outcomes data are from UCDP through 2003; I updated through 2009 and corrected a few cases based on case-specific research.[80]

The measure of the main independent variable, whether a rebel group uses terrorist tactics, comes from Stanton's coding of "high casualty terrorism," a measure of a group's systematic use of "small-scale bombs . . . to attack unambiguously civilian targets" excluding attacks on infrastructure (for example, power stations, pipelines, bridges) which impose costs on civilians, but in which casualties are rare.[81] I use this more restrictive, high-casualty-only measure of terrorism because it best captures the deliberate and indiscriminate killing of civilians on which my definition and theory focus. Of the 104 cases examined here, twenty-four (23 percent) use high-casualty terrorism.

This measure captures groups generally classified as "terrorist" by other sources, such as the LTTE in Sri Lanka, the Taliban in Afghanistan (after 2003), the FARC in Colombia, the Provisional IRA in Northern Ireland, and so on. One advantage of Stanton's data over databases more commonly used in the terrorism literature is that this minimizes some of the well-known geographical biases in the terrorism data, particularly their overrepresentation of terrorism in Western democracies and underrepresentation or spotty coverage of groups in Africa and other strategically less important (to the U.S.) places. The main disadvantage of this measure is that it is limited to full-scale civil wars active between 1989 and 2004, thus providing the bounds of the empirical analysis. Merging the Stanton and time varying CGS data yields 104 cases and 566 observations over time.[82] * * *

Stanton found surprisingly little variation over time within conflicts in the types of strategies rebels and governments used in terms of targeting civilians. With very few exceptions, groups that used terrorism did so throughout the conflict, whereas those who eschewed the tactic early on continued to avoid it later.[83] This in itself is quite interesting, and suggests that rebel organizations' choices about using terrorism are remarkably "sticky."

The CGS data include a five-point indicator of rebel group strength relative to the government, ranging from much weaker to much stronger. This variable summarizes assessments of the rebel group's ability to mobilize supporters, arms procurement ability, and fighting capacity, which Cunningham and colleagues argue capture the rebel group's ability to target government forces, or "offensive strength."[84] To capture the effects of war aims, I include two dummy variables. The first marks whether the group seeks full independence and is taken from Coggins's data on secessionist movements.[85] The second differentiates among groups fighting for control of the center, marking those who aim to transform society in fundamental ways. This I coded myself, based on case descriptions in the CGS data coding notes, Minorities at Risk (MAR), START's Terrorist Organization Profiles (TOPs), UCDP's case summaries, and case-specific sources.[86] Together, the independence and transform society dummy variables can be compared with an omitted category of relatively "moderate" rebels who aim either for autonomy, or who are engaged in power struggles at the top without a desire to transform society.[87] Because this is a newly coded variable, Figures 6.5 and 6.6 provide information about its relationship with both terrorism and war outcomes, respectively. From this bivariate look at the data, we see that moderate rebels appear to be less likely to use terrorism and more likely to succeed, making inclusion of this variable particularly important to avoid spuriousness.

■ ■ ■

Which Groups Use Terrorism?

Before turning to tests of the hypotheses, I take a brief detour to address the issue of spuriousness, examining the effects of potentially confounding variables on the use of terrorism. Of the rebel groups examined in this study, fewer than a quarter used terrorism as a tactic in their fight against the government, whereas the rest did not. What accounts for this variation? [The data, not shown in this excerpt,] shows the results of logistic analysis with terrorist rebel group as the dependent variable.

* * * Analysis of terrorism as the dependent variable, rather than the independent variable as it

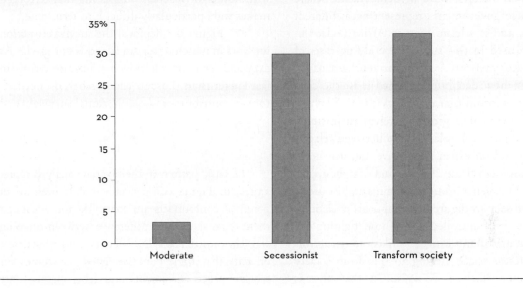

Figure 6.5. War Aims and Percent Terrorist

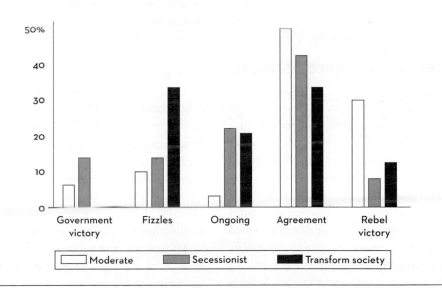

Figure 6.6. War Aims and Percent in Each War Outcome

is in the rest of the article, suggests that terrorism is most likely in civil wars in democracies, where rebels face governments representing a different religion, and is seldom seen in Africa (indeed in the data used in this study, there are no cases of high-casualty terrorism by African rebel groups).[88]

Given how deeply entrenched it is, the conventional wisdom that terrorism is more likely to be used by weaker groups receives surprisingly weak support. The relationship between relative strength and terrorism is negative, but it is never statistically significant.[89] I also find that the apparent link between a group's war aims and its use of terrorism seen in Figure 6.5 disappears once other variables are controlled for. Those fighting for secession are, if anything, less likely to use terrorism, whereas those aiming to transform society appear more likely to do so, but neither effect is significant. Together, these findings indicate that the extremity of a group's aims are not necessarily associated with the extremity of its tactics. * * *

Do Terrorist Rebels Win? The Effects of Terrorism on War Outcomes

Figure 6.7 shows the percentage of terrorist and nonterrorist rebellions ending in each outcome. Although these bivariate relationships obviously do not yet take into account potentially confounding variables, the figures do suggest preliminary support for H1 to H3. Most tellingly, of the groups examined here none of those that deliberately killed large numbers of civilians through terrorist attacks won its fight outright.[90] Peace agreements, which I argue represent significant concessions to the rebel cause, are also much less frequent when rebels use terrorism. Meanwhile, government victories and wars ending through low or no activity are slightly more common in civil wars involving terrorism. Wars in which rebels used terror were much more

likely to be ongoing as of 2009 than were wars with nonterrorist rebels, suggesting that terrorism makes wars particularly difficult to terminate.

* * * Figure 6.8 depict[s] the survival function for wars in which terrorism is and is not used.[91] As expected, civil wars in which rebels use terrorism last longer than those in which rebels do not; terrorism contributes to organizational survival.

■   ■   ■

The basic pattern in the bivariate analysis represented in Figure 6.7 generally holds, even when potential confounders are controlled for. Although there is no significant difference between ongoing war (the omitted baseline category) and rebel defeat or wars that fizzle out, the "good" outcomes for rebels—peace agreements and rebel victory—are both significantly less likely, relative to ongoing war, when rebels employ terrorism as a tactic, supporting H1 and H2. * * * The predicted probability of a war ending in an agreement is 6.6 percent for rebels that do not resort to terrorism, but only 1 percent for those who do. The predicted probability of a rebel victory is low for all rebellions, but drops from 3.4 to 0 percent for those who employ terrorism.

I also test these hypotheses with a competing risks model. * * * This analysis indicates that the use of terrorism increases the risk of government defeat by more than four times. Unlike the multinomial logit results, this effect is statistically significant. Terrorism has no appreciable effect on the likelihood of war fizzling out. Meanwhile, the use of terrorism reduces the likelihood that rebels reach a negotiated agreement by 80 percent, and given that there are no cases of rebel victories by terrorist rebels, the competing risks model predicts that terrorism reduces the chance of a rebel victory to zero; both results easily pass tests of statistical significance. In other words, I again find strong support for H1 and H2.

■   ■   ■

Figure 6.7. Terrorism and Percent in Each War Outcome

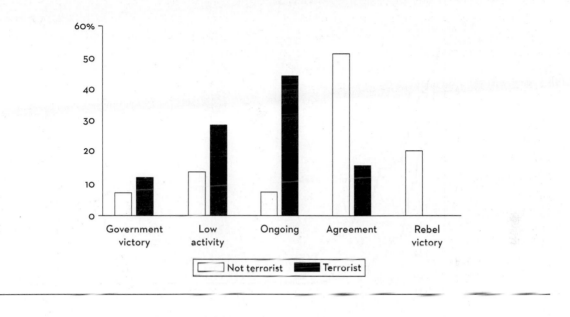

Figure 6.9 shows the results of the competing risks analysis graphically, plotting the cumulative incidence rate of each outcome over time for terrorist and nonterrorist rebels, holding other variables at their mean or modal values. As can be seen, the incidence of the best outcomes for rebels, negotiated agreement and rebel victory, are lower for those who resort to terrorism, whereas the worst outcome, government victory, is higher for terrorist rebels. In sum, rebel groups who deliberately and indiscriminately kill civilians are, all else equal, much less likely to win outright or to achieve concessions in the form of an agreement than are nonterrorist rebel groups, but are no less likely to fizzle out or be defeated rather than to live to fight another day.

I turn, finally, to analysis of the relative effects of terrorism against democratic and nondemocratic governments. An initial look at the cases is consistent with H4; of the terrorist rebel groups that succeeded in reaching a negotiated agreement, three out of four fought democratic governments.[92] * * *

■   ■   ■

[However,] I find only mixed support for H4 overall. The negative effects of terrorism are smaller against democracies, but not always significantly so. Terrorist rebels may be somewhat more likely to succeed against democratic governments than nondemocratic governments, but they are still less likely to succeed than rebels who do not use terrorism

Conclusion

Research on terrorism has exploded since 2001 for obvious reasons. However, the ability of this literature to answer fundamental questions has been hampered by a lack of variation on the phenomenon. This project uses variation within civil wars, namely the fact that some rebel groups use terrorism whereas others do not, to help resolve the debate about the effectiveness of terrorism.

I argue that when it comes to achieving a rebel group's political goals, the disadvantages of terrorism

Figure 6.8. Terrorism and the Duration of War

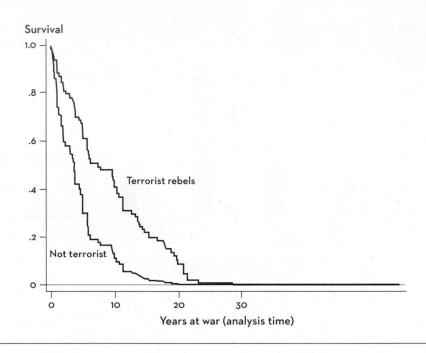

generally outweigh its advantages. It is a cheap way to inflict pain on the other side, and terrorist groups are hard to eliminate completely, but it is useless for taking or holding territory. It may help signal commitment to a cause, but because it is cheap, it signals weakness rather than strength. It may be useful for provoking an overreaction by the government, but it also helps justify draconian measures to crush the rebellion. Its outrageous nature may help bring attention to a cause, but it also undermines legitimacy and alienates potential supporters. Terrorism may help achieve tactical results, but these apparently do not translate into strategic success. It may also be useful at lower levels of conflict or for groups that do not have the ability to wage full-scale war (a question I cannot yet address with available data). Empirically, I find much more support for the argument that terrorism is likely to backfire than for the notion that it is effective. Rebels who use terrorism do not win outright, and they are less likely to achieve concessions in a negotiated outcome. This negative effect may be somewhat attenuated when rebels fight against democracies rather than autocracies. But even in democratic states, terrorist rebel groups do not achieve victory and are unlikely to obtain concessions at the negotiating table. The short answer to the question "Do terrorist rebels win?" is "No."

If terrorism is so ineffective, one might reasonably ask why rebel groups use it, especially rebels who are not fighting democratic governments.[93] The answer may lie in the finding that civil wars in which terrorism is used last significantly longer than others. The use of terrorism contributes to rebels' organizational survival. Rebels thus appear to face a dilemma—using terrorism as a tactic is good for the immediate goal of survival, but comes at the expense of the long-term political goals for which they are, ultimately (or ostensibly) fighting.

This study begins to shed light on the causes of terrorism, as well as its effects. I examine this question only briefly in this article, focusing on variables

Figure 6.9. Terrorism and War Outcomes (Competing Risks)

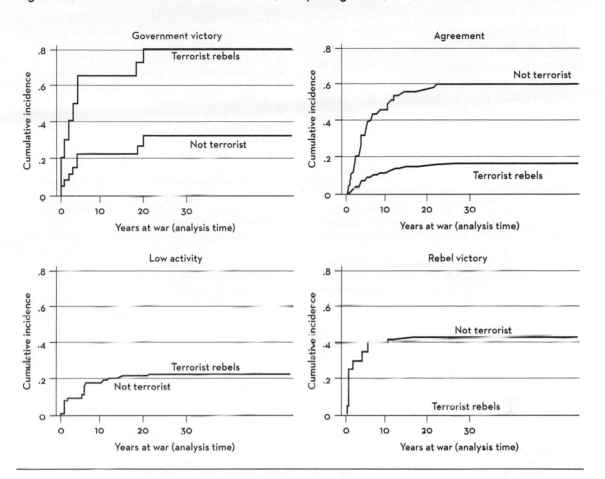

that might also affect war outcomes, to avoid spurious results. The results are intriguing, however. They cast doubt on the conventional wisdom that terrorism is a "weapon of the weak." Among rebels fighting full-fledged civil wars, there is surprisingly little evidence that weaker groups are more likely to use terrorism than stronger ones. Nor is terrorism more likely, again contrary to conventional wisdom, in secessionist wars, or when rebels profess extreme aims. Terrorism is more likely, however, in civil wars in democracies, as many have argued, and where religion divides rebels from the government they fight. It is much less likely to be used in Africa, a finding that remains to be explained theoretically.

Expanding the analysis of why some groups turn to terrorism whereas others do not is an obvious avenue for further research.

Extensions of this study to further our understanding both of where terrorism arises, and how successful it is, will require new data. Data are currently available for only a relatively short period (1989–2004) and for full-fledged civil wars. Extending the analysis temporally before the end of the Cold War and to include more recent conflicts, and especially to lower level conflicts will strengthen the analysis, and in particular allow fuller testing, for example, of the notion that terrorism is a "weapon of the weak." Further research is also needed to establish how rebel groups navigate the tradeoff between organizational survival and political efficacy.

In the meantime, the empirical evidence presented in this study suggests that terrorism is likely to be a persistent problem—elongating the destruction and suffering that civil wars entail—but not a potent force for political change. Terrorism may help rebel groups survive, but it does not help them get what they want politically.

NOTES

1. This study examines only rebels' use of terrorism, not governments' use of such tactics (state terrorism), thus sidestepping the question of whether the definition of terrorism should be limited to nonstate actors.
2. Pape 2003, 351. Pape is ambiguous on whether his argument applies to terrorism more broadly, arguing that suicide terrorism is to terrorism as lung cancer is to cancer—a particularly virulent strain. Author discussion with Pape, 11 November 2010; and Pape and Feldman 2010.
3. Kydd and Walter 2006, 49–50.
4. Thomas 2014, 807–9.
5. See Bueno de Mesquita and Dickson 2007; Gould and Klor 2010; and Wood and Kathman 2014.
6. See Abrahms 2005, 2006, 43, and 2012.
7. Jones and Libicki 2008, 32–33.
8. See Merari 1993, 238–39; and Cronin 2009, 11. See also Acosta 2014.
9. See Krause 2013.
10. See Jones and Libicki 2008, 34; Abrahms 2006, 53–54; and Pape 2003, 355.
11. Wood and Kathman 2014; and Thomas 2014 are exceptions. Abrahms's work is a partial exception, however because he examines only groups designated as "foreign terrorist organizations" by the U.S. State Department, variation on the independent variable is truncated.
12. Exceptions include Sambanis 2008; Findley and Young 2012a; and Boulden 2009.
13. See Enders, Sandler, and Gaibulloev 2011, 323; LaFree and Dugan 2007, 187; and Asal and Rethemeyer 2008a, 447.
14. McCormick 2003, 473. For a good discussion of definitions, see Merari 1993.
15. Some draw a distinction, often based on group size or strength or even the regime type of the opponent, between terrorism and guerrilla warfare or insurgency. These definitions exclude all rebel groups, and preclude the examination of the relationship, for example, between terrorism and group strength. See Schmid and Jongman 1988, especially 13–18; Silke 1996; Cronin 2006, 31–32; and Sambanis 2008.
16. Many definitions in the literature are so broad as arguably to encompass all rebel groups in all civil wars. Indeed, much of the terrorism literature could easily substitute *rebellion* or *insurgency* for *terrorism*. See, for example, Hoffman 2006, 40.
17. Cronin 2003, 32–33.
18. See Stanton 2009, 31. Kydd and Walter 2006, 66–69, refer to this as "intimidation." See also Kalyvas 2006.
19. See Crenshaw 1981, 379; and McCormick 2003, 474.
20. See Stanton 2009, 34–35, emphasis in the original. In more recent work, Stanton refers to this strategy as "terrorism." Stanton 2013.
21. Ibid., 8–9, 90–93. Some of the groups that engage in these strategies also engage in coercion (Stanton's strategies are not mutually exclusive), so are captured under my definition in any case. Investigating the causes and effectiveness of these other types of strategies of violence against civilians is beyond the scope of this article.
22. On the relative morality of terrorism, see Crenshaw 1983, 3; and Merari 1993, 227–31.
23. Some agreements are reached when rebels are largely defeated (for example, the RUF in Sierra Leone), but in the vast majority of cases, agreements represent political gains for the rebels. Terrorism is also sometimes used to prevent agreements between the government and another more moderate group (see my discussion on spoiling). Kydd and Walter 2002. However, an agreement represents a relatively successful outcome for the group that negotiates it.
24. Some conflicts admittedly fizzle out because rebel demands have been partially met (for example, de facto autonomy for Kurds in Iraq after the Persian Gulf War). However, in most low/no activity cases, rebels were all but defeated militarily, making this category a reasonable proxy.
25. Cunningham, Gleditsch, and Salehyan 2009b, 350.
26. Abrahms 2006.
27. Jones and Libicki 2008.
28. See Wilson 1974, 10; and Acosta 2014.
29. Terrorist groups may also attack civilians in other more discriminating ways, as discussed earlier (for example, to punish collaboration with the enemy). Groups that attack only civilians and no military targets do not reach the threshold of civil war—on selection effects, see section on selection effects.
30. Bueno de Mesquita and Dickson 2007, 369.
31. See Kydd and Walter 2006; Thornton 1964; and Crenshaw 1981 and 2011. Kydd and Walter also discuss intimidation, which as I explained is not considered terrorism in this study.
32. See also Goodwin 2006, especially 2038.
33. See Pape 2003, 346; and Kydd and Walter 2006. See also Arreguín-Toft 2001, especially 105.
34. Quoted in Nina Easton, "Condi: The Should-Be Face of the GOP," *Fortune* (Internet ed.), 22 September 2009.
35. Gould and Klor 2010.
36. See Kydd and Walter 2006, 59–60; Merari 1993; and Wood and Kathman 2014.
37. Bapat 2006, 214.
38. Abrahms 2012, 22.
39. This can make terrorism a self-perpetuating tactic. Laitin and Shapiro 2008, 222–23.
40. Walter 2002.
41. Mao 1937. See also Arreguín-Toft 2001, 104.
42. See, for example, Pape 2003; Bueno de Mesquita and Dickson 2007; and DeNardo 1985.

43. To my knowledge, there is no empirical work supporting the contention that terrorism mobilizes support more effectively than other forms of resistance.
44. See Crenshaw 2011, 118; and Thornton 1964, 82–83.
45. The international reaction may be particularly pronounced after 11 September 2001 and the U.S.-led strengthening of the norm against terrorism.
46. Abrahms 2012, 21.
47. Cronin 2009, 93. Stephan and Chenoweth 2008 argue that violence in general decreases legitimacy and discourages broad-based participation.
48. See Kydd and Walter 2006, especially 69–72; Lake 2002; and Crenshaw 2011, 119.
49. Bueno de Mesquita and Dickson suggest that the aggrieved cannot credibly threaten to punish "extremists" for provoking the government's crackdown because the crackdown itself (by diminishing economic opportunities) makes the population inclined toward direct struggle. Bueno de Mesquita and Dickson 2007, 375. But why should the population react to diminished opportunities brought on by the conflict by choosing to continue it, rather than settle?
50. Hence the attempt by almost all governments to label rebels as "terrorists" whether they employ terrorist tactics or not.
51. Kydd and Walter 2006, 70.
52. Arreguín-Toft 2001, 109.
53. Bloom 2005.
54. Kydd and Walter 2006.
55. Terrorist attacks are likely to signal lack of popular support to the aggrieved, rather than strength. Laitin and Shapiro 2008, 216.
56. Kydd and Walter 2002.
57. See Stanton 2009; and Heger 2010.
58. See Cronin 2006, 31; Crenshaw 1981, 383; Pape 2003, 349–50; and Eubank and Weinberg 1994. But see also Lyall 2010.
59. Goodwin 2006, 2027.
60. It is not clear what the equivalent nonterrorist actors would be for a comparison with transnational terrorist groups.
61. Battle deaths exclude civilian deaths, so this could in theory exclude highly lethal terrorist groups that did not also engage in significant attacks on military targets. I checked the Global Terrorism Database to ensure that no domestic terrorist group responsible for 1,000 deaths was omitted from the study. LaFree and Dugan 2007.
62. In some terrorism databases, the majority of "terrorist" groups have never killed anyone. See Asal and Rethemeyer 2008b; and Sánchez-Cuenca and de la Calle 2009, 35.
63. Cronin 2003, 39–40.
64. Cunningham, Gleditsch, and Salehyan 2009a.
65. Fortna 2014.
66. Among many examples, see Crenshaw 1981, 387; McCormick 2003, 483; Merari 1993, 231; Pape 2003, 349; Sánchez-Cuenca and de la Calle 2009; and DeNardo 1985, 230. Little empirical work has tested this conventional wisdom directly, however. The few existing studies come to contradictory conclusions. See Stanton 2009 and 2013; Goodwin 2006; and Metelits 2010.
67. For a good overview, see Chenoweth 2010 and 2013.
68. Fortna 2014.
69. See Pape 2005, 23; and Stanton 2009, especially chapter 5.
70. Fazal 2013.

71. See Pape 2005, 22; Svensson 2007; Asal and Rethemeyer 2008a; Stanton 2013; and Satana, Inman, and Birnir 2013.
72. See Chenoweth 2010; Sánchez-Cuenca and de la Calle 2009; Burgoon 2006; Li and Schaub 2004; and Abadie 2006.
73. Boulden 2009, 13.
74. Laitin and Shapiro 2008, 213.
75. See Lawrence 2010; Bloom 2005; and Nemeth 2014. But see also Findley and Young 2012b; and Stanton 2009, 232–33.
76. On the relationship between these variables and war outcomes, see Cunningham, Gleditsch, and Salehyan 2009a; DeRouen and Sobek 2004; Fortna 2008; Balch-Lindsay, Enterline, and Joyce 2008; and Mason, Weingarten, and Fett 1999.
77. Cunningham, Gleditsch, and Salehyan 2009a, version 2.4.
78. See Gleditsch et al. 2002.
79. Note that although the overall conflict must reach the 1,000 battle death threshold, it is not the case that each rebel group/government dyad included in this study reaches this threshold.
80. For example, I updated Sri Lanka versus LTTE to reflect the government victory in 2009. This updating introduces possible inconsistencies since some variables are coded only through 2003. I also recoded cases in which a peace agreement was reached shortly after. UCDP codes a war as terminated in low activity (for example, the Good Friday Agreement settling the Northern Ireland conflict). This change improves the outcomes for two terrorist rebel groups (Provisional IRA and the MNLF in the Philippines) thus working against the argument made here. I also corrected two clearly miscoded cases: Burundi versus CNDD, and UK versus Real IRA. Cases affected by these changes are dropped in robustness tests.
81. Stanton 2013, 1014–15. For further discussion, see also Stanton 2009. In some cases, Stanton's coding for a single case was applicable to more than one dyad in the CGS data (for example, Stanton codes Fatah and Hamas together in a single conflict against Israel).
82. Because thirty-four cases involve wars that began before 1989, there are another 449 observations in the data that are used for some robustness checks.
83. The PKK turned to terrorism after 1993 (a shift reflected in the time-varying data used here). The MILF (Philippines) did so after 1986 (before the start of the data). E-mail correspondence with Stanton, 25 July 2008. The Taliban did not use terrorism in its fight against the Rabbani government of Afghanistan in the 1990s, but used terrorism against the Karzai government and its Western backers in the 2000s. These are treated as separate conflicts here.
84. Cunningham, Gleditsch, and Salehyan 2009a, 574–75.
85. Coggins 2011.
86. See Minorities at Risk Project 2009; National Consortium for the Study of Terrorism and Responses to Terrorism 2008; and Uppsala Conflict Data Program 2012. Detailed coding notes available from the author.
87. This moderate category is dominated by power struggle cases, of which there are twenty-three, because there are only a handful (five) of cases of rebel groups fighting for autonomy only.
88. More recent use of terrorism in Nigeria and Somalia may, unfortunately, temper this finding.
89. This could be the result of selection effects; this analysis covers only the strongest opposition groups, those involved in full-scale civil

wars. However, among these relatively strong groups, it is clearly not the case that only weak groups resort to terrorism.

90. See Fortna 2014.

91. Nor have any of the cases of terrorist rebel groups that were ongoing as of 2010 ended in rebel victory since then (at least as of this writing [January 2015]).

92. These include Fatah versus Israel, IRA versus the UK, and the MNLF versus Philippines (all in 1993). The only case of an agreement with terrorist rebels in a nondemocracy is the CPN-M/UPF versus Nepal in 2003.

93. Forty-two percent of the rebels who use terrorism were engaged in civil war in a nondemocratic state (measured in the year the war started).

■   ■   ■

REFERENCES

Abadie, Alberto. 2006. Poverty, Political Freedom, and the Roots of Terrorism. *American Economic Review* 96 (2):50–56.

Abrahms, Max. 2005. Review of *Dying to Win: The Strategic Logic of Suicide Terrorism* by Robert A. Pape. *Middle East Policy* 12 (4):176–78.

———. 2006. Why Terrorism Does Not Work. *International Security* 31 (2):42–78.

———. 2012. The Political Effectiveness of Terrorism Revisited. *Comparative Political Studies* 45 (3):366–93.

Acosta, Benjamin. 2014. Live to Win Another Day: Why Many Militant Organizations Survive yet Few Succeed. *Studies in Conflict and Terrorism* 37 (2):135–61.

Arreguín-Toft, Ivan. 2001. How the Weak Win Wars: A Theory of Asymmetric Conflict. *International Security* 26 (1):93–128.

Asal, Victor, and R. Karl Rethemeyer. 2008a. The Nature of the Beast: Organizational Structures and the Lethality of Terrorist Attacks. *Journal of Politics* 70 (2):437–49.

———. 2008b. Dilettantes, Ideologues, and the Weak: Terrorists Who Don't Kill. *Conflict Management and Peace Science* 25 (3):244–63.

Balch-Lindsay, Dylan, Andrew J. Enterline, and Kyle A. Joyce. 2008. Third-Party Intervention and the Civil War Process. *Journal of Peace Research* 45 (3):345–63.

Bapat, Navin A. 2006. State Bargaining with Transnational Terrorist Groups. *International Studies Quarterly* 50 (1):213–29.

Bloom, Mia. 2005. *Dying to Kill: The Allure of Suicide Terror.* New York: Columbia University Press.

Boulden, Jane. 2009. Terrorism and Civil Wars. *Civil Wars* 11 (1):5–21.

Bueno de Mesquita, Ethan, and Eric S. Dickson. 2007. The Propaganda of the Deed: Terrorism, Counterterrorism, and Mobilization. *American Journal of Political Science* 51 (2):364–81.

Burgoon, Brian. 2006. On Welfare and Terror: Social Welfare Policies and Political-Economic Roots of Terrorism. *Journal of Conflict Resolution* 50 (2):176–203.

Chenoweth, Erica. 2010. Democratic Competition and Terrorist Activity. *Journal of Politics* 72 (1):16–30.

———. 2013. Terrorism and Democracy. *Annual Review of Political Science* 16:355–78.

Coggins, Bridget. 2011. Friends in High Places: International Politics and the Emergence of States from Secessionism. *International Organization* 65 (3):433–67.

Crenshaw, Martha. 1981. The Causes of Terrorism. *Comparative Politics* 13 (4):379–99.

———. 1983. *Terrorism, Legitimacy, and Power: The Consequences of Political Violence.* Middletown, CT: Wesleyan University Press.

———. 2011. *Explaining Terrorism: Causes, Processes, and Consequences.* New York: Routledge.

Cronin, Audrey K. 2003. Behind the Curve: Globalization and International Terrorism. *International Security* 27 (3):30–58.

———. 2006. How al-Qaida Ends: The Decline and Demise of Terrorist Groups. *International Security* 31 (1):7–48.

———. 2009. *How Terrorism Ends: Understanding the Decline and Demise of Terrorist Campaigns.* Princeton, NJ: Princeton University Press.

Cunningham, David E., Kristian Skrede Gleditsch, and Idean Salehyan. 2009a. It Takes Two: A Dyadic Analysis of Civil War Duration and Outcome. *Journal of Conflict Resolution* 53 (4):570–97. Data available at http://privatewww.essex.ac.uk/~ksg/eacd.html Version 2.4. Accessed 13 January 2010.

———. 2009b. Data Coding Notes. Available at http://jcr.sagepub.com/content/53/4/570/suppl/DC1. Accessed 25 January 2010.

DeNardo, James. 1985. *Power in Numbers: The Political Strategy of Protest and Rebellion.* Princeton, NJ: Princeton University Press.

DeRouen, Karl, and David Sobek. 2004. The Dynamics of Civil War Duration and Outcome. *Journal of Peace Research* 41 (3):303–20.

Dow, Jay K., and James W. Endersby. 2004. Multinomial Probit and Multinomial Logit: A Comparison of Choice Models for Voting Research. *Electoral Studies* 23 (1):107–22.

Enders, Walter, Todd Sandler, and Khusrav Gaibulloev. 2011. Domestic Versus Transnational Terrorism: Data, Decomposition, and Dynamics. *Journal of Peace Research* 48 (3):319–37.

Eubank, William L., and Leonard Weinberg. 1994. Does Democracy Encourage Terrorism? *Terrorism and Political Violence* 6 (4):417–63.

Fazal, Tanisha M. 2013. Secessionism and Civilian Targeting. Paper presented at the 2013 Annual Meeting of the American Political Science Association, August, Chicago.

Findley, Michael G., and Joseph K. Young. 2012a. Terrorism and Civil War: A Spatial and Temporal Approach to a Conceptual Problem. *Perspectives on Politics* 10 (2):285–305.

———. 2012b. More Combatant Groups, More Terror? Empirical Tests of an Outbidding Logic. *Terrorism and Political Violence* 24 (5):706–21.

Fortna, Virginia Page. 2008. *Does Peacekeeping Work? Shaping Belligerents' Choices after Civil War.* Princeton, NJ: Princeton University Press.

———. 2014. Choosing Terror: Rebels' Use of Terrorism in Internal Armed Conflict, 1970–2010. Unpublished manuscript, Columbia University, New York.

Gleditsch, Nils P., Peter Wallensteen, Mikael Eriksson, Margareta Sollenberg, and Hoavard Strand. 2002. Armed Conflict 1946–2001: A New Dataset. *Journal of Peace Research* 39 (5):615–37. Data available at http://www.pcr.uu.se/research/ucdp/datasets/ucdp_prio_armed_conflict_dataset/. Accessed 1 April 2010.

Goodwin, Jeff. 2006. A Theory of Categorical Terrorism. *Social Forces* 84 (4):2027–46.

Gould, Eric D., and Esteban F. Klor. 2010. Does Terrorism Work? *Quarterly Journal of Economics* 125 (4):1459–510.

Heger, Lindsay L. 2010. In the Crosshairs: Explaining Violence Against Civilians. PhD diss., University of California, San Diego.

Hoffman, Bruce. 2006. *Inside Terrorism*. New York: Columbia University Press.

Jones, Seth G., and Martin C. Libicki. 2008. *How Terrorist Groups End: Lessons for Countering al Qa'ida*. Santa Monica, CA: Rand Corporation.

Kalyvas, Stathis N. 2006. *The Logic of Violence in Civil War*. New York: Cambridge University Press.

Krause, Peter. 2013. The Political Effectiveness of Non-State Violence: A Two-Level Framework to Transform a Deceptive Debate. *Security Studies* 22 (2):259–94.

Kydd, Andrew H., and Barbara F. Walter. 2002. Sabotaging the Peace: The Politics of Extremist Violence. *International Organization* 56 (2):263–96.

———. 2006. The Strategies of Terrorism. *International Security* 31 (1):49–80.

LaFree, Gary, and Laura Dugan. 2007. Introducing the Global Terrorism Database. *Terrorism and Political Violence* 19 (2):181–204.

Laitin, David D., and Jacob N. Shapiro. 2008. The Political, Economic, and Organizational Sources of Terrorism. In *Terrorism, Economic Development, and Political Openness*, edited by Philip Keefer and Norman Loayza, 209–32. New York: Cambridge University Press.

Lake, David A. 2002. Rational Extremism: Understanding Terrorism in the Twenty-First Century. *Dialogue IO* 1 (1):15–29.

Lawrence, Adria S. 2010. Triggering Nationalist Violence: Competition and Conflict in Uprisings Against Colonial Rule. *International Security* 35 (2):88–122.

Li, Quan, and Drew Schaub. 2004. Economic Globalization and Transnational Terrorism: A Pooled Time-Series Analysis. *Journal of Conflict Resolution* 48 (2):230–58.

Lyall, Jason. 2010. Do Democracies Make Inferior Counterinsurgents? Reassessing Democracy's Impact on War Outcomes and Duration. *International Organization* 64 (1):167–92.

Mao, Tse-Tung. 1961 [1937]. *On Guerrilla Warfare*. Translated by Samuel B. Griffith. New York: Praeger.

Mason, T. David, Joseph P. Weingarten, and Patrick J. Fett. 1999. Win, Lose, or Draw: Predicting the Outcome of Civil Wars. *Political Research Quarterly* 52 (2):239–68.

McCormick, Gordon H. 2003. Terrorist Decision Making. *Annual Review of Political Science* 6:473–507.

Merari, Ariel. 1993. Terrorism as a Strategy of Insurgency. *Terrorism and Political Violence* 5 (4):213–51.

Metelits, Claire. 2010. *Inside Insurgency: Violence, Civilians, and Revolutionary Group Behavior*. New York: New York University Press.

Minorities at Risk Project. 2009. Minorities at Risk Dataset: "Minority Group Assessments" and "Chronologies." College Park, MD: Center for International Development and Conflict Management. Available at http://www.cidcm.umd.edu/mar/data.asp. Accessed 29 November 2012.

National Consortium for the Study of Terrorism and Responses to Terrorism (START). 2008. Terrorist Organization Profiles (TOPs). Available at http://www.start.umd.edu/start/data_collections/tops/. Accessed 29 November 2012.

Nemeth, Stephen. 2014. The Effect of Competition on Terrorist Group Operations. *Journal of Conflict Resolution* 58 (2):336–62.

Pape, Robert A. 2003. The Strategic Logic of Suicide Terrorism. *American Political Science Review* 97 (3): 343–61.

———. 2005. *Dying to Win: The Strategic Logic of Suicide Terrorism*. New York: Random House.

Pape, Robert A., and James K. Feldman. 2010. *Cutting the Fuse: The Explosion of Suicide Terrorism and How to Stop It*. Chicago: University of Chicago Press.

Sambanis, Nicholas. 2008. Terrorism and Civil War. In *Terrorism, Economic Development, and Political Openness*, edited by Philip Keefer and Norman Loayza, 174–208. Cambridge, UK: Cambridge University Press.

Sánchez-Cuenca, Ignacio, and Luis de la Calle. 2009. Domestic Terrorism: The Hidden Side of Political Violence. *Annual Review of Political Science* 12:31–49.

Satana, Nil S., Molly Inman, and Johanna K. Birnir. 2013. Religion, Government Coalitions, and Terrorism. *Terrorism and Political Violence* 25 (1):29–52.

Schmid, Alex P., and Albert J. Jongman. 1988. *Political Terrorism: A New Guide to Actors, Authors, Concepts, Data Bases, Theories, and Literature*. Rev. ed. Amsterdam: North Holland.

Silke, Andrew. 1996. Terrorism and the Blind Man's Elephant. *Terrorism and Political Violence* 8 (3):12–28.

Stanton, Jessica A. 2009. Strategies of Violence and Restraint in Civil War. PhD diss., Department of Political Science, Columbia University, New York.

———. 2013. Terrorism in the Context of Civil War. *Journal of Politics* 75 (4):1009–22.

Stephan, Maria J., and Erica Chenoweth. 2008. Why Civil Resistance Works: The Strategic Logic of Nonviolent Conflict. *International Security* 33 (1):7–44.

Svensson, Isak. 2007. Fighting with Faith: Religion and Conflict Resolution in Civil Wars. *Journal of Conflict Resolution* 51 (6):930–49.

Thomas, Jakana. 2014. Rewarding Bad Behavior: How Governments Respond to Terrorism in Civil War. *American Journal of Political Science* 58 (4):804–18.

Thornton, Thomas P. 1964. Terror as a Weapon of Political Agitation. In *Internal War: Problems and Approaches*, edited by Harry Eckstein, 71–99. London: Free Press.

Uppsala Conflict Data Program. 2012. UCDP Conflict Encyclopedia. Uppsala, Sweden: Uppsala University. Available at www.ucdp.uu.se /database. Accessed 29 November 2012.

Walter, Barbara F. 2002. *Committing to Peace: The Successful Settlement of Civil Wars*. Princeton, NJ: Princeton University Press.

Wilson, James Q. 1974. *Political Organizations*. Princeton, NJ: Princeton University Press.

Wood, Reed M., and Jacob D. Kathman. 2014. Too Much of a Bad Thing? Civilian Victimization and Bargaining in Civil War. *British Journal of Political Science* 44 (3):1–22.

7 INTERNATIONAL COOPERATION AND INTERNATIONAL LAW

Cooperation is a central facet of states' interactions in the international system today, and states often comply with international law. This occurs even though the international system is anarchic and states that cooperate can be exploited by others. There is no world government or world police to enforce international law, to make states cooperate with one another, or to protect states from coercion by other states. This raises an interesting question that many scholars have sought to address: If no one is making them do so, why do states often follow international law and cooperate despite the fact that this may make them vulnerable to opportunistic behavior by other states? The works in this chapter tackle this question from different approaches.

In his article "Cooperation under the Security Dilemma," Robert Jervis uses the game-theoretic framework of the prisoner's dilemma to identify conditions that can help ameliorate the impact of anarchy and assuage states' fear of being exploited or coerced. He uses the example of arms control to show that states cooperate in situations where defending against an attack is easier than carrying out an attack, and when states agree to only deploy armaments that are distinguishably better at defending than attacking.

Harold Hongju Koh, an international lawyer in Barack Obama's State Department, asks why states often comply with international law despite the absence of a coercive enforcement power. He emphasizes the "transnational legal process" through which global norms of international law are debated, interpreted, and then internalized in the routine work of states' domestic legal systems and government bureaucracies.

Robert Jervis

COOPERATION UNDER THE SECURITY DILEMMA

I. Anarchy and the Security Dilemma

The lack of an international sovereign not only permits wars to occur, but also makes it difficult for states that are satisfied with the status quo to arrive at goals that they recognize as being in their common interest. Because there are no institutions or authorities that can make and enforce international laws, the policies of cooperation that will bring mutual rewards if others cooperate may bring disaster if they do not. Because states are aware of this, anarchy encourages behavior that leaves all concerned worse off than they could be, even in the extreme case in which all states would like to freeze the status quo. This is true of the men in Rousseau's "Stag Hunt." If they cooperate to trap the stag, they will all eat well. But if one person defects to chase a rabbit—which he likes less than stag—none of the others will get anything. Thus, all actors have the same preference order, and there is a solution that gives each his first choice: (1) cooperate and trap the stag (the international analogue being cooperation and disarmament); (2) chase a rabbit while others remain at their posts (maintain a high level of arms while others are disarmed); (3) all chase rabbits (arms competition and high risk of war); and (4) stay at the original position while another chases a rabbit (being disarmed while others are armed). Unless

From *World Politics* 30, no. 2 (January 1978): 167–214. Some of the author's notes have been omitted.

each person thinks that the others will cooperate, he himself will not. And why might he fear that any other person would do something that would sacrifice his own first choice? The other might not understand the situation, or might not be able to control his impulses if he saw a rabbit, or might fear that some other member of the group is unreliable. If the person voices any of these suspicions, others are more likely to fear that he will defect, thus making them more likely to defect, thus making it more rational for him to defect. Of course in this simple case—and in many that are more realistic—there are a number of arrangements that could permit cooperation. But the main point remains: although actors may know that they seek a common goal, they may not be able to reach it.

Even when there is a solution that is everyone's first choice, the international case is characterized by three difficulties not present in the Stag Hunt. First, to the incentives to defect given above must be added the potent fear that even if the other state now supports the status quo, it may become dissatisfied later. No matter how much decision makers are committed to the status quo, they cannot bind themselves and their successors to the same path. Minds can be changed, new leaders can come to power, values can shift, new opportunities and dangers can arise.

The second problem arises from a possible solution. In order to protect their possessions, states often seek to control resources or land outside their own territory. Countries that are not self-sufficient must try to assure that the necessary

399

supplies will continue to flow in wartime. This was part of the explanation for Japan's drive into China and Southeast Asia before World War II. If there were an international authority that could guarantee access, this motive for control would disappear. But since there is not, even a state that would prefer the status quo to increasing its area of control may pursue the latter policy.

When there are believed to be tight linkages between domestic and foreign policy or between the domestic politics of two states, the quest for security may drive states to interfere pre-emptively in the domestic politics of others in order to provide an ideological buffer zone. * * *

More frequently, the concern is with direct attack. In order to protect themselves, states seek to control, or at least to neutralize, areas on their borders. But attempts to establish buffer zones can alarm others who have stakes there, who fear that undesirable precedents will be set, or who believe that their own vulnerability will be increased. When buffers are sought in areas empty of great powers, expansion tends to feed on itself in order to protect what is acquired. * * *

Though this process is most clearly visible when it involves territorial expansion, it often operates with the increase of less tangible power and influence. The expansion of power usually brings with it an expansion of responsibilities and commitments; to meet them, still greater power is required. The state will take many positions that are subject to challenge. It will be involved with a wide range of controversial issues unrelated to its core values. And retreats that would be seen as normal if made by a small power would be taken as an index of weakness inviting predation if made by a large one.

The third problem present in international politics but not in the Stag Hunt is the security dilemma: many of the means by which a state tries to increase its security decrease the security of others. In domestic society, there are several ways to increase the safety of one's person and property without endangering others. One can move to a safer neighborhood, put bars on the windows, avoid dark streets, and keep a distance from suspicious-looking characters. Of course these measures are not convenient, cheap, or certain of success. But no one save criminals need be alarmed if a person takes them. In international politics, however, one state's gain in security often inadvertently threatens others. In explaining British policy on naval disarmament in the interwar period to the Japanese, Ramsey MacDonald said that "Nobody wanted Japan to be insecure."[1] But the problem was not with British desires, but with the consequences of her policy. In earlier periods, too, Britain had needed a navy large enough to keep the shipping lanes open. But such a navy could not avoid being a menace to any other state with a coast that could be raided, trade that could be interdicted, or colonies that could be isolated. When Germany started building a powerful navy before World War I, Britain objected that it could only be an offensive weapon aimed at her. As Sir Edward Grey, the Foreign Secretary, put it to King Edward VII: "If the German Fleet ever becomes superior to ours, the German Army can conquer this country. There is no corresponding risk of this kind to Germany; for however superior our Fleet was, no naval victory could bring us any nearer to Berlin." The English position was half correct: Germany's navy was an anti-British instrument. But the British often overlooked what the Germans knew full well: "in every quarrel with England, German colonies and trade were . . . hostages for England to take." Thus, whether she intended it or not, the British Navy constituted an important instrument of coercion.[2]

II. What Makes Cooperation More Likely?

Given this gloomy picture, the obvious question is, why are we not all dead? Or, to put it less starkly,

Figure 7.1. Stag Hunt and Prisoner's Dilemma

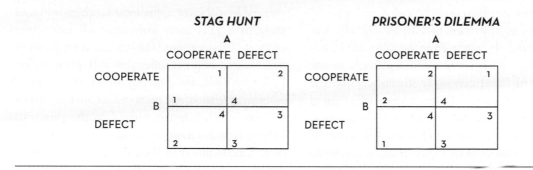

what kinds of variables ameliorate the impact of anarchy and the security dilemma? The working of several can be seen in terms of the Stag Hunt or repeated plays of the Prisoner's Dilemma.[3] The Prisoner's Dilemma differs from the Stag Hunt in that there is no solution that is in the best interests of all the participants; there are offensive as well as defensive incentives to defect from the coalition with the others; and, if the game is to be played only once, the only rational response is to defect [Figure 7.1]. But if the game is repeated indefinitely, the latter characteristic no longer holds and we can analyze the game in terms similar to those applied to the Stag Hunt. It would be in the interest of each actor to have others deprived of the power to defect; each would be willing to sacrifice this ability if others were similarly restrained. But if the others are not, then it is in the actor's interest to retain the power to defect.[4] The game theory matrices for these two situations are given [above], with the numbers in the boxes being the order of the actor's preferences.

We can see the logical possibilities by rephrasing our question: "Given either of the above situations, what makes it more or less likely that the players will cooperate and arrive at CC?" The chances of achieving this outcome will be increased by: (1) anything that increases incentives to cooperate by increasing the gains of mutual cooperation (CC) and/or decreasing the costs the actor will pay if he cooperates and the other does

not (CD); (2) anything that decreases the incentives for defecting by decreasing the gains of taking advantage of the other (DC) and/or increasing the costs of mutual noncooperation (DD); (3) anything that increases each side's expectation that the other will cooperate.[5]

The Costs of Being Exploited (CD)

The fear of being exploited (that is, the cost of CD) most strongly drives the security dilemma; one of the main reasons why international life is not more nasty, brutish, and short is that states are not as vulnerable as men are in a state of nature. People are easy to kill, but as Adam Smith replied to a friend who feared that the Napoleonic Wars would ruin England, "Sir, there is a great deal of ruin in a nation."[6] The easier it is to destroy a state, the greater the reason for it either to join a larger and more secure unit, or else to be especially suspicious of others, to require a large army, and, if conditions are favorable, to attack at the slightest provocation rather than wait to be attacked. If the failure to eat that day—be it venison or rabbit—means that he will starve, a person is likely to defect in the Stag Hunt even if he really likes venison and has a high level of trust in his colleagues. (Defection is especially likely if the others are also starving or if they know that he is.) By contrast, if the costs of CD are lower, if people are well-fed or states are resilient, they can afford to take a more relaxed view of threats.

A relatively low cost of CD has the effect of transforming the game from one in which both players make their choices simultaneously to one in which an actor can make his choice after the other has moved. He will not have to defect out of fear that the other will, but can wait to see what the other will do. States that can afford to be cheated in a bargain or that cannot be destroyed by a surprise attack can more easily trust others and need not act at the first, and ambiguous, sign of menace. Because they have a margin of time and error, they need not match, or more than match, any others' arms in peacetime. They can mobilize in the prewar period or even at the start of the war itself, and still survive. For example, those who opposed a crash program to develop the H-bomb felt that the U.S. margin of safety was large enough so that even if Russia managed to gain a lead in the race, America would not be endangered. The program's advocates disagreed: "If we let the Russians get the super first, catastrophe becomes all but certain."[7]

When the costs of CD are tolerable, not only is security easier to attain but, what is even more important here, the relatively low level of arms and relatively passive foreign policy that a status-quo power will be able to adopt are less likely to threaten others. Thus it is easier for status-quo states to act on their common interests if they are hard to conquer. All other things being equal, a world of small states will feel the effects of anarchy much more than a world of large ones. Defensible borders, large size, and protection against sudden attack not only aid the state, but facilitate cooperation that can benefit all states.

Of course, if one state gains invulnerability by being more powerful than most others, the problem will remain because its security provides a base from which it can exploit others. When the price a state will pay for DD is low, it leaves others with few hostages for its good behavior. Others who are more vulnerable will grow apprehensive, which will lead them to acquire more arms and will reduce the chances of cooperation. The best situation is one in which a state will not suffer greatly if others exploit it, for example, by cheating on an arms control agreement (that is, the costs of CD are low); but it will pay a high long-run price if cooperation with the others breaks down—for example, if agreements cease functioning or if there is a long war (that is, the costs of DD are high). The state's invulnerability is then mostly passive; it provides some protection, but it cannot be used to menace others. As we will discuss below, this situation is approximated when it is easier for states to defend themselves than to attack others, or when mutual deterrence obtains because neither side can protect itself.

The differences between highly vulnerable and less vulnerable states are illustrated by the contrasting policies of Britain and Austria after the Napoleonic Wars. Britain's geographic isolation and political stability allowed her to take a fairly relaxed view of disturbances on the Continent. Minor wars and small changes in territory or in the distribution of power did not affect her vital interests. An adversary who was out to overthrow the system could be stopped after he had made his intentions clear. And revolutions within other states were no menace, since they would not set off unrest within England. Austria, surrounded by strong powers, was not so fortunate; her policy had to be more closely attuned to all conflicts. By the time an aggressor-state had clearly shown its colors, Austria would be gravely threatened. And foreign revolutions, be they democratic or nationalistic, would encourage groups in Austria to upset the existing order. So it is not surprising that Metternich propounded the doctrine summarized earlier, which defended Austria's right to interfere in the internal affairs of others, and that British leaders rejected this view. Similarly, Austria wanted the Congress system to be a relatively tight one, regulating most disputes. The British favored a less centralized system. In other words, in order to protect herself, Austria had either to threaten or to harm others, whereas Britain did not. For Austria and her neighbors the security dilemma was acute; for Britain it was not.

The ultimate cost of CD is of course loss of sovereignty. This cost can vary from situation to situation. The lower it is (for instance, because the two states have compatible ideologies, are similar ethnically, have a common culture, or because the citizens of the losing state expect economic benefits), the less the impact of the security dilemma; the greater the costs, the greater the impact of the dilemma. Here is another reason why extreme differences in values and ideologies exacerbate international conflict.

■   ■   ■

SUBJECTIVE SECURITY DEMANDS

Decision makers act in terms of the vulnerability they feel, which can differ from the actual situation; we must therefore examine the decision makers' subjective security requirements. Two dimensions are involved. First, even if they agree about the objective situation, people can differ about how much security they desire—or, to put it more precisely, about the price they are willing to pay to gain increments of security. The more states value their security above all else (that is, see a prohibitively high cost in CD), the more they are likely to be sensitive to even minimal threats, and to demand high levels of arms. And if arms are positively valued because of pressures from a military-industrial complex, it will be especially hard for status-quo powers to cooperate. By contrast, the security dilemma will not operate as strongly when pressing domestic concerns increase the opportunity costs of armaments. In this case, the net advantage of exploiting the other (DC) will be less, and the costs of arms races (that is,

one aspect of DD) will be greater; therefore the state will behave as though it were relatively invulnerable.

The second aspect of subjective security is the perception of threat (that is, the estimate of whether the other will cooperate). A state that is predisposed to see either a specific other state as an adversary, or others in general as a menace, will react more strongly and more quickly than a state that sees its environment as benign. Indeed, when a state believes that another not only is not likely to be an adversary, but has sufficient interests in common with it to be an ally, then it will actually welcome an increase in the other's power.

■   ■   ■

Geography, Commitments, Beliefs, and Security through Expansion

* * * Situations vary in the ease or difficulty with which all states can simultaneously achieve a high degree of security. The influence of military technology on this variable is the subject of the next section. Here we want to treat the impact of beliefs, geography, and commitments (many of which can be considered to be modifications of geography, since they bind states to defend areas outside their homelands). In the crowded continent of Europe, security requirements were hard to mesh. Being surrounded by powerful states, Germany's problem—or the problem created by Germany—was always great and was even worse when her relations with both France and Russia were bad, such as before World War I. In that case, even a status-quo Germany, if she could not change the political situation, would almost have been forced to adopt something like the Schlieffen Plan. Because she could not hold off both of her enemies, she had to be prepared to defeat one quickly and then deal

with the other in a more leisurely fashion. If France or Russia stayed out of a war between the other state and Germany, they would allow Germany to dominate the Continent (even if that was not Germany's aim). They therefore had to deny Germany this ability, thus making Germany less secure. Although Germany's arrogant and erratic behavior, coupled with the desire for an unreasonably high level of security (which amounted to the desire to escape from her geographic plight), compounded the problem, even wise German statesmen would have been hard put to gain a high degree of security without alarming their neighbors.

■　　■　　■

III. Offense, Defense, and the Security Dilemma

Another approach starts with the central point of the security dilemma—that an increase in one state's security decreases the security of others—and examines the conditions under which this proposition holds. Two crucial variables are involved: whether defensive weapons and policies can be distinguished from offensive ones, and whether the defense or the offense has the advantage. The definitions are not always clear, and many cases are difficult to judge, but these two variables shed a great deal of light on the question of whether status-quo powers will adopt compatible security policies. All the variables discussed so far leave the heart of the problem untouched. But when defensive weapons differ from offensive ones, it is possible for a state to make itself more secure without making others less secure. And when the defense has the advantage over the offense, a large increase in one state's security only slightly decreases the security of the others, and status-quo powers can all enjoy a high level of security and largely escape from the state of nature.

Offense-Defense Balance

When we say that the offense has the advantage, we simply mean that it is easier to destroy the other's army and take its territory than it is to defend one's own. When the defense has the advantage, it is easier to protect and to hold than it is to move forward, destroy, and take. If effective defenses can be erected quickly, an attacker may be able to keep territory he has taken in an initial victory. Thus, the dominance of the defense made it very hard for Britain and France to push Germany out of France in World War I. But when superior defenses are difficult for an aggressor to improvise on the battlefield and must be constructed during peacetime, they provide no direct assistance to him.

The security dilemma is at its most vicious when commitments, strategy, or technology dictate that the only route to security lies through expansion. Status-quo powers must then act like aggressors; the fact that they would gladly agree to forego the opportunity for expansion in return for guarantees for their security has no implications for their behavior. Even if expansion is not sought as a goal in itself, there will be quick and drastic changes in the distribution of territory and influence. Conversely, when the defense has the advantage, status-quo states can make themselves more secure without gravely endangering others.[8] Indeed, if the defense has enough of an advantage and if the states are of roughly equal size, not only will the security dilemma cease to inhibit status-quo states from cooperating, but aggression will be next to impossible, thus rendering international anarchy relatively unimportant. If states cannot conquer each other, then the lack of sovereignty, although it presents problems of collective goods in a number of areas, no longer forces states to devote their primary attention to self-preservation. Although, if force were not usable, there would be fewer restraints on the use of nonmilitary instruments, these are rarely powerful enough to threaten the vital interests of a major state.

Two questions of the offense-defense balance can be separated. First, does the state have to spend more or less than one dollar on defensive forces to offset each dollar spent by the other side on forces that could be used to attack? If the state has one dollar to spend on increasing its security, should it put it into offensive or defensive forces? Second, with a given inventory of forces, is it better to attack or to defend? Is there an incentive to strike first or to absorb the other's blow? These two aspects are often linked: if each dollar spent on offense can overcome each dollar spent on defense, and if both sides have the same defense budgets, then both are likely to build offensive forces and find it attractive to attack rather than to wait for the adversary to strike.

These aspects affect the security dilemma in different ways. The first has its greatest impact on arms races. If the defense has the advantage, and if the status-quo powers have reasonable subjective security requirements, they can probably avoid an arms race. Although an increase in one side's arms and security will still decrease the other's security, the former's increase will be larger than the latter's decrease. So if one side increases its arms, the other can bring its security back up to its previous level by adding a smaller amount to its forces. And if the first side reacts to this change, its increase will also be smaller than the stimulus that produced it. Thus a stable equilibrium will be reached. Shifting from dynamics to statics, each side can be quite secure with forces roughly equal to those of the other. Indeed, if the defense is much more potent than the offense, each side can be willing to have forces much smaller than the other's, and can be indifferent to a wide range of the other's defense policies.

The second aspect—whether it is better to attack or to defend—influences short-run stability. When the offense has the advantage, a state's reaction to international tension will increase the chances of war. The incentives for pre-emption and the "reciprocal fear of surprise attack" in this situation have been made clear by analyses of the dangers that exist when two countries have first-strike capabilities.[9] There is no way for the state to increase its security without menacing, or even attacking, the other. Even Bismarck, who once called preventive war "committing suicide from fear of death," said that "no government, if it regards war as inevitable even if it does not want it, would be so foolish as to leave to the enemy the choice of time and occasion and to wait for the moment which is most convenient for the enemy."[10] In another arena, the same dilemma applies to the policeman in a dark alley confronting a suspected criminal who appears to be holding a weapon. Though racism may indeed be present, the security dilemma can account for many of the tragic shootings of innocent people in the ghettos.

Beliefs about the course of a war in which the offense has the advantage further deepen the security dilemma. When there are incentives to strike first, a successful attack will usually so weaken the other side that victory will be relatively quick, bloodless, and decisive. It is in these periods when conquest is possible and attractive that states consolidate power internally—for instance, by destroying the feudal barons—and expand externally. There are several consequences that decrease the chance of cooperation among status quo states. First, war will be profitable for the winner. The costs will be low and the benefits high. Of course, losers will suffer; the fear of losing could induce states to try to form stable cooperative arrangements, but the temptation of victory will make this particularly difficult. Second, because wars are expected to be both frequent and short, there will be incentives for high levels of arms, and quick and strong reaction to the other's increases in arms. The state cannot afford to wait until there is unambiguous evidence that the other is building new weapons. Even large states that have faith in their economic strength cannot wait, because the war will be over before their products can reach the army. Third, when wars are quick, states will have to recruit allies in advance.[11] Without the opportunity for bargaining and re-alignments during the opening stages of hostilities, peacetime diplomacy loses a degree of the fluidity that facilitates balance-of-power policies. Because alliances must be secured during peacetime, the international system is more likely to become bipolar. It is hard to say whether war therefore becomes more or less likely, but this bipolarity increases tension between the two camps and makes it harder for status-quo states to gain the benefits of cooperation. Fourth, if wars are frequent, statesmen's perceptual thresholds will be adjusted accordingly and they will be quick to perceive ambiguous evidence as indicating that others are aggressive. Thus, there will be more cases of status-quo powers arming against each other in the incorrect belief that the other is hostile.

When the defense has the advantage, all the foregoing is reversed. The state that fears attack does not pre-empt—since that would be a wasteful use of its military resources—but rather prepares to receive an attack. Doing so does not decrease the security of others, and several states can do it simultaneously; the situation will therefore be stable, and status-quo powers will be able to cooperate. * * *

More is involved than short-run dynamics. When the defense is dominant, wars are likely to become stalemates and can be won only at enormous cost. Relatively small and weak states can hold off larger and stronger ones, or can deter attack by raising the costs of conquest to an unacceptable level. States then approach equality in what they can do to each other. Like the .45-caliber pistol in the American West, fortifications were the "great equalizer" in some periods. Changes in the status quo are less frequent and cooperation is more common wherever the security dilemma is thereby reduced.

Many of these arguments can be illustrated by the major powers' policies in the periods preceding the two world wars. Bismarck's wars surprised statesmen by showing that the offense had the advantage, and by being quick, relatively cheap, and quite decisive. Falling into a common error, observers projected this pattern into the future. The resulting expectations had several effects. First, states sought semi-permanent allies. In the early stages of the Franco-Prussian War, Napoleon III had thought that there would be plenty of time to recruit Austria to his side. Now, others were not going to repeat this mistake. Second, defense budgets were high and reacted quite sharply to increases on the other side. * * * Third, most decision makers thought that the next European war would not cost much blood and treasure.[12] That is one reason why war was generally seen as inevitable and why mass opinion was so bellicose. Fourth, once war seemed likely, there were strong pressures to pre-empt. Both sides believed that whoever moved first could penetrate the other deep enough to disrupt mobilization and thus gain an insurmountable advantage. (There was no such belief about the use of naval forces. Although Churchill made an ill-advised speech saying that if German ships "do not come out and fight in time of war they will be dug out like rats in a hole,"[13] everyone knew that submarines, mines, and coastal fortifications made this impossible. So at the start of the war each navy prepared to defend itself rather than attack, and the short-run destabilizing forces that launched the armies toward each other did not operate.)[14] Furthermore, each side knew that the other saw the situation the same way, thus increasing the perceived danger that the other would attack, and giving each added reasons to precipitate a war if conditions seemed favorable. In the long and the short run, there were thus both offensive and defensive incentives to strike. This situation casts light on the common question about German motives in 1914: "Did Germany unleash the war deliberately to become a world power or did she support Austria merely to defend a weakening ally," thereby protecting her own position?[15] To some extent, this question is misleading. Because of the perceived advantage of the offense, war was seen as the best route both to gaining expansion and to avoiding drastic loss of influence. There seemed to be no way for Germany merely to retain and safeguard her existing position.

Of course the war showed these beliefs to have been wrong on all points. Trenches and machine guns gave the defense an overwhelming advantage. The fighting became deadlocked and produced horrendous casualties. It made no sense for the combatants to bleed themselves to death. If they had known the power of the defense beforehand, they would have rushed for their own trenches rather than for the enemy's territory. Each side could have done this without increasing the other's incentives to strike. War might have broken out anyway, * * * but at least the pressures of time and the fear of allowing the other to get the first blow would not have contributed to this end. And, had both sides known the costs of the war, they would have negotiated much more seriously. The obvious question is why the states did not seek a negotiated settlement as soon as the shape of the war became clear. Schlieffen had said that if his plan failed, peace should be sought.[16] The answer is complex, uncertain, and largely outside of the scope of our concerns. But part of the reason was the hope and sometimes the expectation that breakthroughs could be made and the dominance of the offensive restored. Without that hope, the political and psychological pressures to fight to a decisive victory might have been overcome.

The politics of the interwar period were shaped by the memories of the previous conflict and the belief that any future war would resemble it. Political and military lessons reinforced each other in ameliorating the security dilemma. Because it was believed that the First World War had been a mistake that could have been avoided by skillful conciliation, both Britain and, to a lesser extent, France were highly sensitive to the possibility that interwar Germany was not a real threat to peace,

and alert to the danger that reacting quickly and strongly to her arms could create unnecessary conflict. And because Britain and France expected the defense to continue to dominate, they concluded that it was safe to adopt a more relaxed and non-threatening military posture.[17] Britain also felt less need to maintain tight alliance bonds. The Allies' military posture then constituted only a slight danger to Germany; had the latter been content with the status quo, it would have been easy for both sides to have felt secure behind their lines of fortifications. Of course the Germans were not content, so it is not surprising that they devoted their money and attention to finding ways out of a defense-dominated stalemate. *Blitzkrieg* tactics were necessary if they were to use force to change the status quo.

The initial stages of the war on the Western Front also contrasted with the First World War. Only with the new air arm were there any incentives to strike first, and these forces were too weak to carry out the grandiose plans that had been both dreamed and feared. The armies, still the main instrument, rushed to defensive positions. Perhaps the allies could have successfully attacked while the Germans were occupied in Poland.[18] But belief in the defense was so great that this was never seriously contemplated. Three months after the start of the war, the French Prime Minister summed up the view held by almost everyone but Hitler: on the Western Front there is "deadlock. Two Forces of equal strength and the one that attacks seeing such enormous casualties that it cannot move without endangering the continuation of the war or of the aftermath."[19] The Allies were caught in a dilemma they never fully recognized, let alone solved. On the one hand, they had very high war aims; although unconditional surrender had not yet been adopted, the British had decided from the start that the removal of Hitler was a necessary condition for peace.[20] On the other hand, there were no realistic plans or instruments for allowing the Allies to impose their will on the other side. The British Chief of the Imperial General Staff noted, "The French have no intention of carrying out an offensive for years, if at all"; the British were only slightly bolder.[21] So the Allies looked to a long war that would wear the Germans down, cause civilian suffering through shortages, and eventually undermine Hitler. There was little analysis to support this view—and indeed it probably was not supportable—but as long as the defense was dominant and the numbers on each side relatively equal, what else could the Allies do?

To summarize, the security dilemma was much less powerful after World War I than it had been before. In the later period, the expected power of the defense allowed status-quo states to pursue compatible security policies and avoid arms races. Furthermore, high tension and fear of war did not set off short-run dynamics by which each state, trying to increase its security, inadvertently acted to make war more likely. The expected high costs of war, however, led the Allies to believe that no sane German leader would run the risks entailed in an attempt to dominate the Continent, and discouraged them from risking war themselves.

TECHNOLOGY AND GEOGRAPHY

Technology and geography are the two main factors that determine whether the offense or the defense has the advantage. As Brodie notes, "On the tactical level, as a rule, few physical factors favor the attacker but many favor the defender. The defender usually has the advantage of cover. He characteristically fires from behind some form of shelter while his opponent crosses open ground."[22] Anything that increases the amount of ground the attacker has to cross, or impedes his progress across it, or makes him more vulnerable while crossing, increases the advantage accruing to the defense. When states are separated by barriers that produce these effects, the security dilemma is eased, since both can have forces adequate for defense without being able to attack. * * *

Oceans, large rivers, and mountain ranges serve the same function as buffer zones. Being hard to cross, they allow defense against superior numbers. The defender has merely to stay on his side of the barrier and so can utilize all the men he can bring up to it. The attacker's men, however, can cross only a few at a time, and they are very vulnerable when doing so. If all states were self-sufficient islands, anarchy would be much less of a problem. A small investment in shore defenses and a small army would be sufficient to repel invasion. Only very weak states would be vulnerable, and only very large ones could menace others. As noted above, the United States, and to a lesser extent Great Britain, have partly been able to escape from the state of nature because their geographical positions approximated this ideal.

Although geography cannot be changed to conform to borders, borders can and do change to conform to geography. Borders across which an attack is easy tend to be unstable. States living within them are likely to expand or be absorbed. Frequent wars are almost inevitable since attacking will often seem the best way to protect what one has. This process will stop, or at least slow down, when the state's borders reach—by expansion or contraction—a line of natural obstacles. Security without attack will then be possible. Furthermore, these lines constitute salient solutions to bargaining problems and, to the extent that they are barriers to migration, are likely to divide ethnic groups, thereby raising the costs and lowering the incentives for conquest.

Attachment to one's state and its land reinforce one quasi-geographical aid to the defense. Conquest usually becomes more difficult the deeper the attacker pushes into the other's territory. Nationalism spurs the defenders to fight harder; advancing not only lengthens the attacker's supply lines, but takes him through unfamiliar and often devastated lands that require troops for garrison duty. These stabilizing dynamics will not operate, however, if the defender's war materiel is situated near its borders, or if the people do not care about their state, but only about being on the winning side. * * *

■   ■   ■

The other major determinant of the offense-defense balance is technology. When weapons are highly vulnerable, they must be employed before they are attacked. Others can remain quite invulnerable in their bases. The former characteristics are embodied in unprotected missiles and many kinds of bombers. (It should be noted that it is not vulnerability *per se* that is crucial, but the location of the vulnerability. Bombers and missiles that are easy to destroy only after having been launched toward their targets do not create destabilizing dynamics.) Incentives to strike first are usually absent for naval forces that are threatened by a naval attack. Like missiles in hardened silos, they are usually well protected when in their bases. Both sides can then simultaneously be prepared to defend themselves successfully.

In ground warfare under some conditions, forts, trenches, and small groups of men in prepared positions can hold off large numbers of attackers. * * *

■   ■   ■

Concerning nuclear weapons, it is generally agreed that defense is impossible—a triumph not of the offense, but of deterrence. Attack makes no sense, not because it can be beaten off, but because the attacker will be destroyed in turn. In terms of the questions under consideration here, the result is the equivalent of the primacy of the defense. First, security is relatively cheap. Less than one percent of the GNP is devoted to deterring a direct attack on the United States; most of it is spent on acquiring redundant systems to provide a lot of insurance against the worst conceivable contingencies. Second, both sides can simultaneously gain security in the form of second-strike capability. Third, and related to the foregoing, second-strike capability can be maintained in the face of wide variations in the other side's military posture. There is no purely military reason why each side has to react quickly and strongly to the other's increases in arms. Any spending that the other devotes to trying to achieve first-strike capability can be neutralized by the state's spending much smaller sums on protecting its second-strike capability. Fourth, there are no incentives to strike first in a crisis.

■   ■   ■

Offense-Defense Differentiation

The other major variable that affects how strongly the security dilemma operates is whether weapons and policies that protect the state also provide the capability for attack. If they do not, the basic postulate of the security dilemma no longer applies. A state can increase its own security without decreasing that of others. The advantage of the defense can only ameliorate the security dilemma. A differentiation between offensive and defensive stances comes close to abolishing it. Such differentiation does not mean, however, that all security problems will be abolished. If the offense has the advantage, conquest and aggression will still be possible. And if the offense's advantage is great enough, status-quo powers may find it too expensive to protect themselves by defensive forces and decide to procure offensive weapons even though this will menace others. Furthermore, states will still have to worry that even if the other's military posture shows that it is peaceful now, it may develop aggressive intentions in the future.

Assuming that the defense is at least as potent as the offense, the differentiation between them allows status-quo states to behave in ways that are clearly different from those of aggressors. Three beneficial consequences follow. First, status-quo powers can identify each other, thus laying the foundations for cooperation. Conflicts growing out of the mistaken belief that the other side is expansionist will be less frequent. Second, status-quo states will obtain advance warning when others plan aggression. Before a state can attack, it has to develop and deploy offensive weapons. If procurement of these weapons cannot be disguised and takes a fair amount of time, as it almost always does, a status-quo state will have the time to take countermeasures. It need not maintain a high level of defensive arms as long as its potential adversaries are adopting a peaceful posture. * * *

■ ■ ■

* * * [I]f all states support the status quo, an obvious arms control agreement is a ban on weapons that are useful for attacking. As President Roosevelt put it in his message to the Geneva Disarmament Conference in 1933: "If all nations will agree wholly to eliminate from possession and use the weapons which make possible a successful attack, defenses automatically will become impregnable, and the frontiers and independence of every nation will become secure."[23] The fact that such treaties have been rare * * * shows either that states are not always willing to guarantee the security of others, or that it is hard to distinguish offensive from defensive weapons.

■ ■ ■

IV. Four Worlds

The two variables we have been discussing—whether the offense or the defense has the advantage, and whether offensive postures can be distinguished from defensive ones—can be combined to yield four possible worlds [see Figure 7.2].

The first world is the worst for status-quo states. There is no way to get security without menacing others, and security through defense is terribly difficult to obtain. Because offensive and defensive postures are the same, status-quo states acquire the same kind of arms that are sought by aggressors. And because the offense has the advantage over the defense, attacking is the best route to protecting what you have; status-quo states will therefore behave like aggressors. The situation will be unstable. Arms races are likely. Incentives to strike first will turn crises into wars. Decisive victories and conquests will be common. States will grow and shrink rapidly, and it will be hard for any state to maintain its size and influence without trying to increase them. Cooperation among status-quo powers will be extremely hard to achieve.

There are no cases that totally fit this picture, but it bears more than a passing resemblance to Europe before World War I. Britain and Germany, although in many respects natural allies, ended up as enemies. Of course much of the explanation lies in Germany's ill-chosen policy. And from the perspective of our theory, the powers' ability to avoid war in a series of earlier crises cannot be easily explained. Nevertheless, much of the behavior in this period was the product of technology and beliefs that magnified the security dilemma. Decision makers thought that the offense had a big advantage and saw little difference between offensive and defensive military postures. The era was characterized by arms races. And once war seemed likely, mobilization races created powerful incentives to strike first.

In the nuclear era, the first world would be one in which each side relied on vulnerable weapons that were aimed at similar forces and each side understood the situation. In this case, the incentives to strike first would be very high—so high that status-quo powers as well as aggressors would be sorely tempted to pre-empt. And since the forces could be used to change the status quo as well as to preserve it, there would be no way for both sides to increase their security simultaneously. Now the familiar logic of deterrence leads both sides to see the dangers in this world.

Figure 7.2. The Security Dilemma

	Offense Has the Advantage	Defense Has the Advantage
Offensive Posture Not Distinguishable from Defensive One	1 Doubly dangerous.	2 Security dilemma, but security requirements may be compatible.
Offensive Posture Distinguishable from Defensive One	3 No security dilemma, but aggression possible. Status-quo states can follow different policy than aggressors. Warning given.	4 Doubly stable.

Indeed, the new understanding of this situation was one reason why vulnerable bombers and missiles were replaced. Ironically, the 1950s would have been more hazardous if the decision makers had been aware of the dangers of their posture and had therefore felt greater pressure to strike first. This situation could be recreated if both sides were to rely on MIRVed ICBMs.

In the second world, the security dilemma operates because offensive and defensive postures cannot be distinguished; but it does not operate as strongly as in the first world because the defense has the advantage, and so an increment in one side's strength increases its security more than it decreases the other's. So, if both sides have reasonable subjective security requirements, are of roughly equal power, and the variables discussed earlier are favorable, it is quite likely that status-quo states can adopt compatible security policies. * * *

This world is the one that comes closest to matching most periods in history. Attacking is usually harder than defending because of the strength of fortifications and obstacles. But purely defensive postures are rarely possible because fortifications are usually supplemented by armies and mobile guns which can support an attack. In the nuclear era, this world would be one in which both sides relied on relatively invulnerable ICBMs and believed that limited nuclear war was impossible. * * *

In the third world there may be no security dilemma, but there are security problems. Because states can procure defensive systems that do not threaten others, the dilemma need not operate. But because the offense has the advantage, aggression is possible, and perhaps easy. If the offense has enough of an advantage, even a status-quo state may take the initiative rather than risk being attacked and defeated. If the offense has less of an advantage, stability and cooperation are likely because the status-quo states will procure defensive forces. They need not react to others who are similarly armed, but can wait for the warning they would receive if others started to deploy offensive weapons. But each state will have to watch the others carefully, and there is room for false suspicions. The costliness of the defense and the allure of the offense can lead to unnecessary mistrust, hostility, and war, unless some of the variables discussed earlier are operating to restrain defection.

■ ■ ■

The fourth world is doubly safe. The differentiation between offensive and defensive systems permits a way out of the security dilemma; the advantage of the defense disposes of the problems discussed in the previous paragraphs. There is no reason for a status-quo power to be tempted to procure offensive forces, and aggressors give notice of their intentions by the posture they adopt. Indeed, if the advantage of the defense is great enough, there are no security problems. The loss of the ultimate form of the power to alter the status quo would allow greater scope for the exercise of nonmilitary means and probably would tend to freeze the distribution of values.

■ ■ ■

NOTES

1. Quoted in Gerald Wheeler, *Prelude to Pearl Harbor* (Columbia: University of Missouri Press 1963), 167.

2. Quoted in Leonard Wainstein, "The Dreadnought Gap," in Robert Art and Kenneth Waltz, eds., *The Use of Force* (Boston: Little, Brown 1971), 155. * * *

3. In another article, Jervis says: "International politics sometimes resembles what is called a Prisoner's Dilemma (PD). In this scenario, two men have been caught red-handed committing a minor crime. The district attorney knows that they are also guilty of a much more serious offense. He tells each of them separately that if he confesses and squeals on his buddy, he will go free and the former colleague will go to jail for thirty years. If both of them refuse to give any information, they will be prosecuted for the minor crime and be jailed for thirty days; if they both squeal, plea-bargaining will get them ten years. In other words, as long as each criminal cares only about himself, he will confess to the more serious crime no matter what he thinks his colleague will do. If he confesses and his buddy does not, he will get the best possible outcome (freedom); if he confesses and his buddy also does so, the outcome will not be good (ten years in jail), but it will be better than keeping silent and going to jail for thirty years. Since both can

see this, both will confess. Paradoxically, if they had both been irrational and kept quiet, they would have gone to jail for only a month." (Robert Jervis, "A Political Science Perspective on the Balance of Power and the Concert," *American Historical Review* 97, no. 3 (June 1992): 720.)

4. Experimental evidence for this proposition is summarized in James Tedeschi, Barry Schlenker, and Thomas Bonoma, *Conflict, Power, and Games* (Chicago: Aldine 1973), 135–41.

5. The results of Prisoner's Dilemma games played in the laboratory support this argument. See Anatol Rapoport and Albert Chammah, *Prisoner's Dilemma* (Ann Arbor: University of Michigan Press 1965), 33–50. Also see Robert Axelrod, *Conflict of Interest* (Chicago: Markham 1970), 60–70.

6. Quoted in Bernard Brodie, *Strategy in the Missile Age* (Princeton: Princeton University Press 1959), 6.

7. Herbert York, *The Advisors: Oppenheimer, Teller, and the Superbomb* (San Francisco: Freeman 1976), 56–60.

8. Thus, when Wolfers [*Discord and Collaboration* (Baltimore: Johns Hopkins Press 1962),] 126, argues that a status-quo state that settles for rough equality of power with its adversary, rather than seeking preponderance, may be able to convince the other to reciprocate by showing that it wants only to protect itself, not menace the other, he assumes that the defense has an advantage.

9. Schelling, [*The Strategy of Conflict* (New York: Oxford University Press 1963),] chap. 9.

10. Quoted in Fritz Fischer, *War of Illusions* (New York: Norton 1975), 377, 461.

11. George Quester, *Offense and Defense in the International System* (New York: John Wiley 1977), 105–06; Sontag [*European Diplomatic History, 1871–1932* (New York: Appleton-Century-Crofts 1933)], 4–5.

12. Some were not so optimistic. Gray's remark is well-known: "The lamps are going out all over Europe; we shall not see them lit again in our life-time." The German Prime Minister, Bethmann Hollweg, also feared the consequences of the war. But the controlling view was that it would certainly pay for the winner.

13. Quoted in Martin Gilbert, *Winston S. Churchill*, III, *The Challenge of War, 1914–1916* (Boston: Houghton Mifflin 1971), 84.

14. Quester (fn. 33), 98–99. Robert Art, *The Influence of Foreign Policy on Seapower*, II (Beverly Hills: Sage Professional Papers in International Studies Series 1973), 14–18, 26–28.

15. Konrad Jarausch, "The Illusion of Limited War: Chancellor Bethmann Hollweg's Calculated Risk, July 1914," *Central European History*, II (March 1969), 50.

16. Brodie (fn. 6), 58.

17. President Roosevelt and the American delegates to the League of Nations Disarmament Conference maintained that the tank and mobile heavy artillery had re-established the dominance of the offensive, thus making disarmament more urgent (Boggs, [*Attempts to Define and Limit "Aggressive" Armament in Diplomacy and Strategy* (Columbia: University of Missouri Studies, XVI, No. 1, 1941)], pp. 31, 108), but this was a minority position and may not even have been believed by the Americans. The reduced prestige and influence of the military, and the high pressures to cut government spending throughout this period also contributed to the lowering of defense budgets.

18. Jon Kimche, *The Unfought Battle* (New York: Stein 1968); Nicholas William Bethell, *The War Hitler Won: The Fall of Poland, September 1939* (New York: Holt 1972), Alan Alexandroff and Richard Rosecrance, "Deterrence in 1939," *World Politics,* XXIX (April 1977), 404–24.

19. Roderick Macleod and Denis Kelly, eds., *Time Unguarded: The Ironside Diaries, 1937–1940* (New York: McKay 1962), 173.

20. For a short time, as France was falling, the British Cabinet did discuss reaching a negotiated peace with Hitler. The official history ignores this, but it is covered in P.M.H. Bell, *A Certain Eventuality* (Farnborough, England: Saxon House 1974), 40–48,

21. Macleod and Kelly (fn. 19), 174. In flat contradiction to common sense and almost everything they believed about modern warfare, the Allies planned an expedition to Scandinavia to cut the supply of iron ore to Germany and to aid Finland against the Russians. But the dominant mood was the one described above.

22. Brodie (fn. 6), 179.

23. Quoted in Merze Tate, *The United States and Armaments* (Cambridge: Harvard University Press 1948), 108.

Harold Hongju Koh

HOW IS INTERNATIONAL HUMAN RIGHTS LAW ENFORCED?

I am greatly honored to deliver this distinguished lecture, particularly given the illustrious list of lecturers who have preceded me to this podium.[1] My own path to this podium began in Washington, D.C., where as a private lawyer I specialized in issues of international business and trade law: what most American law schools now think of as "international business transactions."[2] But even while working on these matters, I became increasingly diverted toward the novel, growing field of international human rights. While in private practice in the early 1980s, I became involved in the representation of the American hostages who had been held for 444 days in the U.S. embassy in Tehran.[3] Once starting an academic career, I took occasional forays into international human rights advocacy,[4] but my main focus remained on the law of international business transactions and United States foreign policy, two examples of what Henry Steiner and Detlev Vagts have felicitously dubbed "Transnational Legal Problems."[5]

As this decade began, international human rights law became the primary focus of both my theoretical and academic work, when I became involved with my students in a number of lawsuits in U.S. courts against human rights violators. In 1992, my students and I brought suits on behalf of the Haitian and Cuban refugees against the U.S. government[6] and a number of lawsuits against for-

eign human rights violators who had come to the United States—the former Guatemalan Minister of Defense, the former dictator of Haiti, an Indonesian general responsible for the 1991 Dili massacre in East Timor, and most recently a suit that is still ongoing in the Southern District of New York against Radovan Karadzic, the leader of the Bosnian Serbs.[7]

In each of these legal lives, as a scholar and a lawyer, I have asked the question that titles this lecture, namely, "How is International Human Rights Law Enforced?" I wouldn't be surprised if many of you hearing that question were to give a pessimistic answer: international human rights law is *not* enforced, you might say. Just take a look at the massive human rights violations in Bosnia, violations that have gone unredressed in Cambodia and Iraq; the continuing crises in the Congo, Sierra Leone, Algeria, and Burundi. Look at indicted war criminals, like Radovan Karadzic in Republica Srpska, who continue to flout the jurisdictions of the Bosnian war crimes tribunal. Look, you might say, at the world's willingness to overlook human rights violations committed by more powerful nations, such as Russia's activities in Chechnya, or China's continuing repression after Tienanmen Square. International human rights law is not enforced, you might say, because human rights norms are vague and aspirational, because enforcement mechanisms are toothless, because treaty regimes are notoriously weak, and because national governments lack the economic self-interest or the political will to restrain their own human rights violations. So if the question is "how is international human rights law

From *Indiana Law Journal* 74, no. 4 (Fall 1999): 1397–1417. This lecture was originally delivered as the January 1998 Addison C. Harris Lecture at Indiana University Bloomington's Maurer School of Law.

enforced?," many of you might answer: "not at all, or hardly at all." If you hold to this common, skeptical view of human rights enforcement, you would say that international human rights law is not enforced, like "real" domestic law; instead, it is only occasionally "complied with," by nation-states acting out of transparent convenience or self-interest.

In this lecture, let me take a somewhat different tack, asking first, "What do we mean when we say that *any* laws are enforced?" Are any laws perfectly enforced? Even here in Bloomington, Indiana, the height of civilization, are the parking laws or burglary laws perfectly enforced? Of course, you would concede, parking violations occur here in Bloomington, and burglaries occur, perhaps even daily; sometimes egregiously. But those facts alone hardly mean that there is no enforcement of laws against parking violations or burglary. Here in Indiana, the laws against burglary may be under-enforced, they may be imperfectly enforced, but they are enforced, through a well-understood *domestic legal process* of legislation, adjudication, and executive action. That process involves prosecutors, statutes, judges, police officers, and penalties that interact, interpret legal norms, and work to internalize those norms into the value sets of citizens like ourselves.

But if we are willing to give that answer to the question "how is domestic law enforced?", why not similarly answer the question whether *international human rights* law is enforced? In this lecture, I will argue that in much the same way, these international norms of international human rights law are underenforced, imperfectly enforced; but they *are* enforced through a complex, little-understood legal process that I call *transnational legal process*. As I have elaborated in other writing,[8] for shorthand purposes, transnational legal process can be thought of in three phases: the institutional *interaction* whereby global norms of international human rights law are debated, *interpreted*, and ultimately *internalized* by domestic legal systems. To

claim that this complex transnational legal process of enforcing international human rights law via *interaction, interpretation*, and *internalization* exists is not to say that it always works or even that it works very well. As I will be the first to concede, this process works sporadically, and that we often most clearly see its spectacular failures, as in Cambodia, Bosnia, and Rwanda. But the process of enforcing international human rights law also sometimes has its successes, which gives us reason not to ignore that process, but to try to develop and nurture it. Just as doctors used early successes in addressing polio to push our understanding of how the prevention and healing process works, lawyers can try to globalize the lessons of human rights enforcement. So if the question is "how is international human rights enforced?", my short answer is through a transnational legal process of institutional *interaction, interpretation* of legal norms, and attempts to *internalize* those norms into domestic legal systems.

With that introduction, let me divide the balance of these remarks into two parts: First, how, in theory, does transnational legal process promote national obedience of international human rights law? Second, how does transnational legal process—this process that I call "interaction, interpretation and internalization"—work in real cases?

The Theory of Transnational Legal Process

The first question, why do nations obey international human rights law, is really a subset of a much broader question: why do nations obey international law of any kind? That timeless question has troubled thinkers over historical eras dating back to the Roman Empire. * * * "Why Nations Obey?". My forthcoming book examines both the theoretical and the historical answers to that question.[9]

From Compliance to Obedience

Let us start by asking what it means to "obey" international law at all. Imagine four kinds of relationships between rules and conduct: coincidence, conformity, compliance, and obedience. For example, I have lived my whole life in the United States; but a few years ago, I took a sabbatical year in England. While there, I noticed that everybody drives on the left side of the road, as a matter of both practice and of law. Yet what is the relationship between the law and the observed practice?

One remote possibility is *coincidence*. It could be coincidence that the law is that everyone must drive on the left and that in practice everybody follows that norm. Yet coincidence might explain why one person follows a rule, but not why millions of people throughout the country do the same. That suggests a second possibility: *conformity*. If people know of the rule that you must drive on the left, they may well choose to conform their conduct to that rule when convenient; but feel no obligation to do so when inconvenient. (Perhaps some Scots, for example, swerve over and drive on the right, in remote unpopulated areas of the Hebrides.) But, is there a third possibility, *compliance*? Perhaps people are both aware of the rule and accept the rule for a variety of external reasons, for example, to get specific rewards, to receive insurance benefits, or to avoid certain kinds of bad results, such as traffic tickets, or getting hit by an oncoming car. These are instrumental reasons why someone might decide to comply with a rule even if they felt no moral obligation to obey it. Finally, there is a fourth possibility, *obedience:* the notion that a person or an organization adopts the behavior that is prescribed by the rule because he or it has somehow internalized that rule and made it a part of their internal value system.

Notice that as we move down this scale from coincidence to conformity to compliance to obedience, we see an increase of what I will call

"norm-internalization." As you move from grudgingly accepting a rule one time only to habitually obeying it, the rule transforms from being some kind of external sanction to becoming an internal imperative. We see this evolutionary process regularly in our daily lives: when you put on a bicycle helmet; when you snap on your seatbelt; when you recycle a tin can; when you do not smoke in the law school cafeteria. All of these are examples of people moving from conformity with a rule to compliance and gradually obedience, which is driven by a sense of an internalized norm. Over time, we also witness a rise in what one might call "normativity." If you see someone driving 100 mph, and then suddenly they see a police car and slow dramatically to 60 mph, you might say they are complying with; but not really obeying the speed limit. But, if one witnesses people routinely driving at the speed limit (without witnesses around), or routinely disposing of litter, or recycling without being told, we are seeing an *internalized normative form of behavior*—an increase in normativity, if you will—which derives from the incorporation of external norms or values into a person's or organization's internal value set.

There is a further point as well: namely, that the most effective form of *law-enforcement* is not the imposition of external sanction, but the inculcation of internal obedience. Most traffic laws, litter laws, tax laws and the like are enforced primarily not by enforcement officers, but by the social internalization of norms of obedience! Indeed, enforcement is maximized when a norm is so widely obeyed that external sanctions become virtually unnecessary. As my Yale colleague Bob Ellickson has demonstrated, when everyone in a community follows certain social norms out of felt internal normativity, order can be maintained without rigid systems of external legal enforcement, because self-enforcement is both more effective and more efficient than third-party controls.[10] Social psychologists who study why individuals obey the law have reached the same conclusion.[11]

The Relationship Between Enforcement and Obedience

With this background, let us now turn to the question of how *international human rights law* is enforced, which is a subset of the larger question: why do nations obey international law of any kind? In earlier writing, I have suggested that, over time, five distinct explanations have emerged to answer the question "why nations obey?": *power*; *self-interest* or rational choice; *liberal explanations* based on rule-legitimacy or political identity; *communitarian explanations*; and *legal process explanations* at the state-to-state level (what I will call "horizontal" or "international legal process" explanations) and from the international-to-national level (what I will call "vertical" or "transnational legal process explanations").[12]

In their current form, each of these five approaches gives their own short answer to the question "how is international human rights law enforced?" Let me start with the realists, who date back to Thomas Hobbes, but include such modern-day theorists as George Kennan, Hans Morgenthau, and Henry Kissinger. To the question "why do nations obey international law?", their short answer is *power*: nations never truly "obey" international law, they only comply with it, because someone else makes them. Why, for example, why did Iraq ultimately respect the borders of Kuwait? In the end, because the other nations of the world came in and drove Saddam out! Under this view, nations can be coerced or bribed to follow certain rules, or even induced to bargain in the shadow of such incentives. But in the end, the critical factor is neither altruistic or normative, only the realist values of power and coercion.[13] Thus, the familiar power explanation traces back to Thucydides: the strong states do what they can, the weak states suffer what they must, but in the end there is no real "obedience" of international law, only such coincidence between national conduct and international rules that results from power and coercion.

There is a second, kinder and gentler explanation, based on the self-interest rationales favored by the vibrant school of "rational choice" theory.[14] Under this explanation, nations may choose rationally to follow certain global rules out of a sense of self-interest. After participating in game-theoretic discussions, to avoid multi-party prisoners' dilemma, nations may decide to cooperate around certain rules, which lead them to establish what international relations theorists call "regimes": governing arrangements in which certain governing norms, rules, and decisionmaking procedures come to predominate because the nations in their long-term self-interests have calculated that they should follow a presumption favoring compliance with such rules.

This "self-interest" rationale helps explains why, for example, complex global rules have emerged in a whole variety of international areas in which nations have established regimes structured around legal rules born of self-interested cooperation. In the contemporary era, for example, talented international relations scholars such as Robert Keohane, Duncan Snidal, and Oran Young have applied increasingly sophisticated rational choice techniques to argue for such an instrumental, interest-based view of international law. Recently, a number of legal scholars, most prominently Kenneth Abbott, Alan Sykes, and John Setear have espoused a similar, "rationalistic" legal vision. Under the rationalist account, participants in a given issue area will develop a set of governing arrangements, along with a set of expectations, rules, and decisionmaking procedures—in other words, a regime—both to restrain the participants and to provide means for achieving their common aims. Within these regimes, international law stabilizes expectations and promotes compliance by reducing transaction costs, providing dispute-resolution procedures, performing signaling functions, triggering negative responses, and promoting information disclosure.

Recently, more sophisticated instrumentalists have begun to disaggregate the state into its component parts, to introduce international institutions and transnational actors, to incorporate long-term self-interest, and to consider the issue within massively iterated multi-party games.[15] Subtler instrumentalists even recognize that global rules form part of the environment faced by a state and thus alter the incentives of domestic interest groups and organizations. But even so, their analysis remains thin.

The rationalists recognize *nonstate actors* as players in the transnational system, but too often ignore them because of the complexity their inclusion adds to their *game-theoretic* analysis. Nor do these analysts tell much of a domestic politics story, because they tend to operate largely at the horizontal level of the international system. Their chosen issue areas thus tend to be areas like trade and arms control, where nation-states remain the primary players and traditional realist assumptions still largely prevail. Such rationalistic, state-centric theories thus work less well, for example, in such areas as human rights, debt restructuring, or international commercial transactions, where nonstate actors abound, pursue multiple goals in complex nonzero-sum games, and interact repeatedly within institutions nested within broader informal regimes. Rationalists see law as regulating behavior by changing incentives, not altering interests or identities. The role of norms, in their view, is to reduce transactions costs in dynamic interactions among exogenously constituted actors. Shared norms, and the interactive processes by which those norms are interpreted, have little effect on state policies. In effect, they see international law as a kind of mechanical device, a switching mechanism, which facilitates the interactions of autonomous states, not as a communal decisionmaking structure that helps generate options, modify preferences, and build a normative interpretive community.

In short, my major complaint about the self-interest explanation is that it does not take account of what I consider to be an important factor—the "vertical" internalization of international norms into domestic legal systems. The rationalists' picture takes too little account of the internalizing, normative, or constitutive impact of participating in the transnational legal process. For the rationalists, the decision to obey the law remains perpetually calculated, never internally felt. Compliance always remains an instrumental computation, never an internalized normative imperative.[16]

This brings me to a third possible explanation for why international human rights laws are enforced, so-called "liberal" theories, which I divide into those scholars who follow principles of "rule legitimacy" and those who focus on national "political identity." Both sets of theorists derive their analysis from Immanuel Kant's pamphlet in 1795, *Perpetual Peace.* Rule-legitimacy theorists, led by Thomas Franck of NYU, argue that nations do feel some sort of internal "compliance pull" toward certain rules that they feel are legitimate; for example, the rules against genocide or the rules favoring diplomatic immunity. When nations perceive that rules are legitimate, either because they meet some procedural standard of legitimacy or some substantive notion of due process or distributive justice, they will obey that rule because they are "normatively pulled" toward that rule by its legitimacy.[17]

In my view, this rule-legitimacy approach is problematic because it claims to draw its power from the legitimacy of rules themselves, rather than from communitarian and legal process pressures. In fact, most of us do not litter when others are watching, but not because the no-littering *rule* itself has such compliance pull, but because of a combination of internal impulse and felt peer pressure. In the same way, Franck's rule-legitimacy ends up being another way of saying that a state obeys a norm because it has been both internalized, and is being enforced by "communitarian peer pressure" (which, I will argue below, is really a form of transnational legal process).[18]

A second view, pressed strongly by other members of this liberal school, argues that whether or not nations comply with international law depends crucially on the extent to which their political identity is based on liberal democracy. This approach derives from a branch of international relations literature known as the "Democratic Peace" literature, pioneered by Michael Doyle of Princeton, my Yale colleague Bruce Russett, and many others who have sought to verify a basic tenet of Kant's writing that liberal democracies do not go to war with each other. The many adherents of this view include President Clinton, who in October of 1995 opined that promoting democracies that participate in the new global marketplace is the right thing to do because we know that these democracies are less likely to go to war.

Transposing this basic maxim to international law, several Harvard theorists, Anne-Marie Slaughter and Andrew Moravcsik, have flipped this maxim, arguing not so much that democracies do not fight each other, but rather, that democracies are more inclined to "do law" with one another. For these analysts, the key variable for whether a nation will or will not obey international law is whether they can be characterized as "liberal" in identity, i.e., having certain democratic attributes such as a form of representative government, civil and political rights, and an independent judicial system dedicated to the rule of law. Not surprisingly, many liberal scholars focus on European Union law, noting that the European system of human rights works because it is largely composed of liberal democracies, who share reasons for collective obedience. This helps explain why, for example, the embryonic African human rights system—a collection of democracies and authoritarian systems—does not work nearly as well.

What is troubling about this view is that it suggests that liberal states interact mainly in a zone of law, while liberal and illiberal states interact in a zone of politics. But in my view, any analysis that treats a state's identity as somehow exogenously or permanently given, is overly essentialist. National identities, like national interests, are socially constructed products of culture, ideology, learning, and knowledge. As we have witnessed, nations like South Africa, Nigeria, Indonesia, Poland, Argentina, Chile, and the Czech Republic are neither permanently liberal nor illiberal, but transition back and forth from dictatorship to democracy. As Laurence Whitehead has argued, democratization has powerful international dimensions, potentially spreading from one country to another by contagion, control, or consent.[19] Liberal identity analysis does not directly address the impact of compliance on democratization, and thus leaves unanswered a critical, constructivist question: to what extent does compliance with international law itself help *constitute the identity* of a state as law-abiding, and hence, as "liberal" or not? The notion that "only liberal states do law with one another" can be empirically falsified, particularly in such areas as international commercial law, where even rogue states like Libya tend to abide fastidiously by private international law rules on letters of credit without regard to whether they are representative democracies. Finally, like the "cultural relativist" argument in human rights, the claim that nonliberal states somehow do *not* participate in a zone of law denies the universalism of international law and effectively condones dealing with nonliberal states within a realist world of power politics.

In more recent writings, some liberal authors have revised their positions to say that they view liberal states not as actors, but as representative *agents* for various institutions and groups within civil society. These institutions and groups are more likely to engage in transborder cooperation with one another, thus predicting greater levels of transnational legal relations among liberal states. But if this is so, what it suggests is that the density of a state's *interactions* in the transnational legal process—not its label as liberal or illiberal—is the key to explaining its level of compliance with international law.

A fourth possible explanation—"communitarian" reasons—can be found in the English "International Society" school of International Relations, particularly in the work of Martin Wight and Hedley Bull, who traced their international origins back to the Dutch international law scholar Grotius. These theorists argue that nations obey international law because of the values of the international society of which they are a part. So, for example, the Czech Republic, Poland and Hungary now feel peer pressure to obey international law because of their community ties, now as NATO nations. The idea is that one's membership in a community helps to define how one views the obligations of that community. So, for example, when someone becomes a member of a church, they decide they will conduct their lives differently because they now view themselves as Catholic, Jewish, or Muslim. Similarly, under this view, the governments of Russia, Ukraine, and Turkey should all feel communitarian pressure to obey the European Convention on Human Rights—the "rules of their church"—because they have all now become members of the Council of Europe.

Unlike a liberal approach, this communitarian, constructivist approach at least recognizes the *positive transformational effects* of a state's repeated participation in the legal process. At the same time, however, the approach gives too little study to the vertical "transmission belt" whereby the norms created by international society infiltrate into *domestic* society. The *existence* of international community may explain the *horizontal* pressures to compliance generated among nation-states on the global plane, but it does not clarify the *vertical process* whereby transnational actors interact in various fora, generate and interpret international norms, and then seek to internalize those norms domestically, as future determinants of why nations obey.

Fifth and finally, there are so-called "legal process" explanations for why nations obey international law. Let me distinguish here between what I call "international legal process" or horizontal reasons for compliance, which tend to function at a government-to-government level,[20] and the so-called "vertical" explanation, which focuses on the relationship between the international and the domestic legal systems. Suppose, for example, that the government of Canada wishes to urge Japan to join the global land mine treaty. Initially, the two governments will engage in government-to-government discussions at the "horizontal" nation-state level within an intergovernmental process organized by the United Nations. But at the same time, there is also a "vertical," transnational process whereby governments, intergovernmental organizations, nongovernmental organizations, and private citizens argue together about why nations should obey international human rights law. Through this vertical dynamic, international rules that are developed at a government-to-government level gradually work their way down and become internalized into domestic legal structure. Take, for example, recent legal enactments whereby global norms regarding genocide, war crimes, torture, and religious freedom have become internalized into American legal rules.

What I have just recounted is a very compressed version of a small bookshelf of political science and international law and literature. But my broader point, simply speaking, is that all five explanations—power, self-interest, liberal theories, communitarian theories, and legal process explanations—work together to help explain why nations obey international law. These five explanatory strands work together as complementary conceptual lenses to give a richer explanation of why compliance with international law does, or does not, occur in particular cases.

To clarify, let me ask the parallel question, how is domestic law enforced? What is the explanation, for example, for why we now buckle our seatbelts, even though nobody wore seatbelts only a quarter of a century ago? Of course, there are many reasons, but if you thought to explain the change in compliance, you probably would give a variety of explanations. If you organized those explanations in your own mind, they would likely fall under five headings: power or coercion, self-interest, liberal theories, communitarian explanations, and legal process explanations.

Why do I now wear a seatbelt, when I never did before? First, because after the seatbelt rule was issued, a lot of tickets were given out and I felt coerced to comply: a power explanation. A second factor: self-interest. People calculated that it is more rational to wear your seatbelt to avoid injury, sanction, or to gain insurance benefits. Third, the seatbelt rule acquired "rule-legitimacy" and over time developed a compliance pull. Over time, this became part of one's sense of personal identity. Individuals calculated: "If I am a law-abiding person, I ought to obey the seatbelt laws." Partly, the rationale was communitarian. Authorities exhorted people with slogans such as "Seatbelts Save Lives." And fifth and finally, the seatbelt rule was inculcated via legal process. Seatbelts were required by state laws, required by federal highway standards; incorporated into federal automotive standards and became part of the way the automobiles were made. Now you cannot get into a car and drive without buckling your seatbelt without every bell and whistle and electronic voice in the car erupting into a cacophony of noise, making your life miserable until you buckle your seatbelt!

So in short, how are seatbelt laws enforced? Not by any one of these factors acting alone, but by all of them acting in combination. As we move through the five explanations—from power to legal process—we also move from external enforcement of legal rules to internal obedience with legal rules. True compliance is not the result of externally imposed sanctions so much as internally felt norms. In other words, as we move from external to internal factors, we also move from coercive to constitutive behavior. My children, who have been wholly socialized to wear seatbelts, have wholly internalized the norm. They view wearing seatbelts as an integral part of what it means to be a law-

abiding person. As always, the best way to enforce legal norms is not to coerce action, not to impose sanctions, but to change the way that people think about themselves: whether as teetotalers, safe drivers, or regular taxpayers. In short, our prime way to enforce the law is to encourage people to bring rules home, to internalize rules inside themselves, to transform themselves from lawless into law-abiding individuals.

What does this have to do with international human rights law? I would argue that in the international arena, we are seeing the exact same process at work; a process by which norms and rules are generated and internalized and become internal rules, normative rules, and rules that constitute new nations. The best example we have is South Africa, a country which for many years was an outlaw, was subjected to tremendous external pressure and coercive mechanisms over a long period of time. Through a gradual process, South Africa has converted itself into a country that has undergone a fundamental political transformation. It has now reconstituted itself as a law-abiding country that through its constitutional processes has internalized new norms of international human rights law as domestic law.

In the same way, if the United States is attempting to encourage China to follow norms of international human rights law, the analysis above suggests the need to act at all five levels: at the level of power and coercion, to apply external and political sanctions; at the level of self-interest, to develop carrots that can be offered to China in terms of trade benefits or other kinds of economic incentives; at the level of liberal theory, to encourage Hong Kong's liberal legal identity to bubble up to the Beijing government; at the level of communitarian values, to seek to encourage China to ratify the International Covenant on Civil and Political Rights and other multilateral communities of international human rights observance; and finally, from a legal process perspective, to seek to engage the Chinese people and groups in civil society in a variety of international interactions that will cause them to internalize norms of international human rights law. As with the seatbelt example, our goal is not simply to coerce conduct. More fundamentally, we seek to encourage a change in the nature of the Chinese political identity to reconstitute China as a nation that abides by core norms of international human rights law. In short, a theory of transnational legal process seeks to enforce international norms by motivating nation-states to *obey* international human rights law—out of a sense of internal acceptance of international law—as opposed to merely conforming to or complying with specific international legal rules when the state finds it convenient.

How Is International Human Rights Law Enforced?

Against this background, how should we now understand the recent history of international human rights enforcement? Here let me contrast the two "process" stories, the one that everyone usually looks at and the one that I think people should look at. Let me contrast what I will call the horizontal story of enforcement with what I prefer: the vertical, transnational story of human rights enforcement.

The "Horizontal" Story

The conventional "horizontal" story about international human rights law enforcement is that international human rights law was born about fifty years ago, the product of the U.N. Charter, the Nuremberg and Tokyo war crimes trials, and the Universal Declaration of Human Rights. Under this view, the principal enforcers of human rights law have always been nation-states, who have always interacted with one another on an interstate, government-to-government level. The U.N. Charter introduced into this picture U.N. organizations and U.N. norms, which soon led to regional human rights systems as well: in Europe, the Strasbourg (Council of Europe) and Helsinki (Organization of Security and Cooperation in Europe) process; in the Americas, the Inter-American Commission and Court of Human Rights; and far less well-developed regional human rights systems in Africa, the Middle East, and Asia.

In this post-war order, an international regime developed in which governments and intergovernmental organizations began to put pressure on each other—always at a horizontal, intergovernmental level—to comply with human rights, invoking such universal treaty norms as the international covenants on civil and political and economic, social and cultural rights. U.N. organizations, such as the U.N. Human Rights Commission, and treaty-based organizations, such as the U.N. Human Rights Committee, participated as intergovernmental actors in this horizontal international regime, which addressed all manner of global issues: worker rights, racial discrimination, the rights of children, women, and indigenous peoples. As we soon saw, the difficulties of this horizontal, state-to-state enforcement mechanism were legion: the rules were largely declaratory and precatory, and the few mechanisms created had virtually no enforcement. Occasionally new mechanisms would be created: judicial fora, such as the Yugoslav and Rwandan War Crimes Tribunal, or new executive actors, such as the U.N. High Commissioner on Human Rights, or new quasi-legislative fora, such as the Vienna Conference on Human Rights or the 1995 Beijing Women's Conference. Despite these occasional advances, the overall picture of this standard enforcement story is one of impotence, ineffectiveness, of a horizontal system where the key actors are nation-states and intergovernmental organizations, the key forums are governmental forums, and the key transactions are transactions between states and other states.

The "Vertical" Story

If one accepts the horizontal story as the entire picture of human rights enforcement, then the glass is indeed more than half empty. But what is the vertical picture? The "vertical" story of human rights enforcement, I would argue, is a much richer picture: one that focuses on a transnational legal process that includes a different set of actors, fora, and transactions. As I have recently argued in my Frankel Lecture, "Bringing International Law Home," the key agents in this transnational legal process are transnational norm entrepreneurs, governmental norm sponsors, transnational issue networks, interpretive communities and law-declaring fora, bureaucratic compliance procedures, and issue linkages among issue areas.[21]

Many efforts at human rights norm-internalization are begun not by nation-states, but by "transnational norm entrepreneurs," private transnational organizations or individuals who mobilize popular opinion and political support within their host country and abroad for the development of a universal human rights norm. Such norm entrepreneurs first became prominent in the nineteenth century, when activists such as Lord William Wilberforce and the British and Foreign Anti-Slavery Society pressed for treaties prohibiting the slave trade,[22] Jean-Henri Dunant founded the International Committee of the Red Cross,[23] and Christian peace activists, such as America's William Ladd and Elihu Burritt, promoted public international arbitration and permanent international criminal courts.[24] Modern-day entrepreneurs have included individuals as diverse as Eleanor Roosevelt, Jesse Jackson, the Dalai Lama, Aung Sang Suu Kyi, and Princess Diana. These nongovernmental actors seek to develop *transnational issue networks*[25] to discuss and generate political solutions among concerned individuals at the domestic, regional and international levels, among government agencies, intergovernmental organizations, international and domestic, academics, and private foundations. Moreover, these norm entrepreneurs seek national government officials and bureaucracies concerned with the same issue areas and seek to enlist them as allies in their transnational cause. These *governmental norm sponsors*—for example, U.N. Human Rights Commissioner Mary Robinson, Presidents Oscar Arias of Costa Rica, Jimmy Carter of the United States, and the Pope, to take just a few prominent ones, use their official positions to promote normative positions. These transnational actors then seek governmental and nongovernmental fora competent to declare both general norms of international law (e.g., treaties) and *specific interpretation* of those norms in particular circumstances (e.g., particular interpretations of treaties and customary international law rules). Such law-declaring fora thus include treaty regimes; domestic, regional, and international courts; ad hoc tribunals; domestic and regional legislatures; executive entities; international publicists; and nongovernmental organizations: law-declaring fora that create an "interpretive community" that is capable of defining, elaborating and testing the definition of particular norms and their violation.[26]

The next vertical step is for national governments to internalize norm-interpretations issued by the global interpretive community into their domestic bureaucratic and political structures. Within national governments and intergovernmental organizations, for example, in-house lawyers and legal advisers acquire institutional mandates to ensure that the government's policies conform to international legal standards that have become imbedded in domestic law. Such institutional mandates to justify noncompliance with international legal norms may be found within the legal advising apparatus of national governments, in the Executive Branch, (e.g., the Legal Adviser's Office at the U.S. State Department), the legislature, as well as in intergovernmental organizations (e.g., the United Nations, the OAS, etc.).[27]

In the same way as corporations develop standard operating procedures to address new domestic mandates regarding corporate sentencing guidelines, occupational health and safety, and sexual harassment, domestic institutions adopt standard operating procedures, and other internal mechanisms to maintain habitual compliance with the internalized international norms. These institutions evolve in path-dependent routes that avoid conflict with the internalized norms.[28] Thus, over time, domestic decisionmaking structures become "enmeshed" with international legal norms, so that institutional arrangements for the making and maintenance of an international commitment become entrenched in domestic legal and political processes.[29] Gradually, legal ideologies come to prevail among domestic decisionmakers so that they seek to avoid perceptions that their actions will be perceived as domestically unlawful. Finally, strong process linkages exist across issue areas. Thus, when the United States adopts a twelve-mile limit in the ocean law area, for example, it is bound by it when dealing with refugees sailing toward U.S. shores.[30] Because international legal obligations tend to be closely interconnected, even a single deviation tends to lead noncompliant nations into vicious cycles of treaty violation. These institutional habits soon lead nations into default patterns of compliance. These patterns act like riverbeds, which channel conduct along compliant pathways. When a nation deviates from that pattern of presumptive compliance, frictions are created.

By so saying, I do not mean to suggest that international legal violations never occur. I merely suggest viewing human rights enforcement through vertical, "transnational legal process" lenses can help explain why in Louis Henkin's famous phrase, "almost all nations observe almost all principles of international law almost all of the time."[31] To avoid such frictions in its continuing interactions, a nation's bureaucracies or interest groups may press their leaders to shift over time from a policy of violation into one of compliance. Thus it is through this repeated cycle of interaction, interpretation, and internalization—this transnational legal process—that international law acquires its "stickiness," and that nations come to "obey" international human rights law out of a perceived self-interest that becomes institutional habit.

The Pattern Illustrated

By telling the vertical story of transnational legal enforcement, I am not saying that the "horizontal," international legal process picture is wrong. I am just saying it is incomplete. A state-to-state process account simply does not capture the full picture of how international human rights norms are currently generated, brought into domestic systems, and then brought back up to the international level. Take, for example, the recent international drive to limit the use of landmines, which began almost twenty years ago.[32] Despite the development and ratification of a treaty earlier this century banning the use of landmines against civilians, an international norm against the practice had not developed.

Instead, the key step toward a global ban on landmines was taken by nongovernmental organizations in conjunction with the efforts of one U.S. senator. At the end of 1991, a group of nongovernmental activists met in Washington, D.C. and decided to create the International Campaign to Ban Landmines, which had the elimination of landmines as its goal.[33] The organization enlisted the support of a governmental norm entrepreneur, Sen. Patrick J. Leahy, who introduced a measure, passed by the Congress and signed by President Bush in 1992, which prohibited the export of landmines by the United States for one year.[34] Soon, the nongovernmental organizations received the support of other transnational figures, including Pope John Paul II,[35] Princess Diana,[36] and the International Committee of the Red Cross. Frustrated with what they perceived to be a lack of progress toward a total ban through the U.N.-sponsored efforts, nongovernmental organizations and other countries created a new law-declaring forum, the so-called "Ottawa process," in the process enlisting another governmental sponsor, Canadian Foreign Minister Lloyd Axworthy. In the end, the Ottawa process reached agreement on the Convention on the Prohibition of the Use, Stockpiling, Production and Transfer of Anti-Personnel Mines and on Their Destruction,[37] which has now been signed by more than 120 countries. Although the United States initially declined to sign the Convention, the new regime prodded the United States to enact a moratorium on the sale of landmines, to develop new technologies to aid in mine detection and demining, and to increase the amount of money that it spends on these programs to at least $100 million per year.[38] The United States further committed itself to stop using all antipersonnel mines except in Korea by 2003, and to sign the treaty itself by the year 2006. Although it remains to be seen whether the Senate will soon ratify the Convention, the United States government may, within the next decade, *obey* the Convention by fully internalizing the Convention's norms into the governing practices of the U.S. government.

Note that under the vertical, transnational enforcement story that I have told, the central actors are not so much governmental entities as nongovernmental organizations and individuals. Today, modern transnational norm entrepreneurs include most of our recent Nobel Peace Prize winners: Burma's Aung San Suu Kyi, East Timor's Bishop Belo and Jose Ramos-Horta, Tibet's Dalai Lama, Britain's Amnesty International, and America's Martin Luther King Jr. and Jody Williams of the Landmines Coalition. These are people who without governmental portfolio are able to transact a different kind of process, focusing at times on creating new forums to develop new international norms. Their focus is less on the horizontal process among nation-states as upon what I call "vertical" or transnational process. Their effort is to try to bring human rights law home, by trying to internalize it into domestic systems through a process of interaction, interpretation, and internalization.

How, precisely, is this internalization accomplished? In earlier work, I have sought to distinguish among social, political and legal internalization:

- *Social internalization*, I argue, occurs when a norm acquires so much public legitimacy that there is widespread general adherence to it.
- *Political internalization* occurs when the political elites accept an international norm, and advocate its adoption as a matter of government policy.
- *Legal internalization* occurs when an international norm is incorporated into the domestic legal system through executive action, legislative action, judicial interpretation, or some combination of the three. Some legal systems establish their receptivity to internalization of international norms through constitutional law rules regarding the extent to which treaties are or are not self-executing and rules of customary international law are or are not automatically incorporated into domestic law.[39] Virtually all legal systems also have explicit mechanisms whereby executive, legislative, and judicial institutions may domesticate international norms. Thus, the landmines case exemplified the incorporation of an emerging norm of international law into U.S. law and policy largely through the *executive action* of the President and his agencies. *Legislative* internalization occurs when international law norms are embedded into constitutional norms or binding domestic legislation that officials of a noncomplying government must obey as part of the domestic legal fabric. *Judicial internalization* occurs when litigation in domestic courts provokes judicial incorporation of international law norms into domestic law, statutes, or constitutional norms.

The precise sequencing among political, legal, and social internalization, and among the different forms of legal internalization, will vary from case to case. Sometimes an international norm is socially internalized long before it is politically or legally internalized. Thus, for example, the United States was the moving force behind the drafting and signature of the Genocide Convention in 1948, but the U.S. Senate did not formally ratify the Convention and implement it as U.S. domestic law until November 1988, long after the norm against genocide had acquired widespread social legitimacy.[40] In other cases, *legal* norm-internalization prompted by a transnational legal process of interaction and internalization helps to trigger the process of political and social internalization of global norms. By domesticating international rules, transnational legal process thereby spurs internal acceptance of international human rights principles.

The process can be viewed as having four phases: interaction, interpretation, internalization, and obedience. One or more transnational actors provokes an *interaction* (or series of interactions) with another in a law-declaring forum, which forces an *interpretation* or enunciation of the global norm applicable to the situation. By so doing, the moving party seeks not simply to coerce the other party, but to *internalize* the new interpretation of the international norm into the other party's internal normative system. Its aim is to "bind" that other party to obey the interpretation as part of its internal value set. That party's perception that it now has an internal obligation to follow the international norm as it has been domestically interpreted leads it to step four: *obedience to* the newly interpreted norm.

Take, for example, the efforts of U.S. courts to define a U.S. law of torture under the Alien Tort Statute since *Filartiga v. Pena-Irala*.[41] The U.S. Senate has been traditionally reluctant to ratify human rights treaties, even though the U.S. government was one of the primary drafters of these treaties in the postwar era. The Torture Convention, the Genocide Convention, and many others lay unratified by the U.S. government despite this initial input. In 1980, beginning with *Filartiga*, private U.S. human rights lawyers began to bring a series of domestic lawsuits against foreign violators to promote domestic judicial incorporation of the norm against torture under a little-known eighteenth-century statute, the Alien Tort Statute. Over fifteen decades, a string of U.S. courts have ruled that torture is a violation not only of international law, but also of U.S. law. In the early 1990s, these legal internalizations of the norm against torture were cited as precedents for Congress to enact a Torture Victim Protection Act,[42] a statute whose drafting and enactment helped persuade skeptical officials of the Bush Administration to acquiesce in U.S. ratification of the U.N. Torture Convention. Once again, an international law norm trickled down, was internalized, and bubbled back up into new international law.

In the United Kingdom, the issue of legislative internalization has similarly been brought to the forefront in recent years by the election of the Labour party, which promised, if elected, to incorporate the European Convention on Human Rights into United Kingdom law. This issue has been a major human rights issue in British politics since the Clement Attlee Government first ratified the Convention in the early 1950's. Since then, the Convention has been internalized in part through judicial construction. When total judicial incorporation efforts failed, a political internalization movement arose, which at this writing will shortly bring about *legal* internalization of the European Convention into U.K. law by an act of Parliament.[43]

Or, take finally the cases of the Haitian and Cuban boat people, in which my students and I were involved for several years. The United States had signed and ratified the Refugee Convention of 1951,[44] a multilateral treaty at the "horizontal" level whereby it agreed not to return refugees to their persecutors. But when the Haitian refugees began fleeing to the United States in 1991, it effectively reneged on that commitment and began to return the refugees, claiming that the Refugee Convention did not bar extraterritorial repatriations. In fact, Congress had passed a statute as part of the Immigration and Nationality Act which required unequivocally that refugees not be returned to their persecutors, thus ostensibly internalizing the treaty into domestic statute. And so on behalf of the Haitian refugees my students and I brought a lawsuit in which we argued that the courts should enforce the extraterritorial nonreturn rule as a matter of U.S. domestic law. We used a "judicialization strategy" to try to reinforce the concept of legal internalization of the international norm against extraterritorial repatriations.

In the end, the Supreme Court rejected our arguments, leaving the United States legally free to continue the extraterritorial return policy.[45] But other international forums, such as the U.N. High Commission on Refugees, the Inter-American Commission on Human Rights, and other bodies began to condemn the U.S. action. Various legislative efforts were made to overturn the Supreme Court's ruling, and the issue later became the subject of domestic political pressure from the African-American community, the Congressional Black Caucus, and Trans-Africa, all of whom began to promote the notion of a safe haven for Haitian refugees. Finally, in the fall of 1994, the U.S. government changed its Haitian policy, and intervened to return the refugees. When the issue arose again the following year, with regard to fleeing Cuban refugees, the Administration first resisted, then ultimately admitted into the United States those Cuban refugees being detained at offshore refugee camps. Although the U.S. stated policy remains problematic, at this writing, the actual practice of the U.S. government has moved into greater compliance with international law.

Conclusion

Let me close with two thoughts. First, the foregoing analysis teaches something about our duty, as citizens, to participate in transnational legal process. It is sometimes said that someone who, by acquiring medical training, comes to understand the human body acquires as well a moral duty not just to observe disease, but to try to cure it. In the same way, I would argue, a lawyer who acquires knowledge of the body politic acquires a duty not simply to observe transnational legal process, but to try to influence it. Once one comes to understand the process by which international human rights norms can be generated and internalized into domestic legal systems, one acquires a concomitant duty, I believe, to try to influence that process, to try to change the feelings of that body politic to promote greater obedience with international human rights norms.

In that effort, every citizen counts. To this, many Americans might say, "What can one person really do? Isn't such influence beyond the capacity of any one person?" But if you look at these people I have mentioned in this lecture—Aung Sun Suu Kyi, Jody Williams, Nelson Mandela, Martin Luther King Jr.—could they have not said the same thing? In response, many students might say: "But surely, I am not such a world historical figure," to which I would answer, "You don't need to be a Nobel Prize winner to make a difference. Just look at Rosa Parks, or Linda Brown, or Fred Korematsu, ordinary people who simply said that they would not go to the back of the bus, or attend a segregated school, or live in a Japanese internment camp." In short, we need look no further than those individuals who have triggered these legal processes in our own lifetime to promote the enforcement of human rights norms.

The struggle of these individuals reminds us again of the remarkable words of Robert Kennedy, which are etched on his grave in Arlington Cemetery:

Each time a man stands up for an ideal, or acts to improve the lot of others, or strikes out against injustice, he sends forth a tiny ripple of hope, and crossing each other from a million different centers of energy and daring, those ripples build a current that can sweep down the mightiest walls of oppression and resistance.

What he is talking about, in the end, is the need for individuals to activate transnational legal process. As proof that what he says is indeed possible, one need look only at the country in which he said those words: South Africa, in 1966, a country which only three decades later has now been totally transformed by international human rights law.

So, in closing, if my question is "how is international human rights law enforced?", my answer is simple. International human rights law is enforced, I would say, not just by nation-states, not just by government officials, not just by world historical figures, but by people like us, by people with the courage and commitment to bring international human rights law home through a transnational legal process of interaction, interpretation, and internalization.[46] Thank you very much.

NOTES

1. Past Harris lecturers include my former Harvard professors Paul Bator and Charles Fried, as well as my current Yale colleagues Guido Calabresi, Owen Fiss, Jules Coleman, and Robert Gordon.

2. *See generally* Harold Hongju Koh, *International Business Transactions in United States Courts*, 261 Recueil des Cours 13 (1996).

3. *See* Persinger v. Islamic Republic of Iran, 729 F.2d 835 (D.C. Cir. 1984).

4. *See, e.g.,* David Cole et al., *Interpreting the Alien Tort Statute: Amicus Curiae Memorandum of International Law Scholars and Practitioners in* Trajano v. Marcos, 12 Hastings Int'l & Comp. L. Rev. 1 (1988).

5. *See generally* Henry J. Steiner et al., *Transnational Legal Problems* (4th ed. 1994).

6. *See* Cuban-American Bar Ass'n v. Christopher, 43 F.3d 1413 (11th Cir. 1995); Haitian Ctrs. Council, Inc. v. McNary, 969 F.2d 1326 (2d Cir. 1992), *vacated as moot sub nom.* Sale v. Haitian Ctrs. Council, Inc., 509 U.S. 155 (1993); Haitian Ctrs. Council, Inc. v. Sale, 823 F. Supp. 1028 (E.D.N.Y. 1993). For an account of these cases, written by three of my students, see Victoria Clawson et al., *Litigating as Law Students: An Inside Look at* Haitian Centers Council, 103 Yale L.J. 2337 (1994).

7. *See* Xuncax v. Gramajo, 886 F. Supp. 162 (D. Mass. 1995); Todd v. Panjaitan, No. 92-12255WD (D. Mass. decided Oct. 25, 1994) ($14 million judgment awarded); Doe v. Karadzic, 886, F. Supp. 734 (S.D.N.Y. 1994), *rev'd sub nom.* Kadic v. Karadzic, 70 F.3d 232 (2d Cir. 1995); Paul v. Avril, 812 F. Supp. 207 (S.D. Fla. 1993) ($41 million judgment awarded); Ortiz v. Gramajo, No. 91-11612WD (D. Mass. filed Sept. 17, 1992) ($47.5 million judgment awarded).

8. For fuller discussion of transnational legal process, see Harold Hongju Koh, *Transnational Legal Process*, 75 Neb. L. Rev. 181 (1996); Harold Hongju Koh, *The 1998 Frankel Lecture: Bringing International Law Home*, 35 Hous. L. Rev. 623 (1998) [hereinafter Koh, *Frankel Lecture*], and Harold Hongju Koh, *Why Do Nations Obey International Law?*, 106 Yale L.J. 2599 (1997) [hereinafter Koh, *Why Do Nations Obey International Law?*].

9. For the gist of [the] answer, see Koh, *Why Do Nations Obey International Law?, supra* note 8.

10. *See* Robert C. Ellickson, Order Without Law: How Neighbors Settle Disputes 132 (1991) ("A person who has 'internalized' a social norm is by definition committed to self-enforcement of a rule. . . ."); *id.* at 126 n.8 (1991) ("Whatever the origin of self-enforced moral rules, there is broad agreement that the overall system of social control must depend vitally on achieving cooperation through self-enforcement."); Robert C. Ellickson, *Bringing Culture and Human Frailty to Rational Actors: A Critique of Classical Law and Economics*, 65 Chi-Kent L. Rev. 23, 44 (1989) (arguing that the primary system of social control is a "*first-party* system of social control that would operate without external enforcers") (emphasis in original).

11. *See, e.g.,* Tom R. Tyler, Why People Obey the Law (1990) (concluding, after extensive empirical study, that people comply with law not so much because they fear punishment as because they feel that legal authorities are legitimate); *see also id.* at 4 (urging authorities who seek to promote voluntary compliance with laws to apply "[a] normative perspective [which] leads to a focus on people's internalized norms of justice and obligation," rather than "an instrumental perspective [which] regards compliance as a form of behavior occurring in response to external factors").

12. Both the historical and theoretical analysis are fleshed out in Koh, *Why Do Nations Obey International Law?, supra* note 8, from which this portion of the lecture derives.

13. The "power" rationale is captured in a famous joke often told about Henry Kissinger, who after he ceased to be the Secretary of State, reportedly went to work as a zoo keeper. After the first day, zoo patrons noticed an amazing phenomenon: that after all of these centuries, the lion was finally lying down with the lamb. The patrons ran excitedly to Dr. Kissinger, and asked, "How have you achieved this miraculous result?" The famous realist replied, "It's simple. A lamb a day!"

14. *See, e.g.,* Kenneth W. Abbott, *Modern International Relations Theory: A Prospectus for International Lawyers*, 14 Yale J. Int'l L. 335 (1989); Kenneth W. Abbott, *The Trading Nation's Dilemma: The Functions of the Law of International Trade*, 26 Harv. Int'l L.J. 501 (1985); Kenneth W. Abbott, *'Trust But Verify': The Production of Information in Arms Control Treaties and Other International Agreements*, 26 Cornell Int'l L.J. 1 (1993).

15. Duke's Robert Keohane is the leading exemplar of such a sophisticated approach. *See* Robert O. Keohane, *When Does International Law Come Home?*, 35 Hous. L. Rev. 699 (1998).

16. It would be as if every time you got into a car, you calculated *for the first time* whether or not to put on a seatbelt or to stop for a red light, rather than relying upon internalized norms of obedience.

17. Franck calls this the "compliance pull" of particular international legal rules. *See generally* Thomas M. Franck, The Power of Legitimacy Among Nations (1990).

18. Franck defines rule-legitimacy as "a property of a rule which exerts a pull towards compliance on those addressed normatively, because they believe that the rule has come into being and operates in accordance with generally accepted principles of right process," that is, an internalized view of fair legal process. *Id.* at 24 (emphasis omitted).

19. Laurence Whitehead, *Three International Dimensions of Democratization, in* The International Dimensions of Democratization 3, 5–22 (Laurence Whitehead ed., 1996) ("In the contemporary world, there is no such thing as democratization in one country, and perhaps there never was.").

20. The best exemplar of this international process view is Abram Chayes & Antonia Handler Chayes, The New Sovereignty: Compliance with International Regulatory Agreements (1995), which treats the primary instrument for maintaining compliance with treaties as "an *iterative process of discourse* among the parties, the treaty organization, and the wider public," *id.* at 4 (emphasis added).

21. *See* Koh, *Frankel Lecture, supra* note 8, at 647–70.

22. On the transnational work of Wilberforce and the British anti-slavery movement, see generally Betty Fladeland, Men and Brothers: Anglo-American Anti-Slavery Cooperation (1972), and Ethan A. Nadelmann, *Global Prohibition Regimes: The Evolution of Norms in International Society*, 44 Int'l Org. 479, 495 (1990).

23. On the work of Dunant and the International Committee of the Red Cross, which spurred the Geneva Convention of 1864 and the Hague Convention of 1899 and the movement toward codified rules of conduct in warfare, see generally Pierre Boissier, History of the International Committee of the Red Cross: From Solferino to Tsushima (1985), and Martha Finnemore, National Interests in International Society 69–88 (1996).

24. On the work of Ladd and Burritt, see Mark W. Janis, *Protestants, Progress and Peace in the Influence of Religion, in* The Influence of Religion on the Development of International Law 223 (Mark W. Janis ed., 1991).

25. *See* Kathryn Sikkink, *Human Rights, Principled Issue-Networks, and Sovereignty in Latin America*, 47 Int'l Org. 411 (1993).

26. The norm with respect to the recent genocide in Bosnia, for example, has been interpreted before such law-declaring fora as the U.N. General Assembly, the U.N. Security Council, the International Court of Justice, the International Criminal Tribunal for the Former Yugoslavia and Rwanda; the International Court of Justice, numerous scholarly groups, human rights organizations, as well as both the Congress of the United States and a U.S. federal appellate court.

27. *See* Antonio Cassese, *The Role of Legal Advisers in Ensuring that Foreign Policy Conforms to International Legal Standards*, 14 Mich. J. Int'l L. 139 (1992); Robert C. Clark, *Why So Many Lawyers? Are They Good or Bad?*, 61 Fordham L. Rev. 275, 282 (1992) (calling lawyers "specialists in normative ordering").

28. *See* Mark J. Roe, *Chaos and Evolution in Law and Economics*, 109 Harv. L. Rev. 641, 643–44 (1996) (explaining path-dependence).

29. *See* Robert O. Keohane, *Compliance with International Commitments: Politics Within a Framework of Law, International Law and International Relations Theory: Building Bridges,* 86 Am. Soc'y Int'l L. Proc. 167, 179 (1992) (discussing "institutional enmeshment," which "occurs when domestic decision making with respect to an international commitment is affected by the institutional arrangements established in the course of making or maintaining the commitment").

30. For example, Presidential Proclamation 5928, which extended the U.S. territorial sea from three to twelve miles in breadth, has since been followed throughout the U.S. executive branch as if it were internal law, and has become the basis for binding, internal Coast Guard standard operating procedures. In May 1992, the United States adopted a policy of interdicting fleeing Haitians on the high seas and repatriating them summarily to Haiti, while bringing into the United States for exclusion proceedings those Haitians who entered territorial waters. In November 1992, the U.S. Coast Guard interdicted a boat containing fleeing Haitian refugees ten miles off the coast of Florida, and began making plans to repatriate the occupants. When the 1988 opinion of the Justice Department's Office of Legal Counsel was drawn to the Deputy Associate Attorney General's attention, the Coast Guard consulted with the State and Justice Departments and brought the boat into shore, rather than repatriating the occupants. *See* Harold Hongju Koh, *Protecting the Office of Legal Counsel from Itself*, 15 Cardozo L. Rev. 513, 517–18 (1993).

31. Louis Henkin, How Nations Behave 47 (2d ed. 1979).

32. For a fuller account of this campaign, see Koh, *Frankel Lecture, supra* note 8, at 655–63.

33. *See* Raymond Bonner, *How a Group of Outsiders Moved Nations to Ban Land Mines*, N.Y. Times, Sept. 20, 1997, at A5.

34. *See id.*

35. *See id.*

36. *See, e.g.,* Roxanne Roberts, *From London, a Blitz with Glitz; Princess Diana Dazzles a Red Cross Benefit for Land Mine Victims,* Wash. Post, June 18, 1997, at D1. Princess Diana visited landmine victims in Angola and Bosnia in early 1997. *See* Raymond Bonner, *Pentagon Weighs Ending Opposition to a Ban on Mines*, N.Y. Times, Mar. 17, 1996, at A1.

37. Sept. 18, 1997, 36 I.L.M. 1507 (1997).

38. *See* Anthony DePalma, *Some See Opportunity in Global Push to Remove Land Mines*, N.Y. Times, Dec. 7, 1997, at A14.

39. The national constitutions of Ireland, the Netherlands, and Italy, for example, refer to the recognition of international legal principles as a broad policy goal, thereby requiring policymakers to take account of foreign policy guidelines deriving from international law. *See* Irish Const. art. 29, § 3; Grondwet [Constitution] [Grw. Ned.] art. 90 (Netherlands); Constituzione [Constitution] [Cost.] art. 10 (Italy).

40. *See* Genocide Convention Implementation Act of 1987 (The Proxmire Act), Pub. L. No. 100–606, 102 Stat. 3045 (codified in 18 U.S.C. §§ 1091–1093 (1994)).

41. Filartiga v. Pena-Irala, 630 F.2d 876 (2d Cir. 1980) (holding that Paraguayan human rights victims may sue Paraguayan officials under Alien Tort Statute, 28 U.S.C. § 1350 (1994), in U.S. court for civil damages arising from official torture). For a theoretical analysis of this line of doctrine, see Harold Hongju Koh, *Transnational Public Law Litigation*, 100 Yale L.J. 2347 (1991).

42. Pub. L. No. 102–256, 106 Stat. 73 (1992) (codified at 28 U.S.C. § 1350 (1994)).

43. The debate over incorporation of the European Human Rights Convention is the subject of a voluminous literature. For a political history of the incorporation effort, see generally Michael Zander, A Bill of Rights? (4th ed. 1997). For a comparative study, see Andrew Z. Drzemczewski, European Human Rights Convention in Domestic Law: A Comparative Study 177–87 (1983); Aspects of Incorporation of the European Convention of Human Rights into Domestic Law (J.P. Gardner ed., 1993); Jorg Polakiewicz & Valerie Jacob-Foltzer, *The European Human Rights Convention in Domestic Law*, 12 Hum. Rts. J. 65, 65–85, 125–42 (1991). For discussion of compliance without incorporation, see David Kinley, The European Convention on Human Rights: Compliance Without Incorporation (1993). *See also* 8(2) Halsbury's Laws of England (4th ed. 1996) (including human rights law as part of constitutional law). For bills urging incorporation, see Human Rights Bill, *as approved by the House of Lords*, 577 Parl. Deb., H.L. (5th Ser.) 1726 (1997). For

arguments as to why the Convention should be incorporated, see generally Human Rights in the United Kingdom (Richard Gordon & Richard Wilmot-Smith eds., 1996); Hon. Sir John Laws, *Is the High Court the Guardian of Fundamental Constitutional Rights?*, 1992 Pub. L. 59; Lord Lester, *The Mouse that Roared: The Human Rights Bill 1995*, 1995 Pub. L. 198; Rt. Hon. Lord Browne-Wilkinson, *The Infiltration of a Bill of Rights*, 1992 Pub. L. 397.

44. Convention Relating to the Status of Refugees, July 28, 1951, 19 U.S.T. 6259, 189 U.N.T.S. 137.

45. For analysis of the opinions, see Clawson et al., *supra* note 6.

46. Author's note: Since I wrote these words, my life has fundamentally changed. In November 1998, I took an oath as our nation's chief human rights official. At this writing, I have now spent eight months in office, traveling to some twenty-five countries. As I have traveled from Belgrade to Beijing, Colombia to Kosovo, I have become increasingly convinced of the correctness of the basic thesis I have expressed in this lecture. Although I now spend my time as a "governmental norm sponsor," rather than as a private "transnational norm entrepreneur," I continue to witness, and to attempt to influence, the transnational legal process described herein. I look forward to returning to academic life before too long, not only to finish my book manuscript on "Why Nations Obey," but also to illustrate my basic thesis with reference to my governmental experiences in Kosovo, China, Colombia, Indonesia, and elsewhere.

8

INTERNATIONAL POLITICAL ECONOMY

Economic issues are critical to understanding international relations in the twenty-first century. In the first selection here, a classic from *U.S. Power and the Multinational Corporation* (1975), Robert Gilpin concisely discusses the relationship between economics and politics. He examines the three basic conceptions of political economy (liberalism, radicalism, and mercantilism), comparing their perspectives on the nature of economic relations, their theories of change, and how they characterize the relationship between economics and politics. With trade rivalries among the major economic powers on the rise, Gilpin's classic analysis of mercantilism is more timely than ever.

One political barrier to economic cooperation between states is the holdup problem. For example, a weaker state might consider making major long-term investments to take advantage of an opportunity for trade with a stronger partner, but then shy away from the deal out of fear that the partner would condition continued trade on political demands. Allison Carnegie shows that an important contribution of international organizations is to raise the cost of holdups by embedding unequal bilateral relationships in a cooperative system of general rules.

An increasingly significant barrier to economic cooperation is populist backlash against trade and immigration. Dani Rodrik shows how these political effects are filtered through the cultural impact of general economic distress, and he notes the conditions under which populists sometimes favor international cooperation.

The coronavirus pandemic revealed another vulnerability endangering international economic cooperation: the lack of slack and redundancy in complex, fragile, globalized supply chains. Henry Farrell and Abraham Newman point out the destructive "beggar thy neighbor" policies that states adopt in the scramble to manage their own vulnerabilities.

Robert Gilpin

THE NATURE
OF POLITICAL ECONOMY

The international corporations have evidently declared ideological war on the "antiquated" nation state. . . . The charge that materialism, modernization and internationalism is the new liberal creed of corporate capitalism is a valid one. The implication is clear: the nation state as a political unit of democratic decision-making must, in the interest of "progress," yield control to the new mercantile mini-powers.[1]

While the structure of the multinational corporation is a modern concept, designed to meet the requirements of a modern age, the nation state is a very old-fashioned idea and badly adapted to serve the needs of our present complex world.[2]

These two statements—the first by Kari Levitt, a Canadian nationalist, the second by George Ball, a former United States undersecretary of state—express a dominant theme of contemporary writings on international relations. International society, we are told, is increasingly rent between its economic and its political organization. On the one hand, powerful economic and technological forces are creating a highly interdependent world economy, thus diminishing the traditional significance of national boundaries. On the other hand, the nation-state continues to command men's loyalties and to be the basic unit of political decision making. As

one writer has put the issue, "The conflict of our era is between ethnocentric nationalism and geocentric technology."[3]

Ball and Levitt represent two contending positions with respect to this conflict. Whereas Ball advocates the diminution of the power of the nation-state in order to give full rein to the productive potentialities of the multinational corporation, Levitt argues for a powerful nationalism which could counterbalance American corporate domination. What appears to one as the logical and desirable consequence of economic rationality seems to the other to be an effort on the part of American imperialism to eliminate all contending centers of power.

Although the advent of the multinational corporation has put the question of the relationship between economics and politics in a new guise, it is an old issue. In the nineteenth century, for example, it was this issue that divided classical liberals like John Stuart Mill from economic nationalists, represented by Georg Friedrich List. Whereas the former gave primacy in the organization of society to economics and the production of wealth, the latter emphasized the political determination of economic relations. As this issue is central both to the contemporary debate on the multinational corporation and to the argument of this study, this chapter analyzes the three major treatments of the relationship between economics and politics—that is, the three major ideologies of political economy.

From Robert Gilpin, *U.S. Power and the Multinational Corporation* (New York: Basic Books, 1975), chap. 1.

The Meaning of Political Economy

The argument of this study is that the relationship between economics and politics, at least in the modern world, is a reciprocal one. On the one hand, politics largely determines the framework of economic activity and channels it in directions intended to serve the interests of dominant groups; the exercise of power in all its forms is a major determinant of the nature of an economic system. On the other hand, the economic process itself tends to redistribute power and wealth; it transforms the power relationships among groups. This in turn leads to a transformation of the political system, thereby giving rise to a new structure of economic relationships. Thus, the dynamics of international relations in the modern world is largely a function of the reciprocal interaction between economics and politics.

First of all, what do I mean by "politics" or "economics"? Charles Kindleberger speaks of economics and politics as two different methods of allocating scarce resources: the first through a market mechanism, the latter through a budget.[4] Robert Keohane and Joseph Nye, in an excellent analysis of international political economy, define economics and politics in terms of two levels of analysis: those of structure and of process.[5] Politics is the domain "having to do with the establishment of an order of relations, a structure. . . ."[6] Economics deals with "short-term allocative behavior (i.e., holding institutions, fundamental assumptions, and expectations constant). . . ."[7] Like Kindleberger's definition, however, this definition tends to isolate economic and political phenomena except under certain conditions, which Keohane and Nye define as the "politicization" of the economic system. Neither formulation comes to terms adequately with the dynamic and intimate nature of the relationship between the two.

In this study, the issue of the relationship between economics and politics translates into that between wealth and power. According to this statement of the problem, economics takes as its province the creation and distribution of wealth; politics is the realm of power. I shall examine their relationship from several ideological perspectives, including my own. But what is wealth? What is power?

In response to the question, What is wealth?, an economist-colleague responded, "What do you want, my thirty-second or thirty-volume answer?" Basic concepts are elusive in economics, as in any field of inquiry. No unchallengeable definitions are possible. Ask a physicist for his definition of the nature of space, time, and matter, and you will not get a very satisfying response. What you will get is an *operational* definition, one which is usable: it permits the physicist to build an intellectual edifice whose foundations would crumble under the scrutiny of the philosopher.

Similarly, the concept of wealth, upon which the science of economics ultimately rests, cannot be clarified in a definitive way. Paul Samuelson, in his textbook, doesn't even try, though he provides a clue in his definition of economics as "the study of how men and society *choose* . . . to employ *scarce* productive resources . . . to produce various commodities . . . and distribute them for consumption."[8] Following this lead, we can say that wealth is anything (capital, land, or labor) that can generate future income; it is composed of physical assets and human capital (including embodied knowledge).

The basic concept of political science is power. Most political scientists would not stop here; they would include in the definition of political science the purpose for which power is used, whether this be the advancement of the public welfare or the domination of one group over another. In any case, few would dissent from the following statement of Harold Lasswell and Abraham Kaplan:

The concept of power is perhaps the most fundamental in the whole of political science:

the political process is the shaping, distribution, and exercise of power (in a wider sense, of all the deference values, or of influence in general.)[9]

Power as such is not the sole or even the principal goal of state behavior. Other goals or values constitute the objectives pursued by nation-states: welfare, security, prestige. But power in its several forms (military, economic, psychological) is ultimately the necessary means to achieve these goals. For this reason, nation-states are intensely jealous of and sensitive to their relative power position. The distribution of power is important because it profoundly affects the ability of states to achieve what they perceive to be their interests.

The nature of power, however, is even more elusive than that of wealth. The number and variety of definitions should be an embarrassment to political scientists. Unfortunately, this study cannot bring the intradisciplinary squabble to an end. Rather, it adopts the definition used by Hans Morgenthau in his influential *Politics among Nations*: "man's control over the minds and actions of other men."[10] Thus, power, like wealth, is the capacity to produce certain results.

Unlike wealth, however, power cannot be quantified; indeed, it cannot be overemphasized that power has an important psychological dimension. Perceptions of power relations are of critical importance; as a consequence, a fundamental task of statesmen is to manipulate the perceptions of other statesmen regarding the distribution of power. Moreover, power is relative to a specific situation or set of circumstances; there is no single hierarchy of power in international relations. Power may take many forms—military, economic, or psychological—though, in the final analysis, force is the ultimate form of power. Finally, the inability to predict the behavior of others or the outcome of events is of great significance. Uncertainty regarding the distribution of power and the ability of the statesmen to control events plays an important role in international relations.

Ultimately, the determination of the distribution of power can be made only in retrospect as a consequence of war. It is precisely for this reason that war has had, unfortunately, such a central place in the history of international relations. In short, power is an elusive concept indeed upon which to erect a science of politics.

■   ■   ■

The distinction * * * between economics as the science of wealth and politics as the science of power is essentially an analytical one. In the real world, wealth and power are ultimately joined. This, in fact, is the basic rationale for a political economy of international relations. But in order to develop the argument of this study, wealth and power will be treated, at least for the moment, as analytically distinct.

To provide a perspective on the nature of political economy, the next section of the chapter will discuss the three prevailing conceptions of political economy: liberalism, Marxism, and mercantilism. Liberalism regards politics and economics as relatively separable and autonomous spheres of activities; I associate most professional economists as well as many other academics, businessmen, and American officials with this outlook. Marxism refers to the radical critique of capitalism identified with Karl Marx and his contemporary disciples; according to this conception, economics determines politics and political structure. Mercantilism is a more questionable term because of its historical association with the desire of nation-states for a trade surplus and for treasure (money). One must distinguish, however, between the specific form mercantilism took in the seventeenth and eighteenth centuries and the general outlook of mercantilistic thought. The essence of the mercantilistic perspective, whether it is labeled economic nationalism, protectionism, or the doctrine of the German Historical School, is the subservience of the economy to the state and its interests—interests that range from matters of domestic welfare to those of international security. It is this more general meaning of mercantilism that is implied by the use of the term in this study.

■   ■   ■

Three Conceptions of Political Economy

The three prevailing conceptions of political economy differ on many points. Several critical differences will be examined in this brief comparison. (See Table 8.1.)

The Nature of Economic Relations

The basic assumption of liberalism is that the nature of international economic relations is essentially harmonious. Herein lay the great intellectual innovation of Adam Smith. Disputing his mercantilist predecessors, Smith argued that international economic relations could be made a positive-sum game; that is to say, everyone could gain, and no one need lose, from a proper ordering of economic relations, albeit the distribution of these gains may not be equal. Following Smith, liberalism assumes that there is a basic harmony between true national interest and cosmopolitan economic interest. Thus, a prominent member of this school of thought has written, in response to a radical critique, that the economic efficiency of the sterling standard in the nineteenth century and that of the dollar standard in the twentieth century serve "the cosmopolitan interest in a national form."[11] Although Great Britain and the United States gained the most from the international role of their respective currencies, everyone else gained as well.

Liberals argue that, given this underlying identity of national and cosmopolitan interests in a free market, the state should not interfere with economic transactions across national boundaries.

Table 8.1. Comparison of the Three Conceptions of Political Economy

	LIBERALISM	MARXISM	MERCANTILISM
Nature of economic relations	Harmonious	Conflictual	Conflictual
Nature of the actors	Households and firms	Economic classes	Nation-states
Goal of economic activity	Maximization of global welfare	Maximization of class interests	Maximization of national interest
Relationship between economics and politics	Economics should determine politics	Economics does determine politics	Politics determines economics
Theory of change	Dynamic equilibrium	Tendency toward disequilibrium	Shifts in the distribution of power

Through free exchange of commodities, removal of restrictions on the flow of investment, and an international division of labor, everyone will benefit in the long run as a result of a more efficient utilization of the world's scarce resources. The national interest is therefore best served, liberals maintain, by a generous and cooperative attitude regarding economic relations with other countries. In essence, the pursuit of self-interest in a free, competitive economy achieves the greatest good for the greatest number in international no less than in the national society.

Both mercantilists and Marxists, on the other hand, begin with the premise that the essence of economic relations is conflictual. There is no underlying harmony; indeed, one group's gain is another's loss. Thus, in the language of game theory, whereas liberals regard economic relations as a nonzero-sum game, Marxists and mercantilists view economic relations as essentially a zero-sum game.

The Goal of Economic Activity

For the liberal, the goal of economic activity is the optimum or efficient use of the world's scarce resources and the maximization of world welfare. While most liberals refuse to make value judgments regarding income distribution, Marxists and mercantilists stress the distributive effects of economic relations. For the Marxist the distribution of wealth among social classes is central; for the mercantilist it is the distribution of employment, industry, and military power among nation-states that is most significant. Thus, the goal of economic (and political) activity for both Marxists and mercantilists is the redistribution of wealth and power.

The State and Public Policy

These three perspectives differ decisively in their views regarding the nature of the economic actors.

In Marxist analysis, the basic actors in both domestic and international relations are economic classes; the interests of the dominant class determine the foreign policy of the state. For mercantilists, the real actors in international economic relations are nation-states; national interest determines foreign policy. National interest may at times be influenced by the peculiar economic interests of classes, elites, or other subgroups of the society; but factors of geography, external configurations of power, and the exigencies of national survival are primary in determining foreign policy. Thus, whereas liberals speak of world welfare and Marxists of class interests, mercantilists recognize only the interests of particular nation-states.

Although liberal economists such as David Ricardo and Joseph Schumpeter recognized the importance of class conflict and neoclassical liberals analyze economic growth and policy in terms of national economies, the liberal emphasis is on the individual consumer, firm, or entrepreneur. The liberal ideal is summarized in the view of Harry Johnson that the nation-state has no meaning as an economic entity.[12]

Underlying these contrasting views are differing conceptions of the nature of the state and public policy. For liberals, the state represents an aggregation of private interests: public policy is but the outcome of a pluralistic struggle among interest groups. Marxists, on the other hand, regard the state as simply the "executive committee of the ruling class," and public policy reflects its interests. Mercantilists, however, regard the state as an organic unit in its own right: the whole is greater than the sum of its parts. Public policy, therefore, embodies the national interest or Rousseau's "general will" as conceived by the political élite.

The Relationship between Economics and Politics; Theories of Change

Liberalism, Marxism, and mercantilism also have differing views on the relationship between economics and politics. And their differences on this issue are directly relevant to their contrasting theories of international political change.

Although the liberal ideal is the separation of economics from politics in the interest of maximizing world welfare, the fulfillment of this ideal would have important political implications. The classical statement of these implications was that of Adam Smith in *The Wealth of Nations*.[13] Economic growth, Smith argued, is primarily a function of the extent of the division of labor, which in turn is dependent upon the scale of the market. Thus he attacked the barriers erected by feudal principalities and mercantilistic states against the exchange of goods and the enlargement of markets. If men were to multiply their wealth, Smith argued, the contradiction between political organization and economic rationality had to be resolved in favor of the latter. That is, the pursuit of wealth should determine the nature of the political order.

Subsequently, from nineteenth-century economic liberals to twentieth-century writers on economic integration, there has existed "the dream . . . of a great republic of world commerce, in which national boundaries would cease to have any great economic importance and the web of trade would bind all the people of the world in the prosperity of peace."[14] For liberals the long-term trend is toward world integration, wherein functions, authority, and loyalties will be transferred from "smaller units to larger ones; from states to federalism; from federalism to supranational unions and from these to superstates."[15] The logic of economic and technological development, it is argued, has set mankind on an inexorable course toward global political unification and world peace.

In Marxism, the concept of the contradiction between economic and political relations was enacted into historical law. Whereas classical liberals—although Smith less than others—held that the requirements of economic rationality *ought* to determine political relations, the Marxist position was that the mode of production does in fact determine the superstructure of political relations. Therefore, it is argued, history can be understood as the product of the dialectical process—the contradiction between the evolving techniques of production and the resistant sociopolitical system.

Although Marx and Engels wrote remarkably little on international economics, Engels, in his famous polemic, *Anti-Duhring*, explicitly considers whether economics or politics is primary in determining the structure of international relations.[16] F. K. Duhring, a minor figure in the German Historical School, had argued, in contradiction to Marxism, that property and market relations resulted less from the economic logic of capitalism than from extraeconomic political factors: "The basis of the exploitation of man by man was an historical act of force which created an exploitative economic system for the benefit of the stronger man or class."[17] Since Engels, in his attack on Duhring, used the example of the unification of Germany through the Zollverein or customs union of 1833, his analysis is directly relevant to this discussion of the relationship between economics and political organization.

Engels argued that when contradictions arise between economic and political structures, political power adapts itself to the changes in the balance of economic forces; politics yields to the dictates of economic development. Thus, in the case of nineteenth-century Germany, the requirements of industrial production had become incompatible with its feudal, politically fragmented structure. "Though political reaction was victorious in 1815 and again in 1848," he argued, "it was unable to prevent the growth of large-scale industry in Germany and the growing participation of German commerce in the world market."[18] In summary, Engels wrote, "German unity had become an economic necessity."[19]

In the view of both Smith and Engels, the nation-state represented a progressive stage in human development, because it enlarged the political realm of economic activity. In each successive economic epoch, advances in technology and an increasing scale of production necessitate an enlargement of political organization. Because the city-state and feudalism restricted the scale of production and the division of labor made possible by the Industrial Revolution, they prevented the efficient utilization of resources and were, therefore, superseded by larger political units. Smith considered this to be a desirable objective; for Engels it was an historical necessity. Thus, in the opinion of liberals, the establishment of the Zollverein was a movement toward maximizing world economic welfare;[20] for Marxists it was the unavoidable triumph of the German industrialists over the feudal aristocracy.

Mercantilist writers from Alexander Hamilton to Frederick List to Charles de Gaulle, on the other hand, have emphasized the primacy of politics; politics, in this view, determines economic organization. Whereas Marxists and liberals have pointed to the production of wealth as the basic determinant of social and political organization, the mercantilists of the German Historical School, for example, stressed the primacy of national security, industrial development, and national sentiment in international political and economic dynamics.

In response to Engels's interpretation of the unification of Germany, mercantilists would no doubt agree with Jacob Viner that "Prussia engineered the customs union primarily for political reasons, in order to gain hegemony or at least influence over the lesser German states. It was largely in order to make certain that the hegemony should be Prussian and not Austrian that Prussia continually opposed Austrian entry into the Union, either openly or by pressing for a customs union tariff lower than highly protectionist Austria could stomach."[21] In pursuit of this strategic interest, it was "Prussian might, rather than a common zeal for political unification arising out of economic partnership, (that) . . . played the major role."[22]

In contrast to Marxism, neither liberalism nor mercantilism has a developed theory of dynamics. The basic assumption of orthodox economic analysis (liberalism) is the tendency toward equilibrium; liberalism takes for granted the existing social order and given institutions. Change is assumed to be gradual and adaptive—a continuous process of dynamic equilibrium. There is no necessary connection between such political phenomena as war and revolution and the evolution of the economic system, although they would not deny that misguided statesmen can blunder into war over economic issues or that revolutions are conflicts over the distribution of wealth; but neither is inevitably linked to the evolution of the productive system. As for mercantilism, it sees change as taking place owing to shifts in the balance of power; yet, mercantilist writers such as members of the German Historical School and contemporary political realists have not developed a systematic theory of how this shift occurs.

On the other hand, dynamics is central to Marxism; indeed Marxism is essentially a theory of social *change*. It emphasizes the tendency toward *dis*equilibrium owing to changes in the means of production, and the consequent effects on the everpresent class conflict. When these tendencies can no longer be contained, the sociopolitical system breaks down through violent upheaval. Thus war and revolution are seen as an integral part of the economic process. Politics and economics are intimately joined.

Why an International Economy?

From these differences among the three ideologies, one can get a sense of their respective explanations for the existence and functioning of the international economy.

An interdependent world economy constitutes the normal state of affairs for most liberal economists. Responding to technological advances in transportation and communications, the scope of the market mechanism, according to this analysis, continuously expands. Thus, despite temporary setbacks, the long-term trend is toward global economic integration. The functioning of the international economy is determined primarily by considerations of efficiency. The role of the dollar as the basis of the international monetary system, for example, is explained by the preference for it among traders and nations as the vehicle of international commerce.[23] The system is maintained by the mutuality of the benefits provided by trade, monetary arrangements, and investment.

A second view—one shared by Marxists and mercantilists alike—is that every interdependent international economy is essentially an imperial or hierarchical system. The imperial or hegemonic power organizes trade, monetary, and investment relations in order to advance its own economic and political interests. In the absence of the economic and especially the political influence of the hegemonic power, the system would fragment into autarkic economies or regional blocs. Whereas for liberalism maintenance of harmonious international market relations is the norm, for Marxism and mercantilism conflicts of class or national interests are the norm.

■ ■ ■

NOTES

1. Kari Levitt, "The Hinterland Economy," *Canadian Forum* 50 (July–August 1970): 163.
2. George W. Ball, "The Promise of the Multinational Corporation," *Fortune*, June 1, 1967, p. 80.
3. Sidney Rolfe, "Updating Adam Smith," *Interplay* (November 1968): 15.
4. Charles Kindleberger, *Power and Money: The Economics of International Politics and the Politics of International Economics* (New York: Basic Books, 1970), p. 5.
5. Robert Keohane and Joseph Nye, "World Politics and the International Economic System," in *The Future of the International Economic Order: An Agenda for Research*, ed. C. Fred Bergsten (Lexington, MA: D. C. Heath, 1973), p. 116.
6. Ibid.
7. Ibid., p. 117.
8. Paul Samuelson, *Economics: An Introductory Analysis* (New York: McGraw-Hill, 1967), p. 5.
9. Harold Lasswell and Abraham Kaplan, *Power and Society: A Framework for Political Inquiry* (New Haven: Yale University Press, 1950), p. 75.
10. Hans Morgenthau, *Politics among Nations* (New York: Alfred A. Knopf), p. 26. For a more complex but essentially identical view, see Robert Dahl, *Modern Political Analysis* (Englewood Cliffs, NJ: Prentice-Hall, 1963).
11. Kindleberger, *Power and Money*, p. 227.
12. For Johnson's critique of economic nationalism, see Harry Johnson, ed., *Economic Nationalism in Old and New States* (Chicago: University of Chicago Press, 1967).
13. Adam Smith, *The Wealth of Nations* (New York: Modern Library, 1937).
14. J. B. Condliffe, *The Commerce of Nations* (New York: W. W. Norton, 1950), p. 136.
15. Amitai Etzioni, "The Dialectics of Supranational Unification" in *International Political Communities* (New York: Doubleday, 1966), p. 147.
16. The relevant sections appear in Ernst Wangermann, ed., *The Role of Force in History: A Study of Bismarck's Policy of Blood and Iron*, trans. Jack Cohen (New York: International Publishers, 1968).
17. Ibid., p. 12.
18. Ibid., p. 13.
19. Ibid., p. 14.
20. Gustav Stopler, *The German Economy* (New York: Harcourt, Brace and World, 1967), p. 11.
21. Jacob Viner, *The Customs Union Issue*, Studies in the Administration of International Law and Organization, no. 10 (New York: Carnegie Endowment for International Peace, 1950), pp. 98–99.
22. Ibid., p. 101.
23. Richard Cooper, "Eurodollars, Reserve Dollars, and Asymmetrics in the International Monetary System," *Journal of International Economics* 2 (September 1972): 325–44.

Allison Carnegie

STATES HELD HOSTAGE
Political Hold-Up Problems and the Effects of International Institutions

Theories of international institutions typically contend that these institutions support cooperation among all members. Some scholars have criticized this claim, suggesting that benefits accrue most to the powerful states that created the institutions, potentially at the expense of weak states.[1] In this paper, I argue that the distribution of benefits can be most productively understood by examining the effects of institutions on the relationships between certain pairs of states. States have more trouble cooperating with some partners than with others, and pairs that find cooperation difficult gain the most from membership in international institutions.

To analyze how membership in international institutions affects particular types of states, I examine the specific case of the World Trade Organization (WTO) and its predecessor, the General Agreement on Tariffs and Trade (GATT).[2] The distribution of benefits from WTO membership depends on the types of problems that the WTO can solve. Existing theories contend that the WTO can ameliorate time inconsistency problems, which occur when a country's *ex ante* incentives differ from its *ex post* incentives, but these theories offer ambiguous predictions about the differential impact of WTO membership.[3] By contrast, I determine the pairs of states that benefit most from WTO membership by identifying a specific type of

From *American Political Science Review* 108, no. 1 (February 2014): 54–57, 60–61, 67–70.

time inconsistency problem that is pervasive in international relations: the "political hold-up problem." Political hold-up problems occur when one state fails to undertake an investment due to the increased ability it would provide another state to extract political concessions. For example, states often hesitate to construct oil and natural gas pipelines because once they invest in building the pipelines, their partners can obtain political concessions by threatening to terminate oil or gas exports. I demonstrate that these problems are most acute for politically dissimilar pairs of states, in which one state has the ability and incentive to extract concessions from its potential trading partner. However, I show that the WTO can solve political hold-up problems by helping to enforce dynamic agreements, allowing countries to trade based on their economic incentives, rather than for political reasons. In so doing, the WTO can mitigate the impact of a variety of political asymmetries between countries, providing the largest benefits for politically dissimilar pairs of states. I first formalize this claim and then empirically test the implications derived from the model, finding that the WTO increases trade most between country pairs that differ in terms of capabilities, regime types, and alliances, by preventing states from holding up their trading partners for foreign policy concessions.

To understand how political hold-up problems form, consider the historical trade relations between the United States and Hawaii. In 1876, the United States signed a trade agreement with the Kingdom of Hawaii, which eliminated high U.S. sugar tariffs. Hawaii responded by ramping up sugar production for export to the United States, such that Hawaiian sugar exports to the United States rose from 21 million pounds in 1876 to 114 million pounds in 1883 (La Croix and Grandy 1997). Increasing sugar production required a large investment: sugar producers adopted new sugar processing technology, bought government and private land, undertook large-scale irrigation projects, and invested in fertilizers. The Hawaiian government signed the treaty expecting other markets for its sugar exports to open up by the time of the treaty's renewal (La Croix and Grandy 1997). However, when the treaty expired in 1883, Hawaii had no viable alternative export market (Kuykendall 1953).[4] Thus, during negotiations over the treaty's renewal, the United States demanded exclusive rights to Pearl Harbor; otherwise, the United States threatened to reinstate the high sugar tariff. The Hawaiian government conceded.

Why couldn't the United States obtain access to Pearl Harbor when the treaty was initially signed?[5] At that point, the Hawaiian government would have weighed the cost of granting access to Pearl Harbor plus the cost of the sugar investment against the economic gains from increased sugar exports. By the time the treaty was up for renewal, however, the sugar investment had already been made. Thus, the government weighed only the cost of giving up Pearl Harbor against the benefits of trading more sugar. The United States was therefore able to hold up Hawaii for the value of the sugar investment.

In general, I show that states anticipate their partners' opportunistic behavior and therefore underinvest in the production of goods for trade with these partners. While the Hawaiian government was aware that it could be held up when it chose to sign the initial agreement, it hoped that it could open other markets for its sugar by the time the treaty was renewed.[6] A less optimistic country could have refused to undertake the investment in the first place. Because states cannot commit to refrain from holding up other states, their partners underinvest, decreasing the welfare of both parties.[7]

Note that the opportunity to demand political concessions dramatically increases states' incentives to use their trade policies opportunistically. In the aforementioned example, if the U.S. government had no interest in Pearl Harbor, it may have had no reason to hold Hawaii up. Because imports of Hawaiian sugar benefited U.S. consumers, it is not clear that the U.S. government would have wanted to raise its sugar tariffs. The opportunity to link economic and political policies, however, meant that the U.S. government had a large incentive to hold Hawaii up to gain access to Pearl Harbor.

Political hold-up problems create the need for enforceable long-term trade agreements, which allow countries to credibly promise not to raise tariffs to extract political concessions. However, long-term agreements are often unenforceable in a bilateral setting. Luckily, international institutions can help to enforce these agreements, permitting countries to commit to not use their trade policies for political leverage. Countries benefit from tying their hands through the resulting increases in trade and investment. International institutions enable countries to abide by dynamic agreements through a variety of mechanisms; as argued by Axelrod and Keohane (1985, 235), members "(1) can identify defectors; (2) they are able to focus retaliation on defectors; and (3) they have sufficient long-run incentives to punish defectors."

The WTO in particular provides transparency and a loss of reputation for violators through its Dispute Settlement Body (DSB), which adjudicates disputes between WTO members. The DSB provides WTO participants with "a guarantee for the right to negotiate, a common standard for evaluating outcomes, the option for several countries to join a dispute, and incentives for states to change a policy found to violate trade rules" (Davis 2006). By developing norms and behaviors that states are expected to follow and by specifying which states are noncompliant, the DSB influences members' reputations, which serves as an effective restraint in many settings (Tomz 2007). The WTO publicizes which countries cooperate with agreements, which allows members to establish reputations for cooperation and encourages continued cooperation in the future. Conversely, if countries are known to violate agreements frequently, their partners may reduce cooperation with them by withdrawing trade concessions, becoming more reluctant to enter agreements, or becoming less cooperative in related areas (Maggi 1999). WTO rulings can also provide countries with domestic political cover for adhering to agreements (Allee and Huth 2006; Staiger and Tabellini 1999) and the ability to develop domestic reputations for compliance (Mansfield, Milner, and Rosendorff 2002). Additionally, if a country frequently breaches WTO law, what is to prevent its trading partners from recurrent violations? This could lead to a breakdown of the system as a whole, an outcome which many states have strong incentives to avoid.

The loss of reputation before the large audience of WTO members appears to be a strong deterrent, as there are many examples of the WTO helping to uphold agreements between powerful and weak states. Powerful states have high rates of compliance with WTO rulings on cases brought by weak states (Busch and Reinhardt 2003, 2004; Davis 2006; Wilson 2007). Additionally, Busch, Raciborski, and Reinhardt (2009) show that large WTO members reduce protectionist practices against small WTO members in particular. By improving members' abilities to commit to agreements, the WTO can thus help countries to limit political hold-up problems, thereby decoupling trade and politics.

Yet previous work on hold-up problems in the context of the WTO is rare and focuses largely on the determinants of institutional design, rather than on state behavior. For example, Yarbrough and Yarbrough (1992) and Goldstein and Gowa (2002) use the logic of economic hold-up problems to explain the selection of trade institutions.[8] Prior examinations of the role of the WTO point to other types of inefficiencies the WTO can help alleviate. For example, the WTO can also resolve a terms-of-trade prisoner's dilemma, where governments of large countries have an incentive to set tariffs at inefficiently high levels due to their ability to pass some of the cost onto their trading partners through the impact of their tariffs on world prices (Bagwell and Staiger 1999). Further, the WTO can allow countries to avoid succumbing to domestic political pressures (Büthe and Milner 2008; Maggi and Rodriguez-Clare 1998; Mansfield and Pevehouse 2008). Although solving hold-up problems is an important function of the WTO, it is by no means the only time inconsistency problem that the WTO can remedy. But while other theories often offer ambiguous empirical predictions, the logic of political hold-up problems generates clear, testable hypotheses.

In the next section, I present a formal model which shows that hold-up problems occur most frequently when one country has the ability and the incentive to hold up a partner country. The model demonstrates that powerful countries have a greater ability to hold up weaker countries, since weaker countries are less able to retaliate. If a weak country tries to hold up the United States, for example, the United States can threaten it with military, financial, economic, or political penalties, while a weak country would find it more difficult to punish the United States. The model also implies that countries have greater incentives to hold up nonallies and countries with dissimilar regime types, since these countries have more disparate policy goals. Because politically dissimilar countries are most susceptible to hold-up problems, trade and investment should be inefficiently low between these countries in the absence of the WTO. The main benefit of WTO membership, increased trade, should therefore accrue most heavily to these country pairs. In what follows, I formally derive these predictions and then substantiate the claims empirically, finding that the WTO increases trade most for politically dissimilar pairs of countries, which are most vulnerable to hold-up problems. Finally, I provide evidence of the causal mechanism driving the results, demonstrating that WTO membership increases fixed capital investment and that WTO members are more likely to trade goods which rely on contract enforceability.

A Model of Political Hold-Up Problems

Overview

I present a model which shows that the WTO most benefits politically dissimilar country pairs by improving contract enforcement. The model demonstrates that long-term agreements solve political hold-up problems, but are difficult to abide by in a bilateral setting, particularly for dissimilar pairs of states. By contrast, WTO membership allows countries to commit to long-term agreements, resulting in greater levels of investment and trade.

The model features two countries that bargain over the terms of a trade agreement. A two-player model permits a focus on political hold-up problems, since these problems occur when one party makes a relationship-specific investment, or an investment whose returns depend on the continuation of the relationship with a particular partner (Crawford 1990).[9] A viable alternative trading partner may not exist for several reasons: First, the country's investment may only physically permit trade with a specific market, such as roads that connect the country of origin to the destination. Second, investment may produce a good that is demanded by a unique market, such as a factory designed to build automobiles that meet a partner's especially stringent emissions standards. Third, investment may promote trade in goods for which switching partners is too costly, either because a state's market size is so large that a suitable substitute does

not exist (as in the Hawaii example discussed previously), or because the good is supplied at such a favorable price that a feasible alternative is not available.

In the model, one state may choose to make a relationship-specific investment in order to produce a good for export to a partner state. The exporter may desire a lower tariff than the importer wishes to set, so in exchange for a lower tariff, the exporter may offer foreign policy concessions such as human rights improvements, democratization, technology sharing, access to military bases, etc. States could, of course, bargain over tariffs and other economic concessions instead. However, the model's purpose is to demonstrate the conditions under which hold-up problems occur, and economic hold-up problems are typically much less prevalent between countries than political hold-up problems. The model indicates that hold-up problems arise when a state has the ability to hold up its partner; that is, when one state is much more powerful than another. In these cases, the economic concessions that a large state may receive from a small state are often much less valuable than the political concessions the large state can obtain. While trade with a small state tends to represent a minor share of a large state's market, the political importance of small states can be extremely high. For this reason, large states commonly use their trade policies to attempt to obtain political concessions from their partners, both today and historically. Consider a few examples: the renewals of India and Nepal's short-term trade treaties of 1991 and 1996 were contentious due to Indian opposition to Nepal's acquisition of Chinese weapons (Heitzman and Worden 1996); trade agreements concluded by the EU with Mongolia, Sri Lanka, Vietnam, and Nepal make respect for human rights a key condition for yearly renewal; China often ties the renewal of short-term agreements to its partner's support for Taiwan (Dumbaugh 2008); the United States frequently linked the renewal of trade agreements with China, Vietnam, and Cambodia to human rights and other political concessions before these states joined the WTO; Russia would only renew the 1797 Anglo-Russian Treaty of Commerce if Britain provided a military diversion (Roach 1983).

While the aforementioned examples all occurred in the context of short-term trade agreements, the model indicates that political hold-up problems can be solved with perfectly enforceable, long-term agreements, which allow states to commit not to behave opportunistically. However, long-term agreements can be difficult to abide by in the absence of the WTO, as discussed previously. Indeed, the empirical pattern of agreements seems to match the theoretical expectation. For example, while all agreements signed within the WTO are long-term agreements, short-term agreements remain common outside of the WTO.[10] Further, I coded the duration of all current United States trade agreements as well as all current Australian trade agreements and found that 116 out of 236 of the United States' trade agreements and 32 out of 73 of Australia's agreements have limited durations. Additionally, most of these short-term agreements were signed before the advent of the GATT, with a non-WTO member, or between large countries for whom hold-up problems are rare.[11] The model demonstrates that these short-term agreements cause political hold-up problems, but that the WTO alleviates such problems by helping to enforce long-term agreements.[12]

■   ■   ■

An Example: U.S. MFN Designation

The insights generated by the theoretical model can be observed in practice in the trade relations between many pairs of states. Examples of countries holding up asymmetric, nonmember trading partners for political concessions abound. For example, the United States often threatens to raise its tariff levels in order to extract political concessions from non-WTO members. When the U.S. Congress disapproves of policies enacted by these trading partners, it often offers the renewal of most favored nation (MFN) status in exchange for policy concessions. MFN status entitles countries to nondiscriminatory trade policies such that a country cannot lower tariffs for a partner with MFN status without lowering tariffs for all partners with MFN status.[13] While all WTO members must grant each other MFN status, extending MFN status to non-WTO members is optional. Members of the U.S. Congress have explicitly acknowledged that the renewal of MFN status is a valuable tool to obtain political concessions from non-WTO members. For example, Rep. Loretta Sanchez advocated threatening to revoke MFN status from Vietnam in order to extract human rights concessions, stating, "If we insist that Vietnam improve its human rights record as a condition to trading with America, we would gain human rights advances in Vietnam, so I think it is a tragic mistake for the United States to decline to use this tool that is available to us" (*The Congressional Record* 2001, 14673). As predicted by the model, the U.S. typically has relied on these short-term MFN agreements to govern trade with former Communist countries, which, at the time, were nonallies with dissimilar regime types.[14] Also in line with the theory, there is considerable evidence that the repeated renewal of the agreements discouraged investment (Devereaux, Lawrence, and Watkins 2006) since the United States could not commit to refrain from using its MFN policies to hold up its nonmember partners.

As a more detailed illustration, consider the case of U.S.-China trade relations. In 1979, China signed a bilateral trade agreement with the United States, granting China short-term MFN status, which was renewed yearly by the U.S. The fall of the USSR created a unique point in U.S.-Chinese history when the United States had considerable leverage over China (Kissinger 2011), such that U.S. bargaining power, α, was large due to several factors: First, the potential impact of raising U.S. tariffs on the Chinese economy was severe, as the United States was China's most important export market. No other market was large enough to absorb such a high volume of Chinese goods. Second, China had acquired a diminished strategic importance due to the end of the Cold War (Lilley and Willkie 1994, 127). Policy preference dissimilarity, γ, was also high because the Tiananmen Square incident increased the salience of differences in human rights policy preferences.

Due to this dip in China's power relative to that of the United States, the U.S. Congress repeatedly threatened China with tariff increases unless China addressed the United States' concerns regarding human rights, weapons proliferation, and trade (Lilley and Willkie 1994, 24). China made many policy concessions in exchange for low U.S. tariffs. Between 1990 and 1993, China released 881 Tiananmen prisoners, lifted martial law, disclosed information on high profile political prisoners, agreed not to export products made with prison labor, allowed the Red Cross to visit prisoners, sent two human rights delegations to the United States, and gave passports to many families of political exiles (Lilley and Willkie 1994, 86). Investment in China declined over this period (Walmsley, Hertel, and Ianchovichina 2006), suggesting that while the United States' bargaining power, α, and foreign policy preference dissimilarity, γ, were high and while China was not a WTO member, hold-up problems were prevalent. Membership in the WTO was recognized as a means to increase investment in China. U.S. Senator Wellstone argued, "I think the evidence is pretty clear. [Permanent MFN status] will result in . . . more investment" (*The Congressional Record* 2000, S8676). Indeed, once China joined the WTO, investment and capital stocks grew dramatically (Walmsley, Hertel, and Ianchovichina 2006), as political hold-up problems were likely alleviated.

■ ■ ■

Conclusion

This paper shows that international institutions can help to solve political hold-up problems by reducing states' abilities to hold up their partners for foreign policy concessions. While scholars have identified a variety of mechanisms through which international institutions encourage cooperation, I generate novel insights by incorporating the logic of political hold-up problems, which has not been systematically theorized in the international institutions literature. Using the example of the WTO to illustrate the argument, the paper develops a formal model which shows that hold-up problems are most acute for politically dissimilar pairs of states, in which one state has the ability and incentive to extract concessions from its partner. The WTO allows states to solve political hold-up problems by enforcing long-term agreements, increasing trade and investment between states that differ in terms of capabilities, regime types, and alliances. The hypotheses derived from the model are tested using bilateral trade data over a 56-year time span. The empirical analysis strongly supports the theoretical predictions, demonstrating that international institutions can normalize relations between politically asymmetric states.

These findings add to the current understanding of the WTO's benefits. The canonical justification for the existence of the WTO focuses on the WTO's ability to solve a terms-of-trade prisoner's dilemma. This emphasis on economics has led previous researchers to overlook important political benefits of membership: The WTO can decouple economic and political relations by facilitating trade between states that would otherwise face large impediments to economic exchange due to political dissimilarities.

The theoretical framework presented here can also shed light on many additional questions in international relations. Future work might examine the implications of political hold-up problems on other institutions or issue areas, such as the indirect effects of international institutions. This paper shows that the WTO prevents the use of trade policies for political leverage. However, it seems unlikely that states abandon their attempts to wield political influence over their partners. Instead, states may substitute towards the use of alternative, less constrained policies, such as foreign aid or diplomatic tools. Future scholarship may therefore investigate whether, by increasing cooperation in the area it governs, an international institution can politicize other policy areas outside of the institution's domain.

NOTES

1. The literature on the benefits of institutions was pioneered by Keohane (1984). The view that benefits tend to fall disproportionately to powerful states has been advanced by Krasner (1991) and Mearsheimer (1994), among others.
2. In 1995, the WTO replaced the GATT. Throughout the paper, I use the term WTO to refer to both the GATT and the WTO unless otherwise specified.
3. Although see Gowa and Kim (2005) for an argument that predicts that large states are the main beneficiaries.
4. For example, Australia had become a sugar exporter, and the Canadian population was too small to serve as a substitute (La Croix and Grandy 1997). Additionally, continental Europe had begun producing large quantities of beet sugar as a substitute for imported cane sugar (Rolph 1917).
5. See La Croix and Grandy (1997, 175–179) for evidence that the United States did not initially have enough bargaining power to extract this concession, but its bargaining power had increased by the time of the renewal due to Hawaii's extensive investment in its sugar industry.
6. La Croix and Grandy (1997, 177) quote Charles de Varigny, the Foreign Minister of the Kingdom of Hawaii, explaining, "Seven years [the length of time before the treaty's renewal] would give us time to establish our sugar production on a solid basis. After all, we would have an opportunity through similar negotiations to open up other markets."
7. The argument presented here differs from ordinary issue linkage, or the "simultaneous discussion of two or more issues for joint settlement" (Poast 2012, 2). Unlike issue linkage (or the closely related concept of conditionality), wherein both countries can be made better off through the bargain (Davis 2004, 2009; Dreher, Sturm, and Vreeland 2009; Koremenos, Lipson, and Snidal 2001), hold-up problems can result in both countries being made worse off due to underinvestment.
8. Other work on hold-up problems between governments tends to remain outside of the context of the WTO. See Davis and Meunier (2011) for an application to trade and conflict, Lake (1999) for an application to alliances, Wallander (2000) for hold-up problems in the context of NATO, Cooley and Spruyt (2009) for hold-up problems in sovereign transfers, and Rector (2009) for an application to

federations. Additionally, McLaren (1997) argues that the potential for hold-up problems can have perverse effects on the design of agreements. However, I focus on the effect of long-term agreements on investment behavior, arguing that these agreements can remedy political hold-up problems.
9. The key feature of such an investment is described by McLaren (1997) as "irreversibility, or costly reversibility, of investment decisions. Thus, after reorienting production towards a particular trading partner, it would be very costly to return to the status quo."
10. Note that for my purposes, long-term, bilateral agreements are considered multilateral if they use the WTO's dispute settlement body for adjudication. By contrast, bilateral short-term agreements do not rely on this type of multilateral adjudication, and are therefore not considered multilateral.
11. Future work might examine this pattern more systematically. The texts of these agreements were obtained from a variety of sources including the U.S. Trade Compliance Center website and the Australia Government Department of Foreign Affairs and Trade website. This pool of agreements includes bilateral preferential trade agreements, bilateral investment treaties, trade relations agreements, intellectual property rights agreements, agreements covering specific goods, and friendship, commerce, and navigation treaties.
12. Note that a short-term agreement is usually much easier to enforce, since states may simply wait until the agreement's expiration to alter its terms or extract concessions. By contrast, states typically must terminate a long-term agreement in order to change its provisions.
13. There are many exceptions to this rule. Under the GATT, exceptions include the following: Article 1:2–4 based on Historical Preferences, Article IV(c) for Cinematographic Films, Article XX for General Exceptions such as those relating to morals or the environment, Article XXIV:3 for Frontier Traffic, Article XXIV:5 for FTAs and Customs Unions, Article XXI for Security Exceptions, the 1979 Enabling Clause, and the Marrakesh Agreement Article IX:3 Waiver. Many of these exceptions, such as the security clause, are rarely used, while others, such as the FTA exception, are used frequently. Similar MFN exceptions exist under the General Agreement for Trade in Services (GATS) and Trade-Related Aspects of Intellectual Property Rights (TRIPS).
14. In 1972, Senator Jackson sponsored a bill known as the "Jackson-Vanik amendment," which blocks MFN status for countries that disallow freedom of emigration. The amendment requires the president to grant yearly MFN waivers to countries disallowing emigration and for Congress to renew MFN agreements every three years. In practice, the amendment has been applied mainly to former Communist countries (Lilley and Willkie 1994, 124).

REFERENCES

Allee, T. L., and P. K. Huth. 2006. "Legitimizing Dispute Settlement: International Legal Rulings as Domestic Political Cover." *American Political Science Review* 100 (2): 219.

Axelrod, R., and R. O. Keohane. 1985. "Achieving Cooperation Under Anarchy: Strategies and Institutions." *World Politics: A Quarterly Journal of International Relations* 38 (1): 226–54.

Bagwell, K., and R. W. Staiger. 1999. "An Economic Theory of GATT." *The American Economic Review* 89 (1): 215–48.

Busch, M. L., and E. Reinhardt. 2003. "Developing Countries and General Agreement on Tariffs and Trade/World Trade Organization Dispute Settlement." *Journal of World Trade* 37 (4): 719–36.

Busch, M. L., and E. Reinhardt. 2004. "The WTO Dispute Settlement Mechanism and Developing Countries." *Trade Brief Swedish International Development and Cooperation Agency.*

Busch, M. L., R. Raciborski, and E. Reinhardt. 2009. "Does the Rule of Law Matter? The WTO and US Antidumping Investigations." Working Paper.

Büthe, T., and H. V. Milner. 2008. "The Politics of Foreign Direct Investment into Developing Countries: Increasing FDI Through International Trade Agreements?" *American Journal of Political Science* 52 (4): 741–62.

Cooley, A., and H. Spruyt. 2009. *Contracting States: Sovereign Transfers in International Relations.* Princeton, NJ: Princeton University Press.

Crawford, Vincent P. 1990. "Relationship-Specific Investment." *The Quarterly Journal of Economics* 105 (2): 561–74.

Davis, C. L. 2004. "International Institutions and Issue Linkage: Building Support for Agricultural Trade Liberalization." *American Political Science Review* 98 (1): 153–69.

Davis, C. L. 2006. "Do WTO Rules Create a Level Playing Field? Lessons from the Experience of Peru and Vietnam." *Negotiating Trade, Developing Countries in the WTO and NAFTA,* 219–56.

Davis, C. L. 2009. "Linkage Diplomacy: Economic and Security Bargaining in the Anglo-Japanese Alliance, 1902–23." *International Security* 33 (3): 143–79.

Davis, C. L., and S. Meunier. 2011. "Business as Usual? Economic Responses to Political Tensions." *American Journal of Political Science* 55 (3): 628–46.

Devereaux, C., R. Z. Lawrence, and M. D. Watkins. 2006. *Case Studies in US Trade Negotiation, Volume 1: Making the Rules.* Washington, DC: Institute for International Economics.

Dreher, A., J. E. Sturm, and J. R. Vreeland. 2009. "Global Horse Trading: IMF Loans for Votes in the United Nations Security Council." *European Economic Review* 53 (7): 742–57.

Dumbaugh, K. 2008. "China's Foreign Policy: What Does It Mean for US Global Interests?" *Congressional Research Service.*

Eaton, Jonathan, and Samuel Kortum. 2001. "Trade in Capital Goods." *European Economic Review* 45 (7): 1195–235.

Eaton, Jonathan, and Akiko Tamura. 1995. Bilateralism and Regionalism in Japanese and US Trade and Direct Foreign Investment Patterns. Technical report, National Bureau of Economic Research.

Eicher, Theo S., and Christian Henn. 2011. "In Search of WTO Trade Effects: Preferential Trade Agreements Promote Trade Strongly, but Unevenly." *Journal of International Economics* 83 (2): 137–53.

Goldstein, J., and J. Gowa. 2002. "US National Power and the Post-War Trading Regime." *World Trade Review* 1 (2): 153–70.

Gowa, J., and S. Y. Kim. 2005. "An Exclusive Country Club: The Effects of the GATT on Trade, 1950–94." *World Politics* 57 (4): 453–78.

Heitzman, J., and R. L. Worden. 1996. *India: A Country Study.* Washington, DC: Bernan Press.

Herz, Bernhard, and Marco Wagner. 2006. Do the World Trade Organization and the Generalized System of Preferences Foster Bilateral Trade? Available at SSRN 1002846.

Keohane, R. O. 1984. *After Hegemony: Cooperation and Discord in the World Political Economy.* Princeton, NJ: Princeton University Press.

Kissinger, H. 2011. *On China.* New York: Penguin Press.

Koremenos, B., C. Lipson, and D. Snidal. 2001. "The Rational Design of International Institutions." *International Organization* 55 (4): 761–99.

Krasner, S. D. 1991. "Global Communications and National Power: Life on the Pareto Frontier." *World Politics: A Quarterly Journal of International Relations* 43 (3): 336–66.

Kuykendall, R. S. 1953. *The Hawaiian Kingdom: 1854–1874: Twenty Critical Years.* Vol. 2. Honolulu, University of Hawaii Press.

La Croix, S. J., and C. Grandy. 1997. "The Political Instability of Reciprocal Trade and the Overthrow of the Hawaiian Kingdom." *The Journal of Economic History* 57 (1): 161–89.

Lake, D. A. 1999. *Entangling Relations: American Foreign Policy in its Century.* Princeton, NJ: Princeton University Press.

Leeds, B., J. Ritter, S. Mitchell, and A. Long. 2002. "Alliance Treaty Obligations and Provisions, 1815–1944." *International Interactions* 28: 237–60.

Lilley, J. R., and W. L. Willkie. 1994. *Beyond MFN: Trade with China and American Interests.* Washington, DC: American Enterprise Institute.

Maggi, G. 1999. "The Role of Multilateral Institutions in International Trade Cooperation." *The American Economic Review* 89 (1): 190–214.

Maggi, G., and A. Rodriguez-Clare. 1998. "The Value of Trade Agreements in the Presence of Political Pressures." *Journal of Political Economy* 106 (3): 574–601.

Mansfield, E. D., H. V. Milner, and B. P. Rosendorff. 2000. "Free to Trade: Democracies, Autocracies, and International Trade." *American Political Science Review* 94 (2): 305–21.

Mansfield, E. D., H. V. Milner, and B. P. Rosendorff. 2002. "Why Democracies Cooperate More: Electoral Control and International Trade Agreements." *International Organization* 56: 477–513.

Mansfield, E. D., and J. C. Pevehouse. 2008. "Democratization and the Varieties of International Organizations." *Journal of Conflict Resolution* 52 (2): 269.

McLaren, J. 1997. "Size, Sunk Costs, and Judge Bowker's Objection to Free Trade." *The American Economic Review* 87 (3): 400–20.

Mearsheimer, J. J. 1994. "The False Promise of International Institutions." *International Security* 19 (3): 5–49.

Poast, P. 2012. "Does Issue Linkage Work? Evidence from European Alliance Negotiations, 1815 to 1945." *International Organization* 66 (2): 277–310.

Rector, C. 2009. *Federations: the Political Dynamics of Cooperation.* New York: Cornell University Press.

Roach, E. E. 1983. "Anglo-Russian Relations from Austerlitz to Tilsit." *The International History Review* 5 (2): 181–200.

Rolph, G. M. 1917. *Something About Sugar: Its History, Growth, Manufacture and Distribution.* San Francisco: J.J. Newbegin.

Singer, J. D. 1988. "Reconstructing the Correlates of War Dataset on Material Capabilities of States, 1816–1985." *International Interactions* 14 (2): 115–32.

Staiger, R. W., and G. Tabellini. 1999. "Do GATT Rules Help Governments Make Domestic Commitments?" *Economics and Politics* 11 (2): 109–44.

The Congressional Record. 2000. Quoted by Sen. Paul Wellstone.

The Congressional Record. 2001. Quoted by Rep. Loretta Sanchez.

Tomz, M. 2007. *Reputation and International Cooperation: Sovereign Debt Across Three Centuries.* Princeton, NJ: Princeton University Press.

Tomz, M., J. L. Goldstein, and D. Rivers. 2007. "Do We Really Know That the WTO Increases Trade? Comment." *The American Economic Review* 97 (5): 2005–18.

Wallander, C. A. 2000. "Institutional Assets and Adaptability: NATO After the Cold War." *International Organization* 54 (4): 705–35.

Walmsley, T. L., T. W. Hertel, and E. Ianchovichina. 2006. "Assessing the Impact of China's WTO Accession on Investment." *Pacific Economic Review 11* (3): 315–39.

Wilson, B. 2007. "Compliance by WTO Members with Adverse WTO Dispute Settlement Rulings: The Record to Date." *Journal of International Economic Law* 10 (2): 397–403.

World Bank. 2011. *World Development Indicators.* Washington, DC: World Bank.

Yarbrough, B. V., and R. M. Yarbrough. 1992. *Cooperation and Governance in International Trade: The Strategic Organization Approach.* Princeton, NJ: Princeton University Press.

Yarbrough, B. V., and R. M. Yarbrough. 1986. "Reciprocity, Bilateralism, and Economic 'Hostages': Self-Enforcing Agreements in International Trade." *International Studies Quarterly* 30 (1): 7–21.

Dani Rodrik

WHY DOES GLOBALIZATION FUEL POPULISM?

Economics, Culture, and the Rise of Right-Wing Populism

Introduction

Globalization figures prominently in discussions of populism. Especially in its post-1990s variant—which might be better called "hyperglobalization—international economic integration seems to have produced domestic *dis*integration in many countries, deepening the divide between the winners and losers of exposure to global competition. There is nothing particularly surprising about this from the standpoint of economic theory. Standard trade theory is quite clear about the sharp redistributive effects of free trade, and open economy macroeconomics has long grappled with the instability of global financial markets. Economic history is equally suggestive. The high points of globalization in previous eras have also been marked by a populist backlash.[1]

But there are still many open questions. First, what are the mechanisms through which globalization fuels populism? Answering this question requires a more fully fleshed out model of political economy. Second, globalization is not just one thing: we can distinguish among international trade, international finance, and international labor flows specifically. How do each one of these facets of globalization work their way through the

From National Bureau of Economic Research, Working Paper 27526, July 2020. Published in expanded form in *Annual Review of Economics* 13 (August 2021): 133–70.

political system? Third, globalization is clearly not the only economic shock that creates redistributive effects or economic anxiety—and it may not even be the most important economic force to do so. Why does globalization appear to have an outsized effect on politics compared to, say, technological change or regular business cycles?

Fourth, the populist response so far seems to have taken a mostly right-wing form. On the face of it, this is surprising since left-wing populist movements with their redistributive economic agendas could have been the more obvious beneficiary of economic dislocations. Why have nativist, ethnonationalist populists been instead the ones to take advantage? Fifth, and related to the previous question, what about the roles of culture, values, and identities? Could it be that populism is rooted not in economics but in a cultural divide—social conservatives versus social liberals, traditionalists versus modernists, nationalists versus cosmopolitans, ethnically homogenous dominant communities versus "outsider" minorities of various kinds?

The economics-versus-culture question has been a source of controversy in discussions of populism. The literature on the economic determinants of populism—globalization in particular—is quite rich, as the studies I will discuss in this paper attest to. On the other side, Sides, Tesler, and Vavreck (2018), Norris and Inglehart (2019), and Margalit (2019), among others, have made strong cases for the culture thesis. In the United States, the culture argument revolves around the strong undercurrent of racism in American society. In Europe, the argument centers on aversion to Muslim and African immigrants, which has long been the basis of support for far-right parties such as the French National Front.

Some of the disagreement revolves around empirical methods. For example, observational studies tend to favor the economics argument, while survey experiments give greater credence to culture (Naoi 2019). But there is a key conceptual difference at the heart of the matter as well. The relative importance one ascribes to economics versus culture depends crucially on whether we are interested in a question about levels or about changes—whether we ask "why do so many people vote for the populist candidate?" or we ask "why did the populist vote share increase so much?" (Margalit 2020).[2] My focus in this paper, as in much of the economics-centered literature, is on the latter question. Since culture transforms slowly, and a constant cannot explain a change, culture is unlikely to do a good job answering the question in changes form. Economic shocks, such as those related to globalization, are a more likely candidate for the answer.

In any case, I do not aim to resolve the economics-versus-culture debate here. My goal is more limited. By unpacking globalization and specifying the channels through which its different components work their way into politics, I try to bring greater clarity to the discussion on the contribution globalization has made to the rise of populist politics. There is compelling evidence, from diverse settings, that globalization shocks, often working through culture and identity, have played an important role in driving up support for populist, particularly right-wing populist movements. The argument does not dismiss the possibility that purely cultural factors too may have been at play as well, and I will briefly discuss some of the historical evidence on immigration in the United States that leans that way. While I draw on an extensive literature, this is by no means a survey paper. For a recent survey on the political economy of populism, see Guriev and Papaioannou (2020). The political science literature on the relationship between globalization and the rise of the far right is surveyed by Bornschier (2018).

I start the paper in the next section with an empirical look at the 2016 presidential election in the United States. I focus on the characteristics of both Trump voters in general and "switchers"—voters who supported Obama in 2012 but voted for Trump in 2016. This relatively unstructured data analysis shows that globalization-related attitudinal variables were important correlates of the switch to Trump, even in survey data. [Third, I present] a conceptual framework to clarify the various channels through which globalization can stimulate populism. I distinguish here between the demand and supply sides of politics, and the different causal pathways that link globalization shocks to political outcomes. I identify four mechanisms in particular, two each on the demand and supply sides: (a) a direct effect from economic dislocation to demands for anti-elite, redistributive policies; (b) an indirect demand-side effect, through the amplification of cultural and identity divisions; (c) a supply-side effect through political candidates adopting more populist platforms in response to economic shocks; and (d) another supply-side effect through political candidates adopting platforms that deliberately inflame cultural and identity tensions in order to shift voters' attention away from economic issues.

[I then] review the empirical literature with the help of this framework, discussing trade, financial globalization, and immigration separately. The existing literature has focused mostly on the first two channels, with the second two (and especially the last) receiving considerably less attention. [The next section] focuses specifically on the outsized political response to globalization shocks and the reasons why right-wing populists have benefited disproportionately. The answers to these two questions may be related, having to do with the way in which globalization shocks interact with latent cultural divisions. [I] conclude the paper with a discussion that reversed the direction of causation and examines some apparent exceptions where populists have been against, rather than in favor of, trade protection.

Evidence on the Empirical Correlates of Voting Patterns in the 2016 U.S. Presidential Election

In this section I provide the results of some explanatory data analysis of the 2016 presidential election in the United States. I focus on two types of voters: Trump voters in general and "switchers," i.e., those who voted for Obama in 2012 and switched to Trump in 2016. I try to answer three questions. First, what were the distinguishing characteristics of Trump voters? Second, what were the distinguishing characteristics of switchers? Third, how did the switchers differ from other Obama voters from 2012? * * *

I use data from American National Election Studies (2019), which is a representative survey of Americans before and after the 2016 presidential elections. Of the 4,270 individuals in the survey, 1,245 report having voted for Trump in 2016 and 1,728 recall having voted for Obama in 2012. There are 154 respondents in the intersection of these two groups, who constitute the switchers. The survey includes a broad range of demographic and attitudinal questions. Note that the regressions reported below have fewer than 4,270 observations because not all respondents answered all of the questions.

As my primary indicator of economic insecurity I use the question "how worried are you about your current financial situation?" The five possible

valid responses for this question range from "not at all worried" to "extremely worried." I supplement this measure with views on trade, immigration, and banks to gauge the strength of economic correlates. To measure social identity I use respondents' self-assessment of the social class to which they belong. This is a 4-point measure using the values 1="lower class," 2="working class," 3="middle class," and 4="upper class."

To measure racial attitudes I use the same index as Sides et al. (2018, appendix to Chap. 8). Sides et al. (2018) combine answers to four questions, gauging agreement/disagreement with the following statements:

- "Over the past few years, Blacks have gotten less than they deserve."
- "Irish, Italian, Jewish, and many other minorities overcame prejudice and worked their way up. Blacks should do the same without any special favors."
- "It's really a matter of some people not trying hard enough; if Blacks would only try harder they could be just as well off as Whites."
- "Generations of slavery and discrimination have created conditions that make it difficult for Blacks to work their way out of the lower class."

The five-fold responses to these questions are averaged to obtain a single indicator of attitude to racial inequality, with a higher value indicating greater hostility to racial equality.

My benchmark specification is a logit regression with attitudes to racial inequality, social class, and economic insecurity (financial worries) as the main regressors in addition to basic demographic variables (age, gender, race, and education). For each dependent variable, I start with this specification and then add specific regressors related to globalization individually. The latter are binary (0-1) variables meant to capture attitudes towards different aspects of economic globalization. They gauge the respondents' support for (i) trade agreements,

(ii) immigration, and (iii) regulation of banks. Note that there are no questions in ANES that gauge views on financial globalization specifically; I use the "bank regulation" variable as a proxy for support for financial globalization. A final, kitchen-sink regression shows the results when all regressors are included.

* * * Trump voters were more likely to be white, older, and college-educated * * *. More germane to our analysis, they were significantly more hostile to racial equality and perceived themselves to be of higher social class. The estimated coefficient on racial attitudes is particularly large: a one-point increase in the index of racial hostility—which theoretically ranges from 1 to 5—is associated with a 0.28 percentage point increase in the probability of voting for Trump. By contrast, economic insecurity does not seem to be associated with a propensity to vote for Trump.

The finding that Trump voters thought of themselves as belonging to upper social classes may seem surprising. But this largely reflects the role played by party identification in shaping voting preferences. When we control for Republican party identification, the estimated coefficient for social class drops sharply and ceases to be statistically significant. In other words, Republican party identification is a strong correlate of support for Trump, and Republicans tend to be wealthier than Democrats. Note, however, that racial hostility remains significant, although its estimated coefficient becomes smaller.

The remaining [data] examine attitudes toward globalization. All three of our measures are statistically significant: Trump voters disliked trade agreements and immigration; they were also against bank regulation (presumably in line with the general anti-regulation views of the Republican party). These indicators remain significant in the kitchen-sink version where they are all entered together.

In none of these regressions does economic insecurity (financial worries) enter significantly. This changes when we move from Trump voters in general to switchers from Obama to Trump. There are two essential differences from the baseline specification: financial worries now becomes statistically significant, and switchers do not identify with the upper social classes. Switchers, in other words, view their economic and social status very differently from, and as much more precarious than, run-of-the-mill Republican voters for Trump.

With respect to attitudes towards globalization, there are interesting parallels and differences as well. Switchers are similar to Trump voters insofar as they too dislike trade agreements and immigration. But they are dissimilar in that they view regulation of banks favorably. Hence switchers appear to be against all aspects of globalization—trade, immigration, finance. Economic insecurity remains statistically significant when these globalization indicators are added to the regression. But in the kitchen-sink regression—with all the regressors included simultaneously—economic insecurity is no longer significant while the globalization attitudes all retain their statistical significance.

Finally, I focus on how switchers differ from other Obama voters. For this purpose, I restrict the sample to those respondents who report having voted for Obama in 2012. * * *

The baseline regression shows that switchers are both generally more hostile to racial equality and feel greater economic insecurity; they don't seem to differ from other Obama voters in their self-assessed social class. They are also significantly more anti-trade and anti-immigration. Their views on bank regulation are not distinctive. When all indicators are included, trade and immigration attitudes enter significantly while economic insecurity loses statistical significance.

These results suggest switchers to Trump are different both from Trump voters and from other Obama voters in identifiable respects related to social identity and views on the economy in particular. They differ from regular Trump voters in that they exhibit greater economic insecurity, do not associate themselves with an upper social class, and look favorably on financial regulation. They differ from others who voted for Obama in 2012 in that they exhibit greater racial hostility, more economic insecurity, and more negative attitudes toward trade agreements and immigration.

A Conceptual Framework

These empirical results suggest, as a first pass, that the vote for Trump was influenced by perceptions on economic conditions as well as by social and racial attitudes. Anti-globalization views appear to be strongly associated with the decision to vote for Trump instead of Hillary Clinton. But these are merely suggestive empirical associations. Parsing the specific causal relationships between economic and attitudinal variables, on the one hand, and political outcomes, on the other, requires a more fully fleshed-out structural model. In particular, social identities, cultural sensitivities, and racial attitudes may well be endogenous, determined in part by objective economic conditions. Economic conditions, in turn, are shaped by a number of different forces, including globalization shocks. In addition, voters' political preferences may be formed also by narratives and messages ("propaganda") emanating from political parties and leaders. And political leaders may choose to formulate their campaign messages in response to economic conditions as well.

Figure 8.1 sketches a causal framework that highlights the key causal relationships, emphasizing the mechanisms through which globalization may drive support for populism. I distinguish between the demand and supply sides of politics, allowing a role for political leaders' programs and strategies as well as individual voters' preferences. Different types of globalization shocks—trade, immigration, finance—enter the system through their impact on economic conditions—economic dislocation, in particular. Economic dislocation, in turn, can influence political outcomes—here, electoral success of populist politicians—through four different causal pathways. These four causal explanations are identified as (A), (B), (C), and (D) in Figure 8.1.

First, and most directly, it can determine voters' preferences for policies and leaders (A). A voter in a region where employment prospects have been adversely affected by a rise in imports may choose to cast his vote for a politician who advocates protectionism and a tougher line against foreign exporters. Second, it may shape voters' preferences indirectly through the effect it has on identity or the salience of certain cultural values (B). Concretely, economic shocks can heighten feelings of insecurity, inducing voters to make sharper distinctions between insiders ("us") and ethnic, religious, or racial outsiders ("them"). They can lead voters to yearn for an earlier era of prosperity and stability, increasing the political salience of traditional cultural values and hierarchies. And to the extent that they generate wider economic and social gaps within a nation, economic shocks may reinforce more local, less encompassing identities. To the extent that such effects operate, political preferences that appear to be driven by cultural values will in fact have deeper, economic roots.

These two causal pathways operate on the demand side of the political equilibrium. The other two channels work through the supply side. Hence a third possibility is that economic shocks affect the ideology of political candidates or the platforms of competing political parties (C). Even if voters' preferences remain unchanged, they may find themselves confronted with parties or candidates that are more polarized on issues such as trade protection or immigration. The fourth and final channel is that economic shocks may induce some parties—typically those on the right—to try to render culture and identity more salient in voters' decisions at the polling booth (D). For example, suppose greater economic inequality results in the loss of median-voter support for a right-wing party. The party may counter by attempting to shift the

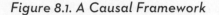

Figure 8.1. A Causal Framework

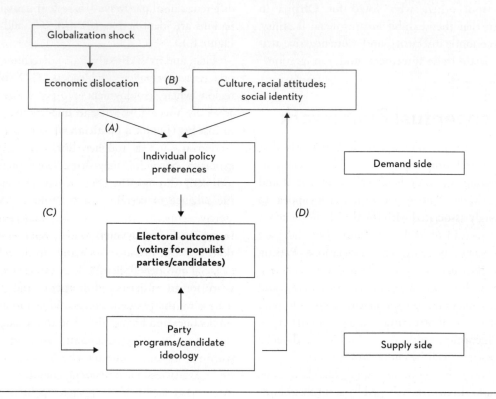

electoral competition away from economics to issues of identity and culture. If such a strategy is successful, it will appear as if electoral outcomes are driven by voters' cultural preferences. But the ultimate determinant will be economics—via party strategies—rather than voters' cultural values per se.

Hence globalization shocks can feed into support for populism directly (*A*) as well as indirectly (*B, C, D*); it can activate supply-side (*C*) as well as demand-side (*A, B, D*) causal pathways. A full causal explanation of the rise of populism—and its links to globalization—would not only have to separately identify each one of these channels, but also gauge their importance vis-à-vis all the other causal pathways in Figure 8.1, including, most crucially,

those that originate from cultural or identity determinants that are orthogonal to economic dislocation. This is a tall order. Perhaps not surprisingly, no single piece of empirical work has attempted to provide such a comprehensive analysis. What we have instead are empirical papers that focus on some of the individual pieces of the larger puzzle. Collectively, they paint a consistent picture on the importance of globalization shocks on the demand side, both directly (*A*) and indirectly (*B*). Supply-side causal pathways have received less attention than others. In particular, there has been virtually no systematic empirical work on channel (*D*), even though the informal evidence (discussed below) is quite suggestive. And convincing tests of the * * * economics-versus-culture hypotheses have proved elusive.

Empirical Studies

The empirical literature on determinants of populism is summarized [below]. * * * Since the present paper hones in on globalization and economic insecurity, I have tried to be comprehensive in those areas, but less so with respect to culture and identity. * * *

Trade

Autor et al.'s (2013) original paper analyzing the local labor market effects of the China trade shock has spawned a small cottage industry of papers using a similar approach to document the political consequences of trade shocks. This paper developed a plausibly exogenous instrument for the increase in imports from China by combining (a) the contemporaneous change in imports from China in eight other developed countries, and (b) the industrial composition of production within commuting zones. Since some commuting zones have more industries exposed to Chinese competition than others, this approach allows an examination of the effects of Chinese imports across different localities. In subsequent work, Autor, Dorn, Hanson, and Majlesi (ADHM, 2019) have mapped commuting zone data to congressional districts and established several interesting findings.

First, they document that Chinese Import penetration had an impact on political preferences. Localities where the China trade shocks were greater experienced an increase in the market share of Fox News (at the expense of viewership for CNN and MSNBC), stronger conservative beliefs (as measured by Pew Surveys), and greater campaign contributions by both left- and right-leaning donors (relative to moderate donors at the center of the ideological spectrum). In the authors' words, "localized economic shocks stemming from rising trade pressure in the 2000s increased the relative demand for conservative media content, support for conservative viewpoints, and campaign contributions by more ideologically extreme donors" (ADHM, 2019). Next, they show that the China trade shock increased the likelihood that GOP legislators would get elected in Congressional elections, especially after 2008. This is so even though the shock appears to have reduced the GOP vote share somewhat overall; the increase in Republican support in *competitive* districts more than compensated. When candidates are classified according to political ideology, the biggest winners were those on the farthest right (conservative Republicans). The paper also uncovers an interesting interaction with race. GOP candidates were especially helped by trade shocks in majority White districts, where many Democratic voters switched to the Republican candidates. In majority non-white districts, the switch was from moderate to liberal Democrats—not a net gain for the Democratic party.

ADHM (2019) also show that the China import shock produced a boost for the GOP in the Presidential elections of 2008 and 2016 (relative to 2000). In a particularly interesting side note which builds on the results of this paper, the authors estimate that a reduction of the China trade shock by half between 2000 and 2014 would have produced a majority for the Democrats in 2016 in the key battleground states of Pennsylvania, Wisconsin, and Michigan (instead of a defeat) and would have swept Hillary Clinton to the Oval Office in lieu of Donald Trump (Autor et al., 2017). This is a particularly stark illustration of the electoral consequences of trade, and of trade shocks driving populists into office.

The ADHM China trade shock instrument has been used in a number of other papers looking at the effect of trade on political preferences. Ballard-Rosa et al. (2017) find that individuals living in relatively diverse regions where the China trade shock was more powerful have more authoritarian values. They interpret this as evidence that economic dislocation shapes political identity by producing "social-norm conformity" among historically dominant groups. This paper is an illustration of causal pathway *B* in Figure 8.1. By contrast, the original ADHM paper is largely agnostic on whether trade shocks work directly (*A*) or through their effects on culture and identity (*B*).

Another paper that sheds light on the mechanisms through which economic insecurity may drive support for right-wing populists is Cerrato et al. (2018). These authors focus explicitly on the cultural backlash produced by the China trade shock. Interestingly, they argue that the political impact of the ADHM trade shock works primarily through (negative) attitudes towards immigrants and racial/ethnic minorities. Attitudes towards international trade per se do not seem to be affected by Chinese import penetration. One specific finding is indicative of what the authors call the "pure" cultural backlash effect: greater import penetration produces negative sentiment towards Muslims.[3] Since Muslims are a tiny share of the labor market, it is difficult to provide this finding an alternative, economic interpretation. In terms of Figure 8.1, channel (*B*) trumps channel (*A*). Using text analysis of campaign speeches, Cerrato et al. (2018) also provide evidence of the anti-immigrant and anti-trade shift in Republican party presidential candidates over 2008–2016, which would be consistent with mechanism (*C*) being at play as well. The import of these findings is that they suggest the cultural determinants of support for populists highlighted in some studies (e.g., Inglehart and Norris 2016, 2019) may themselves have economic underpinnings. They again illustrate the need for a fully fleshed out structural causal model a la Figure 8.1.

The ADHM approach has been used in a growing number of studies on Europe as well, demonstrating an apparently causal impact of trade shocks on the rise of the populist right. Chinese import penetration has been linked to increased support for nationalist, far-right parties in empirical analyses covering regions within 15 European countries (Colontane and Stanig, 2018c), Italian municipalities (Barone and Kreuter, 2019), German counties (Dippel et al., 2018), and Franch cantons (Malgouyres, 2017). It is significantly associated with the strength of the pro-Brexit vote in Britain's 2016 referendum (Colontane and Stanig, 2018a). It is also found to lead to lower support for democracy and liberal values in a study of regions covering 15 European nations and to cultural, but not economic concerns, on immigration (Colontane and Stanig, 2018b). This last finding parallels the Cerrato et al. (2018) results for the United States.[4]

It is somewhat surprising that so many studies covering different European nations have found such strong causal effects from Chinese import penetration to political preferences. Safety nets and labor market protections are much stronger in Europe than in the United States. Imports from China and other low-cost nations have not figured prominently in political campaigns, as they have in the United States. While public opposition to trade agreements has been on the rise in Europe, this opposition generally revolves around trade with the United States and Canada, specifically the proposed Transatlantic Trade and Investment Partnership (TTIP) and the Canada-Europe Comprehensive Economic and Trade Agreement (CETA) (Young, 2019). The apparent fact that the local labor markets effects of Chinese imports have left a measurable political imprint even in Europe is suggestive of an oversized sensitivity to trade shocks, a question I will return to later in the paper.

In view of the appeal of the Autor et al. (2013) instrument, causal studies on the political impact of trade have focused largely on the Chinese trade shock. A notable recent exception is a study by Choi, Kuziemko, Washington, and Wright which applies a similar method to the passage of NAFTA in the United States (Choi et al., 2020). These authors develop a measure of localities' ex ante vulnerability to NAFTA based on industrial composition and pre-existing tariff levels. Using an event-study method, they find that areas with greater exposure to Mexican exports experienced large employment reductions subsequent to the 1993 completion of the Agreement. These areas also shifted sharply towards the Republican party. Interestingly, prior to NAFTA the counties most exposed to Mexico, mainly in the upper South, tended to vote for the Democratic party. By 2000, these same counties had turned heavily Republican. Choi et al. (2020) use a wide variety of regressors to control for possibly confounding secular trends. They also include Autor et al.'s (2013) China trade shock variable. They note that the NAFTA trade shock preceded the China shock, which came in the 2000s. While many of the same localities were hit by the two shocks, the correlation with NAFTA exposure across commuting zones is low for the raw Chinese import penetration measure (0.17) and higher, but considerably less than one, for the instrumented version (0.42).

Immigration and Refugees

The relationship between presence of immigrants and support for populism is clearly a contingent one. Large metropolitan areas and highly diverse cities such as NYC and London with a large immigrant footprint are not where populists get their votes. In Germany, electoral support for the anti-immigrant AfD is concentrated in the eastern part of the country where there are few immigrants. The identity of source countries, recent changes in the volume of immigration, and spatial patterns of immigrant presence can be more important than the numbers of immigrants per se. In particular, a political backlash on account of either economics or culture seems more likely when there is a rapid increase in foreign presence, when immigrants are low-skilled and come from countries with different racial, ethnic, or religious characteristics, and when there is a high level of spatial segregation.[5] The empirical studies * * * are generally consistent with these ideas. While these studies cover a large number

of countries and time periods, the majority are drawn from Europe, which has experienced a recent wave of increase in low-skilled migrants from Muslim and African countries or from East European countries that recently acceded to the EU. The general message * * * is that this influx has been a boon to right-wing, anti-immigrant parties in Europe. The evidence on the United States, by contrast, is decidedly mixed (Mayda et al., 2019; Hill et al., 2019).

What are the specific mechanisms through which immigration generates political consequences? Figure 8.1 suggests a number of possibilities. Consider the following three mechanisms in particular. First, a sudden influx of foreigners may generate a cultural backlash that has nothing to do with economics. This would be the case of xenophobia or anti-immigrant sentiment that arises purely out of psychological and identity-related processes: "we dislike and reject foreigners because they are not like 'us'." Analysts who give culture a primary independent role in driving populism have this mechanism in mind (e.g., Margalit, 2019). Alternatively, the influx may generate a backlash because it creates economic dislocations. Such dislocations arise from competition in local labor markets or in public-goods provision. Immigrants, especially of the low-skill type, can drive local wages down. They can reduce the availability of government services such as public housing or social transfers to native-born citizens. As Figure 8.1 shows, these economic factors can in turn play out politically in two different ways—either directly, or indirectly through culture and identity. These are variants (A) and (B), respectively. The direct channel refers to the case where political support for populist, anti-immigrant parties increases because these parties allay the economic anxieties of voters (A). The indirect channel refers to the case where economic dislocation activates affirmation of traditional, dominant identities and triggers hostility towards perceived out-groups on cultural grounds (B). In the latter case, anti-immigrant preferences appear to be driven by culture, but the roots are in economics. These two cases provide the other two possible mechanisms, in addition to the purely cultural case.[6]

The empirical literature on the political consequences of immigration has generally not scrutinized these different channels separately. The vast majority of studies * * * focus directly on a "reduced form" relationship between immigrant/refugee presence and voting for populist parties (mostly of the extreme right). For example, Becker et al. (2016) find that the increase in immigrants from 12 recent EU accession countries is associated positively with a vote in favor of Brexit across British localities, though the *level* of migrants is negatively (and insignificantly) correlated with the Brexit vote. Dustmann et al. (2016) and Dinas et al. (2019) find that an increase in the local concentration of refugees increases support for far-right, anti-immigrant parties, in Denmark and Greece respectively. For the United States, Mayda et al. (2019) find that an increase in low-skilled immigrants increases the Republican vote share, while an increase in high-skilled immigrants decreases it. Historical evidence, also for the United States, suggests the association between immigrant influx and support for populist politicians is not a recent phenomenon (Eichengreen et al., 2017, and Tabellini, 2019).

The study by Tabellini (2019) is notable because it is one of the few that explicitly tries to unpack the economic versus cultural roots of the anti-immigrant backlash. Tabellini looks at U.S. cities between 1910 and 1930, a period when immigrant levels were very high and anti-immigrant legislation began to be implemented. He uses a shift-share instrument that predicts each city's number of immigrants by interacting 1900 numbers with subsequent (total) migration flows from each sending region, net of the individuals that settled in that city.[7] The regressions include city fixed effects, so that the results are estimated from *changes* in immigrant numbers within cities, compared to other cities. Tabellini shows that greater immigration was associated with the election of more conservative representatives and loss of support for the Democratic party (the more pro-immigration party). He finds no evidence that immigration had adverse labor market effects. In fact, more immigration was associated with higher employment levels, even in occupations where immigrants provided greatest competition, and also with greater occupational upgrading (a proxy for wages). Tabellini reasons that the positive employment effects may have been due to this being a period of rapid economic expansion in the United States, with labor shortages an important constraint on economic activity. Furthermore, the political reaction seems to have been directed primarily at Catholics and Jews, even though these groups' economic impact would have been no different than in the case of immigrants from Protestant countries. Tabellini concludes that the political backlash was rooted not in economic dislocation—i.e., neither in channel (*A*) nor in (*B*)—but in purely cultural factors.

Recall that one of the mechanisms through which globalization shocks can influence political outcomes is the effect on politicians' programs (causal pathway (*C*)). An interesting paper by Moriconi et al. (2019) focuses in part on this channel. Using the Manifesto Project Database, the paper quantifies each European political party's attitude towards redistribution through the welfare state. The authors find that an increase in less-skilled immigration results in national party platforms to shift towards less redistribution, while high-skilled immigration has the opposite (but statistically insignificant) effect. * * * [A]n earlier paper by the same authors shows that different types of immigration have opposite-signed effects on nationalist sentiments as well: low-skill immigration strengthens nationalism, while high-skill immigration weakens it (Moriconi et al., 2018).

Financial Globalization

Unlike trade and immigration, financial globalization has not received much attention in popular discussions as a source of the populist backlash. This is surprising in some ways. The free flow of short-term finance across national borders and the buildup of significant foreign liabilities have played a significant role in triggering the financial crisis of 2008–2009, which was the most severe economic shock experienced by advanced nations since the Great Depression of the 1930s until the more recent COVID-19 pandemic. The fiscal austerity that deepened and lengthened the employment impact of the crisis, particularly in Europe, was the result of conducting economic policy according to the perceived requirements of financial markets. Yet there has not been much apparent political reaction against financial globalization. Global banks and financial speculators have not become targets in the way Chinese exports or Mexican and Muslim immigrants have. This stands in sharp contrast to the original wave of populism in the late-nineteenth-century United States, during which the northeastern financial establishment drew much ire as the upholders of the Gold Standard and hard money.

The scholarly empirical literature on the relationship between financial crises/globalization and populism is correspondingly thin, and disproportionately historical * * *. Funke et al. (2016) look at the electoral consequences of financial crises in 20 developed countries since 1870. They find that financial crises increase the vote share of far-right parties (but not far-left parties) by around 4 percentage points on average (a 30 percent increase) and that the results are statistically stronger for the post–World War II period. Interestingly, regular business-cycle recessions or macro shocks that do not involve financial crises do not produce similar effects. Doerr et al. (2019) focus more narrowly on Germany during the 1930s and show that exposure to bank failures increased support for the Nazi party, with localities with a history of anti-Semitism showing larger effects.

Two other papers cover the interesting recent cases of Hungary and Poland. These Eastern European countries are intriguing because they were not subject to the kind of trade and immigration shocks experienced by the United States and Western Europe. Yet, they have experienced similar electoral gains by right-wing ethno-nationalist populist movements. These papers suggest external financial shocks may have played a more prominent role there. Gyöngyösi and Verner (2020) study the rise of the far-right Jobbik party in Hungary after the financial crisis of 2008. Many Hungarian households had borrowed in foreign currencies (primarily the Swiss franc). The sharp depreciation of the Hungarian forint after the crisis left these borrowers in severe distress. Gyöngyösi and Verner (2020) show that the far-right populist vote increased especially strongly in localities where foreign currency debt exposure was higher, with this financial channel accounting for as much as 20 percent of the increase in the far-right vote.

Ahlquist et al. (2018) carry out an analysis similar in spirit for the Polish parliamentary elections of 2015, which brought the right-wing populist party PiS to power. These elections followed the Swiss National Bank's decision to allow the Swiss Franc to appreciate. This meant a large and unexpected adverse financial shock to Polish borrowers who had taken out low interest-rate mortgages denominated in Swiss Francs. Using a survey carried out just before the elections, Ahlquist et al. (2018) study Polish voters' policy preferences. They document that those exposed to the shock were more likely to demand government action that would make banks pay a larger share of the cost. Among former government voters, Swiss Franc borrowers were more likely to desert the government and vote for PiS. As the authors also make clear, the PiS actively courted these voters by broadening its nationalist, anti-immigrant platform to include policies that would shift the cost of the Zloty depreciation to the banks and protect the borrowers—proposals designed to appeal to the economic interests of the affected voters. So this case appears to be an example of both channel (*A*) and channel (*C*) in operation.

Economic Insecurity in General

Whether they take the form of increased import penetration, influx of immigrants, or financial crises, globalization shocks can cause significant economic distress in various segments of the population. But they are certainly not the only source of economic dislocation. As a cause of job loss, income volatility, and economic insecurity in general, their role is easily dwarfed by other cyclical and secular economic movements. Automation, deindustrialization, de-unionization, flexibilization of labor markets, rising economic inequality, the expansion of the gig economy, expansion of part-time work, and spatial concentration of productive economic activities have all loomed large in labor markets in recent decades. In general, these trends have produced greater economic anxiety and a squeeze of middle-class livelihoods (see Center for American Progress, 2014, on the United States, and Eurofound, 2017, on Europe).[8] Globalization is related of course to many of these trends, but it is far from the only cause. * * *

Some of the studies * * * take as their independent variable unemployment or declines in incomes, without scrutinizing what may lie behind. But two types of non-globalization shocks in labor markets merit particular mention: automation and labor market de-regulation.

On automation, Anelli, Colantone, and Stanig (2019) study 14 West European nations between 1993 and 2016, looking at individual or regional exposure to automation (instrumented by robot adoption in other countries) based on ex ante industrial structure or occupation. They find greater exposure to robots increases support for right-wing populist parties, both among individuals and across regions. They report that these results are robust to controlling separately for a wide set of cultural values at the individual level (though, as they point out, these attitudinal variables are arguably "post-treatment" indicators, influenced by labor market shocks). Interestingly, they also include the Autor et al. (2017) China trade shock variable, which they find has a small and statistically insignificant effect on the rightward political shift. They attribute the result on trade to be due to the fact that the present study covers a later period than the earlier Colantone and Stanig (2018b) paper, which found a large effect for an almost identical sample of countries.[9]

Dal Bó et al. (2019) focus on the rise of the far-right Sweden Democrats. The authors hone in on the reforms of labor market and welfare state arrangements in 2006 alongside the economic insecurity generated by the financial crisis. These reforms produced greater inequality in Sweden and a deeper divide between labor market insiders who benefited from stable, well-paying jobs and outsiders with stagnant incomes and unpredictable employment opportunities. The paper finds that support for Sweden Democrats correlates strongly, across and within municipalities, with the presence of losers from the reforms and from the financial crisis. Interestingly, and in contrast to many other studies cited earlier, this paper does not find any direct correlation between patterns of local immigration and support for the far right. The authors note, however, that labor market reforms made outsider, anti-immigration voters shift towards Sweden Democrats. As they summarize the results, "our results rhyme well with the idea that an economic shock which creates insecurity may interact with pre-existing, latent, traits among some voters, and lead them to switch their political allegiance." In other words, channel (*B*) seems to operate alongside channel (*A*).

This paper is also one of the few to make an explicit distinction between the demand and supply sides of politics (along with Guiso et al., 2018, and Rodrik, 2018) in accounting for the rise of populists. The authors find that politicians from the Sweden Democrats are more likely to be drawn from "outsiders and vulnerable insiders" compared to other parties. To recall Figure 8.1, this is another instance of economic shocks driving the supply-side of politics (causal pathway (C)). They speculate that this might be the reason it has been the extreme right rather than the left that has been able to capitalize on labor market dislocation.

Globalization and Economics as Cultural Flash Points

The rich empirical literature I have discussed in the previous section raises two questions. First, why does globalization elicit such an outsized political backlash, when it is just one of the forces that have buffeted labor markets and the macro economy in recent decades? As I have noted, technological change, de-industrialization, and the usual churn of firm contraction and closure impart a much stronger footprint on labor markets than trade or immigration. Yet, empirical evidence leaves no doubt that globalization has played a significant role in the rise of populism in recent years. Second, why has the political backlash taken a largely right-wing, nativist form? The studies I have discussed find that the backlash has overwhelmingly benefited right-wing populists. Left-wing populists who may have been programmatically better positioned to take advantage of the labor market shocks, with their redistributionist agendas, do not seem to have been much advantaged.

The two questions may be related. As many studies note, globalization shocks play on latent cultural and identity divisions in society, both activating and magnifying them. Trade, immigration and financial shocks present obvious "outsider" targets: foreign exporters, culturally different workers, international banks. Economic anxieties and inse-

curities threats can be recast as threats on the dominant group's traditional way of life, deepening the divide between "us" and "them." This can be a particularly potent channel if the regions of the country or segments of the labor market adversely affected by globalization are less diverse and culturally homogenous, where traditional identities and cultural values are strong to begin with. In terms of Figure 8.1, this argument suggests the indirect channel (B) may be quite powerful, stronger even than the direct channel (A).

Consider first some direct evidence on the outsized response to globalization shocks. Di Tella and I carried out an online survey where we provided respondents with what looked like a newspaper story on a planned factory closure in a fictitious local community (di Tella and Rodrik, 2020). All of our subjects (except those in the control group) were told 900 jobs were at risk. But they were separated into distinct treatment groups with different explanations for why the factory may close. One group was told the factory closure was due to automation (technology shock). The second group was told there had been a shift in consumer preferences away from the products manufactured in the plant (demand shift). A third was told the problem was due to management failure (bad management). Finally, the other treatment groups were told the factory might close because of outsourcing to a foreign country. All respondents were then asked whether they thought the government should do anything in response, and if yes, whether they favored transfers to those who become unemployed (compensation) or import protection.

Figure 8.2 summarizes the results. First note that both technology and demand shocks elicit a protectionist response of 5 percentage points or so. The increase in desired compensation is of the same order of magnitude, if somewhat smaller. Bad management, by contrast, elicits a demand for transfers to workers, but not a statistically significant protectionist response. This stands to reason insofar as respondents want to assist workers

Figure 8.2. Preferred Responses to Labor Market Displacement Shocks

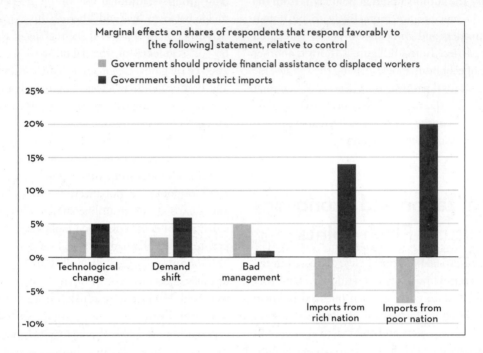

Source: Di Tella and Rodrik, "Labour Market Shocks and the Demand for Trade Protection: Evidence from Online Surveys," *The Economic Journal* (2020).

but not managers and owners when the fault lies with the latter. What really stands out in the chart, however, is the magnitude of the protectionist response when subjects are told the reason for the prospective plant closure is international trade. The last two treatments in the chart differ by one word only. In one case subjects are told the outsourcing is to France; in the other case, they are told it is to Cambodia. The percentage of respondents who ask for import protection more than doubles in the first case (France), compared to the technology and demand shocks. It quadruples in the second case (Cambodia). And the demand for transfers falls in both cases. Not only is the demand for trade protection highly elastic with respect to negative trade shocks, respondents apparently treat trade with advanced nations very differently than trade with developing nations.

Consider why there is such a big difference in the way that our subjects approach trade with France versus trade with Cambodia. From an economic-utilitarian perspective, we might have expected respondents to look more favorably on imports from a developing nation. A poorer nation stands to lose more from cutoffs in market access to the United States. Therefore, a utilitarian calculus would have produced a greater willingness to restrict imports from the richer nation. A cultural-differences perspective, however, yields a different answer. Our American respondents might have thought of Cambodians as much less "like us" than the French, and less worthy of sympathy. They would then have exhibited a greater willingness to penalize them. The results we obtained suggest strongly that the cultural perspective was the dominant one among our respondents. Furthermore, when we divided our sample (in the pre-treatment phase of the experiment) between subjects who had favored Trump in the 2016 presidential elections and subjects who had favored Hillary Clinton, we found that the additional protectionist boost in the case of Cambodia was concentrated among those who favored Trump (di Tella and Rodrik, 2020, Table 5). In other words, what was presumably a cultural aversion to Cambodia was magnified among those respondents who were already likely to be more intolerant of cultural differences.

Labor market shocks that drive a greater wedge between winners and losers can inflame latent cultural tensions. Grossman and Helpman (2019) develop a model that describes one possible mechanism. In their model, cultural associations of lower-skill individuals are driven by two conflicting forces. On the one hand, they benefit from identifying with "the nation as a whole," a category which includes the high-skilled individuals with higher social status. On the other hand, they pay a cognitive-dissonance cost to the extent their material circumstances differ from the average member of the national aggregate. A trade shock such as greater Chinese import penetration increases the latter cost by generating a bigger earnings gap between skill groups. That in turn can induce a change in social and cultural identification patterns whereby lower-skill individuals no longer view themselves as members of the nation as a whole, but as members of a narrower group. When racial or ethnic characteristics are also associated with group identities, this segmentation of identities can also exhibit itself in cultural terms.

Wilkinson (2019) provides an interesting account of how spatial sorting may serve to reinforce the interaction between economics and values to produce a populist backlash. Less educated, socially conservative whites have a lower propensity to migrate to urban areas. Meanwhile, globalization, technological change, and other economic trends have disproportionally benefited urban areas, in particular mega-cities. The China trade shock has hit smaller urban areas and white middle-class communities particularly hard. In Wilkinson's words, "rural stagnation is widening the already significant gap in cultural and moral values produced by the increasing spatial separation of urbanizers and rooted holdouts" (Wilkinson, 2019, 6). This kind of spatial segregation is particularly conducive to generating distrust and magnifying aversion to cultural outsiders (Enos, 2017). Hence economic adversity that exacerbates a pre-existing cultural divide can turn into a powerful force for right-wing populists to leverage in the political sphere. While Wilkinson's story focuses on the United States, it is clear that Europe shares similar features as well. Spatial segregation, between liberals in urban centers and socially conservative residents of outlying areas, has clearly added fuel to the populist backlash (see also Norris and Inglehart, 2019).

Such effects can be amplified through dynamic feedback loops. If globalization shocks make identity more salient and the result is party platforms that reduce transfers to the poor (both whites and minorities), then the increased economic insecurity of poor whites may increase their aversion to minorities and intensify their desire to cut transfers to them further. This is akin to the mechanism described at length in Arlie Hochschild's ethnographic study of "white anger" in *Strangers in Their Own Land* (Hochschild).

These stories are all demand-side stories (focusing on causal pathway (*B*) in Figure 8.1). Economic shocks trigger natural psycho-social processes that alter individual preferences and identities. But economics can inflame culture wars through the supply side as well, by inducing political leaders or parties to adopt campaign strategies deliberately designed to prime latent ethno-religious sensitivites and divides. This is the possibility highlighted by causal pathway (*D*) in Figure 8.1.

In Mukand and Rodrik (2018) we provide one possible mechanism. In this model, political entrepreneurs or parties compete for political support by appealing to either voters' economic interests or to voters' ideas, with the latter including ideas about cultural identities or "who they are." One of the results in the paper is that as economic inequality increases in society, a party representing the rich is more likely to invest in strategies that appeal to identity and culture. Greater inequality means the median voter grows more distant from the rich in terms of where she stands on economic policy interests. For the party of the rich, there is now higher return from a political narrative that catalyses identity around issues such as racial resentment, gay marriage, women's rights, and immigration, all of which can give low-income voters a reason to vote against their purely material interests.

Hacker and Pierson (2020) argue that this is exactly the strategy the Republican Party pursued as U.S. inequality began to rise after the 1970s. The puzzle they address is how the Party was able to advance a right-wing policy agenda—tax reduction, deregulation, weakening of labor market protections, cuts in social insurance—that benefited the wealthy and was increasingly unpopular on its own terms. The answer is that the Party adopted a racially charged narrative to enhance the appeal of regressive policies to middle- and lower-middle-class white voters. Hacker and Pierson (2020) cite an interview in which Republican political operative Lee Atwater lays out the strategy explicitly.[10] Republicans must use language that is a "lot more" abstract than using the n-word, Atwater told the interviewer. Policies that benefited the rich had to be packaged in terms that would resonate with poorer, white voters. For example, "we want to cut this" would convey "blacks get hurt worse than whites" (Hacker and Pierson, 2020, 112). As Hacker and Pierson put it, "Republicans used white identity to defend wealth inequality." Their account makes clear that America's version of right-wing populism predates Trump.[11]

Concluding Remarks: Is Populism Always at Odds with Globalization?

This paper has focused on the causal links between globalization and other economic shocks, on the one hand, and the rise of populism, on the other. Before closing, it is worth spending a moment on the reverse linkage, from populism to globalization. The present-day literature takes it as almost axiomatic that populists are against globalization. And to the extent that globalization, in its many facets, is a driver of globalization, this seems like a sensible presumption. But when we disaggregate the two concepts, we can see some interesting departures from received wisdom.

British proponents of Brexit are normally classified with other populists. And in their opposition to immigration, they shared a common bugaboo with populists in other nations. But they were also, at least nominally, free traders. One of the arguments put forth by "Economists for Brexit" (2016) was that the EU was a protectionist bloc, maintaining high barriers to protect its agriculture and manufacturing. They argued Brexit would enable Britain to reduce those barriers and reap significantly larger gains by trading at world market prices. What the Brexiteers opposed first and foremost was the European Union and the supranational rules emanating from it. Restoring national democratic sovereigny over economic policy would allow Britain to devise its own rules, which in the case of trade, were expected to be more liberal.

The Brexit case illustrates the general principle that populists are not always and necessarily protectionist. What they oppose are the elites—domestic or foreign—that they claim over-ride the popular will at home. Their views on globalization are often mediated through the relationship of those elites to the international economy.

A second case in point is the U.S. populist movement during the late nineteenth century. The movement arose out of the plight of farmers in the southern and western parts of the country who were being squeezed by decline in agriculture prices, on the one hand, and high debt burdens, on the other. The Gold Standard was seen as responsible, since it kept credit conditions tight and prevented an increase in the money supply. The People's Party's ire was directed at the supporters of the Gold Standard, Northeastern bankers, and the financial elite. William Jennings Bryan's famous rallying cry of 1896 is a ringing statement of populists' hostility to the financial globalization of their day: "You shall not crucify mankind upon a cross of gold."

Late-nineteenth-century American populists may have been against bankers and global finance, but they also opposed tariffs. The United States had at the time quite high import tariffs, due to the Civil War tariffs that were further raised by the McKinley tariff of 1890. Republicans generally favored high tariffs, which they viewed as important for developing American industry. Democrats and Populists thought import tariffs were a regressive tax that hurt ordinary people and benefited mainly the northeastern industrial classes (Irwin 2017, 244ff). Populists sought to replace the tariff with a progressive income tax instead (Mehrotra, 2002, 178). As one labor advocate put it at the time, the import tariff was

> devised to draw the money from the working people chiefly, and then to cover up the amount so taken, that they might be squeezed without knowing it. It was seen that if a man should be taxed ten dollars for the privilege of wearing an overcoat, he would rebel against such an outrage, but if, by any hocus-pocus, he could be prevailed on to buy the garment, with the tax added to its original cost, he would not suspect the extent of his robbery. . . . (quoted in Mehrotra, 2002, 183)

Hence American populists of an earlier era had a much more sound understanding of the workings of import tariffs than many apparently do today. Populists lost this particular battle, and their crusade against the Gold Standard did not bear fruit either. But their ideas were long-lived. Income taxation became a permanent fixture of the U.S. economy after the passage of a constitutional amendment in 1913. Franklin D. Roosevelt took the country out of the Gold Standard eventually in 1933.

Populists in late-nineteenth-century America wanted freer trade because they believed protection helped the country's elites and hurt ordinary people. Today's populists want protection for the same reason, namely that globalization benefits the rich and wealthy but harms the middle class. There are of course many differences between the People's Party back then and Trumpist Republicans today. But in terms of attitudes towards globalization, what has changed in the meantime is not the nature of populism, but the relationship of the American elite to the world economy.

NOTES

1. See Rodrik (1997, 2011) on the economic and social rifts created by advanced stages of globalization, and Rodrik (2018) for an earlier overview of the relationship between globalization and populism.
2. Margalit (2019) calls these "outcome" versus "explanatory" significance, but I am not sure if this nomenclature is quite appropriate. The difference has to do more with the kind of outcome we are trying to explain. The level and change in support for populists are both outcomes, and we could be interested in explaining either.
3. In a similar vein, Steiner and Harms (2020) find Chinese import shocks lead respondents in Britain to develop more nationalistic attitudes, but not greater affinity to redistributive economic policies.
4. As in the U.S., trade shocks seem to have boosted the electoral fortunes of mostly right-wing populist movements in Europe and not the left. One exception is the study by Rommel and Walter (2017), which finds that a measure of offshorability of occupation of European respondents is associated with support for leftist and center-right parties but not right-wing populists.
5. On the importance of geography and spatial segregation, see Enos (2017).
6. Figure 8.1 contains other possibilities, on the supply side, which I ignore for the moment. An increase in immigration can also alter

party platforms (C) and induce political candidates to "prime" racial/ethnic/religious identities. I will return to this channel in a later section of the paper.

7. Tabellini performs a number of checks to control against threats to his instrument's validity—early immigrant numbers may predict subsequent political outcomes.

8. Economic insecurity can be hard to disentangle from anxiety with regard to loss of social status. See however Gidron and Hall (2017) and Kurer (2020).

9. The Anelli et al. (2019) study covers a more recent period in which the China shock had dissipated somewhat and the financial crisis and austerity policies had a much larger footprint. The authors report that when they restrict their time coverage to the pre-crisis period, they recover a strong China trade shock effect, while automation retains its significance. Caselli et al. (2020) also find that China trade shock does not have a significant effect on vote shares for far-right parties in Italy after 2008.

10. Atwater was promised lifetime anonymity for his comments, which came into the public domain after his untimely death in 1991.

11. As Hopkins (2019) points out, Trump's presidential campaign contained strong undertones of anti-Latino priming as well. Yet Hopkins (2019) finds anti-Latino prejudice was not strongly predictive of the shift to Trump, while anti-Black prejudice was a strong predictor. Another indication that party strategies to prime ethnic divisions may not always be successful comes from Schwartz et al. (2020), who report that anti-immigrant and anti-refugee sentiments among their sample of UK respondents actually softened after the Brexit referendum.

REFERENCES

Ahlquist, John, Mark Copelovitch, and Stefanie Walter. "The Political Consequences of External Economic Shocks: Evidence from Poland." *American Journal of Political Science*, 2020. https://doi.org /10.1111/ajps.12503.

Algan, Yann, Sergei Guriev, Elias Papaioannou, and Evgenia Passari. "The European Trust Crisis and the Rise of Populism." *Brookings Papers on Economic Activity*, 2017, 309.

American National Election Studies. *User's Guide and Codebook for the ANES 2016 Time Series Study*. University of Michigan and Stanford University, 2019.

Anelli, Massimo, Italo Colantone, and Piero Stanig. "We Were the Robots: Automation and Voting Behavior in Western Europe." *SSRN Electronic Journal*, 2019. https://doi.org/10.2139/ssrn .3419966.

Autor, David, David Dorn, Gordon Hanson, and Kaveh Majlesi. "A Note on the Effect of Rising Trade Exposure on the 2016 Presidential Election." Appendix to Autor, Dorn, Hanson, and Majlesi, "Importing Political Polarization? The Electoral Consequences of Rising Trade Exposure," 2017.

———. "Importing Political Polarization? The Electoral Consequences of Rising Trade Exposure." *American Economic Review* 110, no. 10 (2020): 3139–83.

Autor, David H., David Dorn, and Gordon H. Hanson. "The China Syndrome: Local Labor Market Effects of Import Competition in the United States." *American Economic Review* 103, no. 6 (2013): 2121–2168. https://doi.org/10.1257/aer.103.6.2121.

Ballard-Rosa, Cameron, Amalie Jensen, and Kenneth Scheve. "Economic Decline, Social Identity, and Authoritarian Values in the United States," *International Studies Quarterly*, 2021. https:// doi.org/10.1093/isq/sqab027.

Barone, Guglielmo, Alessio D'Ignazio, Guido de Blasio, and Paolo Naticchioni. "Mr. Rossi, Mr. Hu and Politics: The Role of Immigration in Shaping Natives' Voting Behavior." *Journal of Public Economics* 136 (2016): 1–13.

Barone, Guglielmo, and Helena Kreuter. "Low-Wage Import Competition and Populist Backlash: The Case of Italy." Working Paper. FiFo Discussion Paper, 2019. https://www.econstor.eu/handle/10419 /210375.

Becker, Sascha O, and Thiemo Fetzer. "Did Eastern European Immigration Cause an Increase in Anti-European Sentiment in the UK?," August 22, 2017, 77.

Becker, Sascha O., Thiemo Fetzer, and Dennis Novy. "Who Voted for Brexit? A Comprehensive District-Level Analysis." *Economic Policy* 32, no. 92 (2017): 601–650. https://doi.org/10.1093/epolic/eix012.

Bergh, Andreas, and Anders Gustafsson. "Globalization and Populism in Europe." *SSRN Electronic Journal*, 2019. https://doi.org/10.2139 /ssrn.3489924.

Bornschier, Simon. "Globalization, Cleavages and the Radical Right," in Jens Rydgren, ed., *The Oxford Handbook of the Radical Right*, Oxford University Press, 2018.

Bromhead, Alan de, Barry Eichengreen, and Kevin H. O'Rourke. "Political Extremism in the 1920s and 1930s: Do German Lessons Generalize?" *The Journal of Economic History* 73, no. 2 (June 2013): 371–406. https://doi.org/10.1017/S0022050713000302.

Brunner, Beatrice, and Andreas Kuhn. "Immigration, Cultural Distance and Natives' Attitudes Towards Immigrants: Evidence from Swiss Voting Results." *Kyklos* 71, no. 1 (2018): 28–58. https://doi.org/10 .1111/kykl.12161.

Caselli, Mauro, Andrea Fracasso, and Silvio Traverso. "Globalization, Robotization and Electoral Outcomes: Evidence from Spatial Regressions for Italy." *Journal of Regional Science* 61, no. 1 (2021): 86–111. https://doi.org/10.1111/jors.12503.

Center for American Progress. "The Middle-Class Squeeze: A Picture of Stagnant Incomes, Rising Costs, and What We Can Do to Strengthen America's Middle Class," September 2014. https://cdn .americanprogress.org/wp-content/uploads/2014/09 /MiddeClassSqueeze.pdf.

Cerrato, Andrea, Federico Maria Ferrara, and Francesco Ruggieri. "Why Does Import Competition Favor Republicans? Localized Trade Shocks, Voting Behavior, and Scapegoating in the U.S." *SSRN Electronic Journal*, 2018. https://doi.org/10.2139/ssrn.3147169.

Che, Yi, Yi Lu, Jusin R. Pierce, Peter K. Schott, and Zhigang Tao. "Did Trade Liberalization with China Influence U.S. Elections?," National Bureau of Economic Research 2017.

Chen, Shuai. "Unemployment, Immigration, and Populism: Evidence from Two Quasi-Natural Experiments in the United States," GLO Discussion Paper Series 652, Global Labor Organization (GLO), 2018.

Choi, Jiwon, Ilyana Kuziemko, Ebonya Washington, and Gavin Wright. "Local Employment and Political Effects of Trade Deals: Evidence from NAFTA," February 2, 2020.

Colantone, Italo, and Piero Stanig. "Global Competition and Brexit." *The American Political Science Review* 112, no. 2 (2018): 201–218. https://doi.org/10.1017/S0003055417000685.

———. "The Economic Determinants of the 'Cultural Backlash': Globalization and Attitudes in Western Europe." *SSRN Electronic Journal*, 2018. https://doi.org/10.2139/ssrn.3267139.

———. "The Trade Origins of Economic Nationalism: Import Competition and Voting Behavior in Western Europe." *American Journal of Political Science* 62, no. 4 (2018): 936–953. https://doi.org/10.1111/ajps.12358.

Dal Bó, Ernesto, Frederico Finan, Olle Folke, Torsten Persson, and Johanna Rickne. "Economic Losers and Political Winners: Sweden's Radical Right." Working Paper, University of California, Berkeley, February 2019, 64.

Dauth, Wolfgang, Sebastian Findeisen, and Jens Suedekum. "The Rise of the East and the Far East: German Labor Markets and Trade Integration." *Journal of the European Economic Association* 12, no. 6 (December 1, 2014): 1643–75. https://doi.org/10.1111/jeea.12092.

Di Tella, Rafael, and Dani Rodrik. "Labour Market Shocks and the Demand for Trade Protection: Evidence from Online Surveys." *The Economic Journal*, 2020. https://doi.org/10.1093/ej/ueaa006.

Dinas, Elias, Konstantinos Matakos, Dimitrios Xefteris, and Dominik Hangartner. "Waking Up the Golden Dawn: Does Exposure to the Refugee Crisis Increase Support for Extreme-Right Parties?" *Political Analysis* 27, no. 2 (2019): 244–254. https://doi.org/10.1017/pan.2018.48.

Dippel, Christian, Robert Gold, Stephan Heblich, and Rodrigo R. Pinto. "Instrumental Variables and Causal Mechanisms: Unpacking the Effect of Trade on Workers and Voters." *CESifo Working Paper Series*, no. 6816 (January 17, 2018). https://escholarship.org/uc/item/4kp5c6jj.

Doerr, Sebastian, Stefan Gissler, José-Luis Peydró, and Hans-Joachim Voth. "From Finance to Fascism." *Barcelona GSE Working Paper No. 1092*, April 2020.

Dustmann, Christian, Kristine Vasiljeva, and Anna Piil Damm. "Refugee Migration and Electoral Outcomes." *The Review of Economic Studies* 86, no. 5 (2018): 2035–91. https://doi.org/10.1093/restud/rdy047.

Economists for Brexit. *The Economy after Brexit*, 2016. https://www.economistsforfreetrade.com/wp-content/uploads/2017/08/Economists for Brexit The Economy after Brexit.pdf.

Edo, Anthony, Yvonne Giesing, Jonathan Öztunc, and Panu Poutvaara. "Immigration and Electoral Support for the Far-Left and the Far-Right." *European Economic Review* 115 (June 2019): 99–143. https://doi.org/10.1016/j.euroecorev.2019.03.001.

Eichengreen, Barry, Michael Haines, Matthew Jaremski, and David Leblang. "Populists at the Polls: Economic Factors in the 1896 Presidential Election." *NBER Working Paper Series*, 2017, 23932. https://doi.org/10.3386/w23932.

Enke, Benjamin. "Moral Values and Voting," *Journal of Political Economy* 128, no. 10 (October 11, 2019).

Enos, Ryan D. *The Space Between Us: Social Geography and Politics*. Cambridge, United Kingdom; New York, NY: Cambridge University Press, 2017.

Eurofound. *Income Inequalities and Employment Patterns in Europe before and after the Great Recession*. Luxembourg: Publications Office of the European Union, 2017. https://op.europa.eu/en/publication-detail/-/publication/ab252b03-150c-11e7-808e01aa75ed71a1/language-en.

Fetzer, Thiemo. "Did Austerity Cause Brexit?" *American Economic Review* 109, no. 11 (November 2019): 3849–86. https://doi.org/10.1257/aer.20181164.

Funke, Manuel, Moritz Schularick, and Christoph Trebesch. "Going to Extremes: Politics after Financial Crises, 1870–2014." *European Economic Review* 88 (2016): 227–260. https://doi.org/10.1016/j.euroecorev.2016.03.006.

Gerdes, Christer, and Eskil Wadensjö. "The Impact of Immigration on Election Outcomes in Danish Municipalities." *SULCIS Working Papers*. SULCIS Working Papers. Stockholm University, Linnaeus Center for Integration Studies–SULCIS, March 10, 2010. https://ideas.repec.org/p/hhs/sulcis/2010_003.html

Gibbons, Joseph. "The Space between Us: Social Geography and Politics." *Contemporary Sociology: A Journal of Reviews* 48, no. 2 (2019): 163–165. https://doi.org/10.1177/0094306119828696i.

Gidron, Noam, and Peter A. Hall. "The Politics of Social Status: Economic and Cultural Roots of the Populist Right." *British Journal of Sociology* 68, no. S1 (2017): S57–S84. https://doi.org/10.1111/1468-4446.12319.

Gomez, Raul, and Luis Ramiro. "Beyond the 2008 Great Recession: Economic Factors and Electoral Support for the Radical Left in Europe," *Party Politics* (July 10, 2017): 1–11. https://doi.org/10.1177%2F1354068817718949.

Guiso, Luigi, Helios Herrera, Massimo Morelli, and Tommaso Sonno. "Populism: Demand and Supply," EIEF Working Papers Series 1703, Einaudi Institute for Economics and Finance (EIEF), revised February 2017.

Guriev, Sergei, and Elias Papaioannou. "The Political Economy of Populism," CEPR Discussion Paper DP14433, February 2020.

Gyöngyösi, Gyozo, and Emil Verner. "Financial Crisis, Creditor-Debtor Conflict, and Populism," VfS Annual Conference 2018 (Freiburg, Breisgau): Digital Economy 181587, February 2020.

Hacker, Jacob S., and Paul Pierson. *Let Them Eat Tweets: How the Right Rules in an Age of Extreme Inequality*. New York and London: Liveright Publishing, 2020.

Halla, Martin, Alexander F. Wagner, and Josef Zweimüller. "Immigration and Voting for the Far Right." *Journal of the European Economic Association* 15, no. 6 (2017): 1341–1385. https://doi.org/10.1093/jeea/jvx003.

Harmon, Nikolaj A. "Immigration, Ethnic Diversity, and Political Outcomes: Evidence from Denmark." *The Scandinavian Journal of Economics* 120, no. 4 (2018): 1043–74. https://doi.org/10.1111/sjoe.12239.

Hill, Seth J., Daniel J. Hopkins, and Gregory A. Huber. "Local Demographic Changes and US Presidential Voting, 2012 to 2016," *PNAS*, December 2019. www.pnas.org/cgi/doi/10.1073/pnas.1909202116.

Hobolt, Sara B., and James Tilley. "Fleeing the Centre: The Rise of Challenger Parties in the Aftermath of the Euro Crisis." *West European Politics* 39, no. 5 (June 16, 2016): 971–91. https://doi.org/10.1080/01402382.2016.1181871.

Hochschild, Arlie Russell. *Strangers in Their Own Land: Anger and Mourning on the American Right*. New York: The New York Press, 2016.

Hopkins, Daniel J. "The Activation of Prejudice and Presidential Voting: Panel Evidence from the 2016 U.S. Election," *Political Behavior*, online publication, September 2019.

Im, Zhen Jie, Nonna Mayer, Bruno Palier, and Jan Rovny. "The 'Losers of Automation': A Reservoir of Votes for the Radical Right?" *Research & Politics* 6, no. 1 (2019). https://doi.org/10.1177/2053168018822395.

Inglehart, Ronald, and Pippa Norris. "Trump, Brexit, and the Rise of Populism: Economic Have-Nots and Cultural Backlash." *SSRN Electronic Journal*, 2016. https://doi.org/10.2139/ssrn.2818659.

Irwin, Douglas A. *Clashing over Commerce: A History of US Trade Policy.* Chicago: The University of Chicago Press, 2017.

Iversen, Torben, David Soskice, and Alice Xu. "Transition to the Knowledge Economy and the Rise of Populism: A Human Capital Perspective." Working Paper, Harvard University, 2017.

Jensen, J. Bradford, Dennis P. Quinn, and Stephen Weymouth. "Winners and Losers in International Trade: The Effects on US Presidential Voting." *International Organization* 71, no. 3 (2017): 423–457. https://doi.org/10.1017/S0020818317000194.

Kurer, Thomas. "The Declining Middle: Occupational Change, Social Status and the Populist Right," *Comparative Political Studies*, 2020.

Malgouyres, Clement. "Trade Shocks and Far-Right Voting: Evidence from French Presidential Elections." *SSRN Electronic Journal*, 2017. https://doi.org/10.2139/ssrn.2942173.

Margalit, Yotam. "Costly Jobs: Trade-Related Layoffs, Government Compensation, and Voting in U.S. Elections." *American Political Science Review* 105, no. 1 (2011): 166–188. https://doi.org/10.1017/S000305541000050X.

———. "Economic Insecurity and the Causes of Populism, Reconsidered." *Journal of Economic Perspectives* 33, no. 4 (2019): 152–170. https://doi.org/10.1257/jep.33.4.152.

Mayda, Anna Maria, Giovanni Peri, and Walter Steingress. "The Political Impact of Immigration: Evidence from the United States." *American Economic Journal: Applied Economics*, February 6, 2019.

Mehrotra, Ajay K. "'More Mighty than the Waves of the Sea': Toilers, Tariffs, and the Income Tax Movement, 1880–1913." *Labor History* 45, no. 2 (2004): 165–198. https://doi.org/10.1080/0023656042000217246.

Mendez, Ildefonso, and Isabel M. Cutillas. "Has Immigration Affected Spanish Presidential Elections Results?" *Journal of Population Economics* 27, no. 1 (January 2014): 135–71. https://doi.org/10.1007/s00148-013-0471-y.

Mian, Atif, Amir Sufi, and Francesco Trebbi. "Resolving Debt Overhang: Political Constraints in the Aftermath of Financial Crises." *American Economic Journal: Macroeconomics* 6, no. 2 (2014): 1–28. https://doi.org/10.1257/mac.6.2.1.

Moriconi, Simone, Giovanni Peri, and Riccardo Turati. "Skill of the Immigrants and Vote of the Natives: Immigration and Nationalism in European Elections 2007–2016." *NBER Working Paper Series*, 2018, 25077. https://doi.org/10.3386/w25077.

Mukand, Sharun, and Dani Rodrik. "The Political Economy of Ideas: On Ideas Versus Interests in Policymaking," National Bureau of Economic Research March 2018. https://drodrik.scholar.harvard.edu/publications/ideas-versus-interests.

Mutz, Diana C. "Status Threat, Not Economic Hardship, Explains the 2016 Presidential Vote." *Proceedings of the National Academy of*

Sciences of the United States of America 115, no. 19 (2018): E4330–39. https://doi.org/10.1073/pnas.1718155115.

Naoi, Megumi. "Survey Experiments in International Political Economy: What We (Don't) Know About the Backlash Against Globalization," *Annual Review of Political Science* 23 (2020): 333–56.

Norris, Pippa, and Ronald Inglehart. *Cultural Backlash: Trump, Brexit and Authoritarian Populism.* Cambridge, UK: Cambridge University Press, 2019.

Otto, Alkis Henri, and Max Friedrich Steinhardt. "Immigration and Election Outcomes—Evidence from City Districts in Hamburg." *Regional Science and Urban Economics* 45 (March 2014): 67–79. https://doi.org/10.1016/j.regsciurbeco.2014.01.004.

Rodrik, Dani. *Has Globalization Gone Too Far?* Institute for International Economics, Washington, D.C., 1997.

———. *The Globalization Paradox: Democracy and the Future of the World Economy*, New York: W. W. Norton, 2011.

———. "Populism and the Economics of Globalization," *Journal of International Business Policy* 1, no. 1–2 (2018): 12–33. https://doi.org/10.1057/s42214-018-0001-4.

Rommel, Tobias, and Stefanie Walter. "The Electoral Consequences of Offshoring: How the Globalization of Production Shapes Party Preferences." *Comparative Political Studies* 51, no. 5 (2018): 621–658. https://doi.org/10.1177/0010414017710264.

Rothwell, Jonathan T., and Pablo Diego-Rosell. "Explaining Nationalist Political Views: The Case of Donald Trump." *SSRN Electronic Journal*, 2016. https://doi.org/10.2139/ssrn.2822059.

Roupakias, Stelios, and Michael Chletsos. "Immigration and Far-Right Voting: Evidence from Greece," *The Annals of Regional Science*, 2020.

Schwartz, Cassilde, Miranda Simon, David Hudson, and Jennifer van-Heerde-Hudson. "A Populist Paradox? How Brexit Softened Anti-Immigrant Attitudes," *British Journal of Political Science*, 2020.

Sides, John, Michael Tesler, and Lynn Vavreck. *Identity Crisis: The 2016 Presidential Campaign and the Battle for the Meaning of America.* Princeton, NJ: Princeton University Press, 2018.

Steiner, Nils D., and Philipp Harms. "Local Trade Shocks and the Nationalist Backlash in Political Attitudes: Panel Data Evidence from Great Britain," Gutenberg School of Management and Economics, May 2020.

Swank, Duane, and Hans-Georg Betz. "Globalization, the Welfare State and Right-Wing Populism in Western Europe." *Socio-Economic Review* 1, no. 2 (2003): 215–245. https://doi.org/10.1093/soceco/1.2.215.

Tabellini, Marco. "Gifts of the Immigrants, Woes of the Natives: Lessons from the Age of Mass Migration." *The Review of Economic Studies* 87, no. 1 (2019): 454–86. https://doi.org/10.1093/restud/rdz027.

Vertier, Paul, and Max Viskanic. "Dismantling the 'Jungle': Migrant Relocation and Extreme Voting in France." SSRN Scholarly Paper. Rochester, NY: Social Science Research Network, January 9, 2019. https://doi.org/10.2139/ssrn.2963641.

Wilkinson, Will. "The Density Divide: Urbanization, Polarization, and Populist Backlash." Executive Summary. Washington, D.C.: Niskanen Center, June 2019.

Young, Alasdair R. "Two Wrongs Make a Right? The Politicization of Trade Policy and European Trade Strategy." *Journal of European Public Policy* 26, no. 12 (2019): 1883–1899. https://doi.org/10.1080/13501763.2019.1678055.

Henry Farrell and Abraham L. Newman

WILL THE CORONAVIRUS END GLOBALIZATION AS WE KNOW IT?
The Pandemic Is Exposing Market Vulnerabilities No One Knew Existed

The new coronavirus is shaping up to be an enormous stress test for globalization. As critical supply chains break down, and nations hoard medical supplies and rush to limit travel, the crisis is forcing a major reevaluation of the interconnected global economy. Not only has globalization allowed for the rapid spread of contagious disease but it has fostered deep interdependence between firms and nations that makes them more vulnerable to unexpected shocks. Now, firms and nations alike are discovering just how vulnerable they are.

But the lesson of the new coronavirus is not that globalization failed. The lesson is that globalization is fragile, despite or even because of its benefits. For decades, individual firms' relentless efforts to eliminate redundancy generated unprecedented wealth. But these efforts also reduced the amount of unused resources—what economists refer to as "slack"—in the global economy as a whole. In normal times, firms often see slack as a measure of idle, or even squandered, productive capacity. But too little slack makes the broader system brittle in times of crisis, eliminating critical fail-safes.

Lack of fail-safe manufacturing alternatives can cause supply chains to break down, as they have in some medical and health-related sectors as a result of the new coronavirus. Producers of vital medical supplies have been overwhelmed by a surge in global demand, pitting countries against one another in a competition for resources. The outcome has been a shift in power dynamics among major world economies, with those that are well prepared to combat the new virus either hoarding resources for themselves or assisting those that are not—and expanding their influence on the global stage as a result.

Fragile Efficiency

The conventional wisdom about globalization is that it created a thriving international marketplace, allowing manufacturers to build flexible supply chains by substituting one supplier or component for another as needed. Adam Smith's *The Wealth of Nations* became the wealth of the world as businesses took advantage of a globalized division of labor. Specialization produced greater efficiency, which in turn led to growth.

But globalization also created a complex system of interdependence. Companies embraced global supply chains, giving rise to a tangled web of production networks that wove the world economy together. The components of a given product could now be made in dozens of countries. This drive toward specialization sometimes made substitution difficult, especially for unusual skills or products. And as production went global, countries also

From *Foreign Affairs* (online), March 16, 2020.

became more interdependent, because no country could possibly control all the goods and components its economy needed. National economies were subsumed into a vast global network of suppliers.

The pandemic of the disease caused by the new coronavirus, COVID-19, is exposing the fragility of this globalized system. Some economic sectors—particularly those with a high degree of redundancy and in which production is spread across multiple countries—could weather the crisis relatively well. Others could be pushed close to collapse if the pandemic prevents a single supplier in a single country from producing a critical and widely used component. For example, car manufacturers across western Europe worry about shortages of small electronics because a single manufacturer, MTA Advanced Automotive Solutions, has been forced to suspend production at one of its plants in Italy.

In an earlier age, manufacturers might have built up stockpiles of supplies to protect themselves in a moment like this. But in the age of globalization, many businesses subscribe to Apple CEO Tim Cook's famous dictum that inventory is "fundamentally evil." Instead of paying to warehouse the parts that they need to manufacture a given product, these companies rely on "just-in-time" supply chains that function as the name suggests. But in the midst of a global pandemic, just-in-time can easily become too late. Partly as a result of supply chain problems, global production of laptops fell by as much as 50 percent in February, and production of smartphones could fall by 12 percent this coming quarter. Both products are built with components produced by specialized Asian manufacturers.

Critical Shortages

Production bottlenecks like the ones in electronics manufacturing are also hampering the fight against the new coronavirus. Critical medical supplies such as reagents, a key component of the test kits that laboratories use to detect viral RNA, are either running low or out of stock in many countries. Two companies dominate the production of the necessary reagents: the Dutch company Qiagen (recently purchased by the U.S. giant Thermo Fisher Scientific) and Roche laboratories, which is based in Switzerland. Both have been unable to keep up with the extraordinary surge in demand for their products. The shortfall has delayed the production of test kits in the United States, which finds itself having to get in line behind other countries to buy the chemicals it needs.

As the new virus spreads, some governments are giving in to their worst instincts. Even before the COVID-19 outbreak began, Chinese manufacturers made half of the world's medical masks. These manufacturers ramped up production as a result of the crisis, but the Chinese government effectively bought up the country's entire supply of masks, while also importing large quantities of masks and respirators from abroad. China certainly needed them, but the result of its buying spree was a supply crunch that hobbled other countries' response to the disease.

European countries didn't behave much better. Russia and Turkey prohibited the export of medical masks and respirators. Germany did the same, even though it is a member of the European Union, which is supposed to have a "single market" with unrestricted free trade among its member states. The French government took the simpler step of seizing all available masks. EU officials complained that such actions undermined solidarity and prevented the EU from adopting a common approach to combating the new virus, but they were simply ignored.

These beggar-thy-neighbor dynamics threaten to escalate as the crisis deepens, choking off global supply chains for urgent medical supplies. The problem is dire for the United States, which has been late to adopt a coherent response to the pandemic and is short on many of the supplies it will need. The United States has a national stockpile of masks, but it hasn't been replenished since 2009 and contains only a fraction of the number that could be required. Unsurprisingly, President Donald Trump's trade adviser, Peter Navarro, has used this and other shortages to threaten allies and to justify a further withdrawal from global trade, arguing that the United States needs to "bring home its manufacturing capabilities and supply chains for essential medicines." As a result, Germany is reportedly worried that the Trump administration will make the aggressive move of completely buying out a new vaccine under development by a German company in order to use it in the United States. Berlin is now considering whether to make a counterbid on the vaccine or ban the U.S. transaction.

Viral Influence

Whereas the Trump administration has used the pandemic to pull back on global integration, China is using the crisis to showcase its willingness to lead. As the first country hit by the new coronavirus, China suffered grievously over the last three months. But now it is beginning to recover, just as the rest of the world is succumbing to the disease. That poses a problem for Chinese manufacturers, many of which are now up and running again but facing weak demand from countries in crisis. But it also gives China an enormous short-term opportunity to influence the behavior of other states. Despite early mistakes that likely cost the lives of thousands of people, Beijing has learned how to fight the new virus, and it has stockpiles of equipment. These are valuable assets—and Beijing has deployed them with skill.

In early March, Italy called on other EU countries to provide emergency medical equipment as critical shortages forced its doctors to make heartbreaking decisions about which patients to try to save and which to let die. None of them responded. But China did, offering to sell ventilators, masks, protective suits, and swabs. As the China experts Rush Doshi and Julian Gewirtz have argued, Beijing seeks to portray itself as the leader of the global fight against the new coronavirus in order to promote goodwill and expand its influence.

This is awkward for the Trump administration, which has been slow to respond to the new virus (and which thinks banning travelers from Europe is the best defense against a disease that is already spreading rapidly on its soil). Far from serving as a global provider of public goods, the United States has few resources that it can offer to other states. To add insult to injury, the United States may soon find itself receiving Chinese charity: the billionaire cofounder of Alibaba, Jack Ma, has offered to donate 500,000 test kits and one million masks.

The New Geopolitics of Globalization

As policymakers around the world struggle to deal with the new coronavirus and its aftermath, they will have to confront the fact that the global economy doesn't work as they thought it did. Globalization calls for an ever-increasing specialization of labor across countries, a model that creates extraordinary efficiencies but also extraordinary vulnerabilities. Shocks such as the COVID-19 pandemic reveal these vulnerabilities. Single-source providers, or regions of the world that specialize in one particular product, can create unexpected fragility in moments of crisis, causing supply chains to break down. In the coming months, many more of these vulnerabilities will be exposed.

The result may be a shift in global politics. With the health and safety of their citizens at stake, countries may decide to block exports or seize critical supplies, even if doing so hurts their allies and neighbors. Such a retreat from globalization would make generosity an even more powerful tool of influence for states that can afford it. So far, the United States has not been a leader in the global response to the new coronavirus, and it has ceded at least some of that role to China. This pandemic is reshaping the geopolitics of globalization, but the United States isn't adapting. Instead, it's sick and hiding under the covers.

9 INTERGOVERNMENTAL ORGANIZATIONS AND NONGOVERNMENTAL ORGANIZATIONS

International organizations such as the United Nations (UN) are major actors in international relations. Samantha Power argued in her Pulitzer Prize–winning book *A Problem from Hell* (2002), as excerpted here from *The Atlantic*, that one of the key tasks of international organizations and powerful states should be to prevent massive atrocities. This policy objective, called the "responsibility to protect," or R2P, has subsequently been formally adopted by the United Nations. Power explains why neither the UN nor the United States did more to stop the 1994 genocide in Rwanda. Despite the adoption of R2P, her explanations still resonate in light of the international community's more recent failures to intervene to stop atrocities in the Syrian civil war and the expulsion of the Rohingya minority from Myanmar.

By way of contrast, John J. Mearsheimer, the quintessential realist, is skeptical about the impact of international institutions. He delineates the flaws of liberal institutionalist theory, arguing that international institutions exert no independent influence of their own because they simply reflect the underlying power and interests of states. Also critical of international organizations, but from a difficult angle of view, Michael N. Barnett and Martha Finnemore draw on constructivism to study the "pathologies" of international organizations that can lead to unintended consequences.

Erik Voeten explains the often misunderstood nature of deliberations in the United Nations Security Council. Its task is not mainly to apply international law to disputes or to bring specialized technical or analytic expertise to political problem solving. Rather, says Voeten, the value and effectiveness of the Security Council is as a venue for forging a broader consensus around major powers' desired projects for regional security and interventions, stipulating acceptable limits on goals and means.

In addition to intergovernmental organizations (IGOs) and international law, research on nongovernmental organizations (NGOs), social movements, and transnational advocacy networks has expanded since the 1990s. Using a constructivist approach, Margaret E. Keck and Kathryn Sikkink, in an excerpt from their award-winning book *Activists beyond Borders: Advocacy Networks in International Politics* (1998), show how such networks develop by "building new links among actors in civil societies, states, and international organizations."

Samantha Power

BYSTANDERS TO GENOCIDE
Why the United States Let the Rwandan Tragedy Happen

I. People Sitting in Offices

In the course of a hundred days in 1994 the Hutu government of Rwanda and its extremist allies very nearly succeeded in exterminating the country's Tutsi minority. Using firearms, machetes, and a variety of garden implements, Hutu militiamen, soldiers, and ordinary citizens murdered some 800,000 Tutsi and politically moderate Hutu. It was the fastest, most efficient killing spree of the twentieth century.

A few years later, in a series in *The New Yorker,* Philip Gourevitch recounted in horrific detail the story of the genocide and the world's failure to stop it. President Bill Clinton, a famously avid reader, expressed shock. He sent copies of Gourevitch's articles to his second-term national-security adviser, Sandy Berger. The articles bore confused, angry, searching queries in the margins. "Is what he's saying true?" Clinton wrote with a thick black felt-tip pen beside heavily underlined paragraphs. "How did this happen?" he asked, adding, "I want to get to the bottom of this." The President's urgency and outrage were oddly timed. As the terror in Rwanda had unfolded, Clinton had shown virtually no interest in stopping the genocide, and his Administration had stood by as the death toll rose into the hundreds of thousands.

Why did the United States not do more for the Rwandans at the time of the killings? Did the President really not know about the genocide, as

his marginalia suggested? Who were the people in his Administration who made the life-and-death decisions that dictated U.S. policy? Why did they decide (or decide not to decide) as they did? Were any voices inside or outside the U.S. government demanding that the United States do more? If so, why weren't they heeded? And most crucial, what could the United States have done to save lives?

So far people have explained the U.S. failure to respond to the Rwandan genocide by claiming that the United States didn't know what was happening, that it knew but didn't care, or that regardless of what it knew there was nothing useful to be done. The account that follows is based on a three-year investigation involving sixty interviews with senior, mid-level, and junior State Department, Defense Department, and National Security Council officials who helped to shape or inform U.S. policy. It also reflects dozens of interviews with Rwandan, European, and United Nations officials and with peacekeepers, journalists, and nongovernmental workers in Rwanda. Thanks to the National Security Archive (www.nsarchive.org), a nonprofit organization that uses the Freedom of Information Act to secure the release of classified U.S. documents, this account also draws on hundreds of pages of newly available government records. This material provides a clearer picture than was previously possible of the interplay among people, motives, and events. It reveals that the U.S. government knew enough about the genocide early on to save lives, but passed up countless opportunities to intervene.

From *The Atlantic* (September 2001): 84–108.

In March of 1998, on a visit to Rwanda, President Clinton issued what would later be known as the "Clinton apology," which was actually a carefully hedged acknowledgment. He spoke to the crowd assembled on the tarmac at Kigali Airport: "We come here today partly in recognition of the fact that we in the United States and the world community did not do as much as we could have and should have done to try to limit what occurred" in Rwanda.

This implied that the United States had done a good deal but not quite enough. In reality the United States did much more than fail to send troops. It led a successful effort to remove most of the UN peacekeepers who were already in Rwanda. It aggressively worked to block the subsequent authorization of UN reinforcements. It refused to use its technology to jam radio broadcasts that were a crucial instrument in the coordination and perpetuation of the genocide. And even as, on average, 8,000 Rwandans were being butchered each day, U.S. officials shunned the term "genocide," for fear of being obliged to act. The United States in fact did virtually nothing "to try to limit what occurred." Indeed, staying out of Rwanda was an explicit U.S. policy objective.

With the grace of one grown practiced at public remorse, the President gripped the lectern with both hands and looked across the dais at the Rwandan officials and survivors who surrounded him. Making eye contact and shaking his head, he explained, "It may seem strange to you here, especially the many of you who lost members of your family, but all over the world there were people like me sitting in offices, day after day after day, who *did not fully appreciate* [pause] the depth [pause] and the speed [pause] with which you were being engulfed by this *unimaginable* terror."

Clinton chose his words with characteristic care. It was true that although top U.S. officials could not help knowing the basic facts—thousands of Rwandans were dying every day—that were being reported in the morning papers, many did not

"fully appreciate" the meaning. In the first three weeks of the genocide the most influential American policymakers portrayed (and, they insist, perceived) the deaths not as atrocities or the components and symptoms of genocide but as wartime "casualties"—the deaths of combatants or those caught between them in a civil war.

Yet this formulation avoids the critical issue of whether Clinton and his close advisers might reasonably have been expected to "fully appreciate" the true dimensions and nature of the massacres. During the first three days of the killings U.S. diplomats in Rwanda reported back to Washington that well-armed extremists were intent on eliminating the Tutsi. And the American press spoke of the door-to-door hunting of unarmed civilians. By the end of the second week informed nongovernmental groups had already begun to call on the Administration to use the term "genocide," causing diplomats and lawyers at the State Department to begin debating the word's applicability soon thereafter. In order not to appreciate that genocide or something close to it was under way, U.S. officials had to ignore public reports and internal intelligence and debate.

The story of U.S. policy during the genocide in Rwanda is not a story of willful complicity with evil. U.S. officials did not sit around and conspire to allow genocide to happen. But whatever their convictions about "never again," many of them did sit around, and they most certainly did allow genocide to happen. In examining how and why the United States failed Rwanda, we see that without strong leadership the system will incline toward risk-averse policy choices. We also see that with the possibility of deploying U.S. troops to Rwanda taken off the table early on—and with crises elsewhere in the world unfolding—the slaughter never received the top-level attention it deserved. Domestic political forces that might have pressed for action were absent. And most U.S. officials opposed to American involvement in Rwanda were firmly convinced that they were doing all they could—and, most important, all they *should*—in light of competing American interests and a highly circumscribed understanding of what was "possible" for the United States to do.

One of the most thoughtful analyses of how the American system can remain predicated on the noblest of values while allowing the vilest of crimes was offered in 1971 by a brilliant and earnest young foreign-service officer who had just resigned from the National Security Council to protest the 1970 U.S. invasion of Cambodia. In an article in *Foreign Policy*, "The Human Reality of Realpolitik," he and a colleague analyzed the process whereby American policymakers with moral sensibilities could have waged a war of such immoral consequence as the one in Vietnam. They wrote,

> The answer to that question begins with a basic intellectual approach which views foreign policy as a lifeless, bloodless set of abstractions. "Nations," "interests," "influence," "prestige"—all are disembodied and dehumanized terms which encourage easy inattention to the real people whose lives our decisions affect or even end.

Policy analysis excluded discussion of human consequences. "It simply is not *done*," the authors wrote. "Policy—good, steady policy—is made by the 'tough-minded.' To talk of suffering is to lose 'effectiveness,' almost to lose one's grip. It is seen as a sign that one's 'rational' arguments are weak."

In 1994, fifty years after the Holocaust and twenty years after America's retreat from Vietnam, it was possible to believe that the system had changed and that talk of human consequences had become admissible. Indeed, when the machetes were raised in Central Africa, the White House official primarily responsible for the shaping of U.S. foreign policy was one of the authors of that 1971 critique: Anthony Lake, President Clinton's first-term national-security adviser. The genocide in Rwanda presented Lake and the rest of the Clinton team with an opportunity to prove that "good, steady policy" could be made in the interest of saving lives.

II. The Peacekeepers

Rwanda was a test for another man as well: Romeo Dallaire, then a major general in the Canadian army who at the time of the genocide was the commander of the UN Assistance Mission in Rwanda. If ever there was a peacekeeper who believed wholeheartedly in the promise of humanitarian action, it was Dallaire. A broad-shouldered French-Canadian with deep-set sky-blue eyes, Dallaire has the thick, calloused hands of one brought up in a culture that prizes soldiering, service, and sacrifice. He saw the United Nations as the embodiment of all three.

Before his posting to Rwanda Dallaire had served as the commandant of an army brigade that sent peacekeeping battalions to Cambodia and Bosnia, but he had never seen actual combat himself. "I was like a fireman who has never been to a fire, but has dreamed for years about how he would fare when the fire came," the fifty-five-year-old Dallaire recalls. When, in the summer of 1993, he received the phone call from UN headquarters offering him the Rwanda posting, he was ecstatic. "It was answering the aim of my life," he says. "It's *all* you've been waiting for."

Dallaire was sent to command a UN force that would help to keep the peace in Rwanda, a nation the size of Vermont, which was known as "the land of a thousand hills" for its rolling terrain. Before Rwanda achieved independence from Belgium, in 1962, the Tutsi, who made up 15 percent of the populace, had enjoyed a privileged status. But independence ushered in three decades of Hutu rule, under which Tutsi were systematically discriminated against and periodically subjected to waves of killing and ethnic cleansing. In 1990 a group of armed exiles, mainly Tutsi, who had been clustered on the Ugandan border, invaded

Rwanda. Over the next several years the rebels, known as the Rwandan Patriotic Front, gained ground against Hutu government forces. In 1993 Tanzania brokered peace talks, which resulted in a power-sharing agreement known as the Arusha Accords. Under its terms the Rwandan government agreed to share power with Hutu opposition parties and the Tutsi minority. UN peacekeepers would be deployed to patrol a cease-fire and assist in demilitarization and demobilization as well as to help provide a secure environment, so that exiled Tutsi could return. The hope among moderate Rwandans and Western observers was that Hutu and Tutsi would at last be able to coexist in harmony.

Hutu extremists rejected these terms and set out to terrorize Tutsi and also those Hutu politicians supportive of the peace process. In 1993 several thousand Rwandans were killed, and some 9,000 were detained. Guns, grenades, and machetes began arriving by the planeload. A pair of international commissions—one sent by the United Nations, the other by an independent collection of human-rights organizations—warned explicitly of a possible genocide.

But Dallaire knew nothing of the precariousness of the Arusha Accords. When he made a preliminary reconnaissance trip to Rwanda, in August of 1993, he was told that the country was committed to peace and that a UN presence was essential. A visit with extremists, who preferred to eradicate Tutsi rather than cede power, was not on Dallaire's itinerary. Remarkably, no UN officials in New York thought to give Dallaire copies of the alarming reports from the international investigators.

The sum total of Dallaire's intelligence data before that first trip to Rwanda consisted of one encyclopedia's summary of Rwandan history, which Major Brent Beardsley, Dallaire's executive assistant, had snatched at the last minute from his local public library. Beardsley says, "We flew to Rwanda with a Michelin road map, a copy of the Arusha agreement, and that was it. We were under the impression that the situation was quite straightforward: there was one cohesive government side and one cohesive rebel side, and they had come together to sign the peace agreement and had then requested that we come in to help them implement it."

Though Dallaire gravely underestimated the tensions brewing in Rwanda, he still felt that he would need a force of 5,000 to help the parties implement the terms of the Arusha Accords. But when his superiors warned him that the United States would never agree to pay for such a large deployment, Dallaire reluctantly trimmed his written request to 2,500. He remembers, "I was told, 'Don't ask for a brigade, because it ain't there.'"

Once he was actually posted to Rwanda, in October of 1993, Dallaire lacked not merely intelligence data and manpower but also institutional support. The small Department of Peacekeeping Operations in New York, run by the Ghanaian diplomat Kofi Annan, now the UN secretary general, was overwhelmed. Madeleine Albright, then the U.S. ambassador to the UN, recalls, "The global nine-one-one was always either busy or nobody was there." At the time of the Rwanda deployment, with a staff of a few hundred, the UN was posting 70,000 peacekeepers on seventeen missions around the world. Amid these widespread crises and logistical headaches the Rwanda mission had a very low status.

Life was not made easier for Dallaire or the UN peacekeeping office by the fact that American patience for peacekeeping was thinning. Congress owed half a billion dollars in UN dues and peacekeeping costs. It had tired of its obligation to foot a third of the bill for what had come to feel like an insatiable global appetite for mischief and an equally insatiable UN appetite for missions. The Clinton Administration had taken office better disposed toward peacekeeping than any other Administration in U.S. history. But it felt that the Department of Peacekeeping Operations needed fixing and demanded that the UN "learn to say no" to chancy or costly missions.

Every aspect of the UN Assistance Mission in Rwanda was run on a shoestring. UNAMIR (the acronym by which it was known) was equipped with hand-me-down vehicles from the UN's Cambodia mission, and only eighty of the 300 that turned up were usable. When the medical supplies ran out, in March of 1994, New York said there was no cash for resupply. Very little could be procured locally, given that Rwanda was one of Africa's poorest nations. Replacement spare parts, batteries, and even ammunition could rarely be found. Dallaire spent some 70 percent of his time battling UN logistics.

Dallaire had major problems with his personnel, as well. He commanded troops, military observers, and civilian personnel from twenty-six countries. Though multinationality is meant to be a virtue of UN missions, the diversity yielded grave discrepancies in resources. Whereas Belgian troops turned up well armed and ready to perform the tasks assigned to them, the poorer contingents showed up "bare-assed," in Dallaire's words, and demanded that the United Nations suit them up. "Since nobody else was offering to send troops, we had to take what we could get," he says. When Dallaire expressed concern, he was instructed by a senior UN official to lower his expectations. He recalls, "I was told, 'Listen, General, you are NATO-trained. This is not NATO.'" Although some 2,500 UNAMIR personnel had arrived by early April of 1994, few of the soldiers had the kit they needed to perform even basic tasks.

The signs of militarization in Rwanda were so widespread that even without much of an intelligence-gathering capacity, Dallaire was able to learn of the extremists' sinister intentions. In January of 1994 an anonymous Hutu informant, said to be high up in the inner circles of the Rwandan government, had come forward to describe the rapid arming and training of local militias. In what is now referred to as the "Dallaire fax," Dallaire relayed to New York the informant's claim that Hutu extremists "had been ordered to register all the Tutsi in Kigali." "He suspects it is for their extermination," Dallaire wrote. "Example he gave was that in 20 minutes his personnel could kill up to 1000 Tutsis." "Jean-Pierre," as the informant became known, had said that the militia planned first to provoke and murder a number of Belgian peacekeepers, to "thus guarantee Belgian withdrawal from Rwanda." When Dallaire notified Kofi Annan's office that UNAMIR was poised to raid Hutu arms caches, Annan's deputy forbade him to do so. Instead Dallaire was instructed to notify the Rwandan President, Juvénal Habyarimana, and the Western ambassadors of the informant's claims. Though Dallaire battled by phone with New York, and confirmed the reliability of the informant, his political masters told him plainly and consistently that the United States in particular would not support aggressive peace-keeping. (A request by the Belgians for reinforcements was also turned down.) In Washington, Dallaire's alarm was discounted. Lieutenant Colonel Tony Marley, the U.S. military liaison to the Arusha process, respected Dallaire but knew he was operating in Africa for the first time. "I thought that the neophyte meant well, but I questioned whether he knew what he was talking about," Marley recalls.

III. The Early Killings

On the evening of April 6, 1994, Romeo Dallaire was sitting on the couch in his bungalow residence in Kigali, watching CNN with Brent Beardsley. Beardsley was preparing plans for a national Sports Day that would match Tutsi rebel soldiers against Hutu government soldiers in a soccer game. Dallaire said, "You know, Brent, if the shit ever hit the fan here, none of this stuff would really matter, would it?" The next instant the phone rang. Rwandan President Habyarimana's Mystère Falcon jet, a gift from French President François Mitterrand, had just been shot down, with

Habyarimana and Burundian President Cyprien Ntaryamira aboard. Dallaire and Beardsley raced in their UN jeep to Rwandan army headquarters, where a crisis meeting was under way.

Back in Washington, Kevin Aiston, the Rwanda desk officer, knocked on the door of Deputy Assistant Secretary of State Prudence Bushnell and told her that the Presidents of Rwanda and Burundi had gone down in a plane crash. "Oh, shit," she said. "Are you sure?" In fact nobody was sure at first, but Dallaire's forces supplied confirmation within the hour. The Rwandan authorities quickly announced a curfew, and Hutu militias and government soldiers erected roadblocks around the capital.

Bushnell drafted an urgent memo to Secretary of State Warren Christopher. She was concerned about a probable outbreak of killing in both Rwanda and its neighbor Burundi. The memo read,

> If, as it appears, both Presidents have been killed, there is a strong likelihood that widespread violence could break out in either or both countries, particularly if it is confirmed that the plane was shot down. Our strategy is to appeal for calm in both countries, both through public statements and in other ways.

A few public statements proved to be virtually the only strategy that Washington would muster in the weeks ahead.

Lieutenant General Wesley Clark, who later commanded the NATO air war in Kosovo, was the director of strategic plans and policy for the Joint Chiefs of Staff at the Pentagon. On learning of the crash, Clark remembers, staff officers asked, "Is it Hutu and Tutsi or Tutu and Hutsi?" He frantically called for insight into the ethnic dimension of events in Rwanda. Unfortunately, Rwanda had never been of more than marginal concern to Washington's most influential planners.

America's best-informed Rwanda observer was not a government official but a private citizen, Alison Des Forges, a historian and a board member of Human Rights Watch, who lived in Buffalo, New York. Des Forges had been visiting Rwanda since 1963. She had received a Ph.D. from Yale in African history, specializing in Rwanda, and she could speak the Rwandan language, Kinyarwanda. Half an hour after the plane crash Des Forges got a phone call from a close friend in Kigali, the human-rights activist Monique Mujawamariya. Des Forges had been worried about Mujawamariya for weeks, because the Hutu extremist radio station, Radio Mille Collines, had branded her "a bad patriot who deserves to die." Mujawamariya had sent Human Rights Watch a chilling warning a week earlier: "For the last two weeks, all of Kigali has lived under the threat of an instantaneous, carefully prepared operation to eliminate all those who give trouble to President Habyarimana."

Now Habyarimana was dead, and Mujawamariya knew instantly that the hard-line Hutu would use the crash as a pretext to begin mass killing. "This is it," she told Des Forges on the phone. For the next twenty-four hours Des Forges called her friend's home every half hour. With each conversation Des Forges could hear the gunfire grow louder as the militia drew closer. Finally the gunmen entered Mujawamariya's home. "I don't want you to hear this," Mujawamariya said softly. "Take care of my children." She hung up the phone.

Mujawamariya's instincts were correct. Within hours of the plane crash Hutu militiamen took command of the streets of Kigali. Dallaire quickly grasped that supporters of the Arusha peace process were being targeted. His phone at UNAMIR headquarters rang constantly as Rwandans around the capital pleaded for help. Dallaire was especially concerned about Prime Minister Agathe Uwilingiyimana, a reformer who with the President's death had become the titular head of state. Just after dawn on April 7 five Ghanaian and ten Belgian peacekeepers arrived at the Prime Minister's home in order to deliver her to Radio Rwanda, so that she could broadcast an emergency appeal for calm.

Joyce Leader, the second-in-command at the U.S. embassy, lived next door to Uwilingiyimana. She spent the early hours of the morning behind the steel-barred gates of her embassy-owned house as Hutu killers hunted and dispatched their first victims. Leader's phone rang. Uwilingiyimana was on the other end. "Please hide me," she begged.

Minutes after the phone call a UN peacekeeper attempted to hike the Prime Minister over the wall separating their compounds. When Leader heard shots fired, she urged the peacekeeper to abandon the effort. "They can see you!" she shouted. Uwilingiyimana managed to slip with her husband and children into another compound, which was occupied by the UN Development Program. But the militiamen hunted them down in the yard, where the couple surrendered. There were more shots. Leader recalls, "We heard her screaming and then, suddenly, after the gunfire the screaming stopped, and we heard people cheering." Hutu gunmen in the Presidential Guard that day systematically tracked down and eliminated Rwanda's moderate leadership.

The raid on Uwilingiyimana's compound not only cost Rwanda a prominent supporter of the Arusha Accords; it also triggered the collapse of Dallaire's mission. In keeping with the plan to target the Belgians which the informant Jean-Pierre had relayed to UNAMIR in January, Hutu soldiers rounded up the peacekeepers at Uwilingiyimana's home, took them to a military camp, led the Ghanaians to safety, and then killed and savagely mutilated the ten Belgians. In Belgium the cry for either expanding UNAMIR's mandate or immediately withdrawing was prompt and loud.

In response to the initial killings by the Hutu government, Tutsi rebels of the Rwandan Patriotic Front—stationed in Kigali under the terms of the Arusha Accords—surged out of their barracks and resumed their civil war against the Hutu regime.

But under the cover of that war were early and strong indications that systematic genocide was taking place. From April 7 onward the Hutu-controlled army, the gendarmerie, and the militias worked together to wipe out Rwanda's Tutsi. Many of the early Tutsi victims found themselves specifically, not spontaneously, pursued: lists of targets had been prepared in advance, and Radio Mille Collines broadcast names, addresses, and even license-plate numbers. Killers often carried a machete in one hand and a transistor radio in the other. Tens of thousands of Tutsi fled their homes in panic and were snared and butchered at checkpoints. Little care was given to their disposal. Some were shoveled into landfills. Human flesh rotted in the sunshine. In churches bodies mingled with scattered hosts. If the killers had taken the time to tend to sanitation, it would have slowed their "sanitization" campaign.

IV. The "Last War"

The two tracks of events in Rwanda—simultaneous war and genocide—confused policymakers who had scant prior understanding of the country. Atrocities are often carried out in places that are not commonly visited, where outside expertise is limited. When country-specific knowledge is lacking, foreign governments become all the more likely to employ faulty analogies and to "fight the last war." The analogy employed by many of those who confronted the outbreak of killing in Rwanda was a peacekeeping intervention that had gone horribly wrong in Somalia.

On October 3, 1993, ten months after President Bush had sent U.S. troops to Somalia as part of what had seemed a low-risk humanitarian mission, U.S. Army Rangers and Delta special forces in Somalia attempted to seize several top advisers to the warlord Mohammed Farah Aideed. Aideed's faction had ambushed and killed two dozen Pakistani peacekeepers, and the United States was striking back. But in the firefight that ensued the Somali militia killed eighteen Americans, wounded seventy-three, and captured one Black Hawk helicopter pilot. Somali television broadcast both a video interview with the trembling, disoriented pilot and a gory procession in which the corpse of a U.S. Ranger was dragged through a Mogadishu street.

On receiving word of these events, President Clinton cut short a trip to California and convened an urgent crisis-management meeting at the White House. When an aide began recapping the situation, an angry President interrupted him. "Cut the bullshit," Clinton snapped. "Let's work this out." "Work it out" meant walk out. Republican Congressional pressure was intense. Clinton appeared on American television the next day, called off the manhunt for Aideed, temporarily reinforced the troop presence, and announced that all U.S. forces would be home within six months. The Pentagon leadership concluded that peacekeeping in Africa meant trouble and that neither the White House nor Congress would stand by it when the chips were down.

Even before the deadly blowup in Somalia the United States had resisted deploying a UN mission to Rwanda. "Anytime you mentioned peacekeeping in Africa," one U.S. official remembers, "the crucifixes and garlic would come up on every door." Having lost much of its early enthusiasm for peacekeeping and for the United Nations itself, Washington was nervous that the Rwanda mission would sour like so many others. But President Habyarimana had traveled to Washington in 1993 to offer assurances that his government was committed to carrying out the terms of the Arusha Accords. In the end, after strenuous lobbying by France (Rwanda's chief diplomatic and military patron), U.S. officials accepted the proposition that UNAMIR could be the rare "UN winner." On October 5, 1993, two days after the Somalia firefight, the United States reluctantly voted in the Security Council to authorize Dallaire's mission.

Even so, U.S. officials made it clear that Washington would give no consideration to sending U.S. troops to Rwanda. Somalia and another recent embarrassment in Haiti indicated that multilateral initiatives for humanitarian purposes would likely bring the United States all loss and no gain.

Against this backdrop, and under the leadership of Anthony Lake, the national-security adviser, the Clinton Administration accelerated the development of a formal U.S. peacekeeping doctrine. The job was given to Richard Clarke, of the National Security Council, a special assistant to the President who was known as one of the most effective bureaucrats in Washington. In an interagency process that lasted more than a year, Clarke managed the production of a presidential decision directive, PDD-25, which listed sixteen factors that policymakers needed to consider when deciding whether to support peacekeeping activities: seven factors if the United States was to vote in the UN Security Council on peace operations carried out by non-American soldiers, six additional and more stringent factors if U.S. forces were to participate in UN peacekeeping missions, and three final factors if U.S. troops were likely to engage in actual combat. In the words of Representative David Obey, of Wisconsin, the restrictive checklist tried to satisfy the American desire for "zero degree of involvement, and zero degree of risk, and zero degree of pain and confusion." The architects of the doctrine remain its strongest defenders. "Many say PDD-25 was some evil thing designed to kill peacekeeping, when in fact it was there to save peacekeeping," Clarke says. "Peacekeeping was almost dead. There was no support for it in the U.S. government, and the peacekeepers were not effective in the field." Although the directive was not publicly released until May 3, 1994, a month into the genocide, the considerations encapsulated in the doctrine and the Administration's frustration with peacekeeping greatly influenced the thinking of U.S. officials involved in shaping Rwanda policy.

V. The Peace Processors

Each of the American actors dealing with Rwanda brought particular institutional interests and biases to his or her handling of the crisis. Secretary of State Warren Christopher knew little about Africa. At one meeting with his top advisers, several weeks after the plane crash, he pulled an atlas off his shelf to help him locate the country. Belgian Foreign Minister Willie Claes recalls trying to discuss Rwanda with his American counterpart and being told, "I have other responsibilities." Officials in the State Department's Africa Bureau were, of course, better informed. Prudence Bushnell, the deputy assistant secretary, was one of them. The daughter of a diplomat, Bushnell had joined the foreign service in 1981, at the age of thirty-five. With her agile mind and sharp tongue, she had earned the attention of George Moose when she served under him at the U.S. embassy in Senegal. When Moose was named the assistant secretary of state for African affairs, in 1993, he made Bushnell his deputy. Just two weeks before the plane crash the State Department had dispatched Bushnell and a colleague to Rwanda in an effort to contain the escalating violence and to spur the stalled peace process.

Unfortunately, for all the concern of the Americans familiar with Rwanda, their diplomacy suffered from three weaknesses. First, ahead of the plane crash diplomats had repeatedly threatened to pull out UN peacekeepers in retaliation for the parties' failure to implement Arusha. These threats were of course counterproductive, because the very Hutu who opposed power-sharing wanted nothing more than a UN withdrawal. One senior U.S. official remembers, "The first response to trouble is 'Let's yank the peacekeepers.' But that is like believing that when children are misbehaving, the proper response is 'Let's send the baby-sitter home.'"

Second, before and during the massacres U.S. diplomacy revealed its natural bias toward states and toward negotiations. Because most official contact occurs between representatives of states, U.S. officials were predisposed to trust the assurances of Rwandan officials, several of whom were plotting genocide behind the scenes. Those in the U.S. government who knew Rwanda best viewed the escalating violence with a diplomatic prejudice that left them both institutionally oriented toward the Rwandan government and reluctant to do anything to disrupt the peace process. An examination of the cable traffic from the U.S. embassy in Kigali to Washington between the signing of the Arusha agreement and the downing of the presidential plane reveals that setbacks were perceived as "dangers to the peace process" more than as "dangers to Rwandans." American criticisms were deliberately and steadfastly leveled at "both sides," though Hutu government and militia forces were usually responsible.

The U.S. ambassador in Kigali, David Rawson, proved especially vulnerable to such bias. Rawson had grown up in Burundi, where his father, an American missionary, had set up a Quaker hospital. He entered the foreign service in 1971. When, in 1993, at age fifty-two, he was given the embassy in Rwanda, his first, he could not have been more intimate with the region, the culture, or the peril. He spoke the local language—almost unprecedented for an ambassador in Central Africa. But Rawson found it difficult to imagine the Rwandans who surrounded the President as conspirators in genocide. He issued pro forma demarches over Habyarimana's obstruction of power-sharing, but the cable traffic shows that he accepted the President's assurances that he was doing all he could. The U.S. investment in the peace process gave rise to a wishful tendency to see peace "around the corner." Rawson remembers, "We were naive policy optimists, I suppose. The fact that negotiations can't work is almost not one of the options open to people who care about peace. We were looking for the hopeful signs, not the dark signs. In fact, we were looking away from the dark signs . . . One of the things I learned and should have already known is that once you launch a process, it takes on its own momentum. I had said, 'Let's try this, and then if it doesn't work, we can back away.' But bureaucracies don't allow that. Once the Washington side buys into a process, it gets pursued, almost blindly." Even after the Hutu government began exterminating Tutsi, U.S. diplomats focused most of their efforts on "re-establishing a cease-fire" and "getting Arusha back on track."

The third problematic feature of U.S. diplomacy before and during the genocide was a tendency toward blindness bred by familiarity: the few people in Washington who were paying attention to Rwanda before Habyarimana's plane was shot down were those who had been tracking Rwanda for some time and had thus come to expect a certain level of ethnic violence from the region. And because the U.S. government had done little when some 40,000 people had been killed in Hutu-Tutsi violence in Burundi in October of 1993, these officials also knew that Washington was prepared to tolerate substantial bloodshed. When the massacres began in April, some U.S. regional specialists initially suspected that Rwanda was undergoing "another flare-up" that would involve another "acceptable" (if tragic) round of ethnic murder.

Rawson had read up on genocide before his posting to Rwanda, surveying what had become a relatively extensive scholarly literature on its causes. But although he expected internecine killing, he did not anticipate the scale at which it occurred. "Nothing in Rwandan culture or history could have led a person to that forecast," he says. "Most of us thought that if a war broke out, it would be quick, that these poor people didn't have the resources, the means, to fight a sophisticated war. I couldn't have known that they would do each other in with the most economic means." George Moose agrees: "We were psychologically and imaginatively too limited."

■   ■   ■

VII. Genocide? What Genocide?

Just when did Washington know of the sinister Hutu designs on Rwanda's Tutsi? Writing in *Foreign Affairs* last year [2000], Alan Kuperman argued that President Clinton "could not have known that a nationwide genocide was under way" until about two weeks into the killing. It is true that the precise nature and extent of the slaughter was obscured by the civil war, the withdrawal of U.S. diplomatic sources, some confused press reporting, and the lies of the Rwandan government. Nonetheless, both the testimony of U.S. officials who worked the issue day to day and the declassified documents indicate that plenty was known about the killers' intentions.

A determination of genocide turns not on the numbers killed, which is always difficult to ascertain at a time of crisis, but on the perpetrators' intent: Were Hutu forces attempting to destroy Rwanda's Tutsi? The answer to this question was available early on. "By eight AM the morning after the plane crash we knew what was happening, that there was systematic killing of Tutsi," Joyce Leader recalls. "People were calling me and telling me who was getting killed. I knew they were going door to door." Back at the State Department she explained to her colleagues that three kinds of killing were going on: war, politically motivated murder, and genocide. Dallaire's early cables to New York likewise described the armed conflict that had resumed between rebels and government forces, and also stated plainly that savage "ethnic cleansing" of Tutsi was occurring. U.S. analysts warned that mass killings would increase. In an April 11 memo prepared for Frank Wisner, the undersecretary of defense for policy, in advance of a dinner with Henry Kissinger, a key talking point was "Unless both sides can be convinced to return to the peace process, a massive (hundreds of thousands of deaths) bloodbath will ensue."

Whatever the inevitable imperfections of U.S. intelligence early on, the reports from Rwanda were severe enough to distinguish Hutu killers from ordinary combatants in civil war. And they certainly warranted directing additional U.S. intelligence assets toward the region—to snap satellite photos of large gatherings of Rwandan civilians or of mass graves, to intercept military communications, or to infiltrate the country in person. Though there is no evidence that senior policymakers deployed such assets, routine intelligence continued to pour in. On April 26 an unattributed intelligence memo titled "Responsibility for Massacres in Rwanda" reported that the ringleaders of the genocide, Colonel Théoneste Bagosora and his crisis committee, were determined to liquidate their opposition and exterminate the Tutsi populace. A May 9 Defense Intelligence Agency report stated plainly that the Rwandan violence was not spontaneous but was directed by the government, with lists of victims prepared well in advance. The DIA observed that an "organized parallel effort of *genocide* [was] being implemented by the army to destroy the leadership of the Tutsi community."

From April 8 onward media coverage featured eyewitness accounts describing the widespread targeting of Tutsi and the corpses piling up on Kigali's streets. American reporters relayed stories of missionaries and embassy officials who had been unable to save their Rwandan friends and neighbors from death. On April 9 a front-page *Washington Post* story quoted reports that the Rwandan employees of the major international relief agencies had been executed "in front of horrified expatriate staffers." On April 10 a *New York Times* front-page article quoted the Red Cross claim that "tens of thousands" were dead, 8,000 in Kigali alone, and that corpses were "in the houses, in the streets, everywhere." The *Post* the same day led its front-page story with a description of "a pile of corpses six feet high" outside the main hospital. On April 14 the *New York Times* reported the shooting and hacking to death of nearly 1,200

men, women, and children in the church where they had sought refuge. On April 19 Human Rights Watch, which had excellent sources on the ground in Rwanda, estimated the number of dead at 100,000 and called for use of the term "genocide." The 100,000 figure (which proved to be a gross underestimate) was picked up immediately by the Western media, endorsed by the Red Cross, and featured on the front page of the *Washington Post*. On April 24 the *Post* reported how "the heads and limbs of victims were sorted and piled neatly, a bone-chilling order in the midst of chaos that harked back to the Holocaust." President Clinton certainly could have known that a genocide was under way, if he had wanted to know.

Even after the reality of genocide in Rwanda had become irrefutable, when bodies were shown choking the Kagera River on the nightly news, the brute fact of the slaughter failed to influence U.S. policy except in a negative way. American officials, for a variety of reasons, shunned the use of what became known as "the g-word." They felt that using it would have obliged the United States to act, under the terms of the 1948 Genocide Convention. They also believed, understandably, that it would harm U.S. credibility to name the crime and then do nothing to stop it. A discussion paper on Rwanda, prepared by an official in the Office of the Secretary of Defense and dated May 1, testifies to the nature of official thinking. Regarding issues that might be brought up at the next interagency working group, it stated,

> 1. Genocide Investigation: Language that calls for an international investigation of human rights abuses and possible violations of the genocide convention. *Be Careful. Legal at State was worried about this yesterday—Genocide finding could commit [the U.S. government] to actually "do something."* [Emphasis added.]

At an interagency teleconference in late April, Susan Rice, a rising star on the NSC who worked under Richard Clarke, stunned a few of the officials present when she asked, "If we use the word 'genocide' and are seen as doing nothing, what will be the effect on the November [congressional] election?" Lieutenant Colonel Tony Marley remembers the incredulity of his colleagues at the State Department. "We could believe that people would wonder that," he says, "but not that they would actually voice it." Rice does not recall the incident but concedes, "If I said it, it was completely inappropriate, as well as irrelevant."

The genocide debate in U.S. government circles began the last week of April, but it was not until May 21, six weeks after the killing began, that Secretary Christopher gave his diplomats permission to use the term "genocide"—sort of. The UN Human Rights Commission was about to meet in special session, and the U.S. representative, Geraldine Ferraro, needed guidance on whether to join a resolution stating that genocide had occurred. The stubborn U.S. stand had become untenable internationally.

The case for a label of genocide was straightforward, according to a May 18 confidential analysis prepared by the State Department's assistant secretary for intelligence and research, Toby Gati: lists of Tutsi victims' names and addresses had reportedly been prepared; Rwandan government troops and Hutu militia and youth squads were the main perpetrators; massacres were reported all over the country; humanitarian agencies were now "claiming from 200,000 to 500,000 lives" lost. Gati offered the intelligence bureau's view: "We believe 500,000 may be an exaggerated estimate, but no accurate figures are available. Systematic killings began within hours of Habyarimana's death. Most of those killed have been Tutsi civilians, including women and children." The terms of the Genocide Convention had been met. "We weren't quibbling about these numbers," Gati says. "We can never know precise figures, but our analysts had been reporting huge numbers of deaths for weeks. We were basically saying, 'A rose by any other name . . .'"

Despite this straightforward assessment, Christopher remained reluctant to speak the obvious truth. When he issued his guidance, on May 21, fully a month after Human Rights Watch had put a name to the tragedy, Christopher's instructions were hopelessly muddied.

> The delegation is authorized to agree to a resolution that states that "acts of genocide" have occurred in Rwanda or that "genocide has occurred in Rwanda." Other formulations that suggest that some, but not all of the killings in Rwanda are genocide . . . e.g. "genocide is taking place in Rwanda"—are authorized. Delegation is not authorized to agree to the characterization of any specific incident as genocide or to agree to any formulation that indicates that all killings in Rwanda are genocide.

Notably, Christopher confined permission to acknowledge full-fledged genocide to the upcoming session of the Human Rights Commission. Outside that venue State Department officials were authorized to state publicly only that *acts* of genocide had occurred.

Christine Shelly, a State Department spokesperson, had long been charged with publicly articulating the U.S. position on whether events in Rwanda counted as genocide. For two months she had avoided the term, and as her June 10 exchange with the Reuters correspondent Alan Elsner reveals, her semantic dance continued.

ELSNER: How would you describe the events taking place in Rwanda?
SHELLY: Based on the evidence we have seen from observations on the ground, we have every reason to believe that acts of genocide have occurred in Rwanda.
ELSNER: What's the difference between "acts of genocide" and "genocide"?
SHELLY: Well, I think the—as you know, there's a legal definition of this . . . clearly not all of the

killings that have taken place in Rwanda are killings to which you might apply that label . . . But as to the distinctions between the words, we're trying to call what we have seen so far as best as we can; and based, again, on the evidence, we have every reason to believe that acts of genocide have occurred.

ELSNER: How many acts of genocide does it take to make genocide?

SHELLY: Alan, that's just not a question that I'm in a position to answer.

The same day, in Istanbul, Warren Christopher, by then under severe internal and external pressure, relented: "If there is any particular magic in calling it genocide, I have no hesitancy in saying that."

VIII. "Not Even a Sideshow"

Once the Americans had been evacuated, Rwanda largely dropped off the radar of most senior Clinton Administration officials. In the situation room on the seventh floor of the State Department a map of Rwanda had been hurriedly pinned to the wall in the aftermath of the plane crash, and eight banks of phones had rung off the hook. Now, with U.S. citizens safely home, the State Department chaired a daily interagency meeting, often by teleconference, designed to coordinate mid-level diplomatic and humanitarian responses. Cabinet-level officials focused on crises elsewhere. Anthony Lake recalls, "I was obsessed with Haiti and Bosnia during that period, so Rwanda was, in William Shawcross's words, a 'sideshow,' but not even a sideshow—a no-show." At the NSC the person who managed Rwanda policy was not Lake, the national-security adviser, who happened to know Africa, but Richard Clarke, who oversaw peace-keeping policy, and for whom the news from Rwanda only confirmed a deep skepticism about the viability of UN deployments. Clarke believed that another UN failure could doom relations between Congress and the United Nations. He also sought to shield the President from congressional and public criticism. Donald Steinberg managed the Africa portfolio at the NSC and tried to look out for the dying Rwandans, but he was not an experienced infighter and, colleagues say, he "never won a single argument" with Clarke.

■ ■ ■

During the entire three months of the genocide Clinton never assembled his top policy advisers to discuss the killings. Anthony Lake likewise never gathered the "principals"—the Cabinet-level members of the foreign-policy team. Rwanda was never thought to warrant its own top-level meeting. When the subject came up, it did so along with, and subordinate to, discussions of Somalia, Haiti, and Bosnia. Whereas these crises involved U.S. personnel and stirred some public interest, Rwanda generated no sense of urgency and could safely be avoided by Clinton at no political cost. The editorial boards of the major American newspapers discouraged U.S. intervention during the genocide. They, like the Administration, lamented the killings but believed, in the words of an April 17 *Washington Post* editorial, "The United States has no recognizable national interest in taking a role, certainly not a leading role." Capitol Hill was quiet. Some in Congress were glad to be free of the expense of another flawed UN mission. Others, including a few members of the Africa subcommittees and the Congressional Black Caucus, eventually appealed tamely for the United States to play a role in ending the violence—but again, they did not dare urge U.S. involvement on the ground, and they did not kick up a public fuss. Members of Congress weren't hearing from their constituents. Pat Schroeder, of Colorado, said on April 30, "There are some groups terribly concerned about the gorillas . . . But—it sounds terrible—people just don't know what can be done about the people." Randall Robinson, of the nongovernmental organization TransAfrica, was preoccupied, staging a hunger strike to protest the U.S. repatriation of Haitian refugees. Human Rights Watch supplied exemplary intelligence and established important one-on-one contacts in the Administration, but the organization lacks a grass-roots base from which to mobilize a broader segment of American society.

IX. The UN Withdrawal

When the killing began, Romeo Dallaire expected and appealed for reinforcements. Within hours of the plane crash he had cabled UN headquarters in New York: "Give me the means and I can do more." He was sending peacekeepers on rescue missions around the city, and he felt it was essential to increase the size and improve the quality of the UN's presence. But the United States opposed the idea of sending reinforcements, no matter where they were from. The fear, articulated mainly at the Pentagon but felt throughout the bureaucracy, was that what would start as a small engagement by foreign troops would end as a large and costly one by Americans. This was the lesson of Somalia, where U.S. troops had gotten into trouble in an effort to bail out the beleaguered Pakistanis. The logical outgrowth of this fear was an effort to steer clear of Rwanda entirely and be sure others did the same. Only by yanking Dallaire's entire peacekeeping force could the United States protect itself from involvement down the road.

One senior U.S. official remembers, "When the reports of the deaths of the ten Belgians came in, it was clear that it was Somalia redux, and the sense was that there would be an expectation everywhere that the U.S. would get involved. We thought leaving the peacekeepers in Rwanda and having them confront the violence would take us where we'd been before. It was a foregone conclusion that the United States wouldn't intervene and that the concept of UN peacekeeping could not be sacrificed again."

A foregone conclusion. What is most remarkable about the American response to the Rwandan genocide is not so much the absence of U.S. military action as that during the entire genocide the possibility of U.S. military intervention was never even debated. Indeed, the United States resisted intervention of any kind.

The bodies of the slain Belgian soldiers were returned to Brussels on April 14. One of the pivotal conversations in the course of the genocide took place around that time, when Willie Claes, the Belgian Foreign Minister, called the State Department to request "cover." "We are pulling out, but we don't want to be seen to be doing it alone," Claes said, asking the Americans to support a full UN withdrawal. Dallaire had not anticipated that Belgium would extract its soldiers, removing the backbone of his mission and stranding Rwandans in their hour of greatest need. "I expected the excolonial white countries would stick it out even if they took casualties," he remembers. "I thought their pride would have led them to stay to try to sort the place out. The Belgian decision caught me totally off guard. I was truly stunned."

Belgium did not want to leave ignominiously, by itself. Warren Christopher agreed to back Belgian requests for a full UN exit. Policy over the next month or so can be described simply: no U.S. military intervention, robust demands for a withdrawal of all of Dallaire's forces, and no support for a new UN mission that would challenge the killers. Belgium had the cover it needed.

On April 15 Christopher sent one of the most forceful documents to be produced in the entire three months of the genocide to Madeleine Albright at the UN—a cable instructing her to demand a full UN withdrawal. The cable, which was heavily influenced by Richard Clarke at the NSC, and which bypassed Donald Steinberg and was never seen by Anthony Lake, was unequivocal about the next steps. Saying that he had "fully" taken into account the "humanitarian reasons put forth for retention of UNAMIR elements in Rwanda,"

Christopher wrote that there was "insufficient justification" to retain a UN presence.

> The international community must give highest priority to full, orderly withdrawal of all UNAMIR personnel as soon as possible . . . We will oppose any effort at this time to preserve a UNAMIR presence in Rwanda . . . Our opposition to retaining a UNAMIR presence in Rwanda is firm. It is based on our conviction that the Security Council has an obligation to ensure that peacekeeping operations are viable, that they are capable of fulfilling their mandates, and that UN peacekeeping personnel are not placed or retained, knowingly, in an untenable situation.

"Once we knew the Belgians were leaving, we were left with a rump mission incapable of doing anything to help people," Clarke remembers. "They were doing nothing to stop the killings."

But Clarke underestimated the deterrent effect that Dallaire's very few peacekeepers were having. Although some soldiers hunkered down, terrified, others scoured Kigali, rescuing Tutsi, and later established defensive positions in the city, opening their doors to the fortunate Tutsi who made it through roadblocks to reach them. One Senegalese captain saved a hundred or so lives single-handedly. Some 25,000 Rwandans eventually assembled at positions manned by UNAMIR personnel. The Hutu were generally reluctant to massacre large groups of Tutsi if foreigners (armed or unarmed) were present. It did not take many UN soldiers to dissuade the Hutu from attacking. At the Hotel des Mille Collines ten peacekeepers and four UN military observers helped to protect the several hundred civilians sheltered there for the duration of the crisis. About 10,000 Rwandans gathered at the Amohoro Stadium under light UN cover. Brent Beardsley, Dallaire's executive assistant, remembers, "If there was any determined resistance at close quarters, the government guys tended to back

off." Kevin Aiston, the Rwanda desk officer at the State Department, was keeping track of Rwandan civilians under UN protection. When Prudence Bushnell told him of the U.S. decision to demand a UNAMIR withdrawal, he turned pale. "We can't," he said. Bushnell replied, "The train has already left the station."

On April 19 the Belgian Colonel Luc Marchal delivered his final salute and departed with the last of his soldiers. The Belgian withdrawal reduced Dallaire's troop strength to 2,100. More crucially, he lost his best troops. Command and control among Dallaire's remaining forces became tenuous. Dallaire soon lost every line of communication to the countryside. He had only a single satellite phone link to the outside world.

The UN Security Council now made a decision that sealed the Tutsi's fate and signaled the militia that it would have free rein. The U.S. demand for a full UN withdrawal had been opposed by some African nations, and even by Madeleine Albright; so the United States lobbied instead for a dramatic drawdown in troop strength. On April 21, amid press reports of some 100,000 dead in Rwanda, the Security Council voted to slash UNAMIR's forces to 270 men. Albright went along, publicly declaring that a "small, skeletal" operation would be left in Kigali to "show the will of the international community."

After the UN vote Clarke sent a memorandum to Lake reporting that language about "the safety and security of Rwandans under UN protection had been inserted by US/UN at the end of the day to prevent an otherwise unanimous UNSC from walking away from the at-risk Rwandans under UN protection as the peacekeepers drew down to 270." In other words, the memorandum suggested that the United States was *leading* efforts to ensure that the Rwandans under UN protection were not abandoned. The opposite was true.

Most of Dallaire's troops were evacuated by April 25. Though he was supposed to reduce the size of his force to 270, he ended up keeping 503 peacekeepers. By this time Dallaire was trying to deal with a bloody frenzy. "My force was standing knee-deep in mutilated bodies, surrounded by the guttural moans of dying people, looking into the eyes of children bleeding to death with their wounds burning in the sun and being invaded by maggots and flies," he later wrote. "I found myself walking through villages where the only sign of life was a goat, or a chicken, or a songbird, as all the people were dead, their bodies being eaten by voracious packs of wild dogs."

Dallaire had to work within narrow limits. He attempted simply to keep the positions he held and to protect the 25,000 Rwandans under UN supervision while hoping that the member states on the Security Council would change their minds and send him some help while it still mattered.

By coincidence Rwanda held one of the rotating seats on the Security Council at the time of the genocide. Neither the United States nor any other UN member state ever suggested that the representative of the genocidal government be expelled from the council. Nor did any Security Council country offer to provide safe haven to Rwandan refugees who escaped the carnage. In one instance Dallaire's forces succeeded in evacuating a group of Rwandans by plane to Kenya. The Nairobi authorities allowed the plane to land, sequestered it in a hangar, and, echoing the American decision to turn back the *S.S. St. Louis* during the Holocaust, then forced the plane to return to Rwanda. The fate of the passengers is unknown.

Throughout this period the Clinton Administration was largely silent. The closest it came to a public denunciation of the Rwandan government occurred after personal lobbying by Human Rights Watch, when Anthony Lake issued a statement calling on Rwandan military leaders by name to "do everything in their power to end the violence immediately." When I spoke with Lake six years later, and informed him that human-rights groups and U.S. officials point to this statement as the sum total of official public attempts to shame the Rwandan

government in this period, he seemed stunned. "You're kidding," he said. "That's truly pathetic."

At the State Department the diplomacy was conducted privately, by telephone. Prudence Bushnell regularly set her alarm for 2:00 AM and phoned Rwandan government officials. She spoke several times with Augustin Bizimungu, the Rwandan military chief of staff. "These were the most bizarre phone calls," she says. "He spoke in perfectly charming French. 'Oh, it's so nice to hear from you,' he said. I told him, 'I am calling to tell you President Clinton is going to hold you accountable for the killings.' He said, 'Oh, how nice it is that your President is thinking of me.'"

X. The Pentagon "Chop"

The daily meeting of the Rwanda interagency working group was attended, either in person or by teleconference, by representatives from the various State Department bureaus, the Pentagon, the National Security Council, and the intelligence community. Any proposal that originated in the working group had to survive the Pentagon "chop." "Hard intervention," meaning U.S. military action, was obviously out of the question. But Pentagon officials routinely stymied initiatives for "soft intervention" as well.

The Pentagon discussion paper on Rwanda, referred to earlier, ran down a list of the working group's six short-term policy objectives and carped at most of them. The fear of a slippery slope was persuasive. Next to the seemingly innocuous suggestion that the United States "support the UN and others in attempts to achieve a cease-fire" the Pentagon official responded, "Need to change 'attempts' to 'political efforts'—without 'political' there is a danger of signing up to troop contributions."

The one policy move the Defense Department supported was a U.S. effort to achieve an arms embargo. But the same discussion paper acknowledged the ineffectiveness of this step: "We do not envision it will have a significant impact on the killings because machetes, knives and other hand implements have been the most common weapons."

Dallaire never spoke to Bushnell or to Tony Marley, the U.S. military liaison to the Arusha process, during the genocide, but they all reached the same conclusions. Seeing that no troops were forthcoming, they turned their attention to measures short of full-scale deployment which might alleviate the suffering. Dallaire pleaded with New York, and Bushnell and her team recommended in Washington, that something be done to "neutralize" Radio Mille Collines.

The country best equipped to prevent the genocide planners from broadcasting murderous instructions directly to the population was the United States. Marley offered three possibilities. The United States could destroy the antenna. It could transmit "counter-broadcasts" urging perpetrators to stop the genocide. Or it could jam the hate radio station's broadcasts. This could have been done from an airborne platform such as the Air Force's Commando Solo airplane. Anthony Lake raised the matter with Secretary of Defense William Perry at the end of April. Pentagon officials considered all the proposals non-starters. On May 5 Frank Wisner, the undersecretary of defense for policy, prepared a memo for Sandy Berger, then the deputy national-security adviser. Wisner's memo testifies to the unwillingness of the U.S. government to make even financial sacrifices to diminish the killing.

> We have looked at options to stop the broadcasts within the Pentagon, discussed them interagency and concluded jamming is an ineffective and expensive mechanism that will not accomplish the objective the NSC Advisor seeks.
>
> International legal conventions complicate airborne or ground based jamming and the mountainous terrain reduces the effectiveness of either

option. Commando Solo, an Air National Guard asset, is the only suitable DOD jamming platform. It costs approximately $8500 per flight hour and requires a semi-secure area of operations due to its vulnerability and limited self-protection.

> I believe it would be wiser to use air to assist in Rwanda in the [food] relief effort . . .

The plane would have needed to remain in Rwandan airspace while it waited for radio transmissions to begin. "First we would have had to figure out whether it made sense to use Commando Solo," Wisner recalls. "Then we had to get it from where it was already and be sure it could be moved. Then we would have needed flight clearance from all the countries nearby. And then we would need the political go-ahead. By the time we got all this, weeks would have passed. And it was not going to solve the fundamental problem, which was one that needed to be addressed militarily." Pentagon planners understood that stopping the genocide required a military solution. Neither they nor the White House wanted any part in a military solution. Yet instead of undertaking other forms of intervention that might have at least saved some lives, they justified inaction by arguing that a military solution was required.

Whatever the limitations of radio jamming, which clearly would have been no panacea, most of the delays Wisner cites could have been avoided if senior Administration officials had followed through. But Rwanda was not their problem. Instead justifications for standing by abounded. In early May the State Department Legal Advisor's Office issued a finding against radio jamming, citing international broadcasting agreements and the American commitment to free speech. When Bushnell raised radio jamming yet again at a meeting, one Pentagon official chided her for naiveté: "Pru, radios don't kill people. *People* kill people!"

■   ■   ■

However significant and obstructionist the role of the Pentagon in April and May, Defense Department officials were stepping into a vacuum. As one U.S. official put it, "Look, nobody senior was paying any attention to this mess. And in the absence of any political leadership from the top, when you have one group that feels pretty strongly about what *shouldn't* be done, it is extremely likely they are going to end up shaping U.S. policy." Lieutenant General Wesley Clark looked to the White House for leadership. "The Pentagon is always going to be the last to want to intervene," he says. "It is up to the civilians to tell us they want to do something and we'll figure out how to do it."

■ ■ ■

XI. PDD-25 in Action

No sooner had most of Dallaire's forces been withdrawn, in late April, than a handful of nonpermanent members of the Security Council, aghast at the scale of the slaughter, pressed the major powers to send a new, beefed-up force (UNAMIR II) to Rwanda.

When Dallaire's troops had first arrived, in the fall of 1993, they had done so under a fairly traditional peacekeeping mandate known as a Chapter VI deployment—a mission that assumes a ceasefire and a desire on both sides to comply with a peace accord. The Security Council now had to decide whether it was prepared to move from peacekeeping to peace *enforcement*—that is, to a Chapter VII mission in a hostile environment. This would demand more peacekeepers with far greater resources, more-aggressive rules of engagement, and an explicit recognition that the UN soldiers were there to protect civilians.

Two proposals emerged. Dallaire submitted a plan that called for joining his remaining peacekeepers with about 5,000 well-armed soldiers he hoped could be gathered quickly by the Security Council. He wanted to secure Kigali and then fan outward to create safe havens for Rwandans who had gathered in large numbers at churches and schools and on hillsides around the country. The United States was one of the few countries that could supply the rapid airlift and logistic support needed to move reinforcements to the region. In a meeting with UN Secretary General Boutros Boutros-Ghali on May 10, Vice President Al Gore pledged U.S. help with transport.

Richard Clarke, at the NSC, and representatives of the Joint Chiefs challenged Dallaire's plan. "How do you plan to take control of the airport in Kigali so that the reinforcements will be able to land?" Clarke asked. He argued instead for an "outside-in" strategy, as opposed to Dallaire's "inside-out" approach. The U.S. proposal would have created protected zones for refugees at Rwanda's borders. It would have kept any U.S. pilots involved in airlifting the peacekeepers safely out of Rwanda. "Our proposal was the most feasible, doable thing that could have been done in the short term," Clarke insists. Dallaire's proposal, in contrast, "could not be done in the short term and could not attract peacekeepers." The U.S. plan—which was modeled on Operation Provide Comfort, for the Kurds of northern Iraq—seemed to assume that the people in need were refugees fleeing to the border, but most endangered Tutsi could not make it to the border. The most vulnerable Rwandans were those clustered together, awaiting salvation, deep inside Rwanda. Dallaire's plan would have had UN soldiers move to the Tutsi in hiding. The U.S. plan would have required civilians to move to the safe zones, negotiating murderous roadblocks on the way. "The two plans had very different objectives," Dallaire says. "My mission was to save Rwandans. Their mission was to put on a show at no risk."

America's new peacekeeping doctrine, of which Clarke was the primary architect, was unveiled on May 3, and U.S. officials applied its criteria zealously. PDD-25 did not merely circumscribe U.S. participation in UN missions; it also limited U.S.

support for other states that hoped to carry out UN missions. Before such missions could garner U.S. approval, policymakers had to answer certain questions: Were U.S. interests at stake? Was there a threat to world peace? A clear mission goal? Acceptable costs? Congressional, public, and allied support? A working cease-fire? A clear command-and-control arrangement? And, finally, what was the exit strategy?

The United States haggled at the Security Council and with the UN Department of Peacekeeping Operations for the first two weeks of May. U.S. officials pointed to the flaws in Dallaire's proposal without offering the resources that would have helped him to overcome them. On May 13 Deputy Secretary of State Strobe Talbott sent Madeleine Albright instructions on how the United States should respond to Dallaire's plan. Noting the logistic hazards of airlifting troops into the capital, Talbott wrote, "The U.S. is not prepared at this point to lift heavy equipment and troops into Kigali." The "more manageable" operation would be to create the protected zones at the border, secure humanitarian-aid deliveries, and "promot[e] restoration of a ceasefire and return to the Arusha Peace Process." Talbott acknowledged that even the minimalist American proposal contained "many unanswered questions":

> Where will the needed forces come from; how will they be transported . . . where precisely should these safe zones be created; . . . would UN forces be authorized to move out of the zones to assist affected populations not in the zones . . . will the fighting parties in Rwanda agree to this arrangement . . . what conditions would need to obtain for the operation to end successfully?

Nonetheless, Talbott concluded, "We would urge the UN to explore and refine this alternative and present the Council with a menu of at least two options in a formal report from the [Secretary General] along with cost estimates before the Security Council votes on changing UNAMIR's mandate." U.S. policymakers were asking valid questions. Dallaire's plan certainly would have required the intervening troops to take risks in an effort to reach the targeted Rwandans or to confront the Hutu militia and government forces. But the business-as-usual tone of the American inquiry did not seem appropriate to the unprecedented and utterly unconventional crisis that was under way.

On May 17, by which time most of the Tutsi victims of the genocide were already dead, the United States finally acceded to a version of Dallaire's plan. However, few African countries stepped forward to offer troops. Even if troops had been immediately available, the lethargy of the major powers would have hindered their use. Though the Administration had committed the United States to provide armored support if the African nations provided soldiers, Pentagon stalling resumed. On May 19 the UN formally requested fifty American armored personnel carriers. On May 31 the United States agreed to send the APCs from Germany to Entebbe, Uganda. But squabbles between the Pentagon and UN planners arose. Who would pay for the vehicles? Should the vehicles be tracked or wheeled? Would the UN buy them or simply lease them? And who would pay the shipping costs? Compounding the disputes was the fact that Department of Defense regulations prevented the U.S. Army from preparing the vehicles for transport until contracts had been signed. The Defense Department demanded that it be reimbursed $15 million for shipping spare parts and equipment to and from Rwanda. In mid-June the White House finally intervened. On June 19, a month after the UN request, the United States began transporting the APCs, but they were missing the radios and heavy machine guns that would be needed if UN troops came under fire. By the time the APCs arrived, the genocide was over—halted by Rwandan Patriotic Front forces under the command of the Tutsi leader, Paul Kagame.

XII. The Stories We Tell

It is not hard to conceive of how the United States might have done things differently. Ahead of the plane crash, as violence escalated, it could have agreed to Belgian pleas for UN reinforcements. Once the killing of thousands of Rwandans a day had begun, the President could have deployed U.S. troops to Rwanda. The United States could have joined Dallaire's beleaguered UNAMIR forces or, if it feared associating with shoddy UN peacekeeping, it could have intervened unilaterally with the Security Council's backing, as France eventually did in late June. The United States could also have acted without the UN's blessing, as it did five years later in Kosovo. Securing congressional support for U.S. intervention would have been extremely difficult, but by the second week of the killing Clinton could have made the case that something approximating genocide was under way, that a supreme American value was imperiled by its occurrence, and that U.S. contingents at relatively low risk could stop the extermination of a people.

Alan Kuperman wrote in *Foreign Affairs* that President Clinton was in the dark for two weeks; by the time a large U.S. force could deploy, it would not have saved "even half of the ultimate victims." The evidence indicates that the killers' intentions were known by mid-level officials and knowable by their bosses within a week of the plane crash. Any failure to fully appreciate the genocide stemmed from political, moral, and imaginative weaknesses, not informational ones. As for what force could have accomplished, Kuperman's claims are purely speculative. We cannot know how the announcement of a robust or even a limited U.S. deployment would have affected the perpetrators' behavior. It is worth noting that even Kuperman concedes that belated intervention would have saved 75,000 to 125,000—no small achievement. A more serious challenge comes from the U.S. officials who argue that no amount of leadership from the White House would have overcome congressional opposition to sending U.S. troops to Africa. But even if that highly debatable point was true, the United States still had a variety of options. Instead of leaving it to mid-level officials to communicate with the Rwandan leadership behind the scenes, senior officials in the Administration could have taken control of the process. They could have publicly and frequently denounced the slaughter. They could have branded the crimes "genocide" at a far earlier stage. They could have called for the expulsion of the Rwandan delegation from the Security Council. On the telephone, at the UN, and on the Voice of America they could have threatened to prosecute those complicit in the genocide, naming names when possible. They could have deployed Pentagon assets to jam—even temporarily—the crucial, deadly radio broadcasts.

Instead of demanding a UN withdrawal, quibbling over costs, and coming forward (belatedly) with a plan better suited to caring for refugees than to stopping massacres, U.S. officials could have worked to make UNAMIR a force to contend with. They could have urged their Belgian allies to stay and protect Rwandan civilians. If the Belgians insisted on withdrawing, the White House could have done everything within its power to make sure that Dallaire was immediately reinforced. Senior officials could have spent U.S. political capital rallying troops from other nations and could have supplied strategic airlift and logistic support to a coalition that it had helped to create. In short, the United States could have led the world.

Why did none of these things happen? One reason is that all possible sources of pressure—U.S. allies, Congress, editorial boards, and the American people—were mute when it mattered for Rwanda. American leaders have a circular and deliberate relationship to public opinion. It is circular because public opinion is rarely if ever aroused by foreign crises, even genocidal ones, in the absence of political leadership, and yet at the same time, American leaders continually cite the absence of public support as grounds for inaction. The relationship is deliberate because American leadership is not absent in such circumstances: it was present regarding Rwanda, but devoted mainly to suppressing public outrage and thwarting UN initiatives so as to avoid acting.

Strikingly, most officials involved in shaping U.S. policy were able to define the decision not to stop genocide as ethical and moral. The Administration employed several devices to keep down enthusiasm for action and to preserve the public's sense—and, more important, its own—that U.S. policy choices were not merely politically astute but also morally acceptable. First, Administration officials exaggerated the extremity of the possible responses. Time and again U.S. leaders posed the choice as between staying out of Rwanda and "getting involved everywhere." In addition, they often presented the choice as one between doing nothing and sending in the Marines. On May 25, at the Naval Academy graduation ceremony, Clinton described America's relationship to ethnic trouble spots: "We cannot turn away from them, but our interests are not sufficiently at stake in so many of them to justify a commitment of our folks."

Second, Administration policymakers appealed to notions of the greater good. They did not simply frame U.S. policy as one contrived in order to advance the national interest or avoid U.S. casualties. Rather, they often argued against intervention from the standpoint of people committed to protecting human life. Owing to recent failures in UN peacekeeping, many humanitarian interventionists in the U.S. government were concerned about the future of America's relationship with the United Nations generally and peacekeeping specifically. They believed that the UN and humanitarianism could not afford another Somalia. Many internalized the belief that the UN had more to lose by sending reinforcements and failing than by allowing the killings to proceed. Their chief priority, after the evacuation of the Americans, was looking after UN peacekeepers, and they justified the withdrawal of the peacekeepers on the grounds that it would ensure a future for humanitarian intervention. In other words, Dallaire's peacekeeping mission in Rwanda had to be destroyed so that peacekeeping might be saved for use elsewhere.

A third feature of the response that helped to console U.S. officials at the time was the sheer flurry of Rwanda-related activity. U.S. officials with a special concern for Rwanda took their solace from mini-victories—working on behalf of specific individuals or groups (Monique Mujawamariya; the Rwandans gathered at the hotel). Government officials involved in policy met constantly and remained "seized of the matter"; they neither appeared nor felt indifferent. Although little in the way of effective intervention emerged from midlevel meetings in Washington or New York, an abundance of memoranda and other documents did.

Finally, the almost willful delusion that what was happening in Rwanda did not amount to genocide created a nurturing ethical framework for inaction. "War" was "tragic" but created no moral imperative.

What is most frightening about this story is that it testifies to a system that in effect worked. President Clinton and his advisers had several aims. First, they wanted to avoid engagement in a conflict that posed little threat to American interests, narrowly defined. Second, they sought to appease a restless Congress by showing that they were cautious in their approach to peacekeeping. And third, they hoped to contain the political costs and avoid the moral stigma associated with allowing genocide. By and large, they achieved all three objectives. The normal operations of the foreign-policy bureaucracy and the international community permitted an illusion of continual deliberation, complex activity, and intense concern, even as Rwandans were left to die.

John J. Mearsheimer
THE FALSE PROMISE OF INTERNATIONAL INSTITUTIONS

∎ ∎ ∎

What Are Institutions?

There is no widely-agreed upon definition of institutions in the international relations literature.[1] The concept is sometimes defined so broadly as to encompass all of international relations, which gives it little analytical bite.[2] For example, defining institutions as "recognized patterns of behavior or practice around which expectations converge" allows the concept to cover almost every regularized pattern of activity between states, from war to tariff bindings negotiated under the General Agreement on Tariffs and Trade (GATT), thus rendering it largely meaningless.[3] Still, it is possible to devise a useful definition that is consistent with how most institutionalist scholars employ the concept.

I define institutions as a set of rules that stipulate the ways in which states should cooperate and compete with each other.[4] They prescribe acceptable forms of state behavior, and proscribe unacceptable kinds of behavior. These rules are negotiated by states, and according to many prominent theorists, they entail the mutual acceptance of higher norms, which are "standards of behavior defined in terms of rights and obligations."[5] These rules are typically formalized in international agreements, and are usually embodied in organizations with their own personnel and budgets.[6] Although rules are usually incorporated into a formal international organization, it is not the organization *per se* that compels states to obey the rules. Institutions are not a form of world government. States themselves must choose to obey the rules they created. Institutions, in short, call for the "decentralized cooperation of individual sovereign states, without any effective mechanism of command."[7]

∎ ∎ ∎

Institutions in a Realist World

Realists * * * recognize that states sometimes operate through institutions. However, they believe that those rules reflect state calculations of self-interest based primarily on the international distribution of power. The most powerful states in the system create and shape institutions so that they can maintain their share of world power, or even increase it. In this view, institutions are essentially "arenas for acting out power relationships."[8] For realists, the causes of war and peace are mainly a function of the balance of power, and institutions largely mirror the distribution of power in the system. In short, the balance of power is the independent variable that explains war; institutions are merely an intervening variable in the process.

NATO provides a good example of realist thinking about institutions. NATO is an institution, and it certainly played a role in preventing World War III and helping the West win the Cold War. Nevertheless, NATO was basically a manifestation of the bipolar distribution of power in Europe during the

From *International Security* 19, no. 3 (Winter 1994/95): 5–49. Some of the author's notes have been edited.

Cold War, and it was that balance of power, not NATO *per se*, that provided the key to maintaining stability on the continent. NATO was essentially an American tool for managing power in the face of the Soviet threat. Now, with the collapse of the Soviet Union, realists argue that NATO must either disappear or reconstitute itself on the basis of the new distribution of power in Europe.[9] NATO cannot remain as it was during the Cold War.

■   ■   ■

Liberal Institutionalism

Liberal institutionalism does not directly address the question of whether institutions cause peace, but instead focuses on the less ambitious goal of explaining cooperation in cases where state interests are not fundamentally opposed.[10] Specifically, the theory looks at cases where states are having difficulty cooperating because they have "mixed" interests; in other words, each side has incentives both to cooperate and not to cooperate.[11] Each side can benefit from cooperation, however, which liberal institutionalists define as "goal-directed behavior that entails mutual policy adjustments so that all sides end up better off than they would otherwise be."[12] The theory is of little relevance in situations where states' interests are fundamentally conflictual and neither side thinks it has much to gain from cooperation. In these circumstances, states aim to gain advantage over each other. They think in terms of winning and losing, and this invariably leads to intense security competition, and sometimes war. But liberal institutionalism does not deal directly with these situations, and thus says little about how to resolve or even ameliorate them.

Therefore, the theory largely ignores security issues and concentrates instead on economic and, to a lesser extent, environmental issues.[13] In fact, the theory is built on the assumption that international politics can be divided into two realms—security and political economy—and that liberal institutionalism mainly applies to the latter, but not the former. * * *

■   ■   ■

According to liberal institutionalists, the principal obstacle to cooperation among states with mutual interests is the threat of cheating.[14] The famous "prisoners' dilemma," which is the analytical centerpiece of most of the liberal institutionalist literature, captures the essence of the problem that states must solve to achieve cooperation.[15] Each of two states can either cheat or cooperate with the other. Each side wants to maximize its own gain, but does not care about the size of the other side's gain; each side cares about the other side only so far as the other side's chosen strategy affects its own prospects for maximizing gain. The most attractive strategy for each state is to cheat and hope the other state pursues a cooperative strategy. In other words, a state's ideal outcome is to "sucker" the other side into thinking it is going to cooperate, and then cheat. But both sides understand this logic, and therefore both sides will try to cheat the other. Consequently, both sides will end up worse off than if they had cooperated, since mutual cheating leads to the worst possible outcome. Even though mutual cooperation is not as attractive as suckering the other side, it is certainly better than the outcome when both sides cheat.

The key to solving this dilemma is for each side to convince the other that they have a collective interest in making what appear to be short-term sacrifices (the gain that might result from successful cheating) for the sake of long-term benefits (the substantial payoff from mutual long-term cooperation). This means convincing states to accept the second-best outcome, which is mutual collaboration. The principal obstacle to reaching this cooperative outcome will be fear of getting suckered, should the other side cheat. This, in a nutshell, is the problem that institutions must solve.

To deal with this problem of "political market failure," institutions must deter cheaters and protect victims.[16] Three messages must be sent to potential cheaters: you will be caught, you will be punished immediately, and you will jeopardize future cooperative efforts. Potential victims, on the other hand, need early warning of cheating to avoid serious injury, and need the means to punish cheaters.

Liberal institutionalists do not aim to deal with cheaters and victims by changing fundamental norms of state behavior. Nor do they suggest transforming the anarchical nature of the international system. They accept the assumption that states operate in an anarchic environment and behave in a self-interested manner.[17] * * * Liberal institutionalists instead concentrate on showing how rules can work to counter the cheating problem, even while states seek to maximize their own welfare. They argue that institutions can change a state's calculations about how to maximize gains. Specifically, rules can get states to make the short-term sacrifices needed to resolve the prisoners' dilemma and thus to realize long-term gains. Institutions, in short, can produce cooperation.

Rules can ideally be employed to make four major changes in "the contractual environment."[18] First, rules can increase the number of transactions between particular states over time.[19] This *institutionalized iteration* discourages cheating in three ways. It raises the costs of cheating by creating the prospect of future gains through cooperation, thereby invoking "the shadow of the future" to deter cheating today. A state caught cheating would jeopardize its prospects of benefiting from future cooperation, since the victim would probably retaliate. In addition, iteration gives the victim the opportunity to pay back the cheater: it allows for reciprocation, the tit-for-tat strategy, which works to punish cheaters and not allow them to get away with their transgression. Finally, it rewards states that develop a reputation for faithful adherence to agreements, and punishes states that acquire a reputation for cheating.[20]

Second, rules can tie together interactions between states in different issue areas. *Issue-linkage* aims to create greater interdependence between states, who will then be reluctant to cheat in one issue area for fear that the victim—and perhaps other states as well—will retaliate in another issue area. It discourages cheating in much the same way as iteration: it raises the costs of cheating and provides a way for the victim to retaliate against the cheater.

Third, a structure of rules can increase the amount of *information* available to participants in cooperative agreements so that close monitoring is possible. Raising the level of information discourages cheating in two ways: it increases the likelihood that cheaters will be caught, and more importantly, it provides victims with early warning of cheating, thereby enabling them to take protective measures before they are badly hurt.

Fourth, rules can reduce the *transaction costs* of individual agreements.[21] When institutions perform the tasks described above, states can devote less effort to negotiating and monitoring cooperative agreements, and to hedging against possible defections. By increasing the efficiency of international cooperation, institutions make it more profitable and thus more attractive for self-interested states.

Liberal institutionalism is generally thought to be of limited utility in the security realm, because fear of cheating is considered a much greater obstacle to cooperation when military issues are at stake.[22] There is the constant threat that betrayal will result in a devastating military defeat. This threat of "swift, decisive defection" is simply not present when dealing with international economics. Given that "the costs of betrayal" are potentially much graver in the military than the economic sphere, states will be very reluctant to accept the "one step backward, two steps forward" logic which underpins the tit-for-tat strategy of conditional cooperation. One step backward in the security realm might mean destruction, in which case there will be no next step—backward or forward.[23]

* * * There is an important theoretical failing in the liberal institutionalist logic, even as it applies

to economic issues. The theory is correct as far as it goes: cheating can be a serious barrier to cooperation. It ignores, however, the other major obstacle to cooperation: relative-gains concerns. As Joseph Grieco has shown, liberal institutionalists assume that states are not concerned about relative gains, but focus exclusively on absolute gains.[24] * * *

This oversight is revealed by the assumed order of preference in the prisoners' dilemma game: each state cares about how its opponent's strategy will affect its own (absolute) gains, but not about how much one side gains relative to the other. In other words, each side simply wants to get the best deal for itself, and does not pay attention to how well the other side fares in the process.[25] Nevertheless, liberal institutionalists cannot ignore relative-gains considerations, because they assume that states are self-interested actors in an anarchic system, and they recognize that military power matters to states. A theory that explicitly accepts realism's core assumptions—and liberal institutionalism does that—must confront the issue of relative gains if it hopes to develop a sound explanation for why states cooperate.

One might expect liberal institutionalists to offer the counterargument that relative-gains logic applies only to the security realm, while absolute-gains logic applies to the economic realm. Given that they are mainly concerned with explaining economic and environmental cooperation, leaving relative-gains concerns out of the theory does not matter.

There are two problems with this argument. First, if cheating were the only significant obstacle to cooperation, liberal institutionalists could argue that their theory applies to the economic, but not the military realm. In fact, they do make that argument. However, once relative-gains considerations are factored into the equation, it becomes impossible to maintain the neat dividing line between economic and military issues, mainly because military might is significantly dependent on economic might. The relative size of a state's economy has profound consequences for its standing in the international balance of military power. Therefore,

relative-gains concerns must be taken into account for security reasons when looking at the economic as well as military domain. The neat dividing line that liberal institutionalists employ to specify when their theory applies has little utility when one accepts that states worry about relative gains.[26]

Second, there are non-realist (i.e., non-security) logics that might explain why states worry about relative gains. Strategic trade theory, for example, provides a straightforward economic logic for why states should care about relative gains.[27] It argues that states should help their own firms gain comparative advantage over the firms of rival states, because that is the best way to insure national economic prosperity. There is also a psychological logic, which portrays individuals as caring about how well they do (or their state does) in a cooperative agreement, not for material reasons, but because it is human nature to compare one's progress with that of others.[28]

Another possible liberal institutionalist counterargument is that solving the cheating problem renders the relative-gains problem irrelevant. If states cannot cheat each other, they need not fear each other, and therefore, states would not have to worry about relative power. The problem with this argument, however, is that even if the cheating problem were solved, states would still have to worry about relative gains because gaps in gains can be translated into military advantage that can be used for coercion or aggression. And in the international system, states sometimes have conflicting interests that lead to aggression.

There is also empirical evidence that relative-gains considerations mattered during the Cold War even in economic relations among the advanced industrialized democracies in the Organization for Economic Cooperation and Development (OECD). One would not expect realist logic about relative gains to be influential in this case: the United States was a superpower with little to fear militarily from the other OECD states, and those states were unlikely to use a relative-gains advantage to threaten the United States.[29] Furthermore, the OECD states were important American allies during the Cold War, and thus the United States benefited strategically when they gained substantially in size and strength.

Nonetheless, relative gains appear to have mattered in economic relations among the advanced industrial states. Consider three prominent studies. Stephen Krasner considered efforts at cooperation in different sectors of the international communications industry. He found that states were remarkably unconcerned about cheating but deeply worried about relative gains, which led him to conclude that liberal institutionalism "is not relevant for global communications." Grieco examined American and EC efforts to implement, under the auspices of GATT, a number of agreements relating to non-tariff barriers to trade. He found that the level of success was not a function of concerns about cheating but was influenced primarily by concern about the distribution of gains. Similarly, Michael Mastanduno found that concern about relative gains, not about cheating, was an important factor in shaping American policy towards Japan in three cases: the FSX fighter aircraft, satellites, and high-definition television.[30]

I am not suggesting that relative-gains considerations make cooperation impossible; my point is simply that they can pose a serious impediment to cooperation and must therefore be taken into account when developing a theory of cooperation among states. This point is apparently now recognized by liberal institutionalists. Keohane, for example, acknowledges that he "did make a major mistake by underemphasizing distributive issues and the complexities they create for international cooperation."[31]

CAN LIBERAL INSTITUTIONALISM BE REPAIRED?

Liberal institutionalists must address two questions if they are to repair their theory. First, can institutions facilitate cooperation when states seriously care about relative gains, or do institutions only matter when states can ignore relative-gains considerations and focus instead on absolute gains?

I find no evidence that liberal institutionalists believe that institutions facilitate cooperation when states care deeply about relative gains. They apparently concede that their theory only applies when relative-gains considerations matter little or hardly at all.[32] Thus the second question: when do states not worry about relative gains? The answer to this question would ultimately define the realm in which liberal institutionalism applies.

Liberal institutionalists have not addressed this important question in a systematic fashion, so any assessment of their efforts to repair the theory must be preliminary. * * *

■ ■ ■

PROBLEMS WITH THE EMPIRICAL RECORD

Although there is much evidence of cooperation among states, this alone does not constitute support for liberal institutionalism. What is needed is evidence of cooperation that would not have occurred in the absence of institutions because of fear of cheating, or its actual presence. But scholars have provided little evidence of cooperation of that sort, nor of cooperation failing because of cheating. Moreover, as discussed above, there is considerable evidence that states worry much about relative gains not only in security matters, but in the economic realm as well.

This dearth of empirical support for liberal institutionalism is acknowledged by proponents of that theory.[33] The empirical record is not completely blank, however, but the few historical cases that liberal institutionalists have studied provide scant support for the theory. Consider two prominent examples.

Keohane looked at the performance of the International Energy Agency (IEA) in 1974–81, a period that included the 1979 oil crisis.[34] This case does not appear to lend the theory much support. First, Keohane concedes that the IEA failed outright when put to the test in 1979: "regime-oriented efforts at cooperation do not always succeed, as the fiasco of IEA actions in 1979 illustrates."[35] He claims, however, that in 1980 the IEA had a minor success "under relatively favorable conditions" in responding to the outbreak of the Iran-Iraq War. Although he admits it is difficult to specify how much the IEA mattered in the 1980 case, he notes that "it seems clear that 'it [the IEA] leaned in the right direction,'" a claim that hardly constitutes strong support for the theory.[36] Second, it does not appear from Keohane's analysis that either fear of cheating or actual cheating hindered cooperation in the 1979 case, as the theory would predict. Third, Keohane chose the IEA case precisely because it involved relations among advanced Western democracies with market economies, where the prospects for cooperation were excellent.[37] The modest impact of institutions in this case is thus all the more damning to the theory.

Lisa Martin examined the role that the European Community (EC) played during the Falklands War in helping Britain coax its reluctant allies to continue economic sanctions against Argentina after military action started.[38] She concludes that the EC helped Britain win its allies' cooperation by lowering transaction costs and facilitating issue linkage. Specifically, Britain made concessions on the EC budget and the Common Agricultural Policy (CAP); Britain's allies agreed in return to keep sanctions on Argentina.

This case, too, is less than a ringing endorsement for liberal institutionalism. First, British efforts to maintain EC sanctions against Argentina were not impeded by fears of possible cheating, which the theory identifies as the central impediment to cooperation. So this case does not present an important test of liberal institutionalism, and thus the cooperative outcome does not tell us much about the theory's explanatory power. Second, it was relatively easy for Britain and her allies to strike a deal in this case. Neither side's core interests were threatened, and neither side had to make significant sacrifices to reach an agreement. Forging an accord to continue sanctions was not a

difficult undertaking. A stronger test for liberal institutionalism would require states to cooperate when doing so entailed significant costs and risks. Third, the EC was not essential to an agreement. Issues could have been linked without the EC, and although the EC may have lowered transaction costs somewhat, there is no reason to think these costs were a serious impediment to striking a deal.[39] It is noteworthy that Britain and America were able to cooperate during the Falklands War, even though the United States did not belong to the EC.

There is also evidence that directly challenges liberal institutionalism in issue areas where one would expect the theory to operate successfully. The studies discussed above by Grieco, Krasner, and Mastanduno test the institutionalist argument in a number of different political economy cases, and each finds the theory has little explanatory power. More empirical work is needed before a final judgment is rendered on the explanatory power of liberal institutionalism. Nevertheless, the evidence gathered so far is unpromising at best.

In summary, liberal institutionalism does not provide a sound basis for understanding international relations and promoting stability in the post–Cold War world. It makes modest claims about the impact of institutions, and steers clear of war and peace issues, focusing instead on the less ambitious task of explaining economic cooperation. Furthermore, the theory's causal logic is flawed, as proponents of the theory now admit. Having overlooked the relative-gains problem, they are now attempting to repair the theory, but their initial efforts are not promising. Finally, the available empirical evidence provides little support for the theory.

Conclusion

■ ■ ■

The attraction of institutionalist theories for both policymakers and scholars is explained, I believe, not by their intrinsic value, but by their relationship to realism, and especially to core elements of American political ideology. Realism has long been and continues to be an influential theory in the United States.[40] Leading realist thinkers such as George Kennan and Henry Kissinger, for example, occupied key policymaking positions during the Cold War. The impact of realism in the academic world is amply demonstrated in the institutionalist literature, where discussions of realism are pervasive.[41] Yet despite its influence, Americans who think seriously about foreign policy issues tend to dislike realism intensely, mainly because it clashes with their basic values. The theory stands opposed to how most Americans prefer to think about themselves and the wider world.[42]

There are four principal reasons why American elites, as well as the American public, tend to regard realism with hostility. First, realism is a pessimistic theory. It depicts a world of stark and harsh competition, and it holds out little promise of making that world more benign. Realists, as Hans Morgenthau wrote, are resigned to the fact that "there is no escape from the evil of power, regardless of what one does."[43] Such pessimism, of course, runs up against the deep-seated American belief that with time and effort, reasonable individuals can solve important social problems. Americans regard progress as both desirable and possible in politics, and they are therefore uncomfortable with realism's claim that security competition and war will persist despite our best efforts to eliminate them.[44]

Second, realism treats war as an inevitable, and indeed sometimes necessary, form of state activity. For realists, war is an extension of politics by other means. Realists are very cautious in their prescriptions about the use of force: wars should not be fought for idealistic purposes, but instead for balance-of-power reasons. Most Americans, however, tend to think of war as a hideous enterprise that should ultimately be abolished. For the time being, however, it can only justifiably be used for lofty moral goals, like "making the world safe for democracy"; it is morally incorrect to fight wars to change or preserve the balance of power. This makes the realist conception of warfare anathema to many Americans.

Third, as an analytical matter, realism does not distinguish between "good" states and "bad" states, but essentially treats them like billiard balls of varying size. In realist theory, all states are forced to seek the same goal: maximum relative power.[45] A purely realist interpretation of the Cold War, for example, allows for no meaningful difference in the motives behind American and Soviet behavior during that conflict. According to the theory, both sides must have been driven by concerns about the balance of power, and must have done what was necessary to try to achieve a favorable balance. Most Americans would recoil at such a description of the Cold War, because they believe the United States was motivated by good intentions while the Soviet Union was not.[46]

Fourth, America has a rich history of thumbing its nose at realism. For its first 140 years of existence, geography and the British navy allowed the United States to avoid serious involvement in the power politics of Europe. America had an isolationist foreign policy for most of this period, and its rhetoric explicitly emphasized the evils of entangling alliances and balancing behavior. Even as the United States finally entered its first European war in 1917, Woodrow Wilson railed against realist thinking. America has a long tradition of anti-realist rhetoric, which continues to influence us today.

Given that realism is largely alien to American culture, there is a powerful demand in the United States for alternative ways of looking at the world, and especially for theories that square with basic American values. Institutionalist theories nicely meet these requirements, and that is the main source of their appeal to policymakers and scholars. Whatever else one might say about these theories, they have one undeniable advantage in the eyes of their supporters: they are not realism. Not only do institutionalist theories offer an alternative to realism, but they explicitly seek to undermine it. Moreover, institutionalists offer arguments that reflect basic American values. For example, they are optimistic about the possibility of greatly reducing, if not eliminating, security competition among states and creating a more peaceful world. They certainly do not accept the realist stricture that war is politics by other means. Institutionalists, in short, purvey a message that Americans long to hear.

There is, however, a downside for policymakers who rely on institutionalist theories: these theories do not accurately describe the world, hence policies based on them are bound to fail. The international system strongly shapes the behavior of states, limiting the amount of damage that false faith in institutional theories can cause. The constraints of the system notwithstanding, however, states still have considerable freedom of action, and their policy choices can succeed or fail in protecting American national interests and the interests of vulnerable people around the globe. The failure of the League of Nations to address German and Japanese aggression in the 1930s is a case in point. The failure of institutions to prevent or stop the war in Bosnia offers a more recent example. These cases illustrate that institutions have mattered rather little in the past; they also suggest that the false belief that institutions matter has mattered more, and has had pernicious effects. Unfortunately, misplaced reliance on institutional solutions is likely to lead to more failures in the future.

NOTES

1. Regimes and institutions are treated as synonymous concepts in this article. They are also used interchangeably in the institutionalist literature. See Robert O. Keohane, "International Institutions: Two Approaches," *International Studies Quarterly*, Vol. 32, No. 4 (December 1988), p. 384; Robert O. Keohane, *International Institutions and State Power: Essays in International Relations Theory* (Boulder, CO: Westview Press, 1989), pp. 3–4; and Oran R. Young, *International Cooperation: Building Regimes for Natural Resources and the Environment* (Ithaca, NY: Cornell University Press, 1989),

chaps. 1 and 8. The term "multilateralism" is also virtually synonymous with institutions.

2. See Arthur A. Stein, *Why Nations Cooperate: Circumstance and Choice in International Relations* (Ithaca, NY: Cornell University Press, 1990), pp. 25–27. Also see Susan Strange, "*Cave! Hic Dragones:* A Critique of Regime Analysis," in Stephen D. Krasner, ed., *International Regimes,* special issue of *International Organization*, Vol. 36, No. 2 (Spring 1982), pp. 479–96.

3. Oran R. Young, "Regime Dynamics: The Rise and Fall of International Regimes," in Krasner, *International Regimes*, p. 277.

4. See Douglass C. North and Robert P. Thomas, "An Economic Theory of the Growth of the Western World," *The Economic History Review,* 2nd series, Vol. 23, No. 1 (April 1970), p. 5.

5. Krasner, *International Regimes,* p. 186. Non-realist institutions are often based on higher norms, while few, if any, realist institutions are based on norms. The dividing line between norms and rules is not sharply defined in the institutionalist literature. See Robert O. Keohane, *After Hegemony: Cooperation and Discord in the World Political Economy* (Princeton, NJ: Princeton University Press, 1984), pp. 57–58. For example, one might argue that rules, not just norms, are concerned with rights and obligations. The key point, however, is that for many institutionalists, norms, which are core beliefs about standards of appropriate state behavior, are the foundation on which more specific rules are constructed. This distinction between norms and rules applies in a rather straightforward way in the subsequent discussion. Both collective security and critical theory challenge the realist belief that states behave in a self-interested way, and argue instead for developing norms that require states to act more altruistically. Liberal institutionalism, on the other hand, accepts the realist view that states act on the basis of self-interest, and concentrates on devising rules that facilitate cooperation among states.

6. International organizations are public agencies established through the cooperative efforts of two or more states. These administrative structures have their own budget, personnel, and buildings. John Ruggie defines them as "palpable entities with headquarters and letterheads, voting procedures, and generous pension plans." Ruggie, "Multilateralism[: The Anatomy of an Institution]," [*International Organization*, Vol. 46, No. 3 (Summer 1992),] p. 573. Once rules are incorporated into an international organization, "they may seem almost coterminous," even though they are "distinguishable analytically." Keohane, *International Institutions and State Power,* p. 5.

7. Charles Lipson, "Is the Future of Collective Security Like the Past?" in George W. Downs, ed., *Collective Security beyond the Cold War* (Ann Arbor: University of Michigan Press), p. 114.

8. Tony Evans and Peter Wilson, "Regime Theory and the English School of International Relations: A Comparison," *Millennium: Journal of International Studies*, Vol. 21, No. 3 (Winter 1992), p. 330.

9. See Gunther Hellmann and Reinhard Wolf, "Neorealism, Neoliberal Institutionalism, and the Future of NATO," *Security Studies*, Vol. 3, No. 1 (Autumn 1993), pp. 3–43.

10. Among the key liberal institutionalist works are: Robert Axelrod and Robert O. Keohane, "Achieving Cooperation under Anarchy:

Strategies and Institutions," *World Politics*, Vol. 38, No. 1 (October 1985), pp. 226–54; Keohane, *After Hegemony*; Keohane, "International Institutions: Two Approaches," pp. 379–96; Keohane, *International Institutions and State Power*, chap. 1; Lisa L. Martin, *Coercive Cooperation: Explaining Multilateral Economic Sanctions* (Princeton, NJ: Princeton University Press, 1992); Kenneth A. Oye, "Explaining Cooperation Under Anarchy: Hypotheses and Strategies," *World Politics*, Vol. 38, No. 1 (October 1985), pp. 1–24; and Stein, *Why Nations Cooperate*.

11. Stein, *Why Nations Cooperate*, chap. 2. Also see Keohane, *After Hegemony*, pp. 6–7, 12–13, 67–69.

12. Milner, "International Theories of Cooperation [among Nations: Strengths and Weakness]," [*World Politics*, Vol. 44, No. 3 (April 1992),] p. 468.

13. For examples of the theory at work in the environmental realm, see Peter M. Haas, Robert O. Keohane, and Marc A. Levy, eds., *Institutions for the Earth: Sources of Effective International Environmental Protection* (Cambridge, MA: MIT Press, 1993), especially chaps. 1 and 9.

14. Cheating is basically a "breach of promise." Oye, "Explaining Cooperation Under Anarchy," p. 1. It usually implies unobserved non-compliance, although there can be observed cheating as well. Defection is a synonym for cheating in the institutionalist literature.

15. The centrality of the prisoners' dilemma and cheating to the liberal institutionalist literature is clearly reflected in virtually all the works cited in footnote 10. As Helen Milner notes in her review essay on this literature: "The focus is primarily on the role of regimes [institutions] in solving the defection [cheating] problem." Milner, "International Theories of Cooperation," p. 475.

16. The phrase is from Keohane, *After Hegemony*, p. 85.

17. Kenneth Oye, for example, writes in the introduction to an issue of *World Politics* containing a number of liberal institutionalist essays: "Our focus is on non-altruistic cooperation among states dwelling in international anarchy." Oye, "Explaining Cooperation Under Anarchy," p. 2. Also see Keohane, "International Institutions: Two Approaches," pp. 380–81; and Keohane, *International Institutions and State Power*, p. 3.

18. Haas, Keohane, and Levy, *Institutions for the Earth*, p. 11. For general discussions of how rules work, which inform my subsequent discussion of the matter, see Keohane, *After Hegemony*, chaps. 5–6; Lisa L. Martin, "Institutions and Cooperation: Sanctions During the Falkand Islands Conflict," *International Security*, Vol. 16, No. 4 (Spring 1992), pp. 143–78; and Milner, "International Theories of Cooperation," pp. 474–78.

19. See Axelrod and Keohane, "Achieving Cooperation Under Anarchy," pp. 248–50; [Charles] Lipson, "International Cooperation [in Economic and Security Affairs]," [*World Politics*, Vol. 37, No. 1 (October 1984),] pp. 4–18.

20. Lipson, "International Cooperation," p. 5.

21. See Keohane, *After Hegemony*, pp. 89–92.

22. This point is clearly articulated in Lipson, "International Cooperation," especially pp. 12–18. The subsequent quotations in this paragraph are from ibid. Also see Axelrod and Keohane, "Achieving Cooperation Under Anarchy," pp. 232–33.

23. See Roger B. Parks, "What if 'Fools Die'? A Comment on Axelrod," Letter to *American Political Science Review*, Vol. 79, No. 4 (December 1985), pp. 1173–74.

24. See Grieco, "Anarchy and the Limits of Cooperation[: A Realist Critique of the Newest Liberal Institutionalism,]" [*International Organization*, Vol. 42, No. 3 (Summer 1988)]. Other works by Grieco bearing on the subject include: Joseph M. Grieco, *Cooperation among Nations: Europe, America, and Non-Tariff Barriers to Trade* (Ithaca, NY: Cornell University Press, 1990).

25. Lipson writes: "The Prisoner's Dilemma, in its simplest form, involves two players. Each is assumed to be a self-interested, self-reliant maximizer of his own utility, an assumption that clearly parallels the Realist conception of sovereign states in international politics." Lipson, "International Cooperation," p. 2. Realists, however, do not accept this conception of international politics and, not surprisingly, have questioned the relevance of the prisoners' dilemma (at least in its common form) for explaining much of international relations. See Stephen D. Krasner, "Global Communications and National Power: Life on the Pareto Frontier," *World Politics*, Vol. 43, No. 3 (April 1991), pp. 336–66.

26. My thinking on this matter has been markedly influenced by Sean Lynn-Jones, in his June 19, 1994, correspondence with me.

27. For a short discussion of strategic trade theory, see Robert Gilpin, *The Political Economy of International Relations* (Princeton, NJ: Princeton University Press, 1987), pp. 215–21. The most commonly cited reference on the subject is Paul R. Krugman, ed., *Strategic Trade Policy and the New International Economics* (Cambridge, MA: MIT Press, 1986).

28. See Robert Axelrod, *The Evolution of Cooperation* (New York: Basic Books, 1984), pp. 110–13.

29. Grieco maintains in *Cooperation among Nations* that realist logic should apply here. Robert Powell, however, points out that "in the context of negotiations between the European Community and the United States . . . it is difficult to attribute any concern for relative gains to the effects that a relative loss may have on the probability of survival." Robert Powell, "Absolute and Relative Gains in International Relations Theory," *American Political Science Review*, Vol. 85, No. 4 (December 1991), p. 1319, footnote 26. I agree with Powell. It is clear from Grieco's response to Powell that Grieco includes non-military logics like strategic trade theory in the realist tent, whereas Powell and I do not. See Grieco's contribution to "The Relative-Gains Problem for International Relations," *American Political Science Review*, Vol. 87, No. 3 (September 1993), pp. 733–35.

30. Krasner, "Global Communications and National Power," pp. 336–66; Grieco, *Cooperation among Nations*; and Michael Mastanduno, "Do Relative Gains Matter? America's Response to Japanese Industrial Policy," *International Security*, Vol. 16, No. 1 (Summer 1991), pp. 73–113.

31. Keohane, "Institutional Theory and the Realist Challenge," [in Baldwin, *Neorealism and Neoliberalism*,] p. 292.

32. For example, Keohane wrote after becoming aware of Grieco's argument about relative gains: "Under specified conditions—where mutual interests are low and relative gains are therefore particularly important to states—neoliberal theory expects neorealism to

explain elements of state behavior." Keohane, *International Institutions and State Power*, pp. 15–16.

33. For example, Lisa Martin writes that "scholars working in the realist tradition maintain a well-founded skepticism about the empirical impact of institutional factors on state behavior. This skepticism is grounded in a lack of studies that show precisely how and when institutions have constrained state decisionmaking." Martin, "Institutions and Cooperation," p. 144.

34. Keohane, *After Hegemony*, chap. 10.

35. Ibid., p. 16.

36. Ibid., p. 236. A U.S. Department of Energy review of the IEA's performance in the 1980 crisis concluded that it had "failed to fulfill its promise." Ethan B. Kapstein, *The Insecure Alliance: Energy Crises and Western Politics Since 1944* (New York: Oxford University Press, 1990), p. 198.

37. Keohane, *After Hegemony*, p. 7.

38. Martin, "Institutions and Cooperation." Martin looks closely at three other cases in *Coercive Cooperation* to determine the effect of institutions on cooperation. I have concentrated on the Falklands War case, however, because it is, by her own admission, her strongest case. See ibid., p. 96.

39. Martin does not claim that agreement would not have been possible without the EC. Indeed, she appears to concede that even without the EC, Britain still could have fashioned "separate bilateral agreements with each EEC member in order to gain its cooperation, [although] this would have involved much higher transaction costs." Martin, "Institutions and Cooperation," pp. 174–75. However, transaction costs among the advanced industrial democracies are not very high in an era of rapid communications and permanent diplomatic establishments.

40. See Michael J. Smith, *Realist Thought from Weber to Kissinger* (Baton Rouge: Louisiana State University Press, 1986), chap. 1.

41. Summing up the autobiographical essays of 34 international relations scholars, Joseph Kruzel notes that "Hans Morgenthau is more frequently cited than any other name in these memoirs." Joseph Kruzel, "Reflections on the Journeys," in Joseph Kruzel and James N. Rosenau, eds., *Journeys through World Politics: Autobiographical Reflections of Thirty-four Academic Travelers* (Lexington, MA: Lexington Books, 1989), p. 505. Although "Morgenthau is often cited, many of the references in these pages are negative in

tone. He seems to have inspired his critics even more than his supporters." Ibid.

42. See Keith L. Shimko, "Realism, Neorealism, and American Liberalism," *Review of Politics*, Vol. 54, No. 2 (Spring 1992), pp. 281–301.

43. Hans J. Morgenthau, *Scientific Man vs. Power Politics* (Chicago: University of Chicago Press, 1974), p. 201. Nevertheless, Keith Shimko convincingly argues that the shift within realism, away from Morgenthau's belief that states are motivated by an unalterable will to power, and toward Waltz's view that states are motivated by the desire for security, provides "a residual, though subdued optimism, or at least a possible basis for optimism [about international politics]. The extent to which this optimism is stressed or suppressed varies, but it is there if one wants it to be." Shimko, "Realism, Neorealism, and American Liberalism," p. 297. Realists like Stephen Van Evera, for example, point out that although states operate in a dangerous world, they can take steps to dampen security competition and minimize the danger of war. See Van Evera, *Causes of War* [Vol. II: *National Misperception and the Origins of War*, forthcoming].

44. See Reinhold Niebuhr, *The Children of Light and the Children of Darkness: A Vindication of Democracy and a Critique of Its Traditional Defense* (New York: Charles Scribner's, 1944), especially pp. 153–90. See also Samuel P. Huntington, *The Soldier and the State: The Theory and Politics of Civil-Military Relations* (New York: Vintage Books, 1964).

45. It should be emphasized that many realists have strong moral preferences and are driven by deep moral convictions. Realism is not a normative theory, however, and it provides no criteria for moral judgment. Instead, realism merely seeks to explain how the world works. Virtually all realists would prefer a world without security competition and war, but they believe that goal is unrealistic given the structure of the international system. See, for example, Robert G. Gilpin, "The Richness of the Tradition of Political Realism," in Keohane, ed., *Neorealism and Its Critics* [New York: Columbia University Press, 1986], p. 321.

46. Realism's treatment of states as billiard balls of different sizes tends to raise the hackles of comparative politics scholars, who believe that domestic political and economic factors matter greatly for explaining foreign policy behavior.

Michael N. Barnett and Martha Finnemore

THE POLITICS, POWER, AND PATHOLOGIES OF INTERNATIONAL ORGANIZATIONS

Do international organizations really do what their creators intend them to do? In the past century the number of international organizations (IOs) has increased exponentially, and we have a variety of vigorous theories to explain why they have been created. Most of these theories explain IO creation as a response to problems of incomplete information, transaction costs, and other barriers to Pareto efficiency and welfare improvement for their members. Research flowing from these theories, however, has paid little attention to how IOs actually behave after they are created. Closer scrutiny would reveal that many IOs stray from the efficiency goals these theories impute and that many IOs exercise power autonomously in ways unintended and unanticipated by states at their creation. Understanding how this is so requires a reconsideration of IOs and what they do.

In this article we develop a constructivist approach rooted in sociological institutionalism to explain both the power of IOs and their propensity for dysfunctional, even pathological, behavior. Drawing on long-standing Weberian arguments about bureaucracy and sociological institutionalist approaches to organizational behavior, we argue that the rational-legal authority that IOs embody gives them power independent of the states that created them and channels that power in particular directions. Bureaucracies, by definition, make rules, but in so doing they also create social knowledge.

From *International Organization* 53, no. 4 (Autumn 1999): 699–732.

They define shared international tasks (like "development"), create and define new categories of actors (like "refugee"), create new interests for actors (like "promoting human rights"), and transfer models of political organization around the world (like markets and democracy). However, the same normative valuation on impersonal, generalized rules that defines bureaucracies and makes them powerful in modern life can also make them unresponsive to their environments, obsessed with their own rules at the expense of primary missions, and ultimately lead to inefficient, self-defeating behavior. We are not the first to suggest that IOs are more than the reflection of state preferences and that they can be autonomous and powerful actors in global politics.[1] Nor are we the first to note that IOs, like all organizations, can be dysfunctional and inefficient.[2] However, our emphasis on the way that characteristics of bureaucracy as a generic cultural form shape IO behavior provides a different and very broad basis for thinking about how IOs influence world politics.[3]

Developing an alternative approach to thinking about IOs is only worthwhile if it produces significant insights and new opportunities for research on major debates in the field. Our approach allows us to weigh in with new perspectives on at least three such debates. First, it offers a different view of the power of IOs and whether or how they matter in world politics. This issue has been at the core of the neoliberal-institutionalists' debate with neorealists for years.[4] We show in this article how neoliberal-institutionalists actually disadvantage themselves in their argument with realists by looking at only one facet of IO power. Global organizations do more than just facilitate cooperation by helping states to overcome market failures, collective action dilemmas, and problems associated with interdependent social choice. They also create actors, specify responsibilities and authority among them, and define the work these actors should do, giving it meaning and normative value. Even when they lack material resources, IOs exercise power as they constitute and construct the social world.[5]

Second and related, our perspective provides a theoretical basis for treating IOs as autonomous actors in world politics and thus presents a challenge to the statist ontology prevailing in international relations theories. Despite all their attention to international institutions, one result of the theoretical orientation of neoliberal institutionalists and regimes theorists is that they treat IOs the way pluralists treat the state. IOs are mechanisms through which others (usually states) act; they are not purposive actors. The regimes literature is particularly clear on this point. Regimes are "principles, norms, rules, and decision-making procedures"; they are not actors.[6] Weber's insights about the normative power of the rational-legal authority that bureaucracies embody and its implications for the ways bureaucracies produce and control social knowledge provide a basis for challenging this view and treating IOs as agents, not just as structure.

Third, our perspective offers a different vantage point from which to assess the desirability of IOs. While realists and some policymakers have taken up this issue, surprisingly few other students of IOs have been critical of their performance or desirability.[7] Part of this optimism stems from central tenets of classical liberalism, which has long viewed IOs as a peaceful way to manage rapid technological change and globalization, far preferable to the obvious alternative—war.[8] Also contributing to this uncritical stance is the normative judgment about IOs that is built into the theoretical assumptions of most neoliberal and regimes scholars and the economic organization theories on which they draw. IOs exist, in this view, only because they are Pareto improving and solve problems for states. Consequently, if an IO exists, it must be because it is more useful than other alternatives since, by theoretical axiom, states will pull the plug on any IO that does not perform. We find this assumption unsatisfying. IOs often produce undesirable and even self-defeating outcomes repeatedly, without punishment much less dismantlement, and we, as theorists, want to understand why. International relations scholars are familiar with principal-agent problems and the ways in which bureaucratic politics can compromise organizational effectiveness, but these approaches have rarely been applied to IOs. Further, these approaches by no means exhaust sources of dysfunction. We examine one such source that flows from the same rational-legal characteristics that make IOs authoritative and powerful. Drawing from research in sociology and anthropology, we show how the very features that make bureaucracies powerful can also be their weakness.

The claims we make in this article flow from an analysis of the "social stuff" of which bureaucracy is made. We are asking a standard constructivist question about what makes the world hang together or, as Alexander Wendt puts it, "how are things in the world put together so that they have the properties they do."[9] In this sense, our explanation of IO behavior is constitutive and differs from most other international relations approaches. This approach does not make our explanation "mere description," since understanding the constitution of things does essential work in explaining how those things behave and what causes outcomes. Just as understanding how the double-helix DNA molecule is constituted materially makes possible causal arguments about genetics, disease, and other biological processes, so understanding how bureaucracies are constituted socially allows us to hypothesize about the behavior of IOs and the effects this social form might have in world politics. This type of constitutive explanation does not allow us to offer law-like statements such as "if X happens, then Y must follow." Rather, by providing a more complete understanding of what bureaucracy is, we can provide explanations of how certain kinds of bureaucratic behavior are possible, or even probable, and why.[10]

We begin by examining the assumptions underlying different branches of organization theory and exploring their implications for the study of IOs. We argue that assumptions drawn from economics that undergird neoliberal and neorealist treatments of IOs do not always reflect the empirical situation of most IOs commonly studied by political scientists. Further, they provide research hypotheses about only some aspects of IOs (like why they are created) and not others (like what they do). We then introduce sociological arguments that help remedy these problems.

In the second section we develop a constructivist approach from these sociological arguments to examine the power wielded by IOs and the sources of their influence. Liberal and realist theories only make predictions about, and consequently only look for, a very limited range of welfare-improving effects caused by IOs. Sociological theories, however, expect and explain a much broader range of impacts organizations can have and specifically highlight their role in constructing actors, interests, and social purpose. We provide illustrations from the UN system to show how IOs do, in fact, have such powerful effects in contemporary world politics. In the third section we explore the dysfunctional behavior of IOs, which we define as behavior that undermines the stated goals of the organization. International relations theorists are familiar with several types of theories that might explain such behavior. Some locate the source of dysfunction in material factors, others focus on cultural factors. Some theories locate the source of dysfunction outside the organization, others locate

it inside. We construct a typology, mapping these theories according to the source of dysfunction they emphasize, and show that the same internally generated cultural forces that give IOs their power and autonomy can also be a source of dysfunctional behavior. We use the term *pathologies* to describe such instances when IO dysfunction can be traced to bureaucratic culture. We conclude by discussing how our perspective helps to widen the research agenda for IOs.

Theoretical Approaches to Organizations

Within social science there are two broad strands of theorizing about organizations. One is economistic and rooted in assumptions of instrumental rationality and efficiency concerns; the other is sociological and focused on issues of legitimacy and power.[11] The different assumptions embedded within each type of theory focus attention on different kinds of questions about organizations and provide insights on different kinds of problems.

The economistic approach comes, not surprisingly, out of economics departments and business schools for whom the fundamental theoretical problem, laid out first by Ronald Coase and more recently by Oliver Williamson, is why we have business firms. Within standard microeconomic logic, it should be much more efficient to conduct all transactions through markets rather than "hierarchies" or organizations. Consequently, the fact that economic life is dominated by huge organizations (business firms) is an anomaly. The body of theory developed to explain the existence and power of firms focuses on organizations as efficient solutions to contracting problems, incomplete information, and other market imperfections.[12]

This body of organization theory informs neoliberal and neorealist debates over international institutions. Following Kenneth Waltz, neoliberals and neorealists understand world politics to be analogous to a market filled with utility-maximizing competitors.[13] Thus, like the economists, they see organizations as welfare-improving solutions to problems of incomplete information and high transaction costs.[14] Neoliberals and realists disagree about the degree to which constraints of anarchy, an interest in relative versus absolute gains, and fears of cheating will scuttle international institutional arrangements or hobble their effectiveness, but both agree, implicitly or explicitly, that IOs help states further their interests where they are allowed to work.[15] State power may be exercised in political battles inside IOs over where, on the Pareto frontier, political bargains fall, but the notion that IOs are instruments created to serve state interests is not much questioned by neorealist or neoliberal scholars.[16] After all, why else would states set up these organizations and continue to support them if they did not serve state interests?

Approaches from sociology provide one set of answers to this question. They provide reasons why, in fact, organizations that are not efficient or effective servants of member interests might exist. In so doing, they lead us to look for kinds of power and sources of autonomy in organizations that economists overlook. Different approaches within sociology treat organizations in different ways, but as a group they stand in sharp contrast to the economists' approaches in at least two important respects: they offer a different conception of the relationship between organizations and their environments, and they provide a basis for understanding organizational autonomy.

IOS AND THEIR ENVIRONMENT

The environment assumed by economic approaches to organizations is socially very thin and devoid of social rules, cultural content, or even other actors beyond those constructing the organization. Competition, exchange, and consequent pressures for efficiency are the dominant environmental characteristics driving the formation and behavior of organizations. Sociologists, by contrast, study organizations in a wider world of nonmarket situations, and, consequently, they begin with no such assumptions. Organizations are treated as "social facts" to be investigated; whether they do what they claim or do it efficiently is an empirical question, not a theoretical assumption of these approaches. Organizations respond not only to other actors pursuing material interests in the environment but also to normative and cultural forces that shape how organizations see the world and conceptualize their own missions. Environments can "select" or favor organizations for reasons other than efficient or responsive behavior. For example, organizations may be created and supported for reasons of legitimacy and normative fit rather than efficient output; they may be created not for what they do but for what they are—for what they represent symbolically and the values they embody.[17]

Empirically, organizational environments can take many forms. Some organizations exist in competitive environments that create strong pressures for efficient or responsive behavior, but many do not. Some organizations operate with clear criteria for "success" (like firms that have balance sheets), whereas others (like political science departments) operate with much vaguer missions, with few clear criteria for success or failure and no serious threat of elimination. Our point is simply that when we choose a theoretical framework, we should choose one whose assumptions approximate the empirical conditions of the IO we are analyzing, and that we should be aware of the biases created by those assumptions. Economistic approaches make certain assumptions about the environment in which IOs are embedded that drive researchers who use them to look for certain kinds of effects and not others. Specifying different or more varied environments for IOs would lead us to look for different and more varied effects in world politics.[18]

IO AUTONOMY

Following economistic logic, regime theory and the broad range of scholars working within it generally treat IOs as creations of states designed to further state interests.[19] Analysis of subsequent IO behavior focuses on processes of aggregating member state preferences through strategic interaction within the structure of the IO. IOs, then, are simply epiphenomena of state interaction; they are, to quote Waltz's definition of reductionism, "understood by knowing the attributes and the interactions of [their] parts."[20]

These theories thus treat IOs as empty shells or impersonal policy machinery to be manipulated by other actors. Political bargains shape the machinery at its creation, states may politick hard within the machinery in pursuit of their policy goals, and the machinery's norms and rules may constrain what states can do, but the machinery itself is passive. IOs are not purposive political actors in their own right and have no ontological independence. To the extent that IOs do, in fact, take on a life of their own, they breach the "limits of realism" as well as of neoliberalism by violating the ontological structures of these theories.[21]

The regimes concept spawned a huge literature on interstate cooperation that is remarkably consistent in its treatment of IOs as structure rather than agents. Much of the neoliberal institutionalist literature has been devoted to exploring the ways in which regimes (and IOs) can act as intervening variables, mediating between states' pursuit of self-interest and political outcomes by changing the structure of opportunities and constraints facing states through their control over information, in particular.[22] Although this line of scholarship accords IOs some causal status (since they demonstrably change outcomes), it does not grant them autonomy and purpose independent of the states that comprise them. Another branch of liberalism has recently divorced itself from the statist ontology and focuses instead on the preferences of social groups as the causal engine of world politics, but, again, this view simply argues for attention to a different group of agents involved in the construction of IOs and competing for access to IO mechanisms. It does not offer a fundamentally different conception of IOs.[23]

The relevant question to ask about this conceptualization is whether it is a reasonable approximation of the empirical condition of most IOs. Our reading of detailed empirical case studies of IO activity suggests not. Yes, IOs are constrained by states, but the notion that they are passive mechanisms with no independent agendas of their own is not borne out by any detailed empirical study of an IO that we have found. Field studies of the European Union provide evidence of independent roles for "eurocrats."[24] Studies of the World Bank consistently identify an independent culture and agendas for action.[25] Studies of recent UN peacekeeping and reconstruction efforts similarly document a UN agenda that frequently leads to conflict with member states.[26] Accounts of the UN High Commission on Refugees (UNHCR) routinely note how its autonomy and authority has grown over the years. Not only are IOs independent actors with their own agendas, but they may embody multiple agendas and contain multiple sources of agency—a problem we take up later.

Principal-agent analysis, which has been increasingly employed by students of international relations to examine organizational dynamics, could potentially provide a sophisticated approach to understanding IO autonomy.[27] Building on theories of rational choice and of representation, these analysts understand IOs as "agents" of states ("principals"). The analysis is concerned with whether agents are responsible delegates of their principals, whether agents smuggle in and pursue their own preferences, and how principals can construct various mechanisms to keep their agents honest.[28] This framework provides a means of treating IOs as actors in their own right with independent interests and capabilities. Autonomous action by IOs is to be expected in this perspective. It would also explain a number of the nonresponsive and pathological behaviors that concern us because we know that monitoring and shirking problems are pervasive in these principal-agent relationships and that these relationships can often get stuck at suboptimal equilibria.

The problem with applying principal-agent analysis to the study of IOs is that it requires a priori theoretical specification of what IOs want. Principal-agent dynamics are fueled by the disjuncture between what agents want and what principals want. To produce any insights, those two sets of interests cannot be identical. In economics this type of analysis is usually applied to preexisting agents and principals (clients hiring lawyers, patients visiting doctors) whose ongoing independent existence makes specification of independent interests relatively straightforward. The lawyer or the doctor would probably be in business even if you and I did not take our problems to them. IOs, on the other hand, are often created by the principals (states) and given mission statements written by the principals. How, then, can we impute independent preferences a priori?

Scholars of American politics have made some progress in producing substantive theoretical propositions about what U.S. bureaucratic agencies want. Beginning with the pioneering work of William Niskanen, scholars theorized that bureaucracies had interests defined by the absolute or relative size of their budget and the expansion or protection of their turf. At first these interests were imputed, and later they became more closely investigated, substantiated, and in some cases modified or rejected altogether.[29]

Realism and liberalism, however, provide no basis for asserting independent utility functions for IOs. Ontologically, these are theories about states. They provide no basis for imputing interests to IOs beyond the goals states (that is, principals) give them. Simply adopting the rather battered Niskanen hypothesis seems less than promising given the glaring anomalies—for example, the opposition of many NATO and OSCE (Organization for Security and Cooperation in Europe) bureaucrats to those organizations' recent expansion and institutionalization. There are good reasons to assume that organizations care about their resource base and turf, but there is no reason to presume that such matters exhaust or even dominate their interests. Indeed, ethnographic studies of IOs describe a world in which organizational goals are strongly shaped by norms of the profession that dominate the bureaucracy and in which interests themselves are varied, often in flux, debated, and worked out through interactions between the staff of the bureaucracy and the world in which they are embedded.[30]

Various strands of sociological theory can help us investigate the goals and behavior of IOs by offering a very different analytical orientation than the one used by economists. Beginning with Weber, sociologists have explored the notion that bureaucracy is a peculiarly modern cultural form that embodies certain values and can have its own distinct agenda and behavioral dispositions. Rather than treating organizations as mere arenas or mechanisms through which other actors pursue interests, many sociological approaches explore the social content of the organization—its culture, its legitimacy concerns, dominant norms that govern behavior and shape interests, and the relationship of these to a larger normative and cultural environment. Rather than assuming behavior that corresponds to efficiency criteria alone, these approaches recognize that organizations also are bound up with power and social control in ways that can eclipse efficiency concerns.

The Power of IOs

IOs can become autonomous sites of authority, independent from the state "principals" who may have created them, because of power flowing from at least two sources: (1) the legitimacy of the rational-legal authority they embody, and (2) control over technical expertise and information. The first of these is almost entirely neglected by the political science literature, and the second, we argue, has been conceived of very narrowly, leading scholars to overlook some of the most basic and consequential forms of IO influence. Taken together, these two features provide a theoretical basis for treating IOs as autonomous actors in contemporary world politics by identifying sources of support for them, independent of states, in the larger social environment. Since rational-legal authority and control over expertise are part of what defines and constitutes any bureaucracy (a bureaucracy would not be a bureaucracy without them), the autonomy that flows from them is best understood as a constitutive effect, an effect of the way bureaucracy is constituted, which, in turn, makes possible (and in that sense causes) other processes and effects in global politics.

Sources of IO Autonomy and Authority

To understand how IOs can become autonomous sites of authority we turn to Weber and his classic study of bureaucratization. Weber was deeply ambivalent about the increasingly bureaucratic world in which he lived and was well-attuned to the vices as well as the virtues of this new social form of authority.[31] Bureaucracies are rightly considered a grand achievement, he thought. They provide a framework for social interaction that can respond to the increasingly technical demands of modern life in a stable, predictable, and nonviolent way; they exemplify rationality and are technically superior to previous forms of rule because they bring precision, knowledge, and continuity to increasingly complex social tasks.[32] But such technical and rational achievements, according to Weber, come at a steep price. Bureaucracies are

political creatures that can be autonomous from their creators and can come to dominate the societies they were created to serve, because of both the normative appeal of rational-legal authority in modern life and the bureaucracy's control over technical expertise and information. We consider each in turn.

Bureaucracies embody a form of authority, rational-legal authority, that modernity views as particularly legitimate and good. In contrast to earlier forms of authority that were invested in a leader, legitimate modern authority is invested in legalities, procedures, and rules and thus rendered impersonal. This authority is "rational" in that it deploys socially recognized relevant knowledge to create rules that determine how goals will be pursued. The very fact that they embody rationality is what makes bureaucracies powerful and makes people willing to submit to this kind of authority. According to Weber,

> in legal authority, submission does not rest upon the belief and devotion to charismatically gifted persons . . . or upon piety toward a personal lord and master who is defined by an ordered tradition. . . . Rather submission under legal authority is based upon an *impersonal* bond to the generally defined and functional "duty of office." The official duty—like the corresponding right to exercise authority: the "jurisdictional competency"—is fixed by *rationally established* norms, by enactments, decrees, and regulations in such a manner that the legitimacy of the authority becomes the legality of the general rule, which is purposely thought out, enacted, and announced with formal correctness.[33]

When bureaucrats do something contrary to your interests or that you do not like, they defend themselves by saying "Sorry, those are the rules" or "just doing my job." "The rules" and "the job" are the source of great power in modern society. It is because bureaucrats in IOs are performing "duties of office" and implementing "rationally established norms" that they are powerful.

A second basis of autonomy and authority, intimately connected to the first, is bureaucratic control over information and expertise. A bureaucracy's autonomy derives from specialized technical knowledge, training, and experience that is not immediately available to other actors. While such knowledge might help the bureaucracy carry out the directives of politicians more efficiently, Weber stressed that it also gives bureaucracies power over politicians (and other actors). It invites and at times requires bureaucracies to shape policy, not just implement it.[34]

The irony in both of these features of authority is that they make bureaucracies powerful precisely by creating the appearance of depoliticization. The power of IOs, and bureaucracies generally, is that they present themselves as impersonal, technocratic, and neutral—as not exercising power but instead as serving others; the presentation and acceptance of these claims is critical to their legitimacy and authority.[35] Weber, however, saw through these claims. According to him, the depoliticized character of bureaucracy that legitimates it could be a myth: "Behind the functional purposes [of bureaucracy], of course, 'ideas of culture-values' usually stand."[36] Bureaucracies always serve some social purpose or set of cultural values. That purpose may be normatively "good," as Weber believed the Prussian nationalism around him was, but there was no a priori reason to assume this.

In addition to embodying cultural values from the larger environment that might be desirable or not, bureaucracies also carry with them behavioral dispositions and values flowing from the rationality that legitimates them as a cultural form. Some of these, like the celebration of knowledge and expertise, Weber admired. Others concerned him greatly, and his descriptions of bureaucracy as an "iron cage" and bureaucrats as "specialists without spirit" are hardly an endorsement of the bureaucratic form.[37] Bureaucracy can undermine personal freedom in important ways. The very impersonal, rule-bound character that empowers bureaucracy also dehumanizes it. Bureaucracies often exercise their power in repressive ways, in the name of general rules because rules are their raison d'être. This tendency is exacerbated by the way bureaucracies select and reward narrowed professionals seeking secure careers internally—people who are "lacking in heroism, human spontaneity, and inventiveness."[38] Following Weber, we investigate rather than assume the "goodness" of bureaucracy.

Weber's insights provide a powerful critique of the ways in which international relations scholars have treated IOs. The legitimacy of rational-legal authority suggests that IOs may have an authority independent of the policies and interests of states that create them, a possibility obscured by the technical and apolitical treatment of IOs by both realists and neoliberals. * * *

Examples of the ways in which IOs have become autonomous because of their embodiment of technical rationality and control over information are not hard to find. The UN's peacekeepers derive part of their authority from the claim that they are independent, objective, neutral actors who simply implement Security Council resolutions. UN officials routinely use this language to describe their role and are explicit that they understand this to be the basis of their influence. As a consequence, UN officials spend considerable time and energy attempting to maintain the image that they are not the instrument of any great power and must be seen as representatives of "the international community" as embodied in the rules and resolutions of the UN.[39] The World Bank is widely recognized to have exercised power over development policies far greater than its budget, as a percentage of North/South aid flows, would suggest because of the expertise it houses. While competing sites of expertise in development have proliferated in recent years, for decades after its founding the World Bank was a magnet for the "best and brightest" among "development experts." Its staff had and continues to have impressive credentials from the most prestigious universities and the elaborate models, reports, and research groups it has sponsored over the years were widely influential among the "development experts" in the field. This expertise, coupled with its claim to "neutrality" and its "apolitical" technocratic decision-making style, have given the World Bank an authoritative voice with which it has successfully dictated the content, direction, and scope of global development over the past fifty years.[40] Similarly, official standing and long experience with relief efforts have endowed the UNHCR with "expert" status and consequent authority in refugee matters. This expertise, coupled with its role in implementing international refugee conventions and law ("the rules" regarding refugees), has allowed the UNHCR to make life and death decisions about refugees without consulting the refugees, themselves, and to compromise the authority of states in various ways in setting up refugee camps.[41] Note that, as these examples show, technical knowledge and expertise need not be "scientific" in nature to create autonomy and power for IOs.

The Power of IOs

If IOs have autonomy and authority in the world, what do they do with it? A growing body of research in sociology and anthropology has examined ways in which IOs exercise power by virtue of their culturally constructed status as sites of authority; we distill from this research three broad types of IO power. We examine how IOs (1) classify the world, creating categories of actors and action; (2) fix meanings in the social world; and (3) articulate and diffuse new norms, principles, and actors around the globe. All of these sources of power flow from the ability of IOs to structure knowledge.[42]

CLASSIFICATION

An elementary feature of bureaucracies is that they classify and organize information and knowledge. This classification process is bound up with power. "Bureaucracies," writes Don Handelman, "are ways of making, ordering, and knowing social worlds." They do this by "moving persons among social categories or by inventing and applying such categories."[43] The ability to classify objects, to shift their very definition and identity, is one of bureaucracy's greatest sources of power. This power is frequently treated by the objects of that power as accomplished through caprice and without regard to their circumstances but is legitimated and justified by bureaucrats with reference to the rules and regulations of the bureaucracy. Consequences of this bureaucratic exercise of power may be identity defining, or even life threatening.

Consider the evolving definition of "refugee." The category "refugee" is not at all straightforward and must be distinguished from other categories of individuals who are "temporarily" and "involuntarily" living outside their country of origin—displaced persons, exiles, economic migrants, guest workers, diaspora communities, and those seeking political asylum. The debate over the meaning of "refugee" has been waged in and around the UNHCR. The UNHCR's legal and operational definition of the category strongly influences decisions about who is a refugee and shapes UNHCR staff decisions in the field—decisions that have a tremendous effect on the life circumstance of thousands of people.[44] These categories are not only political and legal but also discursive, shaping a view among UNHCR officials that refugees must, by definition, be powerless, and that as powerless actors they do not have to be consulted in decisions such as asylum and repatriation that will directly and dramatically affect them.[45] Guy Gran similarly describes how the World Bank sets up criteria to define someone as a peasant in order to distinguish them from a farmer, day laborer, and other categories. The classification matters because only certain classes of people are recognized by the World Bank's development machinery as having knowledge that is relevant in solving development problems.[46] Categorization and classification are a ubiquitous feature of bureaucratization that has potentially important implications for those being classified. To classify is to engage in an act of power.

THE FIXING OF MEANINGS

IOs exercise power by virtue of their ability to fix meanings, which is related to classification.[47] Naming or labeling the social context establishes the parameters, the very boundaries, of acceptable action. Because actors are oriented toward objects and objectives on the basis of the meaning that they have for them, being able to invest situations with a particular meaning constitutes an important source of power.[48] IOs do not act alone in this regard, but their organizational resources contribute mightily to this end.

There is strong evidence of this power from development studies. Arturo Escobar explores how the institutionalization of the concept of "development" after World War II spawned a huge international apparatus and how this apparatus has now spread its tentacles in domestic and international politics through the discourse of development. The discourse of development, created and arbitrated in large part by IOs, determines not only what constitutes the activity (what development is) but also who (or what) is considered powerful and privileged, that is, who gets to do the developing (usually the state or IOs) and who is the object of development (local groups).[49]

Similarly, the end of the Cold War encouraged a reexamination of the definition of security.[50] IOs have been at the forefront of this debate, arguing that security pertains not only to states but also to individuals and that the threats to security may be economic, environmental, and political as well as military.[51] In forwarding these alternative definitions of security, officials from various IOs are empowering a different set of actors and legitimating an alternative set of practices. Specifically, when security meant safety from invading national armies, it privileged state officials and invested power in military establishments. These alternative definitions of security shift attention away from states and toward the individuals who are frequently threatened by their own government, away from military practices and toward other features of social life that might represent a more immediate and daily danger to the lives of individuals.

One consequence of these redefined meanings of development and security is that they legitimate, and even require, increased levels of IO intervention in the domestic affairs of states—particularly Third World states. This is fairly obvious in the realm of development. The World Bank, the International Monetary Fund (IMF), and other development institutions have established a web of interventions that affect nearly every phase of the economy and polity in many Third World states. As "rural development," "basic human needs," and "structural adjustment" became incorporated into the meaning of development, IOs were permitted, even required, to become intimately involved in the domestic workings of developing polities by posting in-house "advisors" to run monetary policy, reorganizing the political economy of entire rural regions, regulating family and reproductive practices, and mediating between governments and their citizens in a variety of ways.[52]

■   ■   ■

DIFFUSION OF NORMS

Having established rules and norms, IOs are eager to spread the benefits of their expertise and often act as conveyor belts for the transmission of norms and models of "good" political behavior.[53] There is nothing accidental or unintended about this role.

Officials in IOs often insist that part of their mission is to spread, inculcate, and enforce global values and norms. They are the "missionaries" of our time. Armed with a notion of progress, an idea of how to create the better life, and some understanding of the conversion process, many IO elites have as their stated purpose a desire to shape state practices by establishing, articulating, and transmitting norms that define what constitutes acceptable and legitimate state behavior. To be sure, their success depends on more than their persuasive capacities, for their rhetoric must be supported by power, sometimes (but not always) state power. But to overlook how state power and organizational missionaries work in tandem and the ways in which IO officials channel and shape states' exercise of power is to disregard a fundamental feature of value diffusion.[54]

Consider decolonization as an example. The UN Charter announced an intent to universalize sovereignty as a constitutive principle of the society of states at a time when over half the globe was under some kind of colonial rule; it also established an institutional apparatus to achieve that end (most prominently the Trusteeship Council and the Special Committee on Colonialism). These actions had several consequences. One was to eliminate certain categories of acceptable action for powerful states. Those states that attempted to retain their colonial privileges were increasingly viewed as illegitimate by other states. Another consequence was to empower international bureaucrats (at the Trusteeship Council) to set norms and standards for "stateness." Finally, the UN helped to ensure that throughout decolonization the sovereignty of these new states was coupled with territorial inviolability. Colonial boundaries often divided ethnic and tribal groups, and the UN was quite concerned that in the process of "self-determination," these governments containing "multiple" or "partial" selves might attempt to create a whole personality through territorial adjustment—a fear shared by many of these newly decolonized states. The UN encouraged the acceptance of the norm of sovereignty-as-territorial-integrity through resolutions, monitoring devices, commissions, and one famous peacekeeping episode in Congo in the 1960s.[55]

Note that, as with other IO powers, norm diffusion, too, has an expansionary dynamic. Developing states continue to be popular targets for norm diffusion by IOs, even after they are independent. The UN and the European Union are now actively involved in police training in non-Western states because they believe Western policing practices will be more conducive to democratization processes and the establishment of civil society. But having a professional police establishment assumes that there is a professional judiciary and penal system where criminals can be tried and jailed; and a professional judiciary, in turn, presupposes that there are lawyers that can come before the court. Trained lawyers presuppose a code of law. The result is a package of reforms sponsored by IOs aimed at transforming non-Western societies into Western societies.[56] Again, while Western states are involved in these activities and therefore their values and interests are part of the reasons for this process, international bureaucrats involved in these activities may not see themselves as doing the bidding for these states but rather as expressing the interests and values of the bureaucracy.

Other examples of this kind of norm diffusion are not hard to find. The IMF and the World Bank are explicit about their role as transmitters of norms and principles from advanced market economies to less-developed economies.[57] The IMF's Articles of Agreement specifically assign it this task of incorporating less-developed economies into the world economy, which turns out to mean teaching them how to "be" market economies. The World Bank, similarly, has a major role in arbitrating the meaning of development and norms of behavior appropriate to the task of developing oneself, as was discussed earlier. The end of the Cold War has opened up a whole new set of states to this kind of norm diffusion task for IOs. According to former Secretary of Defense William Perry, one of the functions of NATO expansion is to inculcate "modern" values and norms into the Eastern European countries and their militaries.[58]

■　　■　　■

The Pathologies of IOs

Bureaucracies are created, propagated, and valued in modern society because of their supposed rationality and effectiveness in carrying out social tasks. These same considerations presumably also apply to IOs. Ironically, though, the folk wisdom about bureaucracies is that they are inefficient and unresponsive. Bureaucracies are infamous for creating and implementing policies that defy rational logic, for acting in ways that are at odds with their stated mission, and for refusing requests of and turning their backs on those to whom they are officially responsible.[59] Scholars of U.S. bureaucracy have recognized this problem and have devoted considerable energy to understanding a wide range of undesirable and inefficient bureaucratic behaviors caused by bureaucratic capture and slack and to exploring the conditions under which "suboptimal equilibria" may arise in organizational structures. Similarly, scholars researching foreign policy decision making and, more recently, those interested in learning in foreign policy have investigated organizational dynamics that produce self-defeating and inefficient behavior in those contexts.[60]

IOs, too, are prone to dysfunctional behaviors, but international relations scholars have rarely investigated this, in part, we suspect, because the theoretical apparatus they use provides few grounds for expecting undesirable IO behavior.[61] The state-centric utility-maximizing frameworks most international relations scholars have borrowed from economics simply assume that IOs are reasonably responsive to state interests (or, at least, more responsive than alternatives), otherwise states would withdraw from them. This assumption, however, is a necessary theoretical axiom of these frameworks; it is rarely treated as a hypothesis subject to empirical investigation.[62] With little theoretical reason to expect suboptimal or self-defeating behavior in IOs, these scholars do not look for it and have had little to say about it. Policymakers, however, have been quicker to perceive and address these problems and are putting them on the political agenda. It is time for scholars, too, to begin to explore these issues more fully.

In this section we present several bodies of theorizing that might explain dysfunctional IO behavior, which we define as behavior that undermines the IO's stated objectives. Thus our vantage point for judging dysfunction (and later pathology) is the publicly proclaimed mission of the organization. There may be occasions when overall organizational dysfunction is, in fact, functional for certain members or others involved in the IO's work, but given our analysis of the way claims of efficiency and effectiveness act to legitimate rational-legal authority in our culture, whether organizations actually do what they claim and accomplish their missions is a particularly important issue to examine. Several bodies of theory provide some basis for understanding dysfunctional behavior by IOs, each of which emphasizes a different locus of causality for such behavior. Analyzing these causes, we construct a typology of these explanations that locates them in relation to one another. Then, drawing on the work of James March and Johan Olsen, Paul DiMaggio, and Walter Powell, and other sociological institutionalists, we elaborate how the same sources of bureaucratic power, sketched earlier, can cause dysfunctional behavior. We term this particular type of dysfunction *pathology*.[63] We identify five features of bureaucracy that might produce pathology, and using examples from the UN system we illustrate the way these might work in IOs.

Extant theories about dysfunction can be categorized in two dimensions: (1) whether they locate the cause of IO dysfunction inside or outside the organization, and (2) whether they trace the causes to material or cultural forces. Mapping theories on these dimensions creates the typology shown in Figure 9.1.

Within each cell we have identified a representative body of theory familiar to most international relations scholars. Explanations of IO dysfunction that emphasize the pursuit of material interests within an organization typically examine how competition among subunits over material resources leads the organization to make decisions and engage in behaviors that are inefficient or undesirable as judged against some ideal policy that would better allow the IO to achieve its stated goals. Bureaucratic politics is the best-known theory here, and though current scholars of international politics have not widely adopted this perspective to explain IO behavior, it is relatively well developed in the older IO literature.[64] Graham Allison's central argument is that the "name of the game is politics: bargaining along regularized circuits among players positioned hierarchically within the government. Government behavior can thus be understood as . . . results of these bargaining games."[65] In this view, decisions are not made after a rational decision process but rather through a competitive bargaining process over turf, budgets, and staff that may benefit parts of the organization at the expense of overall goals.

Another body of literature traces IO dysfunctional behavior to the material forces located outside the organization. Realist and neoliberal theories might posit that state preferences and constraints are responsible for understanding IO dysfunctional behavior. In this view IOs are not to blame for bad outcomes, states are. IOs do not have the luxury of choosing the optimal policy but rather are frequently forced to chose between the bad and the awful because more desirable policies are denied to them by states who do not agree among themselves and/or do not wish to see the IO fulfill its mandate in some particular instance. As Robert Keohane observed, IOs often engage in policies not because they are strong and have autonomy but because they are weak and have none.[66] The important point of these theories is that they trace IO dysfunctional behavior back to the environmental conditions established by, or the explicit preferences of, states.

Cultural theories also have internal and external variants. We should note that many advocates of cultural theories would reject the claim that an organization can be understood apart from its environment or that culture is separable from the material world. Instead they would stress how

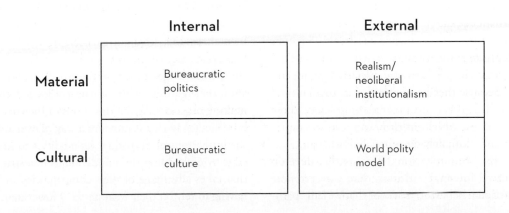

Figure 9.1. Theories of International Organization Dysfunction

	Internal	External
Material	Bureaucratic politics	Realism/ neoliberal institutionalism
Cultural	Bureaucratic culture	World polity model

the organization is permeated by that environment, defined in both material and cultural terms, in which it is embedded. Many are also quite sensitive to the ways in which resource constraints and the material power of important actors will shape organizational culture. That said, these arguments clearly differ from the previous two types in their emphasis on ideational and cultural factors and clearly differ among themselves in the motors of behavior emphasized. For analytical clarity we divide cultural theories according to whether they see the primary causes of the IO's dysfunctional behavior as deriving from the culture of the organization (internal) or of the environment (external).

The world polity model exemplifies theories that look to external culture to understand an IO's dysfunctional behavior. There are two reasons to expect dysfunctional behavior here. First, because IO practices reflect a search for symbolic legitimacy rather than efficiency, IO behavior might be only remotely connected to the efficient implementation of its goals and more closely coupled to legitimacy criteria that come from the cultural environment.[67] For instance, many arms-export control regimes now have a multilateral character not because of any evidence that this architecture is the most efficient way to monitor and prevent arms exports but rather because multilateralism has attained a degree of legitimacy that is not empirically connected to any efficiency criteria.[68] Second, the world polity is full of contradictions; for instance, a liberal world polity has several defining principles, including market economics and human equality, that might conflict at any one moment. Thus, environments are often ambiguous about missions and contain varied, often conflicting, functional, normative, and legitimacy imperatives.[69] Because they are embedded in that cultural environment, IOs can mirror and reproduce those contradictions, which, in turn, can lead to contradictory and ultimately dysfunctional behavior.

Finally, organizations frequently develop distinctive internal cultures that can promote dysfunctional behavior, behavior that we call "path-

ological." The basic logic of this argument flows directly from our previous observations about the nature of bureaucracy as a social form. Bureaucracies are established as rationalized means to accomplish collective goals and to spread particular values. To do this, bureaucracies create social knowledge and develop expertise as they act upon the world (and thus exercise power). But the way bureaucracies are constituted to accomplish these ends can, ironically, create a cultural disposition toward undesirable and ultimately self-defeating behavior.[70] Two features of the modern bureaucratic form are particularly important in this regard. The first is the simple fact that bureaucracies are organized around rules, routines, and standard operating procedures designed to trigger a standard and predictable response to environmental stimuli. These rules can be formal or informal, but in either case they tell actors which action is appropriate in response to a specific stimuli, request, or demand. This kind of routinization is, after all, precisely what bureaucracies are supposed to exhibit—it is what makes them effective and competent in performing complex social tasks. However, the presence of such rules also compromises the extent to which means-ends rationality drives organizational behavior. Rules and routines may come to obscure overall missions and larger social goals. They may create "ritualized behavior" in bureaucrats and construct a very parochial normative environment within the organization whose connection to the larger social environment is tenuous at best.[71]

Second, bureaucracies specialize and compartmentalize. They create a division of labor on the logic that because individuals have only so much time, knowledge, and expertise, specialization will allow the organization to emulate a rational decision-making process.[72] Again, this is one of the virtues of bureaucracy in that it provides a way of overcoming the limitations of individual rationality and knowledge by embedding those individuals in a structure that takes advantage of their competencies without having to rely on their weaknesses. However, it, too, has some negative consequences. Just as rules can eclipse goals, concentrated expertise and specialization can (and perhaps must) limit bureaucrats' field of vision and create subcultures within bureaucracy that are distinct from those of the larger environment. Professional training plays a particularly strong role here since this is one widespread way we disseminate specialized knowledge and credential "experts." Such training often gives experts, indeed is designed to give them, a distinctive worldview and normative commitments, which, when concentrated in a subunit of an organization, can have pronounced effects on behavior.[73]

Once in place, an organization's culture, understood as the rules, rituals, and beliefs that are embedded in the organization (and its subunits), has important consequences for the way individuals who inhabit that organization make sense of the world. It provides interpretive frames that individuals use to generate meaning.[74] This is more than just bounded rationality; in this view, actors' rationality itself, the very means and ends that they value, are shaped by the organizational culture.[75] Divisions and subunits within the organization may develop their own cognitive frameworks that are consistent with but still distinct from the larger organization, further complicating this process.

All organizations have their own culture (or cultures) that shape their behavior. The effects of bureaucratic culture, however, need not be dysfunctional. Indeed, specific organizational cultures may be valued and actively promoted as a source of "good" behavior, as students of business culture know very well. Organizational culture is tied to "good" and "bad" behavior, alike, and the effects of organizational culture on behavior are an empirical question to be researched.

To further such research, we draw from studies in sociology and anthropology to explore five mechanisms by which bureaucratic culture can breed pathologies in IOs: the irrationality of rationalization, universalism, normalization of deviance, organizational insulation, and cultural contestation.

The first three of these mechanisms all flow from defining features of bureaucracy itself. Consequently, we expect them to be present in any bureaucracy to a limited degree. Their severity may be increased, however, by specific empirical conditions of the organization. Vague mission, weak feedback from the environment, and strong professionalism all have the potential to exacerbate these mechanisms and to create two others, organizational insulation and cultural contestation, through processes we describe later. Our claim, therefore, is that the very nature of bureaucracy—the "social stuff" of which it is made—creates behavioral predispositions that make bureaucracy prone to these kinds of behaviors.[76] But the connection between these mechanisms and pathological behavior is probabilistic, not deterministic, and is consistent with our constitutive analysis. Whether, in fact, mission-defeating behavior occurs depends on empirical conditions. We identify three such conditions that are particularly important (mission, feedback, and professionals) and discuss how they intensify these inherent predispositions and activate or create additional ones.

IRRATIONALITY OF RATIONALIZATION

Weber recognized that the "rationalization" processes at which bureaucracies excelled could be taken to extremes and ultimately become irrational if the rules and procedures that enabled bureaucracies to do their jobs became ends in themselves. Rather than designing the most appropriate and efficient rules and procedures to accomplish their missions, bureaucracies often tailor their missions to fit the existing, well-known, and comfortable rulebook.[77] Thus, means (rules and procedures) may become so embedded and powerful that they determine ends and the way the organization defines its goals. One observer of the World Bank noted how, at an operational level, the bank did not decide on development goals and collect data necessary to pursue them. Rather, it continued to use existing data-collection procedures and formulated goals and development plans from those data alone.[78] UN-mandated elections may be another instance where means become ends in themselves. The "end" pursued in the many troubled states where the UN has been involved in reconstruction is presumably some kind of peaceful, stable, just government. Toward that end, the UN has developed a repertoire of instruments and responses that are largely intended to promote something akin to a democratic government. Among those various repertoires, elections have become privileged as a measure of "success" and a signal of an operation's successful conclusion. Consequently, UN (and other IO) officials have conducted elections even when evidence suggests that such elections are either premature or perhaps even counterproductive (frequently acknowledged as much by state and UN officials).[79] In places like Bosnia elections have ratified precisely the outcome the UN and Outside powers had intervened to prevent—ethnic cleansing—and in places like Africa elections are criticized as exacerbating the very ethnic tensions they were ostensibly designed to quell.

■   ■   ■

BUREAUCRATIC UNIVERSALISM

A second source of pathology in IOs derives from the fact that bureaucracies "orchestrate numerous local contexts at once."[80] Bureaucrats necessarily flatten diversity because they are supposed to generate universal rules and categories that are, by design, inattentive to contextual and particularistic concerns. Part of the justification for this, of course, is the bureaucratic view that technical knowledge is transferable across circumstances. Sometimes this is a good assumption, but not always; when particular circumstances are not appropriate to the generalized knowledge being applied, the results can be disastrous.[81]

Many critics of the IMF's handling of the Asian financial crises have argued that the IMF inappropriately applied a standardized formula of budget cuts plus high interest rates to combat rapid currency depreciation without appreciating the unique and local causes of this depreciation. These governments were not profligate spenders, and austerity policies did little to reassure investors, yet the IMF prescribed roughly the same remedy that it had in Latin America. The result, by the IMF's later admission, was to make matters worse.[82]

■   ■   ■

NORMALIZATION OF DEVIANCE

We derive a third type of pathology from Diane Vaughan's study of the space shuttle *Challenger* disaster in which she chronicles the way exceptions to rules (deviance) over time become routinized and normal parts of procedures.[83] Bureaucracies establish rules to provide a predictable response to environmental stimuli in ways that safeguard against decisions that might lead to accidents and faulty decisions. At times, however, bureaucracies make small, calculated deviations from established rules because of new environmental or institutional developments, explicitly calculating that bending the rules in this instance does not create excessive risk of policy failure. Over time, these exceptions can become the rule—they become normal, not exceptions at all: they can become institutionalized to the point where deviance is "normalized." The result of this process is that what at time t_1 might be weighed seriously and debated as a potentially unacceptable risk or dangerous procedure comes to be treated as normal at time t_n. Indeed, because of staff turnover, those making decisions at a later point in time might be unaware that the now-routine behavior was ever viewed as risky or dangerous.

We are unaware of any studies that have examined this normalization of deviance in IO decision making, though one example of deviance normalization comes to mind. Before 1980 the UNHCR viewed repatriation as only one of three durable solutions to refugee crises (the others being third-country asylum and host-country integration). In its view, repatriation had to be both safe and voluntary because forced repatriation violates the international legal principle of nonrefoulement, which is the cornerstone of international refugee law and codified in the UNHCR's convention. Prior to 1980, UNHCR's discussions of repatriation emphasized that the principles of safety and voluntariness must be safeguarded at all costs. According to many commentators, however, the UNHCR has steadily lowered the barriers to repatriation over the years. Evidence for this can be found in international protection manuals, the UNHCR Executive Committee resolutions, and discourse that now weighs repatriation and the principle of nonrefoulement against other goals such as peace building. This was a steady and incremental development as initial deviations from organizational norms accumulated over time and led to a normalization of deviance. The result was a lowering of the barriers to repatriation and an increase in the frequency of involuntary repatriation.[84]

INSULATION

Organizations vary greatly in the degree to which they receive and process feedback from their environment about performance. Those insulated from such feedback often develop internal cultures and worldviews that do not promote the goals and expectations of those outside the organization who created it and whom it serves. These distinctive worldviews can create the conditions for pathological behavior when parochial classification and categorization schemes come to define reality—how bureaucrats understand the world—such that they routinely ignore information that is essential to the accomplishment of their goals.[85]

Two causes of insulation seem particularly applicable to IOs. The first is professionalism. Professional training does more than impart technical knowledge. It actively seeks to shape the normative orientation and worldviews of those who are trained. Doctors are trained to value life

above all else, soldiers are trained to sacrifice life for certain strategic objectives, and economists are trained to value efficiency. Bureaucracies, by their nature, concentrate professionals inside organizations, and concentrations of people with the same expertise or professional training can create an organizational worldview distinct from the larger environment. Second, organizations for whom "successful performance" is difficult to measure—that is, they are valued for what they represent rather than for what they do and do not "compete" with other organizations on the basis of output—are protected from selection and performance pressures that economistic models simply assume will operate. The absence of a competitive environment that selects out inefficient practices coupled with already existing tendencies toward institutionalization of rules and procedures insulates the organization from feedback and increases the likelihood of pathologies.

■   ■   ■

Conclusion

■   ■   ■

Viewing IOs through a constructivist or sociological lens, as we suggest here, reveals features of IO behavior that should concern international relations scholars because they bear on debates central to our field—debates about whether and how international institutions matter and debates about the adequacy of a statist ontology in an era of globalization and political change. Three implications of this alternative approach are particularly important. First, this approach provides a basis for treating IOs as purposive actors. Mainstream approaches in political science that are informed by economic theories have tended to locate agency in the states that comprise IO membership and treat IOs as mere arenas in which states pursue their policies. By exploring the normative support for bureaucratic authority in the broader international culture and the way IOs use that authority to construct the social world, we provide reasons why IOs may have autonomy from state members and why it may make sense analytically to treat them as ontologically independent. Second, by providing a basis for that autonomy we also open up the possibility that IOs are powerful actors who can have independent effects on the world. We have suggested various ways to think about how IOs are powerful actors in global politics, all of which encourage greater consideration of how IOs affect not only discrete outcomes but also the constitutive basis of global politics.

Third, this approach also draws attention to normative evaluations of IOs and questions what appears to us to be rather uncritical optimism about IO behavior. Contemporary international relations scholars have been quick to recognize the positive contributions that IOs can make, and we, too, are similarly impressed. But for all their desirable qualities, bureaucracies can also be inefficient, ineffective, repressive, and unaccountable. International relations scholars, however, have shown little interest in investigating these less savory and more distressing effects. The liberal Wilsonian tradition tends to see IOs as promoters of peace, engines of progress, and agents for emancipation. Neoliberals have focused on the impressive way in which IOs help states to overcome collective action problems and achieve durable cooperation. Realists have focused on their role as stabilizing forces in world politics. Constructivists, too, have tended to focus on the more humane and other-regarding features of IOs, but there is nothing about social construction that necessitates "good" outcomes. We do not mean to imply that IOs are "bad"; we mean only to point out theoretical reasons why undesirable behavior may occur and suggest that normative evaluation of IO behavior should be an empirical and ethical matter, not an analytic assumption.

NOTES

1. For Gramscian approaches, see Cox 1980, 1992, and 1996; and Murphy 1994. For Society of States approaches, see Hurrell and Woods 1995. For the epistemic communities literature, see Haas 1992. For IO decision-making literature, see Cox et al. 1974; Cox and Jacobson 1977; Cox 1996; and Ness and Brechin 1988. For a rational choice perspective, see Snidal 1996.
2. Haas 1990.
3. Because the neorealist and neoliberal arguments we engage have focused on intergovernmental organizations rather than nongovernmental ones, and because Weberian arguments from which we draw deal primarily with public bureaucracy, we, too, focus on intergovernmental organizations in this article and use the term *international organizations* in that way.
4. Baldwin 1993.
5. See Finnemore 1993 and 1996b; and McNeely 1995.
6. Krasner 1983b.
7. See Mearsheimer 1994; and Helms 1996.
8. See Commission on Global Governance 1995; Jacobson 1979, 1; and Doyle 1997.
9. See Ruggie 1998; and Wendt 1998.
10. Wendt 1998.
11. See Powell and DiMaggio 1991, chap. 1; and Grandori 1993.
12. See Williamson 1975 and 1985; and Coase 1937.
13. Waltz 1979.
14. See Vaubel 1991, 27; and Dillon, Ilgen, and Willett 1991.
15. Baldwin 1993.
16. Krasner 1991.
17. See DiMaggio and Powell 1983; Scott 1992; Meyer and Scott 1992, 1–5; Powell and DiMaggio 1991; Weber 1994; and Finnemore 1996a.
18. Researchers applying these economistic approaches have become increasingly aware of the mismatch between the assumptions of their models and the empirics of IOs. See Snidal 1996.
19. Note that empirically this is not the case; most IOs now are created by other IOs. See Shanks, Jacobson, and Kaplan 1996.
20. Waltz 1979, 18.
21. Krasner 1983a, 355–68; but see Finnemore 1996b; and Rittberger 1993.
22. See Keohane 1984; and Baldwin 1993.
23. Moravcsik 1997.
24. See Pollack 1997; Ross 1995; and Zabusky 1995; but see Moravcsik 1999.
25. See Ascher 1983; Ayres 1983; Ferguson 1990; Escobar 1995; Wade 1996; Nelson 1995; and Finnemore 1996a.
26. Joint Evaluation of Emergency Assistance to Rwanda 1996.
27. See Pollack 1997; Lake 1996; Vaubel 1991; and Dillon, Ilgen, and Willett 1991.
28. See Pratt and Zeckhauser 1985; and Kiewit and McCubbins 1991.
29. See Niskanen 1971; Miller and Moe 1983; Weingast and Moran 1983; Moe 1984; and Sigelman 1986.
30. See Ascher 1983; Zabusky 1995; Barnett 1997b; and Wade 1996.
31. See Weber 1978, 196–97; Weber 1947; Mouzelis 1967; and Beetham 1985 and 1996.

32. See Schaar 1984, 120; Weber 1978, 973; and Beetham 1985, 69.

33. Gerth and Mills 1978, 299 (italics in original).

34. See Gerth and Mills 1978, 233; Beetham 1985, 74–75; and Schaar 1984, 120.

35. We thank John Boli for this insight. Also see Fisher 1997; Ferguson 1990; Shore and Wright 1997; and Burley and Mattli 1993.

36. Gerth and Mills 1978, 199.

37. See Weber [1930] 1968, 181–83; and Clegg 1994a, 152–55.

38. Gerth and Mills 1978, 216, 50, 299. For the extreme manifestation of this bureaucratic characteristic, see Arendt 1977.

39. See David Rieff, "The Institution that Saw No Evil," *The New Republic,* 12 February 1996, 19–24; and Barnett 1997b.

40. See Wade 1996; Ayres 1983; Ascher 1983; Finnemore 1996b; and Nelson 1995.

41. See Malkki 1996; Hartigan 1992; and Harrell-Bond 1989.

42. See Foucault 1977, 27; and Clegg 1994b, 156–59. International relations theory typically disregards the negative side of the knowledge and power equation. For an example, see Haas 1992.

43. Handelman 1995, 280. See also Starr 1992; and Wright 1994, 22.

44. See Weiss and Pasic 1997; Goodwin-Gill 1996; and Anonymous 1997.

45. See Harrell-Bond 1989; Walkup 1997; and Malkki 1996.

46. Gran 1986.

47. See Williams 1996; Clegg 1994b; Bourdieu 1994; Carr [1939] 1964; and Keeley 1990.

48. Blumer 1969.

49. See Gupta 1998; Escobar 1995; Cooper and Packard 1998; Gran 1986; Ferguson 1990; and Wade 1996.

50. See Matthews 1989; and Krause and Williams 1996.

51. See UN Development Program 1994; and Boutros-Ghali 1995.

52. See Escobar 1995; Ferguson 1990; and Feldstein 1998.

53. See Katzenstein 1996; Finnemore 1996b; and Legro 1997.

54. See Alger 1963, 425; and Claude 1966, 373.

55. See McNeely 1995; and Jackson 1993.

56. Call and Barnett [1999].

57. Wade 1996.

58. See Perry 1996; and Ruggie 1996.

59. March and Olsen 1989, chap. 5.

60. See Haas 1990; Haas and Haas 1995; and Sagan 1993.

61. Two exceptions are Gallarotti 1991; and Snidal 1996.

62. Snidal 1996.

63. Karl Deutsch used the concept of pathology in a way similar to our usage. We thank Hayward Alker for this point. Deutsch 1963, 170.

64. See Allison 1971; Haas 1990; Cox et al. 1974; and Cox and Jacobson 1977.

65. See Allison 1971, 144; and Bendor and Hammond 1992.

66. Personal communication to the authors.

67. See Meyer and Rowan 1977; Meyer and Zucker 1989; Weber 1994; and Finnemore 1996a.

68. Lipson 1999.

69. McNeely 1995.

70. See Vaughan 1996; and Lipartito 1995.

71. See March and Olsen 1989, 21–27; and Meyer and Rowan 1977.

72. See March and Olsen 1989, 26–27; and March 1997.

73. See DiMaggio and Powell 1983; and Schein 1996.

74. See Starr 1992, 160; Douglas 1986; and Berger and Luckmann 1966, chap. 1.

75. See Campbell 1998, 378; Alvesson 1996; Burrell and Morgan 1979; Dobbin 1994; and Immergut 1998, 14–19.

76. Wendt 1998.

77. Beetham 1985, 76.

78. See Ferguson 1990; and Nelson 1995.

79. Paris 1997.

80. Heyman 1995, 262.

81. Haas 1990, chap. 3.

82. See Feldstein 1998; Radelet and Sach 1999; and Kapur 1998.

83. Vaughan 1996.

84. See Chimni 1993, 447; Amnesty International 1997a,b; Human Rights Watch 1997; Zieck 1997, 433, 434, 438–39; and Barbara Crossette, "The Shield for Exiles Is Lowered," *The New York Times,* 22 December 1996, 4–1.

85. See Berger and Luckmann 1966, chap. 1; Douglas 1986; Bruner 1990; March and Olsen 1989; and Starr 1992.

REFERENCES

Alger, Chadwick. 1963. United Nations Participation as a Learning Process. *Public Opinion Quarterly* 27 (3):411–26.

Allison, Graham. 1971. *Essence of Decision.* Boston: Little, Brown.

Alvesson, Mats. 1996. *Cultural Perspectives on Organizations.* New York: Cambridge University Press.

Amnesty International. 1997a. In Search of Safety: The Forcibly Displaced and Human Rights in Africa. AI Index, 20 June, AFR 01/05/97. Available from www.amnesty.org/ailib/aipub/1997/10100597.htm.

———. 1997b. Rwanda: Human Rights Overlooked in Mass Repatriation. Available from www.amnesty.org/ailib/aipub/1997/AFR/147002797.htm.

Anonymous. 1997. The UNHCR Note on International Protection You Won't See. *International Journal of Refugee Law* 9 (2):267–73.

Arendt, Hannah. 1977. *Eichmann in Jerusalem: A Report on the Banality of Evil.* New York: Penguin.

Ascher, William. 1983. New Development Approaches and the Adaptability of International Agencies: The Case of the World Bank. *International Organization* 37 (3):415–39.

Ayres, Robert L. 1983. *Banking on the Poor: The World Bank and World Poverty.* Cambridge, MA: MIT Press.

Baldwin, David, ed. 1993. *Neorealism and Neoliberalism.* New York: Columbia University Press.

Barnett, Michael. 1997a. The Politics of Indifference at the United Nations and Genocide in Rwanda and Bosnia. In *This Time We Knew: Western Responses to Genocide in Bosnia,* edited by Thomas Cushman and Stjepan Mestrovic, 128–62. New York: New York University Press.

———. 1997b. The UN Security Council, Indifference, and Genocide in Rwanda. *Cultural Anthropology* 12 (4):55–78.

Beetham, David. 1985. *Max Weber and the Theory of Modern Politics.* New York: Polity.

———. 1996. *Bureaucracy.* 2d ed. Minneapolis: University of Minnesota Press.

Bendor, Jonathan, and Thomas Hammond. 1992. Rethinking Allison's Models. *American Political Science Review* 82 (2):301–22.

Berger, Peter, and Thomas Luckmann. 1966. *The Social Construction of Reality.* New York: Doubleday.

Blumer, Herbert. 1969. *Symbolic Interactionism: Perspective and Method.* Englewood Cliffs, NJ: Prentice-Hall.

Bourdieu, Pierre. 1994. On Symbolic Power. In *Language and Symbolic Power,* edited by Pierre Bourdieu, 163–70. Chicago: University of Chicago Press.

Boutros-Ghali, Boutros. 1995. *Agenda for Peace.* 2d ed. New York: UN Press.

Bruner, Jerome. 1990. *Acts of Meaning.* Cambridge, MA: Harvard University Press.

Burley, Anne-Marie, and Walter Mattli. 1993. Europe Before the Court: A Political Theory of Integration. *International Organization* 47 (1):41–76.

Burrell, Gibson, and Gareth Morgan. 1979. *Sociological Paradigms and Organizational Analysis.* London: Heinemann.

Call, Chuck, and Michael Barnett. [1999]. Looking for a Few Good Cops: Peacekeeping, Peacebuilding, and [CIVPOL]. *International Peacekeeping* [6 (4):43–68].

Campbell, John. 1998. Institutional Analysis and the Role of Ideas in Political Economy. *Theory and Society* 27:377–409.

Carr, Edward H. [1939] 1964. *The Twenty Years' Crisis.* New York: Harper Torchbooks.

Chimni, B. 1993. The Meaning of Words and the Role of UNHCR in Voluntary Repatriation. *International Journal of Refugee Law* 5 (3):442–60.

Claude, Inis L., Jr. 1966. Collective Legitimization as a Political Function of the United Nations. *International Organization* 20 (3):337–67.

Clegg, Stewart. 1994a. Power and Institutions in the Theory of Organizations. In *Toward a New Theory of Organizations*, edited by John Hassard and Martin Parker, 24–49. New York: Routledge.

———. 1994b. Weber and Foucault: Social Theory for the Study of Organizations. *Organization* 1 (1): 149–78.

Coase, Ronald. 1937. The Nature of the Firm. *Economica* 4 (November):386–405.

Commission on Global Governance. 1995. *Our Global Neighborhood.* New York: Oxford University Press.

Cooper, Frederick, and Randy Packard, eds. 1998. *International Development and the Social Sciences.* Berkeley: University of California Press.

Cox, Robert. 1980. The Crisis of World Order and the Problem of International Organization in the 1980s. *International Journal* 35 (2):370–95.

———. 1992. Multilateralism and World Order. *Review of International Studies* 18 (2):161–80.

———. 1996. The Executive Head: An Essay on Leadership in International Organization. In *Approaches to World Order*, edited by Robert Cox, 317–48. New York: Cambridge University Press.

Cox, Robert, and Harold Jacobson. 1977. Decision Making. *International Social Science Journal* 29 (1):115–33.

Cox, Robert, Harold Jacobson, Gerard Curzon, Victoria Curzon, Joseph Nye, Lawrence Scheinman, James Sewell, and Susan Strange. 1974. *The Anatomy of Influence: Decision Making in International Organization.* New Haven, CT: Yale University Press.

Deutsch, Karl. 1963. *The Nerves of Government: Models of Political Communication and Control.* Glencoe, IL: Free Press.

Dillon, Patricia, Thomas Ilgen, and Thomas Willett. 1991. Approaches to the Study of International Organizations: Major Paradigms in Economics and Political Science. In *The Political Economy of International Organizations: A Public Choice Approach,* edited by Ronald Vaubel and Thomas Willett, 79–99. Boulder, CO: Westview Press.

DiMaggio, Paul J., and Walter W. Powell. 1983. The Iron Cage Revisited: Institutional Isomorphism and Collective Rationality in Organizational Fields. *American Sociological Review* 48:147–60.

Dobbin, Frank. 1994. Cultural Models of Organization: The Social Construction of Rational Organizing Principles. In *The Sociology of Culture,* edited by Diana Crane, 117–42. Boston: Basil Blackwell.

Douglas, Mary. 1986. *How Institutions Think.* Syracuse, NY: Syracuse University Press.

Doyle, Michael. 1997. *Ways of War and Peace.* New York: Norton.

Escobar, Arturo. 1995. *Encountering Development: The Making and Unmaking of the Third World.* Princeton, NJ: Princeton University Press.

Feld, Werner J., and Robert S. Jordan, with Leon Hurwitz. 1988. *International Organizations: A Comparative Approach.* 2d ed. New York: Praeger.

Feldstein, Martin. 1998. Refocusing the IMF. *Foreign Affairs* 77 (2):20–33.

Ferguson, James. 1990. *The Anti-Politics Machine: "Development," Depoliticization, and Bureaucratic Domination in Lesotho.* New York: Cambridge University Press.

Finnemore, Martha. 1993. International Organizations as Teachers of Norms: The United Nations Educational, Scientific, and Cultural Organization and Science Policy. *International Organization* 47:565–97.

———. 1996a. Norms, Culture, and World Politics: Insights from Sociology's Institutionalism. *International Organization* 50 (2):325–47.

———. 1996b. *National Interests in International Society.* Ithaca, NY: Cornell University Press.

Fisher, William. 1997. Doing Good? The Politics and Antipolitics of NGO Practices. *Annual Review of Anthropology* 26:439–64.

Foucault, Michel. 1977. *Discipline and Punish.* New York: Vintage Press.

Gallaroti, Guilio. 1991. The Limits of International Organization. *International Organization* 45 (2):183–220.

Gerth, H. H., and C. Wright Mills. 1978. *From Max Weber: Essays in Sociology.* New York: Oxford University Press.

Goodwin-Gill, Guy. 1996. *Refugee in International Law.* New York: Oxford Clarendon.

Gran, Guy. 1986. Beyond African Famines: Whose Knowledge Matters? *Alternatives* 11:275–96.

Grandori, Anna. 1993. Notes on the Use of Power and Efficiency Constructs in the Economics and Sociology of Organizations. In *Interdisciplinary Perspectives on Organizational Studies*, edited by S. Lindenberg and H. Schreuder, 61–78. New York: Pergamon.

Gupta, Akhil. 1998. *Postcolonial Developments: Agriculture in the Making of Modern India.* Durham, NC: Duke University Press.

Haas, Ernst. 1990. *When Knowledge Is Power.* Berkeley: University of California Press.

Haas, Ernst, and Peter Haas. 1995. Learning to Learn: Improving International Governance. *Global Governance* 1 (3):255–85.

Haas, Peter, ed. 1992. Epistemic Communities. *International Organization* 46 (1). Special issue.

Handelman, Don. 1995. Comment. *Current Anthropology* 36 (2):280–8l.

Harrell-Bond, Barbara. 1989. Repatriation: Under What Conditions Is It the Most Desirable Solution for Refugees? *African Studies Review* 32 (1):41–69.

Hartigan, Kevin. 1992. Matching Humanitarian Norms with Cold, Hard Interests: The Making of Refugee Policies in Mexico and Honduras, 1980–89. *International Organization* 46:709–30.

Helms, Jesse. 1996. Saving the UN. *Foreign Affairs* 75 (5):2–7.

Heyman, Josiah McC. 1995. Putting Power in the Anthropology of Bureaucracy. *Current Anthropology* 36 (2):261–77.

Hirsch, John, and Robert Oakley. 1995. *Somalia and Operation Restore Hope: Reflections on Peacemaking and Peacekeeping.* Washington, DC: USIP Press.

Human Rights Watch. 1997. Uncertain Refuge: International Failures to Protect Refugees. Vol. 1, no. 9 (April).

Hurrell, Andrew, and Ngaire Woods. 1995. Globalisation and Inequality. *Millennium* 24 (3):447–70.

Immergut, Ellen. 1998. The Theoretical Core of the New Institutionalism. *Politics and Society* 26 (1):5–34.

Jackson, Robert. 1993. The Weight of Ideas in Decolonization: Normative Change in International Relations. In *Ideas and Foreign Policy,* edited by Judith Goldstein and Robert O. Keohane, 111–38. Ithaca, NY: Cornell University Press.

Jacobson, Harold. 1979. *Networks of Interdependence.* New York: Alfred A. Knopf.

Joint Evaluation of Emergency Assistance to Rwanda. 1996. *The International Response to Conflict and Genocide: Lessons from the Rwanda Experience.* 5 vols. Copenhagen: Steering Committee of the Joint Evaluation of Emergency Assistance to Rwanda.

Kapur, Devesh. 1998. The IMF: A Cure or a Curse? *Foreign Policy* 111:114–29.

Katzenstein, Peter J., ed. 1996. *The Culture of National Security: Identity and Norms in World Politics.* New York: Columbia University Press.

Keeley, James. 1990. Toward a Foucauldian Analysis of International Regimes. *International Organization* 44 (1):83–105.

Keohane, Robert O. 1984. *After Hegemony.* Princeton, NJ: Princeton University Press.

Kiewiet, D. Roderick, and Matthew McCubbins. 1991. *The Logic of Delegation.* Chicago: University of Chicago Press.

Krasner, Stephen D. 1991. Global Communications and National Power: Life on the Pareto Frontier. *World Politics* 43 (3):336–66.

———. 1983a. Regimes and the Limits of Realism: Regimes as Autonomous Variables. In *International Regimes,* edited by Stephen Krasner, 355–68. Ithaca, NY: Cornell University Press.

Krasner, Stephen D., ed. 1983b. *International Regimes.* Ithaca, NY: Cornell University Press.

Krause, Keith, and Michael Williams. 1996. Broadening the Agenda of Security Studies: Politics and Methods. *Mershon International Studies Review* 40 (2):229–54.

Lake, David. 1996. Anarchy, Hierarchy, and the Variety of International Relations. *International Organization* 50 (1):1–34.

Legro, Jeffrey. 1997. Which Norms Matter? Revisiting the "Failure" of Internationalism. *International Organization* 51 (1):31–64.

Lipartito, Kenneth. 1995. Culture and the Practice of Business History. *Business and Economic History* 24 (2):1–41.

Lipson, Michael. 1999. International Cooperation on Export Controls: Nonproliferation, Globalization, and Multilateralism. Ph.D. diss., University of Wisconsin, Madison.

Malkki, Liisa. 1996. Speechless Emissaries: Refugees, Humanitarianism, and Dehistoricization. *Cultural Anthropology* 11 (3):377–404.

March, James. 1988. *Decisions and Organizations.* Boston: Basil Blackwell.

———. 1997. Understanding How Decisions Happen in Organizations. In *Organizational Decision Making,* edited by Z. Shapira, 9–33. New York: Cambridge University Press.

March, James, and Johan P. Olsen. 1989. *Rediscovering Institutions: The Organizational Basis of Politics.* New York: Free Press.

Matthews, Jessica Tuchman. 1989. Redefining Security. *Foreign Affairs* 68 (2):162–77.

McNeely, Connie. 1995. *Constructing the Nation-State: International Organization and Prescriptive Action.* Westport, CT: Greenwood Press.

Mearsheimer, John. 1994. The False Promise of International Institutions. *International Security* 19 (3):5–49.

Meyer, John W., and Brian Rowan. 1977. Institutionalized Organizations: Formal Structure as Myth and Ceremony. *American Journal of Sociology* 83:340–63.

Meyer, John W., and W. Richard Scott. 1992. *Organizational Environments: Ritual and Rationality.* Newbury Park, CA: Sage.

Meyer, Marshall, and Lynne Zucker. 1989. *Permanently Failing Organizations.* Newbury Park: Sage Press.

Miller, Gary, and Terry M. Moe. 1983. Bureaucrats, Legislators, and the Size of Government. *American Political Science Review* 77 (June):297–322.

Moe, Terry M. 1984. The New Economics of Organization. *American Journal of Political Science* 28: 739–77.

Moravcsik, Andrew. 1997. Taking Preferences Seriously: Liberal Theory and International Politics. *International Organization* 51 (4):513–54.

———. 1999. A New Statecraft? Supranational Entrepreneurs and International Cooperation. *International Organization* 53 (2):267–306.

Mouzelis, Nicos. 1967. *Organization and Bureaucracy.* Chicago: Aldine.

Murphy, Craig. 1994. *International Organizations and Industrial Change.* New York: Oxford University Press.

Nelson, Paul. 1995. *The World Bank and Non-Governmental Organizations.* New York: St. Martin's Press.

Ness, Gayl, and Steven Brechin. 1988. Bridging the Gap: International Organizations as Organizations. *International Organization* 42 (2):245–73.

Niskanen, William A. 1971. *Bureaucracy and Representative Government.* Chicago: Aldine.

Paris, Roland. 1997. Peacebuilding and the Limits of Liberal Internationalism. *International Security* 22 (2):54–89.

Perry, William. 1996. Defense in an Age of Hope. *Foreign Affairs* 75 (6):64–79.

Pollack, Mark. 1997. Delegation, Agency, and Agenda-Setting in the European Community. *International Organization* 51 (1):99–134.

Powell, Walter W., and Paul J. DiMaggio, eds. 1991. *The New Institutionalism in Organizational Analysis.* Chicago: University of Chicago Press.

Pratt, John, and Richard J. Zeckhauser. 1985. *Principals and Agents: The Structure of Business.* Boston: Harvard Business School Press.

Radelet, Steven, and Jeffrey Sach. 1999. What Have We Learned, So Far, from the Asian Financial Crisis? Harvard Institute for International Development, 4 January. Available from www.hiid.harvard.edu/pub/other/aea122.pdf.

Rittberger, Volker, ed. 1993. *Regime Theory and International Relations.* Oxford: Clarendon Press.

Ross, George. 1995. *Jacques Delors and European Integration.* New York: Oxford University Press.

Ruggie, John. 1996. *Winning the Peace.* New York: Columbia University Press.

———. 1998. What Makes the World Hang Together. *International Organization* 52 (3):855–86.

Sagan, Scott. 1993. *The Limits of Safety: Organizations, Accidents, and Nuclear Weapons.* Princeton, NJ: Princeton University Press.

Schaar, John. 1984. Legitimacy in the Modern State. In *Legitimacy and the State,* edited by William Connolly, 104–33. Oxford: Basil Blackwell.

Schien, Edgar. 1996. Culture: The Missing Concept in Organization Studies. *Administrative Studies Quarterly* 41:229–40.

Scott, W. Richard. 1992. *Organizations: Rational, Natural, and Open Systems.* 3d ed. Englewood Cliffs, NJ: Prentice-Hall.

Shanks, Cheryl, Harold K. Jacobson, and Jeffrey H. Kaplan. 1996. Inertia and Change in the Constellation of Intergovernmental Organizations, 1981–1992. *International Organization* 50 (4):593–627.

Shapira, Zur, ed. 1997. *Organizational Decision.* New York: Cambridge University Press.

Shore, Cris, and Susan Wright. 1997. Policy: A New Field of Anthropology. In *Anthropology of Policy: Critical Perspectives on Governance and Power,* edited by Cris Shore and Susan Wright, 3–41. New York: Routledge Press.

Sigelman, Lee. 1986. The Bureaucratic Budget Maximizer: An Assumption Examined. *Public Budgeting and Finance* (spring):50–59.

Snidal, Duncan. 1996. Political Economy and International Institutions. *International Review of Law and Economics* 16:121–37.

Starr, Paul. 1992. Social Categories and Claims in the Liberal State. In *How Classification Works: Nelson Goodman Among the Social Sciences,* edited by Mary Douglas and David Hull, 154–79. Edinburgh: Edinburgh University Press.

UN Development Program. 1994. *Human Development Report 1994.* New York: Oxford University Press.

UN Peacekeeping Missions. 1994. The Lessons from Cambodia. Asia Pacific Issues, Analysis from the East-West Center, No. 11, March.

Vaubel, Roland. 1991. A Public Choice View of International Organization. In *The Political Economy of International Organizations,* edited by Roland Vaubel and Thomas Willett, 27–45. Boulder, CO: Westview Press.

Vaughan, Diane. 1996. *The Challenger Launch Decision.* Chicago: University of Chicago Press.

Wade, Robert. 1996. Japan, the World Bank, and the Art of Paradigm Maintenance: The East Asian Miracle in Political Perspective. *New Left Review* 217:3–36.

Walkup, Mark. 1997. Policy Dysfunction in Humanitarian Organizations: The Role of Coping Strategies, Institutions, and Organizational Culture. *Journal of Refugee Studies* 10 (1):37–60.

Waltz, Kenneth. 1979. *Theory of International Politics.* Reading, MA: Addison-Wesley.

Weber, Max. 1947. *Theory of Social and Economic Organization.* New York: Oxford University Press.

———.[1930] 1968. *The Protestant Ethic and the Spirit of Capitalism.* New York: Routledge.

———. 1978. Bureaucracy. In *From Max Weber: Essays in Sociology,* edited by H. H. Gerth and C. Wright Mills. New York: Oxford.

Weber, Steven. 1994. Origins of the European Bank for Reconstruction and Development. *International Organization* 48 (1):1–38.

Weingast, Barry R., and Mark Moran. 1983. Bureaucratic Discretion or Congressional Control: Regulatory Policymaking by the Federal Trade Commission. *Journal of Political Economy* 91 (October):765–800.

Weiss, Thomas. 1996. Collective Spinelessness: U.N. Actions in the Former Yugoslavia. In *The World and Yugoslavia's Wars*, edited by Richard Ullman, 59–96. New York: Council on Foreign Relations Press.

Weiss, Tom, and Amir Pasic. 1997. Reinventing UNHCR: Enterprising Humanitarians in the Former Yugoslavia, 1991–95. *Global Governance* 3 (1):41–58.

Wendt, Alexander. 1995. Constructing International Politics. *International Security* 20 (1):71–81.

———. 1998. Constitution and Causation in International Relations. *Review of International Studies* 24 (4):101–17. Special issue.

Williams, Michael. 1996. Hobbes and International Relations: A Reconsideration. *International Organization* 50 (2):213–37.

Williamson, Oliver. 1975. *Markets and Hierarchies, Analysis and Antitrust Implications: A Study in the Economics of Internal Organization.* New York: Free Press.

———. 1985. *The Economic Institutions of Capitalism: Firms, Markets, Relational Contracting.* New York: Free Press.

Wright, Susan. 1994. "Culture" in Anthropology and Organizational Studies. In *Anthropology of Organizations,* edited by Susan Wright, 1–31. New York: Routledge.

Zabusky, Stacia. 1995. *Launching Europe.* Princeton, NJ: Princeton University Press.

Zieck, Marjoleine. 1997. *UNHCR and Voluntary Repatriation of Refugees: A Legal Analysis.* The Hague: Martinus Nijhoff.

Erik Voeten

THE POLITICAL ORIGINS OF THE UN SECURITY COUNCIL'S ABILITY TO LEGITIMIZE THE USE OF FORCE

In a 1966 article, Claude observed that the function of collective legitimization in global politics is increasingly conferred on international organizations (IOs), and that the United Nations (UN) has become the primary custodian of this legitimacy. Claude argued that "the world organization has come to be regarded, and used, as a dispenser of politically significant approval and disapproval of the claims, policies, and actions of states."[1] This assertion is even more relevant now than it was in 1966. States, including the United States, have shown the willingness to incur significant cost in terms of time, policy compromise, and side-payments simply to obtain the stamp of approval from the UN Security Council (SC) for military actions. To be sure, if the attempt to achieve a SC compromise proved unsuccessful, the United States has not shied away from using other means to pursue its ends. Nevertheless, the failure to acquire SC approval is generally perceived as costly, giving SC decisions considerable clout in international politics.

Given its lack of enforcement capabilities, the SC's leverage resides almost entirely in the perceived legitimacy its decisions grant to forceful actions.[2] Governments across the globe appear more willing to cooperate voluntarily once the SC has conferred its blessing on a use of force. Why has the SC become the most impressive source of international

From *International Organization* 59 (Summer 2005): 527–57. Some of the author's notes have been omitted.

legitimacy for the use of military force? That it would be so is far from obvious. Claude, for instance, thought of the UN General Assembly (GA) as the ultimate conferrer of legitimacy.[3] Franck argued in his influential 1990 treatise on legitimacy that if one were interested in identifying rules in the international system with a strong compliance pull, the provisions in the UN Charter that grant the SC military enforcement powers (Chapter VII) should be set aside.[4] Since then, these provisions have been invoked with great regularity to legitimize uses of force.

The development is also puzzling from a theoretical perspective. Most theorists seek the origins of modern institutional legitimacy in legal or moral principles. However, the SC has been inconsistent at best in applying legal principles; its decision-making procedures are not inclusive, transparent, or based on egalitarian principles; its decisions are frequently clouded by the threat of outside action; and the morality of its (non-) actions is widely debated. Hence, it is unlikely that the institution has the ability to appear depoliticized, an argument that motivates most constructivist accounts of institutional legitimacy in the international arena.[5]

On the other hand, scholars who study the strategic aspects of international politics have largely dismissed the UN from their analyses.[6] This article provides a firmer base for the role of the SC in strategic interactions. I argue that when governments and citizens look for an authority to legitimize the use of force, they generally do not seek an independent judgment on the appropriateness of an intervention; rather, they want political reassurance about the consequences of proposed military adventures. The rationale is based on an analysis of the strategic dilemmas that impede cooperation in a unipolar world. In the absence of credible limits to power, fears of exploitation stifle cooperation. Because no single state can credibly check the superpower, enforcing limits on the superpower's behavior involves overcoming a complex coordination dilemma. A cooperative equilibrium that implies self-enforcing limits to the exercise of power exists but is unlikely to emerge spontaneously given that governments have conflicting perceptions about what constitute legitimate actions and fundamental transgressions by the superpower. The SC provides a focal solution that has the characteristics of an elite pact: an agreement among a select set of actors that seeks to neutralize threats to stability by institutionalizing nonmajoritarian mechanisms for conflict resolution. The elite pact's authority depends on the operation of a social norm in which SC approval provides a green light for states to cooperate, whereas its absence triggers a coordinated response that imposes costs on violators. The observance of this norm allows for more cooperation and restraint than can be achieved in the absence of coordination on the SC as the proper institutional device. Hence the extent to which the SC confers legitimacy on uses of force depends not on the perceived normative qualities of the institution, but on the extent to which actors in international politics believe that norm compliance produces favorable outcomes.

The attractiveness of the elite pact account resides partly in its ability to explain the emergence of a limited degree of governance in the international system without assuming the existence of a collective global identity that generates an ideological consensus over appropriate forms of global governance. There is little evidence that such a consensus exists. Thus accounts that require only a limited set of a priori common values appear more plausible. Furthermore, the elite pact model better fits the SC's institutional design than alternative accounts and provides a plausible explanation for the sudden surge in authority following the Gulf War. Finally, the model stresses that elite pacts need to be self-enforcing. This opens a more promising avenue for analyzing norm stability than the constructivist assumption that norms are internalized.

The article proceeds with a broad overview of temporal fluctuations in the extent to which states have historically put weight on SC decisions. The next section explains why SC authority stems from its ability to legitimize uses of force and provides an operational definition. While there is a large literature that asserts that SC decisions confer legitimacy on uses of force, explanations for this phenomenon are rarely made explicit. One of the contributions of this article is to more precisely identify the various plausible roles of the SC in the international system. After discussing the four most common (though often implicit) explanations, the elite pact argument is introduced more elaborately. The conclusion discusses the implications for theories of international legitimacy and the future of SC legitimacy.

The Security Council and Its Authority over Uses of Force

When states sign the UN Charter, they pledge not to use or threaten force "against the territorial integrity or political independence of any state, or in any manner inconsistent with the Purposes of the United Nations."[7] The Charter delegates significant authority to the SC to decide whether particular uses of force meet these purposes. This delegation is necessitated by the incompleteness of any contract that seeks to regulate the use of force but falls short of forbidding it outright. The Charter provides some guidance by explicitly specifying two general circumstances in which force may be exercised.

First, Article 51 of the Charter affirms the inherent right of states to use force in individual or collective self-defense against armed attacks. In principle, states are not obliged to obtain the approval of the SC for invoking this right.[8] However, states routinely resort to expanded conceptions of self-defense in attempts to justify unilateral uses of force. SC resolutions conceivably provide judgments on the merit of self-defense claims. An example is Resolution 1373, which reaffirms the right of the United States to act forcefully in its self-defense against terrorist activities and de facto legitimized the U.S. military action in Afghanistan.[9] This resolution, however, was quite exceptional. In nearly all other controversial claims to self-defense the SC has been unable or unwilling to rule on the legitimacy of self-defense claims; instead allowing the GA to adopt highly politicized and mostly ignored resolutions about the legitimacy of uses of force.[10]

Second, Chapter VII of the Charter defines a more active role for the SC in the management of international security. This chapter lays out a set of procedures through which the SC can authorize uses of force in response to the "existence of any threat to the peace, breach of the peace, or act of aggression."[11] Before 1990, the SC adopted only twenty-two resolutions under Chapter VII, most of which authorized sanctions rather than uses of force.[12] The two most important exceptions were the Congo peacekeeping force and the Korean War (1950). In the latter case, authorization was possible only because of the temporary absence of the Union of Soviet Socialist Republics (USSR) to protest the exclusion of the People's Republic of China from the Council. In anticipation of deadlock when the USSR would retake its seat, the SC adopted the 1950 "Uniting for Peace Resolution,"

which allowed the GA to take responsibility in security affairs if the SC were unable to act. It has been invoked ten times, most notably in 1956 to order the French and British to stop their military intervention in the Suez Canal and to create the UN Emergency Force to provide a buffer between Egyptian and Israeli forces.

Although the UN's effectiveness and decisiveness were often limited, the UN was actively involved in the management of many international conflicts in the first twenty-five years of its existence. Decisions by the UN's political organs carried some weight, even to realists such as Hans Morgenthau, who argued that the United States should be willing to compromise to "to keep the United Nations in existence and make it an effective instrument of international government."[13] Between the late-1960s and 1989, however, neither the GA nor the SC exercised much influence over when or whether states resorted to force, a development characterized by Haas as evidence for "regime decay."[14] States, including the great powers, repeatedly intervened militarily without considering UN authorization and routinely ignored resolutions condemning their actions. Most obviously, this holds for major Cold War interventions, such as the Soviet invasion of Afghanistan and the U.S. military action in Vietnam. But it also pertains to smaller conflicts. U.S. President Ronald Reagan famously claimed that the 1983 GA resolution condemning the United States for its intervention in Grenada "didn't upset his breakfast at all."[15] This disregard for the authority of the UN over uses of force continued at least until December 1989, when the United States invaded Panama without considering asking approval from any IO. A GA resolution deploring the intervention had no discernable impact on domestic public or elite support for the intervention, and neither did a SC resolution that the United States vetoed.[16]

The successful cooperation between states in the first Persian Gulf War abruptly turned the SC into the natural first stop for coalition building.[17] It is important to appreciate the magnitude of the sudden shift in SC activity immediately after operation Desert Storm. Between 1977 and the start of the Gulf War, the SC had adopted only two resolutions under Chapter VII.[18] Between 1990 and 1998, the Council approved 145 Chapter VII resolutions.[19] The number of UN commanded missions that used force beyond traditional peacekeeping principles went from one (Congo) before 1990 to five thereafter.[20] The number of missions where the authority to exercise force was delegated to interested parties went from one (Korea) to twelve.[21] Since 1990, the SC has authorized uses of force by coalitions of able and willing states in Europe (for example, the former Yugoslavia), Africa (for example, Sierra Leone, Somalia, the Great Lakes Region), Latin America (for example, Haiti), Oceania (for example, East-Timor), and Asia (for example, Afghanistan).

This spurt in activity does not simply reflect a newfound harmony in the preferences of the five veto powers. China and Russia frequently abstained from SC votes and often accompanied their abstentions with statements of discontent.[22] Reaching agreement often involved difficult compromises that had a noticeable impact on the implementation of operations, as exemplified most prolifically by the Bosnia case.[23] On several occasions, the United States made significant side-payments to obtain SC blessing for operations it could easily, and de facto did, execute alone or with a few allies. For instance, in exchange for consent for the U.S. intervention in Haiti, China and Russia obtained sizeable concessions, including a favorable World Bank loan and U.S. support for peacekeeping in Georgia.[24] Thus, attaining SC approval for a use of force is no easy task.

Governments outside the United States have also placed considerable weight on SC decisions. SC authorization was crucial to Australia's willingness to intervene in East-Timor.[25] India has since 1992 committed to a "pro-active" approach toward UN peacekeeping missions, providing generous troop contributions across the globe to UN-approved missions while refusing to supply troops for non-UN approved missions.[26] New interpretations of Basic Law provisions that restrict German military activity abroad have made exceptions for German participation in UN peacekeeping and peacemaking missions, as well as North Atlantic Treaty Organization (NATO) and West European Union (WEU) operations directed at implementing SC resolutions.[27] Japan has adopted a law that makes military contributions of most kinds conditional on SC authorization.[28] Thus even for these powerful states that lack permanent membership, SC approval has become almost imperative for participation in cooperative military endeavors.

The increased significance of SC authorization is also apparent in public opinion, both in the United States and elsewhere. There is a wealth of evidence that Americans consistently prefer UN actions to other types of multilateral interventions and even more so to unilateral initiatives. For example, in a January 2003 poll, the Program on International Policy Attitudes (PIPA) asked respondents whether they "think the UN Security Council has the right to authorize the use of military force to prevent a country that does not have nuclear weapons from acquiring them." Of all respondents, 76 percent answered affirmatively to this question, whereas only 48 percent believes the United States without UN approval has this right.[29] What is impressive about these findings is their consistency across interventions, question formats, and time.[30] Public opinion outside the United States tends to insist even more strongly on UN authorization.[31] This suggests that SC authorization may facilitate foreign leaders to participate in military actions.

The observation that, since the Persian Gulf War, it has become costly to circumvent the authority of the SC is not completely undermined by the two main cases where this authority has been ignored: the Kosovo intervention and the 2003 Iraq intervention. The absence of SC authorization for the Kosovo intervention was generally (and explicitly) perceived as unfortunate by the U.S. administration and even more so by its allies in the North Atlantic Treaty Organization (NATO).[32] NATO motivated its actions by referring to previous SC resolutions and obtained SC authorization for the peacekeeping mission and transitional authority that were set up in the immediate aftermath of the military campaign. Similarly, the United States went to considerable length to persuade the SC to authorize the Iraq intervention, argued repeatedly that it was implementing past SC resolutions, and returned to the SC in the immediate aftermath of the intervention.[33] Moreover, the absence of SC authorization is often used domestically in the argument that the lack of allies makes the war unnecessarily expensive. That NATO and the United States eventually went ahead without SC authorization does demonstrate, however, that the SC may raise the costs of unilateral action but can not prevent it altogether.[34] As former U.S. Secretary of Defense William Cohen said about SC authorization for the Kosovo intervention: "It's desirable, not imperative."[35]

Legitimacy

The previous section illustrates that since the Persian Gulf War, the main states in world politics have behaved "as if" it is costly to circumvent the authority of the SC when deciding on uses of force. How can one explain this observation given that the SC lacks independent capabilities to enforce its decisions? Several commonplace explanations for IO authority apply poorly to the SC. There are few, if any, institutional mechanisms that allow states to create credible long-term commitments to the institution, making it an unlikely candidate for locking in policies, along the lines suggested by Ikenberry.[36] The tasks that the SC performs are not routine and do not require high levels of specific expertise or knowledge. Thus, delegation of decision-making authority to the SC does not result in similar gains from specialization that plausibly explain why states are willing to delegate authority to IOs such as the World Bank[37] and the International Monetary Fund (IMF).[38]

In the absence of obvious alternative sources, the origins of the SC authority are usually assumed to lie in the legitimacy it confers on forceful actions.[39] Actions that are perceived as legitimate are obeyed voluntarily rather than challenged. Hence, obtaining legitimacy for proposed interventions is valuable. This clearly implies that legitimacy resides entirely in the subjective beliefs of actors.[40] This contrasts with the conception that legitimacy properly signifies an evaluation on normative grounds, usually derived from democratic theory. In this view, if an institution fails to meet a set of specified standards it is illegitimate, regardless of how individual actors perceive the institution. While it is important to evaluate how democratic principles ought to be extended to a global arena,[41] such a normative approach is unlikely to generate much insight into the question why SC decisions confer the legitimacy they do.

I define legitimacy perceptions as the beliefs of actors that the convention or social norm that the SC authorizes and forbids discretionary uses of force by states against states should be upheld. Discretionary uses of force are those that do not involve direct and undisputed self-defense against an attack. Thus the authority of the SC resides in the beliefs of actors that violating this social norm is costly, undesirable, or inappropriate. This focus on perceptions and on the social aspect of legitimacy is consistent with constructivist approaches.[42] It also fits rationalist accounts of self-enforcing conventions and social norms.[43]

The primary actors are governments, who decide on uses of force and are the members of the UN. However, because governments, especially democratically elected ones, rely on the support of citizens, the perceptions of individuals also matter in an indirect way. In addition, it may well be that actors in the state with the intent to use force, most often the United States in our examples, and actors in other states may have different motivations for insisting on SC authorization.[44]

Explanations

Why do state actors believe that a failure to achieve SC authorization is undesirable? What sustains these beliefs? To find convincing answers to these questions one needs to appreciate not only why states demand some form of multilateralism, but also the reasons that would lead actors to rely on the SC rather than alternatives, such as the GA, regional institutions (for example, NATO), or multilateral coalitions that are not embedded in formal IOs. Thus, pointing to a general inclination toward multilateralism does not form a satisfactory explanation of the empirical pattern.[45] Besides institutional form, a persuasive account must provide useful insights about the sources for temporal variation in the authority of the SC, including its sudden surge following the Gulf War. Moreover, it should give a plausible explanation for how these beliefs can be sustained given the behavior of the SC.

Most theoretical accounts argue that the legitimacy of international institutions resides in their ability to appear depoliticized by faithfully applying a set of rules, procedures, and norms that are deemed desirable by the international community.[46] I discuss three variants of this general argument that each stresses a different role for institutions: consistently applying legal rules, facilitating deliberation, and increasing accountability and fairness. Alternatively, the origins of the SC's legitimacy may lie in beliefs that granting the SC the authority to legitimize force generally lead to more desirable outcomes. The public goods explanation discussed below fits this mold, as does the elite pact account.

Legal Consistency

Much legal scholarship assumes that the SC derives its ability to legitimize and delegitimize the use of force from its capacity to form judgments about the extent to which proposed actions fit a legal framework that defines a system of collective security. Although the SC is explicitly a political institution rather than a court, there is a body of customary and written international law that provides a basis for determinations about the legality of self-defense actions and other uses of force.[47] The indiscriminatory nature of legal norms potentially makes legal uses of force more acceptable to governments and citizens than actions that do not meet legal standards. To maintain its standing as a legitimate conferrer of legal judgments, an institution must thus strive for consistency in its rulings and motivate deviations from past practice with (developing) legal principles. This standard has usefully been applied to other bodies, such as dispute resolution mechanisms in trade organizations[48] and the European Court of Justice (ECJ).[49] That legal consistency is the institutional behavior that reinforces legitimacy beliefs also motivates concerns by legal scholars that the SC squanders its legitimacy when it behaves in ways that are inconsistent with general principles of international law.[50]

There is, however, no empirical evidence that legal consistency has been a driving force behind SC decisions. During the Cold War, the judgments by UN bodies on the legality of self-defense actions were widely perceived as politically motivated and not persuasive on the issue of lawfulness.[51] The SC has not developed a consistent doctrine on this matter since the end of the Cold War. The most noteworthy decision is the previously noted Resolution 1373, which affirms the right of the United States to act forcefully in its self-defense against terrorist activities. The extensive scope of the resolution has led some to question its legal foundations.

As Farer puts it: "At this point, there is simply no cosmopolitan body of respectable legal opinion that could be invoked to support so broad a conception of self-defense."[52]

With regard to Chapter VII authorizations, the most basic determination is whether a situation presents a threat to international peace and security. Such "Article 39 determinations" have been stretched on multiple occasions to accommodate immediate political objectives. For example, Iraqi actions in Kurdish areas in 1991, the humanitarian tragedy in Somalia in 1992, the civil war in Angola in 1993, the failure to implement election results in Haiti in 1994, and Libya's unwillingness to surrender its citizens accused of terrorism have all been deemed threats to international peace.[53] Most importantly, there has been no serious effort at motivating the Article 39 determination on these resolutions. As Kirgis points out: "[I]f we are concerned about the responsible use of power by a marginally representative international organ that at present is not subject to recall or judicial review, we should expect the Security Council to be conscious of how and why it is expanding the definition. It should also contemplate the limits to be applied to the broader definition. It should, in other words, make principled Article 39 determinations, publicly explicated, that do not set unlimited or unintended precedents."[54]

Legal scholars have noted a variety of other difficulties considering SC decisions, including the common practice to delegate the use of force to individual states or groupings of states, the failure to define a greater role for judicial review through the International Court of Justice, and the extent to which the Charter obliges states to seek peaceful resolutions before authorizing force.[55] Glennon has concluded that coherent international law concerning intervention by states no longer exists.[56] Others counter that the Charter does not impose meaningful restrictions on the set of cases in which the SC can legally authorize forceful means.[57] Clearly, either view precludes that legal consistency

is the driving force behind the SC's legitimizing ability. This does not mean that legal norms do not affect the use of force. The norm to ask for approval from the SC for the use of force can itself be understood as a legal norm. The observation that this norm is mostly obeyed even though the SC itself has shown little regard for legal principles warrants an explanation.

Forum for Deliberation

A second set of scholars claim that while legal arguments are not decisive in the SC, law plays a broader role in the process of justificatory discourse.[58] This view relies on the notion that governments generally feel compelled to justify their actions on something other than self-interest. This may be so because governments seek to acquire the support of other governments, domestic political actors, or public opinion. Or, it may be that governments have internalized standards for appropriate behavior that are embedded in international legal norms. The importance of law in persuasion resides in its ability to put limits on the set of arguments that can acceptably be invoked.[59] Moreover, professional experts (international lawyers) help distinguish good arguments from poor ones in the evaluation of truth claims. Of course, the extent to which legal specialists can perform this function depends on the presence of a relatively coherent body of international law that regulates uses of force.

Alternatively, discourse in the SC may be guided by rules that the international community collectively understands to guide the process of acquiring approval for uses of force, even if not codified by law.[60] This thesis relies on the presence of easily recognizable common values that facilitate the evaluation of arguments.

The above view provides a promising account for why states frequently appeal to legal arguments, precedents, and collective security rules, even if final decisions often violate those rules. However, this view does not provide a plausible explanation for the role of the SC in this discursive process. It is widely recognized that the SC falls far short of Habermasian conditions for effective communicative action.[61] There is only a shallow set of common values, participants are unequal, and the SC relies extensively on unrecorded and informal consultations between subsets of the permanent members.[62] U.S. Secretary of State Colin Powell's public exposition of evidence for the case against Iraq was highly unusual and of questionable efficacy as a persuasive effort.[63] More frequently, the most visible efforts at persuasion occur outside of the institutional context of the SC. SC debates are usually recitations by representatives of statements prepared by their state departments. Strategic incentives further impede deliberation. There are clear and obvious incentives for states to misrepresent their positions, as the stakes are clear and the relevant actors few. In short, it is hard to see how the institutional setting of the SC contributes to the process of justificatory discourse and why, if deliberation were so important, institutional reforms have not been undertaken or alternative venues such as the GA have not grown more relevant.

Appropriate Procedures

An institution's decisions may be seen as legitimate because the institution's decision-making process corresponds to practice deemed desirable by members of the community. Beliefs about the appropriateness of a decision-making process constitute an important source of authority for domestic political institutions, particularly in democracies. Citizens may attach inherent value to procedures that conform to principles widely shared in a society. As a consequence, decisions of an institution may be perceived as legitimate even if these produce outcomes deemed undesirable.[64]

In a similar vein, accountability, procedural fairness, and broad participation are often seen as inherent elements of the legitimacy of IOs.[65] This assumption underlies the common argument that the main threat to SC legitimacy is that the institution is dominated by a few countries and that its procedures are opaque and unfair.[66] The assertion is that the SC's decision would carry greater legitimacy if its procedures more closely matched liberal norms, which allegedly have become increasingly important in international society.[67]

The many attempts to reform the SC indicate that the legitimacy of the SC may be enhanced from the perspective of some if its decision-making procedures more closely corresponded to liberal principles. But one cannot plausibly explain the legitimacy the SC does confer on uses of force from the assumption that governments and citizens demand appropriate process. As outlined earlier, SC practice sets a low standard if measured against any reasonable set of liberal principles. One may object that a use of force authorized by the SC more closely approximates standards of appropriate procedure than unilateral actions. But if demands for appropriate procedure were strong, one would surely expect a greater use of more inclusive IOs, such as a return to the "uniting for peace" procedure popular in the 1950s and 1960s, perhaps under a weighted voting system. Instead, the GA has grown increasingly irrelevant for legitimizing uses of force. Alternatively, one might have expected reforms that increase transparency and accountability, which have been moderately successful in international financial institutions. Some argue that accountability has worsened in the 1990s, as the GA can no longer hold the SC accountable through the budget by qualified majority rule,[68] and because of the increasingly common practice of delegating the authority to use force to states and regional organizations.[69]

It is equally implausible that the general public appreciates the SC for its procedures. The public knows little about how the SC makes its decisions.

Even in the midst of the Iraq controversy, 32 percent of the U.S. public claimed that the United States does not have the right to veto SC decisions,[70] and only 16 percent could name the five members with veto power.[71] Knowledge is not much better elsewhere, with correct identification of permanent members varying in a nine-country study from 5 percent in Portugal to 24 percent in Germany.[72]

Finally and most fundamentally, there is no set of common values that generate consensus about what constitutes appropriate global governance. Disagreements have become especially apparent in debates about voting rules and membership questions, but they have also surfaced in virtually any other area where meaningful reforms have been proposed.[73] Even liberal democracies generally disagree on if and how liberal principles ought to be extended to global governance.[74] Explanations that emphasize strong common values are less likely to be successful for a diverse global organization than for an institution with more homogenous membership.

Global Public Goods

An alternative view is that the SC helps solve collective action problems that arise in the production of global public goods.[75] Successful peacekeeping operations reduce suffering and save lives. Globalization and the end of the Cold War may have increased demands for international actions that produce such effects.[76] In addition, UN-authorized interventions may provide a measure of stability and security that benefits virtually all nations. For example, the first Gulf War reinforced the norm that state borders not be changed forcibly and secured the stability of the global oil supply.[77] These benefits accrue to all status quo powers and are not easily excludable.

Models of public good provision predict that poor nations will be able to free ride off the contributions of wealthier nations and that the public good will be underprovided because contributors do not take into account the spillover benefits that their support confers to others. The SC may help alleviate underprovision and free riding in three ways. First, the fixed burden-sharing mechanism for peacekeeping operations provides an institutional solution that helps reduce risks of bargaining failures and lessens transaction costs.[78] Second, the delegation of decision-making authority to a small number of states may facilitate compromise on the amount of public good that ought to be produced.[79] Third, the SC helps states pool resources.[80] The existence of selective incentives induces some states to incur more than their required share of the peacekeeping burden. For example, Kuwait paid two-thirds of the bill for the UN Iraq-Kuwait Observation Mission through voluntary contributions. Australia proved willing to shoulder a disproportionate share of the peacekeeping burden in East-Timor. States are more likely to make such contributions when these add to the efforts of others in a predictable manner.

The absence of enforcement mechanisms implies that the survival of this cooperative solution depends on a social norm. This norm first and foremost requires states to pay their share of the burden. The more states believe that this norm is followed, the fewer incentives they have to free ride in any particular case. In individual instances, states must be willing to shoulder a larger share of the burden than they would with a voluntary mechanism, because they believe that the benefits from upholding the social norm (greater public good production in the long run) exceed the short-term benefits of shirking. Hence, interventions authorized by the SC could be perceived as more legitimate in the sense that they signal a longer-term commitment to global public good production.

Although this argument is plausible theoretically, it fails to account for some noticeable empirical patterns. First, the belief among rational actors that the SC plays this role should and probably has weakened considerably since the early 1990s. The much-publicized failures in Somalia, Rwanda, and Bosnia should have reduced beliefs that the SC is the appropriate mechanism for coordination that helps solve problems of public good production. Moreover, several wealthy states, most notably the United States, have failed repeatedly to meet their peacekeeping assessments. As of 31 January 2003, the United States had $789 million in peacekeeping arrears.[81] Other states owe the UN $1.4 billion in payments for peacekeeping. These arrears constitute a sizeable portion of the total peacekeeping budget.[82] Under the collective action model, the failure of states to meet their assessments gives other states clear incentives to shirk.

Second, the public goods rationale does not explain why states value SC authorization even when they do not use its fixed burden-sharing mechanism. Between 1996 and 2000, estimated expenditures on non–UN-financed peacekeeping missions have exceeded spending on UN-financed operations by $11.5 billion.[83] Interestingly, many of these non–UN-financed operations have taken place with the explicit authorization of the SC. For example, the mandates of the various peacekeeping and peacemaking forces in Bosnia, Kosovo, and Afghanistan were all authorized at some point by SC resolutions,[84] but none of them are financed primarily through the UN system or executed by the UN.

Third, the decision-making procedures grant veto power to states that contribute little to UN operations and exclude some of the most significant contributors. Japan and Germany are the second and third largest contributors but have no permanent seat at the table. China contributes less than small European states such as Belgium, Sweden, and the Netherlands, but has the right to veto any resolution.[85] If public good provision were the prime concern, reform of these decision-making mechanisms would be in every state's best interest. It would prevent large contributors from abandoning the institution or refusing to pay their dues. International financial institutions, such as the World Bank and the IMF, have adopted weighted voting rules that better fit these objectives.

The value states attach to SC authorization rests not entirely in the extent to which it forms an institutional solution to free-rider problems that lead to under-production of public goods. However, the public good argument is not completely without merit. Several SC-authorized peacekeeping missions have helped resolve conflicts and have contributed to the implementation of peace agreements.[86] Moreover, a global alternative is not readily available. The elite pact rationale suggests that the main function of the SC in this may be that it addresses a distributional issue that frequently impedes successful collective action.

The Security Council as an Elite Pact

An alternative perspective is that the SC is an institutional manifestation of a central coalition of great powers.[87] This view does not proclaim that the SC enforces a broad system of collective security, but rather that it may serve as a useful mechanism that facilitates cooperative efforts in an anarchic world characterized by the security dilemma.[88] Concerts were historically designed to deal with situations of multipolarity that followed the defeat of hegemony. However, similar incentives for cooperation exist in a unipolar world characterized by interdependence. There are substantial potential gains from cooperation between the superpower and other states on economic issues such as trade and financial stability. Moreover, many governments face common security threats such as terrorism and states with the capacity and intention to challenge status quo boundaries or produce nuclear weapons. The main impediment to cooperation under the security dilemma is fear of exploitation.[89] Such fears are also relevant in a unipolar world where the superpower can use its preponderant capabilities to extract concessions, set the terms for cooperation, and act against the interests of individual states without being checked by a single credible power.

In such asymmetrical situations, credible limits to the use of force potentially benefit both the superpower and the rest of the world.[90] In the absence of credible guarantees, one observes suboptimal levels of cooperation as states pay a risk premium, captured for instance by increased military expenditure or other actions targeted at limiting the superpower's relative primacy. Institutions, such as NATO, help increase the credibility of security guarantees by raising the cost of reneging from a commitment. However, the absence of an outside threat and strong collective identity make such arrangements much more difficult to achieve at the global level.

Game-theoretic analyses that treat institutions as self-enforcing equilibria suggest an alternative route by which institutions help achieve better outcomes: they aid in solving the coordination dilemma among those actors that fear exploitation. Potential individual challenges are unlikely to deter a superpower from engaging in transgressions. However, the prospect of a coordinated challenge may well persuade the superpower to follow restraint. For this to succeed, states would have to agree on a mechanism that credibly triggers a coordinated response. For example, Greif, Milgrom, and Weingast argue that merchant guilds during the late medieval period provided a credible threat of costly boycotts if trade centers violated merchants' property rights.[91] Without these guilds, trade centers were unable to credibly commit to not exploit individual merchants and consequentially, merchants traded less than desired by the trade centers. As such, cooperation with the guilds became self-enforcing: it was in the self-interest of all actors to abide by the cooperative norm and defend against violations of the norm. Therefore, breaches of the norm came to be seen as illegitimate actions.

There is, however, a complicating factor in applying this analogy to the international arena.

One can reasonably assume that merchants agreed on a common definition of what constituted a fundamental transgression by a trade center. Such consensus surely does not exist in the global arena. As the recent conflict over Iraq illustrates, what some states perceive as a proper use of force, others see as an encroachment. This introduces a political component to the problem. The strategic dilemma in the international system therefore more closely resembles that of achieving limited governance and rule of law in the context of ethnically, linguistically, and religiously heterogeneous societies, as analyzed by Weingast.[92]

In heterogeneous societies, actors usually have conflicting interests about many aspects of governance. Weingast's model assumes that each actor can classify each move by the superpower[93] as either a transgression or a legitimate action. However, actors do not necessarily agree on these classifications. A superpower can exploit this by rewarding a subset of actors and infringing on the interests of the others. Although there are many such uncooperative equilibria, in a dynamic setting the Pareto-optimal cooperative outcome is also an equilibrium. In this equilibrium, no transgressions occur and states can cooperate beneficially. However, this equilibrium entails that states agree on a mechanism that triggers a coordinated response against an identifiable action by the superpower. It also requires that states use trigger strategies to punish one another for failing to cooperate in a coordinated challenge. The heterogeneous actors that occupy the international system are unlikely to resolve their coordination dilemma in a wholly decentralized manner.

In accordance with the literature on comparative politics, Weingast suggests that the most effective manner to induce limited governance in divided societies is through elite pacts.[94] An elite pact is an agreement among a select set of actors that seeks to neutralize threats to stability by institutionalizing nonmajoritarian mechanisms for conflict resolution. The SC can usefully be understood as such a pact that functions as a focal point that helps state actors coordinate what limits to the exercise of power should be defended. If the SC authorizes a use of force, the superpower and the states that cooperate should not be challenged. If, however, the United States exercises force in the absence of SC authorization, other states should challenge it and its allies, for instance, by reducing cooperation elsewhere. This equilibrium behavior can be understood as a social norm or convention. For a convention to be successful, it needs to be self-enforcing. This means that actors should find it in their interest to punish unilateral defections from the pact, for example, because they believe that deviations have the potential to steer international society down a conflict-ridden path. SC authorizations thus legitimize uses of force in that they form widely accepted political judgments that signal whether a use of force transgresses a limit that should be defended. This fits with the conventional interpretation that legitimate power is limited power.

To domestic publics this convention performs a signaling function. Citizens are generally unprepared to make accurate inferences about the likely consequences of forceful actions. If the convention operates as specified above, SC agreement provides the public with a shortcut on the likely consequences of foreign adventures. SC authorization indicates that no costly challenges will result from the action. The absence of SC authorization on the other hand, signals the possibility of costly challenges and reduced cooperation. A U.S. public that generally wants the United States to be involved internationally but is fearful of overextension[95] may value such a signaling function. To foreign publics, SC approval signals that a particular use of force does not constitute an abuse of power that should lead to a coordinated, costly response.[96] Clearly this conception of the SC poses fewer informational demands on general publics than alternatives. Moreover, it does not rely on the assumption that citizens share common values

about the normative qualities of global governance. All citizens need to understand is that SC authorization implies some measure of consent and cooperation, whereas the absence of authorization signals potential challenges. The symbolic (focal point) aspect of SC approval allows for analogies to past experiences in a way that cooperative efforts through ad hoc coalitions do not.

More generally, the elite pact account does not depend on the existence of a broad set of common values that generates a consensus about what global governance should look like. For a cooperative equilibrium to survive, it is not necessary that each actor believe that the norm that sustains the equilibrium is morally appropriate, as long as most nonbelievers assume that other actors would react to violations. This is consistent with Weber's view on why a social order is binding on an individual level.[97] It helps explain the observation that governments insist on SC authorizations of uses of force even if they challenge the normative qualities of the institution. As observed earlier, powerful states such as Germany, Japan, and India, as well as many developing countries, regularly criticize the SC for its composition and decision-making procedures. Yet, they also insist on SC authorization of uses of force and in some cases even adjust their domestic laws to make cooperation conditional on SC.

■ ■ ■

Conclusions

The ability of the SC to successfully restrain the United States is at the heart of its aptitude to play a legitimizing role in international politics. In this conception, a legitimate exercise of power abides by certain accepted limits. SC authorization signals the observance of these limits, which are defined not by legal, moral, or efficiency standards, but by an undemocratic political process that seeks to achieve compromise among elite actors. It is important to understand that although the role of the SC depends entirely on the configuration of state interests, this fact does not make the institution epiphenomenal. There are many potential equilibria and convergence on a particular (semicooperative) equilibrium has important implications. This is true even if the restraint on the exercise of power is limited to raising the cost of unilateralism.

Theoretically, this conception of legitimacy corresponds best to those classical realists who did not consider power and legitimacy to be antithetical, but complementary.[98] Legitimacy, these theorists argued, helps convert power into authority. Authority is a much cheaper regulatory device than the constant exercise of coercion. Therefore, attempts to legitimize power are a persistent feature of political life, even in the anarchical global arena. However, these realists had little faith in legalities or moral values as the source for legitimacy. Instead, the process of legitimation primarily involves the acquisition of political judgments about the proper way in which the exercise of power ought to be limited. As Claude wrote in 1966: "[T]he process of legitimization is ultimately a political phenomenon, a crystallization of judgment that may be influenced but is unlikely to be wholly determined by legal norms and moral principles."[99] This statement contrasts sharply with the view that IOs derive their legitimacy precisely from their ability to appear depoliticized. One way of reconciling these views is that the latter focuses mostly on the role of IOs as bureaucracies or courts, whereas the first stresses their political arena role. The UN encompasses both roles, but the ability of the SC to legitimize the use of force stems from its function as a political meeting place. This political arena function of IOs has hitherto received too little attention in the theoretical literature.

The implications of this argument differ in important ways from alternative accounts. The common claim among scholars of international law that the SC threatens to lose its legitimacy if it adopts resolutions that do not fit a broader legal framework depends strongly on the (usually implicit) assumption that its legitimacy depends primarily on its ability to fulfill the role of legal adjudicator. This is the premise of Glennon's argument that the SC was a "grand attempt to subject the use of force to the rule of law," which has "fallen victim to geopolitical forces too strong for a legalist institution to withstand."[100] If the SC's legitimacy does not critically depend on its functioning as a guardian of a legal system, as I argue here, the legal consistency of SC resolutions should not per se be of great consequence to the legitimacy of the institution.[101]

Others claim that the gravest threat to the legitimacy of the SC is that a few countries dominate it and that its procedures are opaque and unfair.[102] If demand for proper procedures were the motivating factor behind the SC's authority, secretive backroom deals among the great powers would be considered illegitimate. Such deals are part of the elite pact account of legitimacy. This does not imply that actors view the procedural aspects of elite politics as desirable per se, but that these are useful to the higher purpose of stability. This situation suggests that successful reforms to make the SC more transparent may actually have adverse effects in that powerful states may flee the forum.[103] In the public goods rationale, the legitimacy of the SC depends critically on preventing free riding and effectiveness in producing global public goods. This is not necessarily the primary concern in the elite pact rationale, although the proper functioning of the elite pact increases public good production in comparison to uncooperative equilibria. Nevertheless, the failures of the SC in Rwanda and other places and the failure of the United States to meet its peacekeeping burden may have diminished esteem for the institution, but these failures appear to have had little effect on the belief that the SC is the proper authority to legitimize force.

The conclusion from this study should not be that states are not concerned with legal and moral principles or global public goods, but that the existing and persistent belief that the SC is the most desirable institution to approve the use of force cannot be explained persuasively from the assumption that states do. Legitimacy that relies on the effectiveness of an institution to resolve a particular dilemma is often thought to be inherently unstable. For example, it depends on outcomes that could be caused by a multitude of factors, not just the decisions of the institution. I agree that if the SC's legitimacy were based on a convergence of opinions on its normative properties, its legitimacy would be more stable than it is today. However, such agreement does not exist and is unlikely to emerge in the near future. The collective legitimation function of the UN helps shape state behavior because state officials have made it important by their actions and statements.[104] Those actions and statements could also undermine the Council's legitimacy.

NOTES

1. Claude 1966, 367.
2. See Barnett 1997; Caron 1993; and Hurd 1999 and 2002.
3. Claude 1966, 373.
4. Franck 1990, 42.
5. See especially Barnett and Finnemore 1999.
6. Hoffmann 1998, 179.
7. UN Charter, Article 2(4).
8. See Schachter 1989; and Franck 2001. Under the Charter, states do have an obligation to notify the SC.
9. SC Resolution 1373, 28 September 2001.
10. Schachter 1989.
11. UN Charter, Article 39.
12. Bailey and Daws 1998, 271.
13. Morgenthau 1954, 11.
14. Haas 1983.
15. Cited in Luck 2002, 63.
16. Luck 2002, 64.
17. Baker 1995, 278.
18. See SC Resolution 502, 3 April 1982; SC Resolution 598, 20 July 1987; and Bailey and Daws 1998, 272.
19. Bailey and Daws 1998, 271.
20. Jakobsen 2002.
21. Ibid.
22. Voeten 2001.
23. See Christopher 1998.
24. Malone 1998.
25. Coleman 2004.
26. Krishnasamy 2003.
27. Bundesverfassungsgericht [Federal Constitutional Court] 90, 286, 12 July 1994.
28. Law Concerning Cooperation for United Nations Peacekeeping Operations and Other Operations (the International Peace Cooperation Law) originally passed in June 1992. For other examples, see Hurd 1999.
29. PIPA 2003a. Poll conducted among 1,063 American adults, margin of error +/−3 percent. The order of the questions was randomized.
30. Kull 2002.
31. See German Marshall Fund and Compagnia di San Paolo 2003; and Thompson 2004.
32. Daalder and O'Hanlon 2000, 218–19.
33. See also Frederking 2003.
34. See also Hurd 2003, 205.
35. See *New York Times*, 12 June 1998, A1.
36. Ikenberry 2001. Accordingly, Ikenberry focuses on NATO and GATT/WTO.
37. Nielson and Tierney 2003.
38. Martin 2003.
39. See Caron 1993; and Hurd 1999.
40. Weber 1978.
41. For example, Held 1995.
42. See especially Hurd 1999.
43. See Lewis 1969; and Young 1993.
44. See also Thompson 2004.
45. See Ruggie 1993.
46. Barnett and Finnemore 1999, 708.
47. See Murphy 1997 for an overview.
48. Kelemen 2001.
49. Burley and Mattli 1993.
50. See Alvarez 1995; Farer 2002; Glennon 2001; and Kirgis 1995.
51. Schachter 1989.
52. Farer 2002, 359.
53. See SC Resolution 688, 5 April 1991; SC Resolution 794, 3 December 1992; and SC Resolution 940, 31 July 1994.
54. Kirgis 1995, 517. See also Gordon 1994.
55. See Alvarez 1995; Glennon 2001; and Kirgis 1995.
56. Glennon 1999 and 2001.
57. Franck 1999.
58. See Johnstone 2003; and Sandholtz and Stone Sweet 2004.
59. Johnstone 2003.
60. Frederking 2003.
61. See Johnstone 2003; and Risse 2000.
62. See Bailey and Daws 1998; Woods 1999; and Wood 1996.
63. Colin Powell, "Remarks to the United Nations Security Council," New York City, 5 February 2003.
64. Gibson 1989.
65. For example, see Keohane and Nye 2001; and Woods 1999.
66. See especially Caron 1993.
67. See the discussion in Barnett 1997.
68. Woods 1999.
69. Blokker 2000.
70. According to PIPA 2003b, 55 percent thought that the United States does have that right.
71. German Marshall Fund and Compagnia di San Paolo 2003.
72. Ibid.

73. Luck 2003.
74. See Schmitz and Sikkink 2002, 521; and Slaughter 1995.
75. For analyses along these lines see Khanna, Sandler, and Shimizu 1998; Bobrow and Boyer 1997; and Shimizu and Sandler 2002.
76. Jakobsen 2002.
77. Bennett, Lepgold, and Unger 1994.
78. This system was put in place in 1973 by General Assembly Resolution 310.
79. Martin 1992, 773.
80. Abbott and Snidal 1998.
81. See (http://www.globalpolicy.org/finance/tables/core/un-us-03.htm). Accessed 10 March 2005.
82. In the 2000–2002 period, yearly peacekeeping budgets were around $2.6 billion.
83. Based on data from Shimizu and Sandler 2002.
84. Initial SC resolutions for respective missions were SC Resolution 1031, 15 December 1995; SC Resolution 1088, 12 December 1996; SC Resolution 1244, 10 June 1999; and SC Resolution 1386, 20 December 2001.
85. Based on data in Shimizu and Sandler 2002.
86. Doyle and Sambanis 2000.
87. Rosecrance 1992.
88. Jervis 1985. Other realists believe that concerts were mostly epiphenomenal. See Downs and Iida 1994.
89. Jervis 1985, 69.
90. Ikenberry 2001.
91. Greif, Milgrom, and Weingast 1994.
92. The informal discussion here relies on the formal analysis provided by Weingast 1997.
93. Sovereign in Weingast's case.
94. For example, see Lijphart 1969; Rustow 1970; and Tsebelis 1990.
95. Holsti 2004.
96. For a similar argument, see Thompson 2004.
97. Weber 1978.
98. On the UN see: Claude 1964, 1966; and Morgenthau 1954, 10–11. Unfortunately, contemporary Realists have mostly ignored legitimacy. See Barnett 1997, 529.
99. Claude 1966, 369.
100. Glennon 2003, 16.
101. Slaughter 2003; and Hurd 2003 make similar arguments in response to Glennon.
102. Caron 1993.
103. Drezner 2003 argues that reforms in the IMF have had such an effect. For a proposal of procedural reform that takes such incentives into account, see Buchanan and Keohane 2004.
104. See also Claude 1966, 543.

REFERENCES

Abbot, Kenneth, and Duncan Snidal. 1998. Why States Act Through Formal International Organizations. *Journal of Conflict Resolution* 42 (1):3–32.

Alvarez, Jose E. 1995. The Once and Future Security Council. *The Washington Quarterly* (spring):3–20.

Bailey, Sidney D., and Sam Daws. 1998. *The Procedure of the UN Security Council*. 3d ed. Oxford: Clarendon Press.

Baker, James A. III. 1995. *The Politics of Diplomacy: Revolution, War and Peace 1989–1992*. New York: Putnam's Sons.

Barnett, Michael N. 1997. Bringing in the New World Order: Liberalism, Legitimacy, and the United Nations. *World Politics* 49 (4):526–51.

Barnett, Michael N., and Martha Finnemore. 1999. The Politics, Power, and Pathologies of International Organizations. *International Organization* 53 (4):699–732.

Bennett, Andrew, and Joseph Lepgold. 1993. Reinventing Collective Security after the Cold War and the Gulf Conflict. *Political Science Quarterly* 108 (2):213–237.

Bennett, Andrew, Joseph Lepgold, and Danny Unger. 1994. Burden-Sharing in the Persian Gulf War. *International Organization* 48 (1):39–75.

Blokker, Niels. 2000. Is the Authorization Authorized? Powers and Practice of the UN Security Council to Authorize the Use of Force by 'Coalitions of the Able and Willing.' *European Journal of International Law* 11 (3):541–68.

Bobrow, Davis B., and Mark A. Boyer. 1997. Maintaining System Stability: Contributions to Peace keeping Operations. *Journal of Conflict Resolution* 41 (6):723–48.

Buchanan, Allen, and Robert O. Keohane. 2004. The Preventive Use of Force: A Cosmopolitan Institutional Proposal. *Ethics and International Affairs* 18 (1):1–23.

Burley, Anne-Marie, and Walter Mattli. 1993. Europe Before the Court: A Political Theory of Legal Integration. *International Organization* 47 (1):41–76.

Caron, David C. 1993. The Legitimacy of the Collective Authority of the Security Council. *American Journal of International Law* 87 (4):552–88.

Christopher, Warren. 1998. *In the Stream of History: Shaping Foreign Policy for a New Era*. Stanford, Calif.: Stanford University Press.

Claude, Inis L. 1964. *Swords into Plowshares: The Problems and Progress of International Organization*. 3d ed. New York: Random House.

———. 1966. Collective Legitimation as a Political Function of the United Nations. *International Organization* 20 (3):367–79.

Coleman, Katharina P. 2004. States, International Organizations, and Legitimacy: The Role of International Organizations in Contemporary Peace Enforcement Operations. Ph.D. diss., Princeton University, Princeton, N.J.

Daalder, Ivo H., and Michael E. O'Hanlon. 2000. *Winning Ugly: NATO's War to Save Kosovo*. Washington, D.C.: Brookings Institution.

Downs, George, and Keisuke Iida. 1994. *Collective Security Beyond the Cold War*. Ann Arbor: University of Michigan Press.

Doyle, Michael W., and Nicholas Sambanis. 2000. International Peacebuilding: A Theoretical and Quantitative Analysis, *American Political Science Review* 94 (4):779–801.

Drezner, Daniel. 2003. Clubs, Neighborhoods, and Universes: The Governance of Global Finance. Unpublished manuscript, University of Chicago, Chicago.

Farer, Tom. 2002. Beyond the Charter Frame: Unilateralism or Condominium Frame? *American Journal of International Law* 96 (2):359–64.

Franck, Thomas M. 1990. *The Power of Legitimacy Among Nations.* Oxford: Oxford University Press.

———. 1999. Sidelined in Kosovo? The United Nation's Demise Has Been Exaggerated. *Foreign Affairs* 78 (4):116–18.

———. 2001. Terrorism and the Right of Self-Defense. *American Journal of International Law* 95 (4):839–43.

Frederking, Brian. 2003. Constructing Post–Cold War Collective Security. *American Political Science Review* 97 (3):363–78.

German Marshall Fund and Compagnia di San Paolo. 2003. *Transatlantic Trends 2003.* Washington, D.C.: German Marshall Fund of the United States.

Gibson, James L. 1989. Understandings of Justice: Institutional Legitimacy, Procedural Justice and Political Tolerance. *Law and Society Review* 23 (3):469–96.

Glennon, Michael J. 1999. The New Interventionism. *Foreign Affairs* 78 (3):2–7.

———. 2001. *Limits of Law, Prerogatives of Power: Intervention After Kosovo.* New York: Palgrave.

———. 2003. Why the Security Council Failed. *Foreign Affairs* 82 (3):16–35.

Gordon, Ruth. 1994. United Nations Intervention in Internal Conflicts: Iraq, Somalia, and Beyond. *Michigan Journal of International Law* 15(2):519–89.

Greif, Avner, and David Laitin. 2004. A Theory of Endogenous Institutional Change. *American Political Science Review* 98 (4):633–52.

Greif, Avner, Paul Milgrom, and Barry R. Weingast, 1994. Coordination, Commitment, and Enforcement: The Case of the Merchant Guild. *Journal of Political Economy* 102 (4):745–76.

Haas, Ernst B. 1983. Regime Decay: Conflict Management and International Organizations, 1945–1981. *International Organization* 37 (2):189–256.

Held, David, 1995. *Democracy and the Global Order: From the Modern State to Cosmopolitan Governance.* Cambridge: Polity Press.

Hoffmann, Stanley. 1998. *World Disorders: Troubled Peace in the Post–Cold War Era.* Lanham, Md.: Rowman & Littlefield.

Holsti, Ole. 2004. *Public Opinion and American Foreign Policy.* Ann Arbor: University of Michigan Press.

Hurd, Ian. 1997. Security Council Reform: Informal Membership and Practice. In *The Once and Future Security Council,* edited by Bruce Russett and Ian Hurd, 135–52. New York: St. Martin's Press.

———. 1999. Legitimacy and Authority in International Politics. *International Organization* 53 (2):379–408.

———. 2002. Legitimacy, Power, and the Symbolic Life of the UN Security Council. *Global Governance* 8(1):35–51.

———. 2003. Stayin' Alive: The Rumours of the UN's Death Have Been Exaggerated: Too Legit to Quit. *Foreign Affairs* 82 (4):204–5.

Ikenberry, John. 2001. *After Victory.* Princeton, N.J.: Princeton University Press.

Jakobsen, Peter Viggo. 2002. The Transformation of United Nations Peace Operations in the 1990s. *Cooperation and Conflict* 37 (3):267–82.

Jervis, Robert. 1985. From Balance to Concert: A Study of International Security Cooperation. *World Politics* 38 (1):58–79.

Johnstone, Ian. 2003. Security Council Deliberations: The Power of the Better Argument. *European Journal of International Law* 14 (3):437–80.

Kelemen, R. Daniel. 2001. The Limits of Judicial Power: Trade-Environment Disputes in the GATT/WTO and the EU. *Comparative Political Studies* 34 (6):622–50.

Keohane, Robert O., and Joseph S. Nye Jr. 2001. Democracy, Accountability, and Global Governance. Politics Research Group Working Paper 01–04. Cambridge, Mass.: Harvard University.

Khanna, Jyoti, Todd Sandler, and Hirofumi Shimizu. 1998. Sharing the Financial Burden for U.N. and NATO Peacekeeping, 1976–1996. *The Journal of Conflict Resolution* 42 (2):176–95.

Kirgis, Frederic L. 1995. The Security Council's First Fifty Years. *The American Journal of International Law* 89 (3):506–39.

Krishnasamy, Kabilan. 2003. The Paradox of India's Peacekeeping. *Contemporary South Asia* 12 (2):263–64.

Kull, Steven. 2002. Public Attitudes Towards Multilateralism. In *Multilateralism and U.S. Foreign Policy,* edited by Stewart Patrick and Shepard Forman, 99–120. London: Lynne Rienner.

Lesch, Ann M. 1991. Contrasting Reactions to the Persian Gulf Crisis: Egypt, Syria, Jordan, and the Palestinians. *Middle East Journal* 45 (1):30–50.

Lewis, David. 1969. *Convention, A Philosophical Study.* Cambridge, Mass.: Harvard University Press.

Lijphart, Arend. 1969. Consociational Democracy. *World Politics* 21 (2):207–25.

Luck, Edward C. 2002. The United States, International Organizations, and the Quest for Legitimacy. In *Multilateralism and U.S. Foreign Policy,* edited by Stewart Patrick and Shepard Forman, 47–74. London: Lynne Rienner.

———. 2003. Reforming the United Nations: Lessons from a History in Progress. International Relations Studies and the United Nations Occasional Paper 2003:1. Waterloo, Canada: Academic Council on the United Nations System.

Malone, David M. 1998. *Decision-Making in the UN Security Council: The Case of Haiti, 1990–1997.* New York: Oxford University Press.

Martin, Lisa L. 1992. Interests, Power, and Multilateralism. *International Organization* 46 (4):765–92.

———. 2003. Distribution, Information, and Delegation to International Organizations: The Case of IMF Conditionality. Unpublished manuscript, Harvard University, Cambridge, Mass.

Morgenthau, Hans. 1954. The United Nations and the Revision of the Charter. *Review of Politics* 16 (1):3–21.

Morrow, James D. 1994. Modeling the Forms of International Cooperation: Distribution Versus Information. *International Organization* 48 (3):387–423.

Murphy, John F. 1997. Force and Arms. In *The United Nations and International Law,* edited by Christopher C. Joyner, 97–130. Cambridge: Cambridge University Press.

Nielson, Daniel, and Michael Tierney. 2003. Delegation to International Organizations: Agency Theory and World Bank Environmental Reform. *International Organization* 57 (2):241–76.

Program on International Policy Attitudes (PIPA). 2003a. PIPA Knowledge Networks Poll: Americans on Iraq and the UN Inspections I, 21–26 January 2003.

———. 2003b. PIPA Knowledge Networks Poll: Americans on Iraq and the UN Inspections II, 21 February 2003.

Risse, Thomas. 2000. "Let's Argue!": Communicative Action in World Politics. *International Organization* 54 (1):1–40.

Rosecrance, Richard. 1992. A New Concert of Powers. *Foreign Affairs* 71 (2):64–82.

Ruggie, John Gerard. 1993. Multilateralism: The Anatomy of an Institution. In *Multilateralism Matters*, edited by John G. Ruggie, 3–48. New York: Columbia University Press.

Russett, Bruce, and James Sutterlin. 1991. The UN in a New World Order. *Foreign Affairs* 70 (2):69–83.

Rustow, Dankwart. 1970. Transitions to Democracy: Toward a Dynamic Model. *Comparative Politics* 2 (3):337–63.

Sandholtz, Wayne, and Alec Stone Sweet. 2004. Law, Politics and International Governance. In *The Politics of International Law*, edited by Christian Reus-Smit, 238–71. Cambridge: Cambridge University Press.

Schachter, Oscar. 1989. Self-Defense and the Rule of Law. *American Journal of International Law* 83(2):259–77.

Schmitz, Hans Peter, and Kathryn Sikkink. 2002. International Human Rights. In *Handbook of International Relations*, edited by Walter Carlsnaes, Thomas Risse-Kappen, and Beth A. Simmons, 517–37. London: Sage Publications.

Shimizu, Hirofumi, and Todd Sandler. 2002. Peacekeeping and Burden-Sharing, 1994–2000. *Journal of Peace Research* 39 (6):651–68.

Slaughter, Anne-Marie. 1995. International Law in a World of Liberal States. *The European Journal of International Law* 6 (4):503–38.

———. 2003. Misreading the Record. *Foreign Affairs* 82 (4):202–4.

Thompson, Alexander. 2004. Understanding IO Legitimation. Unpublished paper, Ohio State University, Columbus.

Tsebelis, George. 1990. *Nested Games: Rational Choice in Comparative Politics*. Berkeley: University of California Press.

Urquhart, Brian. 1991. Learning from the Gulf. *New York Review of Books* 38 (5):34–37.

Voeten, Erik. 2001. Outside Options and the Logic of Security Council Action. *American Political Science Review* 95 (4):845–58.

Weber, Max. 1978. The Types of Legitimate Domination. In *Economy and Society: An Outline of Interpretive Sociology*, edited by Guenther Roth and Claus Wittich, 212–301. Berkeley: University of California Press.

Weingast, Barry. 1997. The Political Foundations of Democracy and the Rule of Law. *American Political Science Review* 91 (2):245–63.

Weingast, Barry, and William J. Marshall. 1988. The Industrial Organization of Congress; or, Why Legislatures, like Firms, Are Not Organized as Markets. *Journal of Political Economy* 96 (1):132–63.

Wood, Michael. 1996. Security Council Working Methods and Procedure: Recent Developments. *International and Comparative Law Quarterly* 45 (1):150–61.

Woods, Ngaire. 1999. Good Governance in International Organizations. *Global Governance* 5 (1):39–61.

Young, H. Peyton. 1993. The Evolution of Conventions. *Econometrica* 61 (1):57–84.

Margaret E. Keck and Kathryn Sikkink

TRANSNATIONAL ADVOCACY NETWORKS IN INTERNATIONAL POLITICS

World politics at the end of the twentieth century involves, alongside states, many nonstate actors that interact with each other, with states, and with international organizations. These interactions are structured in terms of networks, and transnational networks are increasingly visible in international politics. [Networks are forms of organization characterized by voluntary, reciprocal, and horizontal patterns of communication and exchange.] Some involve economic actors and firms. Some are networks of scientists and experts whose professional ties and shared causal ideas underpin their efforts to influence policy.[1] Others are networks of activists, distinguishable largely by the centrality of principled ideas or values in motivating their formation.[2] We will call these *transnational advocacy networks*. [A transnational advocacy network includes those relevant actors working internationally on an issue who are bound together by shared values, a common discourse, and dense exchanges of information and services.]

Advocacy networks are significant transnationally and domestically. By building new links among actors in civil societies, states, and international organizations, they multiply the channels of access to the international system. In such issue areas as the environment and human rights, they also make international resources available to new actors in domestic political and social struggles. By thus blurring the boundaries between a state's relations with its own nationals and the recourse both citizens and states have to the international system, advocacy networks are helping to transform the practice of national sovereignty.

■ ■ ■

Transnational advocacy networks are proliferating, and their goal is to change the behavior of states and of international organizations. Simultaneously principled and strategic actors, they "frame" issues to make them comprehensible to target audiences, to attract attention and encourage action, and to "fit" with favorable institutional venues.[3] Network actors bring new ideas, norms, and discourses into policy debates, and serve as sources of information and testimony. * * *

They also promote norm implementation, by pressuring target actors to adopt new policies, and by monitoring compliance with international standards. Insofar as is possible, they seek to maximize their influence or leverage over the target of their actions. In doing so they contribute to changing perceptions that both state and societal actors may have of their identities, interests, and preferences, to transforming their discursive positions, and ultimately to changing procedures, policies, and behavior.[4]

Networks are communicative structures. To influence discourse, procedures, and policy, activists

From Margaret E. Keck and Kathryn Sikkink, *Activists beyond Borders: Advocacy Networks in International Politics* (Ithaca, NY: Cornell University Press, 1998), chaps. 1, 3.

may engage and become part of larger policy communities that group actors working on an issue from a variety of institutional and value perspectives. Transnational advocacy networks must also be understood as political spaces, in which differently situated actors negotiate—formally or informally—the social, cultural, and political meanings of their joint enterprise.

■   ■   ■

Major actors in advocacy networks may include the following: (1) international and domestic nongovernmental research and advocacy organizations; (2) local social movements; (3) foundations; (4) the media; (5) churches, trade unions, consumer organizations, and intellectuals; (6) parts of regional and international intergovernmental organizations; and (7) parts of the executive and/or parliamentary branches of governments. Not all these will be present in each advocacy network. Initial research suggests, however, that international and domestic NGOs play a central role in all advocacy networks, usually initiating actions and pressuring more powerful actors to take positions. NGOs introduce new ideas, provide information, and lobby for policy changes.

Groups in a network share values and frequently exchange information and services. The flow of information among actors in the network reveals a dense web of connections among these groups, both formal and informal. The movement of funds and services is especially notable between foundations and NGOs, and some NGOs provide services such as training for other NGOs in the same and sometimes other advocacy networks. Personnel also circulate within and among networks, as relevant players move from one to another in a version of the "revolving door."

■   ■   ■

We cannot accurately count transnational advocacy networks to measure their growth over time,

but one proxy is the increase in the number of international NGOs committed to social change. Because international NGOs are key components of any advocacy network, this increase suggests broader trends in the number, size, and density of advocacy networks generally. Table 9.1 suggests that the number of international nongovernmental social change groups has increased across all issues, though to varying degrees in different issue areas. There are five times as many organizations working primarily on human rights as there were in 1950, but proportionally human rights groups have remained roughly a quarter of all such groups. Similarly, groups working on women's rights accounted for 9 percent of all groups in 1953 and in 1993. Transnational environmental organizations have grown most dramatically in absolute and relative terms, increasing from two groups in 1953 to ninety in 1993, and from 1.8 percent of total groups in 1953 to 14.3 percent in 1993. The percentage share of groups in such issue areas as international law, peace, ethnic unity, and Esperanto, has declined.[5]

■   ■   ■

How Do Transnational Advocacy Networks Work?

Transnational advocacy networks seek influence in many of the same ways that other political groups or social movements do. Since they are not powerful in a traditional sense of the word, they must use the power of their information, ideas, and strategies to alter the information and value contexts within which states make policies. The bulk of what networks do might be termed persuasion or socialization, but neither process is devoid of conflict. Persuasion and socialization often involve not just reasoning with opponents, but also bringing pressure, arm-twisting, encouraging sanctions, and shaming. * * *

Our typology of tactics that networks use in their efforts at persuasion, socialization, and pressure includes (1) *information politics*, or the ability to quickly and credibly generate politically usable information and move it to where it will have the most impact; (2) *symbolic politics*, or the ability to call upon symbols, actions, or stories that make sense of a situation for an audience that is frequently far away;[6] (3) *leverage politics*, or the ability to call upon powerful actors to affect a situation where weaker members of a network are unlikely to have influence; and (4) *accountability politics*, or the effort to hold powerful actors to their previously stated policies or principles.

A single campaign may contain many of these elements simultaneously. For example, the human

Table 9.1. International Nongovernmental Social Change Organizations (Categorized by the Major Issue Focus of Their Work)

ISSUE AREA (N)	1953 (N = 110)	1963 (N = 141)	1973 (N = 183)	1983 (N = 348)	1993 (N = 631)
Human rights	33	38	41	79	168
	30.0%	27.0%	22.4%	22.7%	26.6%
World order	8	4	12	31	48
	7.3%	2.8%	6.6%	8.9%	7.6%
International law	14	19	25	26	26
	12.7%	13.4%	13.7%	7.4%	4.1%
Peace	11	20	14	22	59
	10.0%	14.2%	7.7%	6.3%	9.4%
Women's rights	10	14	16	25	61
	9.1%	9.9%	8.7%	7.2%	9.7%
Environment	2	5	10	26	90
	1.8%	3.5%	5.5%	7.5%	14.3%
Development	3	3	7	13	34
	2.7%	2.1%	3.8%	3.7%	5.4%
Ethnic unity/ Group rts.	10	12	18	37	29
	9.1%	8.5%	9.8%	10.6%	4.6%
Esperanto	11	18	28	41	54
	10.0%	12.8%	15.3%	11.8%	8.6%

Source: Union of International Associations, *Yearbook of International Organizations* (1953, 1963, 1973, 1983, 1993). We are indebted to Jackie Smith, University of Notre Dame, for the use of her data from 1983 and 1993, and the use of her coding form and codebook for our data collection for the period 1953–73.

rights network disseminated information about human rights abuses in Argentina in the period 1976–83. The Mothers of the Plaza de Mayo marched in circles in the central square in Buenos Aires wearing white handkerchiefs to draw symbolic attention to the plight of their missing children. The network also tried to use both material and moral leverage against the Argentine regime, by pressuring the United States and other governments to cut off military and economic aid, and by efforts to get the UN and the Inter-American Commission on Human Rights to condemn Argentina's human rights practices. Monitoring is a variation on information politics, in which activists use information strategically to ensure accountability with public statements, existing legislation and international standards.

■　　■　　■

Network members actively seek ways to bring issues to the public agenda by framing them in innovative ways and by seeking hospitable venues. Sometimes they create issues by framing old problems in new ways; occasionally they help transform other actors' understanding of their identities and their interests. Land use rights in the Amazon, for example, took on an entirely different character and gained quite different allies viewed in a deforestation frame than they did in either social justice or regional development frames. In the 1970s and 1980s many states decided for the first time that promotion of human rights in other countries was a legitimate foreign policy goal and an authentic expression of national interest. This decision came in part from interaction with an emerging global human rights network. We argue that this represents not the victory of morality over self-interest, but a transformed understanding of national interest, possible in part because of structured interactions between state components and networks. * * *

■　　■　　■

Under What Conditions Do Advocacy Networks Have Influence?

To assess the influence of advocacy networks we must look at goal achievement at several different levels. We identify the following types or stages of network influence: (1) issue creation and agenda setting; (2) influence on discursive positions of states and international organizations; (3) influence on institutional procedures; (4) influence on policy change in "target actors" which may be states, international organizations like the World Bank, or private actors like the Nestlé Corporation; and (5) influence on state behavior.

Networks generate attention to new issues and help set agendas when they provoke media attention, debates, hearings, and meetings on issues that previously had not been a matter of public debate. Because values are the essence of advocacy networks, this stage of influence may require a modification of the "value context" in which policy debates take place. The UN's theme years and decades, such as International Women's Decade and the Year of Indigenous Peoples, were international events promoted by networks that heightened awareness of issues.

Networks influence discursive positions when they help persuade states and international organizations to support international declarations or to change stated domestic policy positions. The role environmental networks played in shaping state positions and conference declarations at the 1992 "Earth Summit" in Rio de Janeiro is an example of this kind of impact. They may also pressure states to make more binding commitments by signing conventions and codes of conduct.

The targets of network campaigns frequently respond to demands for policy change with changes in procedures (which may affect policies in the future). The multilateral bank campaign is largely responsible for a number of changes in internal bank directives mandating greater NGO and local participation in discussions of projects. It also opened access to formerly restricted information, and led to the establishment of an independent inspection panel for World Bank projects. Procedural changes can greatly increase the opportunity for advocacy organizations to develop regular contact with other key players on an issue, and they sometimes offer the opportunity to move from outside to inside pressure strategies.

A network's activities may produce changes in policies, not only of the target states, but also of other states and/or international institutions. Explicit policy shifts seem to denote success, but even here both their causes and meanings may be elusive. We can point with some confidence to network impact where human rights network pressures have achieved cutoffs of military aid to repressive regimes, or a curtailment of repressive practices. Sometimes human rights activity even affects regime stability. But we must take care to distinguish between policy change and change in behavior; official policies regarding timber extraction in Sarawak, Malaysia, for example, may say little about how timber companies behave on the ground in the absence of enforcement.

We speak of stages of impact, and not merely types of impact, because we believe that increased attention, followed by changes in discursive positions, make governments more vulnerable to the claims that networks raise. (Discursive changes can also have a powerfully divisive effect on networks themselves, splitting insiders from outsiders, reformers from radicals.[7]) A government that claims to be protecting indigenous areas or ecological reserves is potentially more vulnerable to charges that such areas are endangered than one that makes no such claim. At that point the effort is not to make governments change their position but to hold them to their word. Meaningful policy change is thus more likely when the first three types or stages of impact have occurred.

Both issue characteristics and actor characteristics are important parts of our explanation of how networks affect political outcomes and the conditions under which networks can be effective. Issue characteristics such as salience and resonance within existing national or institutional agendas can tell us something about where networks are likely to be able to insert new ideas and discourses into policy debates. Success in influencing policy also depends on the strength and density of the network and its ability to achieve leverage. * * *

■   ■   ■

Toward a Global Civil Society?

Many other scholars now recognize that "the state does not monopolize the public sphere,"[8] and are seeking, as we are, ways to describe the sphere of international interactions under a variety of names: transnational relations, international civil society, and global civil society.[9] In these views, states no longer look unitary from the outside. Increasingly dense interactions among individuals, groups, actors from states, and international institutions appear to involve much more than representing interests on a world stage.

We contend that the advocacy network concept cannot be subsumed under notions of transnational social movements or global civil society. In particular, theorists who suggest that a global civil society will inevitably emerge from economic globalization or from revolutions in communication and transportation technologies ignore the issues of agency and political opportunity that we find central for understanding the evolution of new international institutions and relationships.

■   ■   ■

We lack convincing studies of the sustained and specific processes through which individuals and organizations create (or resist the creation of) something resembling a global civil society. Our research leads us to believe that these interactions involve much more agency than a pure diffusionist perspective suggests. Even though the implications of our findings are much broader than most political scientists would admit, the findings themselves do not yet support the strong claims about an emerging global civil society.[10] We are much more comfortable with a conception of transnational civil society as an arena of struggle, a fragmented and contested area where "the politics of transnational civil society is centrally about the way in which certain groups emerge and are legitimized (by governments, institutions, and other groups)."[11]

■ ■ ■

HUMAN RIGHTS ADVOCACY NETWORKS IN LATIN AMERICA

Argentina

Even before the military coup of March 1976, international human rights pressures had influenced the Argentine military's decision to cause political opponents to "disappear," rather than imprisoning them or executing them publicly.[12] (The technique led to the widespread use of the verb "to disappear" in a transitive sense.) The Argentine military believed they had "learned" from the international reaction to the human rights abuses after the Chilean coup. When the Chilean military executed and imprisoned large numbers of people, the ensuing uproar led to the international isolation of the regime of Augusto Pinochet. Hoping to maintain a moderate international image, the Argentine military decided to secretly kidnap, detain, and execute its victims, while denying any knowledge of their whereabouts.[13]

Although this method did initially mute the international response to the coup, Amnesty International and groups staffed by Argentine political exiles eventually were able to document and condemn the new forms of repressive practices. To counteract the rising tide of criticism, the Argentina junta invited AI for an on-site visit in 1976. In March 1977, on the first anniversary of the military coup, AI published the report on its visit, a well-documented denunciation of the abuses of the regime with emphasis on the problem of the disappeared. Amnesty estimated that the regime had taken six thousand political prisoners, most without specifying charges, and had abducted between two and ten thousand people. The report helped demonstrate that the disappearances were part of a deliberate government policy by which the military and the police kidnapped perceived opponents, took them to secret detention centers where they tortured, interrogated, and killed them, then secretly disposed of their bodies.[14] Amnesty International's denunciations of the Argentine regime were legitimized when it won the Nobel Peace Prize later that year.

Such information led the Carter administration and the French, Italian, and Swedish governments to denounce rights violations by the junta. France, Italy, and Sweden each had citizens who had been victims of Argentine repression, but their concerns extended beyond their own citizens. Although the Argentine government claimed that such attacks constituted unacceptable intervention in their internal affairs and violated Argentine sovereignty, U.S. and European officials persisted. In 1977 the U.S. government reduced the planned level of military aid for Argentina because of human rights abuses. Congress later passed a bill eliminating all military assistance to Argentina, which went into effect on 30 September 1978.[15] A number of high-level U.S. delegations met with junta members during this period to discuss human rights.

Early U.S. action on Argentina was based primarily on the human rights documentation provided by AI and other NGOs, not on information received through official channels at the embassy or the State Department.[16] For example, during a 1977 visit, Secretary of State Cyrus Vance carried a list of disappeared people prepared by human rights NGOs to present to members of the junta.[17] When Patricia Derian met with junta member Admiral Emilio Massera during a visit in 1977, she brought up the navy's use of torture. In response to Massera's denial, Derian said she had seen a rudimentary map of a secret detention center in the Navy Mechanical School, where their meeting was being held, and asked whether perhaps under their feet someone was being tortured. Among Derian's key sources of information were NGOs and especially the families of the disappeared, with whom she met frequently during her visits to Buenos Aires.[18]

Within a year of the coup, Argentine domestic human rights organizations began to develop significant external contacts. Their members traveled frequently to the United States and Europe, where they met with human rights organizations, talked to the press, and met with parliamentarians and government officials. These groups sought foreign contacts to publicize the human rights situation, to fund their activities, and to help protect themselves from further repression by their government, and

they provided evidence to U.S. and European policymakers. Much of their funding came from European and U.S.-based foundations.[19]

Two key events that served to keep the case of Argentine human rights in the minds of U.S. and European policymakers reflect the impact of transnational linkages on policy. In 1979 the Argentine authorities released Jacobo Timerman, whose memoir describing his disappearance and torture by the Argentine military helped human rights organizations, members of the U.S. Jewish community, and U.S. journalists to make his case a cause célèbre in U.S. policy circles.[20] Then in 1980 the Nobel Peace Prize was awarded to an Argentine human rights activist, Adolfo Pérez Esquivel. Peace and human rights groups in the United States and Europe helped sponsor Pérez Esquivel's speaking tour to the United States exactly at the time that the OAS was considering the IACHR report on Argentina and Congress was debating the end of the arms embargo to Argentina.

The Argentine military government wanted to avoid international human rights censure. Scholars have long recognized that even authoritarian regimes depend on a combination of coercion and consent to stay in power. Without the legitimacy conferred by elections, they rely heavily on claims about their political efficacy and on nationalism.[21] Although the Argentine military mobilized nationalist rhetoric against foreign criticism, a sticking point was that Argentines, especially the groups that most supported the military regime, thought of themselves as the most European of Latin American countries. The military junta claimed to be carrying out the repression in the name of "our Western and Christian civilization."[22] But the military's intent to integrate Argentina more fully into the liberal global economic order was being jeopardized by deteriorating relations with countries most identified with that economic order, and with "Western and Christian civilization."

The junta adopted a sequence of responses to international pressures. From 1976 to 1978 the military pursued an initial strategy of denying the legitimacy of international concern over human rights in Argentina. At the same time it took actions that appear to have contradicted this strategy, such as permitting the visit of the Amnesty International mission to Argentina in 1976. The "failure" of the Amnesty visit, from the military point of view, appeared to reaffirm the junta's resistance to human rights pressures. This strategy was most obvious at the UN, where the Argentine government worked to silence international condemnation in the UN Commission on Human Rights. Ironically, the rabidly anticommunist Argentine regime found a diplomatic ally in the Soviet Union, an importer of Argentine wheat, and the two countries collaborated to block UN consideration of the Argentine human rights situation.[23] Concerned states circumvented this blockage by creating the UN Working Group on Disappearances in 1980. Human rights NGOs provided information, lobbied government delegations, and pursued joint strategies with sympathetic UN delegations.

By 1978 the Argentine government recognized that something had to be done to improve its international image in the United States and Europe, and to restore the flow of military and economic aid.[24] To these ends the junta invited the Inter-American Commission on Human Rights for an on-site visit, in exchange for a U.S. commitment to release Export-Import Bank funds and otherwise improve US-Argentine relations.[25] During 1978 the human rights situation in Argentina improved significantly. [T]he practice of disappearance as a tool of state policy was curtailed only after 1978, when the government began to take the "international variable" seriously.[26]

The value of the network perspective in the Argentine case is in highlighting the fact that international pressures did not work independently, but rather in coordination with national actors. Rapid change occurred because strong domestic human rights organizations documented abuses and protested against repression, and international pressures helped protect domestic monitors and open spaces for their protest. International groups amplified both information and symbolic politics of domestic groups and projected them onto an international stage, from which they echoed back into Argentina. This classic boomerang process was executed nowhere more skillfully than in Argentina, in large part due to the courage and ability of domestic human rights organizations.

Some argue that repression stopped because the military had finally killed all the people that they thought they needed to kill. This argument disregards disagreements within the regime about the size and nature of the "enemy." International pressures affected particular factions within the military regime that had differing ideas about how much repression was "necessary." Although by the military's admission 90 percent of the *armed* opposition had been eliminated by April 1977, this did not lead to an immediate change in human rights practices.[27] By 1978 there were splits within the military about what it should do in the future. One faction was led by Admiral Massera, a right-wing populist, another by Generals Carlos Suarez Mason and Luciano Menéndez, who supported indefinite military dictatorship and unrelenting war against the left, and a third by Generals Jorge Videla and Roberto Viola, who hoped for eventual political liberalization under a military president. Over time, the Videla Viola faction won out, and by late 1978 Videla had gained increased control over the Ministry of Foreign Affairs, previously under the influence of the navy.[28] Videla's ascendancy in the fall of 1978, combined with U.S. pressure, helps explain his ability to deliver on his promise to allow the Inter-American Commission on Human Rights visit in December.

The Argentine military government thus moved from initial refusal to accept international human rights interventions, to cosmetic cooperation with the human rights network, and eventually to concrete improvements in response to increased international pressures. Once it had invited IACHR and discovered that the commission could not be co-opted or confused, the government ended the practice of disappearance, released political prisoners, and restored some semblance of political participation. Full restoration of human rights in Argentina did not come until after the Malvinas War and the transition to democracy in 1983, but after 1980 the worst abuses had been curtailed.

In 1985, after democratization, Argentina tried the top military leaders of the juntas for human rights abuses, and a number of key network members testified: Theo Van Boven and Patricia Derian spoke about international awareness of the Argentine human rights situation, and a member of the IACHR delegation to Argentina discussed the OAS report. Clyde Snow and Eric Stover provided information about the exhumation of cadavers from mass graves. Snow's testimony, corroborated by witnesses, was a key part of the prosecutor's success in establishing that top military officers were guilty of murder.[29] A public opinion poll taken during the trials showed that 92 percent of Argentines were in favor of the trials of the military juntas.[30] The tribunal convicted five of the nine defendants, though only two—ex-president Videla, and Admiral Massera—were given life sentences. The trials were the first of their kind in Latin America, and among the very few in the world ever to try former leaders for human rights abuses during their rule. In 1990 President Carlos Menem pardoned the former officers. By the mid-1990s, however, democratic rule in Argentina was firmly entrenched, civilian authority over the military was well established, and the military had been weakened by internal disputes and severe cuts in funding.[31]

The Argentine case set important precedents for other international and regional human rights action, and shows the intricate interactions of groups and individuals within the network and the repercussions of these interactions. The story of the Grandmothers of the Plaza de Mayo is an exemplar of network interaction and unanticipated effects. The persistence of the Grandmothers helped create a new profession—what one might call "human rights forensic science." (The scientific skills existed before, but they had never been put to the service of human rights.) Once the Argentine case had demonstrated that forensic science could illuminate mass murder and lead to convictions, these skills were diffused and legitimized. Eric Stover, Clyde Snow, and the Argentine forensic anthropology team they helped create were the prime agents of international diffusion. The team later carried out exhumations and training in Chile, Bolivia, Brazil, Venezuela, and Guatemala.[32] Forensic science is being used to prosecute mass murderers in El Salvador, Honduras, Rwanda, and Bosnia. By 1996 the UN International Criminal Tribunal for the former Yugoslavia had contracted with two veterans of the Argentine forensic experiment, Stover and Dr. Robert Kirschner, to do forensic investigations for its war crimes tribunal. "'A war crime creates a crime scene,' said Dr. Kirschner, 'That's how we treat it. We recover forensic evidence for prosecution and create a record which cannot be successfully challenged in court.'"[33]

■ ■ ■

Conclusions

A realist approach to international relations would have trouble attributing significance either to the network's activities or to the adoption and implementation of state human rights policies. Realism offers no convincing explanation for why relatively weak nonstate actors could affect state policy, or why states would concern themselves with the internal human rights practices of other states even when doing so interferes with the pursuit of other goals. For example, the U.S. government's pressure on Argentina on human rights led Argentina to defect from the grain embargo of the Soviet Union. Raising human rights issues with Mexico could have undermined the successful completion of the free trade agreement and cooperation with Mexico on antidrug operations. Human rights pressures have costs, even in strategically less important countries of Latin America.

In liberal versions of international relations theory, states and nonstate actors cooperate to realize joint gains or avoid mutually undesirable outcomes when they face problems they cannot resolve alone. These situations have been characterized as cooperation or coordination games with particular payoff structures.[34] But human rights issues are not easily modeled as such. Usually states can ignore the internal human rights practices of other states without incurring undesirable economic or security costs.

In the issue of human rights it is primarily principled ideas that drive change and cooperation. We cannot understand why countries, organizations, and individuals are concerned about human rights or why countries respond to human rights pressures without taking into account the role of norms and ideas in international life. Jack Donnelly has argued that such moral interests are as real as material interests, and that a sense of moral interdependence has led to the emergence of human rights regimes.[35] For human rights * * * the primary movers behind this form of principled international action are international networks.

NOTES

1. Peter Haas has called these "knowledge-based" or "epistemic communities." See Peter Haas, "Introduction: Epistemic Communities and International Policy Coordination," *Knowledge, Power and International Policy Coordination*, special issue, *International Organization* 46 (Winter 1992), pp. 1–36.
2. Ideas that specify criteria for determining whether actions are right and wrong and whether outcomes are just or unjust are shared principled beliefs or values. Beliefs about cause-effect relationships are shared casual beliefs. Judith Goldstein and Robert Keohane, eds., *Ideas and Foreign Policy: Beliefs, Institutions, and Political Change* (Ithaca: Cornell University Press, 1993), pp. 8–10.
3. David Snow and his colleagues have adapted Erving Goffman's concept of framing. We use it to mean "conscious strategic efforts by groups of people to fashion shared understandings of the world and of themselves that legitimate and motivate collective action." Definition from Doug McAdam, John D. McCarthy, and Mayer N. Zald, "Introduction," *Comparative Perspectives on Social Movements: Political Opportunities, Mobilizing Structures, and Cultural Framings,* ed. McAdam, McCarthy, and Zald (New York: Cambridge University Press, 1996), p. 6. See also Frank Baumgartner and Bryan Jones, "Agenda Dynamics and Policy Subsystems," *Journal of Politics* 53:4 (1991): 1044–74.
4. With the "constructivists" in international relations theory, we take actors and interests to be constituted in interaction. See Martha Finnemore, *National Interests in International Society* (Ithaca: Cornell University Press, 1996), who argues that "states are embedded in dense networks of transnational and international social relations that shape their perceptions of the world and their role in that world. States are *socialized* to want certain things by the international society in which they and the people in them live" (p. 2).
5. Data from a collaborative research project with Jackie G. Smith. We thank her for the use of her data from the period 1983–93, whose results are presented in Jackie G. Smith, "Characteristics of the Modern Transnational Social Movement Sector," in Jackie G. Smith, et al., eds. *Transnational Social Movements and World Politics: Solidarity beyond the State* (Syracuse: Syracuse University Press, 1997), and for permission to use her coding form and codebook for our data collection for the period 1953–73. All data were coded from Union of International Associations, *The Yearbook of International Organizations,* 1948–95 (published annually).
6. Alison Brysk uses the categories "information politics" and "symbolic politics" to discuss strategies of transnational actors, especially networks around Indian rights. See "Acting Globally: Indian Rights and International Politics in Latin America," in *Indigenous Peoples and Democracy in Latin America,* ed. Donna Lee Van Cott (New York: St. Martin's Press/Inter-American Dialogue, 1994), pp. 29–51; and "Hearts and Minds: Bringing Symbolic Politics Back In," *Polity* 27 (Summer 1995): 559–85.
7. We thank Jonathan Fox for reminding us of this point.
8. M. J. Peterson, "Transnational Activity, International Society, and World Politics," *Millennium* 21:3 (1992): 375–76.
9. See, for example, Ronnie Lipschutz, "Reconstructing World Politics: The Emergence of Global Civil Society," *Millennium* 21:3 (1992): 389–420; Paul Wapner, "Politics beyond the State: Environmental Activism and World Civic Politics," *World Politics* 47 (April 1995): 311–40; and the special issue of *Millennium* on social movements and world politics, 23:3 (Winter 1994).
10. Sidney Tarrow, *Power in Movement: Social Movements and Contentious Politics,* rev. ed. (Cambridge: Cambridge University Press, 1998), Chapter 11. An earlier version appeared as "Fishnets, Internets and Catnets: Globalization and Transnational Collective Action," Instituto Juan March de Estudios e Investigaciones, Madrid: Working Papers 1996/78, March 1996; and Peterson, "Transnational Activity."

11. Andrew Hurrell and Ngaire Woods, "Globalisation and Inequality," *Millennium* 24:3 (1995), p. 468.

12. This section draws upon some material from an earlier co-authored work: Lisa L. Martin and Kathryn Sikkink, "U.S. Policy and Human Rights in Argentina and Guatemala, 1973–1980," in *Double-Edged Diplomacy: International Bargaining and Domestic Politics,* ed., Peter B. Evans, Harold K. Jacobson, and Robert D. Putnam (Berkeley: University of California Press, 1993), pp. 330–62.

13. See Emilio Mignone, *Derechos humanos y sociedad: el caso argentino* (Buenos Aires: Ediciones del Pensamiento Nacional and Centro de Estudios Legales y Sociales, 1991), p. 66; Claudio Uriarte, *Almirante Cero: Biografía No Autorizada de Emilio Eduardo Massera* (Buenos Aires: Planeta, 1992), p. 97; and Carlos H. Acuña and Catalina Smulovitz, "Adjusting the Armed Forces to Democracy: Successes, Failures, and Ambiguities in the Southern Cone," in *Constructing Democracy: Human Rights, Citizenship, and Society in Latin America*, ed. Elizabeth Jelin and Eric Hershberg (Boulder, CO: Westview, 1993), p. 15.

14. Amnesty International, *Report of an Amnesty International Mission to Argentina* (London: Amnesty International, 1977).

15. Congressional Research Service, Foreign Affairs and National Defense Division, *Human Rights and U.S. Foreign Assistance: Experiences and Issues in Policy Implementation (1977–1978)*, report prepared for U.S. Senate Committee on Foreign Relations, November 1979, p. 106.

16. After the 1976 coup, Argentine political exiles set up branches of the Argentine Human Rights Commission (CADHU) in Paris, Mexico, Rome, Geneva, and Washington, DC. In October two of its members testified on human rights abuses before the U.S. House Subcommittee on Human Rights and International Organization. Iain Guest, *Behind the Disappearances: Argentina's Dirty War against Human Rights and the United Nations* (Philadelphia: University of Pennsylvania Press, 1990), pp. 66–67.

17. Interview with Robert Pastor, Wianno, Massachusetts, 28 June 1990.

18. Testimony given by Patricia Derian to the National Criminal Appeals Court in Buenos Aires during the trials of junta members. "Massera sonrió y me dijo: Sabe qué pasó con Poncio Pilatos . . . ?" *Diario del Juicio*, 18 June 1985, p. 3; Guest, *Behind the Disappearances*, pp. 161–63. Later it was confirmed that the Navy Mechanical School was one of the most notorious secret torture and detention centers. *Nunca Más: The Report of the Argentine National Commission for the Disappeared* (New York: Farrar, Straus & Giroux, 1986), pp. 79–84.

19. The Mothers of the Plaza de Mayo received grants from Dutch churches and the Norwegian Parliament, and the Ford Foundation provided funds for the Center for Legal and Social Studies (CELS) and the Grandmothers of the Plaza de Mayo.

20. Jacobo Timerman, *Prisoner without a Name, Cell without a Number* (New York: Random House, 1981).

21. See Guillermo O'Donnell, "Tensions in the Bureaucratic Authoritarian State and the Question of Democracy," in *The New Authoritarianism in Latin America*, ed. David Collier (Princeton: Princeton University Press, 1979), pp. 288, 292–94.

22. Daniel Frontalini and Maria Cristina Caiati, *El Mito de la Guerra Sucia* (Buenos Aires: Centro de Estudios Legales y Sociales, 1984), p. 24.

23. Guest, *Behind the Disappearances*, pp. 118–19, 182–83.

24. *Carta Política*, a news magazine considered to reflect the junta's views, concluded in 1978 that "the principal problem facing the Argentine State has now become the international siege (*cerco internacional*)." "Cuadro de Situación," *Carta Política* 57 (August 1978): 8.

25. Interviews with Walter Mondale, Minneapolis, Minnesota, 20 June 1989, and Ricardo Yofre, Buenos Aires, 1 August 1990.

26. See Asamblea Permanente por los Derechos Humanos, *Las Cifras de la Guerra Sucia* (Buenos Aires, 1988), pp. 26–32.

27. According to a memorandum signed by General Jorge Videla, the objectives of the military government "go well beyond the simple defeat of subversion." The memorandum called for a continuation and intensification of the "general offensive against subversion," including "intense military action." "Directivo 504," 20 April 1977, in "La orden secreta de Videla," *Diario del Juicio* 28 (3 December 1985): 5–8.

28. David Rock, *Argentina, 1516–1987: From Spanish Colonization to Alfonsín* (Berkeley: University of California Press, 1985), pp. 370–71; Timerman, *Prisoner without a Name,* p. 163.

29. *Diario del Juicio* 1 (27 May 1985), and 9 (23 July 1985).

30. *Diario del Juicio* 25 (12 November 1985).

31. Acuña and Smulovitz, "Adjusting the Armed Forces to Democracy," pp. 20–21.

32. Cohen Salama, *Tumbas anónimas [informe sobre la identificación de restos de víctimas de la represión* (Buenos Aires: Catálogos Editora, 1992)], p. 275.

33. Mike O'Connor, "Harvesting Evidence in Bosnia's Killing Fields," *New York Times,* 7 April 1996, p. E3.

34. See, e.g., Arthur A. Stein, "Coordination and Collaboration: Regimes in an Anarchic World," *International Organization* 36:2 (Spring 1982): 299–324.

35. Donnelly, *Universal Human Rights [in Theory and Practice* (Ithaca: Cornell University Press, 1989)], pp. 211–12.

10   HUMAN RIGHTS

For generations, the idea of human rights has been contested. Which rights should be included? Which are excluded? How are rights determined in a culturally diverse world? Amartya Sen develops the argument that human rights need to be viewed as entitlements to capability—the opportunity to have freedom. Eschewing the idea of a fixed listing of capabilities, Sen suggests a process of public reasoning to arrive at an understanding of capability.

Jack Donnelly, in a chapter from *Universal Human Rights in Theory and Practice* (2003), probes whether there can be universal human rights. At the level of concepts, he sees an extensive consensus on a limited set of obligations defined in the Universal Declaration of Human Rights. But, he suggests, the ways those rights are implemented may vary, thus offering logical explanations for the persistence of arguments that rights should vary by culture.

The ethnic conflicts and civil wars of recent decades have been the occasion for rape and sexual violence, crimes of war that have been accorded enhanced prominence on the docket of the International Criminal Court. A common explanation is that rape is being used strategically as a weapon of war to intimidate populations and spur them to flee. In one of the most systematic studies of this problem, Dara Kay Cohen seeks to qualify this claim. She argues that collective rape often serves as a perverse bonding ritual that increases the group cohesion of harshly recruited and poorly disciplined fighters.

Amartya Sen
HUMAN RIGHTS AND CAPABILITIES

Introduction

The moral appeal of human rights has been used for varying purposes, from resisting torture and arbitrary incarceration to demanding the end of hunger and of medical neglect. There is hardly any country in the world—from China, South Africa and Egypt to Mexico, Britain and the United States—in which arguments involving human rights have not been raised in one context or another in contemporary political debates.

However, despite the tremendous appeal of the idea of human rights, it is also seen by many as being intellectually frail—lacking in foundation and perhaps even in coherence and cogency. The remarkable co-existence of stirring appeal and deep conceptual scepticism is not new. The American Declaration of Independence took it to be 'self-evident' that everyone is "endowed by their Creator with certain inalienable rights," and 13 years later, in 1789, the French declaration of 'the rights of man' asserted that "men are born and remain free and equal in rights." But it did not take Jeremy Bentham long to insist, in *Anarchical Fallacies*, written during 1791–1792, that "natural rights is simple nonsense: natural and imprescriptible rights [an American phrase], rhetorical nonsense, nonsense upon stilts" (Bentham, 1792/1843, p. 501). That division remains very alive today, and there are many who see the idea of human rights as no more than "bawling upon paper" (to use another of Bentham's barbed descriptions).

The concepts of human rights and human capabilities have something of a common motivation, but they differ in many distinct ways. It is useful to ask whether considering the two concepts together—capabilities and human rights—can help the understanding of each. I will divide the exercise into four specific questions. First, can human rights be seen as entitlements to certain basic capabilities, and will this be a good way of thinking about human rights? Second, can the capability perspective provide a comprehensive coverage of the content of human rights? Third, since human rights need specificity, does the use of the capability perspective for elucidating human rights require a full articulation of the list of capabilities? And finally, how can we go about ascertaining the content of human rights and of basic capabilities when our values are supposed to be quite divergent, especially across borders of nationality and community? Can we have anything like a universalist approach to these ideas, in a world where cultures differ and practical preoccupations are also diverse?

Human Rights as Entitlements to Capabilities

It is possible to argue that human rights are best seen as rights to certain specific freedoms, and that the correlate obligation to consider the associated duties must also be centred around what others can do to safeguard and expand these freedoms. Since capabilities can be seen, broadly, as freedoms of particular kinds, this would seem to establish a basic connection between the two categories of ideas.

From *Journal of Human Development* 6, no. 2 (July 2005): 151–66.

We run, however, into an immediate difficulty here. I have argued elsewhere that 'opportunity' and 'process' are two aspects of freedom that require distinction, with the importance of each deserving specific acknowledgment.[1] While the opportunity aspect of freedoms would seem to belong to the same kind of territory as capabilities, it is not at all clear that the same can be said about the process aspect of freedom.

An example can bring out the *separate* (although not necessarily independent) relevance of both *substantive opportunities* and *freedom of processes*. Consider a woman, let us call her Natasha, who decides that she would like to go out in the evening. To take care of some considerations that are not central to the issues involved here (but which could make the discussion more complex), it is assumed that there are no particular safety risks involved in her going out, and that she has critically reflected on this decision and judged that going out would be the sensible—indeed the ideal—thing to do.

Now consider the threat of a violation of this freedom if some authoritarian guardians of society decide that she must not go out ('it is most unseemly'), and if they force her, in one way or another, to stay indoors. To see that there are two distinct issues involved in this one violation, consider an alternative case in which the authoritarian bosses decide that she must—absolutely *must*—go out ('you are expelled for the evening—just obey'). There is clearly a violation of freedom even here though Natasha is being forced to do exactly what she would have chosen to do anyway, and this is readily seen when we compare the two alternatives 'choosing freely to go out' and 'being forced to go out'. The latter involves an immediate violation of the *process aspect* of Natasha's freedom, since an action is being forced on her (even though it is an action she would have freely chosen also).

The opportunity aspect may also be affected, since a plausible accounting of opportunities can include having options and it can *inter alia* include valuing free choice. However, the violation of the opportunity aspect would be more substantial and manifest if she were not only forced to do something chosen by another, but in fact forced to do something she would not otherwise choose to do. The comparison between 'being forced to go out' (when she would have gone out anyway, if free) and, say, 'being forced to polish the shoes of others at home' (not her favorite way of spending time, I should explain) brings out this contrast, which is primarily one of the opportunity aspect, rather than the process aspect. In the incarceration of Natasha, we can see two different ways in which she is losing her freedom: first, she is being forced to do something, with no freedom of choice (a violation of her process freedom); and second, what Natasha is being obliged to do is not something she would choose to do, if she had any plausible alternative (a violation of her substantive opportunity to do what she would like to do).[2]

It is important to recognize that both processes and opportunities can figure powerfully in the content of human rights. A denial of 'due process' in being, say, sentenced without a proper trial can be an infringement of human rights (no matter what the outcome of the fair trial might be), and so can be the denial of opportunity of medical treatment, or the opportunity of living without the danger of being assaulted (going beyond the exact process through which these opportunities are made real).

The idea of 'capability' (i.e., the opportunity to achieve valuable combinations of human functionings—what a person is able to do or be) can be very helpful in understanding the opportunity aspect of freedom and human rights.[3] Indeed, even though the concept of opportunity is often invoked, it does require considerable elaboration, and capability can help in this elucidation. For example, seeing opportunity in terms of capability allows us to distinguish appropriately between (i) whether a person is actually able to do things she would value *doing*, and (ii) whether she possesses the *means or instruments or permissions* to pursue what she would like to do (her actual ability to do that pursuing may depend on many contingent circumstances). By shifting attention, in particular, toward the former, the capability-based approach resists an overconcentration on means (such as incomes and primary goods) that can be found in some theories of justice (e.g. in the Rawlsian Difference Principle). The capability approach can help to identify the possibility that two persons can have very different substantial opportunities even when they have exactly the same set of means: for example, a disabled person can do far less than an able-bodied person can, with exactly the same income and other 'primary goods.' The disabled person cannot, thus, be judged to be equally advantaged— with the same opportunities—as the person without any physical handicap but with the same set of means or instruments (such as income and wealth and other primary goods and resources).

The capability perspective allows us to take into account the parametric variability in the relation between the means, on the one hand, and the actual opportunities, on the other.[4] Differences in the capability to function can arise even with the same set of personal means (such as primary goods) for a variety of reasons, such as: (1) *physical or mental heterogeneities among persons* (related, for example, to disability, or proneness to illness); (2) *variations in non-personal resources* (such as the nature of public health care, or societal cohesion and the helpfulness of the community); (3) *environmental diversities* (such as climatic conditions, or varying threats from epidemic diseases or from local crime); or (4) *different relative positions vis-à-vis others* (well illustrated by Adam Smith's discussion, in the *Wealth of Nations*, of the fact that the clothing and other resources one needs "to appear in public without shame" depends on what other people standardly wear, which in turn could be more expensive in rich societies than in poorer ones).

I should, however, note here that there has been some serious criticism of describing these substantive opportunities (such as the capability to live one kind of a life or another) as 'freedoms,' and it has been argued that this makes the idea of freedom too inclusive. For example, in her illuminating and sympathetic critique of my *Development as Freedom*, Susan Okin has presented arguments to suggest that I tend "to overextend the concept of freedom."[5] She has argued: "It is hard to conceive of some human functionings, or the fulfilment of some needs and wants, such as good health and nourishment, as freedoms without stretching the term until it seems to refer to everything that is of central value to human beings" (Okin, 2003, p. 292).

There is, certainly, considerable scope for argument on how extensively the term freedom should be used. But the particular example considered in Okin's counter-argument reflects a misinterpretation. There is no suggestion whatever that a functioning (e.g. being in good health or being well nourished) should be seen as freedom of any kind, such as capability. Rather, capability concentrates on the *opportunity* to be able to have combinations of functionings (including, in this case, the opportunity to be well-nourished), and the person is free to make use of this opportunity or not. A capability reflects the alternative combinations of functionings from which the person can choose one combination. It is, therefore, not being suggested at all that being well-nourished is to be seen as a freedom. The term freedom, in the form of capability, is used here to refer to the extent to which the person is free to choose particular levels of functionings (such as being well-nourished), and that is not the same thing as what the person actually decides to choose. During India's struggle for independence from the Raj, Mahatma Gandhi famously did not use that opportunity to be well fed when he chose to fast, as a protest against the policies of the Raj. In terms of the actual functioning of being well-nourished, the fasting Gandhi did not differ from a starving famine victim, but the freedoms and opportunities they respectively had were quite different.

Indeed, the *freedom to have* any particular thing can be substantially distinguished from actually *having* that thing. What a person is free to have—not just what he actually has—is relevant, I have argued, to a theory of justice.[6] A theory of rights also has reason to be involved with substantive freedoms.

Many of the terrible deprivations in the world have arisen from a lack of freedom to escape destitution. Even though indolence and inactivity had been classic themes in the old literature on poverty, people have starved and suffered because of a lack of alternative possibilities. It is the connection of poverty with unfreedom that led Marx to argue passionately for the need to replace "the domination of circumstances and chance over individuals by the domination of individuals over chance and circumstances."[7]

The importance of freedom can be brought out also by considering other types of issues that are also central to human rights. Consider the freedom of immigrants to retain their ancestral cultural customs and lifestyles. This complex subject cannot be adequately assessed without distinguishing between *doing* something and being free to do that thing. A strong argument can be constructed in favor of an immigrant's having the freedom to retain her ancestral lifestyle, but this must not be seen as an argument in favor of her pursuing that ancestral lifestyle whether she herself chooses that pursuit or not. The central issue, in this argument, is the person's freedom to choose how she should live—including the *opportunity* to pursue ancestral customs—and it cannot be turned into an argument for that person specifically pursuing those customs in particular, irrespective of the alternatives she has.[8] The importance of capability—reflecting opportunities—is central to this distinction.

The Process Aspect of Freedom and Information Pluralism

In the discussion so far I have been concentrating on what the capability perspective can do for a theory of justice or of human rights, but I would now like to turn to what it *cannot* do. While the idea of capability has considerable merit in the assessment of the opportunity aspect of freedom, it cannot possibly deal adequately with the process aspect of freedom, since capabilities are characteristics of individual advantages, and they fall short of telling us enough about the fairness or equity of the processes involved, or about the freedom of citizens to invoke and utilise procedures that are equitable.

The contrast of perspectives can be brought out with many different types of illustrations; let me choose a rather harsh example. It is, by now, fairly well established that, given symmetric care, women tend to live longer than men. If one were concerned only with capabilities (and nothing else), and in particular with equality of the capability to live long, it would have been possible to construct an argument for giving men more medical attention than women to counteract the natural masculine handicap. But giving women less medical attention than men for the same health problems would clearly violate an important requirement of process equity, and it seems reasonable to argue, in cases of this kind, that demands of equity in process freedom could sensibly override a single-minded concentration on the opportunity aspect of freedom (and on the requirements of capability equality in particular). While it is important to emphasise the relevance of the capability perspective in judging people's substantive opportunities (particularly in comparison with alternative approaches that focus on incomes, or primary goods, or resources), that point does not, in any way, go against seeing the relevance also of the process aspect of freedom in a theory of human rights—or, for that matter, in a theory of justice.

In this context, I should comment briefly also on a misinterpretation of the general relevance of the capability perspective in a theory of justice. A theory of justice—or more generally an adequate theory of normative social choice—has to be alive both to the fairness of the processes involved and to the equity and efficiency of the substantive opportunities that people can enjoy.[9] In dealing with the latter, capability can indeed provide a very helpful perspective, in comparison with, say, the Rawlsian concentration on 'primary goods.' But capability can hardly serve as the sole informational basis for the *other* considerations, related to processes, that must also be accommodated in normative social choice theory.

Consider the different components of Rawls's (1971) theory of justice. Rawls's 'first principle' of justice involves the priority of liberty, and the first part of the 'second principle' involves process fairness, through demanding that 'positions and offices be open to all.' The force and cogency of these Rawlsian concerns (underlying his first principle and the first part of the second principle) can neither be ignored nor be adequately addressed through relying only on the informational base of capabilities. We may not agree with Rawls's own way of dealing with these issues, but these issues have to be addressed, and they cannot be sensibly addressed within the substantive boundaries of capability accounting.

On the other hand, the capability perspective comes into its own in dealing with the *remainder* of the second principle; namely, 'the Difference Principle'—a principle that is particularly concerned with the distribution of advantages that different people enjoy (a consideration that Rawls tried to capture, I believe inadequately, within the confines of the accounting of 'primary goods'). The territory that Rawls reserved for primary goods, as used in his Difference Principle, would

indeed, I argue, be better served by the capability perspective. That does not, however, obliterate in any way the relevance of the rest of the territory of justice (related to the first principle and the first part of the second principle), in which process considerations, including liberty and procedural equity, figure.

A similar plurality of informational base has to be invoked in dealing with the multiplicity of considerations that underlie a theory of human rights. Capabilities and the opportunity aspect of freedom, important as they are, have to be supplemented by considerations of fair processes and the lack of violation of people's right to invoke and utilize them.

Listing Capabilities

I turn now to the controversial question of the listing of capabilities. In its application, the capability approach allows considerable variations in application. Martha Nussbaum has discussed powerfully the advantages of identifying an overarching 'list of capabilities,' with given priorities. My own reluctance to join the search for such a canonical list arises partly from my difficulty in seeing how the exact lists and weights would be chosen without appropriate specification of the context of their use (which could vary), but also from a disinclination to accept any substantive diminution of the domain of public reasoning. The framework of capabilities helps, in my judgment, to clarify and illuminate the subject matter of public reasoning, which can involve epistemic issues (including claims of objective importance) as well as ethical and political ones. It cannot, I would argue, sensibly aim at displacing the need for continued public reasoning.

Indeed, I would submit that one of the uses of the capability perspective is to bring out the need for transparent valuational scrutiny of individual advantages and adversities, since the different *functionings* have to be assessed and weighted in relation to each other, and the opportunities of having different *combinations* of functionings also have to be evaluated.[10] The richness of the capability perspective broadly interpreted, thus, includes its insistence on the need for open valuational scrutiny for making social judgments, and in this sense it fits in well with the importance of public reasoning. This openness of transparent valuation contrasts with burying the evaluative exercise in some mechanical—and valuationally opaque—convention (e.g. by taking market-evaluated income to be the invariable standard of individual advantage, thereby giving implicit normative priority to institutionally determined market prices).

The problem is not with listing important capabilities, but with insisting on one predetermined canonical list of capabilities, chosen by theorists without any general social discussion or public reasoning. To have such a fixed list, emanating entirely from pure theory, is to deny the possibility of fruitful public participation on what should be included and why.

I have, of course, discussed various lists of capabilities that would seem to demand attention in theories of justice and more generally in social assessment, such as the freedom to be well nourished, to live disease-free lives, to be able to move around, to be educated, to participate in public life, and so on. Indeed, right from my first writings on using the capability perspective (for example, the 1979 Tanner Lecture 'Equality of what?'; Sen, 1980), I have tried to discuss the relevance of specific capabilities that are important in a particular exercise. The 1979 Tanner Lecture went into the relevance of "the ability to move about" (I discussed why disabilities can be a central concern in a way that an income-centered approach may not be able to grasp), along with other basic capabilities, such as "the ability to meet one's nutritional requirements, the wherewithal to be clothed and sheltered, the power to participate in the social life of the community." The contrast between lists of capabilities and commodities was a central concern

in *Commodities and Capabilities* (Sen, 1985a). The relevance of many capabilities that are often neglected were discussed in my second set of Tanner Lectures, given at Cambridge University under the title *The Standard of Living* (Hawthorn, 1987).

My skepticism is about fixing a cemented list of capabilities that is seen as being absolutely complete (nothing could be added to it) and totally fixed (it could not respond to public reasoning and to the formation of social values). I am a great believer in theory, and certainly accept that a good theory of evaluation and assessment has to bring out the relevance of what we are free to do and free to be (the capabilities in general), as opposed to the material goods we have and the commodities we can command. But I must also argue that pure theory cannot 'freeze' a list of capabilities for all societies for all time to come, irrespective of what the citizens come to understand and value. That would be not only a denial of the reach of democracy, but also a misunderstanding of what pure theory can do, completely divorced from the particular social reality that any particular society faces.

Along with the exercise of listing the relevant capabilities, there is also the problem of determining the relative weights and importance of the different capabilities included in the relevant list. Even with a given list, the question of valuation cannot be avoided. There is sometimes a temptation not only to have one fixed list, but also to have the elements of the list ordered in a lexicographic way. But this can hardly work. For example, the ability to be well-nourished cannot in general be put invariably *above* or *below* the ability to be well-sheltered (with the implication that the tiniest improvement of the higher ranked capability will always count as more important than a large change in the lower ranked one). The judgment must take into account the extent to which the different abilities are being realized or violated. Also, the weighting must be contingent on circumstances. We may have to give priority to the ability to be well-nourished when people are dying of hunger in their homes, whereas the freedom to be sheltered may rightly receive more weight when people are in general well-fed, but lack shelter and protection from the elements.

Some of the basic capabilities (with which my 1979 Tanner Lecture was particularly concerned) will no doubt figure in every list of relevant capabilities in every society. But the exact list to be used will have to take note of the purpose of the exercise. There is often good sense in narrowing the coverage of capabilities for a specific purpose. Jean Drèze and I have tried to invoke such lists of elementary capabilities in dealing with 'hunger and public action,' and in a different context, in dealing with India's economic and social achievements and failures (Drèze and Sen, 1989, 2002). I see Martha Nussbaum's powerful use of a given list of capabilities for some minimal rights against deprivation as being extremely useful, in the same practical way. For another practical purpose, we may need quite a different list.

For example, when my friend Mahbub ul Haq asked me, in 1989, to work with him on indicators of human development, and in particular to help develop a general index for global assessment and critique, it was clear to me that we were involved in a particular exercise of specific relevance. So the 'Human Development Index' was based on a very minimal listing of capabilities, with a particular focus on getting at a minimally basic quality of life, calculable from available statistics, in a way that the Gross National Product or Gross Domestic Product failed to capture (United Nations Development Programme, 1990). Lists of capabilities have to be used for various purposes, and so long as we understand what we are doing (and, in particular, that we are getting a list for a particular reason, related to assessment, evaluation, or critique), we do not put ourselves against other lists that may be relevant or useful for other purposes.

All this has to be contrasted with insisting on one 'final list of capabilities that matter.' To decide that some capability will not figure in the list of relevant capabilities at all amounts to putting a zero weight on that capability for every exercise, no matter what the exercise is concerned with, and no matter what the social conditions are. This could be very dogmatic, for many distinct reasons.

First, we use capabilities for different purposes. What we focus on cannot be independent of what we are doing and why (e.g. whether we are evaluating poverty, specifying certain basic human rights, getting a rough and ready measure of human development, and so on).

Second, social conditions and the priorities that they suggest may vary. For example, given the nature of poverty in India as well as the nature of available technology, it was not unreasonable in 1947 (when India became independent) to concentrate on elementary education, basic health, and so on, and to not worry too much about whether everyone can effectively communicate across the country and beyond. However, with the development of the internet and its wide-ranging applications, and the advance made in information technology (not least in India), access to the web and the freedom of general communication has become a very important capability that is of interest and relevance to all Indians.

Third, even with given social conditions, public discussion and reasoning can lead to a better understanding of the role, reach, and the significance of particular capabilities. For example, one of the many contributions of feminist economics has precisely been to bring out the importance of certain freedoms that were not recognized very clearly—or at all—earlier on; for example, freedom from the imposition of fixed and time-honored family roles, or immunity from implicit derogation through the rhetoric of social communication.

To insist on a 'fixed forever' list of capabilities would deny the possibility of progress in social understanding, and also go against the productive role of public discussion, social agitation, and open debates. I have nothing against the listing of capabilities (and take part in that activity often enough), but I have to stand up against any proposal of a grand mausoleum to one fixed and final list of capabilities.

Public Reasoning, Cultural Diversity, and Universality

I turn now to the final question. If the listing of capabilities must be subject to the test of public reasoning, how can we proceed in a world of differing values and disparate cultures? How can we judge the acceptability of claims to human rights and to relevant capabilities, and assess the challenges they may face? How would such a disputation—or a defence—proceed? I would argue that, like the assessment of other ethical claims, there must be some test of open and informed scrutiny, and it is to such a scrutiny that we have to look in order to proceed to a disavowal or an affirmation. The status that these ethical claims have must be ultimately dependent on their survivability in unobstructed discussion. In this sense, the viability of human rights is linked with what John Rawls has called 'public reasoning' and its role in 'ethical objectivity.'[11]

Indeed, the role of public reasoning in the formulation and vindication of human rights is extremely important to understand. Any general plausibility that these ethical claims—or their denials—have is, on this theory, dependent on their ability to survive and flourish when they encounter unobstructed discussion and scrutiny (along with adequately wide informational availability). The force of a claim for a human right would be seriously undermined if it were possible to show that they are unlikely to survive open public scrutiny. But contrary to a commonly offered reason for skepticism and rejection, the case for human rights cannot be discarded simply by pointing to the possibility that in politically and socially repressive regimes, which do not allow open public discussion, many of these human rights are not taken seriously at all.

Open critical scrutiny is essential for dismissal as well as for defence. The fact that monitoring of violations of human rights and the procedure of 'naming and shaming' can be so effective (at least, in putting the violators on the defensive) is some indication of the wide reach of public reasoning when information becomes available and ethical arguments are allowed rather than suppressed.

It is, however, important not to keep the domain of public reasoning confined to a given society only, especially in the case of human rights, in view of the inescapably universalist nature of these rights. This is in contrast with Rawls's inclination, particularly in his later works, to limit such public confrontation within the boundaries of each particular nation (or each 'people,' as Rawls calls this regional collectivity), for determining what would be just, at least in domestic affairs.[12] We can demand, on the contrary, that the discussion has to include, even for domestic justice (if only to avoid parochial prejudices and to examine a broader range of counter-arguments), views also from 'a certain distance.' The necessity of this was powerfully identified by Adam Smith:

> We can never survey our own sentiments and motives, we can never form any judgment concerning them; unless we remove ourselves, as it were, from our own natural station, and endeavour to view them as at a certain distance from us. But we can do this in no other way than by endeavouring to view them with the eyes of other people, or as other people are likely to view them.[13]

Questions are often raised about whether distant people can, in fact, provide useful scrutiny of local issues, given what are taken to be 'uncrossable' barriers of culture. One of Edmund Burke's criticisms of the French declaration of the 'rights of man' and its universalist spirit was concerned with disputing the acceptability of that notion in other cultures. Burke argued that "the liberties and the restrictions vary with times and circumstances, and admit of infinite modifications, that cannot be settled upon any abstract rule."[14] The belief that the universality that is meant to underlie the notion of human rights is profoundly mistaken has, for this reason, found expression in many other writings as well.

A belief in uncrossable barriers between the values of different cultures has surfaced and resurfaced repeatedly over the centuries, and they are forcefully articulated today. The claim of magnificent uniqueness—and often of superiority—has sometimes come from critics of 'Western values,' varying from champions of regional ethics (well illustrated by the fuss in the 1990s about the peerless excellence of 'Asian values'), or religious or cultural separatists (with or without being accompanied by fundamentalism of one kind or another). Sometimes, however, the claim of uniqueness has come from Western particularists. A good example is Samuel Huntington's (1996) insistence that the "West was West long before it was modern," and his claim that "a sense of individualism and a tradition of individual rights and liberties" are "unique among civilized societies." Similarly, no less a historian of ideas than Gertrude Himmelfarb has argued that ideas of 'justice,' 'right,' 'reason,' and 'love of humanity' are "predominantly, perhaps even uniquely, Western values" (1996, pp. 74–75).

I have discussed these diagnoses elsewhere (for example Sen, 1999). Contrary to cultural stereotypes, the histories of different countries in the world have shown considerable variations over time as well as between different groups within the same country. When, in the twelfth century, the Jewish philosopher Maimonides had to flee an intolerant Europe and its Inquisitions to try to safeguard his human right to stick to his own religious beliefs and practice, he sought shelter in Emperor Saladin's Egypt (via Fez and Palestine),

and found an honored position in the court of this Muslim emperor. Several hundred years later, when, in Agra, the Moghal emperor of India, Akbar, was arguing—and legislating—on the government's duty to uphold the right to religious freedom of all citizens, the European Inquisitions were still going on, and Giordano Bruno was burnt at the stake in Rome, in 1600.

In his autobiography, *Long Walk to Freedom*, Nelson Mandela (1994, p. 21) describes how he learned about democracy and individual rights, as a young boy, by seeing the proceedings of the local meetings held in the regent's house in Mqhekezweni:

> Everyone who wanted to speak did so. It was democracy in its purest form. There may have been a hierarchy of importance among the speakers, but everyone was heard, chief and subject, warrior and medicine man, shopkeeper and farmer, landowner and laborer.

Not only are the differences on the subject of freedoms and rights that actually exist between different societies often much exaggerated, but also there is, typically, little note taken of substantial variations *within* each local culture—over time and even at a point of time (in particular, right now). What are taken to be 'foreign' criticisms often correspond to internal criticisms from non-mainstream groups.[15] If, say, Iranian dissidents are imprisoned by an authoritarian regime precisely because of their heterodoxy, any suggestion that they should be seen as 'ambassadors of Western values' rather than as 'Iranian dissidents' would only add serious insult to manifest injury. Being culturally non-partisan requires respecting the participation of people from any corner of the earth, which is not the same thing as accepting the prevailing priorities, especially among dominant groups in particular societies, when information is extremely restricted and discussions and disagreements are not permitted.

Scrutiny from a 'distance' may have something to offer in the assessment of practices as different from each other as the stoning of adulterous women in the Taliban's Afghanistan and the abounding use of capital punishment (sometimes with mass jubilation) in parts of the United States. This is the kind of issue that made Smith insist that "the eyes of the rest of mankind" must be invoked to understand whether "a punishment appears equitable."[16] Ultimately, the discipline of critical moral scrutiny requires, among other things, "endeavoring to view [our sentiments and beliefs] with the eyes of other people, or as other people are likely to view them" (*The Theory of Moral Sentiments*, III, 1, 2; in Smith, 1976, p. 110).

Intellectual interactions across the borders can be as important in rich societies as they are in poorer ones. The point to note here is not so much whether we are *allowed* to chat across borders and to make cross-boundary scrutiny, but that the discipline of critical assessment of moral sentiments—no matter how locally established they are—*requires* that we view our practices *inter alia* from a certain distance.

Both the understanding of human rights and of the adequacy of a list of basic capabilities, I would argue, are intimately linked with the reach of public discussion—between persons and across borders. The viability and universality of human rights and of an acceptable specification of capabilities are dependent on their ability to survive open critical scrutiny in public reasoning.

Conclusions

To conclude, the two concepts—human rights and capabilities—go well with each other, so long as we do not try to subsume either entirely within the other. There are many human rights for which the capability perspective has much to offer. However, human rights to important process freedoms cannot be adequately analyzed within the capability approach.

Furthermore, both human rights and capabilities have to depend on the process of public reasoning, which neither can lose without serious impoverishment of its respective intellectual content. The methodology of public scrutiny draws on Rawlsian understanding of 'objectivity' in ethics, but the impartiality that is needed cannot be confined within the borders of a nation. We have to go much beyond Rawls for that reason, just as we also have to go beyond the enlightenment provided by his use of 'primary goods,' and invoke, in that context, the more articulate framework of capabilities. The need for extension does not, of course, reduce our debt to John Rawls. Neither human rights nor capabilities would have been easy to understand without his pioneering departures.

NOTES

1. See Sen (2002a), particularly the Arrow Lectures ('Freedom and Social Choice') included there (essays 20–22).
2. An investigation of more complex features of the opportunity aspect and the process aspect of freedoms can be found in the Arrow Lectures ('Freedom and Social Choice') in Sen (2002a, essays 20–22).
3. On the concept of capability, see Sen (1980, 1985a, 1985b), Nussbaum and Sen (1993), and Nussbaum (2000). See also the related theories of substantial opportunities developed by Arneson (1989), Cohen (1989), and Roemer (1996), among other contributions.
4. The relevance of such parametric variability for a theory of justice is discussed in Sen (1990).
5. See Okin (2003, p. 293). On related issues see also Joshua Cohen (1994, especially pp. 278–80), and G. A. Cohen (1995, especially pp. 120–25).
6. See Sen (1980, 1985a, 1985b). In contrast, G. A. Cohen has presented arguments in favor of focusing on achieved functionings—related to his concept of 'midfare'—rather than on capability (see Cohen, 1989, 1993).
7. See Marx (1845–1846/1977, p. 190).
8. There is a substantial difference between: (1) valuing multiculturalism because of the way—and to the extent that—it enhances the freedoms of the people involved to choose to live as they would like (and have reason to like); and (2) valuing cultural diversity *per se*, which focuses on the descriptive characteristics of a social pattern, rather than on the freedoms of the people involved. The contrast receives investigation in the *Human Development Report 2004* (United Nations Development Programme, 2004).

9. On the plurality of concerns that include processes as well as opportunities, which is inescapably involved in normative social choice (including theories of justice), see Sen (1970, 1985b). Since I have often encountered the diagnosis that I propound a "capability-based theory of justice," I should make it clear that this could be true only in the very limited sense of naming something according to one *principal* part of it (comparable with, say, using England for Britain). It is only one part of the informational base of a theory of justice that the capability perspective can expect to fill.

10. I cannot emphasise adequately how important I believe it is to understand that the need for an explicit valuational exercise is an advantage, rather than a limitation, of the capability approach, because valuational decisions have to be explicitly discussed, rather than being derived from some mechanical formula that is used, without scrutiny and assessment. For arguments *against* my position on this issue, see Beitz (1986) and Williams (1987). My own position is more fully discussed in Sen (1999, 2004).

11. See Rawls (1971, 1993, especially pp. 110–13).

12. See particularly John Rawls (1999). See also Rawls's formulation of the original position in *Political Liberalism* (Rawls, 1993, p. 12): "I assume that the basic structure is that of a closed society: that is, we are to regard it as self-contained and as having no relations with other societies. . . . That a society is closed is a considerable abstraction, justified only because it enables us to focus on certain main questions free from distracting details."

13. See Smith (1759/1790, III, 1, 2). Smith (1976, p. 110). I have tried to discuss and extend the Smithian perspective on moral reasoning in Sen (2002b).

14. Quoted in Lukes (1997, p. 238).

15. On this see Nussbaum and Sen (1988).

16. Smith (1978/1982, p. 104).

REFERENCES

Arneson, R. (1989) 'Equality and equal opportunity for welfare,' *Philosophical Studies*, 56, pp. 77–93.

Beitz, C. (1986) 'Amartya Sen's resources, values and development,' *Economics and Philosophy*, 2, pp. 282–90.

Bentham, J. (1792) *Anarchical Fallacies; Being an Examination of the Declaration of Rights Issued during the French Revolution* [Republished in J. Bowring (Ed.) (1843) *The Works of Jeremy Bentham*, volume II, William Talt, Edinburgh].

Cohen, G.A. (1989) 'On the currency of egalitarian Justice,' *Ethics*, 99, pp. 906–44.

Cohen, G.A. (1993) 'Equality of what? On welfare, resources and capabilities,' in M. Nussbaum and A. Sen (Eds.), *The Quality of Life*, Clarendon Press, Oxford.

Cohen, G.A. (1995) 'Review: Amartya Sen's unequal world,' *The New Left Review*, January, pp. 117–29.

Cohen, J. (1994) 'Review of Sen's *Inequality Reexamined*,' *Journal of Philosophy*, 92, pp. 275–88.

Drèze, J. and Sen, A. (1989) *Hunger and Public Action*, Clarendon Press, Oxford.

Drèze, J. and Sen, A. (2002) *India: Participation and Development*, Oxford University Press, Delhi.

Hawthorn, G. (Ed.) (1987) *Amartya Sen et al., The Standard of Living*, Cambridge University Press, Cambridge.

Himmelfarb, G. (1996) 'The illusions of cosmopolitanism,' in M. Nussbaum with respondents (Ed.), *For Love of Country*, Beacon Press, Boston.

Huntington, S. (1996) *The Clash of Civilizations and the Remaking of World Order*, Simon and Schuster, New York.

Lukes, S. (1997) 'Five fables about human rights,' in M. Ishay (Ed.), *The Human Rights Reader*, Routledge, London.

Mandela, N. (1994) *Long Walk to Freedom*, Little, Brown & Co., Boston.

Marx, K. (1845–1846) *The German Ideology*, with F. Engels [Republished in D. McLellan (Ed.) (1977) *Karl Marx: Selected Writings*, Oxford University Press, Oxford].

Nussbaum, M. (2000) *Women and Human Development: The Capabilities Approach*, Cambridge University Press, Cambridge.

Nussbaum, M. and Sen, A. (1988) 'Internal criticism and Indian rationalist traditions,' in M. Krausz (Ed.), *Relativism: Interpretation and Confrontation*, University of Notre Dame Press, Notre Dame.

Nussbaum, M. and Sen, A. (Eds.) (1993) *The Quality of Life*, Clarendon Press, Oxford.

Okin, S. (2003) 'Poverty, well-being and gender: what counts, who's heard?,' *Philosophy and Public Affairs*, 31, pp. 280–316.

Rawls, J. (1971) *A Theory of Justice*, Harvard University Press, Cambridge, MA.

Rawls, J. (1993) *Political Liberalism*, Columbia University Press, New York.

Rawls, J. (1999) *The Law of Peoples*, Harvard University Press, Cambridge, MA.

Roemer, J.E. (1996) *Theories of Distributive Justice*, Harvard University Press, Cambridge, MA.

Sen, A. (1970) *Collective Choice and Social Welfare*, Holden-Day, San Francisco [Republished by North-Holland, Amsterdam].

Sen, A. (1980) 'Equality of what?,' in S. McMurrin (Ed.), *Tanner Lectures on Human Values*, volume I, Cambridge University Press, Cambridge; University of Utah Press, Cambridge.

Sen, A. (1985a) *Commodities and Capabilities*, North-Holland, Amsterdam.

Sen, A. (1985b) 'Well-being, agency and freedom: the Dewey Lectures 1984,' *Journal of Philosophy*, 82, pp. 169–221.

Sen, A. (1985/1987) *The Standard of Living*, Tanner Lectures, Cambridge University Press, Cambridge.

Sen, A. (1990) 'Justice: means versus freedoms,' *Philosophy and Public Affairs*, 19, pp. 111–21.

Sen, A. (1999) *Development as Freedom*, Knopf, New York; Oxford University Press, New York.

Sen, A. (2002a) *Rationality and Freedom*, Harvard University Press, Cambridge, MA.

Sen, A. (2002b) 'Open and closed impartiality,' *The Journal of Philosophy*, 99, pp. 445–69.

Sen, A. (2004) 'Elements of a theory of human rights,' *Philosophy and Public Affairs*, 32(4), pp. 315–56.

Smith, A. (1759/1790/1976) *The Theory of Moral Sentiments*, revised edition 1790 [Republished by Clarendon Press, Oxford].

Smith, A. (1776/1979) *An Inquiry into the Nature and Causes of the Wealth of Nations*, Clarendon Press, Oxford [Reprinted by Liberty Press, 1981].

Smith, A. (1978/1982) in R. L. Meek, D. D. Raphael and P. G. Stein (Eds.), *Lectures on Jurisprudence*, Clarendon Press, Oxford [Reprinted by Liberty Press, Indianapolis].

United Nations Development Programme (1990) *Human Development Report 1990,* Oxford University Press, Oxford.

United Nations Development Programme (2004) *Human Development Report 2004*, Oxford University Press, Oxford.

Williams, B. (1987) 'The standard of living: interests and capabilities,' in G. Hawthorn (Ed.), *Amartya Sen et al., The Standard of Living*, Cambridge University Press, Cambridge.

Jack Donnelly

HUMAN RIGHTS AND CULTURAL RELATIVISM

Cultural relativity is an undeniable fact; moral rules and social institutions evidence astonishing cultural and historical variability. The doctrine of cultural relativism holds that some such variations cannot be legitimately criticized by outsiders. I argue, instead, for a fundamentally universalistic approach to internationally recognized human rights.

In most recent discussions of cultures or civilizations[1]—whether they are seen as clashing, converging, or conversing—the emphasis has been on differences, especially differences between the West and the rest. From a broad cross-cultural or intercivilizational perspective, however, the most striking fact about human rights in the contemporary world is the extensive overlapping consensus on the Universal Declaration of Human Rights. * * * Real conflicts do indeed exist over a few internationally recognized human rights. There are numerous variations in interpretations and modes of implementing internationally recognized human rights. Nonetheless, I argue that culture[2] poses only a modest challenge to the contemporary normative universality of human rights.

1. Defining Cultural Relativism

When internal and external judgments of a practice diverge, cultural relativists give priority to the internal judgments of a society. In its most extreme form, what we can call *radical cultural relativism* holds that culture is the sole source of the validity of a moral right or rule.[3] *Radical universalism*, by contrast, would hold that culture is irrelevant to the (universal) validity, of moral rights and rules. The body of the continuum defined by these end points can be roughly divided into what we can call strong and weak cultural relativism.

Strong cultural relativism holds that culture is the principal source of the validity of a right or rule. At its furthest extreme, strong cultural relativism accepts a few basic rights with virtually universal application but allows such a wide range of variation that two entirely justifiable sets of rights might overlap only slightly.

Weak cultural relativism, which might also be called strong universalism, considers culture a secondary source of the validity of a right or rule. Universality is initially presumed, but the relativity of human nature, communities, and rules checks potential excesses of universalism. At its furthest extreme, weak cultural relativism recognizes a comprehensive set of prima facie universal human rights but allows limited local variations.

We can also distinguish a qualitative dimension to relativist claims. Legitimate cultural divergences from international human rights norms might be advocated concerning the *substance* of lists of human rights, the *interpretation* of particular rights, and the *form* in which those rights are implemented. * * * I will defend a weak cultural relativist (strong universalist) position that permits deviations from international human

From Jack Donnelly, *Universal Human Rights in Theory and Practice* (Ithaca: Cornell University Press, 2003), chap. 6, 89–106.

rights norms primarily at the level of form or implementation.

2. Relativity and Universality: A Necessary Tension

Beyond the obvious dangers of moral imperialism, radical universalism requires a rigid hierarchical ordering of the multiple moral communities to which we belong. The radical universalist would give absolute priority to the demands of the cosmopolitan moral community over other ("lower") communities. Such a complete denial of national and subnational ethical autonomy, however, is rare and implausible. There is no compelling moral reason why peoples cannot accept, say, the nation-state, as a major locus of extrafamilial moral and political commitments. And at least certain choices of a variety of moral communities demand respect from outsiders—not uncritical acceptance, let alone emulation, but, in some cases at least, tolerance.

But if human rights are based in human nature, on the fact that one is a human being, how can human rights be relative in any fundamental way? The simple answer is that human nature is itself relative. * * * There is a sense in which this is true even biologically. For example, if marriage partners are chosen on the basis of cultural preferences for certain physical attributes, the gene pool in a community may be altered. More important, culture can significantly influence the presence and expression of many aspects of human nature by encouraging or discouraging the development or perpetuation of certain personality traits and types. Whether we stress the "unalterable" core or the variability around it—and however we judge their relative size and importance—"human nature," the realized nature of real human beings, is as much a social project as a natural given.

But if human nature were infinitely variable, or if all moral values were determined solely by culture (as radical cultural relativism holds), there could be no human rights (rights that one has "simply as a human being") because the concept "human being" would have no specificity or moral significance. As we saw in the case of Hindu India, * * * some societies have not even recognized "human being" as a descriptive category. The very names of many cultures mean simply "the people" (e.g., Hopi, Arapahoe), and their origin myths define them as separate from outsiders, who are somehow "not-human."

Such views, however, are almost universally rejected in the contemporary world. For example, chattel slavery and caste-based legal and political systems, which implicitly deny the existence of a morally significant common humanity, are almost universally condemned, even in the most rigid class societies.

The radical relativist response that consensus is morally irrelevant is logically impeccable. But many people do believe that such consensus strengthens a rule, and most think that it increases the justifiability of certain sorts of international action. In effect, a moral analogue to customary international law seems to operate. If a practice is nearly universal and generally perceived as obligatory, it is required of all members of the community. Even a weak cosmopolitan moral community imposes substantive limitations on the range of permissible moral variation.

Notice, however, that I contend only that there are a few cross-culturally valid moral *values*. This still leaves open the possibility of a radical cultural relativist denial of human *rights*. Plausible arguments can be (and have been) advanced to justify alternative mechanisms to guarantee human dignity. But few states today attempt such an argument. In all regions of the world, a strong commitment to human *rights* is almost universally proclaimed. Even where practice throws that commitment into question, such a widespread rhetorical "fashion" must have some substantive basis.

That basis * * * lies in the hazards to human dignity posed by modern markets and states. The political power of traditional rulers usually was substantially limited by customs and laws that were entirely independent of human rights. The relative technological and administrative weakness of traditional political institutions further restrained abuses of power. In such a world, inalienable entitlements of individuals held against state and society might plausibly be held to be superfluous (because dignity was guaranteed by alternative mechanisms), if not positively dangerous to important and well-established values and practices.

Such a world, however, exists today only in a relatively small number of isolated areas. The modern state, even in the Third World, not only has been freed from many of the moral constraints of custom but also has a far greater administrative and technological reach. It thus represents a serious threat to basic human dignity, whether that dignity is defined in "traditional" or "modern" terms. In such circumstances, human rights seem necessary rather than optional. Radical or unrestricted relativism thus is as inappropriate as radical universalism.[4] Some kind of intermediate position is required.

3. Internal versus External Judgments

Respect for autonomous moral communities would seem to demand a certain deference to a society's internal evaluations of its practices, but to commit ourselves to acting on the basis of the moral judgments of others would abrogate our own moral responsibilities. The choice between internal and external evaluations is a moral one, and whatever choice we make will be problematic.

Where internal and external judgments conflict, assessing the relative importance attached to those judgments may be a reasonable place to start in seeking to resolve them. Figure 10.1 offers a simple typology.

Case 1—morally unimportant both externally and internally—is uninteresting. Whether or not one maintains one's initial external condemnation is of little intrinsic interest to anyone. Case 2—externally unimportant, internally very important—is probably best handled by refusing to press the negative external judgment. To press a negative external judgment that one feels is relatively unimportant when the issue is of great importance internally usually will be, at best insensitive. By the same token, Case 3—externally very important, internally unimportant—presents the best occasion to press an external judgment (with some tact).

Case 4, in which the practice is of great moral importance to both sides, is the most difficult to handle, but even here we may have good reasons to press a negative external judgment. Consider, for example, slavery. Most people today would agree that no matter how ancient and well established the practice may be, to turn one's back on the enslavement of human beings in the name of cultural relativity would reflect moral obtuseness, not sensitivity. Human sacrifice, trial by ordeal, extrajudicial execution, and female infanticide are other cultural practices that are (in my view rightly) condemned by almost all external observers today.

Underlying such judgments is the inherent universality of basic moral precepts, at least as we understand morality in the West. We simply do not believe that our moral precepts are for us and us alone. This is most evident in Kant's deontological universalism. But it is no less true of the principle of utility. And, of course, human rights are also inherently universal.

Figure 10.1. Type Conflicts over Culturally Relative Practices

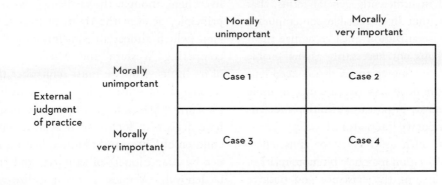

In any case, our moral precepts are *our* moral precepts. As such, they demand our obedience. To abandon them simply because others reject them is to fail to give proper weight to our own moral beliefs (at least where they involve central moral precepts such as the equality of all human beings and the protection of innocents).

Finally, no matter how firmly someone else, or even a whole culture, believes differently, at some point—slavery and untouchability come to mind—we simply must say that those contrary beliefs are wrong. Negative external judgments may be problematic. In some cases, however, they are not merely permissible but demanded.

4. Concepts, Interpretations, Implementations

In evaluating arguments of cultural relativism, we must distinguish between variations in substance, interpretation, and form. Even very weak cultural relativists—that is, strong universalists—are likely to allow considerable variation in the form in which

rights are implemented. For example, whether free legal assistance is required by the right to equal protection of the laws usually will best be viewed as largely beyond the legitimate reach of universal standards. Important differences between strong and weak relativists are likely to arise, however, at the levels of interpretation and, especially, substance.

A. Substance or Concept

The Universal Declaration generally formulates rights at the level of what I will call the *concept*, an abstract, general statement of an orienting value. "Everyone has the right to work, to free choice of employment, to just and favorable conditions of work and to protection against unemployment" (Art. 23). *Only* at this level do I claim that there is a consensus on the rights of the Universal Declaration, and at this level, most appeals to cultural relativism fail.

It is difficult to imagine arguments against recognizing the rights of Articles 3–12, which include life, liberty, and security of the person; the guarantee of legal personality, equality before the law, and privacy, and protections against slavery, arbitrary arrest, detention, or exile, and inhuman or degrading treatment. These are so clearly connected to basic requirements of human dignity, and are stated in sufficiently general terms, that virtually every morally defensible contemporary form of social organization must recognize them (although perhaps not necessarily as inalienable rights). I am even tempted to say that conceptions of human nature or society that are incompatible with such rights are almost by definition indefensible in contemporary international society.

Civil rights such as freedom of conscience, speech, and association may be a bit more relative. Because they assume the existence and positive evaluation of relatively autonomous individuals, they may be of questionable applicability in strong, thriving traditional communities. In such communities, however, they would rarely be at issue. If traditional practices truly are based on and protect culturally accepted conceptions of human dignity, then members of such a community will not have the desire or the need to claim such rights. In the more typical contemporary case, however, in which relatively autonomous individuals face modern states, it is hard for me to imagine a defensible conception of human dignity that does not include almost all of these rights. A similar argument can be made for the economic and social rights of the Universal Declaration.

In twenty years of working with issues of cultural relativism, I have developed a simple test that I pose to skeptical audiences. Which rights in the Universal Declaration, I ask, does your society or culture reject? Rarely has a single full right (other than the right to private property) been rejected. Never has it been suggested to me that as many as four should be eliminated.

Typical was the experience I had in Iran in early 2001, where I posed this question to three different audiences. In each case, discussion moved quickly to freedom of religion, and in particular atheism and apostasy by Muslims (which the Universal Declaration permits but Iran prohibits).[5] Given

the continuing repression of Iranian Bahais—although, for the moment at least, the apparent end to executions—this was quite a sensitive issue. Even here, though, the challenge was not to the principle, or even the right, of freedom of religion (which almost all Muslims support) but to competing "Western" and "Muslim" conceptions of its limits. And we must remember that *every* society places some limits on religious liberty. In the United States, for example, recent court cases have dealt with forced medical treatment for the children of Christian Scientists, live animal sacrifice by practitioners of santaria, and the rights of Jehovah's Witnesses to evangelize at private residences.

We must be careful, however, not to read too much into this consensus at the level of the concept, which may obscure important disagreements concerning definitions and implicit limitations. Consider Article 5 of the Universal Declaration: "No one shall be subjected to torture or to cruel, inhuman or degrading treatment or punishment." The real controversy comes over definitions of terms such as "cruel." Is the death penalty cruel, inhuman, or degrading? Most European states consider it to be. The United States does not. We must recognize and address such differences without overstating their importance or misrepresenting their character.

Implicit limits on rights may also pose challenges to universalist arguments. Most of the rights in the Universal Declaration are formulated in categorical terms. For example, Article 19 begins: "Everyone has the right to freedom of opinion and expression." To use the hackneyed American example, this does not mean that one can scream "Fire!" in a crowded theater. All rights have limits.[6] But if these limits differ widely and systematically across civilizations, the resulting differences in human rights practices might indeed be considerable.

Are there systematic differences in definitions of terms across civilizations? Do cultures differ systematically in the standard limits they put on the exercises of rights? And if these differences are systematic, how significant are they? I have suggested that the answers to these questions are largely negative. For reasons of space—as well as the fact that such negative arguments cannot be conclusively established—I leave this claim as a challenge. Critics may refute my argument with several well-chosen examples of substantial cultural variation either at the level of concepts or in systematic variations at the level of interpretation that undermine the apparent conceptual consensus. So far, at least, I have not encountered anyone capable of presenting such a pattern of contradictory evidence, except in the case of small and relatively isolated communities.[7]

B. Interpretations

What ought to count, for example, as adequate protection against unemployment? Does it mean a guaranteed job, or is it enough to provide compensation to those who are unemployed? Both seem to me plausible interpretations. Some such variations in interpreting rights seem not merely defensible but desirable, and even necessary.

Particular human rights are like "essentially contested concepts," in which there is a substantial but rather general consensus on basic meaning coupled with no less important, systematic, and apparently irresolvable conflicts of interpretations (Gallie 1968). In such circumstances, culture provides one plausible and defensible mechanism for selecting interpretations (and forms).

We should also note that the Universal Declaration lists some rights that are best viewed as interpretations. For example, the right of free and full consent of intending spouses reflects an interpretation of marriage over which legitimate controversy is possible. Notice, however, that the right (as stated in Sec. 2 of Art. 16) is subordinate to the right to marry and to found a family (over which, at this highest level of generality, there is

little international dispute). Furthermore, some traditional customs, such as bride price, provide alternative protections for women that address at least some of the underlying concerns that gave rise to the norm of free and full consent.

I would suggest, however, that defensible variations in interpretations are likely to be relatively modest in number. And not all "interpretations" are equally plausible or defensible. They are *interpretations*, not free associations or arbitrary, let alone self-interested, stipulations. The meaning of, for example, "the right to political participation" is controversial, but an election in which a people were allowed to choose an absolute dictator for life ("one man, one vote, once," as a West African quip put it) is simply indefensible.

We must also note that considerable divergences in interpretation exist not only between but also *within* cultures or civilizations. Consider, for example, differences within the West between Europe and the United States on the death penalty and the welfare state. Japan and Vietnam have rather different interpretations of the rights to freedom of speech and association, despite being East Asians.

Even where there are variations between two cultures, we still need to ask whether culture in fact is the source of cause of these differences. I doubt that we are actually saying much of interest or importance when we talk of, say, Japan as Asian. Consider the common claim that Asian societies are communitarian and consensual and Western societies are individualistic and competitive. What exactly is this supposed to explain, or even refer to, in any particular Asian or Western country? Dutch or Norwegian politics is at least as consensual as Thai politics. The Dutch welfare state is in its own way as caring and paternalistic as the most traditional of Japanese employers. Such examples, which are easily multiplied, suggest that even where variations in practice exist, culture does much less explanatory work than most relativists suggest—or at least that the "culture" in question is more local or national rather than regional or a matter of civilization.

C. Implementation or Form

Just as concepts need to be interpreted, interpretations need to be implemented in law and political practice. To continue with the example of the right to work, what rate of unemployment compensation should be provided, for how long, in what circumstances? The range of actual and defensible variation here is considerable—although limited by the governing concept and interpretation.

Even a number of rights in the International Human Rights Covenants involve specifications at the level of form. For example, Article 10(2)(b) of the International Covenant on Civil and Political Rights requires the segregation of juvenile defendants. In some cultures the very notion of a juvenile criminal defendant (or a penitentiary system) does not exist. Although there are good reasons to suggest such rules, to demand them in the face of strong reasoned opposition seems to me to make little sense—so long as the underlying objectives are realized in some other fashion.

Differences in implementations, however, often seem to have little to do with culture. And even where they do, it is not obvious that cultural differences deserve more (or less) respect than differing implementations attributable to other causes (e.g., levels of economic development or unique national historical experiences).

I stress this three-level scheme to avoid a common misconception. My argument is for universality only at the level of the concept. The Universal Declaration insists that all states share a limited but important range of obligations. It is, in its own words, "a common standard of achievement for all peoples and all nations." The ways in which these rights are implemented, however, so long as they fall within the range of variation consistent with the overarching concept, are matters of legitimate variation. * * *

This is particularly important because most of the "hot button" issues in recent discussions have occurred at the level of implementation. For example, debates about pornography are about the limits—interpretation or implementation—of freedom of expression. Most Western countries permit the graphic depiction of virtually any sex act (so long as it does not involve and is not shown to children). Many other countries punish those who produce, distribute, or consume such material. This dispute, however, does not suggest a rejection of human rights, the idea of personal autonomy, or even the right to freedom of speech.

We should also note that controversy over pornography rages internally in many countries. Every country criminalizes some forms of pornography, and most countries—Taliban Afghanistan being the exception that proves the rule—permit some depictions of sexual behavior or the display of erotic images that another country has within living memory banned as pornographic. Wherever one draws the line, it leaves intact both the basic internationally recognized human right to freedom of speech and the underlying value of personal autonomy.

D. Universality within Diversity

There are at least three ways in which rights that vary in form and interpretation can still be plausibly described as "universal." First, and most important, there may be an overlapping consensus * * * on the substance of the list, despite diversity in interpretations and implementations. Second, even where there are differences at the level of substance or concept, a large common core may exist with relatively few differences "around the edges." Third, even where substantial substantive disagreements occur, we might still be justified in speaking of universal rights if there are strong statistical regularities and the outliers are few and clearly overshadowed by the central tendency.

In contemporary international society, I think that we can say that there are few far outliers (e.g., North Korea) at least at the level of agreed-on concepts. I would admit that overlapping conceptual consensus often is thin. Nonetheless, I think that we can fairly (although not without controversy) say that variations at the level of concepts are infrequent. Somewhat more contentious is the claim that I would also advance that the range of diversity in standard interpretations is modest and poses relatively few serious international political disputes.

We do not face an either-or choice between cultural relativism and universal human rights. Rather, we need to recognize both the universality of human rights and their particularity and thus accept a certain *limited* relativity, especially with respect to forms of implementation. We must take seriously the initially paradoxical idea of the relative universality of internationally recognized human rights.[8]

5. Explaining the Persistence of Culturalist Arguments

If my argument for relative universality is even close to correct, how can we explain the persistence of foundational appeals to culture? If we could explain this puzzle, both for the relativist arguments * * * and for the claims about human rights in traditional societies, * * * the plausibility of a universalist perspective would be enhanced. At least six explanations come to mind.

First, it is surprisingly common for even otherwise sophisticated individuals to take the particular institutions associated with the realization of a right in their country or culture to be essential to that right. Americans, in particular, seem to have unusually great difficulty in realizing that the way we do things here is not necessarily what international human rights norms require.

Second, narrow-minded and ham-handed (Western, and especially American) international human rights policies and statements exacerbate these confusions. Consider Michael Fay, an American teenager who vandalized hundreds of thousands of dollars worth of property in Singapore. When he was sentenced to be publicly caned, there was a furor in the United States. President Clinton argued, with apparently genuine indignation, that it was abominable to cane someone, but he failed to find it even notable that in his own country people are being fried in the electric chair. If this indeed is what universalism means—and I hasten to repeat that it is not—then of course relativism looks far more attractive.

The legacy of colonialism provides a third important explanation for the popularity of relativist arguments. African, Asian, and Muslim (as well as Latin American) leaders and citizens have vivid, sometimes personal, recollections of their sufferings under colonial masters. Even when the statements and actions of great powers stay within the range of the overlapping consensus on the Universal Declaration, there is understandable (although not necessarily justifiable) sensitivity to external pressure. (Compare the sensitivity of the United States to external criticism even in the absence of such a historical legacy.) When international pressures exceed the bounds of the overlapping consensus, that sensitivity often becomes (justifiably) very intense.

Fourth, arguments of relativism are often rooted in a desire to express and foster national, regional, cultural, or civilizational pride. It is no coincidence that the "Asian values" debate * * * took off in the wake of the Asian economic miracle and dramatically subsided after the 1977 financial crisis.

The belief that such arguments have instrumental efficacy in promoting internationally recognized human rights is a fifth important reason. For example, Daniel Bell plausibly argues that building human rights implementation strategies on local traditions (1) is "more likely to lead to long term commitment to human rights"; (2) "may shed light on the groups most likely to bring about desirable social and political change"; (3) "allows the human rights activist to draw on the most compelling justifications"; (4) "may shed light on the appropriate attitude to be employed by human rights activists"; and (5) "may also make one more sensitive to the possibility of alternative" mechanisms for protecting rights (1996: 657–59). I would insist only that we be clear that this is a practical, not a theoretical, argument; that we operate with a plausible theory of culture and an accurate understanding of the culture in question; and that we not assume that culture trumps international norms. "To realize greater social justice on an international scale, activists and intellectuals must take culture seriously, but not in the totalizing, undifferentiated way in which some leaders of non-Western nations have used it as a trump card" (L. Bell 2001: 21).

This leads to the sixth, and perhaps the most important, explanation for the prevalence of culturalist arguments, namely, that they are used by vicious elites as a way to attempt to deflect attention from their repressive policies. And well-meaning Westerners with a well-developed sense of the legacy of Western colonialism indirectly support such arguments when they shy away from criticizing arguments advanced by non-Westerners even when they are empirically inaccurate or morally absurd.

6. Culture and Politics

So far I have proceeded, in line with the standard assumption of cultural relativists, by treating "cultures" as homogenous, static, all-encompassing, and voluntarily accepted "things," the substance of which can be relatively easily and uncontroversially determined. None of these assumptions is defensible.

A. Identifying a "Culture"

Cultures are anything but homogenous. In fact, differences *within* civilizations often are as striking and as important as those between civilizations. "The Western tradition," for example, includes both Caligula and Marcus Aurelius, Francis of Assisi and Torquemada, Leopold II of Belgium and Albert Schweitzer, Jesus and Hitler—and just about everything in between.

We thus face a difficult problem even in determining what is to count as evidence for a claim of the form "civilization x holds belief y." Political authorities are but one (very problematic) source of evidence of the views and practices of a civilization. Nor can we rely on authoritative texts. For example, the Christian Bible has significantly shaped Western civilization. But even when particular practices do not diverge from what one might expect from reading this "foundational" text and setting aside the fact that such expectations change with time, place, and reader—few Western practices are adequately explained in terms of, let alone reducible to, those texts.[9]

Even the long-established practice of leading states may diverge significantly from the norms and values of the civilization of which they are a part. The United States, for example, is in many ways a very *atypical* Western country in its approach to economic and social rights. In characterizing and comparing civilizations, we must not mistake some particular expressions, however characteristic, for the whole. For example, Christianity and secularism are arguably equally important to modern Western civilization. And the balance between secular and religious forces, values, and orientations varies dramatically with time, place, and issue in "the West."

Such cautions are especially important because culturalist arguments regularly rely on appeals to a distant past, such as the precolonial African village, Native American tribes, and traditional Islamic societies. The traditional culture advanced to justify cultural relativism far too often no longer exists—if it ever did in the idealized form in which it is typically presented. In the Third World today we usually see not the persistence of "traditional" culture in the face of "modern" intrusions, or even the development of syncretic cultures and values, but rather disruptive "Westernization," rapid cultural change, or people enthusiastically embracing "modern" practices and values.[10] And the modern nation-states and contemporary nationalist regimes that have replaced traditional communities and practices cannot be judged by standards of a bygone era.

We must also be careful to distinguish "civilization" or "culture" from religion and politics. The United States is a state, a political entity, not a civilization. Islam is not a civilization but a religion, or, as many believers would put it, a true and comprehensive way of life that transcends culture or civilization. An "Islamic civilization"—centered on Mecca and running, say, from the Maghreb to the Indus—does not include all Muslims, or even all majority Muslim countries. The broader Muslim world, running from Dakar to Jakarta, may be an international political unit of growing interest or importance, but it certainly is not a culture or civilization. And tens of millions of Muslims live outside of even this community.

B. The Politics of Cultural Relativism

Cultures are not merely diverse but are contested. In fact, contemporary anthropologists increasingly depict "cultures" not as "things" but as sites of contestation. "Rather than simply a domain of sharing and commonality, culture figures here more as a site of difference and contestation, simultaneously ground and stake of a rich field of cultural-political practices" (Gupta and Ferguson 1997: 5).

Culture is usually viewed by the new cultural theorists as contested—a social context in which power struggles are constantly waged over the meaning and control of what Pierre Bourdieu has called "symbolic capital" as well as over more overtly material forms of wealth and power. In short, culture is not a given, but rather a congeries of ways of thinking, believing, and acting that are constantly in the state of being produced; it is contingent and always unstable, especially as the forces of "modernity" have barreled down upon most people throughout the world over the course of the twentieth century. (Bell, Nathan, and Peleg 2001: 11)

All forms of cultural relativism fundamentally fail to recognize culture as an ongoing historic and institutional process where the existence of a given custom does not mean that the custom is either adaptive, optimal, or consented to by a majority of its adherents. Culture is far more effectively characterized as an ongoing adaptation to a changing environment rather than as a static superorganic entity. In a changing environment, cultural practices routinely outlive their usefulness, and cultural values change either through internal dialogue within the cultural group or through cross-cultural influences. (Zechenter 1997: 332–33)

"Culture" is constructed through selective appropriations from a diverse and contested past and present. Those appropriations are rarely neutral in process, intent, or consequences. Cultural relativist arguments thus regularly obscure often troubling realities of power and politics.

Arguments of cultural relativism are far too often made by (or on behalf of) economic and political elites that have long since left traditional culture behind. Even when this represents an admirable effort to retain or recapture cherished traditional values, it is at least ironic to see "Westernized" elites warning against the values and practices they have adopted. There is also more than a hint of a troubling, even tragic, paternalism. For example, "villagization" in Tanzania, which was supposed to reflect traditional African conceptions, was accomplished only by force, against the strong opposition of much of the population.

Even such troubling sincerity is unfortunately rare. Government officials denounce the corrosive individualism of Western values—while they line their pockets with the proceeds of massive corruption, drive imported luxury automobiles, and plan European or American vacations. Leaders sing the praises of traditional communities—while they wield arbitrary power antithetical to traditional values, pursue development policies that systematically undermine traditional communities, and replace traditional leaders with corrupt cronies and party hacks. Rigged elections, military dictatorships, and malnutrition caused by government incentives to produce cash crops rather than food are just a few of the widespread abuses of internationally recognized human rights that do not express, but rather infringe, indigenous cultural values.

In traditional cultures—at least the kinds of traditional cultures that might justify deviations from international human rights standards—people are not victims of the arbitrary decisions of rulers whose principal claim to power is their control of modern instruments of force and administration. Traditional customs and practices usually provide each person with a place in society and a certain amount of dignity and protection. Furthermore, rulers and ruled (and rich and poor) usually are linked by reciprocal bonds. The human rights violations of most Third World regimes are as antithetical to such cultural traditions as they are to "Western" human rights conceptions.

Relativist arguments became particularly perverse when they support a small elite that has arrogated to itself the "right" to speak for "its" culture or civilization, and then imposes its own self-interested views and practices on the broader society—invoking cultural relativism abroad while ruthlessly trampling on local customs. Consider, for example, Suharto and his cronies in Indonesia, who sought to cloak their version of modern state-based repression and crony capitalism in the aura of traditional culture. In Zaire, President Mobutu created the practice of *salongo*, a form of communal labor with a supposedly traditional basis, which was in fact essentially a revival of the colonial, practice of corvee labor (Callaghy 1980: 490). Macias Nguema of Equatorial Guinea, perhaps the most vicious ruler independent black Africa has seen, called himself "Grand Master of Popular Education, Science, and Traditional Culture," a title that might be comical were the situation not so tragic.

7. Dialogue over Real Differences

The above discussion is intentionally one-sided. I have drawn attention to commonalities and minimized (real) differences. But even if I am correct about the extent of those differences, we must not confuse overlapping consensus with homogeneity.

Furthermore, the fact that differences are *relatively* minor, in the context of the full body of internationally recognized human rights, does not mean that they are unimportant, especially at the level of day-to-day polities. Questions about such issues as capital and corporal punishment, the limits of religious liberty, and the dimensions of gender equality merit intensive discussions both within and between states and civilizations.

Should traditional notions of "family values" and gender roles be emphasized in the interest of children and society, or should families be conceived in more individualistic and egalitarian terms? What is the proper balance between rewarding individual economic initiative and redistributive taxation in the interest of social harmony and support for disadvantaged individuals and groups?

At what point should the words or behaviors of deviant or dissident individuals be forced to give way to the interests or desires of society?

Questions such as these, which in my terminology involve conflicting interpretations, involve vital issues of political controversy in virtually all societies. In discussing them we must often walk the difficult line between respect for the other and respect for one's own values. * * * Here I want to consider a relatively easy case—slavery—in an unconventional way.

Suppose that in contemporary Saudi Arabia a group were to emerge arguing that because slavery was accepted in the early Muslim world it should be reinstituted in contemporary Saudi Arabia. I am certain that almost all Saudis, from the most learned clerics to the most ordinary citizens, would reject this view. But how should these individuals be dealt with?

Dialogue seems to me the appropriate route, so long as they do not attempt to *practice* slavery. Those in the majority who would remonstrate these individuals for their despicable views have, I think, an obligation to use precisely such forceful moral terms. Nonetheless, freedom of belief and speech requires the majority to tolerate these views, in the minimal sense of not imposing legal liabilities on those who hold or express them. Should they attempt to practice slavery, however, the force of the law is appropriately applied to suppress and punish this practice. Condemnation by outsiders also seems appropriate, although so long as the problem is restricted to expressions of beliefs only in Saudi Arabia there probably will be few occasions for such condemnations.

But suppose that the unthinkable were to occur and the practice of slavery were reintroduced in Saudi Arabia—not, let us imagine, as a matter of law, but rather through the state refusing to prosecute slave-holders. Here we run up against the state system and the fact that international human rights law gives states near total discretion to implement internationally recognized human rights within their own territories.

One might argue that slavery is legally prohibited as a matter of *jus cogens*, general principles of law, and customary (as well as treaty) law. But coercive international enforcement is extraordinarily contentious and without much legal precedent. Outsiders, however, remain bound by their own moral principles (as well as by international human rights norms) to condemn such practices in the strongest possible terms. And foreign states would be entirely justified in putting whatever pressure, short of force, they could mobilize on Saudi Arabia to halt the practice.

This hypothetical example illustrates the fact that *some* cultural practices, rather than deserve our respect, demand our condemnation. It also indicates, though, that some beliefs, however despicable, demand our toleration—because freedom of opinion and belief is an internationally recognized human right. So long as one stays within the limits of internationally recognized human rights, one is entitled to at least a limited and grudging toleration and the personal space that comes with that. But such individuals are *owed* nothing more.

Many cases, however, are not so easy. This is especially true where cultures are undergoing substantial or unusually rapid transformation. In much of the Third World we regularly face the problem of "modern" individuals or groups who reject traditional practices. Should we give priority to the idea of community self-determination and permit the enforcement of customary practices against modern "deviants" even if this violates "universal" human rights? Or should individual self-determination prevail, thus sanctioning claims of universal human rights against traditional society?

In discussing women's rights in Africa, Rhoda Howard suggests an attractive and widely applicable compromise strategy (1984: 66–68). On a combination of practical and moral grounds, she argues against an outright ban on such practices as child betrothal and widow inheritance, but she also argues strongly for national legislation that permits women (and the families of female children) to "opt out" of traditional practices. This would permit individuals and families to, in effect, choose the terms on which they participate in the cultures that are of value to their lives. Unless we think of culture as an oppressive external force, this seems entirely appropriate.

Conflicting practices, however, may sometimes be irreconcilable. For example, a right to private ownership of the means of production is incompatible with the maintenance of a village society in which families hold only rights of use to communally owned land. Allowing individuals to opt out and fully own their land would destroy the traditional system. Even such conflicts, however, may sometimes be resolved, or at least minimized, by the physical or legal separation of adherents of old and new values, particularly with practices that are not material to the maintenance or integrity of either culture.

Nevertheless, a choice must sometimes be made, at least by default, between irreconcilable practices. Such cases take us out of the realm in which useful general guidelines are possible. Fortunately, though, they are the exception rather than the rule—although no easier for that fact to deal with when they do arise.

It would be dangerous either to deny differences between civilizations where they do exist or to exaggerate their extent or practical importance. Whatever the situation in other issue areas, in the case of human rights, for all the undeniable differences, it is the similarities across civilizations that are more striking and important. Whatever our differences, now or in the past, all contemporary civilizations are linked by the growing recognition of the Universal Declaration as, in its own words, "a common standard of achievement for all peoples and all nations." Or, as I prefer to put it, human rights are relatively universal.

NOTES

1. Civilizations seems to be emerging as the term of choice in UN-based discussions. 2001 was designated the United Nations Year of Dialogue Among Civilizations. For a sampling of UNESCO sources, see http://www.unesco.org/dialogue2001/en/culturer.htm. I use "culture" and "civilization" more or less interchangeably, although I think that a useful convention would be to treat civilizations as larger or broader: for example, French culture but Western civilization.

2. * * * I begin by taking at face value the common understanding of culture as static, unitary, and integral. * * *

3. I am concerned here only with cultural relativist views as they apply to human rights, although my argument probably has applicability to other relativist claims.

4. We can also note that radical relativism is descriptively inaccurate. Few people anywhere believe that their moral beliefs rest on nothing more than tradition. The radical relativist insistence that they do offers an implausible (and unattractive) account of the nature and meaning of morality.

5. Gender equality, perhaps surprisingly, did not come up (although these were elite, English-speaking audiences, and Iran has, self-consciously, made considerable progress on women's rights issues in recent years). But even when it does, dispute usually focuses on the meaning of nondiscrimination or on particular practices, such as equal rights in marriage.

6. Logically, there can be at most one absolute right (unless we implausibly assume that rights never conflict with one another).

7. The general similarity of regional human rights instruments underscores this argument. Even the African Charter of Human and Peoples' Rights, the most heterodox regional treaty, differs largely at the level of interpretation and, in substance or concept, by addition (of peoples' rights) rather than by subtraction.

8. Coming at a similar perspective from the other end of the spectrum, Richard Wilson notes that human rights, and struggles over their implementation, "are embedded in local normative orders and yet are caught within webs of power and meaning which extend beyond the local" (1997: 23). Andrew Nathan has recently described this orientation as "tempered universalism" (2001).

9. To cite one example of misplaced textualism, Roger Ames (1997) manages to devote an entire article to "the conversation on Chinese human rights" that manages to make only a few passing, exceedingly delicate, mentions of events since 1949. China and its culture would seem to have been unaffected by such forces as decades of brutal party dictatorship or the impact of both socialism and capitalism on land tenure and residence patterns. In fact, although he cites a number of passages from Confucius, Ames does not even attempt to show how traditional Confucian ideas express themselves in contemporary Chinese human rights debates.

10. None of this should be surprising when we compare the legal, political, and cultural practices of the contemporary West with those of ancient Athens, medieval Paris, Renaissance Florence, or even Victorian London.

REFERENCES

Ames, Roger. 1997. "Continuing the Conversation on Chinese Human Rights." *Ethics and International Affairs* 11: 177–205.

Bell, Daniel A. 1996. "The East Asian Challenge to Human Rights: Reflections on an East-West Dialogue." *Human Rights Quarterly* 18 (August): 641–67.

Bell, Lynda, Andrew J. Nathan, and Ilan Peleg. 2001. "Introduction: Culture and Human Rights." In *Negotiating Culture and Human Rights*. Edited by Lynda Bell, Andrew J. Nathan, and Ilan Peleg. New York: Columbia University Press.

Bell, Lynda S. 2001. "Who Produces Asian Identity? Discourses, Discrimination, and Chinese Peasant Women in the Quest for Human Rights." In *Negotiating Culture and Human Rights*. Edited by Lynda Bell, Andrew J. Nathan, and Ilan Peleg. New York: Columbia University Press.

Gallie, W. B. 1968. "Essentially Contested Concepts." In *Philosophy and the Historical Understanding*. New York: Schocken Books.

Gupta, Akhil, and James Ferguson. 1997. "Culture, Power, Place: Ethnography at the End of an Era." In *Culture, Power, Place: Explorations in Critical Anthropology*. Edited by Akhil Gupta and James Ferguson. Durham: Duke University Press.

Howard, Rhoda E. 1984. "Women's Rights in English-Speaking Sub-Saharan Africa." In *Human Rights and Development in Africa*. Edited by Claude E. Welch Jr. and Ronald I. Meltzer. Albany: State University of New York Press.

Kant, Immanuel. 1983. *Perpetual Peace and Other Essays*. Translated by Ted Humphrey. Indianapolis: Hackett.

Nathan, Andrew J. 2001. "Universalism: A Particularistic Account." In *Negotiating Culture and Human Rights*. Edited by Lynda Bell, Andrew J. Nathan, and Ilan Peleg. New York: Columbia University Press.

Wilson, Richard. 1997. "Introduction." In *Human Rights, Culture and Context: Anthropological Perspectives*. Edited by Richard Wilson. London: Pluto Press.

Zechenter, Elizabeth M. 1997. "In the Name of Cultural Relativism and the Abuse of the Individual." *Journal of Anthropological Research* 53 (Fall): 319–47.

Dara Kay Cohen

EXPLAINING RAPE DURING CIVIL WAR
Cross-National Evidence (1980–2009)

Rape during wartime, long dismissed as an inevitable consequence of conflict, is now widely recognized as an important problem of international security. It is arguably one of the most horrifying and least understood aspects of modern conflict. Its ruinous effects on victims, perpetrators, and local communities include forced displacement, the spread of disease, the burden of unwanted children, and deeply traumatized populations. Wartime rape can have devastating repercussions for international security, and it threatens prospects for postconflict peace and reconstruction (e.g., Plümper & Neumayer 2006). Additionally, some researchers suggest that its incidence is increasing (e.g., Green 2006).

Recent scholarship suggests that wartime sexual violence varies widely, in both its form and severity across and within conflicts (Cohen 2010; Leiby 2009; Wood 2008). However, there have been few efforts to gather comprehensive cross-national data on wartime rape, and there is little agreement about why it occurs. Some scholars argue that rape occurs in all or most armed conflicts (Benard 1994), whereas others contend that it is limited in some conflicts and widespread in others (Bourke 2007; Wood 2008), with some researchers claiming that it is most likely to occur in ethnic wars (Bloom 1999; Plümper and Neumayer 2006). Others point to women's relative inequality as an explanation (MacKinnon 1994).

Without a clear comparative understanding of where and to what extent wartime rape occurs, it is difficult to draw defensible conclusions. In this article, I introduce an original dataset of rape during civil wars over the past three decades (1980–2009) and find substantial variation in the prevalence of rape both across and within conflicts. I use the dataset to test existing explanations for rape during conflict, which I organize into three sets of arguments about the causes of wartime rape: opportunism/greed, ethnic hatred, and gender inequality. The evidence does not support much of the conventional wisdom about the causes of wartime rape: It is not more likely to occur during ethnic wars, genocides, or in countries with greater gender inequality.

I offer an alternative explanation for the variation in rape during civil war: *combatant socialization*. One of the most puzzling aspects of wartime rape is that gang rape (rape by multiple perpetrators) is much more common in war than in peacetime (Asher et al. 2004; Bourke 2007; Theidon 2007). Drawing on this observation, I argue that armed groups use wartime rape as a socialization tool. Combatant groups that recruit new members through forcible means, such as abduction or pressganging, must create a coherent fighting force out of a collection of strangers, many of whom were abused in order to compel them to join (Gates 2002). Based on research from economics, sociology, and criminology, I argue that rape—especially gang rape—enables groups with forcibly recruited fighters to create bonds of loyalty and esteem from

From *American Political Science Review* 107, no. 3 (August 2013): 461–477.

initial circumstances of fear and mistrust. I show that both state and insurgent armed groups that have recruited their members through abduction—which subsequently have the lowest levels of internal social cohesion—are more likely to commit widespread rape than are groups that recruited fighters through more voluntary methods.

Although the cross-national analysis demonstrates an association between abduction and rape, I turn to the case of Sierra Leone to explore how extreme forms of forced recruitment—but not weaker forms—are associated with rape, to show how rape creates cohesion in groups that have abducted their fighters, to examine a series of observable implications of the combatant socialization argument, and to demonstrate that an alternative argument does not explain the observed variation. Drawing both on interviews with ex-combatants from fieldwork in Sierra Leone and from existing survey data, I argue that there is substantial evidence that combatant socialization best explains the widespread rape in that conflict. In this article, I provide both cross-national and case study evidence that combatant socialization accounts for variation in wartime rape better than many rival explanations.

Wartime Rape as a Distinct Phenomenon

Following Wood (2006, 308), I define rape as "the coerced (under physical force or threat of physical force against the victim or a third person) penetration of the anus or vagina by the penis or another object, or of the mouth by the penis." Wood (2006, 308) defines sexual violence as "a broader category that includes rape, coerced undressing and non-penetrating sexual assault" as well as a variety of other forms of violence. In this study, I focus on rape rather than the broader category of sexual violence.

Wartime rape may be devastating both to victims and perpetrators, causing psychological and physical harm. Its documented consequences, including trauma, shame, stigma, unwanted children, disease, and displacement, and their plausible effects on the durability of postconflict peace mean that a better understanding of its root causes is urgently needed.

In addition to normative justifications for analyzing rape separately from lethal violence, there are important theoretical reasons. Although scholars have made significant progress in recent years studying violence during conflict, research on the human costs of civil war has focused mainly on deaths. The most influential studies of violence against noncombatants during civil war have analyzed homicide to the exclusion of all other violence (Kalyvas 2006; Valentino, Huth, and Balch-Lindsay 2004; Weinstein 2007), and the standard measure of conflict severity is wartime killing.[1] There is little explicit theoretical justification offered for this operationalization, other than that homicide is easier to measure (Kalyvas 2006, 20) and is presumed to correlate with levels of nonlethal violence, including rape. However, Wood (2009; see also Morris 1996) argues that rape follows a different pattern from homicide and forced displacement. The cross-national data used in this analysis confirm that conflict-level battle death estimates—a combination of soldier and civilian deaths used as a proxy for civilian abuse in the literature—are correlated positively, but weakly, with conflict-level rape.[2]

An additional problem is that wartime homicide is not randomly distributed. Men and boys are significantly more likely to be killed during the course of a conflict than are women and girls (Carpenter 2006; Plümper and Neumayer 2006). Some studies suggest that women and girls are disproportionately more likely to experience nonlethal conflict violence, especially displacement and sexual violence (Human Security Report Project 2005), and are more likely to be affected by the long-term consequences of war, such as food and resource shortages and a lack of medical care (Plümper and Neumayer 2006). Very few studies have focused on rape, a form of violence that is primarily targeted at women (Leiby 2009; Wood 2008, 2009). It is both uncertain and unlikely that theories developed to explain the incidence of homicide can be readily applied to another type of violence that affects a distinct population.

Explanations for wartime rape can be grouped into three main themes: opportunism/greed, ethnic hatred, and gender inequality.[3] The arguments have implications for violence at different levels of analysis (either at the conflict level, or for insurgent-perpetrated or state-perpetrated violence). I have indicated which level is pertinent by underlining it in each hypothesis, and I test these in separate models.

Opportunism/Greed

Arguments for why rape occurs during war follow two related logics that derive from the claim that war affords men an unprecedented opportunity to rape. First, the breakdown of the state that may accompany conflict results in the destruction of social norms and legal prohibitions that exist in peacetime, which unleashes at least some men's latent desire to commit rape (Goldstein 2001). If so, variation in the magnitude of state breakdown may help explain the degree of perceived impunity for crimes against civilians. Hence, state collapse may be a proxy for indiscipline among combatants.

> H1: State collapse is correlated with higher state-perpetrated and insurgent-perpetrated levels of wartime rape.

A related set of arguments focuses on greed and on the types of people who are attracted to violent armed groups as a cause of civilian abuse (Mueller 2000). Weinstein (2007) argues that civilian abuse is more likely when insurgent groups have access to material resources, including contraband or external support. Two mechanisms explain why access to resources lead to violence. First, Weinstein (2007) argues that insurgent groups with access to material resources attract more violence-prone recruits than groups that rely on ideology and thus will be more likely to commit mass-scale civilian abuses. Second, the availability of material resources enables insurgent groups to be unaccountable to the civilian population. Exploitive violence against civilians is an unfortunate consequence of the lack of accountability, not a means to an end. Rape perpetrated by insurgents is hypothesized to be more likely in conflicts where insurgencies are fueled by "economic endowments," especially those easily converted into selective incentives to entice new recruits (Weinstein 2005).[4]

> H2: Rape by insurgents is more likely in conflicts where insurgent groups rely on material resources.

Ethnic Hatred

Ethnic war is a frequently cited environment for extreme violence, including rape (Bloom 1999; Horowitz 1985; Plümper and Neumayer 2006), because ethnic conflicts "engage intense emotions and a sense of existential threat" (Fearon 2006, 682). Proponents of these arguments maintain that rape is most prevalent in conflicts where a major cleavage is based on ethnic differences and that rape plays an important role in humiliating the ethnic opponent. Wartime rape, then, should be correlated with ethnic conflict.

> H3: Ethnic wars are associated with conflict-wide rape.

In contrast, some scholars argue that genocidal wars, rather than ethnic wars, are more likely to feature rape as a "central technique" (Mullins 2009) in genocide. Drawing on MacKinnon (1994), feminist scholars refer to "genocidal rape."[5] Sharlach (2000, 89) argues that, even if the victims are not killed, rape fits the definition of genocide in the 1948 Genocide Convention, which includes "causing serious bodily or mental harm to members of the group and/or deliberately inflicting on the group conditions of life calculated to bring about its physical destruction in whole or in part." Hence, wartime rape should be more likely to be committed by actors who perpetrate genocide.

H4: States or insurgents *who perpetrate genocide are more likely to commit wartime rape than those who do not.*

In a final variation of the ethnic hatred argument, scholars argue that rape is an instrument of ethnic cleansing or of forced expulsion during secessionist wars.[6] Rape can ensure that an ethnic population will flee a disputed territory, guarantee that displaced people will not return, and "sexually contaminate" women of an opposing ethnicity (e.g., Bloom 1999; Farr 2009; Sharlach 2000). One scholar hypothesizes that, in secessionist wars, rape increases hatred and fosters the idea that "life together is finished" (Hayden 2000, 32).

H5: Secessionist wars, especially those featuring ethnic cleansing, are associated with insurgent-perpetrated *rape.*

Gender Inequality

Feminist scholars and human rights advocates have identified a relationship between gender inequality and wartime rape (Hansen 2001; HRW 2004; Koo 2002). Although rape may also be more likely in contexts where women are gaining rights and men feel threatened (Baron and Straus 1989), most arguments about gender and wartime rape predict a correlation between the relative lack of women's rights and widespread rape.

Scholarship on the status of women and rape during war focuses on the symbolic meaning of rape and holds that gender inequality facilitates acceptance of violence against women. In this view, rape is a crime that allows men to inflict psychological harm on women and their communities (Benard 1994; Green 2006; Seifert 1996). It shames not only the victim but also her husband and male relatives, who have failed to protect her (Bastick, Grimm, and Kunz 2007; Hansen 2001). Further, scholars have demonstrated that gender inequality predicts the onset of civil war (Caprioli 2005; Fearon 2010), but have not tested whether gender inequality is correlated with specific forms of violence, including wartime rape.

H6: Greater gender inequality is associated with conflict-wide *rape.*

Forced Recruitment, Cohesion, and Gang Rape

Gang rape is far more common in wartime than in peacetime. Scholars have also noted that gang rape can create bonds between people in social groups and may provide psychological benefits to the perpetrators by improving group morale through inducing feelings of power and victory (Benard 1994; Card 1996; Sanday 2007).[7] However, not all armed groups turn to this form of morale-boosting behavior. I argue that rape may be especially important in groups with low social cohesion.

Even where peacetime rape is thought to be common, researchers have noted a qualitative difference in the nature of peacetime and wartime rape. For instance before the war in the DRC, rape was mainly committed by one perpetrator in private; wartime rape was shocking to local people because of its increased brutality, multiple perpetrators, and public nature (Samset 2011). Although gang rape has received little scholarly attention (Franklin 2004), there are a small number of studies comparing various aspects of gang rape to single-perpetrator rape. In one of the earliest and most influential studies of gang rape, Amir (1971) introduced a "sociological theory of group rape," which he defined as involving three or more perpetrators. He argues that it is a rite of passage in which aggression and humiliation are key features. Gang rape enables the perpetrators to establish status and reputations for toughness. Amir maintains that gang rape occurs only occasionally in such groups, but is found particularly during periods when group members' status is questioned or threatened. Importantly for understanding wartime rape, Amir (1971, 185) writes that gang rape can assist in "solidify[ing] the status claims of a member as well as the cohesiveness of the whole group."

Gaining and maintaining status within a group as a result of committing rape has become a common finding in the literature (Groth and Birnbaum 1979). Psychological and sociological studies of gang rape find that perpetrators experience increased mutual esteem and that rape serves as an act of camaraderie (Brownmiller 1975; Franklin 2004). Deemphasizing the attacks' sexual nature, researchers argue instead that bonding is the primary motivator (Bijleveld and Hendriks 2003; Franklin 2004; Morrow 1993 in Diken and Laustsen 2005). Gang rape is notable for its performance aspects, and perpetrators often watch each other and organize an order of their participation. Researchers believe that the intended "audience" of the performance is the other perpetrators, with the victim serving as their "vehicle" (Sanday 2007; Theidon 2007; see also Bourgois 1996).

The social processes apparent in group rape are in stark contrast to those in rape committed by a lone offender. Single-offender rape is more often driven by personal sexual desire (Hauffe and Porter 2008). Gang rapists are considered less pathological than single rapists (Bijleveld and Hendriks 2003), and perpetrators of group rape are far less

likely to have previously committed sexual offenses than are lone perpetrators (Bijleveld and Hendriks 2003). Additionally, criminologists argue that co-offenders of gang rape have more in common with members of groups that commit other types of violence than with perpetrators of single rape (Bijleveld et al. 2007). Likewise, wartime rape is more likely to be committed by those who might not rape during peacetime (Malamuth 1996; Mezey 1994). The differences between lone perpetrators and group perpetrators shed light on acts of wartime rape, particularly by groups of abducted combatants who are not selected for their propensity to commit violence, but rather are randomly pulled out of their communities to join fighting forces.[8]

Combatant groups with low levels of social cohesion may be more likely to commit rape, especially gang rape. Forced, random recruitment of fighters results in low social cohesion. Groups such as the Revolutionary United Front (RUF) in Sierra Leone, which kidnapped fighters into its ranks, consist of people who do not have much information about their peers and who may not feel particularly congenial toward each other. Being abducted itself is a violent act, often involving beating, forced labor, and, for women, rape and other forms of sexual violence. Interviewees in Sierra Leone reported feeling frightened and isolated when they were first abducted. Hence, armed groups face a central challenge: how to create a coherent force out of a group of frightened strangers who feel no loyalty toward the group of which they are now a member. Gang rape is one such method. Whereas previous literature has emphasized the ease with which social cohesion forms (e.g., Horowitz 1985), I argue that, among fighters who have been abducted by their peers, cohesion is unlikely to form spontaneously.[9]

The military sociology literature finds that violence plays an important role in building group cohesion. Wood (2009) writes that the study of cohesion within military units is based on research on combatants in World War II (Shils and Janowitz 1948). These studies found that combatants' main reason for fighting was a strong sense of commitment to fellow combatants, accomplished by severing previous social ties and building new loyalties (Morris 1996). Wood and Morris both note that socialization among fighters may be formal (through basic training and drills) or informal (through hazing and initiation rites).

Gang rape is another means for increasing group cohesion (Goldstein 2001). Social bonds are also strengthened and reproduced in the process of recounting the violence in the aftermath; scholars have noted that perpetrators may brag about the rapes in which they participated to "revel in a sense of enhanced masculinity" (Sanday 2007, 83). Morris (1996, 706–707) argues that sexual violence is central to some types of (mostly) male groups because of "rape-conducive sexual norms" that are "inadvertently . . . imparted" to members of military organizations. There are multiple examples from related contexts, including urban gangs and fraternities, of (mostly) male groups committing *sexualized violence*—in part, perhaps, because it communicates norms of masculinity, strength, and virility.

Rape is often understood as a type of violence that benefits the individual—a reward analogous to looting—and harms the group through reputational costs.[10] Certainly, rape reaps private benefits for the perpetrator, including sexual gratification, as well as acceptance and prestige among a group of violent strangers. But rape also carries grave risks to the perpetrator: the possibility of contracting debilitating sexually transmitted diseases, the emotional toll of the intimate contact required, and the fact that rape takes longer to commit than other, more time-efficient violations (Cohen 2010). These risks may serve to reinforce the utility of rape as a tool of cohesion. Unlike explanations focused on private motivations, an argument about combatant socialization does not assume that combatants have a biological or latent desire to rape noncombatants nor that rape must have an overt military purpose. The argument merely posits that, when trapped in a group of hostile strangers, individuals are likely to choose participation in costly group behavior over continued estrangement from their new peers.[11]

Anxiety over individuals' status within groups—such as armed groups and street and prison gangs—may lead to performative violence (Humphreys and Weinstein 2006).[12] By participating in group rape—and perhaps by bragging about the individual rapes they have committed—combatants signal to their new peers that they are part of the unit and are willing to take risks to remain in the group. Thus, rape is part of the process of hazing new recruits and of maintaining social order among existing members.[13] The "need" for bonding may be greater in groups that have forcibly recruited their fighters and where the members must immediately begin to depend on each other for protection, food, shelter, and survival despite having little foundation for mutual trust. Perpetrating gang rape and boasting about single-perpetrator rape are effective methods for creating and perpetuating cohesion.

There is some basis for the notion that a small percentage of combatants may actively seek to rape noncombatants in all armed groups. A much cited study of "normal" men's inherent desire to rape found that an average of 35% of respondents reported they would be more than "not at all likely" to "personally . . . rape, if they could be assured of not being caught and punished" (Malamuth 1981, 140). However, rape becomes a widespread practice of an armed group only under certain circumstances and may spread across armed groups as new fighters are recruited due to a growth in the overall size of the group or to replace fighters lost in battle. Whether rape becomes widespread may be explained by differences in recruitment strategies and the resulting variation in internal social cohesion.

Table 10.1 presents the logic underlying the relationship between the recruitment mechanism and violence.[14] Groups that can rely on social ties for in-group cohesion are expected to do so. The Civilian Defense Forces (CDF) in Sierra Leone, for instance, mainly recruited fighters through social and kinship ties within individual communities and committed far less rape than did the RUF. As Gates (2002) argues, ethnically homogeneous groups have stronger "solidary norms." However, when combatant groups rely on the random abduction of strangers, they must turn to alternative methods for creating group cohesion.[15] Extreme forms of forced recruitment, such as abduction, are distinct from weaker forms, such as coercion and conscription, in at least two ways. First, evidence suggests that unlike coercion, abduction is not generally committed by bloc, in which groups of family or friends who are abducted together subsequently serve together.[16] Second, abduction involves direct violence, whereas coercion and conscription more commonly involve implicit or explicit threats of violence—thus allowing fighters a degree of agency in deciding to join. These differences are consequential for the internal cohesion of armed groups. The CDF, for example, relied more heavily on abduction later in the war, and the shift toward extreme forced recruitment corresponded with a predictable increase in rape.

> *H7: Insurgent groups that depend on abduction as a recruitment mechanism are more likely to perpetrate rape than groups that use other, more voluntary methods of recruitment.*

States recruiting their fighters through kidnapping should be likely to suffer from the same problems of low cohesion.

> *H8: States that depend on pressganging as a recruitment mechanism are more likely to perpetrate rape than groups that use other, more voluntary methods of recruitment.*

Rape During Civil War: Cross-National Data

Collecting reliable data on rape—a form of violence associated with shame for the victims that often leaves no visible scars—is challenging. There have been several efforts to create datasets and lists of wartime rape and sexual violence (Bastick, Grimm, and Kunz 2007; Farr 2009; Green 2006), as well as detailed case studies of wartime rape (Bloom 1999; Leiby 2009; Sharlach 2000; Wood 2009).[17] However, these studies did not systematically gather relevant variables of interest across cases of both widespread and limited wartime rape. Therefore, I collected an original dataset that includes all 86 major civil wars between 1980–2009, as defined by Fearon and Laitin (2011), an update of Fearon and Laitin (2003).[18] I used coding procedures similar to those in Butler, Gluch, and Mitchell's (2007) study of state-directed sexual violence, whose coding scheme is in turn based on the widely used Political Terror Scale (PTS), a five-point measure of the level and degree of physical integrity rights violations (Gibney, Cornett, and Wood 2011). I extended the Butler et al. measure by coding reports of rape by both rebel groups and state actors, instead of only state security forces, and by coding all years from 1980 to 2009, instead of just 2003.

Table 10.1. Combatant Socialization: Recruitment, Unit Cohesion, and Violence Outcomes

RECRUITMENT MECHANISM	OUTCOME
Voluntary (strong social ties; high social cohesion)	→ Infrequent acts of costly group behavior that contribute to cohesion
Abduction/Pressganging (weak social ties; low social cohesion)	→ Frequent acts of costly group behavior that contribute to cohesion

---

Using the U.S. State Department Human Rights Country reports (hereafter, State Department reports), I coded both state and nonstate perpetrators by armed group type for the years 1980–2009 in all countries that had experienced a civil war; the unit of analysis is the actor type-conflict-year (e.g., insurgent forces in Sierra Leone in 1995).[19] Instead of Butler et al.'s five-point scale, I used a modified four-point scale that reflects the magnitude of violence.[20] I collected four versions of *Rape,* the dependent variable: I coded the highest levels of rape perpetrated (1) by insurgent groups and (2) by state actors in each conflict-year; (3) I created a variable reflecting the highest level of rape in the conflict-year, using the maximum coded level by either actor type in the conflict-year; and (4) I coded a conflict-level version of the variable reflecting the highest level of rape by actor type in each conflict, to evaluate arguments about cross-conflict variation in robustness checks.

Although not fine-grained, the four-point scale does permit inferences about the relative magnitude of rape across conflicts. Because the dataset uses State Department reports, a coding of zero does not mean that no rape occurred in a particular conflict, only that the State Department received no reports of its occurrence. An alternative measure would be the number of reported victims per conflict-year. However, accurate counts of acts of rape or numbers of victims are only rarely available and are difficult, if not impossible, to construct.

Limitations of the Data

This dataset represents the first systematic effort to create a cross-national measure of rape across civil conflicts by perpetrator group. Three limitations should be noted. First, although the data are drawn from the same source over a period of time and presume consistency in the source's collection methods, there may be inconsistent interest in rape over time. For example, after rape in Bosnia Herzegovina received significant attention, human rights organizations may have increased their focus on rape. Thus an increase in magnitude over time may indicate increased interest rather than increased incidence.

Second, there are no precise measures of the number of victims, so coding was based on descriptors such as "isolated reports" and "widespread occurrence." Of course, a term such as *widespread* may have different meanings in different contexts. Potential biases can also result from both the under- and overreporting of rape. Foreign observers may not have access to conflict zones, or victims may not want to speak about their experiences. Alternatively, victims and NGOs may sense an advantage in emphasizing or perhaps exaggerating certain forms of violence to receive aid (Cohen and Hoover Green 2012).

A third potential source of bias is how the reports are produced. The field offices reporting human rights violations may vary in quality or focus. The global political climate may affect what gets recorded. Reports on human rights abuses from allied countries may be edited to appear less severe due to political pressures (Human Security Report Project 2008). However, even in cases where the United States was a strong supporter of one side in a civil conflict, I found reports of major human rights violations. For example, the government of El Salvador, to which the United States devoted enormous resources to support counterinsurgency efforts, is accused in the State Department reports of committing serious wartime violence against detained suspected insurgents, including beatings, rape, administering electric shocks, and forcing confessions. Finally, there are numerous potential sources of error introduced in the process of coding qualitative reports into a quantitative dataset; to minimize these sources of bias, I checked my coding against all other available sources that examined conflicts with high levels of sexual violence * * * and assessed intercoder reliability.

Additionally, I did not code gang rape specifically because the State Department reports often do not detail the form of rape. However, reports of gang rape are correlated with the reported intensity of wartime rape. Gang rape was specifically reported only during the most severe conflicts and was not reported for other conflicts.[21] Although the combatant socialization argument focuses on gang rape, social cohesion may not depend on it exclusively. The case study describes instances of bragging to peers about single-perpetrator rape.

Despite these limitations, the *relative magnitude* of rape across conflicts can be measured reliably. It is improbable that the variation in reporting and the reality of the occurrence of rape confound the extraction of any meaningful information (Wood 2009); it is doubtful that a conflict with no reports of rape in fact experienced widespread rape. Although the four-point scale is a blunt instrument, it makes a contribution by allowing systematic comparisons of relative levels of rape across a range of conflicts.

Variation during Civil Conflict

The dataset contains all 86 civil wars between 1980–2009, for a total of 983 conflict-years. Civil conflict was unevenly distributed across various geographic regions.[22] The severity of wartime rape varies dramatically as well. Eighteen conflicts were coded as wars with widespread rape (with at least one conflict-year coded as 3), 35 as having many or numerous reports of rape (with at least one conflict-year coded as 2), 18 as having isolated reports (with at least one conflict-year coded as 1), and 15 wars had no reports of rape (all conflict-years coded as 0). The worst conflicts should come as no surprise to those familiar with so-called mass rape wars: Bosnia Herzegovina, Burundi, Democratic Republic of the Congo, Georgia, India (Kashmir and the Northeast), Indonesia/East Timor, Iraq (Kurds), Liberia (NPFL), Rwanda, Sierra Leone, Somalia (post-Barre and Isaaqs), Sudan (SPLA and Darfur), Tajikistan, Uganda (LRA), and Yugoslavia (UCK).

The data indicate that 62% of the conflicts (53 of 86) in the study period involved significant rape in at least one conflict-year (coded 2 or 3). This finding suggests that wartime rape is a major problem in many conflicts, but is not a ubiquitous feature of conflict.

Not only does the severity of wartime rape across conflicts vary but there is also variation within conflicts. Some armed groups exercise restraint, whereas others do not. At least isolated incidents of rape were reported in 71 conflicts—83% of all civil wars—in the period. Most often, both state and nonstate actors committed rape (44, or 62% of conflicts with reported rape). Perpetration of rape by the state only was less common (22, or 31%), and rape by insurgents only was relatively rare (5, or 7%).[23]

Additional Variables and Controls

In addition to measures for magnitude and perpetrators of wartime rape, I collected data on armed groups' recruitment practices. Other variables were drawn from existing quantitative studies and datasets.

Recruitment and Cohesion in Insurgent Groups

Recruitment mechanism is a useful proxy for the level of internal cohesion, as theorized previously. Using State Department reports, I coded two dummy variables: *Abduction* indicates whether abduction specifically was ever reported, and *Forced Recruitment* indicates whether any insurgent group ever used coercive recruitment more generally.[24] Recruitment practices in the State Department reports include descriptions such as the following: "The LRA regularly abducted children of both sexes for impressment into its own ranks" (coded as abduction, from Uganda) and "Guerrillas also committed human rights violations including . . . forced labor and recruitment" (coded as forced recruitment, from Guatemala). Abduction was not coded as such unless it was explicitly reported, as in the Uganda description, and thus it represents a more restrictive measure of forced recruitment.[25]

In 32% of the conflicts in the period, insurgents forced or coerced recruits using methods short of abduction; abduction reports appeared in 13% of the conflicts. Thus 45% (39/86) of insurgencies in the study period recruited their fighters by force. These cases are not well explained by arguments about opportunism and greed (Mueller 2000; Weinstein 2007) because fighters are not selecting to join an armed group, nor are they recruited for their propensity to commit violence.[26]

Recruitment and Cohesion in State Militaries

Forcible recruitment into state armed forces may take two forms: (1) conscription, in which (usually male) citizens are legally required to serve for a specific term, and (2) pressganging, in which fighters are kidnapped into service without notice. Pressganging, typically considered an antiquated practice, is surprisingly common in modern civil wars and frequently occurred in the period (31% of conflicts). Based on State Department reports, I coded a dummy variable, *Pressgang*, for each conflict indicating whether pressganging was ever reported. Examples include statements such as "The Sandanista Army continued military impressment, conducting sweeps of public facilities and forcibly removing youths as young as 12" (from Nicaragua), and "Although a military service decree was issued and youth are being required to register, the authorities still frequently round up youth off the streets or seize them from their homes to press them into military service" (from Ethiopia).

The dichotomous *Conscription* variable (Pickering 2010) indicated whether the state used

conscription. The measure varied by conflict-year, and in some cases, states switched from a volunteer army to a conscripted army (or vice versa) over the course of the war. Because conscription data were available only until 2001, I dropped the eight conflicts that begin after 2001 from the analysis in Model 4 in Table 10.3.[27] Additionally, *Troop Quality* (Pickering 2010), state military expenditures per military personnel, reflected the military's resources and training in each conflict-year.

Other Variables[28]

STATE- AND CONFLICT-LEVEL FACTORS

To measure the magnitude of the failure of state authority, I used *Magfail* from the Political Instability Task Force (PITF) dataset.[29] Following others (Williams and Masters 2011), I added a value of 0 to the original scale to indicate no failure of state authority. To determine ethnic war, I used *Ethwar* (Fearon and Laitin 2011). Finally, I used three separate measures of gender equality[30] from the CIRI dataset—*Political Rights, Social Rights,* and *Economic Rights*. Because the CIRI gender variables have been critiqued for not adequately reflecting women's actual lived experience (Caprioli et al. 2009), I used *Fertility*, from the World Bank, as the main measure of gender inequality.[31] Caprioli et al. argue that the fertility rate captures both cultural factors—such as personal choice and the need for children—and structural inequalities, such as lower levels of education and employment.

INSURGENT-RELATED FACTORS

I used *Aim* (Fearon and Laitin 2011) to capture the rebels' purpose in the war. For cases of significant contraband funding, I used the dichotomous *Drugs* variable (Fearon and Laitin 2011). To measure diaspora funding, I created a dummy variable *Diaspora* to indicate whether the UCDP External Support dataset (2011) reported an insurgent group received diaspora support.

VIOLENCE-RELATED FACTORS

Genocide is a dummy variable based on the PITF (2006) update of Harff's (2003) data on genocide and politicide.[32] Because there are no existing cross-national data on ethnic cleansing, I created a dummy variable, *Ethnic Cleansing*, by combining the variables Ethwar and Aim (both from Fearon and Laitin 2011). The presence of rebel groups with secessionist aims in an ethnic war may be a reliable indicator of ethnic cleansing by insurgents.[33] To account for the possibility that wars with more rape are simply wars with more lethal violence, I controlled for the lethality of the conflict by using multiple measures of wartime deaths. The measure in the main analysis is *Kill* from the CIRI data, a three-level variable reflecting extrajudicial killings by government officials and by private groups if instigated by the state.[34] Second, I used *Battle Deaths* (Lacina and Gleditsch 2005) as a proxy because of the high correlation with civilian deaths (Weinstein 2007, 306).[35]

CONTROLS

I controlled for *Year* in all regressions to capture whether time is a significant factor, either because measurement is improving over time or wartime rape is getting worse. I also calculated the *Duration* of the war as of 2009.[36] Finally, I controlled for *Population* (Penn World Tables 7) and *Democracy* (Polity2), which have both been found to be important factors in previous studies of repression and human rights violations.

Table 10.2 summarizes the arguments, hypotheses and variables.

Table 10.2. *Explaining Wartime Rape: Arguments, Hypotheses, and Data Sources*

ARGUMENTS	HYPOTHESES	INDEPENDENT VARIABLES (SOURCE)
Opportunism/Greed	H1: State collapses → state- and insurgent-perpetrated rape	Magnitude of state failure (PITF)
	H2: Material resources → insurgent-perpetrated rape	Contraband funding (Fearon and Laitin); Diaspora support (UCDP)
Ethnic hatred	H3: Ethnic wars → conflict-wide rape	Ethnic war (Fearon and Laitin)
	H4: Perpetrators of genocide → state- and insurgent-perpetrated rape	Genocide (PITF)
	H5: Secessionist aims/ethnic cleansing → insurgent-perpetrated rape	War aim (Fearon and Laitin); Ethnic cleansing (ethnic-secessionist wars) (Fearon and Laitin)
Gender inequality	H6: Greater gender inequality → conflict-wide rape	Fertility rate (World Bank); Women's rights (CIRI)
Combatant socialization	H7: Abduction by insurgents → insurgent-perpetrated rape	Abduction (original data)
	H8: Pressganging by states → state-perpetrated rape	Pressganging (original data)

Analysis

To evaluate each of the four arguments, I estimated a series of ordered probit regressions, with the standard errors clustered by conflict to account for the fact that they are not statistically independent of each other.[37] Table 10.3 displays the results, with models organized by the level of analysis (conflict level, insurgent-perpetrated violence, or state-perpetrated violence).

Combatant Socialization

First, there is strong evidence in support of the combatant socialization argument (*H7* and *H8*). For insurgent violence (Model 2), the coefficient for abduction is positive and statistically significant at the .05 level, lending support to the argument that abduction is associated with rape. A broader measure of insurgent forced recruitment was not statistically significant (Model 3), suggesting that abduction in particular is associated with increased wartime rape. Similarly, the combatant socialization argument finds strong support for state actors; pressganging is a statistically significant predictor of state-perpetrated rape at the .05 level (Model 4). However, although conscription is negatively associated with wartime rape, it is not statistically significant, whether controlling for troop quality (Model 5) or not (not shown).[38]

That extreme forms of forced recruitment (abduction and pressganging) are associated with rape whereas weaker forms (coercion and conscription) are not is evidence that different forms of impressment have different consequences for cohesion. Because abduction is often random, occurs with little advance notice, and can be so physically violent, it should be expected to have a more damaging effect on the internal cohesion of an armed group than weaker forms of forced recruitment, such as coercion and conscription. Weaker forms of forced recruitment typically occur more gradually and are facilitated by preexisting social ties that allow the fighters some (perhaps very small) degree of agency in deciding to join; as a result, the internal cohesion should be greater in groups that use these weaker forms of forced recruitment. I examine these differences in greater detail in the Sierra Leone case study.

Opportunism/Greed

For overall conflict-wide rape, the opportunism argument (*H1*) is not supported. The magnitude of state collapse is positively associated with overall conflict-wide rape, but the coefficient is not statistically significant (Model 1). However, for insurgent violence, there is support for several strands of the opportunism/greed argument. First, the magnitude of state failure (*H1*) predicts insurgent-perpetrated rape (Models 2 and 3), suggesting that the anarchy of state collapse affords rebel groups the ability to rape without fear of retribution or punishment by the state, perhaps even beyond the general chaos of wartime. Second, insurgent contraband funding (*H2*) is positive and statistically significant, confirming that lootable resources are associated with rape. However, diaspora support of insurgents is not significant either when controlling or not controlling for contraband funding (not shown).

These findings suggest that the type of material support for an insurgency matters. They provide evidence for the argument that forms of support that can easily become a selective incentive may be more likely to attract opportunistic fighters who are prone to violence (Weinstein 2005). They also imply that lootable resources are more corrupting than diaspora support (the variable includes remittances and other types of support, such as sanctuary), perhaps also because they are more easily converted into selective incentives. In addition, it is lootable resources in particular—rather than unaccountable sources of funding more broadly—that are associated with wartime rape. Thus the recruitment mechanism may be more important than the

Table 10.3. *Rape during Civil War: Ordered Probit Results*

	(1) CONFLICT-LEVEL RAPE	(2) RAPE BY INSURGENTS	(3) RAPE BY INSURGENTS	(4) RAPE BY STATE ACTORS	(5) RAPE BY STATE ACTORS
Ethnic war	−0.14 [0.123]	0.24 [0.165]	0.21 [0.175]	−0.14 [0.122]	−0.16 [0.124]
Magnitude of state failure	0.04 [0.105]	0.24** [0.079]	0.20* [0.082]	0.03 [0.077]	0.01 [0.077]
Conflict aim	−0.14 [0.110]	−0.22+ [0.123]	−0.29* [0.127]	−0.09 [0.123]	−0.10 [0.118]
Fertility rate	0.11 [0.076]	0.07 [0.084]	0.07 [0.083]	0.02 [0.078]	0.02 [0.077]
Extrajudicial killings	0.27* [0.115]				
Insurgents					
Genocide (by insurgents)		−0.33 [0.338]	−0.83* [0.343]		
Contraband		0.54* [0.220]	0.76** [0.220]		
Abduction		0.64* [0.304]			
Forced recruitment			0.33 [0.296]		
State Actors					
Genocide (by governments)				0.14 [0.252]	0.26 [0.252]
Troop quality (log)				−0.09 [0.083]	−0.11 [0.088]
Pressganging				0.50* [0.203]	
Conscription					−0.01 [0.165]
Controls					
Polity2	−0.01 [0.019]	−0.01 [0.014]	−0.02 [0.014]	−0.00 [0.019]	−0.01 [0.021]
Duration	−0.00 [0.007]	−0.01 [0.007]	−0.01 [0.009]	−0.00 [0.007]	−0.00 [0.007]

(continued)

	(1) CONFLICT-LEVEL RAPE	(2) RAPE BY INSURGENTS	(3) RAPE BY INSURGENTS	(4) RAPE BY STATE ACTORS	(5) RAPE BY STATE ACTORS
Year	0.09** [0.010]	0.10** [0.013]	0.11** [0.013]	0.10** [0.014]	0.10** [0.014]
Population (log)	0.19** [0.071]	0.05 [0.073]	0.07 [0.076]	0.23** [0.078]	0.18** [0.069]
Cut 1	184.43** [19.233]	210.44** [25.671]	216.01** [25.571]	194.64** [27.410]	197.50** [27.501]
Cut 2	185.37** [19.227]	211.01** [25.687]	216.57** [25.585]	195.57** [27.403]	198.41** [27.490]
Cut 3	186.58** [19.239]	211.98** [25.726]	217.51** [25.628]	196.83** [27.502]	199.63** [27.583]
Observations	855	869	869	692	692
Pseudo R-squared	0.17	0.25	0.23	0.15	0.13

Note: Robust standard errors, clustered by conflict, in brackets; **$p < 0.01$, *$p < 0.05$, +$p < 0.10$.

accountability mechanism for explaining why material resources lead to rape. I consider the recruitment mechanism argument as an alternative to the combatant socialization argument in the case study.

For state forces, and in contrast with insurgent forces, the magnitude of state failure is in the predicted direction, but is not statistically significant. This finding may be the result of the coding for state weakness—the variable is a conservative measure capturing degrees of total state collapse. In those instances, it might be possible that the state no longer exists per se and that state forces have joined other active armed groups to commit violence—in which case, the violence would be coded as insurgent-perpetrated violence.

Ethnic Hatred

Ethnic hatred (H3) is not associated with overall conflict-levels of rape. The coefficient for ethnic war is in the wrong direction and is not statistically

significant (Model 1). This is notable because ethnic hatred is commonly used to explain widespread wartime rape. However, the ethnic war variable is coded broadly, and it is possible that the ethnic cleansing variable more accurately captures the argument.

The ethnic hatred arguments for insurgents are not supported. Although ethnic war is in the predicted direction, it does not reach statistical significance (Models 2 and 3). Insurgent-perpetrated genocide (H4) is not in the hypothesized direction and is only significant in Model 3. The statistically significant coefficient indicates that genocide may actually *decrease* the likelihood of rape—perhaps because of pollution norms, whereby "sexual violence across ethnic boundaries may be understood . . . as polluting the [perpetrator]" (Wood 2008, 341).[39] Additionally, conflict aim (H5) reaches statistical significance, but is also not in the hypothesized direction. These findings suggest that insurgencies aimed at the center are more likely than secessionist insurgencies to perpetrate rape, raising a question about why insurgents intent on leading a country would permit rape, which would only seem to erode public support for their cause.[40] Finally, ethnic cleansing (*H5*) is negatively associated with rape by insurgents; although this variable reaches statistical significance in some specifications (not shown), the variable's sign is consistently negative and thus is not in the hypothesized direction. This may reflect the possibility that ethnic/secessionist wars are not a precise measure of ethnic cleansing. However, until better cross-national data exist on incidents of ethnic cleansing, it is not possible to test this hypothesis more directly.

Lastly, ethnic hatred arguments are also not supported for state actors. Ethnic war (*H3*) is in the opposite direction of the prediction—states are more likely to commit rape in non-ethnic wars—but does not reach statistical significance. Finally, although state-perpetrated genocide (*H4*) is in the predicted direction, it does not reach statistical significance.

Gender Inequality

Although the consistently positive coefficient on fertility indicates that greater gender inequality is associated with higher levels of overall rape (*H6*), neither fertility rates nor any of the measures of women's rights—political, social, and economic—reached statistical significance in any specification (not shown). Once a war has begun, there is no apparent relationship between gender inequality and rape during civil war. However, as previously noted, scholars have found a strong relationship between gender inequality and conflict onset. The insignificant findings may therefore reflect that, for those countries undergoing major civil war, gender inequality is so widespread that it cannot account for the variation in wartime rape. Although it would be inaccurate to argue that gender inequality has no influence on wartime rape, there is no

evidence that conflicts with high levels of rape are distinguished from conflicts with little or no rape by these factors.

Additional Factors and Controls

For overall levels of conflict violence, extrajudicial killing is statistically significant and is positively correlated with overall levels of wartime rape (see robustness checks for more details), supporting arguments that lethal violence and sexual violence may be associated in general, although not always in particular cases.[41] The controls for democracy and duration are consistently negative—suggesting that lower levels of democracy and shorter wars are associated with rape—but insignificant. Population (log) is consistently positive and significant for conflict-level rape and state-perpetrated violence. Larger populations may be more likely to experience state-perpetrated rape, echoing results from earlier studies that found evidence that, all else being equal, larger states may be more likely to repress their citizens (Poe and Tate 1994).

Finally, the variable Year is consistently positive and statistically significant. This finding indicates that time is an important factor in worsening reports of rape. However, it does not settle the debate over whether rape has indeed increased over time or whether monitoring and reporting practices are improving, so what looks to be worsening human rights practices may be at least partially an artifact of measurement (Clark and Sikkink 2013).

Substantive Results

To determine the substantive impact of abduction and pressganging, I calculated the likelihood of each level of rape on the four-point scale with and without abduction by insurgents and with and without pressganging by states using CLARIFY

Figure 10.2. Probability of Insurgent-Perpetrated Wartime Rape with and without Abduction

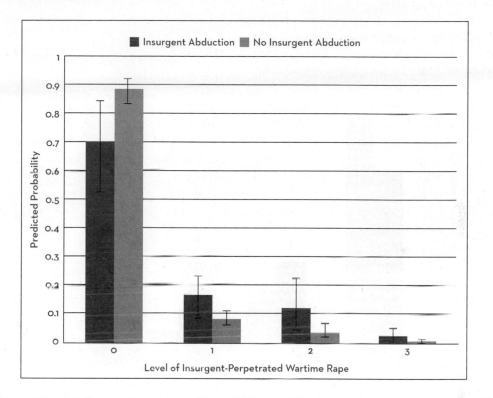

Note: Ordered probit model with standard errors clustered by conflict. Each simulation includes ethnic war, magnitude of state failure, aim, fertility rate, genocide by insurgents, contraband, Polity2, duration, year, and population (log) (all set at their mean values). The error bars represent the 95% confidence interval for each predicted probability value. Estimates calculated using CLARIFY. Two-tailed t-tests show that the differences in the mean predicted probabilities at levels 0, 1, and 2 are statistically significant at the 5% or 10% level. The difference between the mean predicted probability values for level 3 wartime rape falls just short of statistical significance ($p = 0.13$).

(Tomz, Wittenberg, and King 2003). Figure 10.2 shows the mean predicted probabilities, with 95% confidence intervals, of insurgent-perpetrated rape at each level of the dependent variable, given abduction or no abduction. Figure 10.3 displays the same information for state-perpetrated rape. In all cases, abduction and pressganging increase the probability of wartime rape. Rebel groups that rely on abduction are about 2 times, 3.2 times, and 5.5 times more likely to commit wartime rape at levels 1, 2, and 3, respectively, than those groups that do not abduct their fighters. State forces that rely on pressganging are about 1.6 times, 2.5 times, and 4 times more likely to commit wartime rape at levels 1, 2, and 3, respectively, than those government actors that do not pressgang. These findings support the hypothesis that abduction and pressganging have a sizable effect on wartime rape, even when controlling for numerous other factors.

■   ■   ■

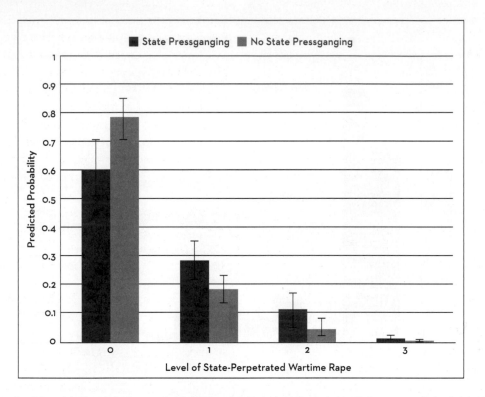

Figure 10.3. Probability of State-Perpetrated Wartime Rape with and without Pressganging

Note: Ordered probit model with standard errors clustered by conflict. Each simulation includes ethnic war, magnitude of state failure, aim, fertility rate, genocide by state actors, troop quality (log), Polity2, duration, year, and population (log) (all set at their mean values). The error bars represent the 95% confidence interval for each predicted probability value. Estimates calculated using CLARIFY. Two-tailed t-tests show that the differences in the mean predicted probabilities at levels 0, 1, and 2 are statistically significant at the 1% or 5% level. The difference between the mean predicted probability values for level 3 wartime rape is not statistically distinguishable from zero ($p = 0.26$).

Micro-Level Evidence from the Sierra Leone Civil War (1990–2002)

Although the statistical analysis demonstrates a correlation between extreme forms of forced recruitment and rape, the nature of the relationship between these variables is best established through a case study. In particular, the case study can help explain why abduction and pressganging are associated with rape, whereas forced recruitment and conscription more generally are not. The case study also shows how rape creates cohesion in groups that have abducted their fighters. Additionally, it explores a series of observable implications of the combatant socialization argument. Finally, I show that an alternative argument that found support in the cross-national data does not explain the observed variation in this case as well as the combatant socialization argument does.

The following brief case study relies on three main data sources: a set of in-depth interviews conducted with ex-combatants in Sierra Leone;[42] the 2004 Sierra Leone War Crimes Documentation (SLWCD) survey (Asher et al. 2004), a nationally representative survey of about 3,600 randomly selected households; and a nationally representative survey of ex-combatants (Humphreys and Weinstein 2004) with data on the combatant groups' demographics, including information on recruitment patterns.

Based on available evidence, the large majority of victims of wartime rape in Sierra Leone identified their perpetrators as members of the Revolutionary United Front (RUF), the main rebel group.[43] That the RUF was reported to have committed the vast majority of rapes is not an artifact of the number of combatants in the group. Among the population of approximately 70,000 demobilized fighters, only about 34% were RUF combatants. The largest armed group was the Civilian Defense Forces (CDF), with about 50% of the total combatants, and the smallest of the major fighting factions was the Sierra Leone Army (SLA), with around 12% (Humphreys and Weinstein 2004). The evidence clearly demonstrates that the RUF disproportionately perpetrated rape; the important question is why.

The armed groups varied dramatically in how they recruited fighters. On joining, RUF combatants "typically knew nobody in their factions," with 77% reporting that they knew neither friends nor family in their unit, leading Humphreys and Weinstein (2004) to conclude that the RUF was a group of "mutual strangers." In contrast, 78% of the CDF reported being recruited by a friend, relative, or a community member, and CDF recruits usually served in units with friends and family members; only 7% knew no one in their unit (Humphreys and Weinstein 2004).

Although many members of the CDF were recruited by kin, they did not necessarily join voluntarily. A detailed conflict-mapping project notes that CDF fighters were coerced even in the early years of the war. For example, the project cites an incident in which a policeman ordered a chief "to gather all the hunters in the section" (Smith, Gambette, and Longley 2004, 164) to be sent to fight, and in another incident, members of a town were "instructed [by an army captain] . . . to give their young men to be trained as vigilantes" (453). Both of these examples demonstrate the use of weaker forms of forced recruitment—coercion and conscription—to garner fighters for the CDF. Notably, the fighters in these cases knew each other and were allowed a degree of agency in deciding to join. As the combatant socialization argument predicts, the CDF was not reported to commit widespread rape in this period.

In the later years of the war, however, individual units comprising the CDF expanded beyond defending only their home chiefdoms. As the CDF units moved into other regions and joined with other fighting forces, they began abducting, and the levels of violence, including rape, committed by the CDF increased. Smith et al. explicitly note this pattern, arguing that a cause of the increase in atrocities by the CDF was that the "new" CDF recruits, who were abducted by force, committed more atrocities than the "old" recruits, some of whom had been carefully selected by their chiefs (Smith, Gambette, and Longley 2004, 54). The CDF grew rapidly during recruitment drives in this period, and commanders reported being unsure how many fighters were under their supervision (Forney 2012). The abduction of large numbers of fighters resulted in a significant loss of internal cohesion. As the CDF began using more extreme forms of recruitment their propensity to commit wartime rape increased accordingly.

The case study also demonstrates a number of observable implications of the combatant socialization argument. The first is that abduction and rape should covary. All factions in Sierra Leone reportedly abducted fighters over the course of the war, but the RUF abducted fighters most often. In addition, RUF was involved in 75% of all attacks and battles throughout the war, but lost almost two-thirds of the battles they fought (186 battles lost of 291 battles total).[44] Both the relatively large number of battles and the high proportion of losses suggest that the RUF, far more often than other fighting groups, needed to constantly draw in new members. Of fighters who reported joining in 1991, 78% said they were abducted, compared with 94% whose first year with the RUF was 1998 (Humphreys and Weinstein 2004). In general, reports of abduction and reports of rape covary over time. Data from the SLWCD survey show two spikes in reported rape in 1998 and 1999, and the number of reported incidents of abduction closely track these increases.[45] If the composition of the group changed little over time, there would be diminishing marginal effectiveness of gang rape. But there were periods of increased need for new fighters due to the nature of the war, including during periods of intense fighting. The loss of fighters and the subsequent abduction and integration of new recruits may be why the RUF invasion of the capital city of Freetown in January 1999 resulted in so many reports of gang rape.

A second observable implication is that, in cases where women are also abducted as fighters, there should be reports of perpetrators of both sexes. The RUF committed the most rape and had the largest proportion of female fighters (24%, according to Humphreys and Weinstein 2004). Of the reported incidents of gang rape in the SLWCD survey, 74% were committed by male-only groups. Mixed-sex perpetrator groups committed 25% of the incidents of gang rape, which comprised 19% of the total reported rape. That is, the survey data indicate that women participated in one in four of the reported incidents of gang rape, or nearly one in five of the total (gang and single-perpetrator) incidents of rape. In interviews, I found that women in the RUF were active perpetrators of gang rape, including restraining the victims and raping them with bottles and sticks.[46]

A third observable implication is that ex-combatants reported that commanders rarely directly ordered them to rape. Few rank-and-file ex-combatants said they were ever commanded to rape, and only a small number of the unit commanders admitted they ever ordered their men to rape. One former RUF fighter said, "Commanders never ordered their men to rape, but they knew it was happening, and they did it themselves."[47] Of the 34 ex-combatant interview subjects, about three-quarters of the sample said they had never seen or heard a commander give an order to rape—an important finding, because this admission is seemingly counter to the fighters' self-interest.

In addition, for rape to serve a bonding function, the violence must be observable to other perpetrators. Of the reported rape in the SLWCD survey, 76% was committed by multiple perpetrators.[48] The survey instrument did not inquire about the exact number of perpetrators, but did distinguish single-perpetrator attacks from those with multiple perpetrators. Evidence from interviews confirms that gang rape happened regularly and was commonly viewed by other combatants and family members or villagers.

Finally, if rape functions as the combatant socialization argument predicts, then it should be a form of violence that creates social bonds between fighters. Interviews with fighters provide abundant detail that rape fostered cohesion rather than causing divisiveness within the group. One particularly revealing answer was the following reply to the question of what types of activities the group would typically do together: "The group rape of women," said one RUF ex-combatant. "Afterward, we would feel good and talk about it a lot, discuss it amongst ourselves, and laugh about it."[49] Others confirmed that rebels would often discuss their sexual prowess with each other, recounting the number of women they had raped during a particular raid. Another ex-combatant stated, "The rebels felt pleased that they were having so much sex, and we would brag to each other about enjoying it so much."[50] Notably, these descriptions were in marked contrast to how ex-combatants recalled conducting other forms of group violence, such as looting and killing. Another measure of cohesion is whether former fighters stayed in contact in the postwar period. Despite the fact that members of the CDF were overwhelmingly recruited into their units by friends or relatives, RUF members were more likely to stay in touch with friends from their faction after the war than CDF members were (Humphreys and Weinstein 2004). This pattern suggests that, although fighters were mostly abducted—quite violently—into their units, the RUF combatants felt strongly socially cohesive with their fellow fighters.

Finally, the cross-national results supported the hypothesis that the availability of material resources predicts the types of recruits attracted to join a group and, in turn, whether civilian abuses will be committed on a mass scale (Weinstein 2007). The argument, at its core, is concerned with combatants' motivations, both for fighting and for committing other acts of violence, for those who "elect to participate" (2007, 7) in armed groups. Because the RUF comprised mostly abducted recruits, the group was made up of a broad variety of different people, few of whom chose to join. Evidence from interviews suggests rape was committed not only by those who joined voluntarily (i.e., those who might be considered "violent types") but also by seemingly ordinary people who were abducted. Despite the availability of material resources, the selection of abusive types does not well explain rape in Sierra Leone, where abductees appear to have perpetrated the majority of rape.

Conclusion

Previous scholarship has shown that the occurrence of rape in war varies widely (e.g., Cohen 2010; Leiby 2009; Wood 2008). What explains this variation? I have argued that the mechanism by which fighters are recruited affects the propensity for combatants to engage in wartime rape. When fighters are forcibly recruited, rape serves to socialize recruits into a coherent force. The findings show that the more extreme forms of forcible recruitment—the random abduction of strangers by insurgents and by states—provide a statistically significant explanation for the occurrence of wartime rape, even when controlling for many other factors, lending support to the combatant socialization argument.

Additionally, circumstances matter. Wartime rape by insurgents is associated with state collapse, which indicates that weak institutions and lack of enforcement of laws create opportunity. Insurgents who fund their operations through contraband are also more likely to commit rape; those relying on diaspora support are not. This finding suggests that access to lootable resources has an especially corrupting influence.

Several common suppositions were not supported. Wartime rape is not more likely during ethnic conflicts nor during genocides. Gender inequality is also not associated with wartime rape.

These findings have important implications for the scholarship on the human costs of war. First, the logics derived from the study of lethal violence may not serve to enhance the understanding of wartime rape. Explaining why rape is widespread in some conflicts but not in others requires further examination of the mechanisms by which fighters are recruited, trained, and socialized.

Second, the findings suggest that high levels of wartime rape may not be part of a military strategy—it may not be an overt "tool" or "weapon" of war—but instead serve to bond recruits together. If so, then the phenomenon often originates at the level of the rank-and-file fighters (see also Goldstein 2001, 368), rather than at the level of commanders.

Reports of abduction by armed groups may serve as an early warning sign of an escalating threat of wartime rape. Such a threat may be especially acute under conditions of state collapse and the presence of lootable resources. In sum, the empirical support for the combatant socialization argument provides the basis for a new direction in academic analyses of wartime rape and possible policy interventions.

NOTES

1. The number of battle deaths is a widely used and also widely criticized measure of the severity of conflict. Lacina and Gleditsch (2005) argue that this measure ignores many forms of nonfatal violence, including sexual violence, and is not an exhaustive measure of the human costs of war.

2. Figure S1 in the Supplemental Appendix (found at http://www .journals.cambridge.org/psr2013016) displays a box plot of battle deaths (log) by the level of wartime rape.

3. Theories *not* tested here include normative explanations for variation in rape across conflicts, such as those advanced by Wood (2008; 2009). I do not dispute Wood's argument, but suggest that the norms of combatant groups are structured by their recruitment choices.

4. Contraband and diaspora support are among the more commonly cited forms of economic endowments used by insurgencies (Weinstein 2005). I explicitly test contraband and diaspora support, arguably the most relevant types of internal and external funding.

5. Genocidal rape may take several forms: occurring immediately before the lethal violence of genocide, as a form of lethal violence itself (a victim may be raped until he or she dies, or the perpetrator may intentionally spread HIV through rape) (Rittner and Roth 2012; Sharlach 2000), or as a way of inflicting long-term trauma (e.g., victims may be physically unable to or be emotionally incapable of having children after a rape) (Koo 2002).

6. For definitions of genocide and ethnic cleansing, see the PITF Problem Set Codebook available at http://globalpolicy.gmu.edu /political-instability-task-force-home/pitf-problem-set-codebook/.

7. These scholars typically trace sexual violence perpetrated by armed factions to norms of masculinity that are imparted to combatants through the training process. Wood (2008) argues that military training is too similar across groups to account for the variation in which militaries commit sexual violence. My argument regarding rape and socialization within the military unit relies not on norms regarding masculinity, but rather on practical needs and strategies.

8. Blattman (2009) uses the near-random nature of LRA abduction in the Ugandan civil war as the basis for a natural experiment comparing ex-combatants and noncombatants.

9. See especially Kier (1998), who argues that task cohesion rather than social cohesion increases military effectiveness. I do not argue that gang rape increases military effectiveness, but only that gang rape increases social cohesion between fighters, which enables the armed unit to sustain itself (see also Gates 2002).

10. Although rape and looting are closely connected crimes in much of the literature, Inal (2013) shows that pillaging was prohibited a century before rape, due in part to the belief that looting was preventable with proper precautions, whereas rape was considered inevitable and too difficult to control.

11. Interviews revealed that many who were abducted felt that they could not leave the armed group. One former RUF fighter said, "The law was that if you escape and get caught, then you will be killed" (Interviewee 11, male RUF ex-combatant, May 28, 2007).

12. Humphreys and Weinstein (2006) argue that groups with low cohesion are unable to "police" effectively fighters' behavior—an innate propensity to be violent is kept in check by strong social ties that shame fighters into less violent behavior. My central argument is briefly outlined as an alternative story in the conclusion of Humphreys and Weinstein (2006: 444), where they raise the possibility that "individuals [may] perform . . . violent acts to establish their position within the organization."

13. When many of the abducted fighters are children, the combatants should have a stronger desire to fit in with group members, because children are more easily influenced by group pressures.

14. The type of recruitment mechanism is exogenously given. The question of how combatant groups choose recruitment mechanisms—which groups abduct and which ask their members to join—has not yet been answered (but see Humphreys and Weinstein [2006], Weinstein [2007] and Beber and Blattman [2013]).

15. Battle itself may serve as a form of costly group bonding. But many wars are not particularly battle heavy—by one count, there were 388 battles over the course of the entire decade-long Sierra Leone war (Bellows and Miguel 2009).

16. This assumption is supported by findings from recent studies (e.g., Humphreys and Weinstein 2004; Vermeij 2009; Weinstein 2005) discussed in the Supplemental Appendix.

17. Table S2 in the Supplemental Appendix summarizes the cases included in previous studies.

18. Data were collected only for those years overlapping with the study period. If a war began before 1980, the data reflect only the period starting in 1980. The State Department Human Rights Country reports began in 1975, and reliable reporting on violence, sexual or otherwise, is unlikely in the first years of reporting. Potential problems posed by this collection strategy are mitigated by controls for the duration of the war.

19. Although the specific armed group, rather than the aggregated group type, may be the ideal unit of analysis, it is challenging to code accurately conflict-year data on wartime rape by individual armed groups on the cross-national level because reports are not always specific about the identities of the perpetrators. There may be reports that "rebels" committed widespread rape, but in cases with more than one active rebel group, it is unclear which particular groups were the perpetrators. If data are collected at the armed group level, reports of "rebels" perpetrating rape in cases with more than one rebel group are uncodable and would be missing from the dataset. A more aggregated dataset of the sort I employ avoids missing these highly relevant, but less specific details reported in the original source.

20. Table S1 in the Supplemental Appendix summarizes the coding rules.

21. See the Supplemental Appendix for further details.

22. See Table S3 in the Supplemental Appendix.

23. Some scholars argue that violence is committed in escalating cycles in which fighters mimic the brutality of their foes; however, rape was asymmetric in about one-third (38%) of the cases.

24. The ideal measure of recruitment would vary by conflict-year, on a scale similar to how wartime rape is measured. However, because of missing data on the conflict-year-armed group level, I instead used a conflict-level dummy variable in the analysis.

25. This measure is not disaggregated by which insurgent group was reported to commit violence in cases where there was more than one insurgency. However, in more than half of the conflict-years in

the study, only one active rebel group is reported in the UCDP/ PRIO data.

26. The conflicts with reported insurgent abduction and forced recruitment and a cross-tabulation between conflict-level reports of insurgent-perpetrated rape and reports of abduction are summarized in Tables S4 and S5 (Supplemental Appendix).

27. Tables S6 and S7 (Supplemental Appendix) summarize conflicts with reports of pressganging and conscription by states, as well as a cross-tabulation between conflict-level reports of state-perpetrated rape and pressganging.

28. An extended discussion of the coding criteria for each variable is available in the Supplemental Appendix, and summary statistics are displayed in Table S11.

29. I also considered two alternative measures of state weakness: first, an index variable reflecting the quality of government (De Soysa and Fjelde 2010), and second, the change in GDP/capita between the current conflict-year and the onset year. Neither proxy changes the substantive results. See the Supplemental Appendix for a discussion and Tables S9 and S10 for results.

30. The UNDP's gender variables—the Gender Empowerment Measure (GEM) and the Gender-Related Development Index (GDI)—were collected beginning in 1995, making them less useful. Both were abandoned in 2010 in favor of a new measure, the Gender Inequality Index, because of their serious limitations and biases, especially for developing countries.

31. Despite the utility of fertility rates as a proxy for gender inequality, they may also be affected by mass wartime rape. However, medical research indicates only a 5% chance of pregnancy per rape (Holmes et al. 1996), so even in cases of widespread rape, it is unlikely that national fertility rates would be affected.

32. Data and brief narratives of each event are available at http.//www .systemicpeace.org/inscr/PITF%20Consolidated%20Case%20 List2010.pdf. Of the 17 conflicts in the period coded as experiencing genocide/politicide, 15 have only state perpetrators and 2 have both state and nonstate perpetrators (Angola [UNITA] and Rwanda).

33. *Ethnic cleansing* takes on a value of 1 when the conflict was ethnic in nature (ethwar=2) *and* rebel groups aimed at regional autonomy (aim=3); all other conflict-years are coded 0.

34. For ease of interpretation, I have reversed the values of 2 and 0 from the original CIRI coding, such that 2 indicates a high level of killing.

35. I used the "best" estimate when it was available, and the low estimate otherwise. There were no death estimates of any type for 187 conflict-years, almost 20% of the dataset. To avoid losing so many observations, I include Battle Deaths in robustness checks but not in the main analysis. Because Kill, Battle Deaths, and Genocide all capture lethal violence, they were not included in the same models.

36. Duration is a constant for each conflict; the main results do not change with an incremental duration variable.

37. I did not perform a fixed-effects analysis for two reasons. First, because the data include only active conflict-years, the panels are both unbalanced (ranging from 1 to 29 observations) and relatively small. Second, there are challenges associated with using fixed effects with nonlinear models with smaller panels, including biased beta coefficients and standard errors. I used the favored approach; namely, an ordered probit model with clustered standard errors.

38. Troop Quality is not significant in any specification, contradicting conventional wisdom that rape by states should be more likely when state military forces are poorly resourced and, as a result, presumably poorly trained.

39. The negative association of genocide with wartime rape may also be an artifact of reporting bias—victims may be raped before being killed, resulting in rape being underreported.

40. The broader question of why insurgencies commit seemingly counterproductive violence against civilians is beyond the scope of this analysis, but has led to numerous recent studies (e.g., Wood 2010.)

41. Using other measures of lethal violence, I estimated a separate model with the inclusion of Battle Deaths (log), in place of extrajudicial killing (in Model 1) and the genocide variables (in Models 2–5) (not shown). The main independent variables retain their statistical significance, and the Battle Deaths variable is consistently positive and significant in some models.

42. I completed 34 in-depth interviews, which included commanders and rank-and-file soldiers from the major armed groups (12 women and 22 men), during fieldwork in Sierra Leone. All but one of the ex-combatant interviews were one-on-one, and each typically lasted two hours. Most were conducted with a translator, who interpreted Krio to English, in Freetown, at the offices of a local NGO that advocates for the rights of former fighters. All interviews were conducted on the condition of anonymity. The interviews are not representative, but illustrate examples of the patterns in the survey data.

43. In the SLWCD, about 85% of the respondents who were raped reported that their attackers were RUF or "rebels." In a survey of IDP camp residents by Physicians for Human Rights (PHR), 84% of respondents reported the perpetrator's faction; 60% of these said that the RUF had raped them (PHR 2002). Of the 626 cases of rape reported to the Truth and Reconciliation Commission, 440 cases, or 70% of the total, were perpetrated by the RUF.

44. Calculated from data from Bellows and Miguel (2009).

45. See Cohen (2010) for a more detailed analysis of abduction and rape over time.

46. See Cohen (2013) for a discussion of female perpetrators in Sierra Leone.

47. Interviewee 7, male RUF ex-combatant, August 1, 2006.

48. The PHR survey found that 33% of rape victims reported gang rape. It is unclear why there is a discrepancy between the two survey results, but both findings suggest, at the very least, that gang rape was common during the war.

49. Interviewee 27, male RUF ex-combatant, March 29, 2008.

50. Interviewee 7, male RUF ex-combatant, August 1, 2006.

REFERENCES

Amir, Menachem. 1971. *Patterns in Forcible Rape.* Chicago: University of Chicago Press.

Asher, Jana, ed., and Human Rights Data Analysis Group of Benetech. 2004. "Sierra Leone War Crimes Documentation Survey (SLWCD) Database v. 2." Data available on request from editor.

Bastick, Megan, Karin Grimm, and Rahel Kunz. 2007. *Sexual Violence in Armed Conflict: Global Overview and Implications for the Security Sector.* Geneva: Geneva Centre for the Democratic Control of Armed Forces.

Baron, Larry, and Murray Straus. 1989. *Four Theories of Rape in American Society: A State-Level Analysis.* New Haven: Yale University Press.

Beber, Bernd, and Christopher Blattman. 2013. "The Logic of Child Soldiering and Coercion." *International Organization* 67 (1): 65104.

Bellows, John, and Edward Miguel. 2009. "War and Local Collective Action in Sierra Leone." *Journal of Public Economics* 93: 1144–57.

Benard, Cheryl. 1994. "Rape as Terror: The Case of Bosnia." *Terrorism and Political Violence* 6 (1): 29–43.

Bijleveld, Catrien, and Jan Hendriks. 2003. "Juvenile Sex Offenders: Differences between Group and Solo Offenders." *Psychology, Crime & Law* 9 (3): 237–45.

Bijleveld, Catrien, Frank Weerman, Daphne Looije, and Jen Hendriks. 2007. "Group Sex Offending by Juveniles: Coercive Sex as a Group Activity." *European Journal of Criminology* 4 (1): 5–31.

Blattman, Christopher. 2009. "From Violence to Voting: War and Political Participation in Uganda." *American Political Science Review* 103 (2): 231–47.

Bloom, Mia. 1999. "War and the Politics of Rape: Ethnic versus Non-Ethnic Conflicts?" Paper prepared for the Annual Meeting of the International Studies Association.

Bourgois, Phillippe. 1996. *In Search of Respect: Selling Crack in El Barrio.* Cambridge: Cambridge University Press.

Bourke, Joanna. 2007. *Rape: Sex, Violence, History.* London: Virago Press.

Brownmiller, Susan. 1975. *Against Our Will: Men, Women and Rape.* New York: Simon and Schuster.

Butler, Christopher, Tali Gluch, and Neil Mitchell. 2007. "Security Forces and Sexual Violence: A Cross-national Analysis of a Principal-agent Argument." *Journal of Peace Research* 44 (6): 669–86.

Card, Claudia. 1996. "Rape as a Weapon of War," *Hypatia* 11(4). Available at http://iupjournals.org/hypatia/hyp11-4.html.

Caprioli, Mary. 2005. "Primed for Violence: The Role of Gender Inequality in Predicting Internal Conflict." *International Studies Quarterly* 49 (2): 161–78.

Caprioli, Mary, Valerie Hudson, Rose McDermott, Bonnie Ballif-Spanvill, Chad Emmett, and S. Matthew Stearmer. 2009. "The WomanStats Project Database: Advancing an Empirical Research Agenda." *Journal of Peace Research* 46 (6): 839–51.

Carpenter, R. Charli. 2006. "Recognizing Gender-based Violence against Civilian Men and Boys in Conflict Situations." *Security Dialogue* 37 (1): 83–103.

Cingranelli, David, and David Richards. 2008. *The Cingranelli-Richards (CIRI) Human Rights Dataset.* Available at http://www.humanrightsdata.org.

Clark, Ann Marie and Kathryn Sikkink. 2013. "Information Effects and Human Rights Data: Is the Good News about Increased Human Rights Information Bad News for Human Rights Measures?" *Human Rights Quarterly* 35 (3).

Cohen, Dara Kay. 2010. *Explaining Sexual Violence during Civil War.* Ph.D. diss. Stanford University.

Cohen, Dara Kay. 2013. "Female Combatants and the Perpetration of Violence: Wartime Rape in the Sierra Leone Civil War," *World Politics* 65 (3): 383–415.

Cohen, Dara Kay, and Amelia Hoover Green. 2012. "Dueling Incentives: Sexual Violence in the Liberian Civil War and the Politics of Human Rights Advocacy." *Journal of Peace Research* 49 (3): 445–58.

De Soysa, Indra, and Hanne Fjelde. 2010. "Is the Hidden Hand an Iron Fist? Capitalism and Civil Peace, 1970–2005." *Journal of Peace Research* 47 (3): 287–98.

Diken, Bulent, and Carsten Bagge Laustsen. 2005. "Becoming Abject: Rape as a Weapon of War." *Body & Society* 11 (1): 111–28.

Farr, Kathryn. 2009. "Extreme War Rape in Today's Civil-War-Torn States: A Contextual and Comparative Analysis." *Gender Issues* 26 (1): 1–41.

Fearon, James D. 2006. "Ethnic Mobilization and Ethnic Violence." In *The Oxford Handbook of Political Economy,* eds. Barry Weingast and Donald Wittman. Oxford: Oxford University Press, pp. 852–868.

Fearon, James D. 2010. "Governance and Civil War Onset," Background paper prepared for the 2011 World Development Report, August 31.

Fearon, James D. and David Laitin. 2011. "A List of Civil Wars, 1945–2009." Revised and Updated Version of the List used for Fearon and Laitin 2003. Stanford University.

Fearon, James D., and David D. Laitin. 2003. "Ethnicity, Insurgency, and Civil War." *American Political Science Review* 97 (1): 75–90.

Forney, Jonathan. 2012. "Who Can We Trust With a Gun? Social Networks and Private Information in Militia Recruitment." Unpublished paper, University of Virginia.

Franklin, Karen. 2004. "Enacting Masculinity: Antigay Violence and Group Rape as Participatory Theater." *Sexuality Research & Social Policy* 1 (2): 25–40.

Gates, Scott. 2002. "Recruitment and Allegiance: The Microfoundations of Rebellion." *Journal of Conflict Resolution* 46 (1): 111–30.

Gibney, Mark, Linda Cornett, and Reed Wood. 2011. *Political Terror Scale 1976–2006.* Available at http://www.politicalterrorscale.org.

Goldstein, Joshua. 2001. *War and Gender: How Gender Shapes the War System and Vice Versa.* Cambridge: Cambridge University Press.

Green, Jennifer Lynn. 2006. "Collective Rape: A Cross-National Study of the Incidence and Perpetrators of Mass Political Sexual Violence, 1980–2003." Ph.D. diss. Ohio State University.

Groth, Nicholas, and Jean Birnbaum. 1979. *Men Who Rape: The Psychology of the Offender.* New York: Plenum.

Hansen, Lene. 2001. "Gender, Nation, Rape: Bosnia and the Construction of Security." *International Feminist Journal of Politics* 3 (1): 55–75.

Harff, Barbara. 2003. "No Lessons Learned from the Holocaust? Assessing Risks of Genocide and Political Mass Murder since 1955." *American Political Science Review* 9 (1): 57–73.

Hauffe, Sarah, and Louise Porter. 2008. "An Interpersonal Comparison of Lone and Group Rape Offences." *Psychology, Crime & Law* 15 (5): 469–91.

Hayden, Robert. 2000. "Rape and Rape Avoidance in Ethno-National Conflicts: Sexual Violence in Liminalized States." *American Anthropologist* 102 (1): 27–41.

Holmes, Melisa, Heidi Resnick, Dean Kilpatrick, and Connie Best. 1996. "Rape-related Pregnancy: Estimates and Descriptive Characteristics from a National Sample of Women." *American Journal of Obstetrics and Gynecology* 175 (2): 320–25.

Horowitz, Donald. 1985. *Ethnic Groups in Conflict.* Berkeley: University of California Press.

Human Rights Watch (HRW). 2004. "In War as in Peace: Sexual Violence and Women's Status." *World Report 2004.* Available at http://hrw.org/wr2k4/15.htm.

Human Security Report Project. 2005. *Human Security Report 2005: War and Peace in the 21ˢᵗ Century.* New York: Oxford University Press.

Human Security Report Project. 2008. *Human Security Brief 2007.* Vancouver: HSRP.

Humphreys, Macartan, and Jeremy Weinstein. 2004. *What the Fighters Say: A Survey of Ex-combatants in Sierra Leone, June-August 2003.* New York: Center on Globalization and Sustainable Development, Columbia University.

Humphreys, Macartan, and Jeremy Weinstein. 2006. "Handling and Manhandling Civilians in Civil War." *American Political Science Review* 100: 429–47.

Inal, Tuba. 2013. *Looting and Rape in Wartime: Law and Change in International Relations.* Philadelphia: University of Pennsylvania Press.

Kalyvas, Stathis. 2006. *The Logic of Violence in Civil War.* Cambridge: Cambridge University Press.

Kier, Elizabeth. 1998. "Homosexuals in the U.S. Military: Open Integration and Combat Effectiveness." *International Security* 23 (2): 5–39.

Koo, Katrina Lee. 2002. "Confronting a Disciplinary Blindness: Women, War and Rape in the International Politics of Security." *Australian Journal of Political Science* 37 (3): 525–36.

Lacina, Bethany, and Nils Petter Gleditsch. 2005. "Monitoring Trends in Global Combat: A New Dataset of Battle Deaths." *European Journal of Population* 21 (2–3): 145–66.

Leiby, Michele. 2009. "Wartime Sexual Violence in Guatemala and Peru." *International Studies Quarterly* 53 (2): 445–68.

MacKinnon, Catharine. 1994. "Rape, Genocide and Women's Human Rights." *Harvard Women's Law Journal* 17 (5): 5–16.

Malamuth, Neil. 1981. "Rape Proclivity among Males." *Journal of Social Issues* 37 (4): 138–57.

Malamuth, Neil. 1996. "The Confluence Model of Sexual Aggression: Feminist and Evolutionary Perspectives." In *Sex, Power, Conflict: Evolutionary and Feminist Perspectives,* eds. David Buss and Neil Malamuth. Oxford: Oxford University Press, pp. 269–295.

Mezey, Gillian. 1994. "Rape in War." *Journal of Forensic Psychiatry* 5 (3): 583–97.

Morris, Madeline. 1996. "By Force of Arms: Rape, War, and Military Culture." *Duke Law Journal* 45 (4): 651–781.

Morrow, Lance. 1993. "Unspeakable: Rape and War." *Time,* February 22.

Mueller, John. 2000. "The Banality of 'Ethnic War.'" *International Security* 25 (1): 42–70.

Mullins, Christopher. 2009. "'He Would Kill Me with His Penis': Genocidal Rape in Rwanda as a State Crime." *Critical Criminology* 17 (1): 15–33.

Physicians for Human Rights. 2002. *War-Related Sexual Violence in Sierra Leone: A Population Based Assessment.* Boston: PHR.

Pickering, Jeffrey. 2010. "Dangerous Drafts? A Time-series, Cross-national Analysis of Conscription and the Use of Military Force, 1946–2001." *Armed Forces and Society* 36 (2): 1–22.

Plümper, Thomas, and Eric Neumayer. 2006. "The Unequal Burden of War: The Effect of Armed Conflict on the Gender Gap in Life Expectancy." *International Organization* 60 (3): 723–54.

Poe, Steven, and C. Neal Tate. 1994. "Repression of Human Rights to Personal Integrity in the 1980s: A Global Analysis." *American Political Science Review* 88 (4): 853–72.

Rittner, Carol, and John K. Roth. eds. 2012. *Rape: Weapon of War and Genocide.* St. Paul: Paragon House.

Samset, Ingrid. 2011. "Sexual Violence: The Case of Eastern Congo." In *The Peace in Between: Post-War Violence and Peacebuilding,* eds. Mats Berdal and Astri Suhrke. New York: Routledge, pp. 229–247.

Sanday, Peggy Reeves. 2007. *Fraternity Gang Rape: Sex, Brotherhood, and Privilege on Campus,* 2nd ed. New York: New York University Press.

Seifert, Ruth. 1996. "The Second Front: The Logic of Sexual Violence in Wars." *Women's Studies International Forum* 19 (1/2): 35–43.

Sharlach, Lisa. 2000. "Rape as Genocide: Bangladesh, the Former Yugoslavia, and Rwanda." *New Political Science* 22 (1): 89–102.

Shils, Edward, and Morris Janowitz. 1948. "Cohesion and Disintegration in the Wehrmacht in World War II." *Public Opinion Quarterly* 12 (2): 280–315.

Smith, Alison, Catherine Gambette, and Thomas Longley. 2004. "Conflict Mapping in Sierra Leone: Violations of International Humanitarian Law from 1991 to 2002." *No Peace without Justice.* Available at http://www.specialcourt.org/SLMission/CMFullReport.html.

Theidon, Kimberly. 2007. "Gender in Transition: Common Sense, Women, and War." *Journal of Human Rights* 6 (4): 453–78.

Tomz, Michael, Jason Wittenberg, and Gary King. 2003. *CLARIFY: Software for Interpreting and Presenting Statistical Results. Version 2.1.* Cambridge, MA: Harvard University.

Valentino, Benjamin, Paul Huth, and Dylan Balch-Lindsay. 2004. "Draining the Sea: Mass Killing, Guerrilla Warfare." *International Organization* 58 (2): 375–407.

Vermeij, Lotte. 2009. "Children of Rebellion: Socialization of Child Soldiers within the Lord's Resistance Army." Master's Thesis. University of Oslo.

Weinstein, Jeremy. 2005. "Resources and the Information Problem in Rebel Recruitment." *Journal of Conflict Resolution* 49 (4): 598–624.

Weinstein, Jeremy. 2007. *Inside Rebellion: The Politics of Insurgent Violence.* Cambridge: Cambridge University Press.

Williams, Lethia, and Daniel Masters. 2011. "Assessing Military Intervention and Democratization: Supportive versus Oppositional Military Interventions." *Democracy and Security* 7 (1): 18–37.

Wood, Elisabeth Jean. 2006. "Variation in Sexual Violence during War." *Politics and Society* 34 (3): 307–42.

Wood, Elisabeth Jean. 2008. "Sexual Violence during War: Toward an Understanding of Variation." In *Order, Conflict and Violence,* eds. Ian Shapiro, Stathis Kalyvas, and Tarek Masoud. New York: Cambridge University Press, pp. 325–51.

Wood, Elisabeth Jean. 2009. "Armed Groups and Sexual Violence: When Is Wartime Rape Rare?" *Politics and Society* 37 (1): 131–61.

Wood, Reed. 2010. "Rebel Capability and Strategic Violence against Civilians." *Journal of Peace Research* 47 (5): 601–14.

11 THE ENVIRONMENT

In his pathbreaking 1968 article, Garrett Hardin describes "the tragedy of the commons," a situation in which a public good is free for all to use, and nobody is required to pay to maintain it. An example is common grazing land, which is soon destroyed by overuse. Climate change is a quintessential example of a "tragedy of the commons." The whole earth is affected, and the efforts of people and governments worldwide are needed to solve the problem. William Nordhaus's article, based on his Nobel Prize acceptance speech, explains his plan to create incentives for countries and people to limit the carbon emissions that cause global climate change: form a large club of economically significant, concerned states that agree to adhere to a high minimum price for any fuel or activity that releases carbon into the atmosphere, and charge a high tariff on all imports from countries that refuse to join the club.

Hamish van der Ven and Yixian Sun note that climate change and the coronavirus pandemic are both examples of tragedies of global interdependence. They explain why the pandemic spurred an urgent, large-scale response while action on climate change has been glacial.

Garrett Hardin
THE TRAGEDY OF THE COMMONS

The population problem has no technical solution; it requires a fundamental extension in morality.

At the end of a thoughtful article on the future of nuclear war, Wiesner and York[1] concluded that: "Both sides in the arms race are . . . confronted by the dilemma of steadily increasing military power and steadily decreasing national security. *It is our considered professional judgment that this dilemma has no technical solution.* If the great powers continue to look for solutions in the area of science and technology only, the result will be to worsen the situation."

I would like to focus your attention not on the subject of the article (national security in a nuclear world) but on the kind of conclusion they reached, namely that there is no technical solution to the problem. An implicit and almost universal assumption of discussions published in professional and semipopular scientific journals is that the problem under discussion has a technical solution. A technical solution may be defined as one that requires a change only in the techniques of the natural sciences, demanding little or nothing in the way of change in human values or ideas of morality.

In our day (though not in earlier times) technical solutions are always welcome. Because of previous failures in prophecy, it takes courage to assert that a desired technical solution is not possible. Wiesner and York exhibited this courage; publishing in a science journal, they insisted that the solution to the problem was not to be found in the natural

sciences. They cautiously qualified their statement with the phrase, "It is our considered professional judgment. . . ." Whether they were right or not is not the concern of the present article. Rather, the concern here is with the important concept of a class of human problems which can be called "no technical solution problems," and, more specifically, with the identification and discussion of one of these.

It is easy to show that the class is not a null class. Recall the game of tick-tack-toe. Consider the problem, "How can I win the game of tick-tack-toe?" It is well known that I cannot, if I assume (in keeping with the conventions of game theory) that my opponent understands the game perfectly. Put another way, there is no "technical solution" to the problem. I can win only by giving a radical meaning to the word "win." I can hit my opponent over the head; or I can drug him; or I can falsify the records. Every way in which I "win" involves, in some sense, an abandonment of the game, as we intuitively understand it. (I can also, of course, openly abandon the game—refuse to play it. This is what most adults do.)

The class of "No technical solution problems" has members. My thesis is that the "population problem," as conventionally conceived, is a member of this class. How it is conventionally conceived needs some comment. It is fair to say that most people who anguish over the population problem are trying to find a way to avoid the evils of overpopulation without relinquishing any of the privileges they now enjoy. They think that farming the seas or developing new strains of wheat will solve the problem—technologically. I try to show here that the solution they seek cannot be found. The population problem cannot be solved

From *Science* 162, no. 3859 (December 13, 1968): 1243–48. This seminal essay remains essential for the discussion of collective goods in the international system and is untainted by the personal views of its author.

in a technical way, any more than can the problem of winning the game of tick-tack-toe.

What Shall We Maximize?

Population, as Malthus said, naturally tends to grow "geometrically," or, as we would now say, exponentially. In a finite world this means that the per capita share of the world's goods must steadily decrease. Is ours a finite world?

A fair defense can be put forward for the view that the world is infinite; or that we do not know that it is not. But, in terms of the practical problems that we must face in the next few generations with the foreseeable technology, it is clear that we will greatly increase human misery if we do not, during the immediate future, assume that the world available to the terrestrial human population is finite. "Space" is no escape.[2]

A finite world can support only a finite population; therefore, population growth must eventually equal zero. (The case of perpetual wide fluctuations above and below zero is a trivial variant that need not be discussed.) When this condition is met, what will be the situation of mankind? Specifically, can Bentham's goal of "the greatest good for the greatest number" be realized?

No—for two reasons, each sufficient by itself. The first is a theoretical one. It is not mathematically possible to maximize for two (or more) variables at the same time. This was clearly stated by von Neumann and Morgenstern,[3] but the principle is implicit in the theory of partial differential equations, dating back at least to D'Alembert (1717–1783).

The second reason springs directly from biological facts. To live, any organism must have a source of energy (for example, food). This energy is utilized for two purposes: mere maintenance and work. For man, maintenance of life requires about 1600 kilo-calories a day ("maintenance calories"). Anything that he does over and above merely staying alive will be defined as work, and is supported by "work calories" which he takes in. Work calories are used not only for what we call work in common speech; they are also required for all forms of enjoyment, from swimming and automobile racing to playing music and writing poetry. If our goal is to maximize population it is obvious what we must do: We must make the work calories per person approach as close to zero as possible. No gourmet meals, no vacations, no sports, no music, no literature, no art. . . . I think that everyone will grant, without argument or proof, that maximizing population does not maximize goods. Bentham's goal is impossible.

In reaching this conclusion I have made the usual assumption that it is the acquisition of energy that is the problem. The appearance of atomic energy has led some to question this assumption. However, given an infinite source of energy, population growth still produces an inescapable problem. The problem of the acquisition of energy is replaced by the problem of its dissipation, as J. H. Fremlin has so wittily shown.[4] The arithmetic signs in the analysis are, as it were, reversed; but Bentham's goal is still unobtainable.

The optimum population is, then, less than the maximum. The difficulty of defining the optimum is enormous; so far as I know, no one has seriously tackled this problem. Reaching an acceptable and stable solution will surely require more than one generation of hard analytical work—and much persuasion.

We want the maximum good per person; but what is good? To one person it is wilderness, to another it is ski lodges for thousands. To one it is estuaries to nourish ducks for hunters to shoot; to another it is factory land. Comparing one good with another is, we usually say, impossible because goods are incommensurable. Incommensurables cannot be compared.

Theoretically this may be true; but in real life incommensurables *are* commensurable. Only a criterion of judgment and a system of weighting are needed. In nature the criterion is survival. Is it better for a species to be small and hide-able, or large and powerful? Natural selection commensurates the incommensurables. The compromise achieved depends on a natural weighting of the values of the variables.

Man must imitate this process. There is no doubt that in fact he already does, but unconsciously. It is when the hidden decisions are made explicit that the arguments begin. The problem for the years ahead is to work out an acceptable theory of weighting. Synergistic effects, nonlinear variation, and difficulties in discounting the future make the intellectual problem difficult, but not (in principle) insoluble.

Has any cultural group solved this practical problem at the present time, even on an intuitive level? One simple fact proves that none has: there is no prosperous population in the world today that has, and has had for some time, a growth rate of zero. Any people that has intuitively identified its optimum point will soon reach it, after which its growth rate becomes and remains zero.

Of course, a positive growth rate might be taken as evidence that a population is below its optimum. However, by any reasonable standards, the most rapidly growing populations on earth today are (in general) the most miserable. This association (which need not be invariable) casts doubt on the optimistic assumption that the positive growth rate of a population is evidence that it has yet to reach its optimum.

We can make little progress in working toward optimum poulation size until we explicitly exorcize the spirit of Adam Smith in the field of practical demography. In economic affairs, *The Wealth of Nations* (1776) popularized the "invisible hand," the idea that an individual who "intends only his own gain," is, as it were, "led by an invisible hand to promote . . . the public interest."[5] Adam Smith did not assert that this was invariably true, and perhaps neither did any of his followers. But he contributed to a dominant tendency of thought that has ever

since interfered with positive action based on rational analysis, namely, the tendency to assume that decisions reached individually will, in fact, be the best decisions for an entire society. If this assumption is correct it justifies the continuance of our present policy of laissez-faire in reproduction. If it is correct we can assume that men will control their individual fecundity so as to produce the optimum population. If the assumption is not correct, we need to reexamine our individual freedoms to see which ones are defensible.

Tragedy of Freedom in a Commons

The rebuttal to the invisible hand in population control is to be found in a scenario first sketched in a little-known pamphlet[6] in 1833 by a mathematical amateur named William Forster Lloyd (1794–1852). We may well call it "the tragedy of the commons," using the word "tragedy" as the philosopher Whitehead used it[7]: "The essence of dramatic tragedy is not unhappiness. It resides in the solemnity of the remorseless working of things." He then goes on to say, "This inevitableness of destiny can only be illustrated in terms of human life by incidents which in fact involve unhappiness. For it is only by them that the futility of escape can be made evident in the drama."

The tragedy of the commons develops in this way. Picture a pasture open to all. It is to be expected that each herdsman will try to keep as many cattle as possible on the commons. Such an arrangement may work reasonably satisfactorily for centuries because tribal wars, poaching, and disease keep the numbers of both man and beast well below the carrying capacity of the land. Finally, however, comes the day of reckoning, that is, the day when the long-desired goal of social stability becomes a reality. At this point, the inherent logic of the commons remorselessly generates tragedy.

As a rational being, each herdsman seeks to maximize his gain. Explicitly or implicitly, more or less consciously, he asks, "What is the utility *to me* of adding one more animal to my herd?" This utility has one negative and one positive component.

1) The positive component is a function of the increment of one animal. Since the herdsman receives all the proceeds from the sale of the additional animal, the positive utility is nearly +1.

2) The negative component is a function of the additional overgrazing created by one more animal. Since, however, the effects of overgrazing are shared by all the herdsmen, the negative utility for any particular decision-making herdsman is only a fraction of −1.

Adding together the component partial utilities, the rational herdsman concludes that the only sensible course for him to pursue is to add another animal to his herd. And another; and another. . . . But this is the conclusion reached by each and every rational herdsman sharing a commons. Therein is the tragedy. Each man is locked into a system that compels him to increase his herd without limit—in a world that is limited. Ruin is the destination toward which all men rush, each pursuing his own best interest in a society that believes in the freedom of the commons. Freedom in a commons brings ruin to all.

Some would say that this is a platitude. Would that it were! In a sense, it was learned thousands of years ago, but natural selection favors the forces of psychological denial.[8] The individual benefits as an individual from his ability to deny the truth even though society as a whole, of which he is a part, suffers. Education can counteract the natural tendency to do the wrong thing, but the inexorable succession of generations requires that the basis for this knowledge be constantly refreshed.

A simple incident that occurred a few years ago in Leominster, Massachusetts, shows how perishable the knowledge is. During the Christmas shopping season the parking meters downtown were covered with plastic bags that bore tags reading: "Do not open until after Christmas. Free parking courtesy of the mayor and city council." In other words, facing the prospect of an increased demand for already scarce space, the city fathers reinstituted the system of the commons. (Cynically, we suspect that they gained more votes than they lost by this retrogressive act.)

In an approximate way, the logic of the commons has been understood for a long time, perhaps since the discovery of agriculture or the invention of private property in real estate. But it is understood mostly only in special cases which are not sufficiently generalized. Even at this late date, cattlemen leasing national land on the western ranges demonstrate no more than an ambivalent understanding, in constantly pressuring federal authorities to increase the head count to the point where overgrazing produces erosion and weed-dominance. Likewise, the oceans of the world continue to suffer from the survival of the philosophy of the commons. Maritime nations still respond automatically to the shibboleth of the "freedom of the seas." Professing to believe in the "inexhaustible resources of the oceans," they bring species after species of fish and whales closer to extinction.[9]

The National Parks present another instance of the working out of the tragedy of the commons. At present, they are open to all, without limit. The parks themselves are limited in extent—there is only one Yosemite Valley—whereas population seems to grow without limit. The values that visitors seek in the parks are steadily eroded. Plainly, we must soon cease to treat the parks as commons or they will be of no value to anyone.

What shall we do? We have several options. We might sell them off as private property. We might keep them as public property, but allocate the right to enter them. The allocation might be on the basis of wealth, by the use of an auction system. It might be on the basis of merit, as defined by some agreed-upon standards. It might be by lottery. Or it might be on a first-come, first-served basis, administered to long queues. These, I think, are all the reasonable possibilities. They are all objectionable. But we must choose—or acquiesce in the destruction of the commons that we call our National Parks.

Pollution

In a reverse way, the tragedy of the commons reappears in problems of pollution. Here it is not a question of taking something out of the commons, but of putting something in—sewage, or chemical, radioactive, and heat wastes into water; noxious and dangerous fumes into the air; and distracting and unpleasant advertising signs into the line of sight. The calculations of utility are much the same as before. The rational man finds that his share of the cost of the wastes he discharges into the commons is less than the cost of purifying his wastes before releasing them. Since this is true for everyone, we are locked into a system of "fouling our own nest," so long as we behave only as independent, rational, free-enterprisers.

The tragedy of the commons as a food basket is averted by private property, or something formally like it. But the air and waters surrounding us cannot readily be fenced, and so the tragedy of the commons as a cesspool must be prevented by different means, by coercive laws or taxing devices that make it cheaper for the polluter to treat his pollutants than to discharge them untreated. We have not progressed as far with the solution of this problem as we have with the first. Indeed, our particular concept of private property, which deters us from exhausting the positive resources of the earth, favors pollution. The owner of a factory on the bank of a stream—whose property extends to the middle of the stream—often has difficulty seeing why it is not his natural right to muddy the waters flowing past his door. The law, always behind the times, requires elaborate stitching and fitting to adapt it to this newly perceived aspect of the commons.

The pollution problem is a consequence of population. It did not much matter how a lonely American frontiersman disposed of his waste. "Flowing water purifies itself every 10 miles," my grandfather used to say, and the myth was near enough to the truth when he was a boy, for there were not too many people. But as population became denser, the natural chemical and biological recycling processes became overloaded, calling for a redefinition of property rights.

How to Legislate Temperance?

Analysis of the pollution problem as a function of population density uncovers a not generally recognized principle of morality, namely: *the morality of an act is a function of the state of the system at the time it is performed.*[10] Using the commons as a cesspool does not harm the general public under frontier conditions, because there is no public; the same behavior in a metropolis is unbearable. A hundred and fifty years ago a plainsman could kill an American bison, cut out only the tongue for his dinner, and discard the rest of the animal. He was not in any important sense being wasteful. Today, with only a few thousand bison left, we would be appalled at such behavior.

In passing, it is worth noting that the morality of an act cannot be determined from a photograph. One does not know whether a man killing an elephant or setting fire to the grassland is harming others until one knows the total system in which his act appears. "One picture is worth a thousand words," said an ancient Chinese; but it may take 10,000 words to validate it. It is as tempting to ecologists as it is to reformers in general to try to persuade others by way of the photographic shortcut. But the essen[c]e of an argument cannot be photographed: it must be presented rationally—in words.

That morality is system-sensitive escaped the attention of most codifiers of ethics in the past. "Thou shalt not . . ." is the form of traditional ethical directives which make no allowance for particular circumstances. The laws of our society follow the pattern of ancient ethics, and therefore are poorly suited to governing a complex, crowded, changeable world. Our epicyclic solution is to augment statutory law with administrative law. Since it is practically impossible to spell out all the conditions under which it is safe to burn trash in the back yard or to run an automobile without smog-control, by law we delegate the details to bureaus. The result is administrative law, which is rightly feared for an ancient reason—*Quis custodiet ipsos custodes?*— "Who shall watch the watchers themselves?" John Adams said that we must have "a government of laws and not men." Bureau administrators, trying to evaluate the morality of acts in the total system, are singularly liable to corruption, producing a government by men, not laws.

Prohibition is easy to legislate (though not necessarily to enforce); but how do we legislate temperance? Experience indicates that it can be accomplished best through the mediation of administrative law. We limit possibilities unnecessarily if we suppose that the sentiment of *Quis custodiet* denies us the use of administrative law. We should rather retain the phrase as a perpetual reminder of fearful dangers we cannot avoid. The great challenge facing us now is to invent the corrective feedbacks that are needed to keep custodians honest. We must find ways to legitimate the needed authority of both the custodians and the corrective feedbacks.

Freedom to Breed Is Intolerable

The tragedy of the commons is involved in population problems in another way. In a world governed solely by the principle of "dog eat dog"—if indeed there ever was such a world—how many children a family had would not be a matter of public concern. Parents who bred too exuberantly would leave fewer descendants, not more, because they would be unable to care adequately for their children. David Lack and others have found that such a negative feedback demonstrably controls the fecundity of birds.[11] But men are not birds, and have not acted like them for millenniums, at least.

If each human family were dependent only on its own resources; *if* the children of improvident parents starved to death; *if*, thus, overbreeding brought its own "punishment" to the germ line— *then* there would be no public interest in controlling the breeding of families. But our society is deeply committed to the welfare state,[12] and hence is confronted with another aspect of the tragedy of the commons.

In a welfare state, how shall we deal with the family, the religion, the race, or the class (or indeed any distinguishable and cohesive group) that adopts overbreeding as a policy to secure its own aggrandizement?[13] To couple the concept of freedom to breed with the belief that everyone born has an equal right to the commons is to lock the world into a tragic course of action.

Unfortunately this is just the course of action that is being pursued by the United Nations. In late 1967, some 30 nations agreed to the following[14]:

> The Universal Declaration of Human Rights describes the family as the natural and fundamental unit of society. It follows that any choice and decision with regard to the size of the family must irrevocably rest with the family itself, and cannot be made by anyone else.

It is painful to have to deny categorically the validity of this right; denying it, one feels as uncomfortable as a resident of Salem, Massachusetts, who denied the reality of witches in the seventeenth century. At the present time, in liberal quarters, something like a taboo acts to inhibit criticism of the United Nations. There is a feeling that the United Nations is "our last and best hope," that we shouldn't find fault with it; we shouldn't play into the hands of the archconservatives. However, let us not forget what Robert Louis Stevenson said: "The truth that is suppressed by friends is the readiest weapon of the enemy." If we love the truth we must openly deny the validity of the Universal Declaration of Human Rights, even though it is promoted by the United Nations. We should also join with Kingsley Davis[15] in attempting to get Planned Parenthood-World Population to see the error of its ways in embracing the same tragic ideal.

Conscience Is Self-Eliminating

It is a mistake to think that we can control the breeding of mankind in the long run by an appeal to conscience. Charles Galton Darwin made this point when he spoke on the centennial of the publication of his grandfather's great book. The argument is straightforward and Darwinian.

People vary. Confronted with appeals to limit breeding, some people will undoubtedly respond to the plea more than others. Those who have more children will produce a larger fraction of the next generation than those with more susceptible consciences. The difference will be accentuated, generation by generation.

In C. G. Darwin's words: "It may well be that it would take hundreds of generations for the progenitive instinct to develop in this way, but if it should do so, nature would have taken her revenge, and the variety *Homo contracipiens* would become extinct and would be replaced by the variety *Homo progenitivus*."[16]

The argument assumes that conscience or the desire for children (no matter which) is hereditary—but hereditary only in the most general formal sense. The result will be the same whether the attitude is transmitted through germ cells, or exosomatically, to use A. J. Lotka's term. (If one denies the latter possibility as well as the former, then what's the point of education?) The argument has here been stated in the context of the population problem, but it applies equally well to any instance in which society appeals to an individual exploiting a commons to restrain himself for the general good—by means of his conscience. To make such an appeal is to set up a selective system that works toward the elimination of conscience from the race.

Pathogenic Effects of Conscience

The long-term disadvantage of an appeal to conscience should be enough to condemn it; but has serious short term disadvantages as well. If we ask a man who is exploiting a commons to desist "in the name of conscience," what are we saying to him? What does he hear?—not only at the moment but also in the wee small hours of the night when, half asleep, he remembers not merely the words we used but also the nonverbal communication cues we gave him unawares? Sooner or later, consciously or subconsciously, he senses that he has received two communications, and that they are contradictory: (i) (intended communication) "If you don't do as we ask, we will openly condemn you for not acting like a responsible citizen"; (ii) (the unintended communication) "If you *do* behave as we ask, we will secretly condemn you for a simpleton who can be shamed into standing aside while the rest of us exploit the commons."

Everyman then is caught in what Bateson has called a "double bind." Bateson and his co-workers have made a plausible case for viewing the double bind as an important causative factor in the genesis of schizophrenia.[17] The double bind may not always be so damaging, but it always endangers the mental health of anyone to whom it is applied. "A bad conscience," said Nietzsche, "is a kind of illness."

To conjure up a conscience in others is tempting to anyone who wishes to extend his control beyond the legal limits. Leaders at the highest level succumb to this temptation. Has any President during the past generation failed to call on labor unions to moderate voluntarily their demands for higher wages, or to steel companies to honor voluntary guidelines on prices? I can recall none. The rhetoric used on such occasions is designed to produce feelings of guilt in noncooperators.

For centuries it was assumed without proof that guilt was a valuable, perhaps even an indispensable, ingredient of the civilized life. Now, in this post-Freudian world, we doubt it.

Paul Goodman speaks from the modern point of view when he says: "No good has ever come from feeling guilty, neither intelligence, policy, nor compassion. The guilty do not pay attention to the object but only to themselves, and not even to their own interests, which might make sense, but to their anxieties."[18]

One does not have to be a professional psychiatrist to see the consequences of anxiety. We in the Western world are just emerging from a dreadful two-centuries-long Dark Ages of Eros that was sustained partly by prohibition laws, but perhaps more effectively by the anxiety-generating mechanisms of education. Alex Comfort has told the story well in *The Anxiety Makers*[19]; it is not a pretty one.

Since proof is difficult, we may even concede that the results of anxiety may sometimes, from certain points of view, be desirable. The larger question we should ask is whether, as a matter of policy, we should ever encourage the use of a technique the tendency (if not the intention) of which is psychologically pathogenic. We hear much talk these days of responsible parenthood; the coupled words are incorporated into the titles of some organizations devoted to birth control. Some people have proposed massive propaganda campaigns to instill responsibility into the nation's (or the world's) breeders. But what is the meaning of the word responsibility in this context? Is it not merely a synonym for the word conscience? When we use the word responsibility in the absence of substantial sanctions are we not trying to browbeat a free man in a commons into acting against his own interest? Responsibility is a verbal counterfeit for a substantial *quid pro quo*. It is an attempt to get something for nothing.

If the word responsibility is to be used at all, I suggest that it be in the sense Charles Frankel uses it.[20] "Responsibility," says this philosopher, "is the product of definite social arrangements." Notice that Frankel calls for social arrangements—not propaganda.

Mutual Coercion Mutually Agreed Upon

The social arrangements that produce responsibility are arrangements that create coercion, of some sort. Consider bank-robbing. The man who takes money from a bank acts as if the bank were a commons. How do we prevent such action? Certainly not by trying to control his behavior solely by a verbal appeal to his sense of responsibility. Rather than rely on propaganda we follow Frankel's lead and insist that a bank is not a commons; we seek the definite social arrangements that will keep it from becoming a commons. That we thereby infringe on the freedom of would-be robbers we neither deny nor regret.

The morality of bank-robbing is particularly easy to understand because we accept complete prohibition of this activity. We are willing to say "Thou shalt not rob banks," without providing for exceptions. But temperance also can be created by coercion. Taxing is a good coercive device. To keep downtown shoppers temperate in their use of parking space we introduce parking meters for short periods, and traffic fines for longer ones. We need not actually forbid a citizen to park as long as he wants to; we need merely make it increasingly expensive for him to do so. Not prohibition, but carefully biased options are what we offer him. A Madison Avenue man might call this persuasion; I prefer the greater candor of the word coercion.

Coercion is a dirty word to most liberals now, but it need not forever be so. As with the four-letter words, its dirtiness can be cleansed away by exposure to the light, by saying it over and over without apology or embarrassment. To many, the word coercion implies arbitrary decisions of distant and irresponsible bureaucrats; but this is not a necessary part of its meaning. The only kind of coercion I recommend is mutual coercion, mutually agreed upon by the majority of the people affected.

To say that we mutually agree to coercion is not to say that we are required to enjoy it, or even to pretend we enjoy it. Who enjoys taxes? We all grumble about them. But we accept compulsory taxes because we recognize that voluntary taxes would favor the conscienceless. We institute and (grumblingly) support taxes and other coercive devices to escape the horror of the commons.

An alternative to the commons need not be perfect just to be preferable. With real estate and other material goods, the alternative we have chosen is the institution of private property coupled with legal inheritance. Is this system perfectly just? As a genetically trained biologist I deny that it is. It seems to me that, if there are to be differences in individual inheritance, legal possession should be perfectly correlated with biological inheritance—that those who are biologically more fit to be the custodians of property and power should legally inherit more. But genetic recombination continually makes a mockery of the doctrine of "like father, like son" implicit in our laws of legal inheritance. An idiot can inherit millions, and a

trust fund can keep his estate intact. We must admit that our legal system of private property plus inheritance is unjust—but we put up with it because we are not convinced, at the moment, that anyone has invented a better system. The alternative of the commons is too horrifying to contemplate. Injustice is preferable to total ruin.

It is one of the peculiarities of the warfare between reform and the status quo that it is thoughtlessly governed by a double standard. Whenever a reform measure is proposed it is often defeated when its opponents triumphantly discover a flaw in it. As Kingsley Davis has pointed out,[21] worshippers of the status quo sometimes imply that no reform is possible without unanimous agreement, an implication contrary to historical fact. As nearly as I can make out, automatic rejection of proposed reforms is based on one of two unconscious assumptions: (i) that the status quo is perfect; or (ii) that the choice we face is between reform and no action; if the proposed reform is imperfect, we presumably should take no action at all, while we wait for a perfect proposal.

But we can never do nothing. That which we have done for thousands of years is also action. It also produces evils. Once we are aware that the status quo is action, we can then compare its discoverable advantages and disadvantages with the predicted advantages and disadvantages of the proposed reform, discounting as best we can for our lack of experience. On the basis of such a comparison, we can make a rational decision which will not involve the unworkable assumption that only perfect systems are tolerable.

Recognition of Necessity

Perhaps the simplest summary of this analysis of man's population problems is this: the commons, if justifiable at all, is justifiable only under conditions of low-population density. As the human population has increased, the commons has had to be abandoned in one aspect after another.

First we abandoned the commons in food gathering, enclosing farm land and restricting pastures and hunting and fishing areas. These restrictions are still not complete throughout the world.

Somewhat later we saw that the commons as a place for waste disposal would also have to be abandoned. Restrictions on the disposal of domestic sewage are widely accepted in the Western world; we are still struggling to close the commons to pollution by automobiles, factories, insecticide sprayers, fertilizing operations, and atomic energy installations.

In a still more embryonic state is our recognition of the evils of the commons in matters of pleasure. There is almost no restriction on the propagation of sound waves in the public medium. The shopping public is assaulted with mindless music, without its consent. Our government is paying out billions of dollars to create supersonic transport which will disturb 50,000 people for every one person who is whisked from coast to coast three hours faster. Advertisers muddy the airwaves of radio and television and pollute the view of travelers. We are a long way from outlawing the commons in matters of pleasure. Is this because our Puritan inheritance makes us view pleasure as something of a sin, and pain (that is, the pollution of advertising) as the sign of virtue?

Every new enclosure of the commons involves the infringement of somebody's personal liberty. Infringements made in the distant past are accepted because no contemporary complains of a loss. It is the newly proposed infringements that we vigorously oppose; cries of "rights" and "freedom" fill the air. But what does "freedom" mean? When men mutually agreed to pass laws against robbing, mankind became more free, not less so. Individuals locked into the logic of the commons are free only to bring on universal ruin; once they see the necessity of mutual coercion, they become free to

pursue other goals. I believe it was Hegel who said, "Freedom is the recognition of necessity."

The most important aspect of necessity that we must now recognize, is the necessity of abandoning the commons in breeding. No technical solution can rescue us from the misery of overpopulation. Freedom to breed will bring ruin to all. At the moment, to avoid hard decisions many of us are tempted to propagandize for conscience and responsible parenthood. The temptation must be resisted, because an appeal to independently acting consciences selects for the disappearance of all conscience in the long run, and an increase in anxiety in the short.

The only way we can preserve and nurture other and more precious freedoms is by relinquishing the freedom to breed, and that very soon. "Freedom is the recognition of necessity"—and it is the role of education to reveal to all the necessity of abandoning the freedom to breed. Only so, can we put an end to this aspect of the tragedy of the commons.

NOTES

1. J. B. Wiesner and H. F. York, *Sci. Amer.* 211 (No. 4), 27 (1964).
2. G. Hardin, *J. Hered.* 50, 68 (1959); S. von Hoernor, *Science* 137, 18 (1962).
3. J. von Neumann and O. Morgenstern, *Theory of Games and Economic Behavior* (Princeton Univ. Press, Princeton, NJ, 1947), p. 11.
4. J. H. Fremlin, *New Sci.*, No. 415 (1964), p. 285.
5. A. Smith, *The Wealth of Nations* (Modern Library, New York, 1937), p. 423.
6. W. F. Lloyd, *Two Lectures on the Checks to Population* (Oxford Univ. Press, Oxford, England, 1833), reprinted (in part) in *Population, Evolution, and Birth Control*, G. Hardin, Ed. (Freeman, San Francisco, 1964), p. 37.
7. A. N. Whitehead, *Science and the Modern World* (Mentor, New York, 1948), p. 17.
8. G. Hardin, Ed., *Population, Evolution, and Birth Control* (Freeman, San Francisco, 1964), p. 56.
9. S. McVay, *Sci. Amer.* 216 (No. 8), 13 (1966).
10. J. Fletcher, *Situation Ethics* (Westminster, Philadelphia, 1966).
11. D. Lack, *The Natural Regulation of Animal Numbers* (Clarendon Press, Oxford, 1954).

12. H. Girvetz, *From Wealth to Welfare* (Stanford Univ. Press, Stanford, CA, 1950).
13. G. Hardin, *Perspec. Biol. Med.* 6, 366 (1963).
14. U. Thant, *Int. Planned Parenthood News*, No. 168 (February 1968), p. 3.
15. K. Davis, *Science* 158, 730 (1967).
16. S. Tax, Ed., *Evolution after Darwin* (Univ. of Chicago Press, Chicago, 1960), vol. 2, p. 469.
17. G. Bateson, D. D. Jackson, J. Haley, J. Weakland, *Behav. Sci.* 1, 251 (1956).
18. P. Goodman, *New York Rev. Books* 10(8), 22 (23 May 1968).
19. A. Comfort, *The Anxiety Makers* (Nelson, London, 1967).
20. C. Frankel, *The Case for Modern Man* (Harper, New York, 1955), p. 203.
21. J. D. Roslansky, *Genetics and the Future of Man* (Appleton-Century-Crofts, New York, 1966), p. 177.

William Nordhaus

THE CLIMATE CLUB

How to Fix a Failing Global Effort

Climate change is the major environmental challenge facing nations today, and it is increasingly viewed as one of the central issues in international relations. Yet governments have used a flawed architecture in their attempts to forge treaties to counter it. The key agreements, the 1997 Kyoto Protocol and the 2015 Paris climate accord, have relied on voluntary arrangements, which induce free-riding that undermines any agreement.

States need to reconceptualize climate agreements and replace the current flawed model with an alternative that has a different incentive structure—what I would call the "Climate Club." Nations can overcome the syndrome of free-riding in international climate agreements if they adopt the club model and include penalties for nations that do not participate. Otherwise, the global effort to curb climate change is sure to fail.

In December 2019, the 25th Conference of the Parties (COP25) of the UN Framework Convention on Climate Change (UNFCCC) met in Madrid, Spain. As most independent observers concluded, there was a total disconnect between the need for sharp emission reductions and the outcomes of the deliberations. COP25 followed COP24, which followed COP23, which followed COP22, all the way back to COP1—a series of multilateral negotiations that produced the failed Kyoto Protocol and the wobbly Paris accord. At the end of this long string of conferences, the world in 2020 is no further along than it was after COP1, in 1995:

there is no binding international agreement on climate change.

When an athletic team loses 25 games in a row, it is time for a new coach. After a long string of failed climate meetings, similarly, the old design for climate agreements should be scrapped in favor of a new one that can fix its mistakes.

The Prisoner's Dilemma of Climate Change

Concepts from game theory elucidate different kinds of international conflicts and the potential for international agreements. A first and easy class of agreements are those that are universally beneficial and have strong incentives for parties to participate. Examples include coordination agreements, such as the 1912 accord to coordinate the world measurements of time and, more recently, the agreement to use "aviation English" for civil aviation, which coordinates communications to prevent collisions during air travel. A second class of agreements, of medium difficulty, rely on reciprocity, a central example being treaties on international trade.

A third class of international agreements confront hard problems—those involving global public goods. These are goods whose impacts are indivisibly spread around the entire globe. Public goods do not represent a new phenomenon. But they are becoming more critical in today's world because of rapid technological change and the astounding decline in transportation and communication costs. The quick spread of COVID-19 is a grim reminder of

From *Foreign Affairs* 99, no. 3 (May/June 2020): 10–17.

how global forces respect no boundaries and of the perils of ignoring global problems until they threaten to overwhelm countries that refuse to prepare and cooperate.

Agreements on global public goods are hard because individual countries have an incentive to defect, producing noncooperative, beggar-thy-neighbor outcomes. In doing so, they are pursuing their national interests rather than cooperating on plans that are globally beneficial—and beneficial to the individual countries that participate. Many of the thorniest global issues—interstate armed conflict, nuclear proliferation, the law of the sea, and, increasingly, cyberwarfare—have the structure of a prisoner's dilemma. The prisoner's dilemma occurs in a strategic situation in which the actors have incentives to make themselves better off at the expense of other parties. The result is that all parties are worse off. (The studies of Columbia's Scott Barrett on international environmental agreements lay out the theory and history in an exemplary way.)

International climate treaties, which attempt to address hard problems, fall into the third class, and they have largely failed to meet their objectives. There are many reasons for this failure. Since they are directed at a hard problem, international climate agreements start with an incentive structure that has proved intrinsically difficult to make work. They have also been undermined by myopic or venal leaders who have no interest in long-term global issues and refuse to take the problem seriously. Further obstacles are the scale, difficulty, and cost of slowing climate change.

But in addition to facing the intrinsic difficulty of solving the hard problem of climate change, international climate agreements have been based on a flawed model of how they should be structured. The central flaw has been to overlook the incentive structure. Because countries do not realistically appreciate that the challenge of global warming presents a prisoner's dilemma, they have negotiated agreements that are voluntary and promote free-riding—and are thus sure to fail.

More Knowledge, No Progress

The risks of climate change were recognized in the UNFCCC, which was ratified in 1994. The UNFCCC declared that the "ultimate objective" of climate policy is "to achieve . . . stabilization of greenhouse gas concentrations in the atmosphere at a level that would prevent dangerous anthropogenic interference with the climate system."

The first step in implementing the UNFCCC was taken in the Kyoto Protocol in 1997. Kyoto's most important innovation was an international cap-and-trade system for emissions. Each country's greenhouse gas emissions were limited under the protocol (the cap). But countries could buy or sell their emission rights to other countries depending on their circumstances (the trade). The idea was that the system would create a market in emissions, which would give countries, companies, and governments strong incentives to reduce their emissions at the lowest possible cost.

The Kyoto Protocol was an ambitious attempt to construct an international architecture to harmonize the policies of different countries. Because it was voluntary, however, the United States and Canada withdrew without consequences, and no new countries signed on. As a result, there was a sharp reduction in its coverage of emissions. It died a quiet death, mourned by few, on December 31, 2012—a club that no country cared to join.

The Kyoto Protocol was followed by the Paris accord of 2015. This agreement was aimed at "holding the increase in the global average temperature to well below 2°C above pre-industrial levels." The Paris agreement requires all countries to make their best efforts through "nationally determined contributions." For example, China announced that it would reduce its carbon intensity (that is, its carbon dioxide emissions per unit of GDP), and other countries announced absolute reductions in emissions. The United States, under the Trump administration, declared that it would withdraw from the agreement.

Even before the United States withdrew, it was clear that the national targets in the Paris accord were inconsistent with the two-degree temperature target. The accord has two major structural defects: it is uncoordinated, and it is voluntary. It is uncoordinated in the sense that its policies, if undertaken, would not limit climate change to the target of two degrees. And it is voluntary because there are no penalties if countries withdraw or fail to meet their commitments.

Studies of past trends, as well as the likely ineffectiveness of the commitments in the Paris accord, point to a grim reality. Global emissions would need to decline by about three percent annually in the coming years for the world to limit warming to the two-degree target. Actual emissions have grown by about two percent annually over the last two decades. Modeling studies indicate that even if the Paris commitments are met, the global temperature will almost certainly exceed the two-degree target later in the twenty-first century.

The bottom line is that climate policy has not progressed over the last three decades. The dangers of global warming are much better understood, but nations have not adopted effective policies to slow the coming peril.

Free Riders

Why are agreements on global public goods so elusive? After all, nations have succeeded in forging effective policies for national public goods, such as clean air, public health, and water quality. Why have landmark agreements such as the Kyoto Protocol and the Paris accord failed to make a dent in emission trends?

The reason is free-riding, spurred by the tendency for countries to pursue their national interests. Free-riding occurs when a party receives the benefits of a public good without contributing to the costs. In the case of international climate change policy, countries have an incentive to rely on the emission reductions of others without making costly domestic reductions themselves.

Focusing on national welfare is appropriate when impacts do not spill over national borders. In such cases, countries are well governed if they put their citizens' well-being first rather than promoting narrow interests such as through protectionist tariffs or lax environmental regulations. However, when tackling global problems, nationalist or noncooperative policies that focus solely on the home country at the expense of other countries—beggar-thy-neighbor policies—are counterproductive.

Many global issues induce cooperation by their very nature. Like players on athletic teams, countries can accomplish more when acting together than when going their separate ways. The most prominent examples of positive-sum cooperation are the treaties and alliances that have led to a sharp decline in battle deaths in recent years. Another important case is the emergence of low-tariff regimes in most countries. By reducing barriers to trade, all nations have seen an improvement in their living standards.

However, alongside the successes lie a string of failures on the global stage. Nations have failed to stop nuclear proliferation, overfishing in the oceans, littering in space, and transnational cybercrime. Many of these failures reflect the syndrome of free-riding. When there are international efforts to resolve a global problem, some nations inevitably contribute very little. For example, NATO is committed to defending its members against attacks. The parties to the alliance agreed to share the costs. In practice, however, the burden sharing is not equal: the United States accounted for 70 percent of the total defense spending by NATO members in 2018. Many other NATO members spend only a tiny fraction of their GDPS on defense, Luxembourg being the extreme case, at just 0.5 percent. Countries that do not fully participate in a multiparty agreement on public goods get a free ride on the costly investments of other countries.

Free-riding is a major hurdle to addressing global externalities, and it lies at the heart of the failure to deal with climate change. Consider a voluntary agreement, such as the Kyoto Protocol or the Paris accord. No single country has an incentive to cut its emissions sharply. Suppose that when Country A spends $100 on abatement, global damages decline by $200 but Country A might get only $20 worth of the benefits: its national cost-benefit analysis would lead it not to undertake the abatement. Hence, nations have a strong incentive not to participate in such agreements. If they do participate, there is a further incentive to understate their emissions or to miss ambitious objectives. The outcome is a noncooperative free-riding equilibrium, in which few countries undertake strong climate change policies—a situation that closely resembles the current international policy environment.

When it comes to climate change policies today, nations speak loudly but carry no stick at all.

Membership Benefits

In light of the failure of past agreements, it is easy to conclude that international cooperation on climate change is doomed to fail. This is the wrong conclusion. Past climate treaties have failed because of poor architecture. The key to an effective climate treaty is to change the architecture, from a voluntary agreement to one with strong incentives to participate.

Successful international agreements function as a kind of club of nations. Although most people belong to clubs, they seldom consider their structure. A club is a voluntary group deriving mutual benefits from sharing the costs of producing a shared good or service. The gains from a successful club are sufficiently large that members will pay dues and adhere to club rules to get the benefits of membership.

The principal conditions for a successful club include that there is a public-good-type resource that can be shared (whether the benefits from a military alliance or the enjoyment of low-cost goods from around the world); that the cooperative arrangement, including the costs or dues, is beneficial for each of the members; that nonmembers can be excluded or penalized at relatively low cost to members; and that the membership is stable in the sense that no one wants to leave.

Nations can overcome the syndrome of free-riding in international climate agreements if they adopt the club model rather than the Kyoto-Paris model. How could the Climate Club work? There are two key features of the Climate Club that would distinguish it from previous efforts. The first is that participating countries would agree to undertake harmonized emission reductions designed to meet a climate objective (such as a two-degree temperature limit). The second and critical difference is that nations that do not participate or do not meet their obligations would incur penalties.

Start with the rules for membership. Early climate treaties involved quantitative restrictions, such as emission limits. A more fruitful rule, in line with modern environmental thinking, would focus on a carbon price, a price attached to emissions of carbon dioxide and other greenhouse gases. More precisely, countries would agree on an international target carbon price, which would be the focal provision of the agreement. For example, countries might agree that each will implement policies that produce a minimum domestic carbon price of $50 per metric ton of carbon dioxide. That target price might apply to 2020 and rise over time at, say, three percent per year in real terms. (The World Bank estimates that the global average carbon price today is about $2 per ton of carbon dioxide.)

Why would carbon prices be a better coordinating device than the quantity of emissions? One important reason is that an efficient path for limiting warming would involve equating the incremental (marginal) costs of reductions in all countries and all sectors. This would be accomplished by having equal carbon prices everywhere. A second and equally powerful reason involves bargaining strategy, a point emphasized in the writings of the economist Martin Weitzman. When countries bargain about the target price, this simplifies the negotiations, making them about a single number: dollars per ton. When the bargaining is about each country's emission limit, this is a hopeless matter, because countries want low limits for others and high limits for themselves. A bargain about emission limits is likely to end up with no limits at all.

A treaty focusing on an international target carbon price would not mandate a particular national policy. Countries could use carbon taxes (which would easily solve the problem of setting the price) or a cap-and-trade mechanism (such as is used by the European Union). Either can achieve the minimum price, but different countries might find one or the other approach more suited to its institutions.

The second and critical feature of the Climate Club would be a penalty for nonparticipants. This is what gives the club mechanism its structure of incentives and what distinguishes it from all current approaches to countering climate change: nonparticipants are penalized. Some form of sanction on nonparticipants is required to induce countries to participate in and abide by agreements with local costs but diffuse benefits. Without penalties, the agreement will dissolve into ineffectiveness, as have the Kyoto and Paris schemes.

Although many different penalties might be considered, the simplest and most effective would be tariffs on imports from nonparticipants into club member states. With penalty tariffs on nonparticipants, the Climate Club would create a situation in which countries acting in their self-interest would choose to enter the club and undertake ambitious emission reductions because of the structure of the payoffs.

One brand of penalty could be a countervailing duty on the carbon content of imports. However, this approach would be both complicated and ineffective as an incentive to join a club. The main problem is that much carbon dioxide is emitted in the production of nontraded goods, such as electricity. Additionally, calculating accurately the indirect carbon content of imports is exceedingly complicated.

A second and more promising approach would be a uniform tariff on all imports from nonclub countries into the club. Take as an example a penalty tariff of five percent. If nonparticipant Country A exported $100 billion worth of goods into the club countries, it would be penalized with $5 billion of tariffs. The advantage of uniform tariffs over countervailing duties is simply simplicity. The point is not to fine-tune the tariffs to a nonparticipant country's production structure but to provide powerful incentives for countries to be part of the Climate Club.

Sanctioning the Nonparticipants

There is a small academic literature analyzing the effectiveness of clubs and comparing them to agreements without sanctions. The results suggest that a well-designed climate club requiring strong carbon abatement and imposing trade sanctions on nonparticipants would provide well-aligned incentives for countries to join.

I will illustrate the point using the results of a study I presented in my 2015 Presidential Address to the American Economic Association and summarized in my Nobel Prize lecture. (The former provided a full explanation of the model, the results, the qualifications, and the sensitivity analyses; the latter was a nontechnical discussion of just the key results.) The study divided the world into 15 major regions. Each region has its own abatement costs and damages from climate change. Because of the global nature of climate change, however, the abatement costs are local, whereas virtually all the benefits of a region's emission reductions spill over to other regions. Even for the largest players (the United States and China), at least 85 percent of the benefits of their emission reductions accrue abroad.

The modeling of the study tested alternative uniform tariff rates, from zero to ten percent, and different international target carbon prices, from $12.50 per ton to $100 per ton. It then asked if there were stable coalitions of countries that wanted to join and remain in the club. One case is a regime with a carbon price of $25 per ton and a penalty tariff of three percent. With this regime, it is in the national interest of every region to participate, and it is in the interest of no region to defect and free-ride. The coalition of all regions is stable because the losses from the tariff (for non-participants) are larger than the costs of abatement (for participants).

The Kyoto Protocol and the Paris accord can be thought of as regimes with zero penalty tariffs. Both history and modeling have shown that these induce minimal abatement. Put differently, the analysis predicts—alas, in a way that history has confirmed—that voluntary international climate agreements will accomplish little; they will definitely not meet the ambitious objectives of the Paris accord.

Such detailed modeling results should not be taken literally. Modeling offers insights rather than single-digit accuracy. The basic lesson is that current approaches are based on a flawed concept of how to manage the global commons. The voluntary approach needs to be replaced by a club structure in which there are penalties for nonparticipation—in effect, environmental taxes on those who are violating the global commons.

Toward Effective Policies

The international community is a long way from adopting a Climate Club or a similar arrangement to slow the ominous march of climate change. The obstacles include ignorance, the distortions of democracy by anti-environmental interests, free-riding among those looking to the interests of their country, and shortsightedness among those who discount the interests of the future. Additionally, nations have continued with the losing strategy (zero wins, 25 losses) pursued by the UNFCCC's Conference of the Parties structure. Global warming is a trillion-dollar problem requiring a trillion-dollar solution, and that demands a far more robust incentive structure.

There are many steps necessary to slow global warming effectively. One central part of a productive strategy is to ensure that actions are global and not just national or local. The best hope for effective coordination is a Climate Club—a coalition of nations that commit to strong steps to reduce emissions and mechanisms to penalize countries that do not participate. Although this is a radical proposal that breaks with the approach of past climate negotiations, no other blueprint on the public agenda holds the promise of strong and coordinated international action.

Hamish van der Ven and Yixian Sun

VARIETIES OF CRISES
Comparing the Politics of COVID-19 and Climate Change

At the outset of the COVID-19 pandemic, a number of scholars and activists expressed confusion at the speed and scale of responses to COVID-19 in comparison to the global climate crisis (Bordoff 2020; Dolsak and Prakash 2020; Galbraith and Otto 2020).[1] Granted, there was, and remains, significant variation in the nature of COVID-19 responses by governments (Hale et al. 2020). However, taken as a whole, the disparity between the two crises is enormous. COVID-19 resulted in national governments closing borders, shutting down workplaces, cancelling sports seasons, and confining citizens to their domiciles. Such actions are unthinkable for most governments as responses to the climate crisis. The question, then, is why have there been immediate and far-reaching state responses to COVID-19 but not similar responses to the climate crisis? After all, the climate crisis has been called a "direct existential threat" by the UN Secretary-General, whereas COVID-19 has an average global case fatality rate of just over 5 percent (Guterres 2018).[2] Why the willingness to move mountains for one crisis but not the other?

We argue that COVID-19 and the climate crisis are different varieties of crisis and that the different characteristics of each crisis lead to different types of governance responses. This may initially appear to be an obvious argument. After all, the timescales of these crises differ dramatically and may auger toward different responses. However, we contend that there are other under-considered differences between these crises that account for their different responses. Enumerating these differences is useful for predicting governance responses to future crises and envisioning how perceptions of the climate crisis might be shifted to engender a faster and farther-reaching response. Our central contribution is a conceptual framework that outlines eight inductively derived crisis characteristics and explains how variation in the value of these characteristics may affect the scope and immediacy of state responses to crises. We argue that the higher the value of these eight characteristics, the more likely it is that a crisis will be met with swift and far-reaching responses. We begin by comparing COVID-19 and the climate crisis across these eight categories. We then describe the relationship between crisis characteristics and political responses. We end by discussing implications for the climate crisis.

The Characteristics of Crises

A crisis—be it a pandemic, war, famine, or natural disaster—adversely affects humans in a variety of ways.[3] However, crises tend to vary along a number of consistent dimensions, which we term *crisis characteristics*. The value of each crisis characteristic

From *Global Environmental Politics* 21, no. 1 (February 2021): 13–22.

varies in accordance with an individual's spatial and temporal context. For example, an impending cyclone has different crisis characteristics for a poor farmer in Bangladesh (i.e., immediate and proximate threat to life) than does its aftermath for an affluent investor in Canada (i.e., long-term and distant threat to investments). Below, we consider the values of eight different crisis characteristics for both COVID-19 and the climate crisis from the perspective of policy makers working for a national government in the industrialized world.[4] We adopt this positional vantage since rich countries have historically been important for leading responses to crises generally and the climate crisis specifically (Karlsson et al. 2011).

The crisis characteristics considered here are novel insofar as they mark a first attempt to consider which factors influence political responses specifically, as opposed to business or societal responses more generally (Bjorck 2016). They also include dimensions not considered in other work on political responses to crises, such as the nature of epistemic authority for a given crisis (Adger et al. 2017). While this may not be an exhaustive list of crisis characteristics, we believe they are among the most important ones for understanding political responses.

Immediacy

Immediacy is the perceived speed with which a crisis emerges and expands. COVID-19 initially emerged in late 2019 in China, but in a matter of months it was transmitted across the globe and put millions of lives at risk. The outbreak of the pandemic prompted immediate, unprecedented responses from multiple states (Cheng et al. 2020; Hale et al. 2020). In comparison, policy makers have known about the risks posed by climate change for decades but have thus far mustered only incremental efforts to reduce greenhouse gas

emissions (Rosenbloom and Markard 2020). The perceived immediacy of a crisis is important because it raises the salience of a response for individuals and may allow policy makers to take action before dissent mobilizes. In an immediate crisis like COVID-19, anti-social isolation protests emerged only after mobility restrictions were already in place. High immediacy kept the crisis in the public mind and reduced opposition to drastic responses like shelter-in-place orders. In a slower-moving crisis like climate change, entrenched opponents to climate action have had decades to marshal resources and hone a dissenting message (Brulle 2014; Colgan et al., forthcoming).

Transience

Transience describes the perceived duration of a crisis and its accordant responses. It is an important quality because it affects public support for government policies and therefore the willingness of policy makers to disrupt the lives of citizens or impose new costs on them. Most people will accept significant disruptions to their lives only if they are convinced that things will soon return to normal; long-term disruptions are much less appealing (Oppenheimer 2015). In the case of COVID-19, governments may have reacted quickly and decisively with the hope that measures would only be in place for as long as it took to "flatten the curve," thereby limiting political repercussions. There was a (perhaps false) sense that everything would soon return to normal. By contrast, the climate crisis will extend well beyond the lifetimes of most living humans and will necessitate permanent changes to extant social, political, and economic institutions. There is a broad perception of a transition to an unknown new normal. This makes taking rapid and far-reaching action less palatable, out of concern for garnering the antipathy of voters who may fear the unknown and not see an immediate payback on their investment.

Visibility

Visibility refers to the extent to which a crisis can be captured by visuals that provoke an emotional reaction. Previous research has emphasized the importance of using evocative images to garner support for humanitarian crises (McKay and Perez 2019). COVID-19 is highly visible in the sense that citizens cannot visit the grocery store without seeing shoppers in masks and screens in front of the cashiers. Media images of stadiums filled with hospital beds and daily briefings by senior government officials are equally important for provoking fear. By contrast, the climate crisis seems less visible despite the increasing use of imagery in climate change communication (Wang et al. 2018). Much of the iconography of the climate crisis—from polar bears drowning to glaciers melting—contributes to the idea that its impacts are remote and abstract for most citizens in the world and do not reflect the urgency of this crisis (Schroth et al. 2014; Shields 2019). Even where the images are closer to home, as in the Australian wildfires or Superstorm Sandy, there are lingering questions about causality.

Proximity

Proximity is the degree to which a crisis appears near to an observer. COVID-19 outbreaks have occurred in nearly every country, making this a proximate crisis for many. On the other hand, the climate crisis suffers from a "spatial optimism" dilemma wherein wealthy people in the industrialized world see the consequences of the climate crisis happening primarily elsewhere (Dolsak and Prakash 2020; Tvinnereim et al. 2020). Public opinion research supports the importance of psychological distance as those who witness the effects of the climate crisis in their own backyard are both more concerned and more willing to pay for responsive policies (Kim and Wolinsky-Nahmias 2014; Rickard et al. 2016).

Accountability

Accountability is the degree to which individuals feel personally accountable for their own health and safety during a crisis. For example, the relationship between attending a crowded indoor gathering and potentially catching COVID-19 is direct and evident. This stands in contrast to the murkier relationship between choosing to fly frequently or eat more meat and suffering the effects of a changing climate. Individuals often fail to see a clear connection between their actions and environmental consequences, even those with knowledge of the climate crisis (Dolsak and Prakash 2020; Norgaard 2011). Accountability seems higher in COVID-19 because the pandemic directly threatens individuals and health systems, whereas in the climate crisis, the impacts on human lives are perceived by many as indirect through changes to natural systems (Rosenbloom and Markard 2020).

Universality

Universality refers to the degree to which a crisis is perceived to affect everyone equally. At the outset of the pandemic, COVID-19 was perceived to pose an equal threat to persons in positions of power (e.g., Boris Johnson). In hindsight, we now know that COVID-19 kills people of color and poor individuals at a far higher rate than white and affluent ones, partially because of structural barriers to health care access (Dorn et al. 2020). However, this knowledge emerged only *after* state responses were already in place. Responses to the climate crisis, on the other hand, occur in a context where the non-universality of consequences are widely acknowledged (Roberts and Parks 2007). The climate crisis stands to impact sub-Saharan Africa and small island states far more than wealthy OECD countries. Even within wealthy countries, the impacts of climate change will be felt most acutely by people of color and lower-income communities that lack the resources to adapt. Therefore, the perception of low universality may contribute to less decisive climate governance.

Expertise

Expertise captures the degree of trust in the epistemic community with the most knowledge about a crisis. A pandemic focuses attention on a different epistemic community than an environmental catastrophe. However, not all epistemic communities are viewed as equal in the eyes of policy makers. Responses to COVID-19 draw on the expertise of doctors and epidemiologists, arguably the most authoritative of epistemic communities due to the perceived infallibility of medical research methodologies (Leão and Gil 2019). Indeed, a broader condition of "medicalization" has been observed across a number of global governance issue areas—in which health authorities are empowered to intervene and redefine a problem in medical terms (Elbe 2011). By contrast, there is some degree of mistrust among policy makers when it comes to climate experts drawing on knowledge from multiple disciplines. This mistrust severs the links between knowledge-making authority and decision-making authority (Lovbrand 2009). Climate scientists have been politicized in a way that doctors were not in the early months of the pandemic (Chinn et al. 2020). The degree of trust in experts is closely related to the amount of public dissent over crisis response and, consequently, to the capacity to respond quickly and decisively to crises. In the case of COVID-19, the political cost of attacking doctors was initially much higher than the political cost of attacking academics and climate activists.

Legibility

Legibility is the extent to which a crisis lends itself to simple and straightforward political responses and the degree to which a simple cause-effect relationship can be observed between responses and outcomes (Scott 1998). In a pandemic, individuals must limit their chances of becoming infected, and governments must enact public policy to support this end. The prospects for a savior technology are straightforward: either a vaccine or a viable treatment. To avoid infection, individuals can avoid large group gatherings, wash their hands frequently, and wear a mask. All of these responses have a clear cause-effect relationship to a desired outcome, that is, preventing the spread of the virus. The climate crisis is far less legible at all scales. Climate governance responses often have complex causal chains in which a successful outcome at one scale often depends on conditions at another (Bernstein and Hoffmann 2018). While a number of policy solutions exist—from carbon pricing to voluntary offsetting—the effects of these solutions are often difficult to trace. Consider, for example, the sequence of conditional relationships that links the purchase of a carbon offset for air travel with an actual reduction in carbon emissions. The difficulty of identifying this connection, even for climate experts, illustrates the low legibility of climate governance.

Crisis Characteristics and Governance Responses

These eight crisis characteristics provide a lens through which scholars, activists, and policy makers can compare and contrast crises. However, they also have explanatory and predictive value inasmuch as we can expect crises with high values across multiple characteristics to be associated with faster and farther-reaching governance responses. If one envisions a crisis as falling along a spectrum within each of the eight crisis characteristics, then COVID-19, measured at the starting point of the pandemic from the perspective of a policy maker in the industrialized world, would score higher across all eight categories than the climate crisis measured at the same point in time by the same audience. Thus, COVID-19 invited a swifter and more decisive political response.

Admittedly, there is considerable variation in political responses to both COVID-19 and the climate crisis. Explaining this variation is outside the scope of this article. Our point is that, in general, one can expect stronger and faster responses when crises score higher on these eight characteristics. At the same time, we recognize that these characteristics do not account for all the variation in political responses and that other variables outside this explanatory model should also be taken into account. In this case, the opposition and obstructionism of the fossil fuel lobby play an important role in conditioning political responses to the climate crisis (Colgan et al., forthcoming). One cannot solely attribute this opposition to longer mobilizing time due to low immediacy. Rather, it stems from the fact that certain interest groups profit from the causes of climate change in a way that lacks a parallel in COVID-19.

Crisis characteristics are related to each other such that a change to the value of one crisis characteristic can lead to change in the value of another. Take the relationship between transience and legibility, for example. Climate change, a long slow-moving problem, has given rise to a complex amalgam of overlapping governance systems promoting different actions, or a regime complex, as it has been termed elsewhere (Keohane and Victor 2011). Put more simply, the longer the climate crisis endures, the less legible it becomes. Similar claims can be made for many of the other crisis characteristics, as with visibility and proximity or immediacy and accountability. While the two crises we discuss here present a remarkable contrast across all characteristics, future research should consider more nuanced cases to explore the interaction effects of different characteristics on political responses.

Implications for the Climate Crisis

COVID-19 and climate change are different varieties of crisis, yet they are interconnected in numerous ways. Warming temperatures and deforestation create increased disease vectors that may lead to the next global pandemic. It is fair to say that addressing the climate crisis may play a key role in avoiding future pandemics. What lessons, then, can we learn from COVID-19 to trigger quicker, farther-reaching, and stronger climate policy? First, much more can be done to highlight the growing immediacy, visibility, proximity, and universality of the climate crisis, making the case of an existential threat to gather more support from policy makers and citizens (Colgan et al., forthcoming). Specific strategies for altering the value of these characteristics include changing frames and visuals in climate communication; launching policy campaigns that have broader constituencies, such as the Green New Deal; and mobilizing young people who are more likely to suffer firsthand the impacts of the climate crisis (Klein 2019; Shields 2019). Indeed, before COVID-19, there were already trends in this direction, as reflected by the Fridays for Future movement. It is crucial to continue this momentum in the post-COVID era as changing demographics and more severe and frequent extreme weather events will continue to increase the value of these crisis characteristics for climate change.

Second, policy makers—inasmuch as they have some agency over crisis responses—should increase the legibility of responses to the climate crisis at all scales. As an example, straightforward pledges to phase out coal by a certain date are far more legible (and arguably more effective) than pledging an abstract number as a nationally determined contribution under the Paris Climate Agreement (Rauner et al. 2020). Another strategy is to emphasize the transient properties of some policy interventions. For example, the "pain" from building clean energy capacity or expanding public transit is temporary, but the benefits will accrue over many years, while the costs of the transition will decrease. Wherever possible, policy makers should look to trigger lock-in effects that prevent future reverses and gradually expand the population supporting relevant changes (Levin et al. 2012). Additionally, policy makers can and should make efforts to protect climate experts from political interference. At a minimum, this means allowing scientists the freedom to disseminate their research to the public without political oversight.

Finally, while the focus of this article is on state responses, one cannot forget the unique features of the climate crisis as a multiscale problem (Bernstein and Hoffmann 2018). The strength of the fossil fuel lobby domestically coupled with numerous weak commitments under the Paris Climate Agreement internationally means that states alone are unlikely to provide a solution. For this reason, scholars, policy makers, and concerned citizens should continue to support action outside the state system through local and regional interventions as well as through transnational networks.

There are a few reasons why nonstate action is necessary. First, crisis characteristics vary in relation to the observer. Thus, nonstate actors may have different values of immediacy, proximity, accountability, or other characteristics and be impelled to take swifter or farther-reaching action than states. Consider the immediacy of the climate crisis for the insurance industry or coastal homeowners, for example. Second, polycentric approaches to climate governance can guard against efforts to discredit or defund any single organization. We have already witnessed such efforts with the Trump administration's move to terminate its relationship with the World Health Organization. Given the challenges of state-led, top-down approaches to crisis governance, more emphasis must be placed on bottom-up efforts from nonstate actors.

NOTES

1. We use the term *climate crisis* here to encompass the increasingly urgent threat to human life posed by climate-related phenomena, including natural disasters, extreme weather, sea-level rise, and ocean acidification.
2. As of June 23, 2020, the global case fatality rate was 5.2% according to the World Health Organization; data accessible at https://covid19 .who.int/?gclid=EAIaIQobChMIzpmL5fuZ6gIVVOvtCh1 fXwThEAAYASAAEgIkSvD_BwE, last accessed November 22, 2020.
3. We use the term *crisis* here to refer to a narrower series of phenomena than captured by terms like *focusing events*. We conceptualize crises as unplanned and harmful to human life, whereas focusing events can be planned (i.e., elections) and non-life threatening (Walker and Waterman 2008).
4. While we focus on industrialized countries, our argument can also apply to some emerging economies and developing countries.

REFERENCES

Adger, W. Neil, Catherine Butler, and Kate Walker-Springett. 2017. Moral Reasoning in Adaptation to Climate Change. *Environmental Politics* 26 (3): 371–390. DOI: https://doi.org/10.1080/09644016 .2017.1287624

Bernstein, Steven, and Matthew Hoffmann. 2018. The Politics of Decarbonization and the Catalytic Impact of Subnational Climate Experiments. *Policy Sciences* 51 (2): 189–211. DOI: https://doi.org/10.1007 /s11077-018-9314-8, PMID: 31007288, PMCID: PMC6445480

Bjorck, Albena. 2016. Crisis Typologies Revisited: An Interdisciplinary Approach. *Central European Business Review* 5 (3): 25–37. DOI: https://doi.org/10.18267/j.cebr.156

Bordoff, Jason. 2020. Sorry, but the Virus Shows Why There Won't Be Global Action on Climate Change. *Foreign Policy* (blog), March 27. Available at https://foreignpolicy.com/2020/03/27/coronavirus -pandemic-shows-why-no-global-progress-on-climate-change/, last accessed November 22, 2020.

Brulle, Robert J. 2014. Institutionalizing Delay: Foundation Funding and the Creation of U.S. Climate Change Counter-movement Organizations. *Climatic Change* 122 (4): 681–694. DOI: https://doi .org/10.1007/s10584-013-1018-7

Cheng, Cindy, Joan Barceló, Allison Spencer Hartnett, Robert Kubinec, and Luca Messerschmidt. 2020. COVID-19 Government Response Event Dataset (CoronaNet v.1.0). *Nature Human Behaviour*, 4 (7): 756–768. DOI: https://doi.org/10.1038/s41562-020-0909-7, PMID: 32576982

Chinn, Sedona, P. Sol Hart, and Stuart Soroka. 2020. Politicization and Polarization in Climate Change News Content, 1985–2017. *Science Communication* 42 (1): 112–129. DOI: https://doi.org/10.1177 /1075547019900290

Colgan, Jeff, Jessica F. Green, and Thomas Hale. Forthcoming. Asset Revaluation and the Existential Politics of Climate Change. *International Organization*.

Dolsak, Nives, and Aseem Prakash. 2020. Here's Why Coronavirus and Climate Change Are Different Sorts of Policy Problems. *Forbes* (blog), March 15. Available at https://www.forbes.com/sites/prakashdolsak/2020/03/15/heres-why-coronavirus-and-climate-change-are-different-sorts-of-policy-problems/#391895d39e6f, last accessed November 22, 2020.

Dorn, Aaron van, Rebecca E. Cooney, and Miriam L. Sabin. 2020. COVID-19 Exacerbating Inequalities in the US. *The Lancet* 395 (10232): 1243–1244. DOI: https://doi.org/10.1016/S0140-6736(20)30893-X

Elbe, Stefan. 2011. Pandemics on the Radar Screen: Health Security, Infectious Disease and the Medicalisation of Insecurity. *Political Studies* 59 (4): 848–866. DOI: https://doi.org/10.1111/j.1467-9248.2011.00921.x

Galbraith, Eric, and Ross Otto. 2020. Why We're Seeing a Unified Global Response to Coronavirus but Not Climate Change. *The Narwhal* (blog), March 20. Available at https://thenarwhal.ca/why-were-seeing-a-unified-global-response-to-coronavirus-but-not-climate-change/, last accessed November 22, 2020.

Guterres, António. 2018. Secretary-General's Remarks on Climate Change [as Delivered]. United Nations Secretary-General, September 10. Available at https://www.un.org/sg/en/content/sg/statement/2018-09-10/secretary-generals-remarks-climate-change-delivered, last accessed November 22, 2020.

Hale, Thomas, Sam Webster, Anna Petherick, Toby Phillips, and Beatriz Kira. 2020. Oxford COVID-19 Government Response Tracker. Blavatnik School of Government. Data use policy: Creative Commons Attribution CC BY standard.

Karlsson, Christer, Charles Parker, Mattias Hjerpe, and Bjorn-Ola Linner. 2011. Looking for Leaders: Perceptions of Climate Change Leadership Among Climate Change Negotiation Participants. *Global Environmental Politics* 11 (1): 89–107. DOI: https://doi.org/10.1162/GLEP_a_00044

Keohane, Robert O., and David G. Victor. 2011. The Regime Complex for Climate Change. *Perspectives on Politics* 9 (1): 7–23. DOI: https://doi.org/10.1017/S1537592710004068

Kim, So Young, and Yael Wolinsky-Nahmias. 2014. Cross-National Public Opinion on Climate Change: The Effects of Affluence and Vulnerability. *Global Environmental Politics* 14 (1): 79–106. DOI: https://doi.org/10.1162/GLEP_a_00215

Klein, Naomi. 2019. *On Fire: The Burning Case for a Green New Deal.* Toronto, ON: Knopf.

Leão, Luciana de Souza, and Eyal Gil. 2019. The Rise of Randomized Controlled Trials (RCTs) in International Development in Historical Perspective. *Theory and Society* 48 (3): 383–418. DOI: https://doi.org/10.1007/s11186-019-09352-6

Levin, Kelly, Benjamin Cashore, Steven Bernstein, and Graeme Auld. 2012. Overcoming the Tragedy of Super Wicked Problems: Constraining Our Future Selves to Ameliorate Global Climate Change. *Policy Sciences* 45 (2): 123–152. DOI: https://doi.org/10.1007/s11077-012-9151-0

Lovbrand, Eva. 2009. Revisiting the Politics of Expertise in Light of the Kyoto Negotiations on Land Use Change and Forestry. *Forest Policy and Economics* 11 (5–6): 404–412. DOI: https://doi.org/10.1016/j.forpol.2008.08.007

McKay, Deirdre, and Padmapani Perez. 2019. Citizen Aid, Social Media and Brokerage After Disaster. *Third World Quarterly* 40 (10): 1903–1920. DOI: https://doi.org/10.1080/01436597.2019.1634470

Norgaard, Kari Marie. 2011. *Living in Denial: Climate Change, Emotions, and Everyday Life.* Cambridge, MA: MIT Press. DOI: https://doi.org/10.7551/mitpress/9780262015448.001.0001

Oppenheimer, Michael. 2015. Adapting to Climate Change: Rising Sea Levels, Limiting Risks. *Social Research* 82 (3): 673–680.

Rauner, Sebastian, Nico Bauer, Alois Dirnaichner, Rita Van Dingenen, Chris Mutel, and Gunnar Luderer. 2020. Coal-Exit Health and Environmental Damage Reductions Outweigh Economic Impacts. *Nature Climate Change* 10 (4): 308–312. DOI: https://doi.org/10.1038/s41558-020-0728-x

Rickard, Laura N., Z. Janet Yang, and Jonathon P. Schuldt. 2016. Here and Now, There and Then: How "Departure Dates" Influence Climate Change Engagement. *Global Environmental Change* 38 (May): 97–107. DOI: https://doi.org/10.1016/j.gloenvcha.2016.03.003

Roberts, J. Timmons, and Bradley C. Parks. 2007. *A Climate of Injustice: Global Inequality, North-South Politics, and Climate Policy.* Cambridge, MA: MIT Press.

Rosenbloom, Daniel, and Jochen Markard. 2020. A COVID-19 Recovery for Climate. *Science* 368 (6490): 447. DOI: https://doi.org/10.1126/science.abc4887, PMID: 32355005

Schroth, Olaf, Jeannette Angel, Stephen Sheppard, and Aleksandra Dulic. 2014. Visual Climate Change Communication: From Iconography to Locally Framed 3D Visualization. *Environmental Communication* 8 (4): 413–432. DOI: https://doi.oig/10.1080/17524032.2014.906478

Scott, James C. 1998. *Seeing Like a State: How Certain Schemes to Improve the Human Condition Have Failed.* New Haven, CT: Yale University Press.

Shields, Fiona. 2019. Why We're Rethinking the Images We Use for Our Climate Journalism. *The Guardian,* October 18, sec. Environment. Available at https://www.theguardian.com/environment/2019/oct/18/guardian-climate-pledge-2019-images-pictures-guidelines, last accessed November 22, 2020.

Tvinnereim, Endre, Ole Martin Lægreid, Xiaozi Liu, Daigee Shaw, Christopher Borick, and Erick Lachapelle. 2020. Climate Change Risk Perceptions and the Problem of Scale: Evidence from Cross-National Survey Experiments. *Environmental Politics* 29 (7): 1–21. DOI: https://doi.org/10.1080/09644016.2019.1708538

Walker, Lee Demetrius, and Richard W. Waterman. 2008. Elections as Focusing Events: Explaining Attitudes Toward the Police and the Government in Comparative Perspective. *Law & Society Review* 42 (2): 337–366. DOI: https://doi.org/10.1111/j.1540-5893.2008.00344.x

Wang, Susie, Adam Corner, Daniel Chapman, and Ezra Markowitz. 2018. Public Engagement with Climate Imagery in a Changing Digital Landscape. *WIREs Climate Change* 9 (2): e509. DOI: https://doi.org/10.1002/wcc.509

12 HUMAN SECURITY: MIGRATION, POPULATION, AND GLOBAL HEALTH

Reflecting the worldwide interconnectedness that is now called "globalization," transnational concerns have become part of the global agenda. Such concerns include not only the environment, but migration, refugees, health, and international crime. For many transnational issues, the interests, rights, and responsibilities of the individual, the state, and the international community may be incompatible or even diverge. When do the rights of the individual take precedence over the rights of the community in the use of land and natural resources or in the control of national borders?

Megan Bradley explains the inherent tensions among law, morality, and the national interest of states that complicate the treatment of refugees. Kathleen McNamara and Abraham Newman argue that the coronavirus pandemic shows that "globalization needs to be seen not just as a distributional game of winners and losers but rather a more profoundly transformational game that reshapes identities, redefines channels of power and authority, and generates new sites for contentious politics."

Megan Bradley

UNRESOLVED AND UNRESOLVABLE? TENSIONS IN THE REFUGEE REGIME

The two cardinal norms of the refugee regime are the right to seek asylum and non-refoulement—that is, the right of refugees not to be returned to a country where their lives or freedom would be threatened. In recent decades, however—particularly in the Global North—many politicians and segments of the public have come to view national interests as antithetical to these norms, leading to the erection of ever more elaborate barriers to deter unwanted arrivals. Despite these efforts, the number of refugees and displaced persons worldwide continues to grow, reaching 68.5 million in 2018, the highest levels since World War II.[1] The problem is not just that more and more refugees are forced from their homes but also that fewer and fewer are able to access so-called "durable solutions" to displacement, whether voluntary return to their countries of origin, local integration in host states, or resettlement elsewhere. Instead, millions are locked in limbo, with the average refugee situation now dragging on for over twenty-five years.[2]

This situation has prompted a flurry of efforts to repair the foundering refugee regime, from the negotiation of a new Global Compact on Refugees to a variety of proposals from experts of various stripes.[3] Many of these efforts attempt, implicitly or explicitly, to resolve tensions between legal principles, moral duties, and national interests related to refugees, for example, by stressing refugees' positive economic contributions to their host societies. Notwithstanding the clear need to rethink and revive the refugee regime, this essay questions the drive toward oversimplification that has characterized many debates on reforming responses to refugees. It recognizes that some of the aforementioned tensions are "baked into" the problem of refugeehood, given that the state system exists, at least in part, to draw lines between insiders and outsiders. In this system, the capacity to make effective rights claims is tied to recognition as a legitimate member of the political community of the state—a recognition refugees lack, and have limited power to contest.[4]

Debates on the interplay of law, morality, and national interest related to the refugee regime have typically focused on the obligation to admit refugees, and on "responsibility sharing" through Northern support for states in the Global South, which collectively host more than 85 percent of the world's refugees.[5] I seek to advance the conversation by exploring how legal norms, moral values, and national interests are also entangled in efforts to support durable solutions for refugees, focusing on voluntary repatriation. What does recognition of the intrinsic, and in some senses irreconcilable tensions between law, morality, and national interests mean for efforts to support "solutions" for refugees? Do these tensions render the very notion of solutions chimerical? Acknowledging these fundamental tensions is not to be defeatist about the possibility of strengthening responses to

From *Ethics & International Affairs* 33, no. 1 (Spring 2019): 45–56.

refugees. I argue that advancing durable solutions, however imperfect, does not mean definitively overcoming the tensions that characterize the refugee predicament writ large, but rather that it requires an ongoing process of navigating these tensions to identify and promote context-specific opportunities to reposition refugees as full and equal citizens as a critical step toward reducing (if not eliminating) their precarity.

What Is at Stake?

At first glance, it may appear that in the contemporary refugee regime there has been a decisive tipping of the scales in favor of national interests at the expense of legal norms and moral values, such as equity, compassion, and justice. However, upon closer examination the picture is, unsurprisingly, more complicated.

Legal Norms

Under international law, states have a modest suite of specific obligations toward refugees, encapsulated primarily in the 1951 Convention Relating to the Status of Refugees and its 1967 Protocol. These obligations are limited by the remarkably narrow definition of "refugee" established in these two documents. The Convention indicates that a refugee is an individual who, "owing to a well-founded fear of being persecuted for reasons of race, religion, nationality, membership of a particular social group or political opinion, is outside the country of his nationality and is unable or, owing to such fear, is unwilling to avail himself of the protection of that country."[6] Many who would be considered refugees according to vernacular or common moral understandings of the term— such as those who have fled war but have not suffered direct persecution—do not qualify for protection under this definition.[7] International

refugee law is predicated on the right to *seek* asylum, but this is not matched by a corresponding legal right to be *granted* asylum. The acceptance of refugees is thus fundamentally shaped by political considerations and, to a lesser extent, related moral commitments.

The prohibition on refoulement is the second cardinal legal rule of the refugee regime, and as a principle of customary international law it is binding even on those states that have not signed the refugee convention. Legally, states cannot simply turn refugees away. However, states exercise remarkable and relentless creativity in curtailing access to their territories through the implementation of non-entrée and neo-refoulement measures. Even when refugees enjoy protection from refoulement, this is not a durable solution for their marginalization from the political community of the state.[8]

Moral Values

Existing legal principles on refugee protection naturally reflect the interests and concerns of the states that negotiated and interpret them. For the Western states that drove the original development of the regime's legal architecture, the refugee issue had intertwined moral and geopolitical salience. For example, protecting those fleeing communism and conflicts in the Soviet Union's "sphere of influence" provided a concrete opportunity to demonstrate the moral superiority of liberal democracy. Even still, Western states were determined to limit their obligations. They therefore articulated a relatively spare set of core *legal* commitments to refugees, leaving the broader dimensions of responses to refugees to be framed in moral and political terms. Thus, states typically portray their response to refugee situations as a humanitarian undertaking, an expression of charity or generosity, rather than as a responsibility or an act of justice. Political theorists and activists of many different perspectives vociferously challenge this perspective, arguing that states—particularly wealthy, liberal democracies—are obliged to admit and assist refugees on the basis of, among other things, liberal or cosmopolitan conceptualizations of justice.[9]

While it is impossible to explore these debates in full here, it is noteworthy that a tendency has emerged among some advocates and scholars to discuss the issue in an echo chamber of shared "progressive" opinions, and to dismiss any opposition as inherently racist or xenophobic, or as a parochial reflection of illegitimate national interests.[10] From this perspective, the idea of tensions between legal norms, moral values, and national interests is largely moot because controlling entry to and membership in a state are cast as *obviously* immoral. This move marks a refusal to grapple with some of the more nuanced defenses of a state's right to decide who belongs, offered by scholars such as Michael Walzer (on communitarian grounds) and David Miller (on the basis of liberal nationalism). These defenses jibe with the sincerely held—if highly contestable—values of many citizens in states confronting refugee flows.[11] Roughly put, these perspectives share the idea that nations may constitute distinctive and valuable communities. Thus, to the extent that accepting large numbers of refugees would negatively change or corrode the identities of these groups, and the state's capacity to protect its citizens' rights and to serve their needs, states may have a legitimate interest in restricting the number of refugees they accept. This meshes with Nigel Biggar's observation in his contribution to this roundtable that a government may be understood to have a moral responsibility to promote the legitimate interests of its people, albeit within the bounds of international justice.[12] The proliferation of abuses against refugees that are unconscionable by most moral codes, including the perspectives advanced by scholars such as Walzer and Miller, obscures these more complex disagreements over national interests and moral values relating to refugees.

National Interests

State interests vis-à-vis refugees are enmeshed with moral values, and are also highly variable, depending in part on historical experience, geostrategic considerations, and whether the state creates or hosts refugees, or both. Broadly speaking, the interests of host and donor states in the contemporary refugee regime reflect different blends of five interconnected motivations.[13]

First, states generally seek to limit the number of refugees within their borders, in particular with states in the Global North dedicated to keeping most refugees contained in the Global South. Intertwined with this perceived interest is a moral claim fundamental to the state system: that sovereign states legitimately have the prerogative—with only modest limits—to regulate entry to and membership in the national political community.

Second, states strive to limit the costs—financial, political, and in terms of perceived security risks—of refugee situations. For host states this often entails supporting more financially expensive responses, such as creating camps and withholding work permits (leaving refugees reliant on aid distributions), in order to limit the perceived political costs of taking in refugees. These political costs include the widely held perceptions that refugees not only overburden social welfare systems and "steal" jobs from citizens but also that they may be criminals or terrorists. Southern host states also try to leverage financial and political concessions from donor states in exchange for accommodating refugees.

In many cases states and politicians not only try to limit the political cost of letting refugees in, they also look to maximize the domestic political gains that may be reaped from vilifying refugees. For some leaders these gains appear so significant that they abrogate ostensibly deeply-held values. For example, Australia, a self-proclaimed human rights flag-bearer, embraces policies flagrantly incompatible with human rights, such as indefinitely detaining asylum seekers, in order to pander to voters opposed to the arrival of refugees. For many donor and host states, limiting the overall cost of refugee situations hinges on limiting their duration and precluding the possibility of refugees staying permanently. As I discuss below, this creates an incentive for states to push to end refugee situations as quickly as possible, ideally through what they view as the preferred solution of voluntary repatriation.

A third motivation, particularly for donor states, is that supporting the refugee regime creates a "release valve" that limits a conflict's destructive toll, at least in terms of loss of life, thereby lessening pressure for even more costly and riskier forms of intervention, such as military engagement. Thus, in conflicts such as occurred in Bosnia and Herzegovina in the 1990s, humanitarian support for refugees has served as a cover for Western inaction to stop the violence that was driving the exodus.

Fourth, as Gareth Evans argues in his introduction to this roundtable, countries have an "interest in being, and in being seen to be, a good international citizen."[14] Some countries, such as Canada under the governments of Pierre Elliot Trudeau and Justin Trudeau, have used the refugee regime to cultivate or rehabilitate a virtuous international reputation and to assert a particular interpretation of national identity as compassionate, supportive of diversity, and distinct from other, less generous neighbor countries.

Fifth, states share a broad interest in avoiding heightened accountability toward refugees—both for the abuses that force them from their homes and for violations of their rights while displaced. Demands for accountability for rights violations have been a prominent feature of post–Cold War politics, but refugees have often been sidelined in such struggles. While refugees have certainly contested this exclusion, including by documenting and protesting violations against them and bringing forward legal claims, typically neither the states that create refugees nor those that abuse their rights are held to account for these acts.

Reconciling Tensions, Irreconcilable Tensions

Many recent efforts to revamp the refugee regime and reform states' restrictive policies toward refugees have attempted to reconcile the tensions between these legal principles, moral commitments, and national interests. Some, for example, have appealed to states' interests by celebrating the displaced as assets who can make positive economic, social, creative, and intellectual contributions to their host societies—echoing an earlier UNHCR campaign recalling that "Einstein was a refugee." Others have proposed the creation of new transnational communities in which the displaced can flourish economically and socially.[15]

While assessing the plausibility and potential efficacy of all such proposals is not possible here, I wish to make a few observations on the veritable cottage industry that has emerged around recommendations for reforming the refugee regime. These proposals posit that refugee crises need not be intractable by highlighting opportunities to use persuasion, effective bargaining, and the realignment of interests to reconcile *extrinsic* tensions between legal norms, moral values, and perceived national interests. Perhaps unsurprisingly, they remain largely silent on the *intrinsic* tensions between the state system itself and efforts to uphold refugees' rights.[16] But as David Turton observes, the refugee regime "is the nation-states' response to the refugee problem, from which it follows that the prime purpose of the regime is not to protect refugees but to protect the international system of nation-states by 'normalizing' the figure of the refugee."[17] In her seminal discussion of refugeehood in *The Origins of Totalitarianism,* Hannah Arendt relatedly argues that refugee outflows expose the poverty of human rights claims and the lie in justifying state power on the grounds that states protect human rights. For rights claims to be truly effective, Arendt suggests, they must be made by individuals recognized as legitimate members of the state—a status arbitrated by states themselves. As "stateless, rightless scum of the earth," the displaced have been cast out of the state and thus lack "the right to have rights," and even the power to meaningfully contest their relegation.[18] Contrary to Arendt's expectations, refugees have indeed contested their marginalization and have, in some cases, made their claims heard.[19] Still, the force of her critique continues to resonate: even as refugees and their advocates challenge their marginalization and perhaps make modest gains, the logic of the state system remains one in which the expulsion of refugees by states with virtual impunity remains an ever-present risk. Indeed in some accounts, the creation of refugees is not only a risk in the state system but integral to its very operation.[20]

Durable Solutions and Gradual Progress

Where does the intrinsic tension between the notion of refugees as rights-holders and the nature of the state system itself leave efforts to reform the system, and the possibility of meaningful solutions to displacement?[21] This question is particularly pertinent when we expand the conversation beyond the typical focus on asylum-seeking and non-refoulement to consider tensions associated with durable solutions to displacement, particularly voluntary repatriation.

While the term "durable solution" does not appear in key legal standards, such as the 1951 Refugee Convention, the UNHCR Statute does mandate the agency to seek "permanent solutions for the problem of refugees by assisting Governments . . . to facilitate the voluntary repatriation of such refugees, or their assimilation within new national communities."[22] Durable solutions are often defined simply in terms of the three routes for ending displacement—local integration, resettlement, and voluntary repatriation—instead of in terms of sustainable outcomes. However, a refugee who, for example, returns to her home country only to be displaced anew has clearly not benefited from a solution to her predicament in any meaningful sense. Indeed, although enabling durable solutions is in theory the ultimate goal of refugee protection, there is considerable murkiness surrounding what counts as a durable solution and what these purported solutions aim to achieve. That said, by any definition the search for durable solutions for refugees is failing. Over recent decades, less than 1 percent of refugees worldwide have been resettled each year, and estimates on local integration (refugees formally acquiring citizenship in their host countries) in the Global South are even lower. In 2016, some 552,200 refugees voluntarily repatriated—the highest return rate since 2008, and more than double the number in 2015, but still representing less than 2.5 percent of refugees globally.[23]

Theoretically, durable solutions are to benefit refugees, but states (and other actors) have sharp and sometimes incompatible interests in the process, reflecting the five broad elements of state interest in the refugee regime articulated above. As manifested in the context of efforts to secure durable solutions to displacement, these interests range from closing camps and freeing-up scarce humanitarian funds to preventing the return of unwanted minorities. In some cases, "solutions" advance the interests of discontented host states and overtaxed humanitarian agencies, but may, from the perspectives of refugees, create more problems than they resolve. This reality raises a critical question: Is the enjoyment of full, equal, and effective citizenship rights the gold standard or the *sine qua non* for durable solutions for refugees? Some argue that true solutions require the full restoration of citizenship rights or, for those who never had full citizenship rights, the recognition of the refugee as a full and equal citizen, whether in her host country, in a resettlement state, or in her state of origin.[24] This position is in line with a principled focus on human rights protection, although it arguably cannot overcome Arendt's fundamental critique of these very principles, and the state system itself. Additionally, we must ask whether it is a coherent proposition when refugees pursue durable solutions in states still experiencing or emerging from conflict, in which citizenship rarely translates into reliable, robust human rights protection, regardless of whether one has been displaced. This concern is especially pressing when it comes to the "preferred" solution of voluntary repatriation, given that refugees are usually returning to countries where development prospects are bleak, mechanisms to protect their rights are fragile at best, and former neighbors and officials may be overtly and even violently opposed to their return.

The Right of Return

Despite currently low return rates, voluntary repatriation is often referred to by states and the UNHCR as the "preferred" solution to displacement. In part, this designation reflects the highly limited nature of the international legal framework around durable solutions, which is itself a reflection of states' collective interest in retaining sovereign control over entry and membership. States have no legal obligation to resettle refugees or extend citizenship to those who wish to integrate permanently into their host societies. Indeed, repatriation is the only "solution" to which refugees have a clear legal right. This is based not on the 1951 Convention, but on the broader human rights principle of the right of return, articulated in standards such as the Universal Declaration of Human Rights and the International Covenant on Civil and Political Rights. The problem of course is that many refugees do not want to return, and may not be able to do so without risking their lives. If conditions in a refugee's country of origin change such that return may be possible, a wide array of UN resolutions, peace treaties, and other standards stress that it should be voluntary, and take place in conditions of "safety and dignity."[25]

Beyond being a legal right, repatriation is often portrayed as the preferred solution because it meshes with the sedentary and exclusionary bias of the state system, in which certain people are seen to belong in certain places. From this perspective, repatriation puts refugees back where they belong, squaring the circle of "the refugee problem" by reaffirming the logic of the state system: state power is legitimate because the state protects its citizens—including exiles who return to the fold. Arendt was skeptical, to say the least, both of this logic and of the possibility that states would ever allow refugee repatriation on a large scale. History has disproved some of her arguments on the latter count, as more than twenty-five million refugees have returned over the past twenty years (notwithstanding currently low return rates). With the notable exception of countries such as Myanmar, Bhutan, and Israel, most refugee-creating states do not directly oppose repatriation. Rather, the challenge is whether the security of returnees can be ensured and their citizenship claims made meaningful in places where citizenship has been an "axis of subordination" rather than empowerment.[26]

Host states have often cloaked their own interests in return by insisting that it is, in fact, also the preference of most refugees. While this claim is often disingenuous, careful ethnographic research with different refugee populations also makes clear that many refugees around the world do hope to return—in particular circumstances—to their lost homes and countries.[27] In return movements from El Salvador to post-apartheid South Africa, some refugees have actively engaged in struggles to reform their states and make their citizenship claims meaningful. Such preferences and decisions do not defuse the intrinsic, irreconcilable tensions between law, morality, and national interests that stymie efforts to create a world without refugees. They do, however, point to the value of understanding the pursuit of durable solutions to displacement as an ongoing *process*. In this process, refugees' precarity, and the risk of future refugee flows, are never fully resolved—in this sense Arendt's critique holds true—but may be mitigated and managed, often through refugees' own mobilization efforts and political strategies. Listening to refugees' perspectives and trying to understand the ways in which they struggle toward solutions are not a panacea for the tensions that hamstring the refugee regime. But refugees themselves often have insight into progressive steps that may be taken toward improving their situations and even recasting their fractured citizenships. This suggests that recognition of the persistent and fundamentally irreconcilable tensions between law, morality, and state interests in the refugee regime does not mean that progress—inevitably modest and contingent—toward durable solutions is unattainable.

Conclusion

Optimism about durable solutions for refugees, and about a strengthened refugee regime more broadly, may seem incompatible with recognition that the creation of refugees is integral to the state system itself, reflecting unreconciled and in some senses irreconcilable tensions between law, morality, and state interests. As long as states retain largely unfettered power to determine who can be present within their borders and who is accorded membership, refugee flows will persist, showing all too clearly the costs of this system. But the scarcity—or impossibility—of solutions to the refugee problem *writ large* within the confines of the state system does not rule out improvements to the regime, including gradual, tentative progress toward durable solutions for displaced individuals and communities.

NOTES

1. UNHCR, "Global Trends 2017" (Geneva: UNHCR, 2018), p. 2.
2. UNHCR, "Contribution to the Fifteenth Coordination Meeting on International Migration," February 10, 2017, UN/POP/MIG-15CM/2017/14.
3. See, for example, the World Refugee Council supported by the government of Canada (www.worldrefugeecouncil.org); Alexander Betts and Paul Collier, *Refuge: Rethinking Refugee Policy in a Changing World* (New York: Oxford University Press, 2017); Robin Cohen and Nicholas Van Hear, "Visions of Refugia: Territorial and Transnational Solutions to Mass Displacement," *Planning Theory and Practice* 18, no. 3 (2017), pp. 494–504; and initiatives promoted by leading experts such as James Hathaway and Alexander Aleinikoff.
4. On this dynamic see, for example, Hannah Arendt, *The Origins of Totalitarianism* (New York: Harcourt, 2001); Emma Haddad, *The Refugee in International Society: Between Sovereigns* (Cambridge: Cambridge University Press, 2008); and Megan Bradley, "Rethinking Refugeehood: Statelessness, Repatriation, and Refugee Agency," *Review of International Studies* 40, no. 1 (2014), pp. 101–23.
5. See, for instance, Matthew Gibney, *The Ethics and Politics of Asylum* (Cambridge: Cambridge University Press, 2004); Phil Orchard, *A Right to Flee* (Cambridge: Cambridge University Press, 2014); and Alexander Betts, *Protection by Persuasion* (Ithaca: Cornell University Press, 2009).
6. Article 1(A)(2). Geographic and temporal limitations on the refugee definition in the convention are lifted in the protocol.
7. Regional standards such as the 1969 Organization for African Unity Convention Governing the Specific Aspects of Refugee Problems in Africa offer broader legal definitions, but these agreements are limited in scope. I use the term "refugee" broadly here, including all those who have been forced from their homes.
8. Jennifer Hyndman and Alison Mountz, "Another Brick in the Wall? Neo-*Refoulement* and the Externalization of Asylum by Australia and Europe," *Government and Opposition* 43, no. 2 (2008), p. 250.
9. See, for instance, Joseph Carens, *The Ethics of Immigration* (New York: Oxford University Press, 2013); and Seyla Benhabib, *The Rights of Others: Aliens, Residents, and Citizens* (Cambridge: Cambridge University Press, 2004).
10. For example, see Natasha King, *No Borders: The Politics of Immigration Control and Resistance* (London: Zed Books, 2016).
11. David Miller, *Strangers in Our Midst: The Political Philosophy of Immigration* (Cambridge, Mass.: Harvard University Press, 2016); and Michael Walzer, *Spheres of Justice* (New York: Basic Books, 1983). To clarify, I do not personally concur with these theorists' perspectives.
12. Nigel Biggar, "A Christian View of Humanitarian Intervention," *Ethics & International Affairs* 33, no. 1 (2019), pp. 19–28.
13. Owing to space considerations, in this discussion I do not address in detail the question of refugees' states of origin. On this issue, see, for example, Megan Bradley, *Refugee Repatriation: Justice, Responsibility and Redress* (New York: Cambridge University Press, 2013).
14. Gareth Evans, "Introduction," *Ethics & International Affairs* 33, no. 1 (2019), p. 15.
15. Cohen and Van Hear, "Visions of Refugia."
16. Many of the backers of the myriad reform programs floated in recent years are well aware of the depth and complexity of the refugee predicament and the impossibility of definitively resolving tensions between laws, values, and interests surrounding forced migration, to say nothing of tensions and outright conflicts between the diverse moral claims advanced by refugees, states, and different

citizenries. Yet such complexities are rarely acknowledged by experts as they strive to make pithy, policy-relevant recommendations.

17. David Turton, "Forced Migration and the Nation State," in Jenny Robinson, ed., *Development and Displacement* (New York: Oxford University Press, 2002), pp. 19–76.

18. Arendt, *Origins*, p. 267.

19. See, for instance, Bradley, "Rethinking Refugeehood"; and Megan Bradley, James Milner, and Blair Peruniak, eds., *Refugees' Roles in Resolving Displacement and Building Peace: Beyond Beneficiaries* (Washington, D.C.: Georgetown University Press, 2019).

20. Haddad, *Between Sovereigns*.

21. This section draws on Megan Bradley, "Resolving Refugee Situations: Seeking Solutions Worthy of the Name," World Refugee Council Research Paper (Waterloo: CIGI, 2018).

22. UNHCR Statute, ch. 1, para. 1.

23. UNHCR, "Global Trends 2016" (Geneva: UNHCR, 2017), pp. 3, 24.

24. See, for example, Andrew Shacknove, "Who Is a Refugee?" *Ethics* 95, no. 2 (1985); Bradley, *Refugee Repatriation*; and Lucy Hovil, "Local Integration," in Elena Fiddian-Qasmiyeh et al., eds., *The*

Oxford Handbook of Refugee and Forced Migration Studies (New York: Oxford University Press, 2014).

25. Return may be legally required after the formal revocation of refugee status, following provisions in the 1951 Convention. These provisions are, in practice, rarely applied.

26. Linda Bosniak, *The Citizen and the Alien: Dilemmas of Contemporary Membership* (Princeton: Princeton University Press, 2006), p. 1. From some moral perspectives, enabling refugees to exercise their right of return is all the more important in cases such as the ethnic cleansing of the Rohingya from Myanmar, as this checks the state's power to unilaterally expunge an unwanted group. In such cases, paradoxically, repatriation may be the most preferable option on some moral grounds, precisely when it is riskiest for individual refugees who will unquestionably face hostility upon their return—raising a host of other moral concerns.

27. On the desire of Palestinian refugees to return, and their diverse and complex interpretations of what "return" means, see Diana Allan, *Refugees of the Revolution: Experiences of Palestinian Exile* (Stanford: Stanford University Press, 2014), pp. 191–212.

Kathleen R. McNamara and Abraham L. Newman

THE BIG REVEAL
COVID-19 and Globalization's Great Transformations

On 15 March 2020, the national German newspaper *Die Welt* reported that the Trump administration had offered a "large sum" of money to a German biotech company developing a COVID-19 vaccine.[1] The administration refutes the account but the German government took the threat seriously, buying a 300 million euro stake in the company and deriding U.S. efforts to acquire "exclusive access" to vaccine research.[2] Similar breaking news stories have noted worrying tensions over the mass production of an eventual vaccine and over supply chains for personal protective equipment (PPE).[3]

Such anecdotes from the initial COVID-19 response suggest how the shock of the coronavirus pandemic has made starkly visible the often underappreciated ways in which globalization has transformed global politics. For the last three decades, international flows of information, money, and goods and services proliferated, breaking apart national economies and reengineering them into world spanning networks. Rather than simply creating a Ricardian paradise of win-wins and growing prosperity for all, however, this deeply intertwined interdependence has generated new vulnerabilities and sources of power and authority—globally, between nation-states, firms, non-state actors, and within domestic political systems. In this paper we lay out key elements of

this shifting political landscape and propose a post-pandemic research agenda to better understand our world.

We challenge both those observers who see the pandemic as a definitive break with the past as well as those who see it simply as an extension of ongoing great power competition. Instead, we argue that the pandemic exacerbates underlying trends already at work and forces scholars to open the aperture on how we study globalization. Most centrally, we contend that globalization needs to be seen not just as a distributional game of winners and losers but rather as a more profoundly transformational game. In other words, economic interdependence is altering both the issues and identities that are important as well as actors' opportunities to fight their political battles. We see these transformational dynamics at work in at least four areas: inequality within and across societies, new forms of economic statecraft, existential ecological threats, and the trajectory of the digital revolution.

COVID-19 by itself is not the primary source of the tensions in areas from inequality to climate change, but the virus has effectively exacerbated the trade-offs and made salient the challenges of governing in a tightly connected world. The global pandemic therefore provides a useful lens to reveal how we should be studying, understanding, and engaging with the politics of globalization going forward. This agenda will require scholars to more deeply integrate issues of power and identity into their analysis of global markets, while also recognizing

From *International Organization* 74, Supplement (December 2020): E59–E77.

the ways in which globalization has transformed political authority.

We begin by noting the limits of much of the standard scholarship in international political economy, which emphasizes the distributional impacts of globalization and the sources of policies of openness. We draw on emerging work to sketch out an alternative theoretical frame for thinking about the politics of globalization today, one that probes into the ways economic interdependence is reshaping identities, relocating political authority, and creating new sites for contentious politics. We then turn to assess some of the key policy arenas where the transformative effects of globalization are being felt, highlighting in particular how COVID-19 has made them even more visible. In so doing, we suggest a roadmap to a post-pandemic research agenda for global markets that more fully captures these transformations and their implications for world politics.[4]

Everything Changed but We Weren't Looking

The debate on the post-COVID world tends to gravitate to one of two poles. For some, the pandemic is a crisis that will reshuffle the decks, producing a fundamental reordering of global politics.[5] For others, the basic principles of the international order are likely to remain much the same, underscoring the importance of the emerging bipolar system between the U.S. and China.[6] We find both narratives dissatisfying, as the former overinterprets the causal role of the pandemic itself, while the latter underappreciates the critical ways in which global politics has been transformed from the highly state-centered system of the Cold War.

Unfortunately, standard international political economy accounts have left us with relatively few tools to grapple with such dynamics.[7] The dominant approach used to understand the early years of deepening globalization drew largely on neoclassical, mainstream economics for a depiction of how markets work.[8] Importantly, economic openness reshuffled the distributional consequences for economic sectors, firms, or class groups, but it hardly transformed their political identities and perceived interests.

Early theoretical moves favoring this neoliberal-informed rationalist approach, in combination with the assumption that domestic and international politics were distinct and separate, focused the field on a narrow set of questions concerning the political conditions that favor or oppose openness. Empirically, this work tended to privilege conventional trade in physical goods. Most studies attempted to understand why countries would liberalize their markets to international trade and finance and, relatedly, how international institutions like the World Trade Organization or Bilateral Investment Treaties could facilitate such efforts.[9] Substantively, this approach generated a number of important blind spots as to the consequences of openness, particularly as globalization moved beyond container ships and accelerated through global data, finance, supply chains, and migration (including viral migration of pandemics).

In the face of the global financial crisis and the rise of populist parties, many scholars have shifted their attention to the sources of backlash and drivers of potential closure.[10] Once again, the underlying assumption behind much of this work is that globalization generates distribution consequences among the material winners and losers of economic openness and that international institutions may be well positioned to solve resulting cooperation problems. Empirically, then, this research agenda focused on a specific set of questions such as measures of relative openness (tariff rates, levels of FDI, or gravity models of trade) as well as indicators of cooperation (dispute settlement mechanisms, participation in international organizations, or signing BITs).[11]

Theoretically, scholars have therefore evaded one of the most interesting and consequential implications of the nature of globalization today: the role of power and culture and the institutionalization of transnational political authority in both formal and everyday ways. In a review of international political economy work, Robert Keohane concludes, "I would urge scholars now active in the IPE field to spend more of their time pondering big questions about change, and asking not what the best existing research tells us about them, but what interpretive leaps may be necessary to point the way to more profound and relevant scholarship."[12] Fortunately, there is plenty of promising work across political science and other disciplines that can help us take that leap.

Reimagining Identity & Authority in Global Markets

Our overall contention is that globalization—the interpenetration of markets across national borders—is transforming politics in the twenty-first century in ways drawn in sharp relief by the coronavirus pandemic. The pandemic is fundamentally a product of globalization, as it was carried from country to country on the backs of global transport, migration, and business. But more fundamentally, the impact and response of the pandemic is being filtered by long-term changes sparked by globalization in terms of what is viewed as contentious and where political contention can play out.

Below, we briefly map an account of globalization that focuses on its transformation of identity and authority, before demonstrating the potential of such an account to enable us to understand the post-pandemic political economy. Our account rests on two key assumptions. First, we highlight how global markets are constituted by people with particular sets of intersecting identities that are shaped by social relations and always refracted through power. Deepening globalization has altered and transformed those identities in profoundly consequential ways as

it implicates both what individuals see as important and what they are willing to fight over, even for those with little felt connection to the global economy. Second, whereas in the past, many assumed that such contentious politics were firmly anchored around the political authority of the nation-state—as the international realm meant state-to-state negotiations or technocratic delegation to international organizations—political authority is now exerted and contested from the town level through state levels, regional levels, national levels, transnational, and supranational levels. Globalization has simultaneously broken the monopoly of authority held by the nation-state and created new opportunity structures for change and sites for contestation.[13]

Global Markets and Identity

Our theoretical framework starts with the foundational assumption that markets themselves are constructed through the social interactions of human beings.[14] These identities always structure and are structured by power relations.[15] In this constructivist approach, we can't model, understand, or predict how the politics of global markets will unfold unless we first grasp the identities of the actors involved and how those identities generate specific sets of market cultures, meanings, and interests.[16] As Kathleen McNamara has argued, this approach has transformational potential built in: different times and places will have different cultures, which are fundamental to the way we see the world and to the meanings we ascribe to anything from the value of the dollar to the desirability of free trade.[17]

Using this lens allows us to open up our research to how globalization creates fundamental changes in the outlooks, ideas, and practices of actors as global markets morph and change. For decades, national market systems produced political debates anchored on left-right ideological conflicts over levels of redistribution. As markets have integrated, they have both transformed these ideological debates and raised new fundamental conflicts over the site of control between states and other political authorities.[18] Standard class conflicts have given way to new cleavages that interact economic conditions with local community identities and positions within global society.[19] The pandemic is the latest of globalization's shocks to raise fundamental questions about people's commitments to global public goods, the moral responsibility to others, as well as about the value of liberal market integration.[20] Instead of seeing the pandemic as what economists might call a "negative externality" of market integration, we need to see it as knit into the reality of markets operating within, and driven by, social life. The foundation for such a view of markets already exists, even if it has not gotten much traction in the mainstream international relations study of IPE.[21]

A specific example of how a focus on identity would allow us to better understand the outbreak of and response to the pandemic can be found in the recent literature on "racial capitalism." Nancy Leong describes racial capitalism as "the process of deriving social and economic value from the racial identity of another person [that] is a longstanding, common, and deeply problematic practice."[22] There are a host of questions around how the changing construction of race over time both causes and is shaped by dynamics in the global political economy, but the rational-materialist approach dominating the high status IPE field has left them largely unasked.[23] The Trump administration's insistence on labeling COVID-19 the Wuhan Flu may seem like a simpleton's tactic to avoid blame, but in demonizing China, the tactic further demonstrates the power of race and racism in international politics, and the role such identity construction plays as a political resource.[24]

If we can rebuild our model of markets around social identity, we can begin to grapple with how race matters for the way that markets have been built historically and function today, and how economic wealth and political power accrues to some states over others in the international system.[25]

While scholars outside mainstream IPE have studied colonialization and empire in ways that do bring race in, we need to put race—and all other salient identities—at the core of our study of IPE to more fully account for the outcomes of power and wealth within a globalized world. Such an approach could also contribute to understanding the mass mobilization supporting anti-racism protests in the United States around the Black Lives Matter movement, as well as its spontaneous reverberations cross-nationally.

The fact that racism has been tightly linked to outcomes of the pandemic, as we discuss below, only makes this approach more vital.[26] We need research that takes identity—starting with race but including gender, sexual orientation, ethnicity, class identities, and beyond, and the broader cultures those identities are situated in—as a variable in terms of both causes and outcomes of global markets. Doing so will allow us to better capture the reality of globalization's transformation potential and the types of political conflicts, cleavages, and coalitions that it is generating.

Political Authority Below, Above, and Across the Nation

Globalization is not only shaping what is being contested but where.[27] As the pandemic has demonstrated, the scale and level of political authority is becoming ever more fluid, while at the same time dramatically more contested. Pandemic politics are deeply contentious, both within national communities, above and across nation-states in new, emergent sites of authority and governance, and in the fragmentation of previously robust political communities. We now need to reorient IPE to take account of this politicization and contested authority to find durable solutions to the current global pandemic and longer term challenges raised by globalization.

In some cases, these relationships can be understood by using the lens of hierarchy studies.[28] In this approach, global politics is understood as a hierarchically structured polity rather than through the canonical view that international relations takes place in a world of anarchy or lack of legitimate authority above the state. Hierarchies are "any system through which actors are organized into vertical relations of super- and subordination."[29] They are thus inherently political and intrinsically about power, making up systems that stratify, rank, and organize the relations not only among states but also other kinds of actors, and often even among a mix of different actors within a single structure of differentiation.

In other cases, however, these relationships are less clear. Globalization has generated new sites of authority above the nation-state and also created new channels of collaboration among actors that sit below it.[30] This allows disaffected actors, who were previously stuck in a world of comparative politics, to relitigate their objectives transnationally. Take the case of Brexit. The UK Independence Party was repeatedly denied electoral success under the UK "first past the post" electoral system. It then strategically used the proportional representation system of the European Parliament to gain traction and then raise salience for the Brexit platform.[31] The overlapping rules of competing political authorities, then, generate new opportunity structures in a world of globalization.

This transformation of authority is revealed in how nation-states—generally thought of as sharing coherent and unified interests and national identities—are seeing contestation and a fraying of social solidarity under the stress of the pandemic. In the US, state-level actors such as state governors have clashed with the Trump administration during the pandemic, whether about shelter-in-place orders, PPE sourcing, or face mask requirements, and have reached out globally to seek assistance on their own from other countries and firms.[32] Notably, these cleavages do not simply map onto partisanship. In Italy, stark differences in the severity of the coronavirus in Lombardy and the Veneto meant travel restrictions were imposed between these regions of Northern Italy—even a shared ruling party (the Lega) was not enough to keep their leaders from political strife.[33] Political authority is also being generated in ways that supersede nation-states themselves, for example in the European Union (EU), as well as through transnational linkages joining political actors and movements globally.[34] While initially the EU seemed ill-equipped to respond to the pandemic, it has recently moved in surprising ways towards new powers, such as in the fiscal realm, to address European citizens' needs.[35]

In sum, today's globalization is shaped by political authority that neither fits the traditional models of state control nor constitutes a free-for-all of markets over politics. Instead, economic integration is creating new forms of political authority and creating links between other entities that exist outside of the state. As these sites of contention shift, so too do global politics.

Opening the Aperture on a Post-Pandemic Globalization Agenda

Globalization has not only transformed how we should study global politics theoretically but also has critical implications for the issues we study—starkly revealed in the ways the pandemic has unfolded. Since the initial cases of COVID-19 began multiplying, states have turned supply chains into choke points, certain workers have been redefined as essential, and as governments race to implement contact tracing technologies they find themselves beholden to the technology of transnational firms.[36] While stories of PPE shipments being rerouted or states fighting over future vaccines seem pulled straight out of a Dan Brown novel, the COVID crisis illuminates longer-term trends.[37] We argue that globalization has left the confines of container ships and trade deals and now implicates transformational dynamics in at least four areas: inequality within and across societies, new forms of economic statecraft, existential ecological threats, and the trajectory of the digital revolution. In the following section, we use the COVID crisis to highlight the importance of these issues, and apply our theoretical insights about identity and authority to chart a research agenda for understanding the post-pandemic world.

Inequality in a Globalized World

As the virus spread from China to the world, its path and initial responses to it revealed much about globalization's linkages. European corporate executives at Asian corporate retreats quickly hopscotched the disease through Swiss mountain towns and Italian villages, while grocery store workers fell ill after the disease was brought home.[38] Russian oligarchs purchased personal ventilators and New York City elites fled to their second home retreats, even as elderly in Italy and the New York City borough of Queens faced healthcare rationing. While the US, Germany, and China fight over future rights to a potential vaccine, countries like Brazil and South Africa struggle to maintain basic supplies of PPEs. The virus thus puts into stark relief the structural inequality that has resulted from globalization—the radically and racially different lived experiences within states and across them. In contrast to distributional approaches, which stress the relative winners and losers of trade openness or efforts to mitigate these differences,[39] our transformative approach shifts attention to the ways high levels of stratification of information, money, and goods and services in global economic networks may fundamentally disrupt political contestation, enable the rise of a consequential global plutocracy, and deepen global cleavages among states.

First, inequality alters the nature of political contention within societies, not only because of its material impacts, but because of the way it reshapes people's sense of their political identities and thus their perceived interests. In countries like the US and the UK, where inequality has risen dramatically over the past few decades, the substance of political debates has been transformed from standard left-right redistributive questions to include debates over sovereignty, identity, and immigration.[40] The rise of global populist politics has many roots, but it is certain that dramatic rises in economic inequality interacting with issues of culture and identity have brought about the electoral success of US president Donald Trump and the UK's vote to leave the European Union.[41] Inequality in life opportunities and lived experience, as Kathleen McNamara has argued, is important because it generates very different social realities and thus everyday practices for its citizens, something only heightened with the geographic differences in the fallout from COVID-19.[42] Robert Reich, former US Secretary of Labor, has suggested that new classes of people have emerged during the pandemic, and that each are experiencing the crisis' impact in dramatically different ways; this felt difference will surely impact politics for years to come.[43] Experiences with inequality and decline within countries, varying significantly by class, race, immigration status, and geographical location, and further sharpened by the pandemic, all contribute to the politics unleashed as globalization deepens.[44] Integrating such deep-seated societal segmentation may help to unravel a number of specific empirical puzzles, including why voters seem to support protectionist policies even when such policies punish their own economic interests.[45] Moreover, such an approach could open up a debate on the ways markets create cosmopolitan and parochial identities, which could provide the basis for a political economy of closure.

Second, rising inequality has generated a global class of plutocrats whose political impact transcends borders. During the COVID pandemic, plutocrats have in some cases replaced governments as the primary actors in the response both domestically (for example in many Russian cities) as well as internationally (for example the Gates Foundation and vaccine research).[46] From Bill Gates to Oleg Deripaska, roughly 2,000 billionaires control more wealth than 60 percent of the planet. These plutocrats are not simply rich people; they are transforming politics. The Gates Foundation strives to eliminate disease, while many Russian oligarchs help the Putin government spread disinformation. The Koch brothers and the Mercer family have played a central role in supporting conservative movements and right-wing initiatives across the US and Europe, while George Soros has played a similar role on the left. If IPE were to follow the money, it would quickly realize that a handful of players are having an outsized influence on global affairs.[47] And these actors are not simply attempting to get a bigger slice of the pie but are changing the nature of the game, rewriting formal rules around campaign finance, media ownership, and government regulation. Recognizing the role of plutocrats in IPE would shift our empirical understanding of capital account liberalization, foreign direct investment, and tax havens from debates about how states engage global markets to how individuals use those markets to alter international politics.[48] The rise of global plutocratic politics also embodies our contention that new sites of political authority and new types of global contestation should be studied and understood to be part of the stratified nature of twenty-first century globalization.

Third, the pandemic has underscored the economic inequality between states in the international system and reignited new global cleavages.[49] Highlighting the interaction between inequality and identity, UN Secretary-General Antonio Guterres warned in a 2020 address honoring Nelson Mandela that "[COVID-19] is exposing fallacies and falsehoods everywhere . . . the delusion that we live in a post-racist world, the myth that we are all in the same boat," adding that these global inequalities are pushing the world to a "breaking point."[50] Erin Lockwood has noted that these divi-

sions have gotten little attention in the study of IPE, despite the field's emphasis on the material impacts of openness and the structure of the global economy.[51] Lockwood's intervention also cautions us against overly optimistic readings of liberalization that focus on successes of countries like China but less on more peripheral states. Such inequality is not simply a character of the units, which might be underdeveloped, but a structural condition of globalization, in which some states are shunted into a permanent underclass. The variation in the severity of the pandemic across states demands investigation, particularly in terms of the advanced economies versus the global south and the early intriguing data suggesting that some low-income countries, such as Viet Nam, have done much better than others such as Brazil or India.

Globalization generates winners and losers. But it also has the potential to create extreme levels of material, political, and social stratification. To understand the consequences of this concentration of power over and access to global markets, scholars should investigate how inequality is transforming identities, political authority, and opportunity structures across, between, and within states. The global economy is altering the lived experience of people who are being further pushed by the pandemic into unequal groups that are not only divided by money but by matters of life and death.

New Economic Statecraft

Since the end of the Cold War, a wide consensus emerged among policymakers and scholars that economic networks for money, information, and production went hand in hand with greater political liberalization and in turn, with global peace.[52] A host of current events, however, make this frame more and more difficult to sustain. From secondary sanctions to technological competition, great powers like the US and China increasingly weaponize economic networks for their strategic gain. Since the outbreak of the COVID crisis, these issues have only become more salient as powerful states manipulate medical supply chains for their own self-interest, use cyberattacks to obtain sensitive vaccine research, and engage in pandemic disinformation campaigns.[53] Understanding the security dynamics of globalization, then, will be an urgent priority for the field. Using the frame of shifting political authority in a hierarchical world order allows us to see these dynamics at work much more clearly.

As Henry Farrell and Abraham Newman argue, the security/economy nexus is not simply about asymmetric interdependence, whereby states manipulate bilateral relations to put pressure on one another.[54] Instead, global economic networks themselves have become a channel of coercion as states engage in weaponized interdependence.[55] In many cases, the networks themselves are asymmetric, with some firms more connected to the network than others. This generates new inequalities and power dynamics not only for firms but for the states that control legal access to them. Organizations such as the SWIFT messaging system or global physical infrastructures such as fiber optic cables become tools of coercion and surveillance. Understanding which networks are likely to be deployed in such a fashion will shed light on a range of critical global challenges, including the future of great power rivalry under conditions of interdependence, as well as the logic of the pandemic response.

More generally, a recognition of this new economic statecraft will push IPE to return to fundamental debates concerning the interaction between global markets and power. For much of its early history, work by IPE scholars including Robert Gilpin and Susan Strange focused on the ways markets create power and tools of dominance.[56] Over time, however, approaches emphasizing cooperation and functionalism tended to view markets as a coordination mechanism rather than a form of control. While a few research agendas on issues like monetary politics and sanctions continued to address such questions, conventional IPE largely came to accept a view of markets that decoupled them from state power. We now need to revisit fundamental questions like the relationship between multinational corporations and national security, and how global firms serve as an extension of state power while also potentially undermining it, as with the pharmaceutical companies and potential vaccine supply chains. Moreover, work on foreign direct investment will need to be more closely coupled with security studies as supply chains become a powerful source of potential vulnerability as well as efficiency. As the COVID crisis makes clear, no nation can afford to ignore the new reality without risking the health and safety of its citizenry in a globalized world.

Existential Ecological Threat

As pandemic lockdowns brought the industrial world to a halt, a profound disruption in energy use, shipping, and aviation ensued. With the flip of a switch, the world got a taste of a not so distant zero-carbon future, in which the demand for carbon bottoms out.[57] By April 2020, as lockdowns and travel restrictions became more encompassing, overall planetary emissions dropped by seventeen percent, and aviation saw a nearly forty percent drop. For the first time in history oil futures swung negative, meaning sellers had to pay buyers to take their oil.

This dramatic disruption foreshadows how the fallout from climate change is not an externality to the market, but instead redefines it.[58] As Jeff Colgan, Thomas Hale, and Jessica Green have argued, we are entering a world of existential politics whereby firms face not only distributional implications of policy choices, but also the possibility that their very business models may be eradicated by climate change and the future of alternative energy.[59] As firm identities are transformed along with their carbon future, it is very difficult to find traditional coordination-based solutions such as issue linkage or side payments to model and solve these essential challenges. Moreover, the extent of the challenge motivates actors facing such existential threats to take on radical approaches—including disinformation and institutional decay strategies—which seek to weaken the entire political system in an effort to limit the ability of policy makers to pursue climate mitigation policies.

As the impacts of climate change continue to be manifested in extreme events around us, the international and comparative political economy scholarly community needs to bridge the traditional divide between those who study green politics domestically and those who study global markets. EU policymakers, for example, are addressing the economic ravages of the pandemic by reassessing their emphasis on a competition policy that prioritizes free markets over national subsidies, and are moving to create a European regime of investment, regulations, and industry collaboration to instead promote green technologies along with global competitiveness. The European Central Bank, long one of the bastions of orthodoxy and conservative monetary policy practices, announced in January 2020 that it was undertaking its first ever comprehensive review of its monetary policy strategy, looking across all its policies and introducing environmental sustainability as a new potential rubric for its policy.[60] As political authority moves beyond the nation-state, climate response has shifted beyond inter-state deals and national commitments to supranational and transnational arenas.

Digital Revolution

As societies grapple with the fallout from the pandemic, the pervasive role of digital technology in our lives has become strikingly apparent. From birthday parties to company meetings, daily life is dependent on video conferencing platforms like Zoom and Google Hangouts.[61]

The largest companies by stock market valuation are the so-called FAANG[62], which rely on digital platforms. In many cases, these platforms span jurisdictions, creating truly transnational firms[63] which often enjoy monopoly or monopsony power.[64] This extraordinary business success has been achieved in part by using nontraditional business models, which offer services to consumers for "free" in exchange for their data. What has been termed "surveillance capitalism" relies on a few large firms vacuuming up personal information and turning that information into more advanced algorithms and targeted advertising.[65] This market transformation is not simply an economic affair but is fundamentally altering the nature of markets, actor identities, and the role of national political authorities.

There is a large literature in communication studies which explores how communications technologies shape what and how we interact. The internet, in particular, has altered media engagement and opened up new channels of expression such as social media. While the exact impact on political views is still debated, the companies involved are themselves growing increasingly concerned about effects on political identity.[66] An exposé in the *Wall Street Journal* released internal Facebook reports highlighting how "[Facebook's] algorithms exploit the human brain's attraction to divisiveness," promoting "more and more divisive content in an effort to gain user attention & increase time on the platform."[67] An important research question then examines variation and effectiveness in how political identities may be shaped cross-nationally through these platforms.

At the same time, these technology companies are coming to play an important role in mediating global politics. For example, Twitter and Facebook are facing mounting criticism to more actively tackle disinformation campaigns even as the president of the United States has often amplified these very campaigns, and Zoom recently disconnected a Chinese civil liberties advocate from a global call, bowing to pressure from the Chinese government.[68] And privacy advocates worry that the pandemic means global contact tracing apps will be used by governments and firms to increase surveillance and control over their societies.[69] Equally important, governments find themselves constrained by the technical options made available by transnational firms. Research on private actor governance, which has long emphasized its coordinating function, will need to spend more time looking at issues of power in markets and its normative consequences.

Finally, states are now using the open information networks of globalization to wage political warfare. The Mueller report made clear how the Russian government views such networks. The Chinese government has increasingly turned to similar disinformation campaigns in the context of the pandemic.[70] Hackers backed by the Chinese government have recently been charged with attempting to hack into US and UK vaccine research. While the internet was long viewed primarily as a technology that championed liberal goals of free speech and open markets, states have turned it into a vector of attack.[71] Research on internet governance, then, will need to expand its focus beyond issues of interconnection and standard setting to consider how openness impacts domestic regime stability in democracies.[72]

All that being said, standard IPE has devoted relatively little attention to these issues and how they are transforming global politics.[73] In our review of articles appearing in *International Organization* over the last decade, only three focused on digital technology. It is thus critical for IPE scholars to pay more attention to how information flows are altering political identities, opportunity structures, and sites of authority. This will become even more pressing as authoritarian governments and firms from those states—most importantly China—play a greater role in the provision of key information technologies.

Conclusion

Over the last several decades, globalization has transformed the nature of world politics. Substantively, the issue space has shifted from questions about distribution to questions about profound structural changes related to inequality, security, the environment, and new technology. At the same time, globalization is altering the institutions and opportunity structures available to actors hoping to contest and reset political debates, even as it interacts with the social identities and cultures of those actors. A major implication, then, of our intervention is to focus on the incremental and long-term changes that have been driven by globalization and that are now reinforced by the pandemic.[74] Rather than an exogenous shock or a return to the mean, the pandemic uncovers blind spots in our existing theoretical toolkit and calls for a reexamination of how IPE engages with globalization. We propose a theoretical refocus on the role of identity and shifting political authority in these transformations, so as to better capture the nature of the world around us.

As states restrict exports of key medical goods and governments call for the reshoring of global pharmaceutical supply chains, it may seem seductive to simply put up walls and tear down globalization. Unfortunately, the nationalist path ignores the ways political and economic systems have been deeply intertwined by global economic networks. Ironically, the post-Brexit slogan is "Global Britain," as leaders face the reality that the UK cannot simply withdraw from the world. The best hope for a critically needed vaccine for Americans may come from foreign investment in a German or French company.

Reconstructing global markets in a post-pandemic world cannot rely on old formulas, but instead will demand a reimagining of markets themselves. What constitutes a sustainable and durable set of global market practices that will be durable for the long run? What institutions may be needed to guarantee such behavior? Now is the time for scholars and students of international political economy to address these pivotal questions.

NOTES

1. See Jan Dams, "Diese Erfahrung wird Europa so schnell nicht vergessen." *Die Welt,* 15 March 2020; Katrin Bennhold and David Sanger, "U.S. Offered 'Large Sum' To German Company for Access to Coronavirus Vaccine Research, German Officials say" *New York Times,* 15 March 2020.

2. "Germany to buy stake in CureVac as world races for COVID-19 vaccine," *Reuters,* 15 June 2020.

3. Bill Bostock, "Sanofi walked back a promise to give the US priority access to its coronavirus vaccine after outrage from the French government," *Business Insider,* 15 May 2020.

4. For an elaboration of a programmatic approach to such a roadmap, see the work of the Global Political Economy Project, retrieved from <https://mortara.georgetown.edu/research/global-political -economy-project-gpep/who-we-are/>.

5. Steven Erlanger, "Spread of Virus Could Hasten the Great Coming Apart of Globalization," *New York Times,* 25 Feb 2020.

6. See Daniel Drezner, "The Most Counterintuitive Prediction about World Politics and the Coronavirus," *Washington Post,* 30 March 2020; Drezner 2020.

7. See Lipscy's contribution to this symposium for an extensive discussion of these issues.

8. For a summary, see Lake 2009.

9. See Büthe and Milner 2008; Lake 2009; Mansfield, Milner, and Pevehouse 2007.

10. See Owen and Johnston 2017; Owen and Walter 2017.

11. See Allee and Peinhardt 2011; Allee and Scalera 2012.

12. Keohane 2009.

13. Farrell and Newman 2016; 2019a.

14. Fligstein 2002.

15. Barnett and Duvall 2005.

16. See Abdelal, Blyth, and Parsons 2011; Best and Paterson 2010.

17. See McNamara 1999; McNamara 2002.

18. See Garrett 1998; Mosley 2003.

19. McNamara 2017.

20. Barnett 2020.

21. See McNamara 2009; Smelser and Swedberg 2005. Our research only finds a total of 15 articles with a constructivist perspective published out of a total of 310 articles in *International Organization* since 2010, indicating the limited use of this approach.

22. Leong 2013.

23. See Guisinger 2017; Tilley and Shilliam 2018.

24. Buzas 2020.

25. Persaud and Sajed 2018.

26. For real time data on the differential impacts of COVID-19 on communities of color, see <https://covidtracking.com/race>.

27. The arguments in this section draw from Farrell and Newman's New Interdependence Approach. For greater elaboration see Farrell and Newman 2014; 2016; 2019a.

28. See Mattern and Zarakol 2016; Mcconaughey, Musgrave, and Nexon 2018; Musgrave and Nexon 2018.

29. Mattern and Zarakol 2016, 624.

30. See Farrell and Newman 2014; Farrell and Newman 2016.

31. Farrell and Newman 2017.

32. Galston 2020.

33. Giuffrida 2020.

34. See Hill, Smith, and Vanhoonacker 2017; McNamara 2015; McNamara 2018; Mérand 2008.

35. See McNamara and Matthijs 2020; Ward 2020.

36. See Farrell and Newman 2020a; Farrell and Newman 2020b.

37. Farrell and Newman 2020a.

38. Ian Goldin, "Coronavirus shows how globalization spreads contagion of all kinds," *Financial Times,* 3 March 2020.

39. There are large and important literatures in IPE that examine how groups are economically affected by trade (e.g. Baccini and Pinto 2017), as well as how states attempt to mitigate or fail to mitigate the political repercussions of these distributional consequences (for example, Rudra 2008).

40. Hooghe and Marks 2018.

41. See Grzymala-Busse 2019; Hopkin 2020.

42. See McNamara 2017; Muro, Whiton, and Maxim 2020; Paul Constant, "The Coronavirus exposed the pre-existing inequality of the American economy," *Business Insider,* 14 May 2020.

43. Reich 2020. Reich identifies four key groups, from those who can work remotely with little disruption, to the essential workers employed on the frontline, the unemployed, and those he calls the "forgotten" in places like prisons, immigration detention facilities, migrant farm worker camps, Native American reservations, homeless shelters, and nursing homes.

44. Richard Oppel, Robert Gebeloff, K.K. Rebecca Lai, Will Wright and Mitch Smith, "The Fullest Look Yet at the Racial Inequality of Coronavirus," *New York Times,* 5 July 2020.

45. Rho and Tomz 2017.

46. Anton Troianovski, "As Local Health Systems Buckle, Russia's Oligarchs Take Charge," *New York Times,* 7 May 2020; Carl O'Donnel and Mana Mishra, "J&J in Talks with Japan, Gates Foundation to lock in Deals on COVID-19 Vaccine," *Reuters,* 16 July 2020.

47. Cooley and Sharman 2017.

48. Kalyanpur 2020.

49. See Barnett's contribution to this issue for a fuller exploration of inequality across states and the Global South in the coronavirus pandemic.

50. Antonio Guterres, "Tackling the Inequality Pandemic: A new social contract for a new era," The Nelson Mandela Lecture, 18 July 2020, retrieved from <https://www.un.org/sg/en/content/sg/statement /2020-07-18/secretary-generals-nelson-mandela-lecture -%E2%80%9Ctackling-the-inequality-pandemic-new-social -contract-for-new-era%E2%80%9D-delivered>.

51. Lockwood 2020; see also, Kalyanpur 2018.

52. See Brooks 2011; Friedman 2005.

53. See Barnes 2020; Farrell and Newman 2020a; Rankin 2020; Willsher, Borger, and Holmes 2020.

54. Farrell and Newman 2019a.

55. See Rudra 2008; Keohane and Nye 1977.

56. See Gilpin 1976; Strange 1990.

57. Christiana Figueres, "COVID-19 has given us the chance to build a low-carbon future," *The Guardian,* 1 June 2020.

58. Our survey of IO articles since 2010 shows only 3 (out of 310) with environmental issues as a central topic.

59. Colgan, Green, and Hale 2020.

60. Press Release, European Central Bank, "ECB Launches Review of its Monetary Policy Strategy," 23 January 2020, retrieved from <https://www.ecb.europa.eu/press/pr/date/2020/html/ecb.pr200123-3b8d9fc08d.en.html>.

61. Andrew Burt, "Three Questions on COVID-19 and Digital Technology," Lawfare, 11 May 2020.

62. FAANG stands for the technology giants Facebook, Amazon, Apple, Netflix, and Google.

63. Kalyanpur and Newman 2019.

64. Culpepper and Thelen 2020.

65. Zuboff 2019.

66. Barberá et al. 2019.

67. Jeff Horwitz and Deepa Seetharaman, 2020. Facebook executives shut down efforts to make the site less divisive. *The Wall Street Journal*, May 26.

68. Gerry Shih, "Zoom censors video talks on Hong Kong and Tiananmen, drawing criticism," *Washington Post*, 11 June 2020.

69. See Natasha Singer, "Google Promises Privacy with Virus Application but can still Collect Location Data," 20 July 2020; Umberto Bacchi, "Coronavirus surveillance poses long-term privacy threat, UN expert warns," *Reuters*, 31 March 2020.

70. Molter, Vanessa and Graham Webster, "Virality Project (China): Coronavirus Conspiracy Claims," 31 March 2020, retrieved from <https://cyber.fsi.stanford.edu/news/china-covid19-origin-narrative>.

71. Farrell and Newman forthcoming.

72. Farrell and Schneier 2019.

73. Simmons 2011.

74. See Farrell and Newman 2010; 2019; Floretos 2011; Thelen 2003.

REFERENCES

Abdelal, Rawi, Mark Blyth, and Craig Parsons. 2011. *Constructing the International Economy*. Cornell University Press.

Allee, Todd L., and Jamie E. Scalera. 2012. The Divergent Effects of Joining International Organizations: Trade Gains and the Rigors of WTO Accession. *International Organization* 66 (2):243–76.

Allee, Todd, and Clint Peinhardt. 2011. Contingent Credibility: The Impact of Investment Treaty Violations on Foreign Direct Investment. *International Organization* 65 (3):401–32.

Barberá, Pablo, Andreu Casas, Jonathan Nagler, Patrick J. Egan, Richard Bonneau, John T. Jost, and Joshua A. Tucker. 2019. Who leads? Who follows? Measuring Issue Attention and Agenda Setting by Legislators and the Mass Public Using Social Media Data. *American Political Science Review* 113 (4):883–901.

Barnes, Julian E. 2020. US Accuses Hackers of Trying to Steal Coronavirus Vaccine Data for China. *The New York Times*. Available at <https://www.nytimes.com/2020/07/21/us/politics/china-hacking-corona-virus-vaccine.html>. Accessed 30 July 2020.

Barnett, Michael. 2020. Humanitarian Governance, Global Triage, and the International Liberal Sacrificial Order. *International Organization* 74 (S1). <https://doi.org/10.1017/S002081832000034X>.

Barnett, Michael, and Raymond Duvall. 2005. Power in International Politics. *International Organization* 59 (1):39–75.

Best, Jacqueline, and Matthew Paterson. 2010. *Cultural Political Economy*. Routledge.

Brooks, Stephen G. 2011. *Producing Security: Multinational Corporations, Globalization, and the Changing Calculus of Conflict*. Princeton University Press.

Büthe, Tim, and Helen V. Milner. 2008. The Politics of Foreign Direct Investment into Developing Countries: Increasing FDI through International Trade Agreements? *American Journal of Political Science* 52 (4):741–62.

Buzas, Zoltan. Forthcoming. Racism and Antiracism in the Liberal International Order. *International Organization*.

Colgan, Jeff, Jessica Green, and Thomas Hale. Forthcoming. Asset Revaluation and the Existential Politics of Climate Change. *International Organization*.

Cooley, Alexander, and J.C. Sharman. 2017. Transnational Corruption and the Globalized Individual. *Perspectives on Politics* 15 (3):732–53.

Culpepper, Pepper D., and Kathleen Thelen. 2020. Are We All Amazon Primed? Consumers and the Politics of Platform Power. *Comparative Political Studies* 53 (2):288–318.

Drezner, Daniel. 2020. The Song Remains the Same: International Relations After COVID-19. *International Organization* 74 (S1). <https://doi.org/10.1017/S0020818320000351>.

Farrell, Henry, and Abraham L. Newman. 2010. Making Global Markets: Historical Institutionalism in International Political Economy. *Review of International Political Economy* 17 (4):609–38.

Farrell, Henry, and Abraham L. Newman. 2014. Domestic Institutions Beyond the Nation-State: Charting the New Interdependence Approach. *World Politics* 66 (2):331–63.

Farrell, Henry, and Abraham L. Newman. 2016. The New Interdependence Approach: Theoretical Development and Empirical Demonstration. *Review of International Political Economy* 23 (5):713–36.

Farrell, Henry, and Abraham Newman. 2017. BREXIT, Voice and Loyalty: Rethinking Electoral Politics in an Age of Interdependence. *Review of International Political Economy* 24 (2):232–47.

Farrell, Henry, and Abraham L. Newman. 2019a. *Of Privacy and Power: The Transatlantic Struggle over Freedom and Security*. Princeton University Press.

Farrell, Henry, and Abraham L. Newman. 2019b. Weaponized Interdependence: How Global Economic Networks Shape State Coercion. *International Security* 44 (1):42–79.

Farrell, Henry, and Abraham L. Newman. 2020a. Will the Coronavirus End Globalization as We Know It? *Foreign Affairs*. Available at <https://www.foreignaffairs.com/articles/2020-03-16/will-coronavirus-end-globalization-we-know-it>. Accessed 19 June 2020.

Farrell, Henry, and Abraham L. Newman. 2020b. Will Governments Restrict Foreign Access to Pandemic Supplies? *Harvard Business Review*. Available at <https://hbr.org/2020/03/will-governments-restrict-foreign-access-to-pandemic-supplies>. Accessed 19 June 2020.

Farrell, Henry, and Abraham L. Newman. Forthcoming. The Janus Face of the Liberal International Order: When Global Institutions are Self-Undermining. *International Organization*.

Farrell, Henry, and Bruce Schneier. 2019. Democracy's Dilemma, *Boston Review,* May 15.

Fioretos, Orfeo. 2011. Historical Institutionalism in International Relations. *International Organization* 65 (2):367–99.

Fligstein, Neil. 2002. *The Architecture of Markets: An Economic Sociology of Twenty-first-century Capitalist Societies.* Princeton University Press.

Friedman, Thomas L. 2005. *The World Is Flat: A Brief History of the Twenty-first Century.* Macmillan.

Galston, William A. 2020. Trump or Governors: Who's the Boss? *Brookings.* Available at <https://www.brookings.edu/blog/fixgov/2020/03/25/trump-or-governors-whos-the-boss/>. Accessed 20 June 2020.

Garrett, G. 1998. Global Markets and National Politics. *International Organization* 52 (4):787–824.

Gilpin, Robert. 1976. The Political Economy of the Multinational Corporation: Three Contrasting Perspectives. *American Political Science Review* 70 (1):184–91.

Giuffrida, Angela. 2020. Why Was Lombardy Hit Harder Than Italy's Other Regions? *The Guardian.* Available at <https://www.theguardian.com/world/2020/may/29/why-was-lombardy-hit-harder-covid-19-than-italys-other-regions>. Accessed 20 June 2020.

Grzymala-Busse, Anna. 2019. Introduction. *Polity* 51 (4):631–40.

Guisinger, Alexandra. 2017. *American Opinion on Trade: Preferences Without Politics.* Oxford University Press.

Hill, Christopher, Michael Smith, and Sophie Vanhoonacker. 2017. *International Relations and the European Union.* Third Edition. New European Union Series. Oxford University Press.

Hooghe, Liesbet, and Gary Marks. 2018. Cleavage Theory Meets Europe's Crises: Lipset, Rokkan, and the Transnational Cleavage. *Journal of European Public Policy* 25 (1):109–35.

Hopkin, Jonathan. 2020. *Anti-System Politics: The Crisis of Market Liberalism in Rich Democracies.* Oxford University Press.

Kalyanpur, Nikhil. 2018. Hegemony, Inequality, and the Quest for Primacy. *Journal of Global Security Studies* 3(3):371–84.

Kalyanpur, Nikhil. 2020. *Liberalism Outsourced: Why Oligarchs and Autocrats Fight in Foreign Courts.* Doctoral Dissertation, Washington, DC: Georgetown University.

Kalyanpur, Nikhil, and Abraham L. Newman. 2019. The MNC-Coalition Paradox: Issue Salience, Foreign Firms and the General Data Protection Regulation. *Journal of Common Market Studies* 57 (3):448–67.

Keohane, Robert O. 2009. The Old IPE and the New. *Review of International Political Economy* 16 (1):34–46.

Keohane, Robert and Joseph Nye. 1977. *Power and Interdependence: World Politics in Transition.* Little, Brown.

Lake, David A. 2009. Open Economy Politics: A Critical Review. *The Review of International Organizations* 4 (3):219–44.

Leong, Nancy. 2013. Racial Capitalism. *Harvard Law Review* 126 (8):2151–226.

Lockwood, Erin. 2020. The International Political Economy of Global Inequality. *Review of International Political Economy.* Available at <https://doi.org/10.1080/09692290.2020.1775106>.

Mansfield, Edward D., Helen V. Milner, and Jon C. Pevehouse. 2007. Vetoing Co-operation: The Impact of Veto Players on Preferential Trading Arrangements. *British Journal of Political Science* 37 (3):403–32.

Mattern, Janice Bially, and Ayşe Zarakol. 2016. Hierarchies in World Politics. *International Organization* 70 (3):623–54.

Mcconaughey, Meghan, Paul Musgrave, and Daniel H. Nexon. 2018. Beyond Anarchy: Logics of Political Organization, Hierarchy, and International Structure. *International Theory* 10 (2):181–218.

McNamara, Kathleen. 2002. Rational Fictions: Central Bank Independence and the Social Logic of Delegation. *West European Politics* 25 (1):47–76.

McNamara, Kathleen R. 2018. Authority Under Construction: The European Union in Comparative Political Perspective. *JCMS: Journal of Common Market Studies* 56 (7):1510–25.

McNamara, Kathleen R. 2017. *Explaining the New Class Cleavages: Geography, Post-Industrial Transformations and Everyday Culture.* SSRN Scholarly Paper. Rochester, NY: Social Science Research Network. Available at <https://papers.ssrn.com/abstract=3059222>. Accessed 30 July 2020.

McNamara, Kathleen R. 2009. Of Intellectual Monocultures and the Study of IPE. *Review of International Political Economy* 16 (1):72–84.

McNamara, Kathleen R. 1999. *The Currency of Ideas: Monetary Politics in the European Union.* Cornell Studies in Political Economy. Cornell University Press.

McNamara, Kathleen R. 2015. *The Politics of Everyday Europe: Constructing Authority in the European Union.* Oxford University Press.

McNamara, Kathleen R., and Matthias Matthijs. 2020. Analysis | Europe's Leaders Meet This Week to Confront the Coronavirus. *Washington Post.* Available at <https://www.washingtonpost.com/politics/2020/04/21/europes-leaders-meet-this-week-confront-coronavirus/>. Accessed 20 June 2020.

Mérand, Frédéric. 2008. *European Defence Policy: Beyond the Nation State.* Oxford University Press.

Mosley, Layna. 2003. *Global Capital and National Governments.* Cambridge University Press.

Muro, Mark, Jacob Whiton, and Robert Maxim. 2020. The Places a COVID-19 Recession Will Likely Hit Hardest. *Brookings.* Available at <https://www.brookings.edu/blog/the-avenue/2020/03/17/the-places-a-covid-19-recession-will-likely-hit-hardest/>. Accessed 19 June 2020.

Musgrave, Paul, and Daniel H. Nexon. 2018. Defending Hierarchy from the Moon to the Indian Ocean: Symbolic Capital and Political Dominance in Early Modern China and the Cold War. *International Organization* 72 (3):591–626.

Owen, Erica, and Noel P. Johnston. 2017. Occupation and the Political Economy of Trade: Job Routineness, Offshorability, and Protectionist Sentiment. *International Organization* 71 (4):665–99.

Owen, Erica, and Stefanie Walter. 2017. Open Economy Politics and Brexit: Insights, Puzzles, and Ways Forward. *Review of International Political Economy* 24 (2):179–202.

Persaud, Randolph B., and Alina Sajed, eds. 2018. *Race, Gender, and Culture in International Relations: Postcolonial Perspectives.* Routledge.

Rankin, Jennifer. 2020. EU says China Behind 'Huge Wave' of Covid-19 Disinformation. *The Guardian.* Available at <https://www.theguardian.com/world/2020/jun/10/eu-says-china-behind-huge-wave-covid-19-disinformation-campaign>. Accessed 30 July 2020.

Reich, Robert. 2020. Covid-19 Pandemic Shines a Light on a New Kind of Class Divide and Its Inequalities. *The Guardian*. Available at <https://www.theguardian.com/commentisfree/2020/apr/25/covid-19-pandemic-shines-a-light-on-a-new-kind-of-class-divide-and-its-inequalities>. Accessed 15 June 2020.

Rho, Sungmin, and Michael Tomz. 2017. Why don't trade preferences reflect economic self-interest? *International Organization* 71 (S1): S85–S108.

Rudra, Nita. 2008. *Globalization and the Race to the Bottom in Developing Countries.* Cambridge University Press.

Simmons, Beth A. 2011. International Studies in the Global Information Age. *International Studies Quarterly* 55 (3):589–99.

Smelser, Neil J., and Richard Swedberg, eds. 2005. *The Handbook of Economic Sociology.* Second Edition. Princeton University Press.

Strange, Susan. 1990. Finance, Information and Power. *Review of International Studies* 16 (3):259–74.

Thelen, K. 2003. How Institutions Evolve: Insights from Comparative Historical Analysis. In *Comparative Historical Analysis in the Social Sciences*, 208–40. Cambridge University Press.

Tilley, Lisa, and Robbie Shilliam. 2018. Raced Markets: An Introduction. *New Political Economy* 23 (5):534–43.

Ward, Alex. 2020. What Alexander Hamilton Has to Do with the EU's $850 Billion Coronavirus Stimulus Plan. *Vox*. Available at <https://www.vox.com/2020/7/21/21332541/coronavirus-eu-stimulus-merkel-billion-hamilton>. Accessed 25 July 2020.

Willsher, Kim, Julian Borger, and Oliver Holmes. 2020. US Accused of 'Modern Piracy' after Diversion of Masks Meant for Europe. *The Guardian*. Available at <https://www.theguardian.com/world/2020/apr/03/mask-wars-coronavirus-outbidding-demand>. Accessed 30 July 2020.

Zuboff, Shoshana. 2019. *The Age of Surveillance Capitalism: The Fight for a Human Future at the New Frontier of Power.* PublicAffairs.

CREDITS

Security 38:1 (Summer 2013), pp. 7–51. © 2013 by the President and Fellows of Harvard College and the Massachusetts Institute of Technology. Reprinted with permission.

FIGURES

Figure 2.1: Figure 1.1 from Beth Simmons, Frank Dobbin, and Geoffrey Garrett, *The Global Diffusion of Markets and Democracy* (Cambridge University Press, 2008). © Cambridge University Press 2007. Reproduced with permission of Cambridge University Press through PLSclear.

Maps 6.1 and 6.2: Figures 5.2 and 6.1 from Eric Heginbotham, Michael Nixon, Forrest E. Morgan, et al., *The U.S.-China Military Scorecard: Forces, Geography, and the Evolving Balance of Power, 1996–2017* (RAND Corporation, 2015). https://www.rand.org/pubs/research_reports/RR392.html. Republished with permission of RAND Corporation; permission conveyed through Copyright Clearance Center, Inc.

Map 6.3: Figure 1 from Fionna S. Cunningham and M. Taylor Fravel, "Assuring Assured Retaliation: The Future of U.S.-China Strategic Stability," *International Security* 40:2 (Fall 2015), pp. 7–50. © 2015 by the President and Fellows of Harvard College and the Massachusetts Institute of Technology. Reprinted with permission.